THE PFA
FOOTBALLERS' WHO'S WHO
2003/2004

Editor and Statistician
Barry J Hugman

Assistant Editor
Ian Nannestad

Photographs by
Allsport UK

QUEEN ANNE PRESS

First published in Great Britain in 2003 by
Queen Anne Press
a division of Lennard Associates Limited
Mackerye End, Harpenden
Hertfordshire AL5 5DR

A CIP catalogue record for this book
is available from the British Library

ISBN 1 85291 651 6

Typeset and designed by
Typecast (Artwork & Design)
8 Mudford Road
Yeovil, Somerset BA21 4AA

Printed and bound in Great Britain by
Butler & Tanner, London and Frome

Foreword

I am extremely pleased to give the PFA's full endorsement and recommendation to *Footballers' Who's Who*. In this modern age of such tremendous interest in the professional football game it is good to have at hand the definitive book on statistics and profiles for every one of our members playing in first-team football throughout the Premier League and Football League in England and Wales.

This book gives the background to what the game is all about – the players. Having to deal with 4,000 PFA members, the book gives me a valuable source of information in an easily accessible, attractive and enjoyable format. It is a must for anybody involved in the game as an administrator, player, manager, spectator and commentator and is especially invaluable for any football 'Brain of Britain' or football quiz aspirant!

The publication has been compiled by Barry Hugman, whose record in this field is unsurpassed. Barry has a team of over 90 people who provide him with the invaluable aspects of local information which gives this book such credibility.

Gordon Taylor
Chief Executive, The Professional Footballers' Association

PROFESSIONAL FOOTBALLERS' ASSOCIATION

PFA

PENSIONS
TRANSFERS
LEGAL ADVICE
FINANCIAL HELP
CONTRACTS

ACCIDENT INSURANCE
EDUCATION
YOUTH TRAINING
PERSONAL APPEARANCES
COMMERCIAL AFFAIRS

PLAYERS UNITED

TEN DECADES' SERVICE TO FOOTBALL

FOUNDED AT THE IMPERIAL HOTEL, MANCHESTER IN 1907, THE PROFESSIONAL FOOTBALLERS' ASSOCIATION TODAY COMMANDS AN ENVIABLE REPUTATION AS THE WORLD'S LONGEST-ESTABLISHED PROFESSIONAL SPORTSMEN'S UNION.

This status stands as testament to the unswerving determination, dedication and commitment of all its contributors, from its earliest forefathers such as Billy Meredith right through to its current Management Committee.

The result is that the PFA is now involved in every aspect of a player's career, from financial management and pensions, to education and training, coaching, commercial, accident insurance and medical & benevolent assistance.

The PFA is also a key factor in both the Youth Training/Football Scholarship Scheme and Football In The Community Programme, ensuring that the players of tomorrow receive the best possible start to their careers.

THE PFA - PROTECTING THE PLAYERS, PROTECTING THE GAME.

20 Oxford Court, Bishopsgate, Manchester M2 3WQ

THE PFA SAYS LET'S KICK RACISM OUT OF FOOTBALL

it's only the colour of the shirt that counts

Acknowledgements

Formerly known as the *Factfile* and now in its ninth edition, the *Who's Who* has, hopefully, become an invaluable part-work which, in due course, will cover the season-by-season career record of all professional footballers operating at that time in the Premier and Football Leagues. To this end, I would once again like to express my thanks to **Gordon Taylor**, the chief executive, and all those at the PFA who are genuinely supporting and helping to establish the *Footballers' Who's Who*. Their help is invaluable and much appreciated.

The massive task of editing the text this year was again carried out by the assistant editor, **Ian Nannestad**, who has been a long-standing contributor to the publication on matters regarding Lincoln City. More about Ian can be found within his section.

This year I was fortunate enough to work with **Michael Joyce**, the author of *Football League Players' Records, 1888 to 1939*. This title, which is still available from SoccerData, 4 Adrian Close, Beeston, Nottingham NG9 6FL, slots in perfectly with my *Post-War Premier and Football League Players' Records*. Michael, who despite now living in Norfolk has supported Arsenal for as long he can remember, has accumulated data for a complete Football League database over many years and used it to produce the player indexes for the Definitive series of club histories and several other publications.

The editorial team were also lucky to be able to call upon **David Barber** (English FA), **Sandy Bryson** (Scottish FA), **Rebecca Burnett** (FA Premier League), **Ceri Stennett** (FA of Wales), and **Marshall Gillespie** (editor of the Northern Ireland Football Yearbook). Others who gave their time were **Alan Platt** (Where Did They Go?) and **Jenny Hugman** (proof reading), and many Premier and Football League members up and down the country. I would also like to thank **Jonathan Power** of Jonathan Power Associates for his welcomed support.

For details provided on players, I have listed below, in alphabetical order, the names of the team, without whose help this book would not have been possible to produce. Once again, I thank every one of them for all the hard work they put in.

Audrey Adams (Watford): Producer and statistician for BBC Radio Sport and a Watford supporter since the days of Cliff Holton, Audrey was the club statistician for *The Ultimate Football Guide*. Regardless of how the club performed last season her devotion to the Hornets remains undimmed.

Geoff Allman (Walsall): A retired university lecturer, having worked for 48 years without taking a day off, he saw his first ever game in February 1944, Walsall versus Wolves. Has written for Walsall's programme for over 30 seasons and, at one time or another, has provided articles for more than half of the clubs currently in the Premiership and Football League. A keen cricketer, he says that although making few runs he prided himself on being able to hold his end up. Geoff is also a Methodist local preacher and press officer.

Stuart Basson (Chesterfield): Stuart is pleased to have contributed to the publication since its inception. He is Chesterfield's club historian and has had three successful books on the club published, the most recent selling out within months of its publication. Stuart contributes reports, previews and historical items to the club's website, www.chesterfield-fc.co.uk. Is also a life-member of the Chesterfield Football Supporters Society, the fans' group that saved the club, and ran it through the 2001-02 season.

David Batters (York City): A supporter since 1948, David is the club historian and a contributor to the matchday programme. He is also the author of *York City: A Complete Record, 1922-1990*, the compiler of *Images of Sport: York City FC* and commentates on matches for York Hospital Radio.

Harry Berry (Blackburn Rovers): Harry has followed Blackburn Rovers for over 50 years, having been born only three miles from Ewood Park, living within 15 miles all his life, and a season ticket holder ever since starting work. Has been a road runner for many years and has completed a few marathons. By profession he is a financial director and works for the largest manufacturer in Blackburn.

Eddie Brennan (Sunderland): A season ticket holder at the Stadium of Light, and a former contributor to *The Ultimate Football Guide*, Eddie has been a regular supporter since 1976.

Jim Brown (Coventry City): The club's official statistician and historian and contributor to the programme, he also pens a weekly column in the *Coventry Evening Telegraph* answering readers queries. He is the author of *Coventry City: The Elite Era* (1998 and 2001) and *The Illustrated History* (2000), in addition to being the co-author of the Breedon publication, *Coventry City FC: A Complete Record* (1991). A Coventry fan since 1962, Jim has an almost complete collection of Coventry programmes since the war, as well as having a large library of football writings, and carries out research for a number of commercial bodies. His latest project is a book on the Huddersfield Town triple championships, 1923-1926.

Mark Brown (Plymouth Argyle): Helped by his wife, Nicola, in putting together the profiles for this publication, Mark has been supporting the club for over 25 years, having been introduced to them at the tender age of five by his Argyle-mad family. Follows most of their games, whether home or away, and is a member of the travel club.

Gavin Buckland (Everton): A life-long Everton supporter of over 30 years and co-author of *Everton: The Ultimate Book of Stats and Facts* and two other football quiz books, Gavin has also worked as a researcher and question setter on several TV quiz programmes. As the club statistician, he has a trivia and facts column in every Everton home programme and provides factual data for Radio Merseyside.

Trevor Bugg (Hull City): A supporter of the Tigers for over 30 years, Trevor contributes to Hull City's official web site as well as the matchday programme. He also played a starring role, information wise, for Exxus, prior to their demise.

Bob Cain (Fulham): Bob has supported Fulham for 32 years, during which time he has not missed a single home match in any first-team competition. In all he has clocked up over 1,500 first team games. A strong advocate of all-seater stadiums, he is still hopeful of a return to a redeveloped Craven Cottage following the groundshare at QPR. Has been a contributor to the club programme for over a decade.

Tim Carder (Brighton & Hove Albion): Tim is chairman of both the Supporters' Club and the Albion's Collectors' and Historians' Society. Along with Roger Harris, he co-authored *Seagulls:The Story of Brighton and Hove Albion FC* and *Albion A to Z: A Who's Who of Brighton and Hove Albion FC*. He is also a respected local historian on matters ranging far beyond the Albion. Having waited so long to see a championship

winning side (36 years before the Div 3 win in 2001), the wait this time was not nearly as long, and he watched with pride (and amazement) as the Albion went one better in winning the Div 2 title in 2002.

Wallace Chadwick (Burnley): A Clarets' supporter for over 40 years, and programme contributor for the last 16, Wallace has assisted on several publications about the club. A member of the AFS from 1980 until its untimely demise, he is an accountant by profession, a statistician by nature, and a supporter by unbreakable habit.

Gary Chalk and **Dave Juson** (Southampton): Gary and Dave are members of Hagiology, a collective dedicated to the collation and dissemination of accurate information on the history of Southampton FC. Gary is co-author, with Duncan Holley, of *Saints: A Complete History, 1885-1987*, *The Alphabet of Saints* (1992), and the forthcoming Hagiology publication, *In That Number: A Post-War Chronicle of Southampton FC*. He was also, with Dave, a leading contributor to *Match of the Millennium: The Saints' Most Memorable Matches* (2000). Dave is co-author, with David Bull, of *Full-Time at the Dell* (2001), a narrative history of the Saints which marked the club's move to the Friends Provident St Mary's Stadium.

Paul Clayton (Charlton Athletic): Author of *The Essential History of Charlton Athletic*, Paul wrote a regular feature in the club programme between 1993 and 1998, having previously written other articles for the now defunct Charlton Athletic magazine and *Valiant's Viewpoint* (Supporters Club newsletter/fanzine). He has also provided the Charlton statistics for a number of publications, including *The Ultimate Football Guide* from 1987 to its final publication in 1999, along with the Charlton player information for the *PFA Footballers' Factfile/Who's Who* since its inception in 1995. Paul is a long-standing season ticket holder at The Valley and rarely misses a game, home or away, despite living in Wiltshire.

Grant Coleby (Exeter City): A member of both the Exeter City Supporters' Club and the Association of Football Statisticians, he has been the contributor for Exeter since the book's conception.

David Copping (Barnsley): David is a life-long Barnsley fan who has been a regular columnist in the club matchday programme for many seasons. He is also one of the club statisticians. For many years he commented on both hospital radio and the club videos.

Frank Coumbe (Brentford): Hasn't missed a competitive Brentford home game since December 1977, a club record. He has also been Brentford's statistician for this book since it began and acted in a similar capacity for *The Ultimate Football Guide* until its demise. Frank returned to the Brentford programme team in 2002-03, writing the *Frankly Speaking* column. On the field, following the release of many first-team players survival was all that mattered and this was achieved relatively comfortably.

Peter Cullen (Bury): A Bury fan for more than 30 years, Peter has watched the Shakers play on all but five league grounds. A former Secretary of the Supporters Assocation and the official club historian, he has written three books on the club, edited/contributed to the matchday programme for 20 years and also worked full time at the club ticket office manager/programme editor for two and a half years.

Mick Cunningham (Bournemouth): A supporter since 1966, Mick has been the programme editor and the club photographer since 1995. He also works as a freelancer and has covered every single AFC Bournemouth first-team game since 1993.

John Curtis (Scunthorpe United): A life-long Scunthorpe fan, John is a former editor of the award-winning club matchday programme. He also covered the club's affairs for the *Scunthorpe Telegraph*, where he now works as the chief sub editor.

Carol Dalziel (Tranmere Rovers): Having watched Tranmere for over 30 years, Carol is a regular contributor to the matchday programme and operates the club's electronic scoreboard.

Denise Dann (Aston Villa): In her own words, Denise is a mad, crazy Villa supporter, who follows them up and down the country without fail. With the *PFA Footballers' Factfile/Who's Who* since its inception, her only previous football work was to help with the club's profiles required for the *Premier League: The Players* publication.

Gareth Davies (Wrexham): Gareth is the co-author of *Who's Who on Welsh International Footballers* (1991) with Ian Garland; editor/compiler of *Coast of Soccer Memories*, the centenary publication of the North Wales Coast FA (1994); co-author of *The Racecourse Robins* with Peter Jones; *Who's Who of Wrexham FC, 1921-99* (1999); co-author of Tempus' *Images of Sport: Wrexham FC, 1872-1950* (2000) with Peter Jones and *Wrexham FC, 1950-2001* (2001) with Peter Jones. He is also a contributor to the Wrexham official programme, *The Holyhead Hotspur* (Cymru Alliance) as the club's press officer, the Welsh Football magazine and various articles and info for other magazines and books.

David Downs (Reading): David works at Reading FC as the club's academy welfare and child protection officer and is also a child protection tutor for the FA. A local newspaper recorded his heart rate at the Play-Off semi-final against Wolves and found that it measured 115 immediately before kick off. Away from football, David is a volunteer custody visitor with the Thames Valley Police Authority, and was also the winner of the Project Purley Local History Society Christmas Limerick Competition.

Ray Driscoll (Chelsea): A life-long Blues' fan, born and bred two miles away from Stamford Bridge, his more than 40 years spectating encompasses the era from Jimmy Greaves to Jimmy Floyd Hasselbaink. An all-round sports 'nut', he has contributed to many football books as well as other sports books, such as cricket, golf, rugby and tennis. He has also contributed to more 'cerebral' literature, such as reference books.

Brian Ellis (Luton Town): One of the co-authors of *The Definitive Luton Town*, Brian is currently compiling, with Alan Shurry, a long awaited Who's Who on Luton Town. A supporter since 1967, he went to his first Luton match in 1967 and has regularly attended Luton home matches ever since, occasionally going to away matches. He is also one of those rare supporters who goes to as many reserve and youth team matches as he can, as he finds it fascinating to follow players at every stage of their career.

Dean Enderby and **Eddie Collins** (Nottingham Forest): Dean has been a season ticket holder at the City Ground for the last 13 seasons and despite wishing to get involved in football publications for some time, the *PFA Footballers' Who's Who* is first. Eddie has been watching Forest since 1956 and derives much pleasure from being involved in this publication. He is also a member of the AFS.

Mark Evans (Leeds United): Has supported United for over 30 years and describes his association with the club as one of the loves of his life. The Leeds' statistician for *The Ultimate Football Guide* for nearly nine years, he was also involved in my two editions of *The FA Carling Premiership: The Players*.

Colin Faiers (Cambridge United): A Cambridge United

fan for over 30 years, Colin has witnessed their rise from non-league football. A chartered accountant in the day, he is the club statistician and occasional contributor to the club programme and web site.

Harold Finch (Crewe Alexandra): Club historian for Alexandra, Harold has now completed 69 years of supporting them. Although no longer the programme editor he is still a regular contributor to the programme and provides all club statistics. His publication, *Crewe Alexandra FC: A Pictorial History of the Club* has proved to be extremely popular with collectors.

Mick Ford and **Richard Lindsey** (Millwall): A life-long Millwall fan, Mick has followed the club for more than 50 years and looks forward to the day when the Lions reach the Premiership. Despite living in Worcester, he only misses a handful of games a season and without the understanding of his wife, Sue, would find it difficult to continue his passion. Has an extensive memorabilia collection, which he adds to when the right items come up. Meanwhile, his Who's Who partner, Richard, the author of *Millwall: A Complete Record*, continues to help establish the Millwall FC Museum at the New Den.

Andrew Frazier (Kidderminster Harriers): Has been following the Harriers since 1978, and hasn't missed a game, home or away, for over nine years. Is a contributor to the club programme, is the club statistician, and a member of the Association of Football Statisticians.

Jon Gibbes (Torquay United): Saw his first game on Boxing Day 1970 aged seven, the beginning of an unhealthy obsession with Torquay United which at times leads to the woeful neglect of wife, Julie, and children, Rosie and Tommy. After having disproved the long-held belief that the club was formed in 1898, Jon co-wrote *Torquay United FC: The Official Centenary History, 1899-1999* with Leigh Edwards and John Lovis.

Harry Glasper (Middlesbrough): Harry could not tell you how he came to be smitten by the football bug, but he remembers that his first season following Boro was definitely 1967 and he well remembers going to a home match on the afternoon of his wedding day, his brand-new wife going with him (Boro 2 v Blackburn Rovers 0 to save you writing in). He became the club's official historian/statistician when he got involved in the production of the club's centenary handbook in 1976, the year he also began contributing to the home programme. Harry's first published history of the club, *Middlesbrough: A Complete Record* came out in 1989 under the Breedon Books banner and he has been actively involved in collating information on Middlesbrough FC for some 36 years now. He continues to look forward to the day when the club wins a major competition.

Paul Godfrey (Cheltenham Town): Paul watched his first Cheltenham Town game at the age of ten – the Robins losing 2-1 to Yeovil Town in an FA Cup Fourth Qualifying Round match. He followed similar near misses and disappointments religiously before events took a dramatic turn in the late 1990s. Having become the club's programme editor in 1990, he was able to witness at first hand the transformation at Whaddon Road brought about by Steve Cotterill and the Board, headed by the chairman, Paul Baker. He joined the club on a full-time basis in 2001 and now combines managing the club's website with his role as the secretary. He is still struggling manfully with the task of compiling the club history.

Frank Grande (Northampton Town): Author of *The Cobblers: A History of Northampton Town FC* and *The Northampton Town Who's Who*, Frank also compiled *The Definitive Northampton Town FC, A Centenary History* and a

biography of Tommy Fowler, the club's longest serving player. Currently working on a book related to the 1940s of national interest, he has been a contributor to the club programme for well over 20 years.

Roy Grant (Oxford United): A life-long Oxford United fan, Roy previously produced the Oxford United matchday programme and had a spell as club statistician. A contributor in this publication since its first issue, Roy has also written for several football club programmes as well as contributing to football websites and productions such as *The Official Football League Yearbook* and *The Ultimate Football Guide*.

Michael Green (Bolton Wanderers): Despite being a fanatical Newcastle United supporter, Michael covers Bolton for this publication and his excellent efforts are much appreciated. Having a yearning to get involved in the area of freelance journalism, preferably concerning football or popular entertainment (music, films etc), he has been on a substantial writing course to further himself in this field.

Alan Harding (Swindon Town): Alan has been supporting Swindon Town since 1968, is a season ticket holder, travels home and away, and has been researching match stats and line-up details, plus details of players, since 1981. Is also a member of the AFS.

Roger Harrison (Blackpool): A life-long supporter who has seen the Pool play every other league side, both home and away, and joint programme editor and club statistician, Roger has contributed to other publications, including *Rothmans* Football Yearbook and *The Ultimate Football Guide*.

Richard Hayhoe (Tottenham Hotspur): Involved since the start of this publication, Richard is happy to write about the men who play for his favourite team and hopes that Spurs can get among the elite in the forthcoming season.

Des Hinks (Stockport County): Des has been following his beloved Hatters for 39 years, covering every game, home and away, in his capacity as club webmaster. He is also the sub editor of the official match programme in addition to editing and producing County's award-winning reserve team programme

Steven Hutton (Bradford City): Steven is a NCJT-qualified sports reporter based in Sheffield and for the past four years has worked for Hayters Teamwork Sports Agency. He also writes regularly for the national newspapers and football magazines and contributes features to the FA website. As part of his work, he covers Premiership and Football League games every weekend, particularly in the Yorkshire region.

Mike Jay (Bristol Rovers): Mike, the club's official historian and programme contributor, has had four books published on Rovers, namely *Bristol Rovers: A Complete Record, 1883-1987, Pirates in Profile: A Who's Who of Players, 1920-94* and *Bristol Rovers FC: Images of England Photographic History* (1999). His latest book, in conjunction with Stephen Byrne, is *The Definitive Bristol Rovers, 1883-2003*, and is due out in August 2003. Mike is currently working with Stephen Byrne on a project called *Bristol Rovers: The Men Who Made It*, which is due to be published in 2004-05.

Colin Jones (Swansea City): A fan since the early 1960s, and a contributor to the club programme during the last seven years, Colin played non-league football before being involved in training and coaching. He will be starting his fourth season as programme editor, a role which can be classed as 'more of a labour of love' than the money received in expenses! Prior to the start of the 2000-01 season, he also made a significant contribution in setting out all the stats in grid form for David Farmer's book, *The Swans, Town & City*.

Andrew Kirkham (Sheffield United): A Blades' supporter

since 1953, and a regular contributor to the club programme and handbook since 1984, Andrew is a member of the AFS and 92 Club. He was a contributor to *Sheffield United: The First 100 Years*, and co-author of *A Complete Record of Sheffield United Football Club, 1889-1999*.

Geoff Knights (Macclesfield Town): Geoff is a retired bank manager who has supported Macclesfield Town since the late 1980s. Describing himself as an ordinary supporter who stands on the terraces, and one who enjoys the friendly atmosphere of a small club, he keeps detailed statistics and records on the club, which are used in response to media and other enquiries.

Geoffrey Lea (Wigan Athletic): A life-long supporter for over 30 seasons who first started watching the club during the non-league days, Geoff has been the editor of the matchday programme for the last eight seasons. He is also the official matchday clubcall reporter and, as the club's statistician, he performs a number of jobs for Wigan as a labour of love. Has missed only a handful of games over the last 11 seasons and has also worked for a number of local radio stations and newspapers following the club's progress.

Mark Lea (Rushden & Diamonds): Mark has been covering Diamonds full-time for the *Northamptonshire Evening Telegraph* over the last four seasons, charting their remarkable rise from the Conference to Nationwide League Division Two with two championships, one runners-up spot and a trip to the Millennium Stadium for the Play-Off final. Born in Boston, he also follows the fortunes of his hometown club along with those of West Ham. As a life-long fan, Mark has gone through the limited highs and many lows of the Irons.

Bob Lonkhurst (Arsenal): A life-long Gunners' supporter, having had trials with the club as a 16-year-old goalie, Bob is a regular visitor to Highbury and has a keen interest in the youth team. Is also a successful boxing author, with a large collection of boxiana, being a contributor to two magazines and the author of *Man of Courage*, the story of the ring legend, Tommy Farr; *Gentleman of the Ring*, the life and career of Jack Petersen and *East End Idol*, the amazing story of Terry Spinks, MBE.

Gordon Macey (Queens Park Rangers): Has supported Queens Park Rangers since the early 1960s and has been collecting and compiling statistics on the club, at all levels, for many seasons. He is a life member of the Association of Football Statisticians and is recognised by many areas of the media as the 'expert' on QPR. In 1993, Gordon was appointed as the club's official historian following the publication of his successful *Queens Park Rangers: The Complete Record* and to mark the Millennium he published an update in August 1999. His three children are all regular attendees at the Rangers' games and help with some of the research at newspaper and local archives. Gordon's work, as an implementer of Financial and Logistic Business Systems, involves travel throughout Europe and other parts of the world. This gives him the opportunity of watching football (and his other interest of ice hockey) in a number of different countries.

John Maguire (Manchester United): A one-club man since this publication began, John has been working on several sports related booklets in 2003. The result of those efforts may be found in Sportspages, both in Manchester and London, and range from booklets on Peter Taylor and Bill Nicholson, and a tribute to Marlow in the FA Cup to more high-tech ventures in the world of CD ROM with *A History of the FA Cup*.

Carl Marsden (Oldham Athletic): A life-long supporter, Carl has been involved with his beloved Athletic on several levels. He was chairman of SAFE (Secure Athletic's Future Existence), a website editor and regular fanzine contributor. He now fronts the sports coverage of the *Oldham Advertiser* newspaper and does live radio commentary on the club's matches for the Latics Live service. He can be reached by email on carl@oafc.co.uk).

Carl Marston (Colchester United): Has been reporting on the fortunes of Colchester United since they regained their Football League status in 1992, both for the *East Anglian Daily Times* and the *Green 'Un* newspapers. Carl has only missed a handful of games during the last 11 years, usually when away, running for Suffolk in cross country races.

Wade Martin (Stoke City): A Stoke supporter since birth, he has written numerous books on the club, including *The Definitive Stoke City*, *A Potter's Tale* and a Who's Who series called the *The Master Potters*. Wade acts as the club's historian and was a contributor to the club's programme for many years.

Tony Matthews (West Bromwich Albion): The official statistician and curator at The Hawthorns, his 60 plus publications include complete records/histories of Aston Villa, Birmingham City, Stoke City, Walsall, West Bromwich Albion and Wolverhampton Wanderers; The Essential Histories of Leicester City and Wolverhampton Wanderers, also assisting with same on Aston Villa and West Bromwich Albion; A-Z Encyclopaedias of Aston Villa, Birmingham City, Manchester United, Stoke City, Tottenham Hotspur, West Bromwich Albion, Wolverhampton Wanderers and *Devon Football* (featuring Exeter City, Plymouth Argyle & Torquay United and published in 2002); Who's Whos of Villa, Blues, Manchester United (1945-85), Albion and Wolves; *A Who's Who of England World Cup Players/Managers*, *The World Cup History: 1930-2002*; wartime and photographic books; *Smokin' Joe: The Cyrille Regis Story* (2002); and also contributes to programmes of Premiership/Nationwide League clubs. His latest works are Who's Whos on Nottingham Forest and Stoke City, A-Z Encyclopedias on Bolton Wanderers and Sheffield United and *The 125-year Day-by-Day History of Everton FC*.

Peter Miles and **David Goody** (Southend U): Peter has supported United since 1976 and remains a regular watcher of matches, both home and away, while David has also supported the club from his youth. Peter has had eight books on football published, four of them about the Shrimpers and all co-authored with David. The Southend related titles are *Potted Shrimps: An Encyclopedia*, *Southend United: Images of Sport*, *100 Greats* and the recently finished *Southend United: 50 Classic Matches*.

Paul Morant (Leyton Orient): Working for an insurance company in London, Paul is an out-and-out Orient fan who rarely misses a game, home or away, and takes great pride in being this publication's Orient contributor.

Gerald Mortimer (Derby County): Gerald first visited the Baseball Ground in 1946 and for 32 years, until his retirement from full-time journalism in 2002, covered the club for the *Derby Evening Telegraph*. The main author of *Derby County: A Complete Record* which, in 1984, began an important club series by Breedon Books, he went on to produce an updated version in 1988 and the *Who's Who of Derby County*.

Donald Nannestad (Boston United): Reporting on the fortunes of the Pilgrims for Raymonds Press Agency during the club's first season of Division Three, Donald, who is a journalist by profession, has a second role in life as a local councillor in Lincoln where he was elected to become the city's 797th Mayor in May 2003.

Ian Nannestad (Lincoln City): Ian has followed the Imps for more than 35 years and is co-author with his brother, Donald, of *A Who's Who of Lincoln City, 1892-1994* and *Lincoln City: The Official History*. A freelance writer and book

editor, in April 2002 he established a new quarterly magazine devoted to the history of the game, titled *Soccer History*. Readers wishing to know more about the magazine can contact Ian by writing to 52 Studland Road, Hall Green, Birmingham, B28 8NW. He was previously editor of the AFS Report.

Philip Noble (Manchester City): Aged 28 and a Manchester City fan since 1985, Philip is a regular attendee at City games, both home and away. Having briefly worked for the club as the curator for 18 months during 2000-01, he has one of the largest collections of City memorabilia, his programme collection, home and away, being complete from 1946-7. Has also contributed to around a dozen publications produced on the club over the past ten years.

John Northcutt (West Ham United): Has supported the Hammers since 1959 and is the co-author of *West Ham: A Complete Record* and *The Illustrated History*. A regular contributor to the club programme, John was the club adviser to *The Ultimate Football Guide*. He also answers all the questions put to the *Vintage Claret* section on the club's web site and is currently working on *The West Ham Definitive*, which should be available early in the new season.

Richard Owen (Portsmouth): A life-long supporter and official club historian for Portsmouth, Richard performs several jobs for the club as labour of love and has been a regular contributor to the club programme for the past 25 years, missing only a handful of away games in the past 27 years, having watched Pompey on 109 league grounds. An avid programme collector, with almost a complete set of post-war Portsmouth home and away issues, in 1998 he co-published *The Centenary Pictorial History of Portsmouth FC* and *A Team Collection*, which featured every team picture of Pompey since 1898. His third book, *Pompey's Rise to the Premiership* was published in July 2003 and he is currently working on two further titles. Richard has now built up a full library of club histories on all British Football League clubs.

Steve Peart and **Dave Finch** (Wycombe Wanderers): A former programme editor of the club and a supporter for over 20 years, Steve put together the player profiles, while the club statistics were supplied by Dave, the official Wycombe statistician. Both were authors of *Wycombe Wanderers, 1887-1996: The Official History*, published in 1996. Dave has supported Wycombe regularly since 1964 and is the club's statistician, having been part of their programme editorial team since 1990.

Steve Phillipps (Rochdale): A Rochdale supporter for nearly 40 years, and the club's official historian, Steve is the author of *The Survivors: The Story of Rochdale AFC* (1990), *The Definitive Rochdale* (1995) and, more recently, *The Official History of Rochdale AFC*. A founder member of the AFS, away from football he is a university lecturer.

Terry Phillips (Cardiff City): Chief soccer writer for the *South Wales Echo* since 1994, and a sports journalist for over 30 years – *Kent Evening Post* (1970-1977), *Derby Evening Telegraph* (1977-1986), *Gloucester Citizen* (1986-1994) – Terry has previously covered clubs at all levels, including Brian Clough's Nottingham Forest, Derby County, Gillingham, and Gloucester City. His specialist subjects are Cardiff City FC and Cardiff Devils (Ice Hockey).

Alan Platt (Liverpool): Is a dedicated football statistician and a follower of Liverpool FC since 1960, and whilst resident in London, a member and official of the London branch of the LFC Supporters Club. He has assisted Barry Hugman in an editorial capacity on all his football publications since 1980, namely the four updates of *Football League Players Records*, the two editions of *Premier League: The Players* and, for the

last seven years, the *PFA Footballers' Who's Who* (formerly *The Factfile*) when not working overseas in his profession of transport planner. Now resident in Manchester, his main interest today is in non-league football and he keeps detailed records on all the senior semi-professional leagues, having compiled a database of over 6,000 players participating in that level of football.

Kevan Platt (Norwich City): Kevan is Norwich City's club secretary, a role he combines with that of in-house club historian and statistician. Has now clocked up 35 years of watching his favourite team on a regular basis and remains an avid fan of the Canaries. Norwich City's Centenary Year was an enormous success with the Grand Player Reunion in September 2002 being one of the highlights when Kevan was able to contact all but a handful of the club's former players known to be alive.

Mike Purkiss (Crystal Palace): Having supported Palace since 1950 and producing stats on them since 1960, Mike is the author of *Crystal Palace: A Complete History, 1905-1989*. Was the club statistician for *The Ultimate Football Guide* and also contributed to *Premier League: The Players*.

Mick Renshaw (Sheffield Wednesday): Has followed Wednesday for over 40 years and is a great supporter of European soccer. Mick also produced the club section for *The Ultimate Football Guide*.

Mick Robinson (Peterborough United): Another life-long fan, for a number of years Mick has contributed to the club programme and was the joint editor of *The Posh*, the official Peterborough history. Was also club statistician for *The Ultimate Football Guide*.

Phil Sherwin (Port Vale): Phil is the Port Vale club statistician and has been a fan since 1968, when they had to seek re-election to the old Fourth Division. Travelling to away games since 1973, he has only missed a handful of matches since then and has contributed to the club programme, various books on the club, the now defunct *Football Club Directory*, and the local newspaper, as well as radio and television.

Mike Slater (Wolverhampton Wanderers): The Wolves' contributor to this publication since its inception, Mike wrote a book on the club's history called *Molineux Memories*, which he published in 1988. Well-known as the compiler of *The Brain of Wolves' Quiz*, he also produced a booklet in 1996 containing all of Wolves' competitive results and records against every other club.

Gordon Small (Hartlepool United): Has supported Pools since October 1965 and for the past 30 odd years has collected and compiled statistics on his adopted club. Has contributed to all nine editions of the *PFA Footballers' Who's Who* and, in 1998, was the author of *The Definitive Hartlepool United*. Has a wide range of football interests and, in particular, has ambitions to produce books on the history of soccer in Lancashire.

Dave Smith (Leicester City): Dave has been the official Leicester City statistician and historian for many years and is a regular contributor to both the club programme and the local press. Is also the co-author of a number of successful hardback books on the club history, notably *Of Fossils & Foxes* which was comprehensively updated and redesigned in 2001 and *The Foxes Alphabet*, which was last published in 1995. He also edited the 2002 publication, *Farewell to Filbert Street*, which was published by the club to mark the end of an era at the Foxes' traditional home.

Phil Smith (Wimbledon): As a supporter of Wimbledon FC for the past 20 years, Phil was ideally placed to take over the player contributions for this publication after Darran and

Chris Jennison, whom I would like to thank personally for all their past efforts, decided to relinquish their posts after the announcement was made that the Dons would be moving to Milton Keynes. Is a regular contributor to the club's official programme.

Gerry Somerton (Rotherham United): A contributor to the *Factfile* (now *Who's Who*) since its inception, Gerry took over the role of media and communications officer at the club in July 2002 to continue his long association with the only team he has ever followed, having spent the previous ten years covering the club's fortunes for the *Rotherham Advertiser*. Has written three books about the club, with a fourth – *A Who's Who of Rotherham United* – in the pipeline for production later this year.

Paul Stead (Huddersfield Town): A life-long supporter of his hometown football club, and a regular spectator both home and away, Paul has seen the Terriers' reach the First Division Play-Offs, face two relegations inside three years, then the threat of liquidation, which was followed by the club going into administration, all in the last few years.

David Steele (Carlisle United): David has been involved with the *PFA Footballers' Who's Who* since its inception in 1995. Has also been a regular contributor to the Carlisle matchday programme since 1989, as well as giving assistance to a wide variety of publications on matters connected with the club's history.

Richard Stocken (Shrewsbury Town): Still following Shrewsbury Town for almost 50 years through thick and mostly thin, Richard is a collector of club programmes and memorabilia and has contributed to a number of publications over the years. Due to write a best seller on Shrewsbury come retirement, he is a senior manager with one of the big four banks in his spare time.

Bill Swann (Newcastle United): A supporter since the Jackie Milburn days of the early 1950s, and a long-term shareholder in the club, along with his wife and three children (all season ticket holders), he is a keen collector of memorabilia connected with the club. Has consolidated his information on club matches, teams, scorers, and players into a database for easy access and analysis. Bill assisted in the production of *Newcastle United: A Complete Record*, is a co-author of the forthcoming *Essential History of Newcastle United* and this is his eighth year as a contributor to this publication. His 17-year-old son, Richard, also a Newcastle fanatic, and an England Independent Schools goalkeeper, kept him right on some of the detailed information in the player biographies.

Colin Tattum (Birmingham City): Colin is the chief sports writer of the *Birmingham Evening Mail* with more than 15 years experience to his credit and specialises in coverage of Birmingham City and the England national team for the newspaper.

Paul Taylor (Mansfield Town): A Mansfield Town supporter of over 30 years standing, Paul has contributed to many publications over the last few years, including the club's centenary history published in 1997. He is the club's official historian, the official Mansfield Town statistician for the AFS and is also president of the Stags Supporter's Association (formed this season from the old Stags Supporter's Club and Support Our Stags members club).

Richard and **Sarah Taylor** and **Ian Mills** (Notts County): Richard is a life-long Notts County fan from a Notts County family, travelling the length and breadth of the land in following the Magpies, and has seen them on all but a few

current league grounds and many non-current grounds too. In the summer, he umpires cricket matches to while away the close season. Sarah, like her father and two brothers, became a dedicated fan at an early age and has made regular excursions home from university to support the Magpies. Having seen his first game at Gay Meadow in 1959-60, Ian, who ran the matchday programme sales, has been hooked ever since, missing just one match since 1970.

Les Triggs (Grimsby Town): A retired librarian, Les first saw the Mariners in a wartime league match whilst the club was in exile at Scunthorpe's Old Show Ground and has been a regular supporter since their days as a then First Division club. Became involved in the historical side of the club when asked to assist in the staging of the Centenary Exhibition in 1978. The co-author of *Grimsby Town: A Complete Record* and the Grimsby statistician for the *Ultimate Football Guide*, he is also an occasional contributor to the club fanzine.

Roger Triggs (Gillingham): Roger has been a Gillingham supporter for over 40 years and has been collecting statistics and records on the club since he was a schoolboy. Co-author of the highly acclaimed centenary book, *Home of the Shouting Men*, produced in 1993, Roger has since produced his images collection in conjunction with Tempus Publishing Company and in August 2001 brought out *The Complete Who's Who of Gillingham's Football League Players, 1920-1938 & 1950-2001*.

Frank Tweddle (Darlington): The club's official historian and statistician, Frank has regularly contributed articles to the Darlington programme for the last 28 seasons and has avidly supported the Quakers for well over 40 years. As well as being a member of the 92 Club and the AFS, he is the author of *Darlington's Centenary History* published in 1983 and *The Definitive Darlington 1883 - 2000*, as well as producing work for various other football publications. Now early-retired, he can devote even more time to delving into Darlington's interesting, if undistinguished, past 120 years.

Paul Voller (Ipswich Town): Has been a life-long Ipswich Town fan and started attending matches at Portman Road in 1963. A member of the Ipswich Town Supporters Media Committee, he edits the supporters page in the matchday magazine and the supporters weekly page in the local *Evening Star*. Was the Ipswich statistician for the *Rothmans Football Yearbook* and the *Football Club Directory* during the 1990s and was joint author of *The Essential History of Ipswich Town*.

Tony Woodburn and **Martin Atherton** (Preston North End): Both North End fans for over 30 years, Tony and Martin provide statistical and historical information on the club for various outlets and maintain the National Football Museum's permanent Preston North End collection, as well as writing for the club programme and, of course, the *PFA Footballers' Who's Who*.

David Woods (Bristol City): An Ashton Gate regular since March 1958, and a shareholder since 1972, David is the official Bristol City historian. Has written four books on Bristol City, the most recent being *Bristol City: The Modern Era, 1967-2000*, published by Desert Island, he is currently working on *Bristol City: The Early Years, 1894-1915*, due for publication by Desert Island Books in the Autumn.

Finally, on the production side of the book, my thanks go to **Jean Bastin**, of Typecast (Artwork & Design) for her patience and diligent work on the typesetting and design, which again went far beyond the call of normal duty and was much appreciated.

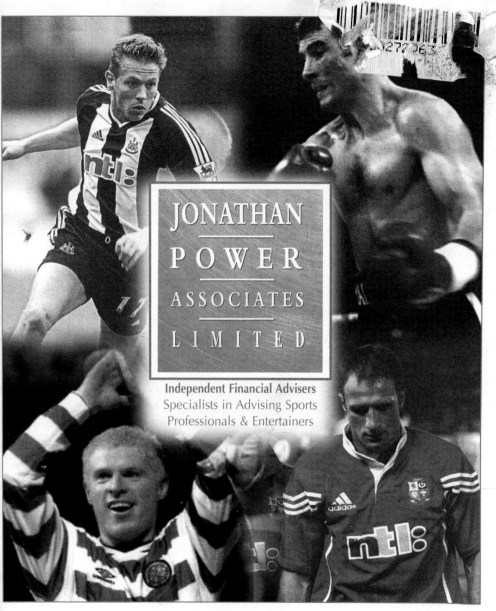

Who are we?

Independent Financial Advisers who specialise in advising professional sports people and entertainers.

Our staff have an extensive knowledge in providing a professional service in all areas of financial planning.

As Independent Financial Advisers our advice to our clients is impartial and independent as we have access to every bank, building society, insurance company, investment company and mortgage lender.

Who are our clients?

The clients who choose us to become their Independent Financial Advisers, represent the widest range of individuals - sports people from the fields of football, cricket, rugby and boxing and clients from the world of entertainment, including pop stars, songwriters, actors and actresses.

Our wide range of services include:

- Sports Injury Insurance -
- Professional Football Association Pension Scheme -
- Mortgage Advice, Remortgage Advice -
- Pension Planning, Retirement Planning -
- Investment Planning (lump sum and regular savings) -
- Protection (life assurance, critical illness and income protection) -
- Tax Planning (including preparation and completion of tax returns) -
- Car Finance -
- General Insurance (motor and household) -
- Will Writing -
- UK and International Finance Planning -
- Overseas Property Purchase -

And finally...

I would like to take this opportunity in thanking the following companies for their kind assistance in co-sponsoring the Footballers Who's Who 2003-2004, Matrix Securities, Scottish Life, J A Hughes Solicitors, Max Bitel Greene Solicitors and Charterhall Associates.

Craig Bellamy

Newcastle United & Wales

"In football you need good financial advice throughout your career and beyond. Jonathan has given me advice that allows me to feel completely confident about my financial future."

Steve Staunton

Aston Villa & Republic of Ireland

"Thanks for your help and advice. I understand the importance of financial planning and feel happy to know that my finances are managed by experts in their field."

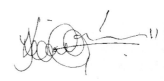

Kevin Campbell

Everton

"Thanks for the great advice. I am happy to recommend Jonathan Power Associates to fellow professionals".

Neil Lennon

Celtic & Northern Ireland

"I am delighted with the work that Jonathan has helped me with and I am delighted in recommending Jonathan to all the players".

Darren Moore

West Bromwich Albion & Jamaica

"Thanks for the great advice Jonathan. Keep up the good work"

Lee Hendrie

Aston Villa & England

*"Jonathan Power Associates have provided me
with excellent advice. I have been very
impressed with their professionalism throughout".*

Robert Earnshaw

Cardiff City & Wales

*"I am delighted to have my advice from Jonathan
Powers Associates. They came highly recommended".*

Frank Sinclair

Leicester City (Former Chelsea) & Jamaica

*"I am delighted to recommend Jonathan Power
Associates. They are experts in their field and
I wish I had met them years ago".*

Jimmy Davis

Manchester United and England U20's

*"Thanks for providing me with great advice
which will help me along in my career".*

Zat Knight

Fulham & England Under 21's

*"Thanks for all your help and advice.
Keep up the good work".*

Alan Shearer, the PFA Player of the Decade

Editorial Introduction

Following on from last year's edition, the *Who's Who* portrays the statistical career record of every FA Barclaycard Premiership and Nationwide League player who made an appearance in 2002-03, whether it be in league football, the Football League Cup (Worthington Cup), FA Cup (Sponsored by AXA), Charity Shield, European Cup, UEFA Cup, Inter-Toto Cup, or in the Play Offs. Not included are Welsh Cup matches. It goes beyond mere statistics, however, with a write up on all of the 2,300 plus players involved, and also records faithfully last season's playing records separately by club.

The work falls into three sections, all inter-relating. Firstly, the main core, PFA Footballers' Who's Who: A-Z (pages 17 to 468); secondly, FA Barclaycard Premiership and Nationwide League Clubs: Summary of Appearances and Goals for 2002-03 (pages 469 to 490); and thirdly, Where Did They Go? (pages 491 to 495); lists all players shown in the previous edition who either moved on or did not play in 2002-03. Below is an explanation on how to follow the *PFA Footballers' Who's Who*.

As the title suggests, all players are listed in alphabetical order and are shown by Surnames first, followed by full Christian names, with the one the player is commonly known by shown in **bold**. Any abbreviation or pseudonym is bracketed.

Birthplace/date: You will note that several players who would be predominately classified as British, were born in places like Germany and India, for example. My book, *Premier and Football League Players' Records*, which covers every man who has played league football since the war, has, in the past, used the family domicile as a more realistic "birthplace". But, for our purposes here, I have reverted to that which has been officially recorded.

Height and Weight: Listed in feet and inches, and stones and pounds, respectively. It must be remembered that a player's weight can frequently change and, on that basis, the recorded data should be used as a guide only, especially as they would have been weighed several times during the season.

Club Honours: Those shown, cover careers from the Conference and FA Trophy upwards. For abbreviations, read:- European Honours: EC (European Cup), ESC (European Super Cup), ECWC (European Cup Winners' Cup) and UEFAC. English Honours: FAC (FA Cup), FLC (Football League Cup), CS (Charity Shield), FMC (Full Members Cup, which takes in the Simod and Zenith Data sponsorships), AMC (Associated Members Cup - Freight Rover, Sherpa Van, Leyland DAF, Autoglass, Auto Windscreens and LDV Vans), AIC (Anglo-Italian Cup), GMVC (GM Vauxhall Conference), FC (Football Conference), NC (Nationwide Conference), FAT (FA Trophy), FAYC (FA Youth Cup). Scottish Honours: SPD (Scottish Premier Division), S Div 1/2 (Scottish Leagues), SC (Scottish Cup), SLC (Scottish League Cup). Please note that medals awarded to P/FL, FLC, and AMC winners relate to players who have appeared in 25%, or over, of matches, while FAC, EC, and UEFAC winners medals are for all-named finalists, including unused subs. For our purposes, however, Charity Shield winners' medals refer

to men who either played or came on as a sub. Honours applicable to players coming in from abroad are not shown at present, but the position will be reviewed in future editions.

International Honours: For abbreviations, read:- E (England), NI (Northern Ireland), S (Scotland), W (Wales) and RoI (Republic of Ireland). Under 21 through to full internationals give total appearances (inclusive of subs), while schoolboy (U16s and U18s) and youth representatives are just listed. The cut-off date used for appearances was up to and including 30 June.

Player Descriptions: Gives position and playing strengths and, in keeping the work topical, a few words on how their season went in 2002-03. This takes into account, in a positive fashion, key performances, along with value to the team, injuries, honours, and other points of interest, etc.

Career Records: Full appearances, plus substitutes and goals, are given for all FA Barclaycard Premiership and Nationwide League games and, if a player who is in the book has played in any of the senior Scottish Leagues, his appearances with the club in question will also be recorded at the point of signing. Other information given, includes the origination of players (clubs in the non-leagues, junior football, or from abroad), registered signing dates (if a player signs permanently following a loan spell, for our purposes, we have shown the initial date as being the point of temporary transfer. Also, loan transfers are only recorded if an appearance is made), transfer fees (these are the figures that have been reported in newspapers and magazines and should only be used as a guide to a player's valuation). Appearances, substitutions and goals are shown by P/FL (Premiership and Football League), PL (Premier League), FL (Football League), FLC (Football League Cup), FAC (FA Cup), and Others. Other matches take in the Play Offs, LDV Vans Trophy, Charity Shield, and European competitions, such as the European Cup, UEFA Cup, European Super Cup and Intertoto Cup. All of these matches are lumped together for reasons of saving space. Scottish appearances for players on loan to P/FL clubs in 2002-03 are shown at the point of transfer and do not include games following their return to Scotland. That also applies to players transferred from England to Scotland. FA Cup appearances, subs and goals are only recorded when they are made playing for a FL club and do not cover appearances made by Conference sides.

> Career statistics are depicted as
> **Appearances + Substitutes/Goals**

Whether you wish to analyse someone for your fantasy football team selection or would like to know more about a little-known player appearing in the lower reaches of the game, the *PFA Footballers' Who's Who* should provide you with the answer.

Barry J. Hugman, Editor, PFA Footballers' Who's Who

ABBEY George Peterson
Born: Port Harcourt, Nigeria, 20 October 1978
Height: 5'10" **Weight:** 10.8
International Honours: Nigeria: 3
Until the latter part of the 2002-03 season there were few opportunities for George in his accustomed role as right back but he made several appearances out of position in the Macclesfield midfield, usually coming on from the substitutes' bench where he used his ability as an attacking player well. In March he replaced Steve Hitchen at right wing back, in a back-five formation, playing enthusiastically, defending and tackling well. While holidaying in Nigeria with his friend Joseph Yobo during the summer break George linked up with the national team and went on to win three full international caps, featuring against Ghana, Cameroon and Malawi, thus making him Macc's most-capped player.
Macclesfield T (Signed from Sharks FC, Port Harcourt, Nigeria on 20/8/1999) FL 56+19/1 FLC 4+1 FAC 2+4 Others 1

ABBEY Nathanael (Nathan)
Born: Islington, 11 July 1978
Height: 6'1" **Weight:** 12.0
Nathan's first act on his Northampton Town debut was to face a penalty after regular 'keeper Lee Harper was dismissed against Swindon. Later in the season when Harper was injured, Nathan also found himself in the treatment room, and he finished the campaign with a total of just five Second Division appearances.
Luton T (From trainee on 2/5/1996) FL 54+1 FLC 3 FAC 8 Others 2
Chesterfield (Free on 10/8/2001) FL 46 FLC 1 FAC 3 Others 3
Northampton T (Free on 6/8/2002) FL 4+1 FLC 1 Others 2

ABBEY Zema
Born: Luton, 17 April 1977
Height: 6'1" **Weight:** 12.11
After suffering a cruciate knee ligament injury at the start of the 2001-02 season, Zema did not return to first-team action for Norwich City until the end of last September. Thereafter he remained an important member of Nigel Worthington's squad. Powerfully built, he is particularly effective in the air using his leap and timing to out jump much taller opponents. Zema gained a regular place

in the Canaries' starting line-up in early March and impressed the fans with his athletic front-running displays.
Cambridge U (Signed from Hitchin T on 11/2/2000) FL 16+6/5 FLC 1+1 FAC 1 Others 1
Norwich C (£350,000 on 15/12/2000) FL 29+27/7 FLC 1 FAC 1+2/1

ABBOTT Pawel Tadeusz Howard
Born: York, 2 December 1981
Height: 6'1" **Weight:** 11.12
This young Preston striker started the 2002-03 season on loan at Bury, where he was a popular recruit. He forged a useful partnership up front with Jon Newby and found the net on a number of occasions before being recalled to Deepdale to cover for an injury crisis. Pawel featured as a substitute against Reading, before scoring within ten minutes of his full debut for North End against Wimbledon. He then had a second spell on loan at Gigg Lane, although he was restricted to just 15 days, which took him up to the maximum 93 days allowed under Football League regulations.
Preston NE (£125,000 + from LKS Lodz, Poland on 16/2/2001) FL 6+10/4 FAC 1
Bury (Loaned on 9/8/2002) FL 13/5 FLC 2 Others 1
Bury (Loaned on 18/3/2003) FL 4/1

ABIDALLAH Nabil
Born: Amsterdam, Holland, 5 August 1982
Height: 5'7" **Weight:** 9.6
International Honours: Morocco: Yth
Nabil was only on the fringes of the Ipswich Town first-team squad last season and his only senior appearance came as a substitute in the FA Cup third round tie with Morecambe. Unable to establish himself because of the competition for midfield places, he was given a free transfer at the end of the campaign.
Ipswich T (Free from Ajax, Holland on 19/7/2000) PL 0+2 FAC 0+1

ACHTERBERG John
Born: Utrecht, Holland, 8 July 1971
Height: 6'1" **Weight:** 13.8
John became the undisputed first choice goalkeeper for Tranmere last term following the departure of Joe Murphy. Once again, he was in outstanding form, keeping 17 clean sheets and making numerous important saves. His campaign got off to a slow start, and after an early period of suspension he suffered concussion in the game against Wigan Athletic. However, John was ever-present from mid-October to early April and his

performances won him the title of 'Players' Player of the Year' at Prenton Park. John is efficient and unflappable but can be vocal when required. His positional sense and handling skills were impressive throughout the season.
Tranmere Rov (Free from PSV Eindhoven, Holland, ex NAC Breda, on 22/9/1998) FL 135+3 FLC 12+1 FAC 13 Others 3

ACIMOVIC Milenko
Born: Ljubljana, Slovenia, 15 February 1977
Height: 6'1" **Weight:** 12.8
International Honours: Slovenia: 46
This extremely talented attacking midfield player returned from a disappointing World Cup with a real point to prove. Milenko made five starts for Tottenham and came off the bench to feature in another 13 games but has yet to reap any reward from his lethal left foot. Goals will be his key objective in 2003-04 as he pushes for a regular first-team spot at White Hart Lane.
Tottenham H (Free from Red Star Belgrade, Yugoslavia, ex Olimpija, on 14/5/2002) PL 4+13 FLC 1

ACUNA Donoso Clarence Williams
Born: Coya Rancagua, Chile, 8 February 1975
Height: 5'8" **Weight:** 11.6
International Honours: Chile: 58; Yth
A torn thigh muscle delayed Clarence's start to the 2002-03 season, and following his recovery he found it difficult to break into Newcastle's first team. He played in the Worthington Cup tie against Everton in November, and then had to wait until New Year's Day to make his first Premiership start of the season at home to Liverpool when he gave an outstanding display. However, after three matches he lost his place again and never regained it. He is an energetic, consistent, box-to-box midfield player who protects his defence well but also finds time to create danger with his runs into the opposition penalty area. Despite his lack of first-team exposure he continued to be selected at international level for Chile.
Newcastle U (£900,000 from Universidad de Chile, ex O'Higgins, on 25/10/2000) PL 35+11/6 FLC 3+1 FAC 6+2/1 Others 0+1

ADAMS Daniel (Danny) Benjamin
Born: Manchester, 3 January 1976
Height: 5'8" **Weight:** 13.9
Danny was virtually ever present in the Macclesfield side during the 2002-03

season. He mostly played as the left wing back in a back-five formation, although for a spell of two months in the middle of the campaign he was the left back in a back four. A forceful player who is not afraid to make hard tackles, he is a solid and consistent all-round performer who has the ability to pass the ball with accuracy. During the away match at Hartlepool last August Danny scored his first-ever league goal with a superb header across the 'keeper.
Macclesfield T (£25,000 from Altrincham on 31/8/2000) FL 119+2/1 FLC 4+1 FAC 8 Others 2

ADAMS Stephen (Steve) Marc
Born: Plymouth, 25 September 1980
Height: 6'0" **Weight:** 11.10
Club Honours: Div 3 '02
Steve was again a mainstay in the heart of Plymouth Argyle's midfield during their Second Division campaign last term. The step up in class did not affect him and his excellent control and sensible passing were often seen at Home Park. He notched two goals, both in November, but unfortunately his season was curtailed for the last few weeks by a cartilage injury. Steve signed a new long-term contract in May.
Plymouth Arg (From trainee on 6/7/1999) FL 89+12/4 FLC 2 FAC 7+3 Others 3+2

ADEBOLA Bamberdele (Dele)
Born: Lagos, Nigeria, 23 June 1975
Height: 6'3" **Weight:** 12.8
Dele linked up with his former boss Trevor Francis when he signed a 12-month contract for Crystal Palace in the summer of 2002. Although hampered by injuries he featured regularly for the Eagles, but although he scored twice in the Worthington Cup victory over Cheltenham Town he generally found goals hard to come by. Dele is a tall and experienced striker with a trusted left foot. He was released by the Eagles in the close season.
Crewe Alex (From trainee on 21/6/1993) FL 98+26/39 FLC 4+3/2 FAC 8+2/3 Others 10+1/2
Birmingham C (£1,000,000 on 6/2/1998) FL 86+43/31 FLC 13+4/8 FAC 2+1/2 Others 1+2/1
Oldham Ath (Loaned on 20/3/2002) FL 5
Crystal Palace (Free on 15/8/2002) FL 32+7/5 FLC 5/2 FAC 4

AGYEMANG Patrick
Born: Walthamstow, 29 September 1980
Height: 6'1" **Weight:** 12.0

Patrick's third season of first-team involvement at Wimbledon could best be described as frustrating. Confined to the bench for most of the campaign due to the form of David Connolly and Neil Shipperley, he produced some marvellous 15-minute cameos when given late tastes of the action. Skilful and very pacy, he often tore tired-looking defences to shreads. His dozen or so starts were less memorable however, as he found it difficult to keep his repertoire of turns and tricks going for any concerted period. Additionally, he was also often asked to start in his less favoured wide position.
Wimbledon (From trainee on 11/5/1999) FL 45+50/13 FLC 2+2/1 FAC 7+3/1
Brentford (Loaned on 18/10/1999) FL 3+9 FAC 1

AINSWORTH Gareth
Born: Blackburn, 10 May 1973
Height: 5'9" **Weight:** 12.5
After coming to the end of his Wimbledon contract during the summer of 2002, Gareth signed on for another year just prior to the start of the new season, but found his first-team opportunities restricted due to the outstanding form of Jobi McAnuff. He went on loan to Walsall where he netted the equaliser at Nottingham Forest with a

neat header in the last game of his loan spell on New Year's Day. He then had a spell back in the Dons' line-up when McAnuff was injured before joining Cardiff in a short-term deal to boost their challenge for the play-offs. Gareth is a brave and pacy right winger who always shows 100 per cent commitment to the cause.
Preston NE (Signed from Northwich Vic, ex Blackburn Rov YTS, on 21/1/1992) FL 2+3 Others 1/1
Cambridge U (Free on 17/8/1992) FL 1+3/1 FLC 0+1
Preston NE (Free on 23/12/1992) FL 76+6/10 FLC 3+2 FAC 3+1 Others 8+1/1
Lincoln C (£25,000 on 31/10/1995) FL 83/37 FLC 8/3 FAC 2 Others 4/1
Port Vale (£500,000 on 12/9/1997) FL 53+2/10 FLC 2/1 FAC 2
Wimbledon (£2,000,000 on 3/11/1998) P/FL 21+15/6 FLC 1+11/4 FAC 5+2/1
Preston NE (Loaned on 28/3/2002) FL 3+2/1
Walsall (Loaned on 5/12/2002) FL 2+3/1
Cardiff C (£50,000 on 17/3/2003) FL 9

AISTON Samuel (Sam) James
Born: Newcastle, 21 November 1976
Height: 6'1" **Weight:** 12.10
Club Honours: Div 1 '96
International Honours: E: Sch
After an injury-interrupted 2001-02

Sam Aiston

campaign this skilful left winger was looking for a much better time at Shrewsbury last term. However, Sam was desperately unlucky to be stretchered off in the first game of the season against Exeter with cruciate ligament problems. He had to wait until late December for his next start, and after that many of his appearances came from the bench. As the Shrews' disastrous season came to an end Sam was reaching his best form. Out of contract, his future at Gay Meadow will depend upon newly appointed manager Jimmy Quinn.

Sunderland *(Free from Newcastle U juniors on 14/7/1995) P/FL 5+15 FLC 0+2 FAC 0+2*
Chester C *(Loaned on 21/2/1997) FL 14 Others 2*
Chester C *(Loaned on 27/11/1998) FL 11 Others 1*
Stoke C *(Loaned on 6/8/1999) FL 2+4 FLC 1*
Shrewsbury T *(Loaned on 24/12/1999) FL 10*
Shrewsbury T *(Free on 21/7/2000) FL 73+25/6 FLC 2 FAC 1+2 Others 0+3*

AKIN Bulent

Born: Brussels, Belgium, 28 August 1979
Height: 6'1" **Weight:** 12.4
International Honours: Turkey U21
Bulent arrived at Bolton with a big reputation in the summer of 2002, signing a three-year deal with the club. However, the move did not turn out to be as successful as Wanderers had hoped, for Bulent struggled to get into the first team and made just one Premiership appearance, in the New Year's Day defeat at Aston Villa. He also made two appearances in domestic cup ties, but it was no surprise when the young midfielder was released in March.
Bolton W *(Free from Galatasaray, Turkey, ex Anderlecht, Genclerbirligi, Salihlispor, Denzlispor, on 30/8/2002) PL 0+1 FLC 1 FAC 1*

AKINBIYI Adeola (Ade) Peter

Born: Hackney, 10 October 1974
Height: 6'1" **Weight:** 12.9
International Honours: Nigeria: 1
Ade spent some time recovering from injury and it was not until the Boxing Day game at Portsmouth that he first appeared for Crystal Palace. He managed just two starts, although he did find the net against Coventry, and in March he linked up with his former manager Tony Pulis when he joined Stoke City on loan. He clearly relished the challenge of trying to keep the Potteries club in the First Division and became popular with the fans after scoring two vital winners. However, he subsequently returned to Selhurst Park when the loan period was up.

Norwich C *(From trainee on 5/2/1993) P/FL 22+27/3 FLC 2+4/2 FAC 0+2 Others 0+1*
Hereford U *(Loaned on 21/11/1994) FL 3+1/2*
Brighton & Hove A *(Loaned on 24/11/1994) FL 7/4*
Gillingham *(£250,000 on 13/1/1997) FL 63/28 FLC 2 FAC 2/1 Others 0+1*
Bristol C *(£1,200,000 on 28/5/1998) FL 47/21 FLC 5/4 FAC 1*
Wolverhampton W *(£3,500,000 on 7/9/1999) FL 36+1/16 FLC 3*
Leicester C *(£5,000,000 on 28/7/2000) PL 49+9/11 FLC 1/1 FAC 5+1/1 Others 2*
Crystal Palace *(£2,200,000 + on 6/2/2002) FL 11+13/3 FAC 0+4*
Stoke C *(Loaned on 27/3/2003) FL 4/2*

ALCIDE Colin James

Born: Huddersfield, 14 April 1972
Height: 6'2" **Weight:** 13.10
This experienced striker began last season on the books at Cambridge, however at the end of August he joined Gainsborough Trinity. The move was initially a loan deal, but he was later released by the U's and remained at the Unibond League club on non-contract forms. In November he signed for Exeter City, for whom he made a single appearance against Hartlepool before being released once more.
Lincoln C *(£15,000 from Emley on 5/12/1995) FL 105+16/26 FLC 7+2/2 FAC 3+3/2 Others 3+1*
Hull C *(Loaned on 4/2/1999) FL 5/1*
Hull C *(Loaned on 10/3/1999) FL 22+2/3 FLC 3+1/2 FAC 0+2*
York C *(£80,000 on 23/11/1999) FL 33+20/7 FLC 1 FAC 2+1/1 Others 2*
Cambridge U *(£30,000 on 8/6/2001) FL 7+1 FLC 1/1 FAC 1 Others 1 (Freed on 4/10/2002)*
Exeter C *(Free from Gainsborough Trinity on 8/11/2002) FL 1*

ALDRIDGE Paul John

Born: Liverpool, 2 December 1981
Height: 5'11" **Weight:** 11.7
Paul signed for Macclesfield in the summer of 2002, but had a most unfortunate time during the 2002-03 campaign. The young midfielder broke the metatarsal bone in his left foot on his debut from the substitutes' bench during the second match of the campaign away at Leyton Orient, and having recovered from this injury he broke the same bone again in a reserve match at Stockport in November. He subsequently underwent surgery and only returned to reserve-team action in April. Paul was released during the close season. He is the son of the former Liverpool star John Aldridge.

Tranmere Rov *(From trainee on 24/3/2000) FL 0+6*
Macclesfield T *(Free on 28/3/2002) FL 0+1*

ALEXANDER Gary George

Born: Lambeth, 15 August 1979
Height: 5'11" **Weight:** 13.0
After a memorable first season with Hull, Gary's second term with the Tigers was something of a contrast, despite a superb hat-trick against Leyton Orient's Lee Thorpe the following month fell through, but he eventually returned to his east London roots when he joined the O's in January. A proven striker with a good goal-scoring record, he took a few games to regain fitness and settle, but then linked up well with Chris Tate and gave the fans a brief glimpse of what they can expect next term with a couple of goals at the end of the season.
West Ham U *(From trainee on 6/7/1998)*
Exeter C *(Loaned on 19/8/1999) FL 37/16 FLC 1 FAC 3/1 Others 4/2*
Swindon T *(£300,000 on 11/8/2000) FL 30+7/7 FLC 3 FAC 2+1 Others 2+1/2*
Hull C *(£160,000 on 21/6/2001) FL 64+4/23 FLC 3/2 FAC 3/2 Others 4/3*
Leyton Orient *(Signed on 27/1/2003) FL 12+5/2*

ALEXANDER Graham

Born: Coventry, 10 October 1971
Height: 5'10" **Weight:** 12.7
Club Honours: Div 2 '00
International Honours: S: 12
This Scottish international fullback had a steady season at Preston, scoring consistently mostly due to his penalty-taking skills. A rare goal from open play clinched a point at Walsall and he benefited from the return of Lee Cartwright, with whom he has an excellent understanding, after Christmas. Dangerous going forward and from dead-ball situations, Graham passed 200 appearances for the club and 550 career games, playing in all but one of North End's matches during the campaign.
Scunthorpe U *(From trainee on 20/3/1990) FL 149+10/18 FLC 11+1/2 FAC 12/1 Others 13+3/3*
Luton T *(£100,000 on 8/7/1995) FL 146+4/15 FLC 17/2 FAC 7+1 Others 6+2*
Preston NE *(£50,000 on 25/3/1999) FL 180/27 FLC 15/4 FAC 10/4 Others 6*

ALEXANDER John David

Born: Middlesbrough, 24 September 1985
Height: 5'11" **Weight:** 12.0
This young trainee made just one

appearance in the Darlington first team last term, coming on as a substitute at Kidderminster in August. John is a promising forward, who played regularly for the Quakers' reserves all season.
Darlington (Trainee) FL 0+1

ALEXANDER Neil
Born: Edinburgh, 10 March 1978
Height: 6'1" **Weight:** 11.0
Club Honours: S Div 2 '99; S Div 1 '01
International Honours: S: U21-10
This agile 'keeper grew in confidence as the 2002-03 season progressed and finished on a major high with three successive clean sheets for Cardiff in the Second Division play-offs. Martyn Margetson had a run of six games in goal during March and April, but Neil returned for the last six, and kept clean sheets in five of them. He earned a regular place in Bertie Vogts' Scotland squad, but was left frustrated as he was still waiting for a first cap by the end of the season.
Stenhousemuir (Free from Edina Hibs on 8/8/1996) SL 48 SLC 1 SC 1 Others 1
Livingston (Signed on 22/8/1998) SL 60 SLC 2 SC 8 Others 5
Cardiff C (£200,000 on 6/8/2001) FL 86 FLC 2 FAC 8 Others 5

ALEXANDERSSON Niclas
Born: Halmstad, Sweden, 29 December 1971
Height: 6'2" **Weight:** 11.8
International Honours: Sweden: 68
After a good World Cup with Sweden, including a goal against England, Niclas occupied the right-wing berth for Everton in four of the first six games of the season, but lost his place in the side following a series of injuries including tendonitis and inflammation behind his knee. He returned in December, but failed to make a first-team start again, although he did score in the infamous FA Cup defeat at Shrewsbury when he came on as a substitute. A skilful winger, he can pass the ball well and is also a good finisher.
Sheffield Wed (£750,000 from Gothenburg, Sweden, ex Halmstad, on 9/12/1997) PL 73+2/8 FLC 4+1/2 FAC 8/2
Everton (£2,500,000 on 20/7/2000) PL 49+9/4 FLC 2 FAC 4+2/1

ALIADIERE Jeremie
Born: Rambouillet, France, 30 March 1983
Height: 6'0" **Weight:** 11.8
Club Honours: FAYC '01
International Honours: France: Yth
Jeremie made his first-team debut for Arsenal as a substitute against

Birmingham City in the opening game of the season. Two matches later, he came off the bench and scored his first senior goal against West Bromwich Albion. A fast and strong young striker with good potential, he then missed three months with a hernia problem before returning to action with the Gunners' reserves. A good finisher, he should make more senior appearances next term, circumstances permitting.
Arsenal (From trainee on 4/4/2000) PL 0+4/1 FLC 0+2

ALJOFREE Hasney
Born: Manchester, 11 July 1978
Height: 6'0" **Weight:** 12.1
International Honours: E: Yth
Hasney began the 2002-03 campaign with Dundee United, but after a single appearance he moved south to join Plymouth Argyle. He enjoyed a good first season with the Pilgrims for whom he proved to be a capable left wing back and a more than competent central defender. Extremely comfortable on the left-hand side, Hasney worked the channel and delivered some telling crosses to create goal-scoring opportunities for his colleagues. He netted his first Plymouth goal with a fine header in the home victory over Notts County in December.
Bolton W (From trainee on 2/7/1996) F/PL 6+8 FLC 4+2 FAC 0+2
Dundee U (Signed on 9/6/2000) SL 52+2/4 SLC 5+1 SC 5+1/3
Plymouth Arg (Signed on 30/8/2002) FL 19/1 FLC 1 FAC 1 Others 1

ALLBACK Marcus
Born: Gothenburg, Sweden, 5 July 1973
Height: 6'0" **Weight:** 12.4
International Honours: Sweden: 32
Marcus struggled to establish a regular place at Aston Villa last season. He marked his debut for the club with a spectacular Intertoto Cup goal against FC Zurich, a stunning right-foot volley that crashed in off the underside of the bar, but subsequently spent most of his time on the bench. Marcus then came on and scored his first Premiership goal for the club against Fulham in November, he started the next game and was then back on the bench again. He is a powerful striker who makes great runs for his colleagues and is particularly effective in the air. Marcus continued to represent Sweden at international level during the campaign.
Aston Villa (£2,000,000 from Heerenveen, Holland, ex Orgryte, on 30/5/2002) PL 9+11/5 FLC 0+2 Others 3/1

ALLEN Bradley James
Born: Romford, 13 September 1971
Height: 5'8" **Weight:** 11.0
International Honours: E: U21-8; Yth
Bradley initially turned down Bristol Rovers in the 2002 close season, electing to take up a short-term contract with Peterborough United. However, he missed the opening games through injury and failed to impress when fully fit. He subsequently joined the Pirates in November and scored an important equaliser in his second appearance after coming off the substitutes' bench against Rochdale. Bradley's experience and ability to hold up the ball were welcome assets but he sustained a stomach injury and was released at the end of the season.
Queens Park R (From juniors on 30/9/1988) F/PL 56+25/27 FLC 5+2/5 FAC 3+2 Others 1
Charlton Ath (£400,000 on 28/3/1996) FL 30+10/9 FLC 3+1/2 FAC 0+2 Others 1+1
Colchester U (Loaned on 24/2/1999) FL 4/1
Grimsby T (Free on 12/7/1999) FL 46+34/15 FLC 5+6/4 FAC 0+2/1
Peterborough U (Free on 31/8/2002) FL 10+1/3 Others 1
Bristol Rov (Free on 28/11/2002) FL 5+3/1 FAC 1+1/1

ALLEN Graham
Born: Bolton, 8 April 1977
Height: 6'1" **Weight:** 12.8
International Honours: E: Yth
A composed defender, Graham was a near ever-present for Tranmere last term, starting either at right back or centre half. Despite a frequently changing line-up around him, his own form was unaffected and he even managed to grab two goals. Graham skippered the side from mid-February and led by example, taking every opportunity to go forward, while remaining rock steady in defence.
Everton (From trainee on 10/12/1994) PL 2+4
Tranmere Rov (Free on 28/8/1998) FL 153+6/9 FLC 12+2/1 FAC 12 Others 2

ALLISON Wayne Anthony
Born: Huddersfield, 16 October 1968
Height: 6'1" **Weight:** 12.6
Club Honours: Div 2 '96
Out of contract, Wayne signed for Sheffield United during the pre-season for one year. He became the regular target man after Iffy Onuora's injury, initially in the starting line-up but used mainly as a substitute later in the season. Powerful in the air, he was at times used as a lone striker, as at Anfield in the Worthington Cup semi-final. His goal tally was only seven but two were well received - against Sunderland (in the Worthington

Cup) and the Owls at Bramall Lane. Whatever the circumstances he always worked hard for the team and was given a year's extension to his contract.

Halifax T *(From trainee on 6/7/1987) FL* 74+10/23 FLC 3/2 FAC 4+1/2 Others 8+1/3
Watford *(£250,000 on 26/7/1989) FL* 6+1
Bristol C *(£300,000 on 9/8/1990) FL* 149+46/48 FLC 4+5/2 FAC 12+1/5 Others 6+2/2
Swindon T *(£475,000 on 22/7/1995) FL* 98+3/31 FLC 9/3 FAC 7/2 Others 3
Huddersfield T *(£800,000 on 11/11/1997) FL* 71+3/15 FLC 3+1/2 FAC 6/2
Tranmere Rov *(£300,000 on 3/9/1999) FL* 85+18/26 FLC 4+3/1 FAC 6+1/5 Others 1
Sheffield U *(Free on 30/7/2002) FL* 15+19/6 FLC 6/1 FAC 2+2 Others 0+2

ALLOTT Mark Stephen
Born: Manchester, 3 October 1977
Height: 5'11" **Weight:** 12.6
Mark began up front for Chesterfield last season but produced his most effective work in midfield, where his ability to lay the ball off and bring others into play was seen to good effect. His versatility helped the club during a difficult campaign and made him a valuable asset to the Spireites.

Oldham Ath *(From trainee on 14/10/1995) FL* 105+49/31 FLC 7+3/2 FAC 8+7 Others 1+3
Chesterfield *(Free on 19/12/2001) FL* 43+11/4 FLC 1+1/1 FAC 1 Others 2/1

ALLSOPP Daniel (Danny)
Born: Australia, 10 August 1978
Height: 6'1" **Weight:** 12.0
International Honours: Australia: U23-7; Yth
This tall and strong-running striker generally had a good season with Notts County last term, He was a regular in the side apart from injuries and his double-figure tally of goals ensured that he became a popular figure with the fans. It was something of a surprise when it was announced that Danny had been sold to Hull City during the summer.

Manchester C *(£10,000 from Carlton, Australia, ex South Melbourne Lakers, on 7/8/1998) P/FL 3+26/4 FLC 0+7/1 Others 1+1/1*
Notts Co *(Loaned on 5/11/1999) FL 3/1*
Wrexham *(Loaned on 25/2/2000) FL 3/4*
Bristol Rov *(Loaned on 12/10/2000) FL 4+2*
Notts Co *(£300,000 on 22/11/2000) FL* 97+8/42 FLC 3/4 FAC 8/4 Others 2+2/3
Hull C *(Signed on 7/5/2003)*

[ALPAY] OZALAN Fehmi
Born: Izmir, Turkey, 29 May 1973
Height: 6'2" **Weight:** 13.7

International Honours: Turkey: 80
Alpay is a tough-tackling defender who is good in the air and hard in the tackle. After missing half of the previous season with a bad ankle injury, he was always going to struggle to maintain a regular place in Aston Villa's side last term. He submitted a transfer request in August and only featured in five games for the club. On the few occasions when he appeared Alpay played as a central defender in either a back-four or back-five formation. On the international front he enjoyed a successful World Cup with Turkey and continued to represent his country during the campaign.

Aston Villa *(£5,600,000 from Fenerbahce, Turkey, ex Altay, Besiktas, on 31/7/2000) PL* 52 FLC 3 FAC 2 Others 8

ALSOP Julian Mark
Born: Nuneaton, 28 May 1973
Height: 6'4" **Weight:** 14.0
Club Honours: Div 3 '00
This tall, powerful striker again finished as top scorer for Cheltenham Town last term, netting 12 goals in all competitions. Julian was virtually ever-present in the first team throughout the season, missing only a handful of matches through illness, and proved invaluable not only for his skills up front, but also for his hard work and defensive abilities at set pieces. He was out of contract in the summer and at the time of writing his future was uncertain.

Bristol Rov *(£15,000 from Halesowen on 14/2/1997) FL 20+13/4 FLC 2/1 FAC 1/1 Others 2*
Swansea C *(Loaned on 20/1/1998) FL 5/2*
Swansea C *(£30,000 on 12/3/1998) FL 73+12/14 FLC 4+2 FAC 6+1/1 Others 5*
Cheltenham T *(Free on 3/7/2000) FL 99+18/35 FLC 4+1 FAC 8+2/6 Others 6+1/3*

AMANKWAAH Kevin Osei-Kuffour
Born: Harrow, 19 May 1982
Height: 6'1" **Weight:** 12.0
International Honours: E: Yth
This powerfully built attacking right back recovered fully from the broken neck he suffered in a car accident and was sent to Torquay on loan to regain match fitness. He showed strength, pace on the overlap and increasing confidence for the Gulls before being recalled to Ashton Gate. Kevin made a welcome return to Bristol City's first-team towards the end of the season and looked like making a difference when coming on as substitute in the second leg of the play-off semi-final against Cardiff City, but alas it was not to be.

Bristol C *(From trainee on 16/6/2000) FL* 30+14/1 FLC 1+1/1 FAC 0+1 Others 4+2/1
Torquay U *(Loaned on 25/1/2003) FL 6*

AMBROSE Darren Paul
Born: Harlow, 29 February 1984
Height: 5'11" **Weight:** 10.5
International Honours: E: U21-2; Yth
Darren made his full debut for Ipswich in the first game of the 2002-03 campaign at Walsall and scored his club's opening goal. However, he was unable to celebrate his success afterwards because he took the full force of the ball in his face later on in the game and needed 11 stitches in his mouth. A versatile midfield player who can play on either flank, he contributed more than his fare share of goals and was used effectively by Joe Royle as a second-half substitute to run at tired defences. In March he was sold to Newcastle United, but a troublesome knee injury prevented him making his debut for the club until the last game of the season when he came off the bench at West Bromwich.

Ipswich T *(From trainee on 3/7/2001) F/PL* 20+10/8 FLC 2/1 FAC 1+1/1 Others 3+1/1
Newcastle U *(£1,000,000 on 25/3/2003) PL 0+1*

AMEOBI Foluwashola (Shola)
Born: Zaria, Nigeria, 12 October 1981
Height: 6'2" **Weight:** 12.0
International Honours: E: U21-17
Shola is a tall, young striker whose first-team opportunities have been limited by the wealth of forward talent available at Newcastle, but who is a valued squad member. When colleagues' suspensions thrust him into leading the attack in Champions' League matches he showed he was able to cope with the pressures at the highest level by crowning an excellent display at Barcelona with a deserved goal and netting twice at Bayer Leverkusen. Very skilful on the ball he is becoming more of a physical threat too as he matures. He played regularly for the England U21 side, scoring twice at home to Portugal in March.

Newcastle U *(From trainee on 19/10/1998) PL* 24+39/7 FLC 2+1/2 FAC 2+2 Others 10+6/6

AMPADU Patrick Kwame
Born: Bradford, 20 December 1970
Height: 5'10" **Weight:** 11.10
Club Honours: AMC '94
International Honours: RoI: U21-4; Yth
The changes in management at Exeter last term did not always do Kwame any

favours as far as a first-team place was concerned. However, his experience was much needed in the defensive midfield position he occupied when recalled towards the end of the season by Gary Peters. Unfortunately he was unable to prevent the Grecians from being relegated from the Third Division.

Arsenal *(From trainee on 19/11/1988) FL 0+2*
Plymouth Arg *(Loaned on 31/10/1990) FL 6/1 Others 1*
West Bromwich A *(£50,000 on 24/6/1991) FL 27+22/4 FLC 6+1 FAC 1 Others 5/1*
Swansea C *(£15,000 on 16/2/1994) FL 128+19/12 FLC 8+1/1 FAC 5+1/1 Others 16/1*
Leyton Orient *(Free on 30/7/1998) FL 69+3/1 FLC 8 FAC 4+1/1 Others 1*
Exeter C *(Free on 18/7/2000) FL 80+15 FLC 2+1/1 FAC 4+1/1 Others 1*

ANDERSEN Trond
Born: Kristiansand, Norway, 6 January 1975
Height: 6'2" **Weight:** 12.8
International Honours: Norway: 29; B-1; U21-30; Yth
A series of niggling injuries meant that Trond missed a quarter of the 2002-03 campaign for Wimbledon, but when available he proved himself to be a key performer, whether playing in midfield or as a central defender. It was in the defensive position that he had his best games, reading the game well and starting many attacks with some thoughtful distribution. He also scored a memorable match-winning goal against Crystal Palace when venturing forward for a corner from that position. The last of the club's Norwegian imports to remain, his impressive displays helped him maintain his place in his country's national squad.
Wimbledon *(£2,500,000 from Molde, Norway, ex Clausenengen, on 9/8/1999) P/FL 136+10/6 FLC 9/1 FAC 12/1*

ANDERSON Iain
Born: Glasgow, 23 July 1977
Height: 5'8" **Weight:** 9.10
Club Honours: Div 2 '00
This winger disappeared almost entirely from the first-team scene at Preston under Craig Brown, making only one start in the Worthington Cup tie at Macclesfield, and his only North End goal was as a substitute in the FA Cup defeat by Rochdale. He joined Tranmere on loan on transfer deadline day, scoring on his debut against Chesterfield. Iain impressed at Prenton Park with his ability to play wide on either wing but returned to

Deepdale at the end of the season.
Dundee *(From juniors on 10/8/1994) SL 90+37/16 SLC 3+5 SC 6+3/2 Others 6+1/2*
(Signed by Toulouse, France on 28/7/1999)
Preston NE *(£500,000 from Toulouse, France on 18/2/2000) FL 46+36/13 FLC 5 FAC 3+1/1 Others 1+2*
Tranmere Rov *(Loaned on 27/3/2003) FL 7/2*

ANDERSON Ijah Massai
Born: Hackney, 30 December 1975
Height: 5'8" **Weight:** 10.6
Club Honours: Div 3 '99
Brentford's attacking left back had a run of ten consecutive games early last season, but was then sidelined by injury. Although recalled at centre back against Wigan in November, he went on loan to Wycombe soon afterwards. He impressed at Adams Park with his pacy forays down the wing before injury struck once more. In February Ijah joined Bristol Rovers in another loan deal and quickly became a firm favourite with the clubs' supporters, many acknowledging him as Ray Graydons' best signing of the season. Although hampered by an ankle problem, he helped the Pirates retain their Football League status and was reported to have signed permanently during the summer break.
Southend U *(From trainee at Tottenham H on 2/8/1994)*
Brentford *(Free on 31/7/1995) FL 196+6/4 FLC 19/1 FAC 5+3 Others 12+1*
Wycombe W *(Loaned on 27/11/2002) FL 5*
Bristol Rov *(Signed on 7/2/2003) FL 14*

ANDERSON John
Born: Greenock, 2 October 1972
Height: 6'2" **Weight:** 12.2
Club Honours: S Div 2 '95; S Div 1 '01
John turned from Lion to Tiger when he joined Hull City from Livingston in the summer of 2002. It was intended that the experienced centre back would partner former Motherwell defender Greg Strong at the heart of the City rearguard. In reality, Greg's misfortune meant that John spent the majority of the term on the left-hand side with his partner changing on a regular basis. However, he proved to be the model of consistency in a campaign dogged by inconsistency and deservedly won the club's 'Player of the Season' award.
Morton *(Signed from Gourock YAC on 25/1/1994) SL 97+3/18 SLC 5/1 SC 9/2 Others 5+1/1*
Livingston *(Signed on 5/6/2000) SL 42+1/3 SLC 3 SC 7/2 Others 4/2*
Hull C *(Free on 17/6/2002) FL 42+1/1 FLC 1 FAC 1*

ANDERTON Darren Robert
Born: Southampton, 3 March 1972
Height: 6'1" **Weight:** 12.5
Club Honours: FLC '99
International Honours: E: 30; B-1; U21-12; Yth
The talented midfielder returned from a knee injury sustained in the summer to take his place in a central midfield position for Tottenham in a 3-5-2 formation. Darren's ability is unquestionable, but his fitness often prevents him from getting a consistent run in the team and that was the case again last season. He went on to make only half of the possible starts and Spurs form dipped as a result. At his best, Darren produces much of the skill and determination that saw him win a regular England place and is a great playmaker as well as a fine finisher.
Portsmouth *(From trainee on 5/2/1990) FL 53+9/7 FLC 3+2/1 FAC 7+1/5 Others 2*
Tottenham H *(£1,750,000 on 3/6/1992) PL 257+22/33 FLC 27+1/6 FAC 25+2/6*

ANDRE Pierre-Yves
Born: Lannion, France, 14 May 1974
Height: 6'1" **Weight:** 12.1
A tall and pacy striker, Pierre-Yves made his debut for Bolton in the away fixture at West Bromwich Albion. Although he did not start a game for Wanderers, he made some very important contributions from the substitutes' bench, particularly as the season drew to a close. He figured in the final six Premiership games and was particularly influential in the crucial home fixture against West Ham. Pierre-Yves seemed to favour dropping deep to use his pace against opposing defenders and his positive displays certainly endeared him to the Reebok faithful.
Bolton W *(Loaned from Nantes, France, ex US Lannion, Rennes, Bastia, on 31/1/2003) PL 0+9*

ANDREWS Keith Joseph
Born: Dublin, 13 September 1980
Height: 5'11" **Weight:** 11.5
Midfield was probably the strongest area of the Wolves' squad and Keith found it hard to break into the side last season. Injury conspired to keep him out of the first 16 matches, and when he made the squad it was initially as a substitute. He continued to pass the ball well but needed a good run in the team to establish himself. Keith made his third start in the FA Cup quarter-final at Southampton when he had the misfortune to suffer a broken leg, which brought his campaign to a premature end.

Nicolas Anelka

Wolverhampton W (From trainee on 26/9/1997) FL 26+18 FAC 3
Oxford U (Loaned on 10/11/2000) FL 4/1 Others 1

ANDREWS Lee David
Born: Carlisle, 23 April 1983
Height: 6'0" Weight: 10.12
After a fine first season in which he was voted 'Player of the Year', Lee had a more patchy campaign with Carlisle in 2002-03. Injury and loss of form kept him out of the team for a long period in mid-season and he later went on loan to Rochdale. He featured both at right wing back and in the centre of a back three for Dale and the change seems to have benefited him, for he was restored to the line-up soon after his return to Brunton Park.
Carlisle U (From trainee on 27/6/2001) FL 48+6 FLC 0+1 FAC 3+1
Rochdale (Loaned on 25/2/2003) FL 8

ANDREWS Wayne Michael Hill
Born: Paddington, 25 November 1977
Height: 5'10" Weight: 11.12
After a slow start, Wayne began to make the most of his second chance in professional football with Oldham Athletic last term. Signed from Ryman League club Chesham United during the summer of 2002, he quickly became a first-team regular and by May he had emerged as the club's most potent striker, scoring 12 goals. Pace was Wayne's chief asset and he likes to attack defenders from wide positions, starting with his back to goal before turning and unleashing his speed.
Watford (From trainee on 5/7/1996) FL 16+12/4 FLC 3+2/1 FAC 0+2 Others 2/1 (Free to St Albans C during 1999 close season)
Cambridge U (Loaned on 2/10/1998) FL 1+1
Peterborough U (Loaned on 5/2/1999) FL 8+2/5
Oldham Ath (Free from Chesham U on 30/5/2002) FL 28+9/11 FLC 1+2 FAC 2+1 Others 3/1

ANELKA Nicolas
Born: Versailles, France, 14 March 1979
Height: 6'0" Weight: 12.3
Club Honours: PL '98; FAC '98; CS '98
International Honours: France: 28
Manchester City's record signing was an ever-present for the Blues in all competitions last season. He started well and after getting his first goals against Everton he netted in the next two matches also. Nicolas enjoyed another good scoring run in November, his tally including the opening goal in the Manchester 'derby' which certainly endeared him to the fans. His return of goals was fairly poor in the remainder of

the second half of the season, although this coincided with a period when the team was struggling at times. However, his two goals on his return to Anfield were the best of the 14 he scored for City, particularly the winner in injury time. A striker of exceptional pace and skill, if a good partner can be found to link up with him next season more goals will follow.
Arsenal (£500,000+ from Paris St Germain on 6/3/1997) PL 50+15/23 FLC 3 FAC 13+1/3 Others 7+1/2 (£22,900,000 to Real Madrid, Spain on 20/8/1999)
Liverpool (Loaned from Paris St Germain on 24/12/2001) PL 13+7/4 FAC 2/1
Manchester C (£13,000,000 from Paris St Germain, France on 16/7/2002) PL 38/14 FLC 2 FAC 1

ANGEL Juan Pablo Aranzo
Born: Medellin, Colombia, 24 October 1975
Height: 6'0" Weight: 11.6
International Honours: Colombia: 19; Yth
Juan Pablo struggled to hold down a regular place in the Aston Villa first team last season. Whilst half of his appearances were made from the substitutes' bench almost all the remainder resulted in him being replaced. Despite this he remained a great favourite amongst the fans. He netted just three times, with his only Premiership goal coming in the home game with Fulham. Juan Pablo is a striker with plenty of technical ability, who is strong in the air and a cool finisher. He was voted supporters' 'Player of the Year' for the campaign.
Aston Villa (£9,500,000 + from River Plate, Argentina, ex Atletico Nacional, on 19/1/2001) PL 41+12/14 FLC 1+3/1 FAC 3/1 Others 2+2/4

ANGEL Mark
Born: Newcastle, 23 August 1975
Height: 5'10" Weight: 12.4
Club Honours: NC '02
International Honours: E: SP-3
A skilful player whose performances on the left side of a four-man midfield gave Boston an added dimension last season. On his best days Mark was able to beat opposing defenders almost at will before producing a supply of dangerous crosses into the box. He finished the campaign as penalty taker, but also came up with some spectacular goals from open play.
Sunderland (Free from Walker Central on 31/12/1993)
Oxford U (Free on 9/8/1995) FL 40+33/4 FLC 4+4 FAC 4+2 Others 2+1/1

West Bromwich A (Free on 2/7/1998) FL 4+21/1 FLC 0+1 FAC 1+1
Darlington (Free on 8/8/2000) FL 1+4 FLC 2+1/1
Queen of the South (Free on 22/1/2001) SL 4+1/1
Boston U (Free on 13/6/2001) FL 24+7/5 FLC 2 FAC 1 Others 2/1

ANGELL Brett Ashley Mark
Born: Marlborough, 20 August 1968
Height: 6'2" Weight: 13.11
Club Honours: Div 2 '00
This experienced striker originally joined Port Vale on trial last August. A burly leader of the line, Brett soon made his presence felt and helped the younger members of the squad along, which was exactly what was required. He still knew where the goal was and managed seven in 17 appearances including a very important brace against Notts County that helped the club to five successive victories. His contract expired in October and he moved on to Queen's Park Rangers. Brett was a regular starter at Loftus Road during Paul Furlong's injury, but when Furlong returned he was relegated to the bench. Surprisingly he failed to increase his career tally of goals for Rangers.
Portsmouth (From trainee on 1/8/1986)
Derby Co (£40,000 from Cheltenham T on 19/2/1988)
Stockport Co (£33,000 on 20/10/1988) FL 60+10/28 FLC 3 FAC 3/1 Others 8/4
Southend U (£100,000 on 2/8/1990) FL 109+6/47 FLC 7+1/4 FAC 3/2 Others 9+1/10
Everton (£500,000 on 17/11/1994) PL 16+4/1 FLC 0+1
Sunderland (£600,000 on 23/3/1995) FL 10 FLC 1/1
Sheffield U (Loaned on 30/1/1996) FL 6/2
West Bromwich A (Loaned on 28/3/1996) FL 0+3
Stockport Co (£120,000 on 19/8/1996) FL 122+4/50 FLC 16+3/7 FAC 7/4 Others 4+1/1
Notts Co (Loaned on 9/12/1999) FL 6/5
Preston NE (Loaned on 24/2/2000) FL 9+6/8
Walsall (Free on 27/7/2000) FL 36+25/16 FLC 2+1 FAC 2+3/2 Others 0+1
Rushden & Diamonds (Free on 8/2/2002) FL 3+2/2 Others 0+2
Port Vale (Free on 7/8/2002) FL 13+2/5 FLC 0+1 Others 1/2
Queens Park R (Free on 22/11/2002) FL 8+5

ANGUS Stevland (Stev) Dennis
Born: Westminster, 16 September 1980
Height: 6'0" Weight: 12.0
Club Honours: FAYC '99
This talented defender continued in the

2002-03 season where he had left off the previous one, and he was a linchpin of the defence throughout the campaign. He formed excellent partnerships with Andy Duncan and Izzy Iriekpen and his consistency was rewarded with 'Player of the Week' awards on more than one occasion.

West Ham U *(From trainee on 2/7/1999)*
Bournemouth *(Loaned on 11/8/2000) FL 7+2*
Cambridge U *(Free on 19/7/2001) FL 81 FLC 3 FAC 7 Others 8+1*

ANTOINE-CURIER Mickael
Born: Orsay, France, 5 March 1983
Height: 6'0" **Weight:** 12.4
This gangly Nottingham Forest striker featured regularly for the reserves last term, but failed to make a breakthrough at first-team level. He joined Brentford on loan in the closing stages of the campaign and initially found it tough going. However, he scored two vital goals at Chesterfield to make the Bees mathematically safe from the drop. Mickael was released by Forest in the summer.

Preston NE *(Signed from Nancy, France on 29/11/2000)*
Nottingham F *(Free on 22/6/2001)*
Brentford *(Loaned on 10/3/2003) FL 11/3*

ANTWI William (Will)
Born: London, 19 October 1982
Height: 6'2" **Weight:** 12.8
This promising young Crystal Palace defender spent much of last season developing in the club's reserves and was only on the fringes of the first team. He made his senior debut in the Worthington Cup tie against Cheltenham in October, and received his only start in the quarter-final tie of the same competition against Sheffield United. Otherwise, Will only managed a handful of first-team appearances from the bench and he was released in the summer.

Crystal Palace *(From trainee on 12/7/2002) FL 0+4 FLC 1+2*

APPLEBY Matthew (Matty)
Wilfred
Born: Middlesbrough, 16 April 1972
Height: 5'8" **Weight:** 11.12
Despite Oldham's promotion challenge, first-team captain Matty Appleby endured a somewhat torrid 2002-03 campaign. He was sidelined by a hip problem in September and went on to make just three more league appearances throughout the rest of the season. The 30-year-old may find it hard to regain his first-team place next term in the final year of his contract.

Newcastle U *(From trainee on 4/5/1990) F/PL 18+2 FLC 2+1 FAC 2 Others 2+2*
Darlington *(Loaned on 25/11/1993) FL 10/1 Others 1*
Darlington *(Free on 15/6/1994) FL 77+2/7 FLC 2 FAC 4 Others 8/3*
Barnsley *(£200,000 on 19/7/1996) F/PL 131+8/7 FLC 10+3 FAC 6+2 Others 3*
Oldham Ath *(Free on 15/11/2002) FL 27+2/2*

APPLEBY Richard (Richie)
Dean
Born: Middlesbrough, 18 September 1975
Height: 5'9" **Weight:** 11.4
Club Honours: Div 3 '00
International Honours: E: Yth
Signed by his former Swansea and Kidderminster boss Jan Molby, Richie

Matty Appleby

viewed his move to ambitious Hull on a three-year contract as an excellent opportunity. Unfortunately, his first Tiger term turned out to be extremely frustrating. He missed the start of the season due to tendonitis in a knee joint and, apart from the Worthington Cup tie with Leicester, did not make his City debut until February. Initially intended to operate on the right of a new midfield trio with Ian Ashbee and Stuart Green, Hull undoubtedly missed Richie's bravery and confidence on the ball.

Newcastle U (From trainee on 12/8/1993) Others 2
Ipswich T (Free on 12/12/1995) FL 0+3 Others 1
Swansea C (Free on 16/8/1996) FL 90+30/11 FLC 4+4 FAC 5+1/2 Others 3+4/1
Kidderminster Hrs (Free on 9/11/2001) FL 18+1/4 FAC 1
Hull C (Free on 3/7/2002) FL 6 FLC 1

ARANALDE Zigor

Born: Guipuzcoa, Spain, 28 February 1973
Height: 6'1" **Weight:** 13.5
This enterprising attacking left-sided defender has missed only nine games in his first three seasons with Walsall, and last term he came back bravely just a month after cracking ribs in the Worthington Cup tie at Blackburn, an occasion when he netted his fourth penalty in seven games. Although occasionally struggling defensively he consistently stuck to his game and showed ice-cool temperament when netting a first-minute penalty to earn a point at Derby.

Walsall (Free from CD Logrones, Spain, ex Albacete, Marbella, Seville, on 11/8/2000) FL 126+3/5 FLC 9/1 FAC 10 Others 3

ARBER Mark Andrew

Born: Johannesburg, South Africa, 9 October 1977
Height: 6'1" **Weight:** 12.11
This experienced central defender began last season with Conference club Barnet before moving on to Peterborough United shortly before Christmas. A powerful figure in the air, Mark was eventually appointed captain of the Posh team, leading them up the table to safety. A talented player who is not just a 'boot-it-anywhere' defender, he played on through the last few weeks of the campaign even though he was carrying an injury.

Tottenham H (From trainee on 27/3/1996)

Barnet (£75,000 on 18/9/1998) FL 123+2/15 FLC 4 FAC 3 Others 8/1
Peterborough U (Free on 9/12/2002) FL 24+1/2

ARCA Julio Andres

Born: Quilmes Bernal, Argentine, 31 January 1981
Height: 5'10" **Weight:** 11.6
International Honours: Argentina: Yth (World Yth '01)
Sunderland's Argentine U20 international endured a frustrating season full of niggling injuries and found himself out of favour at times as the club changed management twice. Left-sided, Julio can operate in midfield or on the wing and his trickery on the ball has made him a great favourite with the Wearsiders' fans. His first start of the season against Aston Villa in September saw him produce a magnificent 20-yard cross-field pass for David Bellion to score the winner. Julio scored his only goals of the campaign in cup competitions, including an extra-time strike against Bolton in the FA Cup third round replay.

Sunderland (£3,500,000 from Argentinos Juniors, Argentine on 31/8/2000) PL 53+9/3 FLC 4/2 FAC 6/1

ARDLEY Neal Christopher

Born: Epsom, 1 September 1972
Height: 5'11" **Weight:** 11.9
International Honours: E: U21-10
Neal initially joined Watford on weekly terms, but was quickly signed up on a full contract. A right-sided utility player, he proved a real asset: he missed only three matches and was a model of consistency and reliability. An excellent crosser of the ball and an expert at corner kicks and set pieces, Neal contributed more assists than any other player, and laid on three of the Watford goals in the famous 7-4 victory at Burnley.

Wimbledon (From trainee on 29/7/1991) F/PL 212+33/18 FLC 22+3/5 FAC 27+4/3
Watford (Free on 9/8/2002) FL 42+1/2 FLC 1 FAC 5

ARMSTRONG Alun

Born: Gateshead, 22 February 1975
Height: 6'1" **Weight:** 11.13
Club Honours: Div 1 '98
Alun's season was again disrupted by injury at Ipswich in 2002-03 and he only made the starting line-up on 13 occasions. He helped maintain the club's unbeaten home European record when he notched the equaliser against Sartid in September and his only other goal came in the league game at Watford. A useful

striker when fully fit, he was given a free transfer in the summer.

Newcastle U (From trainee on 1/10/1993)
Stockport Co (£50,000 on 23/6/1994) FL 151+8/48 FLC 22/8 FAC 10+1/5 Others 7
Middlesbrough (£1,500,000 on 16/2/1998) P/FL 10+19/9 FLC 4
Huddersfield T (Loaned on 23/3/2000) FL 4+2
Ipswich T (£500,000 + on 8/12/2000) P/FL 45+27/12 FLC 2+1/1 FAC 2+1/1 Others 5+2/3

ARMSTRONG Steven Craig

Born: South Shields, 23 May 1975
Height: 5'11" **Weight:** 12.10
This left-sided midfielder had a rather disappointing season at Sheffield Wednesday in 2002-03. Craig was a regular member of the side early on and always produced steady, hard-working displays, but he was then sidelined by injury towards the end of November and he failed to return to first-team action before the summer break. His only goal for the Owls came in the home defeat by Rotherham in August.

Nottingham F (From trainee on 2/6/1992) P/FL 24+16 FLC 6+2/2 FAC 1
Burnley (Loaned on 29/12/1994) FL 4
Bristol Rov (Loaned on 8/11/1996) FL 4
Bristol Rov (Loaned on 28/3/1996) FL 9+1
Gillingham (Loaned on 18/10/1996) FL 10 FLC 2 Others 1
Watford (Loaned on 24/1/1997) FL 3
Watford (Loaned on 14/3/1997) FL 12
Huddersfield T (£750,000 on 26/2/1999) FL 101+6/5 FLC 7+1 FAC 2 Others 1+1
Sheffield Wed (£100,000 on 15/2/2002) FL 24+1/1 FLC 2

ARMSTRONG Christopher (Chris)

Born: Newcastle, 5 August 1982
Height: 5'10" **Weight:** 10.8
International Honours: E: Yth
This Newcastle-born player had an excellent season for Oldham Athletic in 2002-03. Outstanding as either the left-sided centre half in a back three or on the left side of midfield, he attracted the attentions of several higher-league clubs. Chris, whose older brother Gordon plays for Burnley, is a determined defender with tremendous drive who carries the ball from defence to great effect. Capped by England at U20 level in the Toulon Tournament in the summer of 2002, he is developing into an exciting prospect.

Bury (From trainee on 2/3/2001) FL 33/1 FLC 1 Others 3
Oldham Ath (£200,000 on 22/10/2001) FL 64+1/1 FLC 2 FAC 6 Others 6

ARMSTRONG Christopher (Chris) Peter
Born: Newcastle, 19 June 1971
Height: 6'0" **Weight:** 13.3
Club Honours: Div 1 '94; FLC '99
International Honours: E: B-1
Chris initially joined Bolton Wanderers on a short-term contract in August 2002. Early reserve-team showings confirmed that he was a little short of match fitness, although he made his first-team debut in the Worthington Cup defeat at home to local rivals Bury in October. This turned out to be his only taste of senior action and, whilst appearing with some regularity throughout the season for the second string, his future at the Reebok was unsure at the end of the season.
Wrexham (Free from Llay Welfare on 3/3/1989) FL 40+20/13 FLC 2+1 FAC 0+1 Others 5+1/3
Millwall (£50,000 on 16/8/1991) FL 11+17/5 FLC 3+1/2 FAC 0+1 Others 5+1/3
Crystal Palace (£1,000,000 on 1/9/1992)
F/PL 118/45 FLC 8/6 FAC 8/5 Others 2/1
Tottenham H (£4,500,000 on 30/6/1995) PL 117+24/48 FLC 15/10 FAC 9+5/4 Others 3
Bolton W (Free on 28/8/2002) FLC 1

ARMSTRONG Gordon Ian
Born: Newcastle, 15 July 1967
Height: 6'0" **Weight:** 12.11
Club Honours: Div 3 '88
Gordon was very much a bit player in Burnley's 2002-03 campaign, making the starting line-up just once, plus a handful of appearances from the bench. His experience and versatility in defence and midfield have served the Clarets well over the last five seasons since he became one of Stan Ternent's first signings for the club, but it now seems that his age is a barrier to further regular First Division football, and if he is to continue playing it may have to be at a lower level.
Sunderland (From apprentice on 10/7/1985) FL 331+18/50 FLC 25+4/3 FAC 19/4 Others 18+1/4
Bristol C (Loaned on 24/8/1995) FL 6
Northampton T (Loaned on 5/11/1996) FL 4/1 Others 1
Bury (Free on 16/7/1996) FL 49+22/4 FLC 5+2/2 FAC 2+1 Others 1+1
Burnley (Free on 27/8/1998) FL 88+17/5 FLC 2 FAC 3+3

ARMSTRONG Ian
Born: Kirkby, 16 November 1981
Height: 5'7" **Weight:** 10.2
International Honours: E: Yth; Sch
This lightweight Port Vale forward usually operates on the left-hand side but can also play on the right or down the middle if required. Ian looked dangerous last term with his mazy runs, but tended to be in and out of the side due to fitness problems, mostly hamstring trouble. He has a very good shot on him and proved he was a good finisher as he ended up joint-top scorer with eight goals including several spectacular efforts.
Liverpool (From trainee on 16/12/1998)
Port Vale (Free on 2/7/2001) FL 40+20/10 FLC 0+1 FAC 1+1 Others 4+1/3

ARNDALE Neil Darren
Born: Bristol, 26 April 1984
Height: 5'9" **Weight:** 10.0
International Honours: E: Yth
Second-year scholar Neil made his senior debut for Bristol Rovers in the LDV Vans Trophy tie at Exeter City in an unfamiliar right-wing spot and followed this up with his first league start in the following match against Leyton Orient on the left wing. A regular reserve-team member last

Craig Armstrong

term, he is expected to make a strong challenge for a first-team place in the coming season.
Bristol Rov (Trainee) FL 1+1 Others 1

ARNISON Paul Simon
Born: Hartlepool, 18 September 1977
Height: 5'10" **Weight:** 10.12
Although not a Hartlepool first-team regular last term, Paul was a useful squad member whose versatility allowed him to cover in a variety of defensive positions as well as in midfield. Locally born, he will appreciate more than most being part of a Hartlepool promotion team. A rare goal-scorer, he netted with a fine 25-yard volley against Bristol Rovers.
Newcastle U (From trainee on 1/3/1996)
Hartlepool U (Free on 10/3/2000) FL 51+22/3 FLC 2 FAC 2+1 Others 8/2

ARTELL David (Dave) John
Born: Rotherham, 22 November 1980
Height: 6'2" **Weight:** 13.9
This young Rotherham central defender joined Shrewsbury on loan for a month, and this was then extended until the end of the season following Mickey Heathcote's injury. Dave made a very assured debut in the 1-1 draw at Scunthorpe in September and in his third game, at Carlisle, he headed the winner in a 2-1 victory. However, that was probably as good as it got for Dave as Shrewsbury leaked a massive 92 goals in league games.
Rotherham U (From trainee on 1/7/1999) FL 35+2/4 FAC 3 Others 1
Shrewsbury T (Loaned on 26/9/2002) FL 27+1/1 FAC 3 Others 5

ASABA Carl Edward
Born: London, 28 January 1973
Height: 6'2" **Weight:** 13.4
Carl began the season at Sheffield United as one of two strikers, feeding off a target man. He worked hard for the team without looking particularly sharp in front of goal. Coming off the bench at Brighton, following a back injury, he scored a hat-trick in 11 minutes (including two penalties) but he was in and out of the starting line-up until January when an achilles injury sidelined him for three months. Carl returned rejuvenated, working very hard for the side, troubling defenders and scoring vital goals to clinch a play-off place.
Brentford (Free from Dulwich Hamlet on 9/8/1994) FL 49+5/25 FLC 5 FAC 4 Others 7/2
Colchester U (Loaned on 16/2/1995) FL 9+3/2
Reading (£800,000 on 7/8/1997) FL 31+2/8 FLC 7+2/3 FAC 3/1

Gillingham *(£600,000 on 28/8/1998) FL 65+12/36 FLC 3/2 FAC 1+1 Others 9/2*
Sheffield U *(£92,500 + on 8/3/2001) FL 52+15/23 FLC 6+1/1 FAC 2+1 Others 3*

ASAMOAH Derek
Born: Ghana, 1 May 1981
Height: 5'6" **Weight:** 10.12
This forceful Northampton striker was one of the few bright spots in an otherwise poor season at Sixfields. Although most of his appearances were as a substitute he showed the ability to change the course of a game with his clever ball play. Derek has the pace and ability to take on opponents and beat them, while he is proof that there is an abundance of talent in the lower reaches of grassroots football.
Northampton T (Free from Slough T, ex Barking, Hampton & Richmond Borough, on 26/7/2001) FL 23+59/7 FLC 0+3 FAC 2+2/1 Others 2+2/1

ASHBEE Ian
Born: Birmingham, 6 September 1976
Height: 6'1" **Weight:** 13.7
International Honours: E: Yth
Ian had a rather unfortunate start to his Hull career, receiving a red card on his debut Southend at Boothferry Park. However, that was to be an indication of his combative instincts as the Tigers' midfield general proved to be a reassuring presence in their Third Division battles. As well as winning the ball, Ian's intelligent passing regularly prompted the attack. A spectacular volleyed goal in the 4-1 win at Torquay in Peter Taylor's first game in charge was to be his highlight as, after suffering torn ankle ligaments against Shrewsbury in March, he missed the closing stages of the season.
Derby Co (From trainee on 9/11/1994) FL 1
Cambridge U (Free on 13/12/1996) FL 192+11/11 FLC 7 FAC 15 Others 9+1
Hull C (Free on 3/7/2002) FL 31/1 FLC 1/1 FAC 1

ASHBY Barry John
Born: Park Royal, 2 November 1970
Height: 6'2" **Weight:** 13.8
Club Honours: FAYC '89
Barry had another fine season at Gillingham, and it was only when he was missing through injury that his importance as a vital cog in the defence alongside Chris Hope was seen. He is a reliable central defender who is composed on the ball and is always dangerous when joining the attack for set pieces. During the course of the season Barry moved into the top 20 of all-time league appearances for the Gills.

Watford *(From trainee on 1/12/1988) FL 101+13/3 FLC 6 FAC 4 Others 2+1*
Brentford *(Signed on 22/3/1994) FL 119+2/4 FLC 11 FAC 9/1 Others 11+1*
Gillingham *(£140,000 on 8/8/1997) FL 226+2/6 FLC 15 FAC 17/1 Others 9/1*

ASHCROFT Lee
Born: Preston, 7 September 1972
Height: 5'10" **Weight:** 11.10
International Honours: E: U21-1
This versatile striker suffered another difficult season with Wigan Athletic and managed just a single appearance from the bench in the Worthington Cup victory over West Bromwich Albion. Out of favour at the club, Lee joined Port Vale on loan in October, where he acquitted himself well without being offered a permanent deal. He impressed in a similar spell at Huddersfield, but failed to find the net and soon after returning to the JJB Stadium his contract was paid up. Lee spent the remainder of the season at Conference club Southport in the capacity of player-coach.
Preston NE (From trainee on 16/7/1991) FL 78+13/13 FLC 3 FAC 5 Others 6+2/1
West Bromwich A (£250,000 on 1/8/1993) FL 66+24/17 FLC 2+3 FAC 3+1/1 Others 8+3
Notts Co (Loaned on 28/3/1996) FL 4+2
Preston NE (£150,000 on 5/9/1996) FL 63+1/22 FLC 4 FAC 5/5 Others 2+1
Grimsby T (£500,000 on 12/8/1998) FL 52+9/15 FLC 7/2 FAC 1
Wigan Ath (£250,000 on 9/8/2000) FL 37+9/8 FLC 1+1 FAC 3+1/1 Others 0+2
Port Vale (Loaned on 11/10/2002) FL 3 Others 1
Huddersfield T (Loaned on 13/12/2002) FL 4

ASHDOWN Jamie Lawrence
Born: Wokingham, 30 November 1980
Height: 6'3" **Weight:** 14.10
This young 'keeper joined Bournemouth on loan last term and made two impressive appearances for the Cherries. His bravery helped secure a 1-0 win at Macclesfield, but it was at a cost though, and he returned to Reading to have treatment for a knee injury. He subsequently replaced Phil Whitehead as deputy to Marcus Hahnemann, and kept the bench warm as substitute 'keeper for the second half of the campaign. However, Jamie's first-team experience for the Royals was limited to a single appearance, keeping a clean sheet in a 3-0 win at Grimsby.
Reading (From trainee on 26/11/1999) FL 2+1 FAC 1 Others 2
Bournemouth (Loaned on 22/8/2002) FL 2

ASHIKODI Moses
Born: Lagos, Nigeria, 27 June 1987
Height: 6'0" **Weight:** 11.9
International Honours: E: Yth
Moses became the youngest-ever player to appear in a Millwall shirt when he made his debut as a second-half substitute at Brighton in February aged just 15 years and 240 days. The towering striker, capped by England at U16 level, enjoyed a unique season in 2002-03, appearing for the Lions at four levels: U17, U19, reserve and senior. Moses has great pace, a good first touch and a tremendous shot.
Millwall *(Associated Schoolboy) FL 0+5*

ASHINGTON Ryan David
Born: Torbay, 28 March 1983
Height: 5'10" **Weight:** 12.6
After missing the whole of the 2001-02 season through injury, this young Torquay midfielder needed a run of games to get back to full match fitness. However, he managed just a couple of outings from the substitutes' bench before he departed just before Christmas. Ryan subsequently linked up with Dr Martens League club Newport County.
Torquay U *(From trainee on 12/7/2001) FL 9+7 FLC 1+1 FAC 0+2 Others 0+1*

ASHTON Dean
Born: Crewe, 24 November 1983
Height: 6'1" **Weight:** 13.11
International Honours: E: Yth
Dean struggled with injuries and a lack of goal-scoring form early on in the 2002-03 season, but eventually put these problems behind him. He went on to finish with a respectable tally of 16 goals for Crewe, including a hat-trick in the 8-0 win over Doncaster Rovers in the LDV Vans Trophy. Dean is a talented young striker who will be looking to continue in similar vein in the 2003-04 campaign.
Crewe Alex *(From trainee on 6/2/2001) FL 65+26/24 FLC 1+1 FAC 5+3/5 Others 3/5*

ASHTON Jonathan (Jon) James
Born: Nuneaton, 4 October 1982
Height: 6'2" **Weight:** 13.7
This promising young defender occasionally featured from the substitutes' bench for Leicester last season, and was particularly effective when coming on in the Worthington Cup victory at Hillsborough. In December Jon was loaned to Notts County to gain more experience, and certainly did not let anyone down in his outings at centre back. Injury meant that he returned early to Filbert Street and he added another

appearance for the Foxes from the bench in the final home fixture against Norwich, when he had the unusual experience of substituting a substitute. Jon was offered a free transfer at the end of the season.
Leicester C *(From trainee on 29/1/2001) P/FL 3+6 FLC 0+1*
Notts Co *(Loaned on 8/11/2002) FL 4*

ASKEY John Colin
Born: Stoke, 4 November 1964
Height: 6'0" **Weight:** 12.2
Club Honours: GMVC '95, '97; FAT '96
International Honours: E: SP-1
Macclesfield's longest-serving player was used sparingly in his striker's role during the 2002-03 season as he concentrated on his backroom roles of first-team coach and reserve-team manager. Deciding to retire as a player, John made one last appearance from the substitutes' bench during the final match of the season to conclude a playing career of over 670 appearances for Macclesfield at all levels, and scored, just as he did in his very first match for the club back in December 1984. However, John will continue working for the club in his two backroom roles.
Macclesfield T *(Free from Milton U during 1985-86) FL 136+45/31 FLC 9+4/2 FAC 7+2/1 Others 2+1*

ASTAFJEVS Vitalijs (Vitas)
Born: Riga, Latvia, 3 April 1971
Height: 5'11" **Weight:** 12.5
International Honours: Latvia: 93
The experienced Latvian international midfielder gave some impressive performances for Bristol Rovers last term and scored a total of eight goals during the campaign. He was stretchered off at York with ankle ligament damage after scoring a superb 20-yard goal. In the spring he scored four goals in a run of five matches and set up many chances for his colleagues with his accurate passing. Vitas sustained a twisted knee at Oxford on Easter Monday, missing the final two matches, but nevertheless he was voted as the Supporters' Club 'Player of the Season'.
Bristol Rov *(£150,000 from Skonto Riga, Latvia on 28/1/2000) FL 87+22/16 FLC 5 FAC 9+1/1 Others 4/2*

ATANGANA Simon Pierre
Born: Cameroon, 10 July 1979
Height: 5'11" **Weight:** 12.4
International Honours: Cameroon
A bustling front runner, Simon signed on a short-term basis for Colchester and scored at a healthy rate for the reserves.

However, he had very few chances to make an impression in the first team, starting just one game in the 1-1 home draw with Peterborough on Boxing Day. He was released in March and ended the season at Jewson League Premier Division champions Halstead Town.
Dundee U *(Signed from Tonnerre Kalara, Cameroon, ex Olympic, Alfath, on 31/8/2000) SL 8+3 SLC 0+1 (Freed on 3/4/2002)*
Port Vale *(Loaned on 18/11/2002) FL 1+1*
Colchester U *(Free on 8/11/2002) FL 1+5 FAC 0+1*

ATHERTON Peter
Born: Orrell, 6 April 1970
Height: 5'11" **Weight:** 13.12
International Honours: E: U21-1; Sch
Peter recovered from his niggling injury problems to finish the 2002-03 season strongly for Bradford City. He continues to be a robust and solid player in the centre of midfield, although he can also play as a central defender or at right back. Peter's only goal of the campaign proved to be a valuable one, as it aided Bradford to a crucial 2-1 home win over Crystal Palace in March.
Wigan Ath *(From trainee on 12/2/1988) FL 145+4/1 FLC 8 FAC 7 Others 12+1*
Coventry C *(£300,000 on 23/8/1991) F/PL 113+1 FLC 4 FAC 2*
Sheffield Wed *(£800,000 on 1/6/1994) PL 214/9 FLC 16 FAC 18 Others 3*
Bradford C *(Free on 6/7/2000) P/FL 51/1 FLC 3 FAC 1 Others 4*
Birmingham C *(Loaned on 15/2/2001) FL 10 Others 2*

ATKINS Mark Nigel
Born: Doncaster, 14 August 1968
Height: 6'0" **Weight:** 13.2
Club Honours: PL '95
International Honours: E: Sch
This vastly experienced midfield player was ever-present for Shrewsbury until he was sidelined with a knee injury that restricted his appearances in the second half of the campaign. Mark was a key figure in the club's historic FA Cup run, and it is significant that only two games were won from the last 23, when he was mostly absent from the side. He was used in a central defensive position in a number of games, but his midfield strength and ability to make a telling pass were his major contributions. Mark ended his current contract at Gay Meadow by taking charge of the team for the final league game following the resignation of manager Kevin Ratcliffe.
Scunthorpe U *(From juniors on 9/7/1986) FL 45+5/2 FLC 3+1 FAC 5 Others 6+1*

Blackburn Rov (£45,000 on 16/6/1988) F/PL 224+33/35 FLC 20+4/4 FAC 11+3 Others 17+2/1
Wolverhampton W (£1,000,000 on 21/9/1995) FL 115+11/9 FLC 12+1/2 FAC 11+1 Others 2/1
York C (Free on 5/8/1999) FL 10/2 FLC 2 (Free to Doncaster Rov on 4/11/1999)
Hull C (Free on 21/3/2001) FL 8 Others 1+1
Shrewsbury T (Free on 5/7/2001) FL 71+1/3 FLC 2 FAC 5 Others 4/1

ATTWELL Jamie Wayne
Born: Bristol, 8 June 1982
Height: 6'1" **Weight:** 14.12
Signed from Bristol City as cover for Kevin Dearden, this young Torquay 'keeper conceded four on his surprise debut at York. Injury to Dearden then afforded him an extended run but he seemed to lose confidence and after experienced cover was brought in the remainder of his contract was cancelled by mutual consent.
Bristol C (From trainee at Tottenham H on 17/8/2001)
Torquay U (Free on 26/7/2002) FL 2+2 Others 1

AUSTIN Dean Barry
Born: Hemel Hempstead, 26 April 1970
Height: 5'11" **Weight:** 12.4

Dean Austin

This experienced central defender rarely featured for Crystal Palace in the early part of last season. He was restricted to occasional outings from the substitutes' bench and made his only start in the Worthington Cup tie against Plymouth when he was replaced at half time. He subsequently left Selhurst Park and after a brief trial with Watford he joined Conference outfit Woking.
Southend U (£12,000 from St Albans C on 22/3/1990) FL 96/2 FLC 4/1 FAC 2 Others 7
Tottenham H (£375,000 on 4/6/1992) PL 117+7 FLC 7+2 FAC 16+1
Crystal Palace (Free on 8/7/1998) FL 127+15/6 FLC 18+3 FAC 3 Others 2

AUSTIN Kevin Levi
Born: Hackney, 12 February 1973
Height: 6'0" **Weight:** 14.0
International Honours: Trinidad & Tobago: 1
This experienced central defender joined Bristol Rovers in the summer of 2002 linking up once again with his former manager John Still for whom he had played at both Leyton Orient and Lincoln City earlier in his career. Unfortunately he picked up a toe injury in pre-season, which was revealed as tendonitis and sidelined him for the opening two months of the campaign. Kevin recovered and was rewarded for his solid performances with an extended contract until the end of the season.
Leyton Orient (Free from Saffron Walden on 19/8/1993) FL 101+8/3 FLC 4/1 FAC 6 Others 7
Lincoln C (£30,000 on 31/7/1996) FL 128+1/2 FLC 9 FAC 6 Others 4
Brentford (Loaned on 27/10/2000) FL 3
Cambridge U (Free on 21/11/2001) FL 4+2 Others 1
Bristol Rov (Free on 12/7/2002) FL 31+2 FAC 3+1

AUSTIN Neil Jeffrey
Born: Barnsley, 26 April 1983
Height: 5'10" **Weight:** 11.11
International Honours: E: Yth
Neil made his senior debut for Barnsley at right back on the opening day of the 2002-03 season. He became a regular during the campaign and showed his versatility by featuring in a number of defensive roles. Neil was at his best when used on the left-hand side of a three-man central defensive formation. He was called into the England U20 squad on a number of occasions during the season and won the 'Young Player of the Year' award at Oakwell at the season's end.

Barnsley (From trainee on 27/4/2000) FL 32+2 FAC 1

AWUAH Jones
Born: Ghana, 10 July 1983
Height: 6'0" **Weight:** 11.7
This promising young striker was leading scorer for Gillingham's reserve team last season, and went on to make his full senior debut in the final away game at Coventry when he certainly did not let the side down. Quick footed and with a strong shot in either foot, he was rewarded with a one-year professional contract.
Gillingham (Trainee) FL 1+3

AYEGBENI Yakubu
Born: Benin City, Nigeria, 22 November 1982
Height: 6'0" **Weight:** 13.1
Club Honours: Div 1 '03
International Honours: Nigeria
This talented young striker experienced Champions' League action for Maccabi Haifa in the early part of the 2002-03 season, scoring five goals including a hat-trick against Olympiakos. He joined Portsmouth on loan during the January transfer window and was a great success. He netted seven goals from just 12 starts, including a great 30-yard volley against Derby, which was considered by many observers to be one of the best goals scored at Fratton Park in the last ten years. A pacy front man who can kick equally well with either foot, Yakubu also represented Nigeria at international level during the season.
Portsmouth (Loaned from Maccabi Haifa, Israel, ex Okomo Oil, Julius Berger, Hapoel Kfar-Saba, on 13/1/2003) FL 12+2/7

AYRES Lee Terence
Born: Birmingham, 28 August 1982
Height: 6'1" **Weight:** 10.10
Lee won a place in the heart of the Kidderminster defence at the start of 2002-03 when Abdou Sall was sidelined with an injury and made the position his own for the first half of the campaign. Still only young he gained much valuable experience, with the high point of his season being the two goals scored in the 4-3 win over Exeter at Aggborough. He eventually lost his place as tiredness began to show and was one of a number of players waiting to find out whether or not he would get a new contract at the time of writing.
Kidderminster Hrs (Free from Evesham U on 12/6/2001) FL 27+8/2 FLC 2 FAC 2 Others 2+1

B

BAARDSEN Per Espen
Born: San Rafael, USA, 7 December 1977
Height: 6'5" **Weight:** 13.13
Club Honours: FLC '99
International Honours: Norway: 4; U21-31; Yth USA: Yth
Espen joined Everton on a short-term contract at the end of 2002 as cover for injuries to reserve 'keepers Paul Gerrard and Steve Simonsen. He made his debut for the club in the most unlikely of circumstances following an injury to Richard Wright in the warm-up before the game at Tottenham in January. He left Goodison Park in February 2003 having played just that single game.
Tottenham H (Free from San Francisco All Blacks, USA, on 16/7/1996) PL 22+1 FLC 3 FAC 2+1
Watford (£1,250,000 on 3/8/2000) FL 41 FLC 5
Everton (Free on 24/12/2002) PL 1

BABAYARO Celestine
Born: Kaduna, Nigeria, 29 August 1978
Height: 5'8" **Weight:** 11.0
Club Honours: FLC '98; ESC '98; FAC '00; CS '00
International Honours: Nigeria: 26; U23 (OLYM '96); Yth (World-U17 '93)
For the second successive season 'Baba' had an injury-blighted campaign, calf and groin strains conspiring to force him to sit out the middle third of the season and he featured in just half of Chelsea's fixtures. He managed just one Premiership goal, but what a crucial one it was, the only goal of an absorbing match against Middlesbrough, which maintained the Blues' 11-match unbeaten pre-Christmas sequence and lifted them into Champions' League contention.
Chelsea (£2,250,000 from Anderlecht, Belgium on 20/6/1997) PL 110+12/4 FLC 10+2 FAC 14+1 Others 26+3/3

BABB Philip (Phil) Andrew
Born: Lambeth, 30 November 1970
Height: 6'0" **Weight:** 12.3
Club Honours: FLC '95
International Honours: RoI: 35; B-1
Phil had been plying his trade in Portugal with Sporting Lisbon when Sunderland boss Peter Reid snapped him up in the 2002 close season. Quick and strong in the tackle, Phil began the campaign impressively in an overworked rearguard and earned himself a recall to the

international set-up against Russia in September. Unfortunately, his season was cut short in February when a persistent hernia problem required surgery and although he regained full fitness before the campaign ended, he was unable to win his place back.
Millwall (From trainee on 25/4/1989)
Bradford C (Free on 10/8/1990) FL 73+7/14 FLC 5+1 FAC 3 Others 3+1
Coventry C (£500,000 on 21/7/1992) PL 70+7/3 FLC 5/1 FAC 2
Liverpool (£3,600,000 on 1/9/1994) PL 124+4/1 FLC 16 FAC 12 Others 12+2 (Free to Sporting Lisbon, Portugal during 2000 close season)
Tranmere Rov (Loaned on 21/1/2000) FL 4 FLC 1 FAC 2
Sunderland (Free on 11/6/2002) PL 26 FLC 1 FAC 3

BABBEL Markus
Born: Munich, Germany, 8 September 1972
Height: 6'3" **Weight:** 12.10
Club Honours: UEFA '01; FLC '01, '03; FAC '01; ESC '01; CS '01
International Honours: Germany: 51
After making a remarkable recovery from a serious illness in the previous season, it was hoped that the cultured German international defender would quickly ease his way back into the Liverpool first team in 2002-03. His return to first-team action as a substitute for the Charity Shield match against Arsenal at Cardiff was greeted rapturously by the Reds' supporters. However, he had to wait until November for his next opportunity and after six starts in November and December, some uncharacteristic errors seemed to convince manager Gerald Houllier that he was not yet ready for regular first-team duty and he played no further part in the campaign.
Liverpool (Free from Bayern Munich, Germany, ex SV Hamburg, on 10/7/2000) PL 42/3 FLC 7/1 FAC 5/1 Others 17+2/1

BACON Daniel (Danny) Stephen
Born: Mansfield, 20 September 1980
Height: 5'10" **Weight:** 10.12
Much was expected from this skilful striker at Mansfield last term, but his progress was severely hampered by a series of niggling injuries. Towards the end of the season Danny seemed to drop down the pecking order and in March he was loaned out to Unibond League

neighbours Hucknall Town where he became a regular on the score sheet.
Mansfield T (From trainee on 5/1/2000) FL 14+30/4 FLC 1+4 FAC 2+3 Others 1+1/1

BAILEY John Anthony Kenneth
Born: Manchester, 2 July 1984
Height: 5'5" **Weight:** 10.8
International Honours: E: Yth
After sitting on the bench on three occasions without being called upon, Preston's promising young winger made his debut at Selhurst Park in April as a substitute in the defeat at Wimbledon. Eager to take on his man, John can sometimes overdo the trickery, but he has both the skills and pace to trouble any defender as he showed throughout the season in the club's successful reserve side. He will be looking for further first-team opportunities in the near future.
Preston NE (From trainee on 3/7/2001) FL 0+1

BAILEY Mark
Born: Stoke, 12 August 1976
Height: 5'8" **Weight:** 10.12
This right back showed excellent qualities in a Lincoln back five that had the meanest defence in Division Three. Mark always looked dangerous pushing down the flank with his crosses and long throws creating chances for team mates. His only goal was a second half-header in the play-off final at Cardiff.
Stoke C (From trainee on 12/7/1994)
Rochdale (Free on 10/10/1996) FL 49+18/1 FLC 3+1 FAC 1 Others 4 (Free to Winsford U during 1999 close season)
Lincoln C (From Northwich Vic, ex Lancaster C on 8/10/2001) FL 63 FLC 1 FAC 3 Others 4/1

BAINES Leighton John
Born: Liverpool, 11 December 1984
Height: 5'8" **Weight:** 11.10
This promising left back made his senior debut for Wigan Athletic as a substitute in the Worthington Cup victory over Premiership side West Bromwich Albion whilst still a trainee. One of the most promising players to come through the Latics' youth ranks in recent years, he then made the starting line-up for the FA Cup victory over Hereford United. Confident on the ball with accurate distribution and strong tackling, his performances were rewarded with a two-year professional contract in January and he also won the club's 'Young Player of the Year' award.
Wigan Ath (From trainee on 4/1/2003) FL 6 FLC 1+1 FAC 2 Others 1+1

Markus Babbel

BAIRD Christopher (Chris) Patrick

Born: Ballymoney, 25 February 1982
Height: 5'10" **Weight:** 11.11
International Honours: NI: 2; U21-6; Yth
If Chris's rise from anonymity last season was not a fairy story – Southampton did lose the FA Cup final – it was still fabulous. He had yet to reach the subs' bench for Saints until 22 March, when he came on in the closing minutes at St Mary's and played a part in laying on the last gasp equaliser for Kevin Davies. He made his first start in the last game of the season, at Manchester City's Maine Road, and next stop was the Millennium Stadium where he distinguished himself at right back, not only making a goal line clearance early on, but hitting Saints' first effective shot on goal: a 20-yard strike which brought the best out of David Seaman. Chris then capped a memorable time when he won his first full cap for Northern Ireland against Italy in June.
Southampton (From trainee on 15/1/2001)
PL 1+2 FAC 1

BAKER Phillip (Phil)

Born: Birkenhead, 4 November 1982
Height: 6'0" **Weight:** 11.10
After being released by Tranmere, Phil linked up with League of Wales outfit Bangor City in the new year. Towards the end of the campaign he signed for Exeter, establishing himself in the heart of the defence for the closing matches. Despite his pace and awareness Phil was unable to save the club from the drop to the Conference.
Tranmere Rov (From trainee on 3/5/2002. Free to Bangor C on 30/1/2003)
Exeter C (Free on 27/3/2003) FL 5+1

BAKKE Eirik

Born: Sogndal, Norway, 13 September 1977
Height: 6'2" **Weight:** 12.9
International Honours: Norway: 25; U21-34; Yth
Highly rated at Elland Road, Eirik returned from World Cup duty with Norway and was immediately introduced in a midfield 'holding' role by new boss Terry Venables. However, he struggled to settle in the team and it was not until he was moved to a more advanced position that his performances began to improve. He was occasionally used as a central striker, and he was playing in this role when he scored the winner in the FA Cup tie against Gillingham. Eirik is an elegant, forceful midfielder, who is very strong in the air.
Leeds U (£1,000,000 + from Sogndal, Norway on 13/7/1999) PL 99+20/7FLC 6/1 FAC 8+1/6 Others 31+3/5

BALDACCHINO Ryan Lee

Born: Leicester, 13 January 1981
Height: 5'9" **Weight:** 12.3
Ryan's early-season performances for Carlisle resulted in him signing a permanent deal with the club. A right winger of exceptional pace, a hamstring injury then kept him out of the side for a while and disrupted his form. However, he performed strongly in the last three games of the season, particularly in the surprise win at Torquay and will be looking to build on these displays in the 2003-04 campaign.
Blackburn Rov (From trainee on 25/2/1999)
Bolton W (Free on 16/3/2001)
Carlisle U (Free on 9/8/2002) FL 11+11 FAC 1+2 Others 1+3

BALDRY Simon Jonathan

Born: Huddersfield, 12 February 1976
Height: 5'10" **Weight:** 11.6
Simon started the 2002-03 season on the bench for Huddersfield. He soon re-established himself in his normal position on the right side of midfield and his first full start was rewarded with an early goal in the Worthington Cup win against Darlington. He impressed with his close control and accurate crossing, and further goals came at the McAlpine against Port Vale and Northampton. Simon was once again affected by injuries that restricted his appearances.
Huddersfield T (From trainee on 14/7/1994)
FL 87+59/8 FLC 5+5/1 FAC 2+2 Others 3+3/1
Bury (Loaned on 8/9/1998) FL 0+5

BALDWIN Patrick (Pat) Michael

Born: London, 12 November 1982
Height: 6'2" **Weight:** 10.12
Pat provided useful cover in various defensive positions for Colchester United last term and looked a good prospect. The former Chelsea trainee was most at home as a centre half, but several of his appearances were as an emergency left back, due to a lack of options down the left-hand side for new boss Phil Parkinson. Pat found it difficult to dislodge the U's normal central-defensive partnership of Alan White and Scott Fitzgerald, but gave solid displays at Barnsley and against Swindon towards the end of the season, when White was suspended.
Colchester U (Free from trainee at Chelsea on 16/8/2002) FL 13+7 FLC 1 FAC 1

BALIS Igor

Born: Czechoslavakia, 5 January 1970
Height: 5'11" **Weight:** 11.4
International Honours: Slovakia: 41
After holding his position as West Bromwich Albion's right wing back throughout the first half of the season, Igor then lost his place in the side to young Adam Chambers. He fought back, before suffering another injury at Leeds in mid-January and was sidelined for two months, then regained his place at a time when relegation was staring the team straight in the face. Igor had the pleasure of scoring Albion's first penalty of the campaign, in the 2-1 home defeat by Everton a week before Easter.
West Bromwich A (£150,000 from Slovan Bratislava, Slovakia, ex Spartak Trnava, on 14/12/2000) P/FL 60+9/4 FLC 0+1 FAC 3+2

BALMER Stuart Murray

Born: Falkirk, 20 September 1969
Height: 6'0" **Weight:** 12.11
Club Honours: AMC '99
International Honours: S: Yth; Sch
Out of favour at Oldham, Stuart joined Scunthorpe United on loan last October, his experience and organisational skills helping bolster a young defence. He subsequently returned to Boundary Park before linking up with Boston United in December, a move that sparked off a big improvement in the Lincolnshire club's defensive record and helped them finish the campaign in a mid-table position. After an initial loan spell he chose to make the move permanent. His experience in the centre of the back four proved invaluable to the Pilgrims and the only disappointment was that his forays up front failed to produce a goal.
Glasgow Celtic (From juniors on 1/8/1987)
Charlton Ath (£120,000 on 24/8/1990) FL 201+26/8 FLC 15 FAC 9+1 Others 11+1
Wigan Ath (£200,000 on 18/9/1998) FL 99+2/4 FLC 7 FAC 8 Others 12/1
Oldham Ath (Free on 20/7/2001) FL 35+1/6 FLC 2 FAC 4 Others 2
Scunthorpe U (Loaned on 10/10/2002) FL 6 Others 1
Boston U (Free on 13/12/2002) FL 21

BALTACHA Sergei

Born: Kiev, Ukraine, 28 July 1979
Height: 6'5" **Weight:** 12.2
Club Honours: S Div 1 '00
International Honours: S: U21-3
Sergei began 2002-03 with St Mirren, but made no further appearances after

September and was released by the Paisley club. The giant defender subsequently joined Millwall on a non-contract basis in January and made his debut as a centre forward at Grimsby, covering for injuries to his colleagues. However, his preferred position is at right back. Sergei is very strong in the air, but also has good technical ability and can kick with either foot. He is from a strong sporting background: his father, also Sergei, played for Dinamo Kiev, Ipswich and the Soviet Union, whilst his sister Elena is a top-class tennis player.
St Mirren (Signed from Kinnoull juniors on 16/1/1999) SL 49+15/2 SLC 1+2 SC 2+1 Others 4+1/1
Millwall (Free on 16/1/2003) FL 1+1 FAC 0+1

BAMPTON David (Dave) Peter
Born: Swindon, 5 May 1985
Height: 5'8" **Weight:** 11.2
This youngster made his debut for Swindon as a late substitute in the FA Cup defeat at Oxford last December. He was subsequently given three further outings from the bench when he showed himself to be a steady performer in midfield and was selected as the club's 'Young Player of the Year'.
Swindon T (Trainee) FL 0+3 FAC 0+1

BANKOLE Ademola (Ade)
Born: Abeokuta, Nigeria, 9 September 1969
Height: 6'3" **Weight:** 12.10
This experienced goalkeeper found himself as second in line to Clayton Ince at Crewe last season. He spent most of his time on the substitutes' bench and made the starting line-up for just two Second Division matches. However, he played in all the LDV Vans Trophy games and captained the reserves side that defeated Altrincham to win the Cheshire Senior Cup.
Doncaster Rov (Free from Shooting Stars, Ibadan, Nigeria on 30/11/1995)
Leyton Orient (Free on 27/12/1995)
Crewe Alex (Free on 25/9/1996) FL 6 FLC 1
Queens Park R (£50,000 on 2/7/1998) FL 0+1
Crewe Alex (£50,000 on 19/7/2000) FL 51+1 FLC 1+1 FAC 5+1 Others 4

BANKS Steven (Steve)
Born: Hillingdon, 9 February 1972
Height: 6'0" **Weight:** 13.2
Steve again found himself out of the first-team picture at Bolton last term and early in the season he went out on loan to Bradford City, making his debut when he replaced the injured Aidan Davison in the

second half against Coventry. The experienced 'keeper enjoyed a successful loan spell at Valley Parade, saving a last-minute penalty against Norwich, but returned to the Reebok after being sidelined with a knee problem. He subsequently joined Stoke City on loan in December and shortly afterwards signed a short-term contract for the Potters. However, although he generally performed well he was released in the summer.
West Ham U (From trainee on 24/3/1990) Others 1
Gillingham (Free on 25/3/1993) FL 67 FAC 7 Others 2
Blackpool (£60,000 on 18/8/1995) FL 150 FLC 13 FAC 8 Others 10
Bolton W (£50,000 on 25/3/1999) P/FL 20+1 FLC 7 FAC 5 Others 3
Rochdale (Loaned on 14/12/2001) FL 15
Bradford C (Loaned on 30/8/2002) FL 8+1
Stoke C (Free on 6/12/2002) FL 14 FAC 2

BARACLOUGH Ian Robert
Born: Leicester, 4 December 1970
Height: 6'1" **Weight:** 12.2
Club Honours: Div 3 '98
International Honours: E: Yth
Although Ian was principally used as a left back by Notts County during the 2001-02 season, he was given a more varied role last term and produced his most influential performances in midfield, operating either in the centre of the park or down the left-hand side. The highly experienced player was a vital part of the nucleus of the team and scored two goals, netting against Blackpool and Barnsley.
Leicester C (From trainee on 15/12/1988) FAC 1 Others 0+1
Wigan Ath (Loaned on 22/3/1990) FL 8+1/2
Grimsby T (Loaned on 21/12/1990) FL 1+3
Grimsby T (Free on 21/8/1992) FL 68+5/10 FLC 7/1 FAC 4 Others 7
Mansfield T (Free on 6/6/1994) FL 47/5 FLC 7 FAC 4 Others 4
Notts Co (Signed on 13/10/1995) FL 107+4/10 FLC 5+1/1 FAC 8 Others 2
Queens Park R (£50,000 on 19/3/1998) FL 120+5/1 FLC 7 FAC 6
Notts Co (Free on 5/7/2001) FL 63+4/5 FLC 3 FAC 3+1 Others 3

BARKER Christopher (Chris) Andrew
Born: Sheffield, 2 March 1980
Height: 6'0" **Weight:** 11.8
This strong and versatile player had a good first season with Cardiff City. He had spent the previous four seasons in Division One with Barnsley before

dropping a division to sign for the Bluebirds, and jumped straight back with promotion via the play-offs. Chris did well at left back and in the centre of defence, switching comfortably between the two. He made the left-back slot his own at the end of the season, keeping Gary Croft among the substitutes.
Barnsley (Signed from Alfreton on 24/8/1998) FL 110+3/3 FLC 11+1 FAC 4 Others 0+1
Cardiff C (£600,000 on 12/7/2002) FL 32+8 FLC 1 FAC 5 Others 4

BARKER Richard (Richie) Ian
Born: Sheffield, 30 May 1975
Height: 6'0" **Weight:** 13.5
International Honours: E: Yth; Sch
An ever-willing worker for the team, Richie had his most successful season at Rotherham last term, reaching double figures for the first time. That was due to the fact that he established himself as a first-team choice for several months as he forged a good partnership up front with Alan Lee. Effective in the air, he was also a very valuable player in his own penalty area, while his work rate could only be described as prodigious with his ability to run throughout the whole 90 minutes. Richie netted a crucial winner with great skill at Ipswich Town.
Sheffield Wed (From trainee on 27/7/1993) Others 1+1 (Free to Linfield on 22/8/1996)
Doncaster Rov (Loaned on 29/9/1995) FL 5+1 Others 0+1
Brighton & Hove A (Free on 19/12/1997) FL 48+12/12 FLC 1+1/1 FAC 1/1 Others 1
Macclesfield T (Free on 5/7/1999) FL 58/23 FLC 6/2 FAC 3 Others 1/1
Rotherham U (£60,000 on 3/1/2001) FL 41+50/11 FLC 5+1/2 FAC 3/1

BARKER Shaun
Born: Nottingham, 19 September 1982
Height: 6'2" **Weight:** 12.8
A young defender who burst onto the scene at Rotherham last season to solve an injury crisis, Shaun performed so well that he made the right-back position his own with some superb performances. A versatile player who mainly featured at centre half in the junior ranks, his ability to hurl in long-distance throws led to several crucial goals.
Rotherham U (From trainee on 10/7/2002) FL 11

BARLOW Stuart
Born: Liverpool, 16 July 1968
Height: 5'10" **Weight:** 11.0
Club Honours: AMC '99
Although sidelined by injury in the last few months of the season, this

experienced striker still managed to score six goals for Tranmere last term. He struggled to keep his place in the team in the face of some strong challenges from the younger players, but remained capable of producing the unexpected with his extraordinary acceleration. Stuart was released on a free transfer at the end of the season.
Everton (Free from Sherwood Park on 5/6/1990) F/PL 24+47/10 FLC 3+5/1 FAC 4+3/2 Others 0+2
Rotherham U (Loaned on 10/1/1992) Others 4+1
Oldham Ath (£450,000 on 20/11/1995) FL 78+15/31 FLC 5+1 FAC 6+1/1 Others 1
Wigan Ath (£45,000 on 26/3/1998) FL 72+11/40 FLC 6/3 FAC 5/3 Others 9+3/6
Tranmere Rov (Free on 5/7/2000) FL 62+32/19 FLC 6+3/3 FAC 5+5/3 Others 1+1/2

BARMBY Nicholas (Nicky) Jonathan
Born: Hull, 11 February 1974
Height: 5'7" **Weight:** 11.3
Club Honours: FLC '01; UEFAC '01; CS '01
International Honours: E: 23; B-2; U21-4; Yth; Sch
Nicky became Terry Venables first signing for Leeds when he arrived during the 2002 close season. It didn't take him long to win over the United fans, as he scored with a deft touch in the 3-0 opening-day victory over Manchester City. Unfortunately he picked up a serious injury in the pre-match warm up at Tottenham in November, and this kept him out until March. Able to play anywhere across midfield and as a striker, his versatility made him an attractive signing for United.
Tottenham H (From trainee on 9/4/1991) PL 81+6/20 FLC 7+1/2 FAC 12+1/5
Middlesbrough (£5,250,000 on 8/8/1995) PL 42/8 FLC 4/1 FAC 3/1
Everton (£5,750,000 on 2/11/1996) PL 105+11/18 FLC 2+3/3 FAC 12/3
Liverpool (£6,000,000 on 19/7/2000) PL 23+9/2 FLC 3+4/1 FAC 2+3/1 Others 10+4/4
Leeds U (£2,750,000 on 8/8/2002) PL 16+3/4 FLC 1 FAC 0+2 Others 3/1

BARNARD Darren Sean
Born: Rintein, Germany, 30 November 1971
Height: 5'9" **Weight:** 12.3
International Honours: W: 18; E: Sch
One of two players picked up by Grimsby during the 2002 close season from Barnsley, Darren was unable to win a regular place at Blundell Park last term. This was despite regular selection for the Welsh squad and a stunning first goal,

lobbing Derby 'keeper Matt Poom from 40 yards out. The experienced midfielder was eventually ruled out of action by a shoulder injury and missed the vital closing stages of the campaign.
Chelsea (£50,000 from Wokingham T on 25/7/1990) F/PL 18+11/2 FLC 1+1 FAC 1+1
Reading (Loaned on 18/11/1994) FL 3+1
Bristol C (£175,000 on 6/10/1995) FL 77+1/15 FLC 4/1 FAC 6 Others 6/1
Barnsley (£750,000 on 8/8/1997) P/FL 151+19/28 FLC 16+3/5 FAC 9/3 Others 3
Grimsby T (Free on 2/8/2002) FL 21+8/2 FAC 1

BARNARD Donny Gary
Born: Forest Gate, 1 July 1984
Height: 6'0" **Weight:** 11.3
Donny made the right-back slot his own at Leyton Orient last term after Matthew Joseph moved into the sweeper's role. He is a tough-tackling defender who likes to attack with the ball at his feet and is not daunted by older, more experienced opponents. Donny was rewarded with a new contract by the O's during the summer.
Leyton Orient (From trainee on 4/3/2003) FL 28+11 FLC 0+2 FAC 1+1 Others 2/1

Darren Barnard

BARNARD Lee James

Born: Welwyn Garden City, 13 November 1984
Height: 5'10" **Weight:** 10.12
This promising young striker graduated to the professional ranks at Tottenham in the summer of 2002 and in November he joined Exeter City on loan as new head coach Neil McNab attempted to solve his lack of goal power. Lee played three games for the Grecians without registering a goal before heading back to White Hart Lane.
Tottenham H (From trainee on 3/7/2002)
Exeter C (Loaned on 1/11/2002) FL 3 Others 1

BARNES Philip (Phil) Kenneth

Born: Sheffield, 2 March 1979
Height: 6'1'' **Weight:** 11.1
Club Honours: AMC '02
Phil was again first choice 'keeper for Blackpool during 2002-03 when he missed just two Second Division matches. He made several outstanding saves during the campaign, one against Brentford particularly standing out in the memory. He has now reached the landmark figure of 150 senior games and continues to improve with each season.
Rotherham U (From trainee on 25/6/1997) FL 2
Blackpool (£100,000 on 22/7/1997) FL 122 FLC 6 FAC 6 Others 14

BARNESS Anthony

Born: Lewisham, 25 March 1973
Height: 5'10" **Weight:** 13.1
Club Honours: Div 1 '00
Bolton's 'Mr Dependable', Anthony was a regular in the line-up for the majority of the first half of the 2002-03 season, but then a change of team tactics saw him lose his place and he spent much of the remainder of the campaign on the bench. Playing on the right side of an orthodox back four Anthony was his usual consistent self when selected. A solid right back with a minimum of fuss, he proved to be an invaluable squad member and provided experienced defensive cover when needed during the final run in.
Charlton Ath (From trainee on 6/3/1991) FL 21+6/1 FLC 2 FAC 3 Others 1+1/1
Chelsea (£350,000 on 8/9/1992) PL 12+2 FLC 2 Others 2+1
Middlesbrough (Loaned on 12/8/1993) Others 1
Southend U (Loaned on 2/2/1996) FL 5
Charlton Ath (£165,000 on 8/8/1996) P/FL 83+13/3 FLC 5 FAC 3+1 Others 1+1
Bolton W (Free on 6/7/2000) P/FL 57+13 FLC 4 FAC 5 Others 3

BARNETT Leon Peter

Born: Stevenage, 30 November 1985
Height: 6'1" **Weight:** 11.3
Leon became one of the youngest players in Luton's history when he came on as a substitute in the LDV Vans Trophy tie against Woking. Despite only playing a few minutes he gave a good account of himself. Leon started the season playing in defence for the youth team, but was successfully switched to the forward line in the reserves.
Luton T (Trainee) Others 0+1

BAROS Milan

Born: Czechoslovakia, 28 October 1981
Height: 6'0" **Weight:** 11.12
Club Honours: FLC '03
International Honours: Czech Republic: 19; U21-19: Yth
After an anonymous first season at Anfield, the young Czech international striker announced himself to the football world in grand style early in 2002-03 when, in his first start for Liverpool at Bolton, he scored two outstanding goals in the Reds' 3-2 victory. Milan quickly followed up with further goals against West Bromwich Albion and Basle. It seemed that at last Liverpool had found a worthy striking partner for Michael Owen, but manager Gerald Houllier preferred to stick with his established Heskey/Owen pairing for most of the season and nearly half of his appearances were from the bench. Milan was one of the few success stories of the season at Anfield and even greater things can be anticipated for 2003-04.
Liverpool (£3,400,000 from Banik Ostrava, Czechoslovakia, on 24/12/2001) PL 17+10/9 FLC 2+2/2 FAC 0+1 Others 3+8/1

BARRAS Anthony (Tony)

Born: Billingham, 29 March 1971
Height: 6'0" **Weight:** 13.0
In his fourth season at Walsall this brave whole-hearted defender struggled to make an impact early on and was loaned to Plymouth in November. He did well at Home Park, producing a fine display on his debut against Colchester, and it was something of a disappointment when he returned to Bescot. Tony then came back strongly in the last three months of the campaign to give some near flawless displays as Walsall clinched the points that ensured a third successive season in Division One.
Hartlepool U (From trainee on 6/7/1989) FL 9+3 FLC 2 FAC 1 Others 1

Stockport Co (Free on 23/7/1990) FL 94+5/5 FLC 2 FAC 7 Others 19+1
Rotherham U (Loaned on 25/2/1994) FL 5/1
York C (£25,000 on 18/7/1994) FL 167+4/11 FLC 16/2 FAC 10/1 Others 8+1/1
Reading (£20,000 on 19/3/1999) FL 4+2/1
Walsall (£20,000 on 16/7/1999) FL 91+14/9 FLC 9+2/2 FAC 5/1 Others 4
Plymouth Arg (Loaned on 22/11/2002) FL 4

BARRASS Matthew (Matt) Robert

Born: Bury, 28 February 1980
Height: 5'11" **Weight:** 12.0
Matt took his place as an attacking right wing back for Bury's opening Third Division game at Oxford and remained a regular throughout the opening few months of the 2002-03 campaign. Dropped for the game at Carlisle in November, he then faced a battle with Lee Unsworth to regain his place, but in January damaged his left knee in a training injury. Keyhole surgery solved the problem, but it was not until late March that he finally began his comeback at reserve-team level.
Bury (From trainee on 19/5/1999) FL 50+3/1 FLC 3+1 FAC 1 Others 2

BARRETT Adam Nicholas

Born: Dagenham, 29 November 1979
Height: 5'10" **Weight:** 12.0
Adam enjoyed a good first season with Bristol Rovers in 2002-03. Appointed captain on his arrival, he proved to be an effective organiser in the centre of defence and an all-action player who used his height to good effect in both penalty areas. Adam scored his first goal for Rovers with a firm header in the FA Cup replay at Runcorn and also contributed a vital equaliser at Southend. He was runner-up for the Supporters' Club 'Player of the Season' award.
Plymouth Arg (Free from USA football scholarship on 13/1/1999) FL 47+5/3 FLC 6 FAC 6+1 Others 1
Mansfield T (£10,000 on 1/12/2000) FL 34+3/1 FAC 3 Others 2
Bristol Rov (Free on 2/7/2002) FL 45/1 FLC 1 FAC 4/1 Others 1

BARRETT Graham

Born: Dublin, 6 October 1981
Height: 5'10" **Weight:** 11.7
Club Honours: FAYC '00
International Honours: RoI: 1; U21-23; Yth (UEFA-U16 '98); Sch
Graham made a promising bow in international football at the start of the 2002-03 campaign, coming off the bench to score in the Republic of Ireland's 3-0

win in Finland. Immediately afterwards this energetic forward joined Brighton, initially on two months' loan, and ended up staying for the rest of the season before returning to Highbury. Graham scored only one league goal, though, and was more often a substitute than a starter after Christmas. Although not afraid to shoot on sight, his greatest assets are his enthusiasm, running and stamina. He added to his tally of U21 caps during the course of the campaign, and was also included in the full international squad for the trip to Georgia.
Arsenal (From trainee on 14/10/1998) PL 0+2 FLC 1
Bristol Rov (Loaned on 15/12/2000) FL 0+1
Crewe Alex (Loaned on 11/9/2001) FL 2+1 FLC 0+1
Colchester U (Loaned on 14/12/2001) FL 19+1/4
Brighton & Hove A (Loaned on 29/8/2002) FL 20+10/1 FAC 1

BARRETT Paul David
Born: Newcastle, 13 April 1978
Height: 5'11" **Weight:** 11.5
International Honours: E: Yth
An industrious midfielder whose work rate sometimes goes unnoticed, Paul was much more involved in the first-team set up at Wrexham last term. However, injuries did not help his cause at the Racecourse and he required a hernia operation in early February, keeping him out of contention until the latter stages of the campaign. Anxious to make up for lost time he scored the first goal in the 5-0 demolition of Cambridge United in late April.
Newcastle U (From trainee on 20/6/1996)
Wrexham (Free on 24/3/1999) FL 79+14/3 FLC 2+1 FAC 2+1 Others 4+1

BARRETT Scott
Born: Ilkeston, 2 April 1963
Height: 6'0" **Weight:** 14.4
Club Honours: GMVC '92; FAT '92
Scott started the 2002-03 season as goalkeeping coach and third choice 'keeper at Leyton Orient. However, due to injuries and loss of form he made a return to the first-team line-up and when selected did not let anybody down. Always a fans' favourite, he retired just short of his 40th birthday and will be missed by all O's fans. Scott joined Grays Athletic of the Ryman League during the summer as assistant manager.
Wolverhampton W (Signed from Ilkeston T on 27/9/1984) FL 30 FLC 1 FAC 1 Others 3
Stoke C (£10,000 on 24/7/1987) FL 51 FLC 2 FAC 3 Others 4

Colchester U (Loaned on 10/1/1990) FL 13
Stockport Co (Loaned on 22/3/1990) FL 10 Others 2
Gillingham (Free on 14/8/1992) FL 51 FLC 7 FAC 4 Others 4
Cambridge U (Free on 2/8/1995) FL 119 FLC 6 FAC 7 Others 3
Leyton Orient (Free on 25/1/1999) FL 99 FLC 2 FAC 6+1 Others 3

BARRON Michael (Micky) James
Born: Chester le Street, 22 December 1974
Height: 5'11" **Weight:** 11.9
Micky completed his fifth campaign as Hartlepool captain by leading the team to promotion after having experienced three previous seasons of play-off disappointment. For many years a central defender, he played almost all the 2002-03 season at right back and now looks perfectly at ease in his adopted position. A consistent player who always gives his best, he has signed a new two-year contract to lead Pool on to greater things in Division Two.
Middlesbrough (From trainee on 2/2/1993) P/FL 2+1 FLC 1 Others 3+3
Hartlepool U (Loaned on 6/9/1996) FL 16
Hartlepool U (Free on 8/7/1997) FL 218+2/2 FLC 7 FAC 8/1 Others 18

BARROWCLOUGH Carl
Born: Doncaster, 25 September 1981
Height: 5'7" **Weight:** 9.7
After missing the entire 2001-02 season through a foot injury it was hoped that Carl would be available for the new campaign. However, he broke the same bone in his foot again early on in the pre-season. He eventually came on as a late substitute in mid-January after a few appearances for the reserves, but soon afterwards a hamstring injury put him on the sidelines again. When fully fit, Carl is a fast and tricky winger who has undoubted class.
Barnsley (From trainee on 15/3/2001) FL 2+10

BARRY Gareth
Born: Hastings, 23 February 1981
Height: 6'0" **Weight:** 12.6
International Honours: E: 8; U21-25; Yth
Gareth is a versatile player who is as equally comfortable in midfield as he is in defence. He spent the majority of last season in a left-midfield role for Aston Villa, which allowed him to make use of his attacking instincts. Gareth quickly settled into his new position, showing

tremendous ability on the ball and greater levels of fitness and positional sense. When required, he stepped back into his former defensive role with consummate ease, producing timely challenges as well as excellent distribution. He gave superb performances against Manchester United, when his composure and distribution were faultless, and in the FA Cup tie against Blackburn. Gareth was also a regular for England at U21 level, captaining the side during the campaign.
Aston Villa (From trainee on 27/2/1998) PL 138+11/6 FLC 13/1 FAC 11+2 Others 17+1/1

BARRY-MURPHY Brian
Born: Cork, Ireland, 27 July 1978
Height: 6'0" **Weight:** 12.4
International Honours: RoI: U21-6; Yth
Brian failed to feature for Preston in the early part of the 2002-03 season before being loaned to Hartlepool, jumping at the chance of first-team football under manager Chris Turner. He looked good in a two-month spell with the Third Division club, before being recalled due to an injury crisis. Soon afterwards he joined Sheffield Wednesday, linking up with Turner once more, and went straight into the Owls side at left back. Naturally left-footed he used the ball well and proved to be a solid tackler, adding some stability to a shaky defence.
Preston NE (Free from Cork C on 3/8/1999) FL 6+15 FLC 1+3 FAC 1+1 Others 1
Southend U (Loaned on 11/2/2002) FL 8/1
Hartlepool U (Loaned on 30/10/2002) FL 7 FAC 2
Sheffield Wed (Free on 31/1/2003) FL 17

BART-WILLIAMS Christopher (Chris) Gerald
Born: Freetown, Sierra Leone, 16 June 1974
Height: 5'11" **Weight:** 11.6
Club Honours: Div 1 '98
International Honours: E: B-1; U21-16; Yth
Chris started the first seven games for Charlton Athletic last term, but made only a handful of substitute appearances from then on, despite being a regular first-team squad member. He was used mainly as a defensive midfield player and although sometimes lacking in pace, he showed good vision and positional awareness, and proved to have excellent passing skills. Chris is a dead-ball expert, and although he had few chances from set pieces in the games he played, he managed to score from the penalty spot in the away game with Bolton Wanderers.

Leyton Orient (From trainee on 18/7/1991)
FL 34+2/2 FLC 4 Others 2
Sheffield Wed (£275,000 on 21/11/1991)
F/PL 95+29/16 FLC 10+6/4 FAC 9+3/2 Others
1+3/2
Nottingham F (£2,500,000 on 1/7/1995)
F/PL 200+7/30 FLC 16/3 FAC 14/2 Others 7+1
Charlton Ath (free on 3/12/2001) PL
17+12/2 FAC 3+1

BARTHEZ Fabien Alain
Born: Lavelanet, France, 28 June 1971
Height: 5'11" **Weight:** 12.8
Club Honours: PL '01, '03
International Honours: France: 59
This flamboyant goalkeeper's season
started in frustrating fashion when a
niggling hip injury forced him out of
Manchester United's opening five games.
Making a return in the Premiership
against Middlesbrough, he held the
defence together during a particularly
uneasy spell in September. Despite the
odd problem from the hip injury, he
showed no physical signs of weakness as
the campaign wore on, and memorable
highlights included a penalty save against
Fulham at Loftus Road and an inspiring
performance in the 2-0 Premiership win
over Arsenal in December. However, the
injury problems returned late on in the
campaign. Fabien continued to represent
France and was in the team that defeated
Cameroon to win the Confederations Cup
tournament in the summer.
Manchester U (£7,800,000 from AS
Monaco, France, ex Toulouse, Olympique
Marseille, on 7/6/2000) PL 92 FLC 4 FAC 4
Others 39

BARTLETT Thurston **Shaun**
Born: Cape Town, South Africa, 31
October 1972
Height: 6'1" **Weight:** 12.4
International Honours: South Africa: 64
Shaun was given an extended run in the
Charlton side from late September and his
workmanlike performances made him first
choice for the remainder of the 2002-03
season. The South African international
striker only found the net on four
occasions but his overall play was of a high
standard. He scored the winning goals at
Manchester City and West Bromwich
Albion and netted an excellent effort at
Anfield against Liverpool. Shaun is hard
working, has good close control and is
quick, strong and excellent in the air.
Charlton Ath (Signed from FC Zurich,
Switzerland, ex Cape Town Spurs, Colorado
Rapids, NY/NJ Metro Stars, Cape Town Spurs,
on 1/12/2000) PL 51+12/12 FLC 3 FAC 4+1

BARTON Joseph (Joey)
Anthony
Born: Huyton, 2 September 1982
Height: 5'9" **Weight:** 11.2
A product of the Manchester City youth
scheme, Joey burst onto the scene in the
last few matches of the season after some
impressive displays in the reserves. A
promising talent who has been
undaunted by top-flight football, he
earned the 'Man of the Match' award on
a number of occasions. Joey also opened
his goal-scoring account in his third game
against Tottenham.
Manchester C (From trainee on 5/7/2001) PL
7/1

BARTON Warren Dean
Born: Stoke Newington, 19 March 1969
Height: 6'0" **Weight:** 12.0
International Honours: E: 3; B-3
An exemplary captain, willingly
conscientious in his duties on and off the
field, Warren needed all his experience to
cope with Derby's depressing season in
2002-03. He was seen at his best in a
back three when, under temporary
manager George Burley, the structure
became tighter. Until then Warren, either
at right back or in the centre of defence,
was liable to be exposed for lack of pace
by opponents given space to run at him.
This helped to explain an accumulation of

Warren Barton

disciplinary points for an essentially fair player.
Maidstone U (£10,000 from Leytonstone on 28/7/1989) FL 41+1 FLC 0+2 FAC 3/1 Others 7
Wimbledon (£300,000 on 7/6/1990) F/PL 178+2/10 FLC 16/1 FAC 11 Others 2
Newcastle U (£4,500,000 on 5/6/1995) PL 142+22/4 FLC 12/1 FAC 19+3 Others 20+2
Derby Co (Signed on 1/2/2002) P/FL 53 FLC 2 FAC 1

BARTRAM Vincent (Vince)
Lee
Born: Birmingham, 7 August 1968
Height: 6'2" **Weight:** 13.4
Vince found himself on the substitutes' bench for most of the 2002-03 season for Gillingham due to the fine form of regular first-team 'keeper Jason Brown. His only senior action came when Brown was on international duty for Wales U21s, and when he was injured towards the end of the campaign.
Wolverhampton W (From juniors on 17/8/1985) FL 5 FLC 2 FAC 3
Blackpool (Loaned on 27/10/1989) FL 9 Others 2
Bournemouth (£65,000 on 24/7/1991) FL 132 FLC 10 FAC 14 Others 6
Arsenal (£400,000 on 10/8/1994) PL 11 FLC 0+1
Huddersfield T (Loaned on 17/10/1997) FL 12
Gillingham (Free on 20/3/1998) FL 185+1 FLC 12 FAC 13 Others 10

BARWICK Terence (Terry)
Patrick
Born: Doncaster, 11 January 1983
Height: 5'11" **Weight:** 11.2
The 2002-03 campaign was a slightly disappointing one for Terry as he failed to force his way into the first-team picture at Scunthorpe. A tigerish central midfielder with good ball-winning skills, he started just one match – the 'derby' at Hull City – and was substituted at half time. He made a total five substitute appearances during the season, but failed to make the side after November.
Scunthorpe U (From trainee on 2/7/2002) FL 8+8 FLC 1+1 Others 0+1

BASHAM Steven (Steve)
Brian
Born: Southampton, 2 December 1977
Height: 5'11'' **Weight:** 12.0
Club Honours: Div 2 '00
Steve joined Oxford United in the summer of 2002 and after a couple of games on the bench came into the side, scoring on his full debut with a snap-shot winner at

Darlington. His second goal earned a vital point at Bournemouth, but then a hamstring injury kept him out for two months. It took him a while to recover his early form but the goal supply returned and he showed his class as a striker with two goals on the final day of the season that nearly earned a play-off spot.
Southampton (From trainee on 24/5/1996) PL 1+18/1 FLC 0+1
Wrexham (Loaned on 6/2/1998) FL 4+1
Preston NE (£200,000 on 5/2/1999) FL 37+31/15 FLC 5+2/1 FAC 1+2
Oxford U (Free on 8/8/2002) FL 25+6/8 FLC 1 FAC 3 Others 1

BASS Jonathan (Jon) David
Born: Weston super Mare, 1 January 1976
Height: 6'0" **Weight:** 12.2
International Honours: E: Sch
Jon had a frustrating 2002-03 season, playing mainly reserve football for Hartlepool. With manager Chris Turner having assembled a strong squad, he could not break into the first team. He did play in the LDV Vans Trophy match, but this was essentially a Hartlepool reserve side. When new manager Mike Newell was appointed, the slate was wiped clean and he briefly came back into the frame with a couple of first-team appearances, but he failed to make much of an impression.
Birmingham C (From juniors on 27/6/1994) FL 60+8 FLC 7+1 FAC 5
Carlisle U (Loaned on 11/10/1996) FL 3
Gillingham (Loaned on 23/3/2000) FL 4+3
Hartlepool U (Free on 17/7/2001) FL 21+3/1 FLC 1 FAC 1 Others 1

BASTOCK Paul Anthony
Born: Leamington, 19 May 1970
Height: 5'10" **Weight:** 13.12
Club Honours: NC '02
This experienced goalkeeper was a key player in Boston's survival in Division Three last term. He kept 13 clean sheets in league games and his reaction stops often saved the day. Paul was the Pilgrims' only ever-present player and in the final game of the season at Cambridge he equalled the club record of 572 first-team appearances. An extremely popular player, he swept the board in the end of season 'Player of the Year' awards.
Cambridge U (Free from trainee at Coventry C on 22/3/1988) FL 12 FLC 1 (Free to Sabah, Malaysia during 1989 close season)
Boston U (Free from Kettering T, via Fisher Ath, on 3/8/1992) FL 46 FLC 2 FAC 1 Others 2

BATES Thomas (Tom)
Born: Coventry, 31 October 1985
Height: 5'10" **Weight:** 12.0
This young Coventry lad signed for the Sky Blues after impressing as a left-sided midfield player for Bedworth United youth team. After just two reserve appearances he came on as a substitute in the home game with Ipswich but had little opportunity to show his talents.
Coventry C (Signed from Bedworth U on 24/1/2003) FL 0+1

BATTERSBY Anthony (Tony)
Born: Doncaster, 30 August 1975
Height: 6'0" **Weight:** 12.7
This experienced target man struggled to find his form in the early part of the season at Lincoln. His only appearance was in a disappointing defeat at the hands of county rivals Boston United. Tony finally left Sincil Bank in October and subsequently signed for the Pilgrims, quickly making his mark by netting on his debut in an LDV Vans Trophy game with Yeovil. However, he was unable to keep up his scoring record and after losing his place to Richard Logan was released in January, later having a brief spell with Hucknall Town before linking up with Rushden & Diamonds. He spent a month at Nene Park, but failed to find the net and finished the season at Stevenage.
Sheffield U (From trainee on 5/7/1993) FL 3+7/1 FLC 1+1 Others 2+1/1
Southend U (Loaned on 23/3/1995) FL 6+2/1
Notts Co (£200,000 on 8/1/1996) FL 20+19/8 FLC 1 FAC 0+3 Others 4
Bury (£125,000 on 3/3/1997) FL 37+11/8 FLC 3+1/1 FAC 2
Lincoln C (£75,000 on 8/8/1998) FL 95+35/21 FLC 5/2 FAC 3+3/1 Others 8+1/2
Northampton T (Loaned on 24/9/1999) FL 0+3/1
Boston U (Free on 22/10/2002) FL 7+4/1 FAC 1/1 Others 2/1
Rushden & Diamonds (Free on 6/2/2003) FL 2+3

BAUDET Julien
Born: Grenoble, France, 13 January 1979
Height: 6'3" **Weight:** 14.2
Julien was initially signed as a centre half but found himself mainly deployed in a central-midfield role in his second season with Oldham Athletic. An uncompromising player with good passing ability, he contributed two league goals to the club's promotion push but became out of contract during the summer and faced an uncertain future as he awaited Latics' offer of a new deal.

Oldham Ath (Free from Toulouse, France on 9/10/2001) FL 34+10/3 FLC 2 FAC 2+2 Others 2

BAYLISS David Anthony
Born: Liverpool, 8 June 1976
Height: 5'11" **Weight:** 12.4
An injury picked up during the previous season left David out of the first-team reckoning for Luton at the start of last season. He made a brief and successful return to the line-up, but then lost his place. He then spent a frustrating time either injured or in the reserves, until his season was finally ended with an injury picked up at Wigan Athletic. David is a good reader of the game, while his tactical awareness and ability to play in more than one defensive position make him a useful member of the squad.
Rochdale (From trainee on 10/6/1995) FL 169+17/9 FLC 11 FAC 5+3 Others 12+1
Luton T (Free on 7/12/2001) FL 22+9 FLC 1

BAZELEY Darren Shaun
Born: Northampton, 5 October 1972
Height: 5'10" **Weight:** 11.7
Club Honours: Div 2 '98
International Honours: E: U21-1
After being out of first-team football for a season and a half following a torn cartilage, Darren made an immediate impact after linking up with his former boss Colin Lee at Walsall in the summer of 2002. He played 47 consecutive games on the right flank of the defence before moving to the substitutes' bench in April, showing himself to be consistently steady at the back and always willing to go forward. He also showed a very modest attitude, and after netting the vital penalty in the shoot-out in the FA Cup at Reading he immediately transferred the credit to 'keeper Jimmy Walker who had just brought off a penalty save.
Watford (From trainee on 6/5/1991) FL 187+53/21 FLC 13+5/2 FAC 12+1/3 Others 9+1/1
Wolverhampton W (Free on 13/7/1999) FL 69+1/4 FLC 7 FAC 3
Walsall (Free on 16/7/2002) FL 41+2 FLC 3 FAC 4

BEADLE Peter Clifford William James
Born: Lambeth, 13 May 1972
Height: 6'1" **Weight:** 13.10
Club Honours: AMC '03
This chirpy and popular forward returned to action with Bristol City after missing all of the 2001-02 campaign due to injury. He looked like cementing a regular place with some class performances when Lee

Peacock was sidelined with injury, but a thigh strain in the LDV Vans Trophy success against Queen's Park Rangers at Loftus Road in October put him out for a while. Chances were limited after that, and his ability to hold up the front line was often sorely missed in City's ranks. Peter was made available for transfer at the season's end.
Gillingham (From trainee on 5/5/1990) FL 42+25/14 FLC 2+4/2 FAC 1+1 Others 1
Tottenham H (£300,000 on 4/6/1992)
Bournemouth (Loaned on 25/3/1993) FL 9/2
Southend U (Loaned on 4/3/1994) FL 8/1
Watford (Signed on 12/9/1994) FL 12+11/1 FLC 1
Bristol Rov (£50,000 on 17/11/1995) FL 98+11/39 FLC 2+1 FAC 5/2 Others 7+1/1
Port Vale (£300,000 on 6/8/1998) FL 18+5/6 FLC 2 FAC 1
Notts Co (£250,000 on 18/2/1999) FL 14+8/3 FLC 1+3
Bristol C (£200,000 on 19/10/1999) FL 51+31/14 FLC 1+1 FAC 6+4/1 Others 6+6/4

BEAGRIE Peter Sydney
Born: Middlesbrough, 28 November 1965
Height: 5'8" **Weight:** 12.0
International Honours: E: B-2; U21-2
Player-coach Peter remained a key member of the Scunthorpe line-up throughout the 2002-03 campaign, commanding a place on the left wing whenever fit. Still a very tricky ball player, he missed two months of the season after an achilles operation in November but returned to help United into the play-offs with three goals during March. He was out of contract in the summer and at the time of writing his future was uncertain.
Middlesbrough (From juniors on 10/9/1983) FL 24+9/2 FLC 1 Others 1+1
Sheffield U (£35,000 on 16/8/1986) FL 81+3/11 FLC 5 FAC 5 Others 4
Stoke C (£210,000 on 29/6/1988) FL 54/7 FLC 4 FAC 3/1
Everton (£750,000 on 2/11/1989) F/PL 88+26/11 FLC 7+2/3 FAC 7+2 Others 5+1/1
Sunderland (Loaned on 26/9/1991) FL 5/1
Manchester C (£1,100,000 on 24/3/1994) F/PL 46+6/3 FLC 8/1 FAC 4+1/1
Bradford C (£50,000 on 2/7/1997) P/FL 113+18/20 FLC 9/3 FAC 5+1 Others 0+1
Everton (Loaned on 26/3/1998) PL 4+2
Wigan Ath (Free on 16/2/2001) FL 7+3/1 Others 2
Scunthorpe U (Free on 12/7/2001) FL 68+6/16 FLC 1 FAC 3 Others 4/2

BEAN Marcus Tristam
Born: Bournemouth, 2 November 1984
Height: 5'11" **Weight:** 11.6
This right-sided midfield player made his

debut for Queen's Park Rangers in the away game at Wycombe last August. Unfortunately he was one of four players (two from each side) that were sent off on that occasion, however, he returned to the line-up for a brief run in February and will be looking to gain further senior experience in 2003-04.
Queens Park R (Trainee) FL 4+3 Others 0+1

BEARD Mark
Born: Roehampton, 8 October 1974
Height: 5'10" **Weight:** 11.6
Mark is an experienced full back who can also contribute in a midfield role. This wealth of experience was a major asset to a very young Southend team last term and he filled in well at right back when Steve Broad was injured. Full of grit and determination, Mark may not be the most technically accomplished of players, but would run through a brick wall if you asked him to. He was released in the close season.
Millwall (From trainee on 18/3/1993) FL 32+13/2 FLC 3+1 FAC 4/1
Sheffield U (£117,000 on 18/8/1995) FL 22+16 FLC 2+1 FAC 2+2
Southend U (Loaned on 24/10/1997) FL 6+2 Others 1
Southend U (Free on 6/7/1998) FL 74+4/1 FLC 1 FAC 2 Others 1 (Released during 2000 close season)
Southend U (Free from Kingstonian on 11/10/2001) FL 34+16 FLC 1 FAC 4+1 Others 1+2

BEARDSLEY Christopher (Chris) Kelan
Born: Derby, 28 February 1984
Height: 6'0" **Weight:** 12.4
Chris was the leading scorer with Mansfield Town's youth team last season and was called into action at Brentford due to injuries to Andy White and Colin Larkin. He was then given his full debut in the local derby against Chesterfield when Iyseden Christie was suspended. Chris is a promising young striker and will be looking for more first-team experience in 2003-04.
Mansfield T (Trainee) FL 1+4

BEASANT David (Dave) John
Born: Willesden, 20 March 1959
Height: 6'4" **Weight:** 14.3
Club Honours: Div 4 '83, Div 2 '89; Div 1 '98; FAC '88; FMC '90
International Honours: E: 2; B-7
This veteran 'keeper had a brief spell with Bradford City in the early part of the 2002-03 season as cover for injuries, but failed to add to his total of senior

appearances and in October he joined Wigan Athletic on a non-contract basis. Signed as a back-up for John Filan, he became the Latics oldest player in senior football when he appeared in the LDV Vans Trophy match against Doncaster Rovers in November. In February he moved on to Brighton where he assisted in the Seagulls' unsuccessful battle to avoid relegation from the First Division. Dave provided a formidable last line of defence, impressing with his aerial work, the speed and vision of his distribution and his commanding presence.
Wimbledon *(£1,000 from Edgware T on 7/8/1979) FL 340 FLC 21 FAC 27 Others 3*
Newcastle U *(£800,000 on 13/6/1988) FL 20 FLC 2 FAC 2 Others 1*
Chelsea *(£725,000 on 14/1/1989) F/PL 133 FLC 11 FAC 5 Others 8*
Grimsby T *(Loaned on 24/10/1992) FL 6*
Wolverhampton W *(Loaned on 12/1/1993) FL 4 FAC 1*
Southampton *(£300,000 on 4/11/1993) PL 86+2 FLC 8 FAC 9*
Nottingham F *(Free on 22/8/1997) P/FL 139 FLC 8+1 FAC 6*

Portsmouth *(Free on 9/8/2001) FL 8 FLC 1*
Tottenham H *(Free on 16/11/2001)*
Portsmouth *(Free on 11/1/2002) FL 19*
Bradford C *(Free on 27/9/2002)*
Wigan Ath *(Free on 25/10/2002) Others 1*
Brighton & Hove A *(Free on 31/1/2003) FL 16*

BEATTIE James Scott
Born: Lancaster, 27 February 1978
Height: 6'1" **Weight:** 12.0
International Honours: E: 2; U21-5
Always a favourite with the Southampton crowd for both his endeavour and his indomitable approach, James lifted the club's 'Player of the Season' award for the second time in 2002-03. His campaign did not start well, commencing with six blank starts and relegation to the subs' bench before he netted at Aston Villa in October, but from then on he rarely missed a beat, netting 23 Premiership goals and staying in contention for the Golden Boot until the closing day of the season. James' form earned him an England call-up for the friendly against Australia in February.

Blackburn Rov *(From trainee on 7/3/1995) PL 1+3 FLC 2 FAC 0+1*
Southampton *(£1,000,000 on 17/7/1998) PL 118+38/51 FLC 9+3/3 FAC 13+1/2*

BECKETT Luke John
Born: Sheffield, 25 November 1976
Height: 5'11" **Weight:** 11.6
Luke had an excellent season at Stockport and but for an injury that ruled him out for the final games he would have pushed Robert Earnshaw closer for the Division Two Golden Boot. A tally of 27 goals, plus two more in the cups, was a tremendous return and saw the former Chesterfield striker collect all County's 'Player of the Year' awards. He scored his first-ever senior hat-trick against Northampton just before Christmas.
Barnsley *(From trainee on 20/6/1995)*
Chester C *(Free on 11/6/1998) FL 70+4/25 FLC 5/5 FAC 4/2 Others 1*
Chesterfield *(£75,000 on 19/7/2000) FL 58+4/22 FLC 4/2 FAC 3/2 Others 5*
Stockport Co *(£100,000 on 14/12/2001) FL 58+3/34 FLC 2/1 FAC 2/1 Others 1*

Mark Beard (left)

BECKHAM David Robert Joseph
Born: Leytonstone, 2 May 1975
Height: 6'0" **Weight:** 11.12
Club Honours: FAYC '92; PL '96, '97,
'99, '00, '01, '03; FAC '96, '99; CS '96,
'97; EC '99
International Honours: E: 60; U21-9; Yth
This sublime all-round midfielder
possesses a superb range of passing and
shooting skills and began the 2002-03
campaign with some masterful
performances for Manchester United.
After being sidelined by injury in
November and December, he returned to
show a real consistency as United tackled
the glory trail on four fronts. David netted
with a trademark free kick against Real
Madrid in the Champions' League, and a
vital Premiership goal against Charlton,
which kept United on course for yet
another Premiership title. His
performances as skipper of England were
also of a high class, keeping the side on
target for qualification for the Euro 2004
finals. To no one's surprise at all, David
became the latest superstar to join the
exodus to Spain when he finally signed
for Real Madrid during the summer break
after weeks of speculation. David was
awarded an OBE in the Queen's Birthday
Honours list in June.
*Manchester U (From trainee on 29/1/1993)
PL 237+28/62 FLC 10+2/1 FAC 22+2/6
Others 87+6/17*
Preston NE (Loaned on 28/2/1995) FL 4+1/2

BECKWITH Robert
Born: London, 12 September 1984
Height: 6'2" **Weight:** 13.5
This young 'keeper found himself thrown
into the spotlight of the Luton Town first
team when Mark Ovendale pulled out of
the Bristol City game minutes before kick
off. Robert took his chance well pulling
off a string of first-class saves. His
subsequent performances did enough for
him to finish the season as the Hatters'
first choice goalkeeper.
Luton T (Trainee) FL 4

BEDEAU Anthony (Tony)
Charles Osmond
Born: Hammersmith, 24 March 1979
Height: 5'10" **Weight:** 11.0
After struggling to fulfil his potential as a
striker in recent seasons, Tony was
reinvigorated by the appointment of Leroy
Rosenior as Torquay manager. He found
himself deployed wide on the right and
was served with the ball to feet to enable
him to use his speed to run at defenders.
After some scintillating early-season
displays his performances levelled off –

partly due to some close attention from
defenders – but he continued to work
hard and to track back and provide cover
for the full back. His most memorable
moment was a neatly chipped winner in
the local 'derby' at Exeter.
*Torquay U (From trainee on 28/7/1997) FL
163+52/46 FLC 7+1/3 FAC 10+3/1 Others 1+8*
Barnsley (Loaned on 1/2/2002) FL 0+3

BEECH Christopher (Chris)
Born: Congleton, 5 November 1975
Height: 5'10" **Weight:** 11.12
International Honours: E: Yth; Sch
Chris made a promising start to his
Rochdale career last term, but after only
three games he was sidelined with a
broken bone in his foot. This set the tone
for a season that saw him suffer three
lengthy periods out injured. When he was
available, he showed himself to be an
energetic midfielder capable of getting
into attacking positions. His campaign
was perhaps summed up, though, in
Dale's home game against Exeter when
he returned from injury to score a vital
goal but was injured again in the process.
Manchester C (From trainee on 12/11/1992)
*Cardiff C (Free on 7/8/1997) FL 46/1 FLC 2
FAC 6*
*Rotherham U (Free on 30/6/1998) FL
40+15/1 FLC 7 FAC 0+1*

BEECH Christopher (Chris)
Stephen
Born: Blackpool, 16 September 1974
Height: 5'11" **Weight:** 11.12
Chris made a promising start to his
Rochdale career last term, but after
only three games he was sidelined with a
broken bone in his foot. This set the tone
for a season that saw him suffer three
lengthy periods out injured. When he was
available, he showed himself to be an
energetic midfielder capable of getting
into attacking positions. His campaign
was perhaps summed up, though, in
Dale's home game against Exeter when
he returned from injury to score a vital
goal but was injured again in the process.
*Blackpool (From trainee on 9/7/1993) FL
53+29/4 FLC 4+4 FAC 1 Others 3+3/2*
*Hartlepool U (Free on 18/7/1996) FL
92+2/23 FLC 5/1 FAC 3/1 Others 3/1*
*Huddersfield T (£65,000 on 27/11/1998) FL
63+8/12 FLC 6/1 FAC 2/2*
*Rochdale (Free on 22/7/2002) FL 16+2/1
FAC 1/1*

BEEVERS Lee Jonathan
Born: Doncaster, 4 December 1983
Height: 6'1" **Weight:** 12.10
International Honours: W: Yth

This teenaged defender joined Boston
United on loan in March and after
impressing in the reserves he was
promoted to the subs' bench for the last
two first-team games. Lee made his
senior debut when he was introduced for
the final eight minutes of the last-day win
at Cambridge slotting in at right back.
Ipswich T (From trainee on 19/3/2001)
Boston U (Loaned on 27/3/2003) FL 0+1

BEHARALL David (Dave)
Alexander
Born: Jarrow, 8 March 1979
Height: 6'0" **Weight:** 11.12
Dave was highly unfortunate to fall from
the first-team reckoning at Oldham
during the 2002-03 campaign. He started
the season in fine form as part of an
impressive back three with Clint Hill and
Fitz Hall, but the emergence of young
Will Haining and the successful switch of
Chris Armstrong to centre half pushed
him down the pecking order. The
Geordie, who cost Latics a substantial fee,
will be looking to re-establish himself in
the line-up in 2003-04.
*Newcastle U (From trainee on 4/7/1997) PL
4+2*
*Grimsby T (Loaned on 10/8/2001) FL 13+1
FLC 1*
*Oldham Ath (£150,000 on 19/11/2001) FL
48+2/1 FLC 4 FAC 5 Others 2*

BELGRAVE Barrington
Born: Bedford, 16 September 1980
Height: 5'9" **Weight:** 11.8
Last season proved to be a rather
disappointing campaign for this Southend
United striker. He failed to win a regular
place in the starting line-up and at times
struggled to make the substitutes' bench.
However, on his day Barrington can be a
match winner as was demonstrated in the
home game with York City. He was
thrown on to try and break the deadlock
in a turgid encounter and scored a
brilliant injury-time winner. Barrington
was one of a number of players released
by the club at the end of the season.
*Plymouth Arg (From trainee at Norwich C
on 28/7/1999) FL 2+13 FLC 0+1 FAC 0+2
(Free to Yeovil T on 2/8/2000)*
*Southend U (£40,000 on 13/9/2001) FL
38+17/8 FAC 3+1/2 Others 3*

BELL David Anthony
Born: Kettering, 21 April 1984
Height: 5'10" **Weight:** 11.6
Club Honours: Div 3 '03
Premiership clubs quickly took interest in
this young midfielder after he broke into
the Rushden & Diamonds team and went
on to produce a series of eye-catching

displays. He spent two weeks training with Middlesbrough, although the bosses at Nene Park soon moved to end speculation over his future by offering an improved contract at the end of an amazing season for David.
Rushden & Diamonds (From juniors on 24/7/2001) FL 26+5/3 FLC 1 FAC 1+2 Others 1+1

BELL Lee
Born: Crewe, 26 January 1983
Height: 5'10" **Weight:** 11.10
Lee is another of the fine young prospects developing at Crewe and stepped up to make his senior debut from the substitutes' bench at Northampton on the opening day of the 2002-03 season. He scored his first senior goal against Colchester soon afterwards and featured regularly as a substitute during the campaign. Lee is a hard-working midfield player and will be looking to gain further experience at first-team level in 2003-04.
Crewe Alex (From trainee on 6/2/2001) FL 3+14/1 FAC 0+2 Others 1+3

BELL Michael (Mickey)
Born: Newcastle, 15 November 1971
Height: 5'9" **Weight:** 11.4
Club Honours: AMC '03
Despite yet another somewhat mixed bag season for this popular Bristol City wing back he was selected in the PFA divisional team for a fourth successive year. Mickey was unable to match his eight-goal record of the previous term, only managing a couple in league games. A stylish left-sided player, he has a powerful shot.
Northampton T (From trainee on 1/7/1990) FL 133+20/10 FLC 7+2 FAC 5/1 Others 9+2/1
Wycombe W (£45,000 on 21/10/1994) FL 117+1/5 FLC 5 FAC 9/2 Others 3+1
Bristol C (£150,000 on 2/7/1997) FL 230+4/33 FLC 12 FAC 16 Others 14/3

BELLAMY Craig Douglas
Born: Cardiff, 13 July 1979
Height: 5'9" **Weight:** 10.12
International Honours: W: 20; U21-8; Yth; Sch
Striker Craig's start to the 2002-03 season at Newcastle was delayed as he recovered from summer surgery to his knee, and he was then disrupted by a period of suspension. He returned as a substitute at Feyenoord when he scored in the last minute of each half to earn Newcastle their first win in the Champions' League and their passport into the second phase. Despite some problems with referees he had another fine season. His electric pace and livewire activity made him a constant

threat to opposition defences, while he created opportunities and scored regularly himself, including a superb effort at Southampton. He continued to play for Wales, netting the winner against Italy in the home Euro 2004 qualifier and scoring after only 13 seconds against Azerbaijan in March to record the fastest goal in Welsh international history.
Norwich C (From trainee on 20/1/1997) FL 71+13/32 FLC 6/2 FAC 1
Coventry C (£6,500,000 on 17/8/2000) PL 33+1/6 FLC 3/1 FAC 2/1
Newcastle U (£6,000,000 on 11/7/2001) PL 53+3/16 FLC 2+1/4 FAC 4 Others 12/3

BELLION David
Born: Sevres, France, 27 November 1982
Height: 5'11" **Weight:** 11.5
Sunderland's flying young left winger was widely tipped to establish himself at the Stadium of Light last term. Possessing electrifying pace, a thunderous shot, and the ability to turn defenders inside out, David was, however, dogged by a persistent heel injury although he showed just what he was capable of in his first Premiership start against Aston Villa. David is out of contract in the summer and his future was undecided at the time of writing.
Sunderland (Free from AS Cannes, France on 17/8/2001) PL 5+15/1 FLC 3 FAC 0+1

BELMADI Djemel
Born: Champigny sur Marne, France, 27 March 1976
Height: 5'8" **Weight:** 11.3
International Honours: Algeria
An on-loan signing from Marseilles early in 2003 this skilful midfielder or forward had always felt that his style of play would suit the Premiership. However, although he performed well in the reserve team, he did not always match this in his first-team outings. Djemel's produced a great display in first start against Fulham, but he was mysteriously left out of the next match, and only made one further start and another five appearances as substitute.
Manchester C (Loaned from Marseilles, France, ex Paris St Germain, on 3/1/2003) PL 2+6

BENALI Francis Vincent
Born: Southampton, 30 December 1968
Height: 5'10" **Weight:** 11.0
International Honours: E: Sch
Presently Southampton's longest-serving player and a 'legend' with the fans, Francis made his debut at St Mary's against Sunderland last January having been kept out of the side by the

seemingly invulnerable Wayne Bridge since before the Saints' moved from the Dell in the summer of 2001. He slotted straight back into his customary left-back berth and it looked as if he had never been away, as he cajoled his team mates and got stuck in. He relished the two hard fought FA Cup ties with Millwall, in the first of which he distinguished himself with a characteristic header off the goal line. However, Francis was later supplanted as reserve left back by the arrival of Danny Higginbotham at the end of the January transfer window.
Southampton (From apprentice on 5/11/1987) F/PL 271+40/1 FLC 24+7 FAC 23 Others 3+1
Nottingham F (Loaned on 12/1/2001) FL 15

BENARBIA Ali
Born: Oran, Algeria, 8 October 1968
Height: 5'7" **Weight:** 10.7
International Honours: Algeria: Div 1 '02
The little magician struggled a bit more in the Premiership in 2002-03 as age seemed to catch up on him. Ali started 23 games in all competitions and completed only 15. At the start of the season he was named captain of Manchester City but this seemed to affect his performances and by November he was on the substitutes' bench. However two consecutive scoring appearances around Christmas including a cracking strike against Tottenham enabled him to return to the line-up. Ali was virtually an ever-present in the second half of the campaign and showed more of the form that the Blues fans have come to expect from him.
Manchester C (Free from Paris St Germain, France, ex Martigues, AS Monaco, Bordeaux, on 14/9/2001) P/FL 59+12/11 FLC 4 FAC 3

BENEFIELD James (Jimmy) Patrick
Born: Torbay, 6 May 1983
Height: 5'10" **Weight:** 11.2
This promising attacking midfielder had few chances to build on the rapid progress he made at Torquay in 2001-02. He managed a handful of appearances from the substitutes' bench, but failed to make the starting line-up throughout the 2002-03 campaign.
Torquay U (From trainee on 12/7/2001) FL 3+14 FLC 0+1 FAC 0+2 Others 0+1

BENJAMIN Trevor Junior
Born: Kettering, 8 February 1979
Height: 6'2" **Weight:** 13.2
International Honours: Jamaica: 1; E: U21-1

This powerfully built striker started to make a real impact at Leicester last season, finding the net in the away win over Wimbledon and also the Worthington Cup tie at Hillsborough. His whole-hearted approach made him a favourite of the club's fans and he enhanced his standing with his first home strike against Pompey. A run of goal-scoring form followed as his confidence blossomed during the latter part of the campaign and he rounded off the season with a coolly struck spot kick at Molineux. Trevor has now clocked up more career substitute appearances for the Foxes than any other player. He made his debut at international level for Jamaica against Nigeria in November.

Cambridge U *(From trainee on 21/2/1997)*
FL 96+27/35 FLC 7+3/4 FAC 9+1/5 Others 3/2
Leicester C *(£1,000,000 + on 14/7/2000)*
P/FL 29+38/9 FLC 2+3/1 FAC 2+3
Crystal Palace *(Loaned on 20/12/2001) FL 5+1/1*
Norwich C *(Loaned on 8/2/2002) FL 3+3*
West Bromwich A *(Loaned on 27/3/2002) FL 0+3/1*

BENNETT Daniel (Dan) Mark
Born: Great Yarmouth, 7 January 1978
Height: 6'0" **Weight:** 12.0
International Honours: Singapore
Dan returned to the Far East in May 2002 to play for Singapore Armed Forces, assisting them to the championship of the S-League. The cultured centre back then returned to Wrexham in August and featured strongly in the early part of the season. However, he suffered a freak knee injury, twisting ligaments during a weekend run in late December and subsequently found it difficult to get back in the side. Dan made his international debut for Singapore against the Philippines and featured strongly in the Tiger Cup tournament held in December.

Wrexham *(Free from Tanjong Pager U, Malaysia on 31/1/2002) FL 5+1 (Free to Singapore Armed Forces in May 2002)*
Wrexham *(Free on 8/8/2002) FL 14+4 FLC 1 Others 2*

BENNETT Dean Alan
Born: Wolverhampton, 13 December 1977
Height: 5'10" **Weight:** 11.0
Club Honours: NC '00
International Honours: E: SP-1
A lively attacking midfielder, Dean was mostly employed at right wing back for Kidderminster last term. After setting a club record by scoring in seven consecutive games in the previous season he found the target just once – against

---

Leyton Orient on Boxing Day. His performances throughout the campaign, however, marked him out to be one of the most improved players in the Harriers' squad.

West Bromwich A *(Free from Aston Villa juniors on 19/12/1996) FL 0+1 (Free to Bromsgrove Rov on 14/9/98)*
Kidderminster Hrs *(£30,000 on 29/1/1999) FL 102+14/13 FLC 2 FAC 3+3 Others 3+2/1*

BENNETT Ian Michael
Born: Worksop, 10 October 1971
Height: 6'0" **Weight:** 12.10
Club Honours: Div 2 '95; AMC '95
Ian played second fiddle to Nico Vaesen in goal for Birmingham City for most of his testimonial season until returning in January for two games. His saves helped Blues gain a point at Blackburn during a bleak run but he was then dropped following the 4-2 defeat by Bolton. However, Vaesen's knee injury in March gave him another opportunity and he grasped his chance firmly, pulling off some fine stops during the run-in.

Newcastle U *(From trainee at Queens Park R on 20/3/1989)*
Peterborough U *(Free on 22/3/1991) FL 72 FLC 10 FAC 3 Others 4*
Birmingham C *(£325,000 on 17/12/1993) P/FL 281 FLC 38 FAC 16 Others 13*

BENNETT Neil Robert
Born: Dewsbury, 29 October 1980
Height: 6'2" **Weight:** 13.0
Club Honours: SLCC '02
The former Airdrie goalkeeper spent the first part of the 2002-03 season in the reserves at Bradford. In transfer deadline week, though, he moved on non-contract terms to Rochdale to provide some experienced cover for Matthew Gilks. However, he made just one appearance for Dale, when Gilks missed the fixture against Kidderminster due to the after effects of concussion suffered in the previous game.

Sheffield Wed *(From trainee on 20/10/1998. Free to Ossett T during 2000 close season)*
Airdrieonians *(Free on 7/8/2001) SL 10+1 SC 0+1 Others 2 (Free to Barrow during 2002 close season)*
Rochdale *(Free from Drogheda U, via spell at Bradford C, on 27/3/2003) FL 1*

BENNETT Thomas (Tom) McNeill
Born: Falkirk, 12 December 1969
Height: 5'11" **Weight:** 11.8
This vastly experienced midfield player captained the Boston United team in their first few months of League football after signing from Walsall. He produced his

---

best football in the latter stages of the season when his skill on the ball created a plentiful supply of chances for his team mates.

Aston Villa *(From apprentice on 16/12/1987)*
Wolverhampton W *(Free on 5/7/1988) FL 103+12/2 FLC 7 FAC 5+2 Others 3+1*
Stockport Co *(£75,000 on 23/6/1995) FL 105+5/5 FLC 20/2 FAC 10 Others 6+1*
Walsall *(Loaned on 30/12/1999) FL 4/1*
Walsall *(Free on 23/3/2000) FL 75+10/7 FLC 1+1 FAC 5/1 Others 3*
Boston U *(Free on 9/8/2002) FL 29+4 FLC 2 FAC 1 Others 2*

BENT Darren Ashley
Born: Wandsworth, 6 February 1984
Height: 5'11" **Weight:** 11.7
International Honours: E: U21-2; Yth
Darren celebrated his first full season in the Ipswich Town first team by finishing as the club's second-highest scorer with 18 goals in all competitions. One of the more memorable ones came in the home game with Sheffield United when ten-man Town came back from 2-0 down to win 3-2. Darren hit the winning goal when he got on the end of Darren Ambrose's cross and headed home. He is good in the air and has a strong right foot but his best asset is his pace, and this was used to maximum effect by playing him wide on the right-hand side of midfield on occasions.

Ipswich T *(From trainee on 2/7/2001) P/FL 26+14/13 FLC 3+1/3 FAC 0+2/3 Others 1+4/1*

BENT Jason
Born: Toronto, Canada, 8 March 1977
Height: 5'9" **Weight:** 11.7
Club Honours: Div 3 '02
International Honours: Canada: 30; Yth
Following a successful end to the 2001-02 season, Jason started last term in Plymouth's midfield and put in some excellent displays in the opening matches. However, a hamstring tear in the 2-0 victory over Bristol City in August ruled him out until Boxing Day. A firm favourite with the Argyle faithful, Jason scored a solitary league goal, netting in the 6-1 victory against Peterborough United in March.

Plymouth Arg *(Free from Colorado Rapids, USA on 21/9/2001) FL 39+7/4 FAC 3+2/1 Others 1*

BENT Marcus Nathan
Born: Hammersmith, 19 May 1978
Height: 6'2" **Weight:** 12.4
International Honours: E: U21-2
Marcus had a mixed time at Ipswich last term, missing the middle part of the

---

season through injury and struggling to regain his form when he did return to first-team action. His style of play is reminiscent of the traditional centre forward, holding the ball up and then spreading it wide and attempting to get on the end of the resultant cross. He is probably disappointed that he was only able to score 12 goals during the season, although this was still a respectable total.

Brentford *(From trainee on 21/7/1995) FL 56+14/8 FLC 7/1 FAC 8/3 Others 5+1/1*
Crystal Palace *(£150,000 + on 8/1/1998) P/FL 13+15/5 FLC 0+2 FAC 0+1*
Port Vale *(£375,000 on 15/1/1999) FL 17+6/1 FLC 1*
Sheffield U *(£300,000 on 28/10/1999) FL 48/20 FLC 5/3 FAC 3/1*
Blackburn Rov *(£1,300,000 + on 24/11/2000) P/FL 22+15/8 FLC 0+1 FAC 5+1/3*

Ipswich T *(£3,000,000 on 23/11/2001) PL 47+10/20 FLC 0+1 FAC 4/1 Others 2+1/1*

BENTLEY David Michael
Born: Peterborough, 27 August 1984
Height: 5'10" **Weight:** 11.0
International Honours: E:Yth
David is a highly rated young striker with Arsenal who is seen as an exciting prospect by the staff at Highbury. He made his first-team debut as a substitute in the FA Cup match versus Oxford United. Technically very gifted, he scored some fantastic goals in the reserves and also featured in the England U19 squad.
Arsenal *(From trainee on 8/9/2001) FAC 0+1*

BERESFORD David
Born: Middleton, 11 November 1976
Height: 5'5" **Weight:** 11.4
International Honours: E: Yth; Sch
This diminutive winger joined Plymouth Argyle during the 2002 close season and made his debut in the fine victory at Cheltenham Town in August. However, he found it difficult to win a regular place in Argyle's line-up, making the majority of his appearances from the substitutes' bench. Towards the end of the season he returned to the fray and put in some excellent displays with many of his curling, inviting crosses leading to goal-scoring opportunities.
Oldham Ath *(From trainee on 22/7/1994) P/FL 32+32/2 FLC 3+3 FAC 0+1 Others 3*
Swansea C *(Loaned on 11/8/1995) FL 4+2*
Huddersfield T *(£350,000 on 27/3/1997) FL 24+11/3 FLC 2+3 FAC 1+1*
Preston NE *(Loaned on 17/12/1999) FL 1+3 FAC 0+1 Others 1*
Port Vale *(Loaned on 15/9/2000) FL 4*
Hull C *(Free on 4/7/2001) FL 33+8/1 FLC 2 FAC 1 Others 3*
Plymouth Arg *(Free on 23/7/2002) FL 6+10 Others 2*

BERESFORD Marlon
Born: Lincoln, 2 September 1969
Height: 6'1" **Weight:** 13.6
After Marlon represented Burnley in the pre-season Isle of Man tournament, it was something of a shock when the 'keeper began the new campaign at York. He appeared in the opening six games for the Minstermen, playing an important part in their fine start. Within a month he was back at Turf Moor, and his return to the side coincided with the club's' first win of the season, at Derby. Always a popular figure with the Clarets' faithful, his reputation was enhanced with some stunning saves, notably in the Worthington Cup tie at Huddersfield and

Marcus Bent

the FA Cup game at Brentford. However, he was rested following the 7-4 home defeat against Watford, and Nik Michopoulos was restored to first-team duties.
Sheffield Wed *(From trainee on 23/9/1987)*
Bury *(Loaned on 25/8/1989) FL 1*
Northampton T *(Loaned on 27/9/1990) FL 13 Others 2*
Crewe Alex *(Loaned on 28/2/1991) FL 3*
Northampton T *(Loaned on 15/8/1991) FL 15*
Burnley *(£95,000 on 28/8/1992) FL 240 FLC 18 FAC 20 Others 16*
Middlesbrough *(£500,000 on 10/3/1998) P/FL 8+2 FLC 3*
Sheffield Wed *(Loaned on 12/1/2000) FL 4*
Burnley *(Loaned on 31/1/2002) FL 13*
Burnley *(Free on 19/7/2002)*
York C *(Free on 5/8/2002) FL 6*
Burnley *(Free on 10/10/2002) FL 33+1 FLC 4 FAC 5*

BERG Henning

Born: Eidsvell, Norway, 1 September 1969
Height: 6'0" **Weight:** 12.7
Club Honours: PL '95, '99, '00; FLC '02
International Honours: Norway: 95; U21-15; Yth
This consistently dependable player was again a key figure for Blackburn Rovers last term, the team always appearing far more comfortable with a central defensive pairing of Henning with Craig Short than any other combination. His four-month absence with achilles tendon trouble was hugely contributory to the club losing their way in the Premiership, but once he was restored to the line-up the defence was as sound as ever. Although he announced his retirement before the end of the campaign, it is still possible he may continue his career elsewhere.
Blackburn Rov *(£400,000 from Lillestrom, Norway, ex VIF, on 26/11/1993) PL 154+5/4 FLC 16 FAC 10 Others 9*
Manchester U *(£5,000,000 on 12/8/1997) PL 49+17/2 FLC 3 FAC 7 Others 22+5/1*
Blackburn Rov *(£1,750,000 on 8/9/2000) P/FL 90+1/3 FLC 3 FAC 6 Others 1+1*

BERGER Patrik

Born: Prague, Czechoslovakia, 10 November 1973
Height: 6'1" **Weight:** 12.6
Club Honours: FAC '01; UEFAC '01; CS '01
International Honours: Czech Republic: 44; Czechoslovakia: 2; Yth (UEFA-U16 '90)
The Czech international midfielder sadly faded into obscurity at Anfield last season. After two injury-plagued seasons for Liverpool, Patrik desperately needed to

re-establish himself, but instead he was sidelined for half the season with a knee injury. Ironically in his only start in the line-up, against Southampton in the Worthington Cup in November, he hit another of his trademark goals with a skimming 30-yard free kick to open the scoring in a 3-1 victory. This remained his only appearance, barring two brief substitute outings in September, until the end of the season when he was again brought on in the final match at Chelsea, which sealed Liverpool's fate as also-rans for Champions' League qualification.
Liverpool *(£3,250,000 from Borussia Dortmund, Germany, ex Slavia Prague, on 15/8/1996) PL 106+42/28 FLC 9+2/3 FAC 4+4 Others 17+12/4*

BERGKAMP Dennis Nicolaas Maria

Born: Amsterdam, Holland, 18 May 1969
Height: 6'0" **Weight:** 12.5
Club Honours: PL '98, '02; FAC '02, '03; CS '98, '02
International Honours: Holland: 79; U21
Dennis is an extremely talented striker with the ability to score and create goals from nothing. He continued his established partnership with Thierry Henry last term, and whilst he was generally an automatic choice to start games, suspension and minor injuries limited his appearances. Dennis scored his 100th goal for Arsenal in the FA Cup tie against Oxford.
Arsenal *(£7,500,000 from Inter Milan, Italy, ex Ajax, on 3/7/1995) PL 204+30/73 FLC 15/8 FAC 26+5/13 Others 30+6/10*

BERGSSON Gudni

Born: Reykjavik, Iceland, 21 July 1965
Height: 6'1" **Weight:** 12.3
Club Honours: Div 1 '97
International Honours: Iceland: 80; U21-4; Yth
It is not too often that the term 'legend' can be applied to a player, but Gudni has certainly earned that accolade during his eight years with Bolton. Having postponed his impending retirement during the previous two campaigns, it was common knowledge that the 2002-03 season was to be his last as a professional footballer. To say he went out on a high would be an understatement of huge proportions. Playing in his favoured centre-back role, Gudni was a rock at the heart of the Bolton defence, where his assured and confident displays belied his advancing years. His performances were such that he won a recall to Iceland's

national team and he was a major factor in Wanderers retaining their Premiership status. Perhaps the highest compliment that could be attributed to Gudni is that he will be a very tough act to follow in the Bolton rearguard.
Tottenham H *(£100,000 from Valur, Iceland on 15/12/1988) F/PL 51+20/2 FLC 4+2 FAC 2+2 Others 5+1*
Bolton W *(£115,000 on 21/3/1995) P/FL 263+7/23 FLC 23+2/1 FAC 12/1 Others 8+2/2*

BERKOVIC Eyal

Born: Haifa, Israel, 2 April 1972
Height: 5'7" **Weight:** 10.6
Club Honours: SLC '00; Div 1 '02
International Honours: Israel: 75; U21
Eyal produced some brilliant displays in midfield for Manchester City last term, but unfortunately the second half of his season was cut short mainly due to constant niggling injuries. Most of City's best displays were prompted by his enterprise and skill; his movement off the ball and probing passes being particularly effective. Probably his best two performances came in the 'derby' games against Manchester United when he was exceptional, setting up the clinching third goal at home and generally being all over the pitch in both matches. Eyal also appeared for the Israeli national side when fully fit.
Southampton *(Loaned from Maccabi Tel Aviv, Israel on 11/10/1996) PL 26+2/4 FLC 5+1/2 FAC 1*
West Ham U *(£1,700,000 on 30/7/1997) PL 62+3/10 FLC 6 FAC 7+1/2*
Glasgow Celtic *(£5,500,000 on 20/7/1999) SL 29+3/9 SLC 0+2 SC 1 Others 3+3*
Blackburn Rov *(Loaned on 9/2/2001) FL 4+7/2 FAC 3*
Manchester C *(£1,500,000 on 2/8/2001) P/FL 47+5/7 FLC 3+1/1 FAC 3+1/1*

BERNARD Olivier

Born: Paris, France, 14 October 1979
Height: 5'9" **Weight:** 12.6
After a tug of war between Newcastle and West Ham during the summer Olivier remained on Tyneside with a new long-term contract and began the 2002-03 campaign as first choice left back. After a run in the team he had a spell on the bench in the autumn, but was recalled at Old Trafford and thereafter established himself in the side for most of the season, primarily at left back but occasionally left midfield. Strong in the tackle and comfortable on the ball with a good left foot, he particularly enjoys raiding down the touchline, as exemplified at home to Chelsea when he capped a fine display

with a sublime goal chipped over the 'keeper from close in.
Newcastle U *(Signed from Lyon, France, on 26/10/2000) PL 28+18/5 FLC 3 FAC 3 Others 8+5*
Darlington *(Loaned on 13/3/2001) FL 9+1/2*

BERNARD Paul Robert
Born: Edinburgh, 30 December 1972
Height: 5'11" **Weight:** 11.12
Club Honours: SLC '95
International Honours: S: 2; B-1; U21-15
Paul signed non-contract terms for Plymouth Argyle last November after a lengthy period on the sidelines with a career-threatening achilles injury. He made his debut on the left-hand side of midfield against Notts County in December but only managed a further nine appearances during the season. He was released by the Pilgrims in May.
Oldham Ath *(From trainee on 16/7/1991) P/FL 105+7/18 FLC 11+1/2 FAC 11/1 Others 1+1*
Aberdeen *(£800,000 on 27/9/1995) SL 91+9/6 SLC 12 SC 11/2 Others 1 (Freed on 5/11/2001)*
Plymouth Arg *(Free, after recovering from a long-term injury, on 20/12/2002) FL 7+3*

BERTHELIN Cedric
Born: Courrieres, France, 25 December 1976
Height: 6'4" **Weight:** 14.12
Cedric made the transition to English Second Division football with perfect ease last season, and he had the best overall record of all the goalkeepers Luton used. He is a big man, good in the air, superb at being able to position himself when his goal is under threat and above all able to fully dominate his area. He later moved on to Crystal Palace where he featured in a dozen games including the memorable FA Cup win at Liverpool.
Luton T *(Free from RC Lens, France on 1/10/2002) FL 9*
Crystal Palace *(Free on 31/12/2002) FL 9 FAC 2+1*

BERTOS Leonida (Leo)
Christos
Born: Wellington, New Zealand, 20 December 1981
Height: 6'0" **Weight:** 12.6
International Honours: New Zealand: U22; Yth; Sch
Leo scored his first-ever league goal for Barnsley after coming on as a substitute against Bristol City last term. However he suffered a frustrating season on the fringes of the first team. He is a powerful runner with the ball and possesses a

strong shot, but he could not make the break into the side on a regular basis. Leo featured for the New Zealand U22 team against Japan at the end of May.
Barnsley *(Signed from Wellington Olympic, New Zealand on 1/9/2000) FL 4+8/1 FAC 0+1*

BESWETHERICK Jonathan (Jon) Barry
Born: Liverpool, 15 January 1978
Height: 5'11" **Weight:** 11.4
Club Honours: Div 3 '02
This attacking left wing back came to Sheffield Wednesday with a glowing

reputation, but after featuring in several early-season games he lost his place and then fell out of favour. He eventually joined Swindon Town on loan with a view to a permanent move and impressed for the Second Division club on his debut against Queen's Park Rangers. However, he struggled to make an impact thereafter and returned to Hillsborough.
Plymouth Arg *(From trainee on 27/7/1996) FL 133+13 FLC 3 FAC 14+2 Others 4*
Sheffield Wed *(Free on 6/6/2002) FL 5+1 FAC 1*
Swindon T *(Loaned on 21/2/2003) FL 3*

Kevin Betsy

BETSY Kevin Eddie Lewis
Born: Seychelles, 20 March 1978
Height: 6'1" **Weight:** 11.12
International Honours: E: SP-1
Kevin was a permanent fixture in the Barnsley line-up last season until suffering a broken toe in mid-January, but he soon recovered and was back in action in March. He played mostly as a winger, showing plenty of pace and tricks. Kevin was also occasionally used as a striker, and his two goals brought the Reds maximum points against Brentford.
Fulham (£80,000 + from Woking on 16/9/1998) P/FL 3+12/1 FLC 2+1 FAC 0+1 Others 1
Bournemouth (Loaned on 3/9/1999) FL 1+4
Hull C (Loaned on 26/11/1999) FL 1+1 Others 1
Barnsley (£200,000 on 28/2/2002) FL 42+7/5 FLC 1 FAC 1 Others 1

BETTS Robert
Born: Doncaster, 21 December 1981
Height: 5'10" **Weight:** 11.0
This young midfielder failed to make an impression in three first-team outings for Coventry City last term, one of them as a full back, and before the end of the season he had gone on loan to AIK Solna. He did however score his first senior goal for the Sky Blues with a penalty in the 8-0 Worthington Cup win over Rushden & Diamonds. A strong tackler who uses the ball well, he was given a free transfer in the summer.
Doncaster Rov (Trainee) FL 2+1
Coventry C (From trainee on 23/12/1998) P/FL 5+8 FLC 1/1 FAC 2+1
Plymouth Arg (Loaned on 16/2/2001) FL 3+1
Lincoln C (Loaned on 11/10/2001) FL 1+2 Others 0+1

BETTS Simon Richard
Born: Middlesbrough, 3 March 1973
Height: 5'7" **Weight:** 11.6
This experienced defender made the right-back slot his own at Darlington, although he occasionally stepped in on the left flank when required. Simon's quick tackling and sure distribution established him as a key member of the Quakers' defence and he scored his first goal for the club in Hull's emotional last match at Boothferry Park in December, when Darlington spoiled the party with a 1-0 win.
Ipswich T (From trainee on 2/7/1991)
Colchester U (Free, via trials at Wrexham and Scarborough, on 11/12/1992) FL 182+9/11 FLC 9 FAC 8+2 Others 14/2 (Free to Scarborough during 1999 close season)
Darlington (Free from Yeovil T on 26/7/2001) FL 69/1 FLC 1 FAC 7 Others 3

BEVAN Scott
Born: Southampton, 16 September 1979
Height: 6'6" **Weight:** 15.10
This giant goalkeeper joined Huddersfield Town in a season-long loan deal in July 2002 and soon established himself as the club's first-choice 'keeper. A fine shot stopper who commands his goalmouth well, he earned several early-season 'Man of the Match' awards with some outstanding saves. Scott was always quick to turn defence into attack with some long throws and accurate kicking, and he was even keen to join in the attack for those last-minute corners. He faded from the picture late on after suffering a groin injury.
Southampton (From trainee on 16/1/1998)
Huddersfield T (Loaned on 27/7/2002) FL 30 FLC 2 FAC 1 Others 1

BIGNOT Marcus
Born: Birmingham, 22 August 1974
Height: 5'10" **Weight:** 11.2
Club Honours: Div 3 '03
International Honours: E: SP-1
This utility man turned down the offer of a new contract at Queen's Park Rangers last summer and initially joined Rushden & Diamonds on a monthly contract. He immediately stepped into the line-up, featuring at right back on the opening day at Swansea City. Despite suffering a knee injury on his home debut against Torquay United three days later, Marcus impressed enough to earn a permanent contract at Nene Park. He only missed one game after October and earned the club's 'Best Newcomer' award along with a Third Division championship medal.
Crewe Alex (£150,000 + from Kidderminster Hrs on 1/9/1997) FL 93+2 FLC 8 FAC 3
Bristol Rov (Free on 7/8/2000) FL 26/1 FLC 5/2 FAC 1 Others 3
Queens Park R (Signed on 16/3/2001) FL 49+5/1 FLC 1 FAC 1 Others 1
Rushden & Diamonds (Free on 8/8/2002) FL 33 FLC 0+1 FAC 3 Others 1

BILLY Christopher (Chris) Anthony
Born: Huddersfield, 2 January 1973
Height: 5'11" **Weight:** 11.8
After suffering a gashed knee in a pre-season game against Manchester City, Chris missed Bury's opening two games last term. However, he was soon re-installed in his favourite defensive central-midfield position and went on to score four important goals, including a superb left-foot volley at Swansea and the winner at Rushden. He missed three games in March after suffering a knee

injury at home to Bristol Rovers. Chris was reported to have signed for Carlisle United during the summer.
Huddersfield T (From trainee on 1/7/1991) FL 76+18/4 FLC 8+2 FAC 5 Others 15+2/2
Plymouth Arg (Signed on 10/8/1995) FL 107+11/9 FLC 5 FAC 8/1 Others 5+1
Notts Co (Free on 2/7/1998) FL 3+3 FLC 2
Bury (Free on 17/9/1998) FL 165+13/11 FLC 6+1 FAC 7/1 Others 5+1

BIMSON Stuart James
Born: Liverpool, 29 September 1969
Height: 5'11" **Weight:** 11.12
This enthusiastic left-sided defender played an important role in Lincoln's back five last season. Stuart was sharp in the tackle and always keen to get forward. His only goal of the campaign was from the penalty spot when he netted the winner at Hull City.
Bury (£12,500 from Macclesfield T on 6/2/1995) FL 36 FLC 5 Others 3
Lincoln C (Free on 29/11/1996) FL 157+18/4 FLC 2 FAC 7+2 Others 14+1/1

BIRCH Gary Stephen
Born: Birmingham, 8 October 1981
Height: 5'10" **Weight:** 11.6
Gary began the 2002-03 season as a first choice striker for Walsall and set up Moriera Herivelto's goal in the first away game against Wolves at Molineux. His high work rate made him a popular figure whether in attack or midfield and he got his first league goal for the Saddlers with a neat header at Burnley. A mystery groin injury, however, limited him to occasional substitute appearances in the latter part of the season.
Walsall (From trainee on 31/10/1998) FL 6+14/1 FLC 0+1 Others 2/1
Exeter C (Loaned on 22/3/2001) FL 6+3/2
Exeter C (Loaned on 10/8/2001) FL 5+10 Others 1

BIRCH Mark
Born: Stoke, 5 January 1977
Height: 5'10" **Weight:** 12.5
Mark is a whole-hearted performer who featured in midfield and central defence as well as his more accustomed position of right back for Carlisle last season. A popular player with the Brunton Park faithful who appreciate his dedication to the cause, his first-ever goal for the club, which secured victory in the vital relegation battle against Macclesfield, was greeted with unusual acclaim.
Stoke C (From trainee on 8/7/1995. Free to Northwich Vic on 22/7/98)
Carlisle U (£10,000 on 10/8/2000) FL 107+3/1 FLC 4 FAC 8 Others 4+1

BIRCHALL Christopher (Chris)
Born: Stafford, 5 May 1984
Height: 5'9" **Weight:** 12.12
This all-action right winger was still learning his trade for Port Vale last term. Chris was on the bench half-a-dozen times before being called into action at Barnsley just after Christmas. His only other appearance came at Queen's Park Rangers in February, but Vale were getting the run-around at that stage, eventually losing 4-0.
Port Vale (Trainee) FL 0+3 FLC 0+1

BIRCHAM Marc Stephen John
Born: Wembley, 11 May 1978
Height: 5'10'' **Weight:** 12.4
Club Honours: Div 2 '01
International Honours: Canada: 13; U23-1
This central midfield player joined Queen's Park Rangers during the 2002 close season and made his debut in the opening game against Chesterfield when he turned out with his hair dyed in the club colours of blue and white. Soon afterwards he was sidelined by injury for a period of two months, but quickly returned to the side once fit again. He scored just two goals, although his strike against Brentford in December broke a run of over 500 minutes without a goal for the club. Marc was a Rangers supporter in his younger days and became the first member of the Supporters' Association to play for the club at first-team level!
Millwall (From trainee on 22/5/1996) FL 86+18/3 FLC 3+1 FAC 6+1/1 Others 5+1
Queens Park R (Free on 10/7/2002) FL 34+2/2 FAC 2 Others 3

BIRD David Alan
Born: Gloucester, 26 December 1984
Height: 5'8" **Weight:** 12.2
Having spent the best part of two seasons in the Cheltenham Town youth and reserve teams this powerful central midfield player got his chance when defender Antony Griffin was injured in the warm-up before the Division Two fixture at Huddersfield in February. David was pressed into action at right back and did so well that he made the position his own for the final two months of the campaign. He learned the new position quickly and while he still needs to work at his defending, David has a calm temperament and added an extra angle to the attack with some strong running and measured crosses.
Cheltenham T (Signed from Cinderford T on 1/2/2001) FL 12+2

BISCAN Igor
Born: Yugoslavia, 4 May 1978
Height: 6'3" **Weight:** 12.8
Club Honours: FLC '01, '03; ESC '01; CS '01
International Honours: Croatia: 15
Despite having been with Liverpool for two-and-a-half years the Croatian international has yet to make his mark at Anfield. His infrequent appearances last season, although more than in the previous campaign, were mainly from the bench. Although signed as a midfield player, four of his five starts were in central defence, deputising for Stephane Henchoz or Sami Hyppia. This may prove to be his best long-term position, although whether at Anfield remains to be seen.
Liverpool (£3,500,000 from Dynamo Zagreb, Croatia, ex Samobar, on 7/12/2000) PL 15+9 FLC 6+1/1 FAC 3+2 Others 1+7

Chris Billy (right)

BISCHOFF Mikkel

Born: Denmark, 3 March 1982
Height: 6'4" **Weight:** 13.5
International Honours: Denmark: U21;
Yth

A close-season signing by Manchester City, this young central defender showed plenty of promise last term. Mikkel produced some good displays for the reserves and made his only Premiership appearance against Blackburn Rovers, although he regularly featured on the bench in the closing stages. He also represented Denmark at U21 level during the campaign.

Manchester C (£750,000 from FC Copenhagen, Denmark on 2/7/2002) PL 1

BISHOP Andrew (Andy) Jamie

Born: Stone, 19 October 1982
Height: 6'0" **Weight:** 11.2

This promising striker joined Kidderminster on loan from Walsall last November and remained at Aggborough for the rest of the season. He made his Football League debut as a substitute at Torquay when he came on with his side 2-0 down and turned the game, setting up the first goal and scoring the equaliser himself. Despite being tall and lanky Andy showed great ball skills, with a good first touch and the ability to take the ball past defenders.

Walsall (From trainee on 9/8/2002)
Kidderminster Hrs (Loaned on 18/11/2002)
FL 22+7/5 Others 0+1

BISHOP Ian William

Born: Liverpool, 29 May 1965
Height: 5'9" **Weight:** 10.12
International Honours: E: B-1

The veteran midfielder started the 2002-03 campaign with a spell at League of Wales outfit Barry Town, where he featured in the qualifying ties for the European Champions' League. He subsequently joined Rochdale on a short-term basis as Paul Simpson looked to add some guile to his side. Ian figured prominently in a victory over Carlisle in September before being injured. He made five more starts, but Dale were going through a bad patch and after another injury he cancelled his contract in January to return to the USA.

Everton (From apprentice on 24/5/1983) FL 0+1
Crewe Alex (Loaned on 22/3/1984) FL 4
Carlisle U (£15,000 on 11/10/1984) FL 131+1/14 FLC 8/1 FAC 5/1 Others 4
Bournemouth (£35,000 on 14/7/1988) FL 44/2 FLC 4 FAC 5 Others 1
Manchester C (£465,000 on 2/8/1989) FL 18+1/2 FLC 4/1 Others 1

West Ham U (£500,000 on 28/12/1989) F/PL 240+14/12 FLC 21+1/1 FAC 22+1/3 Others 4+1/1
Manchester C (Free on 26/3/1998) F/PL 53+25/2 FLC 4+5 FAC 3+2/2 Others 0+1
(Free to Miami Fusion, America on 26/3/2001)
Rochdale (Free from Barry T on 30/8/2002) FL 5+3 Others 1

BJORKLUND Joachim

Born: Vaxjo, Sweden, 15 February 1971
Height: 6'1" **Weight:** 12.10
Club Honours: SPD '97; SLC '96
International Honours: Sweden: 75

This experienced centre back began last season as a first choice for Sunderland, establishing a good partnership with Phil Babb. An effective man marker with pace and good heading ability, he was hampered by a persistent hamstring injury from September onwards and never enjoyed an extended run in the side for any real length of time. His experience could well be important next term as the Black Cats look to bounce back into the Premiership.

Glasgow R (Signed from Vicenza, Italy, ex Osters, Brann Bergen, Goteborg, on 15/7/1996) SL 59 SLC 5 SC 8 Others 13 (Transferred to Valencia, Spain during 1998 close season)
Sunderland ((£1,500,000 on 1/2/2002) PL 30+2 FAC 1+1

BJORNEBYE Stig Inge

Born: Elverum, Norway, 11 December 1969
Height: 5'10" **Weight:** 11.9
Club Honours: FLC '95, '02
International Honours: Norway: 76; B-1; U21; Yth

Attempting to recover from a horrific training ground accident that saw him suffer a fractured eye socket, Stig Inge was further hindered by problems with his foot last term that required crucial surgery. His only first-team appearance for Blackburn came in the Worthington Cup quarter-final tie at Wigan when he played with his customary consistency. Stig Inge announced his retirement before the end of the season but at the time of writing it was a possibility that he might continue to assist Rovers by scouting in Norway.

Liverpool (£600,000 from Rosenborg, Norway, ex Strommen, Kongsvinger, on 18/12/1992) PL 132+7/2 FLC 16 FAC 11+2 Others 2
Blackburn Rov (£300,000 on 28/6/2000) P/FL 53+3/1 FLC 7 FAC 4+1

BLACK Christopher (Chris)

Born: Ashington, 7 September 1982
Height: 6'0" **Weight:** 12.0

A young Sunderland midfielder, Chris was handed his first-team debut by Mick McCarthy in May when he played as a right winger at Aston Villa. A star of the Black Cats' reserve team, the 20-year-old Tynesider is a player who may get a chance to stake a claim for a regular place next term in the Nationwide League.

Sunderland (From trainee on 25/8/2000) PL 2

BLACK Kingsley Terence

Born: Luton, 22 June 1968
Height: 5'9" **Weight:** 11.2
Club Honours: FLC '88; FMC '92; AMC '98
International Honours: E: Sch. NI: 30; B-3; U21-1

This vastly experienced left-sided midfielder's Football League career finally came to an end at Sincil Bank. Kingsley's only appearance was as a late substitute in the Imps' 3-0 home win over Macclesfield at the end of August and he eventually left Lincoln by mutual consent in October.

Luton T (From juniors on 7/7/1986) FL 123+4/26 FLC 16+2/1 FAC 5+1/2 Others 3+2/1
Nottingham F (£1,500,000 on 2/9/1991) F/PL 80+18/14 FLC 19+1/5 FAC 4 Others 4+2/1
Sheffield U (Loaned on 2/3/1995) FL 8+3/2
Millwall (Loaned on 29/9/1995) FL 1+2/1 FLC 0+1
Grimsby T (£25,000 on 16/7/1996) FL 91+50/8 FLC 14+2 FAC 5+2 Others 2+5/1
Lincoln C (Loaned on 13/10/2000) FL 5
Lincoln C (Free on 2/7/2001) FL 30+2/5 FLC 1 FAC 1+1 Others 1

BLACK Thomas (Tommy) Robert

Born: Chigwell, 26 November 1979
Height: 5'7" **Weight:** 11.4

This popular Crystal Palace winger or striker impressed once again with his hard work and mazy dribbling last season. He was a regular in the Eagles' squad, although often featuring from the bench, and enjoyed a golden spell in December when he netted eight league and cup goals and received the PFA 'Player of the Month' award.

Arsenal (From trainee on 3/7/1998) PL 0+1 FLC 1
Carlisle U (Loaned on 25/8/1999) FL 5/1
Bristol C (Loaned on 17/12/1999) FL 4
Crystal Palace (£250,000 + on 21/7/2000) FL 55+46/10 FLC 12+2/5 FAC 3+1/2

BLACKMAN Lloyd Jason
Born: London, 24 September 1983
Height: 5'10" **Weight:** 12.3
This promising young Brentford striker made his debut in the Bees' 5-1 defeat at Peterborough last September. That was his only senior appearance of the season, but he will be looking to see more first-team action in 2003-04.
Brentford (From trainee on 9/7/2002) FL 1

BLACKWELL Dean Robert
Born: Camden, 5 December 1969
Height: 6'1" **Weight:** 12.7
International Honours: E: U21-6
After being given a free transfer by Wimbledon at the end of 2001-02, Dean had a brief trial at Wycombe before joining Brighton on a monthly contract last October. He soon made his presence felt and was quickly signed up on a contract to the end of the season. Playing as the left-sided central defender in a back five, he impressed with his calm, unsung defensive work, although his campaign was interrupted by a hamstring problem. Dean scored his first league goal for 11 years in the 4-1 home win over Wolves, then added a second against Watford.
Wimbledon (From trainee on 7/7/1988) F/PL 180+25/1 FLC 20 FAC 23+1 Others 1
Plymouth Arg (Loaned on 15/3/1990) FL 5+2
Brighton & Hove A (Free on 23/10/2002) FL 18+3/2 FAC 0+1

BLAKE Nathan Alexander
Born: Cardiff, 27 January 1972
Height: 5'11" **Weight:** 13.2
Club Honours: WC '92, '93; Div 3 '93, Div 1 '97
International Honours: W: 23; B-1; U21-5; Yth
Nathan looked a lot sharper for Wolves at the start of the 2002-03 season and was soon amongst the goals. Not only that, he was leading the line in fashion and scored a deserved brace in the 4-0 win over Preston. A hat-trick at Gillingham gave him ten goals in just 15 starts but a couple of games later he was injured against Portsmouth, resulting in serious damage to his foot ligaments. Nathan was absent for a lengthy spell, and Wolves missed a target man in the team. A week after his return he suffered concussion at Reading, but was soon back on the score sheet, against Gillingham. Nathan also came on for the last few minutes for Wales against Italy, to show his international career was not over.

Cardiff C (From trainee at Chelsea on 20/8/1990) FL 113+18/35 FLC 6+2 FAC 10/4 Others 13+2/1
Sheffield U (£300,000 on 17/2/1994) P/FL 55+14/34 FLC 3+1/1 FAC 1 Others 1
Bolton W (£1,500,000 on 23/12/1995) F/PL 102+5/38 FLC 10+1/8 FAC 6/2
Blackburn Rov (£4,250,000 on 30/10/1998) P/FL 37+17/13 FLC 3/1 FAC 5+3/2
Wolverhampton W (£1,400,000 on 13/9/2001) FL 60+2/23 FLC 2/1 FAC 2 Others 5/1

BLAKE Robert (Robbie) James
Born: Middlesbrough, 4 March 1976
Height: 5'9" **Weight:** 12.6
After putting his injury problems of the previous season behind him, Robbie started the 2002-03 season in Burnley's first team and stayed there for most of the campaign. After opening his scoring account in the 2-1 win at Derby, where he showed the full range of his trickery, he quickly became a Turf Moor crowd favourite and went on to find the net regularly. Sometimes employed up front and sometimes just behind the strikers, Robbie established a particularly good understanding with Glen Little, and shared with him the ability to unlock defences with skill on the ball. He also scored one of the Clarets' best goals of the season with his Beckham-style free kick against Preston.
Darlington (From trainee on 1/7/1994) FL 54+14/21 FLC 4+2/1 FAC 3+1 Others 3+1/1
Bradford C (£300,000 on 27/3/1997) P/FL 109+44/40 FLC 8+3/4 FAC 7/1 Others 3+1/2
Nottingham F (Loaned on 22/8/2000) FL 9+2/1 FLC 1
Burnley (£1,000,000 + on 25/11/2002) FL 35+16/13 FLC 4/1 FAC 3+1/2

Robbie Blake

BLANC Laurent Robert
Born: Ales, France, 19 November 1965
Height: 6'4" **Weight:** 13.9
Club Honours: PL '03
International Honours: France: 97
This world-class central defender had been expecting to wave a fond farewell to Old Trafford in the summer following the signing of Rio Ferdinand from Leeds and the continued progression of Wes Brown and John O'Shea in the wings. Somehow, Sir Alex Ferguson persuaded him to stay, and it turned out to be a shrewd decision with key injuries to both Ferdinand and Brown early doors. Stepping ably into the breach, Laurent didn't relinquish his first-team place until late December, by which time United where chasing honours on four fronts. With sporadic appearances coming from thereon in, his main influence appeared to be more behind the scenes at Carrington. A possible coaching role seemed to be in the offing when he retires in the summer, but he may decide to cut his teeth elsewhere.
Manchester U (Free from Inter Milan, Italy, ex Montpelier, Napoli, Nimes, St Etienne, Auxerre, Barcelona, Marseilles, on 3/9/2001) PL 44+4/1 FAC 3 Others 24/3

BLATHERWICK Steven (Steve) Scott
Born: Hucknall, 20 September 1973
Height: 6'1" **Weight:** 14.6
Now one of Chesterfield's longest-serving players, Steve's many eye-catching displays in the centre of defence made him a regular winner of sponsors' 'Man of the Match' awards last season. Tall, athletic and powerful, he is firm and resolute on the pitch, and can be relied on to give his best at all times.
Nottingham F (From trainee at Notts Co on 2/8/1992) FL 10 FLC 2 FAC 1 Others 2
Wycombe W (Loaned on 18/2/1994) FL 2 Others 1
Hereford U (Loaned on 11/9/1995) FL 10/1 Others 2
Reading (Loaned on 27/3/1997) FL 6+1
Burnley (£150,000 on 18/7/1997) FL 16+8 FLC 5 FAC 1+1 Others 3
Chesterfield (Loaned on 18/9/1998) FL 2
Chesterfield (£50,000 on 1/12/1998) FL 115+7/2 FLC 7 FAC 2 Others 7/2

BLAYNEY Alan
Born: Belfast, 9 October 1981
Height: 6'2" **Weight:** 13.12
International Honours: NI: U21-1
This young Southampton goalkeeper joined Stockport County on loan last October as cover for the injured Lee

Jones. Alan made a series of outstanding saves on his debut at Blackpool and made two further appearances before returning to St Mary's. Then in December he had another loan spell, this time at Bournemouth. He made two first-team appearances and also featured on the bench during his spell with the Cherries. Alan made his debut for Northern Ireland at U21 level during the season, coming on as a substitute against Finland.
Southampton (From trainee on 13/7/2001)
Stockport Co (Loaned on 29/10/2002) FL 2 Others 1
Bournemouth (Loaned on 24/12/2002) FL 2

BLINKHORN Matthew David
Born: Blackpool, 2 March 1985
Height: 5'11" **Weight:** 10.10
In the second year of his scholarship, Matthew continued to impress with Blackpool, finishing the season as leading scorer for both the reserve and youth teams. He received his first start in the LDV Vans Trophy tie at Scunthorpe, and scored his first senior goals when netting twice in the 3-3 draw with Mansfield Town at Bloomfield Road. Matthew has been offered a professional contract for the 2003-04 campaign.
Blackpool (Trainee) FL 3+7/2 Others 1

BLOMQVIST Lars **Jesper**
Born: Tavelsjo, Sweden, 5 February 1974
Height: 5'9" **Weight:** 11.6
Club Honours: EC '99; FAC '99; PL '99
International Honours: Sweden: 30
Jesper joined Charlton Athletic on a one-year contract to give him the chance to prove his fitness following persistent knee problems in recent seasons. Unfortunately he was again plagued by injuries during 2002-03 and only started one match, the FA Cup tie against Exeter City, his only other appearances coming from the substitutes' bench. He has undoubted ability, and showed his skill on the ball and positional awareness when in the side, but unfortunately the club decided not to offer him a contract for the coming season.
Manchester U (£3,400,000 from Parma, Italy, via Gothenburg, AC Milan, on 31/7/1998) PL 20+5/1 FLC 0+1 FAC 3+2 Others 6+1
Everton (Free on 10/11/2001) PL 10+5/1 FAC 2+1
Charlton Ath (Free on 30/8/2002) PL 0+3 FAC 1

BLONDEL Jonathan
Born: Belgium, 3 April 1984
Height: 5'8" **Weight:** 10.12
International Honours: Belgium: 1; U21-7; Yth

Jonathan joined Spurs from Royal Excelsior Mouscron and is highly rated in his native Belgium. Despite only making one appearance off the bench last season, he impressed with his ability on the ball and a tenacious attitude. However he will be hoping to make a breakthrough to regular first-team action in 2003-04.
Tottenham H (£900,000 from Royal Excelsior Mouscron, Belgium on 16/7/2002) PL 0+1

BLOOMER Matthew (Matt) Brian
Born: Grimsby, 3 November 1978
Height: 6'0" **Weight:** 13.0
This young centre back was out of the first-team picture at Hull City last term, spending three months on loan at Conference club Telford United. He arrived at Lincoln at the turn of the year on a month-to-month contract. City mostly used him in the unfamiliar role as a target man up front and he netted his first goal for the Imps with a flashing header in the 3-0 home win over Hartlepool.
Grimsby T (From juniors on 3/7/1997) FL 3+9 FLC 0+2 Others 0+1
Hull C (Free on 5/7/2001) FL 0+3 FLC 1
Lincoln C (Loaned on 22/3/2002) FL 4+1
Lincoln C (Free on 31/12/2002) FL 3+10/1 Others 0+1

BOA MORTE Luis Pereira
Born: Lisbon, Portugal, 4 August 1977
Height: 5'10" **Weight:** 11.5
Club Honours: PL '98; Div 1 '01; CS '98, '99
International Honours: Portugal: 5; U21; Yth
A tricky winger whose pace unsettles opposing defences, Luis is always likely to win both free kicks and penalties. He played much of the season on the left-hand side of midfield for Fulham, although he also played up front on occasion. He particularly seemed to enjoy cup action and enjoyed an excellent game in the UEFA Cup tie in Zagreb when he scored a memorable goal. Luis also had an outstanding game against Bolton on the opening day of the season and continued to feature for Portugal at international level.
Arsenal (£1,750,000 + from Sporting Lisbon, Portugal on 25/6/1997) PL 6+19 FLC 3/2 FAC 2+3/1 Others 2+4/1
Southampton (£500,000 + on 27/8/1999) PL 6+8/1 FLC 0+2 FAC 1
Fulham (£1,700,000 on 31/7/2000) P/FL 61+30/21 FLC 7+3/5 FAC 5+1 Others 10+2/2

BOATENG George
Born: Nkawkaw, Ghana, 5 September 1975
Height: 5'9" **Weight:** 11.7

International Honours: Holland: 2; U21-18

After playing in Aston Villa's first Intertoto Cup game against FC Zurich, George moved on to Middlesborough at the beginning of August. A hard-working midfield player with plenty of composure, he featured regularly for Boro' during the campaign, although he has yet to register his first goal for his new club. At the beginning of June it was announced that George had undergone surgery in Holland to remove a piece of floating bone in his ankle stemming from an injury he picked up during the home clash with Charlton.

Coventry C *(£250,000 from Feyenoord, Holland, ex Excelsior, on 19/12/1997) PL 43+4/5 FLC 3/1 FAC 8/1*
Aston Villa *(£4,500,000 on 22/7/1999) PL 96+7/4 FLC 9+1/1 FAC 9 Others 13*
Middlesbrough *(£5,000,000 on 8/8/2002) PL 28*

BOERTIEN Paul
Born: Haltwhistle, 21 January 1979
Height: 5'10" **Weight:** 11.2

Whether at left back or on the left of midfield, Paul guarantees maximum effort and never shirks. Only Adam Bolder played more games for Derby County last term. Other players know his value and there was much pleasure when he scored in the impressive victory at Wimbledon under George Burley. Paul needs to use the ball with greater accuracy, but a more settled team would speed his development.

Carlisle U *(From trainee on 13/5/1997) FL 16+1/1 FLC 0+2 FAC 1 Others 1*
Derby Co *(£250,000 on 25/3/1999) P/FL 72+13/2 FLC 3+1 FAC 3+2*
Crewe Alex *(Loaned on 11/2/2000) FL 2*

BOGARDE Winston
Born: Rotterdam, Holland, 22 October 1970
Height: 6'2" **Weight:** 13.6

International Honours: Holland: 20

The big Dutch central defender made a 22-minute substitute appearance against Gillingham in a Worthington Cup tie, some 23 months after his previous outing at Portman Road on Boxing Day 2000. Claudio Ranieri has built his defence around the great Marcel Desailly with young lions William Gallas and John Terry appearing to be the long-term partnership and German giant Robert Huth also breaking into the first team, Winston's future options look limited. To his eternal credit he has trained hard in an effort to impress the management and battle back into contention at a club he clearly loves.

Chelsea *(Free from Barcelona, Spain, ex Excelsior, Sparta Rotterdam, Ajax, AC Milan, on 1/9/2000) PL 2+7 FLC 1+1 Others 1*

BOKSIC Alen
Born: Makarska, Yugoslavia, 31 January 1970
Height: 6'1" **Weight:** 12.8

Luis Boa Morte

International Honours: Croatia: 40
After featuring for Croatia in the World
Cup finals over the summer, Alen had an
injury-hit season with Middlesbrough in
2002-03. The experienced striker missed
more games than he had played in,
completing only four full Premiership
matches. His only goals of the season
were scored against the two Manchester
clubs and his last game on Teesside was
against Southampton at the Riverside
Stadium in January, but Alen was
substituted yet again.
*Middlesbrough (£2,500,000 from Lazio,
Italy, ex Hajduk Split, AS Cannes, Olympique
Marseille, Lazio, Juventus, on 11/8/2000) PL
59+9/22 FLC 1+1 FAC 4+3*

BOLAND William (Willie)
John
Born: Ennis, Ireland, 6 August 1975
Height: 5'9" **Weight:** 11.2
International Honours: RoI: B-1; U21-
11; Yth; Sch
This tenacious defensive midfield player
followed his best season for Cardiff City
in 2001-02 with another highly
productive campaign, when he was
comfortably the team's most consistent
player. He worked tirelessly, showing
good passing and movement. Willie
scored his first cup goal for the Bluebirds
when he netted against Margate away in
the FA Cup. He fired home directly from a
free kick after borrowing studded boots
from Andy Legg because his own had
been left out of the skip!
*Coventry C (From juniors on 4/11/1992) PL
43+20 FLC 6+1 FAC 0+1*
*Cardiff C (Free on 24/6/1999) FL 125+11/3
FLC 7 FAC 10+4/1 Others 6*

BOLDER Adam Peter
Born: Hull, 25 October 1980
Height: 5'8" **Weight:** 11.0
Adam lacked experience at the start of
last season but went on to become a
fixture in Derby County's midfield. He was
absent from the squad only once and that
was through suspension. Adam's
determination is as obvious as his
willingness to learn and one of his best
features is an ability to make runs beyond
the strikers. He scored twice to earn an
early away win over Grimsby and
repeated this against Sheffield Wednesday
at home. Six League goals from midfield
was a good return and Adam was one of
the few at Pride Park who could look
back on the season with satisfaction. He
is the brother of Grimsby Town's Chris
Bolder.

*Hull C (From trainee on 9/7/1999) FL 18+2
Others 2+1*
*Derby Co (Signed on 3/4/2000) P/FL 40+18/6
FLC 2 FAC 2*

BOLDER Christopher (Chris)
James
Born: Hull, 19 August 1982
Height: 5'11" **Weight:** 12.4
This young Grimsby midfielder made his
senior debut as a substitute at Derby last
season. Chris was on the edge of the
senior squad and received limited
opportunities until injuries to more senior
players during the run-in let him in. He
acquitted himself well as the Mariners
struggled unsuccessfully against
relegation. Chris is the brother of Derby
County's Adam Bolder.
*Grimsby T (From trainee at Hull C on
9/7/2001) FL 7+5 FAC 0+1*

BOLLAND Paul Graham
Born: Bradford, 23 December 1979
Height: 5'11" **Weight:** 11.0
This promising young midfield player
featured regularly for Notts County last
term, although he was hampered by a
series of niggling injuries that restricted
his appearances. Paul was always
energetic and determined, producing
rapid thrusts from the centre or right-
hand side of midfield. He also occasionally
turned out at right back and netted four
valuable goals for the Magpies.
*Bradford C (From trainee on 20/3/1998) FL
4+8 FLC 2*
*Notts Co (£75,000 on 14/1/1999) FL
80+13/4 FLC 1+4 FAC 3+1 Others 1+3/1*

BOND Kain
Born: Torquay, 19 June 1985
Height: 5'8" **Weight:** 10.10
This second-year scholarship boy with
Torquay is a promising striker. He made
his debut on the substitutes' bench at
Boston in October and also featured in
the FA Cup tie against Boreham Wood.
Kain earned a professional contract for
2003-04 and will be aiming to gain
further senior experience.
Torquay U (Trainee) FL 0+1 FAC 0+1

BONNER Mark
Born: Ormskirk, 7 June 1974
Height: 5'10" **Weight:** 11.0
This gutsy and tenacious midfield player
finished the 2002-03 season as a regular
in the squad for Cardiff City, usually
featuring as substitute. He figured in all
three play-off matches, coming on during
extra time in the final against Queen's

Park Rangers. Overall, though, Mark will
reflect on the season with
disappointment. He signed a new two-
year contract at the start of the
campaign, but was hit by injuries and
spent lengthy periods on the sidelines. He
is a player with the determination and
ability to play a full role for the Bluebirds
in Division One.
*Blackpool (From trainee on 18/6/1992) FL
156+22/14 FLC 15+3 FAC 11 Others 10+3/1*
*Cardiff C (Free on 17/7/1998) FL 99+24/2
FLC 6 FAC 7+1 Others 8+3/1*
Hull C (Loaned on 8/11/1999) FL 1/1

BOOK Steven (Steve) Kim
Born: Bournemouth, 7 July 1969
Height: 5'11" **Weight:** 11.1
Club Honours: FAT '98; NC '99
International Honours: E: SP-3
Steve once again spent most of last term
as first choice 'keeper for Cheltenham
Town. He maintained his reputation as an
excellent shot stopper during the early
part of the season when his goal came
under heavy pressure at times, indeed the
more difficult the game the more he
seemed to excel. When Bobby Gould took
over as manager in January he gave both
Steve and his understudy Shane Higgs an
equal opportunity, and it was Higgs who
ended the campaign in the first team.
*Cheltenham T (Signed from Forest Green
Rov on 23/7/1997) FL 167 FLC 6 FAC 12
Others 8*

BOOTH Andrew (Andy) David
Born: Huddersfield, 6 December 1973
Height: 6'0" **Weight:** 13.0
International Honours: E: U21-3
Huddersfield's big target man led the
attack from the beginning to the end of
the 2002-03 season, although thigh and
hamstring injuries kept him on the
sidelines for short spells. Always likely to
win every header, the purposeful striker
holds the ball up well and creates chances
for others. Despite not being the quickest
player around Andy scored his 100th
career league goal in the win at Barnsley
and notched a further five throughout the
season, a tally he would probably have
wished to improve upon.
*Huddersfield T (From trainee on 1/7/1992)
FL 109+14/54 FLC 10+1/3 FAC 8/3 Others
12+1/4*
*Sheffield Wed (£2,700,000 on 8/7/1996)
P/FL 124+9/28 FLC 10+1/1 FAC 9+1/5*
Tottenham H (Loaned on 30/1/2001) PL 3+1
*Huddersfield T (£200,000 on 22/3/2001) FL
70+7/20 FLC 1 FAC 2 Others 7/3*

54

BOOTY Martyn James
Born: Kirby Muxloe, 30 May 1971
Height: 5'8" **Weight:** 11.2
Martyn showed his best form for Chesterfield at right back last term, but was often played in a midfield slot. Despite being given early news of his release this summer, he remained fully committed to the club's cause and played his part in keeping the Spireites up at the season's end. He tackles and reads the game well, and was named club captain for 2002-03.
Coventry C (From trainee on 30/5/1989) FL 4+1 FLC 2 FAC 2
Crewe Alex (Free on 7/10/1993) FL 95+1/5 FLC 6 FAC 8/1 Others 13
Reading (£75,000 on 18/1/1996) FL 62+2/1 FLC 10+1 FAC 7/1
Southend U (Free on 7/1/1999) FL 78+2 FLC 4 FAC 5 Others 2
Chesterfield (Free on 9/8/2001) FL 75+3/2 FLC 3 FAC 4 Others 3

Martyn Booty

BOPP Eugene
Born: Kiev, Ukraine, 5 September 1983
Height: 5'10" **Weight:** 12.4
This young midfielder started last term on the substitutes' bench for Nottingham Forest before coming into the side in September and October as cover. Just as he was cementing a regular place in the line-up he suffered a knee injury against Derby County, and on his return in March he was only used a bit-part player. Eugen will be hoping for more chances in the coming season.
Nottingham F (From trainee on 11/9/2000) FL 22+10/3 FLC 2+2

BORROWDALE Gary Ian
Born: Sutton, 16 July 1985
Height: 6'0" **Weight:** 12.1
International Honours: E: Yth
A product of the Crystal Palace youth system, this promising left back made his senior debut from the substitutes' bench against Grimsby Town last November. Soon afterwards he signed a long-term contract for the Eagles and featured regularly in the first team towards the end of the season. Gary will be looking to win a regular place in the line-up in 2003-04.
Crystal Palace (From trainee on 6/12/2002) FL 8+5 FLC 0+2 FAC 0+1

BOSHELL Daniel (Danny) Kevin
Born: Bradford, 30 May 1981
Height: 5'11" **Weight:** 11.10
A product of Oldham Athletic's youth system, Danny was made available for transfer in October 2002 as part of a cost-cutting exercise. The young midfielder has had terrible luck with injuries during his career but fought his way back into the first-team in February, making an excellent contribution to the club's 2-1 victory at Stockport. However, Danny was stretchered off with an ankle injury the following weekend and didn't feature again.
Oldham Ath (From trainee on 10/7/1998) FL 19+13/1 FLC 3/1 FAC 2 Others 1

BOTHROYD Jay
Born: London, 7 May 1982
Height: 6'3" **Weight:** 13.6
Club Honours: FAYC '00
International Honours: E: U21-1; Yth; Sch
Jay was a regular up front for Coventry City for a large part of last season and finished the campaign as top scorer. An excellent first touch and good close control, allied to outstanding dribbling and an ability to hold the ball up earned

him many plaudits although some fans found his languid style frustrating. He scored several spectacular goals including the winner at Reading, while his best performance was undoubtedly at Stoke when he netted two individual goals that fully demonstrated his immense talent. After an exceptional spell in December playing as a wide player on the right his form dropped off and at the end of the season he was made available on a free transfer.

Arsenal (From trainee on 8/7/1999)
Coventry C (£1,000,000 on 13/7/2000) P/FL 51+21/14 FLC 1+5/2 FAC 5/1

BOUCAUD Andre

Born: Enfield, 9 October 1984
Height: 5'10" **Weight:** 11.4
This talented young Reading midfielder spent most of last season developing in the club's reserve side before joining Peterborough United on loan in March. A very clever ball player who is not frightened to run at the opposition, Barry Fry likened him to a young Paul Gascoigne, while Posh went undefeated during his appearances.

Reading (From trainee on 25/3/2002)
Peterborough U (Loaned on 27/3/2003) FL 5+1

BOULDING Michael Thomas

Born: Sheffield, 8 February 1975
Height: 5'10" **Weight:** 11.4
This pacy winger joined Aston Villa in the summer of 2002 and scored on his home debut against FC Zurich in the Intertoto Cup. However, Michael was out of the first-team picture when the Premiership started and in September he joined Sheffield United on loan with a view to a permanent transfer. He scored in his second game for the Blades in the Worthington Cup tie Wycombe, but returned to Villa Park after being sidelined with ankle ligament damage. In January Michael returned to Grimsby, initially on loan whilst a permanent deal was worked out. He marked his first match with a goal, and scored three more in seven games before being sidelined once again with an injury.

Mansfield T (Signed from Hallam FC on 2/8/1999) FL 28+38/12 FLC 2+2 FAC 2+1 Others 1+1
Grimsby T (Free on 24/8/2001) FL 24+11/11 FLC 0+2 FAC 0+2
Aston Villa (Free on 9/7/2002) Others 2/1
Sheffield U (Loaned on 29/9/2002) FL 3+3 FLC 1/1
Grimsby T (Free on 10/1/2003) FL 10+2/4

BOUND Matthew (Matt) Terence

Born: Melksham, 9 November 1972
Height: 6'2" **Weight:** 14.6
Club Honours: Div 3 '00
Matt was a virtual ever-present in the Oxford defence last term, missing just five games in his first full season at the club. He formed an excellent partnership with Andy Crosby helping the U's keep many clean sheets. He also found time to score a goal, netting with a cracker of a free kick in the draw with Exeter. Solid and dependable Matt is a difficult player to beat, especially in the air.

Southampton (From trainee on 3/5/1991) F/PL 2+3
Hull C (Loaned on 27/8/1993) FL 7/1
Stockport Co (£100,000 on 27/10/1994) FL 44/5 FLC 1 FAC 3/1 Others 3/1
Lincoln C (Loaned on 11/9/1995) FL 3+1 Others 1
Swansea C (£55,000 on 21/11/1997) FL 173+1/9 FLC 8/2 FAC 10 Others 8+1/2
Oxford U (Free on 21/12/2001) FL 63/1 FLC 3 FAC 3 Others 1

BOWDITCH Dean Peter

Born: Bishops Stortford, 15 June 1986
Height: 5'11" **Weight:** 11.7
International Honours: E: Yth
Dean became one of the youngest players to represent Ipswich Town when he came on as a second-half substitute in the 'derby' game at Norwich in March. Within 30 seconds of arriving on the pitch his cross from the left led to Fabian Wilnis scoring the opening goal of the game. It was also Dean's through ball that sent Darren Bent away to seal the win near the end. A product of the Ipswich academy, he made further appearances from the substitutes' bench but has yet to start a game.

Ipswich T (Trainee) FL 0+5

BOWEN Jason Peter

Born: Merthyr Tydfil, 24 August 1972
Height: 5'7" **Weight:** 11.0
Club Honours: AMC '94
International Honours: W: 2; B-1; U21-5; Yth; Sch
Jason is one of the most skilful players at Cardiff City, and able to play in a variety of positions. His best role has always seemed to be sitting just behind the front two, but he is effective wide right and as a striker. Jason's balance and skill can pull defences apart and he was always in or around the Bluebirds' squad. He brought something different to the team, but was not able to get as many first-team appearances as he would have liked.

Swansea C (From trainee on 1/7/1990) FL 93+31/26 FLC 6+1/2 FAC 9+2/1 Others 15+3/8
Birmingham C (£350,000 on 24/7/1995) FL 35+13/7 FLC 4+6/2 FAC 1+4 Others 2/2
Southampton (Loaned on 2/9/1997) PL 1+2
Reading (£200,000 on 24/12/1997) FL 12+3/1 FLC 1+1 FAC 5
Cardiff C (Free on 12/11/1999) FL 105+27/34 FLC 4/2 FAC 15+2 Others 2+2/1

BOWER Mark James

Born: Bradford, 23 January 1980
Height: 5'10" **Weight:** 11.0
Mark was another shining light for Bradford last season as he continued to show terrific ability at the back. A promising central defender who commands the line well, he rightly became a regular feature in the side. He will be more than happy to have made over 30 senior starts for the club after spending a number of years knocking on the first-team door. Mark came on in leaps and bounds, gaining more confidence with each performance he made.

Bradford C (From trainee on 28/3/1998) P/FL 46+4/2 FLC 3 FAC 1+1 Others 1+1
York C (Loaned on 16/2/2000) FL 15/1
York C (Loaned on 30/11/2000) FL 21/1 FAC 3 Others 0+1

BOWRY Robert (Bobby) John

Born: Hampstead, 19 May 1971
Height: 5'9" **Weight:** 10.8
Club Honours: Div 1 '94
International Honours: St Kitts & Nevis
This experienced midfielder was ever-present for Colchester during the first half of the 2002-03 season. Bobby started every game until the 2-0 home defeat by Blackpool at the end of January. He then lost his place, firstly under caretaker manager Geraint Williams, and then new boss Phil Parkinson. Bobby was mostly on the bench from February onwards, but could be relied upon to shore up central midfield whenever required and was a useful back up to young midfielders Kem Izzet and Thomas Pinault.

Crystal Palace (Free from Carshalton on 4/4/1992) F/PL 36+14/1 FLC 10 FAC 1
Millwall (£220,000 on 5/7/1995) FL 125+15/5 FLC 9+1 FAC 6 Others 4
Colchester U (Free on 25/7/2001) FL 60+11/2 FLC 1+2 FAC 2 Others 3

BOWYER Lee David

Born: London, 3 January 1977
Height: 5'9" **Weight:** 10.6
International Honours: E: 1; U21-13; Yth
Amid much speculation over his signing a

new contract for Leeds United, Lee began the season in scintillating form, with two goals in the first four games, including a superb long-range effort at West Bromwich Albion. However as the campaign progressed it became more apparent that he did not want to stay at Elland Road, and in January he joined West Ham. Although Lee had not played for a month he enjoyed a useful debut for the Hammers against Newcastle. His best display came in the 2-0 win against Spurs when his storming runs down the wing

caused all sorts of problems. Unfortunately, he then sustained a knee injury, which forced him to miss the rest of the season. A midfielder who has all-round ability, incredible energy and a fine goal-scoring record, Lee was released in May.

Charlton Ath (From trainee on 13/4/1994) FL 46/8 FLC 6+1/5 FAC 3/1 Others 2
Leeds U (£2,600,000 on 5/7/1996) PL 196+7/38 FLC 7+1/1 FAC 16/3 Others 38/13
West Ham U (£100,000 on 8/1/2003) PL 10 FAC 1

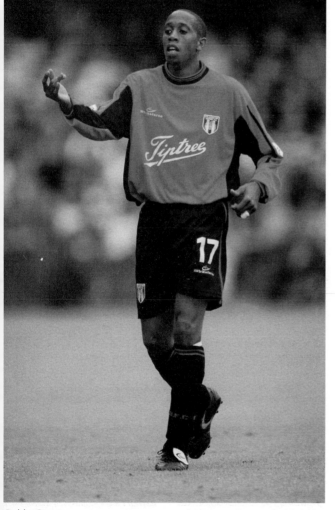

Bobby Bowry

BOXALL Daniel (Danny)
James
Born: Croydon, 24 August 1977
Height: 5'8" **Weight:** 11.10
Club Honours: Div 3 '99
International Honours: RoI: U21-8
Danny enjoyed a good start to his first season at Bristol Rovers last term, holding down a regular place in the side at right back. He linked up well with wide man Wayne Carlisle and provided a useful attacking option. However after an indifferent spell of form in the closing weeks of the season he lost his place in the line-up before showing his versatility by appearing at left back on three occasions.
Crystal Palace (From trainee on 19/4/1995) F/PL 5+3 FLC 1+1
Oldham Ath (Loaned on 21/11/1997) FL 6 Others 1
Oldham Ath (Loaned on 27/2/1998) FL 12
Brentford (Free on 9/7/1998) FL 62+6/1 FLC 6 FAC 4 Others 5+1
Bristol Rov (Free on 2/7/2002) FL 35+4 FLC 1 FAC 4 Others 1

BOYCE Emmerson Orlando
Born: Aylesbury, 24 September 1979
Height: 5'11" **Weight:** 11.10
This full back or central defender enjoyed the best season of his career so far for Luton Town in 2002-03. His concentration has greatly improved, and he was less inclined to run forward from his defensive position, but when he did link up with the play his crosses proved accurate. Only injury delayed Emmerson's progress and prevented him from making more first-team appearances.
Luton T (From trainee on 2/4/1998) FL 129+15/4 FLC 9 FAC 4+3 Others 3

BOYD Adam Mark
Born: Hartlepool, 25 May 1982
Height: 5'9" **Weight:** 10.12
Adam is a talented young striker who has a good goal-scoring record in first-team football. Early in 2002-03 when Gordon Watson was injured, he was handed the opportunity to win a regular first-team place at Hartlepool. When he scored in each of the next three games he looked to have met the challenge, but manager Chris Turner decided to go into the transfer market to sign a new striker in Marcus Richardson. Later in the season Adam had another short first-team run under new manager Mike Newell, but he was again unable to justify a regular place.
Hartlepool U (From trainee on 20/9/1999) FL 24+36/15 FLC 1 FAC 0+2 Others 3+2

BOYD Marc Edward
Born: Carlisle, 22 October 1981
Height: 5'10" **Weight:** 12.4
This skilful midfield player joined Port Vale in the summer of 2002 in a bid to see regular league action. Although very good on the ball, he took a bit of time to adjust to the pace of Second Division football and it was November before he held down a regular place. Marc's first goal came at Shrewsbury in the LDV Vans Trophy and he went on to score three more including an exquisite chip against Chesterfield, which was arguably the club's 'Goal of the Season'. He suffered torn ligaments in the local 'derby' at Crewe, which ended his campaign nine games early.
Newcastle U (From trainee on 22/10/1998)
Port Vale (Free on 1/7/2002) FL 19+1/3 FLC 1 FAC 1 Others 2/1

BRACKENRIDGE Stephen (Steve) James
Born: Rochdale, 31 July 1984
Height: 5'8" **Weight:** 10.7
Steve is a third-year scholarship boy playing regularly in the Macclesfield reserve and youth teams where he has made some quality appearances on the right side of the midfield. He was drafted into the senior side last December when the squad was depleted by injury in 2002, making two cameo appearances from the substitutes' bench, the first of which was his Football League debut in the home match against Rushden & Diamonds.
Macclesfield T (Trainee) FL 0+2

BRACKSTONE Stephen (Steve)
Born: Hartlepool, 19 September 1982
Height: 5'11" **Weight:** 11.2
International Honours: E: Yth
This talented young York City player was an influential figure in midfield in the first half of the 2002-03 campaign, impressing with his passing skills and all-round ability. However, an operation for appendicitis in December put him on the sidelines and it was not until the closing weeks of the campaign that he was able to return to first-team duties. He scored two goals, the best of which was direct from a free kick to earn the Minstermen a dramatic last-minute equaliser against Bristol Rovers in October.
Middlesbrough (From trainee on 7/7/2000)
York C (Signed on 27/2/2002) FL 28+7/2 FLC 1 FAC 2

BRADBURY Lee Michael
Born: Isle of Wight, 3 July 1975
Height: 6'2" **Weight:** 13.10
International Honours: E: U21-3
After recovering from a serious knee injury, Lee joined Sheffield Wednesday on loan to add firepower and know-how to the attack. He made a promising start to his Owls' career, but unfortunately picked up a shoulder injury in the win at Rotherham on New Year's Day. Ironically, he was injured when stopping an opponent from scoring, and his bravery and commitment certainly impressed the Owls' management team. He returned to Portsmouth then went back to Hillsborough for a further month when fit again. In April he was recalled to Fratton Park and played in three games for Pompey towards the end of the season, ironically scoring his only goal against Wednesday. Lee is a bustling striker who works hard and runs tirelessly.
Portsmouth (Free from Cowes on 14/8/1995) FL 41+13/15 FLC 1+2 FAC 4/2
Exeter C (Loaned on 1/12/1995) FL 14/5
Manchester C (£3,000,000 + on 1/8/1997) FL 34+6/10 FLC 6/1
Crystal Palace (£1,500,000 on 29/10/1998) FL 28+4/6 FLC 3+1/1 FAC 1/1
Birmingham C (Loaned on 25/3/1999) FL 6+1 Others 1+1
Portsmouth (£380,000 on 14/10/1999) FL 90+9/28 FLC 3+2 FAC 2/1
Sheffield Wed (Loaned on 24/12/2002) FL 2+1
Sheffield Wed (Loaned on 1/3/2003) FL 8/3

BRADLEY Shayne
Born: Gloucester, 8 December 1979
Height: 5'11" **Weight:** 13.2
International Honours: E: Sch
This striker joined Chesterfield following his release at Mansfield and showed up well to begin with, coming off the bench to use his power to score two goals. In the new year he moved down the pecking order at Saltergate and was then loaned out to Lincoln. He netted the winner from the home game against Kidderminster Harriers but pulled out of the next match after injuring his ankle in the warm-up. Shayne did not play again for Lincoln and quickly returned to Chesterfield.
Southampton (From trainee on 16/1/1998) PL 0+4
Swindon T (Loaned on 25/3/1999) FL 6+1
Exeter C (Loaned on 17/9/1999) FL 6+2/1 FAC 1
Mansfield T (£50,000 + on 22/8/2000) FL 28+14/10 FLC 0+1 FAC 2+2 Others 2
Chesterfield (Free on 12/12/2002) FL 1+8/2
Lincoln C (Loaned on 4/3/2003) FL 3/1

BRADSHAW Gary
Born: Hull, 30 December 1982
Height: 5'6" **Weight:** 10.6
A regular member of the Hull squad under Jan Molby in the opening weeks of the 2002-03 campaign, Gary seemed to be on the verge of fulfilling his undoubted potential. Surprisingly, his fortunes soon went in reverse and new boss Peter Taylor allowed him to go out on loan to Scarborough in February. Gary returned early from his stint with the Conference club with his Tigers contract soon cancelled. A tricky forward, hopefully his enthusiasm will be restored after joining local Northern Counties East outfit, Hall Road Rangers.
Hull C (From trainee on 14/7/2000) FL 10+12/1 FAC 0+1 Others 1

BRAMBLE Tesfaye (Tes)
Born: Ipswich, 20 July 1980
Height: 6'1" **Weight:** 13.10
International Honours: E: U21-10
This burly striker had a somewhat inconsistent campaign for Southend United last term. Tes suffered from a variety of niggling injuries and personal problems, which prevented a consistent run in the side, but nevertheless finished the campaign with a total of 11 goals in all competitions. Undoubtedly a talented player and the side's major goal threat, the front line always looks weaker in his absence.
Southend U (Signed from Cambridge C on 19/1/2001) FL 75+10/24 FLC 1+1 FAC 8/5 Others 4+1+1

BRAMBLE Titus Malachi
Born: Ipswich, 21 July 1981
Height: 6'1" **Weight:** 13.10
International Honours: E: U21-6
Titus arrived on Tyneside in the summer of 2002 to strengthen the Newcastle defence, but he took time to settle at the centre of a back four and following an erratic start found himself on the bench after half-a-dozen games. Recalled for the home Champions' League game against Juventus in late October he had an excellent match followed by another a few days later against Charlton, but he then strained his right hamstring against Dynamo Kiev and this sidelined him for three months. Returning in February he became a regular in the side until the closing stages of the season. Titus is tall and strongly built, uses the ball well and seems to have all the physical attributes required to become a top-class centre back once he develops the necessary consistency.
Ipswich T (From trainee on 24/8/1998) P/FL 41+7/1 FLC 4+1/2 FAC 4+1 Others 4/1

Colchester U (Loaned on 29/12/1999) FL 2
Newcastle U (£5,000,000 on 19/7/2002) PL
13+3 Others 8

BRAMMER David (Dave)

Born: Bromborough, 28 February 1975
Height: 5'10" **Weight:** 12.0
Club Honours: AMC '01
This hard-working midfielder captained
Crewe Alexandra to promotion from the
Second Division last term. He was rarely
absent all season and his experience
proved invaluable to the youngsters
around him. Dave scored two goals
during the campaign, netting in the FA
Cup tie against Mansfield and the 4-0 win
at Cheltenham on Boxing Day.
Wrexham (From trainee on 2/7/1993) FL
118+19/12 FLC 6+2 FAC 8+2/1 Others
13+2/1
Port Vale (£350,000 + on 24/3/1999) FL
71+2/3 FLC 2 FAC 2/1 Others 7
Crewe Alex (£500,000 on 10/8/2001) FL
70+1/3 FLC 4/1 FAC 8/1 Others 2

BRANCH Graham

Born: Liverpool, 12 February 1972
Height: 6'2" **Weight:** 12.2
A player whose Turf Moor career had
looked to be in decline, Graham was the
surprise packet of Burnley's season. Never
previously accepted as a natural left back,
he played in 2002-03 as if born to the
position, and after re-establishing himself
in the side in October he missed few
games. Although his pace was well
known to the Turf Moor faithful, his
speed of recovery and quick thinking in
defensive situations was a revelation, as
was his tackling. His performance in
Burnley's Worthington Cup victory against
Tottenham had a previously sceptical
crowd chanting "Branchy for England"...
unlikely perhaps, but at his best he was
certainly among the First Division's finest
left backs, and towards the end of the
season proved similarly adept in an
unfamiliar central defensive role.
Tranmere Rov (Free from Heswall on
2/7/1991) FL 55+47/10 FLC 4+8/1 FAC 1+2
Others 2+1
Bury (Loaned on 20/11/1992) FL 3+1/1
Others 1
Wigan Ath (Loaned on 24/12/1997) FL 2+1
Stockport Co (Free on 31/7/1998) FL 10+4/3
FLC 1
Burnley (Free on 31/12/1998) FL 110+31/9
FLC 6+3 FAC 8+4 Others 1

BRANCH Paul Michael

Born: Liverpool, 18 October 1978
Height: 5'10" **Weight:** 11.7
International Honours: E: U21-1; Yth; Sch

Out of favour at Wolves, Michael teamed-
up with former Everton colleagues Phil
Jevons and Carl Regan when he joined
Third Division Hull on loan. The life-long
Toffees' fan was signed only days before
former Liverpool legend Jan Molby was
replaced as manager. Therefore, the
speedy forward made his Boothferry Park
debut in front of incoming manager Peter
Taylor (who had selected him for England
U21 duty) and responded with two goals
in the thrilling defeat of Rochdale. He
further endeared himself to the City fans
with a series of fine performances and the
goal that set them on the way to a
Humber 'derby' victory against
Scunthorpe. The move to became a
permanent Tiger appeared to be foiled by
Wolves insistence on a transfer fee.
Everton (From trainee on 24/10/1995) PL
16+25/3 FLC 0+1 FAC 1+2
Manchester C (Loaned on 29/10/1998) FL 4
Wolverhampton W (£500,000 + on
25/11/1999) FL 61+11/10 FLC 2+1 FAC 4
Reading (Loaned on 21/3/2002) FL 0+2
Hull C (Loaned on 4/10/2002) FL 6+1/3

BRANDON Christopher (Chris) William

Born: Bradford, 7 April 1976
Height: 5'7" **Weight:** 10.3
Chris's often intricate, livewire midfield
play made him an immediate favourite at
Chesterfield last term, where he weighed
in with many important and spectacular
goals, including a fine overhead kick
against Port Vale in August. A tendency
to dissent has been eradicated and Chris
is sure to rank among the Second
Division's leading midfielders in 2003-04.
Torquay U (Free from Bradford PA on
5/8/1999) FL 64+7/8 FLC 4/1 FAC 5/1
Others 3
Chesterfield (Free on 9/7/2002) FL 35+1/7
FLC 1+1/1 FAC 1 Others 2/2

BRANIFF Kevin Robert

Born: Belfast, 4 March 1983
Height: 5'11" **Weight:** 12.0
International Honours: NI: U21-7; Yth;
Sch
This Millwall youngster found his
opportunities severely limited last term,
and managed just six starts for the Lions
all season and a similar number of outings
from the substitutes' bench. Kevin is a
very tricky forward who has good pace
and a stinging shot. He featured regularly
for Northern Ireland at U21 level, winning
a further six caps.
Millwall (From trainee on 12/4/2000) FL 7+9
FLC 3+1/1 FAC 1+3

BRANNAN Gerard (Ged) Daniel

Born: Prescot, 15 January 1972
Height: 6'0" **Weight:** 12.3
The versatile player had a somewhat
disappointing season with Wigan Athletic
in 2002-03, suffering a frustrating time
with injuries. After starting the campaign
as a regular in the right-back berth, his
failure to produce consistent form saw
him struggle to keep his place. He
subsequently joined Dunfermline Athletic
in a three-month loan deal at the start of
February before returning to the JJB
Stadium at the end of the season.
Tranmere Rov (From trainee on 3/7/1990) FL
227+11/20 FLC 26+1/4 FAC 10+1 Others
26+1/1
Manchester C (£750,000 on 12/3/1997) FL
38+5/4 FLC 2 FAC 1
Norwich C (Loaned on 21/8/1998) FL 10+1/1
FLC 1
Motherwell (£378,000 on 28/10/1998) SL
81/16 SLC 3+1 SC 7/2
Wigan Ath (£175,000 on 16/2/2001) FL
49+3 FLC 1/1 Others 2
Dunfermline Ath (Loaned on 31/1/2003) SL
8 SC 4

BRANSTON Guy Peter Bromley

Born: Leicester, 9 January 1979
Height: 6'0" **Weight:** 13.12
A strong, powerful left-sided central
defender, the majority of Guy's
appearances for Rotherham came
towards the end of the season. That was
not down to his ability, it was more a
case of those in front of him in the
pecking order showing consistent form.
However, whenever he appeared Guy
always gave his best and few forwards
got the better of him, especially in the
air. He also got on the score sheet a
couple of times to prove his worth at
both ends of the pitch.
Leicester C (From trainee on 3/7/1997)
Colchester U (Loaned on 9/2/1998) FL 12/1
Others 1
Colchester U (Loaned on 7/8/1998) FL 0+1
Plymouth Arg (Loaned on 20/11/1998) FL
7/1 Others 1
Lincoln C (Loaned on 10/8/1999) FL 4 FLC 2
Rotherham U (£50,000 on 15/10/1999) FL
94+2/13 FLC 4+1 FAC 3 Others 2

BRASS Christopher (Chris) Paul

Born: Easington, 24 July 1975
Height: 5'10" **Weight:** 12.6
Chris proved to be an inspirational captain
and leader both on and off the pitch last
term in what was arguably the most
dramatic season in the history of York City

FC. He missed just a handful of matches and was outstanding in the centre of defence where his tackling and organisational skills were well to the fore. Voted as 'Clubman of the Year' he was rather surprisingly appointed as manager in June at just 27 years of age.

Burnley *(From trainee on 8/7/1993) FL 120+14/1 FLC 8+1 FAC 6+1 Others 8+2*
Torquay U *(Loaned on 14/10/1994) FL 7 FAC 2 Others 1*
Halifax T *(Loaned on 22/9/2000) FL 6*
York C *(Free on 15/3/2001) FL 89+2/4 FLC 2/1 FAC 7/1 Others 1+1*

BRAVO Raul
Born: Gandia, Spain, 14 April 1981
Height: 5'9" **Weight:** 11.5
International Honours: Spain: 7
This left-sided defender proved unable to dislodge Roberto Carlos from the Real Madrid line-up and in February he joined Leeds United in a long-term loan deal, as he sought to keep himself in the frame for further caps for his country. He settled in well under Terry Venables, but when Peter Reid took over he was left on the bench and eventually returned to Spain in the summer.

Leeds U *(Loaned from Real Madrid, Spain on 3/2/2003) PL 5 FAC 1*

BRAYSON Paul
Born: Newcastle, 16 September 1977
Height: 5'7" **Weight:** 10.10
International Honours: E: Yth
This talented forward enjoyed mixed fortunes in his first season with Cheltenham Town in 2002-03. He played both up front and wide on the left during the first half of the campaign, his pace and imaginative movement providing a different dimension to the attack. Perhaps his best performance came in the FA Cup second round replay win at Oldham. However, as the team began to struggle Paul found goals hard to come by and he spent the closing stages playing in the reserves.

Newcastle U *(From trainee on 1/8/1995) FLC 1+1*
Swansea C *(Loaned on 30/1/1997) FL 11/5*
Reading *(£100,000 on 26/3/1998) FL 15+26/1 FLC 0+2 FAC 1+1 Others 2*
Cardiff C *(Free on 16/3/2000) FL 48+36/19 FLC 2 FAC 3+4/1 Others 1*
Cheltenham T *(Free on 7/8/2002) FL 14+6/1 FAC 2+1/1 Others 2/2*

BRAZIER Matthew Ronald
Born: Leytonstone, 2 July 1976
Height: 5'8" **Weight:** 11.6
Matthew contested the left-midfield role

for Leyton Orient with John Martin for much of the 2002-03 season, although he also played in central midfield. Matthew is a skilful player and a good passer of the ball, he scored his first goal for the club in the away game at Lincoln.

Queens Park R *(From trainee on 1/7/1994) P/FL 36+13/2 FLC 3+2/1 FAC 3*
Fulham *(£65,000 on 20/3/1998) FL 4+5/1 FAC 2+1 Others 1*
Cardiff C *(Loaned on 28/8/1998) FL 11/2*
Cardiff C *(£100,000 on 9/7/1999) FL 43+13/3 FLC 2+3/1 FAC 5+1/1 Others 2*
Leyton Orient *(Free on 31/1/2002) FL 41/1 FLC 2 FAC 0+1 Others 0+1*

BRECKIN Ian
Born: Rotherham, 24 February 1975
Height: 6'0" **Weight:** 12.9
Club Honours: AMC '96
The most patient player at Wigan Athletic following his close-season signing, suspension and a knee operation disrupted the central defender's early months with the club. A classy and composed defender it was only after the Second Division championship was won that he got back into the side on a regular basis following an injury to Jason De Vos. Strong in the tackle and effective in the air with good positional sense, his 'Man of the Match' performances against Oldham Athletic and Cardiff City proved that when called upon he is more than capable of becoming a regular.

Rotherham U *(From trainee on 1/11/1993) FL 130+2/6 FLC 6 FAC 5 Others 11*
Chesterfield *(£100,000 on 25/7/1997) FL 208+4/8 FLC 16/1 FAC 9/1 Others 12/1*
Wigan Ath *(£150,000 on 25/6/2002) FL 7+2 FAC 2 Others 1*

BREEN Gary Patrick
Born: Hendon, 12 December 1973
Height: 6'2" **Weight:** 12.0
International Honours: RoI: 56; U21-9
Signed by West Ham after some fine performances for the Republic of Ireland in the 2002 World Cup finals, Gary is a right-footed central defender who is effective in the air. He figured prominently in the early-season games, but then lost his place as the Hammers struggled. Although reinstated in December he was left out again following a torrid time in the FA Cup defeat at Old Trafford and was released by the club in May. Gary was also a regular for his country during the campaign.

Maidstone U *(From Charlton Ath juniors on 6/3/1991) FL 19*
Gillingham *(Free on 2/7/1992) FL 45+6 FLC 4 FAC 5 Others 1*

Peterborough U *(£70,000 on 5/8/1994) FL 68+1/1 FLC 6 FAC 6 Others 6/1*
Birmingham C *(£400,000 on 9/2/1996) FL 37+3/2 FLC 4 FAC 1*
Coventry C *(£2,400,000 on 1/2/1997) P/FL 138+8/2 FLC 10+3 FAC 12*
West Ham U *(Free on 30/7/2002) PL 9+5 FLC 2 FAC 2*

BRENNAN James (Jim) Gerald
Born: Toronto, Canada, 8 May 1977
Height: 5'9" **Weight:** 12.5
International Honours: Canada: 33 (Gold Cup 2000); U23-1
Jim was a regular in the Nottingham Forest line-up last term, only missing two league and cup games. Playing on the left-hand side of the defence he forged a good rapport with Andy Reid down the flank. Jim scored his first goal since September 2000 when he netted against Norwich City, thus ending a run of 125 league games without scoring. He also continued to represent Canada, winning further caps against Libya and Estonia.

Bristol C *(Free from Sora Lazio, Canada on 25/10/1994) FL 51+4/3 FLC 6 FAC 1*
Nottingham F *(£1,500,000 on 29/10/1999) FL 117+6/1 FLC 6 FAC 6 Others 2*
Huddersfield T *(Loaned on 21/3/2001) FL 0+2*

BRENNAN Martin Ian
Born: Whipps Cross, 14 September 1982
Height: 6'1" **Weight:** 12.4
Martin joined Cambridge United in the summer of 2002 as back up to first choice 'keeper Shaun Marshall and spent much of the season on the substitutes' bench. He briefly featured in the LDV Vans Trophy tie against Rushden and then replaced the injured Marshall for the second half of the FA Cup tie at Scarborough. He also featured in the 0-0 home draw with leaders Hartlepool when he made some excellent saves, and at the end of the season he could claim that he has yet to concede a goal in first-team football.

Charlton Ath *(From trainee at Tottenham H on 15/11/2000)*
Cambridge U *(Free on 6/8/2002) FL 1 FAC 0+1 Others 0+1*

BRESLAN Geoffrey (Geoff) Francis
Born: Torquay, 4 June 1980
Height: 5'8" **Weight:** 11.0
Geoff failed to win a place in the starting line-up at Exeter last term, despite making plenty of appearances from the substitutes' bench. The promising left-sided midfield player will be hoping to

receive more first-team action in the 2003-04 campaign.
Exeter C (From trainee on 7/1/1999) FL 61+48/6 FLC 4+2 FAC 3+4 Others 7/1

BREVETT Rupis (Rufus) Emanuel
Born: Derby, 24 September 1969
Height: 5'8" **Weight:** 11.6
Club Honours: Div 2 '99; Div 1 '01
Rufus was a regular choice at left back for Fulham in the first half of last season, despite the challenge from new signing Pierre Wome. His performances again epitomised his battling qualities. Strong and commanding in the tackle and rarely beaten for pace by opponents, Rufus loved to join in attacking moves and showed he was a quality crosser of the ball. He moved on to West Ham during the transfer window, adding some much needed steel to the defence. He soon settled into the side, striking up a good partnership with Trevor Sinclair, and was outstanding in the game with Chelsea in May.
Doncaster Rov (From trainee on 8/7/1988) FL 106+3/3 FLC 5 FAC 4 Others 10+1

Queens Park R (£250,000 on 15/2/1991) F/PL 141+11/1 FLC 9+1 FAC 8
Fulham (£375,000 on 28/1/1998) P/FL 171+2/1 FLC 14+2/1 FAC 14 Others 12
West Ham U (Signed on 31/1/2003) PL 12+1

BRIDGE Wayne Michael
Born: Southampton, 5 August 1980
Height: 5'10" **Weight:** 11.11
International Honours: E: 12; U21-8; Yth
Wayne's status continued to grow both as a Southampton player and a member of the England squad in 2002-03. His quality in his favoured left-back position is international class and his ability to run at and beat defenders, hit sweet through balls and telling crosses makes him as dangerous in attack as the best out-and-out wingers, talents equally useful on the left of midfield. He brings with this durability – an injury sustained against Liverpool in January brought an end to a run that had seen him play 113 consecutive league and cup games for Saints, a record that is unlikely to be broken in the near future.
Southampton (From trainee on 16/1/1998) PL 140+12/2 FLC 10+1 FAC 11

BRIDGE-WILKINSON Marc
Born: Nuneaton, 16 March 1979
Height: 5'6 **Weight:** 11.8
Club Honours: AMC '01
This highly rated Port Vale midfield player has the knack of scoring spectacular goals. Not the tallest of players, Marc is very skilful and ended the season as the club's leading scorer in the league, albeit with just eight goals. As usual some of these were top quality, in particular one from a free kick at Colchester and a brace at Swindon Town. A goal that proved to be mighty important came in the last minute at Peterborough to clinch a 2-1 victory when a plunge into the relegation zone appeared likely. Marc can also take penalties, and despatched three out of three.
Derby Co (From trainee on 26/3/1997) PL 0+1
Carlisle U (Loaned on 5/3/1999) FL 4+3
Port Vale (Free on 4/7/2000) FL 84+8/24 FLC 2/1 FAC 2/1 Others 8/3

BRIDGES David Stephen
Born: Huntingdon, 22 September 1982
Height: 6'0" **Weight:** 12.0

Wayne Bridge

This promising Cambridge midfielder or striker had his season disrupted by injury last term. After finishing the previous campaign on a high with his first senior goal, David featured a number of times early on before being sidelined. When he returned to action he found it difficult to find a place in the starting line-up and he was then left on crutches following an ankle injury.
Cambridge U (From trainee on 20/3/2002) FL 7+17/3 FLC 2 FAC 1+2 Others 2+1

BRIDGES Michael
Born: North Shields, 5 August 1978
Height: 6'1" **Weight:** 10.11
Club Honours: Div 1 '96, '99
International Honours: E: U21-3; Yth; Sch
After missing the whole of the 2001-02 campaign through injury, this talented young striker was hoping for better fortune under new Leeds United boss Terry Venables. In September he came on as a substitute in the 1-0 UEFA Cup first leg victory over Metalurg Zaporizhia, setting up the winning goal for Alan Smith. Michael went on to make a further six substitute appearances, but in only his second full game, he appeared to turn and collapse with no one around him in the UEFA Cup second leg against Malaga. The result was that he missed the remainder of the campaign with yet another long-term injury.
Sunderland (From trainee on 9/11/1995) P/FL 31+48/16 FLC 8+3/5 FAC 2
Leeds U (£4,500,000 + on 29/7/1999) PL 39+7/19 FLC 2+1 FAC 1+1 Others 17+2/2

BRIGGS Keith
Born: Ashton under Lyne, 11 December 1981
Height: 5'10" **Weight:** 11.6
Keith broke into the Stockport County first team in the first half of the 2002-03 campaign and started 11 matches in a run of 13. He scored the only goal of the game against Darlington in the LDV Vans Trophy clash in October and added another at Huddersfield in December. He was eventually sold to Norwich City early in the new year where he found his opportunities somewhat limited, although he made an impressive full debut against Preston on the final day of the season. Primarily regarded as a right back, Keith can also play in midfield or in other defensive positions.
Stockport Co (From trainee on 27/8/1999) FL 47+11/2 FLC 4/1 FAC 3+1 Others 2/1
Norwich City (£65,000 on 16/1/2003) FL 1+1

BRIGHTWELL Ian Robert
Born: Lutterworth, 9 April 1968
Height: 5'10" **Weight:** 12.5
International Honours: E: U21-4; Yth
This experienced utility player originally joined Port Vale on trial in the 2002 close season. Ian did well enough to earn a starting place when the serious stuff commenced and when his trial period was over he was given a one-year contract. His know-how helped the younger players along a bit as he operated mainly on the left-hand side of the defence, but he occasionally ventured on to the right.
Manchester C (From juniors on 7/5/1986) F/PL 285+36/18 FLC 29+2 FAC 19+4/11 Others 4+3
Coventry C (Free on 2/7/1998) FLC 1
Walsall (Free on 11/2/2000) FL 77+4 FLC 6 FAC 5 Others 3
Stoke C (Free on 28/3/2002) FL 3+1 Others 0+1
Port Vale (Free on 8/8/2002) FL 34+1 FLC 1 FAC 1 Others 1

BRISCO Neil Anthony
Born: Wigan, 26 January 1978
Height: 6'0" **Weight:** 11.5
Club Honours: AMC '01
This hard-tackling central midfield player missed a large chunk of Port Vale's season with a bad leg injury. From the end of September until mid-February he was forced to watch the club's struggles from the sidelines until his return against Swindon. Neil scored just the one goal, but it was a superb header that clinched a draw against local rivals Crewe Alexandra.
Manchester C (From trainee on 4/3/1997)
Port Vale (Free on 7/8/1998) FL 85+6/2 FLC 2 FAC 3 Others 7+1

BRISCOE Lee Stephen
Born: Pontefract, 30 September 1975
Height: 5'11" **Weight:** 11.12
International Honours: E: U21-5
A near-automatic choice for Burnley when fit, Lee had another solid season, this time appearing regularly in midfield, usually on the left. His goal against Brighton in the opening game put him in the rare position of being the Clarets' leading scorer for a month as their season started disastrously, but his strength was as a worker and creator of space for the forward players, with his own forays into the penalty area an occasional extra. In a season when lack of consistency was Burnley's major problem (particularly in defence), Lee was 'Mr Reliable', a no-nonsense competitor very much in the mould of his manager Stan Ternent.

Sheffield Wed (From trainee on 22/5/1994) PL 48+30/1 FLC 5+2 FAC 0+2 Others 2+1
Manchester C (Loaned on 20/2/1998) FL 5/1
Burnley (Free on 14/7/2000) FL 100+6/7 FLC 7 FAC 6

BRITTON Leon
Born: London, 16 September 1982
Height: 5'5" **Weight:** 9.10
International Honours: E: Yth
Leon joined Swansea City on loan last December, and within a couple of matches he had set the Vetch Field alight with his ball control and gutsy performances in midfield. Despite his small frame he grew in stature as his experience increased, becoming a cult hero with the club's fans. Leon was voted the PFA Division Three 'Player of the Month' for February, but early in the match against Oxford United he was taken off with what turned out to be a severely bruised cheekbone. Two weeks later, however, he returned to action, wearing a protective mask.
West Ham U (From juniors on 21/9/1999)
Swansea C (Loaned on 13/12/2002) FL 25

BRKOVIC Ahmet
Born: Dubrovnik, Croatia, 23 September 1974
Height: 5'7" **Weight:** 10.8
This versatile midfield player once again proved how useful he was by adapting to playing up front when Luton suffered injuries amongst their forwards. He produced some memorable goal-scoring feats including a fastest-ever hat-trick in the LDV match against Stevenage Borough and a fine double in the FA Cup fifth round tie against Grimsby Town.
Leyton Orient (Free from HNK Dubrovnik, Croatia on 14/10/1999) FL 59+10/8 FLC 3/2 FAC 4+2 Others 2+2
Luton T (Free on 4/10/2001) FL 46+11/4 FLC 1 FAC 3/3 Others 3/3

BROAD Joseph (Joe) Reginald
Born: Bristol, 24 August 1982
Height: 5'11" **Weight:** 12.7
A product of Plymouth's youth system, Joe struggled to get into Argyle's first team during their Second Division campaign last term. He made just the one start in league matches but appeared in both of Argyle's LDV Vans Trophy ties. A talented midfield player he will be looking for further opportunities next season.
Plymouth Arg (From trainee on 15/2/2002) FL 2+10 FLC 0+1 Others 2

BROAD Stephen (Steve)
Born: Epsom, 10 June 1980
Height: 6'0" **Weight:** 11.5

Steve started the 2002-03 campaign as the regular choice at right back for Southend United and even managed a rare goal in the home game against Cambridge. He was playing consistently well until injury struck at Bristol Rovers, then a series of hernia and thigh problems kept him out of action. When he returned to match fitness he found his right-back berth had been taken by Daryl Sutch and he was consigned to the reserves. However, a further injury suffered playing for the second string curtailed his season in early April and he was released at the end of the campaign.
Chelsea (From trainee on 9/2/1998)
Southend U (Free on 31/3/2001) FL 57+2/3 FLC 2 FAC 3 Others 1

BROADHURST Karl Matthew
Born: Portsmouth, 18 March 1980
Height: 6'1" **Weight:** 11.7
This popular central defender started the 2002-03 campaign as a regular in the Bournemouth line-up before injuries set in. Karl enjoyed a lengthy run in the side and went on to score his first senior goal in the 2-1 win over Scunthorpe, adding a second a week later in the FA Cup tie against Southend. However, he was then sidelined by ankle problems and when he returned to action suffered a shoulder injury against Swansea in February, and this ruled him out for the rest of the season.
Bournemouth (From trainee on 3/7/1998) FL 83+7/1 FLC 4+1 FAC 8/1 Others 6

BROCK Stuart Alan
Born: West Bromwich, 26 September 1976
Height: 6'1" **Weight:** 13.8
Club Honours: NC '00
Stuart had one of his best seasons between the posts for Kidderminster last term and kept ten clean sheets. He briefly lost his place to Fraser Digby in the spring, but responded well and was in good form on his return to the line-up. By the end of the campaign he was nearing his 200th appearance for the club.
Aston Villa (From trainee on 10/5/1995)
Northampton T (Free on 27/3/1997. Free to Solihull Borough during 1997 close season)
Kidderminster Hrs (Free on 17/9/1997) FL 98 FLC 3 FAC 6 Others 4

BROMBY Leigh
Born: Dewsbury, 2 June 1980
Height: 6'0" **Weight:** 11.8
International Honours: E: Sch
Leigh started the 2002-03 season as one of the two central defenders in a back

four for Sheffield Wednesday. His displays though, were not as forceful as previously, and he seemed to be losing his individual battles with strikers on occasions. He lost his place in the side under new boss Chris Turner, and was then surprisingly sent out on loan to Norwich City. Leigh made his debut for the Canaries in the white-hot atmosphere of a local 'derby' against Ipswich Town and won many admirers at Carrow Road with his polished displays in the heart of the defence. A cultured player, he possesses a very long throw-in and likes to play his way constructively out from the back.
Sheffield Wed (Free from Liversedge on 9/7/1998) FL 69+2/1 FLC 8 FAC 3+1
Mansfield T (Loaned on 10/12/1999) FL 10/1 Others 1
Norwich C (Loaned on 24/2/2003) FL 5

BROOKER Paul
Born: Hammersmith, 25 November 1976
Height: 5'8" **Weight:** 10.0
Club Honours: Div 3 '01; Div 2 '02
Paul enjoyed a relatively prolific if somewhat inconsistent season for Brighton last term, finishing as the club's second highest scorer on six goals. At his best running at defenders as a natural winger, this skilful player was also used as a striker and a midfielder during the campaign. His best form coincided with the club's fine run in the new year, and there was no doubt that when Paul played well the rest of the side responded. A match-winner on his day, he needs only to add consistency to his undoubted talents to become a top-class player.
Fulham (From trainee on 1/7/1995) FL 13+43/4 FLC 1+2/1 FAC 1+3/1 Others 3+3
Brighton & Hove A (£25,000 on 18/2/2000) FL 102+32/15 FLC 5+1 FAC 3+3 Others 3/1

BROOKER Stephen (Steve) Michael Lord
Born: Newport Pagnel, 21 May 1981
Height: 5'10" **Weight:** 12.4
Club Honours: AMC '01
This burly Port Vale striker was hampered by injuries last season. It all began well as he scored on the opening day against Tranmere but a bad groin strain meant that he only started two more league games before Christmas. Steve hit a superb goal at Stockport on New Year's Day and then another at Peterborough, but although he worked hard, he was never really fully fit to regain his old zest. Even so he remained a dangerous threat and opposing defences always knew that he was around. After a

good pre-season this time he will hopefully be firing on all cylinders once again.
Watford (From trainee on 9/7/1999) PL 0+1 FAC 0+1
Port Vale (£15,000 on 5/1/2001) FL 82+8/22 FLC 3 FAC 3/1 Others 8+2/3

BROOMES Marlon Charles
Born: Birmingham, 28 November 1977
Height: 6'0" **Weight:** 12.12
International Honours: E: U21-2; Yth; Sch
Signed at the start of the 2002-03 campaign after spending the summer with Burnley, Marlon made his Preston debut at Gillingham and continued to feature regularly throughout the season. He showed his versatility by playing at left back as well as centre half, either as one of a three-man defence or in a flat back four. A sound and steady defender, good in the air and comfortable with the ball at his feet, Marlon added to the attacking options by carrying the ball out of defence at pace.
Blackburn Rov (From trainee on 28/11/1994) P/FL 24+7/1 FLC 3 FAC 4
Swindon T (Loaned on 22/1/1997) FL 12/1
Queens Park R (Loaned on 25/10/2000) FL 5
Grimsby T (Loaned on 7/9/2001) FL 13+2 FLC 3/2
Sheffield Wed (Free on 13/12/2001) FL 18+1 FAC 1
Burnley (Free on 19/7/2002)
Preston NE (Free on 9/8/2002) FL 21+7 FLC 3 FAC 1

BROUGH John Robert
Born: Ilkeston, 8 January 1973
Height: 6'0" **Weight:** 13.0
Club Honours: NC '99
This versatile player and fans' favourite re-invented himself as a striker for Cheltenham during 2002-2003, nearly three years after his previous appearance in the role. He spent the early part of the season on the bench but was recalled to the defence following an injury to Richard Walker. However, when new boss Bobby Gould found himself short of strikers, John was pressed into action and earned a standing ovation for his non-stop running, link-up play and the amount of balls he won in the air and on the ground. He featured regularly in his new position in the closing stages of the campaign and contributed a goal in the 3-0 local 'derby' win at Swindon Town.
Notts Co (From trainee on 9/7/1991)
Shrewsbury T (Free on 6/7/1992) FL 7+9/1 FLC 1+1 FAC 1 Others 1 (Free to Telford during 1994 close season)

63

*Hereford U (Free on 4/11/1994) FL 70+9/3
FLC 5 FAC 4/1 Others 4+3*
*Cheltenham T (Signed on 16/7/1998) FL
49+48/4 FLC 1+1 FAC 5+2/1 Others 1+1*

BROUGH Michael

Born: Nottingham, 1 August 1981
Height: 6'0" **Weight:** 11.7
International Honours: W: U21-2; Yth
This young Notts County midfielder
continued to show great promise at
Meadow Lane last term, despite being
interrupted by injury. Michael is a hard-
working ball winner in the centre of the
park. He made his debut for Wales at U21
level against Azerbaijan in November and
added a second cap in the return match
in the new year.
*Notts Co (From trainee on 1/7/1999) FL
62+17/2 FAC 4+3 Others 3*

BROUGH Scott

Born: Scunthorpe, 10 February 1983
Height: 5'6" **Weight:** 9.10
An exciting winger who likes to run at
defenders, Scott started last season in
good form for Scunthorpe appearing in
the opening 12 games and scoring a
stunning goal against Kidderminster in
September. However, he then became
frustrated by a lack of first-team
opportunities at Glanford Park and his last
appearance was as a substitute against
Hull in February. He was subsequently
released and joined Unibond League side
Barrow for the closing weeks of the
campaign.
*Scunthorpe U (From juniors on 9/11/2000)
FL 15+31/3 FLC 1+1 FAC 3+2 Others 2+3*

BROUGHTON Drewe Oliver

Born: Hitchin, 25 October 1978
Height: 6'3'' **Weight:** 12.10
Big, bustling centre forward Drewe had a
nightmare start to his 2002-03 season,
missing a late penalty that would have
won Kidderminster's opening game
against Lincoln. He then went on a barren
run that left him without a goal until the
end of October, when he headed in from
close range in the 4-0 win at Swansea to
spark great scenes of celebration. Further
goals were sporadic, however, but he
finished the campaign with a tally of
eight.
*Norwich C (From trainee on 6/5/1997) FL
3+6/1*
Wigan Ath (Loaned on 15/8/1997) FL 1+3
Brentford (£100,000 on 30/10/1998) FL 1
*Peterborough U (£100,000 on 17/11/1998)
FL 19+16/8 FLC 2 Others 1+1/1*
*Kidderminster Hrs (£50,000 on 22/1/2001)
FL 70+24/19 FLC 2 FAC 2/2 Others 5/2*

BROWN Aaron Wesley

Born: Bristol, 14 March 1980
Height: 5'10" **Weight:** 11.12
Club Honours: AMC '03
International Honours: E: Sch
Aaron's pace and skill up front were often
used to good effect by Bristol City last
term when he was called on as a late
substitute. He broke the mould of
previous years, when he had been unable
to open his account until the last game,
by scoring in the 3-1 home success over
Peterborough United in October. Whilst
the addition of more aggression to his
game was to be welcomed, it somewhat
backfired with suspension ruling him out
of the play-offs. He is the older brother of
City's Marvin Brown.
*Bristol C (From trainee on 7/11/1997) FL
106+24/7 FLC 2+2 FAC 7+1 Others 11+4*
Exeter C (Loaned on 6/1/2000) FL 4+1/1

BROWN Jason Roy

Born: Southwark, 18 May 1982
Height: 5'11" **Weight:** 13.3
International Honours: W: U21-3; Yth
Jason confirmed himself as Gillingham's
number one goalkeeper last season and
produced a series of fine performances. A
regular member of the Welsh U21 team,
his form did not go unnoticed elsewhere,
with a number of top clubs said to be
watching him. The only games he missed
were when he was on international duty
and as a result of a shoulder injury
sustained in training. Jason was deservedly
named as the Gills' 'Player of the Year'.
*Gillingham (Free from trainee at Charlton
Ath on 19/3/2001) FL 49 FLC 2 FAC 3*

BROWN Marvin Robert

Born: Bristol, 6 July 1983
Height: 5'9" **Weight:** 11.1
International Honours: E: Yth
This youngster again failed to make a
breakthrough at Bristol City last term and
his only senior football came in loan spells
elsewhere. Marvin made three early-
season appearances for Torquay United,
featuring both in a wide-right role and as
an out-and-out striker before returning to
Ashton Gate. He subsequently joined
Cheltenham Town in a three-month loan
deal early in the new year where he
featured regularly in the line-up, playing
either up front or on the left-hand side of
midfield and scored with a long-range
effort in the 3-1 win over Tranmere
Rovers. Marvin is the younger brother of
his Bristol City colleague Aaron.
*Bristol C (From trainee on 18/7/2000) FL
1+16 FLC 0+1 FAC 0+2 Others 2+3*
Torquay U (Loaned on 26/9/2002) FL 2+2
*Cheltenham T (Loaned on 30/1/2003) FL
11+4/2*

BROWN Michael Robert

Born: Hartlepool, 25 January 1977
Height: 5'9" **Weight:** 11.8
International Honours: E: U21-4
After a few quiet games at the start of
the season, Michael got better and better,
having by far his best season with
Sheffield United, attracting the attention
of Premiership clubs, and, at the time of
writing, making his future at Bramall Lane
uncertain. Very hard working on the left
of midfield, he was an effective ball
winner, his vision and passing created
opportunities for others and his pace and
control going forward down the left flank
created openings. His excellent tally of 22
goals included many memorable long-
range efforts, particularly the one against
local rivals Sheffield Wednesday. He was
deservedly selected for the PFA First
Division team by his peers.
*Manchester C (From trainee on 13/9/1994)
F/PL 67+22/2 FLC 2+4 FAC 10+1/2 Others 4*
Hartlepool U (Loaned on 27/3/1997) FL 6/1
Portsmouth (Loaned on 19/11/1999) FL 4
*Sheffield U (Signed on 17/12/1999) FL
132+4/25 FLC 12+1/3 FAC 6/3 Others 3/2*

BROWN Nathaniel (Nat) Levi

Born: Sheffield, 16 June 1981
Height: 6'2" **Weight:** 12.6
This young defender, who is also an
accomplished striker, made his debut for
Huddersfield Town at Northampton last
season. His performance was full of
confidence and he showed excellent
control, going on to collect the 'Man of
the Match' award. Nat won many aerial
battles, and was always a threat at set
pieces. He went on to fulfil his promise by
establishing himself as a regular in the
first-team set-up for the rest of the
season and will be looking to continue his
progress in 2003-04.
*Huddersfield T (From trainee on 8/7/1999)
FL 36+2 FLC 1 FAC 1 Others 1*

BROWN Ryan Anthony

Born: Stoke, 15 March 1985
Height: 5'9" **Weight:** 10.12
This promising Port Vale left back is still
on a scholarship with the club. He made
his debut on the final day of the season
when he came on as a substitute for the
last 15 minutes at Bristol City. Ryan is an
excellent prospect and was one of the
stars of Vale's run to the fifth round of
the FA Youth Cup, defeating Everton and
Chelsea on the way. He is a pacy
defender who is strong in the tackle.
Port Vale (Trainee) FL 0+1

BROWN Simon James
Born: Chelmsford, 3 December 1976
Height: 6'2" **Weight:** 15.0

Simon was first choice 'keeper for Colchester last term and finished up as the club's 'Player of the Year'. He injured his back during the pre-season, and this caused him to miss the first ten games of the campaign. But he bided his time and after being recalled following the 4-1 defeat at Northampton he never let the team down, producing a string of 'Man of the Match' performances. The U's struggled for much of the season, but Simon gave them a fighting chance of cheating relegation. He dominated his penalty area and really came of age as a 'keeper. He missed the closing stages of the campaign with a groin injury.
Tottenham H (From trainee on 1/7/1995)
Lincoln C (Loaned on 19/12/1997) FL 1
Colchester U (Free on 20/7/1999) FL 101+1 FLC 5 FAC 3 Others 3+1

BROWN Steven (Steve) Byron
Born: Brighton, 13 May 1972
Height: 6'1" **Weight:** 13.10
Club Honours: Div 1 '00

A reliable central defender or right back, Steve found himself further down the pecking order at the Valley with the emergence of Jon Fortune and the signing of Gary Rowett. A great crowd favourite, Steve made three substitute appearances at the start of the season but moved on to Reading in December. He contributed two superb performances at centre back in the space of three days over Christmas and became a rock at the heart of the Royals' defence, with a series of intelligent and brave displays. Steve is strong and commanding in the air and is a very good distributor of the ball. He has a powerful right-foot shot, which is often seen at set pieces, and is also a very capable emergency goalkeeper.
Charlton Ath (From trainee on 3/7/1990) P/FL 194+48/9 FLC 12+4/1 FAC 19+1/1 Others 3+2
Reading (Free on 19/12/2002) FL 21/1 FAC 2 Others 2

BROWN Steven (Steve) Ferold
Born: Northampton, 6 July 1966
Height: 6'0" **Weight:** 11.8

Steve enjoyed another full season at Wycombe Wanderers in his favoured left-midfield position, displaying his usual mix of skill and resolve and still able to last the full 90 minutes. All five of his goals in the league were penalties, his strike in the FA Cup against Brentford being the only one in open play. He passed the 400-appearance mark for the Chairboys and the manager Lawrie Sanchez had little hesitation in awarding another year's contract to one of his most consistent performers. Although not scoring quite so regularly now, he is still managing to keep promising youngsters on the bench.
Northampton T (From juniors on 11/8/1983) FL 14+1/3 (Free to Irthlingborough T in December 1985)
Northampton T (Free on 21/7/1989) FL 145+13/19 FLC 10/1 FAC 11/2 Others 10+1/1

Wycombe W (£60,000 on 9/2/1994) FL 314+32/33 FLC 21+4/3 FAC 24+6/4 Others 11+2/1

BROWN Wayne Lawrence
Born: Barking, 20 August 1977
Height: 6'0" **Weight:** 12.6

Wayne scored his first goal for Ipswich in the home leg of the UEFA Cup tie with Avenir Beggen at the start of last season, but soon after new manager Joe Royle was installed he moved on to join

Steve Brown (Wycombe Wanderers)

Watford. A left-footed central defender or full back who is particularly strong in the air, Wayne was a valuable member of the Hornets' first-team squad without quite holding down a regular place in the side.
Ipswich T (From trainee on 16/5/1996) P/FL 28+12 FLC 3 FAC 2 Others 4+1/1
Colchester U (Loaned on 16/10/1997) FL 0+2
Queens Park R (Loaned on 22/3/2001) FL 2
Wimbledon (Loaned on 14/9/2001) FL 17/1
Watford (Loaned on 30/1/2002) FL 10+1/3
Watford (Free on 18/12/2002) FL 12+1/1 FAC 1

BROWN Wesley (Wes) Michael
Born: Manchester, 13 October 1979
Height: 6'1" **Weight:** 12.4
Club Honours: EC '99; PL '99, '01, '03
International Honours: E: 7; U21-8; Yth; Sch
A solid central defender, who is commanding in the air, Wes fared no better than record signing Rio Ferdinand at the start of last season when he was sidelined with a broken ankle that kept him out until late November. By then, Manchester United had mounted their quest for honours on four fronts, and Wes slipped back comfortably into the side, striking up a particularly good understanding, first with Mikael Silvestre, then with expected partner, Ferdinand in the heart of defence. Though not particularly renowned for his goal-poaching skills, he did manage a valuable contribution in the Champions' League return against Juventus in Turin in February after just eight minutes. Obviously a player with a huge future, Wes's only concern at present is winning a regular place in the England set-up, whilst staving off any more long-term injury woes.
Manchester U (From trainee on 13/11/1996) PL 74+9 FLC 6+1 FAC 4+1 Others 23+5/1

BROWNING Marcus Trevor
Born: Bristol, 22 April 1971
Height: 6'0" **Weight:** 12.10
International Honours: W: 5
This cultured midfielder was a major influence on the Bournemouth team last season when his experience in the middle of the park helped a young squad gain promotion (via the play-offs) at the first attempt. A hard-working player, he scored two goals during the campaign and had the unusual experience of taking over as goalkeeper on two separate occasions. Marcus did particularly well to keep a clean sheet against Hull City when he acted as 'keeper for over 80 minutes.

Bristol Rov (From trainee on 1/7/1989) FL 152+22/13 FLC 7+3 FAC 8/1 Others 13+5/3
Hereford U (Loaned on 18/9/1992) FL 7/5
Huddersfield T (£500,000 on 17/2/1997) FL 25+8 FLC 2+2
Gillingham (Loaned on 20/11/1998) FL 1
Gillingham (£150,000 on 25/3/1999) FL 60+17/3 FLC 6+1 FAC 3+3 Others 0+1
Bournemouth (Free on 9/8/2002) FL 40+3/1 FLC 1/1 FAC 3+1/1 Others 5

BRYAN Marvin Lee
Born: Paddington, 2 August 1975
Height: 6'0" **Weight:** 12.2
The 2002-03 season was not one that Marvin will look back on with too many fond memories because it was a time when he was constantly troubled with injuries, which restricted his appearances for Rotherham United. A right back with an inclination to get forward as much as possible, Marvin's season was cut short by injury which required surgery. Out of contract in the summer, his future was uncertain at the time of writing.
Queens Park R (From trainee on 17/8/1992)
Doncaster Rov (Loaned on 8/12/1994) FL 5/1
Blackpool (£20,000 on 10/8/1995) FL 172+10/4 FLC 10+3 FAC 8 Others 12
Bury (Free on 23/3/2000) FL 6+3
Rotherham U (Free on 10/7/2000) FL 54+9 FLC 2+4 FAC 2 Others 1

BRYANT Simon Christopher
Born: Bristol, 22 November 1982
Height: 5'9" **Weight:** 10.7
Midfielder Simon overcame his injury problems from the previous season and re-established himself in the Bristol Rovers squad last term. He scored his only goal against Rochdale early on and later switched to left back to cover for injuries, acquitting himself well in his new role. However his opportunities to play regularly in his more accustomed central midfield position were restricted following the signing of several new players.
Bristol Rov (From trainee on 17/11/2000) FL 58+17/2 FLC 5+3 FAC 3+1 Others 4+1

BUCKLEY Adam Christian
Born: Nottingham, 2 August 1979
Height: 5'9" **Weight:** 11.6
This left-sided midfield man had few chances to shine in Lincoln's first team last season but performed well in the reserves. His league appearances were all from the substitutes' bench with his only start being in the LDV Vans Trophy when he got on the score sheet. Adam was out of favour in the latter part of the season and was released by the Imps in May.

Grimsby T (Free from West Bromwich A juniors on 7/8/1997) FL 8+7 FLC 0+1 FAC 2
Lincoln C (Free on 23/7/2001) FL 19+15 FLC 0+1 FAC 3 Others 1+2/1

BULL Ronald (Ronnie) Rodney
Born: Hackney, 26 December 1980
Height: 5'8" **Weight:** 10.12
Ronnie is a combative defensive player equally at home for Millwall either at full back or in midfield where he provides effective cover. His appearances were somewhat limited last season due to the consistency of Robbie Ryan at left back, and he made the starting line-up on just nine occasions. Ronnie will be looking to breakthrough to regular first-team football in 2003-04.
Millwall (From trainee on 12/5/1999) FL 37+13 FLC 0+2 Others 3

BULLARD James (Jimmy) Richard
Born: Newham, 23 October 1978
Height: 5'10" **Weight:** 11.10
Club Honours: Div 2 '03
This gifted midfield player was a regular for Peterborough United in the first half of last season, and despite often being heavily marked he continued to show his class. In January he was sold to Wigan Athletic for a bargain fee and he quickly took over the role of midfield playmaker. He delivered some fine defence-splitting passes, and opened his goal account with a stunning 25-yard free kick against Oldham. An inventive and classy performer, he is hard working and alert, always looking to develop positive attacking moves. Jimmy's fellow professionals rewarded him with a place in the PFA's Second Division team for the season.
West Ham U (£30,000 from Gravesend & Northfleet on 10/2/1998)
Peterborough U (Free on 6/7/2001) FL 62+4/11 FLC 2 FAC 6/1 Others 3/2
Wigan Ath (£275,000 on 31/1/2003) FL 17/1

BULLOCK Lee
Born: Stockton, 22 May 1981
Height: 5'9" **Weight:** 11.7
Lee was once again a key figure in midfield for York City last term, showing some impressive all-round footballing skills. He was a near ever-present in the team and netted seven goals including outstanding efforts at home to Leyton Orient in November and at Darlington in March. Despite still being in his early 20s Lee is the joint-longest serving player at Bootham Crescent, having completed five seasons with the club.

York C (From trainee on 29/6/1999) FL
122+14/17 FLC 4+1/1 FAC 9+2/2

BULLOCK Martin John
Born: Derby, 5 March 1975
Height: 5'5" **Weight:** 10.7
Club Honours: AMC '02
International Honours: E: U21-1
Martin is a speedy winger who gets the
crowd excited when he goes on one of
his runs down the flank or through the
middle. He was a regular in the Blackpool
line-up last term, his only goal coming in
the 3-0 win over Peterborough in
December. Martin was also selected for
the PFA Second Division team of the
season.
Barnsley (£15,000 from Eastwood T on
4/9/1993) F/PL 108+77/4 FLC 14+4 FAC
4+11/3 Others 1
Port Vale (Loaned on 14/1/2000) FL 6/1
Blackpool (Free on 10/8/2001) FL 71+10/3
FLC 1+2 FAC 6+1 Others 7/3

BULMAN Dannie
Born: Ashford, Surrey, 24 January 1979
Height: 5'10" **Weight:** 12.3
Once again Dannie was virtually ever
present in the Wycombe central midfield
last season, continuing his very influential
partnership with Michael Simpson. His
work rate is quite extraordinary, but his
high fitness level enables him to finish
games strongly. Although famed for his
fierce tackling, he kept out of trouble and
only received two yellow cards. Possessing
the hardest shot at the club, Dannie likes
to shoot from anywhere near the penalty
area. All four of his goals were scored
away from home, including a 25-yarder at
Crewe.
Wycombe W (£5,000 + from Ashford T on
7/6/1998) FL 130+34/14 FLC 8+1 FAC
2+5/1 Others 9/1

BUNJEVCEVIC Goran Petar
Born: Karlovac, Croatia, 17 February
1973
Height: 6'3" **Weight:** 12.6
International Honours: Yugoslavia: 14
This versatile defender established himself
in his favoured centre-back role in a 3-5-2
formation at Tottenham last season.
Goran adds strength and depth in the
heart of defence and reads the game well
in order to hold the back line together,
whilst turning provider with his accuracy
of pass and willingness to take players on
in midfield.
Tottenham H (£1,400,000 from Red Star
Belgrade, Yugoslavia, ex FK Crvena, Zuezda,
on 25/7/2001) PL 36+5 FLC 3+1

BURCHILL Mark James
Born: Broxburn, 18 August 1980
Height: 5'8" **Weight:** 10.2
Club Honours: SLC '00; Div 1 '03
International Honours: S: 6; U21-15;
Sch
After recovering from a cruciate knee
ligament injury in 2002, Mark seemed out
of favour at Portsmouth last term despite
netting four goals in five starts. At the
turn of the year he returned to Scotland
and spent the second half of the season
on loan at Dundee, where he scored three
times in 15 appearances. Mark is a very
pacy striker with an excellent first touch
and a good eye for goal.
Glasgow Celtic (From Celtic BC on 3/6/1997)
SL 17+34/21 SLC 3+2 SC 1+2/1 Others 4+1/3
Birmingham C (Loaned on 22/9/2000) FL
4+9/4 FLC 3+1/1
Ipswich T (Loaned on 22/1/2001) PL 2+5/1

Portsmouth (£600,000 on 24/8/2001) FL
9+15/8 FLC 1+1
Dundee (Loaned on 31/1/2003) SL 7+4/2 SC
1+3/1

BURGESS Andrew (Andy)
John
Born: Bozcat, 10 August 1981
Height: 6'2" **Weight:** 11.6
Club Honours: NC '01; Div 3 '03
This naturally gifted midfielder, dumped
by boyhood heroes Luton Town before
joining the youth ranks at Nene Park,
missed the start of last season through
suspension and then a fractured foot kept
him out for three months. But Andy
successfully switched from the left wing
to central midfield and became a
revelation in the final weeks of the title
race with creative play full of sensational
skills.

Andy Burgess

67

Rushden & Diamonds *(From juniors on 3/7/1999) FL 47+12/5 FLC 1+1 FAC 1+1 Others 2+1*

BURGESS Benjamin (Ben)
Born: Buxton, 9 November 1981
Height: 6'3" **Weight:** 14.4
International Honours: RoI: U21-2; Yth
Ben took time to settle following his summer move to Stockport and it was not until November that he scored his first goal for the club. Five goals in his next ten games, including a magnificent solo effort against St Albans in the FA Cup, suggested he had turned the corner but another barren spell saw him loaned out to Oldham. Ben started well at Boundary Park, but then faded from the first-team picture and failed to score once for the Latics He became a transfer deadline signing for Hull City, setting a new club record when he became the 44th player used during the season. The big centre forward's fortunes immediately improved and he became the first Tiger to score a hat-trick in their new home of the Kingston Communications Stadium in April.
Blackburn Rov *(From trainee on 25/11/1998) FL 1+1 FLC 1*
Brentford *(Loaned on 16/8/2001) FL 43/17 FLC 2 FAC 2/1 Others 4*
Stockport Co *(£450,000 on 5/8/2002) FL 17+2/4 FLC 0+1 FAC 1+1/2 Others 2*
Oldham Ath *(Loaned on 10/1/2003) FL 6+1*
Hull C *(£100,000 on 27/3/2003) FL 7/4*

BURGESS Daryl
Born: Birmingham, 24 January 1971
Height: 5'11" **Weight:** 12.4
Central defender Daryl had his season at Northampton curtailed by two separate long-term injuries. His experience was sorely missed during his absence and no doubt played its part in the club's demise. After missing all of the period from December to mid-February he returned, but only for a four-match spell. This ended when he suffered the indignation of being carried off and booked at the same time against Colchester.
West Bromwich A *(From trainee on 1/7/1989) FL 317+15/10 FLC 20+2/3 FAC 9 Others 14*
Northampton T *(Free on 5/7/2001) FL 60+1/2 FLC 1 FAC 4 Others 1*

BURGESS Oliver David
Born: Bracknell, 12 October 1981
Height: 5'10" **Weight:** 11.7
This right-sided midfield player was sidelined for the first half of the 2002-03 season whilst recovering from a cruciate

ligament injury suffered back in November 2001. On his return to fitness Oliver failed to win a regular place in the Queen's Park Rangers line-up and had to be mostly content with reserve-team football.
Queens Park R *(Trainee) FL 6+4/1 FAC 2+1 Others 1*

BURLEY Craig William
Born: Irvine, 24 September 1971
Height: 6'1" **Weight:** 13.0
Club Honours: SLC '97; SPD '98
International Honours: S: 46; U21-7; Yth; Sch
Cartilage and achilles tendon operations kept Craig out for exactly a year before he returned for Derby County against Wimbledon last November. Although he made it public that he was unhappy with some of the treatment he received and had to regain match fitness as he went along, Craig soon demonstrated why Derby had missed him. His intelligent positioning added stability in midfield and there was an instant improvement in the delivery from set pieces. His injury-time goal earned a vital point off Leicester City at Pride Park and he was recalled to the Scotland team for a friendly against Austria. Craig announced his retirement from international football a fortnight later and, after six games under his uncle George as interim manager, was released when his Derby contract expired.
Chelsea *(From trainee on 1/9/1989) P/FL 85+28/7 FLC 5 FAC 12+4/4 Others 3*
Glasgow Celtic *(£2,500,000 on 24/7/1997) SL 61+3/20 SLC 7 SC 6/1 Others 12/1*
Derby Co *(£3,000,000 on 2/12/1999) P/FL 73/10 FLC 5/3 FAC 2*

BURNELL Joseph (Joe) Michael
Born: Bristol, 10 October 1980
Height: 5'10" **Weight:** 11.1
Club Honours: AMC '03
Whilst this tenacious performer was a regular in Bristol City's midfield last season many thought that more vision was required in this department. No one could doubt his commitment though and he is likely to be a regular in the club's plans in 2003-04 despite his lack of goals.
Bristol C *(From trainee on 24/7/1999) FL 103+11 FLC 1+2 FAC 3+3 Others 16/2*

BURNS Jacob Geoffrey
Born: Sydney, Australia, 1 April 1978
Height: 5'9" **Weight:** 11.12
International Honours: Australia: 2; U23-19
This self-assured central midfielder was again only on the fringes of the first-team

squad at Leeds last season. He made two Premiership appearances, featuring against Bolton and Tottenham in November, and in the new year he had trials with Feyenoord, with a summer departure looking on the cards.
Leeds U *(£250,000 from Parramatta Power, Australia, ex Sydney U, on 31/8/2000) PL 5+4 FLC 1 Others 3+1*

BURNS James (Jamie) Daniel
Born: Blackpool, 6 March 1984
Height: 5'9" **Weight:** 10.11
This promising Blackpool youngster was a regular in the youth team last term and made his bow in senior football when coming on as a substitute at Huddersfield in August. A left-sided midfield player or winger, he featured a number of times in the closing stages of the campaign. Jamie was in the third year of his scholarship at Bloomfield Road and has been offered a professional contract for the 2003-04 campaign.
Blackpool *(Trainee) FL 4+3*

BURNS John Christopher
Born: Dublin, 4 December 1977
Height: 5'10" **Weight:** 11.6
International Honours: RoI: U21-2; Yth
John was a short-term signing who featured in the early weeks of the season for Carlisle. A hard-working midfield operator, he was unable to secure a long-term deal when his contract ended in mid-September. He later signed for Burton Albion, before finishing the campaign at Unibond League outfit Hucknall Town.
Nottingham F *(Free from Belvedere BC on 4/12/1994) FL 3 FLC 1+1*
Bristol C *(£100,000 + on 5/11/1999) FL 6+5 Others 1+1*
Carlisle U *(Free on 9/8/2002) FL 4+1*

BURNS Liam
Born: Belfast, 30 October 1978
Height: 6'0" **Weight:** 12.12
International Honours: NI: U21-13; Yth
This no-nonsense Port Vale central defender had to wait until October for his first start of the campaign in the victory at Cheltenham. The defence tightened up following Liam's introduction, not conceding a goal in his first three games, and he remained in the team until February when the arrival of Peter Clarke left him on the sidelines once again. Never afraid to go in where it hurts, Liam is a whole-hearted player who tends to operate in the centre of the back line. Still awaiting his first senior goal, he is now Vale's longest-serving player having completed six years service.

Port Vale (From trainee on 2/7/1997) FL 75+16 FLC 1 FAC 4+1 Others 4+1

BURROWS David
Born: Dudley, 25 October 1968
Height: 5'9" Weight: 11.8
Club Honours: CS '89; Div 1 '90; FAC '92
International Honours: E: B-3; U21-7
This vastly experienced central or left-sided defender had a disappointing time at Sheffield Wednesday last term. He started off in central defence and as captain of the side, but was sidelined with an injury after a dozen or so matches. He returned to make a couple more appearances but then played no further part in the Owls' struggle against relegation. His experience and leadership were both sorely missed.
West Bromwich A (From apprentice on 3/11/1986) FL 37+9/1 FLC 3+1 FAC 2 Others 1 F/PL
Liverpool (£550,000 on 20/10/1988) F/PL 135+11/3 FLC 16 FAC 16+1 Others 14
West Ham U (Signed on 17/9/1993) PL 29/1 FLC 3/1 FAC 3

Everton (Signed on 6/9/1994) PL 19 FLC 2 FAC 2
Coventry C (£1,100,000 on 2/3/1995) PL 106+5 FLC 9 FAC 9
Birmingham C (Free on 4/7/2000) FL 17+8 FLC 1+3 FAC 1
Sheffield Wed (Free on 8/3/2002) FL 21 FLC 2

BURT Jamie Paul
Born: Blyth, 29 September 1979
Height: 5'10" Weight: 12.0
Jamie's career at Chesterfield stalled somewhat in the 2002-03 season. He tried so hard to meet the manager's requirement to become more of a 'team' player, but to do so he had to suppress his greatest gifts: individualism, unpredictability and the stroke of match-turning genius. A spell on loan at Carlisle brought a debut goal at Hartlepool and some lively performances, but ended prematurely after a hernia injury flared up.
Chesterfield (Free from Whitby T, ex

Bridlington T, Scarborough, on 14/12/2001) FL 29+11/8 FLC 1+1 FAC 1 Others 2
Carlisle U (Loaned on 31/12/2002) FL 4/1

BURTON Deon John
Born: Ashford, 25 October 1976
Height: 5'9" Weight: 11.9
Club Honours: Div 1 '03
International Honours: Jamaica: 44
Deon started the 2002-03 campaign on loan to his former club Portsmouth and scored three goals in the first four games for Pompey. A foot injury forced him to return to Pride Park, but, having recovered, he showed some of his best form for Derby, starting with a goal when he went on as substitute in the home defeat by Sheffield United. Derby's financial worries meant a transfer remained likely and he rejoined Portsmouth in December, but only managed to score once more, at Watford, in the handful of games he played in. Deon also added a further three caps for Jamaica during the season.

Deon Burton

Portsmouth *(From trainee on 15/2/1994) FL 42+20/10 FLC 3+2/2 FAC 0+2/1*
Cardiff C *(Loaned on 24/12/1996) FL 5/2 Others 1*
Derby Co *(£1,000,000 + on 9/8/1997) P/FL 78+47/25 FLC 6+2/3 FAC 9+1/3*
Barnsley *(Loaned on 14/12/1998) FL 3*
Stoke C *(Loaned on 21/2/2002) FL 11+1/2 Others 2+1/2*
Portsmouth *(Loaned on 9/8/2002) FL 6/3*
Portsmouth *(£75,000 + on 12/12/2002) FL 5+4/1 FAC 0+1*

BURTON Steven (Steve) Paul
Born: Doncaster, 9 October 1983
Height: 6'1" **Weight:** 13.5
This teenaged striker went out on loan to Boston United last August, just days after signing pro forms for Ipswich Town. Steve worked hard up front gaining valuable senior experience during his time at York Street. His only goal came in the Pilgrims' Worthington Cup win at Bristol Rovers and he returned to Portman Road in early October. Steve was later released by Ipswich and finished the season at his home town club of Doncaster Rovers.
Ipswich T (From trainee on 14/8/2002)
Boston U (Loaned on 15/8/2002) FL 6+2 FLC 1+1/1

BURTON Steven (Steve) Peter Graham
Born: Hull, 10 October 1982
Height: 6'1" **Weight:** 11.5
Originally promoted to the senior squad in March 2001, Steve had to wait patiently for his Hull debut. He was sent out on loan to Dr Martens League club Ilkeston Town in September, and returned to make a sparkling debut at left back in a 3-0 defeat of Rochdale with newly-appointed manager Peter Taylor looking on from the stands. Although sparingly used in the Third Division, he impressed sufficiently to be given a contract for a further 12 months. Steve was selected as the Tigers' 'Young Player of the Year'.
Hull C (From trainee on 11/7/2002) FL 2+9 FAC 1 Others 1

BURTON-GODWIN Osagyefo (Sagi) Lenin Ernesto
Born: Birmingham, 25 November 1977
Height: 6'2" **Weight:** 13.6
Club Honours: AMC '01
Sagi featured for Crewe Alexandra during their 2002 pre-season games and made the starting line-up for the fixture against Colchester in August before moving on to join Peterborough United. He featured regularly for the Posh during the remainder of the season, although his

habit of accumulating disciplinary points meant that he missed some games through suspension. A no-nonsense central defender who certainly doesn't mind getting stuck in, he also showed some good skills on the ball.
Crystal Palace (From trainee on 26/1/1996) P/FL 19+6/1 FLC 1 FAC 0+1 Others 0+1
Colchester U (Free on 26/5/1999) FL 9 FLC 2
Sheffield U (Free on 19/11/1999)
Port Vale (Free on 14/1/2000) FL 76+10/2 FLC 3/1 FAC 3 Others 6+1/1
Crewe Alex (Free on 8/8/2002) FL 1

Peterborough U *(Free on 29/8/2002) FL 28+3 FLC 1 FAC 1*

BUTCHER Richard Tony
Born: Peterborough, 22 January 1981
Height: 6'0" **Weight:** 12.12
Richard signed for Lincoln from Conference strugglers Kettering Town last November. He immediately went into the starting line-up and held down a regular place in midfield until the end of the campaign. Richard produced some excellent performances in the second half

Tony Butler

of the season, culminating in a tremendous long-range goal in the 1-0 win at Bournemouth at the end of April.
Rushden & Diamonds (From trainee at Northampton T on 26/11/1999. Freed on 1/10/2001)
Lincoln C (Free from Kettering T on 19/11/2002) FL 23+3/3 Others 3

BUTLER Philip **Anthony (Tony)**
Born: Stockport, 28 September 1972
Height: 6'2" **Weight:** 12.0
Club Honours: AMC '03
This vastly experienced central defender initially came on loan from West Bromwich Albion to add steel to Bristol City's defence. However he did such a good job that he was soon signed up on a two-and-a-half-year contract. Determined and hard-working, he featured regularly during the campaign and helped City win a place in the Second Division play-offs.
Gillingham (From trainee on 13/5/1991) FL 142+6/5 FLC 12 FAC 12+1 Others 5+1/1
Blackpool (£225,000 on 30/7/1996) FL 98+1 FLC 7 FAC 4 Others 4/1
Port Vale (£115,000 on 25/3/1999) FL 19
West Bromwich A (£140,000 on 23/3/2000) FL 65+5/1 FLC 7 FAC 1+1 Others 2
Bristol C (Free on 30/8/2002) FL 38/1 FLC 1 FAC 3 Others 9

BUTLER Martin Neil
Born: Wordsley, 15 September 1974
Height: 5'11" **Weight:** 11.9
The 2002-03 season began as brightly as ever for Martin, with a regular place in the Reading starting line-up, and a typically well-taken striker's goal against Burnley. However, the team's switch to a 4-5-1 formation saw Nicky Forster employed as the one spearhead, with Martin featuring mainly in a substitute's role. He made no first-team appearances from February onwards, and declined the opportunity to go out on loan. He retained his goal-scoring touch however, netting regularly for the reserves, including all four in a 4-2 victory over Plymouth's second string.
Walsall (From trainee on 24/5/1993) FL 43+31/8 FLC 2+1 FAC 2+5/2 Others 2+2/2
Cambridge U (£22,500 on 8/8/1997) FL 100+3/41 FLC 9/5 FAC 9+2/6 Others 3+1/1
Reading (£750,000 + on 1/2/2000) FL 85+15/32 FLC 4+1 FAC 5/2 Others 4+1/2

BUTLER Paul John
Born: Manchester, 2 November 1972
Height: 6'2" **Weight:** 13.0
Club Honours: Div 2 '97; Div 1 '99

International Honours: RoI: 1; B-1
This burly central defender captained Wolves early on, always giving 100 per cent, but lost his place shortly after the start of the season. However, Paul's commitment never wavered, even though his only first-team action in the next 14 games was as a substitute at Burnley, when he scored. On New Year's Day he was back in the starting line-up and remained there, and when Wolves conceded only two in ten league games much of the credit was due to him.
Rochdale (From trainee on 5/7/1991) FL 151+7/10 FLC 8+1 FAC 6+2 Others 12+1
Bury (£100,000 on 22/7/1996) FL 83+1/4 FLC 8 FAC 2 Others 3/1
Sunderland (£600,000 + on 15/7/1998) P/FL 78+1/3 FLC 11+1/1 FAC 4
Wolverhampton W (Loaned on 17/11/2000) FL 5
Wolverhampton W (£1,000,000 on 31/1/2001) FL 81+1/2 FLC 3 FAC 5 Others 5

BUTLER Thomas Anthony
Born: Dublin, Ireland, 25 April 1981
Height: 5'8" **Weight:** 10.8
International Honours: RoI: U21-14; Yth
The diminutive young Sunderland midfielder is one of the club's best prospects, although he experienced a season of distinctly mixed fortunes. Thomas is naturally right footed but operates mainly on the left-hand side of midfield where his eye for a killer pass and ability to commit defenders earned him a regular first-team slot at the beginning of the campaign. However, a series of hamstring injuries kept him on the sidelines from October onwards and when he tore a calf muscle on his return in March, his season was over. Thomas also won his first full caps for the Republic of Ireland whilst continuing to represent the U21s.
Sunderland (From trainee on 25/6/1998) PL 9+10 FLC 0+3
Darlington (Loaned on 13/10/2000) FL 8 FAC 2

BUTT Nicholas (Nicky)
Born: Manchester, 21 January 1975
Height: 5'10" **Weight:** 11.3
Club Honours: FAYC '92; CS '96, '97; PL '96, '97, '99, '00, 01, '03; FAC '96; EC '99
International Honours: E: 27; U21-7; Yth; Sch
A gritty and prodigious midfielder with neat skills and a hardened edge to match, Nicky began the season where he left off for England in the World Cup finals with

some gritty performances in the Manchester United midfield. Just when it seemed that he had reached the peak of his powers, the injury jinx struck again whilst playing for his country against Macedonia in October. Vital surgery was required which kept him out until February, and effectively wrote off a campaign that had started out with so much promise. Returning to full action in the Manchester 'derby' in February, he was an ever-present in the Champions' League and Premiership from then until the end of the campaign. Like Paul Scholes, Nicky remains a quiet man of the side, but his influence remains of the highest order.
Manchester U (From trainee on 29/1/1993) PL 198+51/20 FLC 5+1 FAC 20+4/1 Others 62+12/3

BUTTERFIELD Daniel (Danny) Paul
Born: Boston, 21 November 1979
Height: 5'10" **Weight:** 11.10
Club Honours: AMC '98
International Honours: E: Yth
This tenacious right back proved to be Trevor Francis's best signing for Crystal Palace in his spell as manager of the club. He quickly settled in at Selhurst Park after arriving during the 2002 close season and went on to become an ever-present for the Eagles in First Division matches. He scored his only goal in the 2-1 win at Ipswich.
Grimsby T (From trainee on 7/8/1997) FL 100+24/3 FLC 13+1 FAC 5+2 Others 1+1/1
Crystal Palace (Free on 7/8/2002) FL 46/1 FLC 4+1 FAC 4

BUTTERS Guy
Born: Hillingdon, 30 October 1969
Height: 6'3" **Weight:** 14.2
International Honours: E: U21-3
Signed by Martin Hinshelwood last August to help shore up a leaky Brighton defence, this strapping centre half had initially turned down a move to the Withdean Stadium in the summer. Sadly, he did not prove to be the answer to the club's defensive problems and made just one appearance following the appointment of Steve Coppell as manager in October. In March Guy was allowed to join Conference side Barnet on a month's loan.
Tottenham H (From trainee on 5/8/1988) FL 34+1/1 FLC 2+1 FAC 1
Southend U (Loaned on 13/1/1990) FL 16/3 Others 2
Portsmouth (£375,000 on 28/9/1990) FL 148+6/6 FLC 16+1/1 FAC 7 Others 7+2

*Oxford U (Loaned on 4/11/1994) FL 3/1
Others 1*
*Gillingham (£225,000 on 18/10/1996) FL
155+4/16 FLC 9 FAC 14/1 Others 11*
*Brighton & Hove A (Free on 29/8/2002) FL
6 FLC 1*

BUXTON Jake Fred
Born: Sutton in Ashfield, 4 March 1985
Height: 5'11" **Weight:** 13.0
Jake was Mansfield Town's 'Youth Team
Player of the Year' for 2001-02 and was
given his senior debut in the last few
minutes for the LDV Vans Trophy tie
against Crewe at Field Mill. He made his
first start in the game at Blackpool on
Easter Monday as a central defender. A
valuable member of the Stags' reserve
and youth teams, he will be looking for
more senior experience in 2003-04.
*Mansfield T (Signed from juniors on
21/10/2002) FL 3 Others 0+1*

BUXTON Lewis Edward
Born: Newport, IoW, 10 December 1983
Height: 6'1" **Weight:** 13.10
Lewis had a frustrating time at
Portsmouth last season when he was
restricted to the substitutes' bench and
the reserves. He wore Pompey colours just
once, as a substitute against Walsall. He
had a loan spell at Exeter in October as
head coach Neil McNab sought to stem
the flow of goals conceded, and later
joined Bournemouth in a similar deal. His
best performances for the Cherries came
in the centre of defence, and his
popularity was such that he received a
standing ovation as he left the field for
the last time.
*Portsmouth (From trainee on 9/4/2001) FL
27+3*
*Exeter C (Loaned on 21/10/2002) FL 4
Others 2*
*Bournemouth (Loaned on 10/3/2003) FL
15+2 FAC 1*

BYFIELD Darren
Born: Sutton Coldfield, 29 September 1976
Height: 5'11" **Weight:** 11.11
International Honours: Jamaica: 2
The speedy striker started last season with
a tremendous four-goal blast for
Rotherham in the 6-0 win at Millwall on
the opening day. However, Darren lost his
place in late October and from that point
he struggled to get a decent run in the
side, but nevertheless he had still hit 13
goals by the end of the season. He has a
devastating burst of speed, which often
catches defenders out, but he will be the
first to admit that he would have hoped

for better things. Darren made his debut
for Jamaica in a friendly against South
Africa at the end of April.
*Aston Villa (From trainee on 14/2/1994) PL
1+6 FLC 1 FAC 0+1 Others 1*
*Preston NE (Loaned on 6/11/1998) FL 3+2/1
Others 1*
*Northampton T (Loaned on 13/8/1999) FL
6/1 FLC 1/1*
Cambridge U (Loaned on 17/9/1999) FL 3+1
Blackpool (Loaned on 6/3/2000) FL 3
*Walsall (Free on 21/6/2000) FL 45+32/13 FLC
2+3/2 FAC 4+2/1 Others 2+2/1*
*Rotherham U (£50,000 on 27/3/2001) FL
27+13/15 FLC 0+1*

BYRNE Christopher (Chris)
Thomas
Born: Manchester, 9 February 1975
Height: 5'10" **Weight:** 10.8
Club Honours: GMVC '97
International Honours: E: SP-1
At the beginning of the 2002-03 season
Chris was recovering from a pre-season
achilles injury and this delayed his first
appearance until the end of August. He
made three further appearances for
Macclesfield before incurring a medial
knee ligament injury at Southend in
September. Then whilst recovering from
this Chris was shot in the leg in

Cliff Byrne

November, an injury that required more than one operation. He subsequently struggled to regain fitness and his contract was terminated by mutual consent at the end of March. His ability as an attacking mid-fielder and his spectacular goals will be missed.

Crewe Alex (From trainee on 21/6/1993. Free to Flixton on 1/8/1994) Sunderland (Signed from Macclesfield T on 1/6/1997) FL 4+4 FLC 1+1 Stockport Co (£200,000 on 21/11/1997) FL 3+13/11 FLC 3/1 FAC 1+1 Macclesfield T (Loaned on 27/8/1999) FL 5 Macclesfield T (Free on 16/7/2001) FL 8+7/7 FLC 2 FAC 4/2

BYRNE Clifford (Cliff)
Born: Dublin, 27 April 1982
Height: 6'0" **Weight:** 12.12
International Honours: RoI: U21-8; Yth
This young Sunderland defender joined Scunthorpe on loan last November and spent three excellent months at Glanford Park. A committed central defender, he showed good positional sense and

leadership ability quickly becoming a firm favourite with the Iron's fans. He rejected a permanent move, preferring to try his luck again at the Stadium of Light, but was released by the Wearsiders in the summer. Cliff continued to represent the Republic of Ireland at U21 level during the season.

Sunderland (From trainee on 27/5/1999) Scunthorpe U (Loaned on 21/11/2002) FL 13 FAC 3

BYRNE Desmond (Des)
Born: Dublin, 10 April 1981
Height: 6'1" **Weight:** 12.8
International Honours: RoI: Yth
After some well-publicised off-the-field matters were cleared up, Des left Wimbledon for Carlisle last October. His arrival provided competition for the left-back berth, but unfortunately his contribution was limited by injury. A breach of club discipline later ended his time at Brunton Park and his contract was terminated in March.

Stockport Co (Trainee) FL 2 (Free to St

Patricks Ath on 1/2/1999)
Cambridge U (Loaned on 8/8/2001) FL 3+1 FLC 1
Wimbledon (£20,000 on 2/8/2000) FL 0+1
Carlisle U (Free on 25/10/2002) FL 9+1 FAC 0+1 Others 1

BYRNE Paul
Born: Newcastle, Natal, South Africa, 26 November 1982
Height: 5'9" **Weight:** 11.0
This left-sided midfield player made his first appearance of the 2002-03 season for Port Vale at Stockport on New Year's Day. He generally did well and held his place for half-a-dozen games, but was one of the casualties of the heavy defeat at Queen's Park Rangers. Paul has plenty of skill on the ball and can also play at left back when required, but last season he probably suffered from the team having no reserve side. He has a bright future and will be hoping for more senior appearances in the coming campaign.

Port Vale (From trainee on 1/7/2002) FL 8+3 Others 0+2

Paul Byrne

Danny Cadamarteri

C

CADAMARTERI Daniel (Danny) Leon
Born: Bradford, 12 October 1979
Height: 5'7'' **Weight:** 11.12
Club Honours: FAYC '98
International Honours: E: U21-3; Yth
This powerful striker again failed to hold down a regular place in the Bradford City side last term because of injuries and a loss of form. Danny still possesses great ability and an eye for goal, although he managed to find the net on just one occasion. His pace and strength continue to cause defenders problems, but he really needs to get an injury-free season under his belt.
Everton (From trainee on 15/10/1996) PL 88+55/13 FLC 6+3/2 FAC 6+3
Fulham (Loaned on 4/11/1999) FL 3+2/1
Bradford C (Free on 22/2/2002) FL 28+6/2 FLC 1/1

CADE Jamie William
Born: Durham, 15 January 1984
Height: 5'8'' **Weight:** 10.12
International Honours: E: Yth
Durham-born Jamie came to Middlesbrough as a defender and was successfully converted to an attacking player. An established England U18 player, he progressed through the junior and reserve ranks to the fringe of Premiership football. His breakthrough came in November at Portman Road in the Worthington Cup tie when he became one of three Boro' players to receive a debut, replacing Szilard Nemeth after six minutes.
Middlesbrough (From trainee on 12/7/2001) FLC 0+1

CAHILL Timothy (Tim)
Born: Sydney, Australia, 6 December 1979
Height: 5'10'' **Weight:** 10.11
Club Honours: Div 2 '01
International Honours: W Samoa: Yth
A forceful, strong-running midfielder Tim is remarkably good in the air for a player of only average height. He started the 2002-03 season in excellent form for Millwall, but with only a month gone he suffered a serious cruciate injury, which sidelined him until April. He gave some encouraging performances for the reserves before returning to first-team duties, scoring a late winner with a trademark header against Crystal Palace, and netting three goals from four games. Tim's performances might have won him selection for the Australian national team, but an appearance as a 14-year-old for Western Samoa means that he is ineligible.
Millwall (Signed from Sydney U, Australia on 31/7/1997) FL 172+5/43 FLC 8+1/1 FAC 3+2 Others 10+1/1

CALDWELL Gary
Born: Stirling, 12 April 1982
Height: 5'11'' **Weight:** 12.0
International Honours: S: 4; U21-14; Yth; Sch
This skilful central defender joined Coventry City in a 12-month loan deal, but was initially hampered by a knee injury picked up in pre-season training before making an impressive debut against Nottingham Forest. When the Sky Blues reverted to a back four Gary was switched to right back and he also played a handful of games in central midfield. He impressed management and fans alike with his positive attitude during his loan spell and had very few poor games. He continued to represent Scotland at U21 level during the season.
Newcastle U (From trainee on 19/4/1999)

Jamie Cade

Darlington (Loaned on 20/11/2001) FL 4
Hibernian (Loaned on 31/1/2002) SL 10+1
SLC 1
Coventry C (Loaned on 3/7/2002) FL 36 FLC
3 FAC 2

CALDWELL Stephen (Steve)
Born: Stirling, 12 September 1980
Height: 6'0" **Weight:** 11.5
International Honours: S: 2; U21-5; Yth
It was November before colleagues' injuries gave Steve his first game of the 2002-03 season at the centre of Newcastle's back four in the 'derby' with Middlesbrough, and he capped a fine display with his first ever Premiership goal to help secure a win. Thereafter he remained a squad member for the rest of the campaign. Whenever called upon he never let the side down, always looking a good stopper who is composed, self assured, and comfortable on the ball, perhaps worthy of a longer run in the team. He demonstrated his flexibility when switched to right back during the home game with Tottenham, performing there with distinction. Steve earned his second full cap for Scotland against the Republic of Ireland in February.
Newcastle U (From trainee on 30/10/1997)
PL 17+6/1 FLC 2/1 Others 1+4
Blackpool (Loaned on 12/10/2001) FL 6
Others 1/1
Bradford C (Loaned on 7/12/2001) FL 9

CALVO-GARCIA Alexander (Alex)
Born: Ordizia, Spain, 1 January 1972
Height: 5'10" **Weight:** 11.12
A firm favourite of the Scunthorpe United fans, Alex had rather a mixed time during the 2002-03 campaign. A regular in the midfield until November, he was then restricted mainly to substitute appearances until forcing his way back into the side in April. He marked his return by scoring in the 4-0 trouncing of leaders Hartlepool and also netted twice in the first leg of the play-offs against Lincoln. Still a talented central midfield player, he always looks at his best when given licence to get forward from the middle.
Scunthorpe U (Free from Eibar, Spain on 4/10/1996) FL 197+24/30 FLC 10/4 FAC 19+2/4 Others 12/4

CAMARA Aboubacar (Titi)
Sidiki
Born: Guinea, 17 November 1972
Height: 6'1" **Weight:** 12.8
International Honours: Guinea
After a long injury lay-off this experienced

striker returned to action for West Ham last term looking fitter and more determined. He scored twice in reserve games before returning to first-team action, but managed just four Premiership appearances all from the substitutes' bench. In January he joined the Saudi Arabian team Al-Ittihad on loan for the remainder of the season.
Liverpool (£2,600,000 from Olympique Marseille, France, ex St Etienne, RC Lens, on 14/6/1999) PL 22+11/9 FLC 0+2 FAC 2/1
West Ham U (£1,500,000 on 21/12/2000) PL 5+6 FLC 1 FAC 1+1

CAMARA Ben Ibrahim
Born: Germany, 19 June 1985
Height: 6'2" **Weight:** 12.5
Ben is a second-year scholarship boy with Torquay United. A promising striker he made his senior debut from the substitutes' bench against Scunthorpe in March and also featured in the final game of the season at Lincoln. He was rewarded with a professional contract for the 2003-04 campaign.
Torquay U (Trainee) FL 0+2

CAME Shaun Raymond
Born: Crewe, 15 June 1983
Height: 6'3" **Weight:** 11.12
Shaun found it difficult to break into the Macclesfield Town senior side during the 2002-03 season due to strong performances by more senior central defenders. After making only one first-team appearance his contract was cancelled by mutual consent in the middle of October and shortly afterwards he moved on to Conference club Northwich Victoria. Shaun is the son of the former Bolton Wanderers player Mark Came.
Macclesfield T (From trainee on 5/7/2000) FL 5+4 Others 0+1

CAMERON Colin
Born: Kirkcaldy, 23 October 1972
Height: 5'6" **Weight:** 10.6
Club Honours: S: 11; S Div 1 '93, '95; SLC '94; SC '98
International Honours: Scotland: 19
This midfielder scored twice for Wolves in the first home match of 2002-03 against Walsall, but was injured in his next outing. On his return he netted two in a run of three games, only to be injured again soon afterwards. From early December Colin featured regularly and seemed to cover every blade of grass for the Wolves' cause. He had another few minutes for Scotland in Lithuania and returned to have a fine performance against Rotherham, only to miss a late decisive penalty. He made

amends the next Friday, scoring a lovely goal at Nottingham with the outside of his right foot.
Raith Rov (Signed from Lochore Welfare on 13/7/1990) SL 106+16/23 SLC 8+1/5 SC 6/3 Others 9/2
Heart of Midlothian (£400,000 on 31/3/1996) SL 154+3/48 SLC 13/6 SC 17+1/6 Others 6+3/1
Wolverhampton W (£1,750,000 on 24/8/2001) FL 67+7/11 FAC 5 Others 5

CAMM Mark Liam
Born: Mansfield, 1 October 1981
Height: 5'8" **Weight:** 10.12
This busy, right-sided player appeared in both defence and midfield for Lincoln in the first half of last season. Mark lost his place in the squad after Christmas and went on to spend a couple of months on loan to Unibond League club Gainsborough Trinity.
Sheffield U (From trainee on 5/7/1999)
Lincoln C (Free on 14/8/2000) FL 11+21 FLC 0+1 FAC 1+2 Others 2+2

CAMP Lee Michael John
Born: Derby, 22 August 1984
Height: 5'11" **Weight:** 11.11
International Honours: E: Yth
A loan at the end of January provided Lee with valuable, if hectic, experience behind a Burton Albion defence that was leaking badly in their first Conference season. Derby County's England U19 goalkeeper did well enough for manager Nigel Clough to forecast a good future for him. Although not physically imposing by contemporary standards, Lee attacks crosses and handles confidently. He had a first taste of league action in the second half at Walsall, following an injury to Lee Grant.
Derby Co (From trainee on 16/7/2002) FL 0+1

CAMPBELL Andrew (Andy)
Paul
Born: Stockton, 18 April 1979
Height: 5'11" **Weight:** 11.7
International Honours: E: U21-4; Yth
The finest moment of Andy Campbell's career so far came in the Second Division play-off final at the Millennium Stadium when he netted the extra-time winner in front of nearly 70,000 spectators. Cardiff City had been out of the top two divisions for almost 20 years, and Andy's goal clinched a promotion which means so much to the fans and the club. It was the moment he stole the limelight from Robert Earnshaw, City's record-breaking goal-scorer. Andy had started out as first

choice ahead of Earnshaw, and he took centre stage again in the very last game of the season.
Middlesbrough *(From trainee on 4/7/1996)* F/PL 28+28/4 FLC 5+5/1 FAC 2+3/2
Sheffield U *(Loaned on 10/12/1998)* FL 5/1
Sheffield U *(Loaned on 25/3/1999)* FL 6/2
Bolton W *(Loaned on 9/3/2001)* FL 3+3
Cardiff C *(£950,000 on 25/2/2002)* FL 18+18/10 FLC 1+1 FAC 2+3/2 Others 2+5/2

CAMPBELL Darren
Born: Huntingdon, 16 April 1986
Height: 5'8" **Weight:** 10.8
International Honours: S: Yth
Another graduate of the Reading academy, Darren made a brief 12-minute appearance as a late substitute in the 3-0 win at Watford, although this was sufficient for him to contribute some delightful touches as a wide-right player, and give ample indication of his undoubted potential. The 17-year-old Scottish youth international is nicknamed 'Jinky' by his team mates because of his pace and tricky dribbling skills. Voted the club's 'Under 19 Player of the Year', Darren has now signed a two-year professional contract for the Royals.
Reading *(From trainee on 19/4/2003)* FL 0+1

CAMPBELL Kevin Joseph
Born: Lambeth, 4 February 1970
Height: 6'1" **Weight:** 13.8
Club Honours: FAYC '88; FLC '93; FAC '93; ECWC '94; Div 1 '98
International Honours: E: B-1; U21-4
Looking sharper and fitter than for some time, the big striker topped the Everton overall scoring charts for the fourth time in five years in a season when he featured in all but three matches and captained the team in several games. Kevin started the campaign with six goals in nine games, which was then followed by a match-winning strike at Blackburn. He then suffered something of a goal drought, but finished the season well, contributing admirably to the home wins over Southampton and Aston Villa and scoring the winner at West Bromwich Albion. A clever and muscular leader of the line, he is strong in the air and forged more than useful partnerships with both Tomasz Radzinski and Wayne Rooney.
Arsenal *(From trainee on 11/2/1988)* F/PL 124+42/46 FLC 14+10/6 FAC 13+6/2 Others 15+4/5
Leyton Orient *(Loaned on 16/1/1989)* FL 16/9
Leicester C *(Loaned on 8/11/1989)* FL 11/5 Others 1/1
Nottingham F *(£3,000,000 on 1/7/1995)* F/PL 79+1/32 FLC 2 FAC 11/3 Others 3

(£2,500,000 to Trabzonspor, Turkey on 7/8/1998)
Everton *(£3,000,000 on 25/3/1999)* PL 113+9/44 FLC 5+3/3 FAC 9/3

CAMPBELL Paul Andrew
Born: Middlesbrough, 29 January 1980
Height: 6'1" **Weight:** 11.0
This promising young player made only a handful of appearances for Darlington last term. Paul was unable to establish himself in the line-up for any sustained period and he was mainly on the substitutes' bench towards the end of the season. A creative midfield player with an eye for goal, he was unable to add to his tally. Paul was released at the end of the season.
Darlington *(From trainee on 8/7/1998)* FL 35+26/6 FLC 1+2/1 FAC 2+2/1 Others 4+1

CAMPBELL Stuart Pearson
Born: Corby, 9 December 1977
Height: 5'10" **Weight:** 10.8
Club Honours: FLC '97, '00
International Honours: S: U21-14
Stuart managed to steer clear of the injuries that dogged his career in 2001-02, and as a result was a near ever-present for Grimsby Town last season. Although nominally a central midfielder, he played mostly in a wide-left role. A

skilful and determined player, his ability to get into the box enabled him to finish amongst the Mariners' leading scorers with six goals.
Leicester C *(From trainee on 4/7/1996)* PL 12+25 FLC 2+5 FAC 3+3
Birmingham C *(Loaned on 23/3/2000)* FL 0+2
Grimsby T *(£200,000 on 15/9/2000)* FL 115+1/11 FLC 5 FAC 5

CAMPBELL Sulzeer (Sol) Jeremiah
Born: Newham, 18 September 1974
Height: 6'2" **Weight:** 14.1
Club Honours: FLC '99; PL '02; FAC '02; CS '02
International Honours: E: 54; B-1; U21-11; Yth (UEFA-U18 '93)
Since his arrival at Arsenal Sol has matured into the complete central defender. He is commanding in the air, has a good turn of pace for a big man, and his distribution skills have improved. Dangerous at set pieces in the opposition penalty area, he has scored crucial goals with his head. Sol formed a good defensive partnership with Martin Keown, and is a regular at international level when fit. Mentally, he is highly involved in the motivation of the team. Injury and suspension brought his season to a

Stuart Campbell

premature end. Sol was one of five Gunners' players selected for the PFA Premiership team of the season.
Tottenham H *(From trainee on 23/9/1992) PL 246+9/10 FLC 28/4 FAC 28+2/1 Others 2*
Arsenal *(Free on 10/7/2001) PL 62+2/4 FAC 12/2 Others 21*

CAMPBELL-RYCE Jamal Julian
Born: Lambeth, 6 April 1983
Height: 5'7" **Weight:** 11.10
A skilful winger with electric pace, Jamal spent three months on loan at Leyton Orient at the beginning of last season and did well at Brisbane Road, putting in some fine performances and scoring three goals. He returned to the Valley in November, and was on the verge of breaking into the Charlton side for several months before making his debut as a substitute at Ewood Park in April. Jamal was named by the management team at Charlton as the club's 'Young Player of the Year'.
Charlton Ath *(From trainee on 9/7/2002) PL 0+1*
Leyton Orient *(Loaned on 10/8/2002) FL 16+1/2 FLC 2/1*

CAMPO Ramos Ivan
Born: San Sebastian, Spain, 21 February 1974
Height: 6'1" **Weight:** 12.11
International Honours: Spain: 4
Initially seen as a transfer coup when Sam Allardyce exercised his considerable bargaining powers in August 2002, Ivan took some time to settle into the Bolton team last term. Big things were expected of him, but his initial displays were shaky at best, often appearing as though he was struggling to come to terms with the pace and directness of the English game. All that changed however when he was switched to a holding role between the defence and midfield, and from then on he was a revelation, proving to be one of Wanderers' key performers. The role perfectly suited his tremendous passing range, and his tough tackling added some much needed steel to the team. Also dangerous from set pieces, Ivan scored with a header on his home debut in the 3-2 defeat by Liverpool.
Bolton W *(Loaned from Real Madrid, Spain, ex CD Logrones, Alaves, Vallencia, Valladolid, Real Mallorca, on 31/8/2002) PL 28+3/2 FLC 1 FAC 2*

CANHAM Marc David
Born: Weburg, Germany, 11 September 1982
Height: 5'11" **Weight:** 12.3
Young midfielder Marc skippered the

Colchester United reserve team last season, but had to wait until the beginning of April to enjoy his first league start, away at Plymouth. He also made the line-up for the home match against Luton, but was withdrawn at half time and the U's lost this fixture 5-0. An accurate passer of the ball, Marc is not afraid to shoot from distance. He was released by the U's at the end of the season.
Colchester U *(From trainee on 9/7/2002) FL 2+2*

CANHAM Scott Walter
Born: Newham, 5 November 1974
Height: 5'9" **Weight:** 11.10
Scott signed a one-year contract for Leyton Orient during the summer of 2002 after impressing in the previous season. Although not a first choice in the midfield, he made 12 starts and when he was called upon he always gave 100 per cent. Scott moved to Woking on loan in March and after it was announced his contract was not being renewed he signed permanent forms for the Conference club.
West Ham U *(From trainee on 2/7/1993)*
Torquay U *(Loaned on 3/11/1995) FL 3*
Brentford *(Loaned on 19/1/1996) FL 14*
Brentford *(£25,000 + on 29/8/1996) FL 24+11/1 FLC 4+2 FAC 1+1 Others 1+2*
Leyton Orient *(Free on 10/8/1998) FL 3+6 FLC 0+1 Others 1 (Free to Chesham U on 8/9/2000)*
Leyton Orient *(Free on 9/7/2001) FL 32+8/6 FAC 3/1 Others 1+1*

CANOVILLE Lee
Born: Ealing, 14 March 1981
Height: 6'1" **Weight:** 11.3
International Honours: E: Yth; Sch
After playing the previous season in midfield, Lee settled into the right-back slot for Torquay United last term. He impressed in his new role, looking comfortable on the ball and displaying enterprise when going forward. A spell at centre back showed he still has some defensive lessons to learn, but his poise and pace make him a natural defender.
Arsenal *(From trainee on 3/7/1998) , having earlier been transferred from Millwall juniors for an undisclosed fee on 9/7/1997) FLC 0+1*
Northampton T *(Loaned on 26/1/2001) FL 2*
Torquay U *(Free on 14/9/2001) FL 46+2/1 FLC 1 FAC 1 Others 2*

CANSDELL-SHERIFF Shane Lewis
Born: Sydney, Australia, 10 November 1982
Height: 6'0" **Weight:** 11.12
International Honours: Australia: U23; Yth

This young Leeds reserve central defender went on loan to Rochdale last autumn and made a big impact despite playing in a side on a losing streak. However, after just four games he suffered an injury that forced him to return to Elland Road for an operation on his knee. After he recovered Dale wanted to borrow him again, but Leeds turned them down due to an injury crisis, Shane being named as a substitute for their match against Manchester United.
Leeds U *(Free from NSW Soccer Academy, Australia on 1/2/2000)*
Rochdale *(Loaned on 8/11/2002) FL 3 FAC 1*

CAPALDI Anthony (Tony) Charles
Born: Porsgrunn, Norway, 12 August 1981
Height: 6'0" **Weight:** 11.8
International Honours: NI: U21-11
This young left-sided player spent much of 2002-03 developing in Birmingham City's reserve side. He impressed during a trial with Plymouth Argyle, which included a senior debut in the final game of the season against Wycombe Wanderers, and was signed on a two-year contract. Tony has a good left foot, is excellent with set pieces and also has a useful long throw. He continued to represent Northern Ireland at U21 level during the campaign.
Birmingham C *(From trainee on 9/7/1999)*
Plymouth Arg *(Free on 3/5/2003) FL 1*

CARBON Matthew (Matt) Phillip
Born: Nottingham, 8 June 1975
Height: 6'2" **Weight:** 13.6
International Honours: E: U21-4
This powerful Walsall defender, strong in the air and solid in the tackle, had the bad luck to dislocate a shoulder in the opening away game against Wolves and on his return picked up two further injuries just when he seemed to be settling into a regular first-team place. In between he played powerfully in the FA Cup games against Reading and snatched his second goal in the Saddlers' colours in the win over Burnley in March.
Lincoln C *(From trainee on 13/4/1993) FL 66+3/10 FLC 4/1 FAC 3 Others 4+3*
Derby Co *(£385,000 on 8/3/1996) P/FL 11+9 FLC 1 FAC 0+1*
West Bromwich A *(£800,000 on 26/1/1998) FL 106+7/5 FLC 7+2 FAC 4*
Walsall *(Free on 23/7/2001) FL 42+5/2 FLC 1 FAC 5*

CARBONARI Horacio Angel
Born: Argentina, 2 May 1973
Height: 6'3" **Weight:** 13.4

This central defender, Derby's record buy when he arrived in 1998, appeared to have no future with the club at the start of last season. He had never played under John Gregory until he made a surprise return against Ipswich at the end of September, his 100th appearance for the Rams. He scored the only goal of the game at Portman Road but, after a Worthington Cup defeat by Oldham, injury forced him off at half time in the next First Division game, against Walsall. His contract was cancelled in January and Horacio returned to Argentina.
Derby Co (£2,700,000 from Athletico Rosario Central, Argentina on 1/7/1998) P/FL 39+1/9 FLC 3 FAC 9
Coventry C (Loaned on 22/3/2002) FL 5

CAREY Brian Patrick
Born: Cork, 31 May 1968
Height: 6'3" **Weight:** 14.4
International Honours: RoI: 3; U21-1
A great servant to Wrexham, Brian has given superb service at the heart of the defence and is an inspirational leader of the side. However, he had a bad start to the 2002-03 campaign having to undergo minor surgery to clean out fragments of cartilage following an injury sustained in the first match at Scunthorpe. He returned in October to become an integral part of the defence for the rest of the season. Brian likes nothing better than joining the attack for set pieces often getting on the end of free kicks and corners. He scored three goals in six days in April as the run-in for promotion gathered pace, netting twice against Carlisle United in a 6-1 win and another against Cambridge United in the promotion clincher, both at the Racecourse.
Manchester U (£100,000 from Cork C on 2/9/1989)
Wrexham (Loaned on 17/1/1991) FL 3
Wrexham (Loaned on 24/12/1991) FL 13/1 FAC 3 Others 3
Leicester C (£250,000 on 16/7/1993) F/PL 51+7/1 FLC 3 FAC 0+1 Others 4
Wrexham (£100,000 on 19/7/1996) FL 240+4/13 FLC 11 FAC 21 Others 8+2

CAREY Louis Anthony
Born: Bristol, 20 January 1977
Height: 5'10" **Weight:** 11.10
Club Honours: AMC '03
International Honours: S: U21-1
A knee injury forced this talented Bristol City defender to sit out the first four months of the 2002-03 campaign, but once back in action he didn't take long to

regain his old form. Sometimes too cool, calm and collected for his own good, he rarely let City down at all.
Bristol C (From trainee on 3/7/1995) FL 260+11/4 FLC 13+1 FAC 16+1 Others 17+2/1

CARLISLE Clarke James
Born: Preston, 14 October 1979
Height: 6'1" **Weight:** 12.10
International Honours: E: U21-3
This central defender made his long awaited return to first-team football for

Queen's Park Rangers in mid-September, having missed the whole of the previous season with a cruciate ligament injury. Clarke immediately established himself as a regular in the line-up with strong performances in the heart of the defence. He scored in his second game back and added a second goal later in the season.
Blackpool (From trainee on 13/8/1997) FL 85+8/7 FLC 4+1 FAC 3/1 Others 5
Queens Park R (£250,000 on 25/5/2000) FL 61+2/5 FLC 3 FAC 5 Others 2

Clarke Carlisle

CARLISLE Wayne Thomas

Born: Lisburn, 9 September 1979
Height: 6'0" **Weight:** 11.6
International Honours: NI: U21-9; Yth; Sch

This quick-raiding right winger joined Bristol Rovers on a permanent basis in the 2002 close season and enjoyed his first full campaign at the Memorial Stadium. Despite breaking his hand early on Wayne used his crossing ability to provide goal-scoring opportunities for his team mates and established himself as a crowd favourite for his tremendous work rate. He chipped in with some important goals from free kicks, none more so than the late match-winner against Scunthorpe and another in the penultimate match of the season against Darlington, which effectively saved Rovers from relegation.
Crystal Palace (From trainee on 18/9/1996) FL 29+17/3 FLC 4+3 FAC 1
Swindon T (Loaned on 12/10/2001) FL 10+1/2 FAC 2
Bristol Rov (Free on 28/3/2002) FL 40+6/7 FLC 1 FAC 3+1/1

CARPENTER Richard

Born: Sheerness, 30 September 1972
Height: 6'0" **Weight:** 13.0
Club Honours: Div 3 '01; Div 2 '02

This hard-working midfielder enjoyed a consistent season in a struggling Brighton side last term and was far and away the most impressive performer during the club's terrible run in the autumn. In a midfield that was occasionally overrun, he drove the side on with competitive tackling and hard running. Richard also supported his forwards well and was unlucky to finish with only two goals to his name. An unsung hero renowned for his venomous shooting, he finished third in the club's annual poll for 'Player of the Season' and missed just two games through illness or injury.
Gillingham (From trainee on 13/5/1991) FL 107+15/4 FLC 2+1 FAC 9+1 Others 7/1
Fulham (£15,000 on 26/9/1996) FL 49+9/7 FLC 4/1 FAC 2/1 Others 2
Cardiff C (£35,000 on 29/7/1998) FL 69+6/2 FLC 3+1 FAC 8+1 Others 1
Brighton & Hove A (Free on 4/7/2000) FL 129+2/11 FLC 6 FAC 6/1 Others 1

CARR Michael Andrew

Born: Crewe, 6 December 1983
Height: 5'9" **Weight:** 11.4

Michael is a third-year scholarship boy at Macclesfield, captain of the youth side

and occasional skipper of the reserves. After producing some fine performances as a central defender he was drafted into an injury-hit Macclesfield Town side last December, making his Football League debut in the away match at Darlington when he was unfortunate to receive a red card. Michael went on to make three further appearances, performing well even though playing out of position in the midfield.
Macclesfield T (Trainee) FL 4

CARR Stephen

Born: Dublin, 29 August 1976
Height: 5'9" **Weight:** 12.2
Club Honours: FLC '99
International Honours: RoI: 24; U21-12; Yth; Sch

This hugely influential midfielder was anxious to get the 2002-03 season underway having been out for the whole of the previous campaign with knee problems. However, injury struck again in the season's curtain-raiser at Everton when Stephen pulled up with a hamstring injury which kept him out until October. Without doubt the finest right back in the Premiership, he was selected by his fellow professionals for the PFA Premiership team of the season.
Tottenham H (From trainee on 1/9/1993) PL 190+4/6 FLC 19/1 FAC 13+1 Others 6

CARRAGHER James (Jamie) Lee Duncan

Born: Bootle, 28 January 1978
Height: 6'1" **Weight:** 13.0
Club Honours: FAYC '96; FLC '01, '03; FAC '01; UEFAC '01; ESC '01; CS '01
International Honours: E: 7; B-2; U21-27; Yth

Last term was another solid but unspectacular season for the Liverpool and England international defender who usually fills the right-back slot, although he can play anywhere across the back four and also as a defensive midfielder. Following his summer operation for a knee injury which caused him to miss the 2002 World Cup finals he was rested by manager Gerald Houllier until early September, but once restored to the team he was virtually ever-present for the remainder of the campaign. As a full back he is reluctant to go forward in support of attacks as a paltry total of two goals in 275 appearances testifies.
Liverpool (From trainee on 9/10/1996) PL 182+12/2 FLC 16+3 FAC 15 Others 46+1

CARRAGHER Matthew (Matt)

Born: Liverpool, 14 January 1976
Height: 5'9" **Weight:** 11.4
Club Honours: Div 3 '97; AMC '01

Matt was Port Vale's team captain last term. A versatile player, he can operate anywhere in the defence but is usually to be found either at right back or sweeper. After being out of favour at the start, his first game of the season was at Wigan, where Vale picked up their first points by winning 1-0 against the erstwhile 100 per cent leaders. Matt always gave everything for the cause, changing his role when the team adopted a different formation, and after a spell out injured he returned for a crucial 1-0 victory at Peterborough United. He scored one goal during the season, a low 20-yard shot against Hull City in the LDV Vans Trophy.
Wigan Ath (From trainee on 25/11/1993) FL 102+17 FLC 6+1/1 FAC 10+1/2 Others 7+1
Port Vale (Free on 3/7/1997) FL 190+4/1 FLC 9 FAC 5 Others 12/1

CARRICK Michael

Born: Wallsend, 28 July 1981
Height: 6'0" **Weight:** 11.10
Club Honours: FAYC '99
International Honours: E: 2; U21-13; Yth

This talented West Ham central midfielder enjoyed an excellent season in 2002-03, despite the disappointment of his club's relegation. He showed composure and good passing skills, while he added urgency and bite to his game. Michael was superb in December against Southampton and Middlesbrough, when he was at the hub of most of the Hammers' attacking moves. Unfortunately he missed the last few games of the campaign following a stomach injury in March. He continued to represent England at U21 level during the season adding five more caps.
West Ham U (From trainee on 25/8/1998) PL 94+7/5 FLC 7 FAC 7 Others 0+1
Swindon T (Loaned on 12/11/1999) FL 6/2
Birmingham C (Loaned on 23/2/2000) FL 1+1

CARROLL Roy Eric

Born: Enniskillen, 30 September 1977
Height: 6'2" **Weight:** 12.9
Club Honours: AMC '99; PL '03
International Honours: NI: 13; U21-11; Yth

A highly accomplished goalkeeper, who possesses great presence and a safe pair of hands, Roy was given an early chance to shine for Manchester United both on the European and Premiership stage. After playing in the opening three Premiership

Michael Carrick

games, he then found his way blocked as Fabien Barthez assumed his customary mantle in September. More competition followed with the acquisition of Spanish goalkeeper, Ricardo, which initially forced Roy further down the Old Trafford pecking order. That all changed again as the season progressed, and he bounced back to confine Ricardo to United's third choice 'keeper.
Hull C *(From trainee on 7/9/1995) FL 46 FLC 2 FAC 1 Others 1*
Wigan Ath *(£350,000 on 16/4/1997) FL 135 FLC 11 FAC 8 Others 15*
Manchester U *(£2,500,000 on 27/7/2001) PL 14+3 FLC 3 FAC 2 Others 4*

CARRUTHERS Christopher (Chris) Paul
Born: Kettering, 19 August 1983
Height: 5'10" **Weight:** 12.3
International Honours: E: Yth
Chris was in and out of the Northampton Town line-up last season, when he mostly featured on the left-hand side of defence or in midfield. Chris likes to go forward and has both pace and the ability to deliver pinpoint crosses. He was rewarded with a call-up to the England U20 side during the campaign.
Northampton T *(From trainee on 9/4/2002) FL 33+16/1 FLC 1 FAC 3 Others 1+1*

CARRUTHERS Martin George
Born: Nottingham, 7 August 1972
Height: 5'11" **Weight:** 11.9
Martin broke the 20-goal barrier for the first time in his career when scoring twice against leaders Hartlepool last April and finished the 2002-03 season as one of Division Three's top marksmen with a tally of 21. A virtual ever-present throughout the campaign for Scunthorpe, he also netted the goal which booked them an FA Cup third round tie with Leeds United. A hard-working, predatory striker, he always looks better when playing off a target man.
Aston Villa *(From trainee on 4/7/1990) F/PL 2+2 FAC 0+1 Others 0+1*
Hull C *(Loaned on 31/10/1992) FL 13/6 Others 3*
Stoke C *(£100,000 on 5/7/1993) FL 60+31/13 FLC 7+3/1 FAC 3+1 Others 10+4/6*
Peterborough U *(Signed on 18/11/1996) FL 63+4/21 FLC 5+1/2 FAC 6/4 Others 6*
York C *(Loaned on 29/1/1999) FL 3+3*
Darlington *(Signed on 25/3/1999) FL 11+6/2 FLC 0+2*
Southend U *(£50,000 on 17/9/1999) FL 69+1/26 FLC 2 FAC 5 Others 5+1/3*
Scunthorpe U *(£20,000 on 22/3/2001) FL 80+6/34 FLC 2 FAC 6/4 Others 5+1/1*

CARSLEY Lee Kevin
Born: Birmingham, 28 February 1974
Height: 5'10" **Weight:** 11.11
International Honours: RoI: 28; U21-1
This Republic of Ireland international
enjoyed a consistent season in midfield
for both club and country after waiting
until the end of September before making
a first-team start. Although more used to
a central midfield role where he can
display his fierce tackling ability, a position
in which he was used in the latter half of
the season with Everton, Lee was at his
best in the wide-right position before
Christmas when he scored vital goals in
the wins against West Ham and
Blackburn. This dependable and
committed player had an important role
in the club's rise under David Moyes as
well as establishing himself at
international level.
*Derby Co (From trainee on 6/7/1992) P/FL
122+16/5 FLC 10+3 FAC 12 Others 3*
*Blackburn Rov (£3,375,000 on 23/3/1999)
P/FL 40+6/10 FLC 4/1 FAC 4/1*
*Coventry C (£2,500,000 on 1/12/2000) P/FL
46+1/4 FLC 2/1 FAC 3*
*Everton (£1,950,000 on 8/2/2002) PL
29+3/4 FLC 2 FAC 1*

CARSS Anthony (Tony) John
Born: Alnwick, 31 March 1976
Height: 5'10" **Weight:** 12.0
Tony had another fine campaign for
Oldham Athletic last term despite being
sidelined for three months with damaged
ankle ligaments. He has now made over
200 league appearances but has endured
bad luck with injuries in the past 18
months. Always an energetic performer in
midfield, he again showed his eye for
goal with superb long-range strikes at
Wycombe and Huddersfield. Tony was out
of contract in the summer, but was
hoping to negotiate a new deal with the
Latics at the time of writing.
*Blackburn Rov (From trainee at Bradford C
on 29/8/1994)*
*Darlington (Free on 11/8/1995) FL 33+24/2
FLC 5/1 FAC 2+1 Others 4*
*Cardiff C (Free on 28/7/1997) FL 36+6/1 FLC
2 FAC 5+1 Others 1*
*Chesterfield (Free on 7/9/1998) FL 26+9/1
FLC 2 FAC 1 Others 1+1*
Carlisle U (Free on 11/8/2000) FL 6+1 FLC 2
*Oldham Ath (Free on 13/10/2000) FL
58+17/5 FLC 3/1 FAC 3 Others 1+2*

CARTER Darren Anthony
Born: Solihull, 18 December 1983
Height: 6'2" **Weight:** 12.5
International Honours: E: Yth
Darren had something of an up-and-

down season at Birmingham last term
after his penalty heroics in the 2002 play-
off finals. He made a handful of starts,
but was played out of position at left
wing and left back early on and spent
time developing in the reserves. A strong
runner and tough tackler, Darren was a
regular for England U20s.
*Birmingham C (From trainee on 13/11/2001)
P/FL 15+10/1 FLC 1 Others 1+1*

CARTWRIGHT Lee
Born: Rawtenstall, 19 September 1972
Height: 5'8" **Weight:** 11.0
Club Honours: Div 3 '96; Div 2 '00
Lee was largely out of the first-team
picture at Preston until the new year, only
making his first start at Ipswich in January.
In his 13th season as a first teamer, he
continued to show his abilities on the
right flank, where he supported his full
back in both defence and attack, and
continued to deliver telling crosses into
the box. Never a prolific scorer, Lee
registered his first home league goal for
four years against Millwall, and he later
became only the sixth player in the club's
history to record 450 senior games when
extending his club record of substitute
appearances at Burnley in April. As
always, Lee remained a great favourite
with the North End fans.
*Preston NE (From trainee on 30/7/1991) FL
310+75/22 FLC 18+4/2 FAC 18+6/1 Others
20+5/1*

CARTWRIGHT Mark Neville
Born: Chester, 13 January 1973
Height: 6'2" **Weight:** 13.6
Club Honours: Div 3 '01
Mark left Shrewsbury at the end of the
2001-02 campaign and returned to the
USA to try and complete his studies.
However, he returned home in the new
year and quickly re-signed for the Shrews.
He made his first appearance in the 2-2
draw at home with York, but he ended
on the winning side just once as injury
and a lack of form limited his
appearances during the run-in. Mark is
still under contract for the 2003-04
season and could well play a part in
Town's struggle to regain Football League
status.
*Stockport Co (From trainee at York C on
17/8/1991. Freed during 1992 close season)*
*Wrexham (Signed following a soccer
scholarship at Florida Tech University, USA on
5/3/1994) FL 37 FLC 2 FAC 6 Others 6*
*Brighton & Hove A (Free on 10/8/2000) FL
12+1 FLC 2*
*Shrewsbury T (Free on 4/7/2001) FL 14 FLC
1 (Freed during 2002 close season)*

Shrewsbury T
*(Free from Lindsey Wilson
College, Kentucky, USA on 7/2/2003) FL 13*

CARVALHO Rogerio
Born: Brazil, 28 May 1980
Height: 6'4" **Weight:** 12.3
The first-ever Brazilian to play for York
City, Rogerio had previously played for
Sao Paulo club Ituano. A tall striker, he
made a number of lively if unorthodox
substitute appearances in the early part of
the 2002-03 season but never established
himself in the side. In December he went
out on loan to Unibond League outfit
Harrogate Town before being released by
City the following month.
*York C (Free from Ituano, Brazil on
15/8/2002) FL 0+4 FLC 0+1*

CAS Marcel
Born: Breda, Holland, 30 April 1972
Height: 6'1" **Weight:** 12.8
Very much an old-fashioned right winger,
Marcel showed he had the potential to
cause havoc in opposition defences for
Notts County last term. Unfortunately
financial considerations meant that he
was released in the new year and he
subsequently joined Sheffield United on a
non-contract basis. Although signed as
cover for Peter Ndlovu he settled in at
right wing back, playing particularly well
at Wimbledon, when he showed useful
defensive skills as well as good pace when
going forward. Marcel was reported to
have signed for Grimsby Town during the
summer.
*Notts Co (Free from RBC Roosendaal,
Holland on 4/7/2001) FL 49+9/8 FLC 3 FAC 3
Others 3*
Sheffield U (Free on 4/2/2003) FL 3+3

CASH Brian Dominick
Born: Dublin, 24 November 1982
Height: 5'9" **Weight:** 12.0
International Honours: RoI: U21-3;
This pacy Nottingham Forest right winger
found chances hard to come by last term,
and after making one brief substitute
appearance against Kidderminster in the
Worthington Cup he was allowed to join
Swansea City on loan in October. Brian
gave a good impression in his early games
at the Vetch Field with his pace and ability
to cross the ball, but lacked the
consistency and physical application
required for Third Division football. On his
return to the City Ground he was a
regular in the reserves before making a
late appearance from the bench in the
last game of the season against
Rotherham.

Nottingham F (From trainee on 15/12/1999) FL 0+6 FLC 0+1
Swansea C (Loaned on 19/10/2002) FL 5 Others 1

CASKEY Darren Mark
Born: Basildon, 21 August 1974
Height: 5'8" **Weight:** 11.9
International Honours: E: Yth (UEFA-U18 '93); Sch
This talented midfield playmaker was again the focal point for many of Notts County's attacking movements last season. Darren showed excellent skills on the ball, with good vision and a wide passing range. He is very much an expert with set pieces and his tally of three goals included a superbly struck free kick from 25 yards against Mansfield.
Tottenham H (From trainee on 6/3/1992) PL 20+12/4 FLC 3+1/1 FAC 6+1
Watford (Loaned on 27/10/1995) FL 6/1
Reading (£700,000 on 28/2/1996) FL 180+22/35 FLC 10+2/4 FAC 9+1/5 Others 8+1/1
Notts Co (Free on 4/7/2001) FL 72+9/8 FLC 3 FAC 4 Others 2+1/1

CASTLE Peter
Born: Southampton, 12 March 1987
Height: 6'0" **Weight:** 12.2
International Honours: E: Yth
The record for Reading's youngest League debutant now belongs to Peter, who came on for the final 12 minutes as substitute centre-back in the 3-0 win at Watford, aged 16 years and 49 days. Still a pupil studying for his GCSEs at Western Park Boys School in Southampton, Peter had to ask his headmaster for leave of absence to enable him to play, but he was due to join Reading on a full-time basis in the summer as a scholar at the club's academy. In addition to his first-team outing, Peter also appeared regularly for the reserves, and gained England youth international honours.
Reading (Associated Schoolboy) FL 0+1

CHADWICK Luke Harry
Born: Cambridge, 18 November 1980
Height: 5'11" **Weight:** 11.0
Club Honours: PL '01
International Honours: E: U21-12; Yth
A classy winger who can operate on either flank and score spectacular goals, Luke's impressive run during 2001-02 appeared to have cemented a regular substitute's role for Manchester United in 2002-03, but that failed to materialise, and after just one Premiership appearance from the bench against Leeds, he went on loan to Reading in February. Luke

made an immediate impact, scoring a fine opening goal in the 2-1 win over Gillingham. Although he exhibited immaculate control plus considerable pace and dribbling skills, he looked a little frail for the rigours of the Nationwide League and was frequently substituted during his 17-match spell with the club. The wide-right player returned to Old Trafford following the play-off semi-final defeat against Wolves.
Manchester U (From trainee on 8/2/1999) PL 11+14/2 FLC 5 FAC 1+2 Others 1+5
Reading (Loaned on 7/2/2003) FL 15/1 Others 1+1

CHADWICK Nicholas (Nicky) Gerald
Born: Market Drayton, 26 October 1982
Height: 6'0" **Weight:** 12.8
A dominant presence up-front at reserve level, Nick's first-team opportunities at Everton have been limited. After missing the early part of the season through injury problems, he found himself unable to command a place in the first-team squad and suffered a further blow when a hernia operation in December laid him off until February. He then went on loan to Derby where, although he failed to find the target, he made a good impression. He returned in April and had to wait until the final game of the campaign to make his sole substitute appearance for the Blues. A prolific scorer at every level, Nick will be hoping for regular first-team football in 2003-04.
Everton (From trainee on 29/10/1999) PL 2+8/3 FLC 0+1 FAC 0+1
Derby Co (Loaned on 28/2/2003) FL 4+2

CHALLINOR David (Dave) Paul
Born: Chester, 2 October 1975
Height: 6'1" **Weight:** 12.6
International Honours: E: Yth; Sch
The former Tranmere defender was the only Stockport County player to appear in every Second Division match last season and he only missed the FA Cup Second Round match with Plymouth due to suspension. Dave played a real captain's role as County moved away from the relegation zone over the final weeks of the season. He scored his first Hatters' goal in the final game at Luton.
Tranmere Rov (Signed from Brombrough Pool on 18/7/1994) FL 124+16/6 FLC 17+1 FAC 9+2 Others 1
Stockport Co (£120,000 on 11/1/2002) FL 64/1 FLC 2 FAC 1 Others 2

CHALLIS Trevor Michael
Born: Paddington, 23 October 1975
Height: 5'9" **Weight:** 11.4
International Honours: E: U21-2; Yth
Trevor became Bristol Rovers' longest-serving player at the age of 26 last term, bringing some much needed experience back to a young back four. After appearing at left back in the opening 16 matches he suffered ankle ligament damage at York and although he returned to first-team action briefly, a recurrence of the problem necessitated surgery in February and brought his season to a premature close.
Queens Park R (From trainee on 1/7/1994) F/PL 12+1 FAC 2
Bristol Rov (Free on 15/7/1998) FL 137+8/1 FLC 7 FAC 14+1 Others 5

CHAMBERLAIN Alec Francis Roy
Born: March, 20 June 1964
Height: 6'2" **Weight:** 13.9
Club Honours: Div 1 '96; Div 2 '98
Watford's veteran goalkeeper has now made more than 650 league appearances spread over his five clubs and made his 750th senior appearance in the FA Cup semi-final. Alec had another immaculate season in 2002-03 and missed only four first-team matches. Alert, very fit and always in charge of his penalty area, he played a major part in the Hornets' great FA Cup run, ensuring clean sheets until the semi-final. Despite approaching his 40th year, he remains a model professional and Watford had no hesitation in agreeing a new contract with him.
Ipswich T (Free from Ramsey T on 27/7/1981)
Colchester U (Free on 3/8/1982) FL 188 FLC 11 FAC 10 Others 12
Everton (£80,000 on 28/7/1987)
Tranmere Rov (Loaned on 1/11/1987) FL 15
Luton T (£150,000 on 27/7/1988) FL 138 FLC 7 FAC 7 Others 7
Sunderland (Free on 8/7/1993) FL 89+1 FLC 9 FAC 8 Others 1
Watford (£40,000 on 10/7/1996) P/FL 216+2 FLC 14+1 FAC 14 Others 3

CHAMBERS Adam Craig
Born: West Bromwich, 20 November 1980
Height: 5'10" **Weight:** 11.8
International Honours: E: Yth
Adam had a disappointing season for West Bromwich Albion inasmuch as he played in only 15 senior matches, mainly as a right wing back, owing to a series of niggling injuries to his knee, back, shin

and thigh. When available he was again totally committed, but admitted that at times he found playing in the Premiership was a challenge. Adam is the twin brother of Albion's James Chambers.

West Bromwich A *(From trainee on 8/1/1999) P/FL 38+18/1 FLC 4+1 FAC 5+1 Others 0+1*

CHAMBERS James Ashley
Born: West Bromwich, 20 November 1980
Height: 5'10" **Weight:** 11.8
International Honours: E: Yth
James was once again given very few opportunities in West Bromwich Albion's first team during the course of the season, starting only one game, in the Worthington Cup defeat at Wigan in October when he deputised at right wing back for Igor Balis. He made eight appearances in the Premiership, his debut in the competition coming against Fulham when Albion recorded their first victory of the season. When not on first-team duty he was a regular performer with the reserves. James is the twin brother of his Albion colleague Adam.

West Bromwich A *(From trainee on 8/1/1999) F/PL 40+16 FLC 5+1 FAC 1*

CHAMBERS Luke
Born: Kettering, 29 August 1985
Height: 5'11" **Weight:** 11.0
Luke made his debut in the last match of the season as a substitute for Northampton Town against Mansfield. He won the chance after some sterling displays for the reserves and U19s, and also played in the team that was defeated by Tranmere in the final of the Football League Youth Alliance Cup. A dependable central defender, he will be looking for more senior experience in 2003-04.

Northampton T *(Trainee) FL 0+1*

CHAPLOW Richard David
Born: Accrington, 2 February 1985
Height: 5'9" **Weight:** 9.3
One of several young players drafted into the side as Burnley's season drifted to an injury-hit end, Richard was rewarded for several impressive cameos as a substitute with his first start in the Easter Monday game at Nottingham Forest. A midfielder with good ball skills and a fine range of passing, he also possesses a shot which will surely bring rewards in due course, while the competitive edge to his game will develop as he adds bulk to his frame. If Stan Ternent intends to persevere with youth during the season ahead, then Turf Moor will surely see more of Richard.

Burnley *(Trainee) FL 2+3*

CHAPMAN Benjamin (Ben)
Born: Scunthorpe, 2 March 1979
Height: 5'7" **Weight:** 11.0
Ben had an outstanding season at left back with newly-promoted Boston United. His ferocious tackling and surging runs down the flank earned him plenty of plaudits and he was rewarded when given the captain's arm band in December.

Grimsby T *(From trainee on 11/7/1997) FL 13+8 FLC 3 FAC 3 Others 0+1*
Boston U *(Free on 9/8/2002) FL 37 FAC 1 Others 2*

CHAPMAN Liam James
Born: Leeds, 17 January 1984
Height: 6'2" **Weight:** 11.7
Hull's young central defender was handed his senior debut by Peter Taylor when the Tigers' new boss took the opportunity of a visit to Port Vale in the LDV Vans Trophy to cast an eye over his reserves. Liam's second outing in City colours was a rather more auspicious occasion as he came on for the second half of the Raich Carter Trophy match with Sunderland in December – Hull's inaugural match at their new home at the Kingston Communications Stadium. He was released in April.

Hull C *(Trainee) Others 1*

CHARLTON Simon Thomas
Born: Huddersfield, 25 October 1971
Height: 5'8" **Weight:** 11.10
International Honours: E: Yth
Simon began the 2002-03 season in fine form for Bolton. A string of consistently impressive performances at left back (and, when occasionally required, at centre back and left midfield) saw him retain a first-team place until March, when a thigh injury forced him out of the picture for a handful of games. Such was the quality of Bolton's squad at this time, he then found it hard to regain his place in the starting line-up when he returned to fitness, and he had to be content with a place on the bench at the very end of the season.

Huddersfield T *(From trainee on 1/7/1989) FL 121+3/1 FLC 9/1 FAC 10 Others 14*
Southampton *(£250,000 on 8/6/1993) PL 104+10/2 FLC 9+4/1 FAC 8+1*
Birmingham C *(£250,000 on 5/12/1997) FL 69+3 FLC 3 FAC 3*
Bolton W *(Free on 12/7/2000) P/FL 80+9 FLC 1 FAC 3+1 Others 3*

CHARNOCK Philip (Phil) Anthony
Born: Southport, 14 February 1975
Height: 5'11" **Weight:** 11.2
This left-sided midfielder or defender

joined Port Vale prior to the start of the 2002-03 campaign. Early on he was a regular in the side, varying his roles from left back to the left-hand side of midfield, but as the team struggled for results he tended to be in and out. He did not make the starting line-up between Christmas and Easter, but returned before the end of the season, and scored his only goal from a free kick against Huddersfield. Good on the ball and not bad in the air, he will be hoping to make more of an impression next time around.

Liverpool *(From trainee on 16/3/1993) FLC 1 Others 0+1*
Blackpool *(Loaned on 9/2/1996) FL 0+4*
Crewe Alex *(Signed on 30/9/1996) FL 136+21/8 FLC 13+2 FAC 5 Others 6*
Port Vale *(Free on 8/8/2002) FL 14+4/1 FAC 1 Others 3*

CHETTLE Stephen (Steve)
Born: Nottingham, 27 September 1968
Height: 6'1" **Weight:** 13.3
Club Honours: FMC '89, '92; FLC '89, '90; Div 1 '98
International Honours: E: U21-12
This vastly experienced central defender started the 2002-03 season as an automatic first choice for Grimsby Town. Unfortunately a back injury then ruled him out for several weeks and he was then unable to dislodge young Simon Ford from the side. Steve scored just once for the Mariners during the campaign, netting in the home defeat by Crystal Palace in April.

Nottingham F *(From apprentice on 28/8/1986) F/PL 398+17/11 FLC 49+3/1 FAC 35+1 Others 21+2/2*
Barnsley *(Free on 26/11/1999) FL 91+1/2 FLC 4 FAC 3 Others 3*
Walsall *(Loaned on 25/9/2001) FL 6*
Grimsby T *(Free on 2/8/2002) FL 18+2/1 FLC 1 FAC 1+1*

CHEYROU Bruno
Born: Suresnes, France, 10 May 1978
Height: 6'1" **Weight:** 12.8
Club Honours: FLC '03
One of Liverpool's five summer signings in 2002, Bruno was considered to be one of France's brightest young talents when signed by Gerald Houllier. His first season at Anfield did little to advance his reputation, however, although in mitigation he was never given an extended run in the team and of his 14 games in the starting line up he was substituted in ten. Featuring on the left side of midfield or in the 'hole' behind the front two he probably suffered from playing an unfamiliar role to that he

enjoyed as 'playmaker' at Lille. His first, and to date, only goal for the Reds was scored in the Champions' League against Spartak Moscow in October.

Liverpool (£4,000,000 from Lille, France, ex RC Lens, Racing Club Paris, on 12/7/2002) PL 8+11 FLC 1+1 FAC 2 Others 3+3/1

CHILLINGWORTH Daniel (Dan) Thomas

Born: Cambridge, 13 September 1981
Height: 6'0" **Weight:** 12.6
After missing a large part of the previous season through injury, Dan returned to first-team action for Cambridge last September. Playing up front he was mainly on the fringe of the squad, making more appearances from the substitutes' bench than in the starting line-up. He failed to add to his tally of goals in senior football.

Cambridge U (From trainee on 14/2/2000) FL 21+25/2 FLC 0/4 FAC 1+4 Others 5+5/1
Darlington (Loaned on 19/11/2001) FL 2+2/1 FAC 1/1

CHILVERS Liam Christopher

Born: Chelmsford, 6 November 1981
Height: 6'1" **Weight:** 13.5
Club Honours: FAYC '00
This promising Arsenal defender spent the first half of last season on loan at Belgian club Beveren. In January he returned to join Colchester United, also on loan, where he enjoyed an excellent spell. He plugged the gap at left back, and played an important role in the U's gradual climb away from the relegation zone over the following month. Liam played six games before damaging knee ligaments, which prompted an early return to Highbury.

Arsenal (From trainee on 18/7/2000)
Northampton T (Loaned on 22/12/2000) FL 7
Notts Co (Loaned on 1/11/2001) FL 9/1 FAC 2
Colchester U (Loaned on 24/1/2003) FL 6

CHIPPO Youssef

Born: Boujaad, Morocco, 10 June 1973
Height: 5'10" **Weight:** 10.10
International Honours: Morocco
Famed for his darting runs and defence-splitting passes, Youssef found it difficult to adapt to the needs of First Division football with Coventry City and an inability to impose himself on games sometimes limited his effectiveness. He was played on the right side of midfield in the early part of the season but had a tendency to wander inside thus reducing the team's width. He later spent several weeks on the sidelines with cracked ribs

and in March went on a six-month loan to Qatar club side Al-Sadd.

Coventry C (£1,200,000 from FC Porto, Portugal, ex Al Arabi, on 16/7/1999) P/FL 100+22/6 FLC 7+1/2 FAC 3/2

CHOPRA Rocky Michael

Born: Newcastle, 23 December 1983
Height: 5'8" **Weight:** 9.6
A product of Newcastle's academy, this young striker came to Watford on loan in March and announced himself in the most spectacular way possible, scoring four goals in the Hornets' remarkable 7-4 victory at Burnley. That performance guaranteed his place in the starting line-up for the FA Cup semi-final against Southampton, and although he failed to score that day, he signed off with a great volley against Derby to make his tally five goals in six matches. He also made four substitute appearances for the Magpies during the season, including a cameo at the Nou Camp, and netted a double for England U20s against Italy in November. Neat and quick around the box, Michael has a natural predator's instinct for goal and is surely a big star of the future.

Newcastle U (From trainee on 4/1/2001) PL 0+1 FLC 0+1 Others 0+2
Watford (Loaned on 25/3/2003) FL 4+1/5 FAC 1

CHORLEY Benjamin (Ben) Francis

Born: Sidcup, 30 September 1982
Height: 6'3" **Weight:** 13.2
Club Honours: FAYC '01
This highly rated young Arsenal centre half started the 2002-03 season on loan at Brentford. However, he found it difficult to force his way into the line-up, making just three appearances. Ben returned to Highbury following the Bees' 5-1 reverse at Peterborough, later joining Wimbledon in another loan deal. He made his debut for the Dons against Millwall and showed up well in a 2-0 win. The departure of Mark Williams soon afterwards gave Ben plenty of late-season opportunities, and he showed himself to be a vocal, no-nonsense type of defender very comfortable in playing the way he was facing. He was released by the Gunners and was reported to have signed permanently for Wimbledon in the summer.

Arsenal (From trainee on 2/7/2001)
Brentford (Loaned on 14/8/2002) FL 2 FLC 1
Wimbledon (Free on 3/3/2003) FL 8+2

CHRISTIE Iyseden

Born: Coventry, 14 November 1976
Height: 6'0" **Weight:** 12.6

Iyseden returned to Mansfield after a three-year absence and took his place on the substitutes' bench at the start of the 2002-03 season. However, he went into the starting line-up following the injury to Colin Larkin and became a regular in the side. He finished as the Stags' leading scorer with 19 goals in all competitions, the highlight of his campaign being a four-goal haul against Colchester in November. Iyseden's strength and unpredictability made him a handful for most opponents and his goal-scoring feats ensured that he earned an extension to his contract at Field Mill.

Coventry C (From trainee on 22/5/1995) PL 0+1 FLC 0+1
Bournemouth (Loaned on 18/11/1996) FL 3+1
Mansfield T (Loaned on 7/2/1997) FL 8
Mansfield T (Free on 16/6/1997) FL 44+37/18 FLC 4/5 FAC 0+4 Others 2+1
Leyton Orient (£40,000 on 2/7/1999) FL 32+26/12 FLC 4+1/1 FAC 1+2/1 Others 1
Mansfield T (Free on 9/8/2002) FL 29+8/18 FLC 1 FAC 2/1 Others 1

CHRISTIE Malcolm Neil

Born: Stamford, 11 April 1979
Height: 5'6" **Weight:** 11.4
International Honours: E: U21-11
Although he left in January, Malcolm was still Derby County's joint-leading scorer, at the end of the season. He appeared set to join Middlesbrough in the summer but an offer was rejected. This had an unsettling effect, but he continued to run tirelessly and was always the likeliest source of a goal. He eventually made his move during the January transfer window and quickly slotted into the Boro' forward line, his return of four goals from only 12 Premiership outings making him an instant favourite. The Riverside crowd will hope for more goals of the calibre of his opening strike against relegation-bound West Bromwich Albion in early April. Malcolm was due to have an operation on a groin injury in the summer.

Derby Co (£50,000 + from Nuneaton Borough on 2/11/1998) P/FL 90+26/30 FLC 6+2/3 FAC 5/2
Middlesbrough (£1,500,000 + on 31/1/2003) PL 11+1/4

CISSE Aliou

Born: Zinguinchor, Senegal, 24 March 1976
Height: 5'11" **Weight:** 12.8
International Honours: Senegal
Senegal's World Cup captain arrived at St Andrew's for a substantial fee and became an immediate hit with his no-nonsense approach and tough tackling in

midfield. His partnership with Robbie Savage was a key feature of Birmingham City's early-season play. Tragically Aliou lost several members of his family and friends in a ferry disaster back home, but played on at West Ham in the Blues next game, keeping it secret from the club. However, he missed most of the second half of the campaign through injury.

Birmingham C *(£1,500,000 from Montpelier, France, ex Lille, Sedan, Paris St Germain, on 26/7/2002) PL 21*

CISSE Edouard

Born: Pau, France, 30 March 1978
Height: 6'1" **Weight:** 11.12
International Honours: France: U21
Signed from Paris St Germain on a season-long loan, this classy central midfielder was in and out of first-team action at West Ham last term. He worked hard, screening the midfield and winning many tackles, but regularly suffered from being substituted late on to be replaced by an extra defender as the Hammers unsuccessfully fought against relegation. Despite getting into some good positions he did not score any goals. Edouard returned to France in May.

West Ham U *(Loaned from Paris St Germain, France, ex Pau, Paris St Germain, Rennes, on 8/8/2002) PL 18+7 FLC 1 FAC 2*

CLAPHAM James (Jamie) Richard

Born: Lincoln, 7 December 1975
Height: 5'9" **Weight:** 10.11
Jamie was an ever-present for Ipswich Town last season until he joined Birmingham during the January transfer window, a move necessitated by the club's financial position. A natural left-footed player Jamie has tended to operate as a left wing back or on the left side of midfield, but new boss Joe Royle gave him a roving midfield role, while at St Andrew's he slotted in at left back and helped improve the Blues supply lines down the flank.

Tottenham H *(From trainee on 1/7/1994) PL 0+1 Others 4*
Leyton Orient *(Loaned on 29/1/1997) FL 6*
Bristol Rov *(Loaned on 27/3/1997) FL 4+1*
Ipswich T *(£300,000 on 9/1/1998) P/FL 187+20/10 FLC 19+1/4 FAC 4+3/1 Others 16+2/1*
Birmingham C *(£1,000,000 + on 10/1/2003) PL 16*

CLARE Daryl Adam

Born: Jersey, 1 August 1978
Height: 5'9" **Weight:** 11.12
Club Honours: AMC '98; NC '02

International Honours: RoI: B-1; U21-6
This busy striker found it difficult to continue his prolific scoring record following Boston United's promotion to the Football League. He began the 2002-03 season in the starting line-up but after a well publicised dispute with the club's management he moved on to Chester City. Darryl's only goal for Boston was an important one as it clinched the club's home victory over neighbours Lincoln City.

Grimsby T *(From trainee on 9/12/1995) FL 34+45/9 FLC 1+8/1 FAC 1+4 Others 4+2*
Northampton T *(Loaned on 12/11/1999) FL 9+1/3*

Steve Claridge

Northampton T *(Loaned on 24/11/2000) FL 3+1 Others 0+1*
Cheltenham T *(Loaned on 30/12/2000) FL 4*
Boston U *(Free on 26/7/2001) FL 7/1 FLC 1*

CLARE Robert (Rob)

Born: Belper, 28 February 1983
Height: 6'1" **Weight:** 11.7
International Honours: E: Yth
Last season saw this Stockport County youngster really mature as a player. The defender was a rock in the defence and also managed his first goal for the club, netting in the Worthington Cup victory at Lincoln in September. A number of

Premiership clubs have been monitoring his progress and it would be no surprise to see him move on over the course of the new season. Rob captained the England U20 side against Italy in May.
Stockport Co (From trainee on 10/3/2000) FL 71+10 FLC 2/1 FAC 3 Others 1

CLARIDGE Stephen (Steve) Edward

Born: Portsmouth, 10 April 1966
Height: 5'11" **Weight:** 12.10
Club Honours: Div 3 '91, Div 2 '95; AMC '95; FLC '97

An inspirational performer, Steve was once again an important figure in the Millwall attack and finished as the club's joint-top scorer with a total of 12 goals in all competitions. The image of Steve, arms and legs pumping with his socks round his ankles is one that has endeared him to supporters up and down the country, and like a fine wine, he simply gets better with age! His first touch is the best and his reading of the game is exceptional. A great role model for any youngster, the Millwall faithful accorded him the adulation he deserved. He was reported to have joined Weymouth during the close season.
Bournemouth (Signed from Fareham on 30/11/1984) FL 3+4/1 Others 1 (£10,000 to Weymouth in October 1985)
Crystal Palace (Signed on 11/10/1988)
Aldershot (£14,000 on 13/10/1988) FL 58+4/19 FLC 2+1 FAC 6/1 Others 5/2
Cambridge U (£75,000 on 8/2/1990) FL 56+23/28 FLC 2+4/2 FAC 1 Others 6+3/1
Luton T (£160,000 on 17/7/1992) FL 15+1/2 FLC 2/3 Others 2/1
Cambridge U (£195,000 on 20/11/1992) FL 53/18 FLC 4/3 FAC 4 Others 3
Birmingham C (£350,000 on 7/1/1994) FL 86+2/35 FLC 14+1/2 FAC 7 Others 9+1/5
Leicester C (£1,200,000 on 1/3/1996) P/FL 53+10/16 FLC 8/2 FAC 4/1 Others 3+1/1
Portsmouth (Loaned on 23/1/1998) FL 10/2
Wolverhampton W (£400,000 on 26/3/1998) FL 4+1 FAC 1
Portsmouth (£200,000 on 10/8/1998) FL 94+10/34 FLC 4+2 FAC 2+2/1
Millwall (Free on 21/3/2001) FL 76+15/29 FLC 1+2/1 FAC 4+1/3 Others 1+1

CLARK Benjamin (Ben)

Born: Consett, 24 January 1983
Height: 6'2" **Weight:** 13.0
International Honours: E: Yth; Sch

A young Sunderland centre back who captains England's U19 side, Ben also made the jump into his country's U20 side last term, when he showed his versatility by performing admirably in midfield.

Powerfully built and a natural leader on the pitch, Ben made his first start of the season at right back in the FA Cup tie at Blackburn, the day after his 20th birthday, and followed this up three days later with his only Premiership appearance of the campaign against Southampton. Following relegation, and its financial implications, Ben could well find himself with the opportunity to firmly establish himself next season at the Stadium of Light.
Sunderland (From trainee on 5/7/2000) PL 0+1 FLC 1 FAC 1

CLARK Ian David

Born: Stockton, 23 October 1974
Height: 5'11" **Weight:** 11.7

After ending the previous season as leading scorer for Darlington, Ian started last term up front alongside Barry Conlon. However, the goals did not come as easily as before, with only eight all season, and so in the second half of the campaign he was used mainly as a substitute. Ian continued to show his enthusiasm and versatility by appearing in a variety of positions, but he is probably at his best attacking down the left flank with his tricky footwork and direct running.
Doncaster Rov (Free from Stockton on 11/8/1995) FL 23+22/3 FLC 1+2 FAC 1+1 Others 4/1
Hartlepool U (Free on 24/10/1997) FL 109+29/17 FLC 4 FAC 4+2 Others 11+2/1
Darlington (£10,000 on 14/11/2001) FL 51+10/20 FLC 1 FAC 4+2/1

CLARK Lee Robert

Born: Wallsend, 27 October 1972
Height: 5'8" **Weight:** 11.7
Club Honours: Div 1 '93, '99, '01
International Honours: E: U21-11; Yth; Sch

Lee continued to suffer the injury jinx that had disrupted so much of the previous campaign and when he was fit often found himself unable to displace the more regular midfield choices in the Fulham line-up. He made a goal-scoring return to first-team action in the 4-2 defeat at Southampton in October beginning a brief run in the side before sustaining another injury. A central midfielder whose commitment to the cause can never be doubted, he is a strong tackler and an excellent distributor of the ball. Lee was brought back into the side by caretaker-manager Chris Coleman for the final games and scored an all-important winning goal against his former club Newcastle.
Newcastle U (From trainee on 9/12/1989)

F/PL 153+42/23 FLC 17 FAC 14+2/3 Others 7+5/1
Sunderland (£2,750,000 on 25/6/1997) FL 72+1/16 FLC 4+1 FAC 4 Others 3
Fulham (£3,000,000 on 13/7/1999) P/FL 101+6/17 FLC 15/2 FAC 5 Others 1+1

CLARK Peter James

Born: Romford, 10 December 1979
Height: 6'1" **Weight:** 12.7

Shortly after producing a 'Man of the Match' performance for Stockport on the opening day of the 2002-03 season at Colchester, Peter fell out of favour and was loaned out to Mansfield. At Field Mill he covered for injuries to Allen Tankard and Dave Jervis, but just when he seemed to be settling in well in his new surroundings he picked up an injury. Peter then returned to the Hatters' line-up in February and went on to score with a superb left-foot volley into the top corner in the 1-1 draw with Cardiff City. He was reported to have signed for Northampton Town during the summer.
Carlisle U (From trainee at Arsenal on 6/8/1998) FL 77+2/1 FLC 2 FAC 2 Others 3
Stockport Co (£75,000 on 7/7/2000) FL 66+6/3 FLC 2 FAC 3
Mansfield T (Loaned on 6/9/2002) FL 2+1 FLC 1

CLARK Steven (Steve) Terence

Born: Stepney, 10 February 1982
Height: 6'1" **Weight:** 12.4

Steve performed inconsistently on the wing for Southend last season. In some games his electric pace proved too hot to handle, yet on other occasions he let himself down with poor control and weak crosses. He is clearly a confidence player and the tail end of the campaign saw an upturn in performances as he won over the fans with a string of hard-working and determined displays.
West Ham U (From trainee on 21/7/2001)
Southend U (£12,000 + on 19/11/2001) FL 29+16/1 FLC 0+1 FAC 1+3 Others 1

CLARKE Andrew (Andy) Weston

Born: Islington, 22 July 1967
Height: 5'10" **Weight:** 11.7
Club Honours: GMVC '91
International Honours: E: SP-2

This veteran striker had an amazing season at Peterborough last term. Ironically he might not have got his chance had Leon McKenzie not been injured during the pre-season, but nevertheless Andy grabbed the opportunity with both hands and went on to finish the campaign as the club's

87

leading scorer with 19 goals in all competitions. His pace caused all kinds of trouble for opposition defenders and he remained enthusiastic about his game throughout.
Wimbledon (£250,000 from Barnet on 21/2/1991) F/PL 74+96/17 FLC 13+12/4 FAC 9+8/2
Port Vale (Loaned on 28/8/1998) FL 2+4
Northampton T (Loaned on 15/1/1999) FL 2+2
Peterborough U (Free on 4/5/1999) FL 129+23/45 FLC 2+2/2 FAC 12+1/5 Others 7/4

CLARKE Christopher (Chris) Edward
Born: Leeds, 18 December 1980
Height: 6'3" **Weight:** 12.10
This powerful young defender featured regularly for Blackpool in the first half of last season, although he was often on the substitutes' bench. However, injury problems restricted his appearances in the new year. Chris scored his only goal of the campaign in the 1-1 draw with Notts County in November. He is the twin brother of Darlington defender Matthew Clarke.
Halifax T (From trainee at Wolverhampton W on 5/7/1999) FL 50+1/1 FLC 2 FAC 3 Others 1
Blackpool (£120,000 on 18/2/2002) FL 22+6/1 FAC 3 Others 2/1

CLARKE Clive Richard
Born: Dublin, 14 January 1980
Height: 6'1" **Weight:** 12.3
Club Honours: AMC '00
International Honours: RoI: U21-11; Yth
Clive endured a season interrupted by injury at Stoke City last term. He was sidelined at Gillingham in November and missed out on first-team action for a little over three months. The arrival of Marcus Hall during his absence ensured that on his return Clive was able to show his adaptability, with appearances in wide midfield and at the heart of the defence.
Stoke C (From trainee on 25/1/1997) FL 122+17/5 FLC 9+3 FAC 5+1 Others 17/1

CLARKE Darrell James
Born: Mansfield, 16 December 1977
Height: 5'10" **Weight:** 11.6
Darrell is a consistent performer in midfield for Hartlepool, yet one who rarely gets the credit he deserves. A lively and inventive player, he went through the 2002-03 season missing only one league game as Pool gained promotion from Division Three. An attacking midfielder who likes to get amongst the goals, he had a lean time in the early months of the

season, but later on he scored a number of times as promotion was obtained.
Mansfield T (From trainee on 3/7/1996) FL 137+24/24 FLC 7/2 FAC 4+1/1 Others 2+2
Hartlepool U (Signed on 17/7/2001) FL 69+9/14 FLC 1+1 FAC 2/1 Others 2

CLARKE James (Jamie) William
Born: Sunderland, 18 September 1982
Height: 6'2" **Weight:** 12.9
Jamie made his bow for Mansfield Town last season in the 5-0 home defeat by Crewe Alexandra. He was brought on to play at left back to stem the Railwaymen's flow down that side. With more injuries in defence he was soon switched to his usual right-back position and remained in the side for a short run. However, after November he was no longer a regular and was in and out of the line-up thereafter.
Mansfield T (From trainee on 5/7/2002) FL 18+4/1 FLC 1 FAC 2 Others 1

CLARKE Lee
Born: Peterborough, 28 July 1983
Height: 5'11" **Weight:** 10.10
International Honours: NI: U21-1
This young Peterborough striker made just one senior appearance last term, coming off the bench late on in the home game with Oldham in August. He subsequently continued his development in the club's reserve side before going out on loan to Conference outfit Kettering Town in the closing weeks of the campaign. Colin made his debut for Northern Ireland U21s against Spain in June.
Peterborough U (Signed from Yaxley on 15/10/2001) FL 0+2 Others 0+1

CLARKE Matthew (Matt) John
Born: Sheffield, 3 November 1973
Height: 6'4" **Weight:** 13.10
This big, strong imposing 'keeper began the 2002-03 campaign as first choice for Crystal Palace. However, after appearing in the first six games of the season he was sidelined by a knee ligament injury. Corrective surgery was required and Matt did not return to first-team action for the Eagles before the summer break.
Rotherham U (From trainee on 28/7/1992) FL 123+1 FLC 4 FAC 3 Others 11
Sheffield Wed (£325,000 + on 10/7/1996) PL 2+2
Bradford C (Free on 5/7/1999) PL 38 FLC 2 FAC 2 Others 3
Bolton W (Loaned on 20/3/2001) FL 8 Others 3
Crystal Palace (£1,350,000 on 7/9/2001) FL 34 FLC 2

CLARKE Matthew Paul
Born: Leeds, 18 December 1980
Height: 6'3" **Weight:** 12.7
This giant central defender joined Darlington in the summer of 2002 and soon established a useful partnership with skipper Craig Liddle in the heart of the defence. Matthew is extremely powerful in the air and surprisingly tricky on the ground for such a tall player. When pressed into service as a striker against Kidderminster in January, he scored two excellently taken goals (a header and a volley) to turn the game around and gain a vital win. Matthew is the twin brother of Blackpool's Chris Clarke.
Halifax T (From trainee at Wolverhampton W on 5/7/1999) FL 42+27/2 FAC 5+1 Others 2+2
Darlington (Free on 9/7/2002) FL 35+3/3 FLC 1 FAC 2 Others 1

CLARKE Nathan
Born: Halifax, 30 November 1983
Height: 6'2" **Weight:** 11.5
This young Huddersfield Town defender will want to forget the 2002-03 campaign as soon as possible. Knee and cartilage injuries kept him firmly on the sidelines for all but two games of the season, those against Wycombe and Barnsley. Nathan will be aiming to extend his first-team experience in 2003-04.
Huddersfield T (From trainee on 6/9/2001) FL 38+1/1 FAC 1 Others 4

CLARKE Peter Michael
Born: Southport, 3 January 1982
Height: 6'0" **Weight:** 12.0
International Honours: E: U21-5; Yth; Sch
Peter spent much of the 2002-03 season out on loan. A three-month spell at Blackpool in the autumn saw him create an excellent impression, particularly after he scored twice on his home debut against Luton. He spent the second half of the campaign at Port Vale where he helped the defence become tighter and provided a threat in the air from set pieces. Sandwiched in between, this talented central defender made a single appearance for Everton, lining up in the FA Cup defeat at Shrewsbury. Peter also featured regularly for England at U21 level throughout the campaign.
Everton (From juniors on 19/1/1999) PL 5+3 FAC 4
Blackpool (Loaned on 8/8/2002) FL 16/3
Port Vale (Loaned on 20/2/2003) FL 13/1

CLARKE Ryan James
Born: Bristol, 30 April 1982
Height: 6'1" **Weight:** 12.0

Ryan's patience finally paid off last October when he received his first league start for Bristol Rovers against Lincoln City. The Pirates' reserve 'keeper won many admirers for his mature performance and he kept his place for the next two matches before reverting back to the bench. He continued to make steady progress in the club's reserve team and is expected to challenge strongly for the goalkeeper's jersey in 2003-04.

Bristol Rov (From trainee on 4/7/2001) FL 2+1 Others 1

CLEGG George Gerald
Born: Manchester, 16 November 1980
Height: 5'10" **Weight:** 11.12
This Bury midfielder started the 2002-03 season in scintillating form, scoring in the Shakers opening game against Oxford and also a week later against Swansea. Able to perform anywhere on the left side, George appeared both in midfield and defence, and enjoyed much success from set pieces. Never afraid to take on his man and get in a telling cross, he suffered serious medial ligament damage in a Worthington Cup tie at Bolton in October but returned 12 weeks later to reclaim his place in the side and remained a regular thereafter.

Manchester U (From trainee on 5/7/1999)
Wycombe W (Loaned on 2/3/2001) FL 2+8 FAC 1
Bury (Free on 10/8/2001) FL 53+9/9 FLC 2 FAC 0+1 Others 3+1/1

CLEGG Michael Jaime
Born: Ashton under Lyne, 3 July 1977
Height: 5'8" **Weight:** 11.8
Club Honours: FAYC '95
International Honours: E: U21-2
This former Manchester United defender began the 2002-03 campaign looking as if he had forced his way into Oldham manager Iain Dowie's plans. Michael started the opening five games of the season and helped the side keep four clean sheets. However, he was dropped for the trip to Notts County in early September, and managed just one more start. A long-term injury to his replacement, Josh Low, offered hope but Paul Murray was instead switched from midfield to Michael's favoured right-wing-back slot.

Manchester U (From trainee on 1/7/1995) PL 4+5 FLC 7+1 FAC 3+1 Others 1+2
Ipswich T (Loaned on 16/2/2000) FL 3
Wigan Ath (Loaned on 23/3/2000) FL 6
Oldham Ath (Free on 19/2/2002) FL 12+2 FLC 1 Others 0+1

CLEMENCE Stephen Neal
Born: Liverpool, 31 March 1978
Height: 5'11" **Weight:** 11.7
Club Honours: FLC '99
International Honours: E: U21-1; Yth; Sch
After returning from injury, Stephen found it hard to win a regular first-team place at Spurs as competition for places increased. With ambitions of international football, Stephen decided to cut his losses and make a move to the midlands to join Birmingham. He formed a terrific partnership in central midfield alongside Robbie Savage at St Andrew's and scored his first Blues' goal with a header in the 2-1 win over Liverpool. His driving play and ability to get around the pitch were key factors in the club's late run of good results.

Tottenham H (From trainee on 3/4/1995) PL 68+22/2 FLC 7+1 FAC 7+1/1 Others 2+1
Birmingham C (£250,000 + on 10/1/2003) PL 15/2

CLEMENT Neil
Born: Reading, 3 October 1978
Height: 6'0" **Weight:** 12.3
International Honours: E: Yth; Sch
West Bromwich Albion's left wing back was not at his best in the 2002-03 season. Neil found it difficult to adjust to a higher level of football and was not allowed to attack down the flank as much as he would have liked. Nevertheless, he still produced some competent displays, although late on in the campaign he lost his place (albeit briefly) to Iffy Udeze. Neil's terrific left foot came into operation only occasionally, notably when he blasted home stunning free kicks in the home games against Manchester City and Tottenham Hotspur.

Chelsea (From trainee on 8/10/1995) PL 1 FLC 0+2 FAC 0+1
Reading (Loaned on 19/11/1998) FL 11/1 Others 1
Preston NE (Loaned on 25/3/1999) FL 4
Brentford (Loaned on 23/11/1999) FL 7+1
West Bromwich A (£100,000 + on 23/3/2000) P/FL 131+3/14 FLC 7+1/2 FAC 7/2 Others 2

CLIFFORD Mark Robert
Born: Nottingham, 11 September 1977
Height: 5'10" **Weight:** 10.8
Club Honours: NC '02
This right back missed the start of the 2002-03 season through injury and then found it difficult to break into an established Boston United back four. In the new year Mark went on loan to Chester City, Ilkeston Town and then

Nuneaton for whom he was reported to have signed permanently during the summer.

Mansfield T (From trainee on 3/7/1996) FL 4 FLC 1 (Free to Ilkeston T during 1997 close season)
Boston U (£7,500 on 9/2/2001) FL 5+2 FLC 1 Others 1

CLIST Simon James
Born: Shaftesbury, 13 June 1981
Height: 5'9" **Weight:** 11.0
Many Bristol City followers were mystified as to the omission of this skilful player from a midfield that was crying out for his talents all season long. Simon went on loan to Torquay United with great success. He worked hard and produced some neat and tidy performances on the left side of midfield, highlighted by a superbly taken goal against Scunthorpe. A broken rib ended his season early.

Bristol C (From trainee at Tottenham H on 24/7/1999) FL 53+17/6 FLC 2+1/1 FAC 6+1/2 Others 4+3
Torquay U (Loaned on 22/2/2003) FL 11/2

CLOSE Brian Aidan
Born: Belfast, 27 January 1982
Height: 5'10" **Weight:** 12.6
International Honours: NI: U21-8; Yth
Following his progress through the junior and reserve ranks at Middlesbrough, Brian realised his ambition of playing first-team football when he made a brief appearance in Boro's 3-1 Worthington Cup defeat at Ipswich Town. He was allowed to join Chesterfield on loan in March to gain further experience and he put in many eye-catching displays for the Spireites, mostly at right back. A fiercely determined, no-nonsense exterior masks good ball skills and a keen eye for goal, putting one in mind of a young Roy Keane. Brian won five caps at U21 level for Northern Ireland during the season.

Middlesbrough (Free from St Oliver Plunkett BC on 11/10/1999) FLC 0+1
Chesterfield (Loaned on 7/3/2003) FL 8/1

CLYDE Mark Graham
Born: Limavady, 27 December 1982
Height: 6'1" **Weight:** 12.0
International Honours: NI: U21-5
This tall central defender had a successful loan spell at Kidderminster in the early part of the 2002-03 season, settling in well. He returned to Molineux and went straight into the Wolves' first team, soon establishing a fine defensive partnership with Joleon Lescott. Mark is strong on the ball, does not get flustered easily and reads the game well. He was rested after

a run in the side, but still had the occasional first-team involvement thereafter. Mark continued to represent Northern Ireland at U21 level, winning a further four caps.
Wolverhampton W (From trainee on 6/8/2001) FL15+2 FAC 0+1
Kidderminster Hrs (Loaned on 13/9/2002) FL 4

COATES Jonathan Simon
Born: Swansea, 27 June 1975
Height: 5'8" **Weight:** 10.4
Club Honours: Div 3 '00
International Honours: W: B-1; U21-5; Yth
This wide-left midfield player joined Cheltenham Town on an extended trial basis in the early part of the 2002-03 season. He made several appearances for the reserves and was given one first-team outing, appearing in the 4-1 LDV Vans Trophy first round win over Colchester United. Jonathan subsequently moved on to Conference club Woking before returning to Swansea on transfer deadline day. He went on to make a couple of appearances for the Swans in the closing stages of the campaign.
Swansea C (From trainee on 8/7/1993) FL 218+32/23 FLC 11+2/1 FAC 10 Others 11+3/1
Cheltenham T (Free on 18/10/2002) Others 1 (Free to Woking on 15/11/2002)
Swansea C (Free on 27/3/2003) FL 2+1

COID Daniel (Danny) John
Born: Liverpool, 3 October 1981
Height: 5'11" **Weight:** 11.7
Club Honours: AMC '02
This left-sided player was used in defence and midfield by Blackpool last season when he was a regular in the line-up. Danny scored just once for the Seasiders, netting against Colchester in January. He later signed a new two-year contract to keep him at Bloomfield Road for the foreseeable future.
Blackpool (From trainee on 24/7/2000) FL 113+18/6 FLC 6 FAC 11 Others 12+1

COLDICOTT Stacy
Born: Redditch, 29 April 1974
Height: 5'8" **Weight:** 11.8
After missing a large part of the previous season due to injury Stacy became an almost ever present in the Grimsby line-up last term, clocking up his 150th league appearance early on. Unfortunately he suffered a broken leg at Burnley towards the end of March and this ruled him out of the vital closing stages. He is a combative midfielder who is particularly

effective in the tackle. Stacy was out of contract in the summer and his future was uncertain at the time of writing.
West Bromwich A (From trainee on 4/3/1992) FL 64+40/3 FLC 6+1 FAC 2+2/1 Others 7+3
Cardiff C (Loaned on 30/8/1996) FL 6
Grimsby T (£125,000 on 6/8/1998) FL 156+19/3 FLC 12/1 FAC 6+1

COLE Andrew (Andy) Alexander
Born: Nottingham, 15 October 1971
Height: 5'11" **Weight:** 11.12
Club Honours: Div 1 '93; PL '96, '97, '99, '00, '01; FAC '96, '99; CS '97; EC '99; FLC '02
International Honours: E: 15; B-1; U21-8; Yth, Sch
Andy performed strongly as a 'hold-up' man for Blackburn Rovers last term, showing that he was able to retain possession of the ball despite the attentions of opposition defenders. He firmly established himself as a regular in the first-team line-up and finished the season as the club's joint-leading scorer in all competitions with a total of 13 goals. His tally included Rovers' 'Goal of the Season', struck from long range at Liverpool on Boxing Day.
Arsenal (From trainee on 18/10/1989) FL 0+1 Others 0+1
Fulham (Loaned on 5/9/1991) FL 13/3 Others 2/1
Bristol C (£500,000 on 12/3/1992) FL 41/20 FLC 3/4 FAC 1 Others 4/1
Newcastle U (£1,750,000 on 12/3/1993) F/PL 69+1/55 FLC 7/8 FAC 4/1 Others 3/4
Manchester U (£6,000,000 on 12/1/1995) PL 161+34/94 FLC 2 FAC 19+2/9 Others 49+8/19
Blackburn Rov (£7,500,000 on 29/12/2001) PL 47+2/16 FLC 7/7 FAC 4/3 Others 2+1

COLE Ashley
Born: Stepney, 20 December 1980
Height: 5'8" **Weight:** 10.8
Club Honours: FAC '02, '03; PL '02; CS '02
International Honours: E: 19; U21-3; Yth
An automatic choice at left back for Arsenal, Ashley continued to develop both at club and international level. He is a quick-tackling, strong defender, who made a number of goal line clearances both with head and feet. His strength and speed are his greatest assets, and his surging runs down the left flank caused problems for most defences. A great crosser of the ball, he is also capable of strikes at goal from distance. A hernia

operation in February kept him out of the team for a number of weeks, but he made a good recovery before the end of the season. Ashley was one of five Arsenal players voted into the PFA Premiership team of the season.
Arsenal (From trainee on 23/11/1998) PL 75+3/6 FLC 1+1 FAC 12+1 Others 24+2
Crystal Palace (Loaned on 25/2/2000) FL 14/1

COLE Carlton Michael
Born: Croydon, 12 November 1983
Height: 6'3" **Weight:** 13.4
International Honours: E: U21-3; Yth
This exciting young centre forward began the season with a bang following a successful summer with England's U19 side in the UEFA Championships in Norway. Carlton came off the bench to turn Chelsea's opening fixture at the Valley into a 3-2 victory after they had trailed by two goals, firstly by equalising following a mazy dribble and a thumping edge-of-the-box shot, and then intelligently creating the winner for Frank Lampard. His progress was interrupted by injury and he was loaned to Wolves to regain match fitness. Carlton produced some deft touches and cool finishing at Molineux and on his return made a valuable contribution to the Blues' quest for a Champions' League slot by scoring winning goals in consecutive fixtures against Sunderland and Bolton respectively.
Chelsea (From trainee on 23/10/2000) PL 4+12/4 FLC 1/2 FAC 0+2/1
Wolverhampton W (Loaned on 28/11/2002) FL 5+2/1

COLE Joseph (Joe) John
Born: Islington, 8 November 1981
Height: 5'9" **Weight:** 11.0
Club Honours: FAYC '99
International Honours: E: 10; U21-8; Yth; Sch
The 2002-03 campaign saw Joe mature considerably as a player. The central midfielder was a model of consistency when helping West Ham in their relegation battle. He showed bravery and commitment and an added determination after being made captain. His goal-scoring improved as he weighed in with a total of five goals, his early-season strike against Arsenal being the most memorable. After having been 'Man of the Match' on numerous occasions he deservedly won the 'Hammer of the Year' award. Joe added further full caps for England against Portugal and South Africa and also appeared regularly for the U21s.

Ashley Cole

West Ham U (From trainee on 11/12/1998)
PL 108+18/10 FLC 7+1/1 FAC 10+1/2 Others 2+3

COLEMAN Kenneth (Kenny) James

Born: Cork, 20 September 1982
Height: 6'0" **Weight:** 12.3
International Honours: RoI: Yth

Kenny was one of a string of loan players at Kidderminster last season, arriving as a replacement for Mark Clyde in October and staying for the remainder of the campaign. After a shaky debut he proved himself more than capable at either right back or in the centre of the defence. He missed the closing stages through injury and after being released by Wolves in the summer he was tipped for a possible permanent move to Aggborough.
Wolverhampton W (From trainee on 17/7/2000)
Kidderminster Hrs (Loaned on 11/10/2002) FL 13+2 FAC 2 Others 3

COLES Daniel (Danny) Richard

Born: Bristol, 31 October 1981
Height: 6'1" **Weight:** 11.5
Club Honours: AMC '03

Bristol City's young central defender formed a promising partnership with Tony Butler last season. He suffered a dip in form mid-season, which coincided with the club's poor spell, but after a period out of the side he returned to produce some stirring displays. Danny was voted as the 'Young Player of the Year' by the Bristol City Supporters' Club.
Bristol C (From trainee on 7/6/2000) FL 59+6/2 FAC 4 Others 13/1

COLLETT Andrew (Andy) Alfred

Born: Stockton, 28 October 1973
Height: 6'0" **Weight:** 12.10

Andy's fourth campaign at Darlington was interrupted by a recurrence of a rib injury that kept him out for a spell around the turn of the year. No fewer than four 'keepers were tried in his absence and there was relief when he was able to return to the side in January and play for the remainder of the season. Andy soon returned to his best form and was solely responsible for the Quakers obtaining points on more than one occasion, notably in the home 'derby' game with league leaders Hartlepool.
Middlesbrough (From trainee on 6/3/1992) PL 2 Others 3
Bristol Rov (Loaned on 18/10/1994) FL 4
Bristol Rov (£10,000 on 23/3/1995) FL 103 FLC 4 FAC 7 Others 8
Darlington (Free on 6/8/1999) FL 116 FLC 6 FAC 9 Others 4

COLLINS Aidan

Born: Chelmsford, 18 October 1986
Height: 6'2" **Weight:** 11.10

A tall central defender who likes to tackle and head the ball, Aidan is a product of the Ipswich Town youth set-up. He stepped up to make his senior debut when he came on as a second-half substitute in the last match of the season at Derby and had the task of marking Fabrizio Ravenelli!
Ipswich T (Associated Schoolboy) FL 0+1

COLLINS James Michael

Born: Newport, 23 August 1983
Height: 6'2" **Weight:** 13.0
International Honours: W: U21-3; Yth

One of Cardiff City's most promising young professionals, James celebrates his 20th birthday soon after the start of the 2003-04 season. He went on as substitute in the opening game of 2002-03, in a 2-1 win at Oldham, but only appeared once more in league action, at Brentford. James scored two FA Cup goals against Tranmere, the first in the 2-2 draw at Prenton Park and the second in the replay. He made his debut for Wales at U21 level and featured regularly in the squad during the campaign.
Cardiff C (From trainee on 5/4/2001) FL 2+10/1 FAC 2+5/2 Others 4+2

COLLINS John Angus Paul

Born: Galashiels, 31 January 1968
Height: 5'7" **Weight:** 10.10
Club Honours: SC '95; Div 1 '01
International Honours: S: 58; U21-8; Yth

John is a talented and experienced midfielder who can bring influence to those around him. Surprisingly he failed to start a Premiership game for Fulham last season and appeared on only a handful of occasions as a substitute. He was, however, selected in a number of the Intertoto Cup games. A committed midfielder who reads the game well he played no small part in helping the reserves have a fine season.
Hibernian (Free from Hutchison Vale BC on 9/8/1984) SL 155+8/16 SLC 7+3/1 SC 17/3 Others 4/1
Glasgow Celtic (Signed on 13/7/1990) SL 211+6/47 SLC 22/3 SC 21/3 Others 13/1
(Free to AS Monaco, France on 2/7/1996)
Everton (£2,500,000 on 7/8/1998) PL 52+3/3 FLC 3+2/1 FAC 4
Fulham (£2,000,000 on 21/7/2000) P/FL 54+12/3 FLC 4/1 FAC 5+1 Others 3+2

COLLINS Lee

Born: Bellshill, 3 February 1974
Height: 5'8" **Weight:** 11.6
Club Honours: AMC '02

This hard-tackling midfield player had a disappointing time at Blackpool last term when he was affected by injuries, and even when fit rarely featured in the first-team squad. He spent the closing stages of the campaign with Conference club Morecambe, helping them reach the end-of-season play-offs where they fell to Dagenham & Redbridge.
Albion Rov (Signed from Pollock on 25/11/1993) SL 43+2/1 SLC 2 SC 2 Others 2
Swindon T (£15,000 on 15/11/1995) FL 52+11/2 FAC 4 Others 1
Blackpool (Free on 24/7/2000) FL 48+18/2 FLC 4 FAC 5+1 Others 5+1

COLLINS Samuel (Sam) Jason

Born: Pontefract, 5 June 1977
Height: 6'3" **Weight:** 14.0

This big central defender joined Port Vale in the summer of 2002, but had a difficult time settling in. Sam scored five goals, including a very cool finish at Blackpool and with cracking shots in both games against his former club Huddersfield. Effective in the air, he also has the secret weapon of being a long-throw expert. Sam scored the decisive penalty in a shoot-out victory over Chesterfield in the LDV Vans Trophy. He was rewarded for the progress he made when he won a variety of the supporters' 'Player of the Year' awards for the season.
Huddersfield T (From trainee on 6/7/1994) FL 34+3 FLC 6+1 FAC 3
Bury (£75,000 on 2/7/1999) FL 78+4/2 FLC 5 FAC 0+2 Others 1
Port Vale (Free on 15/7/2002) FL 44/5 FLC 1 FAC 1 Others 3

COLLINS Wayne Anthony

Born: Manchester, 4 March 1969
Height: 6'0" **Weight:** 12.0
Club Honours: Div 2 '97

Wayne suffered more than his fair share of injuries during the 2002-03 campaign and spent much of the time on the sidelines. He made just one appearance for Crewe Alexandra last term, coming on as a substitute in the LDV Vans Trophy game against Blackpool, and was released by the club towards the end of the season. When fully fit Wayne is a stylish midfield player.
Crewe Alex (£10,000 from Winsford U on 29/7/1993) FL 102+15/14 FLC 5/1 FAC 8+1 Others 14+1/2
Sheffield Wed (£600,000 on 1/8/1996) PL 16+15/6 FLC 2 FAC 1

Fulham *(£400,000 + on 23/1/1998) FL 37+21/4 FLC 10+1/2 FAC 6+2/2 Others 4*
Crewe Alex *(Free on 9/8/2001) FL 13+7 FLC 2 FAC 1 Others 0+1*

COLY Ferdinand
Born: Dakar, Senegal, 10 September 1973
Height: 5'10" **Weight:** 12.9
International Honours: Senegal
Signed by Birmingham City on loan from Lens during the transfer window, Ferdinand took time to adjust to Premiership football. He made his debut in a 4-0 hammering by Arsenal and then played in the FA Cup defeat at Fulham. However he came out of the team thereafter and despite some strong, aggressive performances in the reserves, he did not figure again at first-team level.
Birmingham C *(Loaned from RC Lens, France, ex Poitiers, Chateauroux, on 1/1/2003) PL 1 FAC 1*

COMMONS Kristian (Kris) Arran
Born: Mansfield, 30 August 1983
Height: 5'6" **Weight:** 9.8
Kris literally exploded into the Stoke City first team at the start of the 2002-03 campaign when given his chance by new manager Steve Cotterill. The Premiership scouts were soon beating a path to the Britannia Stadium to look at the left-sided midfielder but after less than a dozen games Kris injured his cruciate ligament and his season ended in September. He will be looking to recover fitness and regain his place in the side during 2003-04.
Stoke C *(From trainee on 25/1/2001) FL 6+2/1 FLC 1 Others 1*

CONLON Barry John
Born: Drogheda, 1 October 1978
Height: 6'3" **Weight:** 13.7
International Honours: Rol: U21-7
Barry continued to be the sort of target man up front that Darlington have needed for years with his strong aerial presence and ability to bring down the ball lay it off to others. He demonstrated during 2002-03 that as well as these attributes, he also has an eye for goal, finishing the season as the Quakers' leading scorer with 17 goals.
Manchester C *(From trainee at Queens Park R on 14/8/1997) FL 1+6 FLC 0+1*
Plymouth Arg *(Loaned on 26/2/1998) FL 13/2*
Southend U *(£95,000 on 4/9/1998) FL 28+6/7 FAC 1 Others 1*
York C *(£100,000 on 20/7/1999) FL 33+15/11 FLC 2+2 FAC 1 Others 0+1*

Colchester U *(Loaned on 9/11/2000) FL 23+3/8 FAC 1 Others 1*
Darlington *(£60,000 on 6/7/2001) FL 76/25 FLC 2 FAC 3/3 Others 2*

CONNELL Alan John
Born: Enfield, 15 February 1983
Height: 5'11" **Weight:** 10.8
This young striker proved to be the find of the season for Bournemouth. After scoring on his full debut at Macclesfield Alan found the net in five of the next six games. Unfortunately a knee injury at Leyton Orient sidelined him for the rest of the campaign. The youngster managed a comeback for the reserves late in the season, but it was too late to feature in the play-offs.
Bournemouth *(Free from Ipswich juniors on 9/7/2002) FL 10+3/6 FLC 1/1*

CONNELL Lee Anthony
Born: Bury, 24 June 1981
Height: 6'0" **Weight:** 12.0
Bury utility man Lee experienced mixed fortunes during the 2002-03 season. He appeared in midfield in the opening two games, but then lost his place with the arrival of Terry Dunfield and struggled to regain it. When Lee Unsworth was suspended for the game at Cambridge in February, Lee made a rare appearance at right back and his season prospered in the closing months when he held on to his place. His enthusiastic form as a highly effective attacking right wing back earned him ten successive starts, during which time he also notched two goals, including the headed winner in a 2-1 success at Southend.
Bury *(From trainee on 9/7/1999) FL 23+7/3 FAC 0+1 Others 3*

CONNELLY Sean Patrick
Born: Sheffield, 26 June 1970
Height: 5'10" **Weight:** 11.10
Signed by Tranmere in October, Sean stepped into the team immediately and proved to be a reliable and mature right back. He was calm, clear-headed, hard but fair in the tackle and never slow to help his younger colleagues when needed. Although troubled by some niggling injuries during the season, he was a regular in the starting line-up and his experience was valuable during the ultimately unsuccessful campaign to reach the play-offs. Off the field, and perhaps with an eye on the future, Sean is a chartered physiotherapist.
Stockport Co *(Free from Hallam on 12/8/1991) FL 292+10/6 FLC 29/1 FAC 15+2 Others 15+1*

Wolverhampton W *(Free on 21/3/2001) FL 11+3 FLC 1*
Tranmere Rov *(Free on 11/10/2002) FL 33 FAC 1 Others 3*

CONNOLLY David James
Born: Willesden, 6 June 1977
Height: 5'8" **Weight:** 11.4
International Honours: Rol: 37; U21
Wimbledon's 2002-03 season could have been very different had David been available from the start. A knee injury sustained in a pre-season friendly at Swindon kept him out for the first dozen matches from which the Dons took just ten points. After he returned against Millwall in mid-October, he scored 24 league goals from just 28 games, including seven in consecutive matches against Norwich and Bradford City, and he was a major contributor towards the club's progress up the league table. Together with Neil Shipperley, he formed one of the best striking partnerships in the First Division. His all-round game was exceptional, his commitment to the cause was total, and his form also firmly maintained his place in the Republic of Ireland national squad.
Watford *(From trainee on 15/11/1994) FL 19+7/10 FLC 1 FAC 3+3/4 Others 1/1 (Free to Feyenoord during 1997 close season)*
Wolverhampton W *(Loaned on 21/8/1998) FL 18+14/6 FLC 2 FAC 0+1*
Wimbledon *(Free from Feyenoord, Holland on 27/7/2001) FL 63/42 FLC 1 FAC 4*

CONNOLLY Karl Andrew
Born: Prescot, 9 February 1970
Height: 5'10" **Weight:** 11.2
Club Honours: WC '95
This left-sided midfielder was another Queen's Park Rangers player to return after a long spell out injured last season. Karl started the campaign as the first choice for the left-midfield spot, but unfortunately he was then sidelined by a foot problem. He returned to action with the reserve side in February, but failed to make any more first-team appearances.
Wrexham *(Free from Napoli, in local Sunday League, on 8/5/1991) FL 337+21/88 FLC 22/4 FAC 37+1/16 Others 32+1/6*
Queens Park R *(Free on 31/5/2000) FL 53+19/12 FLC 2 FAC 4+2 Others 2*

CONNOLLY Paul
Born: Liverpool, 29 September 1983
Height: 6'0" **Weight:** 11.9
A talented youngster who developed through the youth ranks at Plymouth Argyle, Paul made a couple of league starts last season. He featured on the

right-hand side of defence and impressed with some cultured and assured performances. Paul was voted as Argyle's 'Young Player of the Season' and he will be pushing for more first-team opportunities in 2003-04.
Plymouth Arg (From trainee on 23/7/2002) FL 2+1 Others 1

CONNOR Daniel (Dan) Brian
Born: Dublin, 31 January 1981
Height: 6'2" **Weight:** 12.9
International Honours: Rol: U21-1; Yth
This young 'keeper was again back-up to Mark Tyler at Peterborough last term and when his rival was sidelined with a broken arm Dan was given a run of four games in the side. However, boss Barry Fry then opted to bring in more experienced cover and Dan was released shortly before the end of the season. He subsequently signed for Eircom League side Waterford United, the move proving a success as he went on to make his debut for the Republic of Ireland U21s against Georgia in June.
Peterborough U (From trainee on 29/4/1998) FL 6+2 FLC 1 Others 2

CONNOR Paul
Born: Bishop Auckland, 12 January 1979
Height: 6'1" **Weight:** 11.5
Club Honours: AMC '00
After a wretched time with injuries the previous term, Paul scored a last-minute winner in the opening game of the 2002-03 season and soon re-established himself as a key member of Rochdale's attack. A skilful striker, equally at home with the close-range finish and when running at defenders, he missed only a handful of games and hit 15 goals in all games. Perhaps his finest goal was a spectacular effort at Swansea, but his best remembered will be that in the giant-killing FA Cup victory over Coventry.
Middlesbrough (From trainee on 4/7/1996)
Hartlepool U (Loaned on 6/2/1998) FL 4+1
Stoke C (Free on 25/3/1999) FL 18+18/7 FLC 3+3/3 FAC 0+1 Others 2+3
Cambridge U (Loaned on 9/11/2000) FL 12+1/5 FAC 1
Rochdale (£100,000 on 9/3/2001) FL 55+15/23 FLC 2 FAC 7+1/3 Others 0+2

CONSTANTINE Leon
Born: Hackney, 24 February 1978
Height: 6'2" **Weight:** 11.10
This tall, laid back striker joined Brentford in the 2002 close season. Used primarily as a substitute, his build-up play was neat, but he rarely threatened when in front of goal. Leon will be aiming to win

a regular place in the starting line-up in 2003-04.
Millwall (Signed from Edgware T on 31/8/2000) FL 0+1 Others 1
Leyton Orient (Loaned on 27/8/2001) FL 9+1/3 Others 0+1
Partick Thistle (Loaned on 11/1/2002) SL 2 SC 1
Brentford (Free on 8/8/2002) FL 2+15 FLC 1+1

CONVERY Mark Peter
Born: Newcastle, 29 May 1981
Height: 5'6" **Weight:** 10.5
Mark made only one first-team appearance for Darlington last term, coming on as a substitute at Stockport County in the LDV Vans Trophy game in October. Despite some good performances in the reserves this busy right-sided midfielder was unable to break into the squad and was released at the end of the season.
Sunderland (From trainee on 24/3/1999)
Darlington (Free on 30/1/2001) FL 11+17/1 FLC 1 FAC 0+2 Others 1+1

COOK James (Jamie) Steven
Born: Oxford, 2 August 1979
Height: 5'10" **Weight:** 11.6
Club Honours: NC '02
This busy player was used by Boston United in a wide role up front last term. He made half a dozen starts early in the season but was relegated to the bench in October following the signing of Tony Battersby. He later lost his place in the first-team squad and finished the season at Conference club Stevenage Borough.
Oxford U (From trainee on 1/7/1997) FL 33+44/7 FLC 1+4 FAC 3+4 Others 3
Boston U (Free on 23/2/2001) FL 6+10/2 FLC 0+1 FAC 1

COOK Lee
Born: Hammersmith, 3 August 1982
Height: 5'9" **Weight:** 11.7
Watford's young left winger had limited opportunities at the start of last season and was sent out on loan to York where he scored on his debut and impressed with his dribbling skills. In November he joined Queen's Park Rangers in a three-month loan deal. Here too he quickly won over the fans, and perhaps the highlight of his time at Loftus Road was a memorable performance in his final game when he also scored. On his return to the Hornets he showed he had benefited from his experiences, demonstrating a renewed commitment and an improved appreciation of team

play, especially of his defensive responsibilities. Skilful on the ball and a good crosser, Lee played five first-team matches towards the end of the season, including a substitute appearance in the FA Cup semi-final at Villa Park.
Watford (Signed from Aylesbury U on 19/11/1999) FL 11+7 FAC 0+1
York C (Loaned on 2/10/2002) FL 7/1 Others 1/1
Queens Park R (Loaned on 20/12/2002) FL 13/1

COOK Lewis Leon
Born: High Wycombe, 28 December 1983
Height: 5'7" **Weight:** 11.1
This pacy young left winger gave one of the outstanding performances by a Wycombe player last season when he tore apart the Chesterfield defence at Adams Park in October. The performance was all the more remarkable because it was Lewis's debut in professional football, but time and time again he dribbled through and delivered perfect crosses. He was used very sparingly for the remainder of the season, just three starts in all, not helped by the fine form of veteran Steve Brown keeping him out of the side.
Wycombe W (From trainee on 28/1/2003) FL 4+13 FAC 0+1 Others 3/1

COOK Paul Anthony
Born: Liverpool, 22 June 1967
Height: 5'11" **Weight:** 11.0
Paul Cook repeatedly showed during 2002-03 that, even when approaching 36 years of age, he was still more than capable of performing at First Division level. His season started badly, with a red card against Wolves, although his foul hardly appeared a sending-off offence. His first-team appearances were sporadic, and he rarely lasted the 90 minutes, but his passing abilities still compared with the very best and as a midfield competitor he often belied his age. His best run in the side came in February and March, but this proved to be his swansong; following an injury picked up in the home game against Bradford City which ruled him out of the end of the Clarets' season, Paul announced his retirement from the club.
Wigan Ath (Signed from Marine on 20/7/1984) FL 77+6/14 FLC 4 FAC 6+1 Others 5+1/1
Norwich C (£73,000 on 23/5/1988) FL 3+3 Others 1+1
Wolverhampton W (£250,000 on 1/11/1989) FL 191+2/19 FLC 7/1 FAC 5+2 Others 6+1/1
Coventry C (£600,000 on 18/8/1994) PL 35+2/3 FLC 3 FAC 3

*Tranmere Rov (£250,000 on 29/2/1996) FL
24+6/4 FLC 8 FAC 1*
*Stockport Co (£250,000 on 24/10/1997) FL
28+1/3 FLC 1+1 FAC 2*
*Burnley (Free on 12/3/1999) FL 140+7/12
LC 5+4 FAC 11+2/3*
Wigan Ath (Loaned on 30/11/2001) FL 6

COOKE Andrew (Andy) Roy
Born: Shrewsbury, 20 January 1974
Height: 6'0" **Weight:** 12.8
Andy endured a season interrupted by injury and managerial changes at Stoke in 2002-03. As always, his work rate, commitment to the cause and an honest hard-working style made him a firm favourite with the club's fans. Although he experienced a regular shuffling of partners up front his six goals made him the Potters' leading scorer in league games.
Burnley (Signed from Newtown on 15/1995) FL 134+37/52 FLC 8+2/6 FAC 7+3/2 Others 9+2/2
Stoke C (£350,000 on 1/12/2000) FL 21+17/21 FLC 1+1 FAC 2+2/1 Others 4+4/1

COOKE Stephen Lee
Born: Walsall, 15 February 1983
Height: 5'8" **Weight:** 9.8
International Honours: E: Yth
This promising creative midfield player was once again on the fringes of the first-team squad, and indeed was handed a squad number at the beginning of last season. His senior experience last term was limited to just a handful of appearances from the substitutes' bench and he will be hoping to feature more regularly under new boss David O'Leary in 2003-04.
Aston Villa (From trainee on 22/12/2000) PL 0+3 Others 0+1
Bournemouth (Loaned on 8/3/2002) FL 6+1

COOKE Terence (Terry) John
Born: Birmingham, 5 August 1976
Height: 5'7" **Weight:** 11.4
Club Honours: FAYC '95
International Honours: E: U21-4; Yth
After impressing with Grimsby Town during the previous season's short-term contract, Terry's move was made permanent during the summer. A fast and skilful winger and an accurate crosser of the ball, he was, however, unable to establish himself and was in and out of the side throughout the campaign. This was something of a puzzle to many fans, with whom he remained a firm favourite.
Manchester U (From trainee on 1/7/1994) PL 4+3 FLC 1+2/1 Others 0+1
Sunderland (Loaned on 29/1/1996) FL 6

Birmingham C (Loaned on 29/11/1996) FL 1+3
Wrexham (Loaned on 30/10/1998) FL 10 Others 1
Manchester C (£1,000,000 on 13/1/1999) FL 27+7/7 FLC 3+1/1 Others 3
Wigan Ath (Loaned on 7/3/2000) FL 10/1
Sheffield Wed (Loaned on 21/9/2000) FL 12+1/1
Sheffield Wed (Loaned on 15/12/2000) FL 4 FLC 1 FAC 2/1
Grimsby T (Free on 28/3/2002) FL 18+10/1 FLC 1 FAC 2/1

COONEY Sean Patrick
Born: Australia, 31 October 1983
Height: 6'2" **Weight:** 13.0
This young Australian was a regular for Coventry City reserves for most of the 2002-03 season and got his first-team chance in the final home game when he came on as a substitute. A strong uncompromising tackler with good heading ability, Sean was selected to play for his country in the FIFA U20 championship tournament that was subsequently postponed until the autumn.
Coventry C (From trainee on 18/1/2003) FL 0+1

COOPER Colin Terence
Born: Sedgefield, 28 February 1967
Height: 5'10" **Weight:** 11.9
Club Honours: Div 1 '98
International Honours: E: 2; U21-8
It is hard to believe that Colin's first professional game was way back in November 1985 and now, some 18 years later, the Middlesbrough defender is determined that he will get at least one more season before he finally hangs up his boots. Colin featured in 20 Premiership matches last season but he was out of contract in the summer and, with a future career in the world of television beckoning him, he was confident that he could squeeze in another season of top-flight football.
Middlesbrough (From juniors on 17/7/1984) FL 183+5/6 FLC 18 FAC 13 Others 19+1/2
Millwall (£300,000 on 25/7/1991) FL 77/6 FLC 6 FAC 2 Others 2
Nottingham F (£1,700,000 on 21/6/1993) F/PL 179+1/20 FLC 14/2 FAC 12/1 Others 7
Middlesbrough (£2,500,000 on 22/8/1998) PL 111+12/5 FLC 10+1 FAC 4+1

COOPER Kevin Lee
Born: Derby, 8 February 1975
Height: 5'7" **Weight:** 10.7
Kevin can play in midfield or on the wing, and is thus a valuable member of any squad. He made his first two appearances of the 2002-03 campaign for Wolves as a

substitute, scoring in both against Burnley and Derby respectively. He was then given two starts but made less impact. Kevin played in most games up until January but was used seldom afterwards, filling in gaps when needed as substitute. His only start in the new year came at Sheffield United in April.
Derby Co (From trainee on 2/7/1993) FL 0+2 FLC 0+2 Others 0+1
Stockport Co (£150,000 on 24/3/1997) FL 146+22/21 FLC 7+5/2 FAC 6 Others 1
Wimbledon (£800,000 + on 15/3/2001) FL 50+1/13 FLC 1 FAC 2
Wolverhampton W (£1,000,000 on 26/3/2002) FL 17+14/3 FAC 0+1 Others 2+1/1

COOPER Richard Anthony
Born: Nottingham, 27 September 1977
Height: 5'9" **Weight:** 10.12
International Honours: E: Yth; Sch
After nearly a year out of action with a broken leg, Richard returned to first-team duty with York City last December and marked the occasion with a spectacular equaliser against Lincoln City after coming off the substitutes' bench. He was soon back in the starting line-up and retained his place for the remainder of the season. He mostly featured in a central-midfield role and showed that he had lost none of his enthusiasm or tenacity.
Nottingham F (From trainee on 2/10/1996) FL 0+3
York C (Free on 2/3/2001) FL 58+5/2 FLC 1 FAC 5+1 Others 1

COOTE Adrian
Born: Great Yarmouth, 30 September 1978
Height: 6'2" **Weight:** 12.0
International Honours: NI: 6; B-1; U21-14
Adrian had a very frustrating season for Colchester United last term, which yielded no goals, very few appearances, and a host of injuries. The ex-Norwich City target man spent most of the year on the bench, or on the treatment table, starting just seven games. He jumped at the chance of a loan period at Bristol Rovers and went on to score for the Pirates with a powerful header in his second outing against Leyton Orient. Adrian also showed his versatility by playing as a central defender for part of one match before returning to Layer Road.
Norwich C (From trainee on 3/7/1997) FL 20+34/3 FLC 1+5 FAC 0+1

Colchester U (£50,000 on 21/12/2001) FL 12+23/4
Bristol Rov (Loaned on 21/10/2002) FL 4+1/1 Others 1

COPPINGER James
Born: Middlesbrough, 10 January 1981
Height: 5'7" **Weight:** 10.6
International Honours: E: Yth
James was one of the few successes at Exeter last term. He was employed both as a forward and winger and managed to link up well with the midfield and front line. His determination and enthusiastic attitude on the pitch made him a favourite with the City fans and he netted five valuable goals. Unfortunately, despite his efforts, the club were relegated to the Conference.
Newcastle U (£250,000 + from trainee at Darlington on 27/3/1998) PL 0+1
Hartlepool U (Loaned on 10/3/2000) FL 6+4/3 Others 1
Hartlepool U (Loaned on 25/1/2002) FL 14/2
Exeter C (Free on 2/8/2002) FL 35+8/5 FLC 1 FAC 3 Others 2

CORAZZIN Giancarlo (Carlo) Michele
Born: Canada, 25 December 1971
Height: 5'10" **Weight:** 12.7
International Honours: Canada: 56 (Gold Cup '00)
Carlo again failed to find his goal-scoring touch for Oldham last term, netting just five goals. He linked up well in an early-season partnership with Clyde Wijnhard and in November headed Latics' winner in a shock 1-0 Worthington Cup victory at West Ham. Carlo was released by Oldham at the end of the season.
Cambridge U (£20,000 from Vancouver 86ers, Canada on 10/12/1993) FL 104+1/39 FLC 4/2 FAC 5 Others 3/2
Plymouth Arg (£150,000 on 28/3/1996) FL 61+13/22 FLC 2+1 FAC 2+2/1 Others 2+1
Northampton T (Free on 2/7/1998) FL 63+15/30 FLC 5+2/1 FAC 3 Others 1/1
Oldham Ath (Free on 31/7/2000) FL 82+28/20 FLC 5+3/2 FAC 6+2/1 Others 1+2

CORBETT James (Jim) John
Born: Hackney, 6 July 1980
Height: 5'10" **Weight:** 12.0
Although he was a regular for the Blackburn Rovers reserves last term, Jim was never in consideration for a first-team place. In February he joined Darlington on loan, making his debut from the bench at home to Exeter. His nimble control and devastating burst of speed brought him his first Quakers goal against Bury in late March, when he outpaced the defence to

slot home. Jim struck up a good understanding with target man Barry Conlon, and also scored in the final match at Feethams on the last day of the season.
Gillingham (From trainee on 13/1/1998) FL 8+8/2 FLC 0+1 Others 0+1
Blackburn Rov (£525,000 + on 22/5/1998)
Darlington (Loaned on 28/2/2003) FL 9+1/2

CORDEN Simon Wayne
Born: Leek, 1 November 1975
Height: 5'9" **Weight:** 11.3
Wayne signed a new three-year contract for Mansfield Town, but he was in and out of the side at the beginning of the season. Probably one of the most gifted footballers at the club he soon recaptured some of the previous season's terrific form. A skilful winger, he prefers to play wide on the left from where he can cut inside to unleash his shot, as a 'blinder' against Notts County at Field Mill in February demonstrated. Wayne ended the season with a personal-best tally of 13 goals.
Port Vale (From trainee on 20/9/1994) FL 30+36/1 FLC 4 FAC 2+1/1
Mansfield T (Free on 3/7/2000) FL 114+10/24 FLC 6/2 FAC 6/1 Others 3

CORICA Stephen (Steve) Christopher
Born: Queensland, Australia, 24 March 1973
Height: 5'8" **Weight:** 11.0
International Honours: Australia: 31; U23; Yth
Steve began the 2002-03 season in his usual key midfield role for Walsall and early on he netted with a rare header in the 2-0 win at Brighton. However, he seemed to struggle at times on the heavy Bescot pitch before it was relayed. He added another vital goal in the thrilling 2-2 draw at Derby and on his day was one of the classiest little players in Division One.
Leicester C (£325,000 from Marconi, Australia on 11/8/1995) FL 16/2 FAC 2
Wolverhampton W (£700,000 on 16/2/1996) FL 80+20/5 FLC 5+1 FAC 3+1 (Free to Sanfrecce Hiroshima, Japan on 20/3/2000)
Walsall (Free on 8/2/2002) FL 46+8/7 FLC 3 FAC 2+2

CORNELLY Christopher (Chris)
Born: Huddersfield, 7 July 1976
Height: 5'7" **Weight:** 11.7
This pacy wide striker showed plenty of promise after signing for Lincoln in

December on a part-time basis from Unibond League club Ashton United. Chris performed equally well on either flank showing he has the ability to beat defenders and set up chances.
Lincoln C (Free from Ashton U, ex Ossett A, Ashton U, Leigh RMI, on 12/12/2002) FL 9+7 Others 0+1

CORNWALL Lucas (Luke) Clarence
Born: Lambeth, 23 July 1980
Height: 5'11" **Weight:** 11.6
This pacy striker arrived on loan at Lincoln City in January but had few chances to show what he could do. Luke started just one game for the Imps and was on the substitutes' bench for the remainder of his time at Sincil Bank. He subsequently returned to Fulham to continue his development in the club's reserve team.
Fulham (From trainee on 6/7/1998) FL 1+3/1 FLC 2+1
Grimsby T (Loaned on 13/3/2001) FL 9+1/4
Lincoln C (Loaned on 17/1/2003) FL 1+2

CORREIA Albano Joao Soares
Born: Guinea-Bissau, 18 October 1981
Height: 6'2" **Weight:** 12.13
This skilful young forward only appeared twice last season in Bristol City's first team, both occasions being for LDV Vans Trophy games. Albano spent time with Conference club Hereford United in the closing stages of the campaign, making a number of appearances.
Bristol C (Signed from Oriental Lisbon, Portugal on 18/9/2000) Others 0+3

CORT Carl Edward Richard
Born: Southwark, 1 November 1977
Height: 6'4" **Weight:** 12.7
International Honours: E: U21-12
Carl's career at Newcastle was again plagued by injury as a thigh strain delayed his start to the 2002-03 season and then a hamstring injury in April ended it early, whilst in between he suffered a series of setbacks which disrupted his fitness and kept him out of the squad. His sole senior start came against Everton in the Worthington Cup tie in November, and he also featured as a substitute at Bayer Leverkusen in February. A big strong striker he will be hoping to stay free of injury in 2003-04 to enable him to contest a first-team place again.
Wimbledon (From trainee on 7/6/1996) PL 54+19/16 FLC 8+2/7 FAC 6+4/2
Lincoln C (Loaned on 3/2/1997) FL 5+1/1
Newcastle U (£7,000,000 on 6/7/2000) PL 19+3/7 FLC 3/1 FAC 2 Others 0+1

CORT Leon Terence Anthony
Born: Bermondsey, 11 September 1979
Height: 6'2" **Weight:** 13.4
Leon was Southend United's 'Player of the Year' by some considerable distance last term and it is hard to recall him putting a foot wrong all season. Dominant in the air and a real threat at set pieces, he contributed seven goals during the campaign, including a remarkable hat-trick of headers in the 4-2 defeat of league newcomers Boston United. He cut out the occasional errors that peppered his first season at the club, and is widely regarded as one of the Third Division's top defenders. Leon is the younger brother of Newcastle's Carl Cort.
Millwall (Free from Dulwich Hamlet on 23/1/1998)
Southend U (Free on 11/7/2001) FL 89+2/10 FLC 2 FAC 8/1 Others 2

COSTELLO Peter
Born: Halifax, 31 October 1969
Height: 6'0" **Weight:** 11.7
Club Honours: NC '02
This veteran was used as a squad player last term after being a key man in Boston's rise from the Dr Martens League into Division Three. He played a few games on the right side of midfield but his best performances came when he was switched to right back. After being released at the end of the campaign he was reported to have signed for Stevenage Borough.
Bradford C (From trainee on 28/7/1988) FL 11+9/2 FLC 0+1 FAC 1 Others 1
Rochdale (£10,000 on 9/7/1990) FL 31+3/10 FLC 4/1 FAC 2/2 Others 3
Peterborough U (£30,000 on 28/3/1991) FL 3+5 FLC 1+2/1 Others 3+2/2
Lincoln C (Loaned on 12/9/1991) FL 3
Lincoln C (£15,000 on 23/9/1992) FL 28+10/7 FLC 2+2 FAC 2/1 Others 4/1 (Free to Dover on 29/7/1994)
Boston U (Free from Hong Kong, ex Nuneaton Borough, Instant Dict (HK), Kettering T, on 1/8/1999) FL 13+5

COTTERILL James Michael
Born: Barnsley, 3 August 1982
Height: 6'0" **Weight:** 12.4
James started last season as one of the first-choice central defenders for Scunthorpe but his big chance ended after just seven games when he broke a leg in the local 'derby' at Lincoln early in September. He returned to action after six months out but only managed two substitute appearances as he fought to regain full fitness. A committed defender

who can also play at right back, he was out of contract in the summer.
Scunthorpe U (From trainee on 3/7/2001) FL 19+4 Others 1

COUGHLAN Graham
Born: Dublin, 18 November 1974
Height: 6'2" **Weight:** 13.6
Club Honours: S Div 1 '01; Div 3 '02
Graham was again a rock in the heart of Plymouth Argyle's defence last season when he was a near ever-present. He has excellent technique in the air and a good eye for goal especially at set pieces, as demonstrated by his five goals during the

campaign. His defensive partnership with Paul Wotton has been an important part in the recent success of the club.
Blackburn Rov (£100,000 from Bray W on 14/10/1995)
Swindon T (Loaned on 25/3/1997) FL 3
Livingston (Free on 29/3/1999) SL 53+3/2 SLC 4 SC 2 Others 5
Plymouth Arg (Free on 21/6/2001) FL 88/16 FLC 2 FAC 8 Others 1

COUNAGO Pablo Gonzalez
Born: Pontevedra, Spain, 9 August 1979
Height: 5'11" **Weight:** 11.12
The 2002-03 campaign proved to be the

Pablo Counago

season when Pablo showed that he could score goals regularly in the English game and he finished as Ipswich Town's leading goal-scorer. He seems to have the knack of being in the right place at the right time, and many of his goals occurred when he was the first to react to a rebound off the 'keeper or a flick-on inside the box. Pablo netted his first hat-trick for Ipswich in the UEFA Cup tie against Avenir Beggin.

Ipswich T (Free from Celta Vigo, Spain on 19/7/2001) P/FL 29+23/17 FLC 3/1 FAC 2+1 Others 7+2/3

COWAN Thomas (Tom)
Born: Bellshill, 28 August 1969
Height: 5'9" **Weight:** 11.10
Tom joined York City during the 2002 close season and featured regularly in the line-up at left back throughout 2002-03. His chief assets proved to be his strength of tackle, heading ability and long throw and all were key factors in helping the Minstermen maintain a strong bid for the Third Division promotion play-offs.

Clyde (Free from Netherdale BC on 11/7/1988) SL 16/2 SC 2
Glasgow R (Signed on 9/2/1989) SL 8+4 SC 0+1 Others 2
Sheffield U (£350,000 on 1/8/1991) F/PL 45 FLC 5 FAC 2 Others 1
Stoke C (Loaned on 1/10/1993) FL 14 FLC 1 Others 3
Huddersfield T (£150,000 on 24/3/1994) FL 137/8 FLC 13/1 FAC 9/1 Others 6
Burnley (£20,000 on 12/3/1999) FL 17+3/1 FLC 2 Others 0+1
Cambridge U (Loaned on 22/2/2000) FL 4
Cambridge U (Free on 20/7/2000) FL 44+2/3 FLC 1 FAC 1
Peterborough U (Loaned on 18/1/2002) FL 4+1/1
York C (Free on 5/7/2002) FL 31+2/1 FLC 1

COX Ian Gary
Born: Croydon, 25 March 1971
Height: 6'0" **Weight:** 12.2
International Honours: Trinidad & Tobago: 5
This was not a particularly happy season for Ian, as he was in and out of Burnley's side thanks to a succession of injuries. After the inconsistencies of the previous campaign, he appeared to be back at his best, but knee and hamstring injuries kept him sidelined for much of the middle part of the season. His return to the side in the 1-0 win at Coventry saw him back at his best, cool and commanding at the heart of defence and heading in the winning goal for good measure. Unfortunately, he

was not always so reliable, and was subsequently ruled out by yet another injury for the closing stages of the season.
Crystal Palace (£35,000 from Carshalton on 8/3/1994) F/PL 2+13 FAC 1+2/1
Bournemouth (Free on 28/3/1996) FL 172/16 FLC 14 FAC 10 Others 11/1
Burnley (£500,000 on 4/2/2000) FL 107+8/5 FLC 7 FAC 8+1

COX Neil James
Born: Scunthorpe, 8 October 1971
Height: 6'0" **Weight:** 13.7
Club Honours: FLC '94; Div 1 '95
International Honours: E: U21-6
Neil had an outstanding season with Watford as both captain and stalwart central defender last term. He clearly enjoyed the respect of both his team mates and his manager, showing excellent leadership qualities both on and off the pitch. Commanding and consistent, he also contributed nine goals, which made him the club's joint-second-leading scorer, and it could have been more had he not missed a couple of penalties. Neil concluded a memorable season by signing a new two-year contract to the delight of manager and fans alike.
Scunthorpe U (From trainee on 20/3/1990) FL 17/1 FAC 4 Others 4+1
Aston Villa (£400,000 on 12/2/1991) F/PL 26+16/3 FLC 5+2 FAC 4+2/1 Others 2
Middlesbrough (£1,000,000 on 19/7/1994) P/FL 103+3/3 FLC 14+1 FAC 5/1 Others 2
Bolton W (£1,200,000 on 27/5/1997) P/FL 77+3/7 FLC 6/1 FAC 1+1 Others 3
Watford (£500,000 on 5/11/1999) P/FL 142+3/16 FLC 10 FAC 8

COYNE Christopher (Chris) John
Born: Brisbane, Australia, 20 December 1978
Height: 6'1" **Weight:** 13.10
Chris was voted as the 'Player of the Year' by Luton Town's supporters after turning in some commanding performances last term. Always cool when on the ball, he was effective in the air and willing to join up with attacks in the opposition area. Chris is young enough to turn into one of the best central defenders in the lower divisions.
West Ham U (£150,000 from Perth SC, Australia on 13/1/1996) PL 0+1
Brentford (Loaned on 21/8/1998) FL 7 FLC 1
Southend U (Loaned on 25/3/1999) FL 0+1
Dundee (Signed on 31/3/2000) SL 16+4 SLC 0+2 SC 4 Others 2
Luton T (£50,000 on 18/9/2001) FL 67+4/4 FLC 1 FAC 2 Others 1

COYNE Daniel (Danny)
Born: Prestatyn, 27 August 1973
Height: 5'11" **Weight:** 13.0
International Honours: W: 2; B-1; U21-9; Yth; Sch
Grimsby Town's first choice goalkeeper once again enjoyed a great season between the sticks. He was an ever-present during the campaign and performed heroically behind an often-insecure defence, bearing no responsibility for the Mariners' unimpressive goals-against record. Although Danny was a regular member of Mark Hughes' Welsh squad, he added no further caps to his total.
Tranmere Rov (From trainee on 8/5/1992) FL 110+1 FLC 13 FAC 2 Others 2
Grimsby T (Free on 12/7/1999) FL 181 FLC 13 FAC 7

CRADDOCK Jody Darryl
Born: Redditch, 25 July 1975
Height: 6'1" **Weight:** 12.4
Sunderland's 'Player of the Season' for 2001-02, centre back Jody made his first start of the season in late September, turning in a typically solid performance against Aston Villa as the Black Cats recorded their first home win. A solid stopper who is dominant in the air and quick on the ground, Jody was Sunderland's 'Player of the Month' for October and went past the 150 league-appearance mark during the campaign. Hugely popular with the Wearside fans, he notched his only goal with a spectacular diving header at Arsenal.
Cambridge U (Free from Christchurch on 13/8/1993) FL 142+3/4 FLC 3/1 FAC 6 Others 5
Sunderland (£300,000 + on 4/8/1997) P/FL 140+6/2 FLC 8+2 FAC 7+2 Others 3
Sheffield U (Loaned on 27/8/1999) FL 10

CRAIG Tony Andrew
Born: Greenwich, 20 April 1985
Height: 6'0" **Weight:** 10.13
This young Millwall full back produced some fine performances in the academy and reserve sides last season, before stepping up to make his first-team debut at Nottingham Forest. He made an excellent start, acquitting himself well against quality opposition, and went on to score on his second appearance for the Lions at home to Coventry. Tony is a tough, hard-tackling defender and a great motivator, very much an old head on young shoulders.
Millwall (From trainee on 13/3/2003) FL 2/1

CRAMB Colin
Born: Lanark, 23 June 1974
Height: 6'0" **Weight:** 12.6
Club Honours: B&Q '93

It was generally felt that the prodigal son had returned home when Colin Cramb rejoined Bury from Fortuna Sittard last January, but after making his debut in a 4-2 defeat at Kidderminster the veteran striker struggled to regain his fitness during his early months back at Gigg Lane. As a result he failed to recapture his best form but nevertheless maintained a starting berth in attack throughout most of the second half of the season as his experience and aggression helped the Shakers into the play-offs.

Hamilton Academical (From juniors on 1/6/1993) SL 29+19/10 SC 0+1 Others 1+3
Southampton (£75,000 on 8/6/1993) PL 0+1
Falkirk (Signed on 30/8/1994) SL 6+2/1 SLC 0+1
Heart of Midlothian (Signed on 1/3/1995) SL 3+3/1
Doncaster Rov (£25,000 on 15/12/1995) FL 50+2/25 FLC 2/1 FAC 1/1 Others 1/1
Bristol C (£250,000 on 10/7/1997) FL 48+15/9 FLC 3+1 FAC 1/1 Others 1+1
Walsall (Loaned on 27/2/1999) FL 4/4 Others 2
Crewe Alex (£200,000 on 6/8/1999) FL 43+7/10 FLC 5+1/1 FAC 2 (Free to Fortuna Sittard, Germany on 16/7/2001)
Notts Co (Loaned on 11/9/2000) FL 2+1
Bury (Loaned on 16/2/2001) FL 15/5
Bury (Free on 24/1/2003) FL 17+1/3 Others 2

CRANE Anthony (Tony) Steven
Born: Liverpool, 8 September 1982
Height: 6'1" **Weight:** 12.6
International Honours: E: Yth

Tony found himself out of favour at Sheffield Wednesday at the start of the 2002-03 campaign, and then injuries kept him on the sidelines until November. However, after this he broke into the first team and proved his worth to the side. Initially playing in his normal midfield role, he switched firstly to central defence and then became an emergency striker. Being tall and well built the youngster made the most of his chance up front, and his late equaliser at Bradford City proved invaluable at the time.

Sheffield Wed (From trainee on 15/9/1999) FL 24+25/4 FLC 3+5/1 FAC 1+3

CRESSWELL Richard Paul Wesley
Born: Bridlington, 20 September 1977
Height: 6'0" **Weight:** 11.8
International Honours: E: U21-4

Richard carried on his good form of the previous season and once again ended as Preston's leading scorer in 2002-03. This was despite suffering a variety of injury problems which saw him miss several matches, the most worrying being when he was extremely lucky to avoid serious facial injuries in a collision with the perimeter fence at Bradford. His first goals of the season claimed a win and a draw in injury time of successive games, and other highlights included the 50th league goal of his career against Grimsby, and a brilliant individual effort at Brighton to mark his 100th appearance for North End. A tireless worker, able to finish with either foot and improving in the air, Richard combines well with his fellow strikers and his blossoming partnership with Ricardo Fuller promises much for 2003-04.

York C (From trainee on 15/11/1995) FL 72+23/21 FLC 3+3 FAC 4+2/3 Others 4
Mansfield T (Loaned on 27/3/1997) FL 5/1
Sheffield Wed (£950,000 + on 25/3/1999) PL 7+24/2 FLC 1+1/1 FAC 0+3

Richard Cresswell

*Leicester C (£750,000 on 5/9/2000) PL 3+5
FLC 1 FAC 0+2/1 Others 0+2
Preston NE (£500,000 on 12/3/2001) FL
74+19/31 FLC 4+2/1 FAC 1+1/2 Others 1+2*

CROFT Gary
Born: Burton on Trent, 17 February 1974
Height: 5'9" **Weight:** 11.8
International Honours: E: U21-4
Gary first arrived at Cardiff City on loan in
2001-02 and returned to Ninian Park for
the start of last season. He established
himself at left back and occasionally
switched to the right. By the time it came
to the run-in, though, Chris Barker was
stepping in on the left-hand side and
Gary spent time among the substitutes.
During the play-offs he twice replaced the
injured Rhys Weston, in the semi-final
second leg at Bristol City and in the final
against Queen's Park Rangers at the
Millennium Stadium. Gary scored City's
winner at Notts County, his only goal of
the campaign.
*Grimsby T (From trainee on 7/7/1992) FL
139+10/3 FLC 7 FAC 8+2/1 Others 3
Blackburn R (£1,700,000 on 29/3/1996)
PL 33+7/1 FLC 6 FAC 4+2
Ipswich T (£800,000 on 21/9/1999) P/FL
20+9/1 FLC 3+1 FAC 1 Others 2+1
Wigan Ath (Loaned on 17/11/2002) FL 7
Cardiff C (Free on 28/3/2002) FL 42+7/2 FLC
2 FAC 3+1 Others 2+2*

CROFTS Andrew Lawrence
Born: Chatham, 29 May 1984
Height: 5'9" **Weight:** 10.8
International Honours: W: Yth
Andrew's season at Gillingham was
interrupted by a series of injuries last
term. Firstly he suffered an ankle ligament
problem that forced him to pull out of
training with the Welsh U19 squad and
was then sidelined with a broken ankle. A
promising young striker, his only first-
team outing came in the Worthington
Cup win at Stockport when he appeared
as a substitute.
Gillingham (Trainee) FL 0+1 FLC 0+1

CRONIN Glenn
Born: Dublin, 14 September 1981
Height: 5'8" **Weight:** 11.4
International Honours: RoI: Yth
Glenn played in nearly every game for
Exeter last term, a considerable feat
bearing in mind the changes in
management at the club. The promising
midfielder often featured from the bench,
but impressed with his passing and
awareness of his team mates.
*Exeter C (From trainee on 18/7/2000) FL
52+17 FLC 1 FAC 3+2 Others 2+1*

CROOKS Lee Robert
Born: Wakefield, 14 January 1978
Height: 6'0" **Weight:** 12.1
International Honours: E: Yth
Lee again suffered another season that
was littered with niggling injuries at
Barnsley. He did, however, show his
versatility and played in a number of
roles. Initially used sparingly by manager
Steve Parkin as the holding player in
midfield, he returned to the line-up under
new boss Glyn Hodges as the middle man
in a back three. Lee produced his best
football for the Reds in this role, before a
toe injury brought a premature end to his
season in mid-April.
*Manchester C (From trainee on 14/1/1995)
P/FL 52+24/2 FLC 5+2 FAC 5 Others 3
Northampton T (Loaned on 26/12/2000) FL
3
Barnsley (£190,000 on 2/3/2001) FL 30+14
FLC 2 FAC 1*

CROPPER Dene James
Born: Chesterfield, 5 January 1983
Height: 6'1" **Weight:** 13.0
Dene had a promising first season with
Lincoln City after the disappointment of
being red carded on his debut. He proved
skilful at holding up the ball in his role as
a target man and also showed the ability
to beat defenders. Dene missed much of
the second half of the season with a knee
injury, but recovered to play his part in the
final few matches.
*Lincoln C (Free from trainee at Sheffield Wed
on 7/8/2002) FL 24+5/3 FLC 1 FAC 1 Others
3+1*

CROSBY Andrew (Andy)
Keith
Born: Rotherham, 3 March 1973
Height: 6'2" **Weight:** 13.7
Club Honours: Div 3 '01
The Oxford team captain, Andy was an
ever-present last term, playing in all of the
team's 53 matches and scoring seven
goals. Six of those came from the penalty
spot giving him a 100 per cent success
rate. A solid, dependable centre back
around whom the team was built, Andy
will be hoping for another good season,
perhaps this time leading the club into
Division Two.
*Doncaster Rov (From trainee at Leeds U on
4/7/1991) FL 41+10 FLC 1+1 FAC 2 Others
4+1/1
Darlington (Free on 10/12/1993) FL 179+2/3
FLC 10 FAC 11/1 Others 9
Chester C (Free on 8/7/1998) FL 41/4 FLC 3
FAC 1 Others 1
Brighton & Hove A (£10,000 on 28/7/1999)
FL 64+8/5 FLC 3 FAC 1+1 Others 7*

*Oxford U (Free on 13/12/2001) FL 68+1/7
FLC 3 FAC 3 Others 1/1*

CROSSLEY Mark Geoffrey
Born: Barnsley, 16 June 1969
Height: 6'0" **Weight:** 16.0
International Honours: W: 6; B-1; E:
U21-3
Mark had a mixed season at
Middlesbrough last term, for he signed a
new one-year contract but, because of
Mark Schwarzer's inspiring form in Boro's
goal, he was restricted to just two
Worthington Cup games. Mark had two
periods out on loan at Stoke City but he
played only one game in his first spell, a
1-1 draw at Gillingham in late November,
before being recalled because of a hand-
injury scare to Schwarzer. He was more
successful the second time in March when
he produced some outstanding
performances and earned a series of 'Man
of the Match' awards. Mark returned to
the Welsh international scene with a
substitute appearance against Bosnia
Herzegovina in February.
*Nottingham F (From trainee on 2/7/1987)
F/PL 301+2 FLC 39+1 FAC 32 Others 18
Millwall (Loaned on 20/2/1998) FL 13
Middlesbrough (Free on 25/7/2000) PL
21+2 FLC 5 FAC 3
Stoke C (Loaned on 29/11/2002) FL 1
Stoke C (Loaned on 6/3/2003) FL 11*

CROUCH Peter James
Born: Macclesfield, 30 January 1981
Height: 6'7" **Weight:** 11.12
International Honours: E: U21-6; Yth
This tall striker had a disappointing season
for Aston Villa last term, struggling to
hold down a regular place in the side.
Although Peter started the campaign as a
first choice in the line-up he soon found
himself out of the side as he struggled to
find the net. He only managed a handful
of starts and then damaged ankle
ligaments in a reserve-team game, which
left him sidelined for a period of time
during the middle of the season. Peter
added a further cap for England U21s
when he appeared against Macedonia.
*Tottenham H (From trainee on 2/7/1998)
Queens Park R (£60,000 on 28/7/2000) FL
38+4/10 FLC 1+1 FAC 3/2
Portsmouth (£1,250,000 on 11/7/2001) FL
37/18 FLC 1/1 FAC 1
Aston Villa (£4,000,000 + on 28/3/2002) PL
14+7/2 Others 4*

CROWE Dean Anthony
Born: Stockport, 6 June 1979
Height: 5'5" **Weight:** 11.3
Dean had a disappointing season for

uton Town last term, finding goals ifficult to come by. His campaign was onstantly interrupted by minor injuries, nd when fit he generally lost out to Tony horpe for a place in the starting line-up. A broken leg suffered in the away match t Mansfield Town finally put an end to is season.

toke C (From trainee on 5/9/1996) FL 9+31/12 FLC 2+3 Others 2/1
Iorthampton T (Loaned on 11/2/2000) FL +2
ury (Loaned on 23/3/2000) FL 4/1
ury (Loaned on 11/8/2000) FL 1+6/1
lymouth Arg (Loaned on 11/8/2001) FL 0+1
uton T (Free on 29/9/2001) FL 49+12/17 LC 1+1 FAC 1 Others 1

CROWE Jason William
Born: Sidcup, 30 September 1978
Height: 5'9" **Weight:** 10.9
Club Honours: Div 1 '03
International Honours: E: Yth
Jason was on the fringes of the Portsmouth first-team squad last term, nd towards the end of the campaign he was placed on the transfer list. The highlight of his season was a second-half substitute appearance at Crystal Palace when he turned the game by scoring twice after Pompey had been 2-0 down. He also shone when coming off the bench at Stoke, when he contributed another goal. Jason is a talented right wing back with excellent man-to-man marking skills.

Arsenal (From trainee on 13/5/1996) FLC 0+2 FAC 0+1
Crystal Palace (Loaned on 10/11/1998) FL 8
Portsmouth (£750,000 + on 7/7/1999) FL 37+19/5 FLC 4 FAC 1+2
Brentford (Loaned on 12/9/2000) FL 9 FLC 2

RYAN Colin
Born: Dublin, 23 March 1981
Height: 5'10" **Weight:** 13.4
International Honours: RoI: U21-3
The form of the four first choice central defenders meant Colin had few first-team opportunities with Sheffield United last term, and he made just two substitute appearances. In his one lengthy appearance, against Norwich, he produced a solid performance, showing himself to be good in the air with fine anticipation. He was a regular member of the successful reserve side and in October he spent one month on loan at Conference side Scarborough. Colin also featured for the Republic of Ireland at U21 level during the season.

heffield U (From trainee on 6/8/1999) FL +4 FLC 0+2

CUDICINI Carlo
Born: Milan, Italy, 6 September 1973
Height: 6'1" **Weight:** 12.3
Club Honours: FAC '00; CS '00
The astonishing rise of this Chelsea goalkeeper gathered momentum during 2002–03. He began the campaign in sparkling form, keeping five consecutive Premiership clean sheets, during one of which he gave possibly his best performance of the season, defying the Tottenham strikers at White Hart Lane with a string of breathtaking saves. Carlo's run of 62 consecutive matches was ended by a thigh strain on Boxing Day but after just two games he reclaimed his place from Ed de Goey and inspired the Blues to post the second-best defensive record in the Premiership and, by extension, Champions' League qualification. He has all the attributes required for the modern top-flight goalkeeper: a command of the penalty area, agility, anticipation, confident kicking and speed off his line to play as an auxiliary sweeper. Carlo capped a fine season when he was chosen as Chelsea's 'Player of the Year'.

Chelsea (£160,000 from Castel di Sangro, Italy, ex AC Milan, Prato, Lazio, on 6/8/1999) PL 87+2 FLC 9 FAC 16 Others 4+1

CULKIN Nicholas (Nick) James
Born: York, 6 July 1978
Height: 6'2" **Weight:** 13.7
This tall, commanding goalkeeper joined Queen's Park Rangers in the summer of 2002 on a free transfer from Manchester United. He started the season as first choice 'keeper, but in only his third game he suffered a leg injury, which kept him out of action for three months. Nick regained his place and remained in the line-up until he suffered another injury in March. However, on his return to fitness he was unable to dislodge Chris Day and had to settle for a place on the bench for the remainder of the season.

Manchester U (£250,000 from trainee at York C on 27/9/1995) PL 0+1
Hull C (Loaned on 24/12/1999) FL 4
Bristol Rov (Loaned on 14/7/2000) FL 45 FLC 5 FAC 1 Others 3
Queens Park R (Free on 22/7/2002) FL 17

CULLEN David Jonathan (Jon)
Born: Durham City, 10 January 1973
Height: 6'0" **Weight:** 12.0
Jon came to Darlington on trial at the beginning of last season but made just three appearances, although he showed his experience and class in midfield during

his stay at Feethams. He subsequently signed for Spennymoor United then had a brief trial with Malaysian club Selangor in the new year before returning to the north-east to play for Morpeth Town.

Doncaster Rov (From trainee on 16/9/1991) FL 8+1 FLC 2+1/1 FAC 0+1 Others 1 (Free to Spennymoor in September 1993)
Hartlepool U (Free from Morpeth on 27/3/1997) FL 33+1/12 FLC 2 FAC 1 Others 2
Sheffield U (£250,000 on 26/1/1998) FL 0+4
Shrewsbury T (Loaned on 10/9/1999) FL 10/1
Halifax T (Loaned on 17/12/1999) FL 11/5
Peterborough U (£35,000 on 3/3/2000) FL 34+10/5 FLC 1+1 FAC 1+2 Others 4/1
Carlisle U (Loaned on 16/3/2001) FL 10+1
Darlington (Free on 16/8/2002) FL 2+1 FLC 1

CULLIP Daniel (Danny)
Born: Bracknell, 17 September 1976
Height: 6'1" **Weight:** 12.7
Club Honours: Div 3 '01; Div 2 '02
Brighton & Hove Albion's skipper capped another fine season in 2002-03 by winning the club's 'Player of the Season' award for the second time. Although he was on the transfer list at his own request at the start of the campaign, Danny showed just what an invaluable member of the team he was and happily signed a new contract in September. Impressing in the centre of the defence with his speed, agility and reading of the game, he led the side by example. Also a vocal captain and organiser, he is a great favourite with the Seagulls fans, never failing to acknowledge their support, and has a never-say-die attitude.

Oxford U (From trainee on 6/7/1995)
Fulham (Free on 5/7/1996) FL 41+9/2 FLC 8 FAC 2 Others 1
Brentford (£75,000 on 17/2/1998) FL 15 FLC 2
Brighton & Hove A (£50,000 on 17/9/1999) FL 158+1/6 FLC 5/1 FAC 10/2 Others 3/1

CUMMINGS Warren
Born: Aberdeen, 15 October 1980
Height: 5'9" **Weight:** 11.8
International Honours: S: U21-9
After spending the first half of the 2002-03 season on loan at Dundee United, Warren joined Bournemouth on loan in the new year. The left back produced solid performances in every game he played, impressing all with his great vision and passing ability. It was to everyone's delight that he later agreed to join the club permanently.

Chelsea (From trainee on 5/7/1999)
Bournemouth (Loaned on 20/10/2000) FL 10/1 Others 1

West Bromwich A *(Loaned on 21/3/2001)*
FL 1+2
West Bromwich A *(Loaned on 25/7/2001)*
FL 6+8 FLC 0+2
Dundee U *(Loaned on 23/8/2002) SL 7+1*
SLC 1
Dundee U *(Loaned on 16/11/2002) SL 0+3*
Bournemouth *(Free on 3/2/2003) FL 20*
Others 3

CUMMINS Michael (Micky)
Thomas
Born: Dublin, 1 June 1978
Height: 6'0" **Weight:** 11.11
Club Honours: AMC '01
International Honours: RoI: U21-2; Yth

This Port Vale midfield player showed his versatility last term by occupying a variety of other roles, namely left and right wing back and full back. He began the season as a regular in the line-up and scored twice in the 4-2 win over Mansfield Town. Micky suffered a dislocated shoulder against Wigan on Boxing Day, which left him on the sidelines for three months. When he returned he filled an unfamiliar left-wing-back role and scored Vale's equaliser at Oldham Athletic. He is very good in the air but will be disappointed that he managed just four goals last season.
Middlesbrough *(From trainee on 1/7/1995)*
PL 1+1

Port Vale *(Free on 17/3/2000) FL 130+3/15*
FLC 5 FAC 5/1 Others 13/1

CUNNINGHAM Kenneth (Kenny) Edward
Born: Dublin, 28 June 1971
Height: 6'0" **Weight:** 11.8
International Honours: RoI: 48; B-2; U21-4; Yth
The Republic of Ireland captain was outstanding in the heart of the Birmingham City defence last season. He was never ruffled and read play brilliantly, always managing to be on the end of passes and crosses. In the latter stages of the campaign he developed an excellent

Kenny Cunningham

entral defensive partnership with Matthew Upson, the pair being instrumental in helping the Blues avoid relegation. Kenny continued to represent his country and was also deservedly voted as City's 'Players' Player of the Season'.
Millwall *(Signed from Tolka Rov on 8/9/1989) FL 132+4/1 FLC 10 FAC 1 Others 6+1/1*
Wimbledon *(£650,000 on 9/11/1994) P/FL 249+1 FLC 22+1 FAC 32+1*
Birmingham C *(£600,000 on 18/7/2002) PL 81 FLC 1*

CURETON Jamie
Born: Bristol, 28 August 1975
Height: 5'8" **Weight:** 10.7
International Honours: E: Yth
It was a season of mixed fortunes for Jamie. He averaged a goal a game for the first six matches for Reading, including braces against Sheffield Wednesday and Burnley, but the nippy striker's form then dipped, and he had to wait until the end of the year for his next conversion, an injury-time winner in the 2-1 home win over Derby County. Used almost exclusively as a substitute during the second half of the season, he showed that he had lost none of his predatory instinct with some incisive finishing. However, his future with the Royals remains in doubt, and he was given the summer to think over the offer of a one-year contract.
Norwich C *(From trainee on 5/2/1993) P/FL 3+16/6 FLC 0+1 FAC 0+2*
Bournemouth *(Loaned on 8/9/1995) FL 0+5 Others 0+1*
Bristol Rov *(£250,000 on 20/9/1996) FL 65+9/72 FLC 7+1/2 FAC 10/2 Others 6/2*
Reading *(£250,000 on 21/8/2000) FL 74+34/50 FLC 4+1/1 FAC 5+2/2 Others 6+1/2*

CURLE Keith
Born: Bristol, 14 November 1963
Height: 6'1" **Weight:** 12.12
Club Honours: AMC '86; FMC '88
International Honours: E: 3; B-4
Keith joined Barnsley on a three-month contract at the start of last season and made his debut in the Reds first win of the season against Queen's Park Rangers. A good organiser in the centre of defence, he was seen at his best when Chris Morgan was his partner. However, after the club went into administration his contract was cancelled by mutual consent. In December he took over as player-manager of Mansfield Town, getting off to a good start with a 4-0 drubbing of Blackpool, only the Stags

second clean sheet of the campaign. His experience became invaluable as he tried to reverse the club's fortunes and plug a very leaky defence, nevertheless he was unable to prevent them from being relegated to the Third Division.
Bristol Rov *(From apprentice on 20/11/1981) FL 21+11/4 FLC 3 FAC 1*
Torquay U *(£5,000 on 4/11/1983) FL 16/5 FAC 1/1 Others 1*
Bristol C *(£10,000 on 3/3/1984) FL 113+8/1 FLC 7+1 FAC 5 Others 14+1*
Reading *(£150,000 on 23/10/1987) FL 40 FLC 8 Others 5*
Wimbledon *(£500,000 on 21/10/1988) FL 91+2/3 FLC 7 FAC 5 Others 6/1*
Manchester C *(£2,500,000 on 14/8/1991) F/PL 171/11 FLC 18/2 FAC 14 Others 1*
Wolverhampton W *(£650,000 on 2/8/1996) FL 148+2/9 FLC 7/1 FAC 11/1 Others 2*
Sheffield U *(Free on 10/7/2000) FL 53+4/1 FLC 3 FAC 1*
Barnsley *(Free on 16/8/2002) FL 11 FLC 1*
Mansfield T *(Free on 10/12/2002) FL 11+3*

CURRAN Christopher (Chris)
Born: Birmingham, 17 September 1971
Height: 5'11" **Weight:** 12.4
Exeter City's captain had a frustrating time last season when his appearances were restricted by injury and changes of management at the club. Chris was loaned out to Dr Martens League club Tiverton Town to gain match fitness, but his season was ended prematurely when he was sidelined with an achilles injury. His experience was sorely missed in the crucial games at the end of the season, which resulted in the Grecians being relegated to the Conference.
Torquay U *(From trainee on 13/7/1990) FL 144+8/4 FLC 15 FAC 8 Others 10/1*
Plymouth Arg *(£40,000 on 22/12/1995) FL 26+4 FLC 1+1 FAC 1 Others 4*
Exeter C *(£20,000 on 31/7/1997) FL 146+11/6 FLC 8 FAC 10/1 Others 6+1*

CURRIE Darren Paul
Born: Hampstead, 29 November 1974
Height: 5'11" **Weight:** 12.7
The most skilful player at Wycombe Wanderers, Darren is truly two-footed and featured on either flank of midfield last season, delivering those pinpoint crosses which are his trademark. At the turn of the year he lost his place when the manager switched to a wing-back formation which does not favour Darren's style of play. He returned to the first team towards the end of the season and showed many nice touches although he

will probably be disappointed with his goal tally of four.
West Ham U *(From trainee on 2/7/1993)*
Shrewsbury T *(Loaned on 5/9/1994) FL 10+2/2*
Shrewsbury T *(Loaned on 3/2/1995) FL 5*
Leyton Orient *(Loaned on 16/11/1995) FL 9+1*
Shrewsbury T *(£70,000 on 7/2/1996) FL 46+20/8 FLC 2+1/1 FAC 3*
Plymouth Arg *(Free on 26/3/1998) FL 5+2*
Barnet *(Free on 13/7/1998) FL 120+7/19 FLC 5/1 FAC 3/2 Others 6*
Wycombe W *(£200,000 on 11/7/2001) FL 67+17/7 FLC 3 FAC 4+1/3 Others 2*

CURTIS John Charles
Born: Nuneaton, 3 September 1978
Height: 5'10" **Weight:** 11.9
Club Honours: FAYC '95; FLC '02
International Honours: E: B-1; U21-16; Yth; Sch
John was only on the fringes of the Blackburn Rovers first-team squad last season and his brief appearances came only in emergencies. In early March he joined Sheffield United on loan until the end of the season. He quickly slotted in to the right-wing-back role, allowing Phil Jagielka to move to central defence. Being quick and accurate in the tackle, showing good anticipation and linking up well when going forward, John played a key role in United's end of season, including the FA Cup semi-final and the play-off games.
Manchester U *(From trainee on 3/10/1995) PL 4+9 FLC 5 Others 0+1*
Barnsley *(Loaned on 19/11/1999) FL 28/2 Others 1+1*
Blackburn Rov *(£2,250,000 on 1/6/2000) P/FL 61 FLC 10 FAC 6 Others 1*
Sheffield U *(Loaned on 3/3/2003) FL 9+3 FAC 1 Others 3*

CURTIS Thomas (Tom) David
Born: Exeter, 1 March 1973
Height: 5'8" **Weight:** 11.7
Tom found himself out of the first-team picture at Portsmouth last term and in September he joined Tranmere Rovers on loan. He featured regularly in the Rovers' line-up, demonstrating excellent distribution skills and an intelligent reading of the game. The experienced midfielder then signed for Mansfield Town shortly before Christmas, but did not get off to a good start and was substituted at half time in his debut at Barnsley. However, he soon made up for this and added some much needed steel to the Stags' midfield.

Derby Co (From juniors on 1/7/1991)
Chesterfield (Free on 12/8/1993) FL
235+5/12 FLC 20/1 FAC 14/1 Others 11+1
Portsmouth (£150,000 on 4/8/2000) FL 7+6
FLC 1+1
Walsall (Loaned on 20/9/2001) FL 3+1
Tranmere Rov (Loaned on 30/8/2002) FL 8
FLC 2 Others 1
Mansfield T (Free on 20/12/2002) FL 23

CUSACK Nicholas (Nick) John
Born: Maltby, 24 December 1965
Height: 6'0" **Weight:** 12.8
Club Honours: Div 3 '00
After finishing the previous season as
joint-manager with goalkeeper Roger
Freestone, Nick was appointed as player-
manager of Swansea City. The team
made a bright start to the new
campaign, but a dip in form and a lack
of goals saw Nick return to the side,
adding much needed guile, and
application to the front line.
Unfortunately results continued to
disappoint, and in mid-September,
following a defeat at Boston United, he
was relieved of his managerial position.
Nick had continued with his role as
Chairman of the PFA, and following his
move from the Vetch Field he stepped
into a full-time role with the
organisation.
Leicester C (Signed from Alvechurch on
18/6/1987) FL 5+11/1 FAC 0+1 Others 1+1
Peterborough U (£40,000 on 29/7/1988) FL
44/10 FLC 4/1 FAC 4/1 Others 2
Motherwell (£100,000 on 2/8/1989) SL
68+9/17 SLC 5/4 SC 3+1/2 Others 1+1/1
Darlington (£95,000 on 24/1/1992) FL 21/6
Oxford U (£95,000 on 16/7/1992) FL
48+13/10 FLC 3/2 FAC 4+2/1 Others 2+1
Wycombe W (Loaned on 24/3/1994) FL
2+2/1
Fulham (Free on 4/11/1994) FL 109+7/14
FLC 6+4/1 FAC 7+1/1 Others 5+2/3
Swansea C (£50,000 on 30/10/1997) FL
184+14/13 FLC 6+1/1 FAC 11/3 Others 5+1

CUTLER Neil Anthony
Born: Birmingham, 3 September 1976
Height: 6'1" **Weight:** 12.0
International Honours: E: Yth; Sch
Neil started the season as first choice
'keeper for Stoke and turned in some fine
performances. The combination of
changes in management and a string of
poor results that ensued did not enhance
his confidence and he jumped at the
chance of a loan spell at Swansea City
when he lost his place. He showed his
class in his early appearances for the

Swans and stayed until the end of the
season, making a significant contribution
to the club's fight against relegation.
West Bromwich A (From trainee on
7/9/1993)
Chester C (Loaned on 27/3/1996) FL 1
Crewe Alex (Signed on 30/7/1996)
Chester C (Loaned on 30/8/1996) FL 5
Chester C (Free on 8/7/1998) FL 23 FLC 1
FAC 1 Others 1
Aston Villa (Signed on 30/11/1999) PL 0+1
Oxford U (Loaned on 15/12/2000) FL 11
Stoke C (Free on 24/7/2001) FL 56 FLC 2 FAC
4+1 Others 3
Swansea C (Loaned on 28/2/2003) FL 13

CYGAN Pascal
Born: Lens, France, 19 April 1974
Height: 6'3" **Weight:** 13.10
A close season signing from Lille, Pascal
made his Premiership debut for Arsenal at
Leeds following an injury to Martin
Keown. A solid central defender, strong in
the tackle, and with impressive
distribution skills, he has the advantage of
being a naturally left-footed central
defender.
Arsenal (£2,100,000 from Lille, France, ex
Valenciennes, Wasquehal, on 8/8/2002) PL
16+2/1 FAC 2 Others 9+2

Neil Cutler

D

DABIZAS Nikolaos (Nikos)
Born: Amyndaeo, Greece, 3 August 1973
Height: 6'1" **Weight:** 12.7
International Honours: Greece: 61;
U21; Yth
Nicos began the 2002-03 season as first
choice at the centre of Newcastle's back
four playing with his customary
commitment and assurance. However, he
was sent off at Blackburn in October, and
thereafter made only a handful of
appearances as the competition for places
increased following the arrival of
Jonathan Woodgate. A strong tackler
who reads the game well and enjoys
taking any opportunity to join the attack,
he continued to earn selection for the
Greek national side.
*Newcastle U (£1,300,000 from Olympiakos,
Greece on 13/3/1998) PL 119+11/10 FLC 6
FAC 17+1/2 Others 21+1/1*

DACOURT Olivier
Born: Montreuil-sous-Bois, France, 25
September 1974
Height: 5'9" **Weight:** 11.12
International Honours: France: 9; U21
This talented midfield player again added
steel and experience to the Leeds United
midfield last season. However, the club's
financial situation dictated that he should
move on and in January he joined Serie A
club Roma in a loan deal to the end of
the campaign. This was subsequently
reported to have become a permanent
move for an undisclosed fee.
*Everton (£4,000,000 from Strasbourg,
France, ex Thovars, on 7/8/1998) PL 28+2/2
FLC 4/1 FAC 2 (£6,500,000 to RC Lens,
France on 29/6/99)*
*Leeds U (£7,200,000 on 18/7/2000) PL
53+4/3 FLC 2 FAC 1 Others 22*

DAILLY Christian Eduard
Born: Dundee, 23 October 1973
Height: 6'0" **Weight:** 12.10
Club Honours: SC '94
International Honours: S: 46; B-1; U21-
34; Yth; Sch
Due to the constant changes in the West
Ham back line, this Scottish defender only
played in just over half of the club's
Premiership games last term. When
selected his contribution was consistent
and he made many vital clearances. He
had a superb match against Chelsea in
May and helped the Hammers gain a vital
1-0 victory. Christian is very effective in
the air and was unlucky not to score with

headers on a few occasions. He was a
regular for Scotland, winning ten more
caps and skippering the side on
occasions, while he scored a vital goal in
the Euro 2004 qualifier in Iceland.
*Dundee U (From juniors on 2/8/1990) SL
110+33/18 SLC 9/1 SC 10+2 Others 8+1/1*
*Derby Co (£1,000,000 on 12/8/1996) PL
62+5/4 FLC 6 FAC 4+1*
*Blackburn Rov (£5,300,000 on 22/8/1998)
P/FL 60+10/4 FLC 5+1 FAC 4 Others 2*
*West Ham U (£1,750,000 on 18/1/2001) PL
72+4 FLC 2 FAC 7+1*

DALGLISH Paul
Born: Glasgow, 18 February 1977
Height: 5'10" **Weight:** 10.0
International Honours: S: U21-7
Paul signed a 12-month contract for
Blackpool during the summer of 2002
and scored on his home debut in the 5-2
victory over Luton Town. A pacy right
winger or striker, he was in the first-team
squad for most of the season, before
joining Scunthorpe on loan in March. He
made a valuable contribution for the Iron,
netting three goals in the final two games
of the regular season to help them reach
the Third Division play-offs. Paul was
released by Blackpool at the end of the
season. He is the son of the former Celtic
and Liverpool star Kenny Dalglish.
Glasgow Celtic (From juniors on 20/7/1995)
Liverpool (Free on 14/8/1996)
*Newcastle U (Free on 21/11/1997) PL 6+5/1
FLC 2/1*
Bury (Loaned on 21/11/1997) FL 1+11 FAC 1
*Norwich C (£300,000 on 25/3/1999) FL
25+18/2 FLC 3+1 FAC 1*
*Wigan Ath (Free on 22/3/2001) FL 22+13/2
FAC 1*
*Blackpool (Free on 8/8/2002) FL 20+7/11 FLC
1 FAC 2/1 Others 0+1*
*Scunthorpe U (Loaned on 20/3/2003) FL
5+3/3 Others 1+1*

DALY Jonathan (Jon) Marvin
Born: Dublin, Ireland, 8 January 1983
Height: 6'1" **Weight:** 12.4
International Honours: RoI: U21-9; Yth
This young striker proved his worth at
club level with Stockport County last
term. Although just 20 years of age Jon's
physical presence unsettled defenders,
creating many chances for his strike
partners. He also contributed eight goals
himself. His late penalty against Plymouth
Argyle in April, which near enough saved
County from relegation, underlined his
courage and nerves of steel. He continued
to represent the Republic of Ireland at
U21 level during the campaign.
*Stockport Co (From trainee on 18/1/2000) FL
36+16/8 FLC 2/1 FAC 1/1 Others 0+1*

DALY Wesley (Wes) James
Patrick
Born: Hammersmith, 7 March 1984
Height: 5'9" **Weight:** 11.2
This right-sided midfield player featured in
the first game of the season for Queen's
Park Rangers, but failed to establish
himself in the side and managed only a
handful of appearances. Wes was a
regular member of the reserves, but was
only called up to the first team to cover
for injuries to other players.
Queens Park R (Trainee) FL 4+3 Others 1

DANIELSSON Helgi Valur
Born: Rejkjavic, Iceland, 13 July 1981
Height: 6'0" **Weight:** 12.0
International Honours: Iceland: 1; U21-
16;
This young midfielder again struggled and
failed to win a regular first-team place at
Peterborough last term, although he
made the starting line-up on 15
occasions. A talented player on the ball
and with excellent distribution he was
reported to have returned home to sign
for Fylkir during the summer. Helgi
featured regularly for Iceland at U21 level,
winning four more caps.
*Peterborough U (Free from Fylkir, Iceland on
16/10/1998) FL 38+17/2 FLC 2 FAC 2/1
Others 2+1*

DANKS Mark James
Born: Warley, 8 February 1984
Height: 5'9" **Weight:** 10.10
Mark struggled to make an impact at
Bradford City last term after joining the
club at the start of the season on a one-
year contract. The striker had to wait until
November before making his debut as a
late substitute at Nottingham Forest. He
went on to feature in another three
games from the bench and scored in the
FA Cup defeat at West Bromwich Albion.
Mark was allowed to go on loan to Dr
Martens League club Halesowen Town in
March and was released by the Bantams
at the end of the season.
*Bradford C (From trainee at Wolverhampton
W on 11/11/2002) FL 0+3 FAC 0+1/1*

DANNS Neil Alexander
Born: Liverpool, 23 November 1982
Height: 5'9" **Weight:** 12.1
A product of Blackburn Rovers' successful
youth policy, Neil made his bow in senior
football in the UEFA Cup tie against CSKA
Sofia last September, before making his
Premiership bow the following Saturday
against Leeds when he came on as a late
substitute. Although outstanding on his
debut he received few more chances at

first-team level. He is best employed in the centre of midfield where he brings power, pace and aggression, but he was also used in a wide-right role.
Blackburn Rov (From trainee on 3/7/2000)
PL 1+1 FLC 2 FAC 1 Others 1

DARBY Brett Thomas
Born: Leicester, 10 November 1983
Height: 5'8" **Weight:** 11.9
Brett began last season playing with Leicester City's U19 academy side, but after being released early in the new year he joined Southend on a non-contract basis. A slightly built right winger, he initially played in the reserves but gained a regular first-team place towards the end of the campaign. He made some useful contributions and his tenacity and crossing ability were clearly evident. Unfortunately his campaign ended on a sour note when he suffered severe ankle ligament damage in the final game at Exeter.
Leicester C (From trainee on 28/12/2000)
Southend U (Free on 18/2/2003) FL 6+4

DARBY Duane Anthony
Born: Birmingham, 17 October 1973
Height: 5'11" **Weight:** 12.6
Club Honours: NC '01; Div 3 '03
The Rushden & Diamonds fans' favourite is idolised at Nene Park for his hard work and 100 per cent commitment. Duane scored in three successive matches during August and four further efforts in March helped Diamonds to significantly close the gap behind long-time Division Three leaders Hartlepool United. He is currently one goal short of a personal half-century in three years at the club and has recently signed a new two-year deal.
Torquay U (From trainee on 3/7/1992) FL 60+48/26 FLC 4+3/1 FAC 1+4 Others 5+3/2
Doncaster Rov (£60,000 on 19/7/1995) FL 8+9/4 FLC 2 FAC 0+1 Others 1+1
Hull C (Signed on 27/3/1996) FL 75+3/27 FLC 5/1 FAC 4/6 Others 4/2
Notts Co (Free on 2/7/1998) FL 22+6/5 FLC 3+1/1
Hull C (Loaned on 25/3/1999) FL 4+4
Rushden & Diamonds (Free on 21/6/2000) FL 52+15/21 FLC 1+1/1 FAC 3+1 Others 0+1

DARLINGTON Jermaine Christopher
Born: Hackney, 11 April 1974
Height: 5'7" **Weight:** 10.10
The pruning down of Wimbledon's first-team squad meant that a versatile player such as Jermaine received plenty of opportunities last season and he featured in both full-back and both wide-midfield

positions during the course of the campaign. His best spell was probably the period before Christmas when he occupied the left-midfield slot, scoring a late goal in the Dons' thrilling 5-3 win at Bradford City. A very skilful player seen at his best when surging forward, ideally Jermaine would probably prefer the wing-back position. He missed the last month of the season after being injured at Norwich.
Charlton Ath (From trainee on 30/6/1992) FL 1+1 (Free to Dover Ath on 23/9/1993)
Queens Park R (£25,000 from Aylesbury U on 25/3/1999) FL 70+1/2 FLC 2 FAC 6
Wimbledon (£200,000 on 16/7/2001) FL 57+7/2 FLC 2+1 FAC 1

DAVENPORT Calum Raymond Paul
Born: Bedford, 1 January 1983
Height: 6'4" **Weight:** 14.4
International Honours: E: Yth
A product of Coventry's youth scheme, this young centre half won plaudits for his cool and assured performances in the first half of the 2002-03 season. Strong in the air and comfortable on the ball, he was a regular at the start of the campaign. He partnered Mo Konjic through the autumn but lost his place after a couple of inconsistent performances. His latter appearances were in a side short on confidence and Calum, like many of the other young players, sometimes struggled. He was voted 'Young Player of the Season' and was called up on a number of occasions for England U20 squad.
Coventry C (From trainee on 6/1/2000) P/FL 27+9/3 FLC 2 FAC 2+1

DAVIDSON Callum Iain
Born: Stirling, 25 June 1976
Height: 5'10" **Weight:** 11.8
Club Honours: S Div 1 '97
International Honours: S: 16; U21-2
This left-sided full back or wing back made the headlines during the pre-season build-up when suffering a broken jaw in a much publicised incident, but received a hero's welcome when returning to action with Leicester City in late August. Callum finally registered his first strike for two years when following up to crash home the decisive goal in the home win over Grimsby. He was used both at full back and in midfield during the season and was also recalled to the Scotland squad by Berti Vogts. Callum was a revelation in his new midfield role adding extra impetus to the Leicester promotion drive, despite being dogged by a troublesome groin injury throughout the campaign.

St Johnstone (From juniors on 8/6/1994) SL 39+5/4 SLC 1 Others 3
Blackburn Rov (£1,750,000 on 12/2/1998) P/FL 63+2/1 FLC 3+1 FAC 6 Others 1+1
Leicester C (£1,700,000 on 12/7/2000) P/FL 82+6/2 FLC 5+1 FAC 3+1 Others 0+1

DAVIES Andrew
Born: Stockton, 17 December 1984
Height: 6'3" **Weight:** 14.8
International Honours: E: Yth
At the age of 18 Andrew made his Premiership debut for Middlesbrough when he replaced 'flu victim Gareth Southgate against Aston Villa. A young central defender brimming with confidence, he captained the club's juniors through to the FA Youth Cup final for only the second time in their history. Andrew was called up for the England U19 squad for the UEFA championships in the summer. He is the brother of Durham cricketer Mark Davies.
Middlesbrough (From trainee on 6/7/2002) PL 1 FLC 1

DAVIES Gareth
Born: Chesterfield, 4 February 1983
Height: 6'1" **Weight:** 12.13
Gareth enjoyed a promising first season at Chesterfield, operating most often at right wing back. As he gains in confidence though, he may well come to offer more to midfield, where his size and mobility plus effectiveness in the tackle and promising distribution should prove effective. In his second game he scored the opening goal in the win at Mansfield, thus endearing himself immediately to the fans, and he remained popular as the season unfolded.
Chesterfield (Free from Chesterfield College on 15/3/2002) FL 27+7/1 FLC 2 FAC 1/1 Others 2

DAVIES Kevin Cyril
Born: Sheffield, 26 March 1977
Height: 6'0" **Weight:** 13.6
International Honours: E: U21-3; Yth
Kevin had a rather difficult time at Southampton last season and in September he was loaned out to First Division Millwall. He did well in a two-month spell at the New Den, finding the net three times before returning to St Mary's. However, he made just one start all season for the Saints, and that in the penultimate game at Arsenal when James Beattie was rested, otherwise being restricted to outings as a substitute. Ironically, his most memorable appearance was when he came off the bench against Millwall in the FA Cup fourth round tie

and snatched a last-minute equaliser. Kevin is a bustling hard-working striker with plenty of natural talent.
Chesterfield (From trainee on 18/4/1994) FL 113+16/22 FLC 7+2/1 FAC 10/6 Others 9+2/1
Southampton (£750,000 on 14/5/1997) PL 20+5/9 FLC 3+1/3 FAC 1
Blackburn Rov (£7,250,000 on 2/6/1998) P/FL 11+12/1 FLC 3 FAC 2/1 Others 1
Southampton (Signed on 18/8/1999) PL 59+23/10 FLC 3+2/1 FAC 3+5/2
Millwall (Loaned on 13/9/2002) FL 6+3/3

DAVIES Simon
Born: Haverfordwest, 23 October 1979
Height: 5'10" **Weight:** 11.4
International Honours: W: 15; B-1; U21-10; Yth
Probably the hottest prospect in the Premiership, this young attacking midfielder matured immensely at Tottenham during the 2002-03 season. It is no real surprise that his pace and skill on the ball topped off with an astute footballing brain have seen him linked to all of the Premiership big guns. After making a dramatic impact on his entry to the full Wales international side, he went on to score in three successive games and is a real factor in the turn around in his country's fortunes. With a taste for football at the highest level now, Simon's ambitions will be European qualification next season.
Peterborough U (From trainee on 21/7/1997) FL 63+2/6 FLC 4 FAC 3 Others 3
Tottenham H (£700,000 on 10/1/2000) PL 65+18/11 FLC 8+2/3 FAC 4+1/2

DAVIS James (Jimmy) Roger William
Born: Redditch, 9 February 1982
Height: 5'8" **Weight:** 11.10
International Honours: E: Yth; Sch
This Manchester United youngster spent the opening three months of the 2002-03 season on loan at Swindon in order to gain some first-team experience and made an immediate impact, bursting into the box to be brought down for a late penalty in the opening game against Barnsley. Although his loan spell was disrupted by injury he did enough during his time at the County Ground to endear himself to the locals and was given a standing ovation at the end of his final game. Jimmy is a fast, strong-running winger or forward with good close ball control who delights in running at defenders.
Manchester U (From trainee on 9/9/1999) FLC 1
Swindon T (Loaned on 9/8/2002) FL 10+3/2 FLC 1 Others 1/1

DAVIS Kelvin Geoffrey
Born: Bedford, 29 September 1976
Height: 6'1" **Weight:** 14.0
International Honours: E: U21-3; Yth
After two seasons of going close, Kelvin finally grabbed an ever-present tag for Wimbledon in 2002-03, and though the Dons' defence often let in goals for fun during the season, few could be put down directly to the man between the sticks. Once again he performed with great credit, producing a string of memorable saves, and in any contest for pure shot-stopping ability Kelvin would have few serious rivals. After being a regular for three seasons he has now ironed out his few weaknesses, and quite simply no Wimbledon fan would remotely contemplate swapping him for anyone else playing at the same level.
Luton T (From trainee on 1/7/1994) FL 92 FLC 7 FAC 2 Others 6
Torquay U (Loaned on 16/9/1994) FL 2 FLC 1 Others 1
Hartlepool U (Loaned on 8/8/1997) FL 2 FLC 1
Wimbledon (£600,000 + on 14/7/1999) FL 131 FLC 7 FAC 8

DAVIS Sean
Born: Clapham, 20 September 1979
Height: 5'10" **Weight:** 12.0
Club Honours: Div 1 '01
International Honours: E: U21-12
Sean enjoyed an outstanding season, despite missing a number of games through injury and suspension. He operated in a central-midfield role, which enabled him to show his attacking qualities. Sean again scored some vital goals including claiming the first Fulham goal at Loftus Road: a last-minute winner against Sochaux. After serving his international apprenticeship with the U21s he gained selection for the full England squad for the friendly against Australia in February but was not used in this game. Sean, however, shrugged off this disappointment to end the season with a number of excellent performances.
Fulham (From trainee on 2/7/1998) P/FL 106+25/9 FLC 9+5/3 FAC 9+2/1 Others 12/1

DAVIS Solomon (Sol) Sebastian
Born: Cheltenham, 4 September 1979
Height: 5'8" **Weight:** 11.0
Sol made his debut for Luton Town against Plymouth, and was soon able to keep experienced full back Alan Kimble out of the side. He made progress every match until suspension and minor injuries began to hamper him. A natural left-sided

player with the ability to put over telling crosses he is a good tackler and reads the game well.
Swindon T (From trainee on 29/5/1998) FL 100+17 FLC 7 FAC 5+1 Others 1
Luton T (£600,000 + on 16/8/2002) FL 34 FLC 2 FAC 1 Others 1

DAVIS Stephen (Steve) Mark
Born: Hexham, 30 October 1968
Height: 6'2" **Weight:** 14.7
Club Honours: Div 4 '92
Throughout Steve's Burnley career, there have been calls from supporters for him to be employed further upfield. They finally got their wish in 2002-03, with the big man playing several games in the heart of midfield and often impressing there. But this was on the whole not a vintage season for the Clarets' skipper, who was again absent for long spells through injury and, although still a dominant figure at the back and often an example to his team mates, seemed more prone to error than before. His best run of games came at the end of the season, when he was seen to best effect in the midfield position which may well be where he sees out the final part of a notable Turf Moor career.
Southampton (From trainee on 6/7/1987) FL 5+1
Burnley (Loaned on 21/11/1989) FL 7+2
Notts Co (Loaned on 28/3/1991) FL 0+2
Burnley (£60,000 on 17/8/1991) FL 162/22 FLC 10/2 FAC 18/1 Others 13
Luton T (£750,000 on 13/7/1995) FL 137+1/21 FLC 19/3 FAC 6/2 Others 10/1
Burnley (£800,000 on 21/12/1998) FL 152+4/20 FLC 9/2 FAC 6+1 Others 1

DAVISON Aidan John
Born: Sedgefield, 11 May 1968
Height: 6'1" **Weight:** 13.12
Club Honours: AMC '98
International Honours: NI: 3; B-1
Aidan again proved he is an excellent goalkeeper with a number of fine performances for Bradford City last season. He was the club's number one for the majority of the campaign following a knee injury to veteran Gary Walsh. A thigh problem in the home draw to Coventry in September forced him on the sidelines for a while, but he quickly returned to full fitness and finished the season as a first-team regular. A dominant 'keeper who excels at catching high crosses, Aidan was not offered a new contract in the summer.
Notts Co (Signed from Billingham Synthonia on 25/3/1988) FL 1
Bury (£6,000 on 7/10/1989)

Millwall *(Free on 14/8/1991) FL 34 FLC 3 FAC 2 Others 2*
Bolton W *(£25,000 on 26/7/1993) P/FL 35+2 FAC 8 Others 4*
Hull C *(Loaned on 29/11/1996) FL 9 Others 1*
Bradford C *(Free on 14/3/1997) FL 10*
Grimsby T *(Free on 16/7/1997) FL 77 FLC 10 FAC 7 Others 10*
Sheffield U *(Free on 6/8/1999) FL 1+1*
Bradford C *(Free on 4/1/2000) P/FL 49+2 FLC 6 FAC 1 Others 2+1*

DAWS Nicholas (Nick) John
Born: Manchester, 15 March 1970
Height: 5'11" **Weight:** 13.2
Club Honours: Div 2 '97
This experienced Rotherham United midfield player frequently did not get the praise he so richly deserved for his willingness to adopt a role that suited the team's requirements more than his own personal glory. Nick is good at breaking up opponents' attacks and then setting his own in motion, while he is also an expert in dead-ball situations. During the season he reached the very creditable milestone of 500 league and cup appearances, these coming for just two

clubs to display his loyalty. He will probably be disappointed with his return of just one goal, that coming in a defeat at Coventry City in early November.
Bury *(£10,000 from Altrincham on 13/8/1992) FL 356+13/16 FLC 24+2/3 FAC 19/1 Others 15+4/3*
Rotherham U *(Free on 16/7/2001) FL 51+17/2 FLC 5+1 FAC 1+1*

DAWSON Andrew (Andy)
Born: Northallerton, 20 October 1978
Height: 5'9" **Weight:** 10.2
Despite only being on a week-to-week contract all season, Andy had another solid campaign at left back for Scunthorpe last term, only missing three matches. A quick player, who loves to get forward, his attacking game continued to flourish alongside experienced winger Peter Beagrie. He is the older brother of Michael (Nottingham Forest) and Kevin (Chesterfield).
Nottingham F *(From trainee on 31/10/1995) FLC 1*
Scunthorpe U *(£70,000 on 18/12/1998) FL 192+3/8 FLC 6 FAC 12/1 Others 12/2*

DAWSON Kevin Edward
Born: Northallerton, 18 June 1981
Height: 6'0" **Weight:** 10.10
Kevin is suited to either a right-back or central-defensive role. He settled in well at Chesterfield and was a regular until hampered by a hernia problem in the new year. After he recovered from that he was diagnosed as diabetic, but took the news in his stride and, with his kit bag full of Jaffa Cakes, he reclaimed a first-team place. His courage shone like a beacon during the 2002-03 campaign, and inspired everyone at the club. He is the brother of Andy and Mike Dawson.
Nottingham F *(From trainee on 25/6/1998) FL 8+3 FAC 1*
Barnet *(Loaned on 9/3/2001) FL 5*
Chesterfield *(Free on 8/8/2002) FL 26/1 FLC 2 FAC 1 Others 2*

DAWSON Michael Richard
Born: Northallerton, 18 November 1983
Height: 6'2" **Weight:** 12.12
International Honours: E: U21-4; Yth
Michael was the find of the season for Nottingham Forest after replacing Jon

Steve Davis

Olav Hjelde in September. He missed only one more game during the rest of the campaign and went on to become an integral part of the England U21 squad. A tough-tackling central defender, his fellow players named him in the PFA Division One team for the season. Michael is the younger brother of Andy and Kevin Dawson.

Nottingham F *(From trainee on 23/11/2000)* FL 39/5 FLC 2 FAC 1 Others 1

DAY Christopher (Chris) Nicholas

Born: Walthamstow, 28 July 1975
Height: 6'3" **Weight:** 13.6
International Honours: E: U21-6; Yth (UEFA-U18 '93)

Chris missed the first half of the 2002-03 season whilst still recovering from the broken leg he suffered back in November 2001. In October he joined Ryman League club Aylesbury United in a two-month loan deal as part of his return to match fitness. However, Chris had to wait until March to get back in the Queen's Park Rangers first team, replacing the injured Nick Culkin then retaining his place until the end of the season.

Tottenham H *(From trainee on 16/4/1993)* Others 4
Crystal Palace *(£225,000 + on 9/8/1996) FL 24 FLC 2 FAC 2*
Watford *(£225,000 on 18/7/1997) PL 11 FLC 1 Others 1*
Lincoln C *(Loaned on 4/12/2000) FL 14 Others 4*
Queens Park R *(Free on 24/7/2001) FL 28 FLC 1 Others 4*

DAY Rhys

Born: Bridgend, 31 August 1982
Height: 6'2" **Weight:** 13.6
Club Honours: AMC '02
International Honours: W: U21-12; Yth

This promising left-sided or central defender initially joined Mansfield Town on loan from Manchester City at the end of November, just days before the departure of manager Stuart Watkiss. He made his debut in the 4-2 defeat at Port Vale, when he replaced club captain Neil Moore, and subsequently partnered new boss Keith Curle in the centre of defence. Rhys featured regularly for the Stags until a broken jaw brought his campaign to a premature conclusion. He also appeared for Wales at U21 level during the season.

Manchester C *(From trainee on 21/9/1999)*
Blackpool *(Loaned on 31/12/2001) FL 4+5 FAC 0+1 Others 3*
Mansfield T *(Free on 29/11/2002) FL 23/1 FAC 1*

DEANE Brian Christopher

Born: Leeds, 7 February 1968
Height: 6'3" **Weight:** 12.7
International Honours: E: 3; B-3

This experienced striker started the 2002-03 campaign by netting the first ever league goal at the Walkers Stadium. Brian forged a useful partnership with Paul Dickov and continued to find the net regularly for Leicester despite recurring back trouble. Indeed, as the season progressed, the adage that 'when Deane scores, City never lose' began to take a real grip, only to be broken on Easter Monday at the home of his former club, Sheffield United. Brian suffered a compressed fracture of the cheekbone in the defeat at Gillingham in January and later a hamstring injury at Turf Moor in March, but still comfortably reached double figures in the goal charts.

Doncaster Rov *(From juniors on 14/12/1985)* FL 59+7/12 FLC 3 FAC 2+1/1 Others 2+2
Sheffield U *(£30,000 on 19/7/1988) F/PL 197/82 FLC 16/11 FAC 23+1/11 Others 2/2*
Leeds U *(£2,900,000 on 14/7/1993) PL 131+7/32 FLC 8+3/2 FAC 13+3/4 Others 3*
Sheffield U *(£1,500,000 on 29/7/1997) FL 24/11 FLC 4/2 FAC 1 (£1,000,000 to Benfica, Portugal on 15/1/1998)*
Middlesbrough *(£3,000,000 on 16/10/1998) PL 72+15/18 FLC 4+1 FAC 3/1*
Leicester C *(£150,000 on 30/11/2001) P/FL 44+3/19 FAC 2*

DEARDEN Kevin Charles

Born: Luton, 8 March 1970
Height: 5'11" **Weight:** 13.4

This experienced 'keeper struggled to find the consistency he had shown for Torquay United in his first season at Plainmoor. Injury saw him miss several matches in the middle of the campaign and after regaining his place he lost out to Arjan Van Heusden. At the time of writing Kevin was reported to be considering an offer of a player-coach role for the 2003-04 season.

Tottenham H *(From trainee on 5/8/1988) PL 0+1 FLC 1*
Cambridge U *(Loaned on 9/3/1989) FL 15*
Hartlepool U *(Loaned on 31/8/1989) FL 10*
Swindon T *(Loaned on 23/3/1990) FL 1*
Peterborough U *(Loaned on 24/8/1990) FL 7*
Hull C *(Loaned on 10/1/1991) FL 3*
Rochdale *(Loaned on 16/8/1991) FL 2*
Birmingham C *(Loaned on 19/3/1992) FL 12*
Brentford *(Free on 30/9/1993) FL 205 FLC 17 FAC 13 Others 19*
Barnet *(Loaned on 5/2/1999) FL 1*
Wrexham *(Free on 4/6/1999) FL 81 FLC 3 FAC 6*
Torquay U *(Free on 9/8/2001) FL 72+1 FLC 3 FAC 1 Others 1*

DEBEC Fabien

Born: Lyon, France, 18 January 1976
Height: 6'2" **Weight:** 14.0

This goalkeeper joined Coventry City on a 12-month contract and went on to enjoy a quiet debut against Colchester in the Worthington Cup tie. He subsequently had a short run in the line-up but then lost his place after injuring a finger in training. Fabien was released at the end of the season.

Coventry C *(Free from Rennes, France, ex Lyon, on 23/8/2002) FL 11 FLC 2*

DEENEY Joseph (Joe) Eugene

Born: Zimbabwe, 18 March 1984
Height: 6'0" **Weight:** 13.10

Joe made his only first-team appearances for Luton in the LDV Vans Trophy matches, opening the scoring against Woking. The young defender also produced some fine performances in the reserve and youth teams but was released by the Hatters towards the end of the season and linked up with Ryman League club Enfield.

Luton T *(Trainee) Others 2/1*

DEENEY Saul

Born: Londonderry, 12 March 1983
Height: 6'1" **Weight:** 12.10
International Honours: Rol: Yth

This promising young 'keeper continued to make progress with Notts County last term and eventually broke through to feature regularly at first-team level in the closing stages of the season. Saul also won a call-up to the Republic of Ireland U21 squad during the season and he will be hoping to become first choice at Meadow Lane in 2003-04.

Notts Co *(From trainee on 8/9/2000) FL 7*

DEFOE Jermain Colin

Born: Beckton, 7 October 1982
Height: 5'7" **Weight:** 10.4
International Honours: E: U21-19; Yth; Sch

Jermain finished last season as West Ham's leading goal-scorer with 11 goals in all competitions and either made the starting line-up or came on as a substitute in every senior game. The pick of his goals was the wonder strike against Nottingham Forest in the FA Cup when he cut inside a defender and curled a 15-yarder into the corner of the net. A talented young striker, he has electric pace in the box and is a natural finisher. He also showed his versatility by performing well as a target man on occasions, despite his lack of height. Jermain was runner-up in the 'Hammer of the Year' award and added three more

Jermain Defoe

caps for England at U21 level during the season.
West Ham U *(£400,000 + from trainee at Charlton Ath on 15/10/1999) PL 43+31/18 FLC 3+1/2 FAC 4+1/6*
Bournemouth *(Loaned on 26/10/2000) FL 27+2/18 FAC 1/1 Others 1*

DE GOEY Eduard (Ed)

Franciscus
Born: Gouda, Holland, 20 December 1966
Height: 6'6" **Weight:** 15.0
Club Honours: FLC '98; ECWC '98; ESC '98; FAC '00; CS '00 ·
International Honours: Holland: 31; U21-17

The big Dutch 'keeper made a surprise return to first-team action for Chelsea on Boxing Day after a period of 15 months. The knee injury sustained at Craven Cottage in October 2001 has certainly cost him dearly as his replacement, Carlo Cudicini, developed into one of the best 'keepers in the Premiership and claimed the Blues' number one spot. Ed also got an unexpected opportunity in January following Carlo's controversial FA Cup dismissal against Middlesbrough, and he proved that he had lost none of his sharpness by producing a string of fine saves to steer the Blues into round four. Ed had endured a particularly frustrating spell as he is marooned on the bench having had a glittering career between the posts for the Blues.
Chelsea *(£2,250,000 from Feyenoord, Holland, ex Sparta Rotterdam, on 10/7/1997) PL 123 FLC 5 FAC 13+1 Others 37*

DE LA CRUZ Bernardo Ulisses

Born: Piqulucho, Ecuador, 8 February 1974
Height: 5'11" **Weight:** 11.12
International Honours: Ecuador: 60
Ulises is a right-sided midfielder who can also play at the back. He had an encouraging debut for Aston Villa at home to Liverpool, showing his pace and producing a series of fine crosses from the right. However, he generally struggled to hold down a place in the line-up. Perhaps the highlight of his campaign was scoring a superb individual goal against Charlton to open his account in claret and blue; the breathtaking effort saw him burst into the penalty area and sidestep three opponents before beating the 'keeper. Ulises' main strength is in a creative role and his best qualities are his dribbling and crossing. His whole game is about setting up chances for other players and by his own admission he is a maker of goals

rather than a taker of chances. He continued to represent Ecuador at international level during the season.
Hibernian *(£700,000 from Liga Deportiva Universitaria, Ecuador on 18/6/2002) SL 25+7/2 SLC 2 SC 2+2/1 Others 2*
Aston Villa *(£1,500,000 on 2/8/2002) PL 12+8/1 FLC 2+1/1 FAC 1*

DELANEY Damien

Born: Cork, 20 July 1981
Height: 6'3" **Weight:** 13.10
International Honours: RoI: U21-1; Yth
This tall, classy central defender joined Mansfield on loan from near neighbours Leicester City in a bid to stem the flow of goals conceded. He initially played at centre back, but after a couple of matches he moved to left back. Damien did well during his spell at Field Mill and became Peter Taylor's first signing for Hull, thus rejoining his former boss from his Filbert Street days. He earned a place in the club's record books in December when his winner against Boston became the last-ever goal to be scored by a Hull player at Boothferry Park. Although mostly used at left back, Damien was also employed as the left-sided centre back in a back four and in centre midfield.
Leicester C *(£50,000 from Cork C on 9/11/2000) PL 5+3 FLC 1 FAC 1+1*
Stockport Co *(Loaned on 15/11/2001) FL 10+2/1*
Huddersfield T *(Loaned on 28/3/2002) FL 1+1*
Mansfield T *(Loaned on 6/9/2002) FL 7*
Hull C *(£50,000 on 18/10/2002) FL 30/1 FAC 1*

DELANEY Mark Anthony

Born: Fishguard, 13 May 1976
Height: 6'1" **Weight:** 11.7
International Honours: W: 19
Mark had a frustrating time at Aston Villa last term when he was affected by more than his fair share of injuries. He was sidelined for a short spell early in the season and after returning for a run of just five games he then broke his right foot whilst playing for Wales against Azerbaijan in November. Mark then injured a cartilage, requiring surgery, and soon after returning to action he was sidelined yet again, this time with cruciate ligament damage, which brought his season to a premature end. Mark is a reliable defender who normally plays in the right-back position and is well known for his sliding tackles as well as some steady defending. Mark was a regular at international level for Wales when fit and was deservedly voted as the Villa 'Players' Player of the Year'.

Cardiff C *(Free from Carmarthen on 3/7/1998) FL 28 FLC 2 FAC 5/1*
Aston Villa *(£250,000 + on 10/3/1999) PL 79+12/1 FLC 3+3 FAC 4+1 Others 13*

DELANY Dean

Born: Dublin, 15 September 1980
Height: 6'1" **Weight:** 13.2
Club Honours: FAYC '98
International Honours: RoI: U21-6
Dean was second choice 'keeper to Mark Goodlad at Port Vale last term and had to be patient. His chance came in the game against Cardiff City in February and he then had a run of eight games between the sticks when he did well. On one occasion he almost scored himself when an enormous clearance was tipped on to the bar by the fortunate Crewe Alexandra 'keeper. Dean then dropped out the team with 'flu but featured again towards the end of the season. He is good shot stopper who probably suffered from the Vale not having a reserve team.
Everton *(From trainee on 23/9/1997)*
Port Vale *(Free on 16/6/2000) FL 20+2 Others 1*

DELAP Rory John

Born: Sutton Coldfield, 6 July 1976
Height: 6'0" **Weight:** 12.10
Club Honours: AMC '97
International Honours: RoI: 9; B-1; U21-4
An injury sustained against Sunderland in January blighted what was becoming a highly successful season for Rory, who had been more than holding his own in the centre of a much improved Southampton midfield. He made two abortive come backs, against Norwich City in the FA Cup in February and, after two brief appearances as a substitute in April at Birmingham when he lasted 45 minutes. Such was Rory's influence in the first half of the season, when his anticipation, tackling and distribution had often been majestic, he was sorely missed for the rest of the campaign. Prior to his injury problems he had also added to his total of caps for the Republic of Ireland.
Carlisle U *(From trainee on 18/7/1994) FL 40+25/7 FLC 4+1 FAC 0+3 Others 12+2*
Derby Co *(£500,000 + on 6/2/1998) PL 97+6/11 FLC 7/2 FAC 2+1*
Southampton *(£3,000,000 + on 21/7/2001) PL 46+6/2 FLC 2+1 FAC 3+1*

DELGADO Chala Agustin

Born: Ibarra, Ecuador, 23 December 1974
Height: 6'3" **Weight:** 14.2
International Honours: Ecuador: 49
Having made a favourable impression in

Ecuador's 2002 World Cup campaign it was hoped that the 'Tin Man', as he is known at home in the Andes, would finally deliver the goods for Southampton, for whom he had managed two appearances (one of them from the bench) in 2001-02. However, he arrived back at St Mary's late and injured, and finally made his full Premiership bow in November, giving the Arsenal defence a torrid time in Saints' 3-2 victory, forcing them to concede a penalty and jabbing home a goal. He started the following game at West Ham, but had to be substituted and further injury problems then restricted him to just one fleeting appearance from the bench.

Southampton (£3,500,000 from Necaxa, Mexico on 13/11/2001) PL 2+5 FLC 1/1 FAC 1

DELORGE Laurent Jan
Born: Leuven, Belgium, 21 July 1979
Height: 5'10" **Weight:** 12.0
International Honours: Belgium: U21; Yth
A badly gashed leg in the opening game of the 2002-03 campaign kept this right-winger on the sidelines at Coventry City last term and although he featured at wing back against Sheffield Wednesday he very quickly returned to Belgium, signing for Lierse SK.

Coventry C (£1,250,000 from KAA Gent, Belgium, ex Maleisen, Wavre, on 12/11/1998) FL 23+7/4 FLC 1+1 FAC 0+2

DE LUCAS Enrique (Quique)
Born: Llobregat, Spain, 17 August 1978
Height: 5'9" **Weight:** 10.10
International Honours: Spain: U21
Due to the financial meltdown of the European transfer market Chelsea's only acquisition during the 2002 summer close season was Quique who arrived at the club in a four-year deal. The highly rated Spanish U21 international had previously impressed Claudio Ranieri and the Blues moved quickly to secure his signature in the face of stiff opposition. A hard-running, aggressive midfielder, Quique had established himself as one of the hottest properties in the Primera Liga. He packs a powerful shot and was a regular scorer for Espanyol but his only goal for Chelsea came in the UEFA Cup against Viking Stavanger. Although equally at home in central midfield, Quique has been more often employed on the right where his direct, high-octane style gives defences differing problems to Jesper Gronkjaer's more sinuous dribbling.

Chelsea (Free from Espanyol, Spain on 19/7/2002) PL 17+8 FLC 2+1 FAC 1+1 Others 1/1

DEMPSTER John
Born: Kettering, 1 April 1983
Height: 6'0" **Weight:** 11.10
Club Honours: Div 3 '03
This local youngster showed great maturity when he came into the Rushden & Diamonds first team. John scored his first senior goal in the defeat at Bournemouth in September and he is certainly considered as a good prospect within the Nene Park set-up. That was recognised by a three-year contract in the summer to ensure John would not leave on a free transfer.

Rushden & Diamonds (From juniors on 24/7/2001) FL 11+7/1 FLC 1+1 FAC 1

DE OLIVEIRA Filipe Vilaca
Born: Braga, Portugal, 27 May 1984
Height: 5'10" **Weight:** 11.2
International Honours: Portugal: Yth
This youngster impressed during Chelsea's pre-season tour and went on to make five substitute appearances in 2002-03. A creative right-sided midfielder who is also comfortable in the 'hole' behind the front players, Filipe has a bright future and looks certain to feature prominently for the Blues in the coming seasons.

Chelsea (£140,000 from FC Porto, Portugal on 11/9/2001) PL 0+3 FLC 0+1 Others 0+1

DERRY Shaun Peter
Born: Nottingham, 6 December 1977
Height: 5'10" **Weight:** 10.13
Club Honours: Div 3 '98
This experienced player joined Crystal Palace last August and had the misfortune to suffer a broken nose in one of his early games. However, once recovered he settled in quickly at Selhurst Park, featuring regularly in the line-up. Shaun was bought by the Eagles to play in a central midfield 'holding' role, but managed to get forward to find the net against Grimsby, his only goal of the season.

Notts Co (From trainee on 13/4/1996) FL 76+3/4 FLC 4+1 FAC 6+1/1 Others 3
Sheffield U (£700,000 on 26/11/1998) FL 62+10 FLC 4 FAC 7/1
Portsmouth (£300,000 + on 16/3/2000) FL 48+1/1 FLC 4 FAC 1+1
Crystal Palace (£400,000 on 6/8/2002) FL 36+3/1 FLC 2 FAC 4

DESAILLY Marcel
Born: Accra, Ghana, 7 September 1968
Height: 6'1" **Weight:** 13.5
Club Honours: ESC '98; FAC '00; CS '00
International Honours: France: 108 (WC '98, UEFA '00); B-1; U21
One of the finest contemporary central

defenders, Marcel took over the captaincy of France from his former Chelsea team mate Didier Deschamps. Although his country had a dismal World Cup, Marcel returned fully refreshed and resumed his imperious form at the heart of the Chelsea defence. His tackling, aggression and anticipation were crucial factors in the Blues posting the second-lowest goals against total in the Premiership and their progression to the Champions' League, a fitting stage for a player of his calibre. Always a threat at set pieces, his tally was restricted to just two Premiership goals during the season — an exquisitely flicked volley against Sunderland, and the precious equaliser against Liverpool in the match when Champions' League qualification was secured. Marcel was selected as a member of the Premiership 'Team of the Decade' and went on to skipper France to victory in the Confederations Cup tournament in the summer.

Chelsea (£4,600,000 from AC Milan, Italy, ex Nantes, Marseilles, on 14/7/1998) PL 141+2/6 FLC 4 FAC 21 Others 29/1

DEVANEY Martin Thomas
Born: Cheltenham, 1 June 1980
Height: 5'10" **Weight:** 11.12
Martin enjoyed his most consistent campaign at Cheltenham Town by some distance, his impressive performances on the right-hand side of midfield earning him the supporters' 'Player of the Season' award. His pace, trickery on the ball and crossing ability made him one of the more reliable attacking options during a season in which the team found it hard to create and score goals. His form was rewarded with an improved contract at the end of the campaign.

Coventry C (From trainee on 4/6/1997)
Cheltenham T (Free on 5/8/1999) FL 85+40/23 FLC 4 FAC 3+3/2 Others 5+2/1

DEVINE Sean Thomas
Born: Lewisham, 6 September 1972
Height: 6'0" **Weight:** 13.6
Club Honours: FAYC '91
International Honours: RoI: B-1
An accomplished and forceful striker, Sean thankfully had an injury-free season at Wycombe, but after scoring a couple of goals early on he lost his place to Andy Rammell. A hat-trick in the LDV Vans Trophy tie at Torquay followed, but he was in and out of the side and in January he elected to move on to Third Division strugglers Exeter City. He became a fans' favourite at St James' Park with his high

Agustin Delgado

work rate and eye for goal. In a difficult season for the club he justified his signing with some crucial goals, one which stood out was the only goal of the game in the vital end-of-season match at Swansea.
Millwall (From trainee on 4/5/1991. Free to Bromley during the 1992 close season)
Barnet (£10,000 from Famagusta, Cyprus on 5/10/1995) FL 112+14/47 FLC 9/3 FAC 5/5 Others 6
Wycombe W (£220,000 + on 18/3/1999) FL 82+7/41 FLC 5+1/1 FAC 4+1/1 Others 1/3
Exeter C (Signed on 8/1/2003) FL 21+2/8

DEVLIN Paul John
Born: Birmingham, 14 April 1972
Height: 5'9" **Weight:** 11.5
Club Honours: AIC '95
International Honours: S: 8
Paul's strong, aggressive running down the right flank was always a handful for Birmingham City's opponents last season. He scored the Blues first-ever Premiership goal against Leeds at St Andrew's with a 25-yard drive that set up the team's opening league win. A regular member of the first-team squad, Paul was always up for the challenge and determined to work for team. He made his international debut for Scotland against Canada shortly after the start of the season and featured regularly in the national squad thereafter.
Notts Co (£40,000 from Stafford R on 22/2/1992) FL 132+9/25 FLC 11+1/1 FAC 8/1 Others 17+2/4
Birmingham C (Signed on 29/2/1996) FL 61+15/28 FLC 8+1/4 FAC 3+1/2
Sheffield U (£200,000 + on 13/3/1998) FL 122+25/24 FLC 9+3/4 FAC 8/1 Others 2
Notts Co (Loaned on 23/10/1998) FL 5
Birmingham C (£200,000 on 8/2/2002) P/FL 31+14/4 FAC 1 Others 2

DE VOGT Wilko
Born: Breda, Holland, 17 September 1975
Height: 6'2" **Weight:** 12.13
Last season Wilko remained second choice goalkeeper for Sheffield United, this time behind new boy Paddy Kenny. Although performing well in the reserves Wilko was on the bench just four times as manager Neil Warnock preferred five outfield substitutes. His one start was in the FA Cup against Ipswich. He conceded three goals in five minutes but saved well, running back, to push out a long distance lob, before United ran out 4-3 winners. Shortly afterwards Wilko returned to the Netherlands, joining RBC Roosendaal till the end of the season.
Sheffield U (Free from NAC Breda, Holland on 10/7/2001) FL 5+1 FAC 3

DE VOS Jason Richard
Born: Ontario, Canada, 2 January 1974
Height: 6'4" **Weight:** 13.7
Club Honours: Div 2 '03
International Honours: Canada: 39 (Gold Cup 2000); U23-14
An outstanding performer at the heart of the Wigan Athletic defence throughout last season, Jason's effective partnership alongside Matt Jackson provided a sound basis to help the Latics win the Second Division title. An inspirational captain, his towering presence saw him finish up with eight league goals, all of which came from corners. Remarkably he played nearly half the season with a broken bone in his foot, only missing the final three matches once the championship was won. A very solid player who led by example, he was voted 'Player of the Season' by the fans and also won a place in the PFA Division Two team. Jason continued to represent Canada and won a further cap against Libya in February.
Darlington (Free from Montreal Impact, Canada on 29/11/1996) FL 43+1/5 FLC 3/1 FAC 4 Others 1
Dundee (£400,000 on 12/10/1998) SL 91+2/2 SLC 5+1 SC 12
Wigan Ath (£500,000 on 8/8/2001) FL 62+1/13 FLC 6 FAC 1

DE-VULGT Leigh Stewart
Born: Swansea, 17 March 1981
Height: 5'9" **Weight:** 11.2
International Honours: W: U21-2; Yth
Leigh did not feature at the start of last season for Swansea, but following a change of management he was given his opportunity at right back at Oxford in October. He retained his place for the next match against Southend United, but unfortunately had to leave the field with a head injury. Leigh returned to make two more league appearances, and after a spell as a non-playing substitute had his contract paid up in mid-December and left the Vetch Field playing staff. A month later he signed for League of Wales side Carmarthen Town.
Swansea C (From trainee on 5/7/1999) FL 16+7 Others 4

DE ZEEUW Adrianus (Arjan) Johannes
Born: Castricum, Holland, 16 April 1970
Height: 6'1" **Weight:** 13.11
Club Honours: Div 1 '03
Classy and composed, Arjan formed a solid central defensive partnership alongside his colleagues at Portsmouth last season. He scored with a diving

header to snatch the winner against Gillingham, while his firm tackling and good positional sense served the team well. Off the field, Arjan possess a medical degree gained in the Netherlands.
Barnsley (£250,000 from Telstar, Holland, on Vitesse 22, on 3/11/1995) F/PL 138/7 FLC 12 FAC 14
Wigan Ath (Free on 2/7/1999) FL 126/6 FLC 8 FAC 6 Others 6
Portsmouth (Free on 3/7/2002) FL 35+3/1 FLC 1

DIABATE Lassina
Born: Bouake, Ivory Coast, 16 September 1974
Height: 5'9" **Weight:** 12.6
Club Honours: Div 1 '03
International Honours: Ivory Coast:
This talented defensive midfielder settled into the rigours of the English game well and played a large part in Portsmouth's promotion last season. A strong, efficient and quietly effective player, Lassina made his debut at Rotherham in October. Assured and hard in the tackle, he accumulated a number of yellow cards and had to be content with a place on the substitutes' bench in the final third of the season after Pompey signed Tim Sherwood. Lassina won a recall to the Ivory Coast international squad in the new year.
Portsmouth (Free from Auxerre, France, ex Bourges, Perpignan, Bordeaux, on 2/10/2002) FL 16+9 FAC 1

DIALLO Drissa
Born: Nouadhibou, Mauritania, 4 January 1973
Height: 6'1" **Weight:** 12.0
International Honours: Guinea:
After arriving at Turf Moor in January, this big central defender went straight into the Burnley line-up and from that point could probably claim to be the side's best defender, effective in the air, strong in the tackle, and able to play the ball out of trouble. His partnership with Ian Cox was possibly the soundest of several central defensive pairings used by Stan Ternent during the season, and it was perhaps significant that he was absent for both of the Clarets' seven-goal home humiliations during April. Drissa was also useful further upfield on his occasional ventures into attacking positions, and took great delight in scoring his first goal for the club, a powerful header in the FA Cup fifth round victory against Fulham.
Burnley (Free from KV Mechelen, Belgium, ex RC Tilleur, Sedan, AS Brevannes, on 9/1/2003) FL 14/1 FAC 4/1

Paul Devlin

DIAO Salif
Born: Kedougou, Senegal, 10 February 1977
Height: 6'0" **Weight:** 11.7
Club Honours: FLC '03
International Honours: Senegal:
One of the stars of Senegal's remarkable performance in the 2002 World Cup finals, Salif joined Liverpool in the summer, following in the steps of his compatriot El-Hadji Diouf. Although signed as a central midfielder, his first two starts in the Liverpool line-up were in central defence in September, covering for the injured Stephane Henchoz. In his more accustomed role in midfield he scored his first two goals for the club in October, netting in the 5-0 victory over Spartak Moscow and then providing the winner against Leeds. He held his place on and off until January, after which he was generally confined to the bench.
Liverpool (£5,000,000 from Sedan, France, ex Monaco, on 9/8/2002) PL 13+13/1 FLC 3+1 FAC 1+1 Others 5+3/1

DIBBLE Andrew (Andy) Gerald
Born: Cwmbran, 8 May 1965
Height: 6'3" **Weight:** 16.8
International Honours: W: 3; U21-3; Yth; Sch
Wrexham manager Denis Smith was keen to add some much needed experience to his defence and it certainly paid dividends. Andy's commanding presence in goal gave the defenders in front plenty of confidence. He showed remarkable agility for such a big stopper, and was at his best in one-on-one situations. A knee injury kept him out of action from the end of October to January, but his return helped inspire his colleagues to promotion. Andy was also employed as goalkeeping coach at the Racecourse.
Cardiff C (From apprentice on 27/8/1982) FL 62 FLC 4 FAC 4
Luton T (£125,000 on 16/7/1984) FL 30 FLC 4 FAC 1 Others 1
Sunderland (Loaned on 21/2/1986) FL 12
Huddersfield T (Loaned on 26/3/1987) FL 5
Manchester C (£240,000 on 1/7/1988) P/FL 113+3 FLC 14 FAC 8+1 Others 2
Aberdeen (Loaned on 20/10/1990) SL 5
Middlesbrough (Loaned on 20/2/1991) FL 19 Others 2
Bolton W (Loaned on 6/9/1991) FL 13 Others 1
West Bromwich A (Loaned on 27/2/1992) FL 9
Glasgow R (Signed on 11/3/1997) SL 7
Luton T (Free on 15/9/1997) FL 1 FLC 2
Middlesbrough (Free on 30/11/1998) FL 2
(Free to Altrincham during 1998 close season)

Hartlepool U (Free on 25/3/1999) FL 6 FLC 2 Others 2+1
Carlisle U (Loaned on 8/10/1999) FL 2
Stockport Co (Free on 10/8/2000) FL 22+1 FLC 0+1 FAC 1
Wrexham (Free on 9/8/2002) FL 33 FLC 1 Others 1

DI CANIO Paolo
Born: Rome, Italy, 9 July 1968
Height: 5'9" **Weight:** 11.9
Paolo once again rewarded the West Ham faithful with some superb goals last season. Several examples stand out in the memory notably one at Stamford Bridge in September, when he scooped the ball up with his right foot and let fly with a 25-yard volley, a two-goal strike against Leeds in November and a diving header against Aston Villa. A knee injury then forced him to miss eight games and in February he was substituted against West Bromwich Albion following which he was not reinstated in the side until the final home game against Chelsea, when to the delight of his many fans he scored the winning goal. The Italian is a midfield genius and has been one of the finest players ever to wear the claret and blue shirt.
Glasgow Celtic (Signed from AC Milan, Italy, ex AC Milan, Lazio, Ternana, Juventus, Napoli, on 3/7/1996) SL 25+1/12 SLC 2 SC 6/3 Others 2+1
Sheffield Wed (£3,000,000 on 8/8/1997) PL 39+2/15 FLC 4/2 FAC 3
West Ham U (£1,700,000 on 28/1/1999) PL 114+4/47 FLC 8/2 FAC 5/1 Others 10/1

DICHIO Daniele (Danny)
Salvatore Ernest
Born: Hammersmith, 19 October 1974
Height: 6'3" **Weight:** 12.3
Club Honours: Div 1 '99
International Honours: E: U21-1; Sch
This very useful target man finished up as West Bromwich Albion's leading marksman in 2002-03 with eight goals. Most of his efforts came via his head, his best of which came in the home games against Arsenal and Tottenham Hotspur. Danny also netted a hat-trick in the 3-1 FA Cup win over Bradford City, the first Albion player to achieve that feat in competition for 11 years. Always a handful to the marking defenders, he had his off days and after being left out of the side by his manager he asked for a transfer, although he later withdrew his request.
Queens Park R (From trainee on 17/5/1993) P/FL 56+19/20 FLC 6/2 FAC 3+3 (Free to Sampdoria, Italy during 1997 close season)

Barnet (Loaned on 24/3/1994) FL 9/2
Sunderland (£750,000, via loan spell at Lecce, Italy on 28/1/1998) P/FL 20+56/11 FLC 11+1/6 FAC 3+3/1 Others 1+2
West Bromwich A (Loaned on 23/8/2001) FL 3/2
West Bromwich A (£1,250,000 on 30/11/2001) P/FL 42+10/12 FLC 1 FAC 6/4

DICKMAN Jonjo
Born: Hexham, 22 September 1981
Height: 5'8" **Weight:** 10.8
A young Sunderland defender, Jonjo made his Premiership debut for the club at Manchester City in April when he slotted effectively into midfield as a substitute, giving a performance that belied his tender years and inexperience. Jonjo had previously been a mainstay in the Black Cats' reserve and youth sides and is able to operate in any position across the back four.
Sunderland (From juniors on 2/11/1998) PL 0+1

DICKOV Paul
Born: Livingston, 1 November 1972
Height: 5'6" **Weight:** 11.9
Club Honours: ECWC '94
International Honours: S: 4; U21-4; Yth; Sch
This busy forward really endeared himself to the Leicester City faithful with his dynamic all-action style. Paul became the first City player to net 20 goals in a season for seven years. A real handful for any defender, he also earned most of the spot kicks that City were awarded. His smartest efforts were perhaps an overhead kick at Reading and a cool left-foot drive to see off Crystal Palace, although the highlight was a hat-trick in the home clash with Wimbledon. A hernia problem necessitated an operation in March, which denied him the opportunity of a recall to the Scotland squad for their Euro 2004 qualifying campaign. Paul ended the campaign as the club's 'Player of the Year' and was also selected for the PFA Division One team of the season.
Arsenal (From trainee on 28/12/1990) PL 6+15/3 FLC 2+2/3
Luton T (Loaned on 8/10/1993) FL 8+7/1
Brighton & Hove A (Loaned on 23/3/1994) FL 8/5
Manchester C (£1,000,000 on 23/8/1996) P/FL 105+51/33 FLC 9+4/5 FAC 5+4/1 Others 3/2
Leicester C (Signed on 22/2/2002) P/FL 53+1/21 FLC 2/1 FAC 2/2

DIGBY Fraser Charles
Born: Sheffield, 23 April 1967
Height: 6'1" **Weight:** 13.10
Club Honours: Div 2 '96
International Honours: E: U21-5; Yth;
Sch
This experienced goalkeeper started the
2002-03 campaign as second choice to
Nick Culkin at Queen's Park Rangers,
signing a six-month contract to cover for
the injured Chris Day. He made a handful
of first-team appearances at Loftus Road
before moving on to join Kidderminster in
March. Signed to add some experience to
the defence, he responded with two clean
sheets in his first three appearances.
Fraser kept his place for the next eight
games but then lost out to Stuart Brock
and was released from his month-to-
month contract in April.
*Manchester U (From apprentice on
15/4/1985)*
*Swindon T (£32,000 on 25/9/1986) F/PL 417
FLC 33 FAC 21 Others 33+1*
*Crystal Palace (Free on 8/8/1998) FL 56 FLC
7 FAC 1 (Released on 31/10/2000)*
*Huddersfield T (Free from Barry T on
6/8/2001)*

*Queens Park R (Free on 11/10/2001) FL
20+2 FLC 1 FAC 3*
Kidderminster Hrs (Free on 31/1/2003) FL 11

DILLON Daniel (Dan)
Born: Hillingdon, 6 September 1986
Height: 5'9" **Weight:** 10.7
Dan was plucked from the Carlisle United
youth team to appear as a substitute in
the final match of the 2002-03 campaign,
aged only 16 years 8 months. Still a
schoolboy, he was due to start as a
scholarship boy at Brunton Park in the
summer.
Carlisle U (Associated Schoolboy) FL 0+1

DINNING Tony
Born: Wallsend, 12 April 1975
Height: 6'0" **Weight:** 12.11
Club Honours: Div 2 '03
A midfield ball-winner with Wigan
Athletic, this tireless performer was a
major cog in the club's Division Two title-
winning side last term. Playing a holding
role, sitting deep while others got
forward, didn't stop him netting several
league goals including a cracker in the
draw against Cardiff in October and

another in the final match of the season
at home to Barnsley. Hard working with
good anticipation which helps close down
the opposition and create goals, he was
always at the centre of the team's
endeavours turning in some outstanding
performances.
Newcastle U (From trainee on 1/10/1993)
*Stockport Co (Free on 23/6/1994) FL
159+32/25 FLC 12+5/3 FAC 4+7 Others
6+1/2*
*Wolverhampton W (£600,000 + on
22/9/2000) FL 35/6 FLC 1/1 FAC 1*
*Wigan Ath (£750,000 on 7/9/2001) FL
68+3/12 FLC 4 FAC 3*
Stoke C (Loaned on 27/3/2002) FL 5 Others 3

DIOUF El Hadji Ousseynou
Born: Dakar, Senegal, 15 January 1981
Height: 5'11" **Weight:** 11.11
Club Honours: FLC '03
International Honours: Senegal
El Hadji made an explosive start to his
Liverpool career with two goals on his
Anfield debut against Southampton in a
3-0 victory, but only scored four more
(three in the Worthington Cup) during the
remainder of the season. Manager

Paul Dickov (centre)

Houllier soon realised that he was not the answer to Liverpool's problems up front and from September to January he was a peripheral figure in the team, mainly used as a substitute. In January he was restored to the first team on the right-hand side of midfield, a position he occupied to the end of the season. However, although he applied himself with discipline in this new role, it hardly exploited his talents to the full and his trademark twists and turns with the ball rarely created any goals or indeed goal-scoring chances.

Liverpool *(£10,000,000 from RC Lens, France, ex Sochaux, Rennes, on 17/7/2002) PL 21+8/3 FLC 5/3 FAC 3 Others 6+4*

DI PIEDI Michele
Born: Italy, 4 December 1980
Height: 6'6" **Weight:** 13.7
Michele again struggled to make a breakthrough at Sheffield Wednesday last term and managed just one start all season. He spent time on loan in Norway with Odd Grenland to gain more senior experience, but still failed to impress the Hillsborough management on his return. He also spent a month on loan with Bristol Rovers where he worked hard to close down defenders, but otherwise made little impact. Michele is a young striker who is quick and tricky, but needs to develop the habit of goal scoring. He was released by the Owls in the summer.
Sheffield Wed *(Free from Perugia, Italy on 15/8/2000) FL 9+30/5 FLC 1+4/2*
Bristol Rov *(Loaned on 21/2/2003) FL 3+2*

DISLEY Craig Edward
Born: Worksop, 24 August 1981
Height: 5'10" **Weight:** 11.0
Craig was an ever-present for Mansfield Town last term until a dip in form saw him relegated to the substitutes' bench in February. He was mostly used in a central-midfield role, operating from box to box, and made excellent progress in what was only his second season of first-team football.
Mansfield T *(From trainee on 23/6/1999) FL 88+19/11 FLC 2 FAC 6 Others 1*

DISTIN Sylvain
Born: Paris, France, 16 December 1977
Height: 6'4" **Weight:** 13.10
Sylvain joined Manchester City in the summer of 2002 and went on to produce some excellent performances last season. He possesses the ideal attributes for a central defender, being quick, skilful and powerful. Sylvain is also very effective at bringing the ball out of defence and on occasions appeared on the left flank to

fire in crosses. He was a regular in the Blues' line-up and missed only five games, three of which were due to injury.
Newcastle U *(Loaned from Paris St Germain, France, ex Tours, Guegnon, on 14/9/2001) PL 20+8 FLC 2 FAC 5*
Manchester C *(£4,000,000 from Paris St Germain, France on 4/7/2002) PL 34 FLC 1 FAC 1*

DIXON Jonathan (Jonny)
James
Born: Muria, Spain, 16 January 1984
Height: 5'9" **Weight:** 11.2

With a fine goal-scoring record at youth and reserve level, Jonny made his debut in the Wycombe attack in the second game of the 2002-03 season, coming off the bench against Northampton. He scored on his full debut at Queen's Park Rangers on Boxing Day, coolly running onto a through ball to flick past the 'keeper and then netted two more in the next three games, suddenly finding himself as the team's main striker. However, he was then sidelined by a knee injury until March. Jonny possesses two great feet and his laid back style of play hides real pace.

Michele Di Piedi

Wycombe W *(From trainee on 14/2/2003) FL* 14+8/5 Others 0+2

DJETOU Martin Okelo
Born: Brogohlo, Ivory Coast, 15 December 1974
Height: 6'2" **Weight:** 12.8
International Honours: France: 6; U21
Martin joined Fulham in a one-year loan from Parma, although he did not recover match fitness until the end of October when he made his debut as a substitute in the 4-2 defeat at Southampton. His first few games were in midfield where he appeared to struggle, but a switch to central defence saw the team benefit from his excellent reading of the game and he was able to move forward with the ball before distributing telling passes. As the season wore on Martin became far more influential on the side wherever he played. His only Premiership goal proved decisive, earning all three points at home to Leeds United.
Fulham (Loaned from Parma, Italy, ex Creteil, Strasbourg, Monaco, on 24/7/2002) PL 22+3/1 FLC 1+1 FAC 4 Others 3+1

DJORKAEFF Youri
Born: Lyon, France, 9 March 1968
Height: 5'11" **Weight:** 11.6
International Honours: France: 82
Youri had an outstanding season with Bolton in 2002-03, contributing immensely to their survival in the Premiership. He extended his contract to a two-year deal in the summer of 2002 and wasted no time in showing why the Wanderers' management team had been so keen to tie him to the club. His form throughout the campaign was of an extremely high standard. Playing as a deep lying striker, Youri was perhaps, along with Jay-Jay Okocha, the focal point of the team throughout the season. His touch and passing range were a joy to behold and he was also the team's joint-top scorer, weighing in with seven vital goals including a stunning overhead kick in the away draw at Charlton in January.
Bolton W (Free from Kaiserslautern, Germany, ex Grenoble, Strasbourg, AS Monaco, Paris St Germain, on 15/2/2002) PL 48/11 FAC 1

DOANE Benjamin (Ben) Nigel David
Born: Sheffield, 22 December 1979
Height: 5'10" **Weight:** 12.0
Ben was fully involved in Sheffield United's pre-season games and started the 2002-03 campaign as a squad member, usually on the bench. He made

two starts early on, producing solid performances at right wing back, but when Phil Jagielka moved to that position Ben's opportunities were reduced. In January he moved to Mansfield in a three-month loan deal and went straight into the side in the right-back berth. However, he was recalled to Bramall Lane in March due to an injury crisis, starting the game at Wimbledon, but he was himself stretchered off with a leg injury that ended his season early.
Sheffield U (From trainee on 15/7/1998) FL 19+4/1 FLC 1+2
Mansfield T (Loaned on 16/1/2003) FL 11

DOBIE Robert **Scott**
Born: Workington, 10 October 1978
Height: 6'1" **Weight:** 12.8
International Honours: S: 5
This pacy striker made more substitute appearances than any other West Bromwich Albion player during the 2002-03 season. Despite his enthusiasm, Scott failed to hold down a regular place in the side, his best run in the first team being five matches during October and November. He scored five goals, two of them in London against Arsenal and Spurs (the latter a real beauty) and he also struck home a terrific right-footer in the 1-1 draw at Bolton. He did, however, have short, unwanted periods on the treatment table, firstly with a groin strain and then with a niggling thigh injury. Scott remained in the Scotland squad and added four more caps during the campaign.
Carlisle U (From trainee on 10/5/1997) FL 101+35/24 FLC 2+6 FAC 4+1/2 Others 6+1
Clydebank (Loaned on 3/11/1999) SL 6
West Bromwich A (£125,000 + on 11/7/2001) P/FL 42+32/15 FLC 3+1/2 FAC 1+5

DOBSON Michael William
Born: Isleworth, 9 April 1981
Height: 5'11" **Weight:** 12.4
Brentford's solid and reliable right back played in every Second Division match in 2002-03. Named captain at the start of the season, he was an effective, encouraging leader of the young Bees' side. Michael had a few games in central midfield due to injuries and headed home his first league goal from a corner against Cheltenham in April. He is the son of former Brentford winger George Dobson.
Brentford (From trainee on 30/6/1999) FL 106+5/1 FLC 4+1 FAC 6/1 Others 12/3

DODD Jason Robert
Born: Bath, 2 November 1970
Height: 5'10" **Weight:** 12.3

International Honours: E: U21-8
Now very much considered a veteran Saint, Jason continued to provide a calm and confident presence in the Southampton defence when called upon. His appearances have been restricted by injury in recent seasons, and it was the same again in 2002-03, with the result that although he remained club captain he was second choice at right back to Paul Telfer from December. A further injury meant he was unavailable for selection towards the end of the campaign and he was obliged to attend the FA Cup final as a spectator.
Southampton (£50,000 from Bath C on 15/3/1989) F/PL 340+25/9 FLC 40+2/1 FAC 31+1/3 Others 5

DOHERTY Gary Michael Thomas
Born: Carndonagh, 31 January 1980
Height: 6'2" **Weight:** 13.1
International Honours: RoI: 18; U21-7; Yth
Probably the most versatile player in the Premiership having played in all positions bar goalkeeper, Gary established himself as a regular at international level for the Republic of Ireland last season. Seeming more at home in the heart of defence, Gary had it all to prove after coming back from a broken leg, but was only on the fringes of the first team last season. He will be looking to feature regularly in 2003-04.
Luton T (From trainee on 2/7/1997) FL 46+24/12 FLC 0+3/1 FAC 6+2/2 Others 1+1
Tottenham H (£1,000,000 on 22/4/2000) PL 29+17/4 FLC 1+2 FAC 5+1/3

DOHERTY Thomas (Tommy) Edward
Born: Bristol, 17 March 1979
Height: 5'8" **Weight:** 9.13
Club Honours: AMC '03
International Honours: NI: 2
Despite all the goals scored by the effervescent Scott Murray, many thought that Tommy Doherty was the real star of the Bristol City side last season. Coupled with his drive and enthusiasm, this midfielder always gave the impression that he had time and space on the ball. With his stamina improving, he now needs to add to his goal return to become the complete player. Tommy finished the season off in style, winning his first full caps for Northern Ireland.
Bristol C (From trainee on 8/7/1997) FL 102+24/4 FLC 5+1/1 FAC 5+1 Others 12+1/1

DOIG Christopher (Chris) Ross
Born: Dumfries, 13 February 1981
Height: 6'2" **Weight:** 12.6

International Honours: S: U21-13; Yth; Sch
A big powerful central defender who can also operate at left back, Chris returned to action with Nottingham Forest in September after a year out due to a serious knee injury. However, he was only ever on the fringes of the first team and his best run in the side came early in the new year when he replaced Des Walker for four games. Despite not being a regular at club level Chris continued to represent Scotland at U21 level.
Queen of the South (Associated Schoolboy) SL 2+2
Nottingham F (From trainee on 7/3/1998) P/FL 35+11/1 FLC 6+1 FAC 2

DOLAN Joseph (Joe)
Born: Harrow, 27 May 1980
Height: 6'3" **Weight:** 13.5
Club Honours: Div 2 '01
International Honours: NI: U21-6; Yth
This big Millwall centre half returned to action after an 18-month spell on the sidelines through injury and seemed determined to make up for lost time. Joe made his long awaited come back against Stoke in November and everything looked great but in the next game against Bradford City he broke down and once again spent the remainder of the campaign in the treatment room. He will be hoping to steer clear of injuries in 2003-04 and establish himself as a regular member of the first-team squad at the New Den.
Millwall (Free from Chelsea juniors on 15/4/1998) FL 47+1/3 FLC 5 FAC 3/1 Others 5

DONALDSON Clayton Andrew
Born: Bradford, 7 February 1984
Height: 6'1" **Weight:** 11.7
A tall centre forward, Clayton took just 12 minutes to score his first goal for Hull after coming on for Gary Alexander during the LDV Vans Trophy tie at Port Vale in October. Following further games in the Unibond League for Harrogate Town in a work experience stint, he returned to make his league debut with a substitute appearance against Lincoln in February.
Hull C (From trainee on 10/2/2003) FL 0+2 Others 0+1/1

DONNELLY Simon Thomas
Born: Glasgow, 1 December 1974
Height: 5'9" **Weight:** 11.0
Club Honours: SC '95; SPD '98
International Honours: S: 10; U21-11
Simon had another injury-affected season for Sheffield Wednesday in 2002-03. He started the campaign in the line-up and

playing quite well, but soon injury took its toll and although he eventually returned to fitness he still failed to win a regular place in the side. He scored twice for the Owls, netting in consecutive games against Burnley and Ipswich in October.
Glasgow Celtic (From juniors on 27/5/1993) SL 113+33/30 SLC 11+6/4 SC 8+5/2 Others 13+7/6
Sheffield Wed (Free on 9/7/1999) P/FL 27+26/8 FLC 3+3 FAC 0+3

DONOVAN Kevin
Born: Halifax, 17 December 1971
Height: 5'8" **Weight:** 11.2
Club Honours: AMC '98
The knee injury that ended Kevin's 2001-02 season early also delayed his start to the new one as he had to go under the surgeon's knife again. He came back into the first team in early January after a few games in the reserves. He initially played in the centre of midfield, but when new manager Glyn Hodges changed the formation he became the regular right wing back where he enjoyed some success. Kevin always works hard and has the capability to deliver telling crosses.
Huddersfield T (From trainee on 11/10/1989) FL 11+9/1 FLC 1+1 FAC 1/2 Others 4
Halifax T (Loaned on 13/2/1992) FL 6
West Bromwich A (£70,000 on 1/10/1992) FL 139+29/19 FLC 9+2/6 FAC 7+1/3 Others 15+1/4
Grimsby T (£300,000 on 29/7/1997) FL 150+6/24 FLC 13+1/2 FAC 11/1 Others 9/3
Barnsley (Free on 2/7/2001) FL 48+6/1 FLC 2+1 FAC 2

[DORIVA] GUIDONI Dorival
Born: Landeara, Brazil, 28 May 1972
Height: 5'9" **Weight:** 11.7
International Honours: Brazil: 12
Both Juninho and Doriva played in the same Brazil squad that reached and lost the 1998 World Cup final, and Juninho proved to be a key factor in Middlesbrough signing the Brazilian international in a deal that brought him to the Riverside until, at least, the end of the season. He arrived just before the January transfer window closed and then grabbed the opportunity to resurrect his career, making an impressive debut in a 3-0 Riverside win over relegation-bound West Bromwich Albion, when he deputised in midfield for the injured George Boateng.
Middlesbrough (Loaned from Celta Vigo, Spain, ex Sao Paulo, Piracicaba, Atletico Mineiro, Oporto, Sampdoria, on 3/2/2003) PL 3+2

[DOUDOU] MBOMBO Aziana Ebele
Born: Kinshasha, Zaire, 11 September 1980
Height: 5'5" **Weight:** 9.11
This quick wide-right midfielder did not make the same impact for Queen's Park Rangers last term as he had in his first season at Loftus Road. Although a regular for the club's reserve team, his first-team appearances were mainly from the substitutes' bench and he only started three games.
Queens Park R (Free from AS Monaco, France on 17/8/2001) FL 23+23/3 FLC 1+1 FAC 1 Others 0+2

DOUGHTY Matthew (Matt) Liam
Born: Warrington, 2 November 1981
Height: 5'8" **Weight:** 10.8
Matt continued as Rochdale's regular left back and battled hard as the club's only real left-sided player for much of the 2002-03 season. Indeed, he was ever-present until missing the Coventry FA Cup tie in February. He regained his place when his young replacement Stephen Hill was injured and was able to use his enthusiasm for getting forward as Dale switched to a system using wing backs, while he also played some games in midfield.
Chester C (Trainee) FL 19+14/1 FLC 2 FAC 2
Rochdale (Free on 20/7/2001) FL 71+6/1 FLC 1+1 FAC 7/1 Others 5

DOUGHTY Philip (Phil)
Born: Kirkham, 6 September 1986
Height: 6'2" **Weight:** 13.2
A promising young defender who was still at school last season, Philip made his senior debut as a late substitute for Blackpool in the FA Cup second round tie against Torquay, shortly after his 16th birthday. He thus became the youngest player to appear for the club in the competition. Philip was a regular for the Seasiders' youth team during the campaign and was offered a scholarship contract in the summer.
Blackpool (Associated Schoolboy) FAC 0+1

DOUGLAS Jonathan
Born: Monaghan, 22 November 1981
Height: 5'10" **Weight:** 12.12
International Honours: RoI: U21-1; Yth
After recovering from a serious knee injury, Jonathan eventually made his full debut for Blackburn Rovers in the FA Cup fourth round tie against Sunderland last term when he featured at right back. He subsequently joined Chesterfield for the

crucial end-of-season run-in where he proved to be strong, quick, two-footed and able to play in any defensive role, as well as in midfield. He went on to score the goal that earned a point at Blackpool on the last day of the season, thus helping the Spireites to preserve their Division Two status.

Blackburn Rov *(From trainee on 10/2/2000)* *PL 0+1 FLC 0+2 FAC 1+4*
Chesterfield *(Loaned on 26/3/2003) FL 7/1*

DOUGLAS Stuart Anthony
Born: Enfield, 9 April 1978
Height: 5'9" **Weight:** 11.5
A bustling striker whose persistence inside the box brought him a steady supply of goals for Boston United last term. His busy style caused plenty of problems for opposing defenders and he was often introduced from the subs' bench with great effect. Stuart signed on a non-contract basis in August and his subsequent form earned him short-term deals before he was rewarded in February when given a contract until the summer of 2004.

Luton T *(From trainee on 2/5/1996) FL 104+42/18 FLC 11+3/3 FAC 8+2/2 Others +1*
Oxford U *(Loaned on 23/10/2001) FL 1+3*
Rushden & Diamonds *(Loaned on 8/1/2002) FL 4+5*
Boston U *(Free on 20/8/2002) FL 14+15/7 LC 1 FAC 0+1 Others 0+1*

DOUGLIN Troy Alexander
Born: Coventry, 7 May 1982
Height: 6'0" **Weight:** 11.8
After showing immense potential as a youngster it was a great disappointment that this central defender's progress seemed to stall. Unable to break into the starting line-up at Torquay, it became clear that there would be no new contract in the summer and so Troy left early in the new year by mutual consent.

Torquay U *(From trainee on 4/7/2000) FL 45 FLC 4 FAC 1 Others 1+1*

DOVE Craig
Born: Hartlepool, 6 August 1983
Height: 5'8" **Weight:** 11.6
International Honours: E: Yth
Craig, an England U19 midfielder, travelled the short distance from Hartlepool to sign for Middlesbrough. He did not have long to wait to make his first senior appearance as he featured as a playing substitute in both the club's Worthington Cup games. His first taste of senior football came when he replaced Joel Whelan for the final six minutes of

the Worthington Cup success at Brentford. His second outing lasted a little longer, 12 minutes to be exact, when he replaced Robbie Stockdale in the 3-1 defeat at Ipswich Town.

Middlesbrough *(From trainee on 7/7/2000) FLC 0+2*

DOWNER Simon
Born: Romford, 19 October 1981
Height: 5'11" **Weight:** 12.0
Simon returned to action for Leyton Orient last February after spending some 18 months out of action with a knee injury. A ball-playing centre half, he soon showed he had lost none of his pace and timing in the tackle. After a short run in the side he was rested towards the end of the campaign, but he will be looking to gain a regular first-team spot in 2003-04.

Leyton Orient *(From trainee on 4/10/1999) FL 63+13 FLC 3+2 FAC 3+1 Others 5*

DOWNING Stewart
Born: Middlesbrough, 22 July 1984
Height: 5'11" **Weight:** 10.6
International Honours: E: Yth
Local lad Stewart, a left-sided midfielder, did not have many first-team starts for Middlesbrough last season, but he took full advantage of the few chances that came his way. His first taste of action was when he substituted Dean Windass at half time at Griffin Park as Boro' eased past Second Division Brentford in the Worthington Cup winning 4-1, and Stewart scored his first senior goal for the club. He gained valuable first-team experience, again from the bench, in the penultimate game, a 5-1 demolition of Tottenham Hotspur and his final appearance was at the Reebok Stadium. Stewart was selected for the England U19 squad for the UEFA championships in the summer.

Middlesbrough *(From trainee on 6/9/2001) PL 2+3 FLC 0+1/1*

DOYLE Daire Michael
Born: Dublin, 18 October 1980
Height: 5'11" **Weight:** 11.12
A midfielder who never forced his way into the Kidderminster first team on a regular basis last season, Daire managed only five senior appearances and four of those were as a substitute. In January he was loaned out to Conference side Nuneaton Borough and a month later he was released to join them on a permanent basis.

Coventry C *(Signed from Cherry Orchard on 15/9/1998)*

Kidderminster Hrs *(Free on 12/1/2001) FL 14+7 FLC 0+2 FAC 0+1*

DOYLEY Lloyd Collin
Born: Whitechapel, 1 December 1982
Height: 6'0" **Weight:** 11.10
Watford's home-grown right back began the 2002-03 season in the first team and made an excellent impression as a very steady defender. However, a change of formation cost him his place, and instead he had the chance to consolidate in the reserves after what had been a rapid rise from the youth team to the first-team squad. Lloyd had further opportunities at the end of the campaign, and particularly impressed with his improved passing.

Watford *(From trainee on 8/3/2001) P/FL 32+10 FLC 2 FAC 0+1*

DRURY Adam James
Born: Cambridge, 29 August 1978
Height: 5'10" **Weight:** 11.8
Rated by many as one of the best left backs outside of the Premiership, Adam was a virtual ever-present in the Norwich City line-up in 2002-03. He showed tremendous consistency, based on solid defensive techniques, such as well-timed tackling and excellent covering. In addition he showed a greater willingness to get forward as demonstrated by his first goals for the club. Adam was occasionally used as one of three centre backs and he showed himself to be well equipped to handle that role. He was voted 'Player of the Season' by the Canaries' supporters.

Peterborough U *(From trainee on 3/7/1996) FL 138+10/2 FLC 8 FAC 9 Others 10+1*
Norwich C *(£275,000 on 21/3/2001) FL 86/2 FLC 2 FAC 4 Others 3*

DRYSDALE Leon Anthony
Born: Walsall, 3 February 1981
Height: 5'9" **Weight:** 11.6
Leon is a right-sided defender whose main strength is his speed when attacking down the flanks. A fully committed player, he lost out last term as Shrewsbury boss Kevin Ratcliffe searched for the most effective defensive formation and made just 11 starts in Third Division fixtures. His first-ever league goal was worth waiting for: a marvellous individual effort leaving three or four defenders in his wake in the 2-2 draw at Oxford in October. Out of contract, it remains to be seen if new manager Jimmy Quinn will include Leon in his plans.

Shrewsbury T *(From trainee on 2/7/1999) FL 51+14/1 FLC 2+1 FAC 3+2 Others 2+1*

DUBERRY Michael Wayne
Born: Enfield, 14 October 1975
Height: 6'1" **Weight:** 13.6
Club Honours: FLC '98; ECWC '98; ESC '98
International Honours: E: U21-5
Michael was again on the fringes of the first-team squad at Leeds last term and made only a handful of appearances. His first full game was in an injury-ravaged defence in the second leg of the UEFA Cup tie with Hapoel Tel Aviv in November, but after a run of five games he was again out of the picture and returned to a place on the bench. Michael is an experienced central defender whose height and strength make him a formidable opponent.
Chelsea (From trainee on 7/6/1993) PL 77+9/1 FLC 8 FAC 12/2 Others 9
Bournemouth (Loaned on 29/9/1995) FL 7 Others 1
Leeds U (£4,000,000 + on 29/7/1999) PL 31+4/1 FLC 0+4 FAC 2+2 Others 9+1

DUBLIN Dion
Born: Leicester, 22 April 1969
Height: 6'1" **Weight:** 12.4
Club Honours: Div 3 '91
International Honours: E: 4
Dion was transformed from the forgotten man to linchpin of the side as he re-established himself as a first choice striker for Aston Villa last term. He did not even make the bench for the opening five Premiership matches, then went on as a second half substitute against Birmingham before his stunning introduction in Villa's next match against Everton, when he scored the late winner after being on the pitch for just four minutes. That was followed by a brace to dispatch Luton from the Worthington Cup and catapult Dion to the top of Villa's scoring chart. The powerful target man scored his 100th Premiership goal in November in the home fixture against West Ham. Even while he was out of the side, he always maintained a thoroughly professional approach.
Norwich C (Free from Oakham U on 24/3/1988)
Cambridge U (Free on 2/8/1988) FL 133+23/52 FLC 8+2/5 FAC 21/10 Others 14+1/5
Manchester U (£1,000,000 on 7/8/1992) PL 4+8/2 FLC 1+1/1 FAC 1+1 Others 0+1
Coventry C (£2,000,000 on 9/9/1994) PL 144+1/61 FLC 11+2/4 FAC 13/7
Aston Villa (£5,750,000 on 6/11/1998) PL 108+24/45 FLC 10+1/8 FAC 5+2/1 Others 10+2/2
Millwall (Loaned on 28/3/2002) FL 5/2 Others 2/1

DUCROS Andrew (Andy) John
Born: Evesham, 16 September 1977
Height: 5'4" **Weight:** 10.6
International Honours: E: Sch
Often described as a 'luxury player' Andy has the potential to be one of the top players in the Third Division, but successive Kidderminster managers have struggled to find a way to fit him into the team. He was restricted to just three appearances in the 2002-03 season before being loaned out to Nuneaton in the autumn. In February he was released and signed for Conference club Burton Albion.
Coventry C (From trainee on 16/9/1994) PL 2+6 FLC 0+1(Free to Nuneaton Borough on 6/8/99)
Kidderminster Hrs (£100,000 on 24/7/2000) FL 38+12/4 FLC 2 FAC 3+1

DUDEK Jerzy
Born: Rybnik, Poland, 23 March 1973
Height: 6'2" **Weight:** 12.10
Club Honours: FLC '03
International Honours: Poland: 26
After establishing his credentials as the Premiership's safest 'keeper in his debut season for Liverpool, Jerzy had a harder time for the Reds last term. The rot started with a couple of errors in November and his loss of confidence led to him being replaced by Chris Kirkland. However, a cruciate injury ended Kirkland's season in January and Jerzy returned to the side. He was in particularly fine form in the Worthington Cup final against Manchester United in March when a series of outstanding second-half saves preserved Liverpool's fragile 1-0 lead intact and paved the way for the Reds' victory. There was no argument with his being named his 'Man of the Match' award.
Liverpool (£4,850,000 from Feyenoord, Holland, ex GKS Tychy, Sokol Tychy, on 31/8/2001) PL 65 FLC 2 FAC 3+1 Others 24

DUDFIELD Lawrence (Lawrie) George
Born: Southwark, 7 May 1980
Height: 6'1" **Weight:** 13.9
Lawrie endured a difficult second season with Hull after a notably successful first term. Having dropped out of the starting line-up during the first few weeks of Jan Molby's reign, a niggling knee injury required surgery. The operation coincided with the arrival of new boss Peter Taylor – the manager who sold Lawrie to Hull when in charge of Leicester. The tall striker went out on loan to Northampton, where he scored once in ten appearances.
Leicester C (Signed from Kettering T on 6/6/1997) PL 0+2
Lincoln C (Loaned on 15/9/2000) FL 2+1
Chesterfield (Loaned on 14/12/2000) FL 4+10/3 Others 3+1/1
Hull C (£210,000 on 2/7/2001) FL 39+20/13 FLC 2 FAC 2/2 Others 3
Northampton T (Signed on 14/3/2003) FL 8+2/1

DUFF Damien Anthony
Born: Dublin, Ireland, 2 March 1979
Height: 5'10" **Weight:** 12.0
Club Honours: FLC '02
International Honours: RoI: 36; B-1; Yth; Sch
After some fine performances for the Republic of Ireland in the 2002 World Cup finals, Damien had a somewhat frustrating time at Blackburn last season when he was hampered by recurring hamstring problems. As a result he was unable to establish a rhythm to his play until the final weeks of the campaign, and his goal-scoring record then improved dramatically. At his best he is one of the most exciting attacking players in the Premiership, able to beat any number of opponents on mazy runs, perceptive in his play and able to create with precise crosses.
Blackburn Rov (Signed from Lourdes Celtic on 5/3/1996) P/FL 157+27/27 FLC 16+1/5 FAC 13+5/2 Others 4/1

DUFF Michael James
Born: Belfast, 11 January 1978
Height: 6'1" **Weight:** 11.8
Club Honours: FAT '98; NC '99
International Honours: NI: 2
Michael enjoyed another highly consistent season at Cheltenham and was in the running for all the club's 'Player of the Season' awards. It was a difficult campaign for the Robins but Michael worked alongside a series of central defensive partners, including his younger brother Shane, and showed no signs of finding the step up to Division Two at all difficult. He won a second Northern Ireland cap against Cyprus in August 2002 and was named on the bench for the Euro 2004 qualifiers against Armenia and Greece.
Cheltenham T (From trainee on 17/8/1996) FL 159/12 FLC 5 FAC 12 Others 9

DUFF Shane Joseph
Born: Wroughton, 2 April 1982
Height: 6'1" **Weight:** 12.10
International Honours: NI: U21-1
After a wait of nearly three years, Shane finally made his bow in senior football

Dion Dublin

when coming off the bench for Cheltenham at Plymouth on New Year's Day. A spate of injuries allowed him to make his full debut at Cardiff soon afterwards and he went on to establish himself in the centre of defence alongside his brother Michael. A series of impressive performances then earned call-ups to the Northern Ireland U21 squad for the matches in Armenia and at home to Finland. Shane is also a talented cricketer and scored the winning run for Shipton-under-Wychwood to clinch the 2002 National Village Knockout final at Lord's. However, he has now committed himself to football with the Robins after signing a new two-year contract at the end of the season.

Cheltenham T (From juniors on 20/10/2002) FL 15+3

DUFFIELD Peter

Born: Middlesbrough, 4 February 1969
Height: 5'6" **Weight:** 10.4
This neat and skilful striker made an outstanding start to the 2002-03 season netting in the opening six games for York City. He continued to score regularly, taking his tally to 15 in league and cup games before moving on to Boston United in January. Surprisingly he struggled to find the net in his first few games for the Pilgrims but after two months without a goal he responded with a double strike after coming on as a substitute against Wrexham.

Middlesbrough (From apprentice on 4/11/1986)
Sheffield U (Free on 20/8/1987) FL 34+24/14 FLC 2+5/2 FAC 6+2/1 Others 3+2/3
Halifax T (Loaned on 7/3/1988) FL 12/6 Others 1
Rotherham U (Loaned on 7/3/1991) FL 17/4
Blackpool (Loaned on 23/7/1992) FL 3+2/1 FLC 0+1
Crewe Alex (Loaned on 15/1/1993) FL 0+2 FAC 0+1
Stockport Co (Loaned on 19/3/1993) FL 6+1/4 Others 2+1
Hamilton Ac (Signed on 24/9/1993) SL 69+3/39 SLC 2/1 SC 2 Others 3/3
Airdrie (Signed on 21/7/1995) SL 19+5/6 SLC 2+2/2 SC 3/3 Others 1
Raith Rov (Signed on 2/3/1996) SL 37+14/11 SLC 2+1/3 SC 2 Others 1+1
Morton (Signed on 8/11/1997) SL 25/9 SLC 1 SC 1
Falkirk (Signed on 27/8/1998) SL 10+7/3
Darlington (Signed on 15/1/1999) FL 31+16/14 FLC 0+2 FAC 2/1 Others 3
York C (Free on 3/7/2000) FL 41+4/19 FLC 2 FAC 2+1/2
Boston U (Free on 30/1/2003) FL 12+4/4

DUFFY Lee Alan

Born: Oldham, 24 July 1982
Height: 5'7" **Weight:** 10.7
Lee had previously understudied Wayne Evans as Rochdale's right back, but early in the 2002-03 season he was promoted to the first team in a midfield role as a replacement for the injured Chris Beech. He later appeared at right back when Evans was injured and also had a couple of spells at right wing back when Dale switched to playing 3-5-2, thus enabling him to make good use of his all-action style.

Rochdale (From trainee on 6/9/2001) FL 20+8 FLC 1 FAC 3 Others 2+1

DUFFY Robert James

Born: Swansea, 2 December 1982
Height: 6'1" **Weight:** 12.6
Club Honours: Div 3 '03
This young Welsh striker is highly rated by Rushden & Diamonds after coming through the youth ranks with a prolific strike-rate. Last season all three of Robert's goals came in the FA Cup first-round ties against old rivals Kidderminster Harriers. Otherwise he was mainly restricted to a substitutes' role as manager Brian Talbot stuck with Onandi Lowe and Duane Darby up front.

Rushden & Diamonds (From juniors on 7/7/2000) FL 4+16/1 FLC 0+1 FAC 3+1/3 Others 1

DUGARRY Christophe

Born: Bordeaux, France, 24 March 1972
Height: 6'2" **Weight:** 12.4
International Honours: France: 55
Christophe arrived at St Andrew's during the transfer window and quickly became the idol of the Birmingham City fans following his debut at Blackburn, indeed manager Steve Bruce even described him as the club's best-ever player. His poise, control and vision added a missing ingredient to the team and he was a major factor in keeping the Blues up. He scored five goals in four games over Easter including a brilliant back-heeled flick at Charlton. Christophe's immense talents meant that he was sometimes singled out for rough treatment, but he never reacted and at the end of the season he signed a permanent deal that will keep him at the club until June 2005.

Birmingham C (Loaned from Bordeaux, France, ex Bordeaux, AC Milan, Barcelona, Marseilles, on 3/1/2003) PL 16/5

DUGUID Karl Anthony

Born: Letchworth, 21 March 1978
Height: 5'11" **Weight:** 11.7

Karl had the misfortune to suffer medial ligament damage during the opening week of the 2002-03 season playing for Colchester at Tranmere. The right wing back or right winger finally made his return at Luton Town in December, and responded by scoring from a free kick to notch a vital 2-1 win for the U's. Karl missed just one more game, due to suspension, and formed a useful partnership with Sam Stockley down the right flank. He has made more appearances for Colchester than any other player on the current staff.

Colchester U (From trainee on 16/7/1996) FL 182+58/35 FLC 6+3 FAC 7+3/2 Others 3+5

DUKE David

Born: Inverness, 7 November 1978
Height: 5'10" **Weight:** 11.3
This predominantly right-footed player showed solid form in the 2002-03 season when he again won a regular place in the Swindon Town line-up. A consistent performer who only missed two games he won awards from the fans for his consistency and as 'Most Improved Player'. Although extremely versatile he was mainly used as a left wing back from where his attacking style and dangerous crosses were most effective. He also worked hard on the defensive side of his game, best shown in the home draw with Bristol City in March when he managed to keep a tight reign on Scott Murray.

Sunderland (Free from Redby CA on 3/7/1997)
Swindon T (Free on 10/8/2000) FL 104+14/5 FLC 7 FAC 6+2 Others 5+1

DUNBAVIN Ian Stuart

Born: Huyton, 27 May 1980
Height: 6'2" **Weight:** 13.0
This young Shrewsbury 'keeper was first choice at Gay Meadow until the return of Mark Cartwright from the USA in February. His early season form was outstanding, especially in the games at Bury, when he saved a spot-kick, Scunthorpe and Torquay. Ian made a total of 33 league appearances and gained tremendous experience in the club's fine FA Cup run. Woefully protected by the defenders in front of him for much of the time, he had a hard season but although clean sheets were hard to come by he did manage five.

Liverpool (From trainee on 26/11/1998)
Shrewsbury T (Free on 17/1/2000) FL 91+5 FLC 3 FAC 6 Others 7

DUNCAN Andrew (Andy)

Born: Hexham, 20 October 1977
Height: 5'11" **Weight:** 13.0

International Honours: E: Sch
This versatile defender started last season as a first choice for Cambridge United. Solid and reliable, he was one of the more consistent players in the squad. However, he was sidelined by a groin injury in March and this kept him out for the remainder of the campaign.
Manchester U (From trainee on 10/7/1996)
Cambridge U (£20,000 on 9/1/1998) FL 56+7/3 FLC 10+1/1 FAC 12 Others 15

DUNFIELD Terence (Terry)
Born: Canada, 20 February 1982
Height: 5'10" **Weight:** 11.6
International Honours: E: Yth; Canada: Yth
This attacking midfielder played for Manchester City in a pre-season game at Bury and impressed Shakers boss Andy Preece so much that he signed the 20-year-old on loan in August. Terry made a 'Man of the Match' debut in a 3-2 win against Swansea and proceeded to display excellent form over the next two months, showing great vision and the ability to make a pinpoint pass from central midfield. He dislocated his shoulder after falling heavily in a Worthington Cup

game at Fulham though and returned to Maine Road for recuperation. In December he returned to Bury permanently, signing a two-and-a-half-year deal, but after dislocating his shoulder for a second time at Kidderminster Terry struggled to maintain his early consistency and was unable to hold down a starting place by the end of the season.
Manchester C (From trainee on 5/5/1999) PL 0+1
Bury (Loaned on 16/8/2002) FL 15/2 FLC 3
Bury (Free on 13/12/2002) FL 13+1 Others 1/1

DUNN David John Ian
Born: Blackburn, 27 December 1979
Height: 5'10" **Weight:** 12.3
Club Honours: FLC '02
International Honours: E: 1; U21-9; Yth
David had a somewhat frustrating season with Blackburn last term, when he was affected by the constant need to reshuffle the middle line and also by a series of hamstring and calf injuries. His versatility proved an advantage as he featured in wide positions on both flanks and also in his preferred central midfield role. His

strengths are his dribbling, tricks on the ball and strong shooting, although his overall game would improve if he developed greater defensive capabilities. David won his first full cap for England when coming on as a second half substitute in the friendly against Portugal last September. However, at the time of writing he appeared the subject of much transfer speculation, indicating a possible departure from Ewood Park might be on the cards.
Blackburn Rov (From trainee on 30/9/1997)
P/FL 120+16/30 FLC 14+3/5 FAC 11+2/3
Others 3+1

DUNNE Alan James
Born: Dublin, 23 August 1982
Height: 5'10" **Weight:** 12.0
Alan fractured his ankle in July 2002 during pre-season training, but recovered well and made a number of reserve-team appearances for Millwall in his customary right-back spot. After eventually recovering he received a handful of first-team outings and acquitted himself well, gaining the 'Man of the Match' award against Reading. Alan is a promising defender who is strong in the challenge

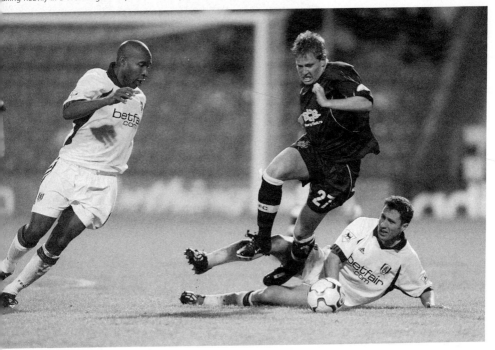

Terry Dunfield (centre)

and has a good engine, which enables him to support the attack.
Millwall (From trainee on 17/3/2000) FL 3+2

DUNNE Richard Patrick
Born: Dublin, 21 September 1979
Height: 6'1'' **Weight:** 14.0
Club Honours: FAYC '98; Div 1 '02
International Honours: RoI: 17; B-1; U21-4; Yth (UEFA-U18 '98); Sch
Richard had an in and out season for Manchester City last term. It was not until late October that he received much of a chance, but once in the team his displays warranted that he kept his place. In fact he became something of a lucky charm for the next three months with the Blues only losing in three of the 15 Premiership games he played in over that period. An experienced right back or defender, he lost his place in February before returning for the last few games. Richard also continued to represent the Republic of Ireland during the campaign.
Everton (From trainee on 8/10/1996) PL 53+7 FLC 4 FAC 8
Manchester C (£3,000,000 on 20/10/2000) P/FL 89+4/1 FLC 4 FAC 6

DUNNING Darren
Born: Scarborough, 8 January 1981
Height: 5'6" **Weight:** 11.12
This promising young Blackburn Rovers midfielder had a spell on loan at Torquay in the autumn. Usually employed in a wide-left midfield role he adapted quickly to Third Division life and looked a tidy and competent all-round player. In January he joined Macclesfield Town in a three-month loan deal and featured regularly. He made a great impression with his telling short-passing game, showed he could be combative when necessary and also proved useful at holding the ball up when required.
Blackburn Rov (From trainee on 25/2/1999) FL 1 FLC 2/1 FAC 1
Bristol C (Loaned on 12/8/2000) FL 9
Rochdale (Loaned on 29/11/2001) FL 4+1
Blackpool (Loaned on 28/3/2002) FL 5
Torquay U (Loaned on 7/11/2002) FL 4+3/1 FAC 1
Macclesfield T (Loaned on 16/1/2003) FL 17

DURKAN Keiron John
Born: Chester, 1 December 1973
Height: 5'11" **Weight:** 12.10
Club Honours: WC '95
International Honours: RoI: U21-3
This experienced winger was again out of favour at Rochdale last term and in

January he moved on to join Swansea City. Unfortunately he suffered an achilles injury midway through his first start for the Swans, sidelining him for a couple of games. When he returned to fitness, his crossing ability from the flanks was soon evident, but he was out of action once more with a recurrence of a back injury, and then an ankle problem put him out for the remainder of the campaign.
Wrexham (From trainee on 16/7/1992) FL 43+7/3 FLC 3+1 FAC 4+2/2 Others 15/1
Stockport Co (£95,000 on 16/2/1996) FL 52+12/4 FLC 10+1 FAC 4/3 Others 4+2
Macclesfield T (£15,000 on 25/3/1998) FL 92+11/13 FLC 4+3 FAC 2+3 Others 1+1
York C (Loaned on 5/10/2000) FL 7

Rochdale (Free on 4/7/2001) FL 16+14/1 FLC 2 FAC 3 Others 1
Swansea C (Free on 10/1/2003) FL 4+2

DURNIN John Paul
Born: Bootle, 18 August 1965
Height: 5'10" **Weight:** 12.3
This experienced midfield player was originally taken on by Port Vale to coach the U17s, only being called upon to play in an emergency. However, injuries dictated that he was involved from the off and he ended up playing in around half of the club's games. He used his experience well to dictate the pace of some games and held the ball up to bring other players into the game. John scored

Richard Dunne

ieron Dyer

one goal last season, the winner at Mansfield in what was a crucial relegation battle.

Liverpool *(Free from Waterloo Dock on 29/3/1986) FLC 1+1*
West Bromwich A *(Loaned on 20/10/1988) FL 5/2*
Oxford U *(£225,000 on 10/2/1989) FL 140+21/44 FLC 7/1 FAC 7/1 Others 4+1/1*
Portsmouth *(£200,000 on 15/7/1993) FL 118+63/31 FLC 14+2/2 FAC 5+2 Others 4+2*
Blackpool *(Loaned on 1/11/1999) FL 4+1/1 FAC 1/1*
Carlisle U *(Free on 3/12/1999) FL 20+2/2 Others 1*
Kidderminster Hrs *(Free on 13/10/2000) FL 28+3/9 FAC 1 (Released during 2001 close season)*
Port Vale *(Free from Rhyl on 14/12/2001) FL 43+4/2 FAC 1 Others 1+1*

DUXBURY Lee Edward
Born: Keighley, 7 October 1969
Height: 5'10" **Weight:** 11.13
This popular Oldham Athletic midfielder and club captain was occasionally used as an emergency centre half during the 2002-03 campaign and performed admirably. In October he was outstanding at Swindon, scoring the winner and steering ten-man Latics to an unlikely victory from the heart of defence. With his 15-year career coming towards an end, Lee has been given coaching responsibilities for the Boundary Park youth team.
Bradford C *(From trainee on 4/7/1988) FL 204+5/25 FLC 18+1/3 FAC 11 Others 13*
Rochdale *(Loaned on 18/1/1990) FL 9+1 FAC 1*
Huddersfield T *(£250,000 on 23/12/1994) FL 29/2 FLC 1 Others 3*
Bradford C *(£135,000 on 15/11/1995) FL 63/7 FLC 2 FAC 5 Others 3*
Oldham Ath *(£350,000 on 7/3/1997) FL 222+26/32 FLC 12/1 FAC 16+2/5 Others 5+1/1*

DYCHE Sean Mark
Born: Kettering, 28 June 1971
Height: 6'0" **Weight:** 13.10
Club Honours: Div 2 '01
Sean was Ray Lewington's first signing for Watford when he arrived from Millwall during the summer of 2002. He proved a sound acquisition at centre half, and by the end of the campaign had passed a career total of 350 Football League appearances. Foot and ankle injuries cost him three months out of action in the middle of the season, but he returned to play a part in the closing stages. A natural leader on the pitch, he generally

channelled his enthusiasm in a positive direction.
Nottingham F *(From trainee on 20/5/1989)*
Chesterfield *(Free on 1/2/1990) FL 219+12/8 FLC 9 FAC 13/1 Others 16*
Bristol C *(£350,000 on 11/7/1997) FL 14+3 FLC 2+1*
Luton T *(Loaned on 4/1/1999) FL 14/1 Others 1*
Millwall *(£150,000 on 5/7/1999) FL 69/3 FLC 2+1 FAC 4*
Watford *(Free on 12/7/2002) FL 23+1 FLC 1*

DYER Bruce Antonio
Born: Ilford, 13 April 1975
Height: 6'0" **Weight:** 11.3
International Honours: E: U21-11
Bruce was again top scorer for Barnsley last season and it was his goals that, more than anything, kept the Reds in the Second Division. He coupled his strong running and high work rate with an eye for goal, and netted a number of spectacular efforts, notably against Peterborough, Oldham and Wycombe. During the second half of the season he became penalty taker and showed himself to be very capable in this capacity. Bruce was voted 'Player of the Season' by the club's supporters for the second successive year. He was out of contract in the summer and his future was uncertain at the time of writing.
Watford *(From trainee on 19/4/1993) FL 29+2/6 FLC 4/2 FAC 1 Others 2/1*
Crystal Palace *(£1,100,000 on 10/3/1994) F/PL 95+40/37 FLC 9+5/1 FAC 7+3/6 Others 3+2*
Barnsley *(£700,000 on 23/10/1998) FL 149+33/59 FLC 11+1/4 FAC 5+2/3 Others 2+1/3*

DYER Kieron Courtney
Born: Ipswich, 29 December 1978
Height: 5'7'' **Weight:** 9.7
International Honours: E: 16; B-2; U21-11; Yth
After three substitute appearances in England's 2002 World Cup campaign, Kieron enjoyed another fine campaign in Newcastle's midfield last term, repeatedly surging forward with the ball under control at pace to supplement his attack. He scored United's first goal of the season at Sarajevo in the Champions' League qualifier, and netted again in the home leg. His finest match came at Leeds where he crowned a superb performance with a brace of goals. Blessed with terrific stamina his all-action game contributed significantly to Newcastle's successful season, recognised by his selection for the PFA Premiership team of the season. He

also captained his club in the absence of Alan Shearer and Gary Speed. England continue to try him in the problematic left midfield position, but he seems better suited to a more central role behind the main strikers, where his pace and control have more impact.
Ipswich T *(From trainee on 3/1/1997) FL 79+12/9 FLC 11/1 FAC 5 Others 5+1/2*
Newcastle U *(£6,000,000 on 16/7/1999) PL 100+9/13 FLC 5+1/3 FAC 8+1/1 Others 14+1/2*

DYER Lloyd
Born: Birmingham, 13 September 1982
Height: 5'10" **Weight:** 11.4
An enthusiastic left wing back with a long, raking stride, Lloyd made just one senior appearance for West Bromwich Albion during the season, taking over from Neil Clement in the 3-1 Worthington Cup defeat at Wigan in October. Still only 21 years of age, he has a lot to offer and Baggies' manager Gary Megson rates him very highly at the Hawthorns.
West Bromwich A *(Signed from Aston Villa juniors on 9/7/2001) FLC 1*

DYKES Daren
Born: Aylesbury, 28 April 1981
Height: 5'11" **Weight:** 12.6
This young attacking midfielder impressed enough during a pre-season trial to be offered a one-year deal by Swindon Town. He was unlucky not to score in his first league start for the Robins when he hit the bar with a spectacular 25-yard volley, before a foot injury brought an end to his debut. He also had a spell on loan at Lincoln, but never really got a chance to shine and after a couple of starts returned to the County Ground.
Swindon T *(Free from Buckingham T on 1/8/2002) FL 1+1 FLC 0+1 Others 1+1*
Lincoln C *(Loaned on 20/12/2002) FL 2+1*

DYSON Jonathan (Jon) Paul
Born: Mirfield, 18 December 1971
Height: 6'1" **Weight:** 12.12
Although released by Huddersfield at the end of the 2001-02 season, this long serving defender rejoined the Terriers on three-month contract in early August to provide extra cover for an injury-depleted squad. Jon went on to appear in a handful of first-team games, displaying a assured approach and some strong tackling. He was released again in mid-January and linked up with Conference outfit Nuneaton Borough.
Huddersfield T *(From juniors on 29/12/1990) FL 184+32/9 FLC 19+4 FAC 11 Others 7+4*

E

EADEN Nicholas (Nicky) Jeremy

Born: Sheffield, 12 December 1972
Height: 5'9" **Weight:** 12.8
Club Honours: Div 2 '03

Very much the bargain buy of the season, Nicky was an ever-present following his move to Wigan Athletic in September, filling the problem position of right back with style. A steady if unspectacular performer, he worked the flank unselfishly and delivered pinpoint crosses, hardly wasting a ball. Sound in defence, he was vital to the club's success in winning the Second Division championship. He celebrated his 400th league appearance during a season which also saw him gain deserved recognition with selection in the PFA Division Two team.
Barnsley (From juniors on 4/6/1991) F/PL 281+12/10 FLC 18+3/3 FAC 20 Others 4+1
Birmingham C (Free on 6/7/2000) FL 68+6/3 FLC 13/1 FAC 1 Others 1+1/1
Wigan Ath (Signed on 20/9/2002) FL 37 FLC 2 FAC 3 Others 1

EARNSHAW Robert

Born: Zambia, 6 April 1981
Height: 5'8" **Weight:** 10.10
International Honours: W: 4; U21-10; Yth

Robert began the season among the substitutes with Andy Campbell starting ahead of him, a situation that lasted for six matches. He made his first start of the campaign in the Worthington Cup tie at Boston United and scored three before going on to finish up with 35 goals in all competitions. He thus broke two long-standing club records: his tally of 31 league goals beat Stan Richards' total of 30 set in 1946-47 and his total of 35 in all competitions broke Hughie Ferguson's record of 32 set in 1926-27. Robert featured again for Wales during the campaign and was also voted into the PFA Second Division team of the season.
Cardiff C (From trainee on 4/8/1998) FL 83+35/63 FLC 3+2/4 FAC 10+2/9 Others 4+1/1
Greenock Morton (Loaned on 20/1/2000) SL 2/2 SC 1

EASTER Jermaine Maurice

Born: Cardiff, 15 January 1982
Height: 5'8" **Weight:** 12.4
International Honours: W: Yth

Jermaine is a young striker with an impressive turn of speed. His second full

season at Hartlepool saw him finish as the reserves top goal-scorer, but he will be disappointed not to have established himself in the first team. Incredibly he has yet to start a first-team game despite having made almost 30 appearances as substitute. However manager Mike Newell assured Jermaine that his promise had been recognised, and he was rewarded with a new two-year contract.
Wolverhampton W (From trainee on 6/7/2000)
Hartlepool U (Free on 17/3/2001) FL 0+24/2 Others 0+3

Nicky Eaden

EASTON Clint Jude
Born: Barking, 1 October 1977
Height: 5'11" **Weight:** 10.8
Club Honours: Div 2 '98
International Honours: E: Yth
This midfielder enhanced his reputation during the 2002-03 season with some excellent performances for Norwich City, playing both wide on the left and also in a more central role. Clint is a creative player, always looking for the telling pass or cross into the penalty area, and on occasions he also displayed the battling qualities necessary to be classed as an all-round midfield player. A lively character with an eye for goal, he is still young enough to become an established member of the Canaries' midfield line-up.
Watford (From trainee on 5/7/1996) P/FL 50+14/1 FLC 4+4/1 FAC 3+1 Others 3
Norwich C (£200,000 on 19/6/2001) FL 33+7/3 FLC 1 FAC 0+2 Others 3

EATON Adam Paul
Born: Wigan, 2 May 1980
Height: 5'11" **Weight:** 11.2
Club Honours: FAYC '98
Adam barely featured at Preston last term, making just one start at Aston Villa in the Worthington Cup before being loaned to Mansfield in December. He performed excellently for the Stags on his debut against Blackpool and was quickly recalled to Deepdale to cover for injuries. However, he appeared just once for North End, coming on as a late substitute at Ipswich, before returning to Field Mill in a deal that was subsequently made permanent in February. He made the left-back position his own, and even occasionally covered in the centre of the defence, before a hernia problem ended his season early.
Everton (From trainee on 2/6/1997)
Preston NE (Free on 29/6/1999) FL 7+7 FLC 2 FAC 1 Others 0+1
Mansfield T (Loaned on 10/12/2002) FL 6
Mansfield T (Signed on 4/2/2003) FL 14

EATON David Franklin
Born: Liverpool, 30 September 1981
Height: 6'1" **Weight:** 12.10
After being released by Everton in the 2002 close season, David initially signed non-contract forms for Macclesfield and was then given a three-month contract, which was later extended to the end of the 2002-03 campaign. He made a dream start to his senior career, scoring with his first touch after coming on from the substitutes' bench in the away win at Kidderminster in October and went on to

hit four more goals. A tall striker, David has good pace and runs at defenders effectively but there are times when he needs to be a little stronger. However, his opportunities were limited towards the end of the season and he was released in the summer.
Everton (From trainee on 4/7/2001)
Macclesfield T (Free on 9/9/2002) FL 8+12/5 FAC 1+2 Others 1

EBDON Marcus
Born: Pontypool, 17 October 1970
Height: 5'10" **Weight:** 12.4
International Honours: W: U21-2; Yth
The Welsh midfielder enjoyed mixed fortunes at Chesterfield last term, playing well when in the team, but missing key games through injury as the side plunged towards the drop zone. Although he was released by the Spireites in the summer

Marcus Ebdon

is clever passing and an ability to buy me on the ball will no doubt interest ther clubs.
verton *(From trainee on 16/8/1989)*
eterborough U *(Free on 15/7/1991) FL*
36+11/15 FLC 14+2 FAC 12+3/1 Others 11+1
hesterfield *(£100,000 on 21/3/1997) FL*
30+12/13 FLC 12+1/1 FAC 7 Others 7+1/3

DDS Gareth James
orn: Sydney, Australia, 3 February 1981
eight: 5'11" **Weight:** 10.12
nternational Honours: Australia: U23; th
areth began the 2002-03 season as first hoice in the right-back role for Swindon own, despite sustaining a fractured nger during pre-season. Early on he gave series of solid, if unspectacular erformances when he looked composed d defensively sound. However, after the eam suffered a poor run Gareth lost his lace in the side and apart from a couple f appearances in the LDV Vans Trophy nd a rare start at Oxford in the FA Cup e was never really in contention for a rst-team spot. Gareth added further ternational honours when appearing for ustralia U23s against Spain last April.
ottingham F *(From trainee on 19/2/1998)* . 11+5/1 FAC 1
windon T *(Free on 9/8/2002) FL 8+6 FLC* +1 FAC 1 Others 2

DGE Roland
orn: Gillingham, 25 November 1978
eight: 5'9" **Weight:** 11.6
nce again, Roland's season was ampered by niggling injuries for illingham, although he was an ever-resent for most of the second half of the ampaign. When fully fit he is a useful ft back who likes to get forward at very opportunity. Roland was out of ontract in the summer and his future vas unclear at the time of writing.
illingham *(From trainee on 10/7/1997) FL* 3+9/1 FLC 6 FAC 12+1 Others 5

DGHILL Richard Arlon
orn: Oldham, 23 September 1974
eight: 5'9" **Weight:** 11.5
nternational Honours: E: B-1; U21-3
vastly experienced full back who can lay on either side, Richard's work rate is ever in question as he covers plenty of round both in defensive duties and vhen pushing forward to help the attack. e joined Wigan Athletic on a non-ontract basis making just one ppearance in an LDV Vans trophy match, hen in January he linked up with heffield United in a similar deal. His one

appearance for the Blades was as a substitute in the defeat at Ipswich when he replaced Wayne Quinn in the left-wing-back position. However, he was released after one month.
Manchester C *(From trainee on 15/7/1992)* PIFL 178+3/1 FLC 17 FAC 8+1 Others 3
Birmingham C *(Loaned on 14/11/2000) FL 3*
Wigan Ath *(Free on 21/10/2002) Others 1*
Sheffield U *(Free on 17/11/2003) FL 0+1*

EDMONDSON Darren Stephen
Born: Coniston, 4 November 1971
Height: 6'0" **Weight:** 12.11
Club Honours: Div 3 '95; AMC '97
The hard-tackling right wing back had another fine season with York City last term and after going nearly three years without scoring he netted an amazing five goals in the space of 12 games in the second half of the campaign. These included outstanding efforts in the home games with Hull City and Scunthorpe and a brilliant strike which earned all three points at Bristol Rovers in March.
Carlisle U *(From trainee on 17/7/1990) FL* 205+9/9 FLC 15/1 FAC 15/3 Others 22/3
Huddersfield T *(£200,000 + on 3/3/1997) FL* 28+9 FLC 2 FAC 2+2
Plymouth Arg *(Loaned on 11/9/1998) FL 4*
York C *(Free on 23/3/2000) FL 100+4/5 FLC 4 FAC 9 Others 1*

[EDU] EDUARDO Cesar Gaspar
Born: Sao Paulo, Brazil, 15 May 1978
Height: 6'1" **Weight:** 11.4
Club Honours: FAC '02; PL '02; CS '02
Although he started the season as first choice on the left side of midfield for Arsenal Edu lost his place following the return to fitness of Freddie Ljungberg and Robert Pires. From that point on he was used as cover or as a substitute. Skilful and versatile with tremendous natural talent, he is a hard-working player who gets forward well and is not afraid to shoot from long range. Edu scored a crucial goal in the 2-0 victory over Manchester United in the fifth round of FA Cup. A cartilage operation kept him out of games at the latter end of season.
Arsenal *(£6,000,000 from Corinthians, Brazil on 18/1/2001) PL 22+15/3 FLC 3/1 FAC 9+2/2 Others 4+6*

EDUSEI Akwasi
Born: London, 12 September 1986
Height: 5'9" **Weight:** 11.0
This promising young striker enjoyed a meteoric rise at Gillingham last term. A product of the club's academy teams, he was promoted to the reserves and after

just two appearances at that level he made his senior debut from the substitutes' bench against Walsall in March. Akwasi was still a school pupil at the time, but has since been taken on by the Gills on scholarship forms.
Gillingham *(Associated Schoolboy) FL 0+2*

EDWARDS Andrew (Andy) David
Born: Epping, 17 September 1971
Height: 6'3" **Weight:** 12.10
Club Honours: Div 3 '03
Fans' favourite Andy appeared regularly for Peterborough last season before his transfer to Rushden & Diamonds in the new year. A commanding central defender who is good in the air and reads the game well, he is well known for his consistency. Andy took a while to settle in at Nene Park, but eventually formed a good partnership with Barry Hunter and went on to help the team seal automatic promotion to Division Two when he scored the vital winner at Carlisle United on Easter Saturday.
Southend U *(From trainee on 14/12/1989) FL 141+6/5 FLC 5 FAC 4 Others 9/2*
Birmingham C *(£400,000 on 6/7/1995) FL 37+3/1 FLC 12/1 FAC 2 Others 5/1*
Peterborough U *(Signed on 29/11/1996) FL 266/10 FLC 24 FAC 21/1 Others 17/1*
Rushden & Diamonds *(Free on 5/3/2003) FL 11+1/1*

EDWARDS Akenhaton **Carlos**
Born: Port of Spain, Trinidad, 24 October 1978
Height: 5'11" **Weight:** 11.9
International Honours: Trinidad & Tobago: 2
Carlos was in charismatic form for Wrexham last term, producing some dazzling wing play down the right flank. Far more consistent than in his previous seasons at the Racecourse, he ran record goal-scorer Andy Morrell close for 'Player of the Year'. Spectacular long distance goals were a feature as was his effort in the promotion clincher at home to Cambridge United and the final league game at Bury. The position of wing back complements his style of play, and he was rewarded with a place in the PFA Third Division team for the season.
Wrexham *(£125,000 from Defence Force, Trinidad on 8/8/2000) FL 84+22/17 FLC 3+2/1 FAC 2 Others 2/1*

EDWARDS Christian Nicholas Howells
Born: Caerphilly, 23 November 1975
Height: 6'2" **Weight:** 12.8

Edu (left)

International Honours: W: 1; B-2; 21-7

hristian was again out of the first-team picture at Nottingham Forest last term. He featured regularly for Tranmere in a two-month loan spell, and later in the campaign joined Oxford United, also on loan. He was initially a little unsure how to settle at the Kassam Stadium, but then showed good form in the heart of the back line. A tall, no-nonsense defender who can use both feet equally well, Christian is powerful in the air and never shirks a tackle.

Swansea C (From trainee on 20/7/1994) FL 13+2/4 FLC 5 FAC 4 Others 9+1
Nottingham F (£175,000 + on 26/3/1998) FL 44+10/3 FLC 1 FAC 1
Bristol C (Loaned on 11/12/1998) FL 3
Oxford U (Loaned on 24/2/2000) FL 5/1
Crystal Palace (Loaned on 16/11/2001) FL 9
Tranmere Rov (Loaned on 17/9/2002) FL 12 FLC 1 FAC 2 Others 2
Oxford U (Loaned on 17/1/2003) FL 5+1

EDWARDS David Alexander
Born: Pontesbury, 3 February 1986
Height: 5'11" **Weight:** 11.2
This promising Shrewsbury Town midfield player did well in the reserve and youth teams last term and stepped up to make his senior debut when he came off the bench in the closing stages of the final home match of the season against Scunthorpe. While he would undoubtedly have preferred to make his bow in happier circumstances, he did well in his first senior action.
Shrewsbury T (Trainee) FL 0+1

EDWARDS Michael
Born: Hessle, 25 April 1980
Height: 6'1" **Weight:** 12.0
Hull's longest-serving player, Michael lost his starting place after the opening two games of the 2002-03 campaign. He returned at Kidderminster in October but suffered a cruciate ligament injury. An exploratory operation revealed that a four-month lay off rather than surgery was required. By the time he returned, new boss Peter Taylor had recruited further defensive cover and Michael decided to accept an offer of settlement of the final year of his Hull contract in March. He was soon snapped up by Colchester on a short-term deal and enjoyed a few outings in the U's defence, mostly as a left back.
Hull C (From trainee on 16/7/1998) FL 55+13/6 FLC 8+1 FAC 11/2 Others 9+1
Colchester U (Free on 27/3/2003) FL 3+2

EDWARDS Nathan Mark
Born: Lincoln, 8 April 1983
Height: 5'11" **Weight:** 12.10
This Swindon Town first-year professional managed three brief outings during the 2002-03 season. He first appeared at Blackpool during August and although a regular on the bench for much of the campaign, he did not see any further first-team action until April when he came on as a substitute at Peterborough and at home to Huddersfield. Nathan is a young midfielder who is often used in a 'holding' role.
Swindon T (From trainee on 3/7/2002) FL 2+8 Others 1

EDWARDS Neil Ryan
Born: Aberdare, 5 December 1970
Height: 5'9" **Weight:** 11.10
International Honours: W: U21-1; Yth; Sch
Rochdale's Welsh goalkeeper started the 2002-03 campaign as the club's undisputed number one and, apart from a couple of games out due to toothache, he performed his usual heroics behind a defence rather less secure than previously. One of the stars of Dale's FA Cup defeat of Coventry, a catalogue of injuries to his knee, groin and hand eventually caught up with him and an operation on his troublesome knee soon afterwards ruled him out for the rest of the season.
Leeds U (From trainee on 10/3/1989) Others 1
Stockport Co (£5,000 on 3/9/1991) FL 163+1 FLC 11 FAC 11 Others 31
Rochdale (£25,000 on 3/11/1997) FL 189 FLC 8 FAC 14+1 Others 11

EDWARDS Paul
Born: Manchester, 1 January 1980
Height: 5'11" **Weight:** 10.12
Signed by Wrexham in the summer of 2002, Paul is a very pacy flank man who can cause no end of problems for defences. He also proved to be quite capable of scoring vital goals, none more so than in November when coming on as a substitute against promotion rivals Bournemouth at the Racecourse. He had much to do before jinking past defenders one way then another, until unleashing an unstoppable shot to bring the house down and ensure a 3-2 win. Together with his namesake Carlos on the other wing they are a formidable pair although Paul could do with brushing up the defensive part of his game.
Doncaster Rov (Free from Ashton U on 2/2/1998) FL 5+4
Swindon T (Free from Altrincham, ex Knutsford T, on 17/8/2001) FL 14+6 FLC 0+1 FAC 1/1 Others 1

Wrexham (Free on 12/7/2002) FL 33+5/4 FLC 2 FAC 0+1 Others 2

EDWARDS Paul
Born: Derby, 10 November 1982
Height: 6'0" **Weight:** 11.0
This promising young Crewe Alexandra striker went out on loan to Dr Martens League club Stafford Rangers and then to Conference outfit Southport in the first half of the 2002-03 season. He returned to make his senior debut as a substitute against Huddersfield Town in January and also featured from the bench at Plymouth. Paul will be looking to gain further senior experience in the 2003-04 campaign.
Crewe Alex (From trainee on 6/2/2001) FL 0+2

EDWARDS Robert (Robbie)
Born: Manchester, 23 February 1970
Height: 5'9" **Weight:** 12.4
Robbie's 2002-03 season was blighted by injury but he remained one of Chesterfield's most consistent performers. Equally at home in a full-back or midfield role, where he can pass with vision as well as break up opposing moves, his experience served the club well as it imported younger players and relied on older heads to hold things together.
Crewe Alex (From trainee on 11/7/1988) FL 110+45/44 FLC 8/5 FAC 13+5/5 Others 9+8/4
Huddersfield T (£150,000 on 8/3/1996) FL 109+29/14 FLC 2+1/1 FAC 7+1/1
Chesterfield (£20,000 on 8/9/2000) FL 89+5/7 FLC 2+1 FAC 5 Others 8

EDWARDS Robert (Rob) Owen
Born: Telford, 25 December 1982
Height: 6'1" **Weight:** 12.0
International Honours: W: 1; Yth
After being handed a first-team squad number in December, Rob was almost immediately plunged into a testing senior appearance as an emergency right back for Aston Villa because of injuries, illness and suspension. He made a highly impressive debut against Middlesborough, adding eight more appearances during the season. Rob also made his international debut for Wales, coming on as a full back in their match against Azerbaijan at the end of March.
Aston Villa (From trainee on 4/1/2000) PL 7+1 FAC 1

EDWARDS Robert (Rob) William
Born: Kendal, 1 July 1973
Height: 6'0" **Weight:** 12.2
Club Honours: Div 2 '00

International Honours: W: 4; B-2; U21-17; Yth

Rob will look back on the 2002-03 season at Preston as one disrupted by injuries, amongst these a groin strain in September, three different injuries including a broken hand against Derby, and an ankle problem over the Christmas period. He is generally sound at left back, able to support his attack with telling crosses as well as possessing a powerful shot. Rob turned in a 'Man of the Match' performance against Grimsby before yet another injury in April kept him on the sidelines towards the end of the season. When recovered he was rested on the bench in favour of Tyrone Mears and he will be hoping for a more settled season in 2003-04.

Carlisle U (From trainee on 10/4/1990) FL 48/5 FLC 4 FAC 1 Others 2+1
Bristol C (£135,000 on 27/3/1991) FL 188+28/5 FLC 16+3/1 FAC 13+2 Others 12+1/2
Preston NE (Free on 5/8/1999) FL 140+5/4 FLC 12 FAC 9 Others 5/1

EDWORTHY Marc

Born: Barnstaple, 24 December 1972
Height: 5'8" **Weight:** 11.10

The experienced full back was initially on loan at Wolves and showed remarkable enthusiasm to join the club. He eventually signed on a permanent basis and after coming on as a substitute against Preston he made his full debut in the 4-4 draw at Rotherham, the first of 16 successive appearances. Marc particularly enjoyed his return to Coventry as Wolves won 2-0, but did not play as often in the new year.

Plymouth Arg (From trainee on 30/3/1991) FL 52+17/1 FLC 5+2 FAC 5+2 Others 2+2
Crystal Palace (£350,000 on 9/6/1995) F/PL 120+6 FLC 8+1/1 FAC 8 Others 8
Coventry C (£850,000 + on 28/8/1998) P/FL 62+14/1 FLC 5 FAC 4
Wolverhampton W (Free on 23/8/2002) FL 18+4 FLC 1

EHIOGU Ugochuku (Ugo)

Born: Hackney, 3 November 1972
Height: 6'2" **Weight:** 14.10
Club Honours: FLC '96
International Honours: E: 4; B-1; U21-15

An excellent reader of the game and an imposing, confident defender, Ugo had a frustrating season thanks to a freak injury. He formed a formidable defensive partnership with his former Aston Villa colleague Gareth Southgate to the extent that Middlesbrough's former leaky defence is now well and truly plugged. His injury nightmare came at Ewood Park

on New Year's Day when he was hospitalised with three broken ribs and a punctured lung following an aerial collision with 'keeper Brad Friedel after the game had been in progress for only eight minutes. Ugo lost a full two months to this particular injury but still managed to feature in 32 Premiership games.

West Bromwich A (From trainee on 13/7/1989) FL 0+2
Aston Villa (£40,000 on 12/7/1991) F/PL 223+14/12 FLC 23+1/1 FAC 22+2/1 Others 18/1
Middlesbrough (£8,000,000 on 20/10/2000) PL 81+1/7 FLC 2 FAC 5/1

ELDERSHAW Simon

Born: Stoke, 5 December 1985
Height: 5'10" **Weight:** 11.3

This promising Port Vale striker is one of a rare breed - a locally born Vale fan who has actually played for the club. Simon's big moment came when he was named as a substitute at Wycombe in December and he was called on for the last few minutes of the game. He made a further appearance from the bench against Wigan on Boxing Day but thereafter returned to the youth team, for whom he was a regular goal-scorer.

Port Vale (Trainee) FL 0+2

ELDING Anthony Lee

Born: Boston, 16 April 1982
Height: 6'1" **Weight:** 13.10
Club Honours: NC '02

This teenaged striker was given his Football League debut in Boston's opening game of the 2002-03 season but lasted only 47 minutes before being carried off with a leg injury. He made only two further league starts finding himself in stiff competition with more experienced front men. Anthony was loaned to Unibond League club Gainsborough Trinity in February and shortly afterwards moved to Conference club Stevenage Borough on a permanent basis.

Boston U (From juniors on 6/7/2001) FL 3+5 FAC 0+1 Others 0+1

EL KARKOURI Talal

Born: Casablanca, Morocco, 8 July 1976
Height: 6'1" **Weight:** 13.10
International Honours: Moroco:

A Moroccan international defender, Talal arrived at Sunderland on loan from Paris St Germain in February. He made his debut at Tottenham in midfield where his composure on the ball and eye for a key pass were immediately evident. Talal then returned to his normal central defensive position where he struck up a good

rapport with Joachim Bjorklund and, although he is not particularly tall, his ability in the air was especially noteworthy.

Sunderland (Loaned from Paris St Germain, France, ex Raja Casablanca, on 31/1/2003) P: 8 FAC 0+1

EL KHALEJ Tahar

Born: Morocco, 16 June 1968
Height: 6'3" **Weight:** 13.8
International Honours: Morocco

Tahar is a very useful and accomplished performer, whether playing in his accustomed role at centre back or in midfield. However, the arrival of Michael Svensson at Southampton at the beginning of the 2002-03 season further curtailed his chances of first-team football, and he was limited to a single appearance on the bench, coming on during the 2–0 defeat at West Bromwich Albion. In January he joined Charlton Athletic on a short-term contract to help bolster the Addicks' injury-hit defence. H made his debut against Aston Villa at the Valley and had a steady game, but did not look quite so assured in his subsequent appearances and was not offered a further contract by the club.

Southampton (£300,000 from Benfica, Portugal, ex KAC Marrakesh, Uniao Leiria, o 10/3/2000) PL 48+10/3 FLC 2+3/1 FAC 1+1
Charlton Ath (Free on 31/1/2003) PL 2+1

ELLENDER Paul

Born: Scunthorpe, 21 October 1974
Height: 6'1" **Weight:** 12.7
Club Honours: NC '02
International Honours: E: SP-1

A versatile performer who produced his best football playing just in front of the back four for Boston United last term, Paul was excellent in the tackle and in winning the ball in the air. He was used a variety of different positions during the season, appearing at centre back, in midfield and as an emergency target ma up front. His only goal of the campaign came while playing as a striker in the Worthington Cup tie against Cardiff City

Scunthorpe U (From trainee on 8/4/1993. Freed during 1994 close season)
Boston U (Signed from Scarborough, ex Gainsborough Trin, Altrincham, on 17/8/2001) FL 25+1 FLC 2/1

ELLINGTON Nathan Levi Fontaine

Born: Bradford, 2 July 1981
Height: 5'10" **Weight:** 12.10
Club Honours: Div 2 '03

This talented striker finished top scorer fo Wigan Athletic last term, netting 22 time

all competitions as the club raced to he Second Division title. One of the highlights was undoubtedly a memorable hat-trick in the Worthington Cup tie against Premiership West Bromwich Ibion. A forward with lightning pace, tricky ball skills and an eye for goal, he was a crucial factor in the club's success despite playing half of the season with a damaged shoulder. He netted important goals in the away wins at Queen's Park Rangers and Crewe and contributed a stunning drive in the FA Cup victory over Luton Town.

Nathan Ellington

Bristol Rov (£150,000 from Walton & Hersham on 18/2/1999) FL 76+40/35 FLC 7/2 FAC 6+1/4 Others 6+1/3
Wigan Ath (£750,000 + on 28/3/2002) FL 44+1/17 FLC 5/5 FAC 2+1/2 Others 0+1

ELLIOTT Marvin Conrad
Born: Wandsworth, 15 September 1984
Height: 5'11" **Weight:** 12.2
Another product of the Millwall academy, Marvin was handed his first-team debut against Nottingham Forest after some excellent performances in the youth and reserve sides. A tall, elegant midfield

player he impressed with some tough tackling and caused problems for the opposition with his forward runs. A fine young prospect, he quickly established his authority on the game and will be looking to receive more experience of senior football in 2003-04.
Millwall (From trainee on 6/2/2002) FL 0+1

ELLIOTT Matthew (Matt) Stephen
Born: Wandsworth, 1 November 1968
Height: 6'3" **Weight:** 14.10
Club Honours: FLC '00
International Honours: S: 18
The right-footed central defender and Leicester City captain powered back to his best form last season partnering either Gerry Taggart or Frank Sinclair. He also got back on the goal trail with some regularity, with the best being a close-range volley at Vicarage Road. Matt's wealth of experience clearly made up for any lack of pace and his astute reading of the game led to masterly defensive performances in the home games against promotion rivals Portsmouth and Nottingham Forest.
Charlton Ath (£5,000 from Epsom & Ewell on 9/5/1988) FLC 1
Torquay U (£10,000 on 23/3/1989) FL 123+1/15 FLC 9/2 FAC 9/2 Others 16/1
Scunthorpe U (£50,000 on 26/3/1992) FL 61/8 FLC 6 FAC 2 Others 8
Oxford U (£150,000 on 5/11/1993) FL 148/21 FLC 16/1 FAC 11/2 Others 6
Leicester C (£1,600,000 on 18/1/1997) P/FL 235+1/27 FLC 20+1/3 FAC 18/3 Others 4

ELLIOTT Robert (Robbie) James
Born: Newcastle, 25 December 1973
Height: 5'10" **Weight:** 11.6
International Honours: E: U21-2; Yth
Robbie is a strong-tackling left back whose opportunities at Newcastle were severely limited last term. He came off the bench in each of the opening two games, a Champions' League qualifier at Sarajevo and the Premiership fixture at home to West Ham, but was then absent until his only start of the season in the Worthington Cup tie at home to Everton in early November, after which he only made a solitary substitute appearance in the home game with Liverpool on New Year's Day.
Newcastle U (From trainee on 3/4/1991) F/PL 71+8/9 FLC 5 FAC 7+3 Others 5+1
Bolton W (£2,500,000 + on 2/7/1997) P/FL 71+15/5 FLC 4+1/2 FAC 5 Others 5+2
Newcastle U (Free on 11/7/2001) PL 26+3/1 FLC 3+1 FAC 3+1 Others 6+1/1

ELLIOTT Steven (Steve) William
Born: Derby, 29 October 1978
Height: 6'1" **Weight:** 14.0
International Honours: E: U21-2
Steve revived his career at Derby last season, although a knee injury suffered in training kept him out for two months in the autumn. He also missed the last six matches because of an ankle operation. When he played at Brighton in November it was his first start for 18 months and the left-sided central defender began to reveal the qualities that had given him such an encouraging start in the game. Steve's first senior goal, against Wimbledon owed something to a deflection from an offside Malcolm Christie, but he should score more from set pieces. His aim is to consolidate a position in the line-up in the new campaign.
Derby Co (From trainee on 26/3/1997) P/FL 56+13/1 FLC 7+1 FAC 3+2

ELLIOTT Stuart
Born: Belfast, 23 July 1978
Height: 5'10" **Weight:** 11.9
International Honours: NI: 16; U21-3
Stuart moved to Hull City during the 2002 close season along with his colleague Greg Strong. A left-sided attacking midfielder who can also play as a striker, he was at his best when running at defenders and delivering quality crosses. Stuart also posed a potent threat in the air. After suffering knee ligament damage at Exeter in August, he was sidelined for six weeks and was then unable to produce consistent form until the closing stages of the campaign. A man of strong religious beliefs, he has pledged to repay the faith shown him by his Hull colleagues and supporters and reinstated his commitment to a three-year City contract. Despite his injury problems, Stuart finished his first Tigers' season as their top scorer.
Motherwell (£100,000 from Glentoran on 20/7/2000) SL 50+20/22 SLC 2+1 SC 1+1/1
Hull C (£230,000 on 12/7/2002) FL 30+6/12 FAC 0+1

ELLIOTT Wade Patrick
Born: Eastleigh, 14 December 1978
Height: 5'9" **Weight:** 11.1
International Honours: E: Sch
This popular right-sided midfielder had a fine season with Bournemouth last term and when on song he showed he could destroy opposition defences. He weighed in with six goals during the campaign including one in the play-off final against Lincoln to help ensure the Cherries

promotion to Division Two. Wade is still completing his degree and such is his popularity at the club that local band The Bewley Brothers released a CD titled 'The Ballad of Wade Elliott' in his honour!
Bournemouth (£5,000 from Bashley on 4/2/2000) FL 112+26/24 FLC 2+1 FAC 11/3 Others 7+2/1

ELLISON Kevin
Born: Liverpool, 23 February 1979
Height: 6'1" **Weight:** 12.8
This former Leicester City winger found himself in and out of the Stockport line-up last season after waiting until mid-September to make his first start. The highlight of his campaign was at Blackpool in late October, when a superb strike from well outside the area sent County on their way to a superb 3-1 victory. The fans certainly took to Kevin endearing him for his aggressive, marauding runs down the left flank.
Leicester C (£50,000 + from Altrincham on 13/2/2001) PL 0+1
Stockport Co (£55,000 on 30/11/2001) FL 23+11/1 FAC 1 Others 1

EMANUEL Lewis James
Born: Bradford, 14 October 1983
Height: 5'8" **Weight:** 11.12
International Honours: E: Yth
Lewis enjoyed his best-ever season with Bradford City last term. He firmly established himself as a regular in the first team with a number of impressive displays at right back. He can also be used at wing back or on the right-hand side of midfield. Lewis, who was a virtual ever present between October and December, is still very young and can only improve with experience.
Bradford C (From trainee on 5/7/2001) FL 33+5 FLC 2 FAC 1+1

EMBERSON Carl Wayne
Born: Epsom, 13 July 1973
Height: 6'2" **Weight:** 14.7
Club Honours: FAYC '91
Despite not always being Luton's first choice goalkeeper last term, Carl played the highest number of matches between the sticks and always performed well. A good shot stopper, who commands his area and the defenders in front of him, it seems likely he will be playing his football away from Kenilworth Road in 2003-04.
Millwall (From trainee on 4/5/1991) Others 1
Colchester U (Loaned on 17/12/1992) FL 13
Colchester U (£25,000 on 6/7/1994) FL 178+1 FLC 9 FAC 8 Others 16

Walsall (Free on 28/6/1999) FL 6+2 FLC 1 Others 2
Luton T (Free on 13/7/2001) FL 51+2 FLC 3 FAC 3 Others 1

EMBLEN Neil Robert
Born: Bromley, 19 June 1971
Height: 6'1" **Weight:** 13.11
After missing almost the entire 2001-02 campaign through injury, Neil was hoping for a full season clear of the treatment table, but a succession of minor injuries prevented him from being a regular member of the Norwich City squad last season. He showed glimpses of his forceful midfield play against Portsmouth and Leicester City at Carrow Road, but early in 2003 he rejoined his former Wolves boss Colin Lee during a month's loan spell at Walsall. Neil made an immediate impact when moving from midfield to defence in the course of a battling goalless draw at Reading, but the loan spell ended less happily when he limped off in the course of the home defeat by Leicester. He was eventually released by Norwich towards the end of the season.
Millwall (£175,000 from Sittingbourne on 8/11/1993) FL 12 Others 1
Wolverhampton W (£600,000 on 14/7/1994) FL 80+8/9 FLC 2+2/1 FAC 7+2 Others 2+1
Crystal Palace (£2,000,000 on 21/8/1997) PL 8+5 FAC 1+1/2
Wolverhampton W (£900,000 on 26/3/1998) FL 102+12/7 FLC 8+1/1 FAC 6+1 Others 2+1
Norwich C (£500,000 + on 12/7/2001) FL 6+8 FLC 0+1
Walsall (Loaned on 10/1/2003) FL 3+2

ENCKELMAN Peter
Born: Turku, Finland, 10 March 1977
Height: 6'2" **Weight:** 12.5
International Honours: Finland: 5; U21-1
Peter finally became the first choice goalkeeper for Aston Villa last term. He was a near ever-present and performed to a high level of consistency throughout the campaign, producing some exceptional saves. The only low point of the season was his miskick from Olof Mellberg's throw-in during the local derby match, which resulted in Birmingham's second goal in the 3-0 defeat. However, to his great credit, he did not allow the incident to affect any of his subsequent performances. Peter is a big goalkeeper who inspires confidence in those in front of him and has a very calm temperament.
Aston Villa (£200,000 from TPS Turku, Finland on 1/2/1999) PL 51+1 FLC 6 FAC 1 Others 7+1

Peter Enckelman

ENGONGA Vicente Mate
Born: Barcelona, Spain, 20 October 1969
Height: 5'11" **Weight:** 13.3
International Honours: Spain: 14
This experienced midfield player joined
Coventry City on a short-term contract
from Real Oviedo in February when it
became apparent that Youssef Safri would
be out for the majority of the rest of the
season. He impressed with his skill but
initially struggled with the pace of the
English game. He later returned to the
line-up and looked more impressive with
his long passing coming to the fore, but
his tackling lacked strength. Vicente was
released in the summer.
*Coventry C (Free from Real Oviedo, Spain,
ex Torrelavega, Sporting Mahones, Valladolid,
Celta Vigo, Valencia, Mallorca, on 13/2/2003)
FL 5+3*

**ERIBENNE Chukwunyeaka
(Chukki)** Osondu
Born: Westminster, 2 November 1980
Height: 5'10" **Weight:** 11.12
This hard-working forward was unable to
win a place in the starting line-up at
Bournemouth last term. He managed six
appearances from the substitutes' bench,
which included a 'Man of the Match'
display against Carlisle. Chukki had a loan
spell with Conference club Hereford
United in October during which time he
netted a brace in the LDV Vans Trophy
match against Northampton Town. He
was released by the Cherries in the
summer.
*Coventry C (From trainee on 19/1/1998)
Bournemouth (Free on 4/7/2000) FL
12+35/1 FLC 2 FAC 0+3 Others 2+1*

ETHERINGTON Matthew
Born: Truro, 14 August 1981
Height: 5'10" **Weight:** 11.2
International Honours: E: U21-3; Yth
This attacking midfield player made good
progress at Tottenham last term and
secured 15 starts in Premiership matches.
Naturally at home on the left wing, Glenn
Hoddle's formation hasn't always allowed
Matthew to express himself as he would
like, however, there is no doubt about his
talent and he remains a key figure in the
team. The future looks bright for
Matthew and his flexibility should bring
more opportunities in 2003-04 as he tries
to secure a regular place in the starting
line-up at White Hart Lane.
*Peterborough U (From trainee on
15/8/1998) FL 43+8/6 FLC 1+1 FAC 2+1
Others 2
Tottenham H (£500,000 on 10/1/2000) PL
20+25/1 FLC 3+1 FAC 1+1/1*

*Bradford C (Loaned on 23/10/2001) FL
12+1/1*

ETUHU Dickson Paul
Born: Kano, Nigeria, 8 June 1982
Height: 6'2" **Weight:** 13.4
Club Honours: Div 1 '02
Injured in pre-season, Dickson had a fitful
start to the 2002-03 campaign at Preston
due to a lack of fitness. At his best in
central midfield, but occasionally used on
either flank to less effect, Dickson scored
a number of important goals, mostly
near-post headers from corners, at which
he used his height effectively. Injured over
Christmas, he turned in some stunning
performances after the arrival of Brian
O'Neil who played alongside him in
midfield. Dickson is powerful on the ball
and in the air, and his surging runs and
willingness to chase a lost cause have
endeared him to the fans, although he
occasionally lets himself down with his
final ball. However, he is still young and
learning the game, and has bags of
potential for the future.
*Manchester C (From trainee on 23/12/1999)
FL 11+1 FLC 1
Preston NE (£300,000 on 24/1/2002) FL
49+6/9 FLC 4 FAC 1*

EUELL Jason Joseph
Born: Lambeth, 6 February 1977
Height: 6'0" **Weight:** 12.7
International Honours: E: U21-6
Jason started the 2002-03 season as a
striker for Charlton but in November he
was switched to a midfield role, playing
just behind the front two, the change
coinciding with a 15-match run when
only one game was lost. Jason is strong,
good in the air and holds the ball up well.
His unselfish play brings others into the
game, and the switch to midfield did not
affect his goal-scoring ability, as he once
again finished top scorer with 11 league
and cup goals. He opened the scoring for
the Addicks in the 2-0 win against
Liverpool on the club's tenth anniversary
back at the Valley, and netted both goals
in the 2-2 draw with at Tottenham. Jason
reverted to a main striker's role in the last
couple of games.
*Wimbledon (From trainee on 1/6/1995) P/FL
118+23/41 FLC 15+2/4 FAC 14+5/2 Others
2+2
Charlton Ath (£4,750,000 on 16/7/2001) PL
66+6/21 FLC 3/1 FAC 4/2*

EUSTACE John Mark
Born: Solihull, 3 November 1979
Height: 5'11" **Weight:** 11.12

After missing most of the previous
campaign through injury, John returned t
full fitness last term, but it was evident
that his long lay-off had reduced his
ability to come from deep to score vital
goals, one of his main strengths.
Although he was always fully committed
he failed to play to his full potential on
the right side of midfield early on and los
his place in the Coventry City line-up. He
did, however, score a superbly struck goa
at Ipswich after coming off the bench. In
January he went on loan to
Middlesbrough with the possibility of a
permanent move but made only one
substitute appearance, featuring in the 1-
1 draw at Anfield. On his return to
Highfield Road John look sharper and ha
an excellent game at Grimsby, but his
confidence waned after this and he lost
his place in the side again.
*Coventry C (From trainee on 5/11/1996) P/F
62+24/7 FLC 6+2/2 FAC 3+2/1
Dundee U (Loaned on 17/2/1999) SL 8+3/1
SC 2
Middlesbrough (Loaned on 17/1/2003) PL
0+1*

EVANS Mark Graham
Born: Chester, 16 September 1982
Height: 6'0" **Weight:** 12.0
Mark found it difficult to break into the
Wrexham first team last season and his
only appearance was as a substitute late
in the game against Leyton Orient in
October. The right back had been signed
on a short-term contract and he was
released at the beginning of January,
subsequently signing for Unibond League
club Colwyn Bay.
*Wrexham (From trainee on 17/7/2002) FL
0+5*

EVANS Michael (Micky)
James
Born: Plymouth, 1 January 1973
Height: 6'1" **Weight:** 13.4
Club Honours: Div 3 '02
International Honours: RoI: 1
Micky again proved an invaluable membe
of Plymouth Argyle's squad last season.
Always giving 100 per cent for the cause
he battled hard up front, holding the pla
up and laying the ball off to the midfield
quartet. His excellent aerial challenges
often unsettled opposing defenders and
resulted in many goal-scoring
opportunities for his team mates. His
return of six goals for the season was a
little disappointing but manager Paul
Sturrock rewarded him for his efforts wit
a new two-year contract in the summer.

lymouth Arg (From trainee on 30/3/1991)
L 130+33/38 FLC 8+1 FAC 10+2/3 Others 0/2
Southampton (£500,000 on 4/3/1997) PL 4+8/4 FLC 2+1/1
West Bromwich A (£750,000 on 7/10/1997) FL 35+28/6 FLC 3+3/2 FAC +2/1
Bristol Rov (£250,000 on 18/8/2000) FL 9+2/4 FLC 2 Others 3/2
Plymouth Arg (£30,000 on 22/3/2001) FL 5+15/15 FLC 1+1 FAC 7/1 Others 0+2/1

ason Euell

EVANS Paul Anthony
Born: Newcastle, South Africa, 28 December 1973
Height: 6'4" **Weight:** 15.6
International Honours: South Africa: U23-8
Paul forced his way into the Sheffield Wednesday team after regular 'keeper Kevin Pressman was injured and impressed so much with his valiant displays that he kept his place even when Pressman was fit again. He went on to play in seven consecutive games before suffering an injury that was to end his season. He will, however, be looking to win a regular place in the Owls' line-up in 2003-04.
Leeds U (£50,000 from Wits University on 29/12/1995. Freed during 1997 close season
Sheffield Wed (Free from Jomo Cosmos, South Africa, ex Wits University, Supersport U, Mamelodi Sundowns, on 9/8/2002) FL 7

EVANS Paul Simon
Born: Oswestry, 1 September 1974
Height: 5'8" **Weight:** 11.6
Club Honours: Div 3 '94, '99
International Honours: W: 2; U21-4; Yth
Paul began the 2002-03 campaign as a regular for Bradford City, scoring from 40 yards in the 2-1 win at Ipswich in August. He was also named in the full Wales squad for their friendly in Croatia. However, he struggled during the middle part of the season and his last appearance for the Bantams was in the 1-0 defeat at Watford in December. He spent the second half of the season on loan at Blackpool, where he made a significant impact before injury curtailed his activities at the beginning of March. Paul is a tenacious midfield player who has the ability to find his striker with a pinpoint pass, and is also dangerous with long-range free kicks.
Shrewsbury T (From trainee on 2/7/1993) FL 178+20/26 FLC 12+2/4 FAC 12+1/2 Others 12/4
Brentford (£110,000 on 3/3/1999) FL 130/31 FLC 8 FAC 3 Others 13/3
Bradford C (Free on 9/8/2002) FL 16+3/2 FLC 1
Blackpool (Loaned on 17/1/2003) FL 10/1

EVANS Rhys Karl
Born: Swindon, 27 January 1982
Height: 6'1" **Weight:** 12.2
International Honours: E: U21-2; Yth; Sch
This promising young 'keeper joined Leyton Orient on a three-month loan deal last August. He proved to be an excellent shot stopper and showed good command of his area. Rhys was unfortunate to receive a leg injury during his period at Brisbane Road and his loan deal was terminated early. Later in the season he made his debut for England U21s against Serbia, but was released by Chelsea in the summer.
Chelsea (From trainee on 8/2/1999)
Bristol Rov (Loaned on 25/2/2000) FL 4
Queens Park R (Loaned on 6/11/2001) FL 11
Leyton Orient (Loaned on 10/8/2002) FL 7

EVANS Richard Glyn

Born: Cardiff, 19 June 1983
Height: 5'9" **Weight:** 11.8

This young winger failed to make a breakthrough at Birmingham City last term and eventually joined Sheffield Wednesday on a short-term contract. He made a good impression at Hillsborough, providing a useful attacking option on the left-hand side and delivering some fine crosses. Richard scored his first goal for the Owls in the 7-2 win at Burnley and will be hoping to sign a longer-term deal over the summer.

Birmingham C (From trainee on 1/7/2002)
Sheffield Wed (Signed on 27/3/2003) FL 3+1/1

EVANS Stephen (Steve) James

Born: Caerphilly, 25 September 1980
Height: 6'1" **Weight:** 11.6
International Honours: W: U21-2; Yth

This tenacious, tough-tackling Brentford central midfielder was unable to break into the Bees' team until late October. However, when he did he soon established himself, winning the fans over by scoring twice against Blackpool at the start of November. A regular until an achilles tendon injury in February saw him miss ten games, he returned for the closing stages of the campaign.

Crystal Palace (From trainee on 31/10/1998) FL 0+6 FLC 0+1
Swansea C (Loaned on 9/11/2001) FL 4 FAC 2
Brentford (Free on 27/3/2002) FL 20+3/3 FLC 1+1 FAC 3 Others 2

EVANS Terence (Terry)

Born: Pontypridd, 8 January 1976
Height: 5'8" **Weight:** 11.0
International Honours: W: U21-4

Terry returned to first-team action for Swansea following his injury problems of the previous season and started the 2002-03 campaign in an unfamiliar role in the centre of a three-man defensive formation. However, following a change of management at the Vetch Field he then switched to his usual right-back position. The second half of his campaign was affected by a string of injuries that curtailed his appearances.

Cardiff C (From trainee on 8/7/1994) FL 12+2 FLC 2 FAC 1 Others 2+2 (Free to Barry T in February 1996)
Swansea C (Free on 30/10/2001) FL 41+2 FLC 1 FAC 3

EVANS Thomas (Tommy) Raymond

Born: Doncaster, 31 December 1976
Height: 6'0" **Weight:** 13.2
International Honours: NI: Yth

Scunthorpe's first choice goalkeeper for the past three seasons, Tommy had his best campaign to date in 2002-03, not missing a game and playing a key role in helping the Iron reach the play-offs. He is a strong shot-stopper who dominates his penalty area and has become a reliable last line of defence. Tommy was rewarded for his efforts with a three-year contract and also won a 'Player of the Season' award.

Sheffield U (From trainee on 3/7/1995)
Crystal Palace (Free on 14/6/1996)
Scunthorpe U (Free on 22/8/1997) FL 190+1 FLC 6 FAC 14 Others 9

EVANS Duncan Wayne

Born: Abermule, 25 August 1971
Height: 5'10" **Weight:** 12.5

Rochdale's 'Mr Consistency' at right back for the previous three seasons, Wayne had a more difficult time in 2002-03. After an early-season injury he was brought back into the side at centre back, and then after a change of formation he was used on the right-hand side of a back three. In March he suffered a blow to the head in a match, but after appearing in the next couple of games he had to be substituted suffering from dizziness after heading the ball. Although he was forced to spend some time on the sidelines he returned to complete 200 appearances for the club in April.

Walsall (Free from Welshpool on 13/8/1993) FL 173+10/1 FLC 14+1/1 FAC 15+1 Others 12+3
Rochdale (Free on 2/7/1999) FL 174/3 FLC 7/1 FAC 13 Others 9

EVATT Ian Ross

Born: Coventry, 19 November 1981
Height: 6'3" **Weight:** 13.11

Ian scored his first senior goal in the Worthington Cup victory at Mansfield and, until he suffered a groin injury in February, was in Derby's squad of 16 for every match. That represented progress for a player whose first start was in the final game of 2001-02 and he could feel himself unlucky to be released at the end of his contract. Although he can turn his hand to a midfield 'holding' role, Ian is by nature a central defender but, whether Derby played with four or three at the

back, all found it hard to settle into a consistent pattern. He returned as a substituted substitute for the final home game against Ipswich Town, a defeat that gave the club much to ponder in the summer.

Derby Co (From trainee on 3/12/1998) P/FL 19+15 FLC 0+2/1 FAC 1
Northampton T (Loaned on 10/8/2001) FL 10+1 FLC 2

EYRE John Robert

Born: Hull, 9 October 1974
Height: 6'0" **Weight:** 12.7

John's second season back at Oldham saw him in unfamiliar territory. Re-signed from Hull City originally as a striker, he was switched into midfield and even stood in as a makeshift wing back. He responded well, producing a series of cultured displays that showed he was one of the most improved players at the club. John was out of contract in the summer, but looked likely to remain at Boundary Park.

Oldham Ath (From trainee on 16/7/1993) P/FL 44+6/1 FLC 0+1
Scunthorpe U (Loaned on 15/12/1994) FL 9/8
Scunthorpe U (£40,000 on 4/7/1995) FL 151+13/43 FLC 9/2 FAC 12/3 Others 8+1/3
Hull C (Free on 5/7/1999) FL 43+9/13 FLC 5/ FAC 4+1/2 Others 3+2/1
Oldham Ath (Free on 25/7/2001) FL 38+13/ FLC 4 FAC 5+1 Others 4+2/1

EYRES David

Born: Liverpool, 26 February 1964
Height: 5'11" **Weight:** 11.8
Club Honours: Div 2 '00

A late starter in football, David is making the most of his career with Oldham Athletic. Playing at left wing back he made more appearances than any other player at the club during the 2002-03 season, scoring an incredible total of 16 goals. Several strikes came from his trademark free kicks and David, who says he has never felt fitter, is set to sign a further 12-month contract to extend his successful spell at Boundary Park.

Blackpool (£10,000 from Rhyl on 15/8/1989) FL 147+11/38 FLC 11+1/1 FAC 11/2 Others 13+2/4
Burnley (£90,000 on 29/7/1993) FL 171+4/37 FLC 17/7 FAC 14/8 Others 9/3
Preston NE (£80,000 on 29/10/1997) FL 85+23/19 FLC 3+4 FAC 10/3 Others 5/3
Oldham Ath (Free on 13/10/2000) FL 110+5/25 FLC 6/1 FAC 10/4 Others 4/2

F

FACEY Delroy Michael
Born: Huddersfield, 22 April 1980
Height: 5'11" **Weight:** 13.10
This fast and powerful striker joined
Bolton Wanderers during the 2002 close
season and in November he was loaned
out to Bradford City to gain further
experience. He made an instant
impression by scoring just eight minutes
into his debut against Wimbledon. Delroy
returned to the Reebok and made his
debut for Wanderers from the bench in
the epic 4-3 win over Newcastle on
Boxing Day. A handful of substitute
appearances followed along with two
starts and he scored his first goal in
Bolton colours in February, coming off the
bench to do so in the crucial home victory
over Birmingham. The highly regarded
youngster will be looking to feature more
often in the Premiership in 2003-04.
Huddersfield T (From trainee on 13/5/1997)
FL 40+35/15 FLC 1+1 FAC 1+2 Others 2
Bolton W (Signed on 4/7/2002) PL 1+8/1
FAC 2
Bradford C (Loaned on 8/11/2002) FL 6/1

FAGAN Craig Anthony
Born: Birmingham, 11 December 1982
Height: 5'11" **Weight:** 11.12
A prolific scorer with Birmingham City
reserves, this feisty striker made his
Premiership debut as a substitute at
Southampton in December. Earlier in the
season he was denied a goal on his senior
debut in the Worthington Cup tie at
Leyton Orient by a great save. Pacy and
aggressive, Craig went on loan to Bristol
City to gain experience, but was unable
to provide the goal-scoring spark that the
Robins were seeking.
Birmingham C (From trainee on 20/12/2001)
FL 0+1 FLC 0+2 FAC 0+1
Bristol C (Loaned on 16/1/2003) FL 5+1/1
Others 1

FALLON Rory Michael
Born: Gisbourne, New Zealand, 20 March
1982
Height: 6'2" **Weight:** 11.10
International Honours: E: Yth
Rory netted his first-ever league goal for
Barnsley last term, providing the winner
against Blackpool and following up with
another in the next game at Stockport.
He had just began to cement his place in
the first team when he suffered a stress
fracture of his foot at the end of February
and it was not until the closing stages

that he rejoined the squad. A tall striker
he was always a danger in the air and the
majority of his goals came from his head.
*Barnsley (From trainee on 23/3/1999) FL
21+15/7 FLC 1+1 FAC 1 Others 1*
*Shrewsbury T (Loaned on 14/12/2001) FL
8+3*

FARR Craig Jonathan
Born: Newbury, 27 June 1984
Height: 5'10" **Weight:** 12.3
Although on the short side for a
goalkeeper Craig is highly rated as a shot
stopper by the Swindon Town coaching
staff. He spent the 2002-03 season as
understudy to Bart Griemink, initially
making his debut in the LDV Vans Trophy.
A late-season full league debut in the
home game against Plymouth Argyle saw
Craig keep a clean sheet giving a
confident performance during which he
dealt with everything that was sent his
way.
*Swindon T (From trainee on 20/8/2002) FL 2
Others 1+1*

FARRELL Craig Wayne
Born: Middlesbrough, 5 December 1982
Height: 6'0" **Weight:** 13.2
One of four Carlisle debutants in the
home fixture with Torquay, Craig was the
only one to eventually secure a
permanent contract. He scored United's
goal that day and eventually finished as
the club's top scorer with 14 in all
competitions. An enthusiastic performer
with an eye for goal, he has plenty of
time on his side to develop his game and
hone his undoubted ability.
Leeds U (From trainee on 7/12/1999)
Carlisle U (Free on 4/10/2002) FL 31+2/11
FAC 1/1 Others 6+1/2

FARRELL David William
Born: Birmingham, 11 November 1971
Height: 5'10" **Weight:** 11.9
Although David featured in the
Peterborough United first-team squad
throughout the 2002-03 campaign he did
not always make the starting line-up and
was regularly used as a substitute. He
became somewhat frustrated with the
situation, but after a run in the reserves as
an out-and-out striker he seemed to
rediscover his enthusiasm for the game.
Previously known as a speedy midfield
player, it will be interesting to see where
David is used in the coming season.
*Aston Villa (£45,000 from Redditch U on
6/11/1992) F/PL 5+1 FLC 2*
*Scunthorpe U (Loaned on 25/1/1993) FL
4+1/1 Others 2*

*Wycombe W (£100,000 on 14/9/1995) FL
44+16/8 FLC 6 FAC 3+2 Others 2*
*Peterborough U (Free on 21/7/1997) FL
196+37/29 FLC 9+2/2 FAC 14+1/3 Others
10/4*

FARRELLY Gareth
Born: Dublin, 28 August 1975
Height: 6'0" **Weight:** 13.0
International Honours: RoI: 6; B-1; U21-
11; Yth; Sch
This cultured midfielder found it extremely
difficult to break into the Bolton first team
last season. His first start was in the
defeat at Arsenal in September, when he
scored what can only be described as a
freakish goal. This prompted a small run
of starting appearances but he struggled
to hold down a place in the first eleven.
He joined Rotherham United on loan in
mid-March where he struggled to
produce his best form, although he still
managed to bring some touches of
quality to the side. Gareth returned to the
Reebok and bolstered the reserve team
for the final two months of the season.
*Aston Villa (From trainee on 21/1/1992) PL
2+6 FLC 0+1*
*Rotherham U (Loaned on 21/3/1995) FL
9+1/2*
*Everton (£700,000 + on 9/7/1997) PL
18+9/1 FLC 2/1 FAC 1*
*Bolton W (Free on 12/11/1999) P/FL 61+17/5
FLC 4 FAC 6+2 Others 3/1*
Rotherham U (Loaned on 14/3/2003) FL 6

FAULCONBRIDGE Craig Michael
Born: Nuneaton, 20 April 1978
Height: 6'1" **Weight:** 13.0
Much was expected of Wycombe's
summer signing and he immediately
made a big impression as a striker. He
scored on his debut at Notts County on
the opening day of the season and netted
twice more in the next three games.
Thereafter Craig hit a bit of a barren spell
and ended up with six goals from his 29
starts before a serious knee injury ended
his season in March. He is expected to
return to training in September. Craig
relies on good crosses, using his height
very well, and many of his goals are far-
post headers.
Coventry C (From trainee on 5/7/1996)
*Dunfermline Ath (Loaned on 27/3/1998) SL
1+12/1 SLC 0+1*
*Hull C (Loaned on 18/12/1998) FL 4+6 FAC 1
Others 1+1*
*Wrexham (Free on 6/8/1999) FL 92+19/31
FLC 4+1/1 FAC 4+2/1 Others 4/1*
*Wycombe W (Free on 24/7/2002) FL 29+5/6
FLC 2 FAC 1 Others 3*

FEATHERSTONE Lee
Born: Chesterfield, 20 July 1983
Height: 6'0" **Weight:** 12.8
Lee impressed playing for Sheffield United reserves against Scunthorpe so the Iron took him on a month's loan, making the deal permanent last November. A hard-working player, he settled down into a left-wing role and enjoyed a good run in the team at the turn of the year. However, his second half of the season fizzled out as injuries restricted him to just four substitute appearances in the closing three months.
Sheffield U (From trainee on 4/7/2001)
Scunthorpe U (Free on 11/10/2002) FL 10+10 FAC 3 Others 0+1

FEENEY Warren
Born: Belfast, 17 January 1981
Height: 5'10" **Weight:** 11.6
International Honours: NI: 3; U21-2; Yth; Sch
This promising striker had a rather frustrating time with injuries at Bournemouth last season. Although never able to enjoy a sustained run in the side, he showed a good goals-per-game record from his appearances. Warren uses his pace to good effect and is always a danger in the box. He won a further full cap for Northern Ireland against Cyprus last August.
Leeds U (Signed from St Andrew's BC on 26/1/1998)
Bournemouth (Free on 22/3/2001) FL 49+19/24 FLC 1 FAC 3+4 Others 2+2/1

FENG Li Wei
Born: Jilin, China, 26 January 1978
Height: 6'0" **Weight:** 11.5
International Honours: China: 57
This experienced defender was brought to Everton, as part of a 12-month loan deal with the club sponsors before the start of last season, but he made just two appearances, including an impressive Premiership debut at centre half at Southampton. He showed himself to be pacy and a good reader of the game, but was unable to command a first-team place due to the good form of his more established colleagues. He returned to China after just seven months in England.
Everton (Loaned from Shenzen Pingan, China on 16/8/2002) PL 1 FLC 1

FENN Neale Michael Charles
Born: Edmonton, 18 January 1977
Height: 5'10" **Weight:** 12.8
International Honours: RoI: B-1; U21-9; Yth
Although considered by many of the

club's fans as the most talented footballer on the books at Peterborough, Neale spent much of last season in the reserves, making the starting line-up on just a handful of occasions. The reason for this was that the tactics employed did not allow for a man to play just behind the front attackers, a role much preferred by Neale. A skilful striker, he makes up for a lack of pace with his ability to hold up the ball and bring other players into the game or deliver a defence-splitting ball.
Tottenham H (From trainee on 1/7/1995) PL 0+8 FLC 1/1 FAC 1
Leyton Orient (Loaned on 30/1/1998) FL 3
Norwich C (Loaned on 26/3/1998) FL 6+1/1
Swindon T (Loaned on 13/11/1998) FL 4
Lincoln C (Loaned on 31/12/1998) FL 0+4 Others 1
Peterborough U (Free on 6/7/2001) FL 33+17/7 FLC 2+1/1 FAC 6+1/2 Others 2

FENTON Graham Anthony
Born: Wallsend, 22 May 1974
Height: 5'10" **Weight:** 12.10
Club Honours: FLC '94, '96, '00; AMC '02
International Honours: E: U21-1
This experienced and proven goal-scorer came on loan to Darlington last September and duly scored on his debut from the substitutes' bench at home against Bournemouth. Graham showed neat control and a good turn of speed, linking well with Barry Conlon up in the forefront of the attack. However, injury problems meant that he made only five more appearances without adding to that goal. He made no first-team appearances for Blackpool during the campaign.
Aston Villa (From trainee on 13/2/1992) PL 16+16/3 FLC 2+5
West Bromwich A (Loaned on 10/1/1994) FL 7/3
Blackburn Rov (£1,500,000 on 7/11/1995) PL 9+18/7 FLC 0+2 FAC 0+1
Leicester C (£1,100,000 on 8/8/1997) PL 13+21/3 FLC 2+5/2 FAC 0+4 Others 0+2
Walsall (Free on 20/3/2000) FL 8+1/1
Stoke C (Free on 11/8/2000) FL 2+3/1 FLC 2
St Mirren (Free on 29/9/2000) SL 26/2 SLC 2 SC 1
Blackpool (Free on 20/8/2001) FL 6+9/5 FLC 0+1 FAC 1 Others 3
Darlington (Loaned on 17/9/2002) FL 4+2/1

FENTON Nicholas (Nicky)
Leonard
Born: Preston, 23 November 1979
Height: 5'10" **Weight:** 10.4
International Honours: E: Yth
This tall, strong centre half was once again a pivotal figure in the Notts County

back line in 2002-03 when he forged an effective partnership with Craig Ireland in the centre of the defence. A near ever-present in the team, he also contributed three valuable goals. Nicky is composed on the ball and very determined in the tackle.
Manchester C (From trainee on 26/11/1996, FL 15 FLC 3+1 Others 1
Notts Co (Loaned on 7/10/1999) FL 13/1 Others 1
Bournemouth (Loaned on 23/3/2000) FL 8
Bournemouth (Loaned on 11/8/2000) FL 4+4
Notts Co (£150,000 on 18/9/2000) FL 111+1/8 FLC 4 FAC 9 Others 3

FERDINAND Leslie (Les)
Born: Acton, 8 December 1966
Height: 5'11" **Weight:** 13.5
Club Honours: FLC '99
International Honours: E: 32; U21-5; Yth
A season of niggling injuries for this experienced striker meant that Spurs missed out on his great aerial ability and strength in attack. Much was expected of the experience that he and Teddy Sheringham could provide in support to Robbie Keane, but after a long lay off Les failed to win a place in the starting line-up and moved on to West Ham in the January transfer window. He struck up a good partnership with young Jermain Defoe who benefitted from his presence at Upton Park. Les leads the line well and was always on hand to help out the defence at set pieces.
Queens Park R (£15,000 from Hayes on 12/3/1987) F/PL 152+11/80 FLC 11+2/7 FAC 6+1/3 Others 1
Brentford (Loaned on 24/3/1988) FL 3
Newcastle U (£6,000,000 on 7/6/1995) PL 67+1/41 FLC 6/3 FAC 4+1/2 Others 5/4
Tottenham H (£6,000,000 on 5/8/1997) PL 97+21/33 FLC 11+4/5 FAC 15+1/1
West Ham U (£200,000 on 21/1/2003) PL 12+2/2

FERDINAND Rio Gavin
Born: Peckham, 8 November 1978
Height: 6'2" **Weight:** 12.1
Club Honours: PL '03
International Honours: E: 27; U21-5; Yth
A consummate central defender, who possesses strength in the air and neat skills on the ground, the fanfares had hardly had chance to die down after Rio's record breaking transfer to Old Trafford in the summer, when he sustained an ankle injury during a pre-season charity game in aid of UNICEF. After recovering from that setback, he made only nine full starts from August to November, before being

142

Rio Ferdinand

sidelined again until late December. Seeing several players excel in his customary position from the sidelines, Rio was back in contention by January, and from thereon in he began to show the kind of form that had persuaded Sir Alex Ferguson to part with that huge cheque. With his influence also showing in the Champions' League against some of the best attacking formations in Europe, Rio's Old Trafford career looks rosy, especially if he can stay clear of injuries.

West Ham U (From trainee on 27/11/1995) PL 122+5/2 FLC 12+1 FAC 9 Others 9
Bournemouth (Loaned on 8/11/1996) FL 10 Others 1
Leeds U (£18,000,000 on 27/11/2000) PL 54/2 FLC 2 FAC 3 Others 14/1
Manchester U (£29,100,000 + on 22/7/2002) PL 27+1 FLC 4 FAC 3 Others 11

FERGUSON Darren
Born: Glasgow, 9 February 1972
Height: 5'10" **Weight:** 11.10
Club Honours: PL '93
International Honours: S: U21-5; Yth
The general feeling amongst the Racecourse faithful is that when Ferguson is on song the whole team are singing! His skilful passing and link play were as always a delight to watch, while there was a buzz of expectation when free kicks were awarded around the edge of the box. The real cog in the Racecourse engine room, with the word 'playmaker' an apt description of his talents, Darren was always on the lookout for goals,

although he only scored two all season. He was rather unfortunate to damage knee ligaments in an end-of-season training ground collision at the beginning of May.

Manchester U (From trainee on 11/7/1990) F/PL 20+7 FLC 2+1
Wolverhampton W (£250,000 on 13/1/1994) FL 94+23/4 FLC 13+2/3 FAC 9+2/3 Others 6
Wrexham (Free on 17/9/1999) FL 158+1/18 FLC 5/1 FAC 8/1 Others 6

FERGUSON Duncan
Born: Stirling, 27 December 1971
Height: 6'4" **Weight:** 14.6
Club Honours: SL '94; SLC '94; FAC '95
International Honours: S: 7; B; U21-7; Yth; Sch
Another season and another injury-plagued campaign for Everton's totemic striker and club captain, who failed to make a single first-team start. A long-term back injury restricted the tall striker to just seven league appearances as a substitute at the tail-end of the season. Although he laboured initially when he returned, an inspirational second-half performance against Aston Villa at Goodison enabled Everton to snatch a victory from the jaws of defeat. At his best the Scot can be near unplayable due to his power in the air and strength on the ground, and all followers of Everton will be hoping that a good pre-season will lead to an improved 2003-04.

Dundee U (Signed from Carse Thistle on 1/2/1990) SL 75+2/28 SLC 2+1/2 SC 8/6

Glasgow R (£4,000,000 on 20/7/1993) SL 8+6/2 SLC 2+2/3 SC 0+3 Others 1
Everton (£4,400,000 on 4/10/1994) PL 110+6/37 FLC 8/1 FAC 8+1/4
Newcastle U (£7,000,000 + on 25/11/1998) PL 24+6/8 FAC 6+2/3 Others 2+1/1
Everton (£3,750,000 on 19/8/2000) PL 26+15/12 FLC 1+1/1 FAC 3/1

FERNANDES Fabrice
Born: Paris, France, 29 October 1979
Height: 5'9" **Weight:** 11.7
Club Honours: Div 1 '01
International Honours: France: U21
Brought on in the dying minutes of the FA Cup final Fabrice, a quick, tricky, player with a weakness for taking on one-too-many defenders, was just the sort of character likely to turn the tables on a tiring Arsenal, but he hardly got a touch. He featured on the left and right of Southampton's four-man midfield during 2002-03, more often, and preferably on the right, from where he could cut in and use his favoured left foot for a slick pass, artful cross or stinging shot.

Fulham (Loaned from Rennes, France on 3/8/2002) FL 23+6/2 FLC 2 FAC 1
Southampton (£1,100,000 from Rennes, France on 27/12/2001) PL 41+7/4 FLC 1/1 FAC 6+2

FERRER Albert Llopes
Born: Barcelona, Spain, 6 June 1970
Height: 5'7" **Weight:** 10.6
Club Honours: ESC '98
International Honours: Spain: 36; U23 (OLYM '92)
The 2002-03 season was a crushing disappointment for this excellent right back who was kept out of the Chelsea line-up by the ever-consistent Mario Melchiot. Albert made just four starts, -al before the turn of the year, and, frankly, his long-term future at the club must be shrouded in doubt. This is a far cry from the situation three years ago when he endeared himself to the Blues' faithful with his intelligent, confident defending and assured counter-attacking.

Chelsea (£2,200,000 from Barcelona, Spain on 15/8/1998) PL 71+5 FLC 2+2 FAC 10+1 Others 22/1

FESTA Gianluca
Born: Cagliari, Italy, 15 March 1969
Height: 6'0'' **Weight:** 13.6
Club Honours: Div 1 '03
This experienced defender made a massive contribution to Portsmouth's success in the First Division last season. Consistent, uncompromising, alert and reliable, he fittingly scored in his last

Darren Ferguson

match for Pompey at Bradford City in a 5-
0 win to round off a splendid season.
Gianluca has now returned to Italy, much
to the sadness of all Pompey supporters.
*Middlesbrough (£2,700,000 from Inter
Milan, Italy, ex Cagliari, on 18/11/1997) F/PL
132+6/10 FLC 18/1 FAC 14+1/1*
*Portsmouth (Signed on 23/8/2002) FL 27/1
FLC 2*

FETTIS Alan William
Born: Belfast, 1 February 1971
Height: 6'1" **Weight:** 12.10
International Honours: NI: 25; B-3; Yth;
Sch

Alan continued to show outstanding form
for York City in the opening half of last
season when he was the club's first choice
'keeper. However, the club's financial
troubles meant that he returned to his
former club Hull City midway through the
campaign. A folk hero in the Tigers'
history as a result of scoring twice as an
outfield player in his first spell at the club,
Alan's consistent displays in his more
orthodox role earned a recall to the
Northern Ireland squad after a five-year
gap. He also became the first Hull player
since Dean Windass in 1994 to be named
in a PFA divisional team of the year.

*Hull C (£50,000 from Ards on 14/8/1991) FL
131+4/2 FLC 7+1 FAC 5 Others 7*
*West Bromwich A (Loaned on 20/11/1995)
FL 3*
*Nottingham F (£250,000 on 13/1/1996) PL
4 FLC 1 FAC 0+1*
*Blackburn Rov (£300,000 on 12/9/1997)
P/FL 9+2 FAC 1*
*York C (Free on 1/3/2000) FL 125 FLC 3
FAC 12*
Hull C (Free on 23/1/2003) FL 17

FEUER Anthony Ian
Born: Las Vegas, Nevada, USA, 20 May
1971
Height: 6'7" **Weight:** 15.6
International Honours: USA: 1

This giant goalkeeper made two early-
season appearances for Tranmere last
term to cover for the suspended John
Achterberg. Soon afterwards he joined
Wolverhampton Wanderers on non-
contract forms as cover, but made no
senior appearances for the First Division
club. Ian is a capable and experienced
'keeper who makes full use of his height.
*West Ham U (£70,000 from Los Angeles
Salsa, USA on 23/3/1994)*
*Peterborough U (Loaned on 20/2/1995)
FL 16*
*Luton T (£580,000 on 11/9/1995) FL 97 FLC
7 FAC 6 Others 5 (Free to New England
Revolution, USA on 24/3/1998)*
*Cardiff C (Free from Colorado Rapids, USA
on 10/1/2000)*
West Ham U (Free on 23/2/2000) PL 3
*Wimbledon (Free on 28/6/2000) FL 2+2 FLC
1 FAC 2*
Derby Co (Loaned on 12/10/2001) PL 2
Tranmere Rov (Free on 12/8/2002) FL 2
Wolverhampton W (Free on 18/9/2002)

FIELDWICK Lee Peter
Born: Croydon, 6 September 1982
Height: 5'11" **Weight:** 12.2
This impressive young Brentford left back
did not really start his season until the
new year due to illness and injury. He
eventually made his senior debut at Luton
in February during an injury crisis, and
helped the Bees to a vital win. Lee added
a handful more appearances before
obtaining a regular seat on the
substitutes' bench.
Brentford (From trainee on 4/7/2001) FL 6+1

FILAN John Richard
Born: Sydney, Australia, 8 February 1970
Height: 5'11" **Weight:** 13.2
Club Honours: Div 2 '03
International Honours: Australia: 1;
U23

Gianluca Festa

145

This experienced 'keeper enjoyed a remarkable season in Wigan Athletic's Second Division title-winning side. Well protected by a back four, the outstanding shot stopper produced the saves when necessary including 'Man of the Match' performances at Blackpool and Cardiff. Ever-present during the campaign, he went over 750 minutes without conceding a goal and again collected the club's 'Players' Player of the Year' award, while being honoured by his fellow professionals with a place in the PFA Second Division team for the season.
Cambridge U *(£40,000 from Budapest St George, Australia on 12/3/1993) FL 68 FLC 6 FAC 3 Others 3*
Coventry C *(£300,000 on 2/3/1995) PL 15+1 FLC 2*
Blackburn Rov *(£700,000 on 10/7/1997) P/FL 61+1 FLC 6 FAC 5*
Wigan Ath *(£450,000 on 14/12/2001) FL 71 FLC 5 FAC 3 Others 1*

FINNAN Stephen (Steve) John
Born: Limerick, 20 April 1976
Height: 5'10" **Weight:** 11.6
Club Honours: Div 3 '98; Div 2 '99; Div 1 '01
International Honours: RoI: 22; B-1; U21-8
After enjoying a successful World Cup with the Republic of Ireland, Steve once again showed the form that has made him a target for a number of the top Premiership sides. He usually operated at right back where he committed tackling and impressive distribution skills helped start a high proportion of Fulham's attacking moves. Occasionally he was employed on the right-hand side of midfield enjoying outstanding games in this position against Manchester United and Arsenal. Now the first choice right back for his country, he remained a regular selection under new boss Brian Kerr.
Birmingham C *(£100,000 from Welling U on 12/6/1995) FL 9+6/1 FLC 2+2 Others 2+1*
Notts Co *(Loaned on 5/3/1996) FL 14+3/2 Others 3/1*
Notts Co *(£300,000 on 31/10/1996) FL 71+9/5 FLC 4 FAC 7/1 Others 1*
Fulham *(£600,000 on 13/11/1998) P/FL 171+1/6 FLC 10+1 FAC 18/1 Others 6*

FINNIGAN John Francis
Born: Wakefield, 29 March 1976
Height: 5'8" **Weight:** 10.11
An all-action central midfield player, John was voted both 'Players' and 'Sponsors'

Player of the Season' at Cheltenham Town in 2002-03. His busy style earned the nickname 'Wasp' from new manager Bobby Gould because of his constant buzzing around the midfield area, never allowing opposition players to settle on the ball. His passing and composure improved noticeably over time, although he managed just one goal, netting in the 2-1 defeat at Cardiff City. He was also badly missed when spending a month out with an injury picked up in a reserve game.
Nottingham F *(From trainee on 10/5/1993)*
Lincoln C *(£50,000 on 26/3/1998) FL 139+4/3 FLC 7 FAC 8+1/1 Others 7*
Cheltenham T *(Free on 7/3/2002) FL 46+3/3 FLC 2 FAC 3 Others 3/1*

FISH Mark Anthony
Born: Capetown, South Africa, 14 March 1974
Height: 6'3" **Weight:** 13.2
International Honours: South Africa: 60 (ANC '96)
Having missed the first few games due to injury, Mark became a regular in the Charlton side for most of the remainder of the 2002-03 season. He was used primarily as a central defender in either a back three or back four, although he also played several games at right back, looking at ease wherever he appeared. Strong and very effective in the air, Mark is extremely comfortable on the ball and has developed a strong partnership with Richard Rufus in the middle of the Addicks' defence. He scored his only goal of the campaign in the home draw with Bolton Wanderers. He missed the last half-dozen games due to a knee injury, but hopefully will be fully fit for the coming season.
Bolton W *(£2,500,000 from Lazio, Italy, ex Orlando Pirates, on 16/9/1997) P/FL 102+1/3 FLC 12+1/1 FAC 6 Others 5*
Charlton Ath *(£700,000 on 10/11/2000) PL 72/2 FLC 2 FAC 4*

FISKEN Gary Stewart
Born: Watford, 27 October 1981
Height: 6'0" **Weight:** 12.7
Gary underwent knee surgery in the summer and then faced a long battle for full fitness, including two further operations. A hard-working and creative midfielder, he finally returned to first-team action for Watford in March, and did enough towards the end of the season to earn himself a new contract.
Watford *(From trainee on 8/2/2000) FL 15+6/1 FLC 2+2 FAC 1*

FITZGERALD Scott Brian
Born: Westminster, 13 August 1969
Height: 6'0" **Weight:** 12.12
International Honours: RoI: B-1; U21-4
Colchester United skipper Scott injured his knee during the pre-season, and this caused him to miss the first four months of the 2002-03 campaign. His first appearance coincided with a 2-1 win at Luton in December, and the ex-Millwall stalwart did not miss another game as the U's climbed the table during the second half of the season. Scott rarely put a foot wrong at the heart of defence, and was often on hand to complete goal line clearances.
Wimbledon *(From trainee on 13/7/1989) F/PL 95+11/1 FLC 13 FAC 5 Others 1*
Sheffield U *(Loaned on 23/11/1995) FL 6*
Millwall *(Loaned on 11/10/1996) FL 7*
Millwall *(£50,000 + on 28/7/1997) FL 79+3/1 FLC 4 FAC 2 Others 5*
Colchester U *(Free on 17/10/2000) FL 92+1 FLC 2 FAC 3 Others 2*

FITZGERALD Scott Peter
Born: Hillingdon, 18 November 1979
Height: 5'11" **Weight:** 11.6
Scott joined Watford on a free transfer last March from Ryman League club Northwood, for whom he had already scored 29 goals in the season. At 23 he was a late starter to professional football, but he was an immediate scorer for the reserves and was given an early chance in the first team. He made his full debut against Sheffield United on the last day of the season and marked the occasion with an opportunist first senior goal. A striker who is quick, enthusiastic and with a natural instinct for goal, he can only improve with the benefit of full-time training.
Watford *(Free from Northwood on 5/3/2003) FL 1+3/1*

FLACK Steven (Steve) Richard
Born: Cambridge, 29 May 1971
Height: 6'2" **Weight:** 13.2
Steve had another good season as he continued to be a first choice striker for Exeter, missing only a handful of games. He finished the campaign as the club's leading scorer with 13 goals and it was only fitting that he should score their last goal prior to relegation when he netted against Southend. He used his height and strength to maximum effect against opposing defences, and coped admirably with having to play alongside a succession of partners up front.
Cardiff C *(£10,000 from Cambridge C on 13/11/1995) FL 6+5/1*

*Exeter C (£10,000 on 13/9/1996) FL
213+55/63 FLC 8+1 FAC 14+4/5 Others
8+2/2*

FLAHAVAN Darryl James
Born: Southampton, 28 November 1978
Height: 5'10" **Weight:** 12.1
Darryl was Southend United's regular
'keeper again last season, although a
thigh injury sustained in the home game
against Scunthorpe meant he missed the
first five matches of the new year. He had
an eventful game at Darlington when,
having been booked, he made amends by
saving a penalty although the Blues went
down 2-1. A supreme shot stopper, his
lack of inches sometimes results in goals
being scored when shots are angled
across him. He kept nine clean sheets, but
nevertheless he was released in the
summer.
*Southampton (From trainee on 14/5/1996.
Free to Woking on 13/8/1998)*
*Southend U (Free on 16/10/2000) FL 111
FLC 2 FAC 12 Others 9*

FLEMING Craig
Born: Halifax, 6 October 1971
Height: 6'0" **Weight:** 12.10
A couple of injuries disrupted Craig's
2002-03 season, but he remained one of
Norwich's most consistent performers,
something which was recognised when
he signed a two-year extension to his
contract in January. Much of his best
work goes unheralded, particularly his
unfussy style and fearless approach to
defending, but his efforts are always
appreciated by his team mates and the
fans. He played the 500th first-team
game of his career in the Easter Monday
home defeat by Wolves.
*Halifax T (From trainee on 21/3/1990) FL
56+1 FLC 4 FAC 3 Others 3+2*
*Oldham Ath (£80,000 on 15/8/1991) F/PL
158+6/1 FLC 12+1 FAC 11 Others 4*
*Norwich C (£600,000 on 30/6/1997) FL
206+7/7 FLC 16 FAC 8+1 Others 3*

FLEMING Curtis
Born: Manchester, 8 October 1968
Height: 5'11" **Weight:** 12.8
Club Honours: Div 1 '95
International Honours: Roi: 10; U23-2;
U21-5; Yth
Curtis began the 2002-03 campaign as
club captain of Crystal Palace and was a
regular in the team in the early weeks of
the season. However, he was then
sidelined with knee problems in October
and spent much of the rest of the season
on the treatment table. He made a brief
return early in the new year, featuring in

the amazing FA Cup win against Liverpool
at Anfield, but managed just one more
appearance from the bench thereafter.
Curtis is a hard-tackling defender who is
effective when pushing forward with the
ball.
*Middlesbrough (£50,000 from St Patricks
on 16/8/1991) F/PL 248+18/3 FLC 24+2/1
FAC 16+1 Others 7+1*
Birmingham C (Loaned on 16/11/2001) FL 6
*Crystal Palace (£100,000 on 31/12/2001) FL
26+2 FLC 1 FAC 1*

FLEMING Terence (Terry)
Maurice
Born: Marston Green, 5 January 1973
Height: 5'9" **Weight:** 10.9
This consistent midfielder was a near ever-
present for Cambridge United last season.
The senior member of what was generally
a young squad, his experience proved
invaluable. Terry found himself used in a
variety of roles with the exception of
goalkeeper and striker, but he was best
employed as a ball winner in the centre of
midfield.
*Coventry C (From trainee on 2/7/1991) F/PL
8+5 FLC 0+1*
*Northampton T (Free on 3/8/1993) FL
26+5/1 FLC 2 FAC 0+1 Others 0+1*
*Preston NE (Free on 18/7/1994) FL 25+7/2
FLC 4 FAC 0+1 Others 3+2*
*Lincoln C (Signed on 7/12/1995) FL 175+8/8
FLC 11+1/2 FAC 11/2 Others 4*
*Plymouth Arg (Free on 4/7/2000) FL 15+2
FLC 2 FAC 2 Others 0+2*
*Cambridge U (Free on 8/3/2001) FL 79+8/3
FLC 3 FAC 6 Others 8+2/1*

FLETCHER Carl Neil
Born: Camberley, 7 April 1980
Height: 5'10" **Weight:** 11.7
Carl was named team captain of
Bournemouth at the start of last season
and responded to the challenge in some
style. A central midfielder, he reverted
back to a central defensive role after an
injury crisis at the club and his form saw
him make a clean sweep of the club
awards. He finished the season
sensationally, scoring twice in the 5-2 win
at the Millennium Stadium against Lincoln
in the play-off final.
*Bournemouth (From trainee on 3/7/1998) FL
140+7/15 FLC 4 FAC 12+1/1 Others 8+1/3*

FLETCHER Darren Barr
Born: Edinburgh, 1 February 1984
Height: 6'0" **Weight:** 13.5
International Honours: S: U21-2
An upright and elegant midfielder, who
possesses good touch and passing skills,
Darren is currently being touted as the

latest big prospect down Old Trafford
way. All those attributes were put to the
test against Basle and Deportivo in the
Champions' League, when he rose to the
occasion in commanding fashion. With
Scotland boss, Berti Vogts also tracking
him, the only downside at present is his
susceptibility to injuries: Darren has
broken the same toe five times and has a
permanent pin inserted.
*Manchester U (From trainee on 3/2/2001)
Others 2*

FLETCHER Gary
Born: Widnes, 4 June 1981
Height: 5'10" **Weight:** 11.7
Gary started the 2002-03 season as a
first-choice striker for Leyton Orient, but
lost his place after his form dipped. He
joined Dagenham & Redbridge on loan in
October and when he returned to
Brisbane Road he switched to playing on
the right-hand side of midfield. He netted
his first goal for the O's at Torquay in April
and will be looking to feature more
regularly at first-team level in 2003-04.
*Hull C (Loaned from Northwich Vic on
16/3/2001) FL 1+4*
*Leyton Orient (£150,000 from Northwich
Vic on 9/7/2001) FL 10+11/1 FLC 1/1 FAC 2*

FLETCHER Steven (Steve)
Mark
Born: Hartlepool, 26 June 1972
Height: 6'2" **Weight:** 14.9
Steve celebrated his 11th season at
Bournemouth by passing the 400-
appearance mark and scoring the opening
goal in the play-off final against Lincoln.
He returned to the first team after missing
nearly a year through injury and proved
again just what an effective target man
he is. Still as popular as ever with the
supporters, Steve had a testimonial match
against Portsmouth in the summer of
2002.
*Hartlepool U (From trainee on 23/8/1990) FL
19+13/4 FLC 0+2/1 FAC 1+2 Others 2+2/1*
*Bournemouth (£30,000 on 28/7/1992) FL
323+25/65 FLC 26/3 FAC 23+1/6 Others
18+2/4*

FLITCROFT David (Dave) John
Born: Bolton, 14 January 1974
Height: 5'11" **Weight:** 13.5
Dave had a terrific season for Rochdale in
2002-03, winning the club's 'Player of the
Year' title and being voted the supporters'
'Player of the Year' by a huge margin. The
combative midfielder was near ever-
present and added a new dimension to
his game with raking passes and through
balls to his front men. Indeed, his value to

147

the side was emphasised when Dale declined to postpone a game when they had three players on international duty so that Dave could complete his suspension and be available for the televised FA Cup tie with Wolves.

Preston NE *(From trainee on 2/5/1992) FL 4+4/2 FLC 0+1 Others 0+1*

Lincoln C *(Loaned on 17/9/1993) FL 2 FLC 0+1*

Chester C *(Free on 9/12/1993) FL 146+21/18 FLC 10+1 FAC 7 Others 8/1*

Rochdale *(Free on 5/7/1999) FL 141+19/4 FLC 5+2 FAC 7+4 Others 9+1*

FLITCROFT Garry William
Born: Bolton, 6 November 1972
Height: 6'0" **Weight:** 12.2
Club Honours: FLC '02
International Honours: E: U21-10; Yth; Sch

Garry was once again a mainstay of the Blackburn Rovers midfield last term. His leadership and aggressive play were invaluable to the team, and whilst he may have limitations in terms of finesse and creativity his presence was essential when facing physically strong opposition. Garry contributed two Premiership goals during the campaign, netting winners against Leeds in September and Manchester United in December.

Manchester C *(From trainee on 2/7/1991) PL 109+6/13 FLC 11+1 FAC 14/2*

Bury *(Loaned on 5/3/1992) FL 12*

Blackburn Rov *(£3,200,000 on 26/3/1996) P/FL 184+10/11 FLC 10+3/1 FAC 11+1/4 Others 3/1*

FLO Tore Andre
Born: Stryn, Norway, 15 June 1973
Height: 6'4" **Weight:** 13.8

Club Honours: FLC '98; ECWC '98; ESC '98; FAC '00; CS '00; SLC '02; SC '02
International Honours: Norway: 68; U21
This 6ft 4in Norwegian international centre forward became Sunderland's record signing when he arrived from Rangers in August. Possessing an excellent first touch and tremendous skill on the ball for such a tall man, he made an immediate impact at the Stadium of Light and a late equaliser against Manchester United gave him a goal on his debut. An ankle injury in January somewhat blighted his hopes of establishing himself in the first team and his appearances were sporadic for the remainder of the campaign.

Chelsea *(£300,000 from Brann Bergen, Norway, ex Sogndal, Tromso, on 4/8/1997) PL 59+53/34 FLC 7+2/3 FAC 5+5/1 Others 23+9/12*

Glasgow R *(£12,000,000 on 23/11/2000) SL 44+9/29 SLC 2+1/1 SC 5/4 Others 10+1/4*

Sunderland *(£6,750,000 on 30/8/2002) PL 23+6/4 FLC 1/2 FAC 1+1*

FLOWERS Timothy (Tim) David
Born: Kenilworth, 3 February 1967
Height: 6'2" **Weight:** 14.0
Club Honours: PL '95; FLC '00
International Honours: E: 11; U21-3; Yth
This experienced goalkeeper joined Manchester City on loan in August 2002 to cover for a crisis, but did not see any action at Maine Road. Otherwise he acted as the regular understudy for Ian Walker at Leicester throughout the season, finally stepping over the touchline for a sentimental farewell with 12 minutes of the campaign remaining at Molineux. Tim assisted with goalkeeping coaching duties with relish. Long-term arthritic problems eventually forced his retirement from the playing side during the summer and a permanent move into coaching beckons.

Wolverhampton W *(From apprentice on 28/8/1984) FL 63 FLC 5 FAC 2 Others 2*

Southampton *(£70,000 on 13/6/1986) F/PL 192 FLC 26 FAC 16 Others 8*

Swindon T *(Loaned on 23/3/1987) FL 2*

Swindon T *(Loaned on 13/11/1987) FL 5*

Blackburn Rov *(£2,400,000 on 4/11/1993) PL 175+2 FLC 14 FAC 13+1 Others 12*

Leicester C *(£1,100,000 + on 30/7/1999) P/FL 54+2 FLC 5+1 FAC 2 Others 2*

Stockport Co *(Loaned on 26/10/2001) FL 4*

Coventry C *(Loaned on 19/2/2002) FL 5*

FLYNN Michael (Mike) Anthony
Born: Oldham, 23 February 1969
Height: 6'0" **Weight:** 11.0
International Honours: W: SP

Dave Flitcroft

This experienced central defender started the season as first choice alongside Chris Morgan for Barnsley. Strong in the air and with a sure tackle, he always gave 100 per cent and was also a good organiser. However, as the team began to struggle he found his chances in the first team becoming more and more limited. In January he joined Blackpool on loan where he impressed with some determined defending and his ability in the air. He featured regularly for the Seasiders and after his contract at Oakwell was cancelled by mutual consent he signed on a permanent basis.
Oldham Ath (From apprentice on 7/2/1987) FL 37+3/1 FLC 1+1 FAC 1 Others 2
Norwich C (£100,000 on 22/12/1988)
Preston NE (£125,000 on 4/12/1989) FL 134+2/7 FLC 6 FAC 6+1/1 Others 13
Stockport Co (£125,000 on 25/3/1993) FL 386+1/16 FLC 34/2 FAC 20/1 Others 19
Stoke C (Loaned on 12/1/2002) FL 11+2
Barnsley (Free on 15/3/2002) FL 20+1
Blackpool (Free on 10/1/2003) FL 21

FLYNN Michael John
Born: Newport, 17 October 1980
Height: 5'10" **Weight:** 12.10
Club Honours: Div 2 '03
A summer signing from Barry Town with whom he had won semi-professional honours for Wales, Michael's first season as a professional saw him contribute to Wigan's Second Division championship campaign. Used mainly as a substitute the lively central midfielder made his first league start in the away win at Notts County. He sealed victory at Blackpool with his first goal for the club and was also on target in the FA Cup against Luton Town.
Wigan Ath (£50,000 from Barry T, ex Newport Co, on 25/6/2002) FL 3+14/1 FLC 0+3 FAC 0+2/1 Others 2

FLYNN Sean Michael
Born: Birmingham, 13 March 1968
Height: 5'8" **Weight:** 11.8
Sean brought a wealth of experience to the Kidderminster midfield when he joined from Tranmere in the summer of 2002, and after being installed as captain he led his troops from the front throughout the campaign. He only found the net on two occasions, the highlight being a 25-yard volley against Carlisle at Aggborough in November. At the time of writing he was one of a number of Harriers' players waiting to find out if he would be offered a new contract.
Coventry C (£20,000 from Halesowen T on 3/12/1991) F/PL 90+7/9 FLC 5/1 FAC 3

Derby Co (£250,000 on 11/8/1995) F/PL 39+20/3 FLC 3 FAC 3
Stoke C (Loaned on 27/3/1997) FL 5
West Bromwich A (£260,000 on 8/8/1997) FL 99+10/8 FLC 11/1 FAC 0+2
Tranmere Rov (Free on 18/7/2000) FL 65+1/6 FLC 8/2 FAC 8/3
Kidderminster Hrs (Free on 8/8/2002) FL 45/2 FLC 1 FAC 1 Others 3

Sean Flynn

FOE Marc-Vivien
Born: Nkolo, Cameroon, 1 May 1975
Height: 6'3" **Weight:** 13.6
International Honours: Cameroon: 64 (ANC 2000)
Marc-Vivien joined Manchester City in a 12-month loan deal, having turned down Champions' League football in favour of action in the Premiership. The tigerish defensive midfield player made a fairly slow start before bursting into life with a run of six goals in six games, including doubles against Charlton and Aston Villa. He was an automatic choice in the team throughout the campaign and finished with a respectable tally of nine goals. However, tragedy struck in the Confederations Cup semi-final between Cameroon and Colombia on 26 June. Marc-Vivien collapsed on the pitch in the closing stages of the match. Shortly afterwards he was pronounced dead. A much-respected player, he will be sorely missed in the football world.
West Ham U (£4,200,000 from RC Lens, France, ex Canon Younde, on 28/1/1999) PL 38/1 FLC 3 FAC 1 Others 5+1/1 (£6,000,000 to Lyon, France during 2000 close season)
Manchester C (Loaned from Lyon, France on 5/7/2002) PL 35/9 FLC 2 FAC 1

FOLAN Caleb Colman
Born: Leeds, 26 October 1982
Height: 6'1" **Weight:** 12.12
Caleb joined Chesterfield from Leeds United last February. Tall and lithe, with good pace, he has some work to do to develop his skills, but he is a level headed, willing individual, who will learn. His bravery on the field was without question and he embraced life at Saltergate with enthusiasm.
Leeds U (From trainee on 2/11/1999)
Rushden & Diamonds (Loaned on 5/10/2001) FL 1+5 Others 1
Hull C (Loaned on 30/11/2001) FL 0+1
Chesterfield (Free on 14/2/2003) FL 9+4/1

FOLEY Dominic Joseph
Born: Cork, 7 July 1976
Height: 6'1" **Weight:** 12.8
International Honours: RoI: 6; U21-8
This tall left-sided striker continued to delight and frustrate in almost equal measure for Watford last season. Hard working and willing, his commitment was never in doubt, but he possibly lacked the necessary ruthlessness in front of goal. In February he went out on loan to Southend, but although clearly a useful target man he added little to the squad. He then spent the closing stages of the campaign at Oxford, where he found the net hard to come by, despite showing some good approach work. Dominic was released by Watford in the summer.
Wolverhampton W (£35,000 from St James' Gate on 31/8/1995) FL 4+16/3 FLC 0+3 FAC 0+1 Others 0+2
Watford (Loaned on 24/2/1998) FL 2+6/1
Notts Co (Loaned on 7/12/1998) FL 2 Others 1
Watford (Free on 11/6/1999) P/FL 12+21/5 FLC 4+3/1
Queens Park R (Loaned on 25/10/2001) FL 1
Swindon T (Loaned on 11/1/2002) FL 5+2/1
Queens Park R (Loaned on 28/3/2002) FL 2+2/1
Southend U (Loaned on 10/2/2003) FL 5
Oxford U (Loaned on 25/3/2003) FL 4+2

FOLEY Kevin Patrick
Born: Luton, 1 November 1984
Height: 5'9" **Weight:** 11.2
Kevin was voted as Luton Town's 'Young Player of the Season' for the second season running in 2002-03. His long-expected first-team league debut came against Bristol City when he acquitted himself very well. A clever full back who has also played in midfield for the reserves, Kevin likes to go forward either through the middle or down the flanks. He scored with a brilliant free kick in the

FA Youth Cup match against Middlesbrough.

Luton T (Trainee) FL 0+2 Others 1+1

FORAN Richard (Richie)
Born: Dublin, 16 June 1980
Height: 6'1" **Weight:** 12.9
International Honours: RoI: U21-2
A key member of the Carlisle United front line, Richie is a hard-working and determined forward who gives defenders a difficult time. Although his season was disrupted at times by injury, he still started the majority of the club's league games. A maker as well as a taker of chances, he forged a promising partnership with top scorer Craig Farrell. Although strong in the air, the pick of Richie's goals was probably the 25-yard volley that secured a late draw at Bury in April.

Carlisle U (£20,000 from Shelbourne on 31/8/2001) FL 64+4/21 FAC 6/2 Others 5+2/2

FORBES Adrian Emmanuel
Born: Ealing, 23 January 1979
Height: 5'8" **Weight:** 11.10
International Honours: E: Yth
Adrian had the misfortune to suffer a serious cruciate knee ligament injury in a pre-season friendly against Southampton. However, his determination and cheerful personality saw him make a relatively quick return to action for Luton and five months later he appeared for the Hatters against Crewe Alexandra. The versatile winger seemed to have lost none of his pace and contributed a useful goal against Cheltenham Town.

Norwich C (From trainee on 21/11/1997) FL 66+46/8 FLC 1+4 FAC 2+2
Luton T (£60,000 on 16/7/2001) FL 18+27/5 FLC 1 FAC 1/1

FORBES Boniek Manuel Gomes
Born: Guinea Bissau, 30 September 1983
Height: 5'10" **Weight:** 11.0
Boniek was again a regular goal-scorer for Leyton Orient's youth and reserve teams last season. A tricky player who likes to get the ball at his feet and take on opponents, he made four brief appearances from the bench for the first team. A switch in positions from striker to the left wing seemed to benefit him and he was rewarded with a new short-term contract during the summer.

Leyton Orient (Trainee) FL 0+3 FAC 0+1

FORBES Terrell Dishan
Born: Southwark, 17 August 1981
Height: 6'0" **Weight:** 12.8
Club Honours: FAYC '99
This right-sided defender continued to

perform to the high standards he set in his first season at Queen's Park Rangers last term. A very popular player with the fans, he was calm in his defensive duties and made some solid contributions to the team's attacking play with his forays down the wing. Terrell was a regular in the first team throughout the campaign, but failed to contribute a goal all season.

West Ham U (From trainee on 2/7/1999)
Bournemouth (Loaned on 18/10/1999) FL 3 FAC 1
Queens Park R (Free on 24/7/2001) FL 81 FLC 2 FAC 2+1 Others 2

FORD Mark Stuart
Born: Pontefract, 10 October 1975
Height: 5'8" **Weight:** 10.10
Club Honours: FAYC '93
International Honours: E: U21-2; Yth
Mark started the season in midfield for Darlington, but lost his place in October to the young Clark Keltie who established himself in the side. Mark never won his place back and was allowed to go out on loan to Leigh RMI in the new year. Extremely quick into the tackle and an accurate passer of the ball, he is also capable of getting forward and grabbing

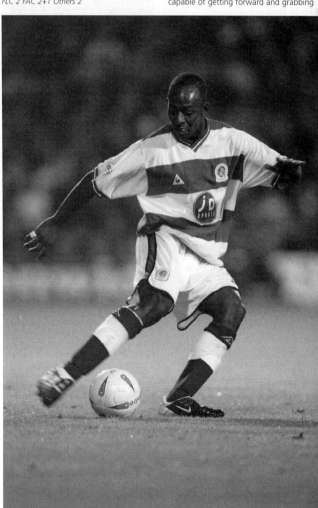

Terrell Forbes

spectacular goals from the edge of the box. He was released at the end of the season.

Leeds U *(From trainee on 5/3/1993)* PL 27+2/1 FLC 7 FAC 5 Others 0+1
Burnley *(£250,000 on 18/7/1997)* FL 43+5/1 FLC 2 FAC 1+1 Others 5+1 *(Free to KFC Commelse, Belgium during 1999 close season)*
Torquay U *(Free on 17/7/2000)* FL 28/3 FLC 2 FAC 2/1 Others 1
Darlington *(£15,000 on 19/2/2001)* FL 55+2/9 FLC 2 FAC 2

FORD Robert (Bobby) John
Born: Bristol, 22 September 1974
Height: 5'9" **Weight:** 11.0
The re-signing of the former Oxford star midfielder six years after he left the club was considered a major coup by the fans and Bobby did not disappoint, becoming one of the best midfield players in the Third Division. A lack of games in pre-season saw him start the early matches from the bench, but he soon became a regular, spraying passes forward to his strikers. He only managed one goal, against Boston, but he was nonetheless an influential player for the U's.
Oxford U *(From trainee on 6/10/1992)* FL 104+12/7 FLC 14+2/1 FAC 10/2 Others 7/1
Sheffield U *(£400,000 on 28/11/1997)* FL 138+17/6 FLC 10+2/1 FAC 14+4 Others 2
Oxford U *(Free on 8/8/2002)* FL 31+6/1 FLC 2 FAC 2

FORD Simon Gary
Born: Newham, 17 November 1981
Height: 6'0" **Weight:** 11.6
Grimsby fans were relieved when this young central defender committed himself to the Mariners for a further two years during the 2002 close season. He was rewarded when he became an automatic first choice for the senior squad from October onwards, retaining his place despite occasional setbacks. Simon benefited from playing alongside Georges Santos and will be looking to make further progress in 2003-04.
Grimsby T *(Free from trainee at Charlton Ath on 12/7/2001)* FL 43+9/3 FLC 0+1 FAC 3

FORINTON Howard Lee
Born: Boston, 18 September 1975
Height: 5'11" **Weight:** 11.4
This experienced striker had an early-season trial at Torquay and was promptly pitched straight into the first team for the 4-3 defeat at York. That proved to be his only appearance for the Gulls and he was soon on his way to Yeovil Town, before

finishing the season with Ryman League outfit Oxford City.
Birmingham C *(Signed from Yeovil T on 14/7/1997)* FL 0+5/1 FLC 2+3
Plymouth Arg *(Loaned on 18/12/1998)* FL 8+1/3
Peterborough U *(£250,000 on 17/9/1999)* FL 34+16/10 FLC 1 FAC 2+5 Others 2
Torquay U *(Free on 15/8/2002)* FL 1

FORLAN Corazo Diego
Born: Montevideo, Uruguay, 19 May 1979
Height: 5'8" **Weight:** 11.11
Club Honours: PL '03
International Honours: Uruguay: 7
A gifted young striker with a good range of skills, Diego finally notched his first goal for Manchester United against Maccabi Haifa in the Champions' League, then followed up with two in successive Premiership games against Aston Villa and Southampton. Legendary status was all but secured amongst the United faithful following his winning brace against Liverpool at Anfield in December. Having then netted the vital goal against Chelsea that put United through to the Worthington Cup semi-finals, he rounded off the year nicely with a strike against Birmingham. Now looking very much a part of the Premiership scene, and able to come off the bench to turn vital matches, he finished the campaign with a total of nine goals from 15 starts. Diego's father, Pablo Forlan represented Uruguay in the 1960s and 1970s, and played in two World Cup final tournaments.
Manchester U *(£7,500,000 from Independiente, Uruguay on 23/1/2002)* PL 13+25/6 FLC 3+2/2 FAC 0+2 Others 6+12/1

FORREST Daniel (Danny) Paul Halafihi
Born: Keighley, 23 October 1984
Height: 5'10" **Weight:** 11.7
International Honours: E: Yth
A product of the youth system at Bradford, Danny broke into the first team last season following injuries to senior players. A pacy, competitive striker who had done well at youth and reserve-team level, his first start came in the Worthington Cup defeat at Wrexham in September. He scored in the 2-0 win over Ipswich and went on to become a valuable member of the squad, netting two more goals in the defeats by Walsall and Norwich. Danny featured for England at U19 level during the season.
Bradford C *(Trainee)* FL 10+7/3 FLC 1

FORREST Martyn William
Born: Bury, 2 January 1979
Height: 5'10" **Weight:** 12.2
This midfield dynamo began the 2002-03 season as Bury's captain and was regarded as an automatic choice in the Shakers' starting line-up. After nine games, however, he was dropped and the captaincy passed to Jon Newby soon after as Martyn found himself unable to hold down a regular place for the remainder of the season. A tigerish player who likes to battle in midfield, he bounced back in March to earn a run of eight league games, but he never really managed to recapture his best form. Martyn is the son of former Bury goalkeeper John Forrest.
Bury *(From trainee on 16/7/1997)* FL 82+24/2 FLC 3+3 FAC 1+1 Others 5+1

FORRESTER Jamie Mark
Born: Bradford, 1 November 1974
Height: 5'6" **Weight:** 11.0
Club Honours: FAYC '93
International Honours: E: Yth (UEFA-U18 '93); Sch
Except for a mid-season spell when he netted six goals in seven games, Jamie never really captured the form that had brought him so many goals for Northampton in recent seasons. He did net his 100th senior goal in an LDV Vans Trophy match against Hereford, but otherwise had an indifferent season. When Terry Fenwick arrived as manager Jamie was allowed to move on to Hull. The crafty forward quickly began to redress the balance and established a promising partnership with young Bolton loanee Jon Walters. However, his season came to an abrupt end in March when he fractured a bone in his foot against Shrewsbury.
Leeds U *(£60,000 from Auxerre, France on 20/10/1992)* PL 7+2 FAC 1+1/2
Southend U *(Loaned on 1/9/1994)* FL 3+2
Grimsby T *(Loaned on 10/3/1995)* FL 7+2/1
Grimsby T *(Signed on 17/10/1995)* FL 27+14/6 FLC 0+1 FAC 3+1/3
Scunthorpe U *(Signed on 21/3/1997)* FL 99+2/37 FLC 6/1 FAC 7/4 Others 7 *(Free to FC Utrecht, Holland on 1/6/1999)*
Walsall *(Loaned on 30/12/1999)* FL 2+3
Northampton T *(£150,000 on 21/3/2000)* FL 109+12/45 FLC 5/1 FAC 7/2 Others 3/2
Hull C *(Signed on 22/1/2003)* FL 11/3

FORSTER Nicholas (Nicky) Michael
Born: Caterham, 8 September 1973
Height: 5'10" **Weight:** 11.5
International Honours: E: U21-4
Leading goal-scorer and lone striker for

Diego Forlan (right)

much of the campaign as Reading employed a 4-5-1 formation, Nicky made a significant contribution towards the club's bid for promotion, and his injury in the play-off semi-final first leg was the turning point against Wolves. He showed that he can play at the highest level, and his pace and control will test the best defenders. A highly intelligent and articulate footballer, he has run his own soccer school, and is studying part-time for a degree at Roehampton University. He collected the match ball after hat-tricks in the home game against Ipswich Town and Preston North End, and remains a vital component of Alan Pardew's future planning.

Gillingham (Signed from Horley T on 22/5/1992) FL 54+13/24 FLC 3+2 FAC 6/2
Brentford (£100,000 on 17/6/1994) FL 108+1/39 FLC 11/3 FAC 8/1 Others 7+1/4
Birmingham C (£700,000 on 31/1/1997) FL 24+44/11 FLC 2+2/1 FAC 3+1
Reading (£650,000 on 23/6/1999) FL 102+25/46 FLC 6 FAC 4+1 Others 4+4/2

FORSYTH Richard Michael
Born: Dudley, 3 October 1970
Height: 5'11" **Weight:** 13.0
Club Honours: GMVC '94
International Honours: E: SP-3
A regular in midfield for Peterborough United in the early part of the 2002-03 season, Richard was loaned out to Cheltenham Town in October and the move became permanent the following month. He arrived at Whaddon Road during a difficult spell for the Robins and his experience in the centre of the park helped to steady the ship after a poor run of results. Richard made an immediate impact with his ball-winning ability and measured passing and was a key figure in the FA Cup wins over Yeovil Town and Oldham Athletic, but suffered a hamstring injury in January and this brought his campaign to a premature end.

Birmingham C (£50,000 from Kidderminster Hrs on 13/7/1995) FL 12+14/2 FLC 7+2 FAC 2 Others 3+1
Stoke C (£200,000 on 25/7/1996) FL 90+5/17 FLC 7/1 FAC 4 Others 1+1
Blackpool (Free on 5/7/1999) FL 10+3 FAC 0+2 Others 0+1
Peterborough U (Free on 14/7/2000) FL 51+9/2 FLC 4/1 FAC 9/1 Others 1+1
Cheltenham T (£15,000 on 11/10/2002) FL 12/2 FAC 3 Others 2/1

FORTUNE Clayton Alexander
Born: Forest Gate, 10 November 1982
Height: 6'3" **Weight:** 13.10
This young defender broke into Bristol

City's first-team last season and impressed well enough to earn a three-year contract. Clayton made ten appearances in Second Division games and will be looking to establish himself in the side in 2003-04.

Bristol C (Free from trainee at Tottenham H on 22/3/2001) FL 7+4 Others 2+2

FORTUNE Jonathan (Jon) Jay
Born: Islington, 23 August 1980
Height: 6'2" **Weight:** 11.4
Jon was a regular in the Charlton Athletic side in the early part of the 2002-03 season, but then lost his place to Mark Fish. He then featured only when the team formation required three central defenders, but eventually broke back into the side early in the new year and was a regular for the remainder of the campaign. Jon has become an accomplished central defender coping adequately with the Premiership's best strikers. Quick and effective in the air, he likes to get into the opposing penalty area for corners, and scored one of the goals in the 2-0 win at West Ham.

Charlton Ath (From trainee on 2/7/1998) PL 36+9/1 FLC 3/1 FAC 3+1
Mansfield T (Loaned on 18/2/2000) FL 4
Mansfield T (Loaned on 31/8/2000) FL 14

FORTUNE Quinton
Born: Cape Town, South Africa, 21 May 1977
Height: 5'11" **Weight:** 11.11
International Honours: South Africa: 43; U23-18
A top class forward or midfielder with pace and good ball skills to match, Quinton seemed to be finding his Premiership feet again as a valuable member of the Manchester United squad when injuries reared their head again and forced him out on the sidelines in November after just nine starts. Sporadic appearances in the Premiership and Champions' League followed, notably at the end of the campaign, but all in all it was a season of frustration for this talented player.

Manchester U (£1,500,000 from Atletico Madrid, Spain on 27/8/1999) PL 23+13/5 FLC 3 Others 8+11/2

FORTUNE-WEST Leopold (Leo) Paul Osborne
Born: Stratford, 9 April 1971
Height: 6'3" **Weight:** 13.10
This big striker played a part in helping Cardiff City to a second promotion in three years, the fourth occasions on which his teams have achieved this

(Gillingham, Rotherham, Cardiff City on two occasions). Leo was among the first signings of the Sam Hammam era at Ninian Park. He helped lift the Bluebirds out of Division Three and left them at the end of last season with the club in Division One. It is the case that City had more enquiries from other clubs about Leo than any other player on their books: a tribute to his effectiveness as a lower division striker.

Gillingham (£5,000 from Stevenage Borough on 12/7/1995) FL 48+19/18 FLC 3+1/2 FAC 3+1/2
Leyton Orient (Loaned on 27/3/1997) FL 1+4
Lincoln C (Free on 6/7/1998) FL 7+2/1 FLC 2
Rotherham U (Loaned on 8/10/1998) FL 5/4
Brentford (£60,000 on 17/11/1998) FL 2+9 FAC 0+1 Others 2+1/1
Rotherham U (£35,000 on 26/2/1999) FL 59/26 FLC 4 FAC 2 Others 2
Cardiff C (£300,000 on 11/9/2000) FL 53+39/23 FLC 2+1 FAC 7+6/3 Others 5/2

FOSTER James Ian
Born: Liverpool, 11 November 1976
Height: 5'7" **Weight:** 11.0
Club Honours: NC '00
International Honours: E: SP-1; Sch
Ian spent most of the 2002-03 campaign on the substitutes' bench at Kidderminster. Although he came into the game on 25 occasions, he found the net only once with a penalty against Darlington back in August. At the end of the season it was announced that his contract would not be renewed and he was given a rousing send off by the Harriers' fans after the last game.

Hereford U (Free from Liverpool juniors on 15/7/1996) FL 4+15 FLC 2+1 Others 0+1 (Free to Barrow during 1998 close season)
Kidderminster Hrs (Free on 13/8/1999) FL 37+35/11 FLC 3 FAC 3+1 Others 4+2

FOSTER Stephen (Steve) John
Born: Warrington, 10 September 1980
Height: 5'11" **Weight:** 11.8
International Honours: E: Sch
Steve again made good progress at Crewe last term and is now an integral member of the team's defence. He showed his versatility by appearing in a number of different roles during the campaign and scored four goals, all following set pieces. Steve has now passed the landmark of 100 first-team starts for the club.

Crewe Alex (From trainee on 19/9/1998) FL 85+15/9 FLC 4+1/1 FAC 8+1/1 Others 4

FOTIADIS Panos **Andrew (Andy)**
Born: Hitchin, 6 September 1977
Height: 5'11" **Weight:** 11.7
International Honours: E: Sch
Andy struggled to find his best form for Luton last term, but rather ironically hit a rich scoring vein shortly before being transferred to Peterborough United in the new year. However, he failed to win a regular first-team place for the Posh either. Nevertheless his season's record showed that he scored seven goals from only 14 Second Division starts. Andy is a skilful striker who can turn opponents and possesses a powerful shot.
Luton T (From juniors on 26/7/1996) FL 50+73/18 FLC 3+6/1 FAC 5+2/1 Others 4+3
Peterborough U (Free on 7/2/2003) FL 6+5/2

FOWLER Jason Kenneth
Born: Bristol, 20 August 1974
Height: 6'3" **Weight:** 11.12
This elegant central midfielder enjoyed a full season for Torquay United last term after several years blighted by illness and injury. He combined well with Alex Russell as the pair embraced new manager Leroy Rosenior's passing philosophy to play to their strengths. Jason is a talented player who possesses excellent vision and distribution.
Bristol C (From trainee on 8/7/1993) FL 16+9 FLC 1+1 Others 1+1
Cardiff C (Signed on 19/6/1996) FL 138+7/14 FLC 8/1 FAC 12+2/4 Others 3/1
Torquay U (Free on 30/11/2001) FL 54/5 FLC 1 FAC 2/1 Others 0+1

FOWLER Lee Anthony
Born: Cardiff, 10 June 1983
Height: 5'7" **Weight:** 10.8
International Honours: W: U21-1; Yth
This young midfielder had a frustrating season at Coventry last term after seeming to have made the breakthrough in the previous campaign. After several impressive games for the reserves he was selected to start against his home town club in the FA Cup replay in January. Not only did he have an excellent game, using his feisty ball-winning skills to good effect but he also scored an impressive goal, chipping the 'keeper when put clean through. Lee added one further senior appearance before joining Cardiff City on loan in March. However, he only made one appearance for the Bluebirds, in the FA Wales Premier Cup tie against Newport County when he injured his foot. Lee also represented Wales at U21 level during the campaign.

Coventry C (From trainee on 7/7/2000) FL 6+8 FAC 1+1/1

FOWLER Robert (Robbie) Bernard
Born: Liverpool, 9 April 1975
Height: 5'11" **Weight:** 11.10
Club Honours: FLC '95, '01; FAC '01; UEFAC '01; ESC '01
International Honours: E: 26; B-1; U21-8; Yth (UEFA-U18 '93)
A hip injury meant that Robbie's season at Leeds didn't start until December. He scored on his return to the line-up in the 3-0 victory at Bolton and remained in the first-team picture while fighting for full fitness. However, the financial situation at Elland Road led to him moving on to Manchester City during the January transfer window. He went on to make 13 appearances at Maine Road, but was struggling to hit his best form for much of the time. The highlights of his season came with the two goals he scored for City against Birmingham and Sunderland and he will be hoping for better things in 2003-04.
Liverpool (From trainee on 23/4/1992) P/FL 210+26/120 FLC 32/27 FAC 21+3/12 Others 26+12/12
Leeds U (£11,000,000 on 30/11/2001) PL 24+6/14 FLC 1+1 Others 0+1
Manchester C (£3,000,000 + on 30/1/2003) PL 12+1/2

FOX Christian
Born: Stonehaven, 11 April 1981
Height: 5'10" **Weight:** 11.5
Christian had a rather disappointing campaign at York City last term when he was beset with injuries including a broken arm sustained in a reserve match. He made the starting line-up on just half-a-dozen occasions and most of his appearances came around the turn of the year. The talented midfielder, still only in his early 20s, battled back to fitness and earned a recall to first-team duty in the final game of the season at Oxford.
York C (From trainee on 29/6/1999) FL 42+23/1 FLC 1 FAC 3 Others 3

FOXE Hayden
Born: Australia, 23 June 1977
Height: 6'4" **Weight:** 13.5
Club Honours: Div 1 '03
International Honours: Australia: 10; U23; Yth
Hayden settled in well at Portsmouth last season and became a solid figure in the club's defensive line. He showed a good first touch and an authoritative style, and always gave 100 per cent for the cause.

Hayden scored his only goal for Pompey in the 3-2 win at Crystal Palace and will be looking forward to the challenge of regular Premiership football at Fratton Park in 2003-04.
West Ham U (Free from Sanfrecce Hiroshima, Japan, ex Ajax, Arminia Bielefeld, on 14/3/2001) PL 7+4 FAC 0+1
Portsmouth (£400,000 on 6/6/2002) FL 30+2/1 FAC 1

FOYEWA Amos
Born: Nigeria, 26 December 1981
Height: 5'8" **Weight:** 11.13
Although Amos had recovered from the broken leg he suffered the previous season, he never managed to establish himself in the Bournemouth line-up last term. The pacy striker made just three appearances from the substitutes' bench during the campaign and was told he could leave when his contract expired in the summer. He subsequently moved on to Conference outfit Woking and scored three times for them in their successful bid to avoid relegation.
Bournemouth (Free from trainee at West Ham U on 12/7/2001) FL 1+8 FLC 0+1 FAC 0+2

FRADIN Karim
Born: St Martin d'Hyeres, France, 2 February 1972
Height: 5'10" **Weight:** 13.0
This box-to-box midfielder didn't appear in a Stockport County shirt last season until the LDV Vans Trophy victory over Darlington in October, the first of ten consecutive starts he enjoyed in the first team. Karim netted his only goal of the season in the FA Cup tie against St Albans, but unfortunately he only managed two more appearances before being released from his contract.
Stockport Co (Free from OGC Nice, France on 19/11/1999) FL 72+9/9 FLC 1 FAC 5+1/2 Others 2

FRAIN John William
Born: Birmingham, 8 October 1968
Height: 5'9" **Weight:** 11.9
Club Honours: AMC '91
This experienced left back had a mixed season at Northampton last term. He missed the opening matches through injury then returned to action for a brief spell in the autumn. However, a leg injury put a stop to any further progress and by the time he returned to match fitness Terry Fenwick was in charge and did not consider him for a first-team spot. Martin Wilkinson thought differently, and when appointed caretaker manager, he brought

John back for the final run-in of games, hoping his experience would help to stave off the threat of relegation.
Birmingham C *(From apprentice on 10/10/1986) FL 265+9/23 FLC 28/1 FAC 12 Others 22/2*
Northampton T *(Free on 24/1/1997) FL 203+4/4 FLC 10 FAC 10/1 Others 16/2*

FRAMPTON Andrew (Andy) James Kerr
Born: Wimbledon, 3 September 1979
Height: 5'11" **Weight:** 10.10
This young left back found it hard to break into the Crystal Palace first team last season, and after one appearance as a substitute against Derby County he moved on to Brentford in October. He proved useful on the ball, but was unable to displace Matt Somner from the Bees' line-up, although he did get some opportunities when Somner played elsewhere. Andy also made a few appearances at centre back due to injuries.
Crystal Palace *(From trainee on 8/5/1998) FL 19+9 FLC 3+1 FAC 2*
Brentford *(Free on 28/10/2002) FL 9+6 FAC 3 Others 3*

FRANCIS Damien Jerome
Born: Wandsworth, 27 February 1979
Height: 6'1" **Weight:** 11.2
Damien began the 2002-03 season as one of the two first choice central midfielders for Wimbledon, but by his own standards had a slow start to the campaign and was on the bench for half-a-dozen games from mid-October. He reclaimed his place at the end of November and quickly recovered his form, combining well with the player who had replaced him, the 18-year-old Nigel Reo-Coker. The start of the year saw Damien in fine goal-scoring form as the Dons pushed up the table, but just when it looked like the play-offs might be a possibility he ruptured an ankle ligament in the away win at Crystal Palace. In his absence the team then lost their next three matches, and with their season prematurely over he was not rushed back into action.
Wimbledon *(From trainee on 6/3/1997) P/FL 80+17/15 FLC 7+4 FAC 9*

FRANCIS Simon Charles
Born: Nottingham, 16 February 1985
Height: 6'0" **Weight:** 12.6
International Honours: E: Yth
Simon was another fine young talent to emerge at Bradford City side last season, showing his versatility by playing in three

different positions in his first three games for the club. A few months after signing scholarship forms, he was used at left back on his debut against Nottingham Forest, at centre half against Sheffield United, before featuring in midfield at Millwall. A solid and enthusiastic player, he was rewarded with a professional contract by the Bantams. Simon was a member of the England U18 squad for the Lisbon Tournament during the season.
Bradford C *(From trainee on 3/5/2003) FL 24+1/1 FAC 1*

FRANCIS Willis David
Born: Nottingham, 26 July 1985
Height: 5'5" **Weight:** 10.10
This promising young midfielder burst into the Notts County first-team squad with

some eye-catching, exuberant displays on the right-hand side of midfield. After impressing in the club's reserve team he made his senior debut from the substitutes' bench at Blackpool in November, and featured in a number of other games towards the end of the season. Willis also captained the Magpies' youngsters to victory over Swindon in the Midland Youth Cup final last term.
Notts Co *(Trainee) FL 2+8*

FRANDSEN Per
Born: Copenhagen, Denmark, 6 February 1970
Height: 6'1" **Weight:** 12.6
Club Honours: Div 1 '97
International Honours: Denmark: 23
Per put in his best performances since

Per Frandsen

returning to Bolton last season. He looked considerably fitter and sharper than in previous campaigns, and his tenacity and tough tackling complimented an effective middle line, helping to accommodate the flair and skills of Youri Djorkaeff and Jay Okocha. Whilst the above-mentioned players scored the majority of goals from midfield, Per also weighed in with some vital contributions, including a 30-yard pile driver in the crucial end-of-season clash against Middlesbrough which effectively sealed Bolton's survival. Per also won a recall to the Denmark international squad towards the end of the season, although he did not add to his total of caps.

Bolton W *(£1,250,000 from FC Copenhagen, Denmark, ex Lille, on 7/8/1996) F/PL 129+1/17 FLC 15+1/4 FAC 4+1 Others 3/1*
Blackburn Rov *(£1,750,000 + on 22/9/1999) FL 26+5/5 FAC 4/1*
Bolton W *(£1,600,000 on 24/7/2000) P/FL 94+8/12 FLC 2+1 FAC 2+2 Others 2+1/1*

FRASER Stuart James
Born: Cheltenham, 1 August 1978
Height: 6'0" **Weight:** 12.6
Stuart was again second choice 'keeper at Exeter last term, and he spent most of the season on the bench as cover for Kevin Miller. His two first-team appearances came as a substitute at Cambridge in November, after Miller was red carded, and in the FA Cup tie against Rushden.

Stoke C *(Signed from Cheltenham T on 8/7/1996) FL 0+1*
Exeter C *(Free on 18/7/2000) FL 15+4 FLC 1 FAC 1 Others 1*

FREEDMAN Douglas (Dougie) Alan
Born: Glasgow, 21 January 1974
Height: 5'9" **Weight:** 11.2
International Honours: S: 2; B-1; U21-8; Sch
Dougie featured regularly up front for Crystal Palace in the early part of 2002-03 and scored the club's 'Goal of the Season' in the home game with Portsmouth in August. However, he was sidelined by a groin injury in November and a hernia operation was required. He returned to the line-up in March and finished the campaign with a respectable tally of 11 goals in all competitions. Dougie is an intelligent striker who turns defenders well and has a good eye for goal.

Queens Park R *(From trainee on 15/5/1992)*
Barnet *(Free on 26/7/1994) FL 47/27 FLC 6/5 FAC 2 Others 2*
Crystal Palace *(£800,000 on 8/9/1995) F/PL*
72+18/31 FLC 3+2/1 FAC 2+1 Others 3+2/2
Wolverhampton W *(£800,000 on 17/10/1997) FL 25+4/10 FAC 5+1/2*
Nottingham F *(£950,000 on 12/8/1998) P/FL 50+20/18 FLC 8+1/4 FAC 3+1/1*
Crystal Palace *(£600,000 on 23/10/2000) FL 77+18/40 FLC 5/3 FAC 1+3*

FREEMAN David Barry
Born: Dublin, 25 November 1979
Height: 5'10" **Weight:** 11.10
International Honours: RoI: U21-1; Yth
David was another short-term loan signing who made a handful of appearances for Carlisle in the early part of the 2002-03 season. The busy little striker had a hand in more than one

United goal in his brief spell at Brunton Park before returning to Nottingham Forest. He subsequently signed for Eircom League club St Patrick's Athletic in the spring.

Nottingham F *(From trainee on 9/12/1996) FL 2+6 FAC 0+1*
Port Vale *(Loaned on 8/9/2000) FL 2+1*
Carlisle U *(Free on 16/9/2002) FL 3+1*

FREESTONE Roger
Born: Newport, 19 August 1968
Height: 6'3" **Weight:** 14.6
Club Honours: Div 2 '89; Div 3 '00; AMC '94
International Honours: W: 1; U21-1; Yth; Sch

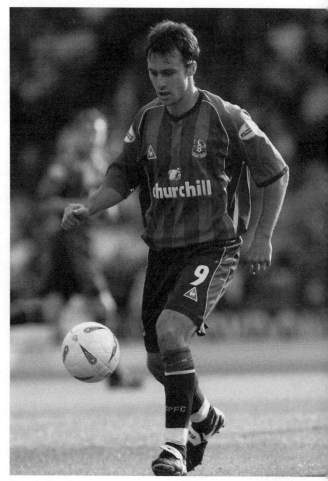

Dougie Freedman

An ankle problem at the start of the
season gave this experienced Swansea
keeper some concern, but he played
through the pain barrier on many
occasions. However, a serious back injury
at Hartlepool in late February left him
sidelined for almost two months, before
he returned to take his place on the
substitutes' bench. Roger moved into
second place in the Swans' all-time
league appearance list during the
campaign.
*Newport Co (From trainee on 2/4/1986) FL
3 Others 1*
*Chelsea (£95,000 on 10/3/1987) FL 42 FLC 2
FAC 3 Others 6*
*Swansea C (Loaned on 29/9/1989) FL 14
Others 1*
Hereford U (Loaned on 9/3/1990) FL 8

*Swansea C (£45,000 on 5/9/1991) FL
514+1/3 FLC 28 FAC 30 Others 44*

FREUND Steffen
Born: Brandenburg, Germany, 19 January
1970
Height: 5'11" **Weight:** 11.6
Club Honours: FLC '99
International Honours: Germany: 21;
U21; Yth
A season blighted by injury meant that
Spurs had to do without this tigerish
midfield anchor man for much of 2002-
03. Steffen is one of the most enthusiastic
players at White Hart Lane and is so fit
that he often seems to run for the full 90
minutes chasing every ball. That said it
was a surprise when Glenn Hoddle
decided not to offer Steffen a new

contract and at the time of writing it
looked like he would be playing his
football elsewhere in 2003-04.
*Tottenham H (£750,000 from Borussia
Dortmund, Germany, ex Motor Sud, Stahl
Brandenburg, Schalke 04, on 29/12/1998) PL
92+10 FLC 14 FAC 11 Others 4*

FRIEDEL Bradley (Brad)
Howard
Born: Lakewood, USA, 18 May 1971
Height: 6'3" **Weight:** 14.7
Club Honours: FLC '02
International Honours: USA: 81
Brad was in superb form for Blackburn
Rovers last term and his efforts were
deservedly recognised with a place in the
PFA Premiership team of the season and
also when he won the club's 'Player of
the Year' trophy by a huge margin.
Whether it was holding the fort under
total onslaught at Arsenal and
Southampton or making a vital save when
having been unoccupied for most of the
game, Brad did it all including a couple of
penalty stops. Absent for just one game,
he achieved a remarkable tally of 15 clean
sheets during the campaign.
*Liverpool (£1,000,000 from Columbus Crew,
USA on 23/12/1997) PL 25 FLC 4 Others 1+1*
*Blackburn Rov (Free on 7/11/2000) P/FL 100
FLC 9 FAC 12 Others 4*

FRIIO David
Born: Thionville, France, 17 February
1973
Height: 6'0" **Weight:** 11.7
Club Honours: Div 3 '02
David proved to be an important member
of Plymouth's consolidation on their
return to the Second Division last term.
His excellent passing skills and ability to
create time on the ball proved invaluable
in the step up in class. His dynamic runs
from the centre of midfield proved that
he still has an eye for goal, and he found
the net seven times, the best of which
was a 35-yard screamer at Wycombe in
September.
*Plymouth Arg (Free from ASOA Valence,
France, ex Epinal, Nimes, on 30/11/2000) FL
100+3/19 FLC 1+1 FAC 7+1/3 Others 2/1*

FRY Russell Harold
Born: Hull, 4 December 1985
Height: 6'2" **Weight:** 12.1
Previously courted by a number of
Premiership clubs, this young midfielder
or striker made his senior debut for Hull
City when he replaced midfielder Scott
Kerr for the closing minutes of the LDV
Vans Trophy defeat at Port Vale in
October. Russell is an excellent prospect

Steffen Freund

and has previously represented Wales at U16 level.

Hull C *(From trainee on 16/12/2002) Others 0+1*

FULLARTON James (Jamie)
Born: Glasgow, 20 July 1974
Height: 5'10" **Weight:** 10.6
International Honours: S: U21-17
This tough-tackling midfielder got off to a mixed start for Brentford last term, scoring on his debut at Huddersfield on the opening day of the season, but then withdrawing with an injury at half time. This set the tone for the campaign with Jamie playing in only just over half the games, missing out due to disc problems and leg injuries, while he failed to add to that early goal.

St Mirren *(Free from Motherwell BC on 13/6/1991) SL 93+9/3 SLC 2 SC 4 Others 4+1 (Transferred to Bastia, France during 1996 close season)*
Crystal Palace *(Free on 7/8/1997) P/FL*

40+7/1 FLC 2+1 FAC 3 Others 1
Bolton W *(Loaned on 25/3/1999) FL 1*
Dundee U *(Free on 11/10/2000) SL 14+2 SLC 1 SC 3*
Brentford *(Free on 9/8/2002) FL 22+5/1 FLC 2 FAC 1 Others 2*

FULLER Ricardo Dwayne
Born: Kingston, Jamaica, 31 October 1979
Height: 6'3" **Weight:** 13.3
International Honours: Jamaica
Ricardo became an instant hit with the Preston fans after arriving in the summer of 2002. He is a natural entertainer: strong on the ball and a lightning fast dribbler for such a big man, hard to dispossess, with a powerful shot and ability in the air. He scored on his home debut and in all recorded 11 goals in his 20 games before a serious knee injury at Coventry ended his season in December, thus putting an end to fears he might be lured away during the transfer window.

The high points of his campaign were probably his two brilliant strikes against Leicester, and all Preston fans will be hoping he returns at the same level of performance that he achieved before his injury.

Crystal Palace *(£1,000,000 from Tivoli Gardens, Jamaica on 19/2/2001) FL 2+6*
Heart of Midlothian *(Loaned on 19/10/2001) SL 27/8 SC 2/2*
Preston NE *(£500,000 on 1/7/2002) FL 18/9 FLC 1+1/2*

FURLONG Paul Anthony
Born: Wood Green, 1 October 1968
Height: 6'0" **Weight:** 13.8
Club Honours: FAT '88
International Honours: E: SP-5
This experienced striker initially joined Queen's Park Rangers on loan at the beginning of last season, but was soon signed up in a permanent deal. He had a number of injury problems early on before becoming a regular in the line-up during the second half of the campaign. Paul showed he still has an eye for goal by finishing up as the club's joint-top scorer with 14 goals, a total which included a run of six goals in six games in the new year.

Coventry C *(£130,000 from Enfield on 31/7/1991) FL 27+10/4 FLC 4/1 FAC 1+1 Others 1*
Watford *(£250,000 on 24/7/1992) FL 79/37 FLC 7/4 FAC 2 Others 4*
Chelsea *(£2,300,000 on 26/5/1994) FL 44+20/13 FLC 3+1 FAC 5+5/1 Others 7/3*
Birmingham C *(£1,500,000 on 17/7/1996) FL 104+27/50 FLC 11+2/3 FAC 5/3 Others 4*
Queens Park R *(Loaned on 18/8/2000) FL 3/1*
Sheffield U *(Loaned on 8/2/2002) FL 4/2*
Queens Park R *(Free on 8/8/2002) FL 27+6/13 FAC 1 Others 3/1*

FUTCHER Benjamin (Ben) Paul
Born: Manchester, 20 February 1981
Height: 6'4" **Weight:** 12.4
Ben was one of the stars of Lincoln's 2002-03 season. Although a central defender he was at his most effective when his height was used up front to finish off set-piece moves. He finished up as the Imps' leading scorer with 11 goals and also picked up the club's 'Young Player of the Year' award. Ben is the son of the former Luton and Barnsley defender Paul Futcher.

Oldham Ath *(From trainee on 5/7/1999) FL 2+8 FAC 0+1 (Free to Stalybridge Celtic on 3/1/2000)*
Lincoln C *(Free from Doncaster Rov on 7/8/2002) FL 41+2/8 FAC 1/1 Others 5/2*

Brad Friedel

G

GAARDSOE Thomas
Born: Randers, Denmark, 23 November 1979
Height: 6'2" **Weight:** 12.8
International Honours: Denmark: U21-10
Thomas blossomed at Ipswich last season as a result of an extended run in the first team and the confidence shown in him by Joe Royle. From his first game in charge Royle seemed to appreciate Thomas's talents and built his defensive tactics around him. An excellent tackler who is effective in the air, he scored four goals including three in successive games against Portsmouth, Leicester and Walsall.
Ipswich T (£1,300,000 from AAB Aalborg on 1/8/2001) P/FL 40+1/5 FLC 2+1/1 FAC 1/1 Others 2+2

GABBIADINI Marco
Born: Nottingham, 20 January 1968
Height: 5'10" **Weight:** 13.4
Club Honours: Div 3 '88
International Honours: E: B-1; U21-2
This experienced striker started the season on fire for Northampton. He netted a goal against Cardiff from around 35 yards out then entered the record books by becoming the oldest Cobbler to score a hat-trick, when he did so against Colchester, aged 34 years 240 days. Unfortunately Marco's goals dried up with the turnover of managers at Sixfields. Firstly, he was asked to play as a lone striker under Terry Fenwick and then dropped to the bench by Martin Wilkinson. An interesting statistic is that Marco played in every game that Northampton won last season, and when he was missing they always lost.
York C (From apprentice on 5/9/1985) FL 52+18/14 FLC 4+3/1 Others 4/3
Sunderland (£80,000 on 23/9/1987) FL 155+2/74 FLC 14/9 FAC 5 Others 9/4
Crystal Palace (£1,800,000 on 1/10/1991) FL 5/5 FLC 6/1 FAC 1 Others 3/1
Derby Co (£1,000,000 on 31/1/1992) F/PL 63+25/50 FLC 13/7 FAC 8+1/3 Others 6+1/8 (Free to Panionios, Greece during 1997 close season)
Birmingham C (Loaned on 14/10/1996) FL 4+2
Oxford U (Loaned on 31/1/1997) FL 5/1
Stoke C (Free on 24/12/1997) FL 2+6 FAC 1/1
York C (Free on 20/2/1998) FL 5+2/1
Darlington (Free on 8/7/1998) FL 81+1/47 FLC 4/1 FAC 4/1 Others 5+1/3

Marco Gabbiadini

Northampton T (Free on 28/6/2000) FL 97+23/25 FLC 4/1 FAC 6+1/3 Others 4+1/1

GABBIDON Daniel (Danny) Leon
Born: Cwmbran, 8 August 1979
Height: 6'1" **Weight:** 11.2
International Honours: W: 4; U21-17; Yth

A depressing season for this talented young defender ended on a high when he helped Cardiff City earn promotion via the Second Division play-offs. Their victory at the Millennium Stadium will rate among the finest moments of his career so far. He missed the Wales trip to the USA because of City's play-off dates, but it proved well worthwhile. Earlier, Danny's campaign was disrupted when he spent more than four months ruled out by a back injury. He needed intensive treatment and did not play again until April when he was in the team at Peterborough.
West Bromwich A (From trainee on 3/7/1998) FL 20 FLC 4+1 FAC 2

Cardiff C (£175,000 + on 10/8/2000) FL 108+3/6 FLC 4 FAC 8 Others 3

GADSBY Matthew John
Born: Sutton Coldfield, 6 September 1979
Height: 6'1" **Weight:** 11.12
Matthew had a trial period at Mansfield in the summer of 2002, playing in several pre-season friendly matches, but on the eve of the new campaign he was recalled to Walsall just when it seemed he would sign for a three-month loan period. He eventually moved to Field Mill on a free transfer in November. Matthew is a right-sided defender or midfielder who can also play at centre back.
Walsall (From trainee on 12/2/1998) FL 23+14 FLC 2 FAC 0+1 Others 2+5
Mansfield T (Free on 8/11/2002) FL 13+7 FAC 2

GAIA Marcio dos **Santos**
Born: Sao Mateus, Brazil, 8 September 1978
Height: 6'1" **Weight:** 12.9
International Honours: Brazil: Yth
Santos became a firm favourite with the Exeter City fans last term, producing some inspired performances in what was generally a nervy defence. Effective in the air, he provided the rearguard with some much needed pace. A highlight of his season was his goal in the FA Cup tie at Charlton. Santos bravely came to the team's aid with a surprise return in the critical game against Swansea towards the end of the season despite suffering from a head injury.
Exeter C (Free from Agremiacao Sportiva Arapiraquense, Brazil on 8/8/2002) FL 33/1 FLC 1 FAC 4/1 Others 1

GAIN Peter Thomas
Born: Hammersmith, 11 November 1976
Height: 6'1" **Weight:** 11.0
International Honours: RoI: U21-1; Yth
This skilful midfield man continued to improve in 2002-03 with his ability on the ball and long-range shooting causing many problems for opposing defenders. He was often switched from his usual left-sided role into the centre of midfield when Lincoln used a 5-2-3 formation.
Tottenham H (From trainee on 1/7/1995)
Lincoln C (Loaned on 31/12/1998) FL 0+1 Others 1
Lincoln C (£15,000 on 26/3/1999) FL 117+27/14 FLC 5/1 FAC 7+1/1 Others 7+2

GALL Kevin Alexander
Born: Merthyr Tydfil, 4 February 1982
Height: 5'9" **Weight:** 11.1

Danny Gabbidon

International Honours: W: U21-4; Yth; Sch

his pacy striker started the 2002-03 season as a regular in the Bristol Rovers first-team squad but was restricted to frequent appearances from the substitutes' bench. He eventually moved on to Yeovil Town in February and went on to score 14 goals as he helped the Conference club win promotion to the Football League. Kevin also featured for Wales at U21 level, netting the winner against Azerbaijan in November to end a unless run stretching back over a period of five-and-a-half years.

Newcastle U (From trainee on 29/4/1999)
*Bristol Rov (Free on 22/3/2001) FL 28+22/5
FLC 2 FAC 2+2 Others 2+2*

GALLACHER Kevin William
Born: Clydebank, 23 November 1966
Height: 5'8" **Weight:** 11.6
International Honours: S: 53; B-2; U21-
6; Yth

Signed on non-contract forms to bolster the Huddersfield attack, Kevin showed all the experience of a top-class player during the handful of appearances he made for the club. He led the front line well, passing purposefully and creating chances for others. However, he failed to find the net in his brief spell at the McAlpine Stadium and departed in October.

*Dundee U (Signed from Duntocher BC on 29/1983) SL 118+13/27 SLC 13/5 SC 20+3/5
Others 15+6/3*
*Coventry C (£900,000 on 29/1/1990) F/PL
9+1/28 FLC 11/7 FAC 4 Others 2*
*Blackburn Rov (£1,500,000 on 22/3/1993)
F/L 132+12/46 FLC 8+2/3 FAC 13/4 Others
+1*
*Newcastle U (£700,000 on 1/10/1999) PL
7+12/4 FLC 2/1 FAC 5+1/1*
*Preston NE (Free on 17/8/2001) FL 1+4/1
LC 0+1/1*
Sheffield Wed (Free on 28/3/2002) FL 0+4
*Huddersfield T (Free on 30/8/2002) FL 5+2
LC 1*

GALLAGHER Paul
Born: Glasgow, 9 August 1984
Height: 6'1" **Weight:** 12.0
International Honours: S: U21-1
his tall, lean striker scored regularly at reserve and youth team level for Blackburn Rovers last term, including a hat-trick against Aston Villa to help his club clinch the FA Academy U19s title. Left-footed with pace and a natural eye for a goal chance, Paul made his senior debut when coming on as a substitute against Arsenal in March. Although born in Scotland he

was brought up in Blackburn and is very much a local discovery.

*Blackburn Rov (From trainee on 5/2/2003)
PL 0+1*

GALLAS William
Born: Paris, France, 17 August 1977
Height: 6'1" **Weight:** 12.7
International Honours: France: 10; U21
This magnificent young central defender had a memorable second season in English football as his all-round class put him at the forefront of Premiership defenders. William has all the attributes for the great modern-day defender and also a penchant for scoring valuable goals-. He figured in every Premiership match of the season and his displays were a vital factor in Chelsea's record of conceding just 38 goals, the second-best

figure in the top flight. Much to his chagrin, William was moved away from his favoured central defensive berth to cover at full back over the last month of the season to accommodate the return of John Terry. To cap an outstanding season William was elected into the PFA Premiership team of the season, and was a member of the French side that won the Confederations Cup in the summer.

*Chelsea (£6,200,000 from Marseilles, France,
ex SM Caen, on 4/7/2001) PL 63+5/5 FLC 7
FAC 9/1 Others 5*

GALLEN Kevin Andrew
Born: Chiswick, 21 September 1975
Height: 5'11" **Weight:** 12.10
International Honours: E: U21-4; Yth
(UEFA-U18 '93); Sch
Kevin enjoyed a resurgence of his old

Kevin Gallen

form for Queen's Park Rangers last term when he was a regular member of the first team, only missing a handful of games due to injury. He formed a useful partnership up front with Paul Furlong and ended the season as joint-top scorer with 14 goals. Kevin was rewarded for his efforts at the end of the season when he swept the board in the club's annual awards, winning supporters' 'Player of the Year', 'Players' Player of the Year' and scorer of the 'Goal of the Season'.

Queens Park R *(From trainee on 22/9/1992) P/FL 126+45/36 FLC 9+3/2 FAC 6+2/2*
Huddersfield T *(Free on 10/8/2000) FL 30+8/10 FAC 1*
Barnsley *(Free on 27/7/2001) FL 8+1/2 FLC 0+1*
Queens Park R *(Free on 20/11/2001) FL 66+15/20 FLC 0+1/1 FAC 0+1 Others 3*

GALLIMORE Anthony (Tony) Mark

Born: Crewe, 21 February 1972
Height: 5'11" **Weight:** 12.6
Club Honours: Div 3 '95; AMC '98
Tony remained an automatic choice at left back for Grimsby Town last term, missing very few games through injury or suspension and occasionally captaining the side. A strong and uncompromising defender with a useful left foot, he is capable of catching opposing goalkeepers unawares with his powerful long-range shot. Tony was out of contract in the summer and his future was uncertain at the time of writing.

Stoke C *(From trainee on 11/7/1990) FL 6+5*
Carlisle U *(Loaned on 3/10/1991) FL 8*
Carlisle U *(Loaned on 26/2/1992) FL 8*
Carlisle U *(£15,000 on 25/3/1993) FL 124/9 FLC 8 FAC 8/1 Others 24/1*
Grimsby T *(£125,000 on 28/3/1996) FL 263+10/4 FLC 20/2 FAC 15 Others 10*

GALLOWAY Michael (Mick) Anthony

Born: Nottingham, 13 October 1974
Height: 5'11" **Weight:** 12.4
After being sidelined for almost the whole of the previous term, Mick found himself back in favour at Carlisle in the early weeks of 2002-03. A creative midfield player with good passing skills, he subsequently had a spell on loan with Conference club Hereford United before his contract was cancelled by mutual agreement. Mick then signed for Scottish League new boys Gretna.

Notts Co *(From trainee on 15/6/1993) FL 17+4 FLC 2 FAC 0+1 Others 4*
Gillingham *(£10,000 + on 27/3/1997) FL 58+17/5 FLC 3+1 FAC 1+2 Others 5*

Lincoln C *(Loaned on 29/9/1999) FL 5*
Chesterfield *(£15,000 on 5/11/1999) FL 18+2/1 FLC 2+1 Others 3*
Carlisle U *(Free on 9/11/2000) FL 30+5/1 FLC 1 FAC 2 Others 0+1*

GARCIA Richard

Born: Perth, Australia, 4 September 1981
Height: 6'1" **Weight:** 11.2
Club Honours: FAYC '99
International Honours: Australia: Yth
Last term proved to be another frustrating campaign for the Australian midfielder. After forcing his way into contention for a place in the West Ham line-up with two substitute appearances early in the season he suffered a set back in November when he fractured a shin. He was back playing for the reserves in February but did not add to his senior experience, although he featured for Australia U23s against Spain in April. Richard is quick with some neat touches and an injury-free season is overdue for him.

West Ham U *(From trainee on 16/9/1998) PL 2+6 FLC 0+2 FAC 0+1*
Leyton Orient *(Loaned on 11/8/2000) FL 18/4 FLC 3*

GARDEN Stuart Robertson

Born: Dundee, 10 February 1972
Height: 6'0" **Weight:** 12.5
Stuart was Notts County's first choice goalkeeper for the opening half of the 2002-03 campaign. However, as the team began to struggle, he suffered a temporary dip in confidence and he lost his place in the line-up following the home defeat by Colchester in November. Although Stuart quickly returned to form with some excellent displays in the reserves, he was unable to dislodge Steve Mildenhall from the 'keeper's jersey before the end of the season.

Dundee *(Signed from Dundee NE on 1/3/1993)*
Brechin C *(Free on 1/9/1995) SL 91+2 SLC 4 SC 8 Others 3*
Forfar Ath *(Free on 4/8/1999) SL 67 SLC 1 SC 1 Others 1*
Notts Co *(Free on 5/7/2001) FL 39 FLC 1 FAC 1 Others 2*

GARDNER Anthony

Born: Stone, 19 September 1980
Height: 6'5" **Weight:** 13.8
International Honours: E: U21-1
This young defender had a real stop-start season at Tottenham last term due to knee and thigh injuries. Height gives him aerial ability and this is coupled with great skill with the ball at his feet. Anthony notched up his first goal for Spurs against

West Ham in September underlining his ability at set pieces. He is a huge prospect for club and country and will be hoping for an injury-free season in 2003-04 and the chance of securing a regular first-team spot at White Hart Lane.

Port Vale *(From trainee on 31/7/1998) FL 40+1/4 FLC 2 FAC 1*
Tottenham H *(£1,000,000 on 28/1/2000) P 27+8/1 FLC 4 FAC 1*

GARDNER Ricardo Wayne

Born: Jamaica, 25 September 1978
Height: 5'9" **Weight:** 11.0
International Honours: Jamaica: 43
One of Bolton's longest-serving players, Ricardo had yet another effective campaign in 2002-03. He missed five weeks after undergoing knee surgery in September, but soon returned to first-team action and retained his place in the side for virtually the rest of the season. Starting out in his traditional left-midfield position, Ricardo actually played for a large part of the second half of the campaign at left wing back, a role in which he appears for the Jamaican national side. His attacking instincts ensured that he could still embark on the mazy runs for which he is renowned, but he also produced some solid performances at the back. He contributed just two goals, although one of these was a fantastic 30-yard free kick in the Boxing Day home victory over Newcastle.

Bolton W *(£1,000,000 from Harbour View, Jamaica on 17/8/1998) P/FL 132+22/15 FLC 11+2/2 FAC 6+3 Others 6/2*

GARNER Darren John

Born: Plymouth, 10 December 1971
Height: 5'9" **Weight:** 12.7
Club Honours: AMC '96
After showing commendable courage by regaining full fitness following a badly broken leg, midfielder Darren rediscovered his form for Rotherham in the first half of the 2002-03 season only to lose his place again. Then came yet another injury which required an operation and ruled him out of the rest of the campaign after early March. His most memorable achievement was to hit a magnificent goal from 30 yards to grab a dramatic last-gasp winner at local neighbours Sheffield Wednesday. That was almost equalled by another superbly struck goal in a draw at Norwich City.

Plymouth Arg *(From trainee on 15/3/1989) FL 22+5/1 FLC 2+1 FAC 1 (Free to Dorchester T on 19/8/1994)*
Rotherham U *(£20,000 on 26/6/1995) FL 221+12/23 FLC 13+2 FAC 15+1/6 Others 9/*

GARNER Glyn
Born: Pontypool, 9 December 1976
Height: 6'2" Weight: 13.6
The close-season departure of goalkeeper Paddy Kenny to Sheffield United gave Glyn Garner the chance to establish himself in the Bury first team last term. He responded well to the challenge and was ever-present in all 56 competitive games for the Shakers. A good shot stopper, he particularly enjoyed fine performances in the Worthington Cup tie against Fulham and at Torquay in February.
Bury (Free from Llanelli on 7/7/2000) FL 44+2 FLC 3 FAC 2 Others 7

GARRARD Luke
Born: Barnet, 22 September 1985
Height: 5'10" Weight: 11.9
This young Swindon Town defender was rewarded for some fine performances in the club's reserve and youth teams by his inclusion on the bench for the closing matches of the campaign. A late substitution during the defeat at Oldham provided Luke with his first ten minutes of League action and he will be looking to progress further during the 2003-04 season.
Swindon T (Free from Tottenham H juniors on 8/7/2002) FL 0+1

GARRY Ryan Felix Mayne
Born: Hornchurch, 29 September 1983
Height: 6'2" Weight: 13.2
Club Honours: FAYC '01
International Honours: E: Yth
This very promising young right-sided defender played in the final two Premiership games of the season for Arsenal. Ryan was a regular member of the Gunners' U19 and reserve squads for whom he has also played in midfield, central defence, and as a striker. He also represented England at U20 level and is highly rated at Highbury.
Arsenal (From trainee on 2/7/2001) PL 1 FLC 0+1

GAVIN Jason Joseph
Born: Dublin, 14 March 1980
Height: 6'1" Weight: 12.7
International Honours: RoI: U21-6; Yth UEFA-U18 '98)
Jason made only a single Worthington Cup appearance for Middlesbrough last season, albeit a full 90 minutes, against Brentford at Griffin Park. The young central defender was loaned out to First Division strugglers Grimsby Town at the beginning of November to cover for an injury crisis. He impressed for the Mariners

with his defensive skills and in March he joined Huddersfield Town, also on loan, again featuring regularly and even managing to find the net with a close-range headed goal at Port Vale.
Middlesbrough (From trainee on 26/3/1997) PL 19+12 FLC 5+1 FAC 1+2
Grimsby T (Loaned on 1/11/2002) FL 8+2
Huddersfield T (Loaned on 14/3/2003) FL 10/1

GAY Daniel (Danny) Karl
Born: Norwich, 5 August 1982
Height: 6'1" Weight: 12.8
This popular youngster was understudy to Southend 'keeper Darryl Flahavan during the 2002-03 campaign. Danny played five games in January when Flahavan was out

with a thigh injury, generally doing well, and also turned in some sterling performances for the reserve team. It was therefore something of a surprise when he was released at the end of the season.
Southend U (Free from trainee at Norwich C on 6/7/2001) FL 10+1

GAYLE Marcus Anthony
Born: Hammersmith, 27 September 1970
Height: 6'1" Weight: 12.9
Club Honours: Div 3 '92
International Honours: E: Yth. Jamaica: 14
After 16 seasons as a left-sided striker, Marcus embarked on a new career as a central defender for Watford in 2002-03.

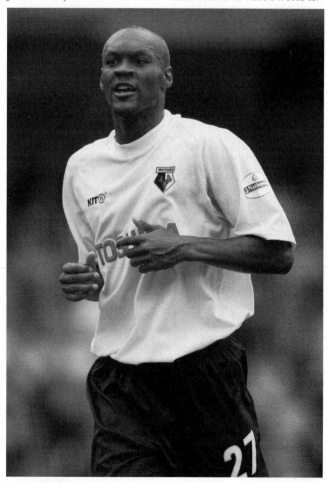

Marcus Gayle

It turned out to be an inspired conversion: Marcus gained assurance with every game he played, formed an excellent partnership with skipper Neil Cox and ended up being voted as the club's 'Player of the Year' after an outstanding season. Tall and commanding in the air, his distribution was excellent, but equally he was not afraid to boot the ball into the stand if the situation demanded it. Marcus played a key role in Watford's FA Cup run: he was 'Man of the Match' against Burnley in the quarter-finals, and scored a splendid headed goal in the semi-final against Southampton. A new contract ensured he would be staying at Vicarage Road for the foreseeable future.
Brentford (From trainee on 6/7/1989) FL 118+38/22 FLC 6+3 FAC 6+2/2 Others 14+6/2
Wimbledon (£250,000 on 24/3/1994) P/FL 198+38/37 FLC 23+1/7 FAC 18+7/3
Glasgow R (£900,000 on 9/3/2001) SL 28+8/4
Watford (£900,000 on 8/8/2001) FL 58+9/4 FLC 3+1/2 FAC 6/2

GEARY Derek Peter
Born: Dublin, 19 June 1980
Height: 5'6" **Weight:** 10.8
Derek began the 2002-03 season in fine form for Sheffield Wednesday and looked on track to win the supporters' 'Player of the Year' title for the second successive season. Unfortunately, injury struck in the new year and he was forced to undergo a cartilage operation which brought his campaign to a premature end. When he is fully fit, Derek is an enthusiastic right back who enjoys pushing down the flank.
Sheffield Wed (Signed from Cherry Orchard on 17/11/1997) FL 54+9 FLC 11+2 FAC 1

GEMMILL Scot
Born: Paisley, 2 January 1971
Height: 5'11" **Weight:** 11.6
Club Honours: FMC '92; Div 1 '98
International Honours: S: 25; B-2; U21-4
After missing the early part of the season through injury, Scot was in Everton's reserve team until Christmas but he retained his place in the Scotland squad during this period. He managed to make his first Premiership start in January and was able to participate in most fixtures before the end of the campaign, passing 100 appearances for the club. A neat and tidy midfielder who links play well and is a good team man, Scot's attitude during his absence from the team remained a credit to his profession.
Nottingham F (From trainee on 5/1/1990)

F/PL 228+17/21 FLC 29+2/3 FAC 19+2/1 Others 13+1/4
Everton (£250,000 on 25/3/1999) PL 79+18/5 FLC 3+1 FAC 7+2

GEORGE Finidi
Born: Nigeria, 15 April 1971
Height: 6'2" **Weight:** 12.7
International Honours: Nigeria:
Finidi had a difficult season at Ipswich last season and was hampered by a series of niggling injuries that kept him sidelined for long periods, such that he was only able to start in a handful of games. He did not seem to be a part of the plans of either manager and in the summer it was reported that he had left the club following a settlement of his contract. When fully fit he is an exciting midfield player or striker who can deliver a useful cross.
Ipswich T (£3,100,000 from Real Mallorca, Spain, ex Port Harcourt, Calabar Rov, Ajax, on 17/8/2001) P/FL 24+11/7 FLC 1+1 Others 5+4/1

GEORGE Liam Brendan
Born: Luton, 2 February 1979
Height: 5'9" **Weight:** 11.3
International Honours: RoI: U21-4; Yth (UEFA-U18 '98)
Liam struggled to earn a first-team place at Bury last term as a result of fierce competition for places. Although frequently to be found on the bench, he was rarely introduced into the action. He started just three league games for the Shakers, his winning strike against Exeter proving to be his only goal for the club. Liam was released in February and joined Boston United on a non-contract basis. He showed some neat touches on the left wing for the Pilgrims but failed to earn a long-term deal and was released after less than a month at York Street, signing for Eircom League club St Patrick's Athletic shortly afterwards.
Luton T (From trainee on 20/1/1997) FL 81+21/20 FLC 3+6 FAC 9+1/4 Others 2+1
Clydebank (Free on 16/3/2002) SL 2 (Free to Stevenage Borough on 27/3/2002)
Bury (Free on 7/8/2002) FL 3+5/1 Others 2
Boston U (Free on 13/2/2003) FL 1+2

[GEREMI] NJITAP FOTSO Geremi Sorele
Born: Cameroon, 20 December 1978
Height: 5'11" **Weight:** 12.8
International Honours: Cameroon: 60
Middlesbrough's on-loan Cameroon international Geremi featured regularly during the 2002-03 campaign, scoring a total of seven valuable goals. A strong

and skilful midfielder who excels at taking free kicks, he impressed during his stay at the Riverside. However, he looked set to leave the club at the time of writing after Steve McClaren and his parent club, Real Madrid, failed to see eye to eye over the value estimation of the player. Geremi continued to feature for Cameroon and was a member of the team narrowly defeated by France in the Confederations Cup final over the summer.
Middlesbrough (Loaned from Real Madrid, Spain, ex Racing Baffousam, Cerro Porteno, Genclerbirligi, on 31/7/2002) PL 33/7 FAC 1

GERRARD Paul William
Born: Heywood, 22 January 1973
Height: 6'2" **Weight:** 14.4
International Honours: E: U21-18
Paul had a frustrating time during 2002-03, managing only two first-team appearances for Everton before rejoining his old boss from Oldham, Joe Royle, at Ipswich on loan in November. He went straight into the team at Watford and kept a clean sheet, but after five appearances a dislocated knee ended his loan spell early. After recovering Paul remained on the substitutes' bench for Everton for the remainder of the season. He remains a fine shot stopper and was linked with a move back to Ipswich in the close season.
Oldham Ath (From trainee on 2/11/1991) P/FL 118+1 FLC 7 FAC 7 Others 2+1
Everton (£1,000,000 + on 1/7/1996) PL 89+1 FLC 6 FAC 3
Oxford U (Loaned on 18/12/1998) FL 16
Ipswich T (Loaned on 16/11/2002) FL 5

GERRARD Steven George
Born: Huyton, 30 May 1980
Height: 6'2" **Weight:** 12.4
Club Honours: FLC '01, '03; FAC '01; UEFAC '01; ESC '01
International Honours: E: 18; U21-4; Yth
After missing the 2002 World Cup finals due to an operation on a groin strain, the stage was set for the fully rested Liverpool and England midfielder to realise his potential as a world-class midfielder. Sadly it did not happen. In the first half of the season his form was patchy and reached its nadir in the vital Champions' League match in Basle when he was substituted at half-time. His form improved in the new year and included two magnificent goals, one a blistering volley from 30 yards which gave Liverpool a fortuitous lead in the Worthington Cup final against Manchester United in March, and the second a glorious solo goal in a rare 3-2 victory at Tottenham later the same

onth. While he remains an automatic
oice for the England team, Steven will
hoping to achieve more consistent
rm in 2003-04.
*verpool (From trainee on 26/2/1998) PL
7+19/16 FLC 10/2 FAC 8+2/1 Others
+1/3*

HENT Matthew Ian
rn: Burton, 5 October 1980
eight: 6'3" **Weight:** 14.1
ternational Honours: E: Yth; Sch
atthew was the second choice
alkeeper to Andy Marriott at Barnsley
much of last season and prior to
arriott's departure his only senior action
me in the LDV Vans Trophy tie at Bury.
took over the 'keeper's jersey in March
d saved a penalty in his second
pearance. He proved to be an excellent
ot stopper, although he needs to
velop more confidence in his own
ilities. Matthew was out of contract in
e summer and his future was uncertain
the time of writing.
ton Villa (From trainee on 13/10/1997)
coln C (Free on 1/12/2000) FL 0+1 FAC 1
ee to Forest Green Rovers in January 2001)
rnsley (Free on 10/8/2001) FL 8 FAC 0+1
hers 1

BB Alistair (Ally) Stuart
rn: Salisbury, 17 February 1976
ight: 5'9" **Weight:** 11.7
e 2002-03 campaign proved to be an
oressive season for this skilful right
dfielder who missed just one league
me for Stockport County. Had it not
en for Luke Beckett's fantastic goal
y, many of them created by Ally, then
would have been a strong contender
walk away with the 'Player of the Year'
ard. His own personal achievement
ne at Blackpool when he scored his
t County goal in a thrilling 3-1 win.
rwich C (From trainee on 1/7/1994)
rthampton T (Loaned on 22/9/1995) FL

*rthampton T (£30,000 on 5/2/1996) FL
+71/3 FLC 8+4 FAC 5+3 Others 6+3*
*ckport Co (£50,000 on 18/2/2000) FL
+5/1 FLC 6 FAC 5 Others 1*

BBS Paul Derek
rn: Gorleston, 26 October 1972
ight: 5'10" **Weight:** 11.10
ul was the regular left back for Barnsley
ing the first half of the 2002-03
son and scored his first-ever goal for
club, netting the winner from the
alty spot against Port Vale in
cember. However, he sustained knee
d then groin injuries in January and was

out of action until late in the campaign
when he was mainly used as a substitute.
Paul possesses an excellent left foot and
this showed in his passing and crossing of
the ball.
*Colchester U (Signed from Diss T on
6/3/1995) FL 39+14/3 FAC 1+1 Others 8+1*
*Torquay U (Free on 26/7/1997) FL 40+1/7
FLC 4/1 FAC 3/1 Others 3/1*
*Plymouth Arg (Free on 7/7/1998) FL 30+4/3
FLC 2*

*Brentford (Free on 10/7/2000) FL 49+5/3
FLC 3 FAC 3/1 Others 6+1*
*Barnsley (Free on 15/3/2002) FL 27+3/1 FAC
1 Others 1*

GIER Robert (Rob) James
Born: Bracknell, 6 January 1980
Height: 5'9" **Weight:** 11.7
After starting the 2002-03 season on the
bench, Rob was given a prolonged run in
the centre of defence for Wimbledon, but

Paul Gibbs

165

Ryan Giggs

total of 13 goals conceded during
November saw him miss a few games
until earning a recall in mid-January for
e 1-1 draw at Wolves. From then on he
as in and out of the first team and
ended the season with four games filling
at right back. A lack of inches does not
elp Rob's cause when defending high
osses, but he is a good tackler, reads the
ame well and always gives of his best.
*imbledon (From trainee on 11/5/1999) FL
*+3 FLC 4+2 FAC 1

IGGS Ryan Joseph
orn: Cardiff, 29 November 1973
eight: 5'11" **Weight:** 10.9
ub Honours: ESC '91; FAYC '92; FLC
2; PL '93, '94, '96, '97, '99, '00, '01,
3; CS '93, '94, '96, '97; FAC '94, '96,
9; EC '99
ternational Honours: W: 40; U21-1;
h. E: Sch
outstanding naturally talented left
nger, who can play equally as well as a
ont line striker, Ryan's season at Old
afford became one of contrasting
rtunes. After celebrating a decade of
st-team action with his 100th goal for
e club in the Premiership clash against
elsea at Stamford Bridge in September,
s form went in fits and starts. However,
showed his influence in the Champions'
ague with impressive strikes against
ympiakos and Juventus. With rumours
ounding over his future, Ryan hit a
olden spell of form late on in the
mpaign with goals in successive games
ainst Liverpool, Newcastle and Arsenal.
anchester U (From trainee on 1/12/1990)
*L 341+41/79 FLC 21+5/6 FAC 39+4/9
*hers 87+6/19

LBERTO SILVA Aparecido
orn: Lagoa da Prata, Brazil, 7 October
76
eight: 6'2" **Weight:** 12.4
ub Honours: CS '02; FAC '03
ternational Honours: Brazil: 16
member of Brazil's World Cup winning
uad, Silva made his debut for Arsenal as
ubstitute in the Charity Shield match
ainst Liverpool and scored the only goal
the match. He settled in quickly at
ghbury, and soon adjusted to the pace
the Premiership. An intelligent player
o is calm, a good passer of the ball,
d able to get forward well on the
erlap, he formed a great partnership in
e centre of midfield with Patrick Vieira.
va scored the fastest-ever Champions'
ague goal (20.07 seconds) for the
inners at PSV Eindhoven.
senal (£4,500,000 from Atletico Mineiro,

Brazil, ex America-MG, on 9/8/2002) PL 32+3
FAC 1+2 Others 11+2/3

GILCHRIST Philip (Phil)
Alexander
Born: Stockton on Tees, 25 August 1973
Height: 5'11" **Weight:** 13.12
Club Honours: FLC '00
This experienced left-sided defender's
season was seriously disrupted by a
double shin and ankle injury that sidelined
him from mid-November to mid-January.
Phil returned to action for West Bromwich
Albion in the home clash with
Manchester United, but was later ruled
out of the remaining half-dozen fixtures
with tendon trouble in his left knee. A
fine positional player, positive in his
actions, Phil, is very solid in the tackle.
Nottingham F (From trainee on 5/12/1990)
Middlesbrough (Free on 10/1/1992)
Hartlepool U (Free on 27/11/1992) FL 77+5
FLC 4+1 FAC 4 Others 5
Oxford U (£100,000 on 17/2/1995) FL
173+4/10 FLC 16 FAC 9/1 Others 3
Leicester C (£500,000 on 10/8/1999) PL
23+16/1 FLC 6+1 FAC 4+1
West Bromwich A (£500,000 on 22/3/2001)
P/FL 73 FLC 3 FAC 5+1 Others 2

GILKS Matthew (Matt)
Born: Oldham, 4 June 1982
Height: 6'1" **Weight:** 12.7
Rochdale's promising young reserve
goalkeeper had to bide his time as his
mentor Neil Edwards returned to fitness
for the start of the 2002-03 season.
However, when a number of injuries
again caught up with Edwards in January,
Matt was plunged back into the fray. He
came off the bench to help Dale to a last-
gasp victory over Oxford and two games
later was facing Wolves in the live
televised FA Cup tie, Matt adding to his
reputation with a brave display. Further
excellent performances, including several
penalty saves, earned him 'Man of the
Match' ratings and ensured that he
remained Dale's number one for the
remainder of the campaign.
Rochdale (From trainee on 4/7/2001) FL
40+2 FLC 1 FAC 3 Others 1

GILL Jeremy (Jerry) Morley
Born: Clevedon, 8 September 1970
Height: 5'7" **Weight:** 11.0
International Honours: E: SP-1
Jerry arrived at Northampton on loan
during the 2002 close season, and
eventually signed permanently in
November. The experienced right back
was one of the few Cobblers' players to
avoid any long-term injuries during the

campaign, and was rarely absent from the
line-up. Jerry is a quality defender who
rescued the side from sticky situations on
more than one occasion.
Leyton Orient (Free from Trowbridge T on
16/12/1998. Free to Weston super Mare on
1/7/1990)
Birmingham C (£30,000 from Yeovil T on
14/7/1997) FL 43+17 FLC 11+1 FAC 3
Others 1
Northampton T (Free on 9/8/2002) FL 41
FLC 1 FAC 2 Others 2

GILL Matthew James
Born: Cambridge, 8 November 1980
Height: 5'11" **Weight:** 12.10
A product of the Peterborough United
youth system, Matthew had his best
season to date last term, starting in 41 of
the club's Division Two fixtures. A versatile
player who features either at full back or
in midfield, he is a ferocious ball winner
although he only has a slight frame. He is
particularly effective at supporting the
forwards when employed in the middle of
the park.
Peterborough U (From trainee on 2/3/1998)
FL 94+24/5 FLC 2+1 FAC 5 Others 2+3

Matthew Gill

GILLESPIE Keith Robert

Born: Bangor, 18 February 1975
Height: 5'10" **Weight:** 11.3
Club Honours: FAYC '92; FLC '02
International Honours: NI: 47; U21-1; Yth; Sch

Although a regular in the Blackburn Rovers first-team squad last season, Keith generally found himself on the substitutes' bench and managed just ten Premiership starts. Still capable of turning games and with the speed to beat a full back, he also showed a willingness to track back and help out in defence. Keith remained a regular in the full Northern Ireland international squad during the campaign.

Manchester U *(From trainee on 3/2/1993) PL 3+6/1 FLC 3 FAC 1+1/1*
Wigan Ath *(Loaned on 3/9/1993) FL 8/4 Others 2*
Newcastle U *(£1,000,000 on 12/1/1995) PL 94+19/11 FLC 7+1/1 FAC 9+1/2 Others 11+5*
Blackburn Rov *(£2,250,000 on 18/12/1998) P/FL 67+46/5 FLC 8+3 FAC 6+4/1 Others 0+3*
Wigan Ath *(Loaned on 1/12/2000) FL 4+1 FAC 2*

GILROY David Miles

Born: Yeovil, 23 December 1982
Height: 5'11" **Weight:** 11.3

This young Bristol Rovers striker mostly featured on the subs' bench last term due to the competition for first-team places from several experienced signings. However, he managed to score his first goal in senior football in the FA Cup replay against Runcorn when he finished coolly from close range. David initially had his contract extended until the end of the season and was then offered a new short-term deal by the Pirates.

Bristol Rov *(From trainee on 2/7/2002) FL 5+10 FAC 0+1/1 Others 0+1*

GIVEN Seamus (Shay) John

Born: Lifford, 20 April 1976
Height: 6'0" **Weight:** 13.4
Club Honours: Div 1 '96
International Honours: RoI: 52; U21-5; Yth

After helping the Republic of Ireland to a fine World Cup Shay was ever-present in Newcastle's Premiership 2002-03 campaign for the second successive season. He again proved himself a 'keeper of the highest quality whose quick feet, safe hands, and shrewd reading of the game enabled him to keep 14 Premiership clean sheets, including one at Birmingham where a stunning save proved vital in securing victory. He generally performed in a quietly confident manner, although

he contributed a memorable headed clearance over his own crossbar in the home draw with Arsenal. Shay continued to be first choice for his country and has now reached 52 caps, 43 of them with Newcastle making him the club's most-capped player ever. The local press chose him as the 'North East Footballer of the Year', while he is also Patron of the Macmillan Cancer Relief's Tyneside appeal.

Blackburn Rov *(From Glasgow Celtic juniors on 8/8/1994) PL 2 FLC 0+1*
Swindon T *(Loaned on 4/8/1995) FL 5*
Sunderland *(Loaned on 19/1/1996) FL 17*
Newcastle U *(£1,500,000 on 14/7/1997) PL 179 FLC 4+1 FAC 18 Others 27*

GLASS Stephen

Born: Dundee, 23 May 1976
Height: 5'9" **Weight:** 11.0
Club Honours: SLC '96
International Honours: S: 1; B-2; U21-11; Sch

Stephen had an excellent season on the left wing for Watford in 2002-03 and deserved better reward. Hard working and a great trier, he also turned out at left back when required and showed an exemplary attitude. He played a full part in the Hornets' fine FA Cup run and scored a memorable goal direct from a free kick in the quarter-final against Burnley – Watford's 'Goal of the Season'. Ironically, he had been told just days before that he would be released at the end of the season, a victim of the club's needs to cut costs.

Aberdeen *(Free from Crombie Sports on 25/10/1994) SL 93+13/7 SLC 10/2 SC 7+2 Others 3/2*
Newcastle U *(£650,000 on 22/7/1998) PL 24+19/7 FLC 3 FAC 3+4 Others 2+3*
Watford *(Free on 5/7/2001) FL 55+9/4 FLC 3 FAC 2/1*

GLENNON Matthew (Matty) William

Born: Stockport, 8 October 1978
Height: 6'2" **Weight:** 14.9

Named by Hull boss Jan Molby as the club's first choice 'keeper at the start of the 2002-03 season, Matty became a casualty of the Tigers' disappointing opening to the campaign when he was dropped after a particularly disastrous home defeat by Macclesfield. He subsequently moved on to Carlisle United for whom he was an automatic choice following his debut in mid-October. He soon proved his worth with a superb last-minute penalty save at Kidderminster in early November, a week later he saved another spot kick in the FA Cup tie

against Lincoln and he was also outstanding in the goalless draw in the LDV Vans Trophy regional final at Shrewsbury. Matty is a goalkeeper who likes to command his area and his positive approach gives confidence to the rest of the defence.

Bolton W *(From trainee on 3/7/1997)*
Bristol Rov *(Loaned on 15/9/2000) FL 1*
Carlisle U *(Loaned on 10/11/2000) FL 29 FAC 3 Others 1*
Hull C *(£50,000 on 20/6/2001) FL 35 FLC 3 FAC 2 Others 2*
Carlisle U *(Free on 18/10/2002) FL 32 FAC Others 7*

GLOVER Edward Lee

Born: Kettering, 24 April 1970
Height: 5'11" **Weight:** 12.1
Club Honours: FLC '89; FMC '92
International Honours: S: U21-3; Yth

After recovering from a hernia operation during the 2002 close season Lee failed make an impression at Macclesfield early on last term and his contract was terminated by mutual agreement at the beginning of September. He then joined Mansfield Town on a non-contract basis but after a couple of appearances from the substitutes' bench he moved on to Conference outfit Burton Albion. Lee is a veteran striker who is most effective with his back to goal from where he can turn and shoot in one action.

Nottingham F *(From apprentice on 2/5/1987) F/PL 61+15/9 FLC 6+5/2 FAC 8+2 Others 4+1*
Leicester C *(Loaned on 14/9/1989) FL 3+2/1*
Barnsley *(Loaned on 18/11/1990) FL 8 FAC 4*
Luton T *(Loaned on 2/9/1991) FL 1*
Port Vale *(£200,000 on 2/8/1994) FL 38+14/7 FLC 5+1/4 FAC 0+2 Others 3+2/2*
Rotherham U *(£150,000 on 15/8/1996) FL 70+15/29 FLC 5 FAC 9+1/3 Others 1+1*
Huddersfield T *(Loaned on 3/3/1997) FL 1*
Macclesfield T *(Free on 5/7/2000) FL 72+13/18 FLC 1+1/1 FAC 4+1/2 Others 2/3*
Mansfield T *(Free on 6/9/2002) FL 0+2*

GNOHERE David Arthur

Born: Ivory Coast, 20 November 1978
Height: 6'2" **Weight:** 12.13

Arthur's season began badly with a red card in Burnley's opening game against Brighton, but on his return from suspension he remained a regular in the side until January. He was often an exciting player to watch, particularly with his seemingly unstoppable forward forays but his defensive displays, formidable at their best, became increasingly unpredictable and he was dropped from

Arthur Gnohere

the side. However, he returned to the line-up towards the end of the season.
Burnley *(Free from SM Caen, France, ex AS Cannes, on 9/8/2001) FL 62+5/5 FLC 5 FAC 5*

GOATER Leonard **Shaun**
Born: Hamilton, Bermuda, 25 February 1970
Height: 6'1" **Weight:** 12.0
Club Honours: AMC '96
International Honours: Bermuda: 19; Yth
Shaun found his position as Manchester City's main striker under threat from new arrival Nicolas Anelka and as the season progressed he found his first-team opportunities were somewhat limited. He remained a very popular figure at Maine Road and his position in City folklore was further confirmed by his three goals in the two 'derby' games against rivals Manchester United. In all he scored seven Premiership goals and after announcing that he wanted a move in the summer he was made captain for the final game of the season, which was also the very last Blues game at Maine Road. Thus it seems that 'The Goat' will no longer be fed in a Manchester City shirt. Shaun was awarded an MBE for services to sport and young people in Bermuda in the Queen's Birthday Honours List in June.
Manchester U *(Free from North Village, Bermuda on 8/5/1989)*
Rotherham U *(Free on 25/10/1989) FL 169+40/70 FLC 13+4/4 FAC 12+3/7 Others 15+5/5*
Notts Co *(Loaned on 12/11/1993) FL 1*
Bristol C *(£175,000 on 17/7/1996) FL 67+8/40 FLC 7/2 FAC 5 Others 5+1/1*
Manchester C *(£400,000 on 26/3/1998) P/FL 164+20/84 FLC 13/9 FAC 9+3/9 Others 3/1*

GODFREY Elliott James
Born: Toronto, Canada, 22 February 1983
Height: 6'1" **Weight:** 12.0
International Honours: Canada: Yth
This promising young centre forward made one substitute appearance for the Watford first team in 2002-03 during a season of consolidation in the reserves. An industrious player who reads the game well, Elliott made his debut for Canada U20s against Costa Rica last October and added two more caps during the season.
Watford *(From trainee on 7/3/2001) FL 0+1*

GOLDBAEK Bjarne
Born: Nykobing Falster, Denmark, 6 October 1968
Height: 5'10" **Weight:** 12.4
Club Honours: Div 1 '01
International Honours: Denmark: 28; B-1, U21; Yth

Bjarne again struggled to gain a first-team place at Fulham, but did not disappoint on those occasions when selected. An excellent crosser of the ball he normally operated on the right-hand side of midfield, using his pace to get in behind the opposing defence to provide vital crosses. His only goal of the season came in an FA Cup tie against Birmingham when he scored a magnificent solo effort. Bjarne was not offered a contract for 2003-04 and was expected to move on.
Chelsea (£350,000 from FC Copenhagen, Denmark, ex Naestved, FC Schalke,

Kaiserslautern, Tennis Borussia, FC Koln, on 10/11/1998) PL 15+14/5 FLC 3 FAC 2+4 Others 1+1
Fulham *(£500,000 + on 18/1/2000) P/FL 73+12/6 FLC 6 FAC 4+3/1 Others 2+2*

GOMA Alain
Born: Sault, France, 5 October 1972
Height: 6'0" **Weight:** 13.0
International Honours: France: 2; B-1; U21; Yth
Alain is a solid and dependable central defender who was missed when absent from the Fulham line-up last season.

Rarely beaten for pace, he reads the game well and is often able to make timely last minute interceptions to deny opponents goal-scoring opportunities. His commanding influence at the back instils confidence in others. Although he suffered a run of niggling injuries in the second half of the season he still made over 40 first-team appearances in all competitions.
Newcastle U (£4,750,000 from Paris St Germain, France, ex Auxerre, on 9/7/1999) P 32+1/1 FLC 4 FAC 2 Others 2
Fulham *(£4,000,000 on 16/3/2001) P/FL 64+1 FLC 1 FAC 9 Others 13*

GOODFELLOW Marc David
Born: Burton, 20 September 1981
Height: 5'8" **Weight:** 10.6
The 2002-03 season started well for Marc as new manager Steve Cotterill included him regularly in the first-team squad from the start of the campaign. However, the arrival of Tony Pulis in the autumn saw a marked reduction in his senior opportunities as the new boss looked to experience. Neverthless Marc continued t progress during the year and he scored regularly at reserve level.
Stoke C (From juniors on 29/1/1999) FL 17+33/6 FLC 1+3/1 FAC 1+6 Others 4/1

GOODHIND Warren Ernest
Born: Johannesburg, South Africa, 16 August 1977
Height: 5'11" **Weight:** 11.6
After struggling with injury the previous season, Warren had a much more settled campaign at Cambridge last time around and was a regular in the defence. He featured mainly at right back, although he was also used to cover as a centre half, and occasionally captained the team.
Barnet (From trainee on 3/7/1996) FL 73+20/3 FLC 5+2 FAC 2 Others 4/1
Cambridge U *(£80,000 on 21/9/2001) FL 45+6 FLC 1 FAC 5 Others 5+3*

GOODLAD Mark
Born: Barnsley, 9 September 1979
Height: 6'0" **Weight:** 13.2
Club Honours: AMC '01
Mark had another good season at Port Vale in 2002-03. Tall and commanding in the air, he remained the first choice 'keeper until February when he was left out for eight games after a temporary loss of form, only to return for a crucial victory at Mansfield in which he made some important saves. Unfortunately he was ill for the next game and so was in and out of the side for the remainder of the season. He scored a penalty in a shoot-

Shaun Goater

ut victory over Chesterfield in the LDV
Vans Trophy and also saved three spot
kicks from the opposition in the same
game.

Nottingham F *(From trainee on 2/10/1996)*
Scarborough (Loaned on 5/2/1999) FL 3
Port Vale (Free on 23/3/2000) FL 119+2 FLC
5 FAC 5 Others 12

GOODMAN Donald (Don) Ralph
Born: Leeds, 9 May 1966
Height: 5'10" **Weight:** 13.2
Club Honours: Div 3 '85
Now very much at the veteran stage of
his career, Don joined Exeter City at the
start of the 2002-03 campaign. His
experience, vision and link-up play with
midfield were evident, but he managed
just one goal, netting for City at Carlisle.
He was loaned out to Doncaster in the
new year and made six appearances as
the Yorkshire club fought their way to the
Conference play-offs and the ultimate
prize of a place in the Third Division.
Bradford C *(Free from Collingham on
0/7/1984) FL 65+5/14 FLC 5+1/2 FAC 2+3/4
Others 4+1/2*
West Bromwich A *(£50,000 on 27/3/1987)*
FL 140+18/60 FLC 11/1 FAC 7/1 Others 5/1
Sunderland *(£900,000 on 6/12/1991) FL
12+4/40 FLC 9/4 FAC 3/1 Others 4/2*
Wolverhampton W *(£1,100,000 on
5/12/1994) FL 115+10/33 FLC 8+1/4 FAC
16+1/2 Others 3 (Free to Hiroshima Antlers,
Japan during 1998 close season)*
Barnsley *(Loaned on 25/12/1998) FL 5+3
FAC 2*
Motherwell *(Signed on 30/3/1999) SL
39+16/9 SLC 4+1 SC 4/3*
Walsall *(Free on 22/3/2001) FL 15+10/3 FLC
1 Others 3/1*
Exeter C *(Free on 6/8/2002) FL 11+2/1 FLC 1*

GOODWIN James (Jim)
Born: Waterford, 20 November 1981
Height: 5'9" **Weight:** 12.2
International Honours: Roi: 1; U21-14
This talented young defender joined
Stockport County in the 2002 close
season and hit his first goals for the club
in the 4-1 demolition of Barnsley in
September, following that up with
County's 'Goal of the Season' at
Northampton. What Jim lacks in skill and
natural talent he makes up for in
abundance with his sheer passion and
aggressiveness on the pitch, qualities that
have endeared him to the club's fans. He
continued to feature for the Republic of
Ireland U21s and became the ninth
County player to win a full international
cap when he came of the bench to
replace Robbie Keane in Finland.

Glasgow Celtic *(From Tramore on
25/11/1997) SL 1*
Stockport Co *(Free on 7/6/2002) FL 22+11/3
FLC 1 FAC 2 Others 2*

GORDON Dean Dwight
Born: Croydon, 10 February 1973
Height: 6'0" **Weight:** 13.4
Club Honours: Div 1 '94
International Honours: E: U21-13
Dean took some time to reach full match
fitness after joining Coventry City in the
summer of 2002, but won plaudits for
his overlapping runs down the left wing
in the early part of the season. He
featured regularly until a torn muscle
kept him out of action early in the new
year, although he returned for the run-
in. There was some evidence of his
powerful shooting but he failed to find
the net until the Ipswich home game in
April, when his vicious left-foot shot
found the target.
Crystal Palace *(From trainee on 4/7/1991)*
*FPL 181+20/20 FLC 16+3/2 FAC 14+1/1
Others 5+1*
Middlesbrough *(£900,000 on 17/7/1998) PL
53+10/4 FLC 5 FAC 3*
Cardiff C *(Loaned on 23/11/2001) FL 7/2*
Coventry C *(Free on 1/8/2002) FL 30/1 FLC 2
FAC 3*

GORDON Kenyatta **Gavin**
Born: Manchester, 24 June 1979
Height: 6'1" **Weight:** 12.0
Gavin returned to action in the autumn,
spending time on loan with Third Division
club Oxford United. He scored with a
powerful header on his debut at York, but
failed to add to his tally before returning
to Ninian Park. He eventually broke into
the Cardiff City first-team squad in the
new year, starting against Port Vale and
Stockport County away. Gavin did well,
but faded and struggled to regain
ground. His battle for a place was rocked
by a disastrous team display as the
Bluebirds crashed to Newport County in
the FA Wales Premier Cup. Gavin made
several appearances as a substitute
towards the end of the season and
started one more game. He is a brave,
agile and pacy striker with an eye for
goal.
Hull C *(From trainee on 3/7/1996) FL
22+16/9 FLC 1+4/1 Others 1+1*
Lincoln C *(£30,000 on 7/11/1997) FL
87+12/28 FLC 2/1 FAC 9/2 Others 4+1*
Cardiff C *(£275,000 + on 18/12/2000) FL
19+16/4 FLC 0+1 FAC 2/1 Others 1+1/6*
Oxford U *(Loaned on 27/9/2002) FL 3+3/1
FLC 0+1*

GORDON Michael Alexander
Born: Wandsworth, 11 October 1984
Height: 5'6" **Weight:** 10.4
Michael is a young forward who was
released by Arsenal at the beginning of
2003 and who signed for Wimbledon a
month or so later after impressing during
some trial matches for the club's U19 and
reserve teams. He was given his league
debut as a substitute in the April home
defeat against Derby County, and during
his half hour showed some signs of
promise in a wide-right role. Very speedy,
he showed up to good effect in
subsequent reserve matches when playing
as a central striker.
Wimbledon *(Free from trainee at Arsenal on
11/3/2003) FL 0+1*

GORRE Dean
Born: Surinam, 10 September 1970
Height: 5'8" **Weight:** 11.7
International Honours: Holland: U21
Dean was a regular for Barnsley in the
early part of last season but suffered more
than most following a poor run of results.
After losing his place in the side he found
it hard to break back into the starting
line-up on a regular basis. At his best
Dean is an attractive playmaker who is
comfortable on the ball and has excellent
distribution. He also has a good eye for
goal, but he finished the season without a
strike to his name.
Huddersfield T *(£330,000 from Ajax,
Holland on 16/9/1999) FL 49+13/6 FLC 4/1
FAC 1+1*
Barnsley *(£50,000 on 24/7/2001) FL
32+14/2 FLC 2 Others 1*

GOULD James Robert
Born: Kettering, 15 January 1982
Height: 5'8" **Weight:** 11.8
Club Honours: NC '02
This left-sided player had the distinction
of being the first Boston United player to
score in the Football League when he
netted on the opening day against
Bournemouth. However, soon afterwards
he lost his left-back position to Ben
Chapman but was later used in a more
forward role on the left-hand side of
midfield. James was released at the end
of the season and was reported to have
signed for Stevenage Borough.
Northampton T *(From trainee on 13/7/2000)
FL 0+1 Others 1+1/1*
Boston U *(Free on 3/7/2001) FL 10+10/2*

GOULD Jonathan Alan
Born: Paddington, 18 July 1968
Height: 6'1" **Weight:** 13.7

Club Honours: SPD '98, '01; SLC '98, '00, '01

Jonathon found himself second choice goalkeeper to Robert Douglas for Celtic last term and made only three appearances in the first half of the season. He subsequently joined Preston North End during the January transfer window and made his debut at Ipswich. From then on he remained first choice other than when injured. Jonathon commands both his box and his defence well, and brought some much needed stability to the side after a mid-season run of poor results. A hamstring injury in March saw him substituted early in two successive games, and he missed five games altogether before regaining his place, which he marked by a stunning save in the home win over Sheffield United.

Halifax T (Free from Clevedon T on 18/7/1990) FL 32 FLC 2 FAC 5 Others 5
West Bromwich A (Free on 30/1/1992)
Coventry C (Free on 15/7/1992) PL 25 FLC 1+1
Bradford C (Free on 29/3/1996) FL 18 FLC 2 Others 3
Gillingham (Loaned on 28/10/1996) FL 3
Glasgow Celtic (Signed on 2/8/1997) SL 109+1 SLC 14+1 SC 12 Others 21
Preston NE (Free on 9/1/2003) FL 13+1

GRABBI Corrado (Ciccio)

Born: Turin, Italy, 29 July 1975
Height: 5'11" **Weight:** 12.12
Club Honours: FLC '02

After spending much of the previous season on loan in Italy, this experienced striker returned to Ewood Park last term and got off to a great start by heading home a glorious equaliser against Liverpool. However most of his senior action came from the substitutes' bench and his only Premiership start came at Chelsea in February. Ciccio also found the net in the UEFA Cup tie against CSKA Sofia and in the Worthington Cup third round tie with Walsall.

Blackburn Rov (£6,750,000 from Ternana, Italy on 12/7/2001) PL 11+14/2 FLC 2+3/1 FAC 1+2/1 Others 1/1

GRAHAM David

Born: Edinburgh, 6 October 1978
Height: 5'10" **Weight:** 11.5
International Honours: S: U21-8

The 2002-03 campaign was certainly a season of two halves for this skilful Torquay striker. Having missed the opening three games through suspension he returned bristling with confidence and enthusiasm to bag 13 goals in 15

league games, and he looked a class act. However, a series of niggling groin and back injuries seemed to cause him to lose his sharpness. The emergence of Jo Kuffour meant that David spent much of the second half of the campaign on the substitutes' bench, but he still finished the campaign as the Gulls' leading scorer.

Glasgow R (From juniors on 1/7/1995) SL 0+3 Others 1+1
Dunfermline Ath (Signed on 15/11/1998) SL 17+23/4 SLC 1 SC 3/1 Others 0+1
Inverness Caledonian Thistle (Loaned on 5/1/2001) SL 0+2 SC 0+2
Torquay U (Free on 22/3/2001) FL 62+13/25 FLC 3/1 FAC 3 Others 1

GRAINGER Martin Robert

Born: Enfield, 23 August 1972
Height: 5'11" **Weight:** 12.0

This experienced Birmingham City full back featured in only a handful of first-team games last season. He injured his knee in September then fell ill, before making a heroic return on New Year's Day at Leeds when the Blues were stripped of players through injury and suspension. However, knee trouble flared up again and kept him out action during the run-in. A solid performer, Martin's dead-ball abilities were sorely missed in his absence.

Colchester U (From trainee on 28/7/1992) FL 37+9/7 FLC 3 FAC 2 Others 3/1
Brentford (£60,000 on 21/10/1993) FL 100+1/12 FLC 6/1 FAC 9/1 Others 8/2
Birmingham C (£400,000 on 25/3/1996) P/FL 202+20/24 FLC 21+2/2 FAC 9+1/1 Others 7

GRAND Simon

Born: Chorley, 23 February 1984
Height: 6'1" **Weight:** 10.12

Considered one of Rochdale's best young prospects, Simon confirmed this judgement as soon as he came into the senior side. A strong, committed central defender not afraid to make his point to more experienced colleagues, he got his chance due to an injury crisis and never looked back. A star of Dale's remarkable FA Cup run - his debut came in the second round at Bristol Rovers - he was virtually ever present for the rest of the 2002-03 season. Simon became one of the club's youngest-ever captains when he led the side at title contenders Rushden, netting his first senior goal in the process.

Rochdale (From trainee on 3/7/2002) FL 22+1/2 FAC 5

GRANT Anthony (Tony) James

Born: Liverpool, 14 November 1974
Height: 5'10" **Weight:** 10.2
Club Honours: CS '95
International Honours: E: U21-1

Burnley's midfield saw numerous changes during 2002-03, and Tony was one of the players whose place could not be guaranteed, although he was usually in the 16-man squad when fit. Tenacious in the tackle, and, along with Paul Cook, Burnley's best passer of the ball, Tony was more often efficient than spectacular but seldom let the side down. His first goal for the Clarets came in a 3-1 home win against Coventry, but he was a provider on several occasions. Stan Ternent frequently used him as a substitute when some extra creativity was required in the engine room.

Everton (From trainee on 8/7/1993) PL 43+18/2 FLC 5+1 FAC 4+4 Others 2+2/1
Swindon T (Loaned on 18/1/1996) FL 3/1
Tranmere Rov (Loaned on 2/9/1999) FL 8+1 FLC 1/1
Manchester C (£450,000 on 24/12/1999) P/FL 11+10 FLC 1 FAC 2+1
West Bromwich A (Loaned on 1/12/2000) FL 3+2
Burnley (£250,000 on 11/10/2001) FL 50+12/1 FLC 3+1 FAC 8

GRANT Lee Anderson

Born: Watford, 27 January 1983
Height: 6'2" **Weight:** 13.4
International Honours: E: U21-1; Yth

After starting out as Derby's third choice goalkeeper, Lee progressed well enough last season to win his first England U21 cap. When Mart Poom joined Sunderland, initially on loan, Lee was given his chance ahead of Andy Oakes. He approached the job in a positive way and although there were errors, he never lost his composure. He handles well and comes out for crosses: experience will refine his judgement. When George Burley took over as temporary manager, Oakes was preferred but Lee gained a great deal from a season behind an ailing defence.

Derby Co (From trainee on 17/2/2001) FL 26+3 FAC 1

GRANVILLE Daniel (Danny) Patrick

Born: Islington, 19 January 1975
Height: 5'11" **Weight:** 12.5
Club Honours: FLC '98, ECWC '98; Div 1 '02
International Honours: E: U21-3

Danny was again first choice at left back for Crystal Palace last term, although he

ee Grant

missed several matches through suspension after accumulating disciplinary points. As well as being sound defensively, he also offers a useful attacking presence with his spirited runs down the wing. A highlight of his season was netting with a brilliant free kick, which proved to be the winner in the home game with local rivals Millwall.

Cambridge U *(From trainee on 19/5/1993)*
FL 89+10/7 FLC 3+2 FAC 2+2 Others 4+2
Chelsea *(£300,000 + on 21/3/1997) PL 12+6*
FLC 3 Others 4+1/1
Leeds U *(£1,600,000 on 8/7/1998) PL 7+2*
FLC 1 FAC 3 Others 0+1
Manchester C *(£1,000,000 on 7/8/1999)*
P/FL 56+14/3 FLC 1+4 FAC 5
Norwich C *(Loaned on 27/10/2000) FL 6*
Crystal Palace *(£500,000 on 28/12/2001) FL*
46+5/3 FAC 3+2

GRAVES Wayne Alan
Born: Scunthorpe, 18 September 1980
Height: 5'8" **Weight:** 12.10
Wayne had an excellent season in the centre of the Scunthorpe midfield where his great work-rate, energy and strong tackling made him a regular. An ever present until the end of November, he scored his only goal of the campaign in the win at York on New Year's Day and stayed clear of the injury problems that have hampered his progress in recent seasons.
Scunthorpe U *(From trainee on 24/3/1999)*
FL 85+29/6 FLC 4+2 FAC 4+5 Others 3+1

GRAVESEN Thomas
Born: Vejle, Denmark, 11 March 1976
Height: 5'10" **Weight:** 12.4
International Honours: Denmark: 37;
U21-6
There are few greater enigmas in the Premiership than this technically gifted midfielder. Coming off the back of a successful World Cup campaign, Thomas was expected to have a decisive influence in Everton's fortunes and this was borne out in an impressive start to the season when he was a consistent star performer, showing some fierce tackling and perceptive passing. A knee injury picked up in training in late October meant he missed three games and following this he rarely showed his early-season form. He continued to thrive on the international scene, scoring a memorable chip from the half way line for his country against Romania in March and adding goals in the wins over Ukraine and Luxembourg.
Everton *(£2,500,000 from SV Hamburg,*
Germany, ex Vejle BK, on 9/8/2000) PL
82+8/5 FLC 2 FAC 3+1

GRAY Andrew (Andy) David
Born: Harrogate, 15 November 1977
Height: 6'1" **Weight:** 13.0
International Honours: S: Yth
Andy enjoyed a terrific first season with Bradford City, finishing the campaign as top scorer with 15 goals and also winning the 'Player of the Year' award. A lively attacking midfield player, his golden touch in front of goal forced the Bantams to use him as an out-and-out striker by the end of the season. He was a virtual ever-present for the club and was rewarded for his great performances with his first full cap for Scotland in the 1-0 defeat by Lithuania in April.
Leeds U (From trainee on 1/7/1995) PL 13+9 FLC 3+1 FAC 0+2
Bury (Loaned on 11/12/1997) FL 4+2/1
Nottingham F (£175,000 on 2/9/1998) P/FL 34+30/1 FLC 3+4 FAC 4+1
Preston NE (Loaned on 23/2/1999) FL 5
Oldham Ath (Loaned on 25/3/1999) FL 4
Bradford C (Free on 9/8/2002) FL 44/15 FLC 1 FAC 1

GRAY Ian James
Born: Manchester, 25 February 1975
Height: 6'2" **Weight:** 13.0
After almost two years of undying patience, Rotherham 'keeper Ian was finally rewarded when he took over from the injured Mike Pollitt for the last few games of the 2002-03 season. What is more, his long spell out of the team had no detrimental effect as he produced some outstanding saves, none more crucial than a late one which defied the odds in the last few minutes of the home game against promoted Leicester City. Ian was given a free transfer at the end of the season.
Oldham Ath (From trainee on 16/7/1993)
Rochdale (Loaned on 18/11/1994) FL 12 Others 3
Rochdale (£20,000 on 17/7/1995) FL 66 FLC 4 FAC 5 Others 4
Stockport Co (£200,000 + on 30/7/1997) F 14+2 FLC 3
Rotherham U (Free on 10/7/2000) FL 38+2 FLC 2 FAC 3 Others 1

GRAY Julian Raymond
Born: Lewisham, 21 September 1979
Height: 6'1" **Weight:** 11.10
This tall, lean left winger featured regularly for Crystal Palace last term, again causing opponents problems with his ability to beat defenders and deliver an accurate cross. The highlights of his campaign came in the FA Cup, he scored one of the goals in the amazing 2-0 win at Anfield and also netted in the following round against Leeds. Julian made his 100th league appearance for the Eagles against Millwall in April.
Arsenal (From trainee on 13/7/1998) PL 0+1
Crystal Palace (£250,000 + on 21/7/2000) FL 76+25/8 FLC 5+6/1 FAC 5/2

GRAY Kevin John
Born: Sheffield, 7 January 1972
Height: 6'0" **Weight:** 14.0
Kevin joined Tranmere Rovers during the 2002 close season and was immediately appointed as team captain. Unfortunately his campaign was affected by a series of injuries, starting with a calf strain in September. Kevin made only 12 first-team appearances for Rovers and scored just once, netting against his former club Huddersfield Town. A full back who is one of life's leaders, he is also a strong tackler and his experience is evident in all aspects of his play.
Mansfield T (From trainee on 1/7/1990) FL 129+12/3 FLC 8/1 FAC 6+1 Others 12+2/2
Huddersfield T (Signed on 18/7/1994) FL 214+16/6 FLC 12+1 FAC 15 Others 11
Stockport Co (Loaned on 11/8/2000) FL 1
Tranmere Rov (Free on 8/7/2002) FL 9+1/1 FLC 1 FAC 1+1 Others 1+1

GRAY Michael
Born: Sunderland, 3 August 1974
Height: 5'7" **Weight:** 10.10
Club Honours: Div 1 '96, '99
International Honours: E: 3
Sunderland's left back and club captain

Wayne Graves

ill have been glad to see the back of the 002-03 season as his home town club vere relegated. On his day Michael is a ompetent attacking full back whose pace nd crossing strengths can be put to ood use. A former England international, e also appeared in midfield last term, a osition he had occupied in his early underland days, and netted his only goal of the season at Bolton in October with a 5-yard drive. Michael made his 400th opearance in a red-and-white shirt at ulham in March.

underland (From trainee on 1/7/1992) P/FL 41+21/16 FLC 22+4 FAC 17+1/1 Others 2

GRAY Stuart Edward
Born: Harrogate, 18 December 1973
Height: 5'11" **Weight:** 11.2
Club Honours: Div 3 '03
International Honours: S: U21-7

After an injury-hit start to his Nene Park career Stuart became an important member of the Rushden & Diamonds midfield last season, scoring seven goals including three penalties. With the freedom allowed by manager Brian Talbot, the former Celtic man often moved inside from the left flank to get more possession and create openings. Stuart is the son of Leeds United legend Eddie Gray.

Glasgow Celtic (Signed from Giffnock North AFC on 7/7/1992) SL 19+9/1 SC 1 Others 2+1
Reading (£100,000 on 27/3/1998) FL 46+6/2 FLC 8 FAC 1+1 Others 2
Rushden & Diamonds (Free on 23/3/2001) FL 46+4/7 FLC 3 FAC 3 Others 2+1

GRAY Wayne William
Born: Camberwell, 7 November 1980
Height: 5'10" **Weight:** 12.10

ulian Gray

This central striker endured a frustrating 2002-03 campaign at Wimbledon thanks to the form of Neil Shipperley and David Connolly. Their sustained goal-scoring form meant that there was never the remotest chance of either being relegated to the bench, which is from where Wayne consequently viewed most of the season, starting no less than 32 league games from that position. When given his opportunities he once again showed plenty of pace, energy and application, and he was leading scorer for the club's reserve team, but for moment being patient at senior level may need to be his greatest quality.

Wimbledon (From trainee on 10/2/1999) P/FL 13+29/2 FLC 1+1 FAC 0+5/1
Swindon T (Loaned on 3/3/2000) FL 8+4/2
Port Vale (Loaned on 6/10/2000) FL 2+1
Leyton Orient (Loaned on 30/11/2001) FL 13+2/5 FAC 2/1
Brighton & Hove A (Loaned on 27/3/2002) FL 3+1/1

GRAYDON Keith
Born: Dublin, 10 February 1983
Height: 5'11" **Weight:** 12.0
International Honours: RoI: Yth
This promising young Sunderland striker did well in the club's reserve team last term and subsequently spent the closing stages of the campaign on loan at Third Division York City. He proved to be a lively forward, scoring from the penalty spot in the 2-2 home draw against Rochdale. Keith also featured for the Republic of Ireland at U20 level during the season.

Sunderland (From trainee on 28/2/2000)
York C (Loaned on 27/3/2003) FL 4+3/1

GRAYSON Simon Nicholas
Born: Ripon, 16 December 1969
Height: 6'0" **Weight:** 13.7
Club Honours: FLC '97
This experienced defender joined Blackpool during the 2002 close season and went on to become a near ever-present last term. Equally sound at full back or in the centre of the defence, he captained the side for the majority of the campaign. Simon also found time to get forward to support the attack and contributed three valuable goals.

Leeds U (From trainee on 13/6/1988) FL 2 Others 1+1
Leicester C (£50,000 on 13/3/1992) F/PL 175+13/4 FLC 16+2/2 FAC 9 Others 13+1
Aston Villa (£1,350,000 on 1/7/1997) PL 32+16 FLC 1+1 FAC 4+1/2 Others 6+3
Blackburn Rov (£750,000 + on 29/7/1999) FL 31+3 FLC 1+1 FAC 2+1
Sheffield Wed (Loaned on 11/8/2000) FL 5

Stockport Co (Loaned on 12/1/2001) FL 13 FAC 1
Notts Co (Loaned on 6/9/2001) FL 10/1 FLC 1 Others 2
Bradford C (Loaned on 15/2/2002) FL 7
Blackpool (Free on 1/8/2002) FL 44+1/3 FLC 1 FAC 3 Others 1

GRAZIOLI Giuliano Stefano Luigi
Born: Marylebone, 23 March 1975
Height: 5'11" **Weight:** 12.11
Giuliano quickly established himself as a crowd favourite with Bristol Rovers supporters last term by scoring eight times in the opening 13 league matches including an impressive hat trick in a stunning 5-2 victory at Shrewsbury Town. The former Blackpool marksman endured a series of minor injuries which interrupted his regular appearances, but he returned in February to score against Carlisle. He finished the season as Rovers' top goal-scorer with a double-figure tally.
Peterborough U (Free from Wembley on 19/10/1995) FL 23+18/16 FLC 1+2 FAC 0+3/1 Others 0+2
Swindon T (Free on 15/7/1999) FL 45+33/18 FLC 3+4 FAC 1+1 Others 1
Bristol Rov (Free on 2/7/2002) FL 28+6/11 FLC 1 FAC 3/1

GREAVES Mark Andrew
Born: Hull, 22 January 1975
Height: 6'1" **Weight:** 13.0
Mark's days at Boothferry Park seemed to be numbered at the start of last term following the arrival of several new faces. Although he featured in three early-season games the assumption proved to be correct and he was quickly offloaded to Boston United. This solid central defender soon established himself as a first-team regular at York Street. He was also used at left back and right midfield before settling into a centre-midfield position. Mark scored just one goal during the campaign, netting a vital winner against Darlington in March.
Hull C (Free from Brigg T on 17/6/1996) FL 152+25/10 FLC 8/1 FAC 11/1 Others 6+2
Boston U (Free on 29/8/2002) FL 24+2/1 FLC 1 Others 2

GREEN Francis James
Born: Nottingham, 25 April 1980
Height: 5'9" **Weight:** 11.6
This young Peterborough United striker was hampered by injury last term and only managed nine starts and 12 outings from the bench. Quick and powerful, he managed two goals during the campaign, both in early-season games. Francis was

released by the Posh in the summer.
Peterborough U (£25,000 + from Ilkeston T on 2/3/1998) FL 51+54/14 FLC 4+2 FAC 5 Others 3+4/2

GREEN Robert Paul
Born: Chertsey, 18 January 1980
Height: 6'2" **Weight:** 12.2
International Honours: E: Yth
Robert kept a clean sheet on the occasion of his 100th senior appearance for Norwich City against Wimbledon at Carrow Road in March. He has now established himself as one of the best young goalkeepers around by virtue of some outstanding displays for the Canaries over the course of the last two seasons. Robert has a tremendous physical presence, is decisive in one-on-one situations, kicks the ball particularly well and is also a top-class shot stopper. He was voted as runner-up in the supporters' 'Player of the Season' awards for 2002-2003.
Norwich C (From juniors on 3/7/1997) FL 96+1 FLC 2 FAC 5 Others 3

GREEN Ryan Michael
Born: Cardiff, 20 October 1980
Height: 5'8" **Weight:** 11.0
International Honours: W: 2; U21-16; Yth
Out of favour at Millwall, Ryan joined Cardiff City but made only one appearance for his home town club, at Exeter City in the LDV Vans Trophy. The promising young full back then joined Sheffield Wednesday in a short-term deal, where he made four first-team appearances, although he has yet to establish himself in the starting line-up. Ryan is a compact defender who is effective when pushing forward.
Wolverhampton W (From trainee on 25/10/1997) FL 6+2 FLC 2 FAC 0+2
Torquay U (Loaned on 2/3/2001) FL 10
Millwall (Free on 19/10/2001) FL 12+1
Cardiff C (Free on 14/8/2002) Others 0+1
Sheffield Wed (Free on 27/11/2002) FL 4

GREEN Scott Paul
Born: Walsall, 15 January 1970
Height: 5'10" **Weight:** 12.5
Club Honours: Div 1 '97; Div 2 '03; AMC '99
A hard-working and versatile footballer who can play in both defence and midfield, Scott was a virtual ever-present in the first half of the season for Wigan Athletic. However, he was due to be out of contract in the summer and in February he was allowed to move on to Wrexham, where he turned out to be an important

signing by Denis Smith. He provided the extra ingredient that made all the difference in the run-in for promotion. He scored a couple of excellent goals in the important 2-0 win over leaders Hartlepool United displaying a calmness in front of goal reminiscent of a predatory striker!
Derby Co (From trainee on 20/7/1988)
Bolton W (£50,000 on 17/3/1990) P/FL 166+54/25 FLC 19+4/1 FAC 20+3/4 Others 16+4/1
Wigan Ath (£300,000 on 30/6/1997) FL 177+22/10 FLC 16+1 FAC 17/1 Others 15+1
Wrexham (Free on 14/2/2003) FL 12+3/3

GREEN Stuart
Born: Carlisle, 15 June 1981
Height: 5'10" **Weight:** 11.4
Stuart's skilful displays were possibly the highlights of a disappointing first half of the season for Hull. He produced a super match-winning performance against leader Hartlepool in City's first league game at their new Kingston Communications Stadium. However, being played wide on the right rather than in his preferred central midfield role, rumours persisted about a move away. He subsequently joined Carlisle United on loan in February and produced an outstanding display in his debut at Rochdale when he scored the game's only goal. Thereafter he seldom showed the form of which he is capable and he eventually returned to Hull.
Newcastle U (From trainee on 8/7/1999)
Carlisle U (Loaned on 14/12/2001) FL 16/3
Hull C (£150,000 on 3/7/2002) FL 27+1/6 FAC 1
Carlisle U (Loaned on 19/2/2003) FL 9+1/2 Others 3

GREENACRE Christopher (Chris) Mark
Born: Halifax, 23 December 1977
Height: 5'11" **Weight:** 12.8
A prolific scorer at Mansfield Town, Chris was Stoke manager Steve Cotterill's main signing in the summer of 2002 but a pre season injury upset his introduction into the side. A committed striker whose main strength is within the six-yard box, his six goals were scant reward for his efforts and he will be looking to increase his tall in 2003-04.
Manchester C (From trainee on 1/7/1995) F 3+5/1 FAC 0+1
Cardiff C (Loaned on 22/8/1997) FL 11/2
Blackpool (Loaned on 5/3/1998) FL 2+2
Scarborough (Loaned on 10/12/1998) FL 10+2/2 Others 1
Mansfield T (Free on 5/11/1999) FL 120+1/49 FLC 5/3 FAC 5/6 Others 2+1
Stoke C (Free on 8/7/2002) FL 18+12/4 FAC 3/2

GREENING Jonathan
Born: Scarborough, 2 January 1979
Height: 5'11" **Weight:** 11.7
Club Honours: EC '99
International Honours: E: U21-10; Yth
Jonathan, an attacking midfielder who can operate as a striker or a winger, had a marvellous season at Middlesbrough and it was pluses all the way for this energetic young man. He missed only 45 minutes of a hectic Premiership season after he was replaced at half time in the final game of the season, at the Reebok Stadium against Bolton Wanderers. He joined the England squad for a training camp in November and, with U21 experience and in view of his excellent season, a full cap must surely be waiting for him on the not too distant horizon.
York C *(From trainee on 23/12/1996) FL 5+20/2 FLC 0+1 Others 1*
Manchester U *(£500,000 + on 25/3/1998) PL 4+10 FLC 6 FAC 0+1 Others 3+3*
Middlesbrough *(£2,000,000 on 9/8/2001) PL 74/3 FLC 1 FAC 4+1*

GREER Gordon
Born: Glasgow, 14 December 1980
Height: 5'10" **Weight:** 12.4
Gordon was a regular for the Blackburn Rovers reserve team last season and spent the closing weeks of the campaign on loan to Stockport. The talented young defender became an instant hit with the County fans at Wycombe. Luke Beckett had just grabbed a late equaliser when Gordon, who had been on the pitch for just eight minutes, powered a header into the top corner to put his side 2-1 up and secure a priceless three points which went a long way to preserving Second Division status.
Clyde *(Free from Port Glasgow on 28/6/2000) SL 27+3 SLC 0+1 SC 1 Others 1*
Blackburn Rov *(£200,000 on 23/5/2001) FLC 1*
Stockport Co *(Loaned on 27/3/2003) FL 4+1/1*

GREGAN Sean Matthew
Born: Guisborough, 29 March 1974
Height: 6'2" **Weight:** 14.7
Club Honours: Div 2 '00
Sean was brought in to bolster up West Bromwich Albion's midfield but during the course of the season, owing to injuries and suspensions, he was used regularly as a central defender, where he performed with great determination and endeavour. A totally committed player, strong in the tackle, he took over the captaincy for a while from Derek McInnes

and his only goal of the campaign was a long-range bobbling effort that earned Albion a 1-0 home victory over Southampton. Sean missed a couple of games early in the new year with an achilles injury.
Darlington *(From trainee on 20/1/1991) FL 129+7/4 FLC 8 FAC 7 Others 10+1/1*
Preston NE *(£350,000 on 29/11/1996) FL 206+6/12 FLC 14 FAC 15/1 Others 10*
West Bromwich A *(£1,500,000 on 6/8/2002) PL 36/1 FAC 2*

GRENET Francois
Born: Bordeaux, France, 8 March 1975
Height: 5'11" **Weight:** 11.11
One of three players signed from France in Colin Todd's brief spell as manager, Francois never settled at Derby, despite his considerable experience as Girondins de Bordeaux's right back. He featured in just a handful of first-team games last term and it was no surprise when he returned to his native country with Stade Rennais,

initially on loan before the deal was made permanent in February.
Derby Co *(£3,000,000 from Bordeaux, France on 6/11/2001) P/FL 14+4 FAC 1*

GRESKO Vratislav
Born: Pressburg, Bratislava, Slovakia, 24 July 1977
Height: 5'11" **Weight:** 11.5
Vratislav joined Blackburn Rovers on loan early in the new year and proved to be a real revelation at full back. The complete defender – strong on the ball, sure in the tackle, constructive in his distribution and never out of position – he slotted straight in and immediately improved the Rovers' back line. Unfortunately sidelined by a foot injury sustained at Leeds at the end of April, it remains to be seen if the club can negotiate his permanent transfer over the summer break.
Blackburn Rov *(Loaned from Parma, Italy, ex Dukla Banska, Inter Bratislava, Bayer Leverkusen, Inter Milan, on 31/1/2003) PL 10*

Bart Griemink

GRIEMINK Bart
Born: Holland, 29 March 1972
Height: 6'4" **Weight:** 15.4
Bart had another consistent season in goal for Swindon Town in 2002-03 and he has now made over 100 appearances for the Robins. He would again have been ever-present in the league but for the manager's desire to give understudy Craig Farr some late-season opportunities. Noted for his shot-stopping ability, he was always capable of pulling off an outstanding save, one particularly memorable effort occurring just before half time in the Robins' 1-0 victory at Tranmere. Although his kicking has improved he still needs to learn to dominate his box.
Birmingham C (Free from WK Emmen, Holland on 9/11/1995) FL 20 FLC 3 FAC 1 Others 1+1
Peterborough U (£25,000 on 11/10/1996) FL 58 FLC 1 FAC 4 Others 4
Swindon T (Loaned on 5/2/2000) FL 4
Swindon T (Free on 27/7/2000) FL 113+1 FLC 7 FAC 7 Others 4

GRIFFIN Andrew (Andy)
Born: Billinge, 7 March 1979
Height: 5'9" **Weight:** 10.10
International Honours: E: U21-2; Yth
This combative right back began the 2002-03 season on Newcastle's bench, making his first start in almost a year when selected at Dynamo Kiev in the Champions' League. His fierce tackling and no-nonsense performances earned him a regular place in the team until an accumulation of yellow cards saw him suspended in January, and thereafter, following an elbow injury, he mixed starts with substitute appearances. He endeared himself to the Toon Army with a sterling performance in the home derby with Sunderland, and after two-and-a-half years without a goal he scored the vital winner at home to Juventus in the Champions' League, followed three days later with a goal at home to Charlton, a strike he described as his best ever.
Stoke C (From trainee on 5/9/1996) FL 52+5/2 FLC 4+1 FAC 2
Newcastle U (£1,500,000 + on 30/1/1998) PL 58+13/2 FLC 7 FAC 6 Others 12/1

GRIFFIN Antony Richard
Born: Bournemouth, 22 March 1979
Height: 5'11" **Weight:** 11.2
The 2002-03 season was a frustrating time for Antony, who was unable to capitalise on the excellent progress he had made at Cheltenham during the previous campaign. He was used sparingly in the

first half of the season, and after being given a chance when new boss Bobby Gould arrived he pulled a hamstring and his replacement, David Bird, went on to hold down the right-back spot for the rest of the campaign. Antony remains the quickest player on the club's books and can operate in either full-back position or on the right-hand side of midfield. He even made a handful of appearances for the reserves as a sweeper in the middle of a five-man defence.
Bournemouth (From trainee on 7/7/1997) FL 1+5
Cheltenham T (£20,000 on 27/7/1999) FL 57+24/1 FLC 3+1 FAC 5 Others 3+2

GRIFFITHS Carl Brian
Born: Welshpool, 15 July 1971
Height: 5'11" **Weight:** 11.10
International Honours: W: B-1; U21-2; Yth
Carl spent most of the 2002-03 season recovering from an injury suffered in the previous campaign. However, after a lot of hard work and patience he was finally able to make his return in the home game with Bristol City in April and his comeback was fully complete when he scored in the Hatters' 5-0 win at Colchester the following week. When fully fit Carl is an experienced striker who is one of the best finishers in the lower divisions.
Shrewsbury T (From trainee on 26/9/1988) FL 110+33/54 FLC 7+4/3 FAC 6/2 Others 7+3/3
Manchester C (£500,000 on 29/10/1993) PL 11+7/4 FLC 0+1 FAC 2
Portsmouth (£200,000 on 17/8/1995) FL 2+12/2 FLC 0+1
Peterborough U (£225,000 on 28/3/1996) FL 6+10/2 FLC 0+2/1 FAC 1+1/1 Others 0+1
Leyton Orient (Loaned on 31/10/1996) FL 5/3
Leyton Orient (£100,000 on 7/3/1997) FL 60+5/29 FLC 7+1/3 FAC 5/1 Others 2
Wrexham (Loaned on 13/1/1999) FL 4/3 Others 1/1
Port Vale (£100,000 on 25/3/1999) FL 3+5/1 FLC 0+2/1
Leyton Orient (£80,000 on 16/12/1999) FL 46+2/18 FLC 2+1 FAC 3/4
Luton T (£65,000 on 10/7/2001) FL 13/8 FLC 1

GRIFFITHS Gareth John
Born: Winsford, 10 April 1970
Height: 6'4" **Weight:** 14.0
The Rochdale skipper was again pretty much an automatic choice at centre half when available last term. He would probably be the first to admit, though,

that his form was sometimes lacking in consistency. Some superb battling performances like the one against Wolves in the televised FA Cup tie, were set against some days he'd probably rather forget, such as the games against Torquay when he was sent off in one and netted an own goal in the other. His power in the air earned him an excellent goals tally for a defender, his most notable being a bullet header in the FA Cup defeat of Coventry City.
Port Vale (£1,000 from Rhyl on 8/2/1993) FL 90+4/4 FLC 8 FAC 7/1 Others 7
Shrewsbury T (Loaned on 31/10/1997) FL 6
Wigan Ath (Free on 2/7/1998) FL 44+9/2 FLC 4/1 FAC 5 Others 5+1
Rochdale (Free on 18/7/2001) FL 82+1/10 FLC 3 FAC 5/1 Others 4

GRIFFITHS Leroy
Born: London, 30 December 1976
Height: 5'11" **Weight:** 13.5
This tall left-sided forward spent the early part of the 2002-03 campaign on loan to Conference sides Farnborough and Margate. Leroy eventually made a return to first-team action with Queen's Park Rangers in February due to injuries to other players, but was unable to retain his place in the side.
Queens Park R (£40,000 from Hampton & Richmond Borough, ex Corinthian Casuals, on 30/5/2001) FL 26+10/3 FAC 1

GRITTON Martin
Born: Glasgow, 1 June 1978
Height: 6'1" **Weight:** 12.7
After failing to gain a regular start with Plymouth Argyle, Martin arrived at Torquay on a trial basis with a point to prove. He won the battle with Marcus Richardson for the centre-forward slot, earning a full contract and striking up an immediate rapport with David Graham. His tremendous work rate, strength and determination and an ability to hold the ball up made him an excellent target man. After Graham's injury, he assumed the mantle of goal scorer with increasingly assured finishing, ending the season with 16 goals in all competitions.
Plymouth Arg (Free from Porthleven on 7/8/1998) FL 15+29/7 FLC 2+2/1 FAC 0+4 Others 3/1
Torquay U (Signed on 8/8/2002) FL 39+4/13 FLC 1 FAC 2/3 Others 1

GRONKJAER Jesper
Born: Nuuk, Denmark, 12 August 1977
Height: 6'1" **Weight:** 12.8
International Honours: Denmark: 37; U21-13

Jesper Gronkjaer

For the first time since his move to Chelsea, Jesper had a comparatively injury-free season and figured prominently for the Blues throughout the campaign. He started out in sparkling form, filling the wide-right midfield berth as Claudio Ranieri opted for two wingers to supply ammunition for Chelsea's predatory strikers. One of the quickest players in the Premiership, Jesper's blistering pace troubled every defence in the top-flight although his dribbling was occasionally spoiled by a wayward final pass. He is particularly effective late in a match when Chelsea used his searing speed as a springboard for a telling counter-attack. The flying Dane's greatest contribution came in the final Premiership match against Liverpool, when he laid on Marcel Desailly's equaliser with a delightful hanging cross and later cut in from the right and drilled a left-footed winner which confirmed the Blues' place amongst the cream of Europe.

Chelsea (£7,800,000 from Ajax, Holland, ex Aalborg BK, on 21/12/2000) PL 37+20/5 FLC 1+1 FAC 6+4/3 Others 2

GROVES Paul

Born: Derby, 28 February 1966
Height: 5'11" **Weight:** 11.5
Club Honours: AMC '98

Paul had something of a rough ride in his first full season as player-manager of Grimsby Town, with a long crop of injuries and lack of funds for team strengthening hampering his efforts to avoid relegation. He returned to a midfield role following the emergence of young Simon Ford, and performed with his usual panache, also contributing the occasional goal. Any plans he had to withdraw to the sidelines were thwarted by the club's injury problems. Paul now ranks third in the Mariners' roll of league outings and notched up his 700th appearance in senior football at Gillingham in February.

Leicester C (£12,000 from Burton A on 18/4/1988) FL 7+9/1 FLC 1/1 FAC 0+1 Others 0+1
Lincoln C (Loaned on 20/8/1989) FL 8/1 FLC 2
Blackpool (£60,000 on 25/1/1990) FL 106+1/21 FLC 6/1 FAC 9/4 Others 13/3
Grimsby T (£150,000 on 12/8/1992) FL 183+1/38 FLC 10+1/2 FAC 12/2 Others 4/1
West Bromwich A (£600,000 on 8/7/1996) FL 27+2/4 FLC 2/1 FAC 1
Grimsby T (£250,000 on 21/7/1997) FL 255+4/33 FLC 25/5 FAC 13/1 Others 10/2

GUDJOHNSEN Eidur Smari

Born: Reykjavik, Iceland, 15 September 1978
Height: 6'1" **Weight:** 13.0
Club Honours: CS '00
International Honours: Iceland: 24; U21-11; Yth

This talented striker had a disjointed first half to the 2002–03 season at Chelsea, as a combination of niggling injuries and Gianfranco Zola's inspired form interrupted his fruitful partnership with Jimmy-Floyd Hasselbaink. But, come the turn of the year and heavier pitches, Eidur grabbed his chance and began to score regularly. Amongst his tally was a gem at Old Trafford when he darted behind the United defence and subtly dinked the ball over the advancing Fabien Barthez. This was but a prelude to his next Premiership goal, the sensational overhead bicycle kick against Leeds, which inspired a famous victory for the Blues after they had trailed twice. His tenth, and final, Premiership goal of the season came on Easter

Paul Groves

180

Monday with a sweet finish that helped to defeat Everton.

Bolton W *(Free from KR Reykjavik, Iceland, x Valur, PSV Eindhoven, on 6/8/1998) FL 8+7/18 FLC 8+1/3 FAC 4+1/4 Others 4/1*
Chelsea *(£4,000,000 on 12/7/2000) PL 3+34/34 FLC 5+3/3 FAC 10+5/6 Others +4/3*

GUDJONSSON Bjarni
Born: Iceland, 26 February 1979
Height: 5'9" **Weight:** 11.9
Club Honours: AMC '00
International Honours: Iceland: 12;

U21-20; Yth
The 2002-03 season was a roller coaster ride for Bjarni, son of former Stoke boss Gudjón Thórdarson. Following the departure of his father he finally won over the club's supporters, while his quality crossing from the right wing was a positive feature in the first two-thirds of the campaign. Unfortunately new boss Tony Pulis preferred others on the right-hand side of his team, no matter what system was being played, and at the end of the season Bjarni was not offered a new contract.

Newcastle U *(£500,000 from Akranes, Iceland on 14/7/1997. £125,000 to KRC Genk on 12/11/1998)*
Stoke C *(£250,000 on 10/3/2000) FL 119+13/11 FLC 7/2 FAC 8+1/1 Others 9+4/2*

GUDJONSSON Johannes (Joey) Karl
Born: Akranes, Iceland, 25 May 1980
Height: 5'8" **Weight:** 11.5
International Honours: Iceland: 13; U21-10; Yth
Out of favour at Real Betis, this aggressive attacking midfielder joined Aston Villa in

Sidur Gudjohnsen

a long-term loan deal last January. Joey made an excellent debut at Middlesborough, marking the occasion with a goal directly from a free kick almost 30 yards out. He featured in most of Villa's games following his arrival and certainly added some strength to the midfield. However, the change in management at Villa Park meant there was little likelihood of a permanent transfer being arranged.
Aston Villa (Loaned from Real Betis, Spain, ex IA Akranes, KRC Genk, MVV Maastricht, RKC Waalwijk, on 27/1/2003) PL 9+2/2

GULLIVER Philip (Phil) Stephen
Born: Bishop Auckland, 12 September 1982
Height: 6'2" **Weight:** 13.6
This promising young Middlesbrough central defender spent most of the 2002-03 season out on loan in a bid to gain experience of first-team football. He joined Blackpool in November, making his senior debut against Notts County. Next stop was Carlisle where he was required as cover for injuries and made just one senior appearance. Phil concluded his travels with a successful spell at Bournemouth. He endured a tough time on his debut at Hull, but improved with every match, culminating with a dominating performance at the Millennium Stadium in the Third Division play-off final.
Middlesbrough (From trainee on 7/7/2000) Blackpool (Loaned on 29/11/2002) FL 2+1 FAC 1
Carlisle U (Loaned on 31/12/2002) FL 1
Bournemouth (Loaned on 27/3/2003) FL 4+2 Others 3

GUNNARSSON Brynjar Bjorn
Born: Iceland, 16 October 1975
Height: 6'1" **Weight:** 11.12

International Honours: Iceland: 37; U21-8; Yth
The 2002-03 campaign proved to be an up and down campaign for Brynjar who failed to hit the heights of earlier seasons with Stoke City. On his day he could be one of the best midfielders in the First Division, but he sometimes lacked consistency. Nevertheless, Brynjar was offered a new contract in the summer despite hints that there was disquiet at his frequent trips abroad to play for Iceland.
Stoke C (£600,000 from Orgryte IS, Sweden on 4/1/2000) FL 128+3/16 FLC 7/1 FAC 7/2 Others 12+1/1

GURNEY Andrew (Andy) Robert
Born: Bristol, 25 January 1974
Height: 5'10" **Weight:** 11.6
Absent from the Swindon Town line-up during the opening games of the 2002-03 season due to suspension, Andy's return to action coincided with an unfortunate run of defeats and his confidence suffered. However, he gradually rediscovered his form and became a vital member of the team as fortunes improved. He again weighed in with a useful contribution of nine goals, including expertly taken free kicks at Plymouth and Tranmere. Comfortable on the ball he is versatile defender who can appear at right back or in midfield if required.
Bristol Rov (From trainee on 10/7/1992) FL 100+8/9 FLC 7/1 FAC 5 Others 15
Torquay U (Free on 10/7/1997) FL 64/10 FLC 6 FAC 5/1 Others 3
Reading (£100,000 on 15/1/1999) FL 55+12/3 FLC 5 FAC 5+1 Others 5+1
Swindon T (Free on 2/7/2001) FL 84/14 FLC 3 FAC 3/1 Others 2+1

GUTTRIDGE Luke Horace
Born: Barnstaple, 27 March 1982
Height: 5'5" **Weight:** 9.7
Luke featured in several midfield positions for Cambridge last season, although he preferred a central role, which allowed him to be fully involved in the game. He continued to work hard and netted four goals during the campaign. One of these provided the 'golden goal' winner in the LDV Vans Trophy tie at Luton when he celebrated in style, removing his shirt in spite of the freezing conditions.
Torquay U (Trainee) FL 0+1
Cambridge U (Free on 15/8/2000) FL 67+6/ FLC 0+2 FAC 3+1 Others 8+3/2

Luke Guttridge

H

HACKETT Christopher (Chris) James
Born: Oxford, 1 March 1983
Height: 6'0" Weight: 11.6
The 2002-03 season was something of a disappointment for this speedy winger who made just two starts, with most of his appearances coming from the substitutes' bench. It was more a case of the Oxford team playing with wing backs that led to Chris being the odd man out, but on his day his pace can prove very decisive.
Oxford U (From trainee on 20/4/2000) FL 6+29/2 FLC 0+1 FAC 1+1 Others 1+2

HACKWORTH Anthony (Tony)
Born: Durham, 19 May 1980
Height: 6'1" Weight: 13.7
International Honours: E: Yth
Tony found his opportunities at Notts County somewhat restricted by the exploits of the likes of Mark Stallard and Paul Heffernan last term. He made ten first-team appearances throughout the campaign, but failed to find the net. Tony is a tall and very capable striker who loves to lead the line as a target man.
Leeds U (From trainee on 23/5/1997) FLC 0+1 Others 0+2
Notts Co (£150,000 on 16/7/2001) FL 13+29/1 FLC 0+2 FAC 2+1 Others 3/1

HADDRELL Matthew (Matt) Charles
Born: Stoke, 19 March 1981
Height: 6'1" Weight: 14.0
Matt signed for Macclesfield from Unibond League side Vauxhall Motors after making a great impression during their amazing FA Cup run last season. A versatile player who usually operates in defence but can also feature in the midfield or up front, Matt made four appearances as a defender, his debut coming at the end of March when he came off the bench against Kidderminster. Matt will be looking to establish himself in the senior side during the 2003-04 campaign.
Macclesfield T (£35,000 from Vauxhall Motors, ex Kidsgrove, Newcastle T, on 21/3/2003) FL 2+2

HADJI Moustapha
Born: Ifrane, Morocco, 16 November 1971
Height: 6'0" Weight: 11.10
International Honours: Morocco
Moustapha had a rather frustrating season at Aston Villa last term when he struggled to win a regular place in the line-up. After being drafted in for the Worthington Cup tie against Liverpool in December, he made quite an impression during his first Premiership start of the season by producing a lively display. He then turned in three excellent performances before coming off early on against Middlesbrough with a hamstring injury. Moustapha is a creative midfielder who can turn a game with a flick of the ball or an ingenious pass. He can play down either flank or up front, but prefers a role just behind the two strikers. He returned to international action with Morocco during the campaign and featured in the friendly match against Mali.
Coventry C (£4,000,000 from Deportivo La Coruna, Spain, ex Nancy, Sporting Lisbon, on 3/8/1999) PL 61+1/12 FLC 4+1 FAC 3/1
Aston Villa (£4,500,000 on 6/7/2001) PL 24+10/2 FLC 3 FAC 0+1 Others 4+5/1

HADLAND Phillip (Phil) Jonathan
Born: Warrington, 20 October 1980
Height: 5'11" Weight: 11.8
This tricky and pacy wide player came to Darlington on trial in the early part of last season and featured mainly out on the left flank. However, he managed only five starts in the first team and two substitute appearances before being allowed to leave. Phil subsequently linked up with Chester City, before signing for Leek Town in March.
Reading (From trainee on 22/6/1999) FLC 1
Rochdale (Free on 8/8/2000) FL 12+20/2 FLC 0+1 FAC 1 Others 1
Leyton Orient (Free on 9/7/2001) FL 0+5/1 FLC 0+1
Carlisle U (Loaned on 19/11/2001) FL 4/1 FAC 1
Brighton & Hove A (Free on 19/3/2002) FL 0+2
Darlington (Free on 16/8/2002) FL 4+2 FLC 1

HAHNEMANN Marcus Stephen
Born: Seattle, USA, 15 June 1972
Height: 6'3" Weight: 16.2
International Honours: USA: 3
Following a successful loan spell the previous season, Marcus signed for Reading in August 2002. After just two games on the bench he replaced Phil Whitehead between the sticks, and then made 46 consecutive appearances during the remainder of the campaign. A tall, powerfully built 'keeper, his agility and bravery has made him a crowd favourite, and their chants of 'USA' whenever he has to face a penalty kick, or has made a great save, show their empathy with the American international. He kept seven consecutive clean sheets at one stage, but he also likes to venture upfield, and recorded Reading's only shot on target in the Boxing Day defeat at Coventry City.
Fulham (£80,000 from Colorado Rapids, USA on 9/7/1999) FL 2 FLC 2
Rochdale (Loaned on 12/10/2001) FL 5 Others 2
Reading (Loaned on 14/12/2001) FL 6
Reading (Free on 14/8/2002) FL 41 FLC 1 FAC 2 Others 2

HAINING William (Will) Wallace
Born: Glasgow, 2 October 1982
Height: 5'11" Weight: 10.10
This young central defender was unexpectedly thrust into first-team action for Oldham Athletic after Clint Hill broke his leg last December. Will's progress was sensational as he helped keep the Latics' defensive record amongst the meanest in the Second Division. A great header of the ball and reader of the game, Will displayed composure and confidence beyond his years in the centre of a back three. The Glasgow-born defender also scored the first senior goal of his career in the FA Cup defeat by Cheltenham Town.
Oldham Ath (From trainee on 17/10/2001) FL 26+4/2 FLC 0+1 FAC 0+1/1 Others 3

HALFORD Gregory (Greg)
Born: Chelmsford, 8 December 1984
Height: 6'4" Weight: 13.10
Greg played for Colchester United juniors in an FA Youth Cup tie at Arsenal last December and looked the part in central midfield. He was a regular for the youth and reserve teams, before being handed a surprise league debut against Luton in April. The U's lost this match 5-0, but Greg belied his tender years with a 'Man of the Match' performance at right back. The talented youngster caused a stir with his long throws into the six-yard box.
Colchester U (Trainee) FL 1

HALL Daniel (Danny) Andrew
Born: Ashton under Lyne, 14 November 1983
Height: 6'2" Weight: 12.7
Youngster Danny received his initial tastes of first-team action for Oldham Athletic during the 2002-03 campaign. The central defender, who can also play in midfield, received his first call up for the

squad that travelled to Luton Town in March, having recently returned from a loan spell at Conference outfit Scarborough where he made one start. After impressing in Latics' reserve side, Danny made two appearances as a late substitute in the games at Northampton and at home to Barnsley.
Oldham Ath (Trainee) FL 0+2

HALL Fitz
Born: Leytonstone, 20 December 1980
Height: 6'1" **Weight:** 13.4
Oldham unearthed a bargain in signing Fitz from Ryman League club Chesham United in March 2002. The former West Ham youth player attracted Premiership scouts aplenty with his stylish displays at centre half. A skilful defender with a silky touch and an eye for a pass, Fitz also poses an attacking threat at set pieces. Seemingly destined to play at a higher level, Fitz was selected by his fellow professionals for the PFA Second Division team of the season.
Oldham Ath (£20,000 + from Chesham U, ex Staines T, on 15/3/2002) FL 44/5 FLC 4 FAC 3/1 Others 2+1

HALL Marcus Thomas
Born: Coventry, 24 March 1976
Height: 6'1" **Weight:** 12.2
International Honours: E: B-1; U21-8
This experienced left back joined Nottingham Forest on weekly contracts in the summer of 2002, but, after suffering an injury only days after the opening game of the season against Portsmouth, he was offered a permanent move to former manager Gordon Strachan's new club Southampton. Marcus understudied Wayne Bridge at St Mary's, but was unable to break into the first team and was released in December to join Stoke City. He proved to be an excellent short-term signing for new manager Tony Pulis who needed a replacement as Clive Clarke faced a long injury lay-off. Marcus soon established himself and his swashbuckling runs up the left flank benefited the team. His performances were rewarded with an offer of contract at the end of the season.
Coventry C (From trainee on 1/7/1994) P/FL 113+19/2 FLC 14+1/2 FAC 8+2
Nottingham F (Free on 7/8/2002) FL 1
Southampton (Free on 30/8/2002)
Stoke C (Free on 6/12/2002) FL 23+1 FAC 3

HALL Paul Anthony
Born: Manchester, 3 July 1972
Height: 5'9" **Weight:** 11.0
Club Honours: Div 3 '03

International Honours: Jamaica: 41
This flying front man was deservedly named in the PFA's Division Three team of the season after showing prolific form for Rushden & Diamonds from a wide position. A total of 16 league goals represented Paul's best-ever, and that tally included the title-winning strike against Hartlepool United on the final day of the season. Despite club commitments he continued to represent Jamaica at international level, winning a further five caps during the campaign.
Torquay U (From trainee on 9/7/1990) FL 77+16/1 FLC 7 FAC 4+1/2 Others 5+1/1
Portsmouth (£70,000 on 25/3/1993) FL 148+40/37 FLC 10+3/1 FAC 7+1/2 Others 6+2/2
Coventry C (£300,000 on 10/8/1998) PL 2+8 FLC 2+1/1
Bury (Loaned on 18/2/1999) FL 7
Sheffield U (Loaned on 17/12/1999) FL 1+3/1
West Bromwich A (Loaned on 10/2/2000) FL 4
Walsall (Free on 17/3/2000) FL 46+6/10 FLC 4+1 FAC 3/1 Others 3
Rushden & Diamonds (Free on 11/10/2001) FL 78+1/24 FLC 2 FAC 4+1 Others 4+1/3

HAMANN Dietmar
Born: Waldsasson, Germany, 27 August 1973
Height: 6'3" **Weight:** 12.2
Club Honours: FLC '01; FAC '01; UEFAC '01; ESC '01; CS '01
International Honours: Germany: 49; U21; Yth
'Didi' returned from the 2002 World Cup finals as one of the heroes of Germany's unexpected success. As the 'holding' midfield player in Liverpool's midfield quartet, playing just in front of the back four, Didi's contribution to the team is often understated and unappreciated, except perhaps when he is absent. He was an automatic choice for most of the season except for six weeks in December and January when he was sidelined with a hamstring injury. An infrequent scorer, although he possesses possibly the most powerful shot of any player at Anfield, he netted two goals and almost inevitably one was against his former club Newcastle in September. Several other goal-bound shots were thwarted by outstanding saves by opposing 'keepers.
Newcastle U (£4,500,000 from Bayern Munich, Germany, ex Wacker Munchen, on 5/8/1998) PL 22+1/4 FLC 1 FAC 7/1
Liverpool (£8,000,000 on 23/7/1999) PL 113+6/6 FLC 4+3 FAC 10/1 Others 35+2

HAMILTON Derrick (Des) Vivian
Born: Bradford, 15 August 1976
Height: 5'11" **Weight:** 13.0
International Honours: E: U21-1
This powerful midfield player spent another frustrating season trying to break into the Cardiff City first team. Again hampered by injuries at the wrong times, Des finished the campaign still unable to produce his best on a regular basis. He made 12 first-team appearances, but only managed two starts in Second Division games.
Bradford C (From trainee on 1/6/1994) FL 67+21/5 FLC 6/1 FAC 6 Others 4+1/2
Newcastle U (£1,500,000 + on 27/3/1997) PL 7+5 FLC 1+1/1 FAC 1 Others 2+1
Sheffield U (Loaned on 16/10/1998) FL 6
Huddersfield T (Loaned on 15/2/1999) FL 10/1
Norwich C (Loaned on 22/3/2000) FL 7
Tranmere Rov (Loaned on 25/10/2000) FL FLC 1
Tranmere Rov (Loaned on 10/1/2001) FL 3+1 FAC 3
Cardiff C (Free on 3/7/2001) FL 16+9 FLC 0+1 FAC 4+1/1 Others 4

HAMMOND Dean John
Born: Hastings, 7 March 1983
Height: 6'0" **Weight:** 12.4
A promising young midfielder, Dean made his league debut for Brighton against Gillingham last September as a substitute and was included in the starting line-up at Watford three weeks later. He also started the Worthington Cup tie at Ipswich, scoring his first senior goal when he drifted in at the far post to knock home a free kick. Although Dean looked a cool, skilful performer when given the chance, experience was preferred for the fight against relegation and he did not figure again, but more opportunities will surely come his way in Division Two.
Brighton & Hove A (From trainee on 10/6/2002) FL 1+3 FLC 1/1 Others 0+1

HAMMOND Elvis Zark
Born: Accra, Ghana, 6 October 1980
Height: 5'10" **Weight:** 10.10
Elvis was one of the success stories at Fulham last season. Top scorer in the reserves he went on to make his Premiership debut as a substitute at West Ham on Boxing Day. Towards the end of the season Elvis was given a more regular place in the starting line-up but was unfortunate to find himself playing alone up front. A player who is quick on the ball and not afraid to have a shot on goal he looks to have a great future ahead of him.

Fulham *(From trainee on 1/7/1999) PL 3+7 FLC 0+1*
Bristol Rov *(Loaned on 31/8/2001) FL 3+4 FLC 0+1*

HAMSHAW Matthew (Matt) Thomas
Born: Rotherham, 1 January 1982
Height: 5'9" **Weight:** 11.9
International Honours: E: Yth; Sch
Matt started the 2002-03 season on the substitutes' bench for Sheffield Wednesday, but eventually worked his way into the starting line-up towards the end of the year. Unfortunately almost as soon as he had managed to get into the side he suffered cruciate ligament damage whilst playing against Nottingham Forest in December and this brought his campaign to a premature end. When fully fit Matt is a pacy, direct right winger and he will be looking to establish himself for the Owls in 2003-04.
Sheffield Wed *(From trainee on 5/1/1999) FL 26+28/1 FLC 6+3/2 FAC 2/2*

HAND Jamie
Born: Uxbridge, 7 February 1984
Height: 5'11" **Weight:** 11.10
International Honours: E: Yth
This strong and combative midfielder made good progress at Watford last season to confirm his high promise and he was deservedly voted the club's 'Young Player of the Year'. A very fit and competitive player who is always looking for the ball and eager to be involved, Jamie came on as a substitute in the FA Cup ties against Burnley and Southampton. He was also a member of the England U19 squad during the season.
Watford *(From trainee on 17/4/2002) FL 24+9 FLC 1 FAC 0+2*

HANDYSIDE Peter David
Born: Dumfries, 31 July 1974
Height: 6'1" **Weight:** 13.8
Club Honours: AMC '98
International Honours: S: U21-7
Peter's two seasons as captain of Stoke City have been without doubt packed with incident. In 2001-02 he led the club to promotion after a play-off, then a last-day-of-the-season win saw the Potters retain First Division status last term. A cultured defender his form waned mid-season but he was once again a stalwart in a defence that was back to its very best for the run-in.
Grimsby T *(From trainee on 21/11/1992) FL 181+9/4 FLC 18+1 FAC 12+1 Others 13+1*
Stoke C *(Free on 10/7/2001) FL 78 FLC 2 FAC 5/1 Others 3*

HANKEY Dean Anthony
Born: Sutton in Ashfield, 23 August 1986
Height: 5'8" **Weight:** 10.10
Dean became the 40th player used by Mansfield Town during the 2002-03 season when he was given a run out from the bench in the final league game of the campaign. This young forward will no doubt benefit from his early baptism into first-team football.
Mansfield T *(Trainee) FL 0+1*

HANKIN Sean Anthony
Born: Camberley, 28 February 1981
Height: 5'11" **Weight:** 12.4
After enjoying his first season as the left-sided centre back in a back five, Torquay's switch to a 4-4-2 formation for the 2002-03 season meant that Sean had to adapt to life as an orthodox left back. After early struggles, he had just come to terms with the new role when his campaign was unfortunately ended early through a knee injury.
Crystal Palace *(From trainee on 29/6/1999) FL 0+1*
Torquay U *(£20,000 on 15/10/2001) FL 44+2/1 FLC 1 FAC 2 Others 1*

HARDIKER John David
Born: Preston, 17 February 1982
Height: 6'0" **Weight:** 11.4
The 2002-03 campaign was a difficult one for the man who achieved folk status in Stockport the previous season for his late brace against Manchester City. Injuries didn't help the young defender who found himself in and out of the side. An

Matt Hamshaw

185

injury against Swindon in January kept him out for two months before he returned to the team in the 1-1 draw with champions-elect Wigan Athletic in March.
Stockport Co *(£150,000 from Morecambe on 28/1/2002) FL 30+5/3 FLC 2 FAC 1 Others 2*

HARDING Daniel (Dan) Andrew
Born: Gloucester, 23 December 1983
Height: 6'0" **Weight:** 11.11

Lee Hardy

This young left back made his league debut for Brighton as a substitute against Norwich City at the Withdean Stadium last August but had little opportunity to impress. His senior experience lasted just 11 minutes in a 2-0 defeat and the third-year scholar was confined to the reserves and the U19 side for the remainder of the season. However, he was rewarded with a two-year professional contract in April and will surely have more chances to make a name for himself in the future.
Brighton & Hove A *(Trainee) FL 0+1*

HARDY Lee
Born: Blackpool, 26 November 1981
Height: 6'1" **Weight:** 12.6
Signed from Oldham Athletic on a one-year contract during the 2002 close season, Lee was unable to force his way into the Macclesfield side on a regular basis last term. Usually playing on the left side of the midfield his appearances were split equally between the starting line-up and the substitutes' bench. He provided pace and made some telling crosses into the box, but nevertheless was released in the summer.
Blackburn Rov *(From trainee on 3/7/2000)*
Oldham Ath *(Free on 19/7/2001) FL 0+1*
Macclesfield T *(Free on 4/7/2002) FL 8+8 FLC 1 FAC 2 Others 0+1*

HAREWOOD Marlon Anderson
Born: Hampstead, 25 August 1979
Height: 6'1" **Weight:** 11.0
Nottingham Forest manager Paul Hart's faith was rewarded in 2002-03 when Marlon became a key member of the side. He formed a lethal partnership with David Johnson that was the First Division's most potent, while his personal tally of 21 goals included a hat-trick against Gillingham and four against Stoke City. Marlon is a big and strong striker with pace to burn and a good eye for goal.
Nottingham F *(From trainee on 9/9/1996) P/FL 105+58/39 FLC 9+4/3 FAC 3+2/1 Others 2*
Ipswich T *(Loaned on 28/1/1999) FL 5+1/1*

HARGREAVES Christian (Chris)
Born: Cleethorpes, 12 May 1972
Height: 5'11" **Weight:** 12.2
Midfield player Chris was used in a variety of roles in the middle of the park last season as the different Northampton Town bosses attempted to cover for injuries and find a winning combination. He missed almost two months with a leg injury himself and by the time he returned to action the Cobblers were struggling with both form and further injuries.
Grimsby T *(From trainee on 6/12/1989) FL 15+36/5 FLC 2+2/1 FAC 1+2/2 Others 2+4*
Scarborough *(Loaned on 4/3/1993) FL 2+1*
Hull C *(Signed on 26/7/1993) FL 34+15 FLC 1 FAC 2+1/1 Others 3+1*
West Bromwich A *(Free on 13/7/1995) FL 0+1 Others 0+1*
Hereford U *(Free on 19/2/1996) FL 57+4/6 FLC 3+1 FAC 1 Others 2*
Plymouth Arg *(Free on 20/7/1998) FL 74+2/5 FLC 4 FAC 11/2 Others 1*
Northampton T *(Free on 7/7/2000) FL 103+6/3 FLC 4 FAC 6/1 Others 4/1*

HARLEY Jonathan (Jon)
Born: Maidstone, 26 September 1979
Height: 5'9" **Weight:** 10.3
Club Honours: FAC '00
International Honours: E: U21-3; Yth
Jon hardly got a look in at Fulham before
the turn of the year and in October he
went out on loan to Sheffield United as
cover for the injured Rob Ullathorne. He
soon settled in at left wing back,
producing some classy performances. He
tackled and defended well, showing very
good anticipation and being prominent in
attack. On his return to Loftus Road he got
back in the side whilst Rufus Brevett served
a suspension and shortly afterwards found
himself first choice after Brevett departed
to West Ham. Jon scored a bizarre winning
goal from 40 yards out against Aston Villa.
*Chelsea (From trainee on 20/3/1997) PL
22+8/2 FLC 0+1 FAC 7 Others 1+3*
Wimbledon (Loaned on 20/10/2000) FL 6/2
*Fulham (£3,500,000 on 8/8/2001) PL 16+5/1
FLC 2 FAC 4+1 Others 4*
*Sheffield U (Loaned on 30/10/2002) FL
8+1/1 FLC 2*

HARPER James Alan John
Born: Chelmsford, 9 November 1980
Height: 5'10" **Weight:** 11.7
A clear winner of the Reading fans'
'Player of the Season' poll, James had an
outstanding campaign in which he
established himself as a first-team regular
and at last fulfilled his potential as a
creative and industrious midfield player.
Although he only netted twice himself, his
vision and range of passing set up
countless opportunities for his colleagues,
and his consistent form attracted the
attention of Premiership clubs. However,
he has pledged his future to Reading
following his battle to win over the fans,
and looks to be an important playmaker in
the Royals line-up for many years to come.
Arsenal (From trainee on 8/7/1999)
Cardiff C (Loaned on 29/12/2000) FL 3
*Reading (£400,000 on 28/2/2001) FL
62+12/4 FLC 3 FAC 3 Others 4+2*

HARPER Kevin Patrick
Born: Oldham, 15 January 1976
Height: 5'6" **Weight:** 10.10
Club Honours: Div 1 '03
International Honours: S: B-1; U21-7;
Sch
This lively and perceptive wing back
showed a tremendous improvement for
Portsmouth last season. Kevin featured
regularly in the squad, although often
used from the substitutes' bench, and
scored four goals including a fine solo
effort at Walsall. He was solid at the back
and troubled opposition defenders with
his penetrating runs down the flank.
*Hibernian (Signed from Hutchison Vale BC
on 3/8/1992) SL 73+23/15 SLC 4+5 SC 9+1/3*
*Derby Co (£300,000 + on 11/9/1998) PL
6+26/1 FLC 1+5 FAC 0+3/1*
Walsall (Loaned on 17/12/1999) FL 8+1/1
*Portsmouth (£300,000 on 6/3/2000) FL
85+27/9 FLC 1+2 FAC 3*

HARPER Lee Charles Phillip
Born: Chelsea, 30 October 1971
Height: 6'1" **Weight:** 13.11
Goalkeeper Lee must have known that
Keith Welch was going to be a hard act
to follow at Northampton. However, he
soon won over the Cobblers' fans with
some fine performances, none more so
than against Barnsley when he firstly
saved a penalty and then made several
point-blank saves that kept the points
intact for his side. Lee was another player
to lose a large chunk of the season
through injury, but returned in time to
help the club's relegation fight.
*Arsenal (£150,000 from Sittingbourne on
16/6/1994) PL 1*

Chris Hargreaves

187

Queens Park R *(£125,000 + on 11/7/1997)*
FL 117+1 FLC 8+1 FAC 4
Walsall *(Free on 20/7/2001) FL 3 FLC 2*
Northampton T *(Free on 18/7/2002) FL 31*
FAC 2 Others 0+1

HARPER Stephen (Steve)
Alan
Born: Easington, 14 March 1975
Height: 6'2" **Weight:** 13.0
Newcastle's reserve goalkeeper
demonstrated his value to the squad
when he signed a new long-term deal in
August 2002. Kept on the bench by first
choice Shay Given's fine form, his
patience and excellent attitude were
rewarded by selection for the home
Champions' League tie with Juventus at
end of October, when he delivered a fine
performance resulting in a clean sheet. He
also featured against Dynamo Kiev a
week later and in the Worthington Cup
tie against Everton, which proved to be
his last first-team appearance of the
season. Locally born, Steve is the longest-
serving player on the club's books and is a
qualified referee.
Newcastle U *(Free from Seaham Red Star on*
5/7/1993) PL 29+2 FLC 8 FAC 7+1 Others 7
Bradford C *(Loaned on 18/9/1995) FL 1*
Hartlepool U *(Loaned on 29/8/1997) FL 15*
Huddersfield T *(Loaned on 18/12/1997) FL*
24 FAC 2

HARRAD Shaun
Born: Nottingham, 11 December 1984
Height: 5'10" **Weight:** 12.4
Shaun is a promising striker with the
Notts County academy set-up and was a
member of the Magpies' youth team that
defeated Swindon to win the Midland
Youth Cup last season. He was rewarded
for some fine performances in the club's
reserves by being called up to the senior
squad, making his debut from the bench
against Tranmere in December and adding
four more appearances as a substitute.
Shaun was selected as County's 'Reserve
Player of the Year'.
Notts Co *(Trainee) FL 0+5*

HARRIES Paul Graham
Born: Sydney, Australia, 19 November
1977
Height: 6'0" **Weight:** 13.7
After spending the closing stages of the
2001-02 campaign with Dr Martens
League outfit Merthyr Tydfil, Paul had an
unsuccessful trial with Partick Thistle last
August. He subsequently signed for Exeter
City the following month, but managed
just one appearance from the substitutes'
bench for the troubled Devon club. He

later had further trials with a number of
clubs without winning the long-term deal
he sought.
Portsmouth *(Signed from NSW Soccer*
Academy, Australia on 8/9/1997) FL 0+1
Crystal Palace *(Free on 7/9/1998)*
Torquay U *(Loaned on 26/2/1999) FL 5*
Carlisle U *(Free on 30/7/1999) FL 6+14/2*
FAC 1/1 Others 0+1 (Free to Wollongong,
Australia on 26/10/2000)
Macclesfield T *(Free on 6/12/2001. Freed*
during 2002 close season)
Exeter C *(Free, via trial at Partick Thistle, on*
10/9/2002) FL 0+1 FLC 0+1

HARRIS Andrew (Andy) David
Douglas
Born: Springs, South Africa, 26 February
1977
Height: 5'10" **Weight:** 11.11
A hard-working central midfielder who
covers every blade of grass on the pitch,
Andy is an expert at breaking up
opposition attacks with his tough
tackling. A near ever-present for Leyton
Orient last term, he also occasionally
appeared at right back. Andy was out of
contract in the summer and after being
released by the O's he was reported to
have signed for Conference outfit Chester
City.
Liverpool *(From trainee on 23/3/1994)*
Southend U *(Free on 10/7/1996) FL 70+2*
FLC 5 FAC 3
Leyton Orient *(Free on 5/7/1999) FL*
143+6/2 FLC 11 FAC 9 Others 3+2

HARRIS Neil
Born: Orsett, 12 July 1977
Height: 5'11" **Weight:** 12.9
Club Honours: Div 2 '01
Neil was back to his best for Millwall last
season following his recent problems with
illness. He featured regularly in the Lions'
starting line-up and finished the season as
the side's leading scorer in First Division
games with a total of 12 goals, thus
bringing him within reach of Teddy
Sheringham's all-time club record tally of
93. Neil is an out-and-out striker with fine
close control and an excellent shot with
either foot.
Millwall *(£30,000 from Cambridge C on*
26/3/1998) FL 155+28/83 FLC 4+1 FAC 6+2/1
Others 11+1/3

HARRIS Richard Lewis Scott
Born: Croydon, 23 October 1980
Height: 5'11" **Weight:** 10.9
Richard had hoped to be pushing hard for
a striker's spot at Wycombe last season.
He did his cause a power of good when
coming off the bench at Oldham in

August and scoring after a smart turn and
dribble. However, he did not start a game
until Luton in January and then scored
two brilliantly taken goals the following
Saturday at home to Notts County. He
suffered a hamstring injury after the
second goal went in, keeping him out for
nine weeks, and he ended the season
with the impressive record of six goals in
six starts. Richard has pace and good
body strength, which he uses to hold off
and turn opponents, and an incredibly
long throw which effectively turns throw-
ins in the final third into corners.
Crystal Palace *(From trainee on 22/12/1997)*
FL 2+7 FLC 2+2
Mansfield T *(Loaned on 28/9/2001) FL 0+6*
Wycombe W *(Free on 26/3/2002) FL 7+18/5*
FLC 0+2/1 FAC 1 Others 2

HARRISON Daniel (Danny)
Robert
Born: Liverpool, 4 November 1982
Height: 5'11" **Weight:** 12.5
Another impressive product of Tranmere's
youth policy, Danny has become a reliable
midfielder with a maturity and calmness
far beyond his years. He positively loves to
go forward, and scored his first senior
goal in spectacular fashion in the 5-0
defeat of Hartlepool in the LDV Vans
Trophy. Danny's astute understanding of
the game coupled with his ability to
remain unmoved in the face of
provocation should help him to establish
himself as a regular for Rovers in 2003-
04.
Tranmere Rov *(From trainee on 16/5/2002)*
FL 8+5 FLC 1 FAC 0+1 Others 2+1/1

HARRISON Lee David
Born: Billericay, 12 September 1971
Height: 6'2" **Weight:** 12.7
Lee began the 2002-03 campaign in the
Conference with Barnet, but in the
autumn he joined Peterborough United
on loan as a replacement for the injured
Mark Tyler. He quickly became a crowd
favourite, producing some fine
performances in goal for the Posh before
returning to London. He subsequently
signed for Leyton Orient shortly before
the transfer deadline where he proved to
be an excellent shot stopper with a good
command of his area. Lee's career has
now gone a complete circle, for he
started out on schoolboy forms with the
O's
Charlton Ath *(From trainee on 3/7/1990)*
Fulham *(Loaned on 18/11/1991) Others 1*
Gillingham *(Loaned on 24/3/1992) FL 2*
Fulham *(Free on 18/12/1992) FL 11+1 FAC 1*
Others 6

arnet *(Free on 15/7/1996) FL 183 FLC 9 FAC Others 12*
eterborough U (Loaned on 12/12/2002) L 12
eyton Orient (Signed on 14/3/2003) FL 6

1ARSLEY Paul
orn: Scunthorpe, 29 May 1978
leight: 5'9" **Weight:** 11.5
his aggressive, tenacious attacking
nidfield player was one of the season's
ew shining lights at Northampton in
002-03. A 100 per cent player with a
never say die' attitude, he also showed

that he was not afraid to have a shot
from outside the area. Paul featured in all
but one of the Cobblers' Second Division
matches and walked away with the club's
'Player of the Year' award at the end of
the campaign.
Grimsby T (From trainee on 16/7/1996)
Scunthorpe U (Free on 7/7/1997) FL
110+18/5 FLC 6 FAC 4+2/1 Others 5+1
Halifax T (Free on 1/7/2001) FL 45/11 FLC 1
FAC 3/1 Others 1
Northampton T (Free on 8/7/2002) FL
41+4/2 FLC 1 FAC 3/1 Others 1+1

HART Gary John
Born: Harlow, 21 September 1976
Height: 5'9" **Weight:** 12.8
Club Honours: Div 3 '01; Div 2 '02
Gary finished the 2001-02 campaign on
the sidelines with a broken leg, but
proved that he was up to the mark when
he came back into the Brighton line-up in
the new year and performed admirably.
An ever-popular right winger or forward,
Gary runs for 90 minutes and never gives
less than 100 per cent. Always willing to
take on defenders, he also tackles back
well and does not shy away from the
physical side of the game. However, he
may well be disappointed with a return of
just four goals from the season.
Brighton & Hove A (£1,000 from Stansted
on 18/6/1998) FL 188+19/36 FLC 6+3 FAC 7
Others 4+1/1

HARTE Ian Patrick
Born: Drogheda, 31 August 1977
Height: 5'10" **Weight:** 11.8
International Honours: RoI: 49; U21-3
After playing a major role for the Republic
of Ireland in the World Cup finals over the
summer, Ian began the new season as a
regular at left back for Leeds. However,
his form seemed to dip as the season
progressed and early in the new year he
found himself replaced by new signing
Raul Bravo. However he was soon back in
the side and went on to contribute three
valuable goals in the closing stages of the
campaign as United narrowly avoided
relegation.
Leeds U (From trainee on 15/12/1995) PL
178+12/27 FLC 8+2/1 FAC 15+2/3 Others
45/6

HASLAM Steven Robert
Born: Sheffield, 6 September 1979
Height: 5'11" **Weight:** 10.10
International Honours: E: Yth; Sch
Steven was looking to establish himself as
a central defender in the Sheffield
Wednesday line-up last term, but a series
of injuries hampered his progress. He
played in the full-back position on a few
occasions in the middle of the season but
it was always going to be difficult to
make an impression in a struggling side.
Steven is a solid performer who prefers to
play the simple ball rather than try the
unexpected.
Sheffield Wed (From trainee on 12/9/1996)
P/FL 99+20/2 FLC 10+1 FAC 7

HASSELBAINK Jerrel (Jimmy Floyd)
Born: Surinam, 27 March 1972
Height: 6'2" **Weight:** 13.4

Neil Harris

Club Honours: CS '00
International Honours: Holland: 23
Chelsea's prolific centre forward had a
low-key beginning to the season, a
combination of his post-operative
recovery from a calf injury and summer
transfer speculation linking him to
Barcelona clearly affected his form,
leading to the unthinkable ... exclusion
from the Blues' line-up. Following his one-
match sabbatical on the bench against
Arsenal, normal service was resumed in
October with a steady stream of goals.
Although a final total of 11 Premiership

goals fell below the high standards that
he sets himself, his tally included some
vital strikes, possibly the most important
being the looping header, which helped
to defeat Everton on Easter Monday. This
took his haul against the Toffees to eight
goals in seven matches.
*Leeds U (£2,000,000 from Boavista,
Portugal, ex Campomaiorense, on 18/7/1997)
PL 66+3/34 FLC 5/2 FAC 9/5 Others 4/1
(£12,000,000 to Atletico Madrid, Spain on
20/8/1999)*
*Chelsea (£15,000,000 on 12/7/2000) PL
97+9/57 FLC 7/5 FAC 13/6 Others 7/2*

Gary Hart

HASSELL Robert (Bobby)
John Francis
Born: Derby, 4 June 1980
Height: 5'9" **Weight:** 12.6
After an excellent 2001-02 campaign for
Mansfield, Bobby picked up a niggling
injury during the pre-season period and
missed the opening matches of 2002-03.
His solid defensive work and support
down the right-hand flank were missed
during his absence. Bobby was back in
action in September, but broke down
again, and from then on he was in and
out of the side. The disruption caused by
injuries meant that the promising right
back was never really able to capture his
best form.
*Mansfield T (From trainee on 3/7/1998) FL
118+8/3 FLC 5+1 FAC 5 Others 1*

HATCHER Daniel (Danny) Ian
Born: Newport, IoW, 24 December 1983
Height: 5'10" **Weight:** 11.8
Danny struggled to make a breakthrough
for Leyton Orient last term, and only
made a handful of first-team appearances
although he was a regular in the reserves
and youth teams. Eventually the pacy
striker's contract was cancelled by mutual
consent and he returned home to join
Newport (IOW).
*Leyton Orient (Trainee) FL 3+13 FAC 1+2
Others 1+2*

HAWKINS Peter Steven
Born: Maidstone, 19 September 1978
Height: 6'0" **Weight:** 11.6
Peter started 42 of Wimbledon's 46
league matches last term, and performed
to a consistent level throughout the
season. Featuring mainly at left back, he
probably had his best 45 minutes of the
campaign when switched to the centre of
defence for the second half of the Dons'
memorable win at Crystal Palace. That
was his main position when coming up
through the club's academy ranks, and
may yet prove to be his best as a senior
player. For the time being, he will
probably continue to be a versatile
member of the defence, being comfortable
with either foot and no slouch when
competing aerially for the ball.
*Wimbledon (From trainee on 6/3/1997) FL
97+5 FLC 5 FAC 9*
York C (Loaned on 22/2/2000) FL 14

HAWORTH Simon Owen
Born: Cardiff, 30 March 1977
Height: 6'2" **Weight:** 13.8
Club Honours: AMC '99
International Honours: W: 5; B-1; U21-
12; Yth

mon was in exceptional form for
anmere Rovers throughout the 2002-03
ampaign. He finished the season as the
ub's leading scorer with a total of 22
oals in all competitions, the first player
o reach the 20-goal mark in one season
or Rovers since John Aldridge. He was
alled up to the Welsh international
quad in the close season, but was unable
o join them as he was still on his
oneymoon. It was no surprise that the
ub's supporters voted him as their
Player of the Year'.
ardiff C (From trainee on 7/8/1995) FL
7+10/9 FLC 4 FAC 0+1 Others 4/1
oventry C (£500,000 on 4/6/1997) PL 5+6
.C 2/1 FAC 0+1
Vigan Ath (£600,000 on 2/10/1998) FL
9+18/44 FLC 8/6 FAC 4/4 Others 12+1/4
ranmere Rov (£125,000 on 28/2/2002) FL
4/25 FLC 1/1 FAC 2/1 Others 2

AY Alexander (Alex) Neil
orn: Birkenhead, 14 October 1981
eight: 5'10" **Weight:** 11.5
rought up through the ranks at
ranmere, this enthusiastic striker scored
is first senior goal for Rovers in the away
ame against Mansfield last season. A
fe-long supporter of the club, Alex
emonstrated his versatility by playing on
oth wings as well as up front and never
ave less than 100 per cent in any of his
tarts. He was a mainstay of the reserve
eam again, but must surely make the
reakthrough to become a first-team
egular in 2003-04.
ranmere Rov (From trainee on 24/3/2000)
. 13+9/3 FLC 2 FAC 0+2 Others 1

AY Daniel (Danny) John
orn: Auckland, New Zealand, 15 May
975
eight: 6'4" **Weight:** 14.11
nternational Honours: New Zealand
fter over a season's absence this tall
efender returned to action with Walsall
the summer of 2002. Danny then
eadily eased his way back to full fitness
fter being rushed into action after Matt
arbon's injury in the opening away game
gainst Wolves. Solid defensive
erformances were punctuated by the
dd mistake and each time Danny
eemed to be embarking on a successful
un something happened, such as the
nkle ligament injury in the last minute of
he vital win at Gillingham in April.
owever, he recovered in time to take his
lace in the New Zealand squad for the
onfederations Cup tournament during
e close season.

Leeds U (£200,000 from Perth Glory,
Australia on 25/8/1999) PL 2+2 FLC 1 Others
0+1
Walsall (Free on 5/8/2002) FL 26+3 FLC 3
FAC 3

HAYES Paul Edward
Born: Dagenham, 20 September 1983
Height: 6'0" **Weight:** 12.2
After impressing in a couple of reserve
games early last season, Scunthorpe took
over Paul's scholarship contract and the
rewards were massive. He broke into the
first team in January and bagged eight
goals in the run-in, the main reason the
Iron made the play-offs. A tall, strong,
quick player with excellent ball control, he
was rewarded with a two-year
professional contract. Paul is the younger
brother of former Arsenal and Celtic star
Martin.
Scunthorpe U (Free from trainee at Norwich
C on 22/3/2003) FL 15+3/8 Others 2

HAYLES Barrington (Barry)
Edward
Born: Lambeth, 17 May 1972
Height: 5'9" **Weight:** 13.0
Club Honours: GMVC '96; Div 2 '99; Div
1 '01
International Honours: Jamaica: 9; E:
SP-2
A competitive forward who always battles
for the cause, Barry holds the ball up well
for others and is always likely to steal in
to grasp a goal-scoring opportunity. Sadly
he did not enjoy the best of seasons in
2002-03 finding himself struggling to
score in the opening weeks of the
campaign. Things got worse when he was
diagnosed with a serious neck injury
following the Worthington Cup tie
against Bury in November. Fortunately an
operation proved successful and Barry
soon returned to training, making a
number of substitute appearances at the
end of the season. He added another cap
for Jamaica against Japan in October,
when he played against team mate
Junichi Inamoto.
Bristol Rov (£250,000 from Stevenage
Borough on 4/6/1997) FL 62/32 FLC 4/1 FAC
5/2 Others 3+2/2
Fulham (£2,100,000 on 17/11/1998) P/FL
106+43/40 FLC 10+2/5 FAC 9+4/5 Others
2+5/2

HAYTER James Edward
Born: Sandown, IoW, 9 April 1979
Height: 5'9" **Weight:** 11.2
The longest-serving Bournemouth player,
James is also one of the hardest working
and much of what he does goes

unnoticed. He can quite happily play as
an out-and-out striker, or tuck in behind
the front two. He was again leading
scorer for the Cherries, and was in great
form at the end of the campaign, netting
four goals in a run of three matches.
Bournemouth (From trainee on 7/7/1997) FL
144+43/31 FLC 2+3/1 FAC 12/3 Others 9+3/5

HAYWARD Steven (Steve) Lee
Born: Pelsall, 8 September 1971
Height: 5'11" **Weight:** 12.5
Club Honours: AMC '97; Div 2 '99
International Honours: E: Yth
Steve had a frustrating time with injuries
at Barnsley last term. After 18 months out
with a serious knee problem he produced
some impressive performances for the
reserves and returned to first-team duties
at Brentford. However, he suffered a foot
injury in that match and did not return
until the end of December. This
industrious midfield came back into the
team around the turn of the year but he
asked for, and was granted, a transfer at
the end of January. Steve did not feature
in the side again after that.
Derby Co (From juniors on 17/9/1988) FL
15+11/1 FLC 0+2 FAC 1 Others 3+4
Carlisle U (£100,000 on 13/3/1995) FL
88+2/13 FLC 6/1 FAC 4 Others 15/1
Fulham (£175,000 on 23/6/1997) FL
108+7/7 FLC 16+3/1 FAC 9+2/3 Others 3
Barnsley (£25,000 on 19/1/2001) FL 16/1

HAZELL Reuben
Born: Birmingham, 24 April 1979
Height: 5'11" **Weight:** 12.0
After establishing a reputation at Torquay
as a central defender with fine positional
sense and excellent timing, Reuben found
the Gulls newly found belief in the
passing game to be something of a mixed
blessing. Although he enjoyed the
freedom to play from the back, he needs
to guard against a tendency to become
over-casual.
Aston Villa (From trainee on 20/3/1997)
Tranmere Rov (Free on 5/8/1999) FL 38+4/1
FLC 8 FAC 3 Others 1
Torquay U (Free on 10/1/2002) FL 65/1 FLC
1 FAC 1 Others 1

HEALD Gregory (Greg) James
Born: Enfield, 26 September 1971
Height: 6'1" **Weight:** 12.8
International Honours: E: SP-1; Sch
Greg spent most of the 2002-03
campaign with Conference club Barnet
before joining Leyton Orient along with
Wayne Purser in March. Signed as an
experienced replacement for the departed
Dean Smith, he featured in the centre of

191

the defence. Greg managed to stabilise the O's back line and was made club captain towards the end of the season. Like Lee Harrison, Greg started his career on schoolboy forms at Brisbane Road.
Peterborough U *(£35,000 from Enfield on 8/7/1994) FL 101+4/6 FLC 8 FAC 8+1 Others 11/2*
Barnet *(Signed on 8/8/1997) FL 141/13 FLC 8/1 FAC 4 Others 7/1*
Leyton Orient *(£9,000 on 27/3/2003) FL 5/1*

HEALY David Jonathan
Born: Downpatrick, 5 August 1979
Height: 5'8" **Weight:** 11.0
International Honours: NI: 26; B-1; U21-8; Yth; Sch
This young Preston striker was only a regular substitute in the early part of the 2002-03 season, as he was unable to displace Ricardo Fuller and Richard Cresswell. His first start against Stoke saw him score, and following Fuller's injury he had the chance to re-establish himself as a first choice, but he looked out of form despite occasional goals. David subsequently spent time on loan at Norwich, firstly in January and then again from March until the end of the season. He seemed to rediscover some of his confidence at Carrow Road, showing awareness in his link up play and good distribution skills. He remained a regular at international level for Northern Ireland, adding a further eight caps.
Manchester U *(From trainee on 28/11/1997) PL 0+1 FLC 0+2*
Port Vale *(Loaned on 25/2/2000) FL 15+1/3*
Preston NE *(£1,500,000 on 29/12/2000) FL 66+24/24 FLC 6 FAC 4+1 Others 3/1*
Norwich C *(Loaned on 30/1/2003) FL 5/1*
Norwich C *(Loaned on 13/3/2003) FL 5+3/1*

HEARD Jamie
Born: Sheffield, 11 August 1983
Height: 5'11" **Weight:** 11.2
Jamie made his senior debut for Hull City in the LDV Vans Trophy tie at Port Vale in October. The promising right back then gained further senior experience when he came on in front of a crowd of 22,000 for the second-half of the Raich Carter Trophy game with Sunderland – the first match to be played at the Kingston Communications Stadium. However, he was released at the end of the season. Jamie is the son of former Hull player Pat Heard.
Hull C *(Trainee) Others 1*

HEARN Charles (Charley) Richard
Born: Ashford, Kent, 5 November 1983
Height: 5'11" **Weight:** 11.9

This very promising midfielder enjoyed a successful season in the Millwall youth and reserve teams last season. A hard-working player with a good engine, he has no trouble getting from box to box and for a youngster he has tremendous vision. He gained further senior experience last term and will be looking to win a regular place in the first-team squad in 2003-04. Charley was selected by the *Sun* newspaper as one of their promising young sportsmen and women for the new millennium in January 2000 and it seems as if he is beginning to fulfil some of that promise.
Millwall *(From trainee on 27/4/2001) FL 6+5 FLC 0+1 FAC 2+2*

HEARY Thomas Mark
Born: Dublin, 14 February 1978
Height: 5'10" **Weight:** 11.12
International Honours: RoI: U21-4; Yth; (UEFA-U18 '98); Sch
Thomas was overlooked by Huddersfield for large periods of the 2002-03 season. He received occasional opportunities as a result of suspension and injuries to others and when selected he performed competently. Strong in the tackle and with a no-nonsense attitude, he is difficult to beat on the ball and he added an extra dimension to the Terriers' midfield engine room.
Huddersfield T *(From trainee on 17/2/1996) FL 68+24 FLC 3+1 FAC 4 Others 9*

HEATH Matthew (Matt) Philip
Born: Leicester, 1 November 1981
Height: 6'4" **Weight:** 13.13
This promising young defender continued to earn rave reviews for Leicester City's reserves throughout the 2002-03 season and featured in both league and cup ties at the heart of the Foxes' back four, including an assured Worthington Cup outing at Hillsborough. He found himself on the score sheet at Millwall, with a header from a rehearsed set piece, and also in the home win over Walsall, whilst his close-range header at Reading effectively put the game out of the Royals' reach.
Leicester C *(From trainee on 17/2/2001) P/FL 12+4/3 FLC 2 FAC 1+2*

HEATH Nicholas (Nick) Alan
Born: Sutton Coldfield, 2 January 1985
Height: 5'9" **Weight:** 11.0
A product of the Kidderminster youth team, Nick was called upon when manager Ian Britton found himself short of players as a result of injuries and suspensions. The young midfielder was

given a taste of Football League action fo the final two minutes of the fixture at Macclesfield and let nobody down in his position wide on the right.
Kidderminster Hrs *(Free from Coventry Marconi on 27/3/2003) FL 0+1*

HEATHCOTE Jonathan
Born: Frimley, 10 November 1983
Height: 5'10" **Weight:** 11.2
Cambridge United's youth-team captain made his bow in senior football in the 5-defeat at Wrexham, and while the result was disappointing, his own performance stood out. He followed this up with a calm and composed display in the final home game of the season against Boston The left-sided defender will be looking fo more senior action in 2003-04.
Cambridge U *(From trainee on 28/4/2003) FL 2*

HEATHCOTE Michael (Mick)
Born: Kelloe, 10 September 1965
Height: 6'2" **Weight:** 12.5
After an excellent season in 2001-02, Shrewsbury Town's experienced central defender was served a devastating blow after only six games last term. A problem with his back initially caused him to miss games and eventually led to his retirement in January. Such was his influence at Gay Meadow that his absence was one of the major factors tha caused the team to struggle, for his strength and composure in the middle of the defence were sorely missed.
Sunderland *(£15,000 from Spennymoor on 19/8/1987) FL 6+3 Others 0+1*
Halifax T *(Loaned on 17/12/1987) FL 7/1 FAC 1*
York C *(Loaned on 4/11/1990) FL 3 Others 1*
Shrewsbury T *(£55,000 on 12/7/1990) FL 43+1/6 FLC 6 FAC 5 Others 4*
Cambridge U *(£150,000 on 12/9/1991) FL123+5/13 FLC 7/1 FAC 5+2/2 Others 7/2*
Plymouth Arg *(£70,000 on 27/7/1995) FL 195+4/13 FLC 9/1 FAC 18/3 Others 9*
Shrewsbury T *(Free on 8/8/2001) FL 39+1/2 FLC 1 FAC 1 Others 1*

HECKINGBOTTOM Paul
Born: Barnsley, 17 July 1977
Height: 5'11" **Weight:** 12.0
Paul joined Norwich on a 'Bosman' free transfer in the summer of 2002, but found his senior opportunities limited by the tremendous consistency of Adam Drury. He was therefore transfer listed at the end of the season to allow him to pursue his career elsewhere. He has the ability to play on the left-hand side of midfield as well as his preferred left-back

le. Paul is strong in the tackle, useful in
ie air and possesses an excellent long
irow.
underland *(From trainee at Manchester U
n 14/7/1995)*
carborough *(Loaned on 17/10/1997) FL
3+1 Others 1*
artlepool U *(Loaned on 25/9/1998) FL 5/1*
arlington *(Free on 25/3/1999) FL 111+4/5*
C 4 FAC 8/1 Others 8
orwich C *(Free on 5/7/2002) FL 7+8 FLC 0+1*

EFFERNAN Paul
orn: Dublin, Ireland, 29 December 1981
eight: 5'10" **Weight:** 10.7
nternational Honours: RoI; U21-3
his promising young Notts County striker
.ade full use of his first-team
opportunities last term. He enjoyed
xtended runs in the line-up and
esponded by registering a double-figure
ally of goals. Paul made excellent
rogress and deservedly received the
lagpies' 'Young Player of the Year'
ward at the end of the season.
otts Co *(Signed from Newtown, Co
icklow on 22/10/1999) FL 43+19/16 FLC
+2/1 FAC 1+1 Others 1+3*

EIKKINEN Markus
orn: Katrineholm, Finland, 13 October
978
eight: 6'1" **Weight:** 13.3
nternational Honours: Finland: 7; U21;
th
his competent defender was a member
f the HJK team that won the Finnish title
a 2002 and during the Scandinavian
ose season he joined Portsmouth in a
ree-month loan deal. However, he was
nable to break into the starting line-up
nd was restricted to outings from the
ubstitutes' bench against Derby and
oventry. Markus also featured for the
nland national team during his stay at
atton Park.
ortsmouth *(Loaned from HJK Helsinki,
nland, ex OPS, Turun Palloseura, MyPa, on
1/1/2003) FL 0+2*

ELGUSON Heidar
orn: Iceland, 22 August 1977
eight: 6'0" **Weight:** 12.2
nternational Honours: Iceland: 23;
21-6; Yth
fter spending most of the previous
eason warming the substitutes' bench,
eidar won a regular place in the Watford
rst team in 2002-03 and responded in
ie best possible way with 13 goals –
nough to make him the club's leading
corer. A brave and very hard-working
riker with the priceless ability to 'hang'

in the air, he was a constant threat to any
defence and starred in the Hornets'
exciting FA Cup run, scoring against both
Macclesfield and West Bromwich Albion.
He added further caps for Iceland during
the campaign and had no hesitation in
agreeing a new contract to commit
himself to Watford for the foreseeable
future.
Watford *(£1,500,000 from SK Lillestrom,
Norway, ex Throttur, on 13/1/2000) P/FL
76+37/31 FLC 2+7/2 FAC 5+2/2*

HENCHOZ Stephane
Born: Billens, Switzerland, 7 September
1974
Height: 6'1" **Weight:** 12.10
Club Honours: FLC '01, '03; FAC '01;
UEFAC '01; ESC '01; CS '01
International Honours: Switzerland: 58;
U21; Yth
Although many reasons can be given for
Liverpool's disappointing form last season,
the enforced absence of this dependable
central defender in two separate spells
was a major factor in a loss of defensive
cohesion. A calf injury in September
proved difficult to shake off and resulted
in a prolonged absence from early
October to late November. Then after
assisting the Reds to their unexpected
triumph in the Worthington Cup final
against Manchester United in March, he
suffered a recurrence of the calf problem,
surgery was required and he was sidelined
for the rest of the season. Thus he only
played in half the games Liverpool
contested in 2002-03 and none of his
replacements provided the defensive
solidity that his excellent partnership with
Sami Hyppia brings to the team.
Blackburn Rov *(£3,000,000 from Hamburg,
Germany, ex FC Bulle, Neuchatel Xamax, on
14/7/1997) PL 70 FLC 3+1 FAC 6 Others 2*
Liverpool *(£3,750,000 on 20/7/1999) PL 117
FLC 12 FAC 11 Others 34*

HENDERSON Darius Alexis
Born: Sutton, 7 September 1981
Height: 6'0" **Weight:** 12.8
Like the previous season, the majority of
Darius's appearances were as a second-
half substitute for Reading, and he is now
averaging just 25 minutes per first-team
outing. However, the powerful young
striker still contributed some important
goals, and his abrasive style of play
helped to take the weight off other
members of the team. On most occasions
he came on in the centre-forward
position, but in the play-off matches he
was used as a wide-left player to counter
the threat of an attacking full back. This

he did competently, and as he adds to his
experience he will feature more
prominently in the starting formation.
Reading *(From trainee on 15/12/1999) FL
5+65/11 FLC 2+2/2 FAC 1+2 Others 4+1/2*

HENDERSON Ian
Born: Norwich, 24 January 1985
Height: 5'8" **Weight:** 10.10
The 2002-03 season was a momentous
one for this Norfolk-born teenager. He
started the campaign as a member of the
Norwich City youth team in the second
year of his scholarship, but ended it with
his first professional contract, 22 first-
team appearances to his name and a first
senior goal at Wimbledon. A hard-
working striker, he is both brave and
quick, never letting his opponent have the
time to settle on the ball. Ian is a good
finisher and is also unselfish in front of
goal. He will be hoping that his rise to
fame continues apace in 2003-04.
Norwich C *(From trainee on 3/2/2003) FL
4+16/1 FAC 0+2*

HENDERSON Kevin Malcolm
Born: Ashington, 8 June 1974
Height: 6'3" **Weight:** 13.2
This hard-working striker received little
return for his efforts in 2002-03. Apart
from a short spell in mid-season, Kevin
was part of the Hartlepool first-team
squad throughout the promotion
campaign, yet he was rarely in the
starting line-up. As an experienced front
man he made some useful contributions
when coming on as substitute. He also set
a new club record in making 25
appearances as substitute in league
games, and now holds the overall record
for a Hartlepool player with a total of 47
appearances from the bench.
Burnley *(Signed from Morpeth T on
17/12/1997) FL 0+14/1 FLC 0+2 Others 0+4/1*
Hartlepool U *(Free on 2/7/1999) FL
81+47/29 FLC 3+2 FAC 1+1 Others 6+3/3*

HENDON Ian Michael
Born: Ilford, 5 December 1971
Height: 6'0" **Weight:** 12.10
Club Honours: FAYC '90; CS '91; Div 3 '98
International Honours: E: U21-7; Yth
This tall, versatile defender, never really
found himself a niche at Sheffield
Wednesday last season. He struggled to
make the match-day squad and in
December he moved on loan to
Conference club Barnet. Ian eventually
left Hillsborough in the new year, signing
a short-term contract for Peterborough.
He featured in a wide role for the Posh
and quickly won over the fans with his

hard tackling and fine ball distribution. However, injury restricted him to just seven starts and at the end of the season he chose to sign as player-coach for Barnet.

Tottenham H *(From trainee on 20/12/1989)* FL 0+4 FLC 1 Others 0+2
Portsmouth *(Loaned on 16/1/1992)* FL 1+3
Leyton Orient *(Loaned on 26/3/1992)* FL 5+1
Barnsley *(Loaned on 17/3/1993)* FL 6
Leyton Orient *(£50,000 on 9/8/1993)* FL 130+1/5 FLC 8 FAC 7 Others 12/1
Birmingham C *(Loaned on 23/3/1995)* FL 4

Notts Co *(£50,000 on 24/2/1997)* FL 82/6 FLC 5/1 FAC 8+1
Northampton T *(£30,000 on 25/3/1999)* FL 60/3 FLC 4 FAC 1/1 Others 1
Sheffield Wed *(£40,000 + on 12/10/2000)* FL 49/2 FLC 2 FAC 2
Peterborough U *(Free on 24/1/2003)* FL 7/1

HENDRIE Lee Andrew
Born: Birmingham, 18 May 1977
Height: 5'10" **Weight:** 10.3
International Honours: E: 1; B-1; U21-13; Yth
Lee had a point to prove at Aston Villa

last season after losing his place in the second half of the previous campaign. He was rarely absent during the campaign, while the arrival of Mark Kinsella resulted in him being able to venture forward more frequently and he revelled in his newly found freedom. Lee was encouraged to shoot on sight, but although he certainly put in more shots, he only managed four goals including a Premiership double against Everton in September. He is a quick-witted midfield who also has the feet to make things happen when moving forward.
Aston Villa *(From trainee on 18/5/1994)* PL 138+35/19 FLC 9+2/3 FAC 8+8 Others 14+5/

HENDRY Edward **Colin** James
Born: Keith, 7 December 1965
Height: 6'1" **Weight:** 12.7
Club Honours: FMC '87; PL '95; SLC '98 SPD '99; SC '99
International Honours: S: 51; B-1
This vastly experienced central defender was out of the first-team picture at Bolto last term and in the new year he joined Blackpool on loan. Colin made a huge impact during his stay at Bloomfield Roa He featured regularly in the line-up and his presence certainly helped his fellow defenders.
Dundee *(Signed from Islavale on 1/7/1983)* SL 17+24/2 SC 2+3/1
Blackburn Rov *(£30,000 on 11/3/1987)* FL 99+3/22 FLC 4 FAC 3 Others 13/1
Manchester C *(£700,000 on 16/11/1989)* F 57+6/5 FLC 3+1/1 FAC 5/2 Others 4/2
Blackburn Rov *(£700,000 on 8/11/1991)* P/FL 229+5/12 FLC 23 FAC 17+1 Others 11
Glasgow R *(£4,000,000 on 5/8/1998)* SL 18+3 SLC 3+1 SC 3 Others 4+1
Coventry C *(£750,000 on 3/3/2000)* PL 10+
Bolton W *(£250,000 on 15/12/2000)* P/FL 25/3 FLC 4 FAC 1 Others 3
Preston NE *(Loaned on 28/2/2002)* FL 2
Blackpool *(Loaned on 20/12/2002)* FL 14

HENRIKSEN Bo
Born: Denmark, 7 February 1975
Height: 5'10" **Weight:** 11.10
The pony-tailed Dane raised his cult statu even higher at Kidderminster last term b becoming the first player to score 20 goals in a season since the club gained entry into the Football League. He also became the first to score a hat-trick, achieving the feat in the game at Exeter City. Despite being a striker he has grea vision and passing skills that can turn a game in an instant.
Kidderminster Hrs *(Free from Herfolge, Denmark, ex Odense BK, on 9/11/2001)* FL 60+2/28 FLC 1 FAC 3 Others 1+1

Ian Hendon

ENRY Karl Levi Daniel
orn: Wolverhampton, 26 November 1982
eight: 6'1" **Weight:** 10.13
ternational Honours: E: Yth
regular in the Stoke City line-up in the
st half of the 2002-03 season, usually in
midfield role, Karl continued to make
ogress in a higher class of football.
owever, managerial changes brought a
cus on experience to preserve the club's
st Division status and his opportunities
ere reduced, but nevertheless time is on
e side of this gifted youngster.
oke C *(From trainee on 30/11/1999) FL*
+18/1 FLC 1+1 FAC 4+1 Others 1+1

ENRY Ronnie Stephen
orn: Hemel Hempstead, 2 January 1984
eight: 5'11" **Weight:** 11.11
is young centre back joined Southend
loan last March to replace Stephen
elly, who had been recalled in order to
ow him to join Queen's Park Rangers.
onnie looked a technically gifted player,
it with Leon Cort and David
cSweeney regulars at centre back, he
as asked to deputise at right back. He
owed considerable application, but his
experience in the role was exposed on
casions.
ttenham H *(From trainee on 3/7/2002)*
uthend U *(Loaned on 27/3/2003) FL 3*

ENRY Thierry
orn: Paris, France, 17 August 1977
eight: 6'1" **Weight:** 12.2
ub Honours: FAC '02, '03; PL '02; CS
2
ternational Honours: France: 51
EFA '00); Yth; (UEFA-U18 '96)
ne of the finest strikers in Europe,
ierry can operate down either flank, or
a lethal hit man as a central striker. He
ossesses incredible dribbling skills, which
able him to make long runs deep into
e opposition half. An excellent team
ayer who can create goals as well as
ore them, he is intelligent and
mbitious, while his electric pace enables
m to go outside defenders before
itting in on goal, or releasing the ball for
am mates. Thierry scored his 100th goal
r the club in the away game at
rmingham. An automatic choice for the
ench national squad, he scored the
ciding goal in the Confederations Cup
al victory over Cameroon in the
mmer. Thierry was voted as the PFA
layer of the Year' and also won a place
the Premiership team for the season.
rsenal *(£8,000,000 from Juventus, Italy, ex*
onaco, on 6/8/1999) PL 121+15/82 FLC 2/1
C 12+5/3 Others 45+5/26

HERIVELTO Moriera
Born: Brazil, 23 August 1975
Height: 5'10" **Weight:** 11.6
This speedy striker registered Walsall's first
goal of the 2002-03 season when netting
in the 3-1 defeat against Wolves at
Molineux, and in the next few weeks he
scored a reserve-team hat-trick against
Bury and hit the crossbar in the thrilling
Worthington Cup tie at Blackburn. This
however, proved to be his last first-team
appearance before being released by the
Saddlers and in the new year he joined
Greek club Ionikos Piraeus along with his
team mate Dani Rodrigues.
Walsall *(Free from Cruzeiro, Brazil, ex CS*
Maritimo, on 9/8/2001) FL 11+17/5 FLC
2+1/1 FAC 1+1

HERRERA Horacio Martin
Born: Rio Puerto, Argentina, 13
September 1970
Height: 6'1" **Weight:** 12.6
Martin joined Fulham in the summer of
2002, but spent much of the season in
the reserves. Injury to Edwin van der Sar
in mid-season saw him promoted to
substitute goalkeeper and he finally saw
Premiership action when Maik Taylor was
red carded at Spurs, going on to make his
full debut at home to Southampton. An
athletic goalkeeper who enjoyed
consistent form in the reserves where he
made a number of crucial saves, his style
was often spectacular.
Fulham *(Free from CP Alaves, Spain, ex Boca,*
Atlanta, Toluca, Ferro, on 5/7/2002) PL 1+1

HERRING Ian
Born: Swindon, 14 February 1984
Height: 6'1" **Weight:** 11.12
A third-year scholarship boy at Swindon,
Ian's future looked in doubt last
December and he was sent out on loan to
Salisbury and Chippenham. However, a
shortage of numbers saw him make his
full professional debut at Crewe in April
where he gave a fine performance at
right wing back. He repeated this in a
home game against Plymouth Argyle
when he claimed an assist in the Robins'
first goal and earned himself a new six-
month contract at the County Ground.
Swindon T *(Trainee) FL 2+3*

HESKEY Emile William Ivanhoe
Born: Leicester, 11 January 1978
Height: 6'2" **Weight:** 13.12
Club Honours: FLC '97, '00, '01, '03;
FAC '01; UEFAC '01; ESC '01; CS '01
International Honours: E: 34; B-1; U21-
16; Yth
Emile remains an enigma as a striker both

for Liverpool and England. Whilst his all-
round play and commitment cannot be
faulted his lack of goals at both club and
international level remains a cause for
concern. Although he can win most aerial
challenges with his power, his knock-
downs rarely seemed to fall to a team
mate. Partly this was due to Liverpool's
deep-lying style of play with too few
midfielders supporting the attack. Whilst
he remained Gerald Houllier's first choice
as partner to Michael Owen he faces
fierce competition from the emerging
Milan Baros. Emile also remained a
regular choice in Sven Goren Eriksson's
England squad although his only
international goal came at the end of the
season in the friendly match in South
Africa.
Leicester C *(From trainee on 3/10/1995) PL*
143+11/40 FLC 25+2/6 FAC 11 Others 5
Liverpool *(£11,000,000 on 10/3/2000) PL*
93+22/32 FLC 5+5 FAC 6+4/5 Others
38+3/11

**HESSENTHALER Andrew
(Andy)**
Born: Dartford, 17 June 1965
Height: 5'7" **Weight:** 11.5
International Honours: E: SP-1
Gillingham's player-manager was once
again a hugely instrumental figurehead as
the team battled to retain their First
Division status last term. A regular
throughout the campaign, he missed the
last few games with a hamstring injury,
but he has decided to play on again in
the 2003-04 season. A competitive
central midfielder, the highlight of his
campaign was making his 500th
professional appearance at the home of
one of his former clubs, Watford.
Watford *(£65,000 from Redbridge Forest on*
12/9/1991) FL 195/12 FLC 13/1 FAC 5/2
Others 4
Gillingham *(£235,000 on 7/8/1996) FL*
218+16/17 FLC 21+1/3 FAC 16+2/2 Others
9+1/3

HEVICON Ryan
Born: Manchester, 3 December 1982
Height: 5'10" **Weight:** 11.2
This young left-sided midfielder spent the
pre-season period with Altrincham, before
joining Carlisle in a short-term deal. He
made an appearance from the bench in
the opening game of the campaign, but
soon afterwards he signed for Unibond
League club Mossley. Later in the season
Ryan also featured for Hyde United and
Trafford.
Blackburn Rov *(From trainee on 5/7/2001)*
Carlisle U *(Free on 9/8/2002) FL 0+1*

Thierry Henry

EWLETT Matthew (Matt)
aul
rn: Bristol, 25 February 1976
eight: 6'2" **Weight:** 11.3
ternational Honours: E: Yth
idfielder Matt had a steady season
uring 2002-03. His career has often
een blighted by injury, but apart for a
ief spell during August he was a
nsistent performer. He has now made
er 100 league appearances for the
wn and doubled his goal tally for the
ub when he netted in the 5-2 win at
ockport during January. Matt captained
e side during April while regular skipper
ndy Gurney was suspended and retained
e armband on his return. A hard-
orking central midfield player, he also
ossesses good passing skills.
istol C (From trainee on 12/8/1993) FL
1+16/9 FLC 10+2 FAC 4+1/2 Others
-2/1
rnley (Loaned on 27/11/1998) FL 2
hers 1
vindon T (Free on 27/7/2000) FL 102+3/2
C 7 FAC 3 Others 1

EYWOOD Matthew (Matty)
ephen
rn: Chatham, 26 August 1979
eight: 6'2" **Weight:** 14.0
atty enjoyed a fine season at Swindon
2002-03 when he was an ever-present
first-team level. Like several of his
low defenders he overcame a slow start
settle down and produce his usual
ol, calm and collected displays at the
eart of the Robins' defence. The only
ght disappointment was that he
anaged to find the net on just two
casions during the campaign.
rnley (From trainee on 6/7/1998) FL 11+2
C 1 Others 1
vindon T (Free on 22/1/2001) FL 109+2/6
C 3 FAC 5/1 Others 5/1

BBERT Anthony (Tony)
mes
rn: Liverpool, 20 February 1981
eight: 5'8" **Weight:** 11.3
ub Honours: FAYC '98
tigerish and sharp-tackling right back,
ny would have been an England U21
gular if it were not for a series of
uries that plagued the second half of
s season at Everton. At his best he can
ovide both pace and width to the right
ank and is expert at creating space for
mself to use his more than useful
ossing ability. After excelling before
hristmas, the youngster had difficulties
covering from a hernia operation that
delined him following the 'derby' game

against Liverpool in December. Although
he returned to the team for four games
before the end of the season, he clearly
lacked match-fitness, and required further
surgery in the summer.
Everton (From trainee on 1/7/1998) PL 31+6
FLC 1+1 FAC 1

**HIGGINBOTHAM Daniel
(Danny)** John
Born: Manchester, 29 December 1978
Height: 6'1" **Weight:** 12.6
As financial pressure mounted on Derby,
Danny always seemed one of their most
marketable players and duly left for

Matty Heywood

197

Southampton, initially on loan, when the transfer window reopened. His central defensive partnership with Chris Riggott had improved enormously and, until the day he left, Danny remained the champion shot-blocker at Pride Park. At St Mary's he immediately took over on the left of the back four, in place of the injured Wayne Bridge. He looked more than comfortable in his first two appearances, but found himself peremptorily relegated to the substitutes' bench on Bridge's return. A permanent move is set to be ratified in the close season.

Manchester U (From trainee on 10/7/1997)
PL 2+2 FLC 1 Others 1+1
Derby Co (£2,000,000 on 12/7/2000) P/FL
82+4/3 FLC 7+1/1 FAC 3+1
Southampton (Loaned on 31/1/2003) PL 3+6 FAC 1

Danny Higginbotham

HIGGINS Alexander (Alex) John

Born: Sheffield, 22 July 1981
Height: 5'9" **Weight:** 11.4
International Honours: E: Yth; Sch

This neat central midfield player signed for Boston United last October after impressing on trial in the reserves. His ball-winning skills and distribution quickly won him a first-team place but unfortunately he collapsed in the Boxing Day and New Year's Day fixtures against York City and Lincoln City respectively. Alex was diagnosed with epilepsy, but after being prescribed medication he was quickly back on the subs' bench. He then picked up a troublesome thigh injury, which kept him out of action in the closing months of the campaign.

Sheffield Wed (From trainee on 16/11/1998)
Queens Park R (Free on 22/3/2001) FL 0+1

(*Free to Chester C during 2001 close season*)
Boston U (Free from Stalybridge Celtic on 10/10/2002) FL 13 FAC 1/1 Others 2

HIGGS Shane Peter

Born: Oxford, 13 May 1977
Height: 6'2" **Weight:** 12.12

After understudying Steve Book for the previous three seasons, Shane finally got chance of a decent run in goal for Cheltenham Town last term. He played in four games during March, was left out for the next two and then returned for the final six games of the campaign. He produced some sure handling and notable saves, particularly in the games against Wycombe Wanderers and Peterborough United that took the Robins so close to securing Second Division survival.

Bristol Rov (From trainee on 17/7/1995) FL 10 Others 2 (Free to Worcester C on 11/7/1998)
Cheltenham T (£10,000 on 21/6/1999) FL 10+2 Others 2

HIGNETT Craig John

Born: Prescot, 12 January 1970
Height: 5'9" **Weight:** 11.10
Club Honours: Div 1 '95; FLC '02

Craig failed to win a regular place at Blackburn last term and subsequently moved on loan to Coventry City. His stay at Highfield Road was a very mixed one. He took time to find his form, but then in December he sparked the Sky Blues into a five-game winning run, featuring in a deep-lying role behind the striker. He scored a stunning 25-yard goal in the home win over Derby but unfortunately suffered a broken leg in an innocuous incident at Bramall Lane at Christmas. He returned to Ewood Park to recover from his injury and once recuperated found himself back on the subs' bench.

Crewe Alex (From trainee at Liverpool on 11/5/1988) FL 108+13/42 FLC 9+1/4 FAC 11+1/8 Others 6+1/3
Middlesbrough (£500,000 on 27/11/1992) F/PL 126+30/33 FLC 19+3/12 FAC 10+2/3 Others 5+1
Aberdeen (Free on 1/7/1998) SL 13/2 SLC 2
Barnsley (£800,000 on 26/11/1998) FL 62+4/28 FLC 2 FAC 6/5 Others 3/2
Blackburn Rov (£2,250,000 on 14/7/2000) P/FL 20+33/8 FLC 5+1/3 FAC 4+4/3 Others 7
Coventry C (Loaned on 1/11/2002) FL 7+1/. FLC 1

HILEY Scott Patrick

Born: Plymouth, 27 September 1968
Height: 5'9" **Weight:** 11.5
Club Honours: Div 4 '90

cott rejoined Exeter City on loan last
eptember, before making the move
ermanent two months later. He was an
ver-present in the right-back berth
uring his spell at St James' Park, where
s experience and composure were much
eeded during a stormy season for the
recians. However, despite his efforts the
ub were relegated to the Conference at
e season's end.
xeter C *(From trainee on 4/8/1986) FL*
05+5/12 FLC 17 FAC 14 Others 16+2
rmingham C (£100,000 on 12/3/1994) FL
9 FLC 7 FAC 1 Others 2
anchester C *(£250,000 on 23/2/1996)*
FL 4+5
outhampton *(Free on 4/8/1998) PL 30+2*
AC 1
ortsmouth *(£200,000 on 3/12/1999) FL*
5+9 FLC 2 FAC 3
xeter C *(Free on 20/9/2002) FL 37 FAC 4*
thers 2

ILL Clinton (Clint) Scott
orn: Huyton, 19 October 1978
eight: 6'0" **Weight:** 11.6
int joined Oldham Athletic in the
ummer of 2002 for a substantial fee. A
omineering centre half, he was an
stant hit with the fans and scored his
st goal for the Latics with a thumping
eader against his former club Tranmere
August. A broken leg sustained at
rystal Palace in the club's Worthington
up exit looked to have ended his
ampaign but Clint battled on and
turned to the back three in the final
ague game of the season at
uddersfield.
anmere Rov *(From trainee on 9/7/1997) FL*
88+2/16 FLC 18/3 FAC 11+1/1
ldham Ath *(Signed on 16/7/2002) FL 17/1*
C 4 FAC 2 Others 2

ILL Kevin
orn: Exeter, 6 March 1976
eight: 5'8" **Weight:** 10.3
evin had a varied time at Torquay last
rm, starting the season as a makeshift
riker and finishing it as a makeshift
rthodox left back. He spent most of the
me in between playing wide on the left-
and side of midfield, but he also had a
ell as left wing back. Wherever he was
eployed, he always showed total
ommitment although his later
erformances were hampered by a knee
jury that required an end-of-season
eration.
orquay U *(Free from Torrington on*
8/1997) FL 212+30/29 FLC 11+1/1 FAC
3/2 Others 8+1/1

HILL Matthew (Matt) Clayton
Born: Bristol, 26 March 1981
Height: 5'7" **Weight:** 12.6
Club Honours: AMC '03
The 2002-03 campaign proved to be
another stirring season for this left-sided
defender who demonstrated that he had
fully recovered from the knee ligament

injury of the previous season. A good
header of the ball, despite a lack of
inches, Matt was a fixture for Bristol City,
so it was a disappointment that he was
left out of the starting line-up for the LDV
Vans Trophy final at the Millennium
Stadium. Fortunately he came on as a
substitute to play a part in City's laboured

Matt Hill

2-0 win over Third Division strugglers Carlisle United.
Bristol C (From trainee on 22/2/1999) FL 119+14/4 FLC 4 FAC 10 Others 14+4

HILL Nicholas (Nicky) Damien
Born: Accrington, 26 February 1981
Height: 6'0" **Weight:** 12.3
This Bury central defender joined the action from the substitutes' bench in the August games against Cambridge and Swansea, but was largely restricted to reserve-team football throughout the remainder of last season. Nicky was loaned out to Leigh RMI in November but suffered a hamstring injury in his second game and returned to Gigg Lane. He appeared in the LDV Vans Trophy games against Rochdale and Barnsley but his sole start in Division Three occurred in the final fixture against Wrexham when the Shakers rested a number of players with one eye on the play-offs.
Bury (From trainee on 9/7/1999) FL 16+6 Others 5+1

HILL Stephen Bryan
Born: Prescot, 12 November 1982
Height: 5'10" **Weight:** 11.2
A strong-tackling left back, Stephen worked his way up through Rochdale's junior sides to make his first-team bow in the 2002-03 pre-season friendlies. His senior debut came as substitute when Dale beat runaway leaders Hartlepool 4-0, and for his first full game he was pitched in against First Division Coventry City in the FA Cup tie, Stephen coming through with flying colours as Dale gained a famous victory. He also played in the next six games before unfortunately suffering a pulled hamstring and then did not reappear until the last couple of weeks of the campaign.
Rochdale (From trainee on 3/7/2002) FL 9+1 FAC 2

HILLIER Ian Michael
Born: Neath, 26 December 1979
Height: 6'0" **Weight:** 11.10
International Honours: W: U21-5
Ian is a very versatile and talented squad player who filled in as a full back, central midfielder and central defender for Luton Town last season, but has yet to find a regular first-team position. A hard worker in whichever position he appeared, he was a little unlucky, picking up injuries once he looked to have established a place in the line-up and these prevented him from having an extended run in the side.
Tottenham H (From trainee on 2/7/1998)

Luton T (Free on 18/8/2001) FL 23+22/1 FLC 0+1 FAC 1+1 Others 2

HILLS John David
Born: Blackpool, 21 April 1978
Height: 5'9" **Weight:** 11.2
Club Honours: AMC '02
This left-sided defender or midfielder always gave 100 per cent effort for Blackpool last season and chipped in with six valuable goals. He turned down the offer of a new contract at Bloomfield Road and was reported to have signed for Gillingham in the summer.
Blackpool (From trainee on 27/10/1995) Everton (£90,000 on 4/11/1995) PL 1+2 Swansea C (Loaned on 30/1/1997) FL 11 Swansea C (Loaned on 22/8/1997) FL 7/1 Blackpool (£75,000 on 16/1/1998) FL 146+16/16 FLC 5 FAC 12/2 Others 13+1/2

HINDS Richard Paul
Born: Sheffield, 22 August 1980
Height: 6'2" **Weight:** 11.0
This versatile player was only on the fringes of the Tranmere first-team squad in 2002-03 and managed just six starts during the campaign. His preferred position is at centre back, but Richard can cover any of the midfield roles as well as possessing the admirable trait of being able to walk away from potential trouble rather than to provoke it. Richard's contract was not renewed by the Birkenhead club at the end of the season.
Tranmere Rov (From juniors on 20/7/1998) FL 42+13 FLC 3+5 FAC 5 Others 1

HINSHELWOOD Adam
Born: Oxford, 8 January 1984
Height: 5'10" **Weight:** 12.10
This well built defender made a surprise debut for Brighton in the opening fixture of the 2002-03 campaign at Burnley, playing alongside Robbie Pethick at the heart of the defence in place of absent skipper Danny Cullip. Adam performed admirably, winning rave reviews in a 3-1 win, and made the starting line-up a further three times during the course of the season, also playing in both full-back positions. In the third year of his scholarship, he was rewarded for his efforts with a two-year professional contract in April. He is the nephew of former Seagulls' boss Martin Hinshelwood.
Brighton & Hove A (Trainee) FL 4+3

HINTON Craig
Born: Wolverhampton, 26 November 1977
Height: 6'0" **Weight:** 12.0
Club Honours: NC '00

Always one of the most consistent defenders in Kidderminster's squad Craig had to prove his versatility last season when he appeared in a variety of positions. Normally a central defender, he spent much of the campaign on the left-hand side of a back three but also appeared in a central role and at right back. His performances suffered as a result and after winning the award for the previous two seasons he had to give up the 'Player of the Year' title to Danny Williams.
Birmingham C (From trainee on 5/7/1996) Kidderminster Hrs (Free on 12/8/1998) FL 131/2 FLC 4 FAC 6 Others 7

HIRSCHFELD Lars
Born: Edmonton, Canada, 17 October 1978
Height: 6'4" **Weight:** 13.8
International Honours: Canada: 12; U23-1
Tottenham Hotspur's third choice goalkeeper joined Luton Town on loan and made a very successful debut in the 1-0 win over Plymouth Argyle. After such a promising start his season was unfortunately ended prematurely following a hamstring injury in the home game against Oldham. Lars is a tall goalkeeper, good in the air and very agile but he needs an extended run of first team football to improve and learn his goalkeeping trade. He continued to add to his total of caps for Canada during the campaign.
Tottenham H (Free from Calgary Storm, Canada, ex Edmonton Drillers, Energie Cottbus, via trial at Portsmouth, on 31/8/2002) Luton T (Loaned on 22/2/2003) FL 5

HISLOP Neil Shaka
Born: Hackney, 22 February 1969
Height: 6'4" **Weight:** 14.4
Club Honours: Div 2 '94; Div 1 '03
International Honours: Trinidad & Tobago: 14; E: U21-1
After joining Portsmouth in the summer of 2002 Shaka immediately established himself as the club's first choice goalkeeper. He went on to become an ever-present in the line-up and to keep 1 clean sheets as Pompey won the First Division title. A great shot stopper who commands his area well, Shaka showed excellent reactions and made some remarkable finger-tip saves. He was deservedly selected for the PFA Division One team of the season.
Reading (Signed from Howard University, USA on 9/9/1992) FL 104 FLC 10 FAC 3 Others 9

ewcastle U *(£1,575,000 on 10/8/1995) PL
R FLC 8 FAC 6 Others 4*
*'est Ham U (Free on 8/7/1998) PL 105 FLC
' FAC 7 Others 9*
*ortsmouth (Free on 3/7/2002) FL 46 FLC 2
AC 1*

ITCHEN Steven (Steve)
mes
orn: Salford, 28 November 1976
eight: 5'8" **Weight:** 11.7
eve was ever-present in the Macclesfield
de until early March, but then found
mself replaced by George Abbey despite
aving hardly put a foot wrong. He
ostly played at right wing back,
though during a mid-season spell when
e manager reverted to a back-four
rmation he was employed at right back.
owever, in both positions he always
efended strongly, tackled well and
stributed the ball with accuracy, yet at
e same time acting as an effective
tacking player.
ackburn Rov (From trainee on 4/7/1995)
*acclesfield T (Free on 14/7/1997) FL
35+7/1 FLC 7+1 FAC 11 Others 3*

ITZLSPERGER Thomas
orn: Munich, Germany, 5 April 1982
eight: 6'0" **Weight:** 12.5
ternational Honours: Germany: U21-
2; Yth
homas was a greatly improved player for
ston Villa last term. Although he
ruggled to maintain a place in the side
t the beginning of the campaign and
as then sidelined by an abdominal
rain, he eventually broke through to
ecome a regular in midfield. Thomas has
powerful shot on him from both open
ay and set pieces, and displays an
npressive ability to score spectacular
oals from distance. His tally included a
uperb swerving left-footer into the top
orner against Arsenal, and a thunderbolt
stoppage time to secure a win against
cal rivals West Bromwich Albion.
homas represented Germany at U21
vel during the campaign.
*ston Villa (Free from Bayern Munich,
ermany on 8/8/2000) PL 35+4/3 FLC 2+1/2
thers 4*
*hesterfield (Loaned on 27/10/2001) FL 5
thers 1*

JELDE Jon Olav
orn: Levanger, Norway, 30 April 1972
eight: 6'1" **Weight:** 13.7
lub Honours: Div 1 '98
on started the 2002-03 campaign playing
ongside Des Walker in the centre of the
ottingham Forest defence, but then lost

his place to Michael Dawson. He
continued to be a valuable member of the
first-team squad never letting anyone
down when called upon. A tall central
defender who is effective in the air and
solid on the ground, he was released at
the end of the season.
*Nottingham F (£600,000 from Rosenborg,
Norway on 8/8/1997) P/FL 136+21/4 FLC 11/2
FAC 5 Others 0+1*

HOBSON Gary
Born: Hull, 12 November 1972
Height: 6'1" **Weight:** 13.3
This experienced defender again showed

great composure at the heart of York
City's defence last season. A regular for
most of the campaign, Gary had a spell
on the sidelines in February and March
but was recalled to the line-up, producing
an outstanding performance in the home
win over Southend and then retaining his
place for the closing matches.
*Hull C (From trainee on 17/7/1991) FL 135+7
FLC 13+1 FAC 2+2 Others 6*
*Brighton & Hove A (£60,000 on 27/3/1996)
FL 92+6/1 FLC 7 FAC 4+1 Others 3*
Chester C (Signed on 7/1/2000) FL 20
*York C (Free on 17/7/2000) FL 46+9 FLC 2
FAC 6*

Thomas Hitzlsperger

HOCKENHULL Darren

Born: St Helens, 5 September 1982
Height: 5'9" **Weight:** 10.10
Rochdale boss Paul Simpson had watched Darren in Blackburn Rovers' academy games and moved in quickly when he became available for a loan deal, signing him on transfer deadline day for the rest of the season. He went straight into the side, making his senior debut at right wing back against Torquay before taking a position on the right-hand side of midfield for the last few games and netting his first senior goal in the victory over Hull.

Blackburn Rov (From trainee on 4/7/2002)
Rochdale (Loaned on 27/3/2003) FL 6+1/1

HOCKING Matthew (Matt)
James
Born: Boston, 30 January 1978
Height: 5'11" **Weight:** 11.12
This defender had an excellent season with his home town club in their inaugural Football League campaign. Matt was equally effective at right back and in the middle of defence. He proved sharp in the tackle and won plenty of ball in the air. His only goal came in the final home game of the season when his header sealed victory over Macclesfield to secure Boston's Division Three status for 2003-04.

Sheffield U (From trainee on 16/5/1996)
Hull C (£25,000 on 19/9/1997) FL 55+2/2 FLC 6 FAC 4 Others 4
York C (£30,000 on 25/3/1999) FL 83+14/2 FLC 2+1 FAC 6+2 Others 2
Boston U (Free on 9/8/2002) FL 44+1/1 FLC 1+1 FAC 1 Others 2

HOCKLESS Graham
Born: Hull, 20 October 1982
Height: 5'7" **Weight:** 10.6
This promising young midfielder did well in Grimsby Town's reserve team last season. Graham stepped up to make his bow in senior football in the penultimate game of the season at Reading and will be aiming to see more first-team action in 2003-04.

Grimsby T (Signed from Hull C juniors on 9/7/2001) FL 1

HOCKLEY Matthew (Matt)
Born: Paignton, 5 June 1982
Height: 5'10" **Weight:** 11.7
This Torquay United utility man proved his dedication and commitment on countless occasions last term. He looked most at home when used as a combative central midfielder, but was unable to wrest a permanent berth from the more creative

players at the club. He also filled in efficiently at right back, and was called from the bench on a number of occasions to shake things up, notably in the penultimate game with Carlisle which saw United's play-off hopes disappear. Matt came on with the Gulls 3-0 down, but inspired a fight back as they narrowly failed to salvage a point.

Torquay U (From trainee on 4/7/2000) FL 41+17/3 FAC 4 Others 2

HODGES Lee Leslie
Born: Plaistow, 2 March 1978
Height: 5'5" **Weight:** 10.2
International Honours: E: Sch
Rochdale fans were delighted with the capture of this tricky winger, but unfortunately he struggled with a series of niggling injuries and rarely figured in boss Paul Simpson's plans. Lee was subsequently loaned to Bristol Rovers where he impressed with his close control and ability to beat opponents and cross accurately from the left flank. He eventually joined the Pirates on a permanent basis at the end of the season.

West Ham U (From trainee on 2/3/1995) PL 0+3 FAC 0+3
Exeter C (Loaned on 13/9/1996) FL 16+1
Leyton Orient (Loaned on 28/2/1997) FL 3
Plymouth Arg (Loaned on 6/11/1997) FL 9 Others 1
Ipswich T (Loaned on 20/11/1998) FL 0+4
Southend U (Loaned on 25/3/1999) FL 10/1
Scunthorpe U (£50,000 on 8/7/1999) FL 97+16/20 FLC 4 FAC 9/2 Others 4/2
Rochdale (Free on 9/8/2002) FL 3+4 Others 1
Bristol Rov (Loaned on 21/3/2003) FL 7+1

HODGES Lee Leslie
Born: Epping, 4 September 1973
Height: 6'0" **Weight:** 12.1
Club Honours: Div 3 '02
International Honours: E: Yth
Lee once again had an impressive season with Plymouth last term. He covered both the left back and the left-hand side of midfield during the campaign and was able to deliver some telling crosses with his cultured left foot. He continued to be dangerous from set plays often causing mayhem in the opposing defence with his aerial ability. Lee netted twice including an injury-time penalty to salvage a draw against Swindon Town in December.

Tottenham H (From trainee on 29/2/1992) PL 0+4
Plymouth Arg (Loaned on 26/2/1993) FL 6+1/2
Wycombe W (Loaned on 31/12/1993) FL 2+2 FAC 1 Others 1

Barnet (Free on 31/5/1994) FL 94+11/26 FLC 6+1 FAC 6+1/4 Others 3+1
Reading (£100,000 on 29/7/1997) FL 58+21/10 FLC 7+3 FAC 7+1/1 Others 0+2
Plymouth Arg (Free on 17/8/2001) FL 80+4/8 FLC 2 FAC 7 Others 1

HODGSON Richard James
Born: Sunderland, 1 October 1979
Height: 5'10" **Weight:** 11.8
Richard struggled to win a regular place in the Darlington line-up last term and it was only during a four-month spell in the middle of the campaign that he featured regularly. He is a skilful, direct left winger who loves to run at defenders and provide accurate crosses for his team mates. He has the knack of tricking defenders and cutting inside from his usual wide berth, which led to him scoring three goals during the season.

Nottingham F (From trainee on 8/10/1996)
Scunthorpe U (Free on 9/3/2000) FL 1
Darlington (Free on 7/8/2000) FL 66+32/6 FLC 3+1 FAC 8+1/3 Others 5+1/1

HOEKSTRA Peter
Born: Groningen, Holland, 4 April 1973
Height: 6'3" **Weight:** 12.8
International Honours: Holland: 5
This gifted left-sided midfielder is adored by the Stoke City fans, his delightful skills proving capable of turning matches at a higher level of football. There were some concerns that he was injury prone but as season he showed he could shake off the knocks and he featured regularly. Peter was offered a new contract at the end of the campaign.

Stoke C (Free from Ajax, Holland, ex PSV Eindhoven, on 27/7/2001) FL 46+8/7 FLC 1+ FAC 4+1/1

HOGG Lewis James
Born: Bristol, 13 September 1982
Height: 5'8" **Weight:** 10.8
This ball-winning midfielder had a rather frustrating season with Bristol Rovers last term, rarely making the starting line-up and generally having to be content with place on the substitutes' bench. When selected he could always be relied upon to give 100 per cent effort, but nevertheless he was released in the summer.

Bristol Rov (From trainee on 14/9/1999) FL 61+13/3 FLC 6/1 FAC 5+2/1 Others 4/1

HOLDEN Dean Thomas John
Born: Salford, 15 September 1979
Height: 6'0" **Weight:** 11.0
International Honours: E: Yth
Dean's 2002-03 season was wrecked by

njury problems. The versatile defender
joined Oldham during the summer from
Bolton Wanderers, having spent most of
the previous season on loan at Boundary
Park. But he suffered tendon damage
during the pre-season and then tore a
thigh muscle, restricting him to just six
appearances, although he did manage to
score in consecutive games in October.
Sean will be hoping to re-establish
himself in the side next term.

Bolton W *(From trainee on 23/12/1997) FL
6+6/1 FLC 3+1 FAC 3+1*
Oldham Ath *(Free on 12/10/2001) FL 22+7/4
FLC 0+1 FAC 1 Others 3*

HOLDSWORTH David Gary

Born: Walthamstow, 8 November 1968
Height: 6'1" **Weight:** 12.10
International Honours: E: U21-1; Yth
David joined Bolton on a short-term
contract in August 2002 and made his
debut in the Worthington Cup defeat
against Bury, when he gave a competent
display at the heart of the defence.
Unfortunately, this was his one and only
appearance for Wanderers and soon
afterwards he was released, subsequently
joining Conference outfit Scarborough.
He is the twin brother of Dean
Holdsworth who was a colleague in his
brief spell at the Reebok.

Watford *(From apprentice on 8/11/1986) FL
149+9/11 FLC 20/2 FAC 14+1/1 Others 8+2*
Sheffield U *(£450,00 on 8/10/1996) FL 93/4
FLC 7 FAC 13/3 Others 5*
Birmingham C *(£1,200,000 on 22/3/1999)
FL 78+7/7 FLC 10/1 FAC 1 Others 4+1*
Walsall *(Loaned on 18/1/2002) FL 9/1 FAC 2*
Bolton W *(Free on 4/9/2002) FLC 1*

HOLDSWORTH Dean Christopher

Born: Walthamstow, 8 November 1968
Height: 5'11" **Weight:** 11.13
Club Honours: Div 3 '92
International Honours: E: B-1
This experienced striker managed just five
starts for Bolton Wanderers last term
before moving on loan to Coventry in
December. Signed as a replacement for
the injured Lee Mills he had an excellent
game playing as a lone striker in the 2-0
win at Molineux, holding the ball up well
to create both goals and was awarded a
short-term deal. Despite some good
performances Dean lost his place to Matt
Hansen in March and on transfer deadline
day he joined Rushden & Diamonds in
another short-term deal. He scored twice
on his full home debut against
Macclesfield Town on Easter Monday, but
was freed at the end of the season.

Watford *(From apprentice on 12/11/1986) FL
2+14/3 Others 0+4*
Carlisle U *(Loaned on 11/2/1988) FL 4/1*
Port Vale *(Loaned on 18/3/1988) FL 6/2*
Swansea C *(Loaned on 25/8/1988) FL 4+1/1*
Brentford *(Loaned on 13/10/1988) FL 2+5/1*
Brentford *(£125,000 on 29/9/1989) FL
106+4/53 FLC 7+1/6 FAC 6/7 Others 12+2/9*
Wimbledon *(£720,000 on 20/7/1992) PL
148+21/58 FLC 16+3/11 FAC 13+7/7*
Bolton W *(£3,500,000 on 3/10/1997) P/FL
97+61/39 FLC 11+5/4 FAC 5+2/3 Others 5/3*
Coventry C *(Free on 29/11/2002) FL 13+4
FAC 3/1*
Rushden & Diamonds *(Free on 27/3/2003)
FL 4+3/2*

HOLLAND Christopher (Chris) James

Born: Clitheroe, 11 September 1975
Height: 5'9" **Weight:** 11.5
International Honours: E: U21-10; Yth
This strong and purposeful midfielder
never stops working throughout a game

Chris Holland

whether he is involved in defensive duties or leading the attack. Now in his third year at Huddersfield, Chris looked to form a keen partnership with his fellow midfield players last term. A hernia injury kept him on the sidelines for a spell, but with the Terriers struggling at the wrong end of the table he found it hard to create chances for his team mates.

Preston NE (Trainee) FL 0+1 Others 1
Newcastle U (£100,000 on 20/1/1994) PL 2+1 FLC 0+1
Birmingham C (£600,000 on 5/9/1996) FL 39+31 FLC 7+5 FAC 4 Others 1+1
Huddersfield T (£150,000 on 3/2/2000) FL 113+4/2 FLC 4 FAC 4 Others 8+1/1

HOLLAND Matthew (Matt)
Rhys
Born: Bury, 11 April 1974
Height: 5'9" **Weight:** 11.12
International Honours: RoI: 33; B-1
Matt had another good season at Ipswich last term, captaining the side with verve and no little amount of skill Both managers played him in midfield and defence and this versatility endeared him to the fans, as did the fact that he would run a lap of the pitch at the end of every game to offer thanks for their support. Matt weighed in with six goals, two of which came from free kicks outside the box, against Wolves and Reading. He was voted the club's 'Player of the Year' and continued to feature at international level for the Republic of Ireland.

West Ham U (From trainee on 3/7/1992)
Bournemouth (Signed on 27/1/1995) FL 97+7/18 FLC 6 FAC 3 Others 3
Ipswich T (£800,000 on 31/7/1997) P/FL 259/38 FLC 23+1/6 FAC 12 Others 17+2/2

HOLLIGAN Gavin Victor
Born: Lambeth, 13 June 1980
Height: 5'10" **Weight:** 12.0
Gavin's season at Wycombe was almost completely spoilt by cartilage damage suffered during pre-season training. He eventually played his first game of the campaign as a substitute in March, then scored two goals in quick succession, both coming off the bench against Brentford and Peterborough, before a further knock kept him out of contention. In spite of just one start last term, his contract was extended for a further year when he will be hoping to steer clear of injuries.

West Ham U (£100,000 from Kingstonian on 5/3/1999) PL 0+1
Leyton Orient (Loaned on 17/9/1999) FL 1 FLC 1
Exeter C (Loaned on 17/10/2000) FL 3

Wycombe W (Free on 9/8/2001) FL 12+18/6 FAC 2 Others 2/1

HOLLOWAY Darren
Born: Crook, 3 October 1977
Height: 5'10" **Weight:** 12.2
International Honours: E: U21-1
Darren's third season with Wimbledon was one he would probably not remember too fondly in days to come. When available for selection, he displayed his usual level of commitment, being strong in the tackle and generally using the ball to good effect. Unfortunately, his availability was frequently limited, for he missed the start of the season due to an ankle injury, the middle period thanks to a cartilage operation, and the final two games with a badly gashed shin. When starting he continued to feature in the right-back position, proving to be one of the stronger members of the club's defensive line.

Sunderland (From trainee on 12/10/1995) P/FL 46+12 FLC 3 FAC 2 Others 3
Carlisle U (Loaned on 29/8/1997) FL 5
Bolton W (Loaned on 14/12/1999) FL 3+1
Wimbledon (£1,250,000 on 2/10/2000) FL 76+3 FLC 3 FAC 6

HOLMES Derek
Born: Lanark, 18 October 1978
Height: 6'0" **Weight:** 13.2
This big striker had to be content with a place on the bench at Bournemouth for the majority of last season. However, when called upon he showed himself to be a natural finisher. Derek is a similar player to Steve Fletcher and at the start of the campaign he formed an effective partnership up front with Alan Connell.

Heart of Midlothian (From juniors on 5/1/1995) SL 1+6/1 SLC 0+2/2 Others 0+3/1
Ross Co (Free on 15/10/1999) SL 39+19/14 SLC 1+1/1 SC 1+1 Others 3
Bournemouth (£40,000 on 14/9/2001) FL 45+21/12 FLC 1 FAC 0+5/1 Others 2+2

HOLMES Lee
Born: Mansfield, 2 April 1987
Height: 5'7" **Weight:** 10.6
International Honours: E: Yth
When Lee went on as a substitute against Grimsby Town on Boxing Day he became the youngest player in Derby County's history at 15 years and 268 days. Nine days later, Lee was the youngest to play for anybody in the FA Cup after the qualifying rounds, as a substitute at Brentford. After that, school commitments and England U17 duty combined to limit the club involvement of the attacking left-sided midfield player.

Derby Co (Associated Schoolboy) FL 0+2 FAC 0+1

HOLMES Paul
Born: Stocksbridge, 18 February 1968
Height: 5'10" **Weight:** 11.3
This vastly experienced defender had a disappointing time at Torquay last season when he succumbed once again to a series of niggling injuries that restricted him to just eight first-team appearances. He was mostly used in his favoured right-back slot, but he also filled in at left back when required.

Doncaster Rov (From apprentice on 24/2/1986) FL 42+5/1 FAC 3+1/1 Others 1
Torquay U (£6,000 on 12/8/1988) FL 127+12/4 FLC 9 FAC 9+2 Others 13+3
Birmingham C (£40,000 on 5/6/1992) FL 12 FAC 1
Everton (£100,000 on 19/3/1993) PL 21 FLC 4 FAC 1 Others 0+2
West Bromwich A (£80,000 on 12/1/1996) FL 102+1/1 FLC 5 FAC 4 Others 3
Torquay U (Free on 11/11/1999) FL 82+5/2 FLC 2 FAC 3 Others 2+1

HOLMES Peter James
Born: Bishop Auckland, 18 November 1980
Height: 5'10" **Weight:** 10.6
International Honours: E: Yth; Sch
Peter again failed to make a significant mark on the Luton Town first team last term, spending the whole season as a fringe player. His performances were mixed and despite scoring a goal against Huddersfield he did not receive an extended run in the line-up. Peter is a lightweight midfielder who is an excellent passer of the ball.

Sheffield Wed (From trainee on 2/12/1997)
Luton T (Free on 1/8/2000) FL 24+18/3 FLC 3+2 FAC 3+1 Others 3+1/1

HOLMES Richard
Born: Grantham, 7 November 1980
Height: 5'10" **Weight:** 10.7
This promising youngster never managed to breakthrough to win a regular place in the Notts County first-team squad last term. When selected he was mostly used at right wing back, which enabled his exhilarating overlaps down the flank to be put to good use. Richard will be hoping to feature more regularly at first-team level in 2003-04.

Notts Co (From trainee on 23/3/1999) FL 47+12 FLC 3+1 FAC 2+2 Others 2+1

HOLMES Shaun Paul
Born: Derry, 27 December 1980
Height: 5'9" **Weight:** 11.3
International Honours: NI: 1; U21-13; Yth; Sch
Shaun missed out somewhat last season

with Wrexham's decision to play a formation using three central defenders and two wing backs. His appearances were more limited, although his defensive qualities were more than useful when asked to come on to shore up a result for the side when under pressure. However, Shaun also displayed attacking instincts, as in the away game at Boston in early April when he was very effective in securing a draw for the Dragons.

Manchester C (From trainee on 10/1/1998)
Wrexham (Free on 9/8/2001) FL 52+18 FLC 4 +2 FAC 2 Others 2+1

HOLT Andrew (Andy)
Born: Stockport, 21 May 1978
Height: 6'1" **Weight:** 12.7
Transfer-listed by Jan Molby shortly before the start of Hull's 2002-03 season, Andy was allowed to go out on a month's loan to Second Division Barnsley with Carl Regan moving in the opposite direction. At Oakwell he helped give the defence a more secure look, but his form dropped off and he returned to Boothferry Park. Back at the Tigers' camp, the burly left back briefly returned to the first team under new boss Peter Taylor at the turn of the year. However, he finished the season on loan at Shrewsbury. Andy's combative style was appreciated by the Gay Meadow fans, but he had the misfortune to arrive during a run of dismal results for the team and he was unable to prevent them from being relegated to the Conference.

Oldham Ath (From trainee on 23/7/1996) FL 104+20/10 FLC 8 FAC 6+4 Others 3
Hull C (£150,000 on 15/3/2001) FL 39+7/2 FLC 1 Others 4+1
Barnsley (Loaned on 15/8/2002) FL 4+3 FLC 1
Shrewsbury T (Loaned on 27/3/2003) FL 9

HOLT Gary James
Born: Irvine, 9 March 1973
Height: 6'0" **Weight:** 12.11
Club Honours: SC '98
International Honours: S: 4
Nicknamed 'three lungs' due to his amazing running power and stamina, Gary enjoyed another full season in the Norwich City engine room. He likes to break forward from midfield, carrying the ball to the opposition and although he is not a regular goal-scorer himself, he does get himself into good scoring positions. Defensively he is almost impossible to run past and has great strength to ease his opponent off the ball. He made his 100th appearance for the Canaries in the away defeat at Derby in April.

Stoke C (Free from Glasgow Celtic N/C on 20/10/1994)

Kilmarnock (Free on 18/8/1995) SL 138+13/9 SLC 10+1 SC 13 Others 8
Norwich C (£100,000 on 22/3/2001) FL 94+1/2 FLC 2 FAC 5 Others 3

HOLT Grant
Born: Carlisle, 12 April 1981
Height: 6'1" **Weight:** 12.7
This young, bustling striker joined Sheffield Wednesday from Unibond League outfit Barrow and after showing some good form for the reserves he won a place on the substitutes' bench for the first team. He made a bright start, scoring on his full debut for the Owls in the vital relegation battle at Brighton, and featured in a handful more games during the season. Grant will be looking to add to

his first-team experience in 2003-04.
Halifax T (Signed from Workington on 16/9/1999) FL 0+6 FLC 1/1 Others 1 (Free to Barrow during 2001 close season)
Sheffield Wed (Free on 27/3/2003) FL 3+4/1

HOLYOAK Daniel (Danny)
Born: London, 27 November 1983
Height: 6'2" **Weight:** 13.5
This young centre back made his debut for Mansfield Town in the 5-0 home defeat by Crewe Alexandra, coming off the bench when the side were four goals in arrears. As was expected from his displays for the youth and reserve sides Danny gave a solid performance, but could not stop the drubbing that was well in progress. However, he then became a

Gary Holt

205

victim of the new manager's clearout in mid-January and his contract was paid up, although he soon fixed himself up at Kettering Town.

Mansfield T *(Trainee) FL 0+2 Others 1*

HOPE Christopher (Chris) Jonathan
Born: Sheffield, 14 November 1972
Height: 6'1" **Weight:** 12.7
Chris was an ever-present for Gillingham for the third consecutive season in 2002-03, and is now closing in on the club record of 192 consecutive first-team appearances. A cool and unruffled central

Geoff Horsfield

defender, he is justly rated as one of the best in his position in the First Division. Chris signed an extension to his contract in March that will keep him at Priestfield until the summer of 2006.

Nottingham F *(From Darlington juniors on 23/8/1990)*
Scunthorpe U *(£50,000 on 5/7/1993) FL 278+9/19 FLC 13+1 FAC 18/1 Others 18/2*
Gillingham *(£250,000 on 12/7/2000) FL 138/7 FLC 10 FAC 8/2*

HOPE Richard Paul
Born: Stockton, 22 June 1978
Height: 6'2" **Weight:** 12.6

Richard was another Northampton Town player to spend most of the season on the treatment table. Primarily a central defender, he had his best spell at the turn of the year before being struck down by injury again. Richard is the son of John Hope the former Sheffield United and Hartlepool goalkeeper.

Blackburn Rov *(From trainee on 9/8/1995)*
Darlington *(Free on 17/1/1997) FL 62+1/1 FLC 3 FAC 1 Others 0+1*
Northampton T *(Signed on 18/12/1998) FL 113+22/7 FLC 3 FAC 5+3 Others 7+1*

HORLOCK Kevin
Born: Erith, 1 November 1972
Height: 6'0" **Weight:** 12.0
Club Honours: Div 2 '96; Div 1 '02
International Honours: NI: 32; B-2
Kevin featured fairly regularly for Manchester City last term, although he was used in a variety of roles, featuring either just in front of the defence or in the centre or left side of midfield. He worked hard and rarely gave the ball away, whilst his ability in the air proved useful at set pieces. Nevertheless he failed to find the net for the Blues during the season and found himself replaced by young Joey Barton in the closing stages of the campaign.

West Ham U *(From trainee on 1/7/1991)*
Swindon T *(Free on 27/8/1992) F/PL 151+12/22 FLC 15+2/1 FAC 12/3 Others 5+2*
Manchester C *(£1,250,000 on 31/1/1997) P/FL 184+20/37 FLC 15+1/3 FAC 9/1 Others 3/1*

HORSFIELD Geoffrey (Geoff) Malcolm
Born: Barnsley, 1 November 1973
Height: 5'10" **Weight:** 11.0
Club Honours: FC '98; Div 2 '99
This all-action striker developed a habit of scoring in crucial matches for Birmingham City last term. He netted in both 'derby' victories against Aston Villa, and headed home in the fifth minute of stoppage time to snatch a winner against West Bromwich Albion at St Andrew's in the crucial bottom-of-the-table game in March. He recovered from a double hernia in just 17 days and also played in goal (taking over from the injured Nico Vaesen at Villa Park), at right back and centre half at various times. Geoff came into his own as Christophe Dugarry's front partner during the last seven games after Clinton Morrison was sidelined with a dislocated shoulder.

Scarborough *(From juniors on 10/7/1992) FL 12/1 FAC 1 Others 0+2 (Free to Halifax T on 31/3/1994)*

*alifax T (Free from Witton A on 8/5/1997)
L 10/7 FLC 4/1
*ulham (£325,000 on 12/10/1998) FL
4+5/22 FLC 6/6 FAC 8+1/3*
*irmingham C (£2,000,000 + on 12/7/2000)
*/FL 73+32/23 FLC 10+1/3 FAC 1+1 Others
/2

HOULT Russell

orn: Ashby de la Zouch, 22 November
972
Height: 6'3" **Weight:** 14.9
ussell had another excellent season
etween the posts for West Bromwich
Albion, and at one point he was even
onsidered as a possible England
andidate following an injury to David
eaman. A fine shot stopper, daring and
crobatic, he more than once kept Albion
n the game with some quite stupendous
aves. He was outstanding in the home
ocal 'derby' with Aston Villa, saving Dion
Dublin's penalty, and put on majestic
lisplays in the away games at Leeds,
Charlton and Sunderland. Russell was
oted 'Midland Footballer of the Year' last
November.
*Leicester C (From trainee on 28/3/1991) FL
0 FLC 3 Others 1*
*Lincoln C (Loaned on 27/8/1991) FL 2 FLC 1
*Bolton W (Loaned on 3/11/1993) FL 3+1
Others 1*
*Lincoln C (Loaned on 12/8/1994) FL 15
Others 1*
*Derby Co (£300,000 on 17/2/1995) F/PL
21+2 FLC 8 FAC 7
*Portsmouth (£300,000 + on 21/1/2000) FL
40 FLC 4
*West Bromwich A (£500,000 on 5/1/2001)
P/FL 95 FLC 3 FAC 6 Others 2

HOWARD Jonathan (Jon)

Born: Sheffield, 7 October 1971
Height: 5'11" **Weight:** 12.6
With Jon's release in the summer, the last
member of Chesterfield's 1996-97 FA Cup
semi-final team left the playing staff. The
ricky forward received few opportunities
n 2002-03 and went on loan to Burton
Albion in March. The Brewers were
mpressed with what they saw, though,
and at the time of writing a permanent
nove looked on the cards.
*Rotherham U (From trainee on 10/7/1990)
*L 25+11/5 FLC 0+1 FAC 4/2 Others 3+1
Free to Buxton on 11/11/94)
*Chesterfield (Free on 9/12/1994) FL
152+84/39 FLC 11+3/1 FAC 14+3/2 Others
11+4/2*

HOWARD Michael Anthony

Born: Birkenhead, 2 December 1978
Height: 5'9" **Weight:** 11.13

Club Honours: Div 3 '00
Michael lost out to new signing David
Smith at the start of the season, but then
regained his place in the Swansea line-up
at left back. A hernia problem midway
through the campaign saw him pencilled
in for an operation during the summer
break, but despite the injury he was
playing as well as ever.
*Tranmere Rov (From trainee on 9/7/1997)
*Swansea C (Free on 6/2/1998) FL 196+7/2
FLC 9 FAC 10 Others 7*

HOWARD Steven (Steve)
John
Born: Durham, 10 May 1976
Height: 6'2" **Weight:** 14.6
For the second successive season Steve
ended up as Luton Town's top goal-scorer.
He developed a fine partnership up front
for the Hatters with Tony Thorpe, which
proved as good as anything in the Second
Division last term. Steve is an old-
fashioned centre forward, good in the air,
difficult to push off the ball and very
physical on the ground. Like any good
striker, Steve knows how to get into goal-
scoring positions and he seems likely to
be a key influence for the Hatters again in
2003-04.
*Hartlepool U (Free from Tow Law on
8/8/1995) FL 117+25/27 FLC 7+1/1 FAC 5/2
Others 7/3*
*Northampton T (£120,000 on 22/2/1999) FL
67+19/18 FLC 4 FAC 2+1 Others 2*
*Luton T (£50,000 on 22/3/2001) FL 95/49
FLC 3/1 FAC 1*

HOWARTH Neil
Born: Farnworth, 15 November 1971
Height: 6'2" **Weight:** 13.6
Club Honours: GMVC '95, '97; FAT '96
International Honours: E: SP-1
Neil began the 2002-03 campaign as first
choice at right back for Cheltenham, and
was a regular for the opening half of the
season, his height and physical presence
proving invaluable to a defence that was
often overworked. However, he suffered a
hamstring injury early in the new year and
once he had recovered he found it
difficult to win his place back, being
restricted to occasional appearances either
at right back or in the centre of defence.
He was released on a free transfer in the
summer following the Robins' relegation
to Division Three.
*Burnley (From trainee on 2/7/1990) FL 0+1
*Macclesfield T (Free on 3/9/1993) FL
49+11/3 FLC 3+1 FAC 2+2 Others 6*
*Cheltenham T (£7,000 on 24/2/1999) FL
106+14/7 FLC 6 FAC 7+1/1 Others 6*

HOWARTH Russell Michael
Born: York, 27 March 1982
Height: 6'1" **Weight:** 13.10
International Honours: E: Yth
Russell was restricted to just one
appearance for York City last term,
appearing in the LDV Vans Trophy game
at Lincoln. Soon afterwards he moved on
to Tranmere, arriving as cover for John
Achterberg. Russell went on to make his
full debut for Rovers at Luton in April,
and appeared four times altogether,
keeping two clean sheets. A confident
'keeper and a good handler and
distributor of the ball, he has bags of
potential and is a more than able deputy
for Achterberg.
*York C (From trainee on 26/8/1999) FL 6+2
FLC 3 Others 3*
*Tranmere Rov (Free on 5/11/2002) FL 2+1
FAC 0+1*

HOWE Edward (Eddie) John
Frank
Born: Amersham, 29 November 1977
Height: 5'10" **Weight:** 11.10
International Honours: E: U21-2
Eddie was again beset by injuries at
Portsmouth last term. He made the line-
up for the opening game of the season
against Nottingham Forest but pulled up
with a knee injury and did not make the
first team again. When fully fit he is a
commanding central defender who is
comfortable on the ball and useful when
moving up to join the attack for set pieces.
*Bournemouth (From trainee on 4/7/1996) FL
183+17/10 FLC 12+1/1 FAC 12/2 Others 8+2*
Portsmouth (£400,000 on 28/3/2002) FL 2

HOWEY Stephen (Steve)
Norman
Born: Sunderland, 26 October 1971
Height: 6'2" **Weight:** 11.12
Club Honours: Div 1 '93, '02
International Honours: E: 4
This likeable central defender was a
regular in the Manchester City line-up
until March, when a combination of injury
and loss of form saw him miss the closing
stages of the campaign. He showed
plenty of promise early on and was
particularly effective in successive home
games against Bolton and Tottenham.
Although he had one year of his Blues
contract remaining, Steve was reported to
have signed for Leicester City during the
summer.
*Newcastle U (From trainee on 11/12/1989)
F/PL 167+24/6 FLC 14+2/1 FAC 21+2 Others
10+2*
*Manchester C (£2,000,000 + on 14/8/2000)
P/FL 94/11 FLC 6 FAC 3*

HOWIE Scott
Born: Motherwell, 4 January 1972
Height: 6'2" **Weight:** 13.7
Club Honours: S Div 2 '93
International Honours: S: U21-5
Scott was again Bristol Rovers' first-choice 'keeper last term and apart from a brief spell in the autumn he was an ever-present in the team. He showed a tremendous attitude throughout as Rovers struggled to avoid the drop to the Conference and enjoyed several 'Man of the Match' performances, notably against Wrexham and in the vital 1-0 victory at Oxford on Easter Monday. He was surprisingly released at the end of the season.
Clyde (Signed from Ferguslie U on 7/1/1992) SL 55 SLC 3 SC 4 Others 1
Norwich C (£300,000 on 12/8/1993) PL 1+1
Motherwell (£300,000 on 13/10/1994) SL 69 SLC 4 SC 5 Others 1
Reading (£30,000 on 26/3/1998) FL 84+1 FLC 6 FAC 4 Others 7
Bristol Rov (Free on 2/8/2001) FL 90 FLC 3 FAC 10 Others 3

Scott Howie

HOWSON Stuart Leigh
Born: Chorley, 30 September 1981
Height: 6'1" **Weight:** 12.12
The loss of Stuart with a broken leg in early March accelerated Chesterfield's decline into relegation trouble last term. Prior to that, he had become an important member of the back line. Naturally left-footed, his best position is i the centre of defence, but he can play at full back too. He shows great composure for one so young, a lightness of touch in the pass conceals a firm tackle, and the Spireites are still surprised that Blackburn let him go.
Blackburn Rov (From trainee on 22/7/1999)
Chesterfield (Free on 15/2/2002) FL 45+1/3 FLC 2 FAC 1 Others 2

HOYTE Justin Raymond
Born: Waltham Forest, 20 November 198₄
Height: 5'11" **Weight:** 10.10
International Honours: E: Yth
Justin is a young midfield player who made his debut in senior football when he came off the bench for Arsenal in the end-of-season Premiership game against Southampton. He has great potential, having played for the Gunners' U17 team whilst still at school, represented England U19s at the age of 16, and played for England U20s against Switzerland last December. He spent most of last season as a regular member in the U19 and reserve teams at Highbury.
Arsenal (From trainee on 1/7/2002) PL 0+1

HREIDARSSON Hermann
Born: Iceland, 11 July 1974
Height: 6'1" **Weight:** 13.1
Club Honours: Div 3 '99
International Honours: Iceland: 49; U21-6
Hermann was used mainly as an attacking left wing back by Ipswich Town last season, thus using his pace and strength to best effect. It was a sight to terrorise opposing defenders: Hermann charging down the left wing to get on the end of a Thomas Gaardsoe long ball and on most occasions making contact, either to head it into the box or to control it and make further inroads down the flank. He damaged knee ligaments in the home game with Stoke and whilst still recovering from this agreed to join Charlton for a bargain fee, although he has yet to make his debut for the Addicks. Hermann continued to represent Iceland at international level during the season.
Crystal Palace (Signed from IBV, Iceland on 9/8/1997) P/FL 32+5/2 FLC 5/1 FAC 4 Others 2

Brentford *(£850,000 on 24/9/1998) FL 41/6*
FLC 2 FAC 2/1 Others 3/1
Wimbledon *(£2,500,000 on 14/10/1999)*
P/FL 25/1 FAC 2
Ipswich T *(£4,000,000 + on 19/8/2000) P/FL*
101+1/2 FLC 11 FAC 6 Others 9/1
Charlton Ath *(£500,000 + on 27/3/2003)*

HUCKERBY Darren Carl
Born: Nottingham, 23 April 1976
Height: 5'10" **Weight:** 11.12
Club Honours: Div 1 '02
International Honours: E: B-1; U21-4
Darren started the 2002-03 season in the
Manchester City squad, coming on as a
substitute in the opening game against
Leeds, then starting (and scoring) in the
first home game against Newcastle.
However, after that he rarely featured in
manager Kevin Keegan's plans and in
January he joined Nottingham Forest on
loan. The move was an immediate success
as he netted five times in his first six
games, but unfortunately he was then
hampered by hamstring problem.
Nevertheless, he helped his home town
club reach the First Division play-offs.
Darren possesses tremendous pace and
skill but has not always been able to
deliver a supply of goals in top-flight
football.
Lincoln C *(From trainee on 14/7/1993) FL*
20+8/5 FLC 2 Others 1/2
Newcastle U *(£400,000 on 10/11/1995) PL*
0+1 FAC 0+1
Millwall *(Loaned on 6/9/1996) FL 6/3*
Coventry C *(£1,000,000 on 23/11/1996) FL*
85+9/28 FLC 2+1 FAC 12/6
Leeds U *(£4,000,000 on 12/8/1999) PL*
41+29/2 FLC 11 FAC 1+2 Others 1+11/2
Manchester C *(£2,250,000 + on*
29/12/2000) P/FL 44+25/22 FLC 2+3/6 FAC
5+1/2
Nottingham F *(Loaned on 24/2/2003) FL 9/5*
Others 2

HUDSON Mark
Born: Bishop Auckland, 24 October 1980
Height: 5'10" **Weight:** 11.3
This promising Middlesbrough midfielder
spent much of last season out on loan. In
August he joined Chesterfield, where he
impressed with some effective tackling,
surging runs and accurate passing. Mark
also spent time with Carlisle, where he
did well, producing a 'Man of the Match'
performance in the Boxing Day clash with
Darlington. He eventually joined
Chesterfield on a permanent basis and
went on to captain the side, leading the
Spireites away from relegation trouble.
Middlesbrough *(From trainee on 5/7/1999)*
PL 0+5 FAC 0+1

Chesterfield *(Loaned on 13/8/2002) FL*
15+1/1 FLC 1 FAC 0+1 Others 0+1
Carlisle U *(Loaned on 10/12/2002) FL 14+1/1*
Chesterfield *(Free on 21/3/2003) FL 8/2*

HUDSON Mark Alexander
Born: Guildford, 30 March 1982
Height: 6'3" **Weight:** 12.6
A composed defender who can operate
at right back or central defence, Mark's
only first-team outing for Fulham came in
the Worthington Cup tie against Bury. He
is unfortunate that there are no fewer
than five other more experienced central
defenders at the club. However, he
continued to play regularly in the
successful Fulham reserve side.
Fulham *(From trainee on 6/4/1999) FLC 2+1*

HUGHES Aaron William
Born: Magherafelt, 8 November 1979
Height: 6'0" **Weight:** 11.2
International Honours: NI: 31; B-2; Yth
Despite growing competition for places
Aaron continued to be a regular in
Newcastle's defence last term, beginning
the season in his preferred right-back role.
The emergence of Andy Griffin in late
September led to a switch to the opposite
flank where he looked equally
comfortable, although he was also
occasionally employed in the centre of the
back four or in midfield to man-mark
opposing playmakers. His only goal of the
campaign was the winner at
Southampton. Calm and composed he
reads the game well and is comfortable
and rarely hurried on the ball. Aaron
continued to be selected regularly for the
Northern Ireland side.
Newcastle U *(From trainee on 11/3/1997) PL*
141+8/3 FLC 8 FAC 12+3/1 Others 17+3/1

HUGHES Andrew (Andy) John
Born: Manchester, 2 January 1978
Height: 5'11" **Weight:** 12.1
Club Honours: Div 3 '98
Last term proved to be another exciting
and successful season for this Reading
midfielder, who missed only four matches
in a long and arduous campaign. Quick
and strong, Andy not only made chances
for others with some perceptive passing,
but also contributed a major share of the
Royals' goal tally for the season, and each
of his strikes was accompanied by a
different and elaborate celebration. His
best finish was the long, dipping 35-yard
volley which brought a 1-0 win at
Molineux, closely followed by a powerful
header which resulted in the only goal of
the game in the Good Friday home win
over Nottingham Forest. For the final

match of the season he played as a lone
striker in place of the injured Nicky
Forster.
Oldham Ath *(From trainee on 20/1/1996) FL*
18+15/1 FLC 1+1 FAC 3+1 Others 1+2
Notts Co *(£150,000 on 29/1/1998) FL*
85+25/17 FLC 6+1/1 FAC 10/2 Others 2
Reading *(Free on 16/7/2001) FL 75+7/15 FLC*
1 FAC 2+1 Others 3

HUGHES Bryan
Born: Liverpool, 19 June 1976
Height: 5'10" **Weight:** 11.2
Club Honours: WC '95
Bryan was left out of the Birmingham City
line-up after the first two months of the
2002-03 campaign and at one point
looked set to sign on loan for Leicester.
However, he was recalled to the side in
April and scored a brilliant lob volley in
the win over Sunderland. He followed
that up with another impressive finish in
the Easter Monday victory over
Southampton, a game that effectively
secured Premiership status for the Blues.
A sleek midfield mover with or without
the ball, Bryan managed to show his
ability late on in the season.
Wrexham *(From trainee on 7/7/1994) FL*
71+23/12 FLC 2 FAC 13+3/7 Others 14+1/3
Birmingham C *(£750,000 + on 12/3/1997)*
P/FL 180+42/31 FLC 17+5/3 FAC 5+4/2
Others 6+2/1

HUGHES Ian
Born: Bangor, 2 August 1974
Height: 5'10" **Weight:** 12.8
Club Honours: Div 2 '97; AMC '02
International Honours: W: U21-12; Yth
This hard-tackling central defender started
the 2002-03 campaign as a regular in the
Blackpool squad, but rarely featured after
October, partly due to injury. He
eventually returned to the starting line-up
against Crewe Alexandra in mid-April and
made a handful more senior appearances
in the closing stages of the season.
Bury *(From trainee on 19/11/1991) FL*
137+24/1 FLC 14+3 FAC 6+2 Others 14+4/1
Blackpool *(£200,000 on 12/12/1997) FL*
139+21/3 FLC 11/1 FAC 8 Others 8+4/1

HUGHES Lee
Born: Smethwick, 22 May 1976
Height: 5'10" **Weight:** 11.6
International Honours: E: SP-4
Lee got on the score sheet twice for
Coventry in the opening games of the
2002-03 campaign, including a penalty
against Crystal Palace, before returning to
his former club West Bromwich Albion.
Unfortunately he failed to reproduce the
form he had shown during his first spell

at the Hawthorns, and in fact failed to register a Premiership goal in 23 appearances, although he did find the net in the Worthington Cup defeat at Wigan. However, a tedious knee injury and a lengthy attack of 'flu did not help his cause. Lee often found space behind defenders, but simply could not put the ball away. Albion fans will be hoping his goal touch returns in 2003-04.
West Bromwich A *(£250,000 + from Kidderminster Hrs on 19/5/1997) FL 137+19/78 FLC 10+3/4 FAC 6/2 Others 2/1* **Coventry C** *(£5,000,000 on 9/8/2001) FL 38+4/15 FLC 1+1* **West Bromwich A** *(£2,500,000 on 30/8/2002) PL 14+9 FLC 1/1*

HUGHES John **Paul**
Born: Hammersmith, 19 April 1976
Height: 6'0" **Weight:** 12.10
International Honours: E: Sch

Ian Hughes

Luton's most gifted player had another season beset with niggling injuries last term. When fully fit the influence he asserts on the game is telling either in defence, midfield or attack. Paul is a creative attacking midfield player who seems to have plenty of untapped potential. He contributed three goals during the campaign.
Chelsea *(From trainee on 11/7/1994) PL 13+8/2 FAC 1 Others 1* **Stockport Co** *(Loaned on 17/12/1998) FL 7* **Norwich C** *(Loaned on 24/3/1999) FL 2+2/1* **Southampton** *(Free on 23/3/2000)* **Luton T** *(Free, via trial at Burnley, on 10/8/2001) FL 42+15/5 FLC 3 FAC 1 Others 2*

HUGHES Richard
Born: Glasgow, 25 June 1979
Height: 5'9" **Weight:** 9.12
International Honours: S: U21-8; Yth
Richard caught the eye for Portsmouth in five central midfield starts early last season, before limping off in the Worthington Cup tie against Peterborough. He developed complications with a hamstring strain before losing the tip of his finger after trapping it in a training-room door. Happier times followed, however, as he was loaned to Grimsby Town in February where he created an immediate impact by setting up a goal for player-manager Paul Groves within minutes of his debut at Ipswich. He quickly became a favourite of the Mariners' fans with his creative support for the front runners, but eventually returned to pursue a first-team place at Fratton Park.
Arsenal *(Free from Atalanta, Italy on 11/8/1997)* **Bournemouth** *(£20,000 on 5/8/1998) FL 123+8/14 FLC 9+1 FAC 8/2 Others 5* **Portsmouth** *(£100,000 on 13/6/2002) FL 4+2 FLC 1* **Grimsby T** *(Loaned on 21/2/2003) FL 12/1*

HUGHES Stephen (Steve) Thomas
Born: London, 26 January 1984
Height: 6'1" **Weight:** 12.10
This young, left-sided midfielder signed professional terms for Brentford in the 2002 close season and made his debut as a substitute against Luton in September. Steve went on to make a handful of first-team appearances after this, his biggest match being the FA Cup fourth round tie against Burnley when he acquitted himself well.
Brentford *(From trainee on 9/7/2002) FL 2+ FAC 1+1 Others 0+1*

HULBERT Robin James
Born: Plymouth, 14 March 1980
Height: 5'9" **Weight:** 10.5
International Honours: E: Yth; Sch
Robin made little impression at Bristol City last term, and only featured in a handful of games before moving out to Shrewsbury Town on loan in March. The midfielder was one of four transfer-deadline-day acquisitions by manager Kevin Ratcliffe as he sought to turn the club's fortunes around. He showed some nice touches on the right-hand side, but it was difficult for him to make an impact in a side that was in free-fall mode.
Swindon T (From trainee on 25/9/1997) FL 2+17 FLC 1+1 FAC 2
Bristol C (£25,000 on 23/3/2000) FL 21+18 LC 1+2 Others 5+2
Shrewsbury T (Loaned on 27/3/2003) FL 1+3

HULSE Robert (Rob) William
Born: Crewe, 25 October 1979
Height: 6'1" **Weight:** 11.4
This talented young striker had an exceptional season at Crewe last term. He proved a real handful for opposition defenders and finished the campaign as the club's leading scorer with a total of 27 in all competitions, including his first hat-trick in the LDV Vans Trophy game at Mansfield. Rob was rewarded for some hard-working performances with a place in the PFA Second Division team of the season.
Crewe Alex (From trainee on 25/6/1998) FL 47+19/46 FLC 6+1/2 FAC 5+1 Others 2/4

HUME Iain
Born: Brampton, Ontario, Canada, 31 October 1983
Height: 5'7" **Weight:** 11.2
International Honours: Canada: 1; Yth
Iain really made his mark at Tranmere last season, winning a regular place in the side in the second half of the campaign. He netted his first senior goal against Peterborough in October and went on to find the net a total of six times, including a spell four in four games. He found his niche playing up front alongside the free-scoring Simon Haworth. Iain is an assured player, blessed with the ability to kick with either foot and was voted both 'Young Player of the Year' and the scorer of the 'Goal of the Season' by Rovers' fans. To complete an excellent campaign he also won his first senior cap for Canada against Libya.
Tranmere Rov (From juniors on 6/11/2000) FL 23+39/6 FLC 0+3 FAC 0+2 Others 1+2

HUMPHREYS Richard (Richie) John
Born: Sheffield, 30 November 1977
Height: 5'11" **Weight:** 14.6
International Honours: E: U21-3; Yth
This attacking midfielder has been outstanding in his two years at Hartlepool. Long considered a great prospect who had failed to live up to his potential as a teenager, Richie really came into his own in 2002-03 as Hartlepool went for promotion. A player who cannot help but entertain the crowd with his occasional showboating, his most memorable performance was in the home game against Swansea when he scored a hat-trick. He was named in the PFA's Division Three team, was chosen as the Hartlepool supporters' 'Player of the Year' and was also named the 'North East Nationwide League Player of the Year'.
Sheffield Wed (From trainee on 8/2/1996) P/FL 34+33/4 FLC 4+2 FAC 5+4/4
Scunthorpe U (Loaned on 13/8/1999) FL 6/2
Cardiff C (Loaned on 22/11/1999) FL 8+1/2 FAC 1 Others 1
Cambridge U (Free on 2/2/2001) FL 7/3
Hartlepool U (Free on 18/7/2001) FL 88+4/16 FLC 2 FAC 3 Others 3

HUNT David
Born: Dulwich, 10 September 1982
Height: 5'11" **Weight:** 11.9
Another product of the Crystal Palace youth system, David made his senior debut as a late substitute in the Worthington Cup tie against Oldham last season. A talented defender with an extra long throw, he also featured twice in the starting line-up in April. David will be looking to extend his senior experience at Selhurst Park in 2003-04.
Crystal Palace (From trainee on 9/7/2002) FL 2 FLC 0+1

HUNT James Malcolm
Born: Derby, 17 December 1976
Height: 5'8" **Weight:** 10.3
James joined Oxford in the summer of 2002 and became a regular in the side under his former Northampton manager, Ian Atkins. A mainly defensive midfielder, he often pushed forward to good effect and managed a couple of goals – one being the winner in the Worthington Cup tie at Bristol City. James was possibly Oxford's best player up to Christmas but playing a lot of the second half of the season with a broken toe did him no favours.
Notts Co (From trainee on 15/7/1994) FL 15+4/1 FAC 0+1 Others 2+2/1

Northampton T (Free on 7/8/1997) FL 150+22/8 FLC 8+2 FAC 7+3/1 Others 10+1/1
Oxford U (Free on 12/7/2002) FL 39/1 FLC 3/1 FAC 2

HUNT Lewis James
Born: Birmingham, 25 August 1982
Height: 5'11" **Weight:** 12.8
Another product of Derby County's youth scheme, Lewis showed a pleasing composure when he graduated to the first team. He made his debut as a substitute in the Worthington Cup victory at Mansfield and, after his first start against Walsall at the beginning of October, began to settle at right back. Sadly, he broke an ankle at Portsmouth the following month and was out of action for four months. Although he was able to return, Lewis then fell victim to a thigh strain that ended his season.
Derby Co (From trainee on 17/2/2001) FL 7+3 FLC 0+2

HUNT Nicholas (Nicky) Brett
Born: Westhoughton, 3 September 1983
Height: 6'1" **Weight:** 10.8
A big and strong central defender, Nicky had another small taste of first-team action last season, starting the FA Cup tie against Sunderland in January and appearing as a substitute in the subsequent replay. A competitive and tough-tackling player who has made quite a name for himself in the Bolton academy and reserve teams, he will be aiming to feature more regularly at senior level in 2003-04.
Bolton W (From trainee on 7/7/2001) FL 0+1 FAC 1+1

HUNT Stephen (Steve)
Born: Port Laoise, Ireland, 1 August 1980
Height: 5'7" **Weight:** 12.6
International Honours: RoI: U21-1
Brentford's exciting outside left enjoyed an excellent season in 2002-03. A real ball-playing winger he only missed out when suffering with an ankle injury in March. Steve scored with terrific free kicks (against Chesterfield and Derby), a great volley (against Crewe) and following a mazy run (against Northampton). The club's penalty-taker, he achieved four out of five.
Crystal Palace (From trainee on 29/6/1999) FL 0+3
Brentford (Free on 6/8/2001) FL 75+2/11 FLC 1+2 FAC 5/2 Others 6/1

HUNTER Barry Victor
Born: Coleraine, 18 November 1968
Height: 6'3" **Weight:** 13.2

Club Honours: Div 3 '03
International Honours: NI: 15; B-2; Yth
This experienced defender certainly had
an eventful season at Rushden &
Diamonds, finishing with a Third Division
championship medal. He was sent off
three times inside the opening two
months of the season, but returned to
play a key role in the club's promotion
campaign, producing a number of 'Star
Man' displays. His experience at the back
was crucial and although Paul
Underwood wore the captain's armband
Barry was the natural leader on the
pitch. He collected no less than four
'Player of the Year' awards at the end of
the campaign.
*Newcastle U (Signed from Coleraine on
2/11/1987. Freed during 1988 close season)*
*Wrexham (£50,000 from Crusaders on
20/8/1993) FL 88+3/4 FLC 6 FAC 7+1/1
Others 15/1*
*Reading (£400,000 on 12/7/1996) FL 76+8/4
FLC 5/1 FAC 3+1/1 Others 6+1*
Southend U (Loaned on 12/2/1999) FL 5/2
*Rushden & Diamonds (Free on 14/9/2001)
FL 63/2 FLC 1 FAC 4*

HUNTER Roy Ian
Born: Saltburn, 29 October 1973
Height: 5'10" **Weight:** 12.8
Roy was a regular squad member for
Oxford United after joining early last
season, initially on non-contract terms.
He moved between midfield and right
wing back and did a good job despite
never being the first choice for either
position. He scored two his only goal in the
3-0 home win over Bournemouth. At the
time of writing Roy had not been offered
a further contract and looked set to
move on.
*West Bromwich A (From trainee on
4/3/1992) FL 3+6/1 Others 4+1*
*Northampton T (Free on 2/8/1995) FL
149+28/17 FLC 10 FAC 11/2 Others 13/1
(Freed during 2002 close season)*
*Oxford U (Free from Nuneaton Borough on
18/10/2002) FL 12+5/1 FAC 1 Others 1*

HURST Glynn
Born: Barnsley, 17 January 1976
Height: 5'10" **Weight:** 11.10
Glynn missed the early part of last season
with tendonitis and returned to action in
a struggling Chesterfield side. Despite
occasional poor service and struggling
with his form he never stopped battling
up front. Now fully fit, his pace and
aerial ability will no doubt be to the fore
again in 2003-04, enabling Spireites' fans
to see the Glynn Hurst of old.

*Barnsley (From trainee at Tottenham H on
13/7/1994) FL 0+8 FLC 1 (Freed on
27/3/1997)*
Swansea C (Loaned on 15/12/1995) FL 2/1
*Mansfield T (Loaned on 18/11/1996) FL 5+1
Others 0+1*
*Ayr U (£30,000 from Emley on 23/3/1998) SL
78/49 SLC 6/2 SC 10 Others 1+2*
*Stockport Co (£150,000 on 16/2/2001) FL
22+4/4 FLC 0+1*
*Chesterfield (Free on 14/12/2001) FL
49+6/16 FAC 0+1*

HURST Mark Patrick
Born: Mansfield, 18 February 1985
Height: 5'11" **Weight:** 11.8
Highly rated by the Mansfield backroom
staff, this young defender was given a
first-team debut earlier than expected,
coming off the bench in the latter stages
of the Worthington Cup tie with Derby
County when the club's playing resources
were severely strained by injury. He made
his full debut in October following
Damien Delaney's departure and Allen
Tankard's injury setback, and also featured
in the LDV Vans Trophy tie.
Mansfield T (Trainee) FL 1 FLC 0+1 Others 1

HURST Paul Michael
Born: Sheffield, 25 September 1974
Height: 5'4" **Weight:** 9.4
Club Honours: AMC '96
A one-club player, Paul's loyalty was
rewarded with a richly deserved
testimonial year, while on the pitch he
continued to prove wrong the doubters
who claimed his smallness of stature
would find him out. Once again he made
the left-back position his own until the
last few games of the season when he
moved forward to play wide on the left of
midfield. His only goal was not enough to
prevent a home defeat at the hands of
Millwall as he took his league
appearances to well over the 300 mark
with the promise of many more to come.
*Rotherham U (From trainee on 12/8/1993)
FL 274+38/12 FLC 9+1 FAC 18+2/2 Others
14+1*

HUTCHINGS Carl Emil
Born: Hammersmith, 24 September 1974
Height: 5'11" **Weight:** 11.0
Carl played most of the 2002-03 season
in a central-midfield role for Leyton
Orient, but he occasionally appeared as a
centre half, a position in which he is also
comfortable. An effective tackler who is
adept at breaking up opposition attacks,
Carl scored one goal during the
campaign. His contract ended during the

summer and he was released on a free
transfer.
*Brentford (From trainee on 12/7/1993) FL
144+18/7 FLC 9+2 FAC 11+1 Others 11+3*
*Bristol C (£130,000 on 6/7/1998) FL 33+9/3
FLC 4+1/2 FAC 2+2 Others 1*
Brentford (Loaned on 11/2/2000) FL 7+1
*Exeter C (Loaned on 30/11/2000) FL 2
Others 1*
*Southend U (Free on 29/12/2000) FL 42+1/4
FLC 1 FAC 4 Others 2/1*
*Leyton Orient (Free on 13/2/2002) FL
30+8/2 FLC 2*

HUTCHINSON Edward (Eddie) Stephen
Born: Kingston, 23 February 1982
Height: 6'1" **Weight:** 12.7
This neat and tidy central midfielder
finally made the breakthrough into the
Brentford first team on a regular basis last
term. Eddie started the first 18 games of
the season before a groin injury kept him
out of action. He found it hard to force
himself back into the side when fit,
before further injuries curtailed his
campaign. Eddie is the twin brother of
the Dundee player Tom Hutchinson.
*Brentford (£75,000 from Sutton U on
21/7/2000) FL 28+11 FLC 2 FAC 0+1 Others
1+1*

HUTCHINSON Jonathan (Joey)
Born: Middlesbrough, 2 April 1982
Height: 6'0" **Weight:** 12.0
Joey made his Premiership debut for
Birmingham City at Leeds on New Year's
Day and certainly did not look out of
place. He also made the starting line-up
for the Worthington Cup defeat by
Preston in November and the FA Cup loss
at Fulham in January. A promising
defender who follows play well and is
good at mopping up on the ground, Joey
is comfortable in possession.
*Birmingham C (From trainee on 1/7/2000)
P/FL 1+3 FLC 2 FAC 1*

HUTCHISON Donald (Don)
Born: Gateshead, 9 May 1971
Height: 6'1" **Weight:** 11.8
International Honours: S: 23; B-1
After being out of the game for ten
months with a knee ligament injury Don
returned to the West Ham side against
Bolton last December. Playing on the right
side of midfield he showed some good
attacking skills and an eye for goal but
was unable to gain a place in the starting
line-up, being restricted to outings from
the substitutes' bench. He continued to
represent Scotland, adding further caps

gainst Republic of Ireland, Iceland,
ithuania and Austria.
*Hartlepool U (From trainee on 20/3/1990) FL
9+5/2 FLC 1+1 FAC 2 Others 1*
*Liverpool (£175,000 on 27/11/1990) F/PL
3+12/7 FLC 7+1/2 FAC 1+2 Others 3+1/1*
*West Ham U (£1,500,000 on 30/8/1994) PL
0+5/11 FLC 3/2 FAC 0+1*
*Sheffield U (£1,200,000 on 11/1/1996) FL
?0+8/5 FLC 3+2 FAC 5/1 Others 2+1*
*Everton (£1,000,000 + on 27/2/1998) PL
58+7/10 FLC 4+1/1 FAC 9*
*Sunderland (£2,500,000 on 19/7/2000) PL
?2+2/8 FLC 2/2 FAC 3*
*West Ham U (£5,000,000 on 31/8/2001) PL
4+10/1 FLC 1 FAC 3*

HUTH Robert
Born: Berlin, Germany, 18 August 1984
Height: 6'2" **Weight:** 12.12
International Honours: Germany: Yth
Although his progress will inevitably be
hampered by the plethora of top-quality
centre backs at Stamford Bridge, Robert
was as always given a mature performance
when called upon to deputise. He made
our of his five seasonal appearances
during an injury crisis in September and
acquitted himself remarkably well. His last
outing came as a late substitute in the
fifth round FA Cup tie at Stoke. The
competition for a first-team place at
Chelsea is obviously tough but the
talented German has the ability to make
the grade.
*Chelsea (From trainee on 23/8/2001) PL 2+1
FAC 0+1 Others 2*

HYDE Graham
Born: Doncaster, 10 November 1970
Height: 5'8" **Weight:** 11.11
Graham again found himself out of the
reckoning at Birmingham City at the start
of last season and had a loan spell at
Peterborough early on. Unfortunately
Posh finished on the winning side only
once in his nine appearances and he
returned to St Andrew's. He subsequently
signed for Bristol Rovers in November and
quickly established himself as a regular in
the centre of midfield. His experience
proved invaluable, while he impressed
with his tremendous work rate and ability
to defend as well as link up with the
attack.
*Sheffield Wed (From trainee on 17/5/1988)
F/PL 126+46/11 FLC 17+3/1 FAC 13+5/2
Others 8/1*
*Birmingham C (Free on 5/2/1999) FL
55+17/1 FLC 2+2/1 FAC 2*
*Chesterfield (Loaned on 18/8/2001) FL
?+1/1*

Robert Huth

Peterborough U *(Loaned on 20/9/2002) FL 8+1*
Bristol Rov *(Free on 28/11/2002) FL 21/1 FAC 2*

HYDE Micah Anthony
Born: Newham, 10 November 1974
Height: 5'9" **Weight:** 11.5
Club Honours: Div 2 '98
International Honours: Jamaica: 8
Micah is an experienced midfielder who has now made more than 200 league appearances for Watford. An influential player with an eye for the telling pass and a firm tackle, Micah's form tends to mirror and dictate that of the team as a whole. He added a further three caps for Jamaica during the season.
Cambridge U (From trainee on 19/5/1993) FL 89+18/13 FLC 3 FAC 7+2 Others 4+1
Watford (£225,000 on 21/7/1997) P/FL 207+13/23 FLC 15/4 FAC 11 Others 3

HYLDGAARD Morten
Lauridsen
Born: Denmark, 27 April 1976
Height: 6'6" **Weight:** 13.6
International Honours: Denmark: U21
Morten starting the 2002-03 season as first choice 'keeper for Coventry City, but then lost his place to Fabien Debec in mid-September. He bounced back, however, and held on to the goalkeeper's jersey until the end of March when the club, realising that further appearances would invoke an extra payment to his former Danish club, announced he would not be retained. A brave, confident shot stopper, Morten was sometimes exposed in the air but improved under the guidance of coach Alan Hodgkinson.
Coventry C (£200,000 from Ikast FS, Denmark on 9/7/1999) FL 27 FLC 1 FAC 3
Scunthorpe U (Loaned on 7/1/2000) FL 5 Others 2

HYLTON Leon David
Born: Birmingham, 27 January 1983
Height: 5'9" **Weight:** 11.3
International Honours: E: Yth
This promising Aston Villa youngster joined Swansea City on loan in February as cover for injuries and suspensions. He did well in his spell at the Vetch Field, impressing in the left-back position with his passing and tackling. He returned to Villa Park to continue his development after a two-month stay. Leon also featured for England at U20 level during the season.
Aston Villa (From trainee on 23/2/2000)
Swansea C (Loaned on 7/2/2003) FL 7+1

HYYPIA Sami
Born: Porvoo, Finland, 7 October 1973
Height: 6'4" **Weight:** 13.5
Club Honours: FLC '01, '03; FAC '01; UEFAC '01; ESC '01; CS '01
International Honours: Finland: 55; U21-27; Yth
This colossus at the heart of Liverpool's defence was virtually ever-present for the Reds last season and as always was one of their most consistent players. However, at times his performances dipped below their usual high standards, perhaps due to the lengthy absences of his accustomed partner, Stephane Henchoz. Sami scored his usual quota of goals with headers from corners and set pieces, but the goal that will give him most satisfaction came in the UEFA Cup match in Auxerre in February when, following a cleared corner, he collected the ball on the edge of the area, sidestepped an opponent and finished with the aplomb of an experienced striker to give his team a valuable 1-0 victory.
Liverpool (£2,600,000 from Willem II, Holland, ex MyPa, on 7/7/1999) PL 146/11 FLC 13/1 FAC 13 Others 41/4

Morten Hyldgaard

BEHRE Jabo Oshevire
Born: Islington, 28 January 1983
Height: 6'2" **Weight:** 12.10
Jabo was never able to command a regular place in the Leyton Orient line-up last term due to injuries, but still managed to score five goals. A quick and strong centre forward, his pace and trickery were often used to good effect from the substitutes' bench. Jabo will be looking to remain free from injury and challenge for a regular first-team place in 2003-04.
Leyton Orient (From trainee on 18/7/2001) FL 33+28/11 FLC 1+2/1 FAC 2+2/1 Others 4+1

FIL Jerel Christopher
Born: Wembley, 27 June 1982
Height: 6'1" **Weight:** 12.11
This young central defender was a regular in Watford's reserve team last season before joining Swindon Town on loan. He produced some steady performances for the Robins and impressed with his blistering pace. One storming run down the right wing late in the game at Tranmere which nearly led to a goal for Eric Sabin will long be remembered by those that saw it. He went on to make his first-team debut for the Hornets against Derby County towards the end of the campaign.
Watford (From trainee on 8/2/2000) FL 1
Huddersfield T (Loaned on 28/3/2002) FL 1+1 Others 2
Swindon T (Loaned on 30/1/2003) FL 5+4

FILL Paul
Born: Brighton, 20 October 1979
Height: 6'0" **Weight:** 12.10
Club Honours: Div 2 '01
A tall, clever player, Paul has won over the Millwall faithful with his pace, trickery on the ball and unpredictability. After starting his career as an out-and-out striker, he successfully switched to a wide-midfield role and is at his best running at opposing defences. He has also improved his defensive responsibilities, as was demonstrated on a number of occasions last season when making vital interceptions inside the danger zone. Paul is a great match winner and was often instrumental in assisting the team to pull out unexpected results.
Millwall (From trainee on 2/6/1998) FL 50+29/28 FLC 5/1 FAC 9/1 Others 8+1

IGOE Samuel (Sammy) Gary
Born: Staines, 30 September 1975
Height: 5'6" **Weight:** 10.0
This diminutive wide-right midfielder had something of a disappointing season at Reading last term, being restricted to just a handful of starts and rarely featuring at all after the turn of the year. Sammy eventually joined Luton Town on loan on the transfer deadline and went straight into the line-up. He brought a fresh enthusiasm to the proceedings and this quickly made him a crowd favourite. However, after just two appearances a training-ground accident brought his season to a premature close.
Portsmouth (From trainee on 15/2/1994) FL 100+60/11 FLC 7+5 FAC 2+3
Reading (£100,000 on 23/3/2000) FL 53+34/7 FLC 4+1 FAC 4+2 Others 6+1
Luton T (Loaned on 27/3/2003) FL 2

IMPEY Andrew (Andy) Rodney
Born: Hammersmith, 13 September 1971
Height: 5'8" **Weight:** 11.2
Club Honours: FLC '00
International Honours: E: U21-1
This right-sided winger or wing back was dogged by injury as the 2002-03 campaign got underway. However, Andy demonstrated his ability on the right of a back four once recapturing his first-team place for Leicester, before a groin injury suffered at Gillingham in mid-January once again interrupted his progress. He regained his place in the team after Frank Sinclair served a suspension, and played so well that Sinclair could not immediately gain a recall. Andy is often underrated but has proved a vital cog in the well-oiled Foxes' machine.
Queens Park R (£35,000 from Yeading on 14/6/1990) F/PL 177+10/13 FLC 15+1/3 FAC 7+3/1 Others 0+2/1
West Ham U (£1,300,000 on 26/9/1997) PL 25+2 FLC 4 FAC 3
Leicester C (£1,600,000 on 25/11/1998) P/FL 121+18/1 FLC 7+4 FAC 9+1 Others 2

INAMOTO Junichi
Born: Kagashima, Japan,, 18 September 1979
Height: 5'11" **Weight:** 11.13
International Honours: Japan: 40
After enjoying a successful World Cup Junichi proved a big hit at Fulham particularly in the early stages of the season. Signed on a 12-month loan deal from J-League side Gamba Osaka he shot to prominence in the Intertoto Cup final against Bologna, following up a

Junichi Inamoto (right)

magnificent solo goal in Italy with a hat-trick in the home leg. A regular at the start of the season he faded a little as the campaign wore on. An excellent ball winner and a good distributor of the ball, he was always in the thick of the action. Junichi continued to win international selection for Japan appearing against both Jamaica and Uruguay, when he scored. He committed himself to Fulham for a further year shortly before the end of the season.
Arsenal (loaned from Gamba Osaka, Japan on 24/7/2001) FLC 2 Others 0+2
Fulham (loaned from Gamba Osaka, Japan on 23/7/2002) PL 9+10/2 FLC 2 FAC 1+1 Others 3+7/4

INCE Clayton
Born: Trinidad, 13 July 1972
Height: 6'3" **Weight:** 14.2
International Honours: Trinidad & Tobago
Clayton finally established himself as first choice goalkeeper for Crewe Alexandra last term when he was a near ever-present in the first team. An extremely popular figure with the fans he takes both the game and his personal performances very seriously, and he helped to create a new club record of clean sheets in a season. Clayton continued to add to his total of caps for Trinidad & Tobago, featuring in the end-of-season friendlies against Kenya and South Africa..
Crewe Alex (£50,000 from Defence Force, Trinidad on 21/9/1999) FL 61+3 FLC 4 FAC 6

INCE Paul Emerson Carlyle
Born: Ilford, 21 October 1967
Height: 5'11" **Weight:** 12.2
Club Honours: CS '93, '94; FAC '90, '94; ECW '91; ESC '91; FLC '92; PL '93, '94
International Honours: E: 53; B-1; U21-2; Yth
This talented midfielder came to Molineux determined to show that he still had a lot to offer. It took a while for him to gain full fitness, starting just one of the first six games, but even then he was an asset to the team in terms of encouragement. He replaced Paul Butler as captain in October, and kept the role when the centre half returned. Paul scored his first Wolves goal on New Year's Day, and lashed in another four days later as Newcastle were defeated in the FA Cup. He continued to impress and his determined running led to both his team's goals in the first leg of the play-off semi-finals against Reading.
West Ham U (From apprentice on 18/7/1985) FL 66+6/7 FLC 9/3 FAC 8+2/1 Others 4/1

Manchester U (£1,000,000 on 14/9/1989) F/PL 203+3/25 FLC 23+1/2 FAC 26+1/1 Others 24/1 (£8,000,000 to Inter Milan, Italy on 13/7/1995)
Liverpool (£4,200,000 on 22/7/1997) PL 65/14 FLC 6/1 FAC 3/1 Others 7/1
Middlesbrough (£1,000,000 on 3/8/1999) PL 93/7 FLC 6/1 FAC 7/1
Wolverhampton W (Free on 6/8/2002) FL 35+2/2 FLC 1+1 FAC 3/1 Others 3

INGHAM Michael
Born: Preston, 9 September 1980
Height: 6'4" **Weight:** 13.12
International Honours: NI: U21-4; Yth
This promising Sunderland 'keeper spent a large part of the 2002-03 season out on loan. In the opening weeks of the season he joined Stockport as back up for Lee Jones, but his only appearance came in the Worthington Cup tie at Lincoln when he had little to do. Next stop was Darlington, where he covered for the injured Andy Collett and performed capably well. Finally, he spent the last three months on loan at York, where he impressed the fans and kept seven clean sheets in his 17 appearances.
Sunderland (£30,000 from Cliftonville on 28/7/1999) FLC 1
Carlisle U (Loaned on 1/10/1999) FL 7
Stockport Co (Loaned on 23/8/2002) FLC 1
Darlington (Loaned on 22/11/2002) FL 3
York C (Loaned on 24/1/2003) FL 17

INGIMARSSON Ivar
Born: Iceland, 20 August 1978
Height: 6'0" **Weight:** 12.7
International Honours: Iceland: 11; U21-14; Yth
This versatile player began the 2002-03 season for Wolves in a midfield role. He produced some dashing displays and often threatened a goal, before scoring in two successive league games, both at Selhurst Park. Ivar was looking good, but he seemed to lose his edge a little, and he faded from the scene after November. In February he joined Brighton on loan to assist the South Coast club's fight against relegation. Ivar turned out principally as one of three central defenders in a back-five line-up for the Seagulls, but also performed in midfield at the end of the campaign. He impressed with his simple but effective style and slotted easily into the team. Ivar continued to represent Iceland at international level during the campaign.
Torquay U (Loaned from IBV Vestmannaeyjar, Iceland on 21/10/1999) FL 4/1
Brentford (£150,000 from IBV Vestmannaeyjar, Iceland on 18/11/1999) FL

109+4/10 FLC 6 FAC 3 Others 13/1
Wolverhampton W (Free on 2/7/2002) FL 10+3/2 FLC 2
Brighton & Hove A (Loaned on 10/2/2003) FL 15

INGRAM Rae
Born: Manchester, 6 December 1974
Height: 5'11" **Weight:** 12.8
This tall left-sided defender began the 2002-03 season in the Port Vale team but was sent off at Swindon after coming on as a substitute and that turned out to be his last appearance of the campaign. Firstly it was injury that kept him out but then he was diagnosed with a strain of meningitis that left him very weak. Fortunately he was able to recover and will be hoping to resume his place in the side in 2003-04.
Manchester C (From trainee on 9/7/1993) P/FL 18+5 FLC 1 FAC 4
Macclesfield T (Free on 19/3/1998) FL 95+8/1 FLC 6 FAC 4+1 Others 1+1
Port Vale (Free on 2/7/2001) FL 25+3 FLC 2 FAC 2 Others 2

INNES Mark
Born: Glasgow, 27 September 1978
Height: 5'10" **Weight:** 12.1
Although Mark was injured for most of the 2002-03 campaign, he was overlooked when fit and did not return to the Chesterfield line-up until the final two games, when the club secured the points necessary for Second Division survival. Naturally left-footed, he has good vision and can create and defend with equal aplomb in a role on the left side of midfield.
Oldham Ath (From trainee on 10/10/1995) FL 52+21/1 FLC 4+3 FAC 4+2 Others 3+1
Chesterfield (Free on 19/12/2001) FL 27+6/2

INVINCIBILE Daniel (Danny)
Born: Australia, 31 March 1979
Height: 6'4" **Weight:** 12.2
International Honours: Australia: Sch
This pacy forward enjoyed another good season with Swindon Town in 2002-03, linking up well with fellow striker Sam Parkin. His speed and ability to run at defenders with the ball always caused problems, although his tally of goals was perhaps not as great as his talent suggested he was capable of. A modest and unassuming player and a great favourite with the Robins' fans, he was out of contract in the summer and at the time of writing seemed likely to move on.
Swindon T (Free from Marconi Stallions, Australia on 10/8/2000) FL 109+19/22 FLC 3+1/1 FAC 8/2 Others 4/2

IPOUA Gui (Guy)

Born: Douala, Cameroon, 14 January 1976
Height: 6'1" **Weight:** 12.0
Although at times Guy could be a frustrating striker, there is no doubt that his performances added to the Gillingham front line last term. He started the campaign in fine style by netting the winning goals against Wimbledon and Millwall, but the competition for places then became fiercer when Rod Wallace and Tommy Johnson became available. In March it was announced that his contract would not be renewed and consequently he did not figure in the final few games of the season.
Bristol Rov (Free from Seville, Spain on 7/8/1998) FL 15+9/3 FLC 1+1 FAC 3+1 Others 1
Scunthorpe U (Free on 27/8/1999) FL 60+15/23 FAC 5/4 Others 2
Gillingham (£25,000 on 19/3/2001) FL 42+40/12 FLC 4+2/1 FAC 2+4/2

IRELAND Craig

Born: Dundee, 29 November 1975
Height: 6'3" **Weight:** 13.9
This powerful defender formed a useful partnership with Nicky Fenton in the centre of defence for Notts County last season. Craig featured regularly in the line-up and scored his only goal of the campaign in the 3-1 win over Blackpool in April. Tall and able to dominate in the air, he is very effective when moving up to assist the attack at set pieces.
Aberdeen (From juniors on 5/10/1994) SLC 1
Dunfermline Ath (Free on 12/2/1996) SL 61+6/2 SLC 0+2 SC 0+1
Dundee (Free on 27/10/1999) SL 14/1 SC 1
Airdrieonians (Loaned on 12/10/2000) SL 12/2 Others 1
Notts Co (£50,000 on 2/2/2001) FL 77+3/2 FLC 2 FAC 1

IRIEKPEN Ezomo (Izzy)

Born: London, 14 May 1982
Height: 6'1" **Weight:** 12.4
Club Honours: FAYC '99

Guy Ipoua

International Honours: E: Yth
Izzy joined Leyton Orient on loan last October and scored after just 11 minutes of his debut, which for a central defender is no mean feat. He never let the side down when called upon before his return to Upton Park, and in the new year he went out on loan again, this time to Cambridge United. Here he formed an excellent central defensive partnership with his former colleague Stev Angus. Izzy was ever-present in his spell for the U's until an injury forced him to miss the last two matches. He was released by West Ham during the summer.
West Ham U (Free from trainee on 25/5/1999)
Leyton Orient (Loaned on 22/10/2002) FL 5/1 FAC 1 Others 2/1
Cambridge U (Loaned on 28/2/2003) FL 13/1

IRONS Kenneth (Kenny)

Born: Liverpool, 4 November 1970
Height: 5'10" **Weight:** 12.2
This central midfielder seemed to struggle to find his best form for Huddersfield Town last term following a change in formation. An experienced player, Kenny has the talent to break down opposition defences with his close control and accurate passing. He managed just one goal during the campaign, netting with a trademark free kick at home to Cheltenham.
Tranmere Rov (From trainee on 9/11/1989) FL 313+39/54 FLC 24+7/7 FAC 14+2/3 Others 28+3/3
Huddersfield T (£450,000 on 18/6/1999) FL 120+29/11 FLC 9/2 FAC 3 Others 7+1

IRWIN Joseph **Denis**

Born: Cork, 31 October 1965
Height: 5'8" **Weight:** 11.0
Club Honours: CS '93, '96, '97; ECWC '91; ESC '91; FLC '92; PL '93, '94, '96, '97, '99, '00, '01; FAC '94, '96; EC '99
International Honours: RoI: 56; B-1; U23-1; U21-3; Yth; Sch
This experienced full back had won so many honours at Manchester United that it was hoped he would bring the winning habit to Wolves. He made an early impression by scoring against Burnley, and he added another goal in October against Grimsby. Both were free kicks that former colleague David Beckham would have been proud of. Denis was also still capable of getting in many telling crosses. He was comfortable on either right or left flank and was still fit enough to appear in virtually every game. Denis was honoured by his fellow professionals with a place in the PFA's First Division team for the season.

Leeds U (From apprentice on 3/11/1983) FL 72/1 FLC 5 FAC 3 Others 2
Oldham Ath (Free on 22/5/1986) FL 166+1/4 FLC 19/3 FAC 13 Others 5
Manchester U (£625,000 on 20/6/1990) F/PL 356+12/22 FLC 28+3 FAC 42+1/7 Others 85+2/4
Wolverhampton W (Free on 25/7/2002) FL 43/2 FLC 1+1 FAC 4 Others 3

ISTEAD Steven Brian
Born: South Shields, 23 April 1986
Height: 5'8" **Weight:** 11.4
This young right winger produced some good displays for Hartlepool in the 2002-03 pre-season build up. He went on to make his first-team debut from the substitutes' bench against Bristol Rovers. At 16 years 187 days, he became Hartlepool's youngest-ever first-team player, and it was a debut that was almost capped with a goal. Shortly after he was given further substitute appearances, before returning to the juniors to continue his development.
Hartlepool U (Trainee) FL 0+6 FAC 0+1

IVERSEN Steffen
Born: Oslo, Norway, 10 November 1976
Height: 6'1" **Weight:** 11.10
Club Honours: FLC '99

International Honours: Norway: 39; U21-23; Yth
Back from injury and with fitness improving each week, Steffen grabbed a place in the Spurs strike force alongside new signing Robbie Keane. He looked lean and athletic and was particularly effective in the air. The 2003-04 season will be a crucial one for Steffen as he seeks to cement a place in the line-up following the departure of Les Ferdinand and Teddy Sheringham.
Tottenham H (£2,700,000 from Rosenborg, Norway, ex Nationalkam, on 7/12/1996) PL 112+31/36 FLC 11+4/6 FAC 10+5/4 Others 4/1

IWELUMO Christopher (Chris) Robert
Born: Coatbridge, 1 August 1978
Height: 6'3" **Weight:** 13.8
Chris made a major contribution to Stoke City retaining their First Division status last term. His fighting qualities were appreciated by the club's fans as he played on despite suffering knee and foot injuries that eventually required surgery during the summer break. Chris scored the Potters' 'Goal of the Season' with a superb volley against Sheffield Wednesday at the Britannia Stadium.

St Mirren (From juniors on 5/8/1996) SL 7+19 SLC 0+3/1 SC 1+1/1 Others 0+2 (Free to Aarhus Fremad, Denmark during 1998 close season)
Stoke C (£25,000 from AGF Aarhus, Denmark on 1/3/2000) FL 37+38/16 FLC 1+3/1 FAC 6+1/4 Others 4+1/1
York C (Loaned on 10/11/2000) FL 11+1/2 FAC 4/1
Cheltenham T (Loaned on 13/2/2001) FL 2+2/1

IZZET Kemal (Kem)
Born: Whitechapel, 29 September 1980
Height: 5'8" **Weight:** 10.5
This tigerish midfielder retained his 'Young Player of the Year' award for Colchester United last term. For the second year running, Kem was outstanding in the centre of the park, missing just one game. He covered just about every blade of grass, and contributed a valuable eight goals, including a brace to beat Chesterfield 2-0 in mid-October. Five months later and he hit the Spireites once more, this time at Saltergate, scoring the first in a 4-0 romp. Despite his lack of height, Kem continued to surprise defenders with his effectiveness in the air, which resulted in several headed goals. He has certainly emerged from the shadow of his more famous older brother Muzzy (Leicester City).
Charlton Ath (From trainee on 11/1/1999)
Colchester U (Signed on 22/3/2001) FL 84+7/12 FLC 3/1 FAC 2 Others 3/1

IZZET Mustafa (Muzzy) Kemal
Born: Mile End, 31 October 1974
Height: 5'10" **Weight:** 10.12
Club Honours: FLC '97, '00
International Honours: Turkey: 7
This right-footed midfielder looked to be one of the classiest midfielders in Division One last season, whether creating or scoring for Leicester City. Muzzy netted with a spectacular overhead kick from outside the penalty area at Grimsby, a strike that had the local press enthusing about the best-ever goal for the Foxes. Unusually, he continued to clock up a string of disciplinary points during the campaign. His drive from midfield was an important feature in the Foxes' late unbeaten run that effectively secured promotion and he earned a well-merited place in the PFA Division One team of the season.
Chelsea (From trainee on 19/5/1993)
Leicester C (£650,000 + on 28/3/1996) P/FL 235+4/36 FLC 24+1/4 FAC 15/4 Others 7/1

Denis Irwin

J

JAASKELAINEN Jussi

Born: Vaasa, Finland, 19 April 1975
Height: 6'3" **Weight:** 12.10
International Honours: Finland: 14;
U21-14; Yth

Bolton's only ever-present player in the Premiership last season, Jussi produced some outstanding performances to enhance his ever-growing reputation. One of the best shot stoppers in the domestic game, he was particularly impressive in the home games against Aston Villa and Chelsea and the away draw at Everton, when the match seemed almost to develop into a one-on-one battle between Jussi and Wayne Rooney. A regular in the Finland international squad (he is embroiled in a battle with Antti Niemi for the number one jersey), Jussi is without doubt the number one 'keeper at the Reebok and should continue to be so for some years to come.
Bolton W (£100,000 + from VPS Vassa, Finland, ex MPS, on 14/11/1997) P/FL 166+1 FLC 10 FAC 5 Others 2

JACK Michael Lawrence

Born: Carlisle, 2 October 1982
Height: 5'8" **Weight:** 10.5
The 2002-03 campaign proved to be a somewhat disappointing time for Michael after the promising start he had made in the previous season. Although he featured in several of Carlisle's early matches, he was then sidelined until the closing stages of the campaign. He eventually won a brief recall to the side due to an injury crisis. Michael was released at the end of the season.
Carlisle U (From trainee on 27/6/2001) FL 9+20 FLC 0+1 FAC 2+1 Others 0+1

JACK Rodney Alphonso

Born: Kingstown, St Vincent, 28 September 1972
Height: 5'7" **Weight:** 10.9
International Honours: St Vincent & Grenadines
Rodney featured regularly for Crewe Alexandra last term and despite missing a number of games through injury, he netted a total of 16 goals in all competitions. A versatile striker, he is best used in a role out wide, where his speed is most effective and he has the opportunity to shoot from distance. Rodney was released by the club in the summer and was reported to have signed for newly promoted Rushden & Diamonds.

Torquay U (Free from Lambada, St Vincent on 10/10/1995) FL 82+5/24 FLC 6/1 FAC 6 Others 6/3
Crewe Alex (£650,000 on 14/8/1998) FL 140+23/33 FLC 12/5 FAC 8+2 Others 3/4

JACKSON John (Johnnie)

Born: Camden, 15 August 1982
Height: 6'1" **Weight:** 13.0
International Honours: E: Yth
This young left-footed midfielder spent three months on loan at Swindon Town at the beginning of the 2002-03 season. His arrival helped the Robins to overcome a seven-game barren spell as he produced some solid, hard-working performances on the left-hand side of a five-man midfield. He scored two goals during his spell, both from well-taken free kicks. Johnnie subsequently joined Colchester United on loan in March. Billed as a cultured midfielder, he showed his

Jussi Jaaskelainen

versatility by operating as an effective left back. He made his U's debut in the 1-1 draw at Brentford, and went on to play eight games, helping the club to preserve their Division Two status for another season. He returned to Tottenham before the end of campaign due to injury.
Tottenham H *(From trainee on 23/3/2000)*
Swindon T *(Loaned on 13/9/2002) FL 12+1/1 FAC 2 Others 2/1*
Colchester U *(Loaned on 11/3/2003) FL 8*

JACKSON Mark Graham
Born: Barnsley, 30 September 1977
Height: 6'0" **Weight:** 11.12
International Honours: E: Yth
Scunthorpe's key central defender, Mark remained one of the first names on the team sheet last season, a result of his mature leadership, aerial dominance and solid defensive work. He missed two months of the campaign following a knee operation in October and was sidelined again in March with ankle trouble before

returning to help United make the Division Three play-offs.
Leeds U *(From trainee on 1/7/1995) PL 11+8 FAC 4*
Huddersfield T *(Loaned on 29/10/1998) FL 5*
Barnsley *(Loaned on 14/11/2000) FL 1*
Scunthorpe U *(Free on 9/3/2000) FL 111+5/4 FLC 2 FAC 10 Others 6*

JACKSON Matthew (Matt) Alan
Born: Leeds, 19 October 1971
Height: 6'1" **Weight:** 12.12
Club Honours: FAC '95; Div 2 '03
International Honours: E: U21-10; Sch
The central defender produced another season full of composed and authoritative displays at the heart of the Wigan Athletic defence last term. His partnership alongside Jason De Vos at the heart of the back four was the bedrock of the team's success in winning the Second Division title. A polished, competitive defender with excellent positional sense,

the campaign also saw him net his first goal for the Latics in the away match at Barnsley.
Luton T *(From juniors on 4/7/1990) FL 7+2 FLC 2 Others 0+1*
Preston NE *(Loaned on 27/3/1991) FL 3+1 Others 1*
Everton *(£600,000 on 18/10/1991) F/PL 132+6/4 FLC 9 FAC 14/2 Others 4*
Charlton Ath *(Loaned on 26/3/1996) FL 8 Others 2*
Queens Park R *(Loaned on 20/8/1996) FL 7*
Birmingham C *(Loaned on 31/10/1996) FL 10*
Norwich C *(£450,000 on 24/12/1996) FL 158+3/6 FLC 6 FAC 5*
Wigan Ath *(Free on 19/10/2001) FL 71/1 FLC 5 FAC 3 Others 2*

JACKSON Michael Douglas
Born: Cheltenham, 26 June 1980
Height: 5'7" **Weight:** 10.10
Michael signed a one-year contract for Swansea during the summer of 2002, but was unable to command a regular place in the starting line-up under either Nick Cusack or Brian Flynn. An energetic central midfielder, his only first-team outings were as a substitute against Southend United, and in the LDV Vans Trophy tie at Stevenage Borough. In October Michael's contract was paid up and he joined Dr Martens League club Bath City.
Cheltenham T *(From trainee on 1/8/1997) FL 2+7 FLC 0+2 FAC 0+1 Others 1*
Swansea C *(Free on 1/7/2002) FL 0+1 Others 0+1*

JACKSON Michael James
Born: Runcorn, 4 December 1973
Height: 6'0" **Weight:** 13.8
Club Honours: Div 2 '97, '00
International Honours: E: Yth
After starting Preston's first three games as one of a three-man central defence, Michael became a regular on the bench. His first goal for a year was the injury-time winner at Macclesfield in the Worthington Cup in a rare start, before he was loaned to Tranmere in December for some first-team action. He made six solid appearances for Rovers and eventually returned to Preston's first team in February with a 'Man of the Match' display against Nottingham Forest. Michael then retained his place alongside Chris Lucketti until the end of what was an up-and-down season for the uncomplicated defender.
Crewe Alex *(From trainee on 29/7/1992) FL 5 FLC 1 FAC 1 Others 2*
Bury *(Free on 13/8/1993) FL 123+2/9 FLC 9/1 FAC 3 Others 12*

Mark Jackson

Preston NE (£125,000 on 26/3/1997) FL
96+6/16 FLC 15/2 FAC 13 Others 8
Tranmere Rov (Loaned on 18/12/2002) FL 6

JACKSON Richard
Born: Whitby, 18 April 1980
Height: 5'8" **Weight:** 10.12
Given a run in the Derby County line-up
at the end of the season, Richard's
increase in confidence was clearly seen.
He was in danger of being typecast as a
stalwart in the reserves, but reinstated
coach Billy McEwan is a strong supporter
of a right back who is neat on the ball
and ready to break into attack. Colin
Addison, manager of Scarborough when
Derby signed Richard, described him as a
young Denis Irwin. If he can improve his
final ball, that description may not be too
fanciful. A regular place is the next aim
after he was offered a new contract.
Scarborough (From trainee on 27/3/1998) FL
21+1 FLC 2
Derby Co (£30,000 + on 25/3/1999) P/FL
23+9 FLC 1

JACOBS Wayne Graham
Born: Sheffield, 3 February 1969
Height: 5'9" **Weight:** 11.2
A reliable and experienced defender,
Wayne remains the longest-serving player
on the books at Bradford City. He rarely
enjoyed long spells in the side during the
2002-03 season due to a number of
niggling injury problems. He missed the
beginning of the campaign after suffering
a hamstring strain in pre-season, but
returned to the starting line-up in
September before going on to make nine
successive appearances. Despite the lack
of starts, Wayne still managed to be an
indispensable member of the squad.
Sheffield Wed (From apprentice on
3/1/1987) FL 5+1 FLC 3 Others 1
Hull C (£27,000 on 25/3/1988) FL 127+2/4
FLC 7 FAC 8 Others 6
Rotherham U (Free on 5/8/1993) FL 40+2/2
FLC 4 FAC 1 Others 2
Bradford C (Free on 5/8/1994) P/FL
278+13/12 FLC 17+2 FAC 13/2 Others 7

JAGIELKA Philip (Phil)
Nikodem
Born: Manchester, 17 August 1982
Height: 5'11" **Weight:** 12.8
International Honours: E: U21-2; Yth
Phil had an excellent season for Sheffield
United, playing consistently well in a
variety of roles. He began in midfield but
injuries to Robert Page and Steve Yates
meant a move to the central defence
where he used his height and anticipation
to good effect and was quick to cover

when required. He spent much of mid-
season as a right wing back showing
speed and accuracy in the tackle, and the
ability to use the ball well when coming
forward. Phil reverted to central defence
towards the end of the season, where,
because of his greater pace, he was
preferred to Shaun Murphy. He played for
England U20 in the Toulon tournament
and in April was voted the Supporters'
Club 'Young Player of the Year'.
Sheffield U (From trainee on 8/5/2000) FL
58+23/3 FLC 11/1 FAC 5/1 Others 3

JAGIELKA Stephen (Steve)
Born: Manchester, 10 March 1978
Height: 5'8" **Weight:** 11.5
Steve was still recovering from cruciate
ligament surgery in the early part of the
2002-03 season and it was not until
November that he returned to action for
Shrewsbury. However, he struggled to
regain his best form and was used as
often from the bench as he appeared in
the starting line-up. A right-sided midfield
player with excellent pace and control, he
scored three vital goals, including two in
the March victory over Rochdale that
turned out to be Shrewsbury's last in the
Football League. Steve is the older brother
of Sheffield United's Phil Jagielka.
Stoke C (From trainee on 15/7/1996)
Shrewsbury T (Free on 30///1997) FL
89+76/17 FLC 4+3 FAC 5+3/1 Others 3+4/1

JAMES David Benjamin
Born: Welwyn Garden City, 1 August
1970
Height: 6'5" **Weight:** 14.5
Club Honours: FAYC '89; FLC '95
International Honours: E: 15; B-1; U21-
10; Yth
Despite playing behind a shaky West Ham
defence for most of the 2002-03 season
David gave many commanding
goalkeeping displays and although prone
to the odd mistake he never lost his
confidence. He was outstanding against
Arsenal at Highbury and also at West
Bromwich in February, when he pulled off
a string of remarkable saves to help the
Hammers gain a vital win against their
fellow relegation candidates. After
gaining a further four England caps he
now has a serious claim to be regarded as
England's number one 'keeper.
Watford (From trainee on 1/7/1988) FL 89
FLC 6 FAC 2 Others 1
Liverpool (£1,000,000 on 6/7/1992) PL
213+1 FLC 22 FAC 19 Others 22
Aston Villa (£1,800,000 on 23/6/1999) PL
67 FLC 6 FAC 8 Others 4
West Ham U (£3,500,000 on 17/7/2001) PL
64 FLC 2 FAC 5

JAMES Kevin Ernest
Born: Southwark, 3 January 1980
Height: 5'9" **Weight:** 10.7
After showing fine form for Gillingham's
reserve team, Kevin gained a regular first-
team spot last September, only to lose his
place two months later. He then suffered
a knee injury in February that required
surgery on his cartilage and left him on
the sidelines. A pacy midfielder or wing
back, Kevin won the Gills' 'Goal of the
Season' award for his wonderful effort
against Watford in October.
Charlton Ath (From trainee on 2/7/1998)
Gillingham (Free on 21/8/2000) FL 6+26/3
FLC 1+1 FAC 1

JANSEN Matthew (Matt)
Brooke
Born: Carlisle, 20 October 1977
Height: 5'11" **Weight:** 10.13
Club Honours: AMC '97; FLC '02
International Honours: E: U21-6; Yth
Matt had the misfortune to suffer a
serious head injury in a motorcycle
accident in the summer of 2002 and it
was not until October that he returned to
first-team action for Blackburn. He
subsequently made occasional
appearances as his recuperation
continued, and netted two goals in the FA
Cup third round victory at Aston Villa. In
February he was loaned to Coventry City
where his skills as a striker were a breath
of fresh air to Sky Blues fans. He scored
opportunist goals against Leicester and
Ipswich and after returning to Ewood
Park he featured on the bench in the final
match of the season at Tottenham.
Carlisle U (From trainee on 18/1/1996) FL
26+16/10 FLC 4+1/3 FAC 1+3 Others 3+3
Crystal Palace (£1,000,000 + on 12/2/1998)
P/FL 23+3/10 FLC 4 FAC 0+1 Others 2
Blackburn Rov (£4,100,000 on 19/1/1999)
P/FL 91+32/40 FLC 8+4/8 FAC 8+4/4
Others 0+1
Coventry C (Loaned on 13/2/2003) FL 8+1/2

JARRETT Jason Lee Mee
Born: Bury, 14 September 1979
Height: 6'0" **Weight:** 12.4
Club Honours: Div 2 '03
A regular in the Wigan Athletic line-up
until the turn of the year, this all-action
player showed a liking for the hard work
and decisive tackling required for the
central-midfield position. Playing
alongside Tony Dinning, Jason looked
comfortable on the ball and benefited
from the freedom the system afforded to
push forward, netting his first goal for the
club in the Worthington Cup win over
Northampton Town. Often used later on

as a substitute, he was a valuable squad member who never let the side down when called upon.
Blackpool *(From trainee on 3/7/1998) FL 2 FAC 0+1 Others 1*
Wrexham *(Free on 8/10/1999) FL 1*
Bury *(Free on 13/7/2000) FL 45+17/4 FLC 0+1 FAC 2+2 Others 3/1*
Wigan Ath *(£75,000 on 27/3/2002) FL 30+10 FLC 5/1 FAC 3 Others 1+1/1*

JARVIS Ryan Robert
Born: Fakenham, 11 July 1986
Height: 5'11" **Weight:** 11.0
International Honours: E: Yth
This Norfolk-born youngster became the youngest-ever player in Norwich City's 100-year history when he came on as a substitute at Walsall in April, aged 16 years 282 days. He followed that up with successive starts against Wolves and Leicester, before ending the season as part of the England U17 UEFA Championship squad in Portugal. An intelligent and thoughtful striker with quick feet and the ability to do the unexpected, Ryan was not at all overawed by his introduction to senior football.
Norwich C *(Trainee) FL 2+1*

JASZCZUN Antony (Tommy) John
Born: Kettering, 16 September 1977
Height: 5'10" **Weight:** 10.10
Club Honours: AMC '02
This left-sided defender was in the Blackpool line-up for the first part of the 2002-03 season but was absent between November and April as a result of injury. He is a hard-working player who likes to get forward to support the attack.
Aston Villa *(From trainee on 5/7/1996) FLC 0+1*
Blackpool *(£30,000 on 20/1/2000) FL 102+13 FLC 7 FAC 4/1 Others 11/1*

JAVARY Jean-Phillipe
Born: Montpellier, France, 10 January 1978
Height: 6'0" **Weight:** 12.6
International Honours: France: Yth (UEFA-U18 '96)
Fully involved for Sheffield United in the pre-season games, Jean-Phillipe spent much of last season in the Blades' successful reserve team or on the first-team bench. The combative midfielder made just two starts but, whenever called upon, he was always looking to be involved, working hard in both attack and defence. In January he spent a month on loan at Walsall but, although on the bench, he did not make a first-team

appearance. He will hope to see more senior action in 2003-04.
Raith Rov *(Signed from Montpellier, France, ex ASOA Valence, RCD Espanyol, on 20/1/2000) SL 11+1*
Brentford *(Free on 18/8/2000) FL 4+2 FLC 2 Others 1*
Plymouth Arg *(Free on 28/2/2001) FL 4 (Freed during 2001 close season)*
Sheffield U *(Free, via trials at Raith Rov and Bradford C on 15/3/2002) FL 8+5/1 FAC 0+1*

JEFFERS Francis
Born: Liverpool, 25 January 1981
Height: 5'10" **Weight:** 10.7
Club Honours: FAYC '98
International Honours: E: 1; U21-13; Yth; Sch
Francis has never been able to command a regular place in the line-up since his move to Arsenal, although a series of injuries badly affected his availability last season. A player with unique intelligence as a striker, it is well known that other players at the club like playing with him. He has a good turn of speed going forward, and excellent delivery skills make him a provider of goals. As a striker, Francis is an excellent goal poacher. He did well for England U21s, scoring twice against Slovakia in October and securing a hat-trick against Macedonia a few days later.
Everton *(From trainee on 20/2/1998) PL 37+12/18 FLC 2+2/1 FAC 6+1/1*
Arsenal *(£8,000,000 + on 27/6/2001) PL 4+18/4 FLC 1/1 FAC 7+1/3 Others 1+6*

JELLEYMAN Gareth Anthony
Born: Holywell, 14 November 1980
Height: 5'10" **Weight:** 10.6
International Honours: W: U21-1; Yth
A pacy attacking full back who enjoys nothing more than pushing down the flank, Gareth looked to have finally established himself as a first-team regular with Peterborough United last term. He clearly benefited from Posh's tactics of playing five at the back and started in 30 of the 46 Second Division games. After having a wretched time with injuries over the previous two seasons he will be looking to consolidate his position in 2003-04.
Peterborough U *(From trainee on 5/8/1998) FL 56+14 FAC 3+2 Others 8+1*

JEMSON Nigel Bradley
Born: Hutton, 10 October 1969
Height: 5'11" **Weight:** 12.10
Club Honours: FLC '90; AMC '96
International Honours: E: U21-1
Nigel is a very experienced striker who is

always difficult to play against! He wins and holds the ball up very well and, despite lacking a little pace, he still scored a total of 17 goals in all competitions during the season. The highlights will surely be the brace that ensured back-page headlines in January as Shrewsbury caused a major upset by beating Everton 2-1, and the hat-trick he netted at Bury in August. Out of contract in the summer, the possibility of him playing a part in the fight for a return to Division Three was in the balance at the time of writing.
Preston NE *(From trainee on 6/7/1987) FL 28+4/8 FAC 2/1 Others 5+1/5*
Nottingham F *(£150,000 on 24/3/1988) FL 45+2/13 FLC 9/4 FAC 3+1/3 Others 1*
Bolton W *(Loaned on 23/12/1988) FL 4+1*
Preston NE *(Loaned on 15/3/1989) FL 6+3/2 Others 2/1*
Sheffield Wed *(£800,000 on 17/9/1991) F/PL 26+25/9 FLC 3+4/1 FAC 3+3/1 Others 2+2/1*
Grimsby T *(Loaned on 10/9/1993) FL 6/2 Others 1*
Notts Co *(£300,000 on 8/9/1994) FL 7+7/1 FLC 2+2/1 Others 1*
Watford *(Loaned on 12/1/1995) FL 3+1*
Rotherham U *(Loaned on 15/2/1996) FL 16/5 Others 3/4*
Oxford U *(£60,000 on 23/7/1996) FL 68/27 FLC 12/6 FAC 2*
Bury *(£100,000 on 5/2/1998) FL 17+12/1 FLC 0+2 FAC 0+1*
Ayr U *(Free on 21/7/1999) SL 9+3/5 SLC 1*
Oxford U *(Free on 27/1/2000) FL 13+5*
Shrewsbury T *(Free on 21/7/2000) FL 107+2/36 FLC 4/1 FAC 6/5 Others 8/1*

JENAS Jermaine Anthony
Born: Nottingham, 18 February 1983
Height: 5'11" **Weight:** 11.2
International Honours: E: 3; U21-7; Yth
In his first full season at Newcastle 'JJ' became a key component of the midfield with performances that belied his tender years. Comfortable on the ball with good pace, he reads the game well and looks increasingly at home at the top level. After going 36 games before his first goal for Newcastle he hit a golden patch in January with four in the next five, including a stunning strike at West Ham, an effort he matched against Manchester United in April. An U21 international, he progressed to make his full England debut as a second-half substitute against Australia in February when his performance earned him the 'Man of the Match' award. Jermaine's talent was recognised by his selection as the PFA 'Young Player of the Year', and he was

lso chosen as Tyne Tees TV's 'North East
oung Player of the Year'.
ottingham F *(From trainee on 19/2/2000)*
L 29/4 FLC 2 FAC 2
ewcastle U *(£5,000,000 on 5/2/2002) PL
9+15/6 FAC 1/1 Others 8*

ENKINS Lee David
orn: Pontypool, 28 June 1979
leight: 5'9" **Weight:** 11.0
lub Honours: Div 3 '00
nternational Honours: W: U21-9; Yth;
ch

ee started the 2002-03 season at right
ving back for Swansea, with occasional
ppearances in midfield, fully recovered
om the injury problems that had
ffected him in the previous campaign.
le featured regularly in the line-up and
ecame one of the club's most consistent
efenders towards the end of the season
when the pressure was on to avoid
elegation.
wansea C *(From trainee on 20/12/1996) FL
17+41/3 FLC 3+1 FAC 3+1 Others 9*

ENKINS Neil
orn: Carshalton, 6 January 1982
leight: 5'6" **Weight:** 10.8
nternational Honours: E: Yth

eil proved to be a more-than-useful
cquisition for Southend United in the
002-03 campaign. Equally at home at
eft back or as a wide-left midfielder, he
ormed a good understanding on the
ank with Damon Searle and the pair
roduced many goal-scoring
pportunities. Neil also chipped in scoring
even times, including a debut goal at
lull which led to a Blues fight back from
wo down to secure a valuable point in
njury time.
Vimbledon *(From trainee on 17/7/2000)*
outhend U *(Free on 7/8/2002) FL 29+5/7
LC 1 FAC 1+1*

ENKINS Stephen (Steve)
:obert
orn: Merthyr Tydfil, 16 July 1972
leight: 5'11" **Weight:** 12.3
lub Honours: AMC '94
nternational Honours: W: 16; U21-2;
th

teve stood out from the rest of the
rowd as one of the better talents in the
econd Division last term. Dependable
nd confident, the composed defender
ooked consistent at the back for
luddersfield, as well as leading the attack
own the flanks. However, financial
onsiderations brought a sale to Cardiff
nd he made his debut at Stockport on St
avid's Day. Steve was due to be among

the substitutes, but moved into the team
when Rhys Weston injured his back
during the warm-up. He was then carried
off following a clash of heads when he
'swallowed' his tongue. Thanks to the
speedy actions of physio Clive Goodyear,
Steve recovered and made three more
first-team appearances.
Swansea C *(From trainee on 1/7/1990) FL
155+16/11 FLC 12+1 FAC 10+1 Others 26*
Huddersfield T *(£275,000 on 3/11/1995) FL
257+1/4 FLC 18 FAC 14 Others 5*
Birmingham C *(Loaned on 15/12/2000) FL 3
FLC 1*
Cardiff C *(Free on 5/2/2003) FL 4*

JENSEN Claus William
Born: Nykobing, Denmark, 29 April 1977
Height: 5'11" **Weight:** 12.6
International Honours: Denmark: 23;
U21-17

Claus was once again one of Charlton
Athletic's most important players in 2002-
03. He has developed a great partnership
with Scott Parker in the Addicks' midfield
and most of the team's attacking moves
stemmed from one or the other. He
scored six goals, including a brilliant 35-
yarder at Old Trafford, a truly spectacular
effort in the home fixture against
Manchester United and a great volley at
West Ham. Claus can run with ease with
the ball at his feet and is not afraid to hit
a 40-yard pass. He is also extremely
dangerous at corners and set pieces, with
the ability to bend a free kick into the
goal from the edge of the penalty area.
He played regularly for Denmark and hit a
hat-trick in the 4-1 win over Egypt in
February.
Bolton W *(£1,600,000 from Lyngby,
Denmark, ex Naestved, on 14/7/1998) FL
85+1/8 FLC 12/2 FAC 6 Others 5*
Charlton Ath *(£4,000,000 on 21/7/2000) PL
85+6/12 FLC 5 FAC 3*

JENSEN Niclas
Born: Denmark, 17 August 1974
Height: 5'11" **Weight:** 12.3
Club Honours: Div 1 '02
International Honours: Denmark: 21

Niclas was a regular for Manchester City
last term and scored only one goal,
although it proved to be one of the goals
of the season: a tremendous left-foot
volley from around 30 yards against Leeds
United. Firmly established in the line-up at
left back, he was excellent at keeping
control in tight situations and also
displayed the knack of finding players
with inch-perfect passes. After showing a
definite improvement in his play at club

level, Niclas also continued to represent
Denmark at international level.
Manchester C *(£700,000 from FC
Copenhagen, Denmark, ex Lyngby, on
16/1/2002) P/FL 48+3/2 FLC 2 FAC 3*

JEPHCOTT Avun Cyd
Born: Coventry, 16 October 1983
Height: 6'2" **Weight:** 14.0
A product of Coventry City's youth
academy, Avun made one substitute
appearance near the end of the season
after a very impressive spell on loan at Dr
Martens League club Tamworth. A tall
striker with a good touch, he was a
regular for the reserves and was awarded
a one-year contract in the spring.
Coventry C *(From trainee on 19/2/2003) FL
0+1*

JERVIS David (Dave) John
Born: Retford, 18 January 1982
Height: 5'9" **Weight:** 11.3
Dave started the 2002-03 season in the
left-back position for Mansfield, but
received a foot injury in the 5-0 defeat by
Crewe in August and was sidelined for
several weeks. He was fully fit again by
November, but his chances were limited
and in January his contract was paid up.
Dave moved to Unibond League outfit
Gainsborough Trinity soon afterwards and
later had a trial with Kettering.
Mansfield T *(From trainee on 3/7/2000) FL
21+9 FAC 2+1 Others 0+1*

JESS Eoin
Born: Aberdeen, 13 December 1970
Height: 5'9" **Weight:** 11.10
Club Honours: SLC '89
International Honours: S: 18; B-2; U21-
14

Eoin had a disappointing 2002-03
campaign after joining Nottingham Forest
just days before the start of the season.
An attacking midfield player, he was an
instant hit with the fans after scoring on
his debut against Preston North End.
However, he was unable to hold down a
regular place in the starting line-up and
made many of his appearances from the
substitutes' bench.
Aberdeen *(Free from Glasgow R juniors on
13/11/1987) SL 167+34/50 SLC 19+2/4 SC
14+2/3 Others 8+2/6*
Coventry C *(£1,750,000 on 24/2/1996) PL
28+11/1 FLC 1 FAC 4/2*
Aberdeen *(£700,000 on 3/7/1997) SL
108+3/29 SLC 8+1/1 SC 6/1*
Bradford C *(Free on 29/12/2000) P/FL
60+2/17 FLC 2 FAC 2*
Nottingham F *(Free on 9/8/2002) FL
17+15/3 FLC 0+1*

JEVONS Philip (Phil)
Born: Liverpool, 1 August 1979
Height: 5'11" **Weight:** 11.10
Club Honours: FAYC '98
After undergoing surgery in the summer to solve a long-standing cartilage problem, Phil returned to action to score Grimsby's goal in a pre-season friendly at Hull. However, the lively striker was out of favour and only managed a handful of outings from the substitutes' bench for the Mariners. He subsequently joined Hull in a season-long loan deal in September. Here he linked up again with former Everton team mates Michael Branch,

Michael Price and Carl Regan. Phil's pace and movement off the ball posed plenty of problems for Third Division defences but he lost his place in the squad in the New Year when opportunities became more limited following the arrival of Jamie Forrester. He returned to Grimsby at the end of the term with a year of his Mariners' contract to run.
Everton (From trainee on 10/11/1997) PL 2+6 FLC 1
Grimsby T (£150,000 + on 26/7/2001) FL 25+9/6 FLC 4/2 FAC 2
Hull C (Loaned on 5/9/2002) FL 13+11/3 FLC 1 FAC 1

JIHAI Sun
Born: Dalian, China, 30 September 1977
Height: 5'10" **Weight:** 10.12
International Honours: China: 62
This right-sided defender mostly featured for Manchester City at right back or right wing back last season. A hugely committed player, he showed great enthusiasm going forward and scored two Premiership goals, netting at Birmingham and at Sunderland in December. He generally kept his place in the line-up until the arrival of David Sommeil during the January transfer window, and will be looking to return to the side in the 2003-04 season.
Crystal Palace (£500,000 from Dalian Wanda, China on 10/9/1998) FL 22+1 FLC 1 FAC 1 (£500,000 to Dalian Wanda, China on 27/7/1999)
Manchester C (£2,000,000 on 26/2/2002) P/FL 27+8/2 FLC 2 FAC 1

JOACHIM Julian Kevin
Born: Boston, 20 September 1974
Height: 5'6" **Weight:** 12.2
International Honours: E: U21-9; Yth; (UEFA-U18 '93)
Injuries again blighted Julian's career at Coventry last term. He started the first four games of the season but then suffered a heel injury that kept him out until February. He then started six successive games and scored twice before being made available for transfer.
Leicester C (From trainee on 15/9/1992) F/P 77+22/25 FLC 7+2/3 FAC 4+1/1 Others 4+2
Aston Villa (£1,500,000 on 24/2/1996) PL 90+51/39 FLC 10+1/3 FAC 8+4/2 Others 6+3/1
Coventry C (Signed on 11/7/2001) FL 14+13/3 FLC 1 FAC 1

JOB Josephe-Desire
Born: Lyon, France, 1 December 1977
Height: 5'10" **Weight:** 11.3
International Honours: Cameroon: 43 (ANC '00)
Joseph-Desire had a mixed season at Middlesbrough last term. He came off the transfer list in mid-September but at the end of November he suffered a slight fracture of the skull in Boro's 1-0 defeat at West Bromwich Albion following an horrific collision. He was getting regular Premiership football until Juninho's return to full fitness, which meant that Joseph-Desire had to settle for a place on the substitutes' bench. The pacy striker eventually found himself competing with a host of talent for one of the forward-line places at the Riverside. He continued to feature for Cameroon and was a

Eoin Jess

ember of the team narrowly defeated y France in the Confederations Cup final ver the summer.

iiddlesbrough *(£3,000,000 from RC Lens, ance, ex Lyon, on 7/8/2000) PL 33+11/7 .C 1+2 FAC 1*

OBSON Richard Ian
orn: Holderness, 9 May 1963
eight: 6'1" **Weight:** 13.5
lub Honours: Div 2 '91
nternational Honours: E: B-2
ichard was appointed Rochdale's
*eserve-team player-coach in the summer,

but when new signing Steve Macauley was injured the veteran central defender regained his place in the side. After another spell back in the reserves, an injury crisis saw Dale call up both Richard and his young partner Simon Grand and they helped the team recover after a string of mid-season defeats with a seven-match unbeaten run. Richard remained on call when needed for the first team as he approached his 40th birthday in May.
Watford *(£22,000 from Burton A on 5/11/1982) FL 26+2/4 FLC 2 FAC 0+1 Others 5+1*

Hull C *(£40,000 on 7/2/1985) FL 219+2/17 FLC 12 FAC 13/1 Others 9*
Oldham Ath *(£460,000 on 30/8/1990) P/FL 188+1/10 FLC 19/1 FAC 13 Others 4*
Leeds U *(£1,000,000 on 26/10/1995) PL 22/1 FLC 3 FAC 1*
Southend U *(Loaned on 23/1/1998) FL 8/1*
Manchester C *(Free on 12/3/1998) FL 49+1/4 FLC 4+1 FAC 2*
Watford *(Loaned on 7/11/2000) FL 2*
Tranmere Rov *(Free on 28/12/2000) FL 17 FAC 5*
Rochdale *(Free on 28/9/2001) FL 49+2/3 FLC 1 FAC 6 Others 4*

JOHANSSON Jonatan (JJ)
Lillebror
Born: Stockholm, Sweden, 16 August 1975
Height: 6'1" **Weight:** 12.8
Club Honours: SPL '99, '00; SLC '99
International Honours: Finland: 51
The 2002-03 campaign was a rather disappointing time for JJ, who was unable to rediscover either his form or his goal-scoring touch on a regular basis and only started ten Premiership games for Charlton Athletic. The Finnish international striker is very quick, possesses a powerful shot and is able to set up goals for other players using his pace and ability to turn defenders. JJ can also play wide on the left, a position he sometimes occupies for his international side, and is an excellent crosser of the ball. He scored twice in the home game against Aston Villa after coming on as a late substitute, but his best game of the season was probably the FA Cup tie against Exeter City when he hit two spectacular goals with overhead kicks.
Glasgow R *(From FC Flora Tallinn, Estonia, ex TPS Turku, on 13/8/1997) SL 22+25/14 SLC 4/1 SC 2+4/3 Others 9+8/7*
Charlton Ath *(£3,250,000 + on 1/8/2000) PL 58+34/19 FLC 5/3 FAC 3+1/2*

JOHANSSON Nils-Eric
Born: Stockholm, Sweden, 13 January 1980
Height: 6'1" **Weight:** 12.7
Club Honours: FLC '02
International Honours: Sweden: 3; U21-21
This young Blackburn defender was regularly switched between left back and a more central defensive role last term before eventually losing his place midway through the campaign. Quick, strong in the tackle and always unflappable, he will be aiming to feature more often in 2003-04. Previously a regular for Sweden at U21 level, Nils-Eric stepped up to make his full international debut when coming

un Jihai

on as a substitute in the friendly against Russia last August and went on to win further caps against Portugal and Czech Republic.

Blackburn Rov *(£2,700,000 from Nuremburg, Germany, ex Brommapojkarna, AIK Solna, Bayern Munich, on 5/10/2001) PL 34+16 FLC 7+1/1 FAC 4+1/1 Others 4*

JOHN Stern
Born: Trinidad, 30 October 1976
Height: 6'1" **Weight:** 12.12

Stern John

International Honours: Trinidad & Tobago
Stern finished the 2002-03 campaign as leading scorer for Birmingham City with a tally of nine goals in all competitions. His hold-up play and ball control were certainly up to Premiership standard, while his eye for a chance often saw him on the end of attacking moves. He bagged a hat-trick in the Worthington Cup tie at Leyton Orient and followed up three days later with a brace in the 2-1 win at West Ham. However, a knee injury

disrupted his good start to the season and he had to battle for a place thereafter. Stern also added a further three caps for Trinidad & Tobago, captaining the side in their Gold Cup qualifying games and finding the net in each of his appearances.

Nottingham F *(£1,500,000 + from Columbus Crew, USA on 22/11/1999) FL 49+23/18 FLC 3/2 FAC 4+1*
Birmingham C *(Free on 8/2/2002) P/FL 35+10/12 FLC 1/3 FAC 0+1/1 Others 3/1*

JOHN-BAPTISTE Alexander (Alex) Aaron
Born: Sutton in Ashfield, 31 January 1986
Height: 5'11" **Weight:** 11.7
Alex became another youth-team regular to be given a senior debut by Mansfield Town last season when he replaced the injured Rhys Day. He did not look out of place in the centre of the Stags' back four and gave some very confident and assured performances. The promising youngster was selected by the Stags' Supporters' Association as 'Youth Team Player of the Year'.

Mansfield T *(From trainee on 5/2/2003) FL*

JOHNROSE Leonard (Lenny)
Born: Preston, 29 November 1969
Height: 5'10" **Weight:** 12.6
Club Honours: Div 2 '97
Despite having been released by Burnley at the end of the 2001-02 campaign, Lenny made a number of appearances in the early part of last season. However, he was unable to win a contract at Turf Moor and in October he joined Bury on a month-to-month deal. Unfortunately, the popular midfield battler spent most of his first month at the club on the treatment table following a hamstring injury and although he displayed his usual tenacity and tough tackling, he was released in January. He subsequently joined Swansea City on a non-contract basis where he showed up well and netted three crucial goals to help the club avoid the drop into the Conference.

Blackburn Rov *(From trainee on 16/6/1988) FL 20+22/11 FLC 2+1/1 FAC 0+3 Others 2*
Preston NE *(Loaned on 21/1/1992) FL 1+2/*
Hartlepool U *(£50,000 on 28/2/1992) FL 59+7/11 FLC 5+1/4 FAC 5/1 Others 5*
Bury *(Signed on 7/12/1993) FL 181+7/19 FL 16+2/2 FAC 9/1 Others 9/1*
Burnley *(£225,000 on 12/2/1999) FL 51+27/4 FLC 2 FAC 1+2/1 Others 1*
Bury *(Free on 21/10/2002) FL 5+1 Others 2*
Swansea C *(Free on 24/1/2003) FL 15/3*

OHNSEN Jean **Ronny**
rn: Norway, 10 June 1969
ight: 6'2" **Weight:** 13.2
ub Honours: PL '97, '99, '01; CS '97; C '99; EC '99
ternational Honours: Norway: 56
ter joining Aston Villa in the summer of 02 Ronny made a surprise debut ainst Charlton in midfield. He was tially forced to operate in the centre of e park because of injury problems, fore having the chance to impress at e back. Unfortunately he himself was o affected by a string of injuries during e campaign to his thigh, ankle and ee. When he was not in the treatment om, Ronny was always in contention for lace in the centre of defence playing ngside Olof Mellberg or Steve aunton. He was as solid and consistent ever and featured again for Norway ring the campaign.
***anchester U** (£1,200,000 from Besiktas, key, ex Lyn, Lillestrom, on 26/7/1996) PL +14/7 FLC 3 FAC 8+2/1 Others 35+3/1*
***ton Villa** (Free on 29/8/2002) PL 25+1 C 3*

OHNSON Andrew (Andy)
rn: Bedford, 10 February 1981
ight: 5'9" **Weight:** 9.7
ternational Honours: E: Yth
dy followed his former boss Trevor ancis to Crystal Palace in the summer of 02 and made a useful contribution to e Eagles campaign. He finished the ason as the club's leading scorer with goals, including hat-tricks in successive mes against Brighton and Walsall in tober. However, the pacy young striker as stretchered off with a pulled mstring against Wimbledon in March d the injury brought his campaign to a emature close.
***mingham C** (From juniors on 11/3/1998) 44+39/8 FLC 6+9/5 FAC 1 Others 1+3*
***ystal Palace** (£750,000 on 5/8/2002) FL +1/11 FLC 3/3 FAC 3*

OHNSON Andrew (Andy)
mes
rn: Bristol, 2 May 1974
ight: 6'0" **Weight:** 13.0
ub Honours: Div 1 '98
ternational Honours: W: 10; E: Yth
is attacking midfielder worked tirelessly West Bromwich Albion last term, but uggled at times through injury. A oken toe, suffered when his colleague e Hughes jumped on his foot after he d grabbed a last gasp equaliser at me to Bolton in early February, kept him out of the side at a crucial stage of the campaign when Albion's squad was already rather depleted. Andy was selected by Wales on three occasions, playing exceedingly well in the 2-0 win over Finland and likewise against Croatia in Zagreb.
***Norwich C** (From trainee on 4/3/1992) F/PL 56+10/13 FLC 6+1/2 FAC 2*
***Nottingham F** (£2,200,000 on 4/7/1997) P/FL 102+17/9 FLC 6+1/1 FAC 2*
***West Bromwich A** (£200,000 on 19/9/2001) P/FL 58+6/5 FAC 6/1*

JOHNSON Damien Michael
Born: Lisburn, 18 November 1978
Height: 5'9" **Weight:** 11.2
Club Honours: FLC '02
International Honours: NI: 1624; U21-11; Yth
Damien was the most consistent player for Birmingham City in the first-half of the 2002-03 campaign, and a highlight was undoubtedly scoring the club's 'Goal of the Season' with a curler against Leeds in August. However, a hamstring injury then knocked him off his stride and he sometimes struggled to find his best form. A versatile player who featured on either flank, and often moved to right back during a game, he proved an unsung hero for the Blues with some fine dribbling skills allied to a quick turn of pace and lots of energy.

Andy Johnson (West Bromwich Albion)

Blackburn Rov *(From trainee on 2/2/1996)*
*P/FL 43+17/3 FLC 12+3/1 FAC 3+4 Others
0+1*
Nottingham F *(Loaned on 29/1/1998) FL 5+1*
Birmingham C *(Signed on 8/3/2002) P/FL
33+5/2 FLC 0+1 FAC 1 Others 1*

JOHNSON David Anthony
Born: Kingston, Jamaica, 15 August 1976
Height: 5'6" **Weight:** 12.3
Club Honours: FAYC '95; Div 2 '97
International Honours: Jamaica: 4; E: B-
1; Sch
Nottingham Forest supporters finally saw

the best of David in the 2002-03 season.
His partnership with Marlon Harewood
proved to be the most potent strike force
in the First Division, and he scored a
personal best of 25 league goals. A fast
and extremely tricky striker, David was
named as supporters 'Player of the Year'
and was also selected for the PFA Division
One team of the season.
Manchester U *(From trainee on 1/7/1994)*
Bury *(Free on 5/7/1995) FL 72+25/18 FLC
8+3/4 FAC 1+1 Others 3+2/1*
Ipswich T *(£800,000 on 14/11/1997) P/FL
121+10/55 FLC 13/5 FAC 7/2 Others 7*

Nottingham F *(£3,000,000 + on 12/1/200*
FL 76+7/30 FLC 4/2 FAC 1+1 Others 2/2
Sheffield Wed *(Loaned on 5/2/2002) FL 7*
Burnley *(Loaned on 12/3/2002) FL 8/5*

JOHNSON Gavin
Born: Stowmarket, 10 October 1970
Height: 5'11" **Weight:** 12.0
Club Honours: Div '92; Div 3 '97
An experienced left-sided defender, Gav
began the 2002-03 season in impressive
form for Colchester United. However, h
campaign unfortunately ended in
September when he broke his left leg a
Port Vale. Gavin tried to battle back to
fitness, but he suffered a setback that
required a second operation in the sprin
He will be spending the summer
recuperating. Gavin has proved a solid
performer over the years for the U's, bu
he has struggled with injuries in recent
times.
Ipswich T *(From trainee on 1/3/1989) P/FL
114+18/11 FLC 10+1/2 FAC 12+1/2 Others
3+1/1*
Luton T *(Free on 4/7/1995) FL 4+1*
Wigan Ath *(£15,000 on 15/12/1995) FL
82+2/8 FLC 4 FAC 3 Others 1*
Dunfermline Ath *(Free on 1/7/1998) SL 1*
SC 0+1
Colchester U *(Free on 12/11/1999) FL
84+8/3 FLC 4+1 FAC 3 Others 2*

JOHNSON Glen McLeod
Born: London, 23 August 1984
Height: 6'0" **Weight:** 12.0
International Honours: E: U21-2; Yth
Glen joined Millwall on loan last Octobe
and spent six weeks as cover for injuries
to the regular defenders. He made an
instant impact, producing some exceller
performances and looking comfortable
full back and in the centre of defence. I
was recalled to Upton Park and came in
the West Ham line-up at right back,
becoming something of a shining light
during the club's fight against relegation
Glen showed a level of maturity beyon
his years and after playing for the Engla
U20 side in December he stepped up t
the U21s in April. As the season ended
deservedly won the 'Young Hammer of
the Year' award.
West Ham U *(From trainee on 25/8/2001)
14+1 FAC 0+1*
Millwall *(Loaned on 17/10/2002) FL 7+1*

JOHNSON Jermaine
Born: Kingston, Jamaica, 25 June 1980
Height: 5'9" **Weight:** 11.5
International Honours: Jamaica
An exciting midfielder full of pace and
trickery, Jermaine found his first-team

David Johnson

ances somewhat limited at Bolton last
ason. His only start came in the
orthington Cup defeat against Bury,
hough he also made two substitute
pearances in the Premiership. A
nsistent scorer at reserve-team level, he
ntinued to appear (and score) for the
maican national side throughout the
urse of the season, and will be hoping
play more of a part in the Wanderers'
st team in the future.
lton W *(£750,000 from Tivoli Gardens,*
maica on 19/9/2001) PL 4+8 FLC 3 FAC 1+1

JOHNSON Leon Dean
rn: Shoreditch, 10 May 1981
eight: 6'0" **Weight:** 12.4
on joined Gillingham soon after being
eased by Southend, but failed to win a
gular place in the Gills' line-up last term
d made most of his appearances from
e substitutes' bench. A promising young
dfielder, he never let the side down
nen selected and will no doubt be
nocking on the door for a first-team spot
ring 2003-04.
uthend U *(From trainee on 17/11/1999)*
43+5/3 FLC 1 FAC 1+3 Others 8
llingham *(Free on 15/8/2002) FL 8+10 FLC*
FAC 1

JOHNSON Marvin Anthony
rn: Wembley, 29 October 1968
eight: 6'0" **Weight:** 13.6
is veteran Luton Town defender was
incipally employed as youth-team coach
Kenilworth Road last term. However,
e managed one first-team appearance in
e LDV Vans Trophy match against
oking. Despite his age and lack of
atch practice, Marvin made some well-
ned tackles that belied his age and kept
e Hatters in the game.
ton T *(From apprentice on 12/11/1986) FL*
2+21/7 FLC 27+2/2 FAC 19+1/1 Others
+1

OHNSON Michael Owen
rn: Nottingham, 4 July 1973
eight: 5'11" **Weight:** 11.12
ub Honours: AIC '95
ternational Honours: Jamaica: 9
ampered by a groin injury, Michael had
wait until Christmas for his first
emiership start in the Birmingham City
efence last season, however he rarely
atured even when fit, managing only
e Premiership starts. A dogged
erformer, he was careful to play to his
rengths of pace and athletic ability and
ke no risks. Michael also returned to the
maican international fold, featuring in

the end-of-season friendlies against South
Africa and Nigeria.
Notts Co *(From trainee on 9/7/1991) FL*
102+5 FLC 9 FAC 4 Others 15+1
Birmingham C *(£225,000 on 1/9/1995) P/FL*
227+35/13 FLC 25+6/5 FAC 6+4 Others 11

JOHNSON Richard Mark
Born: Newcastle, Australia, 27 April 1974
Height: 5'11" **Weight:** 12.4
Club Honours: Div 2 '98
International Honours: Australia: 1
Richard returned to action for Watford in
September after a frustrating two seasons
struggling to overcome a serious knee
injury. A hard-working midfield player
with the vision to dictate play and in
possession of a vicious shot, he was
naturally rusty after such a long lay-off,
and in February went on loan to
Northampton in search of regular first-
team football. His stay at Sixfields was cut
short by another injury, but after
returning to Watford he finished the
campaign strongly with a run of games in
the first team and the prospect of better
things to come in 2003-04.
Watford *(From trainee on 11/5/1992) P/FL*
210+32/20 FLC 13+1/1 FAC 13+2/1 Others
5+1
Northampton T *(Loaned on 7/2/2003) FL*
5+1/1

JOHNSON Roger
Born: Ashford, 28 April 1983
Height: 6'3" **Weight:** 11.0
After impressing so much at the end of
the previous season as a central defender,
Roger was surprisingly only called into
service three times before Christmas last
term. He eventually got his break in
January when Paul McCarthy left the
scene and from then on he became one
of the most impressive performers at
Adams Park. He immediately became the
natural leader in defence, producing some
fully committed performances. Roger was
even appointed captain for one game, the
youngest at the club in recent memory.
Comfortable on the ball, he likes to bring
the play as far as possible before setting
up attacks and he is perfecting the art of
the well-timed tackle.
Wycombe W *(From trainee on 10/7/2001) FL*
33+9/4 FLC 1 Others 1+2

JOHNSON Seth Art Maurice
Born: Birmingham, 12 March 1979
Height: 5'10" **Weight:** 11.0
International Honours: E: 1; U21-15;
Yth
Seth was again frustrated by injuries last
term, restricting his appearances for Leeds

to a mere handful. After an outing from
the bench against Manchester City in the
opening game of the season, his next
game was at Bolton in December. A few
more substitute appearances followed,
before he forced his way into the line-up
and scored his only goal in United's
colours in the 1-0 home victory over West
Ham in February. A further injury ended
his season in February.
Crewe Alex *(From trainee on 12/7/1996) FL*
89+4/6 FLC 5 FAC 2/1 Others 0+3
Derby Co *(£3,000,000 on 21/5/1999) PL*
73/2 FLC 6+1 FAC 0+1
Leeds U *(£7,000,000 + on 19/10/2001) PL*
15+8/1 FAC 3+1

JOHNSON Simon Ainsley
Born: West Bromwich, 9 March 1983
Height: 5'9" **Weight:** 12.0
International Honours: E: Yth
This promising Leeds United striker started
2002-03 on loan at Hull City, and
immediately made a favourable
impression by scoring the equaliser on his
senior debut for the Tigers at Bristol
Rovers. On his return to Elland Road the
livewire forward did well in the reserves
and went on to make his Premiership
debut from the bench in the 6-1 win at
Charlton. Simon featured in a couple
more games before receiving his first start
in the final game of the season against
Aston Villa. He also represented England
at U20 level during the campaign.
Leeds U *(From trainee on 7/7/2000) PL 1+3*
Hull C *(Loaned on 12/8/2002) FL 4+8/2 FLC*
0+1

JOHNSON Thomas (Tommy)
Born: Newcastle, 15 January 1971
Height: 5'11" **Weight:** 12.8
Club Honours: FLC '96; SPD '01; SLC 00;
SC '01
International Honours: E: U21-7
This experienced striker missed a large
chunk of the 2002-03 season for
Gillingham after he broke a bone in his
foot following a collision with a team
mate. When fit Tommy featured regularly
in the squad, although often used from
the substitutes' bench, and showed on a
number of occasions that he still has the
ability to hold his own in the First
Division.
Notts Co *(From trainee on 19/1/1989) FL*
100+18/47 FLC 7+2/5 FAC 3+2/1 Others
14+3/4
Derby Co *(£1,300,000 on 12/3/1992) FL*
91+7/30 FLC 9+1/2 FAC 5/1 Others 16/8
Aston Villa *(£1,450,000 on 1/9/1995) FL*
38+19/13 FLC 5/2 FAC 5+2/1 Others 1+1/1
Glasgow Celtic *(£2,400,000 on 27/3/1997)*

SL 23+12/18 SLC 3+1/3 SC 2+4 Others 0+3/1
Everton *(Loaned on 24/9/1999) PL 0+3*
Sheffield Wed *(Free on 8/9/2001) FL 8/3*
FLC 1
Kilmarnock *(Free on 22/12/2001) SL 7+3/7*
SC 1+1
Gillingham *(Free on 7/8/2002) FL 12+14/2*
FLC 0+2/1 FAC 0+1

JOHNSTON Allan
Born: Glasgow, 14 December 1973
Height: 5'9" **Weight:** 11.0
Club Honours: Div 1 '99
International Honours: S: 17; B-2;
U21-3

Allan was another Riverside fringe player
whose Middlesbrough action was
restricted to the Worthington Cup last
season. His start to the season looked
promising enough with two international
appearances, but he eventually went out
on loan to Sheffield Wednesday in search
of first-team football. Allan scored a fine
goal on his debut in a storming comeback
victory over Reading, his tricky, direct
wing play giving the side some much
needed left-sided balance and
penetration. Unfortunately he broke a toe
in a training collision and returned to the
Riverside to recuperate.

Heart of Midlothian *(Free from Tynecastle*
BC on 23/6/1990) SL 46+38/12 SLC 3+2/2 S
4+1 (Signed for Rennes, France during 1996
close season)
Sunderland *(£550,000 on 27/3/1997) FL*
82+4/19 FLC 8+1/1 FAC 3 Others 3
Birmingham C *(Loaned on 15/10/1999) FL*
7+2 FLC 1
Bolton W *(Free on 21/1/2000) FL 17+2/3*
FAC 2 Others 2/1
Glasgow R *(Free on 13/6/2000) SL 10+4 Sl*
0+2 SC 2+1/1
Middlesbrough *(£1,000,000 on 5/9/2001)*
PL 13+4/1 FLC 3 FAC 2+1
Sheffield Wed *(Loaned on 13/12/2002) FL*
12/2

JONES Andrew (Andy) Stuar
Born: Sutton in Ashfield, 12 February
1986
Height: 5'8" **Weight:** 11.7
Andy was another of the promising crop
of youngsters at Mansfield to make his
bow in senior football last term, coming
off the bench in the game at Queen's
Park Rangers. His debut in midfield did
not last long as he was booked for a
reckless tackle before he had kicked a ba
and sent off for a second challenge nine
minutes after entering the field of play.
Although he did not get another
opportunity in the first team he is
nonetheless highly rated by the
management at Field Mill.
Mansfield T *(Trainee) FL 0+1*

JONES Bradley (Brad)
Born: Armadale, Australia, 19 March 198
Height: 6'3" **Weight:** 12.3
International Honours: Australia: U23; Y
This promising young Middlesbrough
goalkeeper arrived at Stockport on loan
mid-December. He mostly sat on the
substitutes' bench, although he made hi
senior debut in the 4-1 defeat at Bristol
City. It was a difficult occasion, but
despite the score line he seemed to
improve as the game went on. Brad
returned to the Riverside to continue his
development in the reserve team and
made his debut for Australia U23s again
Spain in April.
Middlesbrough *(From trainee on 26/3/199*
Stockport Co *(Loaned on 13/12/2002) FL 1*

JONES Gary Roy
Born: Birkenhead, 3 June 1977
Height: 5'10" **Weight:** 12.0
Gary suffered a back injury on the
opening day of the season and on
resuming training suffered a knee injury.
However, he then returned to the
Barnsley first team after a month out an

Allan Johnston

ent on to become a regular in the line-
p thereafter. A busy midfield player, his
ork rate and ability to get from box to
ox were his strengths. For the second
ason running he only managed one
bal and he will be looking for
provement in that area in 2003-04.
vansea C *(Signed from Caernarfon T on
/7/1997) FL 3+5 FLC 0+1*
pchdale *(Free on 15/1/1998) FL 123+17/22
C 4+1 FAC 6+3 Others 7+2/3*
arnsley *(£175,000 on 30/11/2001) FL 56/2
C 1*

ONES Gary Steven
orn: Chester, 10 May 1975
eight: 6'3" **Weight:** 14.0
ary was re-signed permanently by Ray
lathias for his second spell at Tranmere
llowing a successful month's loan from
ottingham Forest. This came as a
rprise to many, but he justified his
turn with nine goals, carrying on exactly
here he left off last time as a stalwart in
e heart of midfield. Gary is a good team
an, and immediately linked up well with
s new colleagues, his height causing all
rts of problems for the opposition in
e middle of the park.
anmere Rov *(From trainee on 5/7/1993)
117+61/28 FLC 17+4/3 FAC 9+2/3
thers 1+1*
ottingham F *(Free on 3/7/2000) FL
4+12/2 FLC 1+1 FAC 1*
anmere Rov *(Free on 29/8/2002) FL 40/6
C 2 FAC 2 Others 3/2*

ONES Graeme Anthony
orn: Gateshead, 13 March 1970
eight: 6'0" **Weight:** 13.0
ub Honours: Div 3 '97; AMC '99
his veteran striker quickly became a
opular figure at Southend after signing
the 2002 close season. His best
erformance in a Blues shirt came at Bury,
hen he bravely threw himself at a loose
all to head home. However, he was
jured at Carlisle in January and did not
gure in the team again. He subsequently
ined Boston United in March and made
s mark immediately, netting with a 20-
rd volley after just eight minutes of his
ebut after coming on as a substitute
gainst Rushden. Graeme started the next
vo games before a hamstring injury kept
m out of the final matches of the
eason.
oncaster Rov *(£10,000 from Bridlington T
1 2/8/1993) FL 80+12/26 FLC 4+1/1 FAC
+1/2 Others 5/1*
/igan Ath *(£150,000 on 8/7/1996) FL
5+20/44 FLC 4+3/1 FAC 4/1 Others 6+2/6*

St Johnstone *(£100,000 on 19/11/1999) SL
31+10/7 SLC 2 SC 1*
Southend U *(£35,000 on 30/7/2002) FL
18+3/2 FLC 1 FAC 2+1 Others 1/1*
Boston U *(Free on 21/3/2003) FL 2+1/1*

JONES Griffith (Griff) Thomas
Born: Liverpool, 22 June 1984
Height: 5'8" **Weight:** 12.13
Another graduate of the Barnsley
academy, Griff got his chance as a half-
time substitute against Wigan last
September. He continued to perform well
in the academy and reserve teams and
added another two appearances from the
substitutes' bench. Griff is a hard-working
forward who has scored regularly at
junior level for the Reds.
Barnsley *(Trainee) FL 0+2 Others 0+1*

JONES Lee
Born: Pontypridd, 9 August 1970
Height: 6'3" **Weight:** 14.4
Club Honours: AMC '94
Lee started the 2002-03 season in fine
form, winning a series of 'Man of the
Match' awards, after conceding just two
goals in Stockport's first six games as they
made an early push for the play-offs. The
goalkeeper's fortunes went downhill after
this, however, and after starting against
Notts County in January he lost his place
to Ola Tidman for the remainder of the
campaign.
Swansea C *(£7,500 from AFC Porth on
24/3/1994) FL 6 Others 1*
Bristol Rov *(Signed on 7/3/1998) FL 76 FLC 6
FAC 7 Others 4*
Stockport Co *(£50,000 on 19/7/2000) FL
72+3 FLC 5 FAC 4*

JONES Philip Lee
Born: Wrexham, 29 May 1973
Height: 5'9" **Weight:** 10.8
International Honours: W: 2; B-1; U21-
14; Yth
Lee is a striker who likes to play on the
shoulder of opposition defenders where
his pace is an obvious advantage. His
opportunities at Wrexham were limited
last season, and he was nowhere near
involved as he would have liked,
struggling with his fitness through most
of the campaign. A highlight was
coming off the bench to earn a vital
three points at Shrewsbury with a
stunning strike in the 90th minute in
April. A few days later he produced the
break and shot that made the winner
late in the game against Bristol Rovers at
the Racecourse.
Wrexham *(From trainee on 5/7/1991) FL
24+15/10 FLC 2 FAC 1+2/1 Others 4+1/2*

Liverpool *(£300,000 on 12/3/1992) PL 0+3
FLC 0+1*
Crewe Alex *(Loaned on 3/9/1993) FL 4+4/1*
Wrexham *(Loaned on 26/1/1996) FL 20/9*
Wrexham *(Loaned on 31/1/1997) FL 2+4*
Tranmere Rov *(£100,000 on 27/3/1997) FL
58+28/16 FLC 7+3/2 FAC 0+1*
Barnsley *(Free on 3/7/2000) FL 17+23/5 FLC
3+4/2 FAC 0+1 (Free to Oswestry T on
27/3/2002)*
Wrexham *(Free on 28/3/2002) FL 12+15/9
FAC 0+1 Others 2+1/2*

JONES Mark Alan
Born: Wrexham, 15 August 1983
Height: 5'11" **Weight:** 10.10
In his final year as a scholar at Wrexham,
Mark was included on the bench a
number of times last season. He made his
Football League debut against Exeter City
at the Racecourse in mid-September, and
also played the second half of FA Wales
Premier Cup match against Afan Lido.
Mark had to undergo a hernia operation
during the campaign, but was back in
action again during April assisting
Wrexham U19s in their successful season.
He was also a member of the Wales U21
squad against Finland, Italy and
Azerbaijan.
Wrexham *(Trainee) FL 0+1*

JONES Matthew (Matt) Graham
Born: Llanelli, 1 September 1980
Height: 5'11" **Weight:** 11.5
Club Honours: FAYC '97
International Honours: W: 13; B-1;
U21-7; Yth
Matt returned to action for Leicester last
December following a cruciate ligament
injury that had sidelined him for over a
year. The Foxes' mid-season injury crisis
led to him playing a full game at home to
Stoke at a time when he should have
been slowly regaining match fitness, but
he still managed to acquit himself
creditably and quickly earned a recall to
the full Welsh squad. An ankle injury
during the latter part of the season
affected his fitness and denied him the
opportunity to make more of an impact.
A closing-day injury crisis led to a late
recall to the starting line-up, whilst a
further call to international duty at the
season's end was also forthcoming. Matt
was, however, made available on a free
transfer at the end of 2002-03.
Leeds U *(From trainee on 3/9/1997) PL
11+12 FLC 1+1 FAC 0+2 Others 4+2*
Leicester C *(£3,250,000 on 13/12/2000) P/FL
19+8/1 FLC 1+1 FAC 4+2*

JONES Nathan Jason
Born: Rhondda, 28 May 1973
Height: 5'7" **Weight:** 10.12
Club Honours: Div 3 '01
Last term was not a vintage season for this Welsh full back who was in and out of the Brighton & Hove Albion team. Played also occasionally as a wide man in midfield, Nathan enjoyed a 13-match run in the side after returning from knee problems, but made nearly as many appearances as a substitute. Famed for his 'shuffle', he was at his best when given the freedom to attack and roam behind the forwards, but in a struggling side his opportunities were limited. The highlight of his campaign was undoubtedly his performance at Nottingham Forest, which he capped with

a mazy run from the halfway line to finish with a stunning 25-yarder.
Luton T *(£10,000 from Merthyr Tydfil on 30/6/1995. Freed on 20/12/1995)*
Southend U *(Free from Numancia, Spain on 5/8/1997) FL 82+17/2 FLC 6+2 FAC 3+1/1 Others 0+3*
Scarborough *(Loaned on 25/3/1999) FL 8+1*
Brighton & Hove A *(Free on 7/7/2000) FL 72+32/7 FLC 3+2/1 FAC 5+1 Others 3*

JONES Paul Steven
Born: Chirk, 18 April 1967
Height: 6'3" **Weight:** 14.8
International Honours: W: 31
Last season proved successful for Paul as far as international duty for Wales was concerned, but a frustrating time for his career at Southampton, where he found

himself displaced as first choice 'keeper by Antti Niemi. He proved as good as ever when called upon and his undoubted class as a shot stopper was shown in the final Premiership game against Manchester City at Maine Road and also against Arsenal at the Millennium Stadium when he became the first goalkeeper to be brought on as a substitute in an FA Cup match.
Wolverhampton W *(£40,000 from Kidderminster Hrs on 23/7/1991) FL 33 FLC 5 FAC 5 Others 4*
Stockport Co *(£60,000 on 25/7/1996) FL 46 FLC 11 FAC 4 Others 4*
Southampton *(£900,000 on 28/7/1997) PL 184+1 FLC 16 FAC 11+1*

JONES Scott
Born: Sheffield, 1 May 1975
Height: 5'10" **Weight:** 12.8
This versatile defender joined York City on a permanent basis in the summer of 2002, having spent the closing stages of the 2001-02 campaign on loan at Bootham Crescent. However, he took some time to settle in with the Minstermen before eventually finishing the season with a run of good form, chiefly operating in a central defensive role.
Barnsley *(From trainee on 1/2/1994) F/PL 76+7/4 FLC 7/1 FAC 4+3/2*
Mansfield T *(Loaned on 7/8/1997) FL 6 FLC 2*
Bristol Rov *(£200,000 on 10/8/2000) FL 51+7/3 FLC 5 FAC 2 Others 2+1*
York C *(Free on 26/3/2002) FL 26+2/1 Others 1*

JONES Stephen (Steve) Graham
Born: Derry, 25 October 1976
Height: 5'4" **Weight:** 10.9
International Honours: NI: 2
Steve had to be patient at Crewe last term and had to overcome two spells out injured before he won a regular first-team place. A real competitive figure who usually plays in a wide-midfield role, he has a fine turn of speed and managed a double-figure tally of goals. His progress was recognised when he stepped up to win his first full cap for Northern Ireland against Italy in the summer and he also featured in the following game against Spain.
Blackpool *(Free from Chadderton on 30/10/1995)*
Bury *(Free on 23/8/1996. Free to Sligo Rov during 1997 close season)*
Crewe Alex *(£75,000 + from Leigh RMI, ex Bray W, Chorley, on 4/7/2001) FL 19+18/9 FLC 0+1 FAC 2+1/1 Others 2+2/1*
Rochdale *(Loaned on 5/2/2002) FL 6+3/1*

Nathan Jones

~~J~~ONES Stephen (Steve) Robert

Born: Bristol, 25 December 1970
Height: 5'10" **Weight:** 12.2
Club Honours: Div 3 '00

A popular player with players and supporters alike, Steve endured another season blighted by injury at Cheltenham last term. Recalled to the team for the away match at Blackpool in October, he put in an impressive first-half performance before suffering a broken ankle at the start of the second period. He had recovered by February but was unable to attain 100 per cent fitness, although he remained a regular starter for the reserves. An excellent defender with the ability to get forward as well, Steve was released at the end of the season and deserves better luck in the remainder of his career.

Swansea C (£25,000 from Cheltenham T on 24/11/1995) FL 140+6/4 FLC 2+1 FAC 9 Others 8
Cheltenham T (Free on 11/7/2001) FL 7+3

~~J~~ONES Stuart John

Born: Aberystwyth, 14 March 1984
Height: 6'0" **Weight:** 11.8

A third-year scholar with Swansea, this promising central defender performed well with the club's U19 side and was given his senior debut in the LDV Vans Trophy match at Stevenage. He was voted as 'Man of the Match' on that occasion and retained his place in the line-up for the following game at Carlisle. Stuart also featured in the Wales U19 squad during the season and was rewarded with a one-year professional contract by the Swans on completion of his scholarship.

Swansea C (Trainee) FL 5+1 Others 1

~~J~~ONES William (Billy) Kenneth

Born: Chatham, 26 March 1983
Height: 6'0" **Weight:** 11.7

Billy started the 2002-03 season as reserve left back to Matthew Lockwood for Leyton Orient, but when the club had injury problems in central defence he made the adjustment to left-sided central defender with ease. Billy is skilful on the ball and has the vision to spray passes round the pitch. He will be hoping to win a regular first-team place at Brisbane Road in 2003-04.

Leyton Orient (From trainee on 10/7/2001) FL 39+2 FLC 1 FAC 3+1

~~J~~ORDAN Stephen (Steve)

Born: Warrington, 6 March 1982
Height: 6'0" **Weight:** 11.13

This promising Manchester City youngster joined Cambridge United in an extended loan deal last October and made his senior debut for the U's against Wrexham. Primarily used at left back, he was also employed in midfield on occasions. Steve returned to Maine Road and was rewarded with an appearance from the substitutes' bench against Bolton in April. He will be looking for more senior action in 2003-04.

Manchester C (From trainee on 11/3/1999) PL 0+1
Cambridge U (Loaned on 4/10/2002) FL 11 Others 3

JORDAN Thomas (Tom) Michael

Born: Manchester, 24 May 1981
Height: 6'4" **Weight:** 13.5

This tall centre back spent the 2002-03 campaign on a month-to-month contract at Southend, where he was a regular in the reserves. He was unlucky to find a clutch of players ahead of him in the queue for first-team places and received few opportunities. He made his debut in the LDV Vans Trophy and his only other senior action came as a substitute at Bournemouth in April. With limited opportunities at Roots Hall Tom was released at the end of the season. He is the son of former Leeds, Manchester United and Scotland star Joe Jordan.

Bristol C (From trainee on 29/3/2001)
Southend U (Free on 28/8/2002) FL 0+1 Others 1

[JORDAO] BATISTA Adelion Jose Martins

Born: Malange, Angola, 30 August 1971
Height: 6'3" **Weight:** 12.10

This tall, well built central midfielder hardly figured at all in West Bromwich Albion's line-up during the 2002-03 season, making just four senior appearances. He struggled with his fitness, a shoulder injury keeping him out of action during December and January, and had to wait until mid-February at Fulham before making his Premiership debut as a substitute. He did appear in some 20 reserve fixtures, but was not a serious contender for first-team duty.

West Bromwich A (£350,000 from Sporting Braga, Portugal, ex Estrela Amadora, Campomaiorense, Lece, on 25/8/2000) P/FL 47+16/6 FLC 4+1/2 FAC 1 Others 0+2

JORGENSEN Claus Beck

Born: Denmark, 24 April 1979
Height: 5'11" **Weight:** 11.0

Claus had a sensational second half to the season to help Bradford City move clear of the First Division relegation zone. A talented midfield player who can operate in the centre or on the right, he was a constant threat to opposition defences with his late runs into the area. Claus showed his eye for a goal when he set a new club record by scoring in eight consecutive away league games. He was out of contract in the summer and at the time of writing his future was uncertain.

Bournemouth (Free from AC Horsens, Denmark on 12/7/1999) FL 77+10/14 FLC 6/1 FAC 6 Others 1+1
Bradford C (Free on 23/7/2001) FL 41+9/12 FLC 2+1 FAC 1

JOSEPH Marc Ellis

Born: Leicester, 10 November 1976
Height: 6'0" **Weight:** 12.10

This calm defender was a near ever-present for Peterborough in the early part of the 2002-03 season before dropping down a division to join Hull shortly before the Tigers' move from Boothferry Park to the Kingston Communications Stadium. New City manager Peter Taylor brought Marc in on a two-and-a-half year contract to provide competition for right back Carl Regan and experienced cover at centre back. Marc showed that he was more than capable of performing to a high standard in either role as the campaign progressed.

Cambridge U (From trainee on 23/5/1995) FL 136+17 FLC 7 FAC 5+2 Others 7+1
Peterborough U (Free on 3/7/2001) FL 60+1/2 FLC 3 FAC 6 Others 3
Hull C (£40,000 on 22/11/2002) FL 22+1

JOSEPH Matthew Nathanial

Born: Bethnal Green, 30 September 1972
Height: 5'8" **Weight:** 10.7
International Honours: E: Yth.
Barbados: 2

Matthew again started the season as first choice right back for Leyton Orient last term, but switched to sweeper when injuries and player departures left the club short of central defenders. He looked equally at home in either position, and some excellent performances led to him winning both the supporters' and club 'Player of the Year' awards. Matthew signed a new contract during the summer.

Arsenal (From trainee on 17/11/1990)
Gillingham (Free on 7/12/1992)
Cambridge U (Signed on 19/11/1993) FL 157+2/6 FLC 6+1 FAC 7 Others 5
Leyton Orient (£10,000 on 22/1/1998) FL 196+4/2 FLC 9+1 FAC 14+1 Others 5+1

JOY Ian Paul
Born: San Diego, USA, 14 July 1981
Height: 5'10" **Weight:** 11.1
This attacking left-sided midfielder was
unable to force his way into the first team
at Kidderminster last term as a result of
the form of Scott Stamps and Sam Shilton
and was restricted to just a handful of
games. He was released from his contract
by mutual consent in the new year in
order to return to the USA so that he
could try out for MLS outfit Columbus
Crew, but quickly returned to England
and Chester City.
Tranmere Rov (From trainee on 29/7/1998)
Stirling A (Free on 3/8/2000) SL 0+2 Others
1
Montrose (Free on 27/9/2000) SL 24+2/2 SC
3+1
Kidderminster Hrs (Free on 6/8/2001) FL
15+7 FAC 0+1 Others 2

[JUANJO] PEREZ Juanjo
Carricondo
Born: Barcelona, Spain, 4 May 1977
Height: 5'7" **Weight:** 10.10
Juanjo had a somewhat disappointing
season at Bradford City last term, making
the starting line-up on just three
occasions, although he made several
appearances from the substitutes' bench.
A tricky and diminutive attacking player
who is at his best when facing a defender
with the ball at his feet, he last featured
in the Bantams 5-0 home defeat to high-
flying Sheffield United in November. He
was released at the end of the season.
Heart of Midlothian (Free from Barcelona,
Spain on 9/10/1998) SL 32+40/9 SLC 3+3 SC
4+3/2 Others 3
Bradford C (Free on 31/10/2001) FL 7+19/1
FLC 0+1 FAC 2

JUDGE Alan Graham
Born: Kingsbury, 14 May 1960
Height: 5'11" **Weight:** 11.6
Alan became Oxford United's oldest-ever
player at nearly 43 years of age when he
played in goal against Cambridge United
last March. Alan, who appeared for the
U's in the 1986 Milk Cup final, had not
played senior football for anyone for over
ten years but was goalkeeping coach at
the Kassam Stadium. With both 'keepers
injured, Alan got the nod and had an
excellent game, conceding just one goal
and saving a certain winner near the end.
Luton T (From juniors on 3/1/1978) FL 11
FLC 1
Reading (Free on 2/9/1982) FL 77 FLC 4 FAC
3 Others 1
Oxford U (£10,000 on 24/12/1984) FL 80
FLC 11 FAC 5 Others 4

Lincoln C (Loaned on 6/11/1985) FL 2
Cardiff C (Loaned on 20/10/1987) FL 8
Others 1
Hereford U (Free on 25/7/1991) FL 105 FLC
6 FAC 9 Others 8 (Freed during 1994 close
season)
Swindon T (Free from Banbury U on
24/12/2002)
Oxford U (Free on 17/3/2003) FL 1

JUDGE Matthew Peter
Born: Barking, 18 January 1985
Height: 6'0" **Weight:** 11.7
This promising Luton Town striker turned
in some sparkling match-winning
performances for the youth team last
season. He was given his chance to play
up front in the LDV Vans Trophy match
against Woking and showed some nice
touches, certainly enough to earn further
chances of first-team action He came on
as a substitute in the Hatters' FA Cup
defeat by Wigan Athletic and made his
bow in the Second Division at Colchester.
Matthew is quick, good in the air, and has
an eye for goal.
Luton T (Trainee) FL 0+1 FAC 0+1 Others
1+1

JULIAN Alan John
Born: Ashford, 11 March 1983
Height: 6'2" **Weight:** 13.5
Brentford's reserve goalkeeper made his
senior debut in the LDV Vans Trophy tie at
Plymouth last November, keeping a clean
sheet. Alan then made two league
appearances over the Christmas period,
when Paul Smith was ill, and added
another late in the campaign. Tall and
commanding, he will be looking for more
first-team experience in 2003-04.
Brentford (From trainee on 4/7/2001) FL 3
Others 1

[JUNINHO] JUNIOR Oswaldo
Giroldo
Born: Sao Paulo, Brazil, 22 February 1975
Height: 5'5" **Weight:** 10.4
International Honours: Brazil: 49
Middlesbrough's very own little midfield
wizard is the only player in the 127 years
history of the club to have played for
Boro' in three different spells and is clearly
loved by the fans. The 29-year-old
Brazilian damaged his cruciate knee
ligament in a pre-season friendly abroad
which postponed his fairy-tale re-
emergence in the Premiership until March,
but what a rapturous reception he
received when he came on at the start of
the second half in a 1-1 draw at the
Riverside against Everton.
Middlesbrough (£4,750,000 from Sao

Paulo, Brazil, ex Ituano, on 3/11/1995) PL
54+2/14 FLC 9/1 FAC 9/2 Others 3
(£12,000,000 to Atletico Madrid, Spain on
25/8/1997)
Middlesbrough (Loaned from Atletico
Madrid, Spain on 21/9/1999) PL 24+4/4 FLC
4/1 FAC 1
Middlesbrough (Loaned from Atletico
Madrid, Spain on 14/8/2002) PL 9+1/3

[JUNIOR] JUNIOR Guimaraes
Sanibio Jose Luiz
Born: Fortaleza, Brazil, 15 June 1979
Height: 6'0" **Weight:** 13.0
After a summer tour with Bolton this
spectacular striker scored for Walsall in a
pre-season game against Malawi, but
then had to wait for international
clearance before making his first-team
debut against Reading at the end of
August. Soon he was scoring a stunning
goal to win the Worthington Cup tie at
Nottingham Forest's City ground and his
ability to hold the ball up and finishing
power made him a handful for any
defence. He developed an excellent
understanding with Jorge Leitao and his
late-season hat-trick against Derby took
his tally to 16 goals. Junior has expressed
a desire to stay at Bescot and Walsall fans
hope that the complex paperwork can be
completed.
Walsall (Free from Treze, Brazil, via loan
spells at Beveren and Ajaccio, ex U.Espanola,
Cordoba, Aleanza, Beveren, on 3/8/2002) FL
28+8/15 FLC 3/1 FAC 3

JUPP Duncan Alan
Born: Guildford, 25 January 1975
Height: 6'0" **Weight:** 12.12
International Honours: S: U21-9
Duncan was rarely in consideration for a
place at Wimbledon last term and in the
autumn he signed for Notts County on
loan. He played a handful of games on
the right side of midfield and
demonstrated the ability to get dangerous
crosses into the penalty area. Duncan
subsequently followed his former
manager to Luton on a short-term
contract. His experience and composure
steadied the Hatters' defence during an
injury crisis, but despite giving some
confident performances he was not
offered a longer deal.
Fulham (From trainee on 12/7/1993) FL
101+4/2 FLC 10+2 FAC 9+1/1 Others 9+1/1
Wimbledon (£125,000 + on 27/6/1996) P/FL
23+7 FLC 8+2 FAC 3+2
Notts Co (Free on 8/11/2002) FL 6+2 FAC
0+1
Luton T (Free on 28/2/2003) FL 2+3

K

KABBA Stephen (Steve)

Born: Lambeth, 7 March 1981
Height: 5'10" **Weight:** 11.12
Steve began the 2002-03 season in bright form for Crystal Palace, netting the winner in the opening game at Preston after coming off the substitutes' bench. However, he was soon on his way to Grimsby, on loan, where he made a tremendous impact, finding the net regularly. His form alerted other clubs and in November he moved on to Sheffield United for a substantial fee. The skilful and speedy striker proved a popular acquisition at Bramall Lane. Although he showed a tendency to over-elaborate, he created many openings and was particularly effective in the FA Cup victory over Leeds. Steve continued to score regularly and finished the campaign with a total of 18 goals in all competitions for his three clubs.
Crystal Palace (From trainee on 29/6/1999) FL 2+8/1 FLC 0+1
Luton T (Loaned on 28/3/2002) FL 0+3
Grimsby T (Loaned on 23/8/2002) FL 13/6 FLC 1
Sheffield U (£250,000 on 15/11/2002) FL 9+6/7 FAC 5/3 Others 1+2/1

KACHLOUL Hassan

Born: Agadir, Morocco, 19 February 1973
Height: 6'1" **Weight:** 11.12
International Honours: Morocco
This experienced midfielder had a very disappointing season at Aston Villa last term when he made just one appearance for the first team, coming on from the substitutes' bench against FC Zurich in the Intertoto Cup. At his best Hassan is a creative figure in the centre of the park who has a good eye for goal.
Southampton (£250,000 from St Etienne, France, ex Nimes, Dunkerque, Metz, on 20/10/1998) PL 73+13/14 FLC 5 FAC 4+2/1
Aston Villa (Free on 1/7/2001) PL 17+5/2 FLC 2 Others 6+7

KAMARA Malvin Ginah

Born: London, 17 November 1983
Height: 5'11" **Weight:** 13.7
Malvin is another product of Wimbledon's academy set-up, and made his league debut as a substitute in the club's penultimate home game of the season against Preston. He also appeared the following week in the 5-1 win at Ipswich. A right-sided player, he featured in both matches as a wide-midfield replacement,

but right back would probably be his preferred position. Malvin is a very enthusiastic and personable young man who would more than likely have been given his chance earlier but for a hamstring injury that kept him out for several weeks in the spring.
Wimbledon (Trainee) FL 0+2

KANCHELSKIS Andrei

Born: Kirovograd, USSR, 23 January 1969
Height: 5'10" **Weight:** 13.4
Club Honours: ESC '91; FLC '92; PL '93, '94; FAC '94; CS '93, '94; SPD '99, '00; SC '99, '00, '02; SLC '99
International Honours: Russia: 36; CIS 6; USSR: 17 (UEFA-U21 '90)
Andrei came to Southampton to join in training and keep himself fit, but so impressed Gordon Strachan he was given a short-term contract – and allocated the recently retired Matthew Le Tissier's famous number 7 shirt. However, by October he had only featured on the subs' bench twice, making brief appearances on each occasion. Given no further opportunities of first-team outings by February, the experienced winger decided to continue his career with the Al-Halil club, in Saudi Arabia.
Manchester U (£650,000 from Shakhtar Donetsk, Ukraine, ex Dinamo Kiev, on 26/3/1991) F/PL 96+27/28 FLC 15+1/3 FAC 11+1/4 Others 10/1
Everton (£5,000,000 on 25/8/1995) PL 52/20 FLC 2/1 FAC 6/1 (£8,000,000 to Fiorentina, Italy on 29/1/1997)
Glasgow R (£5,500,000 on 15/7/1998) SL 64+12/13 SLC 4/1 SC 13+10/3 Others 10+10/3
Manchester C (Loaned on 30/1/2001) PL 7+3 FAC 1/1
Southampton (Free on 31/8/2002) PL 0+1 FLC 0+1

KANOUTE Frederic (Fredi)

Born: Sainte Foy Les Lyon, France, 2 September 1977
Height: 6'4" **Weight:** 12.10
International Honours: France: B-1; U21
After scoring against Arsenal and Tottenham at the start of the season the talented West Ham striker was sidelined by a bad groin injury. This was a huge setback to the Hammers as his pace and power were sorely missed. He played one further game at Christmas and then went to Canada for treatment. Returning to the line-up in March he showed an impressive sharpness, netting against Sunderland and Aston Villa and contributing the winning goal against Manchester City, while a superb display against Chelsea

was possibly his best-ever performance for the club. One can only wonder if Fredi had been fit all season would the Hammers have been relegated?
West Ham U (£4,000,000 from Lyon, France on 23/3/2000) PL 79+5/29 FLC 3 FAC 5/4

KANU Nwankwo

Born: Owerri, Nigeria, 1 August 1976
Height: 6'4" **Weight:** 13.3
Club Honours: CS '99; FAC '02, '03; PL '02
International Honours: Nigeria: 38; U23 (OLYM '96); Yth (World-U17 '93)
Kanu is another player who failed to secure a regular place in the Arsenal line-up last term, despite his incredible ball skills. He marked his 100th Premiership appearance with two goals in the opening nine minutes at home to Sunderland in October. He had previously scored two at Leeds, and the winner at home to Bolton, yet five goals in three games did not make him an automatic choice. His tricks and talent can be beguiling. On occasions, he displays outrageous ability and wonderful skills. Off the field Kanu was awarded the Order of Niger, the Nigerian equivalent of an OBE, while he also founded the Nwankwo Kanu Heart Foundation to help children with heart disease.
Arsenal (£4,500,000 from Inter Milan, Italy, ex Fed Works, Iwuanyanwu National, Ajax, on 4/2/1999) PL 60+49/29 FLC 4/2 FAC 4+10/3 Others 27+20/7

KARLSSON Par

Born: Sweden, 29 May 1978
Height: 5'8" **Weight:** 10.10
International Honours: Sweden: U21
After selling Kevin Cooper the previous season, Wimbledon were hopeful that Par would be able to fill the vacancy on the left side of midfield last term. He was given a couple of starts early on against Brighton and Nottingham Forest, but failed to impress in either game and was sold to Swedish club Elfsborg just prior to the August transfer window deadline. Par is an undoubtedly talented player, but one whose career with the Dons never really took off after a promising start.
Wimbledon (£40,000 from IFK Gothenburg, Sweden, ex Karlskoya, on 7/9/2000) FL 10+16 FLC 1 FAC 5/1

KAVANAGH Graham Anthony

Born: Dublin, 2 December 1973
Height: 5'10" **Weight:** 12.11
Club Honours: AMC '00
International Honours: RoI: 3; B-1; U21-9; Yth; Sch

Graham Kavanagh

Victory at the Millennium Stadium was a sweet moment for this talented midfielder. After losing in three successive play-off semi-finals, twice for Stoke City and once for Cardiff City, Graham finally made it as he led the Bluebirds to victory against Queen's Park Rangers in the final. He was able to lift the trophy and earn the success and joy he craved. Personally, Graham had a better season in 2001-02, but he played a full part in leading the Bluebirds into Division One. Graham was also selected for the PFA Division Two team of the season.

Middlesbrough *(Signed from Home Farm or 16/8/1991) F/PL 22+13/3 FLC 1 FAC 2+2/1 Others 7*
Darlington *(Loaned on 25/2/1994) FL 5*
Stoke C *(£250,000 + on 13/9/1996) FL 198+8/35 FLC 16+2/7 FAC 6 Others 15/4*
Cardiff C *(£1,000,000 on 6/7/2001) FL 85+2/18 FLC 3 FAC 8/3 Others 5*

KAWAGUCHI Yoshikatsu (Yoshi)
Born: Shizuoka, Japan, 15 August 1975
Height: 5'11" **Weight:** 12.5
International Honours: Japan: 54
Yoshi was second choice 'keeper to Shaka Hislop at Portsmouth last term and was mostly restricted to the substitutes' bench. His only first-team appearance came in the final 45 minutes of the last game of the season at Bradford, when he pulled off two magnificent saves. A vastly experienced 'keeper, he added another cap for Japan when he appeared against Uruguay in March, and also made the squad for the Confederations Cup tournament in the summer.
Portsmouth *(£1,800,000 from Yokohama Antlers, Japan on 24/10/2001) FL 11+1 FAC 1*

KAY Antony Roland
Born: Barnsley, 21 October 1982
Height: 5'11" **Weight:** 11.8
International Honours: E: Yth
This promising Barnsley youngster adapted well to a change of position to centre back last term. Antony came into the first team for the LDV Vans Trophy tie at Bury but then did not reappear until mid-January. By this time the team had switched to a three-man central defensive formation and Antony was employed on the right-hand side. He is strong in the tackle, good with his head and his midfield background means that he reads the game well. Antony can also bring the ball forward and pick out a pass.
Barnsley *(From trainee on 25/10/1999) FL 16+8 Others 1*

Robbie Keane

KEANE Michael Thomas Joseph
Born: Dublin, 29 December 1982
Height: 5'7" **Weight:** 10.10
International Honours: RoI: U21-7; Yth
Preston's tigerish young midfielder had
made only two starts and three
appearances from the bench by October
when a foot injury necessitated a screw
being fitted in a broken bone and
appeared to rule him out for the rest of
the season. However, a quicker than
expected recovery saw him back in
action by February. Whole-hearted in the
tackle, he showed the incisiveness of his
passing when he set up the injury-time
winner for Richard Cresswell against
Stoke, and his recovery was rewarded
with a loan spell to Grimsby on transfer
deadline day. He performed with
enthusiasm and commitment for the
Mariners but was unable to prevent
them from being relegated to the
Second Division.
*Preston NE (From trainee on 7/8/2000) FL
18+9/2 FLC 1+1 FAC 3*
Grimsby T (Loaned on 27/3/2003) FL 7/2

KEANE Robert (Robbie)
David
Born: Dublin, 8 July 1980
Height: 5'9" **Weight:** 11.10
International Honours: RoI: 44; B-1; Yth
(UEFA-U18 '98)
The Republic of Ireland's World Cup hero
came back to Leeds to find himself on the
substitutes' bench at the start of the new
season. Robbie came on and scored with
a mercurial lob on the first day against
Manchester City, but he remained on the
bench and very shortly afterwards joined
Tottenham for a substantial fee.
Undoubtedly the hottest property at Spurs
and Glenn Hoddle's finest buy to date, he
didn't take long to settle and bagged a
hat-trick at home to Everton in probably
his best performance of the season. The
quick thinking and agile striker scored
regularly during the campaign, finishing
up as Spurs' leading scorer with 13
Premiership goals.
*Wolverhampton W (From trainee on
26/7/1997) FL 66+7/24 FLC 7+2/3 FAC 3+2/2*
*Coventry C (£6,000,000 on 20/8/1999) PL
30+1/12 FAC 3 (£13,000,000 to Inter Milan,
Italy on 31/7/1999)*
*Leeds U (£12,000,000 on 22/12/2000) PL
28+18/13 FLC 2/3 FAC 2 Others 6/3*
*Tottenham H (£7,000,000 on 31/8/2002) PL
29/13 FLC 1+1 FAC 1*

KEANE Roy Maurice
Born: Cork, 10 August 1971
Height: 5'10" **Weight:** 12.10

Club Honours: FMC '92; CS '93, '96,
'97; PL '94, '96, '97, '99, '00, '01, '03;
FAC '94, '96, '99
International Honours: RoI: 58; U21-4;
Yth; Sch
An inspirational midfield general, who
possesses excellent skills with a hardened
edge to match, Roy can turn a game with
an inspirational goal. He quickly put the
furore over his autobiography behind him
and played in the Reds first three
Premiership games, opening his goal
account with a strike against Sunderland.
Taking time out to go under the surgeon's
knife for a recurring hip injury, he
returned to the side in late December, and
once again showed why he is so valued
on the United stage. Although he
signalled his retirement from the
international scene, his commitment to
the Reds remains unwavering, particularly
in those blockbusting last few games of
the Premiership campaign when United
needed him at his best. Though many
now see him as possible management
material, Roy proved that he still has a
few miles left in the tank.
*Nottingham F (£10,000 from Cobh
Ramblers on 12/6/1990) F/PL 114/22 FLC 17/6
FAC 18/3 Others 5/2*
*Manchester U (£3,750,000 on 22/7/1993)
PL 252+10/29 FLC 11+2 FAC 36+1/1 Others
80+1/16*

KEARNEY Thomas (Tom)
James
Born: Liverpool, 7 October 1981
Height: 5'9" **Weight:** 11.0
Tom's 2002-03 season was wrecked by a
serious knee injury just four games into
the campaign. He had been a regular in
the Bradford City midfield following the
departure of fans' favourite Stuart
McCall, but the home game with
Grimsby in August proved to be his final
appearance as he underwent major
ligament surgery to save his promising
career. The former Everton youngster
spent a lengthy period at Lilleshall during
his rehabilitation and the Bantams will
be keeping their fingers crossed that Tom
makes a full recovery.
Everton (From trainee on 15/10/1999)
Bradford C (Free on 21/3/2002) FL 9

KEATES Dean Scott
Born: Walsall, 30 June 1978
Height: 5'6" **Weight:** 10.10
This diminutive midfielder initially joined
Hull City on non-contract terms before his
impressive midfield performances earned
a two-year contract. Dean earned a place
in City's history books by netting their first

league goal at the new Kingston
Communications Stadium with a superb
chip in the Boxing Day defeat of
Hartlepool. Usually partnering Ian Ashbee
on the left of the centre-midfield duo, the
Tigers sorely missed his consistency and
tenacity when damaged ankle ligaments
ruled him out of the early weeks of the
new year. He returned to be named
captain in the absence of Justin Whittle
and Ian Ashbee, and also assumed the
duties of penalty taker.
*Walsall (From trainee on 14/8/1996) FL
125+34/9 FLC 15+1/1 FAC 10+4 Others
14+1/3*
Hull C (Free on 23/8/2002) FL 36/4 FLC 1

KEAVENY Jonathan
Born: Swansea, 24 May 1981
Height: 5'9" **Weight:** 11.2
Jonathan was a prolific goal-scorer with
Welsh League outfit Pontardawe Athletic,
and then League of Wales side
Carmarthen Town during 2001-02, and
joined Swansea City in the close season
after impressing in a trial game at the
Vetch. The young striker had a number of
opportunities to impress during the early
part of the campaign, but in October his
contract was paid up by the Swans and
he rejoined Carmarthen.
*Swansea C (Free from Carmarthen T, ex
Pontadarwe A, on 12/7/2002) FL 4+5*

KEEBLE Christopher (Chris)
Mark
Born: Colchester, 17 September 1978
Height: 5'10" **Weight:** 11.8
Chris missed the whole of the 2001-02
season after rupturing his achilles tendon
at Wycombe on the final day of the
previous campaign, and he made just
three substitute appearances for
Colchester last term. The central
midfielder was a regular for the reserves,
but could not break into the first team.
He was released by the U's at the end of
April.
Ipswich T (From trainee on 2/6/1997) FL 0+1
*Colchester U (Free on 23/3/2000) FL
12+12/2 FLC 1+1 Others 1*

KEEN Peter Alan
Born: Middlesbrough, 16 November 1976
Height: 6'0" **Weight:** 12.0
Peter continued as first choice 'keeper for
Carlisle until mid-October when Matty
Glennon returned to Brunton Park. From
then on he saw little first-team action, but
he remained an integral member of the
squad and returned to play in the final
match of the season. A good all-round
performer, Peter's finest moment was

probably his full-length penalty save at Darlington.
Newcastle U *(From trainee on 25/3/1996)*
Carlisle U *(Free on 4/8/1999) FL 58/1 FAC 3 Others 1*
Darlington *(Loaned on 13/3/2001) FL 7*

KEENAN Joseph (Joe) John
Born: Southampton, 14 October 1982
Height: 5'7" **Weight:** 10.8
International Honours: E: Yth
For the second successive season a serious injury interrupted the progress of this promising young midfielder. Joe had the misfortune to suffer a broken leg playing for Chelsea reserves against Arsenal after making just one Premiership substitute appearance for two minutes against Newcastle United. He certainly deserves the rub of the green in the near future to allow him to fulfil his undoubted potential, particularly as coach Claudio Ranieri seems determined to give the Chelsea youngsters their chance.
Chelsea *(From trainee on 15/10/1999) PL 0+2 FAC 0+1*

KEITH Joseph (Joe) Richard
Born: Plaistow, 1 October 1978
Height: 5'7" **Weight:** 10.6
Joe was voted the 'Players' Player of the Year' at Colchester United last term, after another outstanding season at Layer Road. He was the joint-top scorer with nine goals, proving dangerous from free kicks and reliable as a penalty taker. Joe operated down the left flank, starting the season at wing back but ending it as a left-sided midfielder. Never afraid to take on defenders with his mazy runs, his highlights included a wonderful free kick to beat Peterborough in a dour London Road tussle in late August, and a late equaliser at Stockport County in February.
West Ham U *(From trainee on 9/7/1997)*
Colchester U *(Free on 5/7/1999) FL 135+14/17 FLC 6+2/2 FAC 4 Others 3+1*

KEITH Marino
Born: Peterhead, 16 December 1974
Height: 5'10" **Weight:** 12.11
Club Honours: SCC '98; Div 3 '02
Marino struggled to get into Plymouth's first team at the start of last season mainly due to niggling injuries. He made his first start in the LDV Vans Trophy tie against Chester in October and scored in the 2-1 victory. However, towards the end of the season manager Paul Sturrock gave Marino more first-team opportunities and he seized the opportunity with both hands. He went on an excellent goal-

scoring streak including the winner at champions-elect Wigan, ending the campaign as Argyle's leading scorer with 12 goals.
Dundee U *(Free from Fraserburgh on 11/10/1995) SL 0+4 SC 0+1*
Falkirk *(Free on 9/9/1997) SL 53+8/27 SLC 2/1 SC 7/1 Others 1+1*
Livingston *(Signed on 30/7/1999) SL 15+5/7 SLC 1+3 SC 2/3 Others 2*
Plymouth Arg *(Free on 8/11/2001) FL 33+27/20 FAC 3+3 Others 1+1/1*

KELLER Kasey C
Born: Washington DC, USA, 27 November 1969
Height: 6'2" **Weight:** 13.12
Club Honours: FLC '97
International Honours: USA: 62
Injury to Neil Sullivan handed Kasey the goalkeeper's jersey for Tottenham last season and he seized the opportunity with both hands. He produced a number of fine displays, notably in the 'derby' match against Arsenal at White Hart Lane. Kasey's agility and shot-stopping expertise will provide a real challenge to Neil Sullivan's comeback hopes in 2003-04.
Millwall *(Free from Portland University on 20/2/1992) FL 1/6 FLC 14 FAC 8 Others 4*
Leicester C *(£900,000 on 17/8/1996) PL 99 FLC 16 FAC 8 Others 2 (Signed for Rayo Vallecano, Spain during 1999 close season)*
Tottenham H *(Free on 16/8/2001) PL 47 FLC 4 FAC 1*

KELLY Alan Thomas
Born: Preston, 11 August 1968
Height: 6'2" **Weight:** 14.3
International Honours: RoI: 34; U23-1; Yth
Alan had to be content to sit on the bench for Blackburn Rovers for most of last season with regular 'keeper Brad Friedel in such fine form. His only Premiership start came at Charlton in November, although he also managed appearances in the Worthington Cup ties against Walsall and Rotherham. An assured goalkeeper and a more than useful back up, he has signed a further contract that will keep him at Ewood Park for another season.
Preston NE *(From apprentice on 25/9/1985) FL 142 FLC 1 FAC 8 Others 13*
Sheffield U *(£200,000 on 24/7/1992) P/FL 213+3 FLC 15 FAC 22 Others 2*
Blackburn Rov *(£675,000 on 30/7/1999) P/FL 39+1 FLC 6 FAC 4*
Stockport Co *(Loaned on 3/4/2001) FL 2*
Birmingham C *(Loaned on 24/8/2001) FL 6*

KELLY Darren
Born: Derry, 30 June 1979
Height: 6'1" **Weight:** 12.10
This highly rated defender became a fixture in the Carlisle defence following his early-season move from Derry City. Darren's prime attributes include speed and strength in the tackle, but he is also a commanding figure in the air. A fine striker of the ball he was several times close to scoring with pile-driving free kicks, although ironically his only goal was a close-range header against York.
Carlisle U *(£100,000 from Derry C on 21/8/2002) FL 30+2/1 FLC 1 FAC 2 Others 7*

KELLY Garry
Born: Drogheda, 9 July 1974
Height: 5'8" **Weight:** 11.8
International Honours: RoI: 52; U21-5; Yth; Sch
Leeds United's longest-serving player, Garry celebrated ten years at Elland Road with a match against Celtic at the end of 2002 – a game that raised a substantial amount of money for cancer charities. A defender of real pace and with the ability to read the game, he was a squad member all season but did not get a regular run in the side until November, before injury ruled him out in March. A highlight was scoring with a quickly taken free kick in the 2-1 FA Cup victory over Crystal Palace, his first goal for some six years. He also appeared twice for the Republic of Ireland.
Leeds U *(Signed from Home Farm on 24/9/1991) PL 279+11/2 FLC 21+2 FAC 28+1/1 Others 35+1*

KELLY Gary Alexander
Born: Preston, 3 August 1966
Height: 5'11" **Weight:** 13.6
Club Honours: FAYC '85
International Honours: RoI: B-1; U23-1; U21-8
Gary began the 2002-03 season at Oldham, but made no further senior appearances and subsequently moved on to Conference outfit Northwich Victoria. He then joined Sheffield United at the end of March on a non-contract basis as cover for Paddy Kenny. Gary was a regular in the reserves and played in the final league game of the season at Watford, conceding two goals but performing well. He is the older brother of Alan who also kept goal for the Blades, but is now at Blackburn.
Newcastle U *(From apprentice on 20/6/1984) FL 53 FLC 4 FAC 3 Others 2*
Blackpool *(Loaned on 7/10/1988) FL 5*

Bury *(£60,000 on 5/10/1989) FL 236 FLC 14 FAC 13 Others 29*
Oldham Ath *(£10,000 on 27/8/1996) FL 224+1 FLC 13 FAC 19 Others 6 (Freed on 13/12/2002)*
Sheffield U *(Free from Northwich Vic on 26/3/2003) FL 1*

KELLY Stephen Michael
Born: Dublin, 6 September 1983
Height: 5'11" **Weight:** 12.4
International Honours: RoI: U21-3; Yth
This young Tottenham Hotspur defender joined Southend United on loan in February and quickly became a fixture in the line-up playing alongside Leon Cort at centre back. Soon after returning to White Hart Lane he went out on loan again, this time to Queen's Park Rangers where he was used as cover for the injured Terrell Forbes. He quickly impressed the fans and made a strong contribution to the final push for a play-off place. Stephen went on to make his debut for the Republic of Ireland at U21 level during the summer.
Tottenham H *(From juniors on 11/9/2000)*
Southend U *(Loaned on 30/1/2003) FL 10*
Queens Park R *(Loaned on 27/3/2003) FL 7 Others 2*

KELTIE Clark Stuart
Born: Newcastle, 31 August 1983
Height: 6'1" **Weight:** 12.7
After making his debut on the final day of the 2001-02 season, Clark broke into the Darlington first team last October and became firmly established in midfield. He missed only a handful of games from then on, showing commitment in the tackle and mature distribution. Clark possesses a strong shot and scored three cracking goals; all fierce straight drives from well outside the box at Shrewsbury, Scunthorpe and Bristol Rovers.
Darlington *(Free from Walker Central on 19/9/2001) FL 27+4/3 FAC 3 Others 1*

KENNA Jeffrey (Jeff) Jude
Born: Dublin, 27 August 1970
Height: 5'11" **Weight:** 12.2
International Honours: RoI: 27; B-1; U21-8; Yth; Sch
Birmingham City's team captain, Jeff played to a consistent level throughout the 2002-03 season. Steady and undemonstrative, his positional sense at right back was excellent, and even when called to cover at left back due to injuries he never let the side down. A near ever-present in the Blues' line-up, he weighed in with a vital equaliser in the Christmas game at home to Tottenham.
Southampton *(From trainee on 25/4/1989) F/PL 110+4/4 FLC 4 FAC 10+1 Others 3*
Blackburn Rov *(£1,500,000 on 15/3/1995) P/FL 153+2/1 FLC 17+2 FAC 13 Others 7*
Tranmere Rov *(Loaned on 20/3/2001) FL 11*
Wigan Ath *(Loaned on 2/11/2001) FL 6/1 FAC 1*
Birmingham C *(Free on 24/12/2001) P/FL 57+1/1 FLC 1 FAC 1 Others 3*

KENNEDY Mark
Born: Dublin, 15 May 1976
Height: 5'11" **Weight:** 11.9
International Honours: RoI: 34; U21-7; Yth; Sch
Injury ruled the left winger out of the 2002 World Cup finals, and he had not recovered by the start of the 2002-03 season. He eventually returned for Wolves as a substitute against Portsmouth. Mark was then a regular in the team but it took him a few games to get back into things. He retained his place from then on, scoring twice in the 6-0 win over Gillingham. On his day Mark was probably the best winger in the First Division and he contributed greatly to the club's play-off success, scoring the vital goal in the final against Sheffield United at the Millennium Stadium.

Mark Kennedy

Millwall (From trainee on 6/5/1992) FL
37+6/9 FLC 6+1/2 FAC 3+1/1
Liverpool (£1,500,000 on 21/3/1995) PL
5+11 FLC 0+2 FAC 0+1 Others 0+2
Queens Park R (Loaned on 27/1/1998) FL
3/2
Wimbledon (£1,750,000 on 27/3/1998) PL
11+10 FLC 4+1/1 FAC 2
Manchester C (£1,000,000 + on 15/7/1999)
P/FL 56+10/8 FLC 5+4/3 FAC 2

Wolverhampton W (£1,800,000 on
6/7/2001) FL 65+1/8 FLC 1 FAC 5/1 Others
3+1/1

KENNEDY Peter Henry James
Born: Lurgan, 10 September 1973
Height: 5'9" **Weight:** 11.11
Club Honours: Div 2 '98, '03
International Honours: NI: 17; B-1
An important member of Wigan Athletic's

Peter Kennedy

championship-winning side, this left-
footed player favoured a midfield role but
again showed his versatility at left back
when asked to cover for injuries. Blessed
as an excellent crosser and dangerous at
set pieces, he scored with a stunning free
kick to secure a win at Bristol City in
January and seemed to be back to his
best before a bout of chickenpox kept
him sidelined in February. Peter added
two more caps for Northern Ireland
during the season.
Notts Co (£100,000 from Portadown on
28/8/1996) FL 20+2 FLC 1 FAC 2+1/1 Others
0+1
Watford (£130,000 on 10/7/1997) P/FL
108+7/18 FLC 9/2 FAC 7/2 Others 3
Wigan Ath (£300,000 on 18/7/2001) FL
50+3/1 FLC 3 FAC 4 Others 3

KENNY Patrick (Paddy)
Joseph
Born: Halifax, 17 May 1978
Height: 6'1" **Weight:** 14.6
Paddy initially joined Sheffield United on
loan from Bury as cover for the injured
Simon Tracey, but immediately became
first choice 'keeper, signing permanently
in October. He had a superb season,
being excellent as a shot stopper and in
one-on-one situations. He had good
command of his area and regularly acted
as a sweeper behind the defence. It was
in this role that he injured an ankle at
Portsmouth, but he played in several vital
games before resting. Popular with the
supporters, Paddy's consistency won him
the Supporters' Club 'Player of the Year'
award.
Bury (£10,000 + from Bradford PA on
28/8/1998) FL 133 FLC 5 FAC 7 Others 5
Sheffield U (Signed on 26/7/2002) FL 45 FLC
7 FAC 4 Others 3

KENTON Darren Edward
Born: Wandsworth, 13 September 1978
Height: 5'10" **Weight:** 11.11
Darren once again proved himself to be
one of the best defenders outside of the
Premiership with a string of high quality
performances for Norwich City
throughout the 2002-03 campaign. His
early-season form at the heart of the
defence was quite sensational, and he
won a series of 'Man of the Match'
awards. He uses his upper body strength
to good effect to win challenges against
much bigger opponents, he is very good
in the air and the timing of his tackles is
top class. He can also play in either of the
full-back positions, adding versatility to his
list of attributes. After informing the club
that he intended to take advantage of his

'Bosman' status at the end of the season, he was released early from his contract in May.
Norwich C *(From trainee on 3/7/1997) FL 142+16/9 FLC 9+1 FAC 2+2 Others 3*

KEOWN Martin Raymond
Born: Oxford, 24 July 1966
Height: 6'1" **Weight:** 12.4
Club Honours: PL '98, '02; FAC '98, '02, '03; CS '98, '99, '02
International Honours: E: 43; B-1; U21-8; Yth
A fiercely competitive central defender of the highest order, Martin is strong and aggressive in the tackle, and extremely pacy for a big man. His strength in the air makes him a threat from set pieces in the opposition goal area. He formed an excellent central defensive partnership with Sol Campbell both at club and international level. Unfortunately, Martin's season was curtailed somewhat when he sustained a hamstring injury in the Champions' League match against PSV Eindhoven in September, which sidelined him for over two months. Although he recovered full fitness, further injury problems kept him out of the line-up towards the end of the campaign.
Arsenal *(From apprentice on 2/2/1984) FL 22 FAC 5*
Brighton & Hove A *(Loaned on 15/2/1985) FL 21+2/1 FLC 2/1 Others 2/1*
Aston Villa *(£200,000 on 9/6/1986) FL 109+3/3 FLC 12+1 FAC 6 Others 2*
Everton *(£750,000 on 7/8/1989) F/PL 92+4 FLC 11 FAC 12+1 Others 6*
Arsenal *(£2,000,000 on 4/2/1993) PL 279+21/4 FLC 18+2/1 FAC 31+3 Others 45+8/3*

KERR Brian
Born: Motherwell, 12 October 1981
Height: 5'8" **Weight:** 11.2
International Honours: S: 1; U21-11; Yth; Sch
A product of the Newcastle United youth system, Brian shook off a pre-season hamstring problem to make his debut for Scotland U21s against Denmark in August 2002, during which month he also made a substitute appearance in the Champions' League qualifier against Sarajevo. He subsequently went out on loan to Coventry City, where he featured on the right-hand side of midfield, and after his return made his Premiership debut in the home win over Liverpool in January, followed by occasional appearances during the rest of the season. A slight figure who is calm on the ball with good distribution skills he prefers

Dean Kiely

aying as a defensive central midfielder. ian made his full debut for Scotland gainst New Zealand in May.

ewcastle U (From trainee on 4/12/1998) PL +5 FAC 0+2 Others 1+1
oventry C (Loaned on 24/10/2002) FL 2+1 C 1

ERR Scott Anthony
orn: Leeds, 11 December 1981
eight: 5'9" **Weight:** 10.12
cott's stint with Hull City was blighted by serious back injury, and he failed to stablish a place in the first-team squad ue to the considerable turnover of ayers and managers during his recovery eriod. His senior action for City totalled nly 81 minutes of the LDV Vans Trophy e at Port Vale in October. On leaving Hull March the gritty midfielder was soon apped up by Conference club carborough.

radford C (From trainee on 4/7/2000) PL +1 FLC 0+1 Others 1
ull C (Signed on 20/6/2001) Others 1

EWELL Harold (Harry)
orn: Sydney, Australia, 22 September 978
eight: 6'0" **Weight:** 11.10
lub Honours: FAYC '97
ternational Honours: Australia: 14; Yth
y his own standards Harry had a sappointing campaign in 2002-03. Terry enables, his former international anager, played him as a central striker nd he responded by scoring regularly, nd indeed he led the club's scoring harts until Mark Viduka's late prolific urst. Amongst his tally were a number of rilliant efforts, notably in the 2-1 FA Cup ctory over Crystal Palace, when he ceived the ball just inside his opponents' alf with his back to goal and waltzed ound two defenders before unleashing rocket from some 25 yards which hit ne net before the goalkeeper could ove. On the international scene he one in Australia's historic defeat of ngland at Upton Park, scoring one of the oals in a 3-1 victory.

eds U (Signed from the Australian cademy of Sport on 23/12/1995) PL 59+12/45 FLC 8/4 FAC 16/6 Others 34+3/8

HELA Inderpaul
orn: Birmingham, 6 October 1983
eight: 6'0" **Weight:** 12.6
nother product of the Kidderminster uth team, central defender Inderpaul ined the Harriers' senior squad early in e 2002-03 season. However, he had to ait until the end of April before making

his Football League debut when he came on as a substitute at York City, played out of position in midfield he nevertheless almost marked the occasion with a goal. In the months prior to that he had been making a name for himself out on loan at Evesham United in the Dr Martens League.

Kidderminster Hrs (Free from Bedworth U on 28/8/2002) FL 0+1

KIELY Dean Laurence
Born: Salford, 10 October 1970
Height: 6'1" **Weight:** 13.5
Club Honours: Div 2 '97; Div 1 '00
International Honours: RoI: 8; B-1; E: Yth; Sch.
An ever present in goal, Dean had another great season for Charlton Athletic last term, making several outstanding saves and keeping nine clean sheets in league and cup matches. He is very comfortable at dealing with crosses and an excellent shot stopper who commands his area well. Dean announced his retirement from international football in

April having added two more caps for the Republic of Ireland.

Coventry C (From trainee on 30/10/1987)
York C (Signed on 9/3/1990) FL 210 FLC 9 FAC 4 Others 16
Bury (£125,000 on 15/8/1996) FL 137 FLC 13 FAC 4 Others 3
Charlton Ath (£1,000,000 on 26/5/1999) P/FL 146 FLC 7 FAC 10

KIGHTLEY Michael John
Born: Basildon, 24 January 1986
Height: 5'9" **Weight:** 9.12
This former Spurs youngster made excellent progress at Southend last season. Initial promise shown in the U19 academy side led to reserve-team appearances, where the young striker continued to shine. He then made an impressive showing as a substitute in Steve Tilson's testimonial match against an ex-England XI in March. This led to promotion to the first-team substitutes' bench and finally to a brief run out in the final match of the season at Exeter.
Southend U (Trainee) FL 0+1

Kevin Kilbane (left)

KILBANE Kevin Daniel
Born: Preston, 1 February 1977
Height: 6'0" **Weight:** 12.10
International Honours: Rol: 46; U21-11
A tall, pacy left winger, Kevin was called upon to show his versatility last term and appeared in a variety of positions for Sunderland including at left back and central midfield. A regular in the Republic of Ireland side, Kevin scored the first goal of new boss Brian Kerr's reign against Scotland and registered his only goal for the Black Cats at Everton in January. Kevin can also operate as a central striker where his ability to run at and commit defenders can be used.
Preston NE (From trainee on 6/7/1995) FL 39+8/3 FLC 4 FAC 1 Others 1+1
West Bromwich A (£1,000,000 on 13/6/1997) FL 105+1/15 FLC 12/2 FAC 4/1
Sunderland (£2,500,000 on 16/12/1999) PL 97+11/8 FLC 3 FAC 3+4/1

KILFORD Ian Anthony
Born: Bristol, 6 October 1973
Height: 5'10" **Weight:** 11.0
Club Honours: Div 3 '97; AMC '99
After being released by Wigan, Ian spent the first part of the 2002-03 season training with Bury before being handed a trial at Scunthorpe. He quickly impressed in the centre of midfield with good work-rate and excellent passing ability and as a result the move became permanent. He did not miss a match in the second half of the campaign as his experience helped Scunthorpe make the Division Three play-offs.
Nottingham F (From trainee on 3/4/1991) FL 0+1
Wigan Ath (Loaned on 23/12/1993) FL 2+1/2 FAC 0+1
Wigan Ath (Free on 13/7/1994) FL 175+43/30 FLC 14+3/1 FAC 14+2/2 Others 14+2/2
Bury (Free on 16/8/2002)
Scunthorpe U (Free on 8/11/2002) FL 27+1/3 FAC 3+1 Others 2

KILGALLON Matthew
Born: York, 8 January 1984
Height: 6'1" **Weight:** 12.5
International Honours: E: Yth
A product of the Leeds academy, Matthew was already a regular with the reserves before he made his senior debut in the away leg of the UEFA Cup tie against Hapoel Tel Aviv. A tall central defender, quick in the tackle and assured on the ball, he went on to make his Premiership debut in the 1-0 victory over West Ham in February and also featured

on the final day of the season against Aston Villa.
Leeds U (From trainee on 10/1/2001) PL 0+2 Others 0+1

KILHEENEY Ciaran Joseph
Born: Stockport, 9 January 1984
Height: 5'11" **Weight:** 11.9
This promising young striker began last season on the books at Maine Road, but with no first-team place in sight, he opted to join North West Counties League outfit Mossley. The move paid off and in March he returned to the full-time game, signing for Exeter City on a short-term contract. Ciaran impressed in his brief spell at St James' Park, showing plenty of confidence against more experienced defenders. Nevertheless he was unable to keep the club in the Third Division.
Manchester C (From juniors on 1/7/2002. Free to Mossley on 7/1/2003)
Exeter C (Free on 19/3/2003) FL 0+4

KILLEN Christopher (Chris) John
Born: Wellington, New Zealand, 8 October 1981
Height: 5'11" **Weight:** 11.3
International Honours: New Zealand
Kiwi striker Chris joined Oldham Athletic during the summer of 2002 for a fee that could eventually rise to £250,000. He made his debut on the opening day of the season at home to Cardiff and scored the Latics' winner at Peterborough just three days later. However, the unexpected emergence of Wayne Andrews and a niggling ankle injury in mid-March, restricted him to a handful of further appearances. Chris was a regular at international level for New Zealand, featuring in the team that won the Oceania Nations' Cup in July 2002 and also making the squad for the Confederations Cup matches in the summer of 2003.
Manchester C (Free from Miramar Rangers, New Zealand on 8/3/1999) FL 0+3
Wrexham (Loaned on 8/9/2000) FL 11+1/3
Port Vale (Loaned on 24/9/2001) FL 8+1/6 Others 1
Oldham Ath (£200,000 + on 31/7/2002) FL 11+16/3 FLC 2+1/1 FAC 1+2 Others 1

KILLOUGHERY Graham Anthony
Born: London, 22 July 1984
Height: 5'10" **Weight:** 11.7
This Torquay United scholarship boy made his senior debut as a late substitute against Boston United in

March before adding a couple more appearances later in the season. A promising left winger or midfield player he earned a professional contract for the 2003-04 campaign.
Torquay U (Trainee) FL 1+2

KIMBLE Alan Frank
Born: Dagenham, 6 August 1966
Height: 5'9" **Weight:** 12.4
Club Honours: Div 3 '91
Despite being in the veteran stages of hi career and signed predominately as cove Alan always looked classy in his appearances for Luton Town last term. When selected he slotted in well and proved to be a brilliant reader of the game who always knew exactly when to tackle. Alan is an experienced left back who is something of a specialist with set piece kicks.
Charlton Ath (From juniors on 8/8/1984) FL
Exeter C (Loaned on 23/8/1985) FL 1 FLC 1
Cambridge U (Free on 15/3/2002) FL 295+4/24 FLC 23+1 FAC 29/1 Others 22
Wimbledon (£175,000 on 27/7/1993) P/FL 196+19 FLC 22+3/1 FAC 26
Peterborough U (Loaned on 15/3/2002) FL
Luton T (Free on 5/8/2002) FL 8+4 FAC 1 Others 2+1

KINET Christophe
Born: Huy, Belgium, 31 December 1972
Height: 5'8" **Weight:** 10.12
Club Honours: Div 2 '01
Christophe spent much of his time at Millwall on the bench last season, but when he did appear the crowd loved hir for his trickery on the ball and his ability to cause problems for opposition defences. He has a sweet left foot, as Coventry found out to their cost, and w; very effective when brought on to run a' tired defenders.
Millwall (£75,000 from Racing Strasbourg, France, ex Germinal, on 9/2/2000) FL 39+28/7 FLC 4+1/1 FAC 2+4 Others 2+2/3

KING Ledley Brenton
Born: Stepney, 12 October 1980
Height: 6'2" **Weight:** 13.6
International Honours: E: 2; U21-12; Y
Injury kept this most talented defender out of Tottenham's campaign until November, but he was quick to impress upon his return. Surprisingly agile and skilful on the ball, doubts over a niggling achilles problem seem to have vanished and the 2003-04 season looks set to be launch pad for both his Premiership and international career.
Tottenham H (From trainee on 22/7/1998) PL 77+2/1 FLC 7/1 FAC 8+1/1

KING Marlon Francis
Born: Dulwich, 26 April 1980
Height: 6'1" **Weight:** 11.12
Marlon made an emotional return to the Gillingham first-team squad at Ipswich last October following a period of enforced absence. He came off the bench in the dying minutes to be greeted enthusiastically by the huge travelling Gills' army and showed he had lost none of his instincts in front of goal. He went on to notch seven goals in just 12 appearances before he sustained a serious knee injury at Derby in January, which finished his season. Marlon has stated that he will be back in 2003-04, fitter and stronger than ever before and, of course, scoring goals.
Barnet (From trainee on 9/9/1998) FL 36+17/14 FLC 0+2 FAC 0+1 Others 2+2
Gillingham (£255,000 on 28/6/2000) FL 73+17/36 FLC 5+2/3 FAC 5+1/3

KINKLADZE Giorgiou (Giorgi)
Born: Tbilisi, Georgia, 6 November 1973
Height: 5'8" **Weight:** 11.2
International Honours: Georgia: 49
After the turn of the year, Giorgi showed his most consistent form since joining Derby and that was enough to earn him the supporters' vote as 'Player of the Year' with a convincing majority. For all his captivating skill on the ball, knack of picking out passes and ability to play them at the right weight, Giorgi has always been in struggling sides since he entered English football with Manchester City. A succession of managers worried about how to gain maximum returns from his undoubted talent. Quiet, almost shy, off the field, he needs to grab hold of matches more consistently. He has all the equipment and it would be interesting to see him in a genuinely good side. He continued to add to his tally of caps for Georgia.
Manchester C (£2,000,000 from Mretebi Tbilisi, Georgia, ex Mretebi, on 17/8/1995) P/FL 105+1/20 FLC 6 FAC 9/2 (£5,000,000 to Ajax, Holland on 15/5/1998)
Derby Co (Signed on 26/11/1999) P/FL 60+33/7 FLC 3+1/1 FAC 2+1

KINSELLA Mark Anthony
Born: Dublin, 12 August 1972
Height: 5'9" **Weight:** 11.8
Club Honours: GMVC '92; FAT '92; Div 1 '00
International Honours: RoI: 41; B-1; U21-8; Yth
This right-sided midfielder made his debut for Aston Villa in the second game of the season against Tottenham. Mark managed to secure himself a regular place within the side for the first part of the season but then an ear infection caused him to miss the 'derby' clash against West Bromwich Albion in the middle of November and he had to settle for a run of seven games on the bench. However, he struggled to win a place in the side in the second half of the campaign. Mark usually adopted a deep position, allowing the likes of Lee Hendrie to get forward when opportunities arose. Solid, reliable and consistent, he has a good range of passing and a thunderous shot. Mark was a regular for the Republic of Ireland during the season.
Colchester U (Free from Home Farm on 18/8/1989) FL 174+6/27 FLC 11+1/3 FAC 9/2 Others 9+1/5
Charlton Ath (£150,000 on 23/9/1996) P/FL 200+8/19 FLC 4+2 FAC 8+1/3 Others 3
Aston Villa (£750,000 on 23/8/2002) PL 15+4 FLC 2+2 FAC 1

KIRKLAND Christopher (Chris)
Born: Leicester, 2 May 1981
Height: 6'3" **Weight:** 11.7
Club Honours: FLC '03
International Honours: E: U21-7; Yth

Marlon King

Radostin Kishishev (right)

hris seemed destined to play second
ddle to Jerzy Dudek for Liverpool last
eason until fate took a hand. The Pole's
oss of form in November resulted in
hris's elevation to first choice and he
roved a more than capable replacement
maintaining the high standards he
isplayed in his first outing of the season
September against Southampton in the
Vorthington Cup. Sadly his luck took
nother turn in January when he was
arried off in the FA Cup tie against
rystal Palace. The cruciate ligament
jury required an operation and thus
rought his season to a premature end.
evertheless when he is fit again it will be
close call for manager Gerald Houllier to
ecide which of the two 'keepers will be
is first choice in 2003-04.

*oventry C (From trainee on 6/5/1998) P/FL
4 FLC 3+1 FAC 1*
*iverpool (£6,000,000 + on 31/8/2001) PL 9
C 5 FAC 2 Others 3*

KIROVSKI Jovan

Born: Escondido, California, USA, 18
March 1976
Height: 6'1" **Weight:** 12.4
International Honours: USA: 59

Jovan was to some extent a victim of his
own versatility at Birmingham City last
term and received few first-team
opportunities. A skilful, clever player with
an eye for the spectacular, he finally got
into the line-up at Christmas, scoring a
brilliant curled winner at Fulham and
heading an equaliser in the Boxing Day
draw against Everton. An attacking right-
sided player, the arrival of Christophe
Dugarry left him competing for a place on
the substitutes' bench. However, Jovan
had the consolation of being recalled to
the USA national team, scoring in the
end-of-season friendly against New
Zealand and making the squad for the
Confederations Cup tournament in the
summer.

*Crystal Palace (£350,000 from Sporting
Lisbon, Portugal, ex San Diego Nomads,
Borussia Dortmund, on 9/8/2001) FL 25+11/5
FLC 2 FAC 1*
*Birmingham C (Free on 15/8/2002) PL
5+12/2 FLC 1+1 FAC 1*

KISHISHEV Radostin Prodanov

Born: Bulgaria, 30 July 1974
Height: 5'10" **Weight:** 12.4
International Honours: Bulgaria: 50

Having missed most of the previous season
due to knee problems, Radostin featured in
all but four of Charlton Athletic's games in
2002-03. A gifted right-sided midfielder or
wing back, he is an effective tackler who is
very comfortable on the ball and not afraid
to try the unexpected. He scored his first-
ever goal for the Addicks in the home
game with West Ham in January and
added another against Everton also at the
Valley, the following month. Radostin
played regularly for Bulgaria during the

ave Kitson (centre)

campaign, and showed his versatility by appearing in the final three games for Charlton as an orthodox right back when the Addicks' defence was decimated by injury.

Charlton Ath *(£300,000 + from Liteks Lovech, Bulgaria, ex Neftokhimik Burgas, Bursapor, on 14/8/2000) PL 52+12/2 FLC 2 FAC 4+1*

KITSON David (Dave)
Born: Hitchin, 21 January 1980
Height: 6'3" **Weight:** 12.11

Cambridge's tall striker really took off last season, and his displays won plenty of attention from higher league clubs. Strong in the air and very capable on the ground, he hit the target regularly and finished the campaign as leading scorer with 25 goals in all competitions. Dave was voted as the U's 'Player of the Year' and also won a place in the PFA Division Three team for the season.

Cambridge U *(Signed from Arlesey T on 16/3/2001) FL 80+5/30 FLC 3/1 FAC 8/1 Others 7+1/4*

KITSON Paul
Born: Murton, 9 January 1971
Height: 5'11" **Weight:** 10.12
International Honours: E: U21-7

Signed to bring some top-flight experience to the Brighton & Hove Albion strike force, Paul endured a rather unfortunate time at the Withdean Stadium last term. He looked out of sorts from the opening matches and quickly succumbed to a series of injuries that kept him out of the starting line-up for seven months. Even when he did come back he looked short of match fitness and was unable to reproduce the form that had once earned him nearly 30 goals in the Premiership. The highlight was undoubtedly his first goal for the club, a header to seal the points at Reading after he had come on as a substitute.

Leicester C *(From trainee on 15/12/1988) FL 39+11/6 FLC 5/3 FAC 1+1/1 Others 5/1*
Derby Co *(£1,300,000 on 11/3/1992) FL 105/36 FLC 7/3 FAC 5/1 Others 13+1/9*
Newcastle U *(£2,250,000 on 24/9/1994) PL 26+10/10 FLC 3+2/1 FAC 6+1/3 Others 0+1*
West Ham U *(£2,300,000 on 10/2/1997) PL 46+17/18 FLC 2+3/1 FAC 4+1/1 Others 3+5/1*
Charlton Ath *(Loaned on 21/3/2000) FL 2+4/1*
Crystal Palace *(Loaned on 14/9/2000) FL 4*
Brighton & Hove A *(Free on 20/8/2002) FL 7+3/2*

KNIGHT Leon Leroy
Born: Hackney, 16 September 1982
Height: 5'4" **Weight:** 9.10
International Honours: E: Yth

This young striker joined Sheffield Wednesday in a 12-month loan deal covering the 2002-03 campaign, but had a rather disappointing time at Hillsborough. Although he had demonstrated his talents as a goal-scorer at Huddersfield during the previous term, Leon was generally used as a wide midfield player or winger and the expected supply of goals did not arrive. He was in and out of the side and spent much of his time on the substitutes' bench.

Chelsea *(From trainee on 17/9/1999) Others 0+1*
Queens Park R *(Loaned on 9/3/2001) FL 10+1*
Huddersfield T *(Loaned on 23/10/2001) FL 31/16 FAC 2/1 Others 4*
Sheffield Wed *(Loaned on 8/7/2002) FL 14+10/3 FLC 2 FAC 0+1*

KNIGHT Zatyiah (Zat)
Born: Solihull, 2 May 1980
Height: 6'6" **Weight:** 13.8

Leon Knight

International Honours: E: U21-4
Although mostly used as a central
defender where his height is invaluable,
Zat is an excellent passer of the ball and
not out of place in a midfield role. He was
not a first choice for Fulham in 2002-03,
but was called upon on numerous
occasions when the more regular central
defenders were unavailable. His long,
leggy style often enables him to make
last-ditch interceptions to prevent a goal-
scoring opportunity. Zat also enjoys trying
his luck with distance shots on goal, and
though he is yet to score for the first
team he almost opened his account with
an audacious 50-yard effort in the final
minutes at Birmingham.
*Fulham (Signed from Rushall Olympic on
19/2/1999) PL 20+7 FLC 6 FAC 3+1 Others
+2*

Peterborough U (Loaned on 25/2/2000) FL 8

KOLINKO Aleksandrs (Alex)
Born: Latvia, 18 June 1975
Height: 6'3" **Weight:** 13.7
International Honours: Latvia: 38
Although Alex began the 2002-03
campaign as second choice 'keeper at
Crystal Palace, he was soon in action for
the first team following Matt Clarke's
injury. Apart from a couple of spells when
loan players were brought in, he featured
regularly from then on, and was in
particularly good form as the season
closed. The popular player continued to
add to his tally of international
appearances for Latvia, and replaced Eric
Young as the Eagles' most capped player
during the season. He was released in the
summer.

*Crystal Palace (£600,000 from Skonto Riga,
Latvia, ex Metals Riga, on 15/9/2000) FL
79+3 FLC 12 FAC 5*

KONCHESKY Paul Martyn
Born: Barking, 15 May 1981
Height: 5'10" **Weight:** 10.12
International Honours: E: 1; U21-12; Yth
The 2002-03 proved to be an eventful
time for Paul, who won his first full
England international cap when he came
on as a second-half substitute against
Australia at Upton Park in February.
However, he was in the starting line-up
for less than half of Charlton's Premiership
games due to the continuing good form
of the club's other England international
left back, Chris Powell. When Paul did
start it was mostly on the left side of
midfield, and some think his long-term

Paul Konchesky

future may lie in this position. He is quick, strong in the tackle and can play anywhere across the back or in midfield. He has a powerful shot and is a dead-ball specialist. Paul found the net on three occasions, including the Addicks' opening goal of the season at home to Chelsea at the Valley.

Charlton Ath (From trainee on 25/5/1998) P/FL 59+41/4 FLC 5+4/1 FAC 6+1

KONJIC Muhamed (Mo)

Born: Bosnia, 14 May 1970
Height: 6'4" **Weight:** 13.7
International Honours: Bosnia-Herzegovina
Mo's strong physical presence and outstanding heading ability earned him much admiration from the Coventry City fans last term and his mazy up field dribbles began to win him cult status at Highfield Road. He fractured his cheek playing for Bosnia in August, and played on with a protective mask, and then suffered a broken hand against Norwich in October. For the second season running he made more starts than any other Coventry player and his popularity resulted in him being winner of most of the club's 'Player of the Year' awards. Mo was a regular in the Bosnian international side that gained some excellent results during the season.

Coventry C (£2,000,000 from AS Monaco, France, ex Slobada Tuzla, Croatia Belisce, Croatia Zagreb, FC Zurich, on 5/2/1999) P/FL 94+2/2 FLC 7+1 FAC 4

KOUMANTARAKIS George

Born: Athens, Greece, 27 March 1974
Height: 6'4" **Weight:** 13.3
International Honours: South Africa: 11
George arrived at Preston during the January transfer window on a contract until the end of the season. He made his North End debut at home to Nottingham Forest and a lack of match fitness meant he took some time to settle into the style of play. After scoring his first goal in the home match with Derby, the tall and powerful left-footed striker followed up with two in the 5-0 demolition of Walsall and seemed to be developing a real understanding with Richard Cresswell when his season was ended early through a serious knee injury whilst on international duty with South Africa.

Preston NE (Loaned from Basle, Switzerland, ex Manning R, Supersport U, Lucerne, on 23/1/2003) FL 10/3

KOUMAS Jason

Born: Wrexham, 25 September 1979
Height: 5'10" **Weight:** 11.0

International Honours: W: 4
As widely predicted, this talented midfielder moved from Tranmere to West Bromwich Albion early in the 2002-03 season, but not before he had scored two further goals for the Birkenhead club. Jason made his debut for the Baggies in the 1-0 home victory over Fulham and quickly became a huge favourite with the Hawthorns supporters with his driving runs and powerful right-foot shooting. He scored four goals, including a wonderful free kick against Sunderland and a fine effort against Manchester United, when he scampered forward to drive a full-blooded shot past the diving Fabien Barthez. Jason added to his tally of full caps for Wales and was voted as Albion's 'Player of the Year'.

Tranmere Rov (From trainee on 27/11/1997) FL 96+31/25 FLC 9+5/2 FAC 9/5

West Bromwich A (£2,500,000 on 29/8/2002) PL 27+5/4 FLC 1 FAC 2

KOZLUK Robert (Rob)

Born: Mansfield, 5 August 1977
Height: 5'8" **Weight:** 11.7
International Honours: E: U21-2
After recovering from his serious knee injury of the previous season, Rob started the 2002-03 campaign in the right-wing-back position for Sheffield United. He used his pace and anticipation to good effect in defence and was effective coming forward. He lost his place to Phil Jagielka in mid season but in February he took over the problematic left-wing-back slot, becoming a fixture in the line-up. He played some of his best games since joining the Blades, hardly putting a foot wrong. The club's 'joker', he used his long throw to good effect and scored his first senior goal, after more than 100 games, at Grimsby.

Derby Co (From trainee on 10/2/1996) PL 9+7 FLC 3 FAC 2+1

Sheffield U (Signed on 12/3/1999) FL 104+12/1 FLC 4+1 FAC 7 Others 3

Huddersfield T (Loaned on 7/9/2000) FL 14

KUIPERS Michel

Born: Amsterdam, Holland, 26 June 1974
Height: 6'2" **Weight:** 14.10
Club Honours: Div 3 '01; Div 2 '02
The affable Brighton goalkeeper's 2002-03 campaign was ruined by a thigh injury, which niggled for some time before flaring up during a game at Norwich in January, enforcing his substitution. That was the end of his season apart from 45 minutes of reserve football in March, and he underwent an

operation to try to repair the damage. Having also suffered from a back problem earlier in the campaign, Michel will be hoping for better things in 2003-04, as will all his fans at the Withdean Stadium. A magnificent shot stopper, he provides a reliable last line of defence when fully fit.

Bristol Rov (Free from SDW Amsterdam, Holland on 20/1/1999) FL 1

Brighton & Hove A (Free on 4/7/2000) FL 94 FLC 2 FAC 5 Others 5

KUQI Shefki

Born: Albania, 10 November 1976
Height: 6'2" **Weight:** 13.10
International Honours: Finland: 31
This burly striker had a somewhat inconsistent season for Sheffield Wednesday in 2002-03. His pace and commitment were great assets to the side, but although he finished as the club's leading scorer with eight goals he never seemed to fully realise his potential. Although mostly a regular in the starting line-up he lost his place for short spells and also spent time on the substitutes' bench.

Stockport Co (£300,000 from FC Jokerit, Finland, ex HJK Helsinki, on 31/1/2001) FL 32+3/11 FLC 2/1 FAC 1

Sheffield Wed (£700,000 + on 11/1/2002) FL 51+6/14 FLC 2 FAC 1

KYLE Kevin Alistair

Born: Stranraer, 7 June 1981
Height: 6'3" **Weight:** 13.7
International Honours: S: 7; U21-8
A tall powerful young Scottish centre forward, Kevin made a real breakthrough into the Sunderland first team last term, partnering Kevin Phillips in the curtain raiser at Blackburn. At 6ft 4in, the striker could well be a long-term successor to the now retired Niall Quinn and is already a full Scotland international. He scored his first Sunderland goal in the 3-2 Worthington Cup win at Arsenal in November and although still learning his trade, Kevin's aerial power and physical style have already earmarked him as a potential star of the future. Indeed, he was desperately unlucky not to write himself a page in Wearside folklore in April when a last-minute headed equalise against local rivals Newcastle was harshly disallowed.

Sunderland (Free from Ayr Boswell on 25/9/1998) PL 9+14 FLC 2+1/1 FAC 2+2

Huddersfield T (Loaned on 8/9/2000) FL 0+

Darlington (Loaned on 1/11/2000) FL 5/1 FAC 3/1

Rochdale (Loaned on 26/1/2001) FL 3+3

L

LABANT Vladimir
Born: Slovakia, 8 June 1974
Height: 6'0" **Weight:** 11.7
International Honours: Slovakia: 24
The Slovakian left-sided defender only made one appearance for West Ham last term, coming on as a substitute in the season's opening game at Newcastle. He played for Slovakia against Turkey in September but after finding it hard to adjust to the Premiership he rejoined Sparta Prague in a long-term loan deal in December. At his best he is a tough tackler with a cultured left foot.
West Ham U (£900,000 from Sparta Prague, Czechoslovakia, ex Slavia Sofia, on 1/1/2002) PL 7+6 FAC 0+2

LABARTHE Albert **Gianfranco** Jome
Born: Lima, Peru, 20 September 1984
Height: 5'10" **Weight:** 10.7
International Honours: Peru: Yth
This talented young striker joined Huddersfield Town after the January transfer window opened and impressed in the reserves with his close control, pace and an ability to score goals. He went on to make three brief substitute appearances late in the season. Gianfranco also represented Peru in the South American U20 championships early in the new year.
Huddersfield T (Free from Sport Boys, Peru, ex Cantolao, on 30/1/2003) FL 0+3

LACEY Damian James
Born: Bridgend, 3 August 1977
Height: 5'9" **Weight:** 11.3
Club Honours: Div 3 '00
Damian's long-standing foot problems cropped up again in the close season, preventing him from being included in the Swansea line-up for the first couple of games. He was surprisingly given a second-half substitute role in the Worthington Cup first round against Wolves and then retained his place in the team for a number of games in a central-midfield role. However, his foot problems returned in November and in the new year it was confirmed that he was to retire from the game.
Swansea C (From trainee on 1/7/1996) FL 15+29/2 FLC 3+1 FAC 3+1 Others 6/1

LAMBERT Rickie Lee
Born: Liverpool, 16 February 1982
Height: 5'10" **Weight:** 11.2
By and large the 2002-03 campaign

proved to be a season of under achievement at Stockport for the former Macclesfield man. A promising striker or midfielder, it wasn't until January that he scored his first goal, a consolation in the 5-2 drubbing by Swindon Town. His next strike showed some of his potential when he fired in a fantastic free kick in the 2-2 draw with Blackpool in March. Rickie certainly showed glimpses of his undoubted ability, but needs to add more consistency to his game.
Blackpool (From trainee on 17/7/2000) FL 0+3
Macclesfield T (Free on 2/3/2001) FL 36+8/8 FAC 4/2 Others 1
Stockport Co (£300,000 on 30/4/2003) FL 22+7/2 FLC 1 Others 2

LAMPARD Frank James
Born: Romford, 20 June 1978
Height: 6'0" **Weight:** 12.6
International Honours: E: 11; B-1; U21-19; Yth
The disappointment of his omission from the 2002 World Cup squad inspired Frank to produce the best form of his career at Chelsea last term and so force his way back into the England set-up. He has developed into one of the most effective 'box-to-box' midfield players in the Premiership allied to neat, incisive passing and opportunistic goal-scoring making him an intrinsic member of Chelsea's formidable squad. Frank is an automatic choice for the Blues and played in every one of their 48 fixtures, notching eight goals. It is a measure of his consistency and fitness that he has passed the 100-match milestone in his two seasons at Stamford Bridge and the last-gasp Champions' League qualification was a fitting reward for his endeavours.
West Ham U (From trainee on 1/7/1995) PL 132+16/23 FLC 15+1/9 FAC 13/2 Others 10/4
Swansea C (Loaned on 6/10/1995) FL 8+1/1 Others 1+1
Chelsea (£11,000,000 on 3/7/2001) PL 71+4/11 FLC 7 FAC 12+1/2 Others 5+1/2

LANGLEY Richard Barrington Michael
Born: Harlesden, 27 December 1979
Height: 5'10" **Weight:** 11.4
International Honours: Jamaica: 6; E: Yth
This versatile midfield player was a regular fixture for Queen's Park Rangers last term, only missing games when he was injured or suspended. Although not usually a prolific scorer, he netted a respectable tally of ten goals, including a hat-trick in

the away game at Blackpool. Richard again linked up with the Jamaica national squad and added several more caps during the season.
Queens Park R (From trainee on 31/12/1996) FL 122+10/17 FLC 5/1 FAC 7 Others 2/1

LARKIN Colin
Born: Dundalk, Ireland, 27 April 1982
Height: 5'9" **Weight:** 10.4
International Honours: RoI: Yth
Colin was signed by Mansfield Town in the summer of 2002 as a replacement for the departed Chris Greenacre. He soon had the fans saying 'Chris who?' when he started the season in goal-scoring form, netting three times in his first two outings. However, an unfortunate series of injuries meant that he was in and out of the side for most of the season, which made it difficult for him to recapture his earlier form. The pacy young striker will be looking to have a better time in 2003-04.
Wolverhampton W (From trainee on 19/5/1999) FL 1+2 FLC 0+1/1
Kidderminster Hrs (Loaned on 14/9/2001) FL 31+2/6 Others 1+1/1
Mansfield T (£135,000 on 9/8/2002) FL 13+9/7 FAC 2 Others 1

LARRIEU Romain
Born: Mont-de-Marsan, France, 31 August 1975
Height: 6'4" **Weight:** 13.11
Club Honours: Div 3 '02
Romain continued to enhance his reputation as one of the best goalkeepers in Plymouth Argyle's recent history during 2002-03. He again showed some fine form producing several excellent displays. His strengths are his agility and excellent reflexes resulting in many point blank saves. His season was briefly interrupted by two dislocated fingers in October but he was soon back in action and signed an extension to his contract during the campaign.
Plymouth Arg (Free from ASOA Valence, France, ex Montpellier, on 30/11/2000) FL 102+1 FLC 2 FAC 8 Others 3

[LAUREN] LAUREANO Bisan-Etame Mayer
Born: Lodhji Krib, Cameroon, 19 January 1977
Height: 5'11" **Weight:** 11.4
Club Honours: FAC '02, '03; PL '02; CS '02
International Honours: Cameroon: 25 (ANC '00, OLYM '00)
Now in his third season at Arsenal, a

Frank Lampard

series of excellent performances made Lauren the automatic choice at right back following Lee Dixon's retirement. He is a tenacious defender, skilful and resilient, who can also play in the centre or on the right-hand side of midfield if required. A strong tackler, he has become a forceful presence in the Arsenal defence. Lauren also possesses good creative skills, which enable him to start attacking moves in his own half, make surging runs down the right flank and deliver good crosses to the strikers. He is one of the game's quiet men, and off the field is softly spoken and intelligent.

Arsenal (£7,200,000 from Real Mallorca, Spain, ex Cant Sevilla, Utrera, Seville, Levante, on 16/6/2000) PL 68+4/5 FAC 13/2 Others 27+6/1

LAVILLE Florent
Born: Valence, France, 7 August 1973
Height: 6'0" **Weight:** 13.0
Known as 'The Rock' in his native France, Florent quickly lived up to that nickname when signing on loan for Bolton during the January transfer window. He made an outstanding debut in the home draw with Manchester United and subsequently remained in the side until an unfortunate red card against Arsenal resulted in him missing the final game of the season. It is no coincidence that Bolton's record whilst he played resulted in four wins and four draws from ten games, including eight clean sheets. A strong and composed centre back, it was a top priority for Wanderers to sign Florent on a permanent basis once the season ended.
Bolton W (Loaned from Lyon, France on 1/2/2003) PL 10

LAWRENCE Denis William
Born: Trinidad, 1 August 1974
Height: 6'7" **Weight:** 12.7
International Honours: Trinidad & Tobago: 34
'Tall Man', as he is affectionately known by Wrexham fans, finally arrived last season and became nothing short of a cult figure at the Racecourse. After a shaky start when prone to odd errors his lanky frame became a permanent fixture in the starting line-up. He likes nothing better than to venture forward with the ball at his feet, which has the fans in a frenzy. Ungainly, but hugely effective Denis seems to have adjusted to the pace of the Football League, and contributed the second goal at Oxford in February in a vital win towards promotion.
Wrexham (£100,000 from Defence Force,

Trinidad on 10/3/2001) FL 60+7/3 FLC 2 FAC 0+1 Others 2

LAWRENCE James (Jamie) Hubert
Born: Balham, 8 March 1970
Height: 5'11" **Weight:** 12.11
Club Honours: FLC '97
International Honours: Jamaica: 12
Jamie played something of a bit-part role for Bradford in what proved to be his final season at Valley Parade. A fast attacking player, who is more suited to a place on the right-hand side of midfield, he was unable to earn a regular run in the line-up. With his contract due to expire in the summer he was allowed to join Walsall just before the transfer deadline. He impressed in his brief period at Bescot, producing a battling performance in the

vital 1-0 win at Gillingham on his debut, and then showing the sort of power and drive from midfield that the team had been missing for some time.
Sunderland (Signed from Cowes on 15/10/1993) FL 2+2 FLC 0+1
Doncaster Rov (£20,000 on 17/3/1994) FL 16+9/3 FLC 2 FAC 1 Others 3
Leicester C (£125,000 on 6/1/1995) P/FL 21+26/1 FLC 3+4/2 FAC 1+1
Bradford C (£50,000 on 17/6/1997) P/FL 133+22/12 FLC 8+1/1 FAC 4+1/1 Others 0+2
Walsall (Free on 27/3/2003) FL 4+1

LAWRENCE Liam
Born: Retford, 14 December 1981
Height: 5'10" **Weight:** 11.3
This exciting Mansfield Town prospect had an excellent season at Field Mill when he was a near ever-present in the line-up. He

Liam Lawrence

suffered somewhat from the absence of Bobby Hassell, but nevertheless produced some fine form in a wide-midfield role and scored a healthy total of goals. One of an exciting crop of youngsters to make his mark in the promotion side of 2001-02, Liam fully deserved his 'Player of the Year' award from the Stags' Supporters' Association.
Mansfield T (From trainee on 3/7/2000) FL 79+16/16 FLC 2 FAC 4/2 Others 1+2

LAWRENCE Matthew (Matt) James
Born: Northampton, 19 June 1974
Height: 6'1" **Weight:** 12.12
Club Honours: Div 2 '01
International Honours: E: Sch
This tough-tackling, hard-working right back showed tremendous consistency for Millwall last season, preventing rivals for his position getting much of a look-in. Matt linked well with Paul Ifill down the right flank, and put opposition defences under pressure with some excellent crosses. He has now made over 100 senior appearances for the Lions, but has yet to get his name on the score sheet.
Wycombe W (£20,000 from Grays Ath on 19/1/1996) FL 13+3/1 FLC 4 FAC 1 Others 0+1
Fulham (Free on 7/2/1997) FL 57+4 FLC 4+1 FAC 2 Others 5
Wycombe W (£86,000 + on 2/10/1998) FL 63/4 FLC 4 FAC 6 Others 3
Millwall (£200,000 on 21/3/2000) FL 109+4 FLC 6+1 FAC 9 Others 6

LAWSON Ian James
Born: Huddersfield, 4 November 1977
Height: 5'11" **Weight:** 11.5
This Bury striker's season was once again largely wrecked by injury in 2002-03, with an ankle problem keeping him sidelined in pre-season and the early months. Ian battled on and fought his way back into contention in November, emphasising that he had lost none of his prolific finishing power by scoring three goals in four games during January including the winners against Hull and Swansea. Further injury problems in the closing months left Ian attempting to regain his fitness in the reserves.
Huddersfield T (From trainee on 26/1/1995) FL 13+29/5 FLC 1+4 FAC 1+1
Blackpool (Loaned on 6/11/1998) FL 5/3
Blackpool (Loaned on 8/1/1999) FL 4
Bury (£75,000 on 16/7/1999) FL 20+5/11 FLC 2/1 FAC 3+1 Others 1
Stockport Co (£150,000 on 17/2/2000) FL 14+1/4
Bury (Free on 12/9/2001) FL 15+16/7 FAC 2 Others 4/2

LAZARIDIS Stanley (Stan)
Born: Perth, Australia, 16 August 1972
Height: 5'9" **Weight:** 11.12
International Honours: Australia: 56; U23; Yth
Despite the fact that Stan did not make the Birmingham City starting line-up until October, he went on to enjoy his best season to date in a Blues' shirt. He inspired the team to victory at West Ham and later in the campaign forged a great understanding with Christophe Dugarry. In fact Stan's rangy running and supply of crosses and through balls made him the team's most potent attacking weapon. A member of the Australian team that defeated England in February, he was named by Blues' boss Steve Bruce as 'Clubman of the Year'.
West Ham U (£300,000 from West Adelaide, Australia on 8/9/1995) PL 53+16/3 FLC 6+1 FAC 9+1 Others 0+1
Birmingham C (£1,600,000 on 29/7/1999) P/FL 91+33/6 FLC 11+3 FAC 1+1 Others 2+5

LEACOCK Dean
Born: Croydon, 10 June 1984
Height: 6'2" **Weight:** 12.4
International Honours: E: Yth
This talented young defender continued to progress with Fulham last term, making his first-team debut in the Worthington Cup tie at Wigan, and after a shaky start to the game he gave a good account of himself. Towards the end of the season he made the bench as an unused substitute on several occasions. A right back who has excellent positional sense and is firm in the tackle he has represented England at both U19 and U20 levels during the course of the season.
Fulham (From trainee on 17/7/2002) FLC 1

LEARY Michael
Born: Ealing, 17 April 1983
Height: 5'11" **Weight:** 12.3
International Honours: RoI: Yth
Despite only playing one full first-team game for Luton, in the LDV Vans Trophy against Woking, and coming on as a substitute in the FA Cup first round against Grimsby Town, this promising youngster did enough in the reserves to earn his first full professional contract. Michael usually played down the flanks in the second string. He is a good passer and crosser of the ball and likes to get into the play creating chances for the forwards by making diverting runs.
Luton T (From juniors on 3/8/2001) Others 1+1

LEE Alan Desmond
Born: Galway, 21 August 1978
Height: 6'2" **Weight:** 13.9

International Honours: RoI: U21-5
The powerfully built striker was soon into his best form for Rotherham last term, reaching double figures by the end of October and he continued to show improved form throughout the season, although he was often on the receiving end of some harsh refereeing decisions. For a big man, he possesses great speed and opposing defences frequently had trouble in coping with him, while he netted a superbly headed goal against promoted Leicester City and thoroughly deserved his call up to the full Republic of Ireland international squad.
Aston Villa (From trainee on 21/8/1995)
Torquay U (Loaned on 27/11/1998) FL 6+1/2 Others 2/1
Port Vale (Loaned on 2/3/1999) FL 7+4/2
Burnley (£150,000 on 8/7/1999) FL 2+13 FLC 1+1 FAC 0+2 Others 1/1
Rotherham U (£150,000 on 21/9/2000) FL 104+6/37 FLC 4/2 FAC 4+1/1 Others 1/1

LEE Andrew (Andy) Jack
Born: Bradford, 18 August 1982
Height: 5'7" **Weight:** 9.7
Bradford City have high hopes for this left-sided player, who is at home in defence or in midfield. Another product of the club's youth system, Andy's only appearance in the senior side was as a substitute for the last seven minutes at Wimbledon in February. He joined Unibond League outfit Wakefield & Emley on loan for the last three months of the season to get a taste of regular first-team football.
Bradford C (From trainee on 5/7/2001) FL 0+2

LEE David John Francis
Born: Basildon, 28 March 1980
Height: 5'11" **Weight:** 11.8
This Brighton reserve midfielder enjoyed a one-month loan spell at Bristol Rovers last October initially starting for the Pirates up front before being switched to a central midfield role, a position he preferred. A good passer of the ball David enjoyed his spell at the Memorial Stadium before returning to second-string football on the South Coast.
Tottenham H (From trainee on 17/7/1998)
Southend U (Free on 2/8/2000) FL 37+5/8 FLC 2 FAC 3 Others 5/2
Hull C (Free on 1/6/2001) FL 2+9/1 FLC 0+1 FAC 0+1 Others 0+1
Brighton & Hove A (Free on 11/1/2002) FL 0+2
Bristol Rov (Loaned on 16/10/2002) FL 5 Others 1

LEE Graeme Barry
Born: Middlesbrough, 31 May 1978
Height: 6'2" **Weight:** 13.7
A central defender who has occasionally been used as a striker, Graeme is Hartlepool's longest-serving player. He had a most successful 2002-03 campaign, and during the season completed his 200th league appearance. An excellent header of the ball, he was steady at the centre of defence forming a great partnership with Chris Westwood. Graeme was also named in the PFA Division Three side chosen by his fellow professionals.
Hartlepool U (From trainee on 2/7/1996) FL 208+11/19 FLC 7+2/1 FAC 8+1 Others 13+2/2

LEE Jason Benedict
Born: Forest Gate, 9 May 1971
Height: 6'3" **Weight:** 13.8
Club Honours: Div 2 '98
Jason returned to action with Peterborough United last August after missing the whole of the 2001-02 campaign through injury. He initially looked a little rusty, as was to be expected, but he retained his enthusiastic approach and he was still hard to beat in the air. A highlight of his campaign was netting a brace in the 4-1 win over Chesterfield in December, but he was released by Posh in the summer.
Charlton Ath (From trainee on 2/6/1989) FL 0+1 Others 0+2
Stockport Co (Loaned on 6/2/1991) FL 2
Lincoln C (£35,000 on 1/3/1991) FL 86+7/21 FLC 6 FAC 2+1/1 Others 4
Southend U (Signed on 6/8/1993) FL 18+6/3 FLC 1 FAC 1 Others 5+3/3
Nottingham F (£200,000 on 4/3/1994) F/PL 41+35/14 FLC 4+3/1 FAC 0+5 Others 4+2
Charlton Ath (Loaned on 5/2/1997) FL 7+1/3
Grimsby T (Loaned on 27/3/1997) FL 2+5/2
Watford (£200,000 on 16/6/1997) FL 36+1/11 FLC 4 FAC 4 Others 1
Chesterfield (£250,000 on 28/8/1998) FL 17+11/1 FAC 0+2 Others 0+2
Peterborough U (£50,000 on 3/1/2000) FL 49+29/17 FAC 5/1 Others 2+2/1

LEE Martyn James
Born: Guildford, 10 September 1980
Height: 5'6" **Weight:** 9.0
Martyn suffered an ankle injury in pre-season training, which delayed his first start of the season for Wycombe until December. He was then ever-present on the bench until his second and final start of the season in April, before being released in the summer. With a sweet left foot and good passing skills Martyn still has much to offer the full time game.
Wycombe W (From trainee on 30/1/1999) FL 22+19/3 FAC 4+2 Others 3+1
Cheltenham T (Loaned on 28/3/2002) FL 2+3 Others 1+1

LEE Richard Anthony
Born: Oxford, 5 October 1982
Height: 6'0" **Weight:** 12.8
International Honours: E: Yth
This young goalkeeper spent most of the 2002-03 season understudying Alec Chamberlain from the Watford substitutes' bench. He made his first-team debut against Preston in March and was unfortunate to face an early spot kick. However he gained in assurance and confidence after that setback and kept clean sheets in his remaining three matches thanks to sound handling and decision-making and a good command of his area. A regular in Watford's reserve side that won the Barclaycard Premiership Reserve League South, Richard also

Alan Lee

received an England U20 call up at the end of the campaign.
Watford *(From trainee on 7/3/2001) FL 4*

LEE Robert (Rob) Martin
Born: West Ham, 1 February 1966
Height: 5'11" **Weight:** 11.13
Club Honours: Div 1 '93
International Honours: E: 21; B-1; U21-2

Rob, along with Warren Barton one of only two players John Gregory was able to bring in, laboured mightily to make

sense of Derby's midfield. He opened the season with a fine goal against Reading but his shooting was increasingly wayward until he clipped one in against Ipswich Town in the final game. It was a farewell because his contract was not renewed at the end of the season. As an expected push for the play-offs turned into a battle against relegation, Derby increasingly needed Rob's solid virtues, winning the ball and giving it to somebody in a matching shirt. As he passed a 37th birthday, physical demands

were high but, over nine months he was the most consistent player, setting a fine example of professionalism.
Charlton Ath *(Free from Hornchurch on 12/7/1983) FL 274+24/59 FLC 16+3/1 FAC 14/2 Others 10+2/3*
Newcastle U *(£700,00 on 22/9/1992) F/PL 292+11/44 FLC 22+1/3 FAC 27/5 Others 28*
Derby Co *(£250,000 + on 7/2/2002) P/FL 47+1/2 FLC 2*

LEGG Andrew (Andy)
Born: Neath, 28 July 1966
Height: 5'8" **Weight:** 10.7
Club Honours: WC '89, '91; AIC '95
International Honours: W: 6

Andy Legg just loves proving people wrong. He has played more than 600 first-team matches during his career, but will not listen to anybody who suggests his playing days may be coming to an end. He burst back into the Cardiff City team at the end of last season and played a major role in the chase that ended in promotion to Division One. Featuring on the left-hand side of midfield, he started all three play-off games, culminating with an outstanding display against Queen's Park Rangers in the final at the Millennium Stadium. Andy was then rewarded with a new contract, which he quickly agreed.
Swansea C *(Signed from Britton Ferry on 12/8/1988) FL 155+8/29 FLC 9+1 FAC 16/4 Others 15+3/5*
Notts Co *(£275,000 on 23/7/1993) FL 85+4/9 FLC 11 FAC 7+1/2 Others 13+2/6*
Birmingham C *(Signed on 29/2/1996) FL 31+14/5 FLC 3+1 FAC 2+1*
Ipswich T *(Loaned on 3/11/1997) FL 6/1 FLC 1*
Reading *(£75,000 on 20/2/1998) FL 12 FLC 1*
Peterborough U *(Loaned on 15/10/1998) FL 5*
Cardiff C *(Free on 16/12/1998) FL 152+23/12 FLC 8+1 FAC 17+4 Others 4*

LEGWINSKI Sylvain
Born: Clermont-Ferrand, France, 6 October 1973
Height: 6'3" **Weight:** 11.7
International Honours: France: U21

A first choice for Fulham much of last season, Sylvain enjoyed some outstanding games whilst appearing out of sorts in others. Although primarily a central midfielder he was often used on the flanks and his style of play linked defence and attack with ease. He started the season in excellent goal-scoring form with a double in the opening game against Bolton and a dramatic last-minute winner

Andy Legg

gainst Tottenham. His best effort,
ough, was reserved for the crucial
aster home game against Newcastle
hen he demonstrated his lethal long-
stance shooting ability to turn the game
Fulham's favour.
ulham *(£3,500,000 from Bordeaux, France,
x AS Monaco, on 22/8/2001) PL 63+5/7 FLC
+1/1 FAC 8/1 Others 10+2/2*

EIGERTWOOD Mikele
enjamin
orn: Enfield, 12 November 1982
eight: 6'1" **Weight:** 13.11
fter making his league debut in the final
ame of 2001-02, Mikele began last
eason on the bench. However,
/imbledon's poor start meant that he
as given an early chance, which he took
ull advantage of. Sturdily built, he added
uch-needed strength as well as pace to
e back line and the Dons enjoyed their
est run of the season when he was in
e team. An ankle ligament injury in
aining ruled him out of some key
atches in the spring, and by the time he
turned the Dons' play-off hopes had
vaporated. A good tackler and strong in
e air, he scored his first goal for the club
the excellent Worthington Cup win at
ortsmouth.
*/imbledon (From trainee on 29/6/2001) FL
3+1 FLC 3/1 FAC 2*
*eyton Orient (Loaned on 19/11/2001) FL 8
AC 2*

EITAO Jorge Manuel
asconcelos
orn: Oporto, Portugal, 14 January 1974
eight: 5'11" **Weight:** 13.4
orge completed his third campaign at
/alsall with a series of displays
haracterised by his tireless running. He
pened his season's account with a
elightful right-foot shot at Brighton,
en hammered home a left-foot winner
the Worthington Cup tie against
hrewsbury and a few weeks later got a
vo-goal haul in the 4-2 win over Stoke.
orge found a most useful striking partner
Junior, and although he reached double
gures in league and cup games for the
ird successive season many Walsall fans
el that the best of him may not yet have
een seen.
*/alsall (£150,000 from SC Farense,
ortugal, ex Avintes, on 10/8/2000) FL
07+19/37 FLC 8/4 FAC 9+1/3 Others 3*

EONHARDSEN Oyvind
orn: Kristiansund, Norway, 17 August
970
eight: 5'10" **Weight:** 11.2

International Honours: Norway: 86;
U21-14; Yth
Oyvind had to wait a while to get into
Aston Villa's starting line-up last term and
it was not until the end of October that
he started his first game. However, after
breaking through he went on to enjoy a
sustained spell in the side during
November and December. Unfortunately,
he suffered a niggling hamstring injury on
Boxing Day and did not appear in the side
again until the beginning of April. Oyvind
is a talented right-sided midfielder who
sets up many goal-scoring chances for his
colleagues. He continued to feature at
international level for Norway.
*Wimbledon (£660,000 from Rosenborg,
Norway, ex Clausenengen, Molde, on
8/11/1994) PL 73+3/13 FLC 7+2/1 FAC 17/2*
*Liverpool (£3,500,000 on 3/6/1997) PL
34+3/7 FLC 4+2 FAC 1 Others 3+2*
*Tottenham H (£3,000,000 on 6/8/1999) PL
46+8/7 FLC 6+2/2 FAC 3+3/1 Others 4/1*
*Aston Villa (Free on 30/8/2002) PL 13+6/3
FLC 3+1*

LE PEN Ulrich
Born: Auray, France, 21 January 1974
Height: 5'8" **Weight:** 9.12
This experienced left winger featured as a
substitute for Ipswich Town in their UEFA
Cup tie away to Avenir Beggin before
returning to France to sign for Strasbourg
in a 12-month loan deal. He featured
regularly for them at first-team level,
scoring three goals.
*Ipswich T (£1,400,000 from Lorient, France,
ex Rennes, Lavallois, on 15/11/2001) PL 0+1
FAC 0+1 Others 0+1*

LE SAUX Graeme Pierre
Born: Jersey, 17 October 1968
Height: 5'10" **Weight:** 12.2
Club Honours: PL '95; FLC '98; ESC '98;
CS '00
International Honours: E: 36; B-2; U21-4
Although the international career of this
top-class left wing back seems to be over,
Graeme played an influential role in
Chelsea's 2002-03 season. He figured at
left back and left midfield and was later
given a roving commission by coach
Ranieri, which frequently led to him
appearing on the right flank and just
behind the strikers from where he
notched valuable goals against West
Bromwich Albion and Charlton. Whether
whipped in from the right or curled in
from the left, the Blues' front men feasted
on his delightful left-footed crosses. An
articulate, approachable and likeable man,
it is 14 years since Graeme made his
debut for Chelsea and he passed the 300-

match milestone for the club during the
season.
*Chelsea (Free from St Paul's, Jersey on
9/12/1987) F/PL 77+13/8 FLC 7+6/1 FAC 7+1
Others 8+1*
*Blackburn Rov (£750,000 on 25/3/1993) PL
127+2/7 FLC 10 FAC 8 Others 6+1*
*Chelsea (£5,000,000 on 8/8/1997) PL
133+7/4 FLC 10/1 FAC 18+2/2 Others 20+2*

LESCOTT Aaron Anthony
Born: Birmingham, 2 December 1978
Height: 5'8" **Weight:** 10.9
Aaron got better and better for Stockport
County as the 2002-03 season
progressed. A real box-to-box midfielder
he won over the fans with his totally
committed performances that helped the
club move away from the relegation zone,
and scored his first goal for County in the
5-2 defeat by Swindon Town in January.
Aaron is the older brother of Wolves'
Joleon.
*Aston Villa (From trainee on 5/7/1996) FAC
0+1*
Lincoln C (Loaned on 14/3/2000) FL 3+2
*Sheffield Wed (Loaned on 3/10/2000) FL
19+18 FLC 3+1 FAC 2*
*Stockport Co (£75,000 on 14/11/2001) FL
53+5/1 FLC 1+1 FAC 2+1 Others 1*

LESCOTT Joleon Patrick
Born: Birmingham, 16 August 1982
Height: 6'2" **Weight:** 13.0
International Honours: E: U21-2; Yth
This powerful central defender was not at
his best for Wolves early on in the 2002-
03 season, but soon settled down to reel
off some consistently good displays.
Having been helped by the experienced
Paul Butler last season, Joleon showed his
maturity by partnering young Mark Clyde
for a spell. His strength was that he was a
very difficult barrier for opponents to pass
and he produced some truly dominant
performances at the back, rarely missing a
match all season. Joleon was selected as a
member of the PFA First Division team for
the season, won England U21 honours
and was voted as the Wolves 'Player of
the Season'.
*Wolverhampton W (From trainee on
18/8/1999) FL 119+6/8 FLC 6 FAC 6 Others 5*

LESTER Jack William
Born: Sheffield, 8 October 1975
Height: 5'10" **Weight:** 11.8
Club Honours: AMC '98
International Honours: E: Sch
Jack played the majority of his games for
Nottingham Forest in the 'hole' behind
the forwards last season. The role suited
him well and he proved very effective,

contributing seven valuable goals as the club made it to the play-offs. However, disciplinary problems restricted his appearances in the second half of the campaign and he was rather unfortunate to be released by Forest in the summer.
Grimsby T *(From juniors on 8/7/1994)* FL 93+40/17 FLC 13+4/6 FAC 8+1/2 Others 4+4
Doncaster Rov *(Loaned on 20/9/1996)* FL 5+6/1
Nottingham F *(£300,000 on 28/1/2000)* FL 73+26/21 FLC 3/3 FAC 1 Others 0+1

LEVER Mark
Born: Beverley, 29 March 1970
Height: 6'3" **Weight:** 13.5
Club Honours: AMC '98
This experienced centre back linked up with Mansfield Town in the second week of the season to plug gaps in the middle of a very leaky defence. Not fully match fit when he arrived, he was injured in only his second game and was on the treatment table for a couple of weeks. His time at Field Mill was not a happy one as the team, and the defence in particular, struggled. Following the arrival of new manager Keith Curle Mark's contract was paid up and he moved on to Ilkeston Town.
Grimsby T *(From trainee on 9/8/1988)* FL 343+18/8 FLC 21+2 FAC 17+3 Others 18
Bristol C *(Free on 24/7/2000)* FL 28+3/1 FLC 3 FAC 1 Others 1+1
Mansfield T *(Free on 22/8/2002)* FL 15 FAC 1

LEWINGTON Dean Scott
Born: Kingston, 18 May 1984
Height: 5'11" **Weight:** 11.2
Dean was given a five-minute league debut for Wimbledon as a left-midfield substitute in the late-season defeat at Sheffield Wednesday. He regularly featured in both the U19 and reserve teams during the campaign, almost always in the left-back position, and proved to be comfortable on the ball as well as being useful in the air. Very left-footed, he has good positional sense and will be hoping for further opportunities in the near future. Dean is the son of the former Dons' player and current Watford manager Ray Lewington.
Wimbledon *(Trainee)* FL 0+1

LEWIS Edward (Eddie) James
Born: Cerritos, California, USA, 17 May 1974
Height: 5'9" **Weight:** 11.12
International Honours: USA: 49
Eddie's Preston debut following his move from Fulham was delayed due to work permit problems, and, not being fully

match fit, he took some time to settle. Once in his stride, he made steady progress throughout the season on the wide-left flank, and produced a superb performance against Burnley. He scored his first goal at Birmingham in the Worthington Cup, whilst his first league goal was the winner at Coventry, and he topped these with a brilliant free kick at Leicester as he gradually found his shooting boots. Eddie also made a number of goals and opportunities for his team mates with his telling crosses, which he delivered with either foot, often after teasing defenders with his nifty footwork.
Fulham *(£1,300,000 from San Jose Clash, USA on 17/3/2000)* P/FL 8+8 FLC 6/1
Preston NE *(Signed on 5/9/2002)* FL 34+4/5 FLC 3+1/1 FAC 1

LEWIS Karl Junior
Born: Wembley, 9 October 1973
Height: 6'5" **Weight:** 12.4
Club Honours: Div 2 '02
This lanky midfielder forced his way back into first-team reckoning at Leicester for a time last season, and even opened his Foxes' goal-scoring account with a header against his old club Gillingham. Junior rejected a couple of potential loan moves during the transfer window in January in order to try to win his place back but eventually signed up for a loan spell with Swindon Town in March. He gave the Second Division club good service with a series of polished performances which left an excellent impression. Junior also displayed his versatility by appearing as a defender on the left of a back three, where he looked equally at home. He was made available on a free transfer at the end of 2002-03.
Fulham *(From trainee on 3/7/1992)* FL 4+1 FAC 1 *(Free to Dover Ath during 1993 close season)*
Gillingham *(Free from Hendon on 3/8/1999)* FL 47+12/8 FLC 4+2 FAC 7+2 Others 4
Leicester C *(£50,000 on 30/1/2001)* P/FL 24+6/1 FLC 3 FAC 1
Brighton & Hove A *(Loaned on 8/2/2002)* FL 14+1/3
Swindon T *(Loaned on 19/3/2003)* FL 9

LEWIS Matthew (Matt) Thomas
Born: Coventry, 20 March 1984
Height: 6'1" **Weight:** 11.7
A tall, gangly striker, Matt has a lot of promise but he was unable to show it at Kidderminster last term as he was restricted to just two substitute appearances before being farmed out on loan for most of the season. He had a

spell at Evesham United, for whom he scored several goals, before being sent to Bath City and he ended the season at Solihull Borough.
Kidderminster Hrs *(Free from Coventry Marconi on 23/7/2001)* FL 0+4

LIBURD Richard John
Born: Nottingham, 26 September 1973
Height: 5'9" **Weight:** 11.1
Richard appeared regularly for Notts County last term, but never managed to make any one position his own. He featured on both flanks, either as a full back or in midfield, and was also used in a more central role. He scored two goals for the Magpies, netting in the home games against Mansfield and Queen's Park Rangers.
Middlesbrough *(£20,000 from Eastwood T on 25/3/1993)* FL 41/1 FLC 4 FAC 2 Others 5
Bradford C *(£200,000 on 21/7/1994)* FL 75+3/3 FLC 6+2 FAC 2+2 Others 2
Carlisle U *(Free on 26/2/1998)* FL 9
Notts Co *(Free on 4/8/1998)* FL 127+27/9 FLC 5+2 FAC 8+4/2 Others 1+1

LIDDELL Andrew (Andy) Mark
Born: Leeds, 28 June 1973
Height: 5'7" **Weight:** 11.6
Club Honours: AMC '99; Div 2 '03
International Honours: S: U21-12
Wigan Athletic's longest-serving player, Andy was again the club's top scorer in league matches netting 16 goals despite missing around a quarter of the season as a result of injuries. A talented right-footed striker with good pace, he can make or score goals and his versatility allows him to play either up front or on either wing. Amongst the highlights of his season were two stunning strikes in the away win at Notts County, while he also passed the landmark figure of 100 career goals during the campaign.
Barnsley *(From trainee on 6/7/1991)* F/PL 142+56/34 FLC 11+4/3 FAC 5+7/1 Others 2+1
Wigan Ath *(£350,000 on 15/10/1998)* FL 171+6/61 FLC 8/1 FAC 7/1 Others 14+1

LIDDLE Craig George
Born: Chester le Street, 21 October 1971
Height: 5'11" **Weight:** 12.7
Craig was again outstanding in the centre of the defence for Darlington last term when he captained the side. He led by example and his commitment and dedication were great motivators for his colleagues. He is strong in the air, quick into the tackle and a good distributor of the ball from the heart of the defence.

aig also enjoys getting forward for set
eces and was rewarded with five goals
uring the campaign.
ston Villa *(From trainee on 4/7/1990. Free
Blyth Spartans in August 1991)*
iddlesbrough *(Free on 12/7/1994) P/FL*
+5 FLC 3+2 FAC 2 Others 2
arlington *(Free on 20/2/1998) FL 222/12
C 9 FAC 13/1 Others 10/3*

GHTBOURNE Kyle Lavince
orn: Bermuda, 29 September 1968
eight: 6'2" **Weight:** 11.11
ub Honours: AMC '00
ternational Honours: Bermuda: 22;
:h

is experienced striker enjoyed an almost
ury-free season at Macclesfield in 2002-
. He made a useful contribution
owing more pace up front and good
fensive work against set pieces,
pecially in the air, while he scored 13
als, including his 100th Football League
al. However, he was released during
e close season. Kyle is a double
ternational having represented Bermuda
both football and cricket.
arborough *(Signed from Pembroke
amilton, Bermuda on 11/12/1992) FL
+8/3 FLC 1 Others 0+1*
alsall *(Free on 1/9/1993) FL 158+7/65 FLC
2 FAC 16+2/12 Others 7/5*
oventry C *(£500,000 + on 18/7/1997) PL
-6 FLC 3*
lham *(Loaned on 13/1/1998) FL 4/2
hers 1/1*
oke C *(£500,000 on 16/2/1998) FL
+28/21 FLC 7 FAC 3/1 Others 7+2/3*
vindon T *(Loaned on 13/1/2001) FL 2*
ardiff C *(Loaned on 20/2/2001) FL 2+1*
acclesfield T *(Free on 31/7/2001) FL
+12/15 FLC 3/1 FAC 3/2 Others 1*
ull C *(Loaned on 20/3/2002) FL 3+1*

INCOLN Greg Dean
orn: Enfield, 23 March 1980
eight: 5'9" **Weight:** 10.3
ternational Honours: E: Yth
eg joined Northampton Town during
e summer of 2002, but received few
ances under either Kevan Broadhurst or
rry Fenwick. It was the Cobblers' third
oss of the season, Martin Wilkinson,
ho gave him his chance and he took it
th both hands. Greg has a style of play
milar to team mate and fellow
dfielder Paul Harsley: aggressive and
holehearted.
rsenal *(From trainee on 3/7/1998. Freed
ring 2001 close season)*
orthampton T *(Free from Hammarby IF,
veden on 9/7/2002) FL 5+7*

LINDEROTH Tobias
Born: Marseilles, France, 21 April 1979
Height: 5'9" **Weight:** 10.12
International Honours: Sweden: 24;
U21-22
This was a season of missed opportunity
for the Swedish international midfielder,
who was hoping to cement his place in
the Everton first team on the back of a

fine World Cup. After establishing himself
in the starting line-up in October, he
damaged a hamstring in the Worthington
Cup win at Newcastle and then following
his return to fitness he suffered a knee
injury in February that ended his season.
A neat player with fine technical ability,
Tobias can pass the ball well with both
feet and is adept at breaking up play. A

Greg Lincoln

return to full fitness can only be beneficial for Everton.

Everton *(£2,500,000 + from Stabaek, Norway, ex Hassleholm, Elfsborg, on 1/2/2002) PL 6+7 FLC 1 FAC 2+1*

LISBIE Kevin Anthony
Born: Hackney, 17 October 1978
Height: 5'8' **Weight:** 10.12
International Honours: Jamaica: 6; E: Yth

Kevin finally established himself as a first-choice striker for Charlton Athletic last term, keeping Jonatan Johansson and Matt Svensson out of the side for most of the season. He developed a strong partnership with Shaun Bartlett up front with Jason Euell playing just behind the front two in a forward midfield role. Although Kevin only found the net on four occasions, he set up numerous chances for other players. He has electric pace, is very skilful on the ball and can play as a central striker or wide on the right. He holds play up well and is a good crosser of the ball. He added six full international caps for Jamaica during the season.

Charlton Ath *(From trainee on 24/5/1996) P/FL 44+71/11 FLC 2+7/2 FAC 2+5*
Gillingham *(Loaned on 5/3/1999) FL 4+3/4*
Reading *(Loaned on 26/11/1999) FL 1+1*
Queens Park R *(Loaned on 1/12/2000) FL 1+1*

LITA Leroy Halirou
Born: London, 5 June 1985
Height: 5'9" **Weight:** 11.2

This skilful attacker made his mark in Bristol City's first team last season, although he never made the starting line-up. Leroy made a total of 18 substitute appearances, opening his scoring account with a late winner at Port Vale. Further success followed with his two-goal haul at the FA Cup at Heybridge Swifts and he followed up with a late equaliser at Mansfield prior to Christian Roberts' dramatic late winner.

Bristol C *(From trainee on 6/3/2003) FL 0+15/2 FAC 0+1/2 Others 0+2*

LITTLE Colin Campbell
Born: Wythenshawe, 4 November 1972
Height: 5'10" **Weight:** 11.0

Colin received few first-team opportunities at Crewe last season and spent much of the campaign out on loan. In October he had a spell at Mansfield, with Andy White moving in the opposite direction. Colin filled in admirably for the injured Colin Larkin and did everything but score for the Stags. He subsequently

had two loan spells at Macclesfield Town, the first ending in the eighth minute of his first appearance with the recurrence of a hamstring injury. However, he returned on transfer deadline day and played his part in Macc's successful battle against relegation, operating on the left side of midfield. He was reported to have signed a permanent deal for the Moss Rose club in the summer.

Crewe Alex *(£50,000 from Hyde U on 7/2/1996) FL 135+58/33 FLC 16+2/8 FAC 5/1 Others 5/3*
Mansfield T *(Loaned on 24/10/2002) FL 5*
Macclesfield T *(Loaned on 13/12/2002) FL 1*
Macclesfield T *(Loaned on 27/3/2003) FL 3+2/1*

LITTLE Glen Matthew
Born: Wimbledon, 15 October 1975
Height: 6'3" **Weight:** 13.0

Burnley's tricky wingman remained the side's best hope of creating special things, and his introduction at half time at Derby transformed the Clarets from apparent no-hopers to winners. However, he reserved his finest performance of the season for the trip to Hillsborough, when he scored a superb goal after leaving the home defence cold. The period after Christmas, though, was a frustrating one, and Glen subsequently joined Reading on loan, where he played with great purpose. He contributed a stream of crosses and one well-taken goal, a right-foot screamer into the far corner in the 2-1 home win over Grimsby Town. His height also added variety to Reading's attacking options, and he became popular with the fans before returning to Turf Moor at the end of the season.

Crystal Palace *(From trainee on 1/7/1994. Free to Glentoran on 11/11/1994)*
Burnley *(£100,000 on 29/11/1996) FL 178+34/29 FLC 9+4 FAC 9+6/3 Others 4+1/1*
Reading *(Loaned on 27/3/2003) FL 6/1 Others 1*

LITTLEJOHN Adrian Sylvester
Born: Wolverhampton, 26 September 1970
Height: 5'9" **Weight:** 11.0
International Honours: E: Yth

This experienced striker joined Port Vale in February on a short-term contract following a period in China. A small, nippy player Adrian added some pace to the Vale forward line and gave everything for the cause. He had to wait until his ninth appearance for his first goal, but then scored in three successive home games, one against Huddersfield being particularly well taken, whilst his injury-

time winner against Northampton was a crucial strike. A popular player, Adrian will be hoping to clinch a long-term deal for 2003-2004.

Walsall *(From trainee at West Bromwich A juniors on 24/5/1989) FL 26+18/1 FLC 2+1 FAC 1+1 Others 4+1*
Sheffield U *(Free on 6/8/1991) F/PL 44+25/12 FLC 5+1 FAC 3+2/1 Others 2/1*
Plymouth Arg *(£100,000 on 22/9/1995) FL 100+10/29 FLC 6 FAC 6+2/3 Others 6*
Oldham Ath *(Signed on 20/3/1998) FL 16+5/5 FLC 2/1*
Bury *(£75,000 on 13/11/1998) FL 69+30/14 FLC 4/1 FAC 6/1 Others 2+1*
Sheffield U *(Free on 22/10/2001) FL 1+2 (Freed in December 2001)*
Port Vale *(Free, after spells in China and th USA, via a trial at Barnsley, on 19/2/2003) F 12+1/3*

LIVERMORE David
Born: Edmonton, 20 May 1980
Height: 5'11" **Weight:** 12.1
Club Honours: Div 2 '01

One of the shrewdest Millwall purchases in recent seasons, David was a near ever present for the Lions last term. He produced a series of consistent performances in the centre of midfield and even managed to score a goal with his right foot! David plays with a maturit that belies his age, and his tackling and work rate are reminiscent of Terry Hurloc in his Millwall heydays. He is a real unsung hero at the New Den.

Arsenal *(From trainee on 13/7/1998)*
Millwall *(£30,000 on 30/7/1999) FL 152+3 FLC 9/1 FAC 9 Others 5*

LIVESEY Daniel (Danny)
Born: Salford, 31 December 1984
Height: 6'2" **Weight:** 13.0

This locally born central defender made his debut for Bolton as a substitute in th home defeat by Liverpool last Septembe He subsequently made his first start in th experimental side which played Bury in the Worthington Cup, and also started the FA Cup tie against Sunderland, wher he did not look out of place in a back three alongside Anthony Barness and Iva Campo. A consistent performer with the reserve team, Danny will be looking for more first-team opportunities during the 2003-04 season.

Bolton W *(From trainee on 17/8/2002) PL 0+2 FLC 1 FAC 1*

LIVINGSTONE Stephen (Steve) Carl
Born: Middlesbrough, 8 September 196
Height: 6'1" **Weight:** 13.6

ub Honours: AMC '98
fter missing practically the whole of the
001-02 campaign due to injury, Steve
turned to senior football last term only
receive a severe setback when he
actured his skull in only the third game
the season. The versatile Grimsby Town
ayer quickly returned to action and
thin two months he was back. Steve
atured up front for the Mariners,
etting three goals in all. He was out of

contract in the summer and at the time of
writing his future was uncertain.
Coventry C *(From trainee on 16/7/1986) FL
17+14/5 FLC 8+2/10 Others 0+1*
Blackburn Rov *(£450,000 on 17/1/1991)
F/PL 25+5/10 FLC 2 FAC 1/1*
Chelsea *(£350,000 on 23/3/1993) PL 0+1*
Port Vale *(Loaned on 3/9/1993) FL 4+1*
Grimsby T *(£140,000 on 29/10/1993) FL
226+63/43 FLC 15+5/4 FAC 12+5/4 Others
4+3*

avid Livermore

LJUNGBERG Fredrik (Freddie)
Born: Sweden, 16 April 1977
Height: 5'9" **Weight:** 11.6
Club Honours: CS '99; PL '02; FAC '02, '03
International Honours: Sweden: 38; U21-12; Yth
Although he is a cult figure with the Arsenal fans, Freddie is another senior player to have suffered from long-term injuries last season. After recovering from a hip operation for an injury sustained whilst playing for Sweden in the World Cup finals, he returned to first-team duty in the Champions' League game against Borussia Dortmund in September and scored a characteristic goal. He was then sidelined by a further injury that kept him out until the final games of the season, but on his return scored a fine hat-trick at Sunderland. Freddie is a versatile player who offers pace and skill in attack, whilst putting in a high work rate when required to defend. Last December he was presented with the prestigious 'Sportstar of the Year' award by the Scandinavia newspaper *Aftonbladet*.
Arsenal *(£3,000,000 from BK Halmstad, Sweden on 17/9/1998) PL 100+17/31 FLC 2 FAC 16+3/4 Others 37+8/9*

LLEWELLYN Christopher (Chris) Mark
Born: Swansea, 29 August 1979
Height: 5'11" **Weight:** 11.6
International Honours: W: 2; B-1; U21-14; Yth
Chris found it very difficult to force his way into the Norwich City first-team picture last season. An experienced player for his age, he prefers to play in a striking role, but most of his opportunities at Carrow Road have come playing on the left-hand side of midfield. A tremendous athlete, he never gives defenders a moment's peace with his constant foraging. He enjoyed a useful loan spell at Bristol Rovers in the closing weeks of the campaign, scoring three including a spectacular 25-yard volley in his first appearance against Macclesfield at the Memorial Stadium.
Norwich C *(From trainee on 21/1/1997) FL 103+39/17 FLC 7+3 FAC 3+3/1*
Bristol Rov *(Loaned on 21/2/2003) FL 14/3*

LOCK Matthew John
Born: Barnstaple, 10 March 1984
Height: 5'11" **Weight:** 11.4
A first-year professional with Exeter, Matthew made three appearances in Third Division fixtures last term, two of

them from the bench. The promising young midfielder also played twice in FA Cup ties, scoring his first goal in senior football when he netted a late winner against Forest Green. Matthew found it hard to break into the squad, with management looking to experience rather than youth to help the struggling side.

Exeter C (From trainee on 2/8/2002) FL 1+2 FAC 0+2/1

LOCKWOOD Matthew Dominic

Born: Southend, 17 October 1976
Height: 5'9" **Weight:** 10.12
Matthew was a near ever-present for Leyton Orient last term. He started the season as first choice left back, but later switched to playing on the left-hand side of midfield. A highly rated defender, Matthew is the O's dead-ball expert and possesses a tremendous shot. He scored six goals during the campaign.

Queens Park R (From trainee at Southend U on 2/5/1995)
Bristol Rov (Free on 24/7/1996) FL 58+5/1 FLC 2+1 FAC 6 Others 4+2
Leyton Orient (Free on 7/8/1998) FL 170+7/23 FLC 12/2 FAC 13 Others 9/2

LODGE Andrew (Andy) Robert

Born: Peterborough, 17 July 1978
Height: 5'9" **Weight:** 11.9
Club Honours: NC '02
Andy found it difficult to break into the Boston team last season following the club's promotion as Conference champions. His only start was in the home defeat to Cambridge United and by November he had moved on to St Albans City.

Boston U (Free from Stamford, ex Spalding U, Whittlesey U, Bury T, Ely C, on 1/1/2000) FL 1+1

LOGAN Richard Anthony

Born: Barnsley, 24 May 1969
Height: 6'1" **Weight:** 13.3
Richard had another season marred by injury after beginning the campaign in Lincoln's starting line-up. He made a quick recovery after receiving 12 stitches in a head wound against Rochdale, but was unable to regain his place in the centre of defence after picking up a calf injury at Torquay. Richard was loaned to Unibond League club Gainsborough Trinity in November but later suffered back problems. He underwent an operation on a prolapsed disc in February, which put him out of action for the remainder of the season.

Huddersfield T (Free from Gainsborough

Trinity on 15/11/1993) FL 35+10/1 FLC 3 FAC 1 Others 9
Plymouth Arg (£20,000 on 26/10/1995) FL 67+19/12 FLC 4/1 FAC 2+2 Others 8
Scunthorpe U (Free on 2/7/1998) FL 77+3/7 FLC 1 FAC 4 Others 3
Lincoln C (Free on 12/7/2000) FL 14+3/1 FLC 2

LOGAN Richard James

Born: Bury St Edmunds, 4 January 1982
Height: 6'0" **Weight:** 12.5
International Honours: E: Yth; Sch

This big, pacy striker made a substitute appearance for Ipswich Town in the Worthington Cup tie against Middlesbrough but was unable to establish a regular place in the side and soon moved out on loan to Boston United. He scored six goals in his first five starts for the Pilgrims and narrowly missed out on a hat-trick when he failed from the penalty spot in the 6-0 win over Shrewsbury. Richard's loan spell became permanent move in January but his goal became less frequent after he picked up

Steve Lomas

nee injury. He still finished up with a
ouble-figure tally in a successful season.
ıswich T (From trainee on 6/1/1999) FL 0+3
LC 0+1 FAC 0+1
ambridge U (Loaned on 25/1/2001) FL 5/1
orquay U (Loaned on 13/12/2001) FL 16/4
oston U (Free on 30/11/2002) FL 26+1/10

.OMAS Stephen (Steve)
Martin
orn: Hanover, Germany, 18 January
974
eight: 6'0" **Weight:** 12.8
ıternational Honours: NI: 45; B-1; Yth;
ch
his right-sided midfielder once again
ave 100 per cent commitment to a West
am team fighting against relegation. He
attled hard for every ball and covered
'enty of ground in each match. Always
 the thick of the action he bravely
layed on while carrying an ankle injury
nd was unlucky not to add to his goal
tal against Aston Villa in April when his
eader hit the bar and then bounced on
 the post. Steve was also a regular in
ıe Northern Ireland team during the
eason.
Manchester C (From trainee on 22/1/1991)
'FL 102+9/8 FLC 15/2 FAC 10+1/1
West Ham U (£1,600,000 on 26/3/1997) PL
56+3/9 FLC 12/2 FAC 10+1/1 Others 10

.ONERGAN Andrew (Andy)
orn: Preston, 19 October 1983
leight: 6'4" **Weight:** 13.2
ıternational Honours: RoI: Yth; E: Yth
ndy was again out of the first-team
icture at Preston last term apart from the
ccasional outing on the substitutes'
ench. He joined Darlington on loan and
ıade two appearances either side of
hristmas, but unfortunately suffered an
ıjury in his second outing at Carlisle on
oxing Day and returned to Deepdale for
reatment. Andy subsequently had a loan
ıell at Blackpool, without featuring in
ıe side, but made the England U20
ıuad for the Toulon tournament in the
ımmer.
'eston NE (From trainee on 21/10/2000) FL
FLC 1
Darlington (Loaned on 20/12/2002) FL 2

.OPES Osvaldo
torn: Fregus, France, 6 April 1980
leight: 5'10" **Weight:** 11.7
Isvaldo joined Plymouth Argyle on non-
ontract terms last August and made his
ebut in the Worthington Cup tie against
rystal Palace the following month. His
referred position is the right-hand side of
ıidfield where he often showed a

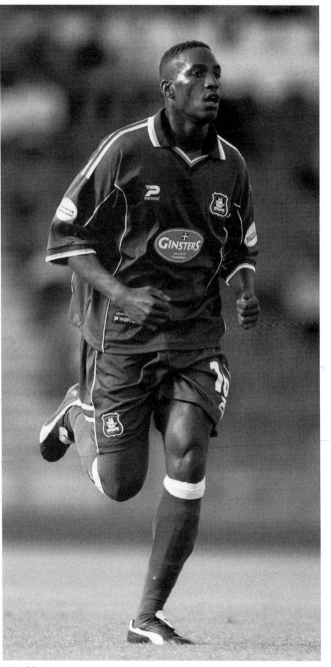

Osvaldo Lopes

delightful touch and a good sense of awareness. However, Osvaldo found it difficult to retain his place in the starting line-up and was eventually released by manager Paul Sturrock at the end of the season.

Plymouth Arg (Free from Draguignan, France, ex Montpelier, on 26/8/2002) FL 4+5 FLC 1 FAC 1 Others 2

LORAN Tyrone

Born: Amsterdam, Holland, 29 June 1981
Height: 6'2" **Weight:** 13.11
International Honours: Holland: U21
Tyrone joined Manchester City during the summer of 2002 but failed to make a breakthrough at Maine Road and in December he went on loan to Tranmere. He began his Rovers career in central defence, but was then sidelined with a facial injury, and when he came back to action in mid-February it was in a more unfamiliar midfield role. However, he adapted well and his return coincided with the beginning of the club's undefeated run. A tough tackler and an intelligent player, Tyrone was reported to have signed permanently for the Birkenhead club in the close season.

Manchester C (£60,000 from Volendam, Holland on 16/7/2002)
Tranmere Rov (Loaned on 31/12/2002) FL 16+1

LOUIS Jefferson Lee

Born: Harrow, 22 February 1979
Height: 6'2" **Weight:** 13.2
This big striker settled well into the professional game for Oxford last term and scored seven times in 40 appearances including 15 starts. Strong and speedy, if not a bit ungainly to watch, he was used to good effect and headed the winner in the FA Cup tie against arch-rivals Swindon.

Oxford U (Free from Thame U, ex Aylesbury U, on 4/3/2002) FL 12+23/6 FLC 1+1 FAC 1+2/1 Others 1

LOUIS-JEAN Matthieu

Born: Mont St Aignan, France, 22 February 1976
Height: 5'9" **Weight:** 10.12
International Honours: France: U21; Yth
This right back continued to be a regular member of the Nottingham Forest side during the 2002-03 season. Comfortable on the ball and effective when attacking down the flank, he is particularly good attacking. Matthieu did well enough to be offered a new contract at the end of the campaign.

Nottingham F (Signed from Le Havre, France on 14/9/1998) P/FL 129+6/2 FLC 10+2 FAC 3 Others 2

[LOURENCO] DA SILVA Louis Carlos Lourenco

Born: Luanda, Angola, 5 June 1983
Height: 5'6" **Weight:** 10.7
International Honours: Portugal: Yth
This Portuguese midfielder joined Oldham Athletic in the summer of 2002 on a one-year loan from Sporting Lisbon. However, 'Jimmy' as he was fondly nicknamed by the players, made just eight appearances during his five-month spell at the club. His only goal for Latics came from a memorable overhead kick in the 4-0 defeat of Huddersfield Town at Boundary Park in September. After talks with manager Iain Dowie, Lourenco returned home at Christmas after struggling to secure a regular first-team place.

Bristol C (Loaned from Sporting Lisbon, Portugal on 22/3/2001) FL 1+2/1
Oldham Ath (Loaned from Sporting Lisbon, Portugal on 31/7/2002) FL 1+6/1 FLC 1+1 Others 1

LOVETT Jay

Born: Brighton, 22 January 1978
Height: 6'2" **Weight:** 12.5
This steady and competent Brentford right back managed just one first-team appearance last season, featuring in the line-up at Oldham in January. Jay also spent time on loan to Conference sides Hereford United and Gravesend in the closing stages of the campaign. Despite his lack of games, he is still a useful player.

Brentford (£75,000 from Crawley on 27/7/2000) FL 24+4 Others 3+2/1

LOW Joshua (Josh) David

Born: Bristol, 15 February, 1979
Height: 6'1" **Weight:** 12.0
International Honours: W: U21-4; Yth
Despite a frustrating campaign dogged by injury problems, Josh had a successful start to his Oldham Athletic career last term. He rebuilt his confidence with some impressive early-season displays before a hamstring injury sidelined him for almost four months. His return to action in mid-March gave the Latics line-up a more balanced look and Josh was soon back in form, using his pace to unsettle defenders from his right-wing-back berth.

Bristol Rov (From trainee on 19/8/1996) FL 11+11 FLC 0+2 FAC 2+2 Others 2
Leyton Orient (Free on 27/5/1999) FL 2+3/1 FLC 1

Cardiff C (Free on 20/11/1999) FL 54+21/6 FLC 1+1 FAC 2+3 Others 3+1
Oldham Ath (Signed on 12/8/2002) FL 19+2/3 FLC 2 FAC 2/1 Others 2

LOWE Onandi

Born: Kingston, Jamaica, 2 December 1973
Height: 6'3" **Weight:** 13.12
Club Honours: Div 3 '03
International Honours: Jamaica
This giant striker again made a big impac at Rushden & Diamonds as Brian Talbot's team won the Third Division title. Much was expected of Onandi after 20 goals had taken Diamonds to the play-off final in May 2002 and therefore he was a marked man all season. However statistic showed that he was by far the best all-round striker in the division with many more attempts on goal than anyone else Onandi added two more caps for Jamaic featuring in friendly matches against the USA and Nigeria.

Port Vale (Loaned from Rochester Rhinos, USA, ex Harbour View, Montreal Impact, Waterhouse, Richmond Kickers, on 1/2/200? FL 4+1/1 Others 1/1
Rushden & Diamonds (Free from Kansas Wizards on 30/11/2001) FL 63+1/34 FAC 2+1/1 Others 4/1

LOWE Ryan Thomas

Born: Liverpool, 18 September 1978
Height: 5'11" **Weight:** 11.10
This young Shrewsbury Town striker mad good progress last season, netting a tota of 13 goals, including the 'golden goal' against Port Vale in the LDV Vans Trophy, and a brace against Crewe in the regiona semi-final of the same competition. However, he reserved the best for Boxinc Day with his first senior hat-trick in the 4 1 home victory over Bury. Used mainly ju behind the front two, Ryan has an excellent turn of pace and good control. He needs to develop a little more consistency in his game and the club's first Conference season may just be the launch pad he requires.

Shrewsbury T (Free from Burscough on 25/7/2000) FL 62+45/20 FLC 1+2 FAC 3+2 Others 7/4

LOWER Scott

Born: Coventry, 9 August 1984
Height: 5'8" **Weight:** 10.5
Promoted from the Kidderminster Harriers' youth team, right back Scott played just once in the first team last term, coming on as a late substitute in the Worthington Cup defeat at Nottingham Forest. He was later sent out

Matthieu Louis-Jean

on loan to Evesham United before being released and he ended the season at Nuneaton Borough.
Kidderminster Hrs (Free from Coventry Marconi on 28/8/2002) FL 0+1

LOWNDES Nathan Peter
Born: Salford, 2 June 1977
Height: 5'11" **Weight:** 11.6

Nathan was signed by Plymouth Argyle after being released by Livingston at the end of the previous season. A pacy striker, he had a rather disappointing campaign for the Pilgrims, netting only two goals, one in the opening game against Mansfield and a second in the final match of the season against Wycombe. In between Nathan struggled

with injuries and lack of form but after impressing in the final month he will be looking to continue in similar vein in 2003-04.
Leeds U (From trainee on 1/4/1995)
Watford (£40,000 on 3/10/1995) FL 1+6 FL 0+1 FAC 1+1 Others 1
St Johnstone (£50,000 on 21/8/1998) SL 30+34/14 SLC 2+2/2 SC 4+2 Others 2+1

David Lucas

ivingston *(Free on 20/7/2001) SL 7+14/3
LC 0+2 SC 0+2*
?otherham U *(Loaned on 28/3/2002) FL 2*
?lymouth Arg *(Free on 23/7/2002) FL
+10/2 FLC 1 Others 2*

.UA LUA Lomano Tresor

3orn: Zaire, 28 December 1980
4eight: 5'8" **Weight:** 12.2
1nternational Honours: DR Congo: 4
he 2002-03 campaign began well for
.omano as Craig Bellamy's lack of fitness
ed to him starting in each of Newcastle's
rst five games, and in the Premiership
.pener at home to West Ham he turned
1 a 'Man of the Match' performance
1cluding a brace of goals. Craig's return
aw Lomano back on the bench where he
.emained for most of the season, but he
, an important squad member offering
.ome exhilarating dribbling skills coupled
.ith a good turn of pace. He continued
.o represent DR Congo and scored his
.rst international goal against Botswana
1 the African Nations Cup last October.
.olchester U *(Signed from Leyton College
n 25/9/1998) FL 37+24/15 FLC 4/4 FAC 1/1
)thers 1*
4ewcastle U *(£2,250,000 on 29/9/2000) PL
2+40/5 FLC 1+3 FAC 0+6 Others 5+10/4*

.UCAS David Anthony

3orn: Preston, 23 November 1977
4eight: 6'2" **Weight:** 13.10
1nternational Honours: E: Yth
?avid started the 2002-03 season as
reston's second choice 'keeper, his first
wo appearances being in Worthington
.up ties. An excellent shot stopper who
.ften comes out on top in one-on-one
.ituations, he finally made his 100th
.eague appearance for North End against
.eading in October, a game in which he
.nade three top-drawer saves and from
.hen he took over as first choice. A
.amstring injury on New Year's Day saw
.onathon Gould arrive from Celtic to
.laim the first-team berth. David missed
.ut on any further senior action until he
.eplaced the injured Gould for six matches
1 April. Still young for a 'keeper, David
.as aspects of his game to work on but
.e remains an asset to the club.
.reston NE *(From trainee on 12/12/1994) FL
16+4 FLC 10 FAC 7 Others 11*
)arlington *(Loaned on 14/12/1995) FL 6*
?arlington *(Loaned on 3/10/1996) FL 7*
.cunthorpe U *(Loaned on 23/12/1996) FL 6*
)thers 2*

.UCIC Teddy

3orn: Biskopsgaard, Sweden, 15 April 1973
4eight: 6'1" **Weight:** 11.10
1nternational Honours: Sweden: 52

This experienced defender joined Leeds
United on a season-long loan deal from
AIK Solna after appearing in the World
Cup finals for Sweden during the
summer. A versatile player who can
operate anywhere across the back four,
Teddy made his debut at centre back in
the home defeat by Liverpool in October
and later played a number of games at
left back. Tough and uncompromising, he
scored his first goal for United when
bundling in a low corner at Chelsea in the
3-2 defeat in January.
*Leeds U (Loaned from AIK Solna, Sweden, ex
Lundby, Vasta Frolunda, Gothenburg,
Bologna, on 31/8/2002) PL 16+1/1 FLC 1 FAC
2+1*

LUCKETTI Christopher (Chris) James

Born: Rochdale, 28 September 1971
Height: 6'0" **Weight:** 13.6
Club Honours: Div 2 '97
Preston's captain led by example
throughout the 2002-03 season, with his
commanding presence in the air and in
the tackle serving as an inspiration to
both those around him and the fans.
Unfortunate to have the 'winner'
disallowed at Bradford from a towering
header, he scored his first goal for 11
months at Walsall with a similar effort
and he was always a threat whenever he
ventured upfield. Despite the team
experiencing a poor run of form around
Christmas, his own game could not be
faulted and it was a case of 'who plays
alongside Chris?' for Preston's other
central defenders. Vastly experienced but
still very fit, he will continue to play a vital
role in organising his fellow defenders
and bringing on the younger players at
the club.
Rochdale (Trainee) FL 1
Stockport Co (Free on 23/8/1990)
*Halifax T (Free on 12/7/1991) FL 73+5/2 FLC
2/1 FAC 2 Others 4*
*Bury (£50,000 on 1/10/1993) FL 235/8 FLC
16 FAC 11/1 Others 15/1*
*Huddersfield T (£750,000 + on 14/6/1999)
FL 68/1 FLC 7/1*
*Preston NE (£750,000 on 23/8/2001) FL
83/4 FLC 5 FAC 4*

LUMSDON Christopher (Chris)

Born: Newcastle, 15 December 1979
Height: 5'7" **Weight:** 10.6
The 2002-03 season will be one that
Chris will want to forget. He started out
as the playmaker in the Barnsley midfield
and scored the winning goal against
Queen's Park Rangers early on. However,
he lost his sparkle as the Reds began to

slide down the table and soon dropped
out of the line-up. From then on he
struggled to find his form and his
appearances were only occasional until
near the season's end when he finally got
a run of games. At his best there is no
better attacking midfielder in the Second
Division.
*Sunderland (From trainee on 3/7/1997) P/FL
2 FLC 1+1*
Blackpool (Loaned on 3/2/2000) FL 6/1
Crewe Alex (Loaned on 11/9/2000) FL 14+2
*Barnsley (£350,000 on 8/10/2001) FL
53+4/10 FLC 2 FAC 2 Others 1*

LUNDEKVAM Claus

Born: Norway, 22 February 1973
Height: 6'3" **Weight:** 12.10
International Honours: Norway: 20;
U21-16
Dominant in the air, swift in the tackle
and a commanding leader of one of the
most parsimonious back fours in the top
flight, it was something of a surprise,
when Claus' game appeared to
deteriorate towards the end of the
season, after a short lay-off for an injury
in April. Prior to that injury he had
enjoyed an outstanding campaign for
Southampton, even by his own
Impeccable standards, and must be rated
among the most accomplished central
defenders in the Premiership.
*Southampton (£400,000 from SK Brann,
Norway on 3/9/1996) PL 219+6 FLC 22+3
FAC 16*

LUNT Kenneth (Kenny) Vincent

Born: Runcorn, 20 November 1979
Height: 5'10" **Weight:** 10.0
International Honours: E: Yth; Sch
This experienced midfielder was once
again ever-present for Crewe
Alexandra last term. A competitive and
skilful player he contributed seven
valuable goals to the club's promotion
campaign. Kenny is Alexandra's longest-
serving player and has now passed the
landmark of 200 Football League
appearances for the club.
*Crewe Alex (From trainee on 12/6/1997) FL
211+28/19 FLC 15+4/1 FAC 12+1 Others 4/1*

LUZHNY Oleg

Born: Ukraine, 5 August 1968
Height: 6'1" **Weight:** 12.3
Club Honours: CS '99; FAC '03
International Honours: Ukraine: 50;
USSR: 8
A valuable squad player at Arsenal, Oleg's
appearances last season were limited, and
generally he replaced first choice team

members suffering from injury. Filling in usually at right back or in the centre of defence, he can also operate on the right-hand side of midfield. Strong in the air and in the tackle, he has a good turn of pace which enables him to overlap, and put in good surging runs down the right flank.

Arsenal *(£1,800,000 from Dinamo Kiev, Ukraine on 9/7/1999) PL 58+17 FLC 4 FAC 9 Others 20+2*

LYNCH Mark John
Born: Manchester, 2 September 1981
Height: 5'11" **Weight:** 11.5
An able Manchester United defender,

Mark was yet another product of the Old Trafford assembly line to be given his head last term, and he comfortably made the fruitful transition into first-team football. A single appearance in the Champions' League against Deportivo in March showed he had the mettle for the big occasion.
Manchester U *(From trainee on 3/7/2001) Others 1*

LYNCH Simon George
Born: Montreal, Canada, 19 May 1982
Height: 6'0" **Weight:** 10.0
International Honours: S: U21-9
This young striker was only on the fringes of the Celtic first-team squad last term and his sole appearance came in the first leg of the UEFA Cup tie away to FK Suduva. Simon moved on to Preston in January and made his debut as a substitute at Ipswich ten days later, before scoring on his home debut the following week. He remained in the squad for the rest of the season, alternating with Pawel Abbott between the bench and the starting line-up over the final few games. A slight player, he possesses surprising strength and quick feet and is rated as a fine finisher, although North End fans have not seen the best of this aspect of his game yet.
Glasgow Celtic *(Signed from juniors on 13/7/1999) SL 2+1/3 Others 1+1*
Preston NE *(£130,000 on 8/1/2003) FL 6+11/1*

LYTTLE Desmond (Des)
Born: Wolverhampton, 24 September 1971
Height: 5'9" **Weight:** 12.13
Club Honours: Div 1 '98
West Bromwich Albion's experienced right wing back hardly got a look all season owing to the form of Igor Balis and young Adam Chambers. Des featured in the Worthington Cup defeat at Wigan, but then had to wait until the visit to Middlesbrough in April before he saw any Premiership action. He was, however, still as enthusiastic as ever when called into the team and turned down two loan moves to stay at the Hawthorns as a squad member.
Leicester C *(From trainee on 1/9/1990)*
Swansea C *(£12,500 from Worcester C on 9/7/1992) FL 46/1 FLC 2 FAC 5 Others 5*
Nottingham F *(£375,000 on 27/7/1993) F/F 177+8/3 FLC 19+1 FAC 16 Others 8*
Port Vale *(Loaned on 20/11/1998) FL 7*
Watford *(Free on 28/7/1999) PL 11 FLC 1*
West Bromwich A *(Free on 21/3/2000) P/FL 61+15/1 FLC 8 FAC 2+1 Others 2*

Chris Lucketti

M

McALLISTER Gary

Born: Motherwell, 25 December 1964
Height: 6'1" **Weight:** 11.12
Club Honours: S Div 1 '85; Div 1 '92; CS
'92, '02; FLC '01; FAC '01; UEFAC '01;
SC '01
International Honours: S: 57; B-2; U21-1
Despite being in the twilight of his playing
career, Gary performed consistently well
in midfield during a long season for
Coventry City last term. He admitted to
finding the lower division much harder
work than the Premiership and he often
seemed to be the target of the
opposition's hard men. He netted a total
of nine goals in all competitions, the best
of which came at home to Derby when
he hit a dipping volley from 25 yards that
went and swivelled into the net. As player-
manager he won the December 'Manager
of the Month' award but this proved to
be the kiss of death and the side only
won one more game until the end of the
season.
*Motherwell (Signed from Fir Park BC on
5/9/1981) SL 52+7/6 SLC 3+1 SC 7/2*
*Leicester C (£125,000 on 15/8/1985) FL
99+2/46 FLC 14+1/3 FAC 5/2 Others 4*
*Leeds U (£1,000,000 on 2/7/1990) F/PL
130+1/31 FLC 26/4 FAC 24/6 Others 14/4*
*Coventry C (£3,000,000 on 26/7/1996) PL
119/20 FLC 11/5 FAC 10/1*
*Liverpool (Free on 6/7/2000) PL 35+20/5 FLC
2+3/1 FAC 4+1 Others 10+11/3*
*Coventry C (Free on 5/7/2002) FL 41/7 FLC
1/1 FAC 3/1*

McANESPIE Kieran

Born: Gosport, 11 September 1979
Height: 5'8" **Weight:** 10.13
International Honours: S: U21-4
Once again Kieran found himself unable
to break into the Fulham line-up last term
and in March he joined Plymouth Argyle
on non-contract terms until the end of
the season. The left-sided utility player
made his debut in the 2-1 defeat at
Stockport when he put in an
accomplished performance, creating a
couple of decent goal-scoring
opportunities for himself. He went on to
make two more appearances, one from
the substitutes' bench, but was released
by the Pilgrims at the end of the season.
*St Johnstone (From juniors on 14/9/1995) SL
24+26/5 SC 3+2 Othrs 3+1*
Fulham (£80,000 on 11/8/2000) FLC 1+1
*Heart of Midlothian (Loaned on 22/1/2001)
SL 3+2 SC 0+1*

*Bournemouth (Loaned on 15/2/2002) FL
3+4/1*
Plymouth Arg (Free on 27/3/2003) FL 2+2

McANUFF Joel (Jobi) Joshua
Frederick
Born: Edmonton, 9 November 1981
Height: 5'11" **Weight:** 11.10
International Honours: Jamaica: 1
Until he picked up a groin injury in the
middle of January, Jobi was a very strong
candidate to be the Wimbledon 'Player of
the Season'. From the outset of the
campaign he showed some stunning form
on the right wing, and time after time he
tore opposing defences to ribbons with
his electric combination of pace, control
and fierce shooting. His performances in
the wins at Portsmouth and Preston in
particular were awesome, and had he
remained fully fit the Dons' season could
well have had a different ending. As it
was, he missed key games late on and
was not put back into the action once the
club's play-off hopes had gone.
*Wimbledon (From trainee on 11/7/2000) FL
51+18/8 FLC 2/1 FAC 1+2/1*

MACARI Paul
Born: Manchester, 23 August 1976
Height: 5'8" **Weight:** 11.12
Paul was mostly on the fringes of the
Huddersfield Town first-team squad last
season, although he had spells on the
substitutes' bench. He was a regular in
the reserves with whom he continued to
impress with his close control and regular
goal scoring. The promising youngster
made five first-team appearances from
the bench during the campaign. Paul is
the son of former Manchester United star
Lou Macari.
Stoke C (From juniors on 26/8/1993) FL 0+3
*Sheffield U (Free on 10/12/1998. Released
during 2000 close season)*
*Huddersfield T (Free on 1/7/2000) FL 0+11
FLC 0+2 Others 0+2*

McATEER Jason Wynn
Born: Birkenhead, 18 June 1971
Height: 5'10" **Weight:** 11.12
International Honours: RoI: 51; B-1
An experienced Republic of Ireland
midfielder, who is equally effective in a
central or wide position, Jason endured a
frustrating campaign at Sunderland due
to persistent injury problems. His season
had started well when he notched the
winning goal for the Black Cats at Leeds
in August, a 1-0 victory that turned out to
be the club's sole away Premiership
success. However, following the 'derby'
defeat at Newcastle the following month,

Jason required surgery on an abdominal
hernia and did not return until late
February, when a hamstring injury
sidelined him again. With his boundless
energy and knack of scoring vital goals, a
fully-fit Jason will be important to
Sunderland's promotion hopes next term.
*Bolton W (Signed from Marine on
22/1/1992) P/FL 109+5/8 FLC 11/2 FAC 11/3
Others 8+1/2*
*Liverpool (£4,500,000 on 6/9/1995) PL
84+16/3 FLC 12+1 FAC 11+1/3 Others 12+2*
*Blackburn Rov (£4,000,000 on 28/1/1999)
P/FL 58+14/4 FLC 4 FAC 7*
*Sunderland (£1,000,000 on 19/10/2001) PL
35/3 FAC 2*

McAULEY Hugh Francis
Born: Plymouth, 13 May 1976
Height: 5'10" **Weight:** 11.4
Hugh began last season playing on the
right-hand side of midfield for
Cheltenham, enjoying a good run when
he scored three times in a run of four
games. However, he was subsequently
switched to the opposite flank and
eventually drifted out of the first-team
picture. He joined local rivals
Kidderminster on transfer deadline day,
but found his opportunities limited and
he was restricted to appearances from the
substitutes' bench which proved
insufficient to earn him a new contract at
the end of the season.
*Cheltenham T (Signed from Leek T on
15/7/1999) FL 70+30/9 FLC 5/1 FAC 6+1
Others 4+2/1*
*Kidderminster Hrs (Free on 27/3/2003) FL
0+4*

MACAULEY Stephen (Steve)
Roy
Born: Lytham, 4 March 1969
Height: 6'1" **Weight:** 12.10
Club Honours: FAYC '86
One of new Rochdale manager Paul
Simpson's first signings, this experienced
central defender started as a first choice
in the back four, but after just six games
he was injured and was unable to reclaim
a place in the side. After another injury
lay-off he spent two successful loan spells
at Macclesfield with a month's interval
between to enable him to have treatment
for a knee injury. Steve produced some
strong performances for Macc showing
ability in the air, making many telling
tackles and some good clearances as well
as scoring the odd goal. He eventually
signed permanently for Macclesfield.
*Manchester C (From trainee on 5/11/1987.
Released during 1988 close season)*
Crewe Alex (£25,000 from Fleetwood T on

269

24/3/1992) FL 247+14/26 FLC 20 FAC 16/1
Others 20/3
Macclesfield T (Loaned on 14/12/2001) FL 4
FAC 1
Macclesfield T (Loaned on 15/2/2002) FL 8
Rochdale (Free on 29/7/2002) FL 6 Others 1
Macclesfield T (Loaned on 22/11/2002) FL
4/1
Macclesfield T (Free on 16/1/2003) FL 16
FAC 1

McBRIDE Brian
Born: Arlington Heights, USA, 19 June
1972
Height: 6'1" **Weight:** 12.7
International Honours: United States:
68
David Moyes brought the USA
international striker to Everton for a
three-month loan spell in January, having
previously signed him whilst at Preston.
Brian made an immediate impact, scoring
after ten minutes of his debut at Spurs
and then twice against Sunderland in his
first home game the following week. He
showed great commitment and honesty
in his time at the club, being an
economical and clinical finisher as well as
good in the air. Although a permanent
deal between the club and Major League
Soccer (who own his contract at home)
was mooted, failure to agree a fee
resulted in Brian returning home in
March.
Preston NE (Loaned from Columbus Crew,
USA, ex St Louis University, VfL Wolfsburg,
on 15/9/2000) FL 8+1/1 FLC 1 FAC 1
Everton (Loaned from Columbus Crew on
5/2/2003) PL 7+1/4

McCALL Andrew **Stuart** Murray
Born: Leeds, 10 June 1964
Height: 5'7" **Weight:** 12.0
Club Honours: Div 3 '85; SPL '92, '93,
'94, '95, '96; SLC '92, '93; SC '92, '93,
'96
International Honours: S: 40; U21-2
Stuart joined Sheffield United as player-
coach in the summer of 2002. However,
after the first three league games he was
almost ever-present before an ankle injury
caused him to miss some games in
March. He was a key player in the Blades'
season, featuring as a defensive
midfielder, picking up and distributing the
loose ball, being available when his side
had possession, closing down opponents
as well as more than occasionally going
forward. Stuart's energetic displays belied
his age and he brought out the best of
the younger midfielders around him.
Bradford C (From apprentice on 1/6/1982) FL
235+3/37 FLC 19/3 FAC 11/3 Others 12+1/3

Everton (£850,000 on 1/6/1988) FL 99+4/6
FLC 11/1 FAC 16+2/3 Others 8+1
Glasgow R (£1,200,000 on 15/8/1991) SL
186+8/14 SLC 15/3 SC 25+2 Others 28/2
Bradford C (Free on 4/6/1998) P/FL 154+3/8
FLC 5+3/1 FAC 5+1 Others 4
Sheffield U (Free on 2/7/2002) FL 32+2 FLC
6 FAC 5 Others 0+1

McCAMMON Mark Jason
Born: Barnet, 7 August 1978
Height: 6'5" **Weight:** 14.5
This tall target man really looked the part
for Brentford last season and led the line
well. The fans took him to their hearts
and raised the roof when he scored his
first goal for 18 months against Swindon.
He also netted twice at Stockport before
being transferred to Millwall at the end of
March. He made his debut for the Lions
against Bradford City and registered his
first goal for the club against Derby.
Excellent in the air, he is powerful on the
ball and can shoot with either foot.
Cambridge U (Free from Cambridge C on
31/12/1996) FL 1+3 FAC 0+1 Others 1
Charlton Ath (Free on 17/3/1999) FL 1+3
FLC 0+1
Swindon T (Loaned on 3/1/2000) FL 4
Brentford (£100,000 + on 18/7/2000) FL
46+29/10 FLC 4/1 FAC 3+1/1 Others 3+5/3
Millwall (Free on 27/3/2003) FL 7/2

McCANN Gavin Peter
Born: Blackpool, 10 January 1978
Height: 5'11" **Weight:** 11.0
International Honours: E: 1
A former England international central
midfielder, Gavin's season at Sunderland
was one of many ups and downs. A fierce
tackler, who distributes the ball efficiently,
the schemer's enthusiasm sometimes
landed him in trouble with referees.
However, two games in particular showed
him at his best: against Liverpool in
December he capped a magnificent
performance with a brilliantly taken solo
goal and against Blackburn the following
month he volleyed home from 20 yards
before rounding off with the winning
spot kick in the subsequent penalty
shoot-out. With relegation confirmed,
Gavin, as one of Sunderland's most
saleable assets, may well be leaving the
club in the summer.
Everton (From trainee on 1/7/1995) PL 5+6
Sunderland (£500,000 on 27/11/1998) P/FL
106+10/8 FLC 4+3/2 FAC 11+1/3

McCANN Grant Samuel
Born: Belfast, 14 April 1980
Height: 5'10" **Weight:** 12.0
International Honours: NI: 7; U21-11

Grant enjoyed a second loan spell at
Cheltenham early on in the 2002-03
campaign, but after being recalled to
West Ham he eventually made a
permanent move to the Robins in the
new year. His arrival coincided with an
improvement in the team's fortunes, but
although he scored a spectacular free-kick
goal in the 2-1 win at Port Vale in March
he was unable to save the club from
relegation. Grant is a left-footed player
who mostly featured out wide in midfield
but also played in a more central role,
while he served Northern Ireland at left
back. He added a further four caps for his
country during the season.
West Ham U (From trainee on 6/7/1998) PL
0+4
Livingston (Loaned on 27/8/1999) SL 0+4
Notts Co (Loaned on 11/8/2000) FL 2 FLC 1
Cheltenham T (Loaned on 17/10/2000) FL
27+3/3 FAC 2 Others 1
Cheltenham T (Loaned on 4/10/2002) FL 8
Others 2/1
Cheltenham T (£50,000 on 29/1/2003) FL 19/4

MACCARONE Massimo
Born: Galliate, Italy, 9 September 1979
Height: 6'0" **Weight:** 11.12
International Honours: Italy 2; U21
Massimo was already a much-travelled
player in the Italian football arena when
his name came to the attention of
Middlesbrough manager Steve McClaren
after his goals had helped Empoli to
secure promotion to the Italian Serie A.
He was also a full international and with
such a pedigree it took a club record
outlay to bring him to the Riverside.
Massimo ended the season as the club's
leading scorer on nine goals but he was
booked in for surgery over the summer
after dislocating his shoulder as a
youngster. Even bigger and better things
are expected of the young Italian next
time round after his year of adjusting to
the rigours of the Premiership.
Middlesbrough (£8,150,000 from Empoli,
Italy, ex AC Milan, Modena, on 20/7/2002) PL
26+8/9

McCARTHY Jonathan (Jon)
David
Born: Middlesbrough, 18 August 1970
Height: 5'9" **Weight:** 11.5
International Honours: NI: 18; B-2
This former Vale favourite rejoined the
club on a week-to-week basis at the
beginning of last season. A right winger
who also operated on the right-hand side
of midfield, Jon started on the substitutes
bench before forcing his way into the
line-up and the team won four of the five

ames he played. He suffered a hamstring rain and was released in October. He hen had brief spells at Doncaster and another former club, York City making a ngle appearance for each. Jon ubsequently joined Carlisle on a monthly ontract where he became an increasingly influential figure in the closing weeks of he campaign and helped the club avoid elegation to the Conference.
artlepool U (From juniors on 7/11/1987) FL +1 (Free to Shepshed Charterhouse in March 1989)

on McCarthy

York C (Free on 22/3/1990) FL 198+1/31 FLC 8/1 FAC 11/3 Others 15/3
Port Vale (£450,000 on 1/8/1995) FL 93+1/11 FLC 10/2 FAC 7/1 Others 8/2
Birmingham C (£1,500,000 on 11/9/1997) FL 107+17/8 FLC 9+1 FAC 4 Others 3+1
Sheffield Wed (Loaned on 28/3/2002) FL 4
Port Vale (Free on 8/8/2002) FL 5+3 FLC 1 (Free to Doncaster Rov on 7/10/2002)
York C (Free on 7/11/2002) FL 1
Carlisle U (Free on 29/11/2002) FL 19+2/1 FAC 2 Others 4/1

McCARTHY Patrick (Paddy)
Born: Dublin, 31 May 1983
Height: 6'1" **Weight:** 12.8
International Honours: RoI: Yth
This highly rated Manchester City defender was loaned to Boston United early on last term only to have the misfortune to be red carded on his debut at Hull. After serving his suspension he quickly won his place back. Paddy settled in at right back and did well enough to earn the offer of a permanent contract, however he chose to return to Maine Road. He was later loaned to Notts County, where he was also used at right back, and impressed the Magpies' fans with some exciting displays. Paddy was a member of the Republic of Ireland U19 team that finished fourth in the UEFA championships in the summer of 2002.
Manchester C (From trainee on 14/6/2000)
Boston U (Loaned on 22/11/2002) FL 11+1
Notts Co (Loaned on 23/3/2003) FL 6

McCARTHY Paul Jason
Born: Cork, 4 August 1971
Height: 5'10" **Weight:** 13.12
International Honours: RoI: U21-10; Yth; Sch
Paul continued his influential role on the left side of central defence and team captain of Wycombe Wanderers last term. A forceful defender, he was an automatic choice until January when he lost his place to teenager Roger Johnson. He made his final appearance for the Chairboys at home to Huddersfield the following month before being released by manager Lawrie Sanchez. A wonderful servant at Adams Park for seven years, Paul quickly joined Oxford United on loan where he proved to be a very useful end-of-season signing. Strong in defence, he was also a threat at set pieces and knocked in a goal in the win over Kidderminster.
Brighton & Hove A (From trainee on 26/4/1989) FL 180+1/6 FLC 11/1 FAC 13 Others 12/1
Wycombe W (£100,000 on 5/7/1996) FL 199+13/9 FLC 17+1/5 FAC 21/5 Others 8
Oxford U (Loaned on 27/3/2003) FL 6/1

McCARTNEY George
Born: Belfast, 29 April 1981
Height: 6'0" **Weight:** 12.6
International Honours: NI: 12; U21-5; Yth; Sch
This Northern Ireland international left back has found his progress at Sunderland restricted in the past, having to understudy skipper Michael Gray. However, George enjoyed an extended

271

run last term under Howard Wilkinson when Gray moved into midfield and the youngster impressed with his confident use of the ball and all-round defending ability. George can also operate at centre back, but is still looking to open his goal-scoring account for the Black Cats.
Sunderland (From trainee on 28/5/1998) PL 29+15 FLC 5+2 FAC 2+3

McCLARE Sean Patrick
Born: Rotherham, 12 January 1978
Height: 5'10" **Weight:** 11.12
International Honours: RoI: U21-3
This midfield player spent the majority of last season on the transfer list at Port Vale. Sean made his first appearance in the victory over Notts County in September and played well at Blackpool before going off injured. He was then sidelined until returning at Barnsley after Christmas. Good on the ball, Sean had a run of five games in the team but was a casualty after the defeat at Queen's Park Rangers and did not appear in the line-up again during the remainder of the campaign.
Barnsley (From trainee on 3/7/1996) FL 29+21/6 FLC 10+3 FAC 5+1/1
Rochdale (Loaned on 22/3/2000) FL 5+4
Port Vale (Free on 20/10/2001) FL 28+12/1 FAC 1+1 Others 2+3

McCLEN James (Jamie) David
Born: Newcastle, 13 May 1979
Height: 5'9" **Weight:** 11.3
The 2002-03 season proved disappointing for Jamie as he made only a brief substitute appearance in the opening Premiership game at home to West Ham, following which he failed to make Newcastle's first-team squad again. An energetic midfield player with good control and distribution skills he will be hoping for more opportunities in 2003-04.
Newcastle U (From trainee on 4/7/1997) PL 7+7 FAC 3/1 Others 0+5
Motherwell (Loaned on 13/10/2000) SL 1+2

McCOMBE Jamie Paul
Born: Scunthorpe, 1 January 1983
Height: 6'5" **Weight:** 12.6
After starting last season on the substitutes' bench, Jamie broke into Scunthorpe's first team for a three-month spell up to Christmas. However, he was in and out of the team from the turn of the year as United turned to a number of loan defenders to help them out. A giant, imposing centre half who is strong in the air, he will be hoping to rediscover the form that led to a trial at Premiership Aston Villa in 2002.

Scunthorpe U (From trainee on 28/11/2001) FL 34+14/1 FAC 5/1 Others 3+1/1

McCOMBE John Paul
Born: Pontefract, 7 May 1985
Height: 6'2" **Weight:** 12.10
A youngster attached to the Huddersfield Town academy, John made his senior debut as a substitute against Oldham Athletic in the final league game of the season. He is a promising defender who will be looking to gain more first-team experience in 2003-04.
Huddersfield T (Trainee) FL 0+1

McCONNELL Barry
Born: Exeter, 1 January 1977
Height: 5'10" **Weight:** 10.3
Barry was the regular right back for Exeter City last season until he lost out to the returning Scott Hiley. He continued to feature regularly in the first half of the campaign, but made few appearances in the closing stages. Barry is one of the most naturally gifted players on the books at St James' Park, one of his main attributes being his consistency.
Exeter C (From trainee on 4/8/1995) FL 108+54/15 FLC 4+3/2 FAC 7+6/1 Others 5+2

McCORMICK Luke Martin
Born: Coventry, 15 August 1983
Height: 6'0" **Weight:** 13.12
A product of Plymouth Argyle's youth system, Luke signed a professional contract for the club at the start of last season. He spent most of the campaign as back-up goalkeeper to Romain Larrieu, receiving his first start in the LDV Vans Trophy tie against Chester City and adding a handful more appearances when his rival was sidelined through injury. Luke is learning all the time and will be hoping for more first-team opportunities in 2003-04.
Plymouth Arg (From trainee on 9/7/2002) FL 3+1 Others 2

McCOURT Patrick (Paddy) James
Born: Derry, 16 December 1983
Height: 5'10" **Weight:** 11.0
International Honours: NI: 1; U21-6
Rochdale's young winger had a slow start to the 2002-03 season, a string of niggling injuries preventing him from reproducing his mercurial best. He managed only three starts before February, though he remained a regular with Northern Ireland at U21 level. He netted a stunning goal against Bristol Rovers in the FA Cup when coming on as substitute, and when he did get back to

fitness turned in some exciting performances, sometimes playing in the 'hole' behind the two strikers to give full rein to his dribbling skills. However, another injury saw him miss the closing games of the campaign.
Rochdale (From trainee on 11/2/2002) FL 22+27/6 FLC 0+1 FAC 0+4/1 Others 0+4

McCREADY Christopher (Chris) James
Born: Runcorn, 5 September 1981
Height: 6'0" **Weight:** 11.11
Chris is one of many youngsters who have come up through the ranks at Crewe Alexandra. He made some good progress last term and featured in a handful of first-team games before injury curtailed his season. Chris is a very capable defender and will be looking to gain further senior experience in 2003-04.
Crewe Alex (From trainee on 30/5/2000) FL 6+3 FLC 1

McCULLOCH Lee Henry
Born: Bellshill, 14 May 1978
Height: 6'5" **Weight:** 13.6
Club Honours: Div 2 '03
International Honours: S: U21-14
Lee's conversion from striker to midfield player was one of the success stories of the 2002-03 season for Wigan Athletic. A tall player with good aerial ability he provided a strong physical presence down the left-hand side, despite finding himself on the end of a few clattering tackles. He was on target twice in the opening three matches, netting six in total in the Latics' championship season. Lee showed his versatility late on in the campaign when reverting to a striker's role and leading the line effectively following injuries to both Nathan Ellington and Andy Liddell.
Motherwell (Signed from Cumbernauld U on 17/8/1995) SL 75+47/28 SLC 5+2/2 SC 11+3/4
Wigan Ath (£700,000 on 2/3/2001) FL 67+15/15 FLC 2 FAC 1+1 Others 1+1

McDERMOTT John
Born: Middlesbrough, 3 February 1969
Height: 5'7" **Weight:** 11.0
Club Honours: AMC '98
This loyal one-club defender completed his 17th season for Grimsby Town last term and continued to create new records, clocking up his 500th league and 600th senior appearance in all competitions for the Mariners. The club captain, he remained first choice at right back for his consistency as a solid defender and his runs forward in support of attack. John was voted as BBC Radio

Humberside 'Sports Personality of the Year'. Out of contract in the summer, his future was unclear at the time of writing.
Grimsby T *(From trainee on 1/6/1987) FL 514+18/8 FLC 36+2 FAC 30+1/2 Others 21*

McDONAGH William (Will)
Born: Dublin, 14 March 1983
Height: 6'1" **Weight:** 11.12
A strongly built midfielder with a knack of grabbing vital goals, Will continued to impress in his first full season in English football. He played a crucial role in the LDV Vans Trophy run by scoring the 'golden goal' in the victories over both Stockport and Bury. He also grabbed a late equaliser in normal time in the latter match. Will was called up for training with the Republic of Ireland U20 squad during the season.
Carlisle U *(Signed from Bohemians, Ireland on 16/10/2001) FL 17+19/3 FAC 3 Others 4+2/3*

MacDONALD Gary
Born: Germany, 25 October 1979
Height: 6'1" **Weight:** 12.12
Although Gary featured regularly for Peterborough United in the early weeks of the 2002-03 campaign he was generally employed in an unfamiliar full-back position. In October he joined Conference outfit Stevenage Borough on loan and the deal was made permanent the following month. A promising central defender, he still has time to return to league football.
Portsmouth *(From trainee on 3/7/1998. Free to Havant & Waterlooville on 22/7/1999)*
Peterborough U *(Signed on 16/2/2001) FL 13+4/1 FLC 2+1 FAC 1*

McDONALD Scott
Born: Melbourne, Australia, 21 August 1983
Height: 5'8" **Weight:** 12.4
International Honours: Australia: U23; Yth
This promising young striker joined Huddersfield Town on loan last season and featured up front alongside stalwart Andy Booth. Despite his limited experience of first-team football he looked at ease in the Second Division and scored for the Terriers against Tranmere Rovers. He subsequently linked up with the Australian U20 squad for the qualifying rounds of the World Youth Championships before joining Bournemouth at the end of March. He impressed for the Cherries with his strength on the ball, skill and determination. Scott was capped at U23 level when he appeared against Spain in April.

Southampton *(Signed from Eastern Pride, Australia on 23/8/2000) PL 0+2 FLC 1*
Huddersfield T *(Loaned on 27/7/2002) FL 7+6/1 FLC 0+1*
Bournemouth *(Free on 27/3/2003) FL 3+4/1 Others 0+1*

McEVELEY James (Jay)
Born: Liverpool, 11 February 1985
Height: 6'1" **Weight:** 12.11
International Honours: E: U21-1
Jay made his bow in senior football for Blackburn Rovers in the Worthington Cup third round tie against Walsall last November and it soon became apparent that he was an outstanding prospect. Although essentially a central defender he was called upon to play at left back and did so well in the problem position that he remained until Vratislav Gresko was signed. His positional play was fine, he tackled sharply, looked confident on the ball and ably supported the attack. His progress was recognised when he made his debut for England U21s against Italy in February.
Blackburn Rov *(From trainee on 8/7/2002) PL 9 FLC 3+1 FAC 2*

McEVILLY Lee Richard
Born: Liverpool, 15 April 1982
Height: 6'0" **Weight:** 13.0
International Honours: NI: 1; U21-6
Lee continued his meteoric rise from non-league to international player in 2002-03 by establishing himself as a regular item for Rochdale and Northern Ireland U21s. A powerful striker sometimes used in a wide role, he was seen to best advantage when using his strength through the middle. His powerful shooting earned him the job of penalty taker in the second half of the season and he finished as Dale's top scorer with 16, to which he added three for his country including the winner against Scotland. More bizarrely he became the first-ever Rochdale goalkeeper to score a league goal; substituting for the injured Gilks against York, he had his penalty saved but netted the rebound to earn a 2-2 draw.
Rochdale *(£20,000 from Burscough on 24/12/2001) FL 40+15/19 FAC 4+1/1 Others 3/1*

McGHEE David (Dave) Christopher
Born: Worthing, 19 June 1976
Height: 5'11" **Weight:** 12.4
Dave only made a few brief appearances for Leyton Orient at the start of last season before snapping his achilles tendon during the Worthington Cup

game against Queen's Park Rangers. The injury caused him to miss the rest of the campaign, but he is now on his way back to full fitness and he will be looking to regain his place in the line-up in 2003-04. Dave is a commanding central defender with a whole-hearted approach to the game.
Brentford *(From trainee on 15/7/1994) FL 95+22/8 FLC 5+2/1 FAC 9/1 Others 8+1 (Freed on 22/1/1999)*
Leyton Orient *(Free from Stevenage Borough on 11/11/1999) FL 98+7/6 FLC 5 FAC 8 Others 6*

McGIBBON Patrick (Pat) Colm
Born: Lurgan, 6 September 1973
Height: 6'2" **Weight:** 13.12
Club Honours: AMC '99
International Honours: NI: 7; B-5; U21-1; Sch
A defender whose preferred position is at centre half, Pat is both swift in the tackle and effective in the air. He linked up with his former Wigan boss Ray Matthias at Tranmere in the early part of the 2002-03 season, where he made four appearances. An efficient player who is also more than competent at right back, Pat subsequently joined Irish league club Portadown, for whom he featured regularly for the rest of the campaign.
Manchester U *(£100,000 from Portadown on 1/8/1992) FLC 1*
Swansea C *(Loaned on 20/9/1996) FL 1*
Wigan Ath *(£250,000 on 3/3/1997) FL 163+10/11 FLC 11+1 FAC 9+1 Others 18*
Scunthorpe U *(Loaned on 15/2/2002) FL 6*
Tranmere Rov *(Free on 12/8/2002) FL 4*

McGILL Brendan
Born: Dublin, 22 March 1981
Height: 5'8" **Weight:** 9.8
International Honours: RoI: Yth (UEFA-U16 '98)
After spending the previous term on loan from Sunderland, Brendan signed a permanent deal for Carlisle early last season. A clever ball player who can operate on either flank, his willingness to run at defences posed a constant threat to opponents. One of his best performances came in early November. Playing against Oxford United, his lively display was capped with a fine individual goal that gave Carlisle only their second home win of the season.
Sunderland *(Signed from River Valley Rangers on 29/7/1998) FLC 0+1*
Carlisle U *(Loaned on 7/9/2001) FL 27+1/2 FAC 3 Others 1*
Carlisle U *(Free on 15/8/2002) FL 22+12/3 FLC 1/1 FAC 2+1 Others 3+2*

McGLEISH Scott

Born: Barnet, 10 February 1974
Height: 5'9" **Weight:** 11.3

Scott ended last season as Colchester United's joint-top scorer with nine goals, level with Joe Keith. He had a quiet start to the campaign, netting just three times before the turn of the year. But the U's front runner then hit good form, scoring the first in the 2-1 win at high-flyers Bristol City in February, and then plundering the only goal against Mansfield six days later. Always a handful in the air, Scott could never be faulted for effort. He figured in all but three games for the U's.

Charlton Ath *(Free from Edgware T on 24/5/1994) FL 0+6*
Leyton Orient *(Loaned on 10/3/1995) FL 4+2/1 Others 1/1*
Peterborough U *(Free on 4/7/1995) FL 3+10 FLC 0+1 FAC 0+1 Others 3+1/2*
Colchester U *(Loaned on 23/2/1996) FL 10+5/6 Others 2*
Cambridge U *(Loaned on 2/9/1996) FL 10/7 FLC 1*
Leyton Orient *(£50,000 on 22/11/1996) FL 36/7 FLC 3/1 FAC 1 Others 1*
Barnet *(£70,000 on 1/10/1997) FL 106+28/36 FLC 5/4 FAC 3 Others 7+2/1*
Colchester U *(£15,000 on 11/1/2001) FL 93+17/28 FLC 3 FAC 3/1 Others 3/1*

McGLINCHEY Brian Kevin

Born: Londonderry, 26 October 1977
Height: 5'7" **Weight:** 10.2
Club Honours: Div 3 '01
International Honours: NI: B-1; U21-14; Yth

This tough-tackling left wing back fought his way back from a broken ankle to regain his first-team place for Plymouth Argyle at the start of 2002-03. He starred in the first four games, netting a well-taken goal in the 2-1 victory against Luton Town in August. Unfortunately his campaign was then interrupted by a series of injuries, but he will be hoping to regain full fitness for the start of the 2003-04 campaign.

Manchester C *(From trainee on 4/12/1995)*
Port Vale *(Free on 1/7/1998) FL 10+5/1 FLC 0+1 FAC 1*
Gillingham *(Free on 3/8/1999) FL 7+7/1 FLC 3+1 FAC 4/1 Others 1*
Plymouth Arg *(Free on 1/12/2000) FL 54+14/2 FLC 1 FAC 3+2 Others 4+1*

McGOVERN Brian

Born: Dublin, 28 April 1980
Height: 6'3" **Weight:** 12.7
International Honours: RoI: U21-2; Yth

This quick and mobile central defender moved on to Peterborough United at the end of November, but his only appearance came in the home game with Barnsley when he was replaced at half time. He was released by Posh in the new year and later signed for Eircom League outfit St Patrick's Athletic, although here too he found it difficult to get in the line-up and within a short period of time he had been sent out on loan to Longford Town.

Arsenal *(Signed from Cherry Orchard on 5/9/1997) PL 0+1*
Queens Park R *(Loaned on 24/12/1999) FL 3+2*
Norwich C *(£50,000 + on 27/7/2000) FL 8+13/1 FLC 3+1*
Peterborough U *(Free on 21/11/2002) FL 1*

McGOVERN Jon-Paul

Born: Glasgow, 3 October 1980
Height: 5'7" **Weight:** 9.6

Jon-Paul joined Sheffield United in a long-term loan deal last season. Playing on the right as an attacking midfielder, he made his debut as a substitute against Portsmouth, starting and scoring a crucial goal in the next game against Walsall. He

Scott McGleish

howed a direct, positive approach, being prepared to take on and beat opponents nd he had a clinical shot. He did not quite maintain his initial impetus and after run of eight starts he was in and out of he side before returning to Parkhead. *Glasgow Celtic (Signed from Heart of Midlothian juniors on 8/6/2000)* *Sheffield U (Loaned on 13/8/2002) FL 1+4/1 FLC 2/1 FAC 1/1*

McGREAL John
Born: Liverpool, 2 June 1972
Height: 5'11" **Weight:** 12.8
John's 2002-03 season was blighted by injury and as a consequence his appearances for Ipswich Town were limited. He missed most of August and re-stablished himself at the heart of the efence when he was fit, but was injured gain in Joe Royle's first game in charge. He reappeared at Brighton but didn't last he 90 minutes and then made a couple f appearances in February when his lack f pace suggested that he was not fully match-fit.
Tranmere Rov (From trainee on 3/7/1990) FL 93+2/1 FLC 20+1 FAC 8 Others 7+2
Ipswich T (£650,000 on 4/8/1999) P/FL 102+3/3 FLC 12 FAC 3 Others 9/1

McGREGOR Mark Dale Thomas
Born: Chester, 16 February 1977
Height: 5'11" **Weight:** 11.5
After just one league appearance in the previous campaign, Mark staked an early laim to a regular place with some fine performances for Burnley at the eginning of 2002-03. His greatest asset, is ability to play anywhere along the ack line, is also something of a liability s he has yet to establish himself as first choice in any position, but injuries and suspensions to other defenders ensured hat he had plenty of first-team pportunities, and he was very reliable, sure in the tackle and adept at playing the ide out of trouble. Mark's first league oal for the Clarets came in the 2-0 home win against Norwich.
Wrexham (From trainee on 4/7/1995) FL 37+7/11 FLC 9 FAC 24+1 Others 11
Burnley (Free on 20/7/2001) FL 26+5/1 FLC /1 FAC 2+2

McGREGOR Paul Anthony
Born: Liverpool, 17 December 1974
Height: 5'10" **Weight:** 11.6
Paul spent time in a wide midfield position and as a striker for Northampton own last term, weighing in with a couple f well taken goals when called on to lay up front. A skilful player who works

hard for the team, he missed much of the campaign with a leg injury.
Nottingham F (From trainee on 13/12/1991) F/PL 7+23/3 FAC 0+3 Others 0+4/1
Carlisle U (Loaned on 25/9/1998) FL 3/2
Carlisle U (Loaned on 20/11/1998) FL 6+1/1 Others 1
Preston NE (Free on 24/3/1999) FL 1+3
Plymouth Arg (Free on 6/7/1999) FL 75+2/19 FLC 2+1/1 FAC 9/4 Others 0+1
Northampton T (Free on 5/7/2001) FL 54+8/5 FLC 2+1/1 FAC 0+4 Others 2/1

McGURK David Michael
Born: Middlesbrough, 30 September 1982
Height: 6'0" **Weight:** 11.10
This tall, young defender made only a

handful of appearances for Darlington as cover for injuries in defence last season after previously impressing with his strong tackling and strength in the air. However, he is still young enough to break through to regular first-team football with the Quakers.
Darlington (From trainee on 9/8/2002) FL 13+3 FLC 1 FAC 0+1 Others 1

MACHO Jurgen
Born: Vienna, Austria, 24 August 1977
Height: 6'4" **Weight:** 13.10
International Honours: Austria: U21
Sunderland's Austrian goalkeeper began the campaign out of favour. However, by the season's end, the giant stopper was many fans' 'Player of the Year' despite the

John McGreal

275

fact he made only 15 starts after grabbing his chance following injuries to both Thomas Sorensen and Thomas Myhre. Jurgen turned in 'Man of the Match' performances away to both Liverpool and Manchester United and repeated the feat against the Merseysiders at the Stadium of Light in December, earning praise from Reds' boss Gerard Houllier. Extremely brave and possessing lightning fast reflexes, Jurgen was Sunderland's 'Player of the Month' for both November and December and one particularly outstanding save from Michael Owen at Anfield was voted North East 'Save of the Season'. His form also attracted the attention of his national selectors and he was awarded his first full cap shortly before Christmas.

Sunderland (Free from First Vienna, Austria, ex Sportklub, Casino Vienna, on 24/7/2000) PL 20+2 FLC 3+1 FAC 1

McHUGH Frazer
Born: Nottingham, 14 July 1981
Height: 5'9" **Weight:** 12.5
This promising young midfielder featured for a number of non-league clubs last term including Gainsborough Trinity, Bromsgrove and Halesowen Town before joining Bradford City on a non-contract basis at the end of March. He made his full debut at Gillingham a month later and kept his place in the side for the following trip to Preston. Frazer signed a one-year contract with the Bantams at the end of May.
Swindon T (From trainee on 5/8/1999) FL

13+6 FLC 0+2 Others 2+1 (Freed during 2001 close season)
Bradford C (Free from Halesowen, ex Tamworth, Gainsborough Trin, Bromsgrove Rov, on 27/3/2003) FL 2

McINNES Derek John
Born: Paisley, 5 July 1971
Height: 5'8" **Weight:** 12.0
Club Honours: S Div 2 '95; SPL '97
International Honours: S: 21
West Bromwich Albion's skipper had an unfortunate start to the club's Premiership campaign, being red carded in the opening game at Old Trafford and then suffering a knee injury in training while suspended. Derek came back and grafted hard and long in midfield alongside Andy Johnson and Jason Koumas. However, his

Jurgen Macho

ppearances were restricted by a string of njuries to his knee, shoulder and thigh. Derek's two goals came in the same ame, a 2-1 victory at Sunderland on aster Saturday. He also gained full nternational honours, winning his first cottish cap as a second-half substitute gainst Denmark in August and later eaturing against Portugal.

Morton *(Signed from Gleniffer Thistle on 3/8/1988) SL 196+25/19 SLC 7+1/1 SC 0+6 Others 10*
Glasgow R *(£250,000 on 13/11/1995) SL 15+20/1 SLC 4+2/1 SC 0+1 Others 7+2/1*
Transferred to Toulouse, France on 7/12/1999)
Stockport Co *(Loaned on 6/11/1998) FL 13 AC 2*
West Bromwich A *(£450,000 on 10/8/2000) I/FL 87+1/6 FLC 7 FAC 5*

McINTOSH Martin Wyllie
Born: East Kilbride, 19 March 1971
Height: 6'2" **Weight:** 12.0
International Honours: S: B-2; Sch

An immaculate left-footed central defender, Martin took over as club captain and showed a perfect example of attitude as he led Rotherham United to unexpected heights in a great season. Strong in the air, Martin also proved to be a good tackler and not many opposing forwards got the better of him, while he also weighed in with a number of goals, his first coming from a long-range free kick in the opening day crushing of Millwall. In the last few matches of the season, he displayed his versatility by playing at left back although he much prefers to be in the middle.

St Mirren *(From trainee at Tottenham H on 30/11/1988) SL 2+2*
Clydebank *(Signed on 17/8/1991) SL 39+6/10 SLC 2 SC 4+1/1 Others 3/1*
Hamilton Academical *(Signed on 1/2/1994) SL 99/12 SLC 5 SC 5 Others 5/1*
Stockport Co *(£80,000 on 15/8/1997) FL 96+3/5 FLC 5+1 FAC 4*
Hibernian *(£250,000 on 10/2/2000) SL 21 SLC 3 SC 2*
Rotherham U *(£125,000 on 17/8/2001) FL 31/9 FLC 4 FAC 3*

MACKAY Malcolm (Malky) George
Born: Bellshill, 19 February 1972
Height: 6'1" **Weight:** 11.7

A pre-season hamstring injury, prevented Malky from winning a regular place in the Norwich City line-up until mid-September. However, he scored as a substitute on his return against Sheffield United and netted six times in all, including a fine effort with

the sweetest of half-volley strikes in the 2-0 victory at Millwall in March. A towering central defender, he is particularly strong in the air and his 'they shall not pass' attitude ensures that no opposing striker has an easy 90 minutes.

Queens Park *(From juniors on 8/12/1989) SL 68+2/6 SLC 3/2 SC 2 Others 2*
Glasgow Celtic *(Signed on 6/8/1993) SL 32+5/4 SLC 5+1 SC 4/1 Others 4+1*
Norwich C *(£350,000 on 18/9/1998) FL 153+14/11 FLC 7+1 FAC 7 Others 3/1*

McKEEVER Mark Anthony
Born: Londonderry, 16 November 1978
Height: 5'9" **Weight:** 11.8
International Honours: NI: Yth. RoI: U21-4

Mark was one of just a handful of players still on the books at Bristol Rovers prior to the arrival of new manager Ray Graydon but then had the misfortune to suffer a pre-season injury. He eventually forced his way back into the line-up on the left wing, although he found it difficult to hold down a regular place in the side and later had to be content with brief appearances from the substitutes' bench. He was released in the summer.

Peterborough U *(Trainee) FL 2+1 FLC 1*
Sheffield Wed *(£500,000 + on 15/4/1997) PL 2+3 FLC 0+1 FAC 0+1*
Bristol Rov *(Loaned on 10/12/1998) FL 5+2*
Reading *(Loaned on 8/3/1999) FL 6+1/2*
Bristol Rov *(Free on 8/2/2001) FL 20+16 FLC 1 FAC 1+1 Others 1*

Mark McKeever

MACKEN Jonathan (Jon) Paul
Born: Manchester, 7 September 1977
Height: 5'10" **Weight:** 12.8
Club Honours: Div 2 '00
International Honours: E: Yth
Jon struggled with a knee injury for most of last term and his season only really started in mid-January when he came on as substitute for Manchester City at Newcastle. However, he then suffered a further set back and it was not until April that he was available again. A striker with good close control and strength he will be hoping to partner Nicolas Anelka up front for City in 2003-04.
Manchester U (From trainee on 10/7/1996)
Preston NE (£250,000 on 31/7/1997) FL 155+29/63 FLC 12+2/8 FAC 10+5/2 Others 9+3/1
Manchester C (£4,000,000 + on 5/3/2002) P/FL 4+9/5

McKENNA Paul Stephen
Born: Chorley, 20 October 1977
Height: 5'7" **Weight:** 11.12
Club Honours: Div 2 '00
Paul failed to meet his own high standards early in the season, but this was largely due to having missed most of pre-season through injury, and he gradually recovered form as his fitness improved. A combative midfielder who is always keen to support his forwards, Paul operates best in the centre of the pitch, from where he gave a 'Man of the Match' performance at Derby, and scored his first goal of season soon afterwards against Burnley. The possessor of a fearsome shot which he could use more often than he does, he scored a last-minute equaliser against Portsmouth from 20 yards, and he was one of several players to benefit from playing alongside Brian O'Neil.
Preston NE (From trainee on 2/2/1996) FL 175+18/15 FLC 12 FAC 6+2/2 Others 6+2

McKENZIE Colin James Francis
Born: North Shields, 29 November 1983
Height: 6'0" **Weight:** 12.5
Colin is a strong running central playmaker who is persistent in his challenges for the ball in midfield. A third-year scholarship boy who had been chosen as Hartlepool's 'Young Player of the Year' in 2001-02, much was expected of him. He made his debut in the LDV Vans Trophy game at Tranmere as Chris Turner experimented by fielding his reserve side. Colin put in a good performance, but returned to the juniors and could not get back in the first team. He was disappointed not to be offered

professional forms, and left the club in April.
Hartlepool U (Trainee) Others 1

McKENZIE Leon Mark
Born: Croydon, 17 May 1978
Height: 5'11" **Weight:** 11.2
Leon broke his ankle in a pre-season game and did not return to first-team action for Peterborough until Boxing Day when he came off the bench against Colchester United. However, it was not until the end of March that he made the starting line-up, his effect on the team's fortunes being immense. There was a complete turn around as a seemingly relegation-bound side rose up the table to a respectable position. A pacy striker with excellent skills on the ball, Leon netted five times in those closing matches.
Crystal Palace (From trainee on 7/10/1995) F/PL 44+41/17 FLC 5+2/1 FAC 2+4
Fulham (Loaned on 3/10/1997) FL 1+2
Peterborough U (Loaned on 13/8/1998) FL 4/3
Peterborough U (Loaned on 30/11/1998) FL 10/5 Others 1/1
Peterborough U (Free on 13/10/2000) FL 64+7/36 FLC 1 FAC 6+1/1 Others 1/1

MacKENZIE Neil David
Born: Birmingham, 15 April 1976
Height: 6'2" **Weight:** 12.12
Club Honours: AMC '02
This experienced midfielder arrived at Mansfield in the summer of 2002 and soon became a favourite at Field Mill, not least because of his no-nonsense attitude. Neil was not afraid to have a go at goal either, although he scored just once, netting with a rocket against Tranmere in October. He was, however, in and out of the side under Stuart Watkiss, and later in the season a knee injury, which required surgery, necessitated another lengthy lay-off.
Stoke C (From trainee at West Bromwich A on 9/11/1995) FL 15+27/1 FLC 1+1 FAC 0+1 Others 0+1
Cambridge U (Loaned on 24/3/1999) FL 3+1/1
Cambridge U (£45,000 on 14/10/1999) FL 20+8 FLC 1+1 FAC 5 Others 0+1
Kidderminster Hrs (Free on 24/11/2000) FL 20+3/3 FAC 0+1 Others 2
Blackpool (Free on 9/7/2001) FL 6+8/1 FLC 1+1 FAC 1+3/1 Others 3/2
Mansfield T (Free on 6/8/2002) FL 16+8/1 FLC 1 FAC 2 Others 1

MACKEY Benjamin (Ben)
Born: Leamington, 27 October 1986
Height: 5'8" **Weight:** 11.9

Ben became the youngest-ever Coventry City player when he came on as a substitute against Ipswich in April aged 16 years and 167 days. His rapid rise to the senior ranks came after a four-goal youth-team appearance and just one outing from the subs' bench for the reserves. A promising young striker, he made two further substitute appearances but looked a little out of his depth.
Coventry C (Associated Schoolboy) FL 0+3

MACKIE John
Born: London, 5 July 1976
Height: 6'0" **Weight:** 12.6
The season could not have begun more brightly for John. First choice centre-back and captain of the Reading team, he seemed set for an exciting campaign, but all that changed after he was sent off in the home game against Norwich City. He lost his place, and the captaincy to Adrian Williams, but he battled his way back into the squad, although his appearances petered out towards the end of the campaign. Even so, it was still something of a surprise when, with a year remaining on his contract, he was told he could leave if he could find a club which would offer him regular first-team football.
Reading (Free from Sutton U on 5/11/1999) FL 54+8/2 FLC 2+1 FAC 5+2 Others 1+2

McKINLAY William (Billy)
Born: Glasgow, 22 April 1969
Height: 5'9" **Weight:** 11.6
International Honours: S: 29; B-1; U21 6; Yth; Sch
Billy attracted national media attention when he initially agreed to play for nothing at Leicester to try to win a contract. He was rewarded with a one-month deal and this was subsequently extended first until Christmas, then until the end of the campaign, as his class began to make an impact in City's midfield. As his match fitness improved, so did his level of performance and he forged a formidable midfield partnership with Muzzy Izzet. Billy impressed the fans with his vision and range of passing. He suffered a toe injury in the FA Cup reverse at Molineux that sidelined him for a while. Then, at Coventry in March, he netted his first senior strike anywhere for six years with a blistering 25-yarder into the top corner.
Dundee U (Signed from Hamilton Thistle on 24/6/1985) SL 210+10/23 SLC 21/3 SC 23+3/4 Others 17/2
Blackburn Rov (£1,750,000 on 14/10/1995) PL 76+14/3 FLC 4/1 FAC 7+1 Others 1
Leicester C (Loaned on 27/10/2000) FLC 1

Bradford C *(Free on 24/11/2000) PL 10+1 FAC 1*
Preston NE *(Free on 25/9/2001)*
Clydebank *(Free on 24/11/2001) SL 8 SC 1*
Leicester C *(Free on 9/8/2002) FL 29+8/1 FLC 0+1 FAC 2*

McKINNEY Richard
Born: Ballymoney, 18 May 1979
Height: 6'3" Weight: 14.0
Richard played second fiddle to Simon Brown in goal for Colchester for most of last season, but when called upon, he produced a number of blinding performances, not least against his former club Swindon Town. He was 'Man of the Match' in the 1-0 win over the Robins at Layer Road in late March, and followed

this up with another clean sheet and a terrific display in the 0-0 draw at Plymouth. A 'keeper who is never afraid to scamper off his goal line to close down strikers, he started the first ten games of the campaign, and also played in the closing fixtures when Brown was injured.
Manchester C *(Free from Ballymena U on 25/8/1999)*
Swindon T *(Free on 18/7/2001) FL 1*
Colchester U *(Free on 9/8/2002) FL 20+1 FLC 1 Others 1*

McLACHLAN Fraser Malcolm
Born: Manchester, 9 November 1982
Height: 5'11" Weight: 12.6
A product of the Stockport County youth system, Fraser's 2002-03 season started

disastrously when he was red-carded at Colchester on the opening day. He kept his place for the next two games but after his suspension did not play again until late October, and then found it hard to keep his place for long spells. Fraser came back strongly, and appeared in the last few games, proving a key member in County's revival and change in fortunes.
Stockport Co *(From trainee on 11/7/2001) FL 29+4/1 FAC 2*

McLAREN Paul Andrew
Born: High Wycombe, 17 November 1976
Height: 6'0" Weight: 13.4
This midfield grafter had a good solid season with Sheffield Wednesday in 2002-03. Although not as prolific as he might be in front of goal, his tireless running and prompting more than made up for this, and he did score a couple of great goals. Paul will be hoping to become one of the players around whom new manager Chris Turner builds his promotion challenge in 2003-04.
Luton T *(From trainee on 5/1/1994) FL 137+30/4 FLC 10+4/1 FAC 11/1 Others 9*
Sheffield Wed *(Free on 11/6/2001) FL 60+11/6 FLC 6+1/1 FAC 1*

McLEAN Aaron
Born: Hammersmith, 25 May 1983
Height: 5'6" Weight: 10.2
Aaron only made a few appearances as substitute for Leyton Orient last season before joining Grays Athletic on loan. The pacy young striker eventually left Brisbane Road in March and signed for Ryman League club Aldershot Town.
Leyton Orient *(From trainee on 9/7/2001) FL 5+35/2 FAC 0+3 Others 1+1/1*

McLEOD Izale (Izzy) Michael
Born: Birmingham, 15 October 1984
Height: 6'0" Weight: 11.2
Izzy had never even started a reserve game for Derby County when he made his senior debut at Ipswich last September. He was plucked straight out of the academy but, from then on, was a permanent part of the squad. The young striker is strong, fast and always ready to embark on runs but, through the nature of his promotion, has much to learn. Happily for Derby he is eager to develop and bowed out with a lively display as substitute in the final home defeat by Ipswich. His aim now is to build on this start.
Derby Co *(From trainee on 7/2/2003) FL 20+9/3 FLC 1*

Billy McKinlay

McLEOD Kevin Andrew
Born: Liverpool, 12 September 1980
Height: 5'11" **Weight:** 11.3
Kevin was one of a number of Everton players who went out on loan last term, moving to Queen's Park Rangers on a temporary basis until the end of the season. Before this, due to the good form of others, Kevin had made just one appearance for the Toffees in the FA Cup. A robust player who can either play left-midfield or as an orthodox left-winger, he made a good impression at Loftus Road and appeared for Rangers in the Second Division play-off final.
Everton (From trainee on 24/9/1998) PL 0+5 FLC 1 FAC 0+1
Queens Park R (Loaned on 21/3/2003) FL 8/2 Others 3

McMAHON Stephen Joseph
Born: Southport, 31 July 1984
Height: 5'9" **Weight:** 10.5
Stephen was in the third year of his scholarship at Blackpool last term and did well enough to earn his debut in senior football when he featured in the line-up for the LDV Vans Trophy tie at Scunthorpe in October. He appeared from the bench against Wigan soon afterwards and then added several appearances in the last few weeks of the season. A promising central midfielder, Stephen is the son of the Seasiders' manager Steve McMahon.
Blackpool (Trainee) FL 3+3 Others 1

McMASTER Jamie
Born: Sydney, Australia, 29 November 1982
Height: 5'10" **Weight:** 11.13
International Honours: E: Yth
This talented young midfielder made his senior debut for Leeds United at Blackburn last September and also featured against Everton, before joining Coventry City on loan in November. Jamie made two appearances for the Sky Blues, but was then sidelined by medial ligament damage and returned to Elland Road to recuperate. He subsequently made further appearances for United from the bench against West Ham and Liverpool.
Leeds U (From trainee on 30/11/1999) PL 0+4
Coventry C (Loaned on 22/11/2002) FL 2

McMILLAN Stephen (Steve) Thomas
Born: Edinburgh, 19 January 1976
Height: 5'10" **Weight:** 11.10
Club Honours: Div 2 '03
International Honours: S: U21-4
Steve once again showed himself to be a valuable member of the Wigan Athletic

squad during their championship-winning season in 2002-03. Injuries prevented the left-sided player enjoying a prolonged run in the side but he never let anyone down, producing some reliable performances at left back and in a midfield role. His pace going forward was again an asset and he loved nothing better than to push up and deliver telling crosses.
Motherwell (Signed from Troon Juniors on 19/8/1993) SL 144+8/6 SLC 9 SC 13+1
Wigan Ath (£550,000 on 2/3/2001) FL 63+4 FLC 4

McNAMEE Anthony
Born: Kensington, 13 July 1984
Height: 5'6" **Weight:** 10.0
International Honours: E: Yth
Watford's precociously gifted left winger started the 2002-03 season with huge and probably unreasonable expectations resting on his slight shoulders. His ball skills and crossing ability made him a great favourite with the fans, who regarded him as a potential match winner, and he proved to be just that when he came on against Walsall. In the end, he started only one match – the last of the season – but came on as a substitute 23 times as manager Ray Lewington sought to protect his young prodigy. Anthony featured regularly for England at U19 level and was selected for the U20s squad for the prestigious Toulon Tournament in the summer.
Watford (From trainee on 17/4/2002) FL 3+27/1 FLC 0+1

McNIVEN Scott Andrew
Born: Leeds, 27 May 1978
Height: 5'10" **Weight:** 12.1
International Honours: S: U21-1; Yth
Scott became a regular in the Oxford line-up and missed just three games in his first season for the club. Consistent in his defending he got into some good crossing positions in his wing-back berth. Scott also played in goal when regular 'keeper Andy Woodman was injured and kept a clean sheet for the remainder of the game. He even managed to score a goal himself when his long-range shot deceived the Bury goalkeeper to earn a vital point.
Oldham Ath (From trainee on 25/10/1995) FL 204+18/3 FLC 13+1 FAC 18+1/1 Others 9+2
Oxford U (Free on 11/7/2002) FL 44/1 FLC 3 FAC 3

McPHAIL Stephen
Born: Westminster, 9 December 1979
Height: 5'10" **Weight:** 12.0

Club Honours: FAYC '97
International Honours: RoI: 5; U21-7; Yth (UEFA-U18 '98)
After a disappointing previous season, Stephen was one of a number of squad players hoping to fare better under new Leeds United manager Terry Venables last term. He received his first start in the 1-0 home victory over Manchester United in September, and from then on he featured regularly until the UEFA Cup defeat by Malaga three months later. Stephen possesses a magical left foot, but needs to add extra steel to his game if he is to make his mark in the Premiership.
Leeds U (From trainee on 23/12/1996) PL 44+22/2 FLC 2+4 FAC 3 Others 15+5
Millwall (Loaned on 14/3/2002) FL 3

McPHEE Christopher (Chris) Simon
Born: Eastbourne, 20 March 1983
Height: 5'10" **Weight:** 12.4
A young striker with a decent first touch, Chris enjoyed just a handful of opportunities for Brighton last season, making four brief appearances as a substitute under Martin Hinshelwood prior to the appointment of Steve Coppell as manager. With one year left on his contract Chris will be hoping for more chances in the Second Division in 2003-04. He scored eight goals for the reserves but will have to work hard if he is to make an impact at the Withdean Stadium.
Brighton & Hove A (From trainee on 10/6/2002) FL 2+6 FLC 0+2 Others 0+1

McPHEE Stephen (Steve)
Born: Glasgow, 5 June 1981
Height: 5'7" **Weight:** 10.8
This Port Vale striker worked hard but seemed to lose his scoring touch last season, managing only three goals. He was occasionally used on the right-hand side of midfield from where his pacy runs caused plenty of problems for opposing defenders. Steve's second goal of the campaign, against Chesterfield in February, was his best being an exquisite chip over the 'keeper after only two minutes.
Coventry C (From juniors on 19/11/1998)
Port Vale (Free on 30/7/2001) FL 79+5/14 FLC 3/2 FAC 3 Others 6/1

McSHEFFREY Gary
Born: Coventry, 13 August 1982
Height: 5'8" **Weight:** 10.10
International Honours: E: Yth
Gary began the 2002-03 campaign by netting a superb winning goal for

oventry against Sheffield United in the pening game. The highlight of his eason came soon afterwards, with a hat- rick in the 8-0 win over Rushden & iamonds in the Worthington Cup. The oventry-born striker renowned for his peed and close control was rarely given ore than two games in a row and was lso played out of position on the left on everal occasions. It was a little isappointing for everyone to learn that e had been placed on the transfer list at he end of the season.
ockport Co (Loaned on 30/11/2001) FL +2/1

IcSPORRAN Jermaine
orn: Manchester, 1 January 1977
eight: 5'8" **Weight:** 10.10
bsent since April 2002 with a cruciate gament injury, 'Jocky' endured a long ehabilitation and eventually reappeared n the Wycombe Wanderers first team in ebruary. He scored on his second start, at ome to Barnsley and fans were relieved hat he had not suffered any loss to his stonishing pace. At the beginning of pril however he had further problems vhen he suffered cruciate ligament amage to the other knee at Stockport nd is now recovering after undergoing n operation at the end of May.
Vycombe W (Signed from Oxford C on /11/1998) FL 88+37/23 FLC 8+1/3 FAC +1/1 Others 3+2/2

IcSWEENEY David
orn: Basildon, 28 December 1981
eight: 5'11" **Weight:** 11.7
avid's 2002-03 season at Southend did ot start until November due to injury and was perhaps a lack of match practice hat led to an accumulation of bookings nd subsequent suspension. On his return o the side he then suffered a freak omestic accident, which saw him idelined for ten games. Restored to the ne-up in late March, he turned in a tring of consistent performances at entre half, which was enough to win the ffer of a new contract in the summer.
outhend U (From trainee on 30/4/2001) FL 8+11 FLC 0+1 FAC 5+2 Others 5+1

IcVEIGH Paul
orn: Belfast, 6 December 1977
eight: 5'6" **Weight:** 10.5
nternational Honours: NI: 10; U21-11; 'th; Sch
aul was Norwich City's leading goal-corer in the 2002-03 season with 15 in

total, after starting the campaign in particularly rich form, scoring six in his first six games. He prefers a central attacking role, which enables him to get into goal-scoring positions, but was often used on the left flank from where he scored some of his more spectacular efforts, cutting in to shoot from long range. He has quick feet and an excellent first touch, which seemingly gives him an extra split-second on the ball. Paul made his 100th appearance for the Canaries at Nottingham Forest in March and remained a regular member of Sammy McIlroy's full Northern Ireland squad.
Tottenham H (From trainee on 10/7/1996) PL 2+1/1

Norwich C (Free on 23/3/2000) FL 81+17/23 FLC 1+1 FAC 5/1 Others 3/1

MADDISON Lee Robert
Born: Bristol, 5 October 1972
Height: 5'11" **Weight:** 12.4
Club Honours: S Div 1 '98
After scarcely featuring in the 2001-02 campaign for Carlisle, Lee found himself restored at left back for much of last season. A capable and experienced defender, he did all that was asked of him. However, he will long remember his first senior goal in England: an extraordinary 30-yard strike against Leyton Orient that was deservedly voted 'Goal of the Season'.

Lee Maddison

281

Bristol Rov (From trainee on 18/7/1991) FL
68+5 FLC 4 FAC 2 Others 6+1
Northampton T (£25,000 on 22/9/1995) FL
55 FLC 3+1 FAC 3 Others 4+1
Dundee (Free on 23/7/1997) SL 59+6/1 SLC
3 SC 3/1
Carlisle U (Free on 13/10/2000) FL 57+5/1
FLC 1 FAC 5 Others 2+2
Oxford U (Loaned on 5/2/2002) FL 11

MADDISON Neil Stanley
Born: Darlington, 2 October 1969
Height: 5'10" **Weight:** 12.0
This experienced midfielder again showed
his class with Darlington last term. Neil
produced quality control and accurate
passing from midfield, but was unable to
claim a regular position in the side due to
the good form of some of the younger
players striving for places. As a result of
this he only played in about half of the
games during the campaign and scored
just one goal, netting in the 5-1 drubbing
of Shrewsbury Town towards the end of
the season.
Southampton (From trainee on 14/4/1988)
F/PL 149+20/19 FLC 9+5 FAC 8+5 Others 1
Middlesbrough (£250,000 on 31/10/1997)
P/FL 32+24/4 FLC 7+1 FAC 4
Barnsley (Loaned on 4/11/2000) FL 3
Bristol C (Loaned on 16/3/2001) FL 4+3/1
Darlington (Free on 26/7/2001) FL 49+9/2
FLC 2 FAC 1+2 Others 2

MADDIX Daniel (Danny)
Shawn
Born: Ashford, 11 October 1967
Height: 5'11" **Weight:** 12.2
International Honours: Jamaica: 2
Danny was injured at the start of the
2002-03 season and took his time to win
his place back in the Sheffield Wednesday
line-up. When he did return he showed
all of his experience in central defence
and helped a struggling, inexperienced
side. He was very unlucky to lose his place
as the Owls switched players around, but
he remained patient and bided his time in
the reserves. He eventually got his chance
again and in the absence of Daryl Powell,
also took over the captaincy.
Tottenham H (From apprentice on
25/7/1985)
Southend U (Loaned on 1/11/1986) FL 2
Queens Park R (Free on 23/7/1987) F/PL
259+35/13 FLC 25/3 FAC 21+2/2 Others 2+3
Sheffield Wed (Free on 11/7/2001) FL
55+4/2 FLC 7/1

MAGENNIS Mark Arthur
Born: Newtonards, 15 March 1983
Height: 5'7" **Weight:** 10.6
International Honours: NI: Yth

Mark arrived at Carlisle on a short-term
contract last October. The young midfield
player showed good pace and netted in
the game against Swansea, but his spell
at Brunton Park ended soon afterwards.
In January he moved on to join Irish

League club Ards, where he made a
number of appearances in the second ha
of the season.
Coventry C (From trainee on 7/4/2001. Free
to Linfield during 2002 close season)
Carlisle U (Free on 4/10/2002) FL 6/1 Others

Danny Maddix

MAGILTON James (Jim)
Born: Belfast, 6 May 1969
Height: 6'0" Weight: 14.2
International Honours: NI: 47; U23-2;
U21-1; Yth; Sch
Jim started the 2002-03 season on the
substitutes' bench for Ipswich Town,
but quickly re-established his pivotal
role in the centre of midfield and
became a regular once Joe Royle took
over the reins. He was mostly used as
the playmaker of the team, picking the
ball up from defence and distributing it
to his strikers. He was often found in
the opposing penalty area supporting
his forwards and in the home game
with Wimbledon he had the
opportunities to score a first-half hat-
trick. Jim was on the score sheet three
times during the season, netting the
equaliser at Brighton, grabbing the vital
third goal against Reading and scoring
directly from a free kick in the final
game at Derby.
Liverpool (From apprentice on 14/5/1986)
*Oxford U (£100,000 on 3/10/1990) FL
150/34 FLC 9/1 FAC 8/4 Others 6/3*

*Southampton (£600,000 on 11/2/1994) PL
124+6/13 FLC 12+2/2 FAC 12/3*
*Sheffield Wed (£1,600,000 on 10/9/1997)
PL 14+13/1 FLC 2 FAC 1*
*Ipswich T (£682,500 on 15/1/1999) P/FL
139+15/11 FLC 10+1/1 FAC 4+1/1 Others
13+1/3*

MAHER Kevin Andrew
Born: Ilford, 17 October 1976
Height: 6'0" Weight: 12.5
International Honours: RoI: U21-4
Kevin was Southend United's captain in
2002-03 and arguably the club's most
influential player. On his day he is a
peerless passer of the ball with few equals
in the Third Division. He turned down a
summer move to local rivals Leyton Orient
to commence his sixth season at Roots
Hall, thus making him by far the club's
longest-serving player. One aspect of
Kevin's game which will need addressing
in his disciplinary record, which saw an
accumulation of yellow cards during the
season.
Tottenham H (From trainee on 1/7/1995)
*Southend U (Free on 23/1/1998) FL
188+7/14 FLC 9 FAC 13 Others 7+1/1*

MAHER Shaun Patrick
Born: Dublin, 20 June 1978
Height: 6'2" Weight: 12.6
This central defender was beginning to
live up to his potential at the starting of
last season. He began in style, netting his
first goal for Bournemouth in their
opening day game at Boston and seemed
to be adapting well to Third Division
football. Unfortunately Shaun suffered a
cruciate injury at Darlington in September
and this brought his season to a
premature close. He signed a new one-
year deal for the Cherries in the summer.
*Fulham (£35,000 from Bohemians on
18/12/1997) Others 2 (Free to Bohemians on
10/9/1998)*
*Bournemouth (Free on 23/8/2001) FL
35+4/2 FLC 2*

MAHON Alan Joseph
Born: Dublin, 4 April 1978
Height: 5'10" Weight: 11.5
Club Honours: FLC '02
International Honours: RoI: 1; U21-18;
Yth; Sch
Alan was never really in the frame at

Kevin Maher (left)

Blackburn Rovers last term, with the exception of the UEFA Cup ties, when he worked as hard as ever but made no great impression. He also rescued the club in extra time in the Worthington Cup tie against Walsall although his shot needed a considerable deflection. In January he joined Cardiff City on loan and netted in the home win over Blackpool and at Wycombe. He played on the left flank, with Gareth Ainsworth on the right, as City opted for the width that had been missing all season. Alan returned to Ewood Park following the home match against Colchester United in April, thus missing out on the Bluebirds' play-off excitement.

Tranmere Rov (From trainee on 7/4/1995) FL 84+36/13 FLC 12+6/1 FAC 4+2 (Free to Sporting Lisbon, Portugal on 1/7/2000)
Blackburn Rov (£1,500,000 on 14/12/2000) P/FL 24+9/1 FLC 4+3 FAC 9
Cardiff C (Loaned on 24/1/2003) FL 13+2/2

MAHON Gavin Andrew
Born: Birmingham, 2 January 1977
Height: 6'0" **Weight:** 13.2
Club Honours: Div 3 '99
Gavin started the 2002-03 season recovering from knee ligament damage sustained at the end of the previous term. He eventually returned to first-team duties with Watford in November and proved to be a useful all-rounder, two footed and sound in the air. Having initially been deployed in right midfield, he ended the season at right back.

Wolverhampton W (From trainee on 3/7/1995)
Hereford U (Free on 12/7/1996) FL 10+1/1 FLC 4
Brentford (£50,000 + on 17/11/1998) FL 140+1/8 FLC 8 FAC 5 Others 12
Watford (£150,000 + on 4/3/2002) FL 19+4 FAC 4+1

MAKIN Christopher (Chris) Gregory
Born: Manchester, 8 May 1973
Height: 5'10" **Weight:** 11.2
Club Honours: Div 1 '99
International Honours: E: U21-5; Yth; Sch
Chris linked up with his former boss from his Oldham days, Joe Royle, and blossomed once again at Ipswich last season. He was handed a central defensive role, playing on the left-hand side of a back three, where he built up good relationships firstly with Hermann Hreidarsson and, latterly, with Matthew Richards. His tackling and pace were features of his game and he even managed to bolster the attack on occasions.

Oldham Ath (From trainee on 2/11/1991) F/PL 93+1/4 FLC 7 FAC 11 Others 1+1 (Transferred to Marseilles, France during 1996 close season)
Wigan Ath (Loaned on 28/8/1992) FL 14+1/2
Sunderland (£500,000 on 5/8/1997) P/FL 115+5/1 FLC 13 FAC 7+1 Others 1+1
Ipswich T (£1,250,000 on 7/3/2001) P/FL 73 FLC 3 FAC 2 Others 7+1

MALBRANQUE Steed
Born: Mouscron, Belgium, 6 January 1980
Height: 5'8" **Weight:** 11.7
International Honours: France: U21
A great favourite with the Fulham fans, Steed enjoyed an excellent season and displayed outstanding goal-scoring form particularly at the turn of the year when he netted nine goals in a run of six matches, starting with a hat-trick in the FA Cup tie against Charlton. Oddly this prolific spell came after he had moved back to his more traditional midfield role following several matches as an emergency striker when he had failed to find the net. A talented player surely

Chris Makin

estined for recognition at full
international level with France, he passes
the ball well and is the club's main dead-
ball specialist.
*ulham (£5,000,000 from Lyon, France on
4/8/2001) PL 68+6/14 FLC 1+2/1 FAC 10/5
Others 12+2/3*

MALCOLM Stuart
Born: Edinburgh, 20 August 1979
Height: 6'1" **Weight:** 12.6
This tall central defender was signed by
Plymouth Argyle at the start of the 2002-
03 season to provide competition for
places in the defence. He made his debut
in the 2-1 victory against Huddersfield
Town in August replacing the injured
Graham Coughlan, but received few more
opportunities and was released by
manager Paul Sturrock in May.
*St Johnstone (Signed from Hutchison Vale
PC on 10/7/1996) SL 0+1*
Cowdenbeath (Loaned on 6/11/1998) SL 4
*Plymouth Arg (Signed on 7/8/2002) FL 3
Others 2*

MANSARAM Darren
Born: Doncaster, 25 June 1984
Height: 6'2" **Weight:** 11.7
Undoubtedly Grimsby Town's discovery of
the 2002-03 season, Darren impressed
with the reserves and was elevated to the
senior squad earlier than anticipated as
injuries plagued the Mariners' slender
playing resources. A striker who is
athletic, speedy and with impressive ball
control skills, he can cause mayhem
amongst opposing defences and is no
mean shot. When Grimsby boss Paul
Groves adopted a defensive policy during
the run-in as relegation loomed, he was
often required to plough a lone furrow as
sole striker usually against more
experienced defenders but always
acquitted himself well. Darren was the
Mariners' 'Young Player of the Year'.
*Grimsby T (From trainee on 16/9/2002) FL
1+13/2 FLC 0+1 FAC 2/1*

MANSELL Lee Richard Samuel
Born: Gloucester, 28 October 1982
Height: 5'9" **Weight:** 10.10
Lee was something of a forgotten man at
Luton last season, and his only first-team
appearances came in the LDV Vans Trophy
matches. A promising central midfield
player, he spent the closing stages of the
campaign on loan to Conference club
Nuneaton Borough, where on all accounts
he did well.
*Luton T (From trainee on 16/5/2001) FL
3+7/6 FLC 1 FAC 1/1 Others 3*

MARGETSON Martyn Walter
Born: Neath, 8 September 1971
Height: 6'0" **Weight:** 14.0
International Honours: W: B-1; U21-7;
Yth; Sch
Martyn proved to be one of Cardiff City's
best signings, yet he wasn't even first
choice as goalkeeper. He arrived as back
up to Neil Alexander at the start of the
2002-03 season and filled that role
superbly. Always professional and always
ready, he produced a string of clean
sheets for the reserves and some high
quality displays for the first team when
called upon.
*Manchester C (From trainee on 5/7/1990)
F/PL 51 FLC 2+2 FAC 3 Others 1*
Bristol Rov (Loaned on 8/12/1993) FL 2+1
*Southend U (Free on 3/8/1998) FL 32 FLC 4
FAC 1 Others 1*
*Huddersfield T (Signed on 6/8/1999) FL
47+1 FLC 1 FAC 2 Others 8*
*Cardiff C (Free on 2/8/2002) FL 6 FLC 1 FAC
1 Others 2*

MARINELLI Carlos Ariel
Born: Buenos Aires, Argentina, 14 March
1982
Height: 5'8" **Weight:** 11.6
International Honours: Argentina: Yth
Carlos was labelled as an exciting player
for the future on his arrival on Teesside
in 1999, but the young Argentine had a
frustrating season last term. His first-
team opportunities at the Riverside
were limited to just a handful of games
and he grabbed the opportunity to play
for Italian Serie A strugglers Torino
when the January transfer window
opened. After impressing in his three
games the Italian side were keen to
negotiate a permanent deal, but
Middlesbrough were not prepared to
accept anything less than the required
£3 million.
*Middlesbrough (£1,500,000 from Boca
Juniors, Argentina on 27/10/1999) PL
17+25/2 FLC 3+2/1 FAC 3+2*

MARLET Steve
Born: Pithiviers, France, 10 January 1974
Height: 5'11" **Weight:** 11.5
International Honours: France: 17
This hard-working forward started the
season in excellent form for Fulham,
scoring vital away goals in the early
rounds of the Intertoto Cup. Steve holds
the ball up well and brings others into the
game, but his form suffered late in the
season when he was substituted a
number of times. His four Premiership
goals all came before the end of

November. Steve continued to make the
occasional appearance for the French
national side.
*Fulham (£13,500,000 from Lyon, France, ex
Paris Red Star, Auxerre, on 3/9/2001) PL
49+5/10 FLC 1 FAC 6+2/3 Others 13+1/5*

MARNEY Daniel (Danny)
Gary
Born: Sidcup, 2 October 1981
Height: 5'9" **Weight:** 10.12
After making his senior debut for
Brighton as a substitute in the opening
fixture at Burnley, this talented young
winger enjoyed seven starts in a
struggling side and showed up well with
his ball-control and running. However,
new manager Steve Coppell opted for
experience and Danny was allowed to go
out on loan to Southend United where he
made the right-midfield position his own
for the next three months. He displayed
genuine pace and got better and better
as his loan deal progressed, while he
created many chances with his crosses.
His presence and dynamism were missed
when he returned to the Withdean in
March.
*Brighton & Hove A (From trainee on
7/8/2001) FL 6+6 FLC 1*
*Southend U (Loaned on 19/12/2002) FL
13+4*

MARNEY Dean Edward
Born: Barking, 31 January 1984
Height: 5'9" **Weight:** 10.7
This young Spurs midfielder joined
Swindon Town for a two-month loan
period at the end of December and
featured at both right back and right
wing back. He impressed during his spell
at the County Ground before eventually
returning to White Hart Lane.
Tottenham H (From trainee on 3/7/2002)
Swindon T (Loaned on 24/12/2002) FL 8+1

MARRIOTT Alan
Born: Bedford, 3 September 1978
Height: 6'1" **Weight:** 12.5
Alan was an ever-present throughout
Lincoln's Third Division campaign last
term showing some excellent form. He
continued to increase his senior
experience as a goalkeeper behind a
defence that was the meanest in division.
Alan saved a penalty kick on the opening
day of the season and went on to make
many more important stops.
Tottenham H (From trainee on 3/7/1997)
*Lincoln C (Free on 5/8/1999) FL 132 FLC 4
FAC 5 Others 6*

MARRIOTT Andrew (Andy)
Born: Sutton in Ashfield, 11 October 1970
Height: 6'1" **Weight:** 12.6
Club Honours: Div 4 '92; FMC '92; WC '95
International Honours: E: U21-1; Yth; Sch. W: 5
Andy was an ever-present for Barnsley prior to his departure in March with the exception of the LDV Vans Trophy tie at Bury. He again showed that he was a capable shot stopper, despite being in a team that struggled throughout the campaign. The consistency of his performances eventually brought a surprise transfer to Premiership club Birmingham City, where he was required as cover following the injury to Nico Vaesen. Andy's one and only appearance for the Blues came at Spurs in April.
Arsenal (From trainee on 22/10/1988)
Nottingham F (£50,000 on 20/6/1989) F/PL 11 FLC 1 Others 1

West Bromwich A (Loaned on 6/9/1989) FL 3
Blackburn Rov (Loaned on 29/12/1989) FL 2
Colchester U (Loaned on 21/3/1990) FL 10
Burnley (Loaned on 29/8/1991) FL 15 Others 2
Wrexham (£200,000 on 8/10/1993) FL 213 FLC 10 FAC 22 Others 21
Sunderland (£200,000 + on 17/8/1998) P/FL 2 FLC 3
Wigan Ath (Loaned on 1/1/2001) Others 2
Barnsley (Free on 13/3/2001) FL 53+1 FLC 2 FAC 1
Birmingham C (Signed on 13/3/2003) PL 1

MARSDEN Christopher (Chris)
Born: Sheffield, 3 January 1969
Height: 5'11" **Weight:** 10.12
Southampton's continued improved performances last term, invariably with Chris wearing the captain's arm band, saw him receive unprecedented press coverage: ubiquitously referred to as a 'journeyman'. But there is more to this much travelled midfielder's game than non-stop running, hard-tackling and determination; he has a sweet left foot and is an astute reader of the game, qualities that have made him, arguably, the most influential member of the side, whether playing in the centre of midfield, or, more usually in the last two seasons, on the left in tandem with Wayne Bridge. So important has been his presence in the team he subjected himself to a series of remedial injections in order to get himself fit to lead Saints for the FA Cup final.
Sheffield U (From apprentice on 6/1/1987) FL 13+3/1 FLC 1 Others 1
Huddersfield T (Signed on 15/7/1988) FL 113+8/9 FLC 15+1 FAC 6+2 Others 10
Coventry C (Loaned on 2/11/1993) PL 5+2
Wolverhampton W (£250,000 on 11/1/1994) FL 8 FAC 3
Notts Co (£250,000 on 15/11/1994) FL 10 FLC 1 Others 1/1
Stockport Co (£70,000 on 12/1/1996) FL 63+2/3 FLC 13 FAC 4 Others 4/1

Steve Marlet

rmingham C *(£500,000 on 9/10/1997) FL*
+1/3 FLC 5/3 FAC 2
uthampton *(£800,000 on 2/2/1999) PL*
)9+7/6 FLC 6+2/1 FAC 10+1/1*

1ARSH Christopher (Chris)
)nathan
)rn: Sedgley, 14 January 1970
eight: 5'11" Weight: 13.2
ıll back Chris was another Northampton
)wn player who lost a large chunk of the
ason through injury. When he was
atch fit he featured at left back, centre
ıck and central midfield. Being
)mething of a utility player Chris is an
eal candidate for the substitutes' bench
, he can be called upon to cover most
)sitions without disrupting the team.
'alsall (From trainee on 11/7/1988) FL
,5+37/23 FLC 23+2 FAC 33+3/3 Others
I+1/3
ycombe W (£30,000 on 23/3/2001) FL
'+1 FLC 0+1
)rthampton T *(£10,000 on 6/9/2001) FL*
* FAC 1 Others 1*

1ARSHALL Andrew (Andy)
)hn
)rn: Bury St Edmunds, 14 April 1975
eight: 6'2" Weight: 13.7
ternational Honours: E: U21-4; Yth
IEFA-U18 '93)
'ith Matteo Serenl on a 12-month loan
Italy Andy had the opportunity to
)nfirm his status as Ipswich Town's
ımber one 'keeper last term but, by his
)vn high standards, he was probably
sappointed with his performances over
e season as a whole. Andy is an
)xcellent shot stopper as he proved
gainst his former club, Norwich when
ılling off a superb diving save to turn a
ıssell pile driver round the post. He was
ade available on a free transfer at the
immer, even though he had one year
ft on his contract.
)rwich C *(From trainee on 6/7/1993) P/FL*
)4+1 FLC 18 FAC 5+1*
)urnemouth *(Loaned on 9/9/1996) FL 11*
illingham *(Loaned on 21/11/1996) FL 5 FLC*
Others 1
swich T *(Free on 4/7/2001) P/FL 53 FLC 2*
C 4 Others 6

1ARSHALL Lee Keith
)rn: Islington, 21 January 1979
eight: 6'0" Weight: 11.11
:ternational Honours: E: U21-1
iis promising attacking midfielder played
)r Leicester in the opening-day fixture at
e new Walkers Stadium before finally
ıining West Bromwich Albion in mid-
ugust. Lee had the pleasure of scoring

the Baggies' first-ever Premiership goal, in
the 3-1 home defeat by Leeds United
after coming on as a late substitute for
skipper Derek McInnes. Thereafter he
struggled with his form and fitness and
managed only ten senior appearances
during the campaign. He lost his place in
the squad due to an irritating hamstring
problem and on regaining full fitness in
December he went into the reserves,
where he remained throughout the
second half of the season.
Norwich C (Signed from Enfield on
27/3/1997) FL 95+22/11 FLC 11+1/2 FAC 2
Leicester C (£600,000 on 21/3/2001) P/FL
37+8 FLC 1 FAC 2
West Bromwich A (£700,000 on 14/8/2002)
PL 4+5/1 FLC 1

MARSHALL Scott Roderick
Born: Edinburgh, 1 May 1973
Height: 6'1" Weight: 12.5
International Honours: S: U21-5; Yth
Scott started his first league game in 20
months at Stockport last October
following a long-term injury and
celebrated with a goal. The Brentford
centre half remained a regular for the rest
of the campaign and played as well as he
has ever done for the Bees. Scott is a solid
defender who reads the game well.
Arsenal (From trainee on 18/3/1991) PL
19+5/1 FLC 1+1
Rotherham U (Loaned on 3/12/1993) FL
10/1 Others 1
Sheffield U (Loaned on 25/8/1994) FL 17
Southampton (Free on 3/8/1998) PL 2
Brentford (£250,000 on 15/10/1999) FL
73+2/3 FLC 5 FAC 7/1 Others 7/3

MARSHALL Shaun Andrew
Born: Fakenham, 3 October 1978
Height: 6'1" Weight: 12.12
Following the departure of Lionel Perez,
Sean staked his claim to be Cambridge
United's first choice 'keeper last season.
He began in fine form and rarely missed a
match all season, his occasional absences
coming as a result of injury and a bout of
'flu. Reliable and competent, he will be
looking to retain his place in the side in
2003-04.
Cambridge U (From trainee on 21/2/1997)
FL 104+5 FLC 3 FAC 12 Others 7

MARTEINSSON Petur
Born: Reykjavik, Iceland, 14 July 1973
Height: 6'1" Weight: 12.4
International Honours: Iceland: 24;
U21-19; Yth
It was very much a mystery to Stoke City
fans as to why Petur was never given the
opportunity of a good run in the first

team despite the club's slide down the
Division One table last term. When
selected he always acquitted himself well,
proving his adaptability by appearing
along the defence or in midfield.
Stoke C (Free from Stabaek IF, Norway, ex
Leftur, Fram, Hammarby IF, Sweden, on
10/1/2002) FL 9+6/2 FAC 1+1

MARTIN John
Born: Bethnal Green, 15 July 1981
Height: 5'6" Weight: 9.12
John contested the left-midfield position
for Leyton Orient with Matt Brazier last
season and featured in the majority of
games, although he was often used from
the substitutes' bench. Despite being only
a small player he is very effective in the
tackle, he is also an excellent passer of
the ball and scored several vital goals
during the campaign. John's contract
expired during the summer and he was
released on a free transfer.
Leyton Orient (From trainee on 6/8/1998) FL
74+18/5 FLC 5+2 FAC 5+1/1 Others 5+3

MARTIN Lee Brendan
Born: Huddersfield, 9 September 1968
Height: 6'0" Weight: 13.0
Club Honours: FC '98
International Honours: E: Sch
Lee only made two senior appearances in
goal for Macclesfield during the 2002-03
campaign, taking over when regular
goalkeeper Steve Wilson was out injured.
He still made an excellent contribution as
the club's reserve-team 'keeper and
goalkeeping coach, but was released
during the 2003 close season.
Huddersfield T (From trainee on 1/7/1987)
FL 54 FAC 4 Others 5
Blackpool (Free on 31/7/1992) FL 98 FLC 8
FAC 4 Others 7
Rochdale (Free on 8/11/1996)
Halifax T (Free on 12/8/1997) FL 37 FLC 4
FAC 1 Others 1
Macclesfield T (Free on 19/7/1999) FL 52+1
FLC 1 FAC 3 Others 1

MARTINEZ Roberto
Born: Balaguer Lerida, Spain, 13 July
1973
Height: 5'10" Weight: 12.2
Club Honours: Div 3 '97
Roberto showed some quality ball skills in
his brief appearances for Walsall early last
the season. He then served manager
Colin Lee for a time in assessing games
from the stand before moving on to
Swansea in February. He immediately
impressed in a central-midfield role,
scoring his first Swans' goal in only his
third game and towards the end of the

287

campaign he was awarded the captaincy, taking over from Jason Smith.
Wigan Ath (Free from CFS Vipla Balaguer, Spain on 25/7/1995) FL 148+39/17 FLC 11+1/1 FAC 13+2/4 Others 7+5/2 (Free to CFS Vipla Balaguer, Spain during 2001 close season)
Walsall (Free on 13/8/2002) FL 1+5
Swansea C (Free on 28/1/2003) FL 19/2

MATHIE Alexander (Alex)
Born: Bathgate, 20 December 1968
Height: 5'10" **Weight:** 11.7
Club Honours: Div 2 '00
International Honours: S: Yth
This experienced striker managed just two starts for York City last term and also featured on a number of occasions from the substitutes' bench. At his best a skilful player with a good eye for goal, Alex was eventually released by the Minstermen in March and subsequently linked up with

Northern Counties East outfit Pickering Town.
Glasgow Celtic (From juniors on 15/5/1987) SL 7+4 SC 1 Others 0+1
Morton (£100,000 on 1/8/1991) SL 73+1/31 SLC 2/1 SC 5/3 Others 7/9
Port Vale (Loaned on 30/3/1993) FL 0+3
Newcastle U (£285,000 on 30/7/1993) PL 3+22/4 FLC 2+2
Ipswich T (£500,000 on 24/2/1995) P/FL 90+19/38 FLC 10+3/8 FAC 2+2 Others 6/1
Dundee U (£700,000 on 16/10/1998) SL 13+10/1 SLC 0+1 SC 4+2
Preston NE (Loaned on 17/9/1999) FL 5+7/2 FLC 2/2 FAC 1+2 Others 1
York C (Free on 27/9/2000) FL 26+26/3 FAC 2+4/1 Others 1+1

MATIAS Pedro Manuel Miguel
Born: Madrid, Spain, 11 October 1973
Height: 6'0" **Weight:** 12.0
International Honours: Spain: U21

Pedro spent much of his fourth season at Walsall on the fringes of the first-team squad and most of his appearances came from the substitutes' bench. Whenever he appeared he gave the team width and he netted three opportunist goals in the last few weeks of the campaign.
Macclesfield T (Free from Logrones, Spain, ex Real Madrid, Almeria, on 3/12/1998) FL 21+1/2 FAC 1
Tranmere Rov (Free on 5/8/1999) FL 1+3
Walsall (Free on 7/10/1999) FL 99+27/23 FL 4+2 FAC 6+4/1 Others 4/2

MATTEO Dominic (Dom)
Born: Dumfries, 24 April 1974
Height: 6'1" **Weight:** 11.12
International Honours: S: 6; E: B-1; U21-4; Yth
Dom began the 2002-03 season as the new skipper of Leeds United and playing in the centre of defence. He showed

Roberto Martinez (left)

ood form early on, but his campaign
as interrupted by a number of injuries.
onically he had stepped down from
ternational duty with Scotland during
e season in the hope that he might stay
ear of the treatment room! An
telligent player his vision, skill and
hleticism were sorely missed when he
as absent.
iverpool *(From trainee on 27/5/1992) PL
12+15/1 FLC 9 FAC 6+2/1 Others 10+1*
underland *(Loaned on 28/3/1995) FL 1*
eeds U *(£4,750,000 on 24/8/2000) PL 82
.C 2 FAC 5 Others 23/2*

1ATTHEWS Lee Joseph

orn: Middlesbrough, 16 January 1979
eight: 6'3" **Weight:** 12.6
ub Honours: FAYC '97
ternational Honours: E: Yth
espite Bristol City ending the season as
e Second Division's top scorers, the
alents of this injury-jinxed striker were
adly missed last season. Sidelined at the
art of the campaign he came back and
ored a great goal at Cheltenham before
ffering a slipped disc during the 3-1
ome defeat at the hands of Queen's Park
angers in September, and this kept him
delined for the rest of the season. All at
shton Gate will be hoping that Lee will
e fit for the start of the 2003-04 season.
eeds U *(From trainee on 15/2/1996) PL 0+3
C 0+1*
otts Co *(Loaned on 24/9/1998) FL 4+1*
illingham *(Loaned on 23/3/2000) FL 2+3*
ristol C *(£100,000 on 16/3/2001) FL
3+22/7 FLC 0+3 Others 2+1/2*

1ATTIS Dwayne Antony

orn: Huddersfield, 31 July 1981
eight: 6'1" **Weight:** 10.10
ternational Honours: RoI: U21-2; Yth
wayne started the 2002-03 season as a
gular choice in the centre of midfield for
uddersfield Town. Keen, eager in the
ckle, and able to deliver accurate and
ensible passes, it was easy to see why
e youngster has passed his 50th senior
ppearance for the club. He scored a
onderful long-range effort in the early-
ason away victory at Peterborough
nited, and also featured in the Republic
f Ireland U21 squad during the
ampaign.
luddersfield T *(From trainee on 8/7/1999)
. 48+16/2 FLC 1+2 FAC 3 Others 4/1*

1AXWELL Layton Jonathan

orn: Rhyl, 3 October 1979
eight: 5'8" **Weight:** 11.6
ternational Honours: W: U21-14; Yth
ayton was unable to break the midfield

dominance of Graham Kavanagh and
Willie Boland at Cardiff last season. On
his day, he can be a forceful and effective
player in the centre, but he was given few
chances in that area. Too often he was
played in a wide of centre that did not
suit him as well. The former Wales U21
international was informed that he could
find another club for 2003-04, but vowed
to see out his contract and fight for a
first-team place.
Liverpool *(From trainee on 17/7/1997) FLC 1/1*
Stockport Co *(Loaned on 17/7/2000) FL
8+12/2 FLC 1+1 FAC 0+1*
Cardiff C *(Free on 7/8/2001) FL 10+23/1 FLC
1+1 FAC 1+3 Others 3+1*

MAY Benjamin (Ben)

Born: Gravesend, 10 March 1984
Height: 6'1" **Weight:** 12.6
This promising young Millwall striker
broke into the reserve team during the
2001-02 campaign and went on to make
his senior debut at Watford last August.
Soon afterwards he netted his first league
goal at home to Ipswich Town and he
featured in a number of early-season
games for the Lions. Although held back
by an injury he made sporadic
appearances in the new year before
joining Colchester United on loan in
March. Ben went on to make half-a-
dozen appearances for the U's but the
closest he came to scoring was when he
hit the bar with a header in the last game
of the season against Queen's Park
Rangers.
Millwall *(From juniors on 10/5/2001) FL
4+6/1 FLC 1 FAC 0+1*
Colchester U *(Loaned on 27/3/2003) FL 4+2*

MAY David

Born: Oldham, 24 June 1970
Height: 6'0" **Weight:** 13.5
Club Honours: CS '94, '96; PL '96, '97,
'99; FAC '96, '99; EC '99
A very able central defender with good
recovery skills and excellent heading
ability to match, David's appearances in a
now over-stocked defensive area at Old
Trafford were limited to just one
Premiership run out against Liverpool in
December, and two Worthington Cup
appearances. Now entering the veteran
stages of his career at the club, and
having covered himself in past glories, it
would come as no surprise if he severed
links with United in the summer.
Blackburn Rov *(From trainee on 16/6/1988)
F/PL 123/3 FLC 12+1/2 FAC 10/1 Others 5*
Manchester U *(£1,400,000 on 1/7/1994) PL
68+17/6 FLC 9/1 FAC 6 Others 15+3/1*
Huddersfield T *(Loaned on 24/12/1999) FL 1*

MAYE Daniel (Danny) Peter Christopher

Born: Leicester, 14 July 1982
Height: 5'9" **Weight:** 10.10
This left-sided midfielder joined Southend
United on a short-term contract at the
beginning of the 2002-03 campaign. He
looked to have something to offer but
was unfortunate to find the left-flank
berth well served by Mark Rawle and Neil
Jenkins. Danny made three appearances
as a substitute, but when his deal expired
in October he was released and after a
brief liaison with Nuneaton Borough he
signed for Corby Town in the new year.
Port Vale *(From trainee on 29/9/2001) FL
0+2 Others 0+1*
Southend U *(Free on 3/7/2002) FL 0+2 FLC
0+1*

MAYLETT Bradley (Brad)

Born: Manchester, 24 December 1980
Height: 5'8" **Weight:** 10.10
Although injury played a large part in
keeping Brad on the sidelines last
season, he never looked likely to make a
major breakthrough into the first-team
reckoning at Burnley. His pace down the
right wing is undeniable, but other
aspects of his game have never really
blossomed. After a successful loan spell
with Swansea, he was unexpectedly
given a start in the Clarets' final home
game, but a 7-2 hammering by already
relegated Sheffield Wednesday was
hardly likely to give him a chance to
shine and he was substituted before the
score line had risen to its embarrassing
conclusion.
Burnley *(From trainee on 19/2/1999) FL
3+42 FLC 1+2 FAC 0+1 Others 1*
Swansea C *(Loaned on 14/3/2003) FL 6*

MAYO Kerry

Born: Haywards Heath, 21 September
1977
Height: 5'10" **Weight:** 13.4
Club Honours: Div 3 '01; Div 2 '02
After struggling initially and losing his
place, Brighton's longest-serving player
came back with a vengeance and proved
he could do a job in the First Division
despite having many doubters. Primarily a
left back, he also played as a left-sided
central defender for a prolonged spell.
While still needing to work on his close-
passing game, he always gave total
commitment and was constantly looking
to attack, especially with his phenomenal
throw-ins. Kerry's finest moment came
when he scored the last-minute winner
against Derby County at the Withdean in
November. He finished second in the

club's 'Player of the Season' poll behind the outstanding Danny Cullip.
Brighton & Hove A (From trainee on 3/7/1996) FL 225+18/10 FLC 7+1 FAC 7+6/2 Others 4+3

MAYO Paul
Born: Lincoln, 13 October 1981
Height: 5'11" **Weight:** 11.9
This left back featured in a number of different positions for Lincoln last season. Paul found himself kept out of his usual position by the form of Stuart Bimson and was loaned to Conference club Dagenham & Redbridge for a while. On his return he found himself appearing at centre back and in midfield in the reserves. He forced his way into the first team in March and finished the season in a striking role. Paul scored his first senior goal in the 5-3 play-off semi-final win over Scunthorpe United.
Lincoln C (From trainee on 6/4/2000) FL 61+14 FLC 3 FAC 3+1 Others 6/1

MAZZINA Jorge Nicolas
Born: Buenos Aires, Argentina, 31 January 1979
Height: 5'10" **Weight:** 11.7
This attacking midfield player or winger was given a short-term contract by York City at the start of the 2002-03 season and initially impressed with his skill on the ball. He made a handful of appearances from the substitutes' bench but was eventually released last November.
Swansea C (Free from AC Kimberley, Argentina on 10/8/2001) FL 3 FLC 1
York C (Free on 2/9/2002) FL 0+3

MEARS Tyrone
Born: Stockport, 18 February 1983
Height: 5'11" **Weight:** 11.10
The fastest player at Preston in recent memory, Tyrone arrived in the summer of 2002, but sustained an injury in pre-season, which delayed his appearance until October. Such was his reputation that a higher-than-average crowd attended his debut in the reserves, and he showed what he could do with a surging run at top speed along the full length of the field, which resulted in a penalty. A good dribbler as well as fast, he is essentially a defender, although he demonstrated his versatility by playing in both full-back positions as well as wide midfield and even up front as a substitute, scoring his only goal at Reading. Given a run at left back in late season due to Rob Edwards' injury, he showed himself to be useful on the overlap and a good tackler.

Manchester C (From juniors on 5/7/2000) FL 0+1
Preston NE (Signed on 10/7/2002) FL 11+11/1 FLC 1+1 FAC 0+1

MEDINA Nicolas Ruben
Born: Buenos Aires, Argentina, 17 February 1982
Height: 5'9" **Weight:** 10.6
Central midfielder Nicholas made his long awaited debut for Sunderland in the FA Cup replay victory over Bolton in January, and immediately impressed with his confident poise on the ball and accurate passing. It was therefore somewhat surprising that he was not seen again for the rest of the campaign. An Argentine U20 international, Nicholas was an important member of the Sunderland reserves title-winning side.
Sunderland (£3,500,000 from Argentinos Juniors, Argentina on 2/7/2001) FAC 1

MELAUGH Gavin Mark John
Born: Derry, 9 July 1981
Height: 5'7" **Weight:** 9.7
International Honours: NI: U21-8
An Aston Villa reserve and captain of Northern Ireland U21s, Gavin joined two of his international team-mates Paddy McCourt and Lee McEvilly at Rochdale when he moved to Spotland on loan last November. He made his league debut against Oxford and became a regular in midfield for Dale, gaining a contract for the rest of the season after his loan spell ended. He scored his first goal in the return game with Oxford, but the highlight of his campaign was surely his goal in the televised FA Cup tie against Wolves.
Aston Villa (From trainee on 17/7/1998)
Rochdale (Free on 7/11/2002) FL 17+2/1 FAC 5/1

MELCHIOT Mario
Born: Amsterdam, Holland, 4 November 1976
Height: 6'1" **Weight:** 11.8
Club Honours: FAC '00; CS '00
International Honours: Holland: 10; U21-13; Yth
Chelsea's powerfully built right back had another solid, consistent season and was a key member of the Blues' back four which was the second meanest in the Premiership. Mario has consolidated his position as first choice ahead of Albert Ferrer and played in virtually every match during the campaign. He mastered every left winger he faced and formed a good partnership on the right with Jesper Gronkjaer. Mario is always ready to join

the attack and is very comfortable on the ball, his probing passes and overlapping giving the Blues a valuable added dimension to their attacking armoury.
Chelsea (Free from Ajax, Holland on 5/7/1999) PL 97+10/2 FLC 7 FAC 11+2 Others 5/1

MELLANBY Daniel (Danny)
Born: Bishop Auckland, 17 July 1979
Height: 5'10" **Weight:** 11.9
Danny suffered a frustrating season at Darlington, as a series of niggling injuries kept him out of the reckoning for much of the campaign. He did not make a league start until March, but then grabbed four goals in four games with h tricky footwork and ability to turn opponents in and around the box. The promising striker will be hoping for a better time in 2003-04.
Darlington (Free from Bishop Auckland, ex West Auckland on 26/7/2001) FL 28+9/8 FLC 1 FAC 3+1 Others 1

MELLBERG Erik Olof
Born: Gullspang, Sweden, 3 September 1977
Height: 6'1" **Weight:** 12.10
International Honours: Sweden: 35
Olof had an excellent season at Aston Villa last term when he was one of the club's most consistent performers, turnin in 'Man of the Match' displays week in, week out. Solid and athletic, he was appointed captain during Steve Stauntons absence and appeared to take to the role with ease. Perhaps not surprisingly for a defender, he scored just one goal during the campaign, a powerful header against Manchester United at Old Trafford. An immense figure in the centre of defence, Olof deservedly won the PFA 'Player of the Month' award for January. He also added a further cap for Sweden against Latvia.
Aston Villa (£5,000,000 from Racing Santander, Spain, ex Degerfors, AIK Solna, o 25/7/2001) PL 70/1 FLC 3 FAC 2 Others 5

MELLIGAN John (JJ) James
Born: Dublin, 11 February 1982
Height: 5'9" **Weight:** 11.4
International Honours: RoI: U21-1; Yth
This talented young midfielder spent almost the whole of 2002-03 on loan at Kidderminster where he was one of the stars of the season. He made an immediate impression, scoring on his second appearance at Southend and at Wrexham over Christmas he netted a cracking 25-yard thunderbolt. JJ returned to Wolves in the closing stages of the

mpaign and made two brief
pearances from the substitutes' bench
ainst Coventry and Nottingham Forest.
s performances won a call-up to the
public of Ireland U21 squad and he
atured from the bench against Scotland
February.
olverhampton W (From trainee on
/7/2000) FL 0+2
urnemouth (Loaned on 30/11/2001) FL
1 FAC 1

Kidderminster Hrs (Loaned on 13/9/2002)
FL 28+1/10 Others 3/2

MELLON Michael (Micky) Joseph
Born: Paisley, 18 March 1972
Height: 5'10" **Weight:** 12.11
Micky played a major part in the engine
room for Tranmere last season, and
proved to be an inspiration to his
colleagues. His greatly-improved

of Mellberg

disciplinary record led to him being
named skipper of the side in the absence
of Kevin Gray, and he at last showed
what a good team man he can be. Micky
provided both stability and guidance to a
youthful midfield, and was never slow to
set up an attacking opportunity or to
make a telling pass. His diligence was
exemplary and it is to be hoped he carries
on in 2003-04 exactly where he left off
last term.
Bristol C (From trainee on 6/12/1989) FL
26+9/1 FLC 3 FAC 1+1 Others 5+3
West Bromwich A (£75,000 on 11/2/1993)
FL 38+7/6 FLC 3+2 FAC 0+1 Others 6/1
Blackpool (£50,000 on 23/11/1994) FL
123+1/14 FLC 9/1 FAC 4 Others 7/2
Tranmere Rov (£285,000 on 31/10/1997) FL
45+12/3 FLC 4 FAC 3+1
Burnley (£350,000 on 8/1/1999) FL 72+12/5
FLC 3+1 FAC 5
Tranmere Rov (Free on 5/3/2001) FL
63+11/3 FLC 5/1 FAC 4+1/1 Others 4

MELLOR Neil Andrew
Born: Sheffield, 4 November 1982
Height: 6'0" **Weight:** 13.7
Club Honours: FLC '03
This young Liverpool striker made his first-
team debut for the Reds in December in
the Worthington Cup tie against Ipswich.
More surprisingly he was given a short
run in the starting line-up in January
during Liverpool's disastrous mid-season
slump, before returning to the reserves
where he was top scorer with 19 goals
from 22 games. Neil is the son of Ian
Mellor who played for several clubs in the
1970s including Manchester City and
Sheffield Wednesday.
Liverpool (From trainee on 8/2/2002) PL 1+2
FLC 2/1 FAC 1

MELTON Stephen (Steve)
Born: Lincoln, 3 October 1978
Height: 5'11" **Weight:** 12.2
Club Honours: Div 3 '01
After impressing during the pre-season
build-up, Steve was chosen in the starting
line-up for Brighton & Hove Albion's
opening fixture at Burnley. However, in
scoring the first goal of the campaign he
was injured and missed out on a chance
to establish himself in the side. Although
he made six more starts thereafter, he
was never quite able to recapture his early
form and in October he was tempted to
Hull City on loan by his former manager,
Peter Taylor, a move that soon became
permanent. The cultured midfielder
celebrated the move by becoming the
player to score the first goal at the Tigers'
magnificent new home, netting after 20

minutes of the official opening game against Sunderland. Before the campaign closed, he had been used in all four of Hull's midfield positions, displaying some outstanding ball control.
Nottingham F *(From trainee on 9/10/1995)* *P/FL 2+1 FLC 1*
Stoke C *(Free on 28/2/2000) FL 0+5 Others 0+2*
Brighton & Hove A *(Free on 2/8/2000) FL 21+25/3 FLC 1+3 Others 4+1/2*
Hull C *(Free on 24/12/2002) FL 19+6*

MELVILLE Andrew (Andy) Roger

Born: Swansea, 29 November 1968
Height: 6'0" **Weight:** 13.10
Club Honours: WC '89; Div 1 '96, '01
International Honours: W: 58; B-1; U21-2
Fulham's club captain enjoyed an outstanding season at the heart of the defence where his experience often proved invaluable. An excellent header of the ball his ability to read the game prevented many an opposition attacking move. He enjoyed particularly good form in the European games where his vast international experience stood him and the club in good stead. Andy continued to represent Wales at international level during the campaign.
Swansea C *(From trainee on 25/7/1986) FL 165+10/22 FLC 10 FAC 14+1/5 Others 13/2*
Oxford U *(£275,000 on 23/7/1990) FL 135/13 FLC 12/1 FAC 6 Others 6/1*
Sunderland *(£750,000 + on 9/8/1993) P/FL 204/14 FLC 18+1 FAC 11 Others 2*
Bradford C *(Loaned on 13/2/1998) FL 6/1*
Fulham *(Free on 1/7/1999) P/FL 141+3/4 FLC 11+1 FAC 13+1 Others 12*

MENDES Albert **Junior** Hillyard Andrew

Born: Balham, 15 September 1976
Height: 5'8" **Weight:** 11.4
This experienced striker featured regularly for St Mirren early on last term and registered a hat-trick in the 3-2 win at Clyde at the end of August. Early in the new year he signed for Mansfield Town and went straight into the line-up, making his debut at Plymouth. Junior featured regularly from then on, although he only found the net once. Operating either in a central role or wide on the right, where he looked more effective, his pace caused problems for most opposition defenders.
Chelsea *(From trainee on 1/7/1995)*
St Mirren *(Free on 29/4/1996) SL 98+22/21 SLC 6 SC 4/1 Others 0+2*
Carlisle U *(Loaned on 18/11/1998) FL 5+1/1*

Paul Merson

unfermline Ath *(£20,000 on 24/7/2000)*
7+7 SLC 2
Mirren (Free on 22/6/2002) SL 15+2/6
C 1 SC 1 Others 3
ansfield T (Free on 30/1/2003) FL 18/1

ENDY Bernard

orn: Evreux, France, 20 August 1981
eight: 5'11" **Weight:** 12.2
ternational Honours: France: U21; Yth
gned by Bolton on a season-long loan
eal, big things were expected from this
ghly rated French right back. However,
s debut in the opening fixture at Fulham
owed that it would take some time for
ernard to adapt to the playing style of
e Premiership and the first half of the
eason was virtually a write-off for him, a
eries of niggling injuries not helping his
ause in the slightest. It was January
hen he forced his way into the line-up
nd he remained there until the end of
e season, his pace proving to be a
errific asset. Playing in a more attacking
ole on the right-hand side, he terrorised
efences providing a major contribution
o the run of good form which saw
Vanderers retain their Premiership status.
olton W (Loaned from Paris St Germain,
ance on 27/7/2002) PL 20+1 FLC 1 FAC 1

ERSON Paul Charles

orn: Harlesden, 20 March 1968
eight: 6'0" **Weight:** 13.2
lub Honours: Div 1 '89, '91, '03; FLC
3; FAC '93; ECWC '94
ternational Honours: E: 21; B-4; U21-
Yth
aul made a single appearance for Aston
illa in the Intertoto match against FC
urich before moving on to Portsmouth.
e was very much the catalyst for
ompey's success last term in a
emarkable campaign in which he scored
2 goals himself and created double that
mount for his colleagues. Instrumental in
o much of their build-up play, he was the
am captain throughout the season and
issed only two first-team games,
nswering critics about his fitness. Paul
as deservedly selected by his fellow
rofessionals for the PFA Division One
eam of the season.
rsenal (From apprentice on 1/12/1985) F/PL
89+38/78 FLC 38+2/10 FAC 28+3/4 Others
7+2/7
rentford (Loaned on 22/1/1987) FL 6+1
thers 1+1
iddlesbrough (£4,500,000 + on
5/7/1997) P/FL 48/11 FLC 7/3 FAC 3/1
ston Villa (£6,750,000 on 10/9/1998) PL
01+16/18 FLC 6+2 FAC 11 Others 8+1/1
ortsmouth (Free on 8/8/2002) FL 44+1/12
LC 2 FAC 1

METTOMO Lucien

Born: Cameroon, 19 April 1977
Height: 6'0" **Weight:** 12.7
Club Honours: Div 1 '02
International Honours: Cameroon: 30
(ANC '00)
Lucien endured another frustrating season
with Manchester City in 2002-03 and
made just five first-team starts plus an
appearance from the bench. A defender
with plenty of steel, he could draw
satisfaction from being part of the team
that defeated local rivals Manchester
United for the first time in over a decade.

From December onwards he failed to
even make the first-team squad and it
looked like his future with the Blues was
in some doubt.
Manchester C (£1,200,000 from St Etienne,
France on 4/10/2001) F/PL 20+7/1 FLC 2+1
FAC 1

MICHOPOULOS Nikalaos (Nik)

Born: Khardsa, Greece, 20 February 1970
Height: 6'3" **Weight:** 14.5
Nik was Burnley's goalkeeper for the first
five matches of the 2002-03 season, but

Nik Michopoulos

then made way for the returning Marlon Beresford. In September he went out on loan to Crystal Palace, where he played half-a-dozen games before going back to Turf Moor. However, he received few opportunities on his return although he produced a superb performance in the 1-0 win at Coventry. Nik eventually won his place back in the closing stages of the campaign, but in the Clarets' final home game he was carried off on a stretcher before half time with the side already three goals down.
Burnley *(Free from PAOK Salonika, Greece on 25/8/2000) FL 85 FLC 3 FAC 5*
Crystal Palace *(Loaned on 27/9/2002) FL 5 FLC 1+1*

MIGLIORANZI Stefani
Born: Pocos de Caldas, Brazil, 20 September 1977
Height: 6'0" **Weight:** 11.12
This talented midfielder spent the 2002-03 season on short-term contracts at Swindon due to a suspected injury problem. Nevertheless he was a near ever-present in the side, missing just a handful of games. A classy player who always looks calm and collected he has good body strength, which enables him to shrug off challenges. He also possesses a fine shot and he scored a cracker on the final day of the campaign to celebrate the offer of a new contract. Stefani finished third in the club's annual 'Player of the Year' contest.
Portsmouth *(Free from St John's University, NY, USA on 8/3/1999) FL 25+10/2 FLC 2+4 FAC 1*
Swindon T *(Free on 1/8/2002) FL 39+2/3 FLC 1 FAC 1 Others 2/1*

MIKE Adrian (Adie) Roosevelt
Born: Manchester, 16 November 1973
Height: 6'0" **Weight:** 12.2
International Honours: E: Yth; Sch
This experienced striker showed some neat touches early in the season at Lincoln. He proved most effective coming on as a substitute, but was allowed to join Gainsborough Trinity before having a couple of months with Irish League club Cliftonville early in 2003.
Manchester C *(From trainee on 15/7/1992) F/PL 5+11/2 FLC 1+1 FAC 0+1*
Bury *(Loaned on 25/3/1993) FL 5+2/1*
Stockport Co *(£60,000 on 18/8/1995) FL 4+5 FAC 0+1 Others 1+1*
Hartlepool U *(Loaned on 4/10/1996) FL 7/1*
Doncaster Rov *(Loaned on 14/2/1997) FL 5/1*
Doncaster Rov *(Free on 5/8/1997) FL 42/4 FLC 2 FAC 1/1 Others 1 (Freed during 1998 close season)*

Lincoln C *(Free from Stalybridge Celtic, ex Leek T, Hednesford, Southport, Northwich Vic, on 23/8/2002) FL 5+12/2 FLC 0+1/1 FAC 0+1 Others 2*

MILDENHALL Stephen (Steve) James
Born: Swindon, 13 May 1978
Height: 6'4" **Weight:** 14.0
Steve was again involved in a contest with Stuart Garden for the Notts County goalkeeper's jersey last term. He began the season on the bench, but eventually forced his way back in the line-up in November, retaining his place until the closing stages when a hand injury forced him to the sidelines. Steve is a tall and commanding 'keeper who has a safe pair of hands and marshals his defence effectively.
Swindon T *(From trainee on 19/7/1996) FL 29+4 FLC 2 FAC 2 Others 1*
Notts Co *(£150,000 on 16/7/2001) FL 46+1 FLC 2/1 FAC 3 Others 2*

MILES John Francis
Born: Bootle, 28 September 1981
Height: 5'10" **Weight:** 10.8
This skilful midfield player joined Crewe on a one-year contract during the 2002 close season and made his debut in the Worthington Cup tie at Port Vale in September. However, he failed to win a regular place in the line-up at Gresty Road and subsequently moved on loan to Macclesfield Town on transfer deadline day. John went on to play a vital role in Macc's successful battle against relegation scoring four crucial goals, including a double strike away at Shrewsbury.
Liverpool *(From trainee on 27/4/1999)*
Stoke C *(Free on 28/3/2002) FL 0+1*
Crewe Alex *(Free on 16/8/2002) FL 0+5/1 FLC 1 FAC 2 Others 0+2*
Macclesfield T *(Signed on 27/3/2003) FL 7+1/4*

MILLEN Keith Derek
Born: Croydon, 26 September 1966
Height: 6'2" **Weight:** 12.4
Club Honours: Div 3 '92; Div 2 '98
After being absent with knee problems throughout the whole of the 2001-02 campaign many thought they had seen the last of this veteran Bristol City defender. Keith signed a one-year contract as player-coach at Ashton Gate, coming into the side at the start of the season, and was playing well when a cyst on his kneecap brought his first-team action to a premature conclusion.
Brentford *(From apprentice on 7/8/1984) FL 301+4/17 FLC 26/2 FAC 18/1 Others 30+1*

Watford *(Signed on 22/3/1994) FL 163+2/9 FLC 10+1 FAC 14 Others 1*
Bristol C *(£35,000 on 12/11/1999) FL 59+1 FLC 1 FAC 8 Others 6*

MILLER Justin James
Born: Johannesburg, South Africa, 16 December 1980
Height: 6'0" **Weight:** 11.10
Justin was an instant hit at Leyton Orient after signing on loan from Ipswich Town last September. He later returned to Portman Road, before signing for the O's permanently in the new year. A talented central defender who is crisp in the tackle, he reminded older fans of a young Glenn Roeder in the way he confidently brought the ball forward.
Ipswich T *(From juniors on 26/11/1999)*
Leyton Orient *(Loaned on 13/9/2002) FL 1 FLC 1 FAC 2 Others 2*
Leyton Orient *(Free on 31/1/2003) FL 6*

MILLER Kenneth (Kenny)
Born: Edinburgh, 23 December 1979
Height: 5'8" **Weight:** 11.3
International Honours: S: 5; U21-7
This slender striker soon won a regular place in the Wolves' starting line-up last season, but initially struggled to find the net. A tally of six by Christmas was not enough, but his confidence soared following the FA Cup victory over Newcastle and he scored in seven successive matches, to equal a post-war club record. After the 0-0 draw with Watford he responded with his first hat-trick, to make it 12 goals in nine games. Kenny continued to find the net regularly thereafter, scoring a total of 24 in all competitions including a vital strike in the play-off final against Sheffield United at the Millennium Stadium.
Hibernian *(Signed from Hutchison Vale BC on 25/5/1996) SL 29+16/12 SLC 1+2/1 SC 5/1*
Stenhousemuir *(Loaned on 25/11/1998) SL 11/8*
Glasgow R *(£2,000,000 on 16/7/2000) SL 12+18/8 SLC 1/1 SC 2+1/1 Others 3+2/1*
Wolverhampton W *(Loaned on 7/9/2001) 3+2/2*
Wolverhampton W *(£3,000,000 on 14/12/2001) FL 37+21/19 FLC 1+1/1 FAC 4+1/3 Others 3+2/1*

MILLER Kevin
Born: Falmouth, 15 March 1969
Height: 6'1" **Weight:** 13.0
Club Honours: Div 4 '90
Kevin rejoined Exeter City during the summer of 2002 and enjoyed an outstanding season for the Grecians,

arting in all 46 Third Division matches. he talented goalkeeper impressed with is confidence, handling ability and omposure. No City fan will forget his enalty save against Southend on the nal, fateful day of the season. Kevin anded in a transfer request in the week ollowing relegation.

xeter C *(Free from Newquay on 9/3/1989)* . 163 FLC 7 FAC 12 Others 18
irmingham C *(£250,000 on 14/5/1993)* FL 4 FLC 4 Others 2
Vatford *(£250,000 on 7/8/1994)* FL128 FLC 0 FAC 10 Others 3
rystal Palace *(£1,000,000 + on 21/7/1997)* FL 66 FLC 3 FAC 5 Others 2
arnsley *(£250,000 on 27/8/1999)* FL 115 LC 11 FAC 4 Others 3
xeter C *(Free on 9/8/2002)* FL 46 FLC 1 FAC Others 2

MILLER Thomas (Tommy)
Villiam
orn: Easington, 8 January 1979
leight: 6'1" **Weight:** 11.12
lthough he started the season as a ringe first-team player for Ipswich,

Tommy eventually fought through to win a regular place in the starting line-up, thriving under new manager Joe Royle's influence. He operated from box to box alongside Jim Magilton, but was always keen to support the attack and notched up ten goals during the campaign. One of his best efforts was when he opened the scoring against Millwall at Portman Road, latching on to the loose ball after a corner and crashing it into the net.

Hartlepool U *(From trainee on 8/7/1997)* FL 130+7/35 FLC 6/3 FAC 5/1 Others 12/5
Ipswich T *(£800,000 + on 16/7/2001)* P/FL 29+9/6 FLC 4/1 FAC 1+1/1 Others 3+3/2

MILLIGAN Jamie
Born: Blackpool, 3 January 1980
Height: 5'6" **Weight:** 9.12
Club Honours: FAYC '98; AMC '02
International Honours: E: Yth
Jamie had a frustrating time with injuries at Blackpool last term and he failed to make the starting line-up in Second Division fixtures. He scored twice, netting from the penalty spot in the LDV Vans Trophy win at Scunthorpe, and after

coming off the bench against Stockport. Jamie is a skilful midfield player with a cultured left foot.
Everton *(From trainee on 13/6/1997)* PL 0+4
Blackpool *(Free on 22/3/2001)* FL 10+20/1 FLC 0+1 FAC 1+1 Others 3+4/1

MILLS Daniel (Danny) John
Born: Norwich, 18 May 1977
Height: 5'11" **Weight:** 11.9
International Honours: E: 17; U21-14; Yth
After playing a major role for England in the World Cup finals during the summer, Danny became one of the most consistent performers at Leeds United last season. Apart from a brief absence in November he was a regular in the line-up. His speed, tackling and battling qualities earned him a new long-term extension to his contract during the campaign. He netted just the one goal, but it was a memorable effort, involving a fine solo run and left-foot drive in the 3-0 win at Bolton. In a season when injury has plagued the club, Danny operated superbly at full back and in central defence when required. He continued to represent England at international level, adding five more caps.
Norwich C *(From trainee on 1/11/1994)* FL 46+20 FLC 3+2/1 FAC 2
Charlton Ath *(£350,000 on 19/3/1998)* P/FL 45/3 FLC 3 FAC 1 Others 2
Leeds U *(£4,370,000 on 1/7/1999)* PL 96+5/3 FLC 4/1 FAC 6+1 Others 27+2

MILLS Garry Leonard
Born: Faversham, 20 May 1981
Height: 5'9" **Weight:** 11.8
Club Honours: NC '01; Div 3 '03
This central midfielder only missed one game for Rushden & Diamonds before the end of December and produced some useful performances to help the club stay in contention at the top of the Third Division. However he was left out of the side by manager Brian Talbot through tiredness and also struggled with a couple of injuries in the final weeks of the season. A product of the club's successful youth system, Garry was rewarded with the offer of a long-term deal in the summer.
Rushden & Diamonds *(From juniors on 3/7/1999)* FL 26+13 FLC 3+1 FAC 2 Others 2

MILLS Rowan Lee
Born: Mexborough, 10 July 1970
Height: 6'1" **Weight:** 13.9
This experienced target man had a rather frustrating campaign in 2002-03. Lee began the season in promising style for Coventry, using his strength to hold the

Kenny Miller (left)

ball up and netting superb goals against Grimsby and Millwall. Unfortunately he injured an ankle in November and found it difficult to regain a place in the side when he was fit. He was recalled briefly in January but soon afterwards he joined Stoke City on loan, later signing a short-term contract. However, although he scored some vital goals for the Potters he had the misfortune to be involved in a motorway road accident that set him back. He was unable to win his place back in the closing stages and was released in the summer.
Wolverhampton W (Signed from Stocksbridge PS on 9/12/1992) FL 12+13/2 FLC 1 FAC 3+1/1 Others 3/1
Derby Co (£400,000 on 24/2/1995) FL 16/7
Port Vale (£200,000 on 1/8/1995) FL 81+28/35 FLC 7+3/5 FAC 0+3 Others 6/4
Bradford C (£1,000,000 on 7/8/1998) P/FL 63+2/28 FLC 5+1/1 FAC 4/1 Others 5/3
Manchester C (Loaned on 10/3/2000) FL 1+2
Portsmouth (£1,000,000 + on 11/8/2000) FL 24+2/4 FLC 3/1
Coventry C (Free on 28/11/2001) FL 30+8/7 FLC 3/3 FAC 1/1
Stoke C (Free on 17/1/2003) FL 7+4/2

MILLS Pablo

Born: Birmingham, 27 May 1984
Height: 6'0" **Weight:** 11.6
International Honours: E: Yth
Of all the young players introduced by Derby in a difficult season, this England U19 defender made the most lasting impression and was a worthy choice as 'Young Player of the Year'. His first starts, at Reading and, in the FA Cup, Brentford were as a right back but he is obviously happier in the centre of defence. There he shows both strength and an ability to use the ball. His composure is also notable for a teenager. Pablo has a good chance of success if he maintains his progress.
Derby Co (From trainee on 16/7/2002) FL 12+4 FAC 1

MILNER James Philip

Born: Leeds, 4 January 1986
Height: 5'11" **Weight:** 11.0
International Honours: E: Yth
In a season of disappointments at Leeds, James was very much a bright spot. He was just 16 years old when he made his debut at West Ham in November, and then became the Premiership's youngest scorer when at 16 years and 356 days he netted the winner at Sunderland on Boxing Day. Two days later he scored a sublime goal against Chelsea, taking the

ball from around 20 yards out of goal, he turned one way and another leaving Marcel Desailly prostrate, before hitting an unstoppable effort past the 'keeper. Even when the injury list improved James remained a vital squad member at Elland Road. He reads the game well, has an abundance of skill and looks to have a good future in the game.
Leeds U (From trainee on 12/2/2003) PL 1+17/2 FAC 0+4

MILOSEVIC Dejan (Danny)

Born: Carlton, Australia, 26 June 1978
Height: 6'3" **Weight:** 14.12
International Honours: Australia: Yth
Third-choice 'keeper at Leeds United, Danny went out on loan to Plymouth Argyle in the autumn to gain experience. He made his senior debut for Argyle against Oldham Athletic but failed to last the full 90 minutes after suffering a knee injury. Later, in the new year, he had a loan spell at Crewe with an almost identical outcome. His first appearance, remarkably, was against Oldham and this time a broken wrist led to him leaving the pitch early in the second half. He returned to Elland Road to recuperate but was back in action for the reserves in the closing stages of the campaign.
Leeds U (£110,000 from Perth Glory, Australia on 24/1/2000)
Plymouth Arg (Loaned on 5/11/2002) FL 1
Crewe Alex (Loaned on 20/1/2003) FL 1

MILTON Russell Maurice

Born: Folkestone, 12 January 1969
Height: 5'8" **Weight:** 12.1
Club Honours: FAT '98; NC '99
International Honours: E: SP-2
This talented ball player with a sweet left foot began the 2002-03 season in the first team at Cheltenham Town, but was unable to sustain a regular place from October onwards. The majority of his appearances were made on the left-hand side of midfield and he scored both in the 2-0 win over Swindon Town and the 2-1 defeat at Luton Town. Russell is one of several long-serving figures at Whaddon Road, having played a big part in the club's rise from non-league football, and there was an emotional farewell for him following the final home game when it was announced that he would be given a free transfer.
Arsenal (From apprentice on 26/2/1987. Free to Double Flower, Hong Kong during 1988 close season)
Cheltenham T (£50,000 from Dover Ath on 12/8/1997) FL 108+9/14 FLC 3 FAC 7+1/3 Others 6+1/1

MINTO Scott Christopher

Born: Heswall, 6 August 1971
Height: 5'9" **Weight:** 12.7
Club Honours: FAC '97
International Honours: E: U21-6; Yth
Having put his injury troubles behind him Scott still found it difficult to break into West Ham's line-up last term, firstly being thwarted by the consistency of Nigel Winterburn and then by new signing Rufus Brevett. Featuring at left back he enjoyed a good spell back in September and had an excellent game at Chelsea when West Ham won their first game of the season. After coming on as a substitute in successive games in January he did not figure again in the first team and was released by the club in May.
Charlton Ath (From trainee on 2/2/1989) FL 171+9/7 FLC 8/2 FAC 8+2 Others 7/1
Chelsea (£775,000 on 28/5/1994) PL 53+1/4 FLC 3/1 FAC 9 Others 5+1 (Free to Benfica, Portugal on 30/6/1997)
West Ham U (£1,000,000 on 15/1/1999) PL 44+7 FLC 4 FAC 2 Others 5

MIRFIN David Matthew

Born: Sheffield, 18 April 1985
Height: 6'2" **Weight:** 14.5
A youngster attached to the Huddersfield Town academy, David made his senior debut as a substitute in the final game of the 2002-03 season against Oldham Athletic at the McAlpine Stadium. David a promising defender with a neat touch, accurate passing and a willingness to push forward at set pieces.
Huddersfield T (Trainee) FL 0+1

MISKELLY David Thomas

Born: Newtonards, 3 September 1979
Height: 6'0" **Weight:** 12.9
International Honours: NI: U21-11; Yth
This Northern Ireland U21 goalkeeper had his busiest season to date at Oldham last term, making a total of 15 appearances in all competitions. He produced a fine display in the Worthington Cup win at Derby and featured for the Latics in the play-offs against QPR. However, despite this his season ended unhappily when it was announced that his contract was not to be renewed.
Oldham Ath (From trainee on 1/7/1997) FL 17+3 FLC 3 FAC 0+1 Others 2

MITCHELL Craig Richard

Born: Mansfield, 6 May 1985
Height: 6'0" **Weight:** 12.4
This promising Mansfield Town striker was one of five youth-team players on the bench for the Chesterfield 'derby' match.

e came on for the last 20 minutes or so
nd did not look out of place in the
ags' attack. Craig's first goal for the
ub came in another 'derby' game
gainst Notts County at Field Mill, when
e hit the ball in to the top of the net
om the edge of the area.
ansfield T (Trainee) FL 3+12/1

ITCHELL Paul Alexander
orn: Stalybridge, 26 August 1981
eight: 5'11" **Weight:** 12.3
ub Honours: Div 2 '03
hard-working, versatile and popular
ayer, Paul was in and out of the Wigan
thletic side during their Second Division
ampionship-winning season last term.
gutsy performer, he never let the side
wn with his no-nonsense approach as a
olding' player in the centre of midfield.
e also showed his versatility with an
xcellent performance when called to play
s an emergency central defender in the
ome victory over Oldham Athletic.

Wigan Ath *(From trainee on 3/7/2000) FL
29+22 FLC 4+2 FAC 1+2 Others 3+2*
Halifax T *(Loaned on 22/3/2001) FL 11*

MOILANEN Teuvo (Tepi)
Johannes
Born: Oulu, Finland, 12 December 1973
Height: 6'5" **Weight:** 13.12
Club Honours: Div 2 '00
International Honours: Finland: 3; U21;
Yth
Preston's giant 'keeper started as first
choice in 2002-03, making four excellent
saves at Rotherham, and he was recalled
to the Finland squad for the Euro 2004
qualifiers. At his best, Tepi is strong on
crosses and an improving shot stopper,
but he suffered a dip in form and was
dropped in October after two unfortunate
errors at Grimsby. He returned as a
second-half substitute at Stoke on New
Year's Day, but after another defeat
against Rochdale in the FA Cup, he was
loaned to Hearts in January.

Preston NE *(£120,000 from FF Jaro, Finland,
ex Ilves, on 12/12/1995) FL 155+3 FLC 12+1
FAC 11 Others 2*
Scarborough *(Loaned on 12/12/1996) FL 4*
Darlington *(Loaned on 17/1/1997) FL 16*
Heart of Midlothian *(Loaned on 24/1/2003)
SL 14 SLC 1*

MOLENAAR Robert
Born: Zaandam, Holland, 27 February
1969
Height: 6'2" **Weight:** 14.4
An experienced no-nonsense defender
who managed to feature in the majority
of Bradford's games for the 2002-03
season, this commanding centre back
makes up for a lack of pace with his
ability to read the game. His only goal of
the season came in the 1-0 win at home
to play-off chasing Nottingham Forest in
December. Robert was out of contract at
the end of the season and was not
offered a new deal by the Bantams.
Leeds U *(£1,000,000 from FC Volendam,*

obert Molenaar (right)

Holland, ex Zilvermeuwen, on 11/1/1997) PL 47+4/5 FLC 4+1 FAC 5/1 Others 4
Bradford C *(£500,000 on 1/12/2000) P/FL 70+1/2 FLC 2+1 FAC 3*

MOLLOY Trevor
Born: Dublin, 14 April 1977
Height: 5'10" **Weight:** 11.6
International Honours: RoI: U21; Yth
This experienced ball-playing striker joined Carlisle in the summer of 2002, but he was unable to settle at Brunton Park. He will best be remembered for his match-winning penalty at Lincoln, when United triumphed despite finishing with only eight players on the pitch. Trevor made a quick return across the Irish Sea, later signing for one of his former clubs, Shamrock Rovers.
Carlisle U *(Free from Shelbourne, ex St Patrick's Ath, Athlone T, Shamrock Rov, Bohemians, on 9/8/2002) FL 7/1 FLC 1*

MONCUR John Frederick
Born: Stepney, 22 September 1966
Height: 5'7" **Weight:** 9.10
This tough-tackling central midfielder finished his career at West Ham still a huge favourite with the fans. He only appeared as a substitute on seven occasions during the 2002-03 campaign but his enthusiasm for the game was always evident. Usually brought on to liven things up he will be missed, but can look back with satisfaction after appearing in around 200 games for the Hammers.
Tottenham H *(From apprentice on 22/8/1984) FL 10+11/1 FLC 1+2*
Doncaster Rov *(Loaned on 25/9/1986) FL 4*
Cambridge U *(Loaned on 27/3/1987) FL 3+1*
Portsmouth *(Loaned on 22/3/1989) FL 7*
Brentford *(Loaned on 19/10/1989) FL 5/1 Others 1*
Ipswich T *(Loaned on 24/10/1991) FL 5+1*
Swindon T *(£80,000 on 30/3/1992) F/PL 53+5/5 FLC 4 FAC 1 Others 4/1*
West Ham U *(£900,000 on 24/6/1994) PL 131+44/6 FLC 13+1/2 FAC 7+1/1 Others 5+1*

MONINGTON Mark David
Born: Bilsthorpe, 21 October 1970
Height: 6'1" **Weight:** 14.0
Club Honours: AMC '96; NC '02
This experienced centre back found himself out of favour at Boston from the start of the 2002-03 season. His only appearance came in the home defeat against Cambridge United when the Pilgrims were missing seven first-choice players through injury or suspension. He subsequently signed for Conference club Halifax Town following a successful loan spell at the Shay.

Burnley *(From juniors on 23/3/1989) FL 65+19/5 FLC 5 FAC 4+1/1 Others 4+2*
Rotherham U *(Signed on 28/11/1994) FL 75+4/3 FLC 3 FAC 1 Others 4*
Rochdale *(Free on 6/7/1998) FL 90+5/12 FAC 8/1 Others 8/3*
Boston U *(Free on 3/7/2001) FL 1*

MONK Garry Alan
Born: Bedford, 6 March 1979
Height: 6'0" **Weight:** 13.0
A quick skilful and tidy central defender Garry has been on Southampton's books since 1999, without ever making a serious breakthrough into the first team. He was signed on for a further year in December, and then joined Sheffield Wednesday on loan, where he stayed three months and showed some excellent form. His appearances for Saints were confined to a single outing on the bench against Chelsea at St Mary's in August and playing at right back in the 2–1 defeat at Charlton.
Torquay U *(Trainee) FL 4+1*
Southampton *(Signed on 23/5/1997) PL 9+2 FLC 1 FAC 0+1*
Torquay U *(Loaned on 25/9/1998) FL 6*
Stockport Co *(Loaned on 9/9/1999) FL 2 FLC 2*
Oxford U *(Loaned on 12/1/2001) FL 5*
Sheffield Wed *(Loaned on 13/12/2002) FL 15*

MONKHOUSE Andrew (Andy) William
Born: Leeds, 23 October 1980
Height: 6'1" **Weight:** 11.6
A left winger who possesses great talent with his ball skills, Martin was rarely able to put his ability to the best possible use for Rotherham last term, as he found it difficult to make himself an automatic choice and often had to be content with a role as a substitute. However, he is still young enough to come through to live up to all the expectations that have been laid at his feet for the last couple of years. A knee injury ruled him out of action for several weeks towards the end of the season but he battled back well to regain his full fitness.
Rotherham U *(From trainee on 14/11/1998) FL 33+42/3 FLC 5/3 FAC 1+4 Others 1+1/1*

MONTGOMERY Gary Stephen
Born: Leamington, 8 October 1982
Height: 6'1" **Weight:** 13.8
Gary was one of three goalkeepers used by Coventry City last season. He replaced Fabien Debec for one game in November and after some excellent performances in the reserve team he became first choice in the closing stages of the campaign. In

only his second start, at Preston, he made a string of impressive saves and despite playing in a struggling side he acquitted himself well. He was surprisingly released at the end of the season and was reported to have signed for Rotherham.
Coventry C *(From trainee on 31/1/2001) FLC 1*
Kidderminster Hrs *(Loaned on 28/3/2002) FL 2*

MONTGOMERY Nicholas (Nick) Anthony
Born: Leeds, 28 October 1981
Height: 5'9" **Weight:** 11.8
International Honours: S: U21-1
Nick was a regular member of the Sheffield United squad last term, but found himself on the bench more often than in the starting line-up. He played in midfield, either as a tireless ball winner or as a man-to-man marker. When coming on as a substitute he was often used in a more attacking role down the right. An ankle injury at Anfield robbed him of the chance to play for Scotland U21, but he was chosen again, playing against Austria in April.
Sheffield U *(From trainee on 7/7/2000) FL 43+38/2 FLC 4+3/1 FAC 3+2*

MOONEY Thomas (Tommy) John
Born: Billingham, 11 August 1971
Height: 5'10" **Weight:** 12.6
Club Honours: Div 2 '98
Tommy found himself completely out of favour at Birmingham last season, and after a five-minute appearance from the substitutes' bench early on he spent the remainder of the campaign out on loan. He certainly improved the Stoke City strike force during his spell at the Britannia Stadium with his pace and commitment, while at Bramall Lane he worked hard. Tommy's final port of call was Derby, where he endeared himself to the fans with some enthusiastic chasing and even featured as a defender in a back three. He will be hoping for a more settled time in 2003-04.
Aston Villa *(From trainee on 23/11/1989)*
Scarborough *(Free on 1/8/1990) FL 96+11/30 FLC 11+2/8 FAC 3 Others 6/2*
Southend U *(£100,000 on 12/7/1993) FL 9+5/5 FLC 1+1 Others 2+3*
Watford *(Signed on 17/3/1994) P/FL 221+29/60 FLC 22/3 FAC 11+1/2 Others 4*
Birmingham C *(Free on 1/7/2001) P/FL 29+5/13 FLC 1/2 FAC 1 Others 3*
Stoke C *(Loaned on 13/9/2002) FL 11+1/3*
Sheffield U *(Loaned on 17/1/2003) FL 2+1 FLC 0+1 FAC 2/1*
Derby Co *(Loaned on 19/3/2003) FL 7+1*

MOOR Reinier Sean
Born: Holland, 12 June 1983
Height: 5'10" **Weight:** 12.0
International Honours: Rol: Yth
This promising young striker found it
difficult to win a place in the Exeter
starting line-up last term, as the various
management teams opted for experience
in what was a difficult season for the
club. He made the bulk of his
appearances from the bench, and
weighed in with his first two senior goals
in the 3-0 win at Boston. Reinier will be
looking for more regular first-team action
in 2003-04.

Reinier Moor

*Exeter C (From trainee on 2/8/2002) FL
2+17/3 FAC 1+3/1 Others 0+1*

MOORE Alan
Born: Dublin, 25 November 1974
Height: 5'10" **Weight:** 11.10
Club Honours: Div 1 '95
International Honours: Rol: 8; U21-4;
Yth; Sch
It was a mixed season for Alan, who
struggled to secure a regular place in the
Burnley line-up and only occasionally
showed his full capabilities as a speedy
and tricky left-winger. With Lee Briscoe
regularly playing on the left side of

midfield and other attacking options there
from Graham Branch and Glen Little,
Alan's role in the side was less well
defined than before. Two of his three
goals came in the FA Cup, most notably
the early strike at Fulham in Burnley's 1-1
draw at Loftus Road. Injury ruled him out
of the run-in, at a time when other
players' absences might have given him
the chance of an extended run in the side.
*Middlesbrough (From trainee on 5/12/1991)
F/PL 98+20/14 FLC 9+6/1 FAC 3+2/2 Others
3+1*
Barnsley (Loaned on 30/10/1998) FL 4+1
*Burnley (Free on 20/7/2001) FL 37+19/4 FLC
2+2/1 FAC 7+1/3*

MOORE Darren Mark
Born: Birmingham, 22 April 1974
Height: 6'2" **Weight:** 15.6
International Honours: Jamaica: 3
West Bromwich Albion's rock-like central
defender was absent from the last eight
matches of the season through injury
suffered in the home defeat by Chelsea in
mid-March, and may well be out of action
until November. His presence was sorely
missed, for at the time he was playing as
well as anyone despite the team's plight.
A positive performer, strong in every
aspect of defensive play, he never shirks a
tackle, wins most of the 50-50 balls in the
air and is a great leader, always urging his
colleagues on from the back. His two
goals in 2002-03 were important
inasmuch they were both winners, against
Fulham at home in August, and at
Manchester City in February.
*Torquay U (From trainee on 18/11/1992) FL
102+1/8 FLC 6 FAC 7/1 Others 8/2*
*Doncaster Rov (£62,500 on 19/7/1995) FL
76/7 FLC 4 FAC 1 Others 3/1*
*Bradford C (£310,000 + on 18/6/1997) FL
62/3 FLC 6/1 FAC 2*
*Portsmouth (£500,000 + on 15/11/1999) FL
58+1/2 FLC 5 FAC 2*
*West Bromwich A (£750,000 on 15/9/2001)
P/FL 60+1/4 FAC 6*

MOORE Ian Ronald
Born: Birkenhead, 26 August 1976
Height: 5'11" **Weight:** 12.0
International Honours: E: U21-7; Yth
With the emergence of Robbie Blake as a
Burnley regular, it was a rather difficult
season for Ian Moore, who remained a
near-automatic choice in the side (or
occasionally on the bench) but was
variously used up front, out wide (usually
on the right), just behind Gareth Taylor, or
even in midfield. Still a popular player
with the Clarets' faithful, Ian could never
be accused of lack of effort but is still

sometimes guilty of over-elaboration. Despite his frequent changes of role, he still reached double figures in goal-scoring, two coming in possibly his best game of the season, the FA Cup replay against Grimsby.
Tranmere Rov *(From trainee on 6/7/1994) FL 41+17/12 FLC 3+2/1 FAC 1+1 Others 0+1*
Bradford C *(Loaned on 13/9/1996) FL 6*
Nottingham F *(£1,000,000 on 15/3/1997) F/PL 3+12/1 FLC 0+2 FAC 1*
West Ham U *(Loaned on 26/9/1997) PL 0+1*
Stockport Co *(£800,000 on 31/7/1998) FL 83+10/20 FLC 8/2 FAC 3/1*
Burnley *(£1,000,000 on 20/11/2000) FL 102+15/24 FLC 2+1 FAC 10/7*

MOORE Neil
Born: Liverpool, 21 September 1972
Height: 6'1" **Weight:** 12.12
This experienced centre half was snapped

up by Mansfield Town in the summer of 2002 and started the new season as a first choice central defender. He was eventually made captain of the side when Lee Williamson stood down. However, with the club's defence leaking goals at an alarming rate, the step back up into the Nationwide League seemed to be too much for him. Neil moved to Southport in December initially on loan to the end of the season, but his contract was paid up early in 2003.
Everton *(From trainee on 4/6/1991) PL 4+1 FLC 0+1*
Blackpool *(Loaned on 9/9/1994) FL 7 Others 1*
Oldham Ath *(Loaned on 16/2/1995) FL 5*
Carlisle U *(Loaned on 25/8/1995) FL 13 Others 2*
Rotherham U *(Loaned on 20/3/1996) FL 10+1*

Norwich C *(Free on 8/1/1997) FL 2*
Burnley *(Free on 29/8/1997) FL 48+4/3 FLC 3+1 FAC 2/1 Others 4*
Macclesfield T *(Free on 10/12/1999) FL 12+3/2 Others 1 (Free to Telford U on 24/3/2000)*
Mansfield T *(Free on 5/7/2002) FL 18 FLC 1/1 FAC 1+1 Others 1*

MOORE Stefan
Born: Birmingham, 28 September 1983
Height: 5'10" **Weight:** 11.0
Club Honours: FAYC '02
International Honours: E: Yth
One of the stars of the Aston Villa team that won the FA Youth Cup in 2001-02, this young striker made his Premiership debut from the substitutes' bench against Charlton. Stefan tormented the opposition with his trickery from the moment he came on and required just nine minutes to mark his appearance with a goal, producing a burst of speed to run past two defenders before applying the coolest of finishes to beat the goalkeeper with a precise right-footer into the bottom corner of the net. He later made his full debut at Old Trafford and handled the occasion very well.
Aston Villa *(From trainee on 9/10/2000) PL 7+6/1 FLC 1+1 Others 0+2*
Chesterfield *(Loaned on 27/10/2001) FL 1+ Others 1*

MORGAN Christopher (Chris) Paul
Born: Barnsley, 9 November 1977
Height: 5'10" **Weight:** 12.9
For the first time in his six seasons in the Barnsley first team Chris missed a series of games through injury last term, when he damaged a knee ligament at Northampton at the end of August. His return at Brentford in October saw the Reds win for only the second time in nine games. Chris then featured regularly in the side once more. A danger at set plays no Reds' fan will forget the two goals he scored against Cardiff. Chris is a combative central defender who is effective in the air and strong in the tackle.
Barnsley *(From trainee on 3/7/1996) P/FL 182+3/7 FLC 14/1 FAC 9 Others 4*

MORGAN Craig
Born: St Asaph, 18 June 1985
Height: 6'1" **Weight:** 12.7
International Honours: W: Yth
This promising Wrexham defender continued to impress on the perimeter of the first team last season and was voted 'Young Player of the Year' by the club's

Darren Moore

upporters. Thrust into the action after only ten minutes against then league leaders Hartlepool United at the Racecourse in March he didn't put a foot wrong. Craig received his first start at Shrewsbury in April and was offered a professional contract soon afterwards.
Wrexham (Trainee) FL 1+7/1 Others 1

MORGAN Dean Lance
Born: Enfield, 3 October 1983
Height: 5'11" **Weight:** 11.2
Dean had a 'Jekyll and Hyde' season for Colchester United. The teenage front runner was brilliant one minute, ordinary the next. He reserved many of his better displays for away trips, although he did strike a terrific long-range goal to sink champions-to-be Wigan at Layer Road in August, one of only two away defeats suffered by the Latics. Dean also netted a wonder goal from 30 yards in the amazing 3-0 win at Cardiff City in mid-April. He was most effective playing in a wide role, and has the ability to beat defenders with an array of skills.
Colchester U (From trainee on 8/8/2001) FL 23+48/6 FLC 1 FAC 0+3 Others 1+1

MORGAN Lionel Anthony
Born: Tottenham, 17 February 1983
Height: 5'11" **Weight:** 12.7
International Honours: E: Yth
Lionel is another of Wimbledon's fine crop of youngsters developed through the academy ranks, but in recent seasons his appearances have been severely restricted due to injuries. He missed the start of the 2002-03 campaign recovering from cruciate ligament surgery, then after regaining his first-team place towards the end of the year suffered a further knee injury that kept him out for two more months. A superbly skilful left-footed midfielder and a current England U20 international, he was the subject of some targeted fierce tackling on his return to action, and finished the season as he started it, on the sidelines.
Wimbledon (From trainee on 10/8/2000) FL 11+16/2 FLC 1+1 FAC 0+1/1

MORGAN Mark **Paul** Thomas
Born: Belfast, 23 October 1978
Height: 6'0" **Weight:** 11.5
International Honours: NI: U21-1
This cultured centre back performed as a sweeper with great effect for Lincoln last term. Paul's form earned him a call-up for the Northern Ireland B squad but he missed out because of the team reaching the play-offs. He captained the Imps with

authority and was voted 'Player of the Year' by the club's supporters.
Preston NE (From trainee on 9/5/1997) FLC 1
Lincoln C (Free on 17/7/2001) FL 77+2/1 FLC 2 FAC 1 Others 5

MORGAN Westley (Wes) Nathan
Born: Nottingham, 21 January 1984
Height: 6'2" **Weight:** 14.0
Wes made an immediate impression following his arrival on loan at Kidderminster last March. His tough-tackling style in the centre of the defence was felt by Scunthorpe forwards within minutes of the start of his Football League debut and two games later he found the net for the first time at Cambridge United.
Nottingham F (Signed from Central Midlands League side, Dunkirk, on 5/7/2002)
Kidderminster Hrs (Loaned on 27/2/2003) FL 5/1

MORISON Steven (Steve)
Born: London, 29 August 1983
Height: 6'2" **Weight:** 12.0
After being on the fringe of the Northampton first team for a while Steve began to establish himself in the squad towards the end of the season, featuring occasionally in the starting line-up. A prolific scorer in the club's youth and reserve sides he is a promising striker who is good in the air and difficult to knock off the ball.
Northampton T (Trainee) FL 4+10/1 Others 0+2

MORLEY Benjamin (Ben)
Born: Hull, 22 December 1980
Height: 5'9" **Weight:** 10.1
This right wing back signed for Boston United in the summer of 2002 and made his debut for the Pilgrims in their opening Football League game against

Andy Morrell

Bournemouth but lasted only 45 minutes before he was forced off with a leg injury. His only other appearance was as a late substitute and he moved on to Conference club Telford United in September.

Hull C (From trainee on 10/12/1998) FL 7+19 FLC 1+2 FAC 2/1 Others 1+2
Boston U (Free on 8/8/2002) FL 1+1

MORRELL Andrew (Andy) Jonathan
Born: Doncaster, 28 September 1974
Height: 5'11" **Weight:** 12.0
Wrexham's 'Player of the Season' and how! Andy may have waited a long time to show the fans that he can score goals on a regular basis, but they hardly envisaged he would break Gary Bennett's post-war scoring record for the club. During his spell at the Racecourse he had previously always been more of an 'assist' man, his hard graft usually making opportunities for others. His haul of 34 goals included two hat-tricks and six doubles. Andy was named in the PFA Division Three team of the season, and was reported to have signed for Coventry City during the summer.
Wrexham (Free from Newcastle Blue Star on 18/12/1998) FL 76+34/40 FLC 3/1 FAC 1+2 Others 2+3/2

MORRIS Glenn James
Born: Woolwich, 20 December 1983
Height: 6'0" **Weight:** 11.3
This young Leyton Orient 'keeper started last season as reserve to Rhys Evans and also played a few games for the U19s before being given his opportunity of first-team football after Evans was sidelined with an injury. He enjoyed a lengthy run in the side, showing maturity beyond his years, before he was replaced following the arrival of the more experienced Lee Harrison in the new year.
Leyton Orient (From trainee on 4/3/2003) FL 24+1 FLC 2 FAC 1 Others 3

MORRIS Jody Steven
Born: Hammersmith, 22 December 1978
Height: 5'5" **Weight:** 10.12
Club Honours: ECWC '98; FAC '00; CS '00
International Honours: E: U21-7; Yth; Sch
The 2002-03 season brought the breakthrough that Jody Morris had threatened at Chelsea since his debut some seven years previously. The summer departures of Slovisa Jokanovic and Sam Dalla Bona gave the U21 international an opportunity that he grabbed with both

hands. Hard work during the close season clearly impressed coach Ranieri and Jody enjoyed a long run in the first team as the Blues challenged for a Champions' League berth. His hard-working style and neat passing game perfectly complemented fellow central midfielders Frank Lampard and Manu Petit plus the wide flank men. Not a noted goal-scorer, he struck a magnificent curling effort from 20 yards out to wrap up the FA Cup tie at Shrewsbury.

Chelsea (From trainee on 8/1/1996) PL 82+42/5 FLC 10+2/2 FAC 10+5/2 Others 11+11

MORRIS Lee
Born: Blackpool, 30 April 1980
Height: 5'10" **Weight:** 11.2
International Honours: E: U21-1; Yth
After battling through injuries since he joined Derby, 2002-03 was a big season for Lee. It went well until he missed 11 of the last 12 matches with a combination

Lee Morris

f back and hamstring trouble but he had
one enough to earn the offer of a new
ontract. Whether played on the left or as
central striker, his preferred position, Lee
as the pace to ruffle opponents. He
nished as joint-leading scorer, with
Malcolm Christie, and would probably
ave had the honour to himself but for
he late unavailability. Supporters like his
ager running and obvious enthusiasm
ut he still has something to prove to
hem.

heffield U (From trainee on 24/12/1997) FL
4+12/6 FAC 2+5/2 Others 0+1
erby Co (£1,800,000 + on 7/6/1999) P/FL
1+27/12 FLC 1+3/1 FAC 1+2
uddersfield T (Loaned on 8/3/2001) FL 5/1

MORRISON Clinton Hubert
orn: Wandsworth, 14 May 1979
eight: 6'1" **Weight:** 11.2
nternational Honours: RoI: 10; U21-2
irmingham City's record signing justified
is fee by scoring a number of vital goals
t crucial moments last season. The
alented striker netted the opener against
ston Villa in September, bagged both in
2-2 draw at Liverpool and then sank
underland at the Stadium of Light in the
st minute. Although he often had to
eed off scraps, for the most part he
ever gave up despite finding the step
om Division One tough at times.
nfortunately Clinton dislocated his
houlder in March and missed the closing
tages of the campaign. He added three
nore caps for the Republic of Ireland,
coring against both Russia and Scotland.
rystal Palace (From trainee on 29/3/1997)
/FL 141+16/62 FLC 16+3/9 FAC 4/1
irmingham C (£4,250,000 + on 3/8/2002)
L 24+4/6 FLC 1 FAC 1

MORRISON John Owen
orn: Londonderry, 8 December 1981
eight: 5'8" **Weight:** 11.12
nternational Honours: NI: U21-7; Yth;
ch
his young forward had a disappointing
eason at Sheffield Wednesday last term,
ot helped by a lengthy series of injuries.
le made only two appearances for the
wls and spent time on loan at Hull City,
ut returned early as he had not yet
egained match fitness. In February Owen
nade a surprise move to local rivals
heffield United on a short-term contract
ntil the end of the season. Playing on
he left as an attacking midfielder, he won
ver the crowd with a lively performance
vhen coming on as a substitute against
righton, nearly scoring with a mazy run
rom the halfway line. His chances were

limited, but he won a further three caps
for Northern Ireland U21s during his stay
at Bramall Lane.
Sheffield Wed (From trainee on 5/1/1999)
P/FL 31+25/8 FLC 8+2/3 FAC 1+2
Hull C (Loaned on 23/8/2002) FL 1+1
Sheffield U (Free on 21/2/2003) FL 3+5

MORTIMER Alexander (Alex) Barry
Born: Manchester, 28 November 1982
Height: 5'10" **Weight:** 10.9
This young full back was released by
Leicester City last October, moving on to
Shrewsbury Town on a three-month
contract. He managed only one first-team
appearance for the Third Division club,
coming off the bench in the 2-1 win at

Carlisle, and after leaving Gay Meadow
he had a brief spell at Kidderminster, then
signed for Dr Martens League club
Stafford Rangers.
Leicester C (From trainee on 10/1/2000)
Shrewsbury T (Free on 10/10/2002) FL 0+1
Kidderminster Hrs (Free on 14/1/2003)

MOSES Adrian (Ade) Paul
Born: Doncaster, 4 May 1975
Height: 5'10" **Weight:** 12.8
International Honours: E: U21-2
Opportunity knocked for this versatile
defender who was a regular all season in
the Huddersfield Town back four, playing
either at centre half, or in the right-back
berth following the departure of club
captain Steve Jenkins. His only absences

Owen Morrison

from the starting line-up were as a result of a cracked rib or suspension. A close-range goal against Notts County and a superb 'Man of the Match' display against his former club Barnsley were the highlights of his campaign.
Barnsley (From juniors on 2/7/1993) F/PL 137+14/3 FLC 15+1 FAC 15
Huddersfield T (£225,000 on 20/12/2000) FL 63+6/1 FLC 1 FAC 2+1/1 Others 5

MOSS Darren Michael
Born: Wrexham, 24 May 1981
Height: 5'10" **Weight:** 11.6
International Honours: W: U21-4; Yth
Darren featured regularly for Shrewsbury last term, making some excellent pacy attacking runs to complement some solid defensive work. A promising right back who is equally at home in midfield, he has an excellent shot that deserved to yield more goals than the three he bagged. Darren made his debut for Wales at U21 level in Finland last September and subsequently featured in a rare victory in Azerbaijan.
Chester C (From trainee on 14/7/1999) FL 33+9 FLC 1+1 FAC 4 Others 1
Shrewsbury T (Free on 24/7/2001) FL 58+13/4 FLC 0+1 FAC 4 Others 7/1

MOSS David Albert
Born: Doncaster, 15 November 1968
Height: 6'2" **Weight:** 13.7
Club Honours: SLCC '97
David impressed during Swansea's pre-season tour of the Netherlands, but missed the opening games of the new campaign because of a groin strain. He scored after coming on as a substitute at Bristol Rovers in late August, and again in the next match against York City. David proved adept at playing either in an attacking midfield role or as a central striker, but he was hampered by a toe problem. In January his contract was paid up and soon afterwards he joined Dr Martens League side Hednesford Town.
Doncaster Rov (Signed from Boston U on 10/3/1993) FL 18/5 FLC 2 Others 0+1
Chesterfield (Free on 8/10/1993) FL 59+12/16 FLC 2/1 FAC 2+1 Others 3
Scunthorpe U (Free on 1/7/1996) FL 4 FLC 1/1
Partick Thistle (Free on 10/9/1996) SL 31/11 SLC 1 SC 1
Falkirk (Signed on 6/8/1997) SL 59+2/25 SLC 3/2 SC 8/6 Others 4
Dunfermline Ath (£120,000 on 9/9/1999) SL 36+13/12 SLC 3/1 SC 3+1/1
Ayr U (Loaned on 1/11/2001) SL 5/1 SLC 1
Falkirk (Free on 22/3/2002) SL 3
Swansea C (Free on 9/8/2002) FL 3+6/2 FLC 1

MOSS Neil Graham
Born: New Milton, 10 May 1975
Height: 6'2" **Weight:** 13.10
Neil had started his career at Bournemouth and it was a very popular decision when he returned on loan from Southampton last season. His performances were superb as he proved how well he reads the game and what a great shot stopper he is. After returning to St Mary's he joined the Cherries on a permanent basis in February and from then on he was ever-present for the side he supported from the terraces as a boy.
Bournemouth (From trainee on 29/1/1993) FL 21+1 FLC 1 FAC 3+1 Others 2
Southampton (£250,000 on 20/12/1995) PL 22+2 FLC 2
Gillingham (Loaned on 8/8/1997) FL 10 FLC 2
Bournemouth (Free on 13/9/2002) FL 33 FAC 2 Others 6

MUGGLETON Carl David
Born: Leicester, 13 September 1968
Height: 6'2" **Weight:** 13.4
International Honours: E: U21-1
Some 16 years after joining the Spireites on loan Carl finally got round to signing a proper contract! He was exactly what the club needed – an experienced head behind a predominantly young defence – and he was sorely missed when he broke a leg at Brentford last December. Happily he returned for the last few games to help keep his club in Division Two.
Leicester C (From apprentice on 17/9/1986) FL 46 FAC 3 Others 5
Chesterfield (Loaned on 10/9/1987) FL 17 Others 2
Blackpool (Loaned on 1/2/1988) FL 2
Hartlepool U (Loaned on 28/10/1988) FL 8 Others 2
Stockport Co (Loaned on 1/3/1990) FL 4
Stoke C (Loaned on 13/8/1993) FL 6 FLC 1 Others 2
Glasgow Celtic (£150,000 on 11/11/1994) SL 12 SC 1
Stoke C (£150,000 on 21/7/1994) 148+1 FLC 17 FAC 5 Others 6
Rotherham U (Loaned on 1/11/1995) FL 6 Others 1
Sheffield U (Loaned on 28/3/1996) FL 0+1
Mansfield T (Loaned on 9/9/1999) FL 9
Chesterfield (Loaned on 9/12/1999) FL 5
Cardiff C (Loaned on 15/3/2001) FL 6
Cheltenham T (Free on 1/7/2001) FL 7 FLC 1
Bradford C (Loaned on 28/12/2001) FL 4 FAC 1
Chesterfield (Free on 9/7/2002) FL 26 FLC 2 FAC 1 Others 2

MUIRHEAD Benjamin (Ben) Robinson
Born: Doncaster, 5 January 1983
Height: 5'9" **Weight:** 10.5
International Honours: E: Yth
A talented winger or striker, Ben was loaned by Manchester United to his home town club Doncaster Rovers in the early part of the 2002-03 campaign. Later released from his contract at Old Trafford he impressed Bradford City manager Nicky Law during two trial games and signed a short-term deal in March. Ben made his first appearance as a substitute in the home defeat by Reading later the same month, and then made the starting line-up at Burnley. He was out of contract in the summer and at the time of writing his future was uncertain.
Manchester U (From trainee on 7/1/2000)
Bradford C (Free on 6/3/2003) FL 5+3

MULLIGAN David James
Born: Bootle, 24 March 1982
Height: 5'8" **Weight:** 9.13
International Honours: New Zealand: Yth
David lost his place in the Barnsley team at the start of last season. However, he was soon back in the line-up, first playing at right back and then when the manager switched to three centre backs he moved to left wing back where he gave a number of assured displays. Always better on the offensive, he managed to score his first-ever senior goal with a spectacular volley at Oldham. David won his first cap for New Zealand against Estonia in October, and after making several more appearances for the All Whites, he featured in the squad for the Confederations Cup matches in the summer.
Barnsley (From trainee on 18/10/2000) FL 57+4/1 FLC 1 FAC 3 Others 1

MULLIN John Michael
Born: Bury, 11 August 1975
Height: 6'0" **Weight:** 11.10
A powerful and strong-running midfield player, John likes to get forward in support of the front men but he will have been disappointed with his return of just three goals for Rotherham last season. He netted twice against Burnley, while his other goal contributed to a crucial Easter Monday win against Ipswich Town. John is also the team's specialist from dead-ball situations with his ability to take free kicks and corners.
Burnley (From trainee on 18/8/1992) FL 7+11/2 FAC 2
Sunderland (£40,000 + on 12/8/1995) P/FL 23+12/4 FLC 5+1 FAC 2+1

Preston NE *(Loaned on 13/2/1998) FL 4+3
Others 1*
Burnley *(Loaned on 26/3/1998) FL 6*
Burnley *(Free on 20/7/1999) FL 38+39/8 FLC
4+1 FAC 5+1/1 Others 1*
Rotherham U *(£150,000 on 5/10/2001) FL
28+10/5 FLC 2 FAC 3/2*

MULLINS Hayden Ian
Born: Reading, 27 March 1979
Height: 6'0" **Weight:** 11.12
International Honours: E: U21-3
This talented midfield player enjoyed an
excellent season at Crystal Palace last
term, being a near ever-present and

winning the club's 'Player of the Year'
award. He took over the captaincy from
the injured Curtis Fleming and netted
three goals for the Eagles, including two
in the 3-3 draw at Watford in September.
Hayden also passed the landmark figure
of 200 league appearances for Palace
during the campaign.
Crystal Palace *(From trainee on 28/2/1997)
FL 209+3/18 FLC 23/2 FAC 9 Others 2*

MULRYNE Phillip (Phil)
Patrick
Born: Belfast, 1 January 1978
Height: 5'8" **Weight:** 10.11

Club Honours: FAYC '95
International Honours: NI: 18; B-1;
U21-3; Yth
Phil eventually decided that his footballing
future lay at Norwich, and signed a new
three-year contract in the summer of
2002 after it appeared he was leaving on
a 'Bosman' free transfer. The Canaries'
playmaker enjoyed an excellent first two-
thirds of the campaign before a series of
niggling injuries disrupted his progress in
the latter stages. A fine passer of the ball,
he has both the vision and ability to play
the defence-splitting pass and his eye for
goal led to the best goal-scoring season
of his career to date – netting eight times
in total. One of the first names on Sammy
McIlroy's Northern Ireland team sheet, he
remains a vital cog for both club and
country.
Manchester U *(From trainee on 17/3/1995)
PL 1 FLC 3 FAC 0+1*
Norwich C *(£500,000 on 25/3/1999) FL
110+7/15 FLC 6 FAC 5/2 Others 3*

MUMFORD Andrew Owen
Born: Neath, 18 June 1981
Height: 6'2" **Weight:** 13.6
International Honours: W: U21-4; Yth
Andrew struggled to make the starting
line-up for Swansea for much of 2002-03,
and generally failed to recapture his form
of the previous season. A talented
defender who is capable of delivering an
accurate ball from set-piece situations, he
will be disappointed at not making a
greater impact. Away from the Vetch Field
Andrew was selected to start for the
Wales U21 team that played in Finland,
and won further caps against Italy and
Azerbaijan.
Swansea C *(Free from Llanelli T on
14/6/2000) FL 47+15/6 FAC 1*

MUNROE Karl Augustus
Born: Manchester, 23 September 1979
Height: 6'1" **Weight:** 11.0
Karl was unable to command a regular
place in the Macclesfield line-up last term,
although he enjoyed two short runs in the
side playing in midfield. However, towards
the end of the season he was given a role
on the left side of the three central
defenders, from where he provided a
strong physical presence. He performed
well in the new role, and indeed
produced some of his best performances
for Macc to date.
Swansea C *(From trainee on 9/7/1998) FL
0+1*
Macclesfield T *(Free on 14/10/1999) FL
59+24/1 FLC 4+2/1 FAC 4 Others 2*

Ben Muirhead

MURDOCK Colin James
Born: Ballymena, 2 July 1975
Height: 6'2" **Weight:** 13.0
Club Honours: Div 2 '00
International Honours: NI: 17; B-3; Yth;
Sch
A rock in the centre of Preston's defence
in early season, Colin then had to share
the position with Marlon Broomes during
mid-season after the team reverted to
two rather than three centre halves.
Excellent in the air, he improved his
ground game during the season and was
rewarded by being made captain at
Ipswich in the absence of Chris Lucketti.
Injured in February, Colin was out for the
rest of the season and was then placed
on the transfer list after refusing a new
contract.
Manchester U (From juniors on 21/7/1992)
*Preston NE (£100,000 on 23/5/1997) FL
163+14/6 FLC 13+1 FAC 9+2 Others 10*

MURPHY Brian
Born: Waterford, 7 May 1983
Height: 6'0" **Weight:** 13.1
International Honours: RoI: Yth
After assisting the Republic of Ireland
U19s to fourth place in the 2002 UEFA
championships Brian was faced with stiff
competition for the 'keeper's jersey at
Maine Road and in January he was loaned
out to Oldham Athletic as cover for
injuries. He made no appearances for the
Latics, but later went out on loan to
Peterborough United for whom he made
his senior debut in the last game of the
season at Brentford. Brian was released by
Manchester City in the summer.
Manchester C (From trainee on 13/5/2000)
Peterborough U (Loaned on 2/5/2003) FL 1

MURPHY Christopher (Chris)
Patrick
Born: Leamington Spa, 8 March 1983
Height: 5'6" **Weight:** 9.8
This diminutive Shrewsbury striker was
looking to establish himself at first-team
level last term, but he found his way
blocked by the form of regular front men
Luke Rodgers and Ryan Lowe. A
promising youngster with excellent pace
and control, Chris managed just five
appearances from the substitutes' bench,
but showed what he could do by setting
up one of the goals in the 3-0 LDV Vans
Trophy victory over Morecambe.
*Shrewsbury T (From trainee on 3/7/2002) FL
0+8 FAC 0+1 Others 0+1*

MURPHY Daniel (Danny)
Benjamin
Born: Chester, 18 March 1977
Height: 5'9" **Weight:** 10.8

Club Honours: FLC '01, '03; FAC '01;
UEFAC '01; ESC '01; CS '01
International Honours: E: 7; U21-5;
Yth; Sch
Danny was the most consistent of
Liverpool's midfield quartet last season,
although at times even he was infected
by the collective malaise which seemed to
affect the team in mid-season. Perhaps he
had more excuse than most, as his
playing position seemed to alternate
between the right and left side of
midfield with every game early on, he
then took over the central-midfield slot,
before switching back to the left-hand
side. He also enjoyed his best season for
goals – 12 in all. Three of these were
strong candidates for Liverpool's 'Goal of
the Season': a curling 25-yard shot
against Tottenham in October, an
opportunistic 20-yarder against Leeds in
March and a thunderbolt against local
rivals Everton in April. Danny remained a
member of the England squad and won
two more caps during the campaign.
*Crewe Alex (From trainee on 21/3/1994) FL
110+24/27 FLC 7 FAC 7/4 Others 15+3/3*
*Liverpool (£1,500,000 + on 17/7/1997) PL
95+44/20 FLC 13+1/9 FAC 10+3/2 Others
32+9/5*
Crewe Alex (Loaned on 12/2/1999) FL 16/1

MURPHY Daniel (Danny)
Thomas
Born: Southwark, 4 December 1982
Height: 5'6" **Weight:** 10.8
International Honours: RoI: Yth
This left-sided defender was unable to
hold on to a regular place in the Queen's
Park Rangers line-up last season. He had a
brief run in the side at the end of the year
and also made a number of appearances
from the substitutes' bench. Although
Danny is not a tall player he is quick to
the tackle and passes the ball well.
*Queens Park R (From trainee on 8/12/1999)
FL 14+9 FAC 0+1*

MURPHY David Paul
Born: Hartlepool, 1 March 1984
Height: 6'1" **Weight:** 12.3
International Honours: E: Yth
Middlesbrough's promising teenaged left
back was another player whose
blossoming potential last season was
hampered by injury. His full Premiership
debut in August at Southampton was
curtailed when he damaged a medial
knee ligament in a 50-50 tackle. David
had returned to first-team duty by
January, but he played his last game of
the season when he collected a thigh

injury in the first half against Charlton
Athletic at the Riverside in March.
*Middlesbrough (From trainee on 20/7/2001)
PL 4+9 FLC 2/1 FAC 0+1*

MURPHY John James
Born: Whiston, 18 October 1976
Height: 6'2" **Weight:** 14.0
Club Honours: AMC '02
John found the net consistently for
Blackpool last term, before injury forced
him on the sidelines at the end of March.
He finished as the Seasiders' top scorer
with 19 goals in all competitions,
including a hat-trick in the 3-1 win at
Luton in February. John is a big strong
striker who is effective in the air and
holds the ball up well.
*Chester C (From trainee on 6/7/1995) FL
65+38/20 FLC 7+3/1 FAC 1+2 Others 3+1*
*Blackpool (Signed on 6/8/1999) FL
144+13/57 FLC 7+1/5 FAC 11/5 Others
11+3/6*

MURPHY Joseph (Joe)
Born: Dublin, Ireland, 21 August 1981
Height: 6'2" **Weight:** 13.6
International Honours: RoI: U21-14;
Yth (UEFA-U16 '98)
Joe saved a penalty (from Michael Owen)
with his first touch in Premiership football
during West Bromwich Albion's 2-0
defeat at Liverpool last September after
coming on when Russell Hoult was red
carded. Signed as cover for Hoult, he
contested a position on the bench with
Brian Jensen for most of the season and
made two more senior appearances, in
the Premiership at Newcastle United and
in the Worthington Cup tie at Wigan. Joe
also won further caps for the Republic of
Ireland at U21 level.
*Tranmere Rov (From trainee on 5/7/1999) FL
61+2 FLC 8 FAC 3 Others 1*
*West Bromwich A (Signed on 17/7/2002) PL
1+1 FLC 1*

MURPHY Matthew (Matt)
Simon
Born: Northampton, 20 August 1971
Height: 6'0" **Weight:** 12.2
Matt joined Swansea City in a 12-month
deal during the summer of 2002 and
started the new season in a central-
midfield role. Following a change of
management, he later appeared as an
out-and-out striker, scoring against
Macclesfield at the Vetch Field, and also
netting against York City and Shrewsbury
Town. Unfortunately he was sidelined
with cruciate ligament damage in mid-
December and this curtailed his activities
for the season.

xford U *(£20,000 from Corby T on
2/2/1993) FL 168+78/38 FLC 10+9/8 FAC
2+3/6 Others 6+3/3*
cunthorpe U *(Loaned on 12/12/1997) FL
+2 Others 1*
ury *(Free on 9/8/2001) FL 5+4 Others 1*
wansea C *(Free on 8/7/2002) FL 9+3/1 FAC
1 Others 0+1*

MURPHY Peter
orn: Dublin, 27 October 1980
eight: 5'11" **Weight:** 12.10
nternational Honours: RoI; Yth
arlisle's 'Player of the Season', Peter
issed only six of United's 57 league and
up games last term. A skilful footballer
ho initially played mostly at left wing
ack, he gave some of his best
erformances in central defence where
s distribution was put to best use. A
ne striker of the dead ball, his 30-yard
ee kick against Bury was a contender for
Goal of the Season'.
Blackburn Rov *(From trainee on 15/7/1998)*
alifax T *(Loaned on 26/10/2000) FL 18+3/1
C 1 Others 2*
arlisle U *(Free on 10/8/2001) FL 77+3/2 FLC
FAC 6 Others 8*

MURPHY Shaun Peter
orn: Sydney, Australia, 5 November
970
eight: 6'1" **Weight:** 12.0
lub Honours: AIC '95
nternational Honours: Australia: 20;
23; Yth
haun was a regular for much of the
heffield United's dramatic season,
laying a vital role as a central defender.
e showed his usual command in the air
nd good all round anticipation. Shaun
as always a danger in the opposition's
enalty area at set pieces, scoring four
mes and setting up chances for others.
wards the end of the season he was
ccasionally caught out when the ball
as played quickly on the ground and
as on the bench in the FA Cup semi
nal. He took no part in the play-offs due
a serious family illness.
otts Co *(Signed from Perth Italia, Australia
n 4/9/1992) FL 100+9/5 FLC 5+2 FAC 6
thers 12+1/1*
Vest Bromwich A *(£500,000 on
/12/1996) FL 60+11/7 FLC 3 FAC 4*
heffield U *(Free on 22/7/1999) FL
7+1/10 FLC 18/1 FAC 6/1*
rystal Palace *(Loaned on 1/2/2002) FL 11*

MURRAY Adam David
orn: Birmingham, 30 September 1981
eight: 5'8" **Weight:** 10.10

International Honours: E: Yth
Although he was leading scorer in the
reserves, Adam has yet to break his duck
in Derby County's senior team. He was
again in and out of the side last season,
needing an injection of confidence to
fulfil the midfield promise he first showed
as a teenager. He has to use the ball more
crisply to compensate for a lack of pace,
one of many virtues he shows in the
second team. Adam's contract expired in
summer but he was offered a new deal
and must seize the opportunity.
Derby Co *(From trainee on 7/10/1998) P/FL
25+31 FLC 3+1 FAC 4*
Mansfield T *(Loaned on 26/2/2002) FL 13/7*

MURRAY Antonio
Born: Cambridge, 15 September 1984
Height: 5'8" **Weight:** 11.0
Another product of the Ipswich Town
academy, Antonio made his debut as a
second-half substitute at Derby in the last
game of the season after impressing for
the reserves. A promising young
midfielder, Antonio is the son of the
former Cambridge United and Brentford
player Jamie Murray.
Ipswich T *(Trainee) FL 0+1*

MURRAY Frederick (Fred)
Anthony
Born: Clonmel, Ireland, 22 May 1982
Height: 5'10" **Weight:** 11.12
International Honours: RoI; Yth
Fred started the season as first choice left
back for Cambridge United until an ankle
injury suffered at Boston ruled him out
from September through to January. He
fought his way back into the line-up and
was then virtually ever-present through to
the end of the campaign.
Blackburn Rov *(From trainee on 25/5/1999)*
Cambridge U *(Free on 14/12/2001) FL 46+4
FLC 1 FAC 1+1 Others 6*

MURRAY Karl Anthony
Born: Islington, 24 June 1982
Height: 5'11" **Weight:** 12.6
Karl is a Shrewsbury midfielder with a
hard-tackling, combative approach who
always pleases the crowd. He has a
cracking shot that produced two goals,
including an early strike at Carlisle in
October that helped yield three points.
As manager Kevin Ratcliffe wrestled with
his defensive formation Karl was
converted to play as a central defender
for the last six games and he did well in
his new role.
Shrewsbury T *(From trainee on 7/2/2000) FL
77+32/5 FLC 5 FAC 4+1 Others 3+2*

MURRAY Matthew (Matt)
William
Born: Solihull, 2 May 1981
Height: 6'4" **Weight:** 13.10
International Honours: E: U21-4; Yth
This tall, agile goalkeeper had previously
shown considerable promise for Wolves,
but had been hampered by long-term
injuries despite his young years. Matt
made his debut at Wimbledon due to an
enforced absence for Michael Oakes, and
at the time it seemed a brief reward for
his patience. Yet it was not long before
Matt was the regular in the team and his
sudden rise to fame continued with two
unexpected outings for England U21s. He
was still in the Wolves team when he
made a third international appearance in
April, making a vital save against Turkey.
He also played his part in the team's run
of 436 minutes without conceding a goal,
before letting one in against Nottingham
Forest.
Wolverhampton W *(From trainee on
6/5/1998) FL 40 FLC 1 FAC 4 Others 3*

MURRAY Paul
Born: Carlisle, 31 August 1976
Height: 5'9" **Weight:** 10.5
International Honours: E: B-1; U21 4; Yth
Paul missed the opening three months of
the 2002-03 season for Oldham after
being injured in pre-season training. Upon
his return he found himself playing in an
unfamiliar position at right wing back
covering for injury-victim Josh Low.
However, he adapted well to the task and
returned to his favoured central-midfield
slot upon Low's return in March. A
naturally two-footed player, the attack-
minded Paul had an excellent campaign
but was disappointed to score only once.
Carlisle U *(From trainee on 14/6/1994) FL
27+14/1 FLC 2 FAC 1 Others 6+1*
Queens Park R *(£300,000 on 8/3/1996) P/FL
115+25/7 FLC 8/1 FAC 9*
Southampton *(Free on 2/8/2001) PL 0+1*
Oldham Ath *(Free on 12/12/2001) FL 52+2/6
FLC 1 FAC 2 Others 3*

MURRAY Scott George
Born: Aberdeen, 26 May 1974
Height: 5'10" **Weight:** 11.0
Club Honours: AMC '03
International Honours: S: B
Chosen by his fellow professionals as a
member of the PFA Second Division team
for the third consecutive season, this
cheerful and enthusiastic right-midfielder
hit the high notes for Bristol City in the
goal-scoring stakes last term. Notching up
a total of 26 goals he ensured that the
poaching skills of the departed Tony

Thorpe were not missed as he almost propelled City to promotion. His talents again caught the eye of Scottish boss Berti Vogts and Scott came on as a substitute for the 'B' side in their 3-3 draw against Germany in December. The Bristol City Supporters' Club members voted Scott as their 'Player of the Year'.
Aston Villa (£35,000 from Fraserburgh on 16/3/1994) PL 4
Bristol C (£150,000 on 12/12/1997) FL 193+31/46 FLC 10+3 FAC 13+1/7 Others 18+2/8

MURTY Graeme Stuart
Born: Saltburn, 13 November 1974
Height: 5'10" **Weight:** 11.10
Winner of the previous season's 'Player of the Year' poll for Reading, Graham was runner-up in 2002-03, a sure sign of the high standards the young defender has set himself and achieved. He made more appearances than any other first-team player, and was a model of consistency in the right-back position, to such an extent that there was even talk of him being considered for international recognition with Scotland. The Royals did have to pay a bonus to York City, Graham's former club, following promotion to Division One, but this was a small inconvenience considering the player's magnificent contribution to a highly successful and enjoyable campaign.
York C (From trainee on 23/3/1993) FL 106+11/7 FLC 10/2 FAC 5+1 Others 6+2
Reading (£700,000 on 10/7/1998) FL 126+10/1 FLC 2 FAC 8+1 Others 6+2

MUSSELWHITE Paul Stephen
Born: Portsmouth, 22 December 1968
Height: 6'2" **Weight:** 14.2
Club Honours: AMC '93
In a season of three distinct parts, Paul can have every reason to feel particularly unlucky. After Hull manager Jan Molby publicly named him as second choice to Matty Glennon, the vastly experienced 'keeper took his opportunity with both hands when he was recalled in September. A run of 21 consecutive games included the 600th appearance of his senior career and indeed he did little wrong, but nevertheless the arrival of Alan Fettis saw him return to the bench. Paul continued to be a credit to his profession and gained some consolation by skippering the reserves team to the Avon Insurance Division One East championship.
Portsmouth (From apprentice on 1/12/1986)
Scunthorpe U (Free on 21/3/1988) FL 132 FLC 11 FAC 7 Others 13

Port Vale (£20,000 on 30/7/1992) FL 312 FLC 15 FAC 21 Others 19
Sheffield Wed (Free, via trials at Scunthorpe U, Darlington, on 25/8/2000)
Hull C (Free on 19/9/2000) FL 77 FAC 3 Others 5

MUSTAFA Tarkan
Born: Islington, 28 August 1973
Height: 5'10" **Weight:** 11.12
Club Honours: NC '01
International Honours: E: SP-2
Tarkan came into the Rushden & Diamonds line-up in August following new signing Marcus Bignot's injury and stayed there until October. But then Bignot impressed on his return and Tarkan fell out of the reckoning. He had a loan period with Doncaster Rovers before moving on to Dagenham & Redbridge, for whom he scored in the Conference play-off final as the Londoners again just missed out on promotion.
Barnet (Free from Kettering T on 5/8/1997) FL 2+9 FLC 0+1 (Free to Kingstonian on 9/9/1998)
Rushden & Diamonds (Signed on 6/6/2000) FL 31+3/1 FLC 4/1 Others 3

MUSTOE Robin (Robbie)
Born: Witney, 28 August 1968
Height: 5'11" **Weight:** 11.12
Club Honours: Div 1 '95
Robbie initially joined Charlton Athletic on a three-month contract, after being released by Middlesbrough. A dynamic midfielder, he was the ideal person to replace injured captain Graham Stuart and his never-say-die approach fitted in well with the Addicks' tactical play. However, after just seven league and cup appearances he received a thigh injury at Everton in November and although his contact was extended until the end of the season he failed to recover and was released by mutual consent in April.
Oxford U (From juniors on 2/7/1986) FL 78+13/10 FLC 2 FAC 2 Others 3
Middlesbrough (£375,000 on 5/7/1990) F/PL 327+38/25 FLC 44+3/7 FAC 29+1/2 Others 12+1/1
Charlton Ath (Free on 30/8/2002) PL 6 FLC 1

MYERS Andrew (Andy) John
Born: Hounslow, 3 November 1973
Height: 5'10" **Weight:** 13.11
Club Honours: FAC '97; ECWC '98
International Honours: E: U21-4; Yth
Andy had a mixed season at Bradford City in 2002-03 and only showed glimpses of the form that had won him the 'Player of the Year' award in the previous campaign. A number of troublesome injury problems

forced him on the sidelines for three months in the middle of the campaign, but he recovered well to again become a regular member of the side. A tough-tackling defender, who can play at left back or in the centre of defence. His pace remains a great asset both in defence and attack.
Chelsea (From trainee on 25/7/1991) F/PL 74+10/2 FLC 2+1 FAC 9+3 Others 4+3
Bradford C (£800,000 on 16/7/1999) P/FL 74+15/3 FLC 5 FAC 1 Others 3+1
Portsmouth (Loaned on 23/3/2000) FL 4+4

MYHILL Glyn (Boaz) Oliver
Born: California, USA, 9 November 1982
Height: 6'3" **Weight:** 14.6
International Honours: E: Yth
This highly-rated Bristol City 'keeper joined Bristol City on loan last August, but failed to make a senior appearance during his stay at Ashton Gate. Boaz then joined Bradford City in a similar deal in November after Steve Banks was forced to end his loan spell because of a knee injury. He made two appearances for the Bantams before returning to Villa Park to continue his development.
Aston Villa (From trainee on 28/11/2000)
Bradford C (Loaned on 22/11/2002) FL 2

MYHRE Thomas
Born: Sarpsborg, Norway, 16 October 1973
Height: 6'4" **Weight:** 13.12
International Honours: Norway: 29; U21; Yth
A Norwegian international goalkeeper, Thomas signed for Sunderland during the 2002 close season and made his Black Cats' bow in the 7-0 Worthington Cup victory at Cambridge in October. Extremely agile with a safe pair of hands, Thomas made his Premiership debut five days later as a substitute for Thomas Sorensen at Arsenal, but was himself subbed by Jurgen Macho in what turned out to be his only other appearance at Bolton the same month, when a thigh injury effectively ended his season. It has since been reported that Thomas has been offered a free transfer by Sunderland.
Everton (£800,000 from Viking Stavanger, Norway on 28/11/1997) PL 70 FLC 3 FAC 9 (£375,000 to Besiktas, Turkey on 1/11/2001)
Glasgow R (Loaned on 24/11/1999) SL 3 SL 1 Others 2
Birmingham C (Loaned on 31/3/2000) FL 7 Others 2
Tranmere Rov (Loaned on 28/11/2000) FL 3 FLC 1
Sunderland (Free on 8/7/2002) PL 1+1 FLC

N

NACCA Francesco (Franco)
Born: Venezuela, 9 November 1982
Height: 5'7" **Weight:** 10.6
Franco made his senior debut for
Cambridge United in the LDV Vans Trophy
tie against Rushden when he looked at
home in a central midfield role. A versatile
player who came up through the ranks as
a right-sided defender, he settled down
well in his new role, getting stuck in and
working hard for the team.
*Cambridge U (From trainee on 21/4/2001)
FL 9+8 FLC 0+2 FAC 1+3 Others 2+3*

NAISBITT Daniel (Danny)
John
Born: Bishop Auckland, 25 November 1978
Height: 6'1" **Weight:** 11.12
Danny joined Carlisle United on loan as
goalkeeping cover, but made just two
appearances during his stay at Brunton
Park. He featured in the Worthington Cup
game at Rotherham and in the following
week's match at Scunthorpe, before
returning to London to resume his career
with Conference outfit Barnet.
*Walsall (From trainee at Middlesbrough on
1/7/1997)
Barnet (Free on 3/8/1999) FL 19+4 FLC 1
FAC 2
Carlisle U (Loaned on 23/8/2002) FL 1 FLC 1*

NARADA] BERNARD
Narada Michael
Born: Bristol, 30 January 1981
Height: 5'2" **Weight:** 10.5
This left-sided defender was only ever on
the fringes of the Bournemouth first-team
squad last season, but never let the team
down when selected. A player with great
pace, he captained the reserve team
throughout the campaign. Narada was
released in the summer.
*Arsenal (From trainee at Tottenham H on
1/7/1999)
Bournemouth (Free on 31/7/2000) FL 13+16
FAC 2+1 Others 6+1*

NARDIELLO Daniel (Danny)
Antony
Born: Coventry, 22 October 1982
Height: 5'11" **Weight:** 11.4
International Honours: E: Yth; Sch
An excellent young forward with a good
range of skills, Danny so impressed the
Welsh boss, Mark Hughes in the
Worthington Cup run for Manchester
United, he was asked to forsake the land
of his birth, for the land of his father,
Donato. Although practically ignored by

Sir Alex Ferguson in the Premiership last
term, his Worthington Cup exploits
certainly had Hughes waxing lyrical.
Danny is the son of former Coventry City
winger Donato Nardiello.
*Manchester U (From trainee on 1/11/1999)
FLC 1+1 Others 0+1*

NASH Carlo James
Born: Bolton, 13 September 1973
Height: 6'5" **Weight:** 14.1
Club Honours: Div 1 '02
International Honours: Canada: 26
(Gold Cup 2000); U23-11
Carlo firmly established himself as the
second choice 'keeper at Manchester City
last season in the absence through injury

of Nicky Weaver. He deputised for Peter
Schmeichel on ten occasions and
although he only kept one clean sheet, at
Birmingham in October, he generally
performed competently. His best display
came in the 'derby' match at Old Trafford
when he was exceptional. With
Schmeichel's retirement in the summer
Carlo will be looking to become the
number one choice for the goalkeeper's
jersey in 2003-04.
*Crystal Palace (£35,000 from Clitheroe on
16/7/1996) FL 21 FLC 1 Others 3
Stockport Co (Free on 7/6/1998) FL 89 FLC 5
FAC 4
Manchester C (£100,000 on 12/1/2001) P/FL
37+1 FLC 2 FAC 1*

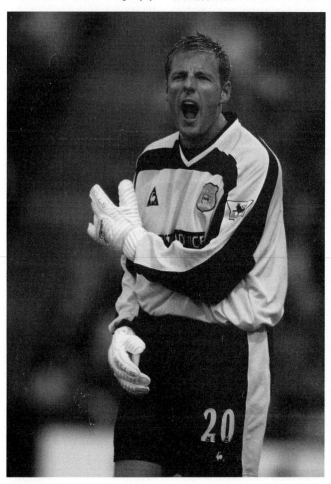

Carlo Nash

NASH Martin John
Born: Regina, Canada, 27 December 1975
Height: 5'11" **Weight:** 12.5
International Honours: Canada: 16 (Gold Cup 2000); U23-11
After spending the 2002 season with US-A League outfit Rochester Raging Rhinos, this attacking midfielder joined Macclesfield Town in the new year and made his debut from the substitutes' bench in the home match against Hartlepool. However, he subsequently managed just one start and three more outings from the bench and was injured towards the end of the campaign. Martin became the first Macclesfield Town player to win full international honours when he played for Canada against Estonia in March. He returned home at the end of the season.
Stockport Co (Free from Regina, Canada on 27/11/1996) FL 0+11 FLC 0+1 Others 2+1/1 (Freed during 1998 close season)
Chester C (Free from Vancouver 86ers, Canada on 24/9/1999) FL 12+4 FAC 3+1 (Freed during 2000 close season)
Macclesfield T (Free from Rochester Raging Rhinos, USA on 17/1/2003) FL 1+4

NAVARRO Alan Edward
Born: Liverpool, 31 May 1981
Height: 5'11" **Weight:** 11.7
Alan had a wretched season in 2002-03 after a seemingly harmless tackle in the home game against Huddersfield in late August ruptured his cruciate ligament and put him out for the remainder of the campaign. He had made five early-season appearances for Tranmere and was beginning to show signs of forming a promising midfield partnership with Micky Mellon. When fit, Alan's tough tackling belies his creativity and he is sufficiently versatile to play in any of the positions across the middle of the park. He made a return for the reserves during the closing month of the season, and must be anxious for the start of the 2003-04 campaign.
Liverpool (From trainee on 27/4/1999)
Crewe Alex (Loaned on 22/3/2001) FL 5+3/1
Crewe Alex (Loaned on 9/8/2001) FL 7 FLC 2
Tranmere Rov (£225.000 on 9/11/2001) FL 26/1 FAC 3/1

NAYLOR Anthony (Tony) Joseph
Born: Manchester, 29 March 1967
Height: 5'7" **Weight:** 10.8
Club Honours: AMC '01
A fans' favourite at Cheltenham, Tony began the 2002-03 campaign hoping to

continue the 'little and large' partnership with Julian Alsop that had brought the pair 44 goals in the previous campaign. The signs were promising when he scored twice in an incredible 3-0 win at Norwich City in the Worthington Cup, but a shin injury then forced him out of the side in the middle of the season. He eventually returned to action and netted with a spectacular strike in the 3-0 win over Blackpool that kept the hopes of survival alive into the final week. He is an imaginative striker with many tricks up his sleeve and a good eye for goal.
Crewe Alex (£20,000 from Droylsden on 22/3/1990) FL 104+18/45 FLC 7+2/5 FAC 9/6 Others 12/9
Port Vale (£150,000 on 18/7/1994) FL 207+46/71 FLC 15+1/8 FAC 12+1/2 Others 12+1/8
Cheltenham T (Free on 16/8/2001) FL 62+12/18 FLC 3/2 FAC 5/5 Others 4/1

NAYLOR Glenn
Born: Goole, 11 August 1972
Height: 5'10" **Weight:** 11.10
Glenn was Darlington's longest-serving player last season, but rarely featured in the first team during the campaign. He managed just one start and spent much of the rest of the time on the bench, although he did increase his goals tally for the Quakers, netting a brace against Carlisle and another against Bury. Glenn was released at the end of the season.
York C (From trainee on 5/3/1992) FL 78+33/30 FLC 2+4 FAC 4+1/2 Others 3+4
Darlington (Loaned on 13/10/1995) FL 3+1/1 Others 1+1
Darlington (Signed on 26/9/1996) FL 157+52/46 FLC 6+2/2 FAC 12+2/5 Others 6+5

NAYLOR Lee Martyn
Born: Walsall, 19 March 1980
Height: 5'9" **Weight:** 11.8
International Honours: E: U21-3; Yth
This left back began the 2002-03 in the Wolves' starting line-up, but lost his place after a run of a dozen games. Lee had a long spell out but returned late in the year, determined to re-establish himself. He always tried his best and the highlight of his season was a beautiful dipping volley that gave Wolves the lead at Ipswich, in a match they went on to win 4-2. Lee also did well in the play-off semi-finals, scoring the winner at home to Reading with a hard, low free kick and then making a vital clearance in the return leg.
Wolverhampton W (From trainee on 10/10/1997) FL 156+18/5 FLC 14 FAC 13/1 Others 3/1

NAYLOR Richard Alan
Born: Leeds, 28 February 1977
Height: 6'1" **Weight:** 13.7
Richard was generally on the fringes of the first team at Ipswich last season until new manager Joe Royle decided that he had the potential to be a better central defender than he was as a striker and gave him a run in this position towards the end of the season. He had an outstanding game in his new position in the 1-0 win at Sheffield Wednesday and will be interesting to see if he switches permanently to the new role. Ironically Richard joined Ipswich as a centre half and was converted to a striker by the club's youth coaches!
Ipswich T (From trainee on 10/7/1995) P/FL 69+73/23 FLC 6+9/1 FAC 2+5 Others 3+6/1
Millwall (Loaned on 29/1/2002) FL 2+1
Barnsley (Loaned on 4/3/2002) FL 7+1

NAYSMITH Gary Andrew
Born: Edinburgh, 16 November 1979
Height: 5'7" **Weight:** 11.8
Club Honours: SC '98
International Honours: S: 15; U21-22; Sch
Nominally an attacking full back, Gary was also employed on the left-hand side of midfield during the season for Everton, a campaign in which he was also one of the few players to emerge with any credit from Scotland's performances at international level. Although he suffered an ankle injury in September that temporarily sidelined him, he was still able to score his first goal for his country against Iceland. Recalled to the Everton line-up in November, he showed typical tenacity and pace for the rest of the campaign, scoring in consecutive matches in December and displaying good crossing ability.
Heart of Midlothian (From Whitehill Welfare on 17/6/1996) SL 92+5/3 SLC 5/1 SC 10 Others 7/1
Everton (£1,750,000 on 20/10/2000) PL 64+8/3 FLC 2+1/1 FAC 6

NDAH George Ehialimolisa
Born: Dulwich, 23 December 1974
Height: 6'1" **Weight:** 11.4
International Honours: E: Yth
The first half of the 2002-03 season saw George in and out of the Wolves' line-up. He scored from a distance against Bradford City and in January he netted three FA Cup goals, including a neat finish after a clever dribble against Leicester. George had been back in favour because of injuries to fellow strikers, but

ronically he was injured again and missed two games. He kept scoring on his return and at Preston he took the ball from near his own penalty area some 60 yards before making it three in three games, and eight in his last nine. George had formed a fast-moving partnership with Kenny Miller but a torn hamstring early on against Palace ruled him out yet again.
Crystal Palace *(From trainee on 10/8/1992) F/PL 33+45/8 FLC 7+6/2 FAC 3+1/1 Others 4+1*
Bournemouth *(Loaned on 13/10/1995) FL 2/2 Others 1*
Gillingham *(Loaned on 29/8/1997) FL 4*
Swindon T *(£500,000 on 21/11/1997) FL 56+1/14 FLC 4/1 FAC 3*
Wolverhampton W *(£1,000,000 on 21/10/1999) FL 44+29/14 FLC 1+1 FAC 3+1/4 Others 1*

NDLOVU Peter
Born: Bulawayo, Zimbabwe, 25 February 1973
Height: 5'8" **Weight:** 10.2
International Honours: Zimbabwe
Peter probably had his best season for Sheffield United last term. He used his speed, ball control and balance to good effect, playing usually on the right, sometimes switching to the left. He was more direct, with less over elaboration, creating a significant number of opportunities for his colleagues as well. He reached double figures himself, including the dramatic last-gasp winner against Leeds in the Worthington Cup. Peter worked tirelessly in midfield, intercepting and harrying and made some vital contributions in defence. He added to his Zimbabwe caps, as captain, scoring a vital winning goal against Eritrea and netting twice from the spot against Seychelles to put his country in a strong position in the African Nations' Cup qualifiers.
Coventry C *(£10,000 from Highlanders, Zimbabwe on 16/8/1991) F/PL 141+36/37 FLC 10/2 FAC 5+4/2 Others 0+1*
Birmingham C *(£1,600,000 on 15/7/1997) FL 78+29/22 FLC 17+2/4 FAC 3+1/1 Others 2+2*
Huddersfield T *(Loaned on 8/12/2000) FL 6/4*
Sheffield U *(Free on 2/2/2001) FL 86+13/16 FLC 5+3/2 FAC 5/2 Others 3*

NEAL Lewis Ryan
Born: Leicester, 14 July 1981
Height: 6'0" **Weight:** 11.2
Although Lewis only started seven league games for Stoke City in 2002-03 this was undoubtedly his break-through season. New manager Tony Pulis did not seem to

want him in the side on a regular basis as the fight against relegation intensified, but his appearances were appreciated by the club's fans who took him to their hearts. Comfortable either wide on the left or in central midfield his immaculate cross for Ade Akinbiyi's winner against Reading to clinch the Potters' First Division status will be long remembered.
Stoke C *(Free from juniors on 17/7/1998) FL 13+15 FAC 2+3 Others 1+2/1*

NEDERGAARD Steen
Born: Denmark, 25 February 1970
Height: 6'0" **Weight:** 11.13
This highly experienced Dane enjoyed another excellent season at Norwich, playing mostly at right back, but also in the wide-right midfield role on occasions. Strong in the air, Steen is a tremendous athlete and a great crosser of the ball,

indeed a large percentage of City's goals in 2002-03 came from his crosses. He scored, arguably, the Canaries' 'Goal of the Season' with a thundering 35-yarder in the 2-0 home win against Coventry in March. Steen decided to return to Denmark in the summer, re-signing for his previous club, OB Odense.
Norwich C *(Free from Odense BK, Denmark on 3/7/2000) FL 81+9/5 FLC 2+2 FAC 3*

NEIL Alexander (Alex)
Born: Bellshill, 4 May 1978
Height: 5'8" **Weight:** 12.10
Alex missed the start of the 2002-03 season for Barnsley after undergoing a hernia operation. However, he returned to first-team contention in mid-October and became a regular in the line-up under the management of Glynn Hodges, playing on the left-hand side of a midfield three.

Steen Nedergaard

311

An industrious player, he will be looking to get on the score sheet more often in the 2003-04 campaign.
Airdrieonians *(Free from Dunfermline Ath juniors on 8/7/1999) SL 15+1/5 SC 0+1*
Barnsley *(£25,000 on 11/7/2000) FL 66+24/2 FLC 2+2 FAC 3 Others 1*

NEILL Lucas Edward
Born: Sydney, Australia, 9 March 1978
Height: 6'1" **Weight:** 12.0
Club Honours: Div 2 '01
International Honours: Australia: 3; U23-12; Yth
Lucas had a useful season at Blackburn last term when he was a near ever-present in Premiership games. A sound defender, strong in the tackle and effective in the air he runs strongly on the overlap and competes throughout. He developed more consistency to add to his undoubted potential, although his tackling was occasionally too zealous for referees and he once again saw more than his fair share of cards. Lucas added a further cap for his country when appearing in the friendly against England in February.
Millwall *(Free from Australian Academy of Sport on 13/11/1995) FL 124+28/13 FLC 6+1 FAC 4 Others 11+1*
Blackburn Rov *(£1,000,000 on 7/9/2001) PL 65/1 FLC 4 FAC 7 Others 4*

NEILSON Alan Bruce
Born: Wegburg, Germany, 26 September 1972
Height: 5'11" **Weight:** 12.10
International Honours: W: 5; B-2; U21-7
Alan once again brought experience and maturity to Luton Town last season. Although not a first-team regular, he helped bring on some of the youngsters. The talented defender is a good reader of the game, and this enabled him to make well-timed tackles or block shots as and when required.
Newcastle U *(From trainee on 11/2/1991) F/PL 35+7/1 FLC 4 Others 4*
Southampton *(£500,000 on 1/6/1995) PL 42+13 FLC 7 FAC 1*
Fulham *(£250,000 on 28/11/1997) FL 24+5/2 FLC 4+2 FAC 4 Others 2*
Grimsby T *(Free on 19/10/2001) FL 8+2 FLC 1 FAC 1*
Luton T *(Free on 22/2/2002) FL 29+5 FLC 0+2 FAC 1+1*

NELSON Michael John
Born: Gateshead, 28 March 1980
Height: 6'2" **Weight:** 13.12
Last term was a season to remember for

this Bury central defender who established himself as the dominant figure in the Shakers' back line. He greatly enhanced his growing reputation with a string of consistent displays, proving to be brave, good in the air and never afraid to dive in for last-gasp tackles or clearances. Michael took over the captaincy from Jon Newby in February and thrived on the added responsibility. His height and presence also enabled him to grab five important goals. It was little surprise when he ran away with the club's 'Player of the Season' award.
Bury *(Free from Bishop Auckland on 22/3/2001) FL 68+4/8 FLC 4 FAC 3 Others 5*

NEMETH Szilard
Born: Kamarna, Slovakia, 14 September 1972
Height: 5'10" **Weight:** 10.10
International Honours: Slovakia: 39
Szilard played 28 Premiership games for Middlesbrough last season but he was personally dismayed that 13 of the 28 appearances were as a substitute. He voiced his discontent at not being given a full 90 minutes on many occasions. Brimming with self confidence and self assurance, Szilard was sure that he would have scored many more than the seven Premiership goals that made him runner-up to leading scorer Massimo Maccarone had he been given the opportunity. On the season's international scene Szilard scored six times in his seven appearances for Slovakia.
Middlesbrough *(Signed from Inter Bratislava, Slovakia, ex Slovan Bratislava, Kosice, on 30/7/2001) PL 26+23/10 FLC 3/2 FAC 3+2/1*

NETHERCOTT Stuart David
Born: Ilford, 21 March 1973
Height: 6'1" **Weight:** 13.8
Club Honours: Div 2 '01
International Honours: E: U21-8
Millwall skipper for the past four seasons, Stuart was an ever-present until last January when injury ruled him out. He then found it difficult to win his place back due to the excellent form of Darren Ward and Paul Robinson. Indeed, it was only when Robinson himself was injured that Stuart got back in the side and once more showed his trademark whole-hearted effort. Stuart is an experienced central defender who is particularly effective in the air.
Tottenham H *(From trainee on 17/8/1991) PL 31+23 FAC 5+3/1*
Maidstone U *(Loaned on 5/9/1991) FL 13/1 Others 1*

Barnet *(Loaned on 13/2/1992) FL 3*
Millwall *(Signed on 22/1/1998) FL 195+6/9 FLC 7 FAC 6 Others 13*

NEVILLE Gary Alexander
Born: Bury, 18 February 1975
Height: 5'11" **Weight:** 12.8
Club Honours: FAYC '92; PL '96, '97, '99, '00, '01, '03; FAC '96, '99; CS '96; EC '99
International Honours: E: 57; Yth (UEFA-U18 '93)
A hard-tackling fullback, who is equally as effective in a central defensive role, the broken foot that scuppered Gary's World Cup placing in the summer, showed no sign of imminent weakness when he returned to first-team action for Manchester United in late September. On consistency alone, his performances were second to none, and it is hard to single out a United player who outstripped him in that department. Once again his continued support behind David Beckham on the right side of the field remained one of United's most potent weapons, and his goal as stand-in skipper against Basle in the Champions' League in March came on his 77th outing in European football, more than any player in the competition's history. Though United now have an abundance of players all vying for places in the back four, Gary remains very much the leader of the pack.
Manchester U *(From trainee on 29/1/1993) PL 249+14/3 FLC 9+1 FAC 28+2 Others 83+6/1*

NEVILLE Philip (Phil) John
Born: Bury, 21 January 1977
Height: 5'11" **Weight:** 12.0
Club Honours: FAYC '95; PL '96, '97, '99, '00, '01, '03; FAC '96, '99; CS '96, '97; EC '99
International Honours: E: 40; U21-7; Yth; Sch
A versatile player who is equally comfortable at full back or as a central defender, Phil saw the start of last season's campaign as being his biggest challenge yet. Though such thoughts might have left him to review his future, he proved to be one of Sir Alex Ferguson's most trusted servants during difficult times in September. Deputising ably in Roy Keane's usual midfield slot, his imminent prospects on the international stage must have been given a huge boost, though he remained unrewarded. On the statistical side of things, his record of never having been on the losing side when he scores a goal is entering legendary status. Phil netted two very

Phil Neville

credible efforts last season. His first against Southampton in the Premiership was followed up with an FA Cup goal against West Ham.

Manchester U *(From trainee on 1/6/1994) PL 169+44/5 FLC 12+1 FAC 19+4/1 Others 42+19/1*

NEWBY Jonathan (Jon) Philip Robert
Born: Warrington, 28 November 1978
Height: 6'0" **Weight:** 12.4
Club Honours: FAYC '96

Bury's hard-working striker found himself in great form alongside loan striker Pavel Abbott in the early part of the 2002-03 season, claiming seven goals by September. When Abbott left Gigg Lane in October and Jon also took on the club captaincy, his form seemed to dip and, as his luck in front of goal seemed to desert him, he was switched to a right-wing role for much of the remainder of the campaign. Jon relinquished the captaincy in February as he attempted to recapture his form and he eventually finished as the club's top scorer with 12 league and cup goals.

Liverpool *(From juniors on 23/5/1997) PL 0+1 FLC 0+1 FAC 0+2*
Crewe Alex *(Loaned on 3/3/2000) FL 5+1*
Sheffield U *(Loaned on 4/8/2000) FL 3+10*
Bury *(£100,000 on 2/2/2001) FL 109/21 FLC 4/1 FAC 3 Others 6/2*

NEWEY Thomas (Tom)
Born: Sheffield, 31 October 1982
Height: 5'10" **Weight:** 10.6

This exciting young left-sided player joined Cambridge on loan in February where he received his first experiences of senior football, covering at left back. He returned to Elland Road, but on the transfer deadline he went out on loan again, this time to Darlington. Tom immediately caught the eye with his tricky footwork and pacy runs down the left flank. He became an instant favourite with the fans and he opened his Quakers' goal account with an excellent strike against Hull City at Feethams on Easter Monday.

Leeds U *(From trainee on 4/8/2000)*
Cambridge U *(Loaned on 14/2/2003) FL 6 Others 1*
Darlington *(Loaned on 27/3/2003) FL 7/1*

NEWMAN Richard (Ricky) Adrian
Born: Guildford, 5 August 1970
Height: 5'10" **Weight:** 12.6

The 0-0 draw away to Rotherham United in September saw Ricky return to first-team duty for Reading after 17 months absence. He had recovered fully from a serious knee injury, and his combative style of defending kept him in the team for most of the remainder of the season. He even captained the side for a four-match spell whilst Adrian Williams was sidelined through injury. A vital ball-winner either at full back or in midfield, his bravery inspires those around him. Ricky is approaching the veteran stage of his career now, but is still a valued member of the Royals' squad.

Crystal Palace *(From juniors on 22/1/1988) F/PL 43+5/3 FLC 5 FAC 5+2 Others 2*
Maidstone U *(Loaned on 28/2/1992) FL 9+1/1*
Millwall *(£500,000 on 19/7/1995) FL 144+6/5 FLC 11 FAC 5 Others 7*
Reading *(Free on 17/3/2000) FL 62+12/1 FL 2 FAC 5/1 Others 1+1*

NEWTON Adam Lee
Born: Grays, 4 December 1980
Height: 5'10" **Weight:** 11.6
Club Honours: FAYC '99
International Honours: E: U21-1

Adam joined Peterborough United in the summer of 2002 and got off to a great

Jon Newby

:art, netting on his debut in the 3-2 win t Luton. Operating mostly on the right-and side of midfield he featured :gularly for Posh, adding a second goal t Wigan in September. Adam must be ne of the quickest players in the Football :ague and on his day can turn a efender inside out with his pace and ball <ills.

Vest Ham U (From trainee on 1/7/1999) PL +2 Others 0+1
ortsmouth (Loaned on 2/7/1999) FL 1+2 .C 2
otts Co (Loaned on 22/11/2000) FL 13+7/1 4C 2
eyton Orient (Loaned on 8/3/2002) FL 10/1
eterborough U (Free on 8/7/2002) FL 1+5/2 FLC 1 FAC 0+1 Others 1

NEWTON Shaun O'Neill
orn: Camberwell, 20 August 1975
Ieight: 5'8" **Weight:** 11.7
lub Honours: Div 1 '00
nternational Honours: E: U21-3
his right-footed winger was a regular for Volves in the early part of the 2002-03 :ason, scoring twice. However, he then ropped back to the bench and briefly >st his place in the match-day squad of '6. Shaun persevered and won his osition back, doing well in the FA Cup un and producing a brace against Millwall, the second with a deft chip. He layed a vital role in the play-off semi-nal first leg when he helped to turn the natch Wolves' way after coming on as a ubstitute.

harlton Ath (From trainee on 1/7/1993) 'FL 189+51/20 FLC 19+1/3 FAC 11+6/2 others 7+1/2
Volverhampton W (£850,000 + on '8/2001) FL 74+4/11 FLC 3/1 FAC 5 Others +1

N'GOTTY Bruno
orn: Lyon, France, 10 June 1971
Ieight: 6'1" **Weight:** 13.8
nternational Honours: France: 6
, rock in the Bolton defence, Bruno :egan the 2002-03 campaign in his ccustomed centre-back role, although a alf injury ensured that he missed a large :art of the mid-season fixtures. Returning o the line-up in January, he saw out the najority of the season at right back and :ontinued to give the same high level of erformance to which the Wanderers' ans have come to expect. Also a threat rom set-piece situations at the other end f the field, Bruno notched an important eader in the home draw with Manchester United in February.

Bolton W (Loaned from Marseilles, France, ex Lyon, Paris St Germain, AC Milan, Venezia, on 11/9/2001) PL 47+2/2 FLC 2+1 FAC 1

NICHOLLS Ashley
Born: Ipswich, 30 October 1981
Height: 5'11" **Weight:** 12.2
International Honours: E: Sch
Ashley impressed on his arrival at Darlington with some effortless running and his skill going past opponents. He went on to firmly establish himself in the Quakers' midfield and was rarely absent from the line-up all season. Ashley gets forward very quickly and covers the ground with deceptive speed and graceful movement, and was rewarded with six goals during the campaign.
Ipswich T (Free from Ipswich W on 5/7/2000)
Darlington (Free on 7/8/2002) FL 40+1/6 FLC 0+1 FAC 3/1 Others 1

NICHOLLS Kevin John Richard
Born: Newham, 2 January 1979
Height: 6'0'' **Weight:** 11.0

Kevin Nicholson

International Honours: E: Yth
Luton's captain was always at the front either urging team mates on or advocating on behalf of colleagues, although this sometimes got him into trouble with referees. Kevin is a dynamo of a player on the pitch always running about and involved in all the action. A combative midfielder who is an expert with dead-ball kicks, his best goal came in the home game against Northampton Town.
Charlton Ath (From trainee on 29/1/1996) FL 4+8/1 FLC 2+2
Brighton & Hove A (Loaned on 26/2/1999) FL 4/1
Wigan Ath (£250,000 + on 22/6/1999) FL 19+9 FLC 2 Others 4/1
Luton T (£25,000 + on 3/8/2001) FL 77+1/12 FLC 2 FAC 1 Others 1

NICHOLSON Kevin John
Born: Derby, 2 October 1980
Height: 5'8" **Weight:** 11.5
International Honours: E: Yth; Sch
Kevin was first choice at left back for

Notts County last term and began the season with some excellent performances. Although his form later dipped somewhat he was rarely absent from the line-up. Kevin is a skilful defender who is always comfortable in possession of the ball, and he is very capable in the air despite his rather small stature.
Sheffield Wed *(From trainee on 22/10/1997) FL 0+1*
Northampton T *(Free on 26/1/2001) FL 6+1*
Notts Co *(Free on 8/3/2001) FL 58+14/3 FLC 2 FAC 0+1 Others 3*

NICHOLSON Shane Michael
Born: Newark, 3 June 1970
Height: 5'10" **Weight:** 12.2
Club Honours: GMVC '88
Shane joined Tranmere Rovers during the

2002 close season and quickly settled in at Prenton Park. Although best known as a left back, he soon adapted to playing in a more unfamiliar role on the left-hand side of midfield. Shane is an experienced and intelligent player and the quality of his passing marked him out. He is also excellent at covering back when his more adventurous team mates cannot resist going forward. Shane became Rovers' regular penalty taker, netting with both his attempts during the campaign.
Lincoln C *(From trainee on 19/7/1988) FL 122+11/7 FLC 8+3 FAC 4/1 Others 7+1*
Derby Co *(£100,000 on 22/4/1992) FL 73+1/1 FLC 4 FAC 4/1 Others 5*
West Bromwich A *(£150,000 on 9/2/1996) FL 50+2 FLC 4 FAC 2 Others 4*

Chesterfield *(Free on 21/8/1998) FL 23+1 Others 1*
Stockport Co *(Free on 4/6/1999) FL 73+4/3 FLC 3 FAC 3*
Sheffield U *(Free on 18/7/2001) FL 21+4/3 FLC 1*
Tranmere Rov *(Free on 17/7/2002) FL 36+2/4 FAC 2 Others 3*

NIELSEN Allan
Born: Esbjerg, Denmark, 13 March 1971
Height: 5'8'' **Weight:** 11.2
Club Honours: FLC '99
International Honours: Denmark: 44; U21
An experienced international midfield player and a model professional, Allan was an influential figure at Watford last term, when he appeared mainly on the right or in central midfield. The team always looked stronger for his presence and benefited from his thoughtful probing, long throws and late runs into the penalty area. A calf strain in March cost him a place in the starting line-up for the FA Cup semi-final, though he came on as a substitute. Financial restraints meant that Allan's contract was not renewed, and he bade an emotional farewell on the last day of the season.
Tottenham H *(£1,650,000 from Brondby, Denmark, ex Esbjerg, Bayern Munich, Sion, Odense, FC Copenhagen, on 3/9/1996) PL 78+19/12 FLC 10+1/3 FAC 5+2/3 Others 1*
Wolverhampton W *(Loaned on 23/3/2000) FL 7/2*
Watford *(£2,250,000 on 3/8/2000) FL 95+6/19 FLC 4+2 FAC 5+1*

NIELSEN David
Born: Denmark, 1 December 1976
Height: 6'0" **Weight:** 11.13
David is an enigmatic striker who, on his day, can frighten defences with his pace and trickery. He is an instinctive player with an unorthodox style who can sometimes make goal-scoring look easy, however, he himself would admit to a lack of consistency in his performances for Norwich last term. He was often used by Nigel Worthington as a high-impact substitute with five of his six goals in 2002-03 coming in matches he started on the bench.
Grimsby T *(Loaned from FC Copenhagen, Denmark on 12/10/2000) FL 16+1/5 FAC 1+1/1*
Wimbledon *(Signed from FC Copenhagen, Denmark on 27/3/2001) FL 15+8/4 FLC 1*
Norwich C *(£200,000 on 14/12/2001) FL 33+23/14 FLC 1 FAC 3 Others 3*

Allan Nielsen

NIEMI Antti
Born: Oulu, Finland, 31 May 1972
Height: 6'1" **Weight:** 13.9
Club Honours: SLC '99
International Honours: Finland: 56;
U21-17; Yth
Finland's first choice goalkeeper, Antti
arrived at Southampton just after the start
of last season, having begun the
campaign with Hearts. His first four
games were spent as Paul Jones's
understudy, before a 1–0 defeat at West
Bromwich Albion prompted Gordon
Strachan to promote him. He became the
automatic first choice from then onwards,
being favourably compared by the
supporters with Peter Shilton and
provoking press gossip on which 'big'
club he might be departing for during the
close season. It is, indeed, difficult to spot
any serious weakness in his overall game.
His season climaxed sadly, and
prematurely, during the second half of the
FA Cup final. With Saints 1–0 in arrears
he tore a calf muscle while taking a free
kick and had to be substituted.
*Glasgow R (Signed from FC Copenhagen,
Denmark, ex HJK Helsinki, on 22/7/1997) SL
3 SLC 1 Others 7+1*
*Heart of Midlothian (£400,000 on
7/12/1999) SL 89 SLC 4 SC 9 Others 4*
*Southampton (£2,000,000 on 28/8/2002) PL
5 FLC 2 FAC 6*

NIGHTINGALE Luke Raymond
Born: Portsmouth, 22 December 1980
Height: 5'10" **Weight:** 12.5
This young Portsmouth striker spent two
months on loan at Swindon last term as
he sought to rebuild an injury-affected
career. Although he made the starting
line-up on two occasions he was replaced
in both without really making a strong
impression. His most effective
performance was after coming on as a
substitute at Stockport when he helped to
set up two late goals in a fine 5-2 victory
for the Robins.
*Portsmouth (From trainee on 23/11/1998) FL
4+31/4 FLC 2+1/3 FAC 2+1/1*
Swindon T (Loaned on 24/12/2002) FL 2+1

NIXON Eric Walter
Born: Manchester, 4 October 1962
Height: 6'4" **Weight:** 14.12
Club Honours: AMC '90
This veteran 'keeper was in his second
season as goalkeeping coach at Tranmere
last term. However, Eric retained his
playing registration and was called on in
the opening game of the season against
Port Vale as substitute for the injured
Keith Welch. He went on to keep a clean
sheet, and came on for Welch for the

second time in the away fixture at Crewe.
A firm favourite at Prenton Park, Eric
continues to be very vocal, whether
between the posts or on the bench.
*Manchester C (£1,000 from Curzon Ashton
on 10/12/1983) FL 58 FLC 8 FAC 10 Others 8*
*Wolverhampton W (Loaned on 29/8/1986)
FL 16*
Bradford C (Loaned on 28/11/1986) FL 3
Southampton (Loaned on 23/12/1986) FL 4
Carlisle U (Loaned on 23/1/1987) FL 16
*Tranmere Rov (£60,000 on 24/3/1988) FL
341 FLC 34 FAC 19 Others 45+1*
Reading (Loaned on 9/1/1996) FLC 1
*Blackpool (Loaned on 5/2/1996) FL 20
Others 2*
Bradford C (Loaned on 13/9/1996) FL 12
*Stockport Co (£100,000 on 28/8/1997) FL
43 FLC 2 FAC 2*
Wigan Ath (Loaned on 28/8/1998) FL 1
Wigan Ath (Free on 24/3/1999) FL 2
*Tranmere Rov (Free on 20/7/1999) FL 1+4
FLC 0+1*
*Kidderminster Hrs (Loaned on 12/10/2001)
FL 2 Others 1*

NIXON Marc Steven
Born: Hexham, 29 January 1984
Height: 5'9" **Weight:** 11.2
Marc is a local product who deputised for
striker Richie Foran in some early-season
fixtures for Carlisle last term. In a side
generally lacking in experience, he
worked hard and did not always have the
best of luck. He was released at the end
of the campaign.
*Carlisle U (From trainee on 16/7/2002) FL
3+4 FLC 1 FAC 0+1*

NOEL-WILLIAMS Gifton
Ruben Elisha
Born: Islington, 21 January 1980
Height: 6'1'' **Weight:** 14.6
Club Honours: Div 2 '98
International Honours: E: Yth
Gifton underwent knee surgery in the
summer of 2002 and was not ready for a
return to first-team action with Watford
until December. His strong physical
presence and ability to hold up the ball
gave the team a more robust look, but he
was unable to hold down a regular place
in the starting line-up and he was
released at the end of the season.
Watford's youngest-ever scorer, he was a
great favourite with the fans who
admired his battling spirit in the face of a
persistent arthritic condition and enjoyed
his cheerful personality. Gifton was
reported to have signed for Stoke City in
the summer.
*Watford (From trainee on 13/2/1997) P/FL
107+62/33 FLC 10+2/3 FAC 10+2/5*

NOGAN Lee Martin
Born: Cardiff, 21 May 1969
Height: 5'9" **Weight:** 11.0
Club Honours: AMC '98
International Honours: W: 2; B-1;
U21-1
Lee's experience, exceptional work rate
and all-round ability were again to the
fore for York City last term. He featured in
every game for the Minstermen, netting
five times in Third Division matches
including a vital late winner against
Kidderminster in December. He played as
a striker for most of the season before
dropping back to more of a midfield role
in the closing stages.
*Oxford U (From trainee on 25/3/1987) FL
57+7/10 FLC 4+1 FAC 2+1/1 Others 4+1/1*
Brentford (Loaned on 25/3/1987) FL 10+1/2
*Southend U (Loaned on 17/9/1987) FL 6/1
FLC 2 Others 1/1*
*Watford (£350,000 on 12/12/1991) FL
97+8/26 FLC 5+2/3 FAC 2/1 Others 1+2*
Southend U (Loaned on 17/3/1994) FL 4+1
*Reading (£250,000 on 12/11/1995) FL
71+20/26 FLC 5+1/1 FAC 2 Others 3/2*
Notts Co (Loaned on 14/2/1997) FL 6
*Grimsby T (£170,000 on 24/7/1997) FL
63+11/10 FLC 9+1/2 FAC 4/2 Others 8/2*
*Darlington (Free on 21/7/1999) FL 3/+12/6
FLC 3/2 FAC 3 Others 1+2/1*
*Luton T (Free on 23/11/2000) FL 7/1 FAC 3/1
Others 0+1*
*York C (Free on 12/2/2001) FL 95+9/24 FLC 2
FAC 7 Others 2/1*

NOLAN Kevin Anthony Jance
Born: Liverpool, 24 June 1982
Height: 6'1" **Weight:** 13.5
International Honours: E: U21-1; Yth
Having played such a major role in the
Bolton team during the 2001-02
campaign, Kevin found last season a little
more frustrating. He made the starting
line-up early on and, for the second
season in a row, scored in a Wanderers
victory at Old Trafford. However, he was
out of the team in September due to a
groin tear and whilst he made some
sporadic first-team starts upon his return,
his involvement for the remainder of the
season came primarily from the subs'
bench. A strong and tough-tackling
central midfielder, Kevin was also a
regular in the England U21 squad.
*Bolton W (From trainee on 22/1/2000) P/FL
74+29/10 FLC 1+2 FAC 5+3/2 Others 2*

NOON Mark Richard
Born: Leamington, 23 September 1983
Height: 5'10" **Weight:** 12.4
A product of Coventry City's academy,
Mark performed well for the reserves last

317

season and was rewarded with a first-team debut as a substitute in the final home game with Gillingham when he replaced Gary McAllister. A tall midfielder with good passing skills, he will be looking to gain more senior experience in 2003-04.

Coventry C (From trainee on 29/8/2001) FL 0+2

NORMANN Runar

Born: Harstad, Norway, 1 March 1978
Height: 6'3" **Weight:** 12.11
International Honours: Norway: U21-3; Yth
After only a handful of appearances in three years this left-sided midfield player got his chance for Coventry last September and came off the bench to score a late headed equaliser against Sheffield Wednesday. He started the next two games but was then dropped and soon afterwards his contract was cancelled. Runar subsequently returned to Norway and signed for Brann Bergen.

Coventry C (£1,000,000 from Lillestrom, Norway, ex Harstad, on 3/8/1999) P/FL 3+10/1 FLC 0+1 FAC 1

NORRIS David Martin

Born: Stamford, 22 February 1981
Height: 5'7" **Weight:** 11.6
David was originally loaned to Plymouth Argyle from Premiership Bolton Wanderers last October and became an instant hero by scoring the winner on his debut at Crewe. The talented midfielder went on to produce some excellent performances as his loan spell was extended, and in December he signed permanent forms for the Pilgrims. He remained in fine form, working tirelessly and receiving several 'Man of the Match' awards.

Bolton W (£50,000 from Boston U on 2/2/2000) FLC 3+1 FAC 1/1
Hull C (Loaned on 4/3/2002) FL 3+3/1
Plymouth Arg (Free on 8/10/2002) FL 29+4/6 FAC 3

NORVILLE Jason

Born: Trinidad, 9 September 1983
Height: 5'11" **Weight:** 11.2
Jason, a promising left-sided striker, was a consistent performer with Watford's reserves last season and was rewarded with a place in the first-team squad towards the end of the campaign. He ended up starting six matches and scored a fine goal at Sheffield Wednesday. Quick and strong, with an ability to hold up the ball, he showed a marked improvement in confidence and awareness.

Watford (From trainee on 17/4/2002) FL 6+8/1 FLC 0+1

NOSWORTHY Nyron Paul Henry

Born: Brixton, 11 October 1980
Height: 6'0" **Weight:** 12.0
A virtual ever present for Gillingham last season, Nyron showed his versatility by playing the last three games up front and was rewarded on the final day when his two goals helped beat Crystal Palace 2-1 to lift the Gills' to a final position of 11th. These were his first goals for the club in over three years. However, for most of the campaign he was employed in his more usual role at right back, where he proved to be both pacy and strong in the tackle.

Gillingham (From trainee on 30/12/1998) FL 89+21/3 FLC 3+2 FAC 5+7 Others 0+3

NOTMAN Alexander (Alex) McKeachie

Born: Edinburgh, 10 December 1979
Height: 5'7" **Weight:** 10.11
International Honours: S: U21-11; Yth; Sch
Alex missed much of the 2002-03 season following a freak ankle injury sustained in the local 'derby' at Ipswich in mid-September, when he injured himself charging down a Mark Venus free kick. He started the campaign regularly, coming off the bench to fill a wide-right midfield position, but had made three successive starts when injury struck. His fight back from injury saw him playing regularly for the reserves at the season's end. The former Scottish U21 international striker will be looking for better things in 2003-04.

Manchester U (From trainee on 17/12/1996) FLC 0+1
Aberdeen (Loaned on 11/2/1999) SL 0+2
Sheffield U (Loaned on 20/1/2000) FL 7+3/3
Norwich C (£250,000 on 28/11/2000) FL 18+35/1 FLC 1 FAC 2+1 Others 0+3

NOWLAND Adam Christopher

Born: Preston, 6 July 1981
Height: 5'11" **Weight:** 11.6
Adam is undoubtedly a skilful and talented player, and would be a regular starter in many teams, but has often found his opportunities limited at Wimbledon due to the system the club usually employs. His best position is at the head of a midfield diamond, just behind the front strikers, and though the Dons experimented with a similar formation late in the season with Adam in that role, more often than not he

found himself either on the bench or watching from the stands. He scored his first goal for the club in an early-season game at Watford, and scored his second late on when impressing in the 5-1 win at Ipswich.

Blackpool (From trainee on 15/1/1999) FL 18+51/6 FLC 1+5/1 FAC 2+2/1 Others 0+2
Wimbledon (Signed on 29/6/2001) FL 11+20/2 FLC 1+1

NUGENT David James

Born: Liverpool, 2 May 1985
Height: 5'11" **Weight:** 12.13
This young striker is regarded very much as a rising star by the Bury fans. He continued to develop in his first full season and was mainly used as a substitute by manager Andy Preece who introduced him into the action on 20 occasions, although David also started 11 games. He has the ability to hold off more muscular opponents and possesses the determination and strong running to cause problems for many defenders. He scored five goals for the Shakers – three from the substitutes' bench – and netted his first-ever league goal with a superb header at home to Darlington.

Bury (From trainee on 8/3/2003) FL 12+24/4 FLC 0+1 FAC 0+1 Others 3+3/1

NUGENT Kevin Patrick

Born: Edmonton, 10 April 1969
Height: 6'1" **Weight:** 13.3
International Honours: RoI: Yth
This experienced striker started the 2002-03 season as a reserve for Leyton Orient, but when called upon he never let the team down and showed he still had a lot to offer, holding the ball up and bringing others into the game. Kevin's highlight was scoring against Premiership club Birmingham City in the Worthington Cup tie. He subsequently joined Swansea City on loan where he score three goals in his first four appearances, and this was enough to win him a short-term contract to the end of the season. Kevin featured regularly for the Swans, but managed just two more goals.

Leyton Orient (From trainee on 8/7/1987) FL 86+8/20 FLC 9+3/6 FAC 9/3 Others 9+1/1
Plymouth Arg (£200,000 on 23/3/1992) FL 124+7/32 FLC 11/2 FAC 10/3 Others 5+3
Bristol C (Signed on 29/9/1995) FL 48+22/14 FLC 2+2 FAC 3+2/1 Others 2+1
Cardiff C (£65,000 on 4/8/1997) FL 94+5/29 FLC 8+1/1 FAC 9/6 Others 1+1/1
Leyton Orient (Free on 31/1/2002) FL 17+11/4 FLC 1/1 FAC 2 Others 1
Swansea C (Free on 17/1/2003) FL 15/5

O

AKES Andrew (Andy) Mark
orn: Northwich, 11 January 1977
eight: 6'4" **Weight:** 12.4
st season was difficult for this slender
erby County goalkeeper. After two years
understudy to Mart Poom, he found
mself behind Lee Grant when the
tonian joined Sunderland. Andy was
ck in favour when George Burley
came interim manager and remains a
urageous shot stopper, ignoring
rsonal danger when he goes in among
rwards' feet. If he can deal with crosses
ore confidently, he can break through as
st choice. He certainly has the
termination to succeed and has already
ercome several disappointments in his
reer.
ull C *(Signed from Winsford U on
12/1998) FL 19 Others 1*
erby Co *(£460,000 on 7/6/1999) P/FL 33
C 2 FAC 1*

AKES Michael Christian
orn: Northwich, 30 October 1973
eight: 6'2" **Weight:** 14.6
ub Honours: FLC '96
ternational Honours: E: U21-6
is goalkeeper looked reliable and
nfident as Wolves did well in their
ening four matches, conceding just two
als. A rib injury made Michael a rare
sentee at Wimbledon but he played in
ven of the first eight matches. However,
e team were conceding more goals and
was dropped after a 4-2 defeat by
ystal Palace. Everyone assumed he
uld soon be back, but by April he had
t made any more appearances, though
was comforting to know Wolves had
vo excellent 'keepers on their books.
ston Villa *(From juniors on 16/7/1991) PL
+2 FLC 3 FAC 2 Others 5*
arborough *(Loaned on 26/11/1993) FL 1
hers 1*
olverhampton W *(£400,000 + on
/10/1999) FL 126 FLC 6 FAC 5 Others 2*

AKES Stefan (Stef) Trevor
orn: Leicester, 6 September 1978
eight: 5'11" **Weight:** 12.4
ub Honours: FLC '00
is left-footed midfielder once again only
d limited opportunities at Leicester
der Micky Adams, but particularly
pressed when appearing from the
nch in the Worthington Cup victory at
llsborough. Stef joined Crewe on loan
March and stayed until the end of the

season, featuring regularly in the squad.
He was released by the Foxes in the
summer.
Leicester C *(From trainee on 3/7/1997) P/FL
39+25/2 FLC 7+1/2 FAC 5+2*
Crewe Alex *(Loaned on 17/3/2003) FL 3+4*

OAKLEY Matthew (Matt)
Born: Peterborough, 17 August 1977
Height: 5'10" **Weight:** 12.1
International Honours: E: U21-4
The main highlights of Matt's 2002-03
campaign were the two cracking goals he
scored for Southampton in the FA Cup
fourth round replay at Millwall, which set
the Saints on course for the final.
Strangely, these proved his entire tally for
the season. His industry in the heart of
midfield together with artful passing and

clever one-twos with colleagues allowed
him to further consolidate his place in the
line-up and moved Gordon Strachan to
select him as captain in the absence of
Jason Dodd and Chris Marsden.
Southampton *(From trainee on 1/7/1995) PL
196+22/11 FLC 21+2/2 FAC 16+2/3*

OATWAY Anthony Philip David
Terry Frank Donald Stanley Gerry
Gordon Stephen James **(Charlie)**
Born: Hammersmith, 28 November 1973
Height: 5'7" **Weight:** 10.10
Club Honours: Div 3 '99, '01; Div 2 '02
Although he only started 21 times in
2002-03, this combative Brighton
midfielder was involved in all but one
senior game. It took him some time to
adjust to the higher standards of First

Charlie Oatway

Division football and he was principally used as a substitute or replacement midfielder after October. Always willing to chase, tackle and generally harass the opposition, Charlie made up for any lack of skill with abundant energy and determination. A popular player with the Withdean fans, he was rewarded for his efforts with a late goal in the last home fixture of the season.
Cardiff C *(Free from Yeading on 4/8/1994) FL 29+3 FLC 2/1 FAC 1+1 Others 3+1*
Torquay U *(Free on 28/12/1995) FL 65+2/1 FLC 3 FAC 1*
Brentford *(£10,000 on 21/8/1997) FL 37+20 FLC 1+2/1 FAC 4 Others 0+1*
Lincoln C *(Loaned on 21/10/1998) FL 3*
Brighton & Hove A *(£10,000 on 9/7/1999) FL 123+18/6 FLC 7 FAC 10/1 Others 2*

O'BRIEN Andrew (Andy)
James
Born: Harrogate, 29 June 1979
Height: 6'3" **Weight:** 12.4
International Honours: Rol: 6; U21-8; E: U21-1; Yth
A shin injury saw Andy begin the 2002-03 season on Newcastle's bench, but he was brought into the side for the home game with Leeds in early September and after this he became a virtual regular, featuring mostly in his preferred role in the centre of a back four, but also occasionally at right back. He jarred his back in the FA Cup defeat at Wolves and was out for over three weeks, but then returned to the squad until his season ended early when he suffered a broken nose in the 'derby' at Sunderland in April. Undemonstrative but solid and consistent, Andy was a regular member of the Republic of Ireland squad during the campaign.
Bradford C *(From trainee on 28/10/1996) P/FL 113+20/3 FLC 5 FAC 8 Others 4*
Newcastle U *(£2,000,000 on 28/3/2001) PL 66+3/3 FLC 3+1 FAC 5+1/1 Others 11+2*

O'CALLAGHAN Brian Patrick
Born: Limerick, 24 February 1981
Height: 6'1" **Weight:** 12.1
International Honours: Rol: U21-4; Yth
Brian settled back into his normal central defensive position for Barnsley last season. However, he was seen more as the first-choice reserve than a regular starter. He likes to bring the ball forward but occasionally this would lead to problems. An imposing figure who reads the game well, he can be a danger at set plays. Brian scored his first and only senior goal to date, netting the winner against

Mansfield Town in a crucial end-of-season battle.
Barnsley *(Signed from Pike Rov on 16/7/1998) FL 33+13/1 FLC 4+2 FAC 1*

O'CONNOR Aaron Derek
Born: Nottingham, 9 August 1983
Height: 5'10" **Weight:** 12.0
This pacy youngster began the 2002-03 season with Ilkeston Town before impressing on the right wing and at centre forward for Scunthorpe reserves. He made his Football League debut as a substitute against Bury in December and added two more brief appearances from the bench for the first team before being released in February and rejoining his former club.
Scunthorpe U *(Free from Ilkeston T on 12/12/2002) FL 0+3*

O'CONNOR Garreth
Born: Dublin, 10 November 1978
Height: 5'7" **Weight:** 11.0
The 2002-03 season proved to be the one when Garreth made his big breakthrough for Bournemouth. He produced a number of superb performances in the second half of the campaign and his display against Darlington was such that he was awarded a rating of ten out of ten by the local paper. A midfielder with an excellent strike rate, he signed a new one-year deal in the summer.
Bournemouth *(Free from Bohemians on 5/6/2000) FL 42+49/9 FLC 1+1 FAC 6+4/1 Others 9+1/3*

O'CONNOR James Kevin
Born: Dublin, 1 September 1979
Height: 5'8" **Weight:** 11.6
Club Honours: AMC '00
International Honours: Rol: U21-9; Yth
'Super James's' committed performances continued to make him a firm favourite with the Stoke City fans last term and indeed he walked away with half of the end-of-season player awards. His combative style made him few friends with referees but he had fewer disciplinary problems than in previous seasons and this ensured his availability for key games. Whilst his passing skills sometimes fall short of his own high standards his ability to get around the field mark him out as a player who is continuing to develop.
Stoke C *(From trainee on 5/9/1996) FL 176/16 FLC 9/3 FAC 8+1 Others 16+1/3*

O'CONNOR Kevin Patrick
Born: Blackburn, 24 February 1982
Height: 5'11" **Weight:** 12.0
International Honours: Rol: U21-3

Kevin spent the majority of the 2002-03 season on Brentford's right wing and making a very good job of it. He also played a few games in central midfield and up front. His excellent form saw him called up to the Republic of Ireland U21 squad and he featured against Georgia and Albania. In the Worthington Cup tie at Bournemouth Kevin converted two penalties in normal time and another in the penalty shoot-out, thus completing an unusual 'hat-trick'.
Brentford *(From trainee on 4/3/2000) FL 68+19/6 FLC 3+1/3 FAC 5+1/1 Others 3+4/1*

O'CONNOR Martin John
Born: Walsall, 10 December 1967
Height: 5'9" **Weight:** 11.8
International Honours: Cayman Isles: 2
The 2002-03 campaign proved to be a very mixed season for the Walsall skipper who suffered several injuries, one of these being a fractured jaw sustained in a training ground accident. Even when struggling however, he battled away in midfield and excelled in the frequent heavy conditions at Bescot with his firm tackling and excellent distribution.
Crystal Palace *(£25,000 from Bromsgrove Rov on 26/6/1992) FL 2 Others 1+1*
Walsall *(Loaned on 24/3/1993) FL 10/1 Others 2/1*
Walsall *(£40,000 on 14/2/1994) FL 94/6 FLC 6/2 FAC 10/2 Others 3/1*
Peterborough U *(£350,000 on 12/7/1996) FL 18/3 FLC 4 FAC 2*
Birmingham C *(£500,000 + on 29/11/1996) FL 181+6/16 FLC 22+1/3 FAC 7 Others 6*
Walsall *(Free on 8/2/2002) FL 45+3/2 FLC 2 FAC 3*

ODUNSI Saheed Adeleke (Leke)
Born: Lambeth, 5 December 1980
Height: 5'9" **Weight:** 11.8
Midfielder Leke started just three games for Colchester United, before surprising everyone by announcing he was leaving the full-time game in November. He spent most of his time on the bench, with his final appearance coming in the 4-2 defeat at Mansfield. He was more of a defensive midfielder than a creator, but was prepared to play in a number of positions. Leke subsequently featured for a number of Ryman League clubs including Kingstonian, Bromley and Carshalton.
Millwall *(From trainee on 24/2/1999) FL 5+12 FLC 1+2 Others 2+1*
Colchester U *(Loaned on 16/8/2002) FL 3+. FLC 0+1 Others 0+1*

FFIONG Richard
orn: South Shields, 17 December 1983
eight: 5'11" **Weight:** 12.0
ternational Honours: E: Yth
is extremely quick and nimble young
riker joined Darlington on loan from
ewcastle United last November and
agged a brace of goals on two
casions, in the FA Cup tie against
evenage and then on Boxing Day at
arlisle. Richard's pace was his main
tribute and he could outstrip most
efenders on the ground, but he was not
comfortable with balls played up in the
. He spent much of the second half of
e campaign on loan at Motherwell,
here he made a number of appearances
om the bench and featured in the
ottish Cup semi-final against Rangers at
ampden. Richard was a member of the

England U20 team for the Toulon
tournament in the summer.
Newcastle U (From trainee on 26/9/2001)
Darlington (Loaned on 29/11/2002) FL 7/2
FAC 2/2
Motherwell (Loaned on 31/1/2003) SL 0+9
SC 0+1

**O'GRADY Christopher
(Chris)** James
Born: Nottingham, 25 January 1986
Height: 6'1" **Weight:** 12.8
International Honours: E: Yth
This promising young striker proved
prolific for the Leicester City U17 team
during the early months of the 2002-03
season. Chris graduated to the England
youth line-up, actually starting against
France, and was promoted to the Foxes'
first-team bench during a period of

injuries and suspensions in April. His
debut came late in the home clash with
Grimsby, but he still found time for one
mazy dribble and shot.
Leicester C (Trainee) FL 0+1

O'HARE Alan Patrick James
Born: Drogheda, Ireland, 31 July 1982
Height: 6'2" **Weight:** 12.2
This young Irish defender enjoyed a
phenomenal improvement in the 2002-03
campaign. Settled in the centre of
Chesterfield's defence, he displayed great
game-reading skills, a timely tackle and a
willingness to play the ball forward. He
picked up a clutch of 'Young Player'
awards from the supporters and has
become quite a favourite at Saltergate.
His shackling of Bristol City's Scott Murray
at Saltergate in April saw the Second
Division's most dangerous midfielder
rendered completely ineffective.
Bolton W (From trainee on 24/11/2001)
Chesterfield (Loaned on 25/1/2002) FL 19
Chesterfield (Free on 9/10/2002) FL 18+4
Others 2

OKAI Parys
Born: London, 23 November 1984
Height: 5'9" **Weight:** 11.5
This promising left winger turned in some
outstanding performances for the Luton
Town reserve and youth teams last season
and he made his senior debut from the
bench in an LDV Vans Trophy match.
Quick, good at winning tackles and
excellent at crossing, Parys still has plenty
to do before he makes the grade at senior
level, however, he will be looking to gain
more first-team experience in 2003-04.
Luton T (Trainee) Others 0+1

O'KANE John Andrew
Born: Nottingham, 15 November 1974
Height: 5'10" **Weight:** 12.2
Club Honours: FAYC '92; Div 2 '97;
AMC '02
This experienced Blackpool defender or
midfield player featured regularly in the
squad in the first half of the 2002-03
season, although he was often used from
the substitutes' bench. However, he was
sidelined by injury in the new year and
was absent for much of the remainder of
the campaign.
Manchester U (From trainee on 29/1/1993)
PL 1+1 FLC 2+1 FAC 1 Others 1
Wimbledon (Loaned on 22/6/1995) Others 3
Bury (Loaned on 25/10/1996) FL 2+2/2
Bury (Loaned on 16/1/1997) FL 9/1 Others 1
Bradford C (Loaned on 31/10/1997) FL 7
Everton (£250,000 + on 30/1/1998) PL 14
FAC 1+2
Burnley (Loaned on 31/10/1998) FL 8

Martin O'Connor

321

*Bolton W (Signed on 19/11/1999) FL 32+6/2
FLC 4 FAC 3+1/1*
*Blackpool (Free on 4/7/2001) FL 42+10/4
FLC 3 FAC 2+4 Others 5+1*

OKOCHA Augustine Azuka (Jay Jay)
Born: Enugu, Nigeria, 14 August 1973
Height: 5'7" **Weight:** 11.2
Club Honours: FAYC '92; Div 2 '97;
AMC '02

Jay Jay Okocha

International Honours: Nigeria
Jay Jay made his debut for Bolton at
Fulham on the opening day of the 2002-
03 campaign and initially seemed to
struggle to come to terms with the
English game. Niggling injuries meant that
he only made sporadic appearances over
the next few months, but he returned to
action in November and gradually began
influencing games more and more from
his roaming midfield role, culminating in a

number of 'Man of the Match'
performances. Quite possibly one of the
most skilful players ever to don the Boltc
shirt, he was a revelation, scoring some
tremendous goals. His strike against Wes
Ham at the Reebok in April was one of
the finest goals scored in the Premiership
during the season. His last-minute penal
against Spurs in March was composure
personified, while his dazzling free kick
against Middlesbrough was as perfect ar
example of a set piece that you could
wish to see.
*Bolton W (Free from Paris St Germain,
France, ex Enugu R, B.Nuenkirchen, Eintrach
Frankfurt, Fenerbahce, on 3/8/2002) PL
26+5/7 FAC 0+1*

OKOLI James Chuks
Born: Nigeria, 11 January 1976
Height: 6'1" **Weight:** 12.3
This versatile defender impressed
sufficiently in pre-season friendlies with
York City to sign a contract in August
2002. He made his debut on the
opening day of the campaign at
Macclesfield but was never able to
establish himself in the side and apart
from a couple of outings from the bend
the only other occasion when he
featured was in the LDV Vans Trophy tie
against Lincoln City. James was released
by the Minstermen in March.
*Motherwell (Signed from Altmar K.Stenda
Germany, via a trial at Watford, ex FC Zwoll
Augsburg, Hertha Berlin, on 15/3/2001) SL .*
*York C (Free following spells at Oxford U,
Shelbourne, Bristol Rov, on 8/8/2002) FL 1+
Others 1*

OKON Paul Michael
Born: Sydney, Australia, 5 April 1972
Height: 5'11" **Weight:** 11.12
International Honours: Australia: 35;
U23; Yth
This well-travelled Australian linked up
with former international boss Terry
Venables at Leeds United last term.
However, injuries prevented him from
making an appearance until December,
his debut coming in the 1-0 defeat at
Fulham. Paul remained in the first team
for a lengthy run, playing as a midfield
anchor man and proving to be consisten
at cleaning up and laying the ball off. He
also made a return to the international
scene as skipper when Australia beat
England 3-1 at Upton Park.
*Middlesbrough (Free from Fiorentina, Italy,
ex Marconi Fairfield, Brugge, Lazio, on
4/8/2000) PL 24+4 FAC 2*
Watford (Free on 10/1/2002) FL 14+1
*Leeds U (Free on 13/8/2002) PL 15 FAC 5
Others 1*

LDFIELD David Charles
orn: Perth, Australia, 30 May 1968
eight: 5'11" **Weight:** 13.4
ternational Honours: E: U21-1
avid was a useful summer signing for
xford when he joined from
eterborough. His knowledge and know-
ow made the team tick and they tended
 create more chances when David was
 the line-up, as he linked the play with
s clever touches. He managed three
oals, including real crackers in the FA
up tie at Dover and at Rushden. He
issed a number of games with injuries
nd at the time of writing his future was
ncertain as he had not been offered a
rther contract.
*uton T (From apprentice on 16/5/1986) FL
+8/4 FLC 4+2/2 FAC 0+1 Others 2+1/2
Manchester C (£600,000 on 14/3/1989) FL
3+8/6 FLC 2+1/2 Others 0+1/1
eicester C (£150,000 on 12/1/1990) F/PL
53+25/26 FLC 10+2/1 FAC 7/3 Others
4 +3/2
illwall (Loaned on 24/2/1995) FL 16+1/6
uton T (£150,000 on 21/7/1995) FL
9+18/18 FLC 11/2 FAC 2 Others 7+2/4
toke C (Free on 2/7/1998) FL 50+15/7 FLC
+1 FAC 2 Others 1+1
eterborough U (Free on 23/3/2000) FL
3+10/4 FLC 3 FAC 8+2/1 Others 4+1
xford U (Free on 8/8/2002) FL 19+9/2 FLC
FAC 2/1 Others 0+1*

'LEARY Kristian Denis
orn: Port Talbot, 30 August 1977
eight: 6'0" **Weight:** 13.4
lub Honours: Div 3 '00
ternational Honours: W: Yth
ristian was Swansea City's captain at the
art of the season and occupied a central
efensive role until losing his place to
an signing Alan Tate. He subsequently
ught his way back into the line-up at
ght back, deputising for Terry Evans,
en switched to central defence after
son Smith's injury.
*wansea C (From trainee on 1/7/1996) FL
42+27/1 FLC 8 FAC 5+1 Others 7+2*

LI Dennis Chiedozie
orn: Newham, 28 January 1984
eight: 6'0" **Weight:** 12.4
his tall striker received a number of first-
am starts for Queen's Park Rangers in
e early part of the 2002-03 campaign.
e continued to keep his place in the
quad after Paul Furlong had returned
om injury, although most of his
ubsequent appearances were from the
ubstitutes' bench.
*ueens Park R (From juniors on 24/10/2001)
 8+12 FLC 0+1 FAC 1+1 Others 1*

OLIVER Luke John
Born: Hammersmith, 1 May 1984
Height: 6'6" **Weight:** 14.6
Originally signed from Middlesex club
Brook House whilst studying for his 'A'
levels, Luke quickly progressed through
the Wycombe Wanderers youth team. He
made his senior debut near the end of
the season, appearing as a substitute
against Cheltenham, and giving a solid
performance. He also made one further
appearance from the bench at Plymouth
on the last day of the season. At 6' 6" he
is the tallest Wycombe player in recent
years and uses his height to good
advantage.
*Wycombe W (Free from Brook House on
2/7/2002) FL 0+2*

OLIVER Michael
Born: Middlesbrough, 2 August 1975
Height: 5'10" **Weight:** 12.4
Michael had something of a mixed season
at Rochdale in 2002-03. After missing the
opening games he then re-established
himself in midfield alongside Dave
Flitcroft, scoring a dramatic injury-time
winner against Cambridge. However, after
being second in the table, Dale hit a rocky
patch and Michael was one of those left
out, subsequently dropping back to a role
on the substitutes' bench. After some
time on the sidelines he regained his
place only to pull a hamstring, and a
recurrence of the injury then ruled him
out for most of the remainder of the
campaign.
*Middlesbrough (From trainee on 19/8/1992)
Others 0+1
Stockport Co (£15,000 on 7/7/1994) FL
17+5/1 FLC 0+2 FAC 2 Others 1
Darlington (Free on 30/7/1996) FL
135+16/14 FLC 7+1/1 FAC 10+2 Others 6+3
Rochdale (Free on 14/7/2000) FL 87+16/9
FLC 5 FAC 6/1 Others 5*

OLSEN James Paul
Born: Bootle, 23 October 1981
Height: 5'10" **Weight:** 12.2
After spending most of the previous
season out of action with a broken neck,
this unfortunate youngster endured yet
another injury-wrecked campaign in
2002-03. A freak accident at Tranmere's
open day resulted in a ball smashing him
in the eye, and leaving him temporarily
blind. By the time he recovered, he found
it impossible to break back into the first
team such was the competition for the
defensive positions. James made only one
start with a further four appearances as
substitute, but was a mainstay of the
reserves.

*Tranmere Rov (From trainee at Liverpool on
22/3/2001) FL 1+3 FLC 0+1 Others 0+1*

**OMOYINMI Emmanuel
(Manny)**
Born: Nigeria, 28 December 1977
Height: 5'6" **Weight:** 10.7
International Honours: E: Sch
Manny had another 'cameo' season for
Oxford last term, appearing every now
and again with some dazzling dribbling
skills. His first goal proved to be the
winner on the opening day but after
October he did not make the starting line-
up, although he often featured from the
substitutes' bench. His best performance
was probably in the Worthington Cup tie
at Charlton when he terrorised the
Premiership club's defence as Oxford went
through on penalties.
*West Ham U (From trainee on 17/5/1995) PL
1+8/2 FLC 0+2 FAC 1+1
Bournemouth (Loaned on 30/9/1996) FL
5+2
Dundee U (Loaned on 20/2/1998) SL 1+3 SC
0+1
Leyton Orient (Loaned on 19/3/1999) FL
3+1/1
Gillingham (Loaned on 3/9/1999) FL 7+2/3
FLC 2
Scunthorpe U (Loaned on 21/12/1999) FL
6/1 Others 1
Barnet (Loaned on 25/2/2000) FL 1+5
Oxford U (Free on 10/7/2000) FL 31+33/9
FLC 2+2 FAC 1+2 Others 2*

ONE Armand
Born: Paris, France, 15 March 1983
Height: 6'4" **Weight:** 14.0
This tall striker was out of favour at
Cambridge last season and joined
Northampton Town on loan. He showed
some neat touches but struggled to find
the net, although he did score an
excellent goal against Colchester just
prior to his departure. He was released
by the U's soon after his return to the
club.
*Cambridge U (£30,000 from Nantes, France
on 7/9/2001) FL 18+14/4 FAC 0+2 Others
4+3/5
Northampton T (Loaned on 10/9/2002) FL
6/1 FLC 0+1*

O'NEIL Brian
Born: Paisley, 6 September 1972
Height: 6'1" **Weight:** 12.4
International Honours: S: 6; U21-7;
Yth; Sch
Injuries so wrecked Brian's two years at
Pride Park that Derby seldom saw the best
of him as a defender or midfield player.
His contract was cancelled in November,

and after a trial period he signed a one-month deal with Preston in January. He looked impressive early on, bringing undoubted quality to the middle line, and his future at Deepdale was secured with a long-term contract. A player who always seems to have plenty of time and to know exactly where his team mates are, Brian plays a simple but effective passing game, and his presence improved the play of many of those around him, most notably Dickson Etuhu.

Glasgow Celtic (Free from Porirua Viard U on 10/7/1997) SL 92+27/8 SLC 6+4/1 SC 10/9 Others 8+3/1
Nottingham F (Loaned on 18/3/1997) PL 4+1
Aberdeen (Free on 3/7/1997) SL 24+4/1 SLC 4 SC 1 (Transferred to Wolfsburg, Germany on 23/7/1998)
Derby Co (Signed on 16/11/2000) P/FL 14+3 FLC 1+1 FAC 2
Preston NE (Free on 3/1/2003) FL 12+3

O'NEIL Gary Paul
Born: Bromley, 18 May 1983
Height: 5'10" **Weight:** 11.0
Club Honours: Div 1 '03
International Honours: E: Yth
This talented youngster was restricted to just 11 starts for Portsmouth last season as manager Harry Redknapp opted for experience over youth. When selected Gary produced some consistent displays, holding the ball up for his colleagues and reading the game well. An exciting midfield player, he is comfortable in possession, has good distribution skills and is effective at closing down opponents.
Portsmouth (From trainee on 5/6/2000) FL 45+30/5 FLC 3+2 FAC 1+1

O'NEILL Matthew (Matt) Paul
Born: Accrington, 25 June 1984
Height: 5'11" **Weight:** 10.9
Of the young players introduced into Burnley's side near the end of the season, it was Matt who probably made the greatest impact. His debut from the bench came late in the home game against Watford, and his speed down the left wing and ability to cross the ball into the penalty area were soon illustrated in one of the few plus points from that 7-4 defeat. Matt made his full debut in the home game against Gillingham two weeks later, and played for most of the Clarets' final home game against Sheffield Wednesday when he again impressed in adversity.
Burnley (Trainee) FL 2+5

O'NEILL Paul Dennis
Born: Farnworth, 17 May 1982
Height: 6'3" **Weight:** 12.4
Most of Paul's appearances for Macclesfield Town last term came in the first half of the season when he featured on the left-hand side of the three centre backs. He performed well, but subsequent opportunities were limited due to competition from more experienced players. He successfully underwent a double hernia operation in March making a quick recovery and returning to action with the reserves in the middle of April. Paul was released during the 2003 close season.
Macclesfield T (From trainee on 5/7/2000) FL 23+13 FLC 1 FAC 1 Others 1+1

ONUORA Ifem (Iffy)
Born: Glasgow, 28 July 1967
Height: 6'1" **Weight:** 13.10
Iffy signed a two-year deal for Sheffield United in the summer of 2002, and was involved in the pre-season games. He was first choice as target man in eight of the opening nine games, using his experience to win, hold and deliver the ball. His one goal was the winner at Burnley but in the game against Rotherham he fell awkwardly, rupturing his achilles tendon, and was unable to play for the remainder of the campaign.
Huddersfield T (Signed from Bradford University on 28/7/1989) FL 115+50/30 FLC 10+6/4 FAC 12+3/3 Others 13+3/3
Mansfield T (£30,000 on 20/7/1994) FL 17+11/8 FAC 0+1 Others 1
Gillingham (£25,000 on 16/8/1996) FL 53+9/23 FLC 6/1 FAC 4/2 Others 1
Swindon T (£120,000 on 13/3/1998) FL 64+9/25 FLC 4 FAC 2+1
Gillingham (£125,000 on 3/1/2000) FL 69+17/26 FLC 3/1 FAC 4+1/1 Others 3/1
Sheffield U (Free on 4/7/2002) FL 7/1 FLC 1

OPARA Junior Lloyd
Born: Enfield, 6 January 1984
Height: 6'1" **Weight:** 13.0
Great things were expected of this young striker at Colchester last term, but he made just six appearances as a substitute in the first couple of months of the season. He moved on to Cambridge United, who took over the final six months of his youth scholarship. Lloyd scored for the U19s and reserves then had a spell on loan at Stevenage, before returning to the Abbey Stadium and making two appearances from the bench. He is a pacy front man with plenty of power.

Colchester U (Trainee) FL 0+6 FLC 0+1 FAC 0+1 Others 0+1
Cambridge U (Free from trainee on 28/4/2003) FL 0+2

ORMEROD Brett Ryan
Born: Blackburn, 18 October 1976
Height: 5'11" **Weight:** 11.4
Club Honours: AMC '02
In a season when Southampton struggle to find an effective replacement for the injured Marian Pahars, Brett strived to impress and his work rate and commitment could not be questioned. Even if the goals failed to flow from him James Beattie certainly prospered from Brett's hard work. He looked to have made the breakthrough in October, scoring a hat-trick against Tranmere Rovers in the Worthington Cup and hitting a Premiership brace at St Mary's against Manchester City in the following game, but he then failed to add to his tally until April. That strike was the crucial opener against Watford in the 2–1 FA Cup semi-final win. During the final he was his usual busy self, looking the most likely player to provide the breakthrough in a shot from a tight angle with eight minutes to go bringing the best out of Arsenal's David Seaman.
Blackpool (£50,000 from Accrington Stanley on 21/3/1997) FL 105+23/45 FLC 8/4 FAC 5+1/5 Others 7+2/8
Southampton (£1,750,000 on 7/12/2001) 30+19/6 FLC 1/3 FAC 5+2/1

OSBORN James
Born: London, 27 April 1984
Height: 5'10" **Weight:** 11.3
James made a long overdue first-team debut for Luton Town in the LDV Vans Trophy tie against Woking, but failed to live up to the promise he had showed in the first year of his scholarship when he was rated as the club's best young payer. He spent the remainder of the campaign developing in the reserves and was released in the summer.
Luton T (Trainee) Others 1

OSBORN Simon Edward
Born: Croydon, 19 January 1972
Height: 5'9" **Weight:** 11.4
Simon's 2002-03 season at Gillingham almost finished before he had even got going. In only the fourth game of the season at Norwich he sustained a ruptured achilles tendon that required an operation, and it was not until March that he returned to duty with the first team. From then on the experienced midfielder

as a virtual ever-present for the Gills and
e showed that he had lost none of his
bility on the ball. Simon was out of
ntract in the summer and his future
as unclear at the time of writing.
ystal Palace (From trainee on 3/1/1990)
PL 47+8/5 FLC 11/1 FAC 2 Others 1+3
eading (£90,000 on 17/8/1994) FL 31+1/5
C 4 Others 3
ueens Park R (£1,100,000 on 7/7/1995) PL
-3/1 FLC 2
olverhampton W (£1,000,000 on
2/12/1995) FL 151+11/11 FLC 7/3 FAC 11+1
thers 2
anmere Rov (Free on 22/3/2001) FL 9/1
rt Vale (Free on 7/9/2001) FL 7 FLC 1
llingham (Free on 12/10/2001) FL 38+8/5
AC 2+1

SBOURNE Isaac Samuel
orn: Birmingham, 22 June 1986
eight: 5'10" **Weight:** 11.12
aac made some impressive appearances
midfield for Coventry City's reserve
am last season. His displays pushed him
the fringes of the first team but he did
ot come off the bench until the final
ome game against Gillingham when he
arted for the first time. A pacy
idfielder with a biting challenge and
ood distribution, he will be looking to
uild on his experience in 2003-04.
oventry C (Trainee) FL 2

**SEI-KUFFOUR Jonathan
o)**
orn: Edmonton, 17 November 1981
eight: 5'7" **Weight:** 10.6
ub Honours: FAYC '00
his tricky and lightning-fast striker joined
rquay United on trial and initially found
mself limited to substitute appearances
starts out of position on the wing.
owever, an injury to David Graham gave
m the opportunity to claim a central
riking berth where he used his natural
tributes to bamboozle defenders and
arn a full contract. Jo showed immense
otential, but still needs to work on his
nishing and his final ball.
rsenal (From trainee on 18/7/2000)
windon T (Loaned on 24/8/2001) FL 4+7/2
C 1 Others 1
orquay U (Free on 18/10/2002) FL 18+12/5
AC 1+1/1 Others 1

'SHAUGHNESSY Paul Joseph
orn: Bury, 3 October 1981
eight: 6'4" **Weight:** 11.12
his central midfielder made his full debut
r Bury in the LDV Vans Trophy game at
ochdale in October and completed his
ll Football League debut in the 2-1 win

at Cambridge four months later. Paul's
main attributes are passion, commitment
and a desire to win, and these are
qualities that have never been missing
when he steps out for his home town
team. He played in five successive league
games in February but was used mainly as
a substitute after this.
Bury *(From trainee on 10/7/2001) FL 6+12
FLC 0+1 FAC 1 Others 3*

O'SHEA John Francis
Born: Waterford, 30 April 1981
Height: 6'3" **Weight:** 11.12
Club Honours: PL '03
International Honours: RoI: 7; U21-13;
Yth; (UEFA-U16 '98)
A highly talented young central defender
who possesses presence, great composure
and silky defensive skills John's hopes of a
regular place in the Manchester United
team seemed to be put on hold following
the signing of Rio Ferdinand in the
summer. The young Irishman soon
showed, however, there where more
defensive strings to his bow when he
adopted full-back duties. Although John

had not played in that role since his
schooldays, he was a revelation, and
despite longing for a return to the centre,
he was more than happy to continue.
John later filled a variety of roles in the
Reds defence due to injuries to key
players.
Manchester U *(Signed from Waterford U on
2/9/1998) PL 30+11 FLC 7 FAC 1 Others 12+7*
Bournemouth *(Loaned on 18/1/2000) FL
10/1 Others 1*

OSMAN Leon
Born: Billinge, 17 May 1981
Height: 5'8" **Weight:** 11.0
Club Honours: FAYC '98
International Honours: E: Yth; Sch
Leon made a surprise debut for Everton in
the game at Tottenham in January when
he filled a vacancy on the bench following
the withdrawal of Richard Wright shortly
before the start, and a further substitute
appearance followed in the home game
against Aston Villa. Prior to this Leon had
enjoyed a successful loan spell at Carlisle,
where he won a succession of 'Man of
the Match' awards. A nimble and skilful

John O'Shea

attacking midfield player who was a regular scorer for the reserve team, such was his form for the second string that there were many calls for David Moyes to install the talented youngster in the starting line-up.

Everton *(From trainee on 18/8/1998) PL 0+2*
Carlisle U *(Loaned on 4/10/2002) FL 10+2/1 Others 3/2*

OSTENSTAD Egil
Born: Haugesun, Norway, 2 January 1972
Height: 6'0'' **Weight:** 13.0
Club Honours: FLC '02
International Honours: Norway: 18; U21-27; Yth
Egil was very much a fringe player at Blackburn last season, although he enjoyed a brief spell of action in the weeks leading up to the turn of the year. He added determination to the Rovers' strike force and after scoring with a tap-in in the second leg of the UEFA Cup tie against CSKA Sofia he added a splendid goal against Tottenham and then helped set up Dwight Yorke for the winner at Highbury with some strong running and a judicious lay off.
Southampton *(£800,000 from Viking Stavanger, Norway on 3/10/1996) PL 80+16/28 FLC 9/3 FAC 3+1/2*
Blackburn Rov *(Signed on 18/8/1999) P/FL 38+24/12 FLC 4+5/1 FAC 4+3 Others 2+1/1*
Manchester C *(Loaned on 9/2/2001) PL 1+3*

OSTER John Morgan
Born: Boston, 8 December 1978
Height: 5'9'' **Weight:** 10.8
International Honours: W: 7; B-1; U21-9; Yth
A clever ball-playing winger, John spent much of the season away from Sunderland in two spells on loan at his former club Grimsby. His excellent form at Blundell Park prompted Howard Wilkinson to recall him in the new year and his first game at Manchester United saw the Black Cats lose to a last-minute goal. John made four further appearances, three of which saw Sunderland avoid defeat.
Grimsby T *(From trainee on 11/7/1996) FL 21+3/3 FAC 0+1/1*
Everton *(£1,500,000 on 21/7/1997) PL 22+18/1 FLC 4+1/1 FAC 2+3/1*
Sunderland *(£1,000,000 on 6/8/1999) PL 7+14 FLC 6+1/1 FAC 2+2*
Barnsley *(Loaned on 19/10/2001) FL 2*
Grimsby T *(Loaned on 1/11/2002) FL 10/5*
Grimsby T *(Loaned on 21/2/2003) FL 7/1*

OTSEMOBOR John
Born: Liverpool, 23 March 1983
Height: 5'10'' **Weight:** 12.7
International Honours: E: Yth

A young reserve-team central defender with Liverpool John made his senior debut in November in the Worthington Cup tie against Southampton. Later in the season he was loaned to Hull City to gain more first team experience, linking up with Peter Taylor who knew him from his days on the England coaching staff. Although more than capable of playing at centre back, the stylish defender prefers the right-back role that gives him the opportunity to use his pace and join in the play further forward. This was amply displayed at Hull where he scored three times, including a towering header on his debut at Rushden.
Liverpool *(From trainee on 23/3/2000) FLC 1*
Hull C *(Loaned on 13/3/2003) FL 8+1/3*

OUADDOU Abdeslam
Born: Morocco, 1 November 1978
Height: 6'3" **Weight:** 12.5
International Honours: Morocco:
Although Abdeslam was not a first choice he let no one down when called into the Fulham side. Comfortable with the ball both on the ground and in the air, most of his first-team appearances came in the opening half of the season in the right-back position where he proved an able deputy for Steve Finnan. Despite his lack of Premiership opportunities Abdeslam continued to appear regularly for Morocco throughout the season.
Fulham *(£2,000,000 from Nancy, France on 10/8/2001) PL 13+8 FLC 4 FAC 1+2 Others 10*

OVENDALE Mark John
Born: Leicester, 22 November 1973
Height: 6'2" **Weight:** 13.2
Mark had a disappointing season at Luton last term and managed only five starts in Second Division matches. He underwent a hip operation at the start of the campaign, which set him back, but even when fit he struggled to break into the team. However, when selected his concentration and experience never let him down. Mark is a clever 'keeper who is good on crosses and possesses excellent reflexes.
Northampton T *(Free from Wisbech on 15/8/1994) FL 6 Others 2 (Free to Barry T during 1995 close season)*
Bournemouth *(£30,000 on 14/5/1998) FL 89 FLC 10 FAC 7 Others 5*
Luton T *(£425,000 on 10/8/2000) FL 44+1 FLC 4 FAC 2 Others 4*

OWEN Michael James
Born: Chester, 14 December 1979
Height: 5'9" **Weight:** 11.2
Club Honours: FAYC '96; FLC '01, '03; FAC '01; UEFA '01; ESC '01; CS '01

International Honours: E: 38; U21-1; Yth; Sch
Michael was once again an automatic first choice as striker for Liverpool and England. He finished as top scorer for the Reds with 19 goals in the Premiership appearances and 28 in all competitions – excellent totals by any standards. Yet in many games he seemed an isolated figure in Liverpool's attack, waiting in vain for his team mates to provide him with an opening. He started the season slowly with a solitary goal to show from his first eight games, but then exploded with hat tricks against Manchester City and Spartak Moscow. However, he then had another barren spell, but towards the end of the season he was back to top form with a four-goal blast at West Bromwich Albion in April. Michael also found the net regularly for England, bringing his total of international goals to 20.
Liverpool *(From juniors on 18/12/1996) PL 164+23/102 FLC 12+2/9 FAC 11+1/7 Others 41+4/21*

OWUSU Lloyd Magnus
Born: Slough, 12 December 1976
Height: 6'1" **Weight:** 14.0
Club Honours: Div 3 '99
Much was expected of Lloyd at Sheffield Wednesday last term, however, illness delayed his start with the Owls and he never really recovered. The highlight of his season was in his first appearance as a substitute against Sheffield United, when he scored with his first touch of the ball and became an instant hero of the fans. Unfortunately, the big striker was unable to build on this and further injuries and illness meant he was never properly match fit long enough for a decent run in the team.
Brentford *(£25,000 from Slough T on 29/7/1998) FL 148+16/64 FLC 3+4/3 FAC 8/. Others 13+3/4*
Sheffield Wed *(Free on 8/7/2002) FL 12+20/4 FLC 1+1*

OYEN Davy
Born: Bilzen, Belgium, 17 July 1975
Height: 6'0" **Weight:** 12.4
International Honours: Belgium: 3
After a trial in December this experienced left back joined Nottingham Forest on a free transfer during the January transfer window. However, Davy failed to break into the first-team line-up and was restricted to a handful of outings from the substitutes' bench before being sidelined by a gastric stomach ulcer.
Nottingham F *(Free from Anderlecht, Belgium, ex KRC Genk, Paris St Germain, on 29/1/2003) FL 0+4*

P

ACKHAM William (Will)
Joseph
Born: Brighton, 13 January 1981
Height: 6'2" **Weight:** 13.0
This wiry custodian played just 63 minutes of senior football for Brighton in the 2002-03 season, coming on as a replacement for Michel Kuipers in an FA Cup tie at Norwich in January. A cheerful personality, he stuck to his task as back-up goalkeeper but must have been disappointed to see a succession of more experienced players brought in on loan or short-term contracts in the absence of Michel Kuipers.
Brighton & Hove A (From trainee on 9/6/1999) FL 1+1 FAC 1+1

PACQUETTE Richard Francis
Born: Paddington, 28 January 1983
Height: 6'0" **Weight:** 12.7
This powerful Queen's Park Rangers striker spent a period on loan at Conference side Stevenage Borough last season in order to gain some senior experience. On his return he played in the first team as a replacement for the injured Paul Furlong and scored three goals in four games. He was unfortunate to lose his place following this, although he regularly featured on the bench thereafter. The Supporters' Club members voted him as their 'Young Player of the Season'.
Queens Park R (From trainee on 1/2/2000) FL 13+16/6 FLC 1+1 FAC 0+1 Others 1+3

PADULA Diego **Gino** Mauro
Born: Buenos Aires, Argentina, 11 July 1976
Height: 5'9" **Weight:** 12.4
This left-sided defender joined Queen's Park Rangers in the summer of 2002, but was initially kept out of the side by Tommy Williams. However, once he made his first start he went on to make the left-wing-back position his own. Gino quickly became a favourite with the fans due to his speed, tackling and ability to produce dangerous cross, while his in-swinging corners resulted in a number of goals in the final weeks of the season.
Walsall (Free from Xerez, Spain, ex River Plate, Argentina, via trial at Bristol Rov, on 1/11/1999) FL 23+2 FAC 2
Wigan Ath (Free on 21/7/2000) FL 2+2 FLC +1 FAC 2
Queens Park R (Free on 8/7/2002) FL 17+4/1 FAC 1+1 Others 2+1

PAGE Robert John
Born: Llwynpia, 3 September 1974
Height: 6'0" **Weight:** 12.5
Club Honours: Div 2 '98
International Honours: W: 28; B-1; U21-6; Yth; Sch
Sheffield United's captain was injured in the season's first game and did not return until mid-September, but was then more or less a fixture in the side. He produced a series of reliable and impressive performances at the centre of defence, showing excellent anticipation and the ability to tackle under pressure. Commanding in the air in defence, he has still failed to find the net despite his presence in the opposition penalty area at set pieces. Robert remained a regular for Wales, although injury restricted his appearances.
Watford (From trainee on 19/4/1993) P/FL 209+7/2 FLC 17 FAC 12+1 Others 6/1
Sheffield U (£350,000 on 8/8/2001) FL 76+1 FLC 6 FAC 7 Others 3

PAHARS Marian
Born: Latvia, 5 August 1976
Height: 5'9" **Weight:** 10.9
International Honours: Latvia: 56
To say that 2002-03 was an unfortunate time for Marian would be something of an understatement. He had a hernia operation during the summer, and although he played the first three games of the campaign he never looked confident. He came on as a substitute and converted a penalty against Everton at St Mary's leading to a return to the starting line-up, but to no great effect and his season, thereafter, was a saga of illness and injury. His ability to run at and beat defenders, either head on or from the wing, and his aplomb in front of goal were both greatly missed. Marian finished the season recovering from another operation, which, it was reported, would prevent him from attending the FA Cup final even as a spectator!
Southampton (£800,000 from Skonto Riga, Latvia on 25/3/1999) PL 99+16/40 FLC 6+2/1 FAC 7/1

PALMER Carlton Lloyd
Born: Rowley Regis, 5 December 1965
Height: 6'2" **Weight:** 13.3
International Honours: E: 18; B-5; U21-4
The 2002-03 campaign proved to be a mixed season on the field for Stockport's player-manager. Several inspirational appearances at the heart of the County defence early in the campaign helped his team reach the play-off zone. However, as

the early promise faded, so did Carlton's form and after making his 711th senior appearance at Cheltenham, when he received a red card, he announced the end of his distinguished playing career to help him focus fully on his managerial role.
West Bromwich A (From apprentice on 21/12/1984) FL 114+7/4 FLC 7+1/1 FAC 4 Others 6
Sheffield Wed (£750,000 on 23/2/1989) F/PL 204+1/14 FLC 31/3 FAC 18+1/1 Others 8+1/1
Leeds U (£2,600,000 on 30/6/1994) PL 100+2/5 FLC 12 FAC 12/1 Others 4/1
Southampton (£1,000,000 on 26/9/1997) PL 44+1/3 FLC 5 FAC 2
Nottingham F (£1,100,000 on 21/11/1999) P/FL 14+2/1
Coventry C (£500,000 on 17/9/1999) PL 27+3/1 FLC 2 FAC 3
Watford (Loaned on 15/12/2000) FL 5
Sheffield Wed (Loaned on 13/2/2001) FL 12
Sheffield Wed (Loaned on 7/9/2001) FL 10
Stockport Co (Free on 13/11/2001) FL 44+1/4 FLC 2/1 FAC 2 Others 0+1

PALMER Stephen (Steve)
Leonard
Born: Brighton, 31 March 1968
Height: 6'1" **Weight:** 12.13
Club Honours: Div 2 '92, '98
International Honours: E: Sch
This versatile Queen's Park Rangers player started last season in the centre of defence but moved forward to a central-midfield role on Clark Carlisle's return to the side. Steve retained the club captaincy and although not a quick player he made up for his lack of pace by reading the game well and marshalling the players around him. He was again an ever-present during the campaign and also contributed a single goal.
Ipswich T (Signed from Cambridge University on 1/8/1989) F/PL 87+24/2 FLC 3 FAC 8+3/1 Others 4+2
Watford (£135,000 on 28/9/1995) P/FL 222+13/8 FLC 18+1/1 FAC 9+2 Others 7
Queens Park R (Free on 17/7/2001) FL 92/5 FLC 2 FAC 3 Others 5

PAPADOPOULOS Demitrios
(Demi)
Born: Kazakhstan, 20 September 1981
Height: 5'11" **Weight:** 10.8
International Honours: Greece: 1; U21
It looked like Demi had made his breakthrough at Burnley when he scored two goals in the Worthington Cup game against Blackpool after coming on from the bench. He was finally given a few league starts, but the success of the

Claret's regular strikers restricted his chances and he spent most of the season making cameo appearances as a substitute and rarely living up to that early promise. He did regain his place late on, but as part of a five-man midfield; his goal from the most acute of angles against Preston, however, was worth waiting for. Demi has pace to burn and is the type of forward who constantly harries defenders. He earned his first full cap for Greece and added to his international reputation with a hat-trick for the U21s.

Burnley (£500,000 from Akratitos, Greece on 25/7/2001) FL 7+33/3 FLC 1+4/3 FAC 1+2

PARKER Scott Matthew
Born: Lambeth, 13 October 1980
Height: 5'7" **Weight:** 10.7
Club Honours: Div 1 '00
International Honours: E: U21-11; Yth; Sch
Scott is undoubtedly one of the most influential and skilful players currently on the books at Charlton and his midfield partnership with Claus Jensen was among the best in the Premiership last term. He has an excellent touch, reads the game well and is a strong tackler. He is very self-assured with good vision, and distributes the ball well. Scott likes to get forward and scored four times, including twice in a 4-2 win over West Ham United at the Valley in January. He also netted a brilliant solo goal to earn victory at Leeds United and added a wonderful effort against Southampton in the penultimate home game of the season. Scott was deservedly voted as the supporters' 'Player of the Year' for 2002-03.

Charlton Ath (From trainee on 22/10/1997) P/FL 84+24/7 FLC 6+2 FAC 4+3
Norwich C (Loaned on 31/10/2000) FL 6/1

PARKER Sonny
Born: Middlesbrough, 28 February 1983
Height: 6'0" **Weight:** 11.12
International Honours: E; Yth
This young central defender initially joined Bristol Rovers on a non-contract basis after impressing in three reserve-team matches. He made his senior debut in Rovers' FA Cup replay at Rochdale, when he made a favourable impression, and retained his place to make his league debut at Cambridge. Following a switch to right back Sonny held down a place for the final 11 matches of the campaign and was selected by the club's supporters as the 'Young Player of the Season'.

Birmingham C (From trainee on 15/4/1999)
Bristol Rov (Free on 18/12/2002) FL 13+2 FAC 1

PARKER Wesley (Wes)
Born: Boston, 7 December 1983
Height: 5'8" **Weight:** 10.5
This Grimsby Town youngster impressed in the reserves last term and broke through to the fringes of the first team. A promising left-sided defender his opportunities were limited by the consistency of Tony Gallimore, but whenever called upon he did not let the side down. Wes will be looking to gain further experience of senior football in 2003-04.

Grimsby T (Trainee) FL 1+4 FAC 1

PARKIN Jonathan (Jon)
Born: Barnsley, 30 December 1981
Height: 6'4" **Weight:** 13.7
Jon became a firm favourite of the fans at Bootham Crescent last term, undoubtedly a result of the commitment he showed to the club. Although considered by some to be at his best in the centre of the defence he played much of the campaign up front for York where his physical presence and strength caused problems for the opposition. He finished with 11 goals to his credit including a brace in an early-season home win over Torquay. Amongst his other strikes were vital efforts in the

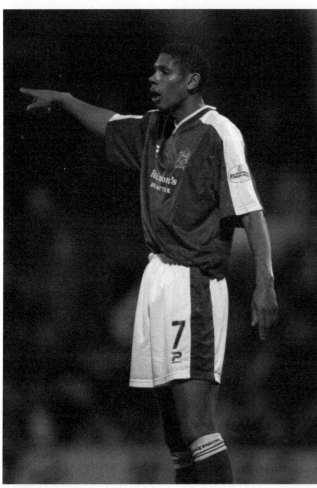

Carlton Palmer

ctories over Shrewsbury, Macclesfield,
eyton Orient and Bournemouth.
arnsley (From trainee on 5/1/1999) FL 8+2
.C 1+1 FAC 0+1
artlepool U (Loaned on 7/12/2001) FL 0+1
ork C (Free on 7/2/2002) FL 55+4/12 FAC 2
thers 1/1

PARKIN Samuel (Sam)
orn: Roehampton, 14 March 1981
eight: 6'2" **Weight:** 13.0
ternational Honours: E: Sch
super Sammy' more than repaid Swindon
own manager Andy King's faith in his
pility by netting 26 goals during the
002-03 campaign. Starting with a hat-
ick on his debut against Barnsley on the
pening day of the season, Sam was to
ecome a regular name on the score
eet throughout the season. Tall, useful
the air and with two good feet, he also
roved to be a cool and clinical finisher in
e box. Understandably he romped away

with the majority of trophies when the
club's 'Player of the Year' awards were
handed out.
Chelsea (From juniors on 21/8/1998)
Millwall (Loaned on 12/9/2000) FL 5+2/4
Wycombe W (Loaned on 24/11/2000) FL
5+3/1 FAC 0+3/1 Others 2/1
Oldham Ath (Loaned on 22/3/2001) FL
3+4/3
Northampton T (Loaned on 4/7/2001) FL
31+9/4 FLC 2/1 FAC 0+2 Others 2
Swindon T (Signed on 8/8/2002) FL 41+2/25
FLC 1 FAC 2 Others 1+1/1

PARKINSON Andrew (Andy)
John
Born: Liverpool, 27 May 1979
Height: 5'8" **Weight:** 10.12
Andy had a frustrating time with injuries
at Tranmere last term and as a result
managed just one start plus a further ten
appearances from the bench. He prefers
to play wide on the right and relishes

nothing more than using his speed to run
at opposing defenders. He was not
offered new terms by Rovers when his
contract expired.
Tranmere Rov (From trainee at Liverpool on
12/4/1997) FL 102+62/18 FLC 15+9/5 FAC
12+2/2 Others 1

PARKINSON Philip (Phil)
John
Born: Chorley, 1 December 1967
Height: 6'0" **Weight:** 12.8
Club Honours: Div 2 '94
A brief run of seven appearances, six of
them as substitute, at the start of the
season saw the curtain come down on
Phil Parkinson's long and distinguished
career as a Reading player. He played with
all his old fervour and commitment, but
now aged 35, it seemed his future lay on
the coaching side of the game. He had
been earmarked for such a role with
Reading, having already worked with the

cott Parker (right)

academy and reserve teams, but was suddenly offered the manager's job at Second Division Colchester United. Typically, he took on the challenge, won the divisional 'Manager of the Month' award in his first four weeks, and lifted the U's out of the relegation zone. He took with him the thanks and best wishes of a generation of Reading supporters.
Southampton *(From apprentice on 7/12/1985)*
Bury *(£12,000 on 8/3/1988) FL 133+12/5 FLC 6+1 FAC 4/1 Others 13/1*
Reading *(£37,500 on 10/7/1992) FL 332+30/20 FLC 28+1/3 FAC 21/1 Others 11+3*

Andy Parkinson

PARLOUR Raymond (Ray)
Born: Romford, 7 March 1973
Height: 5'10" **Weight:** 11.12
Club Honours: FLC '93; ECWC '94; PL '98, '02; FAC '93, '98, '02, '03; CS '98, '99, '02
International Honours: E: 10; B-1; U21-12
A series of niggling injuries and loss of form kept Ray out of the side for long periods, but despite this, he remained an extremely valuable member of the Arsenal squad. A powerful midfield player with tremendous energy and determination, he works box to box, tackles hard, and has a great right-foot shot, particularly from long range. Ray is also a great motivator on the field who involves team mates in all positions with his passing moves and forward surges.
Arsenal *(From trainee on 6/3/1991) F/PL 266+48/22 FLC 20+3 FAC 38+3/4 Others 40+11/6*

PARNABY Stuart
Born: Durham, 19 July 1982
Height: 5'11" **Weight:** 11.4
International Honours: E: U21-3; Yth; Sch
Stuart's 2001-02 season was virtually wiped out through injury but he came back with a bang last term. The player, who can operate in defence or midfield, became a permanent choice in the right-back berth for Middlesbrough in October after first choice Robbie Stockdale was sidelined with a foot injury. However, after five months of regular Premiership football Stuart sustained a torn ligament in Boro's 3-2 win at Leeds. He ended the season by playing in the final two Premiership games and also starred for England U21s in the 3-2 victory over Serbia & Montenegro.
Middlesbrough *(From trainee on 21/7/1999) PL 21 FLC 2 FAC 1*
Halifax T *(Loaned on 23/10/2000) FL 6*

PARRISH Sean
Born: Wrexham, 14 March 1972
Height: 5'10" **Weight:** 11.8
Sean arrived at Kidderminster on a free transfer in the summer of 2002 and brought with him the experience of previous successful promotion campaigns. With competition for places in the Harriers' midfield tough he often found himself on the sidelines, particularly after injury knocked him back when he had begun to establish himself in the team. One of the highlights of his season was the long-range goal that he scored against Wrexham at the Racecourse Ground just before Christmas.
Shrewsbury T *(From trainee on 12/7/1990) FL 1+2 FLC 1 Others 3 (Free to Telford during 1992 close season)*
Doncaster Rov *(£20,000 on 28/5/1994) FL 64+2/8 FLC 3+1 FAC 2 Others 3*
Northampton T *(£35,000 + on 2/8/1996) FL 103+6/13 FLC 8/1 FAC 2 Others 5/2*
Chesterfield *(Free on 19/7/2000) FL 44+11/11 FLC 4/1 FAC 4 Others 4+1*
Kidderminster Hrs *(Free on 8/7/2002) FL 21+8/5 FLC 1 FAC 2 Others 2+1*

PARTON Andrew (Andy)
Born: Doncaster, 29 September 1983
Height: 5'10" **Weight:** 11.12
An impressive pre-season at Scunthorpe

st term put young striker Andy in line
or the opening day starting line-up
before an ankle ligament injury ruled him
out for a month. He never made the first
even after that and was restricted to 12
substitute appearances during the
campaign. A very fast, direct player with a
good left foot, he can operate on either
flank or down the middle.
*Scunthorpe U (Trainee) FL 1+8 FLC 0+1 FAC
1+2 Others 0+1*

PARTRIDGE Richard (Richie)
Joseph
Born: Dublin, 12 September 1980
Height: 5'8" **Weight:** 10.10
International Honours: RoI: U21-8; Yth
UEFA-U18 '98)
The Liverpool winger joined Coventry on
month's loan last September and made
an immediate impression with his electric
pace, direct running and teasing crosses.
His stunning 30-yard goal against
Norwich in his fifth appearance won the
fans over and he went on to net with
another thunderbolt against Reading at
Christmas, while against Leicester he had
a golden 15 minutes when he left the
opposition defence in tatters and could
have scored three. Richie returned to
Anfield in March after an injury curtailed
his loan period. Although he has yet to
win his first full cap for the Republic of
Ireland he appeared in the squad for the
friendly against Greece in November.
*Liverpool (From trainee on 16/9/1997) FLC 1
Bristol Rov (Loaned on 22/3/2001) FL 4+2/1
Coventry C (Loaned on 27/9/2002) FL
3+4/4 FLC 2 FAC 2*

PARTRIDGE Scott Malcolm
Born: Leicester, 13 October 1974
Height: 5'9" **Weight:** 11.2
Club Honours: Div 3 '99
The diminutive striker rarely featured for
Rushden last term and in January he was
loaned out to Exeter City. Scott did well at
St James' Park, and created a small piece
of history by becoming the first away
player to score at Hull City's new Kingston
Communications Stadium. However, he
turned down the chance to return to
Devon and then moved on to Shrewsbury
Town. Mostly used as a deputy for Luke
Rodgers at Gay Meadow, he made little
impact in a struggling side and was
unable to prevent him from being
relegated to the Conference.
*Bradford C (From trainee on 10/7/1992) FL
1+5 FLC 1+1
Bristol C (Free on 18/2/1994) FL 24+33/7 FLC
3+3/1 FAC 1+3
Torquay U (Loaned on 13/10/1995) FL 5/2*

*Plymouth Arg (Loaned on 22/1/1996) FL
6+1/2
Scarborough (Loaned on 8/3/1996) FL 5+2
Cardiff C (£50,000 on 14/2/1997) FL 29+8/2
FLC 2 FAC 2 Others 1
Torquay U (Signed on 26/3/1998) FL
33+1/12 FLC 2 FAC 2/1 Others 2/1
Brentford (£100,000 on 19/2/1999) FL
79+13/21 FLC 3+3 FAC 2+1 Others 7+1/2
Rushden & Diamonds (Free on 13/9/2001)
FL 28+16/5 FLC 1+1 FAC 2+1 Others 3
Exeter C (Loaned on 31/12/2002) FL 2+2/2
Shrewsbury T (Free on 27/3/2003) FL 2+2*

PATTERSON Mark
Born: Leeds, 13 September 1968
Height: 5'10" **Weight:** 12.4
After 18 years in the professional game,
Mark finally called it a day last November,
after making just three first-team
appearances for Gillingham during the
season. The experienced right back picked
up a knee injury in training during
September and, faced with the option of
surgery, opted to bring his full-time career
to a close. Mark subsequently signed for
Dover Athletic and helped them to third
place in the Premier Division of the Dr
Martens League.
*Carlisle U (From trainee on 30/8/1986) FL
19+3 FLC 4 Others 1
Derby Co (£60,000 on 10/11/1987) FL
41+10/3 FLC 5+2 FAC 4 Others 5+1/2
Plymouth Arg (£85,000 on 23/7/1993) FL
131+3/3 FLC 3 FAC 8 Others 9
Gillingham (£45,000 on 30/10/1997) FL
118+6/2 FLC 9+1 FAC 5+2 Others 4*

PATTERSON Rory Christopher
Born: Derry, 16 July 1984
Height: 5'10" **Weight:** 10.13
Another one off Rochdale's conveyor belt
of Irish talent, Rory had played in a pre-
season friendly immediately after arriving
in 2001, and made his first senior
appearance as a substitute in an LDV
Trophy game in October 2002. A striker
or wide player, and a regular scorer for
the reserves, Rory went on to make his
league debut, also as substitute, shortly
afterwards and had several more brief
outings before his first full game – on the
right of midfield – in the excellent 2-2
draw at Hartlepool last April.
Rochdale (Trainee) FL 2+6 Others 0+1

PAYNE Stephen (Steve) John
Born: Pontefract, 1 August 1975
Height: 5'11" **Weight:** 12.5
Club Honours: GMVC '95, '97; FAT '96
International Honours: E: SP-1
Steve missed important parts of the 2002-
03 season through injury but was

nevertheless a reliable and consistent
performer for Chesterfield. As team
captain he marshalled the younger players
around him well, and put in good
performances of his own in his usual
unflappable fashion, often at centre back
but also on the right-hand side of
defence, where his long throw proved to
be a useful attacking weapon.
*Huddersfield T (From trainee on 12/7/1993)
Macclesfield T (Free on 23/12/1994) FL
71+6/2 FLC 6 FAC 6 Others 2
Chesterfield (Signed on 8/7/1999) FL
126+5/7 FLC 4+1 FAC 3 Others 7+2/2*

PAYNTER Owen
Born: Newmarket, 22 October 1982
Height: 5'8" **Weight:** 11.7
A product of the Cambridge United youth
system, Owen made his one and only
first-team appearance as a substitute in
the LDV Vans Trophy game at
Northampton. The young midfielder had
earlier spent time on loan at Ryman
League club Enfield. He was released by
the U's before the end of the season and
later played for Cambridge City and
Mildenhall Town.
*Cambridge U (From trainee on 20/3/2002)
Others 0+1*

PAYNTER William (Billy) Paul
Born: Liverpool, 13 July 1984
Height: 6'1" **Weight:** 12.0
A Scouse teenage goal-scorer who
supports Everton and wears the number
18 shirt? No, not Wayne Rooney but a
promising striker with Port Vale, who,
when he scored his first goal against
Notts County, became the club's youngest
scorer for 24 years. Billy netted three
times in his next five games, but after
Brett Angell departed he lost his way a
bit. After Christmas he was used mainly
as a substitute but he still won the club's
'Young Player of the Year' award.
*Port Vale (From trainee on 1/7/2002) FL
18+21/5 FAC 0+2 Others 2*

PAYTON Andrew (Andy) Paul
Born: Whalley, 23 October 1967
Height: 5'9" **Weight:** 11.13
Two brief appearances from the bench,
plus a farewell pre-match lap of honour
following the announcement of his
departure from Turf Moor, were all that
Burnley supporters saw of the 'Padiham
Predator' last time round. With goal-
scoring rarely a problem and younger
players there to do it, Andy was always
going to be on the fringes, but his
contribution to his home town club will
long be remembered.

*Hull C (From apprentice on 29/7/1985) FL
116+27/55 FLC 9+2/1 FAC 8 Others 3/1*
***Middlesbrough** (£750,000 on 22/11/1991)
FL 8+11/3 FAC 1+3*
***Glasgow Celtic** (Signed on 14/8/1992) SL
20+16/15 SLC 3+2/5 SC 1+1 Others 3*
***Barnsley** (Signed on 25/11/1993) FL
100+8/41 FLC 7/3 FAC 6+1/1*
***Huddersfield T** (£350,000 on 4/7/1996) FL
42+1/17 FLC 7/3 FAC 2*
***Burnley** (Signed on 16/1/1998) FL
115+41/68 FLC 4+2/6 FAC 6+2/3 Others 6/3*
***Blackpool** (Loaned on 6/12/2001) FL 4/1*

PEACOCK Lee Anthony
Born: Paisley, 9 October 1976
Height: 6'0" **Weight:** 12.8
Club Honours: AMC '97, '03
International Honours: S; U21-1; Yth
This well built striker suffered from
injury problems at Bristol City last term
and had a somewhat disappointing
season, despite netting a double-figure
tally of goals. With the end of Mark
Robins' loan spell, Lee was seen as the
key to City's promotion aspirations.
Unfortunately he failed to reproduce the
form that persuaded manager Danny
Wilson to stump up a substantial fee
some three years ago.
***Carlisle U** (From trainee on 10/3/1995) FL
52+24/11 FLC 2+3 FAC 4+1/1 Others 6+4*
***Mansfield T** (£90,000 on 17/10/1997) FL
79+10/29 FLC 4/1 FAC 4 Others 4/2*
***Manchester C** (£500,000 on 5/11/1999) FL
4+4 FAC 1+1*
***Bristol C** (£600,000 on 10/8/2000) FL
92+11/40 FLC 2/1 FAC 8/1 Others 13/5*

PEAD Craig George
Born: Bromsgrove, 15 September 1981
Height: 5'9" **Weight:** 11.6
International Honours: E: Yth
A former star of Coventry City's youth
team, Craig finally overcame a lengthy
run of injuries to make a strong
impression at senior level in 2002-03.
After a couple of substitute
appearances early in the season but in
dropped back to the reserves but in
December came back into the side. His
buzzing style allied to his good
footwork and tenacity impressed the
fans and he filled the problem right-
flank role well. He was a regular first-
team player for the remainder of the
season and scored twice in the 2-2
draw at Preston, his first goals at senior
level for the Sky Blues.
***Coventry C** (From trainee on 17/9/1998) FL
18+7/2 FAC 2*

PEARCE Allan David
Born: Wellington, New Zealand, 7 April
1983
Height: 5'10" **Weight:** 11.5
International Honours: New Zealand: Yth
This nippy striker broke into Lincoln's first-
team squad after impressing in reserve
football. He netted an excellent goal on
his first start to set up a 3-0 home win
over Hartlepool United. Allan's pace and
persistence troubled opposing defences
but after a run of appearances he finished
the campaign back on the substitutes'
bench.
***Lincoln C** (Free from trainee at Barnsley on
25/10/2002) FL 9+7/1*

PEARCE Dennis Anthony
Born: Wolverhampton, 10 September
1974
Height: 5'10" **Weight:** 11.0
Club Honours: Div 3 '98
Dennis made the starting line-up for
Peterborough on just three occasions in
2002-03, all in the early part of the
season. A series of injuries then kept him
on the sidelines and it was not until the
closing stages that he returned to action
with the reserves. When fully fit Dennis is
a dependable full back who is
comfortable on the ball.
***Aston Villa** (From trainee on 7/6/1993)*
***Wolverhampton W** (Free on 3/7/1995) FL
7+2 FLC 1 FAC 1*
***Notts Co** (Free on 21/7/1997) FL 108+10/3
FLC 7+1 FAC 12+1 Others 3*
***Peterborough U** (Free on 10/5/2001) FL
10+1 FLC 1 FAC 1*

PEARCE Ian Anthony
Born: Bury St Edmunds, 7 May 1974
Height: 6'3" **Weight:** 14.4
Club Honours: PL '95
International Honours: E: U21-3; Yth
Ian featured regularly for West Ham last
term but was unable to prevent the club
from being relegated from the
Premiership. Primarily a central defender
he goes about his job admirably, shoring
up the back line and proving effective in
the air. Injuries at Upton Park meant that
he was required to show a degree of
adaptability during the season, firstly
playing at right back and then in
December taking a turn in the forward
line, from where he scored vital goals
against Middlesbrough and Bolton.
***Chelsea** (From juniors on 1/8/1991) F/PL 0+4
Others 0+1*
***Blackburn Rov** (£300,000 on 4/10/1993) PL
43+19/2 FLC 4+4/1 FAC 1+2 Others 6+1*
***West Ham U** (£1,600,000 + on 19/9/1997)
PL 111+7/8 FLC 7 FAC 9+1/1 Others 1+1*

PEARSON Gary
Born: Seaham, 7 December 1976
Height: 5'10" **Weight:** 12.5
This strong-tackling central defender
enjoyed a run in the Darlington line-up
during the final third of the season after
struggling with injury problems earlier.
Gary's robust tackling and committed play
certainly bolstered the defence when it
needed it and he produced one of his
thunderbolt shots from well outside the
box to score against Shrewsbury in April.
***Sheffield U** (From trainee on 3/7/1995. Free
to Stalybridge Celtic on 22/3/1996)*
***Darlington** (Signed from Durham C, ex
Gateshead, Spennymoor U, Seaham RS,
Whitby T, on 8/8/2001) FL 28+2/2 FAC 0+2
Others 1*

PEAT Nathan Neil Martin
Born: Hull, 19 September 1982
Height: 5'9" **Weight:** 10.9
After waiting patiently since breaking into
the Hull first-team squad in December
1999, Nathan finally made his senior
debut when coming on as a substitute in
City's first win of the season at
Cambridge in September. As well as
several appearances on the Tigers bench,
the combative left-sided midfielder also
played for the full 90 minutes of the LDV
Vans Trophy tie at Port Vale in October
and the second half of the FA Cup game
against Macclesfield in November. Nathan
was a regular for the City reserves side
that clinched the Avon Insurance League
Division One East championship in 2002-
03. He was awarded a further year's
contract in April.
***Hull C** (From trainee on 11/7/2002) FL 0+1
FAC 0+1 Others 1*

PEDERSEN Henrik
Born: Denmark, 10 June 1975
Height: 6'1" **Weight:** 13.5
International Honours: Denmark: 1
Henrik made occasional appearances for
Bolton during the first three months of
the 2002-03 season, seemingly
competing with Dean Holdsworth and
Michael Ricketts for a first-team spot.
However, he made a tremendous impact
in the 4-2 victory at Leeds in November,
scoring two goals in a 'Man of the Match'
display. He retained his place in the
starting line-up for the rest of the season,
finishing as the club's joint-top scorer on
seven goals. A hard-working centre
forward, Henrik eventually won over the
fans with some gutsy and tireless displays.
***Bolton W** (£650,000 from Silkeborg,
Denmark on 11/7/2001) PL 36+8/7 FLC 1+2/
FAC 2/1*

PEJIC Shaun Melvyn
Born: Hereford, 16 November 1982
Height: 6'1" **Weight:** 12.3
International Honours: W: U21-3; Yth
A hamstring problem and competition for the central defensive positions curtailed Shaun's involvement for Wrexham after he had been an ever-present up until the turn of the year. The talented central defender has bags of potential and this was recognised when he was called up to the Wales U21 squad during the campaign.
Wrexham (From trainee on 9/8/2002) FL 5+5 FLC 2 FAC 1 Others 2

PELZER Marc Sebastian
Born: Trier, Germany, 24 September 1980
Height: 5'9" **Weight:** 12.8
This young left-sided defender joined Blackburn in the summer of 2002 following an impressive trial, but struggled with hamstring injuries and spent most of last season in the reserve team. His only senior opportunity came in the Worthington Cup third round tie against Walsall when he made the starting line-up but lasted just 30 minutes before injury struck.
Blackburn Rov (£375,000 from Kaiserslautern, Germany on 30/7/2002) FLC 1

PEMBERTON Martin Calvin
Born: Bradford, 1 February 1976
Height: 5'11" **Weight:** 12.6
Last term certainly wasn't the easiest of seasons for this former Mansfield player who found himself challenging Kevin Ellison and Andy Welsh for a place on the left-hand side of the Stockport County midfield. However, although niggling injuries prevented him consolidating a regular place in the line-up Martin made a total of 20 appearances in Second Division games spread over the whole season.
Oldham Ath (From trainee on 22/7/1994) FL 4+5 FLC 0+1 Others 0+1
Doncaster Rov (Free on 21/3/1997) FL 3+2/2 FLC 3+3
Scunthorpe U (Free on 26/3/1998) FL 3+3
Hartlepool U (Free on 3/7/1998) FL 0+4 FLC 0+1 (Free to Harrogate T on 30/9/1998)
Mansfield T (£10,000 + from Bradford PA on 3/8/2000) FL 49+7/5 FLC 1 FAC 2+1 Others 2
Stockport Co (Free on 30/4/2002) FL 15+5 FLC 1+1

PEMBRIDGE Mark Anthony
Born: Merthyr Tydfil, 29 November 1970
Height: 5'8" **Weight:** 12.0
International Honours: W: 48; B-2; U21-1; Sch

Mark provided an industrious and versatile presence in the Everton and Wales midfield in 2002-03. Employed exclusively on the left-hand side of the midfield for his club, he took the 'holding' role in front of the back four for his country. He played a lead part in the Red Dragons' rise under Mark Hughes and had one of the best games of his career in the win over Italy in October 2002. Problems with a calf injury picked up in November meant he could not build on his early season form and he made only five league appearances in the New Year. Mark is a keen competitor and his delivery from the left hand side is consistently under-rated.
Luton T (From trainee on 1/7/1989) FL 60/6 FLC 2 FAC 4 Others 4
Derby Co (£1,250,000 on 2/6/1992) FL 108+2/28 FLC 9/1 FAC 6/3 Others 15/5
Sheffield Wed (£900,000 on 19/7/1995) PL 88+5/11 FLC 6/1 FAC 7/1 Others 1 (Free to Benfica, Portugal on 1/7/1998)
Everton (£800,000 on 6/8/1999) PL 78+9/4 FLC 1 FAC 8+1

PENFORD Thomas (Tom) James
Born: Leeds, 5 January 1985
Height: 5'10" **Weight:** 11.3
Tom made his senior debut for Bradford City as a second-year scholar when he came on for Gus Uhlenbeek at Deepdale last April. He went on to feature from the substitutes' bench in the remaining two games of the season after the Bantams had secured their First Division status. A talented midfield player who can deliver a good cross, he has the confidence to take on defenders and will hope to make more appearances for the club in the 2003-04 campaign.
Bradford C (Trainee) FL 0+3

PENNANT Jermaine
Born: Nottingham, 15 January 1983
Height: 5'6" **Weight:** 10.0
Club Honours: FAYC '00, '01
International Honours: E: U21-17; Yth; Sch
Jermaine returned to Watford for a second loan spell from Arsenal last November. A wide-right player with the ability to beat defenders, he looked stronger than on his previous stay at Vicarage Road and brought some welcome flair to the team. After returning to Highbury in February he showed excellent form in the reserves and when given his first-team chance against Southampton in the closing stages of the campaign he netted a sensational hat-

trick in the Gunners' 6-1 victory. An England U21 international, Jermaine is intelligent, skilful and a good interceptor of the ball.
Notts Co (Associated Schoolboy) FAC 0+1 Others 0+1
Arsenal (From trainee on 16/3/2000, having been signed for £1,500,000 on 14/1/1999) PL 1+4/3 FLC 5+1 Others 0+1
Watford (Loaned on 10/1/2002) FL 9/2
Watford (Loaned on 15/11/2002) FL 12 FAC 2/1

PENNOCK Adrian Barry
Born: Ipswich, 27 March 1971
Height: 6'1" **Weight:** 13.5
After some time attempting to get back to full fitness following a serious knee injury, Adrian decided to announce his retirement from the full-time game last January. He received a fantastic send off from the Gillingham faithful before the home game against Leicester and subsequently joined Gravesend & Northfleet of the Conference. The experienced central defender had made over 300 senior appearances since beginning his career at Norwich almost 15 years previously.
Norwich C (From trainee on 4/7/1989) FL 1
Bournemouth (£30,000 on 4/8/1992) FL 130+1/9 FLC 9 FAC 12/1 Others 8
Gillingham (£30,000 on 4/10/1996) FL 164+4/2 FLC 9 FAC 11/1 Others 11/1

PERICARD Vincent de Paul
Born: Efok, Cameroon, 3 October 1982
Height: 6'1" **Weight:** 13.8
Club Honours: Div 1 '03
This promising young striker joined Portsmouth in a 12-month loan deal to cover the whole of the 2002-03 campaign. He was initially a little slow to adjust to Nationwide League football, but as the season progressed he began to cause more problems for opposition defences. Perhaps his best performance was against Reading, when he scored twice, but his overall tally of ten goals from 19 starts was a very creditable figure. The pacy front man was eventually sidelined by a knee injury.
Portsmouth (Loaned from Juventus, Italy on 22/7/2002) FL 18+14/9 FLC 1+1/1 FAC 0+1

PERPETUINI David Peter
Born: Hitchin, 26 September 1979
Height: 5'8" **Weight:** 10.8
This promising left-sided player broke through to win a regular place in the Gillingham line-up from September to November, but then had to settle for a position on the bench for the rest of the

term. Naturally left-footed, a scarce commodity with the Gills, he will be looking for regular first-team football in 2003-04.

Watford (From trainee on 3/7/1997) P/FL 17+2/1 FLC 1+1

Gillingham (£100,000 on 9/8/2001) FL 38+25/3 FLC 3+2 FAC 4

PERRETT Russell (Russ)
Born: Barton on Sea, 18 June 1973
Height: 6'3" **Weight:** 13.2
Russ spent much of the 2002-03 season out injured and it is arguable that if he had remained fit throughout the season then Luton would have reached the Second Division play-offs. Russ is a classy defender, with good positional sense, a strong tackler, and excellent in the air. He forged a useful central defensive partnership with Chris Coyne during the campaign.

Portsmouth (Signed from Lymington on 30/9/1995) FL 66+6/2 FLC 5 FAC 4

Cardiff C (£10,000 on 21/7/1999) FL 28+1/1 FAC 5/1 Others 1

Luton T (Free on 10/8/2001) FL 58+2/5 FLC 3 FAC 1

PERRY Christopher (Chris)
John
Born: Carshalton, 26 April 1973
Height: 5'8" **Weight:** 11.1
Chris is a traditional defender in every sense: strong, good in the air and with great tenacity in the challenge. However, his campaign was hindered by an early-season injury picked up against West Ham in September. Although he went on to make 17 starts in the Tottenham first team, Chris will be disappointed that recurring injury problems prevented him from becoming a regular in the line-up.

Wimbledon (From trainee on 2/7/1991) PL 158+9/2 FLC 21 FAC 24/1

Tottenham H (£4,000,000 on 7/7/1999) PL 111+9/3 FLC 13 FAC 9 Others 4/1

PESCHISOLIDO Paolo (Paul)
Pasquale
Born: Scarborough, Canada, 25 May 1971
Height: 5'7" **Weight:** 10.12
Club Honours: Div 2 '99
International Honours: Canada: 45; U23-11
A previous toe injury delayed the start of Paul's season with Sheffield United and an achilles injury followed. By December he was a regular member of the squad, generally on the bench, coming on in his customary striking role, and showing anticipation and an eye for goal. Most of

his seven goals came late including a brace against Crystal Palace to put United into the Worthington Cup semi-final, a superb volley against Wolves and a vital effort against Nottingham Forest in the play-off semi-final.

Birmingham C (£25,000 from Toronto Blizzards, Canada on 11/11/1992) FL 37+6/16 FLC 2/1 FAC 0+1 Others 1+1

Stoke C (£400,000 on 1/8/1994) FL 59+7/19 FLC 6/3 FAC 3 Others 5+1/2

Birmingham C (£400,000 on 29/3/1996) FL 7+2/1

West Bromwich A (£600,000 on 24/7/1996) FL 36+9/18 FLC 4+1/3 FAC 1

Fulham (£1,100,000 on 24/10/1997) FL 69+26/24 FLC 7+1/4 FAC 9+1/2 Others 2

Queens Park R (Loaned on 3/11/2000) FL 5/1

Sheffield U (Loaned on 19/1/2001) FL 4+1/2

Norwich C (Loaned on 22/3/2001) FL 3+2

Sheffield U (£150,000 + on 10/7/2001) FL 23+29/9 FLC 3+4/2 FAC 1+3/1 Others 0+2/1

PETERS Mark
Born: Flint, 6 July 1972
Height: 6'0" **Weight:** 11.8
Club Honours: NC '01; Div 3 '03
Mark featured in every match for Rushden & Diamonds from September to February but then lost his place after the 2-2 draw at Darlington. His no-nonsense approach to defending helped Brian Talbot's team to stay near the top of the Third Division table from the start of the season. However Talbot decided to sign Peterborough United's Andy Edwards and an 11-match unbeaten run without Mark in the starting line-up clinched the championship, forcing the Welshman to reconsider his future at Nene Park.

Manchester C (From trainee on 5/7/1990)

Norwich C (Free on 2/9/1992)

Peterborough U (Free on 10/8/1993) FL 17+2 FLC 2 Others 2

Mansfield T (Free on 30/9/1994) FL 107+1/9 FLC 5/1 FAC 8 Others 7

Rushden & Diamonds (Free on 3/7/1999) FL 65+2/1 FLC 4/1 FAC 5 Others 5

PETERS Mark William
Born: Frimley, 4 October 1983
Height: 5'8" **Weight:** 10.10
This diminutive young Brentford striker made a few appearances from the substitutes' bench last term, before eventually making his first start against Queen's Park Rangers in April. Mark responded superbly, netting his first goal when coolly shooting home.

Southampton (From trainee on 4/10/2000)

Brentford (Free on 18/2/2002) FL 3+8/1 FAC 0+1

PETHICK Robert (Robbie)
John
Born: Tavistock, 8 September 1970
Height: 5'10" **Weight:** 11.12
Club Honours: Div 2 '02
A versatile performer, Robbie turned out principally as a central defender for Brighton in 2002-03, although he also made five appearances at right back. However, his season was disrupted firstly by a broken foot and then by an awkward back problem, and he was unable to regain his place in the side thereafter. While still needing to work on his positional play he is blessed with a thunderbolt shot. Robbie filled in well at the start of the campaign as an emergency centre half and January he was rewarded with his first goal for the Seagulls in the FA Cup tie at Norwich.

Portsmouth (£30,000 from Weymouth on 1/10/1993) FL 157+32/3 FLC 13+3 FAC 9 Others 3+1

Bristol Rov (£15,000 on 19/2/1999) FL 60+3/2 FLC 5 FAC 1 Others 2+1

Brighton & Hove A (Free on 10/7/2001) FL 38+12 FLC 1+1 FAC 2/1 Others 3

PETIT Emmanuel (Manu)
Born: Dieppe, France, 22 September 1970
Height: 6'1" **Weight:** 12.8
Club Honours: PL '98; FAC '98; CS '98, '99
International Honours: France: 63 (WC '98, UEFA '00)
The tough-tackling French international midfielder shrugged aside the disappointment of the World Cup to produce a consistent season for Chelsea as they chased a Champions' League spot. Although niggling calf and groin injuries interrupted his campaign, he was a pivotal figure in the Blues' midfield, winning the ball with crunching tackles and laying it off with diligent passing. Manu's central-midfield partnership with Frank Lampard was a crucial factor in the team's successful season. He managed to grab two important goals, the first being a superb half volley on the turn against Everton in the Worthington Cup and the second at his former club Arsenal. Still an integral member of the French national side, Manu has won over the sceptical elements of the Chelsea crowd with his whole-hearted approach and played no small part in the Blues' Champions' League qualification.

Arsenal (£3,500,000 from AS Monaco, France, ex ES Argues, on 25/6/1997) PL 82+3/9 FLC 3 FAC 13/2 Others 16+1 (£15,000,000 to Barcelona, Spain on 28/7/2000)

Chelsea (£7,500,000 on 23/7/2001) PL 9+2/2 FLC 3/1 FAC 11 Others 4

PETRESCU Tomi Christian
Born: Jyvaskyla, Finland, 24 July 1986
Height: 5'9" **Weight:** 10.3
International Honours: Finland: Yth
Tomi is a highly rated academy prospect
with Leicester City who can operate
effectively both on the right of midfield or
as a striker. Signed as a schoolboy
following a scouting trip to Finland, he
was called up for his debut aged 16 years
284 days, the club's fourth youngest-ever
player, at Molineux on the closing day of
the season. He came on as a substitute
for Brian Deane and acquitted himself
with confidence.
Leicester C (Trainee) FL 0+1

PETTEFER Carl James
Born: Burnham, 22 March 1981
Height: 5'7" **Weight:** 10.5
This talented Portsmouth youngster joined
Exeter City on loan last October and
stayed until the end of the season. He
made the left-hand midfield position his
own as the middle berths were chopped
and changed around him. Carl is sharp
and pacy, and scored his first goal in
senior football at Darlington in March.
*Portsmouth (From trainee on 23/11/1998) FL
0+2*
*Exeter C (Loaned on 21/10/2002) FL 30+1/1
FAC 4 Others 2*

PETTERSON Andrew (Andy)
Keith
Born: Freemantle, Australia, 29
September 1969
Height: 6'2" **Weight:** 14.7
Arriving in Brighton in pre-season when
both Michel Kuipers and regular back-up
Will Packham were injured, this
experienced goalkeeper became a first-
team regular during the early part of the
2002-03 campaign. Initially on a monthly
contract, he was signed for a second time
(with a different squad number!) when
Will Packham succumbed to injury, and
made a brief appearance against Bradford
City, coming on at the end of the game
to face a penalty after Michel Kuipers was
sent off. Andy subsequently had a brief
spell at Bournemouth, where he featured
as an unused substitute, before joining
League of Ireland outfit Derry City.
*Luton T (Signed from East Freemantle,
Australia on 30/12/1988) FL 16+3 FLC 2
Others 2*
Ipswich T (Loaned on 26/3/1993) PL 1
*Charlton Ath (£85,000 on 15/7/1994) P/FL
68+4 FLC 6 FAC 3 Others 4*

Bradford C (Loaned on 8/12/1994) FL 3
Ipswich T (Loaned on 26/9/1995) FL 1
Plymouth Arg (Loaned on 19/1/1996) FL 6
Colchester U (Loaned on 8/3/1996) FL 5
Portsmouth (Loaned on 13/11/1998) FL 13
Portsmouth (Free on 5/7/1999) FL 19 FLC 1+1
Torquay U (Loaned on 15/3/2001) FL 6
West Bromwich A (Free on 26/3/2002)
*Brighton & Hove A (Free on 9/8/2002) FL
6+1 FLC 2*
Bournemouth (Free on 23/12/2002)

PETTINGER Paul Alan
Born: Sheffield, 1 October 1975
Height: 6'1" **Weight:** 13.7
Club Honours: FAYC '93

International Honours: E: Yth; Sch
The form of first choice 'keeper Alan
Marriott kept Paul out of Lincoln's 2002-
03 league campaign. His only senior
appearances were in the LDV Vans Trophy
and following a spell on loan at
Conference club Telford United he joined
Gainsborough Trinity in February.
Leeds U (From trainee on 16/10/1992)
Torquay U (Loaned on 23/12/1994) FL 3
Rotherham U (Loaned on 11/8/1995) FL 0+1
Gillingham (Free on 28/3/1996)
Carlisle U (Free on 2/8/1996)
*Rotherham U (Free on 1/8/1997) FL 16 FLC
2 Others 1*
Lincoln C (Free on 11/7/2001) FL 3 Others 0+2

Carl Pettefer

PETTY Benjamin (Ben) James
Born: Solihull, 22 March 1977
Height: 6'0" **Weight:** 12.5
Club Honours: AMC '00
After featuring for Hull in the games against Bury and Hartlepool in the early weeks of the season, Ben soon fell out of the first-team picture under manager Jan Molby. In a bid to boost his confidence, the right-footed versatile defender or midfielder went out on loan to Moor Green. A change of manager at Hull failed to improve his fortunes, and Ben's contract was cancelled by mutual consent in December. He returned to the Midlands and joined the Dr Martens Premier League club Stafford Rangers before finishing the season in the Conference with Burton Albion.
Aston Villa (From trainee on 10/5/1995)
Stoke C (Free on 27/11/1998) FL 26+20 FLC 4+1 FAC 3 Others 7+4/1
Hull C (Free on 18/7/2001) FL 24+5 FLC 1+1 FAC 2 Others 3

PHILLIPS Gareth Russell
Born: Pontypridd, 19 August 1979
Height: 5'8" **Weight:** 9.8
International Honours: W: U21-3; Yth; Sch
Gareth started the season in the midfield engine room for Swansea, but was taken off at half time at Bury with a dead leg. He was then regularly included in first-team games either in the centre of midfield, or at right wing back. However, perhaps his best performance was as a substitute against Oxford United at the Vetch Field when he replaced Leon Britton early on in the match.
Swansea C (From trainee on 9/7/1998) FL 59+29/2 FLC 2+1 FAC 1+2 Others 2

PHILLIPS Kevin Mark
Born: Hitchin, 25 July 1973
Height: 5'7" **Weight:** 11.0
Club Honours: Div 1 '99
International Honours: E: 8; B-1
Sunderland's star striker endured a frustrating campaign as the team slid towards relegation and Kevin was often left to plough a lone furrow. Small and compact, his excellent first touch and instinctive predatory skills make him a first-class front man. Although he did not enjoy a vintage season in terms of goals, two strikes at West Bromwich Albion in December were classic Phillips, the second of which saw him retrieving the ball wide on the touch line before cutting in to fire a 20-yard shot past Russell Hoult. Kevin also set a new post-war FA Cup scoring record for Sunderland when his replay

strike against Blackburn gave him his tenth goal in the competition for the Black Cats. Following relegation, Kevin has formally handed in a transfer request and as Sunderland's most saleable asset, it is likely he will be leaving the Stadium of Light.
Watford (£10,000 from Baldock on 19/12/1994) FL 54+5/24 FLC 2/1 FAC 2 Others 0+2
Sunderland (£325,000 + on 17/7/1997) P/FL 207+1/113 FLC 9+1/5 FAC 14/10 Others 3/2

PHILLIPS Mark Ian
Born: Lambeth, 27 January 1982
Height: 6'2" **Weight:** 13.0
Another product of the Millwall academy, Mark spent much of the 2002-03 season sidelined by injury. He enjoyed a brief run out in the first team during the early part of the campaign before injury intervened. Mark is a promising young central defender, but has also turned out as a striker on occasions for the club's reserve team.
Millwall (From trainee on 3/5/2000) FL 8 FLC 1

PHILLIPS Martin John
Born: Exeter, 13 March 1976
Height: 5'10" **Weight:** 11.10
Club Honours: Div 3 '02
This tricky winger was in and out of Plymouth Argyle's first-team line-up last season due to injury and lack of form. His ball skills have never been in doubt and his crosses continued to prove menacing to opposing defences. He scored twice during the campaign, both coming in home matches early in the new year. Martin was reported to have accepted a new 12-month deal from Argyle during the summer.
Exeter C (From trainee on 4/7/1994) FL 36+16/5 FLC 1+2 FAC 2+2 Others 1+5
Manchester C (£500,000 on 25/11/1995) P/FL 3+12 FLC 0+1
Scunthorpe U (Loaned on 5/1/1998) FL 2+1 Others 1
Exeter C (Loaned on 19/3/1998) FL 7+1
Portsmouth (£50,000 + on 27/8/1998) FL 4+20/1 FLC 2+2 FAC 0+1
Bristol Rov (Loaned on 24/2/1999) FL 2
Plymouth Arg (£25,000 on 11/8/2000) FL 87+18/9 FLC 4 FAC 7+1/2 Others 4

PHILLIPS Steven (Steve) John
Born: Bath, 6 May 1978
Height: 6'1" **Weight:** 11.10
Club Honours: AMC '03
Bristol City's goalkeeper enjoyed a superb season in 2002-03, when he was the

club's only ever-present. Whilst he sometimes still had problems in dealing with crosses he showed great improvement and looks likely to be City's first choice between the sticks for some considerable time to come.
Bristol C (Signed from Paulton Rov on 21/11/1996) FL 145+1 FLC 6 FAC 11 Others 16

PHILLIPS Waynne
Born: Bangor, 15 December 1970
Height: 5'10" **Weight:** 11.2
International Honours: W: B-1
No doubt about it, Waynne must be one of the unluckiest players to have appeared for Wrexham! He suffered a broken leg within seven minutes of the start of the new season at Scunthorpe. And was out for the rest of the campaign. The popular box-to-box midfielder showed a superb attitude in his rehabilitation and hopes to be back in action for the start of the 2003-04 campaign. Waynne used his spare time wisely, working as a match summariser for BBC Radio Wales and the Welsh-language equivalent Radio Cymru.
Wrexham (From trainee on 23/8/1989) FL 184+23/16 FLC 17+1 FAC 12+2/1 Others 18+6/1
Stockport Co (£200,000 on 13/2/1998) FL 14+8 FLC 1 FAC 1
Wrexham (£50,000 on 23/7/1999) FL 35+3/2 FLC 1

PHILPOTT Lee
Born: Barnet, 21 February 1970
Height: 5'10" **Weight:** 12.9
Club Honours: Div 3 '91
Coming on as an added time substitute for Ryan Williams in Hull's opening game of the season against Southend subsequently proved to be this veteran midfielder's only league action of the 2002-03 campaign. Otherwise, apart from being on the bench for two games, a succession of niggling injuries meant left-footed Lee's only other involvement was his full appearance in the LDV Vans Trophy tie at Port Vale when he played in a central midfield role. A member of the Tigers' reserve team that won the Avon Insurance Division One East championship, Lee's contract was not renewed at the end of the season.
Peterborough U (From trainee on 17/7/1986) FL 1+3 FAC 0+1 Others 0+2
Cambridge U (Free on 31/5/1989) FL 118+16/17 FLC 10/1 FAC 19/3 Others 15/2
Leicester C (£350,000 on 24/11/1992) F/PL 57+18/3 FLC 2+1 FAC 6+2 Others 4+1
Blackpool (£75,000 on 22/3/1996) FL 51+20/5 FLC 5/1 FAC 4 Others 0+2

incoln C *(Free on 21/7/1998) FL 33+14/3
LC 1+2 FAC 1+2 Others 1+3*
Hull C *(Free on 10/8/2000) FL 45+9/2 FLC 1
AC 2 Others 1+2*

PIERCY John William
Born: Forest Gate, 18 September 1979
Height: 5'11" **Weight:** 12.4
International Honours: E: Yth
Brought to the South Coast after being
turned out as a defender, midfielder and
forward for Brighton & Hove Albion
reserves and quickly impressed to earn
himself a one-year contract in September.
He went on to score 13 times for the
second string, but found his first-team

opportunities limited, making just two
starts and adding four more appearances
as a substitute. A powerfully built player,
he operates mainly on the left side and
looks to be blessed with a fair amount of
skill.
*Tottenham H (From trainee on 2/7/1998) PL
1+7 FLC 1*
*Brighton & Hove A (Free on 20/9/2002) FL
1+3 FLC 1 FAC 0+1*

PILKINGTON George Edward
Born: Rugeley, 7 November 1981
Height: 5'11" **Weight:** 11.6
International Honours: E: Yth
This promising young Everton defender
joined Exeter City on loan last November

to gain some experience of first-team
football. George made his senior debut in
the 3-0 win at Boston and generally
acquitted himself well, producing some
mature and disciplined displays in the
heart of the Grecians' defence. He was
reported to have signed for Port Vale
during the summer break.
Everton (From trainee on 18/11/1998)
*Exeter C (Loaned on 1/11/2002) FL 7 FAC 4
Others 1*

PILKINGTON Kevin William
Born: Hitchin, 8 March 1974
Height: 6'1" **Weight:** 13.0
Club Honours: FAYC '92
International Honours: E: Sch
Kevin retained his place as regular first
team 'keeper for Mansfield Town at the
start of last season and would have been
an ever-present except for injury. Firstly,
he missed a month through a wrist injury
in September, and then a punctured lung
in February sidelined him for eight weeks.
He was appointed club captain in August,
starting the season in great form and,
even though the Stags conceded 97
Second Division goals, he was rarely at
fault.
*Manchester U (From trainee on 6/7/1992) PL
4+2 FLC 1 FAC 1*
Rochdale (Loaned on 2/2/1996) FL 6
Rotherham U (Loaned on 22/1/1997) FL 17
*Port Vale (Free on 1/7/1998) FL 23 FLC 1
FAC 1 (Freed during 2000 close season)*
*Wigan Ath (Free, via a trial at Macclesfield,
on 31/8/2000. Freed on 4/9/2000)*
*Mansfield T (Free from Aberystwyth T on
8/9/2000) FL 79 FLC 2 FAC 5 Others 2*

PINAULT Thomas
Born: Grasse, France, 4 December 1981
Height: 5'10" **Weight:** 11.1
Thomas continued to produce fine
performances full of flair in central
midfield for Colchester United last term.
However, he also added some goals to his
repertoire, including the opening-day
winner against Stockport County. Later in
the season, he drilled home from long
range to beat Bristol City 2-1 at Ashton
Gate. Thomas tended to get better as the
campaign wore on. A big hit with the U's
supporters, he has the ability to open up
defences with measured passes and
accurate through balls.
*Colchester U (Free from AS Cannes, France
on 5/7/1999) FL 73+20/5 FLC 3+1 FAC 3
Others 3*

PIPE David Ronald
Born: Caerphilly, 5 November 1983
Height: 5'9" **Weight:** 12.4

Steve Phillips

Robert Pires

International Honours: W: 1; U21-1; Yth
David created a buzz in his early games
for Coventry City last term playing either
on the right side of midfield or up front.
Used mainly as a substitute in the first
half of the season, he caused problems
for most defences with his non-stop
running and aggressive style of play. He
scored on his first full start at Gillingham
and although he dropped out of the
reckoning for a while he returned to first-
team duty in March. David featured for
Wales at U21 level during the campaign
and stepped up to make his full
international debut in the friendly against
the USA in May.
Coventry C *(Trainee on 8/11/2000) FL*
1+10/1 FLC 1+1 FAC 0+1

PIPER Matthew (Matt) James
Born: Leicester, 29 September 1981
Height: 6'1" **Weight:** 13.5
An England U21 international right
winger, Matt joined Sunderland from
Leicester in August 2002. Lightning quick
with the ability to deliver dangerous
crosses for his colleagues, Matt looked to
be a tremendous signing before a
succession of injuries ruined his campaign.
Persistent groin trouble was followed by a
stomach problem that ultimately required
surgery. With Sunderland facing life in the
Nationwide League next term, a fully fit
Matt will be crucial to their promotion
hopes.
Leicester C *(From trainee on 12/8/1999) PL*
4+2/1 FLC 1 FAC 0+1
Mansfield T *(Loaned on 20/11/2001) FL 8/1*
Sunderland *(£3,500,000 on 21/8/2002) PL*
+5 FLC 0+1

PIRES Robert
Born: Reims, France, 29 October 1973
Height: 6'1" **Weight:** 12.4
Club Honours: PL '02; FAC '03
International Honours: France: 61
UEFA '00)
Cruciate ligament damage that required
surgery kept Robert out of the Arsenal
team until mid-season. Although he was
back in the reserves in October, returning
to full fitness was a long process. He
scored two goals in a match-winning
performance against Fulham in February,
when he showed he was back to his best.
An extremely talented player, he usually
starts the game on the left side of
midfield but moves about as it progresses.
After regaining his fitness he was picked
again for the French national squad and
came on as a substitute in the final of the
Confederations Cup against Cameroon.
He was one of five Gunners selected for
the PFA's Premiership team of the season.

Arsenal *(£6,000,000 from Olympique*
Marseilles, France, ex Metz, on 24/7/2000) PL
77+10/27 FLC 1/1 FAC 14+3/5 Others 31+2/4

**PISTONE Alessandro
(Sandro)**
Born: Milan, Italy, 27 July 1975
Height: 5'11" **Weight:** 12.1
International Honours: Italy: U21
(UEFA-U21 '96)
An elegant defender who is primarily a
right-footed left back but is comfortable
in any position in the back-four, Sandro
was mostly deployed on the opposite
flank last season as a replacement for
Tony Hibbert in December, after a
hamstring problem had disrupted his
early-season plans. A series of typical
classy displays followed as he showed
Everton supporters the pace and forward
running that sadly had been seen
infrequently due to appalling luck with
injuries. However a hernia operation
following the game at Middlesbrough in
March brought his season to what
seemed a premature end, only for him to
reappear for the final two games of the
campaign.
Newcastle U *(£4,300,000 from Inter Milan,*
Italy, ex Vicenza, Solbiatese, Crevalcore, on
31/7/1997) PL 45+1/1 FLC 1+1 FAC 8 Others 7
Everton *(£3,000,000 on 12/7/2000) PL*
40+7/1 FLC 3 FAC 1

PLATT Clive Linton
Born: Wolverhampton, 27 October 1977
Height: 6'4" **Weight:** 13.0
Clive remained a near automatic choice
for Rochdale for a fourth campaign,
going past 150 league games for the
club, even though his future was unclear
as he declined to make a decision on a
new contract offered to him in mid-
season. Though a target man rather than
an out-and-out goal-scorer, the lanky
striker has also joined the relatively small
band of players with 30 Football League
goals for Rochdale. With Connor and
McEvilly in good scoring form Clive
also put in some sterling performances
when, as an experiment, he was played in
a withdrawn role behind the other two
strikers.
Walsall *(From trainee on 25/7/1996) FL*
18+14/4 FLC 1+2/1 FAC 0+1 Others 1+6
Rochdale *(£70,000 + on 5/8/1999) FL*
151+18/30 FLC 5/1 FAC 13/5 Others 7/1

**PLUMMER Christopher
(Chris)** Scott
Born: Isleworth, 12 October 1976
Height: 6'3" **Weight:** 12.9
International Honours: E: U21-5; Yth

Chris was again affected by injuries,
which restricted his senior football last
season. After recovering from a broken
ankle he joined Bristol Rovers on loan in
November and looked a confident central
defender, but picked up a groin problem
in his third match for the Pirates against
Wrexham. On returning to Loftus Road he
played a few games for Queen's Park
Rangers reserves before making a first-
team appearance as a late substitute at
Northampton. Chris then suffered a
serious hamstring injury in training and
was ruled out for the remainder of the
campaign.
Queens Park R *(From trainee on 1/7/1994)*
F/PL 54+8/2 FLC 2 FAC 7
Bristol Rov *(Loaned on 7/11/2002) FL 2*
FAC 2

POGLIACOMI Leslie (Les)
Amado
Born: Australia, 3 May 1976
Height: 6'4" **Weight:** 14.5
International Honours: Australia: Yth
After signing from Australian Premier
League outfit Parramatta Power during
the summer of 2002, this giant 'keeper
made a stunning impact at Oldham.
Following a slightly nervous start, he
quickly established himself as first choice,
smashing the club record with 19 clean
sheets from 37 league appearances. Les's
strengths lie in his command of his area,
communication with defenders and shot-
stopping ability. A back injury in March
forced him to miss the final six league
games and, with Latics narrowly missing
out on automatic promotion, his absence
proved costly.
Oldham Ath *(Free from Parramatta Power,*
Australia, ex Marconi Stallions, Wollongong
Wolves, Parramatta Power, on 22/7/2002) FL
37 FLC 2 FAC 3 Others 1

POLLET Ludovic (Ludo)
Born: Valenciennes, France, 18 June 1970
Height: 6'1" **Weight:** 12.11
This well-liked centre half was unable to
break up the central defensive partnership
of Paul Butler and Joleon Lescott for
Wolves last season. He looked a bit out of
sorts when called upon for the
Worthington Cup tie at Swansea,
although he did score, but eventually fell
down the pecking order. Ludo
subsequently rejoined his former boss
Colin Lee at Walsall for a brief loan spell
near the turn of the year, and after taking
one game to regain the pace of First
Division football he was never afraid to go
in when it hurt, helping the team to pick
up seven points in the five games he
played. On his return to Molineux he did

not get back in the Wolves team until they were hit by injuries at Portsmouth, and as usual he did not let them down.
Wolverhampton W *(Free from Le Havre, France on 10/9/1999) FL 74+4/7 FLC 2/1 FAC 5 Others 0+1*
Walsall *(Loaned on 14/11/2002) FL 5*

POLLITT Michael (Mike) Francis
Born: Farnworth, 29 February 1972
Height: 6'4" **Weight:** 14.0

Rated as one of Division One's best keepers, Mike had another great season for Rotherham which was capped by an outstanding last-minute penalty save to earn a point from a goalless draw at promotion chasing Wolverhampton Wanderers at the beginning of April. Then he suffered a knee injury that caused him to miss a few games after a sequence of 204 consecutive appearances for the Millers. Commanding in the air, Mike is also an excellent shot stopper and he

Les Pogliacomi

played a vital role in helping his team to consolidate their league position.
Manchester U *(From trainee on 1/7/1990)*
Bury *(Free on 10/7/1991)*
Lincoln C *(Loaned on 24/9/1992) FL 5 FLC 1*
Lincoln C *(Free on 1/12/1992) FL 52 FLC 4 FAC 2 Others 4*
Darlington *(Free on 11/8/1994) FL 55 FLC 4 FAC 3 Others 5*
Notts Co *(£75,000 on 14/11/1995) FL 10 Others 2*
Oldham Ath *(Loaned on 29/8/1997) FL 16*
Gillingham *(Loaned on 12/12/1997) FL 6*
Brentford *(Loaned on 22/1/1998) FL 5*
Sunderland *(£75,000 on 23/2/1998)*
Rotherham U *(Free on 14/7/1998) FL 92 FLC 4 FAC 7 Others 5*
Chesterfield *(Free on 15/6/2000) FL 46 FLC 3 FAC 1 Others 4*
Rotherham U *(£75,000 on 29/5/2001) FL 8. FLC 6 FAC 3*

POOLE Kevin
Born: Bromsgrove, 21 July 1963
Height: 5'10" **Weight:** 12.11
Club Honours: FLC '97
A competent reserve goalkeeper, now classed as 'a veteran', Kevin was second choice at Bolton last season. Whilst he di not make any appearances in the Premiership, he figured in all three of the Wanderers' cup games, particularly excelling in the FA Cup replay at Sunderland, and proving himself to be a suitable deputy to Jussi Jaaskelainen, despite his advancing years.
Aston Villa *(From apprentice on 26/6/1981)*
FL 28 FLC 2 FAC 1 Others 1
Northampton T *(Loaned on 8/11/1984) FL ?*
Middlesbrough *(Signed on 27/8/1987) FL 3*
FLC 4 FAC 2 Others 2
Hartlepool U *(Loaned on 27/3/1991) FL 12*
Leicester C *(£40,000 on 30/7/1991) F/PL 16 FLC 10 FAC 8 Others 12*
Birmingham C *(Free on 4/8/1997) FL 56 FLC 7 FAC 2 Others 2*
Bolton W *(Free on 25/10/2001) PL 3 FLC 1 FAC 2*

POOM Mart
Born: Tallin, Estonia, 3 February 1972
Height: 6'4" **Weight:** 13.6
International Honours: Estonia: 92
Derby rejected Everton's summer bid for Mart who, despite relegation the previou season, remained one of the best goalkeepers in the Premiership. In November he joined Sunderland, initially on loan, as extra cover following an injur crisis, the move being made permanent during the January transfer window. A ta imposing figure and a tremendous shot stopper, he made a long overdue debut a

irmingham in April and with Thomas
orensen expected to leave Wearside,
Mart looks set to become the Black Cats'
umber one. He continued to represent
stonia at international level during the
ampaign.
*Portsmouth (£200,000 from FC Wil,
witzerland, ex Flora, on 4/8/1994) FL 4 FLC 3
Signed by Tallin SC, Estonia on 9/5/1996)
Derby Co (£500,000 on 26/3/1997) P/FL
43+3 FLC 12 FAC 8*
Sunderland (£2,500,000 on 23/11/2002) PL 4

Mike Pollitt

POPOVIC Anthony (Tony)
Born: Australia, 4 July 1973
Height: 6'4" **Weight:** 13.11
International Honours: Australia: 42;
U23; Yth
This talented left-sided central defender
scored twice in the first three games of
the 2002-03 season for Crystal Palace. He
went on to feature regularly in the line-up
throughout the season, contributing three
more goals. However, the highlight of his
campaign occurred in February when he
appeared, and scored, for Australia in
their surprise 3-1 win over England at
Upton Park.
*Crystal Palace (£600,000 from Sanfrecce
Hiroshima, Japan on 24/8/2001) FL 56/5 FLC
6/1 FAC 4*

PORTER Christopher (Chris)
Born: Wigan, 12 December 1983
Height: 6'1" **Weight:** 13.2
This teenaged striker had unsuccessful
trials with Blackpool and Wigan, but then
linked up with Bury in February and
scored twice for the reserve team. He
accepted a three-month contract in March
and made his debut as a substitute at
Macclesfield later that month. A highly
regarded prospect, Chris is a skilful player
who is good with the ball at his feet. He
made his second appearance of the
season as a substitute in the final fixture
against Wrexham.
*Bury (Free from QEGS, Blackburn on
3/3/2003) FL 0+2*

PORTER Christopher (Chris)
Ian
Born: Sunderland, 10 November 1979
Height: 6'2" **Weight:** 13.2
Darlington's second choice 'keeper had a
rather frustrating time last term, as no
fewer than three on-loan goalkeepers
were brought in to cover when Andy
Collett was out injured. However, Chris
did feature in the FA Cup ties against
Stevenage Borough and Farnborough
Town as well as in a couple of league
games at either end of the season when
he impressed with his quick reflexes and
shot-stopping ability.
*Sunderland (From trainee on 1/8/1998. Free
on 8/3/2000)*
*Darlington (Free from Leiftur, Iceland on
21/3/2002) FL 9+1 FAC 2*

POSTMA Stefan
Born: Utrecht, Holland, 10 June 1976
Height: 6'6" **Weight:** 14.12
Stefan joined Aston Villa in the summer
of 2002 and served as second choice
'keeper to Peter Enckelman last term. He
made his debut in the first leg of the
Intertoto Cup tie against Lille, but
otherwise managed just a handful of
appearances covering for injury and
suspension. Stefan deputised well when
called up, but is likely to have to continue
to wait patiently for his chance in
2003-04.
*Aston Villa (£1,500,000 from De
Graafschap, Holland, ex Utrecht, on
28/5/2002) PL 5+1 FLC 1 FAC 1 Others 1*

POTTER Graham Stephen
Born: Solihull, 20 May 1975
Height: 6'1" **Weight:** 11.12
International Honours: E: U21-1; Yth
Graham was again a regular in the York
City line-up last season. Although at his
best in a left-sided role, he also operated
in the centre of midfield in the latter
stages of the campaign. A good crosser
of the ball especially from corners and set
pieces his only goal came in the 2-2 draw
at Shrewsbury in February.
*Birmingham C (From trainee on 1/7/1992) FL
23+2/2 FAC 1 Others 6*
*Wycombe W (Loaned on 17/9/1993) FL 2+1
FLC 1 Others 1*

*Stoke C (£75,000 on 20/12/1993) FL 41+4/1
FLC 3+1 FAC 4 Others 5*
*Southampton (£250,000 + on 23/7/1996)
FL 2+6 FLC 1+1*
*West Bromwich A (£300,000 + on
14/2/1997) FL 31+12 FLC 0+3 FAC 1*
*Northampton T (Loaned on 24/10/1997) FL
4 Others 1*
*Reading (Loaned on 2/12/1999) FL 4
Others 1*
*York C (Free on 7/7/2000) FL 108+6/5 FLC 4
FAC 12/3 Others 1*

POUTON Alan
Born: Newcastle, 1 February 1977
Height: 6'0" **Weight:** 12.8

Stefan Postma

Grimsby Town's combative and
uncompromising midfielder remained the
Mariners' strong man in the centre of the
park last season. Arguably Alan Buckley's
greatest legacy to the club, his hard-
tackling style was liable to incur the wrath
of referees and also meant long spells in
the treatment room, absences which did
not help the club's problems at the foot
of the table especially during the vital run
in. Nevertheless he featured regularly in
the side and contributed five valuable
goals.
*Oxford U (From trainee at Newcastle U on
7/11/1995)*
*York C (Free on 8/12/1995) FL 79+11/7 FLC
5+1 FAC 5/1 Others 2*
*Grimsby T (£150,000 on 5/8/1999) FL
95+21/12 FLC 11+2 FAC 1+1*

POWELL Christopher (Chris)
George Robin
Born: Lambeth, 8 September 1969
Height: 5'10" **Weight:** 11.7
Club Honours: Div 1 '00
International Honours: E: 5
Charlton's most capped England
international is a skilful and unflappable
left-sided defender who can play as an
orthodox left back or as a left wing back
and loves to push forward down the left
wing and get in crosses from the by-line.
Despite the emergence of Paul Konchesky
Chris managed to retain his position in
the Addicks' line-up, missing only one
Premiership game and starting in all but
three. It seems that age is now against
him being recalled into the England
squad, but as ever Chris was a model of
consistency throughout the campaign.
*Crystal Palace (From trainee on 24/12/1987)
FL 2+1 FLC 0+1 Others 0+1*
Aldershot (Loaned on 11/1/1990) FL 11
*Southend U (Free on 30/8/1990) FL 246+2/
FLC 13 FAC 8 Others 21*
*Derby Co (£750,000 on 31/1/1996) F/PL
89+2/1 FLC 5 FAC 5/1*
*Charlton Ath (£825,000 on 1/7/1998) P/FL
179+5/1 FLC 7+1 FAC 8/1*

POWELL Darren David
Born: Hammersmith, 10 March 1976
Height: 6'3" **Weight:** 13.2
Club Honours: Div 3 '99
This tall and commanding central
defender joined Crystal Palace for a
substantial fee in the summer of 2002
and got off to a great start by scoring on
his debut at Preston. Darren settled in
well and went on to become a fixture in
the Eagles' line-up, contributing a second
goal in the Worthington Cup tie against
Plymouth Argyle.

rentford *(£15,000 from Hampton on 7/7/1998) FL 128/6 FLC 7 FAC 4 Others 0+1/2*
rystal Palace *(£400,000 on 8/8/2002) FL 9/1 FLC 5/1 FAC 2*

POWELL Darryl Anthony
orn: Lambeth, 15 November 1971
Height: 6'0" **Weight:** 12.10
nternational Honours: Jamaica: 17
Darryl made his debut for Birmingham City in the 3-0 win over Aston Villa in September. Combative and energetic, he added experienced cover for the Blues but never established himself in the side and in January he was released. He subsequently joined Sheffield Wednesday, adding experience, leadership and stability to the midfield. Darryl was immediately handed the captaincy and added balance to the left-hand side of the middle line, but after settling in well he was sidelined by a leg injury that caused him to miss the rest of the season.
ortsmouth *(From trainee on 22/12/1988) FL 3+49/16 FLC 11+3/3 FAC 10 Others 9+5/4*
Derby Co *(£750,000 on 27/7/1995) F/PL 87+20/10 FLC 11+1/1 FAC 7+1*
Birmingham C *(Free on 12/9/2002) PL 3+8 LC 2 FAC 1*
heffield Wed *(Free on 16/1/2003) FL 8*

POWELL Paul
orn: Wallingford, 30 June 1978
Height: 5'8" **Weight:** 11.6
It was a frustrating time for Paul who was probably the most skilful player at Oxford last season. Unable to get into any sort of playing rhythm he rarely appeared in the line-up, with three of his four starts coming in one run following an injury to Matt Robinson. A tricky winger, Paul mostly featured at full back but despite his infrequent appearances he still scored twice, both vital, point-earning goals. He was released in the summer.
Oxford U *(From trainee on 2/7/1996) FL 43+35/17 FLC 6+4 FAC 8+1/3 Others 3+3/3*

POWER Graeme Richard
orn: Harrow, 7 March 1977
Height: 5'10" **Weight:** 10.10
nternational Honours: E: Yth; Sch
Graeme's fortunes at Exeter last term were very much determined by the changes in management. He was a virtual first choice for the left-back berth under John Cornforth, found himself out of favour with Neil McNab and was then restored to the side under Gary Peters. His never-say-die attitude was needed for the last crucial games of the season, but nevertheless he was unable to prevent the

Grecians from dropping into the Conference.
Queens Park R *(From trainee on 11/4/1995)*
Bristol Rov *(Free on 15/7/1996) FL 25+1 FAC 1 Others 1+2*
Exeter C *(Free on 6/8/1998) FL 165+6/2 FLC 4 FAC 10 Others 7*

POYET Gustavo (Gus)
Augusto
Born: Montevideo, Uruguay, 15 November 1967
Height: 6'2" **Weight:** 13.0
Club Honours: ECWC '98; ESC '98; FAC '00; CS '00
International Honours: Uruguay: 31; Yth
This central midfielder put paid to speculation that his career was over following a serious knee injury, to come back with a fine season for Tottenham last term. Gus favours a central attacking role and despite his years is fit, agile and extremely pacy. Although he creates more than he scores, he has a hunger for the big occasion and seemed to be enjoying his football more than ever. A regular in the squad last term, he contributed five Premiership goals.
Chelsea *(Free from Real Zaragoza, Spain, ex River Plate, Grenoble, Bella Vista, on 15/7/1997) PL 79\26/36 FLC 3+1/2 FAC 8+1/7 Others 20+7/4*
Tottenham H *(£2,250,000 on 10/7/2001) PL 54+8/15 FLC 6/2 FAC 5/3*

PREECE Andrew (Andy) Paul
Born: Evesham, 27 March 1967
Height: 6'1" **Weight:** 12.0
Even at the veteran stage of his career, Bury's player-manager continued to demonstrate a great appetite for the game. He started 11 league games, but chose mainly to make an impression from the substitutes' bench during the closing 20 minutes or so of a match, in fact he did so 18 times. Still powerful in the air, if lacking a little in pace now, Andy bagged four goals during the season, his most spectacular being a curling free kick at Carlisle.
Northampton T *(Free from Evesham on 31/8/1988) FL 0+1 FLC 0+1 Others 0+1 (Free to Worcester C during 1989 close season)*
Wrexham *(Free on 22/3/1990) FL 44+7/7 FLC 5+1/1 FAC 1/2 Others 5/1*
Stockport Co *(£10,000 on 18/12/1991) FL 89+8/42 FLC 2+1 FAC 7/3 Others 12+2/9*
Crystal Palace *(£350,000 on 23/6/1994) PL 17+3/4 FLC 4+2/1 FAC 2+3*
Blackpool *(£200,000 on 5/7/1995) FL 114+12/35 FLC 8+2/1 FAC 2+3/2 Others 12/2*
Bury *(Free on 6/7/1998) FL 77+77/22 FLC 7+6 FAC 2+3 Others 2+3/1*

PRESSMAN Kevin Paul
Born: Fareham, 6 November 1967
Height: 6'1" **Weight:** 15.5
International Honours: E: B-3; U21-1; Yth; Sch
This stalwart custodian has had better seasons form-wise, but still had a good campaign for Sheffield Wednesday in 2002-03. He lost his place through injury then found it difficult to replace Paul Evans, whose own form was outstanding. However, an injury to Evans let in Kevin and he took over with all his old confidence and aplomb; two of his best performances were against bitter rivals Sheffield United and he has now made well over 400 appearances for the Owls.
Sheffield Wed *(From apprentice on 7/11/1985) F/PL 380+3 FLC 46 FAC 18 Others 4*
Stoke C *(Loaned on 10/3/1992) FL 4 Others 2*

PRICE Jason Jeffrey
Born: Pontypridd, 12 April 1977
Height: 6'2" **Weight:** 11.5
Club Honours: Div 3 '00
International Honours: W: U21-7
Jason endured a season dogged by bad luck at Tranmere in 2002-03. He broke his collarbone in the away fixture at Crewe in September then, just one week after his come back, he broke a wrist at Swindon while he also suffered from a number of other niggling injuries throughout his campaign. One of Rovers' most versatile players, Jason can play either in defence, midfield or attack, and frequently caused havoc when brought on as the 'secret weapon' from the bench. Jason was out of contract in the summer and his future was unclear at the time of writing.
Swansea C *(Free from Aberaman on 17/7/1995) FL 133+11/17 FLC 10/1 FAC 4/1 Others 4+1/1*
Brentford *(Free on 6/8/2001) FL 15/1 FLC 2 Others 1*
Tranmere Rov *(Free on 8/11/2001) FL 34+15/11 FAC 5/4*

PRICE Michael David
Born: Wrexham, 29 April 1982
Height: 5'8" **Weight:** 11.4
International Honours: W: U21-11
Although selected in the squad of 16 in six of Hull's first eight games of the 2002-03 campaign, this left back subsequently fell out of favour under both Jan Molby and his successor Peter Taylor. Michael accepted the opportunity of experiencing Conference football with a month's loan at Barnet in November prior to his contract being cancelled on his return to

Hull. He then joined Unibond League club North Ferriby United before returning to the Conference with Scarborough. Despite this he continued to feature for Wales at U21 level.
Everton (From trainee on 17/1/2000)
Hull C (Free on 7/7/2001) FL 1+3 FLC 0+2 Others 1+1

PRIEST Christopher (Chris)
Born: Leigh, 18 October 1973
Height: 5'10" **Weight:** 12.0
Chris appeared regularly for Macclesfield Town in the 2002-03 season when he was yet again an integral part of the

midfield using his experience to the full. He worked tirelessly from box to box and contributed two valuable goals.
Everton (From trainee on 1/6/1992)
Chester C (Loaned on 9/9/1994) FL 11/1 Others 2
Chester C (Free on 11/1/1995) FL 151+5/25 FLC 6 FAC 6/1 Others 6
Macclesfield T (Free on 5/7/1999) FL 114+7/11 FLC 4/1 FAC 8 Others 2

PRIMUS Linvoy Stephen
Born: Forest Gate, 14 September 1973
Height: 6'0" **Weight:** 14.0
Club Honours: Div 1 '03

A fearsome opponent for many First Division strikers last season, Linvoy's self assured and reliable defending helped Portsmouth win the First Division title and he was a major factor in the defence keeping 16 clean sheets. A tough tackler and effective man-to-man marker, he did not make the line-up early on and it was not until Richard Hughes was sidelined by injury that he received his breakthrough. However, from then on he was a regular at full back and finished the campaign in style when he was voted as 'Player of the Season' by the Pompey supporters.
Charlton Ath (From trainee on 14/8/1992) F 4 FLC 0+1 Others 0+1
Barnet (Free on 18/7/1994) FL 127/7 FLC 9+1 FAC 8/1 Others 4
Reading (£400,000 on 29/7/1997) FL 94+1/ FLC 9 FAC 6 Others 4
Portsmouth (Free on 4/8/2000) FL 83+2/2 FLC 5/1 FAC 2

PRINCE Neil Michael
Born: Liverpool, 17 March 1983
Height: 5'11" **Weight:** 10.7
International Honours: E: Yth
This slightly built but skilful left winger or midfielder arrived in the 2002 close season from Liverpool and was in the starting line-up for Torquay's first three games, showing some excellent touches. However, after losing out when David Graham returned from suspension he failed to regain his place in the line-up and in January he moved on to Southport, before finishing the campaign with Leigh RMI.
Torquay U (From trainee at Liverpool on 8/8/2002) FL 3+4 FLC 0+1

PRIOR Spencer Justin
Born: Southend, 22 April 1971
Height: 6'3" **Weight:** 13.4
Club Honours: FLC '97
This experienced defender sometimes struggled to find his best form for Cardiff City last term, but he was outstanding during the run-in as he regained his confidence on the basics: winning the ball in the air, getting in tackles and clearing out of the danger area. His partnership with Danny Gabbidon blossomed, and it was alongside the young Welshman that Spencer played his best football.
Southend U (From trainee on 22/5/1989) FL 135/3 FLC 9 FAC 5 Others 7/1
Norwich C (£200,000 on 24/6/1993) P/FL 67+7/1 FLC 10+1/1 FAC 0+2 Others 2
Leicester C (£600,000 on 17/8/1996) PL 61+3 FLC 7 FAC 5 Others 2
Derby Co (£700,000 on 22/8/1998) PL 48+6/1 FLC 5 FAC 4

Chris Priest

Manchester C *(£500,000 + on 23/3/2000)*
FL 27+3/4 FLC 4 FAC 2+1
Cardiff C (£650,000 on 3/7/2001) FL 68+6/2
LC 2 FAC 7 Others 5

PROCTOR Michael Anthony
Born: Sunderland, 3 October 1980
Height: 5'11" **Weight:** 12.7
This young Sunderland striker started the campaign on loan at Bradford, where he made an excellent impression and scored some valuable goals. Back on Wearside, Michael made his first start in the Worthington Cup win at Arsenal in November and scored his first goal for the

Black Cats the following month when he came off the bench against Liverpool and bagged the winner. More than just a finisher, he can drift out to the wings where his confidence to beat an opponent can be used. With changes of personnel expected at the Stadium of Light in the summer, Michael may well be one of Sunderland's key players next term.
Sunderland *(From trainee on 29/10/1997) PL 11+10/2 FLC 2+1 FAC 3+2/2*
Halifax T *(Loaned on 14/3/2001) FL 11+1/4*
York C *(Loaned on 9/8/2001) FL 40+1/14 FLC 1 FAC 6 Others 1*

Spencer Prior

Bradford C *(Loaned on 23/8/2002) FL 10+2/4*

PROUDLOCK Adam David
Born: Telford, 9 May 1981
Height: 6'0" **Weight:** 13.0
International Honours: E: Yth
After scoring three goals in pre-season friendly matches, Adam featured on the bench for Wolves in a number of early games, before dropping out of the first-team picture. In November he spent time on loan at Tranmere, but failed to find the net and the following month he joined Sheffield Wednesday in a similar deal. He impressed at Hillsborough with two goals from three starts, but then returned to Molineux. Adam subsequently made a number of further appearances from the bench, scoring three times, including a strike against Wednesday.
Wolverhampton W *(From trainee on 15/7/1999) FL 42+29/13 FLC 4+2/2 FAC 2+3/2 Others 0+2*
Clyde *(Loaned on 1/8/2000) SL 4/4 SLC 2/1*
Nottingham F *(Loaned on 19/3/2002) FL 3*
Tranmere Rov *(Loaned on 25/10/2002) FL 5 Others 1*
Sheffield Wed *(Loaned on 13/12/2002) FL 3+2/2*

PROVETT Robert **James (Jim)**
Born: Stockton, 22 December 1982
Height: 5'11" **Weight:** 11.2
This young Hartlepool goalkeeper had a successful loan spell with Spennymoor United at the end of the 2001-02 season. He signed professional forms for 2002-03, but his only first-team appearance came in the LDV Vans Trophy match at Tranmere. He was unfortunate to concede five goals on his senior debut, but there were exceptional circumstances in that manager Chris Turner had chosen to field a reserve team. Apart from this he was an ever-present on the substitutes' bench as Anthony Williams held his position as first choice 'keeper.
Hartlepool U *(From trainee on 3/4/2002) Others 1*

PRUTTON David Thomas
Born: Hull, 12 September 1981
Height: 6'1" **Weight:** 11.10
International Honours: E: U21-22; Yth
David again produced a series of consistent performances in midfield for Nottingham Forest last season. He captained the side before being sold to Southampton at the end of January for a substantial fee. At St Mary's he demonstrated his versatility and became a fixture in the Premiership club's line-up.

He found himself playing in all four places across the midfield as he filled in for injured and suspended team mates. David continued to feature for England at U21 level during the season.
Nottingham F (From trainee on 1/10/1998) FL 141+2/7 FLC 7 FAC 5
Southampton (£2,500,000 on 31/1/2003) PL 9+3

PUGH Daniel (Danny)
Born: Manchester, 19 October 1982
Height: 6'0" **Weight:** 12.10
This young Manchester United midfielder made his mark in the Worthington Cup victory over Burnley last December, and was also given one Premiership and three Champions' League run outs. A steady performer who is bound to be given his first-team head sooner rather than later, Danny has made that important transition with comparative ease.
Manchester U (From trainee on 18/7/2000) PL 0+1 FLC 1 Others 1+2

PULLEN James Daniel
Born: Chelmsford, 18 March 1982
Height: 6'2" **Weight:** 14.2
This promising young goalkeeper made his Ipswich debut in the Worthington Cup tie with Middlesbrough and gave a good performance. Indeed, he was unfortunate to concede a late goal, which spoilt what would have been a deserved clean sheet. He also featured in the First Division game at home to Grimsby, but was given a free transfer at the end of the season.
Ipswich T (Free from Heybridge Swifts on 1/10/1999) FL 1 FLC 1
Blackpool (Loaned on 10/8/2001) FL 16 FLC 1 FAC 1 Others 1

PURCHES Stephen (Steve) Robert
Born: Ilford, 14 January 1980
Height: 5'11" **Weight:** 12.0
This highly versatile player enjoyed an excellent season at Bournemouth, for whom he was a near ever-present apart from a brief spell out injured in the new year. He initially featured at left back, occasionally reverting to right back, but later on he switched to a midfield role. Steve scored a number of spectacular goals, none more so than when he finished off a slick move against Lincoln in the play-off final.
West Ham U (From trainee on 6/7/1998)
Bournemouth (Free on 4/7/2000) FL 109+10/5 FLC 4 FAC 10 Others 7/2

PURSE Darren John
Born: Stepney, 14 February 1977
Height: 6'2" **Weight:** 12.8
International Honours: E: U21-2
Darren formed a solid defensive partnership for Birmingham City with Kenny Cunningham in the opening half of the 2002-03 season. His run was broken following a red card at Fulham in December and soon afterwards he underwent ankle surgery. Unfortunately, complications then set in and he did not return to first-team action again until the final two games of the campaign. Darren is purposeful in the tackle, strong in the air and always gives 100 per cent.
Leyton Orient (From trainee on 22/2/1994) FL 48+7/3 FLC 2 FAC 1 Others 7+1/2
Oxford U (£100,000 on 23/7/1996) FL 52+7/5 FLC 10+1/2 FAC 2
Birmingham C (£800,000 on 17/2/1998) P/FL 134+25/9 FLC 17+2/2 FAC 3 Others 6+1

PURSER Wayne Montague
Born: Basildon, 13 April 1980
Height: 5'9" **Weight:** 11.13
Wayne spent most of last season with Conference outfit Barnet, before joining Leyton Orient in March in a deal which also saw Greg Heald join the O's. Wayne could not have asked for a better start to his career at Brisbane Road, for he netted a hat-trick in the 3-2 home win against Boston United and thus becoming the first Leyton Orient player ever to achieve this feat on his debut. Wayne is a pacy right winger who can also play at centre forward and possesses a useful ability to 'hang' in the air to meet crosses.
Queens Park R (From trainee on 21/4/1997)
Barnet (Free on 18/8/2000) FL 4+14/3 FLC 1+1 FAC 0+2 Others 1+1/1
Leyton Orient (£9,000 on 27/3/2003) FL 7/3

Steve Purches

346

Q

QUASHIE Nigel Francis
Born: Peckham, 20 July 1978
Height: 6'0" **Weight:** 12.4
Club Honours: Div 1 '03
International Honours: E: B-1; U21-4; Yth

This competitive midfielder was a near ever-present for Portsmouth last season and contributed five valuable goals as the team went on to win the First Division title. On many occasions he was the most outstanding player on the pitch and his tally included two long-range efforts against Bradford City in September. Nigel is a determined player with an educated left foot and great vision.
Queens Park R (From trainee on 1/8/1995) PFL 50+7/3 FLC 0+1 FAC 4/2
Nottingham F (£2,500,000 on 24/8/1998) PFL 37+7/2 FLC 7/1 FAC 1+1
Portsmouth (£200,000 + on 7/8/2000) FL 104+4/12 FLC 6/1 FAC 3

QUEUDRUE Franck
Born: Paris, France, 27 August 1978
Height: 6'0" **Weight:** 12.4

Franck is, undoubtedly, an exciting attacking full back to watch but his excitable nature saw him dismissed three times and booked five times. On the positive side a stunning free kick from 25 yards out at the Riverside against Birmingham City gave Nico Vaesen no chance as it flew high into the net and it was enough to prevent the visitors winning their first match at Middlesbrough for 22 years.
Middlesbrough (£2,500,000 from RC Lens, France, ex Meaux, on 12/10/2001) PL 37+2/3 FLC 1/1 FAC 7

QUINN Alan
Born: Dublin, 13 June 1979
Height: 5'9" **Weight:** 11.7
International Honours: RoI: U21-8; Yth (UEFA-U18 '98)

This young winger enjoyed a fine season for Sheffield Wednesday in 2002-03. Alan is a clever, hard-working, whole-hearted player who just needs to add more goals to his repertoire to become the perfect midfielder. He can

play on either flank and is a popular figure with the Owls' fans. Alan was rewarded with a place in the full Republic of Ireland squad, and made his senior debut against Norway in April.
Sheffield Wed (Signed from Cherry Orchard on 6/12/1997) P/FL 124+9/12 FLC 13/1 FAC 6+1

QUINN Barry Scott
Born: Dublin, 9 May 1979
Height: 6'0" **Weight:** 12.2
International Honours: RoI: 3; U21-17; Yth (UEFA-U18 '98)

This young Irish midfield player fought hard to get a first-team place at Coventry last term and took over from Dean Gordon in the unaccustomed left-back position in October. Despite being right footed he produced some steady performances but then suffered a broken toe at Christmas and after recovering he struggled to find his form. Barry failed to add any further caps for the Republic of Ireland during the season.
Coventry C (From trainee on 28/11/1996) P/FL 67+16 FLC 5 FAC 2+1

QUINN Niall John
Born: Dublin, 6 October 1966
Height: 6'4" **Weight:** 15.10
Club Honours: FLC '87; Div 1 '99
International Honours: RoI: 91; B-1; U23-1; U21-6; Yth; Sch

Apart from the club's relegation, the most saddening aspect of 2002-03 for Sunderland fans was the retirement of this giant Republic of Ireland striker. A talismanic figure, Niall had begun the campaign realising that he was only to play a bit-part role on the field and had undertaken coaching duties under Peter Reid, even relinquishing his famous number nine shirt. Following eight substitute appearances, Niall decided to call it a day in November. However, he did not end the season empty handed, picking up the 'North East Sports Personality of the Year' award, not only for his efforts on the field but also for his outstanding gesture in donating all of the proceeds from his May 2002 testimonial to children's charities. Niall will forever be remembered as a true 'Sunderland Great'.
Arsenal (From juniors on 30/11/1983) FL

59+8/14 FLC 14+2/4 FAC 8+2/2 Others 0+1
Manchester C (£800,000 on 21/3/1990) F/PL 183+20/66 FLC 20+2/6 FAC 13+3/4 Others 3/1
Sunderland (£1,300,000 on 17/8/1996) F/PL 168+35/61 FLC 5+1/4 FAC 8+1/2 Others 2/2

QUINN Robert (Rob) John
Born: Sidcup, 8 November 1976
Height: 5'11" **Weight:** 11.2
Club Honours: Div 3 '99
International Honours: RoI: U21-5; B-1

This former Brentford midfielder joined Bristol Rovers in the summer of 2002 and was a near ever-present in the 2002-03 campaign. He quickly settled into the side and produced some hard-working and consistent performances. He netted two goals during the season including an important match-winner at Bury.
Crystal Palace (From trainee on 11/3/1995) F/PL 18+5/1 FLC 2+1/1 Others 2+1
Brentford (£40,000 on 9/7/1998) FL 98+11/2 FLC 9+1 FAC 6/2 Others 7/1
Oxford U (£75,000 on 12/1/2001) FL 23+6/2
Bristol Rov (Free on 15/7/2002) FL 44/2 FLC 1 FAC 4 Others 1

QUINN Wayne Richard
Born: Truro, 19 November 1976
Height: 5'10" **Weight:** 11.12
International Honours: E: B-1; U21-2; Yth

Wayne is primarily a left back although his skill on the ball and ability to deliver telling crosses allow him to play at left midfield on occasion. After appearing as a substitute in Newcastle's opening game, a Champions' League qualifier in Sarajevo, he failed to make the first-team squad again, and early in 2003 he returned to Sheffield United on loan. At Bramall Lane he was used as a left wing back and produced a series of solid performances when the Blades were in need of a left-sided player.
Sheffield U (From trainee on 6/12/1994) FL 131+8/6 FLC 14+1 FAC 12+1 Others 2
Newcastle U (£750,000 + on 1/1/2001) PL 14+1 FLC 1 FAC 0+1 Others 6+1/1
Sheffield U (Loaned on 7/1/2003) FL 6 FLC 2 FAC 2

Barry Quinn

R

RADEBE Lucas
Born: Johannesburg, South Africa, 12
April 1969
Height: 6'1" **Weight:** 11.8
International Honours: South Africa: 70
ANC '96)

espite the fact that he did not feature at
l for Leeds United in the 2001-02
ampaign, Lucas captained the South
frica team during the World Cup finals
the summer. He was reintroduced to
rst-team football at Elland Road last
•rm, but in a season when injuries
ecimated the United defence, he again
uffered his share, indeed, an injury
ustained in the away leg of the UEFA
up tie with Hapoel Tel Aviv caused him
b miss some 18 games. 'The Chief'
•mains one of the best defenders in the
•emiership and one of the finest to pull
n a United shirt since the Revie era.
*eeds U (£250,000 from Kaizer Chiefs, South
frica on 5/9/1994) PL 168+15 FLC 9+4 FAC
9+2/1 Others 27/2*

RADZINSKI Tomasz
Born: Poznan, Poland, 14 December 1973
Height: 5'9" **Weight:** 11.7
International Honours: Canada: 16
No single player embodied Everton's
resurgence under David Moyes than this
Canadian international striker. Following a
moderate first season, the fleet-footed
forward was the club's leading scorer in
the Premiership and was regarded as
'Player of the Season' in most end-of-
season polls. His campaign was cruelly cut
short following a groin injury sustained
against West Ham in March and the fact
that the team dropped three places in his
absence demonstrated his importance to
the side. A perfect foil for Kevin
Campbell, his pacy bursts and selfless
running were a valuable outlet for team
mates, and more precise finishing on
occasions would surely have enhanced his
tally of 11 goals. The highlight of the
campaign was undoubtedly scoring two
late goals to win the home match against
Southampton, the second of which was a
spectacular shot deep into added-time.
*Everton (£4,500,000 from Anderlecht,
Belgium, ex Germinal Ekeren, on 20/8/2001)
PL 50+7/17 FLC 2+1 FAC 3/1*

RAE Alexander (Alex) Scott
Born: Glasgow, 30 September 1969
Height: 5'9" **Weight:** 11.12
Club Honours: Div 1 '99
International Honours: S: B-4; U21-8
This midfielder made a solid start to the
season at Wolves, scoring twice at Derby.
His combination of skill and aggression
was evident, and he was outstanding
when scoring in the win at Coventry. That
was his fifth goal of the season, but he
was not always first choice after
Christmas, partly a tactical move as
Wolves reverted to just two in midfield,
with Paul Ince and Colin Cameron the
preferred pairing. Alex was often on the
bench in the closing stages of the season,
but made his contribution to the club's
promotion campaign with a coolly taken
winner at Reading.
*Falkirk (Free from Bishopbriggs on
15/6/1987) SL 71+12/20 SLC 5/1 SC 2+1
Millwall (£100,000 on 20/8/1990) FL
205+13/63 FLC 13+2/1 FAC 13/6 Others 10/1
Sunderland (£750,000 on 14/6/1996) F/PL
90+24/12 FLC 12+1/3 FAC 7 Others 0+2
Wolverhampton W (£1,200,000 on
21/9/2001) FL 61+13/10 FLC 2/2 FAC 1+2
Others 2+1/1*

Tomasz Radzinski

RAHIM Brent Dominic
Born: Diego Martin, Trinidad, 8 August 1978
Height: 5'8" **Weight:** 10.10
International Honours: Trinidad & Tobago: Signed by Terry Fenwick, who was aware of Brent's talents from his period coaching in Trinidad, this young midfielder looked to be a class find for Northampton Town. However, after a couple of appearances he disappeared on international duty and then returned with a foot injury. Brent remained a regular for Trinidad & Tobago adding six caps during his stay at Sixfields.
West Ham U *(Loaned from Levski Sofia, Bulgaria, ex Joe Public, on 30/8/2002)*
Northampton T *(Loaned from Levski Sofia, Bulgaria on 24/1/2003) FL 6/1*

RAMMELL Andrew (Andy)
Victor
Born: Nuneaton, 10 February 1967
Height: 6'1" **Weight:** 13.12
Wycombe's big target man missed the opening of the 2002-03 season but scored on his first start against Queen's Park Rangers. However, the goals did not flow until he came off the bench against Chesterfield in October to score two fine efforts. Andy then pulled a calf muscle just after Christmas, returned to the team in March and was released to join Bristol Rovers on loan on the transfer deadline. He proved his worth with four vital goals in Rovers' final five matches of the season, including a stunning match-winner at Oxford to secure three points. These ultimately saved the club from relegation to the Conference. Andy is a fine striker in the old-fashioned centre forward mould, with an intimidating physical presence and the precious ability to score regularly if fully fit.
Manchester U *(£40,000 from Atherstone U on 26/9/1989)*
Barnsley *(£100,000 on 14/9/1990) FL 149+36/44 FLC 11+3/1 FAC 12+1/4 Others 8/1*
Southend U *(Signed on 22/2/1996) FL 50+19/13 FLC 3+3/1 FAC 2+1 Others 1*
Walsall *(Free on 15/7/1998) FL 60+9/23 FLC 3/1 FAC 3+1 Others 5/1*
Wycombe W *(£75,000 on 7/9/2000) FL 69+5/25 FLC 3/1 FAC 12/5 Others 3*
Bristol Rov *(Free on 27/3/2003) FL 7/4*

RAMSDEN Simon Paul
Born: Bishop Auckland, 17 December 1981
Height: 6'0" **Weight:** 12.4
This young Sunderland defender progressed successfully to the reserve team in 2001-02 and last term he joined Second Division Notts County in a 12-

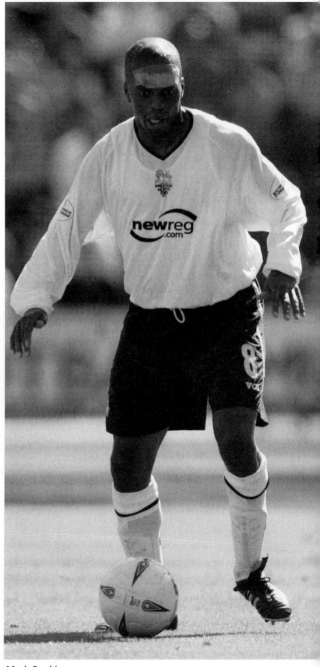

Mark Rankine

onth loan deal. Simon made his debut
senior football from the substitutes'
ench against Wigan and went on to
ature regularly for the Magpies during
e campaign. He became the first choice
right back, producing some convincing
splays and showing a no-nonsense
pproach to defending.
nderland (From trainee on 7/8/2000)
otts Co (Loaned on 16/8/2002) FL 21+11
C 1 FAC 1

ANKIN Isaiah (Izzy)
orn: Edmonton, 22 May 1978
eight: 5'10" **Weight:** 11.6
zy had to settle for a place on the bench
r Barnsley early in the 2002-03 season.
the end he spent most of the campaign
the reserves, the financial needs of the
ub preventing him from playing as
rther appearances would have resulted
an additional fee being due to his
rmer club, Bradford City. Izzy finished
ading scorer for the second string and
ventually came on from the bench to
ore a late winner against Brentford to
eep the club in the Second Division. A
arp and quick striker with an eye for
al, he would benefit from an extended
n of first-team football.
rsenal (From trainee on 12/9/1995) PL 0+1
olchester U (Loaned on 25/9/1997) FL
+1/5 Others 1
radford C (£1,300,000 on 14/8/1998) P/FL
5+22/4 FLC 2/1 FAC 0+2 Others 1+1/1
irmingham C (Loaned on 19/1/2000) FL
1+2/4
olton W (Loaned on 11/8/2000) FL 9+7/2
C 2
arnsley (£350,000 on 19/1/2001) FL
+18/3 FLC 1+1/1

ANKINE Simon Mark
orn: Doncaster, 30 September 1969
eight: 5'9" **Weight:** 12.11
ub Honours: Div 2 '00
his vastly experienced Preston midfielder
arted the opening games of the 2002-
3 season showing his characteristic
etermination and application to the
eam cause, before becoming a regular
ubstitute, then returning to the line-up in
ecember. Unlucky to be sent off at
heffield United, the subsequent
uspension cost him his place as Craig
rown turned to youth, and it was
omewhat ironic when the popular
idfield battler was loaned to the Blades
n deadline day as cover for the run-in.
lark quickly settled into his defensive
idfield duties at Bramall Lane, picking
p and distributing the loose ball, being
vailable when his side had possession

and closing down opponents. He went on
to play a key role in both legs of the play-
off semi-finals against Nottingham Forest.
Doncaster Rov (From trainee on 4/7/1988)
FL 160+4/20 FLC 8+1/1 FAC 8/2 Others 14/2
Wolverhampton W (£70,000 on 31/1/1992)
FL 112+20/1 FLC 9+1 FAC 14+2 Others 7+2
Preston NE (£100,000 on 17/9/1996) FL
217+16/12 FLC 16+4/1 FAC 13/1 Others 6/1
Sheffield U (Loaned on 27/3/2003) FL 5+1
Others 3

RAPLEY Kevin John
Born: Reading, 21 September 1977
Height: 5'9" **Weight:** 10.8
Club Honours: Div 3 '99
Kevin endured a frustrating season at
Colchester United, and was eventually
released by the Essex club at the end of
the campaign. He never actually played
under new manager Phil Parkinson due to
an injury that kept him on the sidelines
from January onwards. The front runner
did score a couple of goals, however,
netting in the 1-1 draw at Huddersfield
and the 4-2 defeat at Mansfield, within
six days of each other.
Brentford (From trainee on 8/7/1996) FL
27+24/12 FLC 3+5/3 FAC 0+2 Others 1
Southend U (Loaned on 20/11/1998) FL 9/4
Notts Co (Loaned on 23/7/1999) FL
21+31/4 FLC 0+3 FAC 1+1/1 Others 1
Exeter C (Loaned on 1/11/2000) FL 6+1 FAC
1 Others 1
Scunthorpe U (Loaned on 17/3/2001) FL
1+4
Colchester U (Free on 3/8/2001) FL
40+16/11 FLC 2+1 FAC 3 Others 2

RASMUSSEN Mark Alan
Born: Newcastle, 28 November 1983
Height: 5'7" **Weight:** 10.10
On the fringes of Burnley's first team
squad for the last two seasons, this right-
sided midfielder finally got his chance
when manager Stan Ternent gave several
of the club's younger players a taste of
the First Division in the home game
against Gillingham in April. Mark had
been a regular in the reserves for some
time and is one of several youngsters who
may be ready to make the step up as the
club must surely make changes in the
season ahead.
Burnley (Free from New Hartley on
3/7/2001) FL 0+2

RAVANELLI Fabrizio
Born: Perugia, Italy, 11 December 1968
Height: 6'1" **Weight:** 13.6
International Honours: Italy: 22
Fabrizio opened the 2002-03 season with
a goal for Derby County in a comfortable

victory over Reading but did not score
again until March. He was hampered by
an achilles tendon injury that eventually
required surgery in Italy and was out of
commission for five months. When he
returned, there were some moments
plucked from the memory bank, a great
turn for the goal against Coventry that
ensured First Division survival and a
devastating free kick at Walsall, but there
were other chances that he would have
swallowed in his pomp. With his great
knowledge of the game, Fabrizio gave
everything to Derby but time marches on
and he was released at the end of the
season. He will be remembered as a good
professional past his best.
Middlesbrough (£7,000,000 from Juventus,
Italy, ex Perugia, Avellino, Casertana, on
15/8/1996) F/PL 35/17 FLC 8/9 FAC 7/6
(£5,300,000 to Marseilles, France on
3/10/1997)
Derby Co (Free from Lazio, Italy on
3/8/2001) P/FL 46+4/14 FLC 2/1 FAC 1/1

RAVEN Paul Duncan
Born: Salisbury, 28 July 1970
Height: 6'1" **Weight:** 12.12
International Honours: E: Sch
This experienced defender was unable to
win a regular place in the Grimsby line-up
last term with the exception of a brief
spell in October. His contract was
eventually cancelled in the spring and he
moved on to Carlisle. Paul proved to be a
crucial signing for the Brunton Park club.
His ability to organise the back line and
read the game produced four clean sheets
in his first five matches. A ligament injury
in mid-April appeared to end his season,
although he bravely returned for the
crucial encounter at Shrewsbury two
weeks later.
Doncaster Rov (From juniors on 6/6/1988)
FL 52/4 FLC 2 FAC 5 Others 2
West Bromwich A (£100,000 on 23/3/1989)
FL 249+10/15 FLC 20/2 FAC 10/3 Others 15/1
Doncaster Rov (Loaned on 27/11/1991) FL 7
Rotherham U (Loaned on 29/10/1998) FL
11/2
Grimsby T (Free on 13/7/2000) FL 21+10 FLC
2 FAC 0+1
Carlisle U (Free on 13/2/2003) FL 11 Others 3

RAWLE Mark Anthony
Born: Leicester, 27 April 1979
Height: 5'11" **Weight:** 12.0
This Southend United striker enjoyed a
solid campaign in 2002-03, just edging
out Tes Bramble for the mantle of top
scorer, he also showed a greatly improved
disciplinary record. Although at times his
ball control was an issue, his

unpredictability made him hard to mark and often won free kicks in dangerous places when defenders resorted to foul tactics. Mark is a real favourite of the Blues' fans who appreciate his willingness to run himself into the ground.
Southend U (£60,000 + from Boston U on 23/2/2001) FL 69+9/15 FLC 2/1 FAC 6+1/3 Others 2/1

REA Simon
Born: Kenilworth, 20 September 1976
Height: 6'1" **Weight:** 13.2
Simon finally won himself a regular place in the Peterborough United line-up last term with some fine and committed displays. He is a left-sided central defender who is strong in the air, dedicated, brave and not without skill. Simon was rewarded for his efforts when he was voted 'Player of the Year' by the Posh Supporters' Club.

Birmingham C (From trainee on 27/1/1995) FL 0+1 Others 1+1
Peterborough U (Free on 24/8/1999) FL 108+9/7 FLC 4+1 FAC 8 Others 5/1

REDDINGTON Stuart
Born: Lincoln, 21 February 1978
Height: 6'2" **Weight:** 13.6
The regular centre back in Mansfield Town's promotion side, Stuart kept his place in the line-up at the start of the 2002-03 campaign. However, he struggling to find his form in the higher division and was loaned out to Burton Albion for a month in October. The loan period proved to be very successful and was extended, before eventually being made permanent.
Chelsea (Signed from Lincoln U on 24/8/1999)
Mansfield T (£20,000 on 16/3/2001) FL 48+6/1 FLC 2 Others 1

REDDY Michael
Born: Kilkenny City, Ireland, 24 March 1980
Height: 6'1" **Weight:** 11.7
International Honours: RoI: U21-8; Yth
This young Sunderland striker spent much of the 2002-03 season out on loan as he sought to gain further experience of senior football. He had a spell at York in mid-season, impressing with his pace, and scoring in the home wins over Carlisle United and Swansea City. Later he signed a one-month deal with Sheffield Wednesday, but did so well he stayed for three months. He was used as a right winger in the 4-2-4 formation employed by the Owls and, although not his favourite role, he played well for the team and managed to get on the score sheet on three occasions.
Sunderland (£50,000 from Kilkenny C on 30/8/1999) PL 0+10/1 FLC 2+1/1 FAC 0+1

Mark Rawle

vindon T *(Loaned on 27/1/2001) FL*
+1/4 Others 1+1/1
ull C *(Loaned on 21/9/2001) FL 1+4/4*
rk C *(Loaned on 1/11/2002) FL 10+1/2*
effield Wed *(Loaned on 30/1/2003) FL*
+2/3

EDFEARN Neil David
rn: Dewsbury, 20 June 1965
eight: 5'9" **Weight:** 13.0
ub Honours: Div 2 '91
is veteran midfield man combined his
aying duties for Boston with the role of
sistant-manager. Neil took time to settle
to the team but was a key figure in the
cond half of the season when the
grims began to move up the table. He
ovided a healthy supply of goals as well
leadership and experience in the
ddle of the park.
olton W *(From Nottingham F juniors on*
/6/1982) FL 35/1 FLC 2 FAC 4
ncoln C *(£8,250 on 23/3/1984) FL*
+4/13 FLC 4 FAC 3/1 Others 7
oncaster Rov *(£17,500 on 22/8/1986) FL*
/14 FLC 2 FAC 3/1 Others 2
rystal Palace *(£100,000 on 31/7/1987) FL*
/10 FLC 6 FAC 1 Others 1
atford *(£150,000 on 21/11/1988) FL*
+2/3 FLC 1 FAC 6/3 Others 5/1
dham Ath *(f150,000 on 12/1/1990) FL*
+6/16 FLC 3/1 FAC 7+1/3 Others 1
rnsley *(£150,000 on 5/9/1991) F/PL*
39+3/71 FLC 21/6 FAC 20/6 Others 5
arlton Ath *(£1,000,000 on 1/7/1998) PL*
)+1/3 FLC 2/1 FAC 1
adford C *(£250,000 on 3/8/1999) PL*
4+3/1 FLC 1+1 FAC 2
igan Ath *(£112,500 on 17/3/2000) FL*
3+4/7 FAC 1 Others 1
alifax T *(Free on 16/3/2001) FL 39+3/6 FLC*
FAC 3 Others 1
oston U *(Free on 3/8/2002) FL 27+4/6 FLC 1*

EDKNAPP Jamie Frank
rn: Barton on Sea, 25 June 1973
eight: 6'0" **Weight:** 12.10
ub Honours: FLC '95; ESC '01
ternational Honours: E: 17; B-1; U21-
), Yth; Sch
ell-documented injury problems
ontinued to blight this talented
idfielder's progress back to international
atus last season. However, Jamie did
ell in his appearances for Tottenham. As
uick on his feet as ever and an
telligent reader of the game, he added
much needed creative presence in
idfield as well as width when playing on
ne flanks. Great ability in attack
roduced only three goals last term and
ne key for his future success is
ndoubtedly an injury-free campaign.

Bournemouth *(From trainee on 27/6/1990)*
FL 6+7 FLC 3 FAC 3 Others 2
Liverpool *(£350,000 on 15/11/1991) F/PL*
207+30/30 FLC 26+1/5 FAC 17+1/2 Others
20+6/4
Tottenham H *(Free on 18/4/2002) PL 14+3/3*

REDMILE Matthew (Matt)
Ian
Born: Nottingham, 12 November 1976
Height: 6'3" **Weight:** 14.10
Club Honours: Div 3 '98
This experienced central defender had a
difficult time at Shrewsbury in 2002-03 as
he struggled to reach his form of the
previous season. A key factor, perhaps,
was the early-season loss of defensive
partner Mick Heathcote to injury and
manager Kevin Ratcliffe never managed
to replace him in a formation that
remained unsettled throughout. An
effective player when coming up to join
the attack for corners, Matt managed just
one goal for the Shrews during the
campaign.
Notts Co *(From trainee on 4/7/1995) FL*
140+7/7 FLC 11 FAC 13/1 Others 4
Shrewsbury T *(£30,000 on 3/11/2000) FL*
107/6 FLC 2 FAC 3 Others 7

REDMOND Stephen (Steve)
Born: Liverpool, 2 November 1967
Height: 5'11" **Weight:** 11.7
Club Honours: FAYC '86
International Honours: E: U21-14; Yth
Despite operating on a rolling monthly
contract throughout the season, purely
down to Bury's finances, veteran central
defender Steve Redmond continually
proved to be a rock at the heart of a
young defence. His experience greatly
benefited Michael Nelson in particular as
he marshalled the back line superbly, and
he also chipped in with two goals. Even if
prone to the odd error, Steve made a
massive contribution to the Shakers'
season and it was a pity that a
disappointing 3-1 play-off defeat at
Bournemouth proved to be his final game
for the club, as he was released in May.
Manchester C *(From apprentice on*
3/12/1984) FL 231+4/7 FLC 24 FAC 17 Others
11
Oldham Ath *(£300,000 on 10/7/1992) P/FL*
195+10/4 FLC 20/1 FAC 10+2 Others 1+1
Bury *(Free on 3/7/1998) FL 145+6/6 FLC 7+1*
FAC 7 Others 9

REED Adam Maurice
Born: Bishop Auckland, 18 February 1975
Height: 6'1" **Weight:** 12.0
Adam had a frustrating time at Darlington
last term, and managed just one

appearance from the bench all season,
featuring at Leyton Orient in September.
The experienced defender can always be
relied upon to produce a reliable
performance with his strength in the air
and calm distribution. Adam was released
at the end of the season.
Darlington *(From trainee on 16/7/1993) FL*
45+7/1 FLC 1+1 FAC 1 Others 3
Blackburn Rov *(£200,000 on 9/8/1995)*
Darlington *(Loaned on 21/2/1997) FL 14*
Rochdale *(Loaned on 5/12/1997) FL 10*
Others 2/1
Darlington *(Free on 17/7/1998) FL 80+14/2*
FLC 6 FAC 6+1 Others 2+3

REEVES Alan
Born: Birkenhead, 19 November 1967
Height: 6'0" **Weight:** 12.0
Swindon Town's veteran defender
enjoyed another fine season in 2002-03.
Although initially not a member of the
side he forced his way back into
contention as the team hit some poor
early-season form and his
uncompromising and committed displays
helped the Robins turn their fortunes
around. Alan is perhaps not the most
polished of defenders but his sheer
persistence and a willingness to throw
himself into the thick of the action were
again evident and he thoroughly deserved
his runner-up spot in the clubs 'Player of
the Season' award. He has now made
over 400 league appearances and
although looking to develop a coaching
role in 2003-04, he should not be written
off as a contender for a first-team spot.
Norwich C *(Free from Heswall on 20/9/1988)*
Gillingham *(Loaned on 9/2/1989) FL 18*
Chester C *(£10,000 on 18/8/1989) FL 31+9/2*
FLC 1+1 FAC 3 Others 3
Rochdale *(Free on 2/7/1991) FL 119+2/9 FLC*
12/1 FAC 6 Others 5
Wimbledon *(£300,000 on 6/9/1994) PL*
52+5/4 FLC 2+2 FAC 8
Swindon T *(Free on 23/6/1998) FL 167+5/11*
FLC 8+2/2 FAC 6 Others 3

REEVES David Edward
Born: Birkenhead, 19 November 1967
Height: 6'0" **Weight:** 12.6
Club Honours: Div 3 '95
With no chance of featuring in Oldham's
plans, David made a surprise loan return
to Chesterfield last August and signed
permanently before the end of the year.
His experience was important in holding
the attack together and he scored six
valuable goals in a seven-game spell in
March. When Dave Rushbury left the
manager's chair close to the season's end

David assumed some coaching duties in the reshuffle.

Sheffield Wed *(Free from Heswall on 6/8/1986) FL 8+9/2 FLC 1+1/1 FAC 1+1 Others 0+1*
Scunthorpe U *(Loaned on 17/12/1986) FL 3+1/2*
Scunthorpe U *(Loaned on 1/10/1987) FL 6/4*
Burnley *(Loaned on 20/11/1987) FL 16/8 Others 2/1*
Bolton W *(£80,000 on 17/8/1989) FL 111+23/29 FLC 14+1/1 FAC 8+5/5 Others 9+2/7*
Notts Co *(£80,000 on 25/3/1993) FL 9+4/2 FLC 1+1*
Carlisle U *(£121,000 on 1/10/1993) FL 127/48 FLC 9/5 FAC 9/4 Others 23/7*
Preston NE *(Signed on 9/10/1996) FL 45+2/12 FLC 3+1/3 FAC 2/3 Others 1*
Chesterfield *(Signed on 6/11/1997) FL 160+8/46 FLC 10+1/4 FAC 6+1/1 Others 10/5*
Oldham Ath *(Free on 19/12/2001) FL 11+2/3*
Chesterfield *(Free on 14/8/2002) FL 36+4/8 FLC 2*

REEVES Martin Lee

Born: Birmingham, 7 September 1981
Height: 6'0" **Weight:** 11.12
This promising midfielder is highly regarded by the academy and reserve staff at Leicester. He appeared from the bench last season and also made one start, in the Worthington Cup win over Sheffield Wednesday. In March he linked up with former boss Peter Taylor at Hull for a loan spell, scoring a goal that, for a time, threatened to end Swansea's league sojourn. He was released by Leicester at the end of 2002-03.

Leicester C *(From trainee on 1/11/2000) P/FL 1+7 FLC 1+1*
Hull C *(Loaned on 7/3/2003) FL 5+3/1*

REGAN Carl Anthony

Born: Liverpool, 9 September 1980
Height: 6'0" **Weight:** 11.5
Club Honours: FAYC '98
International Honours: E: Yth
Following the emergence of Neil Austin at Barnsley, Carl was allowed to go out on loan to Hull with Andy Holt moving in the opposite direction. He soon settled into the right-back slot and, despite the change of manager from Jan Molby to Peter Taylor, was offered an 18-month contract by the Tigers in November. The subsequent arrival of Marc Joseph and Jon Otsemobor provided stiff competition for and he was employed in a right-sided midfield position in the closing weeks of the season.

Everton *(From trainee on 19/1/1998)*

Barnsley *(£20,000 on 15/6/2000) FL 31+6 FLC 5*
Hull C *(Free on 15/8/2002) FL 33+5 FLC 1 FAC 1*

REID Andrew (Andy) Matthew

Born: Dublin, 29 July 1982
Height: 5'7" **Weight:** 11.12
International Honours: RoI: U21-14; Yth (UEFA-U16 '98)
This left winger was a revelation for Nottingham Forest in the second half of the 2002-03 season after mainly being used as a substitute earlier in the campaign. His excellent wing play set up many goals for David Johnson and Marlon Harewood as Forest made it to the play-offs before falling at the semi-final stage to Sheffield United. Andy remained a regular at U21 level for the Republic of Ireland.

Nottingham F *(From trainee on 16/8/1999) FL 50+23/3 FLC 2+2 FAC 2/1 Others 2/1*

REID Brian Robertson

Born: Paisley, 15 June 1970
Height: 6'2" **Weight:** 11.12
Club Honours: AMC '02
International Honours: S: U21-4
This experienced left-sided central defender found himself surplus to requirements at Blackpool last season and was restricted to a single first-team outing in the LDV Vans Trophy tie against Scunthorpe. Brian's contract was cancelled at the end of December and he subsequently returned to Scotland, signing for Falkirk.

Morton *(Free from Renfrew Waverley on 27/7/1988) SL 57/1 SLC 2 SC 7 Others 2/1*
Glasgow R *(Signed on 25/3/1991) SL 5*
Morton *(Signed on 11/3/1996) SL 68/3 SLC 4 SC 3 Others 5*
Burnley *(Signed on 4/9/1998) FL 30+1/3 FAC 1 Others 1*
Dunfermline Ath *(Free on 7/7/1999) SL 23+4/3 SLC 2 SC 1 Others 1*
Blackpool *(Free on 6/10/2000) FL 55/2 FLC 1 FAC 5 Others 8/1*

REID Levi Stanley Junior

Born: Stafford, 19 January 1983
Height: 5'5" **Weight:** 11.1
This adaptable Port Vale midfield player made his debut on the final day of the season at Bristol City when coming on as a substitute for the last half an hour. Levi showed no nerves as he slotted in well in the centre and demonstrated good passing skills. He had been on the bench earlier in the campaign but bided his time until being called upon. Small and nippy, Levi is the eldest of three brothers who

are all on Vale's books in one way or another.

Port Vale *(Trainee) FL 0+1*

REID Paul James

Born: Sydney, Australia, 6 July 1979
Height: 5'10" **Weight:** 10.10
Paul won the admiration of the Bradford City supporters with a fantastic double strike on his full debut in the 2-1 win over Norwich in October. But the enthusiastic central midfielder went on to spend most of the campaign biding his time on the substitutes' bench. His persistence paid off when he earned a run in the side during a hectic fixture schedule in March. Paul was on a monthly contract after joining the club on a trial basis in September and he was rewarded with a new one-year deal in May.

Bradford C *(Free from Wollongong Wolves, Australia on 7/9/2002) FL 7+1/2*

REID Paul Mark

Born: Carlisle, 18 February 1982
Height: 6'2" **Weight:** 12.4
International Honours: E: Yth
This central defender was again unable to make a breakthrough at Ibrox in 2002-03 and spent the second half of the campaign on loan at Northampton. He turned in some impressive displays, despite having to cope with an ever-changing run of partners in the Cobblers' defence. Commanding in the air and sharp on the floor, he was reported to have signed permanently during the summer.

Carlisle U *(From trainee on 19/2/1999) FL 17+2 Others 3*
Glasgow R *(£200,000 on 1/7/2000)*
Preston NE *(Loaned on 29/1/2002) FL 0+1/*
Northampton T *(Loaned on 31/12/2002) FL 19*

REID Paul Robert

Born: Oldbury, 19 January 1968
Height: 5'9" **Weight:** 11.8
Paul opened his account for the Swans with a scorching goal from outside the box in the opening match of the season against Rushden. A tough competitor in the midfield engine room, he took over the captaincy for a short period when Kristian O'Leary was suspended. A change of management at the Vetch Field and a troublesome groin strain saw him struggle to command a place in the starting line-up, and in late March he had his contract paid up. He subsequently joined League of Wales outfit Carmarthen Town.

Leicester C *(From apprentice on 9/1/1986) FL 140+22/21 FLC 13/4 FAC 5+1 Others 6+2*

adford C *(Loaned on 19/3/1992) FL 7*
adford C *(£25,000 on 27/7/1992) FL
+2/15 FLC 3/2 FAC 3 Others 5/1*
addersfield T *(£70,000 on 20/5/1994) FL
+7/6 FLC 9/1 FAC 5+1 Others 1*
dham Ath *(£100,000 on 27/3/1997) FL
/6 FLC 4/1 FAC 8 Others 1*
ry *(Free on 2/7/1999) FL 102+8/9 FLC 5/1
C 5+1 Others 5*
vansea C *(Free on 8/7/2002) FL 18+2/1
C 1 Others 1*

EID Steven John
rn: Kingston, 10 March 1981
eight: 6'1" **Weight:** 12.4
ub Honours: Div 2 '01
ternational Honours: RoI: 9; U21-2; E:
h
even returned to Millwall after featuring
r the Republic of Ireland in the 2002
orld Cup finals, but missed the first four
onths of the new season due to injury.
owever, once fit he quickly returned to
s best form and scored some excellent
als, none better than a 30-yard half
lley against Sheffield Wednesday.
even is a speedy left winger who is very
lful on the ball and has a great eye for
al. His consistency at international level
as recognised when he received the 'FAI
ung Player of the Year' award.
*llwall (From trainee on 18/5/1998) FL
5+24/18 FLC 5+2 FAC 10/1 Others 10+1*

EO-COKER Nigel Shola Andre
rn: Thornton Heath, 14 May 1984
eight: 5'8" **Weight:** 10.5
ternational Honours: E: Yth
gel made his league debut for
imbledon in the last game of the 2001-
' season, and had to wait until the end
October at Sheffield United for his next
ste of first-team action. A barnstorming
splay at Bramall Lane was the outcome,
d from then on he was a virtual ever-
esent in the Dons' starting line-up until
e end of the campaign. An all-action
ntral midfielder, he runs with the ball
perbly and is a tenacious tackler and
oughtful distributor. An overwhelming
oice for the club's 'Young Player of the
ar' award, he also picked up an
gland U19 cap.
*imbledon (From trainee on 15/7/2002) FL
+1/2 FLC 1+1 FAC 1+1*

EPKA Tomas
rn: Zlin, Czechoslovakia, 2 January 1974
eight: 6'0" **Weight:** 12.7
ternational Honours: Czech Republic:
5
he Czech central defender suffered a
an spell in the first part of the 2002-03

season as West Ham slumped to the
bottom of the Premiership. However his
form improved remarkably in the new
year and he produced some inspired
performances, tackling fiercely and
showing excellent positional play. Tomas
was superb in the vital end-of-season
victories against Manchester City and
Chelsea, but nevertheless was unable to
prevent the Hammers from being
relegated.
*West Ham U (£5,500,000 from Fiorentina,
Italy, ex Banik Ostrava, Sparta Prague, on
14/9/2001) PL 63 FLC 1 FAC 3+1*

REUSER Martijn Franciscus
Born: Amsterdam, Holland, 1 February
1975
Height: 5'9" **Weight:** 11.7
International Honours: Holland: 1;
U21-12
Kept out of the Ipswich side by injury for
much of the 2003-03 season, Martijn
often found himself on the substitutes'
bench when he was fully fit. However, he
usually proved effective when brought on,
either scoring himself or laying on
opportunities for his colleagues. Martijn
was made available on a free transfer just

Nigel Reo-Coker

355

before the January transfer window, but continued to play for Ipswich until the end of the season. His powerful shooting brought him both his goals during the season. He hit the vital equaliser against Brighton with a shot from just outside the box and set up the convincing victory over leaders Portsmouth with another long-range effort.

Ipswich T (£1,000,000 + from Vitesse Arnhem, Holland, ex Ajax, on 23/3/2000) P/FL 39+35/11 FLC 4+4/2 FAC 3+1 Others 2+5/2

REVELL Alexander (Alex)
David
Born: Cambridge, 7 July 1983
Height: 6'3" **Weight:** 12.0
This young Cambridge striker suffered a broken foot during the opening weeks of the 2002-03 season and required an operation, keeping him out of action until January. He joined Conference club Cambridge United on loan to help regain match fitness, but on his return to the Abbey Stadium he was restricted to outings from the substitutes' bench.
Cambridge U (From trainee on 21/4/2001) FL 9+28/2 FAC 0+2 Others 1+5

REYNA Claudio
Born: Livingston, New Jersey, USA, 20 July 1973
Height: 5'8" **Weight:** 11.3
Club Honours: SPD '00; SC '99
International Honours: USA: 93
Sunderland's powerhouse American midfielder returned to Wearside from the 2002 World Cup having captained his country to the quarter-finals and been voted into the FIFA All-Star line-up for the competition. A box-to-box schemer whose confidence on the ball is reflected in his incisive and constructive passing, Claudio scored his only goal of the season at Cambridge in the Worthington Cup in October before rupturing a cruciate ligament at Bolton three games later, an injury which ended his season. Claudio was sorely missed by the Black Cats as the team sank into the Nationwide League and although one player alone would have struggled to keep them afloat, his ability at set pieces and undoubted leadership qualities would certainly have made a big difference.
Glasgow R (£2,000,000 from VFL Wolfsburg, Germany, ex Virginia University, Beyer Leverkusen, on 31/3/1999) SL 57+6/9 SLC 2/1 SC 6+1 Others 25/1
Sunderland (£4,500,000 on 7/12/2001) PL 28/3 FLC 1/1

[RICARDO] LOPEZ Ricardo
Felipe
Born: Spain, 30 December 1971
Height: 6'2" **Weight:** 13.9
International Honours: Spain: 1
Ricardo arrived at Manchester United with the aim of succeeding Fabien Barthez as the Reds' number one 'keeper, but after being given an early chance to shine in the Champions' League qualifier against Olympiakos in October he only played in three more European games, and did not make his Premiership debut until late April against Blackburn Rovers at Old Trafford. In the pressure-cooker atmosphere of a must-win game his first contribution was a penalty save from David Dunn after upending the former United favourite, Andy Cole, in the box. Otherwise he competed with Roy Carroll for a regular place on the bench for most of the campaign.
Manchester U (£1,500,000 from Real Valladolid, Spain, ex Atletico Madrid, on 30/8/2002) PL 0+1 Others 3+1

RICHARDS Dean Ivor
Born: Bradford, 9 June 1974
Height: 6'2" **Weight:** 13.5
International Honours: E: U21-4
A defender of the highest quality, Dean is a great battler and holds the back line together using experience and skill. He also has a keen eye for goal at set pieces and likes to push up the field, being comfortable on the ball. A great organiser at the back, he featured regularly for Tottenham last term, but suffered somewhat from playing in an ever-changing defensive combination, a result of injuries more than anything else.
Bradford C (From trainee on 10/7/1992) FL 82+4/4 FLC 7/1 FAC 4/1 Others 3+2
Wolverhampton W (£1,850,000 on 25/3/1995) FL 118+4/7 FLC 11 FAC 10/1 Others 2
Southampton (Free on 28/7/1999) PL 67/3 FLC 7/2 FAC 4+1/2
Tottenham H (£8,100,000 on 24/9/2001) PL 50/4 FLC 1 FAC 4

RICHARDS Justin
Born: West Bromwich, 16 October 1980
Height: 5'10" **Weight:** 11.0
This young striker failed to start a league game for Bristol Rovers last term and took the opportunity to gain further experience with a loan spell at Colchester United, with Adrian Coote moving in the opposite direction. However, Justin was also restricted to outings from the bench at Layer Road, and in December he joined Stevenage Borough, also on loan. He did

well with the Conference club, netting a hat trick in a 5-0 victory over Farnborou and subsequently joined them on a permanent basis.
West Bromwich A (From trainee on 8/1/1999) FL 0+1 FAC 0+1
Bristol Rov (£75,000 on 19/1/2001) FL 3+ Others 0+1
Colchester U (Loaned on 21/10/2002) FL 0+2 Others 0+1

RICHARDS Marc John
Born: Wolverhampton, 8 July 1982
Height: 6'0" **Weight:** 12.7
International Honours: E: Yth
Brought on for Blackburn in extra time i the Worthington Cup tie against Walsall this young striker ended up the hero when he scored the deciding penalty. He was then loaned to Swansea City where he enjoyed a successful spell, scoring seven times from 14 starts. Marc is a live front runner, who has shown that he ha a good eye for goal.
Blackburn Rov (From trainee on 12/7/1999 FLC 1+1
Crewe Alex (Loaned on 10/8/2001) FL 1+3 FLC 0+1/1
Oldham Ath (Loaned on 12/10/2001) FL 3+ Others 1/1
Halifax T (Loaned on 12/2/2002) FL 5
Swansea C (Loaned on 22/11/2002) FL 14+3/7

RICHARDS Matthew
Born: Harlow, 26 December 1984
Height: 5'8" **Weight:** 11.0
Matthew is another successful product c the Ipswich Town academy, having progressed to the first team via the reserve and youth teams. Primarily a left wing back or full back he has an excellen tackle and the pace to match the most fleet-footed attacker. Matthew benefited greatly from the extended opportunities granted by the departure of Jamie Clapham in the new year.
Ipswich T (From trainee on 31/1/2002) FL 10+3 FLC 0+1 FAC 1 Others 1+1

RICHARDSON Frazer
Born: Rotherham, 29 October 1982
Height: 5'11" **Weight:** 12.1
International Honours: E: Yth
This promising young defender made his senior debut for Leeds United in the UEF Cup second leg tie away to Hapoel Tel Aviv, when he came on as a substitute. I January he went out on loan to Stoke City where he was used on the right-har side of midfield rather than his more usual role at right back. Frazer enjoyed a 'Man of the Match' debut against

icester City and went on to make a
tal of seven appearances for the
tteries club before returning to Elland
ad to continue his development.
eds U (From trainee on 2/11/1999) Others
-1
oke C (Loaned on 10/1/2003) FL 6+1

ICHARDSON Ian George
orn: Barking, 22 October 1970
eight: 5'10" **Weight:** 11.1
ub Honours: Div 3 '98
ternational Honours: E: SP-1
great favourite with the Notts County
ns due to his competitive approach to
e game, Ian featured regularly at first-
am level last term. He appeared in a
riety of roles – in the centre of the
efence, at left back and in the centre of
idfield – but wherever he played he
ways gave his best. Ian scored two goals
r the Magpies during the season,
etting in the LDV Vans Trophy tie against
igan and also in the Boxing Day
ncounter with Barnsley.
rmingham C (£60,000 from Dagenham &
edbridge on 23/8/1995) FL 3+4 FLC 3+1
C 2 Others 1+2
otts Co (£200,000 on 19/1/1996) FL
37+16/18 FLC 13 FAC 1/1 Others 8/1

ICHARDSON Kieran Edward
orn: Greenwich, 21 October 1984
eight: 5'9" **Weight:** 10.11
ub Honours: FAYC '03
n excellent midfielder with good all-
und skills, of all the United youngsters
oming through the ranks, Kieran was
ven the seal of approval with first-team
ction coming in all four major
ompetitions last term. Making his debut
gainst Maccabi Haifa in the Champions'
eague in October, he had further fruitful
xploits in the Premiership, Worthington
up and FA Cup. Not to forget of course
s first honour for the Reds in the FA
outh Cup against Middlesbrough. Quite
season for a player who is described as
aving an outstanding future!
anchester U (Trainee) PL 0+2 FLC 0+1/1
AC 1 Others 2+3

ICHARDSON Leam Nathan
orn: Leeds, 19 November 1979
eight: 5'7" **Weight:** 11.4
his promising Bolton Wanderers
efender or midfielder spent most of the
econd half of the 2002-03 campaign on
an at Blackpool. He performed
onsistently in defence for the Seasiders,
nd following the expiry of his contract at
he Reebok he was reported to have

signed permanently for the Second
Division club in the summer.
Blackburn Rov (From trainee on
31/12/1997) FLC 1
Bolton W (£50,000 on 13/7/2000) P/FL 5+8
FLC 3+1 FAC 1
Notts Co (Loaned on 9/11/2001) FL 20+1
FAC 1
Blackpool (Loaned on 20/12/2002) FL 20
FAC 1

RICHARDSON Lee James
Born: Halifax, 12 March 1969
Height: 5'11" **Weight:** 11.0
Lee made only a cameo appearance on
the pitch for Chesterfield last season, but
he was a real asset off it. As assistant to
manager Dave Rushbury he played an
important part in bringing on many of
the club's young players during the year
and he also piloted the Spireites to vital
results as caretaker-manager in the wake
of Rushbury's departure in April. It is
hoped that Chesterfield will continue to
find a role for Lee in the 2003-04
campaign.
Halifax T (From trainee on 6/7/1987) FL
43+13/2 FLC 4 FAC 4+2 Others 6
Watford (£175,000 on 9/2/1989) FL 40+1/1
FLC 1+1 FAC 1
Blackburn Rov (£250,000 on 15/8/1990) FL
50+12/3 FLC 1+1 Others 2+2
Aberdeen (£152,000 on 16/9/1992) SL
59+5/6 SLC 2/1 SC 8/2 Others 3/1
Oldham Ath (£300,000 on 12/8/1994) FL
82+6/21 FLC 6/2 FAC 3/1 Others 4
Stockport Co (Loaned on 15/8/1997) FL 4+2
Huddersfield T (£65,000 on 24/10/1997) FL
29+7/3 FAC 0+2
Bury (Loaned on 27/8/1999) FL 5/1
Livingston (Free on 3/2/2000) SL 6 SC 1
Chesterfield (Free on 11/8/2000) FL 43+1/1
FLC 2+1 FAC 2 Others 5

RICHARDSON Marcus Glenroy
Born: Reading, 31 August 1977
Height: 6'2" **Weight:** 13.2
Marcus began the 2002-03 season on
monthly contracts at Torquay, but after
losing out on a place in the starting line-
up he quickly moved on to join
Hartlepool. A tall striker who is a willing
worker, he partnered his ex-Torquay team
mate Eifion Williams in the attack and
was soon among the goals. Having scored
for the Gulls against Hartlepool early in
the season, he had the satisfaction of
returning the favour in February when
heading the winning goal for Pool against
Torquay!
Cambridge U (Free from Harrow Borough on
16/3/2001) FL 7+9/2 FLC 1

Torquay U (£5,000 on 18/9/2001) FL
21+18/8 FLC 0+1 FAC 1 Others 0+1
Hartlepool U (Free on 1/10/2002) FL 20+4/5
FAC 2/1

RICHMOND Andrew (Andy)
John
Born: Nottingham, 9 January 1983
Height: 6'3" **Weight:** 12.10
Chesterfield's young goalkeeper broke
into the team after injury to Carl
Muggleton and acquitted himself well. His
positional sense and shot stopping were
up to the mark, and his command of the
box and ability to deal with crosses
improved as confidence grew. Although
later replaced by an on-loan 'keeper he
did enough to justify his place at the club
and promised more in a position where
players get better with age.
Chesterfield (From trainee on 9/7/2002) FL
6+1

RICKERS Paul Steven
Born: Pontefract, 9 May 1975
Height: 5'10" **Weight:** 11.0
For this midfield player it was a case of 'it
never rains but what it pours' at
Northampton last term. After recovering
from an injury suffered towards the end
of 2001-02 he came in for a few games
at right back, where he excelled, and then
on the right-hand side of midfield.
However he was then sidelined with a
broken leg and this all but finished his
season.
Oldham Ath (From trainee on 16/7/1993) FL
242+19/20 FLC 13/2 FAC 17+2 Others 5+2
Northampton T (Free on 8/7/2002) FL 8+3
FLC 0+1 FAC 1 Others 2/1

RICKETTS Michael Barrington
Born: Birmingham, 4 December 1978
Height: 6'2" **Weight:** 11.12
International Honours: E: 1
The hero and villain in equal measure, as
far as Bolton fans were concerned,
Michael scored the team's first goal of the
season, a penalty in the 4-1 opening day
defeat at Fulham. However, he struggled
to find his form and it came as no
surprise when he made the move to
Middlesbrough during the January
transfer window. The talented young
striker played nine games for Boro',
finding the net in the final game of the
season, a 3-1 defeat at his old club Bolton
Wanderers, a win which kept the Trotters
in the Premiership.
Walsall (From trainee on 13/9/1996) FL
31+45/14 FLC 2+4 FAC 2+2 Others 3+1/1
Bolton W (£500,000 on 17/7/2000) P/FL
63+35/37 FLC 0+4/3 FAC 4+3/4 Others 1+2/2

Michael Ricketts

*iddlesbrough (£2,200,000 on 31/1/2003)
5+4/1*

ICKETTS Samuel (Sam) erek

orn: Aylesbury, 11 October 1981
eight: 6'0" **Weight:** 11.12
am failed to make an impression in the
xford side last term and made just two
bstitute appearances in a disappointing
ason. He is a willing worker and able to
ay in several positions at the back and
midfield. He enjoyed a successful loan
ell at Nuneaton before coming back to
xford only to break his collarbone in a
serve game.
*xford U (From trainee on 20/4/2000) FL
2+13/1 FLC 1 Others 2*

IDGEWELL Liam Matthew

orn: London, 21 July 1984
eight: 5'10" **Weight:** 11.0
lub Honours: FAYC '02
ternational Honours: E: Yth
member of the Aston Villa team that
on the FA Youth Cup in 2001-02, Liam
as loaned out to Bournemouth in
ctober, making his senior debut against
artlepool. He impressed in his spell with
e Cherries before returning to Villa Park,
here he appeared as a substitute in the
\ Cup tie against Blackburn Rovers. Liam
atured regularly for England at U19
vel during the season.
*ston Villa (From trainee on 26/7/2001) FAC
+1*
*ournemouth (Loaned on 11/10/2002) FL
+3*

IDLER David (Dave) George

orn: Liverpool, 12 March 1976
eight: 6'0'' **Weight:** 12.1
ave featured regularly for Macclesfield
own in the early part of the 2002-03
ampaign, but rarely made the line-up
om November onwards. He added just
wo further appearances before being
eleased on transfer deadline day to join
onference club Scarborough. Dave
sually played on the left side of the three
entre backs but made several
ppearances on the right side, performing
is defensive duties well, although there
vere times when his distribution could
ave been more accurate.
*Vrexham (Free from Rockys on 3/7/1996) FL
04+12/1 FLC 5 FAC 10+2 Others 8+2/1*
*lacclesfield T (Free on 16/7/2001) FL 53+3
LC 2 FAC 4+1 Others 2*

IDLEY Lee

lorn: Scunthorpe, 5 December 1981
leight: 5'9" **Weight:** 11.2

Lee had his best season so far in terms of
appearances for Scunthorpe in 2002-03,
with a good run in the team at the start
of March. Left-sided, his best position is
left back but restricted opportunities saw
him fill in at right back and at centre half,
shining in that role in the away match at
Kidderminster. He is a solid if
unspectacular young defender who works
hard at his game.
*Scunthorpe U (From trainee on 3/7/2001) FL
12+5 FAC 1 Others 0+1*

RIGGOTT Christopher (Chris)

Born: Derby, 1 September 1980
Height: 6'3" **Weight:** 12.2
International Honours: E: U21-9; Yth
This classy central defender featured
regularly for Derby in the first half of the
2002-03 season and it was hoped that
he would be one of the foundations
around whom the team would be
rebuilt. However, he returned to the
Premiership during the January transfer
window, signing for Middlesbrough
along with his colleague Malcolm
Christie. Chris made an immediate
impact for his new club, performing
admirably in a 1-1 draw with Liverpool
in his debut, then he became an instant
hit with his double strike in the Tees-
Wear 'derby' as he sent local rivals
Sunderland plummeting towards
relegation, scoring twice in seven
minutes. The 22-year-old had an
operation to repair damaged cartilage in
March, an injury he picked up in the 1-1
draw against Everton.
*Derby Co (From trainee on 5/10/1998) P/FL
87+4/5 FLC 7/1 FAC 2/1*
*Middlesbrough (£1,500,000 + on
31/1/2003) PL 4+1/2*

RIIHILAHTI Aki

Born: Helsinki, Finland, 9 September
1976
Height: 6'1" **Weight:** 12.6
International Honours: Finland: 45;
U21-2; Yth
This tall and skilful midfield player had a
disappointing time with injuries and loss
of form for Crystal Palace last season. He
was in and out of the side and made the
starting line-up in less than half the
club's matches, scoring his only goal in
the defeat at Sheffield United in
November. Aki continued to represent
Finland at international level during the
campaign.
*Crystal Palace (£200,000 from Valerenga,
Norway, ex HJK Helsinki, on 22/3/2001) FL
69+10/7 FLC 5+1/1 FAC 3*

RIISE Jon Arne

Born: Molde, Norway, 24 September 1980
Height: 6'1" **Weight:** 12.6
Club Honours: ESC '01; CS '01; FLC '03
International Honours: Norway: 25;
U21-17; Yth
This left-sided defender or midfielder
enjoyed another fine season for Liverpool
appearing in more games than any other
Reds' player apart from Danny Murphy.
For the first half of the season he was
employed mostly in midfield where his
natural attacking instincts brought him
several fine opportunistic goals. However
in the latter stages of the campaign he
reverted to left back. His six goals (all in
the Premiership) were all vital match
winners or point-savers, if less spectacular
than some of his dramatic strikes of the
previous campaign. In a team with few
natural goal-scorers his contributions are
much appreciated.
*Liverpool (£3,770,000 from AS Monaco,
France, ex Aalesund, on 26/7/2001) PL
65+10/13 FLC 4 FAC 4+1 Others 26+2/1*

RILEY Paul Anthony

Born: Nottingham, 29 September 1982
Height: 5'9" **Weight:** 10.7
This promising Notts County youngster
struggled to earn a place in the first-team
squad last term, but as soon as he was in
the reckoning he suffered an injury that
forced him onto the sidelines. As a
consequence Paul managed just three
senior appearances during the season. A
left-sided player who possesses bags of
energy, he can play either in a wide-left
midfield role or at left back.
*Notts Co (From trainee on 4/12/2001) FL
5+4 Others 1*

RITCHIE Paul Simon

Born: Kirkcaldy, 21 August 1975
Height: 5'11" **Weight:** 12.0
Club Honours: SC '98; Div 1 '03
International Honours: S: 6; B; U21-7;
Sch
This experienced defender again found
himself out of the first-team reckoning
with Manchester City last term and in
September he joined First Division club
Portsmouth on loan. He performed solidly
during his spell with Pompey filling in the
gaps in an injury-hit back line. In March
he signed for Derby County, also on loan,
where he added some maturity to the
defence and helped to ensure any threat
of relegation was dismissed. Paul is a very
capable player who is strong in the tackle
and a good man-to-man marker.
*Heart of Midlothian (From Links U on
31/7/1992) SL 132+1/5 SLC 10+1 SC 11/3
Others 6*

Bolton W *(Free on 22/12/1999) FL 13+1 FLC 1 FAC 3+1 Others 2*
Glasgow R *(Free on 26/2/2000)*
Manchester C *(£500,000 on 22/8/2000) P/FL 11+9 FLC 3+1 FAC 3*
Portsmouth *(Loaned on 20/9/2002) FL 8+4 FLC 1*
Derby Co *(Loaned on 27/3/2003) FL 7*

RIVERS Mark Alan
Born: Crewe, 26 November 1975
Height: 5'11" **Weight:** 11.2
Mark is an exciting right winger in the old-fashioned mould who likes nothing better than to run directly at his opponent to earn space to deliver a telling cross or a strike at goal. He produced his best form for Norwich in the second half of the campaign with some scintillating displays, including a 'Man of the Match' performance at Portsmouth in early March. Mark thrived in City's attacking 4-3-3 formation, which released him from some of his defensive duties and allowed him to exploit space further up the field.
Crewe Alex *(From trainee on 6/5/1994) FL 177+26/43 FLC 14+1/8 FAC 12/4 Others 6+3/3*
Norwich C *(£600,000 on 28/6/2001) FL 47+15/6 FAC 2+2 Others 3/1*

RIX Benjamin (Ben)
Born: Wolverhampton, 11 December 1982
Height: 5'10" **Weight:** 11.11
This promising young Crewe Alexandra player continued to show progress in 2002-03. The stylish midfielder featured regularly in the starting line-up until he was sidelined after suffering an injury against Brentford in February, but by the end of the campaign he was back in action. Ben scored just one goal during the season, netting in the FA Cup tie against Mansfield.
Crewe Alex *(From trainee on 6/2/2001) FL 23+21 FAC 3+4/2 Others 1+1*

RIZA Omer Kerime
Born: Enfield, 8 November 1979
Height: 5'9" **Weight:** 11.2
International Honours: Turkey: U21
This talented youngster joined Cambridge United during the 2002 close season in a deal that was aided by generous sponsorship from a group of fans. Omer played up front, either as a striker or on the wing and featured in all 46 Second Division matches for the U's, finishing as second top-scorer with 16 goals. He was reported to have turned down the offer of a new contract in favour of a move to Turkey.
Arsenal *(From trainee on 1/7/1998) FLC 0+1*
West Ham U *(£20,000 on 7/12/1999)*

Barnet *(Loaned on 20/10/2000) FL 7+3/4 FAC 1 Others 2/1*
Cambridge U *(Loaned on 2/3/2001) FL 10+2/3*
Cambridge U *(Free on 9/8/2002) FL 43+3/11 FLC 2 FAC 3+2/1 Others 4+1/4*

ROBERT Laurent
Born: Saint-Benoit, France, 21 May 1975
Height: 5'9" **Weight:** 11.2
Laurent's 2002-03 campaign was delayed by a hairline stress fracture of a vertebra in his lower back incurred during pre-season, so it was September before he made his first appearance for the men of Newcastle's midfield. A pacy runner with good close control he delivers crosses whipped in at speed which are very difficult to defend, whilst his dynamic shooting from both open play and dead-ball situations coupled with his surging runs make him an exciting player to watch. He fractured his cheekbone in the Worthington Cup tie against Everton in November and his season ended prematurely when he twisted a knee in the home game with Manchester United in early April.
Newcastle U *(£10,500,000 from Paris St Germain, France, ex Montpellier, Nancy, on 10/8/2001) PL 59+4/13 FLC 3+1/1 FAC 4/1 Others 9+2*

ROBERTS Andrew (Andy) James
Born: Dartford, 20 March 1974
Height: 5'10" **Weight:** 13.0
Club Honours: FAYC '91
International Honours: E: U21-5
This experienced midfield player rejoined Millwall during the 2002 close season and showed Lions' boss Mark McGhee that he still has plenty to offer. A versatile player who can also slot into the back four or operate as a sweeper, Andy would have been an ever-present in the side if it were not for injury. A great favourite with the club's supporters, He has a tremendous right foot, which he showed to full potential with a great strike against Sheffield Wednesday.
Millwall *(From trainee on 29/10/1991) FL 132+4/5 FLC 12/2 FAC 7 Others 4/1*
Crystal Palace *(£2,520,000 on 29/7/1995) F/PL 106+2/2 FLC 7+1 FAC 8 Others 6/1*
Wimbledon *(£1,200,000 + on 10/3/1998) P/FL 92+9/6 FLC 12+1/1 FAC 3+2*
Norwich C *(Loaned on 28/11/2001) FL 4+1*
Millwall *(Free on 16/8/2002) FL 31+2/2 FLC 1*

ROBERTS Benjamin (Ben) James
Born: Bishop Auckland, 22 June 1975
Height: 6'1" **Weight:** 13.0

International Honours: E: U21-1
Ben had another frustrating season at Charlton last term, seeing little first-team action. In August he was loaned to Luton Town where he impressed, keeping three clean sheets in a row and showing excellent reflexes. Then in January he joined Brighton, also on loan as cover for injury. He did well on his debut in the 'derby' match against Portsmouth, but then went down with a stomach bug an returned to the Valley. His chance for the Addicks eventually came in the final gam of the season at home to Fulham when Dean Kiely was sent off for a professional foul and Ben played the final hour of the game. His first task was to face the resultant penalty kick, which he narrowly failed to stop, but he did not concede an further goals and performed well, makin several good saves.
Middlesbrough *(From trainee on 24/3/199. F/PL 15+1 FLC 2+1 FAC 6 Others 1*
Hartlepool U *(Loaned on 19/10/1995) FL 4 Others 1*
Wycombe W *(Loaned on 8/12/1995) FL 15*
Bradford C *(Loaned on 27/8/1996) FL 2*
Millwall *(Loaned on 12/2/1999) FL 11 Others*
Luton T *(Loaned on 24/2/2000) FL 14*
Charlton Ath *(Free on 19/7/2000) PL 0+1*
Reading *(Loaned on 17/1/2002) FL 6*
Luton T *(Loaned on 24/8/2002) FL 5*
Brighton & Hove A *(Loaned on 17/1/2003) FL 3*

ROBERTS Christian John
Born: Cardiff, 22 October 1979
Height: 5'10" **Weight:** 12.8
Club Honours: AMC '03
International Honours: W: U21-1; Yth
This Bristol City striker twice did the business against his boyhood favourites, Cardiff, in the Second Division games, bu failed to find the net against them in the play-offs. There is no denying Christian's potential, but his lack of awareness leave many of the Ashton Gate fans unconvinced of his abilities. He was calle up to the full Welsh squad at the season' end.
Cardiff C *(From trainee on 8/10/1997) FL 6+17/3 FLC 2 FAC 2+3 Others 0+2*
Exeter C *(Free on 24/7/2000) FL 67+12/18 FLC 2+1 FAC 2+1 Others 2*
Bristol C *(Signed on 26/3/2002) FL 35+1/1. FLC 1 FAC 3/3 Others 6+2/1*

ROBERTS Gareth Wyn
Born: Wrexham, 6 February 1978
Height: 5'7" **Weight:** 12.6
Club Honours: FAYC '96
International Honours: W: 4; B-1; U21-1(
Gareth is a firm favourite with the

anmere supporters and enhanced his putation by grabbing four goals in the 002-03 campaign. Although he suffered termittently from shin splints, he formed strong defensive partnership with new gning Shane Nicholson and was equently the creative provider for the ee-scoring Simon Howarth. As always, s commitment, tenacity and steadiness ever faltered as he really made the left-ack berth his own and he was an ever-esent in the team from early February. *verpool (From trainee on 22/5/1996.*

£50,000 to Panionios, Greece on 15/1/1999) *Tranmere Rov (Free on 5/8/1999) FL 148+5/7 FLC 17 FAC 12+1 Others 3/1*

ROBERTS Iwan Wyn
Born: Bangor, 26 June 1968
Height: 6'3" **Weight:** 14.2
International Honours: W: 15; B-1; Yth; Sch
The big Welshman continued to make a huge contribution to Norwich City's progress on the field last term, even though, towards the end of the season he

was often used as a substitute. Iwan's final goals tally of seven took him to third place in Norwich City's all-time goal-scoring lists ahead of Robert Fleck, he also made his 250th appearance for the club. His experience and ability to hold up the ball remain great assets to Nigel Worthington and no one doubts his knack for scoring goals.
Watford (From trainee on 4/7/1988) FL 40+23/9 FLC 6+2/3 FAC 1+6 Others 5
Huddersfield T (£275,000 on 2/8/1990) FL 141+1/50 FLC 13+1/6 FAC 12/4 Others 14/8

aurent Robert

Leicester C (£100,000 on 25/11/1993) P/FL 92+8/41 FLC 5/1 FAC 5/2 Others 1
Wolverhampton W (£1,300,000 + on 15/7/1996) FL 24+9/12 FLC 2 FAC 0+1 Others 2
Norwich C (£900,000 on 9/7/1997) FL 219+18/76 FLC 15+3/10 FAC 5+1/2 Others 0+3/1

ROBERTS Jason Andre Davis
Born: Park Royal, 25 January 1978
Height: 5'11" **Weight:** 12.7
International Honours: Grenada: 6
Despite taking plenty of buffeting from Premiership defenders West Bromwich Albion's hard working, purposeful striker still got on with the game last term. Apart from two spells of suspension, injuries also disrupted his appearances at first-team level and he found goal-scoring pretty hard, managing only three all told: a well-struck effort against Arsenal at Highbury, a clinical finish (and match winner) at West Ham and a late equaliser in the home game with Birmingham City. Jason will perhaps relish another season in the Nationwide League where he will be hoping to regain his scoring form.
Wolverhampton W (£250,000 from Hayes on 12/9/1997)
Torquay U (Loaned on 19/12/1997) FL 13+1/6 Others 1
Bristol C (Loaned on 26/3/1998) FL 1+2/1
Bristol Rov (£250,000 on 7/8/1998) FL 73+5/38 FLC 6/3 FAC 6/7 Others 3
West Bromwich A (£2,000,000 on 27/7/2000) P/FL 75+14/24 FLC 3+1/2 FAC 6 Others 2/1

ROBERTS Neil Wyn
Born: Wrexham, 7 April 1978
Height: 5'10" **Weight:** 11.0
Club Honours: Div 2 '03
International Honours: W: 3; B-1; U21-1; Yth
Neil enjoyed his best season to date with Wigan Athletic last term and was rewarded with a new two-year contract. Although not a prolific scorer, he impressed with his high work-rate, an ability to hold the ball up and a willingness to probe hard for openings. He took advantage of Andy Liddell's early-season injury to become something of a regular in the Latics' front line and he always brought the best out of his fellow striker Nathan Ellington. Recalled to international duties with Wales, he made a substitute appearance in their Euro 2004 qualifying victory in Azerbaijan.
Wrexham (From trainee on 3/7/1996) FL 58+17/17 FLC 1/1 FAC 11+1/4 Others 2+2/2
Wigan Ath (£450,000 on 18/2/2000) FL

55+42/17 FLC 4+2/2 FAC 5/1 Others 3+1
Hull C (Loaned on 25/1/2002) FL 3+3

ROBERTS Stephen (Steve) Wyn
Born: Wrexham, 24 February 1980
Height: 6'0" **Weight:** 12.7
International Honours: W: U21-4; Yth
Although still somewhat injury prone Steve continued to progress in the heart of the Wrexham defence last term. A stylish, controlled type of performer, more of the classic 'play your way out of trouble' centre half than the 'stopper'

variety, he featured regularly in the line-up throughout the season. He also showed that he could get on the score sheet, netting in the 1-1 draw at York City, and one of the five against Cambridge when promotion was confirmed. Both Steve and his brother Neil (of Wigan) featured in promotion-winning teams and both were put on stand by for the Wales friendly in the USA at the end of May.
Wrexham (From trainee on 16/1/1998) FL 85+4/3 FLC 2 FAC 5/1 Others 4+1/1

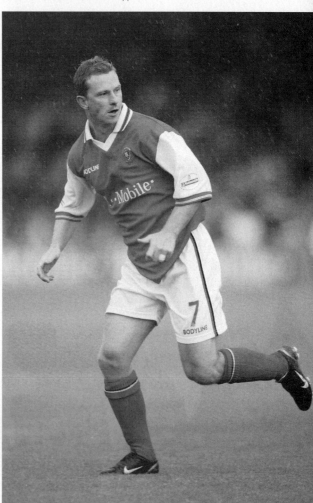

Mark Robins

ROBERTS Stuart Ian
Born: Carmarthen, 22 July 1980
Height: 5'7" **Weight:** 9.8
International Honours: W: U21-13
Wycombe's nippy striker had his season disrupted by two lengthy lay-offs, firstly or ankle ligament damage, which put him on crutches, and then a badly twisted ankle. In between he scored a remarkable hat-trick in the 5-0 win at Northampton in January, only entering the field of play as a 34th minute substitute. The first of his three goals typified his capabilities, cutting in from the left wing and beating two players before coolly shooting home. He was used as both an out-and-out striker and as a wide man on both flanks where his fast feet and tight ball control posed great danger.
Swansea C (From trainee on 9/7/1998) FL 8+34/14 FLC 4+3 FAC 4 Others 7+2
Wycombe W (£102,500 on 19/10/2001) FL 22+22/4 FLC 2 FAC 2+1 Others 0+2

ROBINS Mark Gordon
Born: Ashton under Lyne, 22 December 1969
Height: 5'8" **Weight:** 11.11
Club Honours: FAC '90; ECWC '91; ESC '91; FLC '97
International Honours: E: U21-6
This vastly experienced striker mostly had to be content with a place on the substitutes' bench for Rotherham last season. Nevertheless, whenever he was called upon Mark invariably produced the goods again. He spent a highly successful spell at Bristol City, providing a much needed boost to the strike force. He then returned to Millmoor and scored an important late winner against Ipswich Town in April.
Manchester U (From apprentice on 23/12/1986) FL 19+29/11 FLC 0+7/2 FAC 4+4/3 Others 4+3/1
Norwich C (£800,000 on 14/8/1992) PL 67+10/20 FLC 6+3/1 Others 1+1
Leicester C (£1,000,000 on 16/1/1995) P/FL 40+16/12 FLC 5+4/5 FAC 4+2 Others 4+1
Reading (Loaned on 29/8/1997) FL 5
Signed by Deportivo Orense, Spain on 5/1/1998)
Manchester C (Free from Panionios, Greece on 25/3/1999) FL 0+2
Walsall (Free on 5/8/1999) FL 30+10/6 FLC 1/1 FAC 2/1
Rotherham U (Free on 5/7/2000) FL 32+17/44 FLC 6+1/4 FAC 3+1 Others 1/1
Bristol C (Loaned on 18/2/2003) FL 6/4 Others 1+1/1

ROBINSON Andrew
Born: Birkenhead, 27 March 1982
Height: 5'8" **Weight:** 11.4
This young striker scored plenty of goals for West Cheshire League club Cammell Laird, and soon attracted the attention of bigger clubs. In October he had a trial with Wrexham, featuring in their reserves, and the following month he signed forms for Tranmere Rovers. However, he only made one appearance for the Prenton Park club, coming on as a substitute in the LDV Vans Trophy tie against Bury in December. He was eventually released in the summer.
Tranmere Rov (Free from Cammell Laird on 11/11/2002) Others 0+1

ROBINSON Carl Phillip
Born: Llandrindod Wells, 13 October 1976
Height: 5'10" **Weight:** 12.10
Club Honours: Div 1 '03
International Honours: W: 13; B-2; U21-6; Yth
This industrious midfielder did well in his outings for Portsmouth last term, impressing with his work rate and tidy distribution. However, he was loaned out to Sheffield Wednesday in the new year, making his debut in the 'derby' match against Sheffield United at Bramall Lane. He later rejoined his former boss Colin Lee at Walsall, again in a loan deal, and showed some good form, opening the scoring for the Saddlers at Bradford. Carl continued to represent Wales at international level during the season, winning a further four caps.
Wolverhampton W (From trainee on 3/7/1995) FL 129+35/19 FLC 12+1/1 FAC 14/3
Shrewsbury T (Loaned on 28/3/1996) FL 2+2 Others 1
Portsmouth (Free on 31/7/2002) FL 11+4 FLC 1+1
Sheffield Wed (Loaned on 17/11/2003) FL 4/1
Walsall (Loaned on 20/2/2003) FL 10+1/1

ROBINSON James Gilbert
Born: Whiston, 18 September 1982
Height: 5'10" **Weight:** 11.6
This promising young midfield player is another product of Crewe Alexandra's excellent youth scheme. He was on the fringes of the first-team squad during the second half of the 2002-03 campaign and made his senior debut as a late substitute against Peterborough in March.
Crewe Alex (From trainee on 28/11/2001) FL 0+1

ROBINSON John Robert Campbell
Born: Bulawayo, Rhodesia, 29 August 1971
Height: 5'10" **Weight:** 11.7
Club Honours: Div 1 '00
International Honours: W: 29; U21-5
John is a clever right-footed winger who can play on either flank or as a right wing back. He works tirelessly, loves to take on opponents and can cross with either foot. He only started 10 games during the campaign, and in recognition of his service with the Addicks he was granted a free transfer in the summer, despite having a year to run on his contract. John announced his retirement from international football at the start of last season having won 30 caps for Wales, putting him second in Charlton's all-time international honours list.
Brighton & Hove A (From trainee on 21/4/1989) FL 57+5/6 FLC 5/1 FAC 2+1 Others 1+2/2
Charlton Ath (£75,000 on 15/9/1992) P/FL 296+36/35 FLC 20+4/5 FAC 17+3/3 Others 5+1

ROBINSON Mark
Born: Guisborough, 24 July 1981
Height: 5'9" **Weight:** 11.0
Hartlepool's young left back enjoyed a satisfactory season of regular first-team football last term. Mark is a player with good defensive qualities who continues to grow in confidence. He hits the ball well, and is particularly good at making opportunities for the forwards. He showed great spirit to come back strongly after losing his place for a short spell in mid-season to loan signing Brian Barry-Murphy.
Hartlepool U (From trainee on 2/7/1999) FL 76+5 FLC 2 Others 2

ROBINSON Marvin Leon St Clair
Born: Crewe, 11 April 1980
Height: 6'0" **Weight:** 12.9
International Honours: E: Sch
Marvin received few opportunities at Derby last term and in November he joined Tranmere on loan. A bustling, old-fashioned type of forward, he mostly featured on the bench at Prenton Park, scoring his only goal in his final appearance at Queen's Park Rangers. On returning to Pride Park Marvin managed one appearance as a substitute, but was released in the summer.
Derby Co (From trainee on 8/7/1998) P/FL 3+9/1

363

Stoke C *(Loaned on 13/9/2000) FL 3/1*
Tranmere Rov *(Loaned on 29/11/2002) FL
1+5/1 Others 0+1*

ROBINSON Matthew (Matt)
Richard
Born: Exeter, 23 December 1974
Height: 5'11" **Weight:** 11.8
Matt proved to be a useful signing for
Oxford after arriving in the summer of
2002. He made the left-wing-back spot
his own, missing just a handful of games
all season. A sound defender he also
worked hard on his attacking and his
crosses created a number of chances for
the strikers. He managed one goal himself
when his deflected effort came up trumps
in the win at Bristol Rovers.
Southampton *(From trainee on 1/7/1993) PL
3+11 FAC 1+2*
Portsmouth *(£50,000 on 20/2/1998) FL
65+4/1 FLC 3+2 FAC 3*
Reading *(£150,000 on 28/1/2000) FL 62+3
FLC 3+1 FAC 2 Others 4*
Oxford U *(Free on 12/7/2002) FL 42/1 FLC 3
FAC 3 Others 0+1*

ROBINSON Neil David
Born: Liverpool, 18 November 1979
Height: 5'10" **Weight:** 12.12
This young striker joined Macclesfield in
the summer of 2002 from North West
Counties League side Prescot Cables for
whom he had scored 41 goals in all
competitions during the 2001-02
season. He went on to make his senior
debut at Lincoln in August, although he
found it difficult to break through into
the first team and most of his outings
came from the substitutes' bench.
However, he made some excellent
contributions for the reserves, regularly
appearing on the score sheet and will be
looking to gain further senior experience
in 2003-04.
Macclesfield T *(£6,000 from Prescot Cables
on 29/7/2002) FL 2+8 FLC 0+1*

ROBINSON Paul Derrick
Born: Sunderland, 20 November 1978
Height: 5'11" **Weight:** 11.12
Deemed surplus to requirements at
Wimbledon, Paul returned to Grimsby on
loan at the start of last season. Although
a first choice up front in the opening
weeks, the unexpectedly swift recovery of
Steve Livingstone and the emergence of
Darren Mansaram soon found him
relegated to the substitutes' bench and he
returned to Selhurst Park in November.
Soon afterwards Paul joined Carlisle on
loan, where he mostly featured as a
substitute, although he scored a goal at a

York. He was subsequently released by
the Dons and joined Blackpool on a non-
contract basis in March. Unfortunately the
Seasiders failed to record a win in his
seven appearances for them, although he
did find the net against Notts County at
Meadow Lane.
Darlington *(From trainee on 14/7/1997) FL
7+19/3 FLC 0+1 FAC 2+4/1 Others 0+1*
Newcastle U *(£250,000 + on 27/3/1998) PL
2+9 FLC 0+1 Others 0+4/1*
Wimbledon *(£1,500,000 on 9/8/2000) FL
0+4 FLC 1+1*
Burnley *(Loaned on 10/10/2000) FL 0+4*
Dundee U *(Loaned on 21/2/2001) SL 2+4*
Grimsby T *(Loaned on 28/3/2002) FL 1+4*
Grimsby T *(Loaned on 9/8/2002) FL 5+7/1
FLC 1*
Carlisle U *(Loaned on 22/11/2002) FL 1+4/1
FAC 2 Others 0+1/1*
Blackpool *(Free on 21/3/2003) FL 5+2/1*

ROBINSON Paul Mark James
Born: Barnet, 7 January 1982
Height: 6'1" **Weight:** 12.1
This tall, strong central defender made
good progress in Millwall's reserve team
last season and when injuries presented
him with an opportunity of first-team
football he grabbed it with both hands.
Paul made his senior debut against
Cambridge United in the third round of
the FA Cup, coming on after five minutes
for the injured Stuart Nethercott. He then
stepped into the starting line-up for the
next match against Watford, and followed
this up with a goal in the replay against
Cambridge shortly afterwards. He went
on to enjoy a run of excellent
performances and at the end of the
season he was voted as the club's 'Young
Player of the Year'.
Millwall *(From trainee on 25/10/2000) FL
12+2 FAC 3+1/1*

ROBINSON Paul Peter
Born: Watford, 14 December 1978
Height: 5'9" **Weight:** 11.12
Club Honours: Div 2 '98
International Honours: E: U21-3
Paul, a locally born left back, fell slightly
below his very high standards at Watford
last season. His customary commitment
and effort were in place, but an
accumulation of disciplinary points led to
unwelcome periods of suspension that
disrupted the team. An all-action player
who loves to push forward, Paul has
made more than 200 League appearances
for the Hornets.
Watford *(From trainee on 13/2/1997) P/FL
191+18/8 FLC 14+1/1 FAC 10+2 Others 5*

ROBINSON Paul William
Born: Beverley, 15 October 1979
Height: 6'2" **Weight:** 13.4
Club Honours: FAYC '97
International Honours: E: 2; U21-5
Paul was given his chance at Leeds United
under new manager Terry Venables and
seized the opportunity with both hands to
become an ever-present in all first-team
games. He showed high quality form
consistently throughout the campaign and
fully justified the faith invested in him.
Paul is an excellent shot stopper with
superb reflexes who commands his area
well. He saved the team on many
occasions last term, and United fans will
be hoping that he stays at Elland Road for
the foreseeable future.
Leeds U *(From trainee on 13/5/1997) PL
57+2 FLC 3 FAC 6 Others 12*

ROBINSON Stephen (Steve)
Born: Lisburn, 10 December 1974
Height: 5'9" **Weight:** 11.3
International Honours: NI: 5; B-4; U21-
1; Yth; Sch
Steve enjoyed regular first-team football
at Luton for much of the 2002-03 season
and once he settled in he looked to be a
fixture in the side. However, an injury
picked up at Peterborough put him out
for a while and then he was injured again
in the home game with Oldham and this
ruled him out for the rest of the
campaign. Steve is an attacking midfield
player who possesses subtle skills on the
ball.
Tottenham H *(From trainee on 27/1/1993)
PL 1+1*
Bournemouth *(Free on 20/10/1994) FL
227+13/51 FLC 14/1 FAC 15+1/5 Others 16/.*
Preston NE *(£375,000 on 26/5/2000) FL
6+18/1 FLC 3+1 FAC 0+1*
Bristol C *(Loaned on 18/3/2002) FL 6/1*
Luton T *(£50,000 on 20/6/2002) FL 23+6/1
FLC 1+1 FAC 2 Others 1*

ROBINSON Steven (Steve) E
Born: Nottingham, 17 January 1975
Height: 5'9" **Weight:** 11.3
This non-stop right-sided midfielder was a
consistent performer for Swindon Town
throughout the 2002-03 campaign. A
near ever-present, he was always willing
to work hard for the cause and will have
been pleased to have netted well-taken
goals in the games at Stockport and at
home to Queen's Park Rangers.
Birmingham C *(From trainee on 9/6/1993) F
53+28 FLC 6+2/1 FAC 2+2/1 Others 2*
Peterborough U *(Loaned on 15/3/1996) FL
Swindon T *(£50,000 on 12/2/2001) FL
97+5/4 FLC 2 FAC 4 Others 2*

Paul Robinson (Leeds United)

ROBSON Matthew (Matty)
James
Born: Durham, 23 January 1985
Height: 5'10" **Weight:** 11.2
Matty is a left-sided utility player who can play in defence, midfield, or as a winger. A second-year trainee, he was a non-playing substitute for Hartlepool in a number of early-season games before making his first-team debut against Tranmere in the LDV Vans Trophy match when Chris Turner chose to give his reserve players a run out. Matty played out the season with the reserves and juniors, and his promise was recognised when he was named as the club's 'Young Player of the Year'.
Hartlepool U (Trainee) Others 1

ROCHE Barry Christopher
Born: Dublin, 6 April 1982
Height: 6'4" **Weight:** 12.6
International Honours: RoI: Yth
This promising young 'keeper was second choice to Darren Ward for Nottingham Forest throughout the 2002-03 campaign. He received his only senior opportunity when replacing his rival for the away game at Rotherham on the final day of the regular season.
Nottingham F (From trainee on 29/6/1999) FL 2+1

ROCHE Lee Paul
Born: Bolton, 28 October 1980
Height: 5'10" **Weight:** 10.12
International Honours: E: U21-1; Yth
A young Manchester United full back who possesses a solidness in defence and enterprise in attack, Lee so wooed the Wrexham fans whilst on loan in 2001, he was acclaimed their 'Player of the Year.' In 2002-03 he showed the United fans why. Making his introduction in the eight-goal thriller against Newcastle at Old Trafford in November, Lee's appetite was further whetted against Deportivo in the Champions' League in March. Obviously a player with emerging talent, his biggest frustration might be in playing the waiting game.
Manchester U (From trainee on 11/2/1999) PL 0+1 FLC 1 Others 1
Wrexham (Loaned on 24/7/2000) FL 41 FLC 2 FAC 1 Others 1

RODGER Simon Lee
Born: Shoreham, 3 October 1971
Height: 5'9" **Weight:** 11.9
Club Honours: Div 1 '94
An experienced, left-sided midfielder from nearby Shoreham-by-Sea, it seemed only a matter of time before Simon signed for

Brighton despite his long-term connections with arch rivals Crystal Palace. When ex-Palace manager Steve Coppell took over the Withdean hot seat it was not long before he turned to his former player and signed him up in October. Ironically his debut came as a substitute against his former paymasters in the 5-0 defeat at Selhurst, but as he gained match fitness so Simon's quality and vision became obvious. Although hampered for most of the campaign with a broken toe, he was an automatic choice and scorer of two spectacular goals.
Crystal Palace (£1,000 from Bognor Regis T on 2/7/1990) F/PL 242+34/11 FLC 30+1/2 FAC 9+4 Others 5+3 (Free to Woking during 2002 close season)
Manchester C (Loaned on 28/10/1996) FL 8/1
Stoke C (Loaned on 14/2/1997) FL 5
Brighton & Hove A (Free on 23/10/2002) FL 27+2/2

RODGERS Luke John
Born: Birmingham, 1 January 1982
Height: 5'7" **Weight:** 11.2
Shrewsbury's young striker had another excellent season in 2002-03, when he finished as the club's leading scorer with 20 goals in all competitions. Luke possesses tremendous strength and control on the ball and a superb turn of pace. This lethal mixture of skills enables him to adopt a very positive 'can score, will score' approach. He found the net regularly throughout the season and always gave 100 per cent. Although he didn't score in the FA Cup victory against Everton, his performance caught the eye of many and he was called up to the Republic of Ireland U21 squad, but his debut was delayed to allow him to obtain an Irish passport. Luke had the dubious distinction of scoring Shrewsbury's last goal in the Football League against Scunthorpe as the club made an exit to the Conference.
Shrewsbury T (From trainee on 10/7/2000) FL 87+19/46 FLC 2 FAC 5+1 Others 7+2/4

[RODRIGO] DE ALMEIDA
Juliano Rodrigo
Born: Santos, Brazil, 7 August 1976
Height: 5'8" **Weight:** 11.7
The Brazilian left-sided midfielder had little to show for his time at Everton, a cruciate ligament injury sustained in September effectively ending his season, although he did return in February following recuperation back home. Brought on a one-year deal in 2002 it was decided not to renew his contract. Prior

to his injury he had shown enough skill and flair in four substitute appearances to indicate that he may have been a useful acquisition to the squad.
Everton (Loaned from Botafogo, Brazil on 2/8/2002) PL 0+4

RODRIGUES Daniel (Dani)
Ferreira
Born: Madeira, Portugal, 3 March 1980
Height: 6'0" **Weight:** 11.8
International Honours: Portugal: U21
This Portuguese U21 international suggested that he had come back well from two broken legs when showing blistering pace in Walsall's pre-season friendly at Exeter, but his first-team activity at Bescot was restricted to just 13 minutes as a substitute in the opening game against Ipswich. Dani was released in the new year and was reported to have signed for Greek club Ionikos Piraeus.
Bournemouth (Loaned from CS Farense, Portugal on 1/10/1998) FL 0+5 Others 0+2
Southampton (£170,000 on 3/3/1999) PL 0+2
Bristol C (Loaned on 3/10/2000) FL 3+1
Bristol C (Loaned on 31/12/2001) FL 0+4 Others 0+1
Walsall (Free on 6/8/2002) FL 0+1

RODWELL James (Jim)
Richard
Born: Lincoln, 20 November 1970
Height: 6'1" **Weight:** 14.2
Club Honours: NC '01; '02
Jim made his Division Three debut for Boston when he came off the bench for the second half of the club's opening fixture against Bournemouth. He started the next two games in the centre of defence but then switched back to Conference football and signed for Farnborough Town.
Darlington (Trainee on 1/1/1989) FL 1 (Free to Nettleham during 1989 close season)
Rushden & Diamonds (£40,000 from Halesowen T, ex Boston U, Bedworth U, Hednesford T, Nuneaton Borough, on 15/8/1996) FL 8+1 FLC 2 Others 1
Boston U (Free on 16/4/2002) FL 2+1

ROGERS Alan
Born: Liverpool, 3 January 1977
Height: 5'9" **Weight:** 12.6
Club Honours: Div 1 '98
International Honours: E: U21-3
A pacy left-sided midfielder who can also play at full back or wing back, Alan quickly established himself as a first choice for Leicester City last season. He opened his Foxes' goal-scoring account with a brace in the Worthington Cup

ictory away to Hull City. Alan was an ver-present until suffering a thigh injury t home to Sheffield Wednesday in March, but returned to action with a fine lisplay against Grimsby the following month and generally finished the ampaign in good form.

ranmere Rov (From trainee on 1/7/1995) FL 3+4/2 FLC 1 FAC 1
lottingham F (£2,000,000 on 10/7/1997) /FL 135+2/17 FLC 15/2 FAC 2+1/1
eicester C (£300,000 on 16/11/2001) P/FL 0+4 FLC 3/2 FAC 4

ROGERS Kristian Raleigh John
Born: Chester, 2 October 1980
Height: 6'3" **Weight:** 12.6
International Honours: E: Sch
Kristian found that he had become

third in the ranking of goalkeepers at Wrexham last term behind Andy Dibble and Paul Whitfield. He was between the sticks for the first two games but was then replaced by Dibble, while Whitfield was preferred when the former Welsh international was injured. Kristian regained his place over the Christmas period but when passed over again decided to go on the transfer list. However, with Dibble again struggling with his fitness in mid-April he took to opportunity to show what he can do, making a number of important stops in the run-in for promotion at home to Bristol Rovers and at Leyton Orient.
Wrexham (From Chester C juniors on 14/8/1998) FL 39+1 FLC 2 FAC 1 Others 1

ROGERS Mark Alvin
Born: Guelph, Ontario, Canada, 3 November 1975
Height: 6'1" **Weight:** 12.12
International Honours: Canada: 4
Very much in the 'safe and steady' mould, Wycombe's big central defender is now pretty well established as a first-choice player, normally as a central defender but sometimes filling in at right back. In fact Mark managed to keep the experienced team captain Paul McCarthy out of the starting line up for a while. His occasional goals were always important and his strike at Peterborough in March helped the Chairboys to their last win of the season, all but ensuring survival. He missed the final weeks of the campaign with a hamstring injury. Mark received a

Alan Rogers

call-up to the Canada squad for the friendly in Estonia in March but was an unused substitute.

Wycombe W (Free from Burnaby Canadians, Canada on 23/12/1998) FL 108+16/4 FLC 6/1 FAC 12+1/1 Others 6+1/1

ROGERS Paul Anthony
Born: Portsmouth, 21 March 1965
Height: 6'0" **Weight:** 12.0
Club Honours: Div 3 '97, '01; Div 2 '02; AMC '99
International Honours: E: SP-6

Brighton & Hove Albion's club captain made just one start in his farewell season in the professional game, and added just four more appearances as a substitute. A great club man, Paul gave full support to the young players in the reserves and passed on his experience whenever he could without complaint. Although employed primarily as a midfield harrier, he often turned out as a central defender for the second string. After announcing his retirement as a professional at the end of the campaign Paul was rewarded with a position in the club's commercial department.

Sheffield U (£35,000 from Sutton U on 29/1/1992) F/PL 120+5/10 FLC 8+1/1 FAC 4 Others 1
Notts Co (Signed on 29/12/1995) FL 21+1/2 FAC 1/1 Others 6/1
Wigan Ath (Loaned on 13/12/1996) FL 7+2/3
Wigan Ath (£50,000 on 7/3/1997) FL 85+6/2 FLC 6 FAC 3 Others 8/1
Brighton & Hove A (Free on 8/7/1999) FL 105+14/15 FLC 5+2 FAC 6/1 Others 6

ROGET Leo Thomas Earl
Born: Ilford, 1 August 1977
Height: 6'1" **Weight:** 12.2

Leo's first season for Brentford was an injury-plagued nightmare. He made just 14 league appearances, missing out with an eye injury (August), knee ligament damage (October), hamstring trouble (January) and ankle ligament problems (February). When fully fit he is a powerful, solid central defender.

Southend U (From trainee on 5/7/1995) FL 105+15/7 FLC 8 FAC 6/1 Others 3/1
Stockport Co (Free on 1/3/2001) FL 28+3/1 FLC 2
Reading (Loaned on 14/2/2002) FL 1
Brentford (Free on 9/8/2002) FL 14 FLC 1 FAC 1 Others 1

ROONEY Wayne
Born: Liverpool, 26 October 1985
Height: 5'10" **Weight:** 12.4
International Honours: E: 5; Yth

Few players can have announced themselves to the football world in such a dramatic fashion as this teenaged forward sensation last season. Not content with setting a series of club and domestic records, Wayne capped it all when he became the youngest-ever player to wear the white shirt of England when he came on as a substitute against Australia aged 17 years 111 days in February. An excellent performance against Turkey in his next international confirmed his status as the most talented young English player of his generation. Although initially deployed as a substitute, he first gained national recognition by curling a tremendous right-foot shot past David Seaman to end Arsenal's long unbeaten league run in October. A fortnight later a typical dribble and clinical finish brought the Blues their first league win at Elland Road since 1951 and his iconic position amongst Everton followers was assured.

Everton (From trainee on 20/2/2003) PL 14+19/6 FLC 2+1/2 FAC 1

ROPER Ian Robert
Born: Nuneaton, 20 June 1977
Height: 6'3" **Weight:** 13.4

In his eighth season as a Walsall professional Ian was the personification of the committed central defender and in game after game won virtually everything in the air. A near ever-present in the line-up, he was the supporters' choice as 'Player of the Season' and fitted in with a variety of defensive partners.

Walsall (From trainee on 15/5/1995) FL 170+25/2 FLC 7+6 FAC 9+3/1 Others 11+3

ROSCOE Andrew (Andy) Ronald
Born: Liverpool, 4 June 1973
Height: 5'11" **Weight:** 12.0
Club Honours: AMC '96

Andy vied with Graeme Power for the left-back spot at Exeter last term, and he started in exactly half the club's Third Division fixtures. A sweet hitter of a dead ball, he provided plenty of crosses for the front men. A player who always gives 100 per cent, Andy scored three times for City including the only goal of the game at home to Swansea.

Bolton W (From trainee at Liverpool on 17/7/1991) FL 2+1 Others 1+1
Rotherham U (£70,000 on 27/10/1994) FL 184+18/18 FLC 10 FAC 10/2 Others 11/2
Mansfield T (Free on 5/8/1999) FL 29+10/2 FLC 2 FAC 1 Others 0+1/1
Exeter C (Free on 18/7/2000) FL 91+23/11 FLC 3 FAC 7/1 Others 2

ROSE Matthew David
Born: Dartford, 24 September 1975
Height: 5'11" **Weight:** 11.1
Club Honours: FAYC '94
International Honours: E: U21-2

Matthew was a regular for Queen's Park Rangers from the start of the 2002-03 campaign, initially playing in a central-midfield role and then moving to the right wing. Following the injury to Tommy Williams he moved to the left-wing-back position where he gave his best performances of the season before being sidelined by a medial ligament problem for three months. Matthew regained match fitness before the summer break but only appeared in the reserve side.

Arsenal (From trainee on 19/7/1994) PL 2+3
Queens Park R (£500,000 on 20/5/1997) FL 156+12/6 FLC 7 FAC 4 Others 3

ROSE Richard Alan
Born: Pembury, 8 September 1982
Height: 6'0" **Weight:** 11.9

Richard had a difficult time in gaining a first-team place at Gillingham in 2002-03, although he was a regular for the club's reserve side. In December he was loaned to Bristol Rovers where he enjoyed two successful months. He filled in at left back, defending well and taking every opportunity to push forward and support the attack. He quickly became a favourite of the Pirates' fans, but returned to Priestfield and came off the bench in the final game of the season as a replacement for injured skipper Paul Smith.

Gillingham (From trainee on 10/4/2001) FL 3+6 FLC 0+1
Bristol Rov (Loaned on 13/12/2002) FL 9

ROSENIOR Liam James
Born: Wandsworth, 9 July 1984
Height: 5'9" **Weight:** 11.8
Club Honours: AMC '03

This midfielder or striker impressed so much whenever he got the opportunity for Bristol City last season that many of the fans couldn't understand why he didn't play more often. He certainly livened up a poor City performance in the LDV Vans Trophy final at the Millennium Stadium and deserved to score the second goal. Although his best role is in midfield, last season his zest, enthusiasm and skill were more often used as a striker. Liam is the son of ex-City player and current Torquay boss Leroy Rosenior.

Bristol C (From trainee on 15/8/2001) FL 2+20/2 FAC 0+1 Others 2+3/1

Wayne Rooney

ROSS Neil James
Born: Birmingham, 10 August 1982
Height: 6'1" **Weight:** 12.2
Neil found himself well down the pecking order of strikers at Stockport last term following the arrival of Ben Burgess. His four starts yielded just one goal, against Wycombe, and he eventually left for Macclesfield where he was signed to supplement the strike force. He found it difficult to break into the team on a regular basis and only made the starting line-up on half-a-dozen occasions, but will be looking to establish himself in 2003-04.
Leeds U (From trainee on 12/8/1999)
Stockport Co (Free on 28/1/2000) FL 3+6/2 FLC 1+1 FAC 1 Others 1+1
Bristol Rov (Loaned on 23/10/2001) FL 2+3 Others 1
Macclesfield T (£30,000 on 10/1/2003) FL 6+2

ROSSITER Mark
Born: Sligo, 27 May 1983
Height: 5'11" **Weight:** 12.6
International Honours: RoI: U21-1; Yth
A young right back, Mark made his Sunderland debut last season in the 3-2 Worthington Cup victory at Arsenal in November and impressed with his overlapping runs and boundless energy. It was therefore extremely cruel on the youngster when he ruptured a cruciate knee ligament whilst representing the Republic of Ireland U21s, an injury that will keep him on the sidelines until Christmas.
Sunderland (From trainee on 2/6/2000) FLC 2 FAC 0+1

ROUGIER Anthony (Tony) Leo
Born: Tobago, 17 July 1971
Height: 6'0" **Weight:** 14.1
International Honours: Trinidad & Tobago
Unfortunately Tony was never quite able to win over the Reading fans, or to gain a regular place in the team, and on only three occasions during his 22 appearances did he complete the full 90 minutes. He scored just three times for the Royals, and his most productive spell came when he joined Brighton on loan. Tony made an instant impact on the South Coast, scoring the winner against Millwall within a couple of minutes of coming on as a substitute in February. He went on to force an own goal against Rotherham, repeated the feat against Ipswich, and also scored another himself against the Suffolk side. Although he enjoyed a great

rapport with the club and its supporters, he eventually returned to the Madejski Stadium and was informed he was free to leave at the end of the season.
Raith Rov (Free from Trinity Prospect, Trinidad on 9/3/1995) SL 47+10/2 SLC 3/3 SC 4+1/1 Others 4+1/1
Hibernian (Signed on 10/7/1997) SL 34+11/4 SLC 4
Port Vale (£175,000 on 4/1/1999) FL 41+10/8 FLC 2/1 FAC 1
Reading (£325,000 on 11/8/2000) FL 47+37/6 FLC 2+3 FAC 2+1 Others 3+4
Brighton & Hove A (Loaned on 20/2/2003) FL 5+1/2

ROUTLEDGE Wayne Neville
Born: Sidcup, 7 January 1985
Height: 5'6" **Weight:** 10.7
International Honours: E: Yth
This highly rated winger made good progress at Crystal Palace last season and featured in over half the club's first-team matches. He scored his first senior goal with a great effort against Wolves in September and also represented England at U19 level during the campaign. Wayne was voted as the Eagles' 'Young Player of the Year'.
Crystal Palace (From trainee on 9/7/2002) FL 13+15/4 FLC 2 FAC 0+1

ROWAN Jonathan (Jonny) Robert
Born: Grimsby, 29 November 1981
Height: 5'10" **Weight:** 11.4
Following a promising introduction to the senior squad the previous season, Jonny had a somewhat disappointing time at Grimsby in 2002-03. A loss of form found him almost completely out in the cold and he rarely made it on to the substitutes' bench for the first team. He will be hoping for better things in 2003-04 as the Mariners regroup following their relegation.
Grimsby T (From trainee on 12/7/2000) FL 23+15/4 FLC 2+4/2 FAC 0+1

ROWETT Gary
Born: Bromsgrove, 6 March 1974
Height: 6'0" **Weight:** 12.10
Gary joined Charlton Athletic in the summer of 2002 to bolster the team's defence. A strong, hard-tackling and skilful defender who can play at right back or in central defence, he was expected to become a regular member of the side, but persistent injury problems with his back and later his knee caused him to start only 12 games, and he did not feature at all after Christmas. When

in the side he looked very accomplished and should be an asset for the club in the 2003-04 season. Gary scored his first goal for the Addicks in the 1-1 draw with Sunderland at the Valley.
Cambridge U (From trainee on 10/9/1991) FL 51+12/9 FLC 7/1 FAC 5+2 Others 5/3
Everton (£200,000 on 21/5/1994) PL 2+2
Blackpool (Loaned on 23/1/1995) FL 17
Derby Co (£300,000 on 20/7/1995) P/FL 101+4/2 FLC 8/2 FAC 5+2
Birmingham C (£1,000,000 on 17/8/1998) FL 87/6 FLC 9/3 FAC 3/1 Others 4/1
Leicester C (£3,000,000 + on 7/7/2000) PL 47+2/2 FLC 2 FAC 4/1 Others 2
Charlton Ath (£2,500,000 + on 14/5/2002) PL 12/1

ROWLAND Keith
Born: Portadown, 1 September 1971
Height: 5'10" **Weight:** 10.0
International Honours: NI: 18; B-3; Yth
The injuries that robbed Chesterfield of the best of Keith Rowland in 2001-02 finally put paid to his full-time career last season. The talented midfielder had a trial at Southend in September, returned to make a few appearances for the Spireites in November but was released soon afterwards and eventually joined Barnet in March.
Bournemouth (From trainee on 2/10/1989) FL 65+7/2 FLC 5 FAC 8 Others 3
Coventry C (Loaned on 8/1/1993) PL 0+2
West Ham U (£110,000 on 6/8/1993) FL 63+17/1 FLC 3+2 FAC 5+1
Queens Park R (Signed on 30/1/1998) FL 32+24/3 FLC 1+1 FAC 1+1
Luton T (Loaned on 27/1/2001) FL 12/2
Chesterfield (Free on 10/8/2001) FL 6+6 FLC 1/1 Others 1

ROWLAND Stephen (Steve) John
Born: Wrexham, 2 November 1981
Height: 5'10" **Weight:** 12.4
A Port Vale defender who can play on either the left or right-hand side, Steve began the season as a regular in the team. He did well enough to be called up by Wales U21s for the game in Azerbaijan only to get injured the week before. He returned to the Vale line-up but was sent off at Stockport on New Year's Day and then he was again called up for the U21s only to be pulled out because it clashed with a club fixture. Steve was left out after a defeat at Colchester in March and was only used as a substitute during the remainder of the campaign.
Port Vale (From trainee on 2/7/2001) FL 47+3/1 FAC 2 Others 4

ROWLANDS Martin Charles
Born: Hammersmith, 8 February 1979
Height: 5'9" Weight: 10.10
Club Honours: Div 3 '99
International Honours: RoI: U21-8
This skilful, right-footed Brentford
midfielder had another injury-ravaged
season last term and did not play until
November due to a groin problem. Martin
also suffered with calf and ankle problems
in January before his campaign ended
prematurely as a result of a broken leg in
April. A highlight was his well-taken goal
against Northampton in March, but he
will be hoping to stay clear of the
treatment room in 2003-04.
*Brentford (£45,000 from Farnborough T on
8/8/1998) FL 128+21/20 FLC 8+3/1 FAC 7+2
Others 17/2*

ROYCE Simon Ernest
Born: Forest Gate, 9 September 1971
Height: 6'2" Weight: 12.8
This experienced 'keeper was again out of
the first-team picture at Leicester last term
and at the end of August he joined
Queen's Park Rangers in a three-month
loan deal. He proved to be a very able
deputy for the injured Nick Culkin and the
club wanted to extend the loan period,
but nevertheless he returned to Filbert
Street. At the end of the season it was
announced he was available on a free
transfer, although he still has two years of
his contract remaining.
*Southend U (£35,000 from Heybridge Swifts
on 15/10/1991) FL 147+2 FLC 9 FAC 5
Others 6*
Charlton Ath (Free on 2/7/1998) PL 8
*Leicester C (Free on 17/7/2000) PL 16+3 FLC
FAC 4*
*Brighton & Hove A (Loaned on 24/12/2001)
6*
*Queens Park R (Loaned on 24/8/2002) FL 16
Others 1*

RUBINS Andrejs
Born: Latvia, 26 November 1978
Height: 5'9" Weight: 10.5
International Honours: Latvia: 42
Andrejs again found himself out of favour
at Crystal Palace last term and his first-
team experience was limited to just two
outings from the substitutes' bench. He
was eventually released from his contract
in the autumn and moved on to join
Spartak Moscow. Ironically the small and
speedy winger played almost as much
football for Latvia as he did for Palace
during his stay at Selhurst Park.
*Crystal Palace (£2,000,000 from Skonto
Riga, Latvia on 17/10/2000) FL 17+14 FLC
1+1/2 FAC 2*

RUFUS Richard Raymond
Born: Lewisham, 12 January 1975
Height: 6'1" Weight: 11.10
Club Honours: Div 1 '00
International Honours: E: U21-6
Richard was the mainstay of the Charlton
defence throughout the 2002-03
campaign and it is something of a
mystery that he was not called into the
full England international squad. He is a
strong and determined tackler, very calm
under pressure and extremely quick. He
reads the game very well, has good
distribution and is dominant in the air.
Richard was playing with an injury
towards the end of the season and
missed the last couple of games having
decided to have an operation to cure a
knee problem, but should have fully
recovered for the start of 2003-04.
*Charlton Ath (From trainee on 1/7/1993)
P/FL 284+4/12 FLC 14 FAC 16 Others 5/1*

RUNDLE Adam
Born: Durham, 8 July 1984
Height: 5'10" Weight: 11.2
This exciting young left-winger only made
a handful of appearances for Darlington
at the beginning of last season before
being left out the side. Nevertheless,
Adam became a great favourite of the
club's fans with his dazzling direct runs
down the flank and swerves inside to
shoot for goal. He was surprisingly
allowed to move on to Carlisle United in
mid-season after less than 20 outings for
the Quakers. Adam featured fairly
regularly for the Cumbrian side, scoring
the crucial goal that decided the LDV
Vans Trophy regional final against
Shrewsbury, thus earning the club a trip
to the Millennium Stadium.
Darlington (Trainee) FL 8+9
*Carlisle U (Free on 31/12/2002) FL 19+2/1
Others 3+1/1*

RUSHBURY Andrew (Andy)
James
Born: Carlisle, 7 March 1983
Height: 5'10" Weight: 11.7
No one tried harder for Chesterfield in
2002-03 than Andy Rushbury, who had to
cope with the mantle of being the boss's
son, and then had to watch as his father
left the club near the season's end. A
more than useful wing back or right-sided
midfielder, Andy has the enthusiasm and
determination to make an impression
with the club's new management.
*Chesterfield (From trainee on 25/7/2002) FL
23+12 FLC 2+1 FAC 1+1 Others 0+1*

RUSK Simon
Born: Peterborough, 17 December 1981
Height: 5'11" Weight: 12.8
Club Honours: NC '02
Simon spent much of the 2002-03 season
on the sidelines after picking up a knee
injury and then suffering hamstring
troubles. When fit he proved an effective
player pushing forward on the right side
of midfield for Boston United. He showed
his versatility when called upon to switch
to a more defensive role at right back on
occasions.
*Boston U (Free from Cambridge C on
6/4/2001) FL 12+6/2 FLC 1 FAC 1 Others 1*

RUSSELL Alexander (Alex)
John
Born: Crosby, 17 March 1973
Height: 5'9" Weight: 11.7
This assured midfield general was the
linchpin of Torquay United's team last
season and revelled in the new
commitment to the passing game. Hard
working, he did his share of defensive
duties while contributing ten goals and
creating many more with his unfussy but
accurate passing. Alex deservedly won
recognition from the supporters as
United's 'Player of the Season', and from
his fellow professionals with inclusion in
the PFA Division Three team of the
season.
*Rochdale (£4,000 from Burscough on
11/7/1994) FL 83+19/14 FLC 5/1 FAC 1+1
Others 2+3*
*Cambridge U (Free on 4/8/1998) FL 72+9/8
FLC 7+1 FAC 6 Others 3*
*Torquay U (Free on 9/8/2001) FL 72/16 FLC
3 FAC 2/1 Others 1*

RUSSELL Craig Stewart
Born: Jarrow, 4 February 1974
Height: 5'10" Weight: 12.6
Club Honours: Div 1 '96
Craig began last season at St Johnstone,
but did not feature in the first team after
the end of September. He later moved on
to join Carlisle, where he featured both as
a striker and as an attacking midfielder.
Although he did not make the line-up
regularly, Craig did sufficient to win the
offer of a new contract for the 2003-04
campaign.
*Sunderland (From trainee on 1/7/1992) P/FL
103+47/31 FLC 7+6/1 FAC 6+3/2 Others 2*
*Manchester C (£1,000,000 on 14/11/1997)
FL 22+9/2 FAC 5+1/2*
Tranmere Rov (Loaned on 7/8/1998) FL 3+1
Port Vale (Loaned on 29/11/1999) FL 8/1
Darlington (Loaned on 3/9/1999) FL 11+1/2

Oxford U *(Loaned on 11/2/2000) FL 5+1*
St Johnstone *(Loaned on 29/3/2000) SL 1/1*
St Johnstone *(Free on 12/7/2000) SL 16+19/2 SLC 1+1 SC 1+1/1 Others 2*
Carlisle U *(Free on 16/11/2003) FL 7+6/1 Others 3*

RUSSELL Darel Francis Roy
Born: Stepney, 22 October 1980
Height: 5'11" **Weight:** 11.9
International Honours: E: Yth
Darel rejected Norwich City's offer of a new contract during the summer of 2002, but was retained on weekly terms. His excellent attitude and dedication later ensured that he signed a new one-year deal and another longer-term contract was offered to him for season 2003-04 and beyond. This energetic, bustling midfielder was extremely unfortunate to sustain a nasty foot injury in his first senior start of the campaign, away at Reading in mid-September, but he fought his way back to full fitness and a place in City's starting line-up in the latter stages. Darel is a tremendous athlete with a real appetite for the game, never giving less than 100 per cent: attributes that make him very popular with Canary fans.
Norwich C *(From trainee on 29/11/1997) FL 99+33/7 FLC 8/2 FAC 6+1*

RUSSELL Kevin John
Born: Portsmouth, 6 December 1966
Height: 5'9" **Weight:** 10.12
Club Honours: Div 2 '93
International Honours: E: Yth
One of the Wrexham's great servants, previously on the field but now learning fast off it as assistant-manager to Denis Smith, Kevin came to terms with the knowledge that the 60 minutes he played against Scunthorpe in August was his last in professional football. He won praise from his boss for his role at the Racecourse and in March he was confirmed as a full-time coach, thus bringing his career as a busy and prolific striker to a close.
Portsmouth *(From apprentice at Brighton & Hove A on 9/10/1984) FL 3+1 FLC 0+1 FAC 0+1 Others 1+1*
Wrexham *(£10,000 on 17/7/1987) FL 84/43 FLC 4/1 FAC 4 Others 8/3*
Leicester C *(£175,000 on 20/6/1989) FL 24+19/10 FLC 0+1 FAC 1 Others 5/2*
Peterborough U *(Loaned on 6/9/1990) FL 7/3*
Cardiff C *(Loaned on 17/1/1991) FL 3*
Hereford U *(Loaned on 7/11/1991) FL 3/1 Others 1/1*

Stoke C *(Loaned on 2/1/1992) FL 5/1*
Stoke C *(£95,000 on 16/7/1992) FL 30+10/5 FLC 3 FAC 2 Others 4+1/1*
Burnley *(£150,000 on 28/6/1993) FL 26+2/6 FLC 4/1 FAC 4 Others 1/1*
Bournemouth *(£125,000 on 3/3/1994) FL 30/1 FLC 3/1 FAC 2/1*
Notts Co *(£60,000 on 24/2/1995) FL 9+2*
Wrexham *(£60,000 on 21/7/1995) FL 172+26/17 FLC 6+2/2 FAC 18+5/4 Others 10+1*

RUSSELL Samuel (Sam) Ian
Born: Middlesbrough, 4 October 1982
Height: 6'0" **Weight:** 10.13
A product of the FA School of Excellence, this young Middlesbrough goalkeeper occasionally featured for the reserves and on the substitutes' bench at first-team level last term. At the turn of the year he spent time on loan at Darlington to cover for an injury crisis and he made his bow in senior football in the 1-1 draw against Torquay. This was his only appearance for the Quakers and he subsequently returned to the Riverside to continue his development.
Middlesbrough *(From trainee on 7/7/2000)*
Darlington *(Loaned on 28/12/2002) FL 1*

RUSSELL Simon Craig
Born: Hull, 19 March 1985
Height: 5'7" **Weight:** 10.6
The locally-born midfielder made his Hull City debut when he came on for Ryan Williams after an hour of the Tigers' LDV Vans Trophy tie at Port Vale in October. Although still a regular in the club's youth team, Simon also featured for the City reserves team that won the 2002-03 Avon Insurance Division One East championship. Simon went on to make his Football League debut in the closing stages of City's final home game of the season against Kidderminster.
Hull C *(Trainee) FL 0+1 Others 0+1*

RYAN Keith James
Born: Northampton, 25 June 1970
Height: 5'11" **Weight:** 12.8
Club Honours: FAT '91, '93; GMVC '93
Wycombe's 'Mr Versatility' has had protracted spells in virtually every outfield position in his long career. Last season he had the unusual experience of playing at left back for three months, covering the injured Chris Vinnicombe. He impressed everyone with his whole-hearted displays there, in spite of being predominantly right-footed. Otherwise he was seen

stiffening the centre of midfield with some purposeful tackling, chasing anything and everything.
Wycombe W *(Signed from Berkhamstead T during 1990 close season) FL 254+42/26 FLC 13+2/3 FAC 19+3/4 Others 16+1/1*

RYAN Leon Michael
Born: Sunderland, 8 November 1982
Height: 6'2" **Weight:** 14.0
This former Middlesbrough trainee spen the summer of 2002 in Finland with KTF Kotka and on his return he impressed sufficiently in Scunthorpe's reserves to win a monthly deal. A tall, strongly buil striker, he made two brief substitute appearances for the first team against Lincoln and Carlisle before being released at the start of October followir which he signed for Conference club Halifax Town.
Scunthorpe U *(Free from Kotkan TP, Finland on 6/9/2002) FL 0+2*

RYAN Richard (Richie)
Born: Kilkenny, 6 January 1985
Height: 5'10" **Weight:** 11.3
International Honours: RoI: Yth
This young midfielder made his Sunderland debut after only six reserve appearances last season when he appeared as a substitute amidst the white-hot atmosphere of the Wear-Tyne 'derby' in April. Richie is a left-sided player and having previously represented the Republic of Ireland in age-group teams, he stepped up to the U19 squad last term.
Sunderland *(From trainee on 30/1/2002) PL 0+2*

RYAN Robert (Robbie) Paul
Born: Dublin, 16 May 1977
Height: 5'10" **Weight:** 12.0
Club Honours: Div 2 '01
International Honours: RoI: U21-12; Yth; Sch
One of Millwall's most accomplished and consistent operators in recent seasons, Robbie once again made the left-back position his own last term. Very few wingers get the better of this tough-tackling player and he produced a series of consistent performances. He also managed to score his first-ever goals for the Lions, netting in the Boxing Day gam against Gillingham and the 4-0 win over Watford the following month.
Huddersfield T *(Free from Belvedere YC on 26/7/1994) FL 12+3 FLC 2*
Millwall *(£10,000 on 30/1/1998) FL 181+15/2 FLC 9 FAC 10 Others 5*

S

SABIN Eric
Born: Paris, France, 22 January 1975
Height: 6'1" **Weight:** 12.4
This skilful and pacy forward once again worked hard for the cause at Swindon in the 2002-03 campaign. However, a change in formation from three front men to two meant that his contribution often came from the subs' bench, his blistering speed causing problems for tired defenders. Although not a regular goal-scorer he was popular with the fans and following a trial at Queen's Park Rangers towards the end of the season a permanent departure seemed on the cards at the time of writing.
Swindon T (Free from Wasquehal, France on 3/7/2001) FL 60+13/9 FLC 2 FAC 5 Others +1

SADLER Matthew (Mat)
Born: Birmingham, 26 February 1985
Height: 5'11" **Weight:** 11.6
International Honours: E: Yth
Mat made his senior debut for Birmingham City in the Worthington Cup tie against Leyton Orient and went on to make his Premiership bow when he was pitched into the key game against Bolton at St Andrew's in November, helping the team to a 3-1 victory. However, he then got injured, but returned at Old Trafford over Christmas when he marked Manchester United's David Beckham and held his own. A left back blessed with pace and a cool head, he was selected as the club's 'Young Player of the Season'.
Birmingham C (From trainee on 12/4/2002) FL 2 FLC 2

SADLIER Richard Thomas
Born: Dublin, 14 January 1979
Height: 6'2'' **Weight:** 12.10
Club Honours: Div 2 '01
International Honours: RoI: U21-2; Yth
Richard once again suffered with injuries last term and a hip problem restricted him to just five first-team appearances, three of which were from the substitutes' bench. However, he did manage to score one goal, netting in the 1-1 draw with Burnley in March. Richard is a tall rangy front man who holds the ball up well, is good in the air, deceptively quick and the perfect foil for a poacher such as Neil Harris. He will be looking to stay free of injury and establish himself in the Lions' team in 2003-04.
Millwall (Signed from Belvedere YC on 14/8/1996) FL 103+40/34 FLC 6/2 FAC 4+1/2 Others 7+2/3

SAFRI Youssef
Born: Morocco, 1 March 1977
Height: 5'10" **Weight:** 11.8
International Honours: Morocco:
Youssef produced some excellent performances for Coventry in the autumn, notably at home to Norwich and in the draw at Portsmouth. He impressed with his excellent ball control and passing ability, but playing mainly in the deeper 'holding' midfield role he had limited scoring chances. Youssef suffered a hernia injury at Christmas and although he returned to first-team duty after an operation he suffered a groin strain after two games and sat out the rest of the campaign. His absence was one of the major reasons why the team struggled in the second half of the season. He also featured at international level for Morocco.
Coventry C (Free from Raja Casablanca, Morocco on 25/8/2001) FL 56+4/1 FLC 4

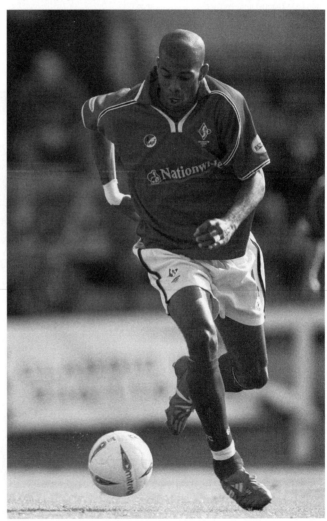

Eric Sabin

SAGARE Jake
Born: Yakima, Washington, USA, 4 May 1980
Height: 5'11" **Weight:** 11.7
This promising young striker came to Grimsby on trial in the autumn and did well enough to earn himself a short-term deal at Blundell Park in the new year. Jake went on to make his bow in English football in the penultimate match of the season when he lined up for the Mariners against Reading. Shortly afterwards he was reported to have rejoined his former club, US-A League outfit Portland Timbers.
Grimsby T (Free from Portland Timbers, USA on 6/11/2002) FL 1

SAHA Louis
Born: Paris, France, 8 August 1978
Height: 5'11" **Weight:** 11.10
Club Honours: Div 1 '01
International Honours: France: U21; Yth (UEFA-U18 '97)
Although Louis has never recaptured the form that saw him score more than 30 goals in his first season at Fulham, he continues to be a thorn in the side of Premiership defences. His pace and silky skills often win free kicks and despite a relative lack of height he is an excellent header of the ball. His ability to sniff out a goal-scoring opportunity was amply demonstrated when he scored with a well-taken header in the last minute against Sunderland. After opening the season with a penalty against Bolton Louis suffered a number of injuries which severely restricted his appearances, before returning with a burst of three Premiership goals in four games, strikes which made a valuable contribution to the fight against dropping into the relegation zone.
Newcastle U (Loaned from Metz, France on 8/1/1999) PL 5+6/1 FAC 1/1
Fulham (£2,100,000 from Metz, France on 29/6/2000) P/FL 80+16/40 FLC 3+3/6 FAC 9+1/1 Others 5+4/1

SALAKO John Akin
Born: Nigeria, 11 February 1969
Height: 5'10" **Weight:** 12.8
Club Honours: FMC '91; Div 1 '94, '00
International Honours: E: 5
A regular on the wide-left side of a five-man midfield for Reading for most of the season, John showed all his old skills in his dribbling and crossing of the ball, even if his pace is beginning to diminish as he enters the veteran stage of his career. His selection as first choice came under threat from the emerging talent of young

Nathan Tyson, by whom he was often substituted, but John weighed in with some important goals, none better than a right-foot curler in the 5-2 win at Burnley. The former England international has begun to establish a media career for himself in preparation for his life after football, and is occasionally seen as a summariser on television.
Crystal Palace (From apprentice on 3/11/1986) F/PL 172+43/22 FLC 19+5/5 FAC 20/4 Others 11+3/2
Swansea C (Loaned on 14/8/1989) FL 13/3 Others 2/1
Coventry C (£1,500,000 on 7/8/1995) PL 68+4/4 FLC 9/3 FAC 4/1
Bolton W (Free on 26/3/1998) PL 0+7
Fulham (Free on 22/7/1998) FL 7+3/1 FLC 2/1 FAC 2+2 Others 1
Charlton Ath (£150,000 on 20/8/1999) P/FL 10+37/2 FLC 1+2 FAC 3+4/1

Reading (£75,000 + on 2/11/2001) FL 64+10/10 FLC 1 FAC 0+2 Others 1

SALL Abdou Hamed
Born: Senegal, 1 November 1980
Height: 6'3" **Weight:** 14.2
Abdou had a disappointing campaign with Kidderminster last term. After picking up an ankle injury in August he was kept on the sidelines until making a brief reappearance to score the 'golden goal' winner against Swindon in the LDV Vans Trophy. He was then loaned to Oxford where he entered the record books as the only player to make two appearances and not touch the ball, both of his brief cameos coming as last-minute tactical moves. Early in the new year the big defender left the Harriers for Conference club Nuneaton Borough.
Kidderminster Hrs (Free from Toulouse,

John Salako

rance on 10/8/2001) FL 31/2 FAC 1 Others 2/1
Oxford U (Loaned on 29/11/2002) FL 0+1
AC 0+1

SALTER Mark Charles
Born: Oxford, 16 March 1980
Height: 6'1" **Weight:** 11.6
Only three years ago Mark was playing village football for Stoke sub Hamdon, but really came to the fore with two prolific goal-scoring seasons at Frome Town. After summer trials at Southend he returned to the Western League club, but eventually signed forms for the Blues in October. He played well in the reserves and made a handful of first-team appearances. The highlight of his campaign came in March when he scored the only goal in the local 'derby' with Leyton Orient. However his slight frame counted against him in the hurly-burly of the Third Division and he was not offered a new deal at the season's end.
Southend U (Free from Frome T on 1/10/2002) FL 5+8/1 Others 0+1

SALVA] BALLESTA Vialcho Salvador
Born: Paese, Spain, 22 May 1975
Height: 6'0" **Weight:** 13.3
International Honours: Spain: 3
A powerful centre forward renowned for his abilities in the air, Salva made his debut for Bolton in the away fixture against West Bromwich Albion last February. He arrived at the Reebok with a big reputation, but unfortunately he was troubled by a niggling ankle injury and he made just one first-team start for the club, in the away defeat at Liverpool. Although he made several appearances from the substitutes' bench it is fair to say that Wanderers' fans did not see the best of a very talented player.
Bolton W (Loaned from Valencia, Spain, ex Espanyol, Seville, Racing Santander, Atletico Madrid, on 31/1/2003) PL 1+5

SAM Hector McLeod
Born: Mount Hope, Trinidad, 25 February 1978
Height: 5'9" **Weight:** 11.5
International Honours: Trinidad & Tobago: 14
Hector was used mainly as a sort of super sub' by Wrexham last term and lived up to his title, scoring some vital late goals. He notched important strikes at home to Oxford United and away to Macclesfield in August and away to Carlisle United in December after coming off the bench. As usual his strength was his unpredictability, always a handful for

defenders who had their work cut out not knowing what he was going to do next. He continued to represent Trinidad & Tobago at international level and won a number of caps during the summer tour of Southern Africa.
Wrexham (£125,000 from CL Financial San Juan Jabloteh, Trinidad on 8/8/2000) FL 34+41/16 FLC 4 FAC 2+1 Others 3+3

SAMBROOK Andrew (Andy) John
Born: Chatham, 13 July 1979
Height: 5'10" **Weight:** 12.4
Club Honours: Div 3 '03
International Honours: E: Sch
Andy is best known as a right back but he also slotted into a midfield role for Rushden & Diamonds later in the season to cover injury problems. He was mainly restricted to substitute appearances due to Marcus Bignot's consistent form in defence. However, despite starting just six games all season, he did enough to impress boss Brian Talbot, earning a new contract in the summer to stay with the Third Division champions.
Gillingham (Associated Schoolboy) FL 0+1
Rushden & Diamonds (Free from Hartwick College, USA on 9/8/2001) FL 31+10 FAC 2 Others 1

SAMPSON Ian
Born: Wakefield, 14 November 1968
Height: 6'2" **Weight:** 13.3
This central defender had a mixed season at Northampton in 2002-03. He too fell victim to the club's injury hoodoo then when he was full fit he could not find a first-team place under Terry Fenwick. However, the arrival of Martin Wilkinson saw the club's longest-serving player not only reinstated but also made team captain again. Ian produced some excellent performances alongside Paul Reid at the back and scored a header from near the edge of the penalty area against Notts County. An interesting statistic is that while at Northampton, Ian has played under seven different managers.
Sunderland (Signed from Goole T on 13/11/1990) FL 13+4/1 FLC 1 FAC 0+2 Others 0+1
Northampton T (Loaned on 8/12/1993) FL 8
Northampton T (Free on 5/8/1994) FL 337+8/24 FLC 16/1 FAC 14/1 Others 19/2
Tottenham H (Loaned on 22/6/1995) Others 3/1

SAMUEL JLloyd
Born: Trinidad, 29 March 1981
Height: 5'11" **Weight:** 11.4

International Honours: E: U21-7; Yth
JLloyd was forced to settle for a place on the substitutes' bench for Aston Villa at the start of last season, but when the team switched to a 3-5-2 formation he returned to the starting line-up as left wing back. He never looked back from then on and was a near ever-present for the rest of the season, occasionally featuring on the right flank as well. JLloyd produced a number of solid performances at club level and also appeared regularly for England U21s.
Aston Villa (From trainee on 2/2/1999) PL 56+17 FLC 4+1 FAC 3 Others 5+2
Gillingham (Loaned on 26/10/2001) FL 7+1

SAMWAYS Vincent (Vinny)
Born: Bethnal Green, 27 October 1968
Height: 5'8" **Weight:** 11.0
Club Honours: FAC '91; CS '91, '95
International Honours: E: U21-5; Yth
Loaned by Walsall from Spanish club Seville in February, Vinny made an outstanding contribution to the Saddlers' First Division survival with his calming influence in front of the back four, his immaculate distribution and a solidity that enabled other midfielders to get forward. Walsall fans were disappointed when he returned to Spain at the end of the season.
Tottenham H (From apprentice on 9/11/1985) F/PL 165+28/11 FLC 27+4/4 FAC 15+1/2 Others 7+1
Everton (£2,200,000 on 2/8/1994) PL 17+6/2 FLC 3/1 Others 2/1 (£600,000 to Las Palmas, Spain on 13/12/1996)
Wolverhampton W (Loaned on 21/12/1995) FL 3
Birmingham C (Loaned on 9/2/1996) FL 12
Walsall (Free from Sevilla, Spain on 26/2/2003) FL 13

SANASY Kevin Roy
Born: Leeds, 2 November 1984
Height: 5'8" **Weight:** 10.5
Kevin was a regular goal-scorer at youth and reserve-team level for Bradford City before being rewarded with a brief senior outing at the end of the 2002-03 season. He replaced Danny Forrest in attack for the last seven minutes in the defeat at Sheffield United in April. A striker with plenty of potential, he will be aiming to gain further senior experience in 2003-04.
Bradford C (Trainee) FL 0+1

SANKOFA Osei Omari Kwende
Born: London, 19 March 1985
Height: 6'0" **Weight:** 12.4
International Honours: E: Yth
Osei made rapid progress during the 2002-03 season, starting in Charlton's

U19 academy squad and finishing the campaign in the first team and winning England U18 honours on the way. A tall defender who can play at right back or in the centre of defence, he made his first-team debut at Old Trafford as a second-half substitute in the penultimate game of the season. Osei is quick, composed and confident, and will get stronger as he gets older.

Charlton Ath (From trainee on 8/11/2002) PL 0+1

SANTOS Georges
Born: Marseille, France, 15 August 1970
Height: 6'3" **Weight:** 14.0
The arrival of Georges Santos at Blundell Park provided one of the few rays of light to illuminate an otherwise dark season for Grimsby Town fans. Initially signed on a one-month contract he played in midfield, but then returned to France to reconsider his position. A deal was worked out and he eventually signed a contract to the end of the season. Georges returned as a central defender to play a vital part in sealing a seriously leaky defence. Strong, powerful in the air and a good reader of the game he is also capable of surging runs through the midfield. He quickly became a firm favourite with the Mariners' fans and was selected as the club's 'Player of the Year'.

Tranmere Rov (Free from Toulon, France on 29/7/1998) FL 46+1/2 FLC 6 FAC 1
West Bromwich A (£25,000 on 23/3/2000) FL 8
Sheffield U (Free on 5/7/2000) FL 37+24/6 FLC 2+3 FAC 1+1
Grimsby T (Free on 27/9/2002) FL 24+2/1 FAC 1

SARA Juan Manuel
Born: Ituzaingo, Argentina, 13 October 1978
Height: 6'0" **Weight:** 11.7
Juan was a regular for Dundee for the first half of 2002-03 before joining Coventry on a temporary transfer in January with a view to staying until the end of the season. The tall, skilful striker had a good goal-scoring record in Scotland and almost found the net with his first touch for the Sky Blues on his debut against Brighton. His only goal in three appearances was a late equaliser at Nottingham Forest when his fast feet saw him keep control to slide home a low shot. He was released at the end of the season.

Dundee (Signed from Cerro Porteno, Paraguay on 1/7/2000) SL 60+18/28 SLC 3/2 SC 6+1/3 Others 2/1

Coventry C (Loaned on 10/1/2003) FL 1+2/1 FAC 0+1

SAUNDERS Mark Philip
Born: Reading, 23 July 1971
Height: 5'11" **Weight:** 11.12
Although out of contract at the start of the season and playing on monthly deals, manager Andy Hessenthaler could still rely on Mark giving his all for the sake of Gillingham. Eventually his performances were rewarded with a new contract and he was a regular until the season's end when he picked up a hamstring injury. Mark is an experienced midfielder who can also play at right back.

Plymouth Arg (Signed from Tiverton T on 22/8/1995) FL 60+12/11 FLC 1+1 FAC 2+3 Others 2
Gillingham (Free on 1/6/1998) FL 106+42/14 FLC 6+2 FAC 9+1/1 Others 3+3

SAVA Facundo
Born: Huzaingo, Argentina, 3 July 1974
Height: 5'11" **Weight:** 12.8
Facundo joined Fulham in the summer of 2002 and made an immediate impression with a hat-trick in his first reserve game at Arsenal. This soon led to a first-team place and he scored in only his second start at Middlesbrough. He went on to hit a total of five Premiership goals, including a spectacular double against Liverpool. A tall player who leads the line well he is particularly quick on the ground and has proved a useful squad player.

Fulham (£2,000,000 from Gymnasia Y. Esgrima la Plata, Argentina on 25/6/2002) PL 13+7/5 FLC 1+1 FAC 3+1/1 Others 6

SAVAGE David (Dave) Thomas Patrick
Born: Dublin, 30 July 1973
Height: 6'1" **Weight:** 12.7
International Honours: RoI: 5; U21-5
Although Dave had been a virtual ever-present in his first season he set out as though he had something to prove last term and had a tremendous campaign in the Oxford midfield. He missed just three games and was the most creative of the U's midfielders, scoring four times, three of them ironically against eventual champions Rushden. Out of contract in the summer, his future was unclear at the time of writing.

Brighton & Hove A (Signed from Kilkenny on 5/3/1991. Free to Longford T in May 1992)
Millwall (£15,000 on 27/5/1994) FL 104+28/6 FLC 11/2 FAC 6+2/2 Others 2/1
Northampton T (£100,000 on 7/10/1998) FL 98+15/18 FLC 3 FAC 5 Others 2+1

Oxford U (Free on 18/8/2001) FL 85/5 FLC 4 FAC 4 Others 2

SAVAGE Robert (Robbie) William
Born: Wrexham, 18 October 1974
Height: 6'1" **Weight:** 11.11
Club Honours: FAYC '92; FLC '00
International Honours: W: 29; U21-5; Yth; Sch
Robbie provided a real heartbeat to the Birmingham City line-up on their return to top-flight football, setting the tempo and example for others to follow. Despite occasionally being singled out for rough treatment by opponents, he inspired those around him to greater heights with his energy levels and will to win. A regular in the line-up in central midfield all season, he also showed some excellent distribution. Robbie was deservedly voted as the Blues' 'Player of the Season'. He continued to represent Wales at international level, winning a further four caps.

Manchester U (From trainee on 5/7/1993)
Crewe Alex (Free on 22/7/1994) FL 74+3/10 FLC 5 FAC 5 Others 8/1
Leicester C (£400,000 on 23/7/1997) PL 160+12/8 FLC 15+2 FAC 12/1 Others 2+1
Birmingham C (£2,500,000 on 30/5/2002) PL 33/4 FAC 1

SCHEMMEL Sebastien
Born: Nancy, France, 2 June 1975
Height: 5'10" **Weight:** 11.12
International Honours: France: U21
Apart from a couple of spells out injured the West Ham wing back was a regular in the side until January. Playing on the right-hand side he was full of energy and determination. A popular figure with the fans he was outstanding in the early-season London 'derbies' against Arsenal and Chelsea, but did not appear in the first team again after January after losing his place to the emerging talent of Glen Johnson.

West Ham U (£465,000 from Metz, France, ex Nancy, on 19/1/2001) PL 60+3/1 FLC 2+1 FAC 7

SCHMEICHEL Peter Boleslaw
Born: Gladsaxe, Denmark, 18 November 1963
Height: 6'4" **Weight:** 16.0
Club Honours: ESC '91; FLC '92; PL '93, '94, '96, '97, '99; FAC '94, '96, '99; CS '93, '94, '96, '97; EC '99
International Honours: Denmark: 129 (UEFA '92)
Peter joined Manchester City on a 12-month contract during the summer of

Robbie Savage

2002 and was very much the club's first choice goalkeeper last term, always looking safe when he stood between the sticks. He continued to produce some great displays, despite being at the veteran stage of his career and his saves were one of the main reasons City managed an unexpected win at Anfield. Having thoroughly enjoyed his season at Maine Road, Peter announced his retirement in the summer and he has already begun to build a new career as a television pundit.

Manchester U *(£550,000 from Brondby on 12/8/1991) P/FL 292 FLC 17 FAC 41 Others 48/1 (Free to Sporting Lisbon, Portugal on 1/7/1999)*
Aston Villa *(Free on 20/7/2001) PL 29/1 FLC 2 FAC 1 Others 4*
Manchester C *(Free on 13/7/2002) PL 29 FLC 1 FAC 1*

SCHOFIELD Daniel (Danny) James

Born: Doncaster, 10 April 1980
Height: 5'10" **Weight:** 11.3
Injury ruled this talented youngster out of the opening fixtures of the 2002-03 campaign for Huddersfield Town, but he returned to the line-up and established himself as a regular in a wide-midfield role. Danny produced some assured displays showing close control and accurate passing skills, and reached his 50th league appearance for the club during the campaign. A double hernia ruled him out of first-team duties for a while, but he returned to the wing and contributed a goal against Notts County.

Huddersfield T *(£2,000 from Brodsworth on 8/2/1999) FL 65+9/10 FLC 2+1 FAC 3+1 Others 6+1/4*

SCHOLES Paul

Born: Salford, 16 November 1974
Height: 5'7" **Weight:** 11.10
Club Honours: PL '96, '97, '99, '00, '01, '03; FAC '96, '99; CS '96, '97
International Honours: E: 56; Yth (UEFA-U18 '93)
A central midfielder whose imaginative distribution made him the fulcrum of the Manchester United team, Paul's continued to display an awe-inspiring influence last term. He enjoyed one of his best goal-poaching seasons in years, more notably in the Premiership, where he notched 13 efforts. The best moment of all came in that amazing eight-goal thriller at St James' Park in April, when Paul scored a majestic hat-trick to put United top of the table. Two more in the following home game against Blackburn,

including his 100th for the club, really put the Premiership up for grabs with challengers, Arsenal. Playing just behind Ruud Van Nistelrooy in a role that he previously disliked, this consummate professional continues to show a great influence for the Reds, despite not always being mentioned in despatches. He was, however, rewarded by his fellow professionals with a place in the PFA team of the season.

Manchester U *(From trainee on 29/1/1993) PL 206+54/69 FLC 10+4/8 FAC 12+8/5 Others 70+11/19*

SCHWARZ Stefan Hans

Born: Malmo, Sweden, 18 April 1969
Height: 5'10" **Weight:** 12.6
International Honours: Sweden: 69; U21
Sunderland's veteran former Swedish international skipper made just two appearances last term, both in the Worthington Cup, including an outing in the 3-2 win at his former club Arsenal, which must have delighted the schemer. A constructive and combative player with a cultured left foot, Stefan ended the season out of contract and has hinted that he may retire from football having been told that he can leave the Stadium of Light.

Arsenal *(£1,750,000 from Benfica, Portugal, ex Malmo, on 31/5/1994) PL 34/2 FLC 4 FAC 1 Others 10/2 (£2,500,000 to Fiorentina, Italy on 27/7/1995)*
Sunderland *(£3,500,000 from Valencia, Spain on 9/8/1999) PL 62+5/3 FLC 2+1 FAC 6*

SCHWARZER Mark

Born: Sydney, Australia, 6 October 1972
Height: 6'5'' **Weight:** 13.6
International Honours: Australia: 21; Yth
Mark, a commanding figure and excellent shot-stopper, reached the landmark figure of 200 league appearances for Middlesbrough last season, when he consolidated his status as one of the best goalkeepers in the Premiership. He would have been an ever-present but the club rested most of the first-team squad for the two Worthington Cup games. Mark wearied of playing understudy to regular Australia 'keeper Mark Bosnich to concentrate on his Boro' career and only recently decide to re-enter the international arena. It must have given him great personal satisfaction to be in goal for the Socceroos when they defeated England 3-1 at Upton Park in February.

Bradford C *(£350,000 from Kaiserslautern,*

Germany, ex Blacktown, Marconi, Dynamo Dresden, on 22/11/1996) FL 13 FAC 3
Middlesbrough *(£1,500,000 on 26/2/1997) F/PL 203 FLC 16 FAC 12*

SCIMECA Ricardo

Born: Leamington Spa, 13 June 1975
Height: 6'1" **Weight:** 12.9
Club Honours: FLC '96
International Honours: E: B-1; U21-9
Ricardo switched from the centre of defence to playing a 'holding' midfield role for Nottingham Forest last season following the arrival of Des Walker. He went on to have his most consistent season to date at the City Ground, being once again a near ever-present and impressing with his long-range shooting. He produced some memorable goals, notably when he netted with a free kick against Coventry City. Forest fans will be hoping he signs the new contract that was offered to him at the end of the season.

Aston Villa *(From trainee on 7/7/1993) PL 50+23/2 FLC 4+3 FAC 9+1 Others 5+2*
Nottingham F *(£3,000,000 on 23/7/1999) F 147+4/7 FLC 8/1 FAC 5 Others 2*

SCOTT Andrew (Andy)

Born: Epsom, 2 August 1972
Height: 6'1" **Weight:** 11.5
Club Honours: Div 3 '99
Andy was top scorer for Oxford last term netting a total of 11 goals although surprisingly only one of them, against Shrewsbury, was at home. These goals helped the U's register a club record for away wins during the season. A strong left-sided striker, he works extremely hard closing down space and is also useful in the air.

Sheffield U *(£50,000 from Sutton U on 1/12/1992) P/FL 39+36/6 FLC 5/2 FAC 2+1 Others 3+1/3*
Chesterfield *(Loaned on 18/10/1996) 4+1/3*
Bury *(Loaned on 21/3/1997) FL 2+6*
Brentford *(£75,000 on 21/11/1997) FL 109+9/28 FLC 8+1/4 FAC 3 Others 6/3*
Oxford U *(£75,000 on 12/1/2001) FL 75+14/24 FLC 3/1 FAC 0+1*

SCOTT Dion Elijah

Born: Birmingham, 24 December 1980
Height: 5'11" **Weight:** 11.3
Signed by Kidderminster boss Ian Britton last February to strengthen the Harriers' defence, Dion slotted straight into the heart of the back line. From then until the end of the season he was ever-present, giving some solid performances, which included helping the team to a clean

heet on his debut and scoring the
qualiser at Carlisle to earn Kidderminster
heir first-ever point at Brunton Park.
lowever, he was not offered a new
ontract in the summer and was reported
o have signed for Nuneaton Borough.
*Walsall (From trainee on 18/5/1999) FL 0+2
thers 2*
*iidderminster Hrs (Free on 31/1/2003) FL
9/1*

COTT Paul
orn: Wakefield, 5 November 1979
leight: 5'11" **Weight:** 12.8
 regular for Huddersfield Town's reserves
st season, this industrious midfielder
lostly featured from the substitutes'
ench at first-team level, although he
lanaged two starts. A sensible and
ccurate passer of the ball Paul was often
rought on towards the end of games to
ark a late push for victory. He was
oted as the club's 'Reserve Player of the
ear' and will be looking to establish
imself in the senior squad in 2003-04.
*uddersfield T (From trainee on 3/7/1998)
. 2+11 FLC 0+1*

COTT Richard Paul
orn: Dudley, 29 September 1974
eight: 5'9" **Weight:** 12.8
'chard began last season at Telford and
ter moved on to Stevenage Borough
efore returning to Peterborough United
n a short-term contract in December.
ble to play at full back or in midfield he
 a good passer of the ball with a fierce
not and exceptional work rate. Richard
as rewarded with an extension to his
ontract at the end of the campaign.
*irmingham C (From trainee on 17/5/1993)
. 11+1 FLC 3+1 Others 3*
*hrewsbury T (Signed on 22/3/1995) FL
1+14/18 FLC 6 FAC 8+1/3 Others 8+1/1*
*eterborough U (Signed on 20/7/1998) FL
5+16/7 FLC 1+3 FAC 1 Others 6+1 (Free to
elford U during 2001 close season)*
*eterborough U (Free from Stevenage
orough on 23/12/2002) FL 13+3/1*

COTT Robert (Rob)
orn: Epsom, 15 August 1973
eight: 6'1" **Weight:** 11.10
ob was an automatic choice in the team
n the right side of the back four for
otherham until Christmas, when he
uffered a dislocated shoulder that kept
m out of action for the rest of the
eason. A pacy former striker, he has the
bility to hurl in long throws and he had
nown good form until his injury. After his
peration Rob worked very hard in an
fort to regain full fitness with his

dedication being rewarded by returning
to full training, so, with a pre-season
behind him, it should be all systems go
again for 2003-04.
*Sheffield U (£20,000 from Sutton U on
1/8/1993) FL 2+4/1 FLC 0+1 Others 2+1*
Scarborough (Loaned on 22/3/1995) FL 8/3
*Northampton T (Loaned on 24/11/1995) FL
5 Others 1*
*Fulham (£30,000 on 10/1/1996) FL
65+19/17 FLC 3+5 FAC 3/1 Others 2+2/1*
Carlisle U (Loaned on 18/8/1998) FL 7/3
*Rotherham U (£50,000 on 17/11/1998) FL
135+5/7 FLC 9+1 FAC 8/1 Others 6*

SCOWCROFT James (Jamie)
Benjamin
Born: Bury St Edmunds, 15 November
1975
Height: 6'1" **Weight:** 12.2
International Honours: E: U21-5
Jamie can operate either as a striker or in
a withdrawn midfield role, but Leicester
City manager Micky Adams generally
used him in the latter position, although
he often switched to a more conventional
striking role later on in games. He headed
the winner in the televised early-season
game at Stoke and also netted with a
fierce low drive against Bradford City,
though he had more than his share of
woodwork-bound efforts, particularly
during the early weeks. Jamie suffered a
stomach strain in mid-season that
required an operation to correct the
situation, but still managed to accumulate
a double-figure goal return.
*Ipswich T (From trainee on 1/7/1994) P/FL
163+39/47 FLC 21+4/7 FAC 9+1 Others 7+4/1*
*Leicester C (£3,000,000 on 31/7/2001) P/FL
64+3/15 FLC 4/1 FAC 2/2*

SCULLY Anthony (Tony)
Derek Thomas
Born: Dublin, 12 June 1976
Height: 5'7" **Weight:** 11.12
International Honours: RoI: B-1; U21-
10; Yth; Sch
This speedy winger was out of favour at
Cambridge last term and was restricted to
a handful of appearances from the bench
before joining Southend United on loan.
He enjoyed a productive spell at Roots
Hall, and made the right-wing berth his
own during his stay. On his return to the
Abbey Stadium Tony received his only
start in the home game with Carlisle
before being released. He subsequently
linked up with Peterborough United
where he featured as a substitute in the
closing stages of the campaign.
*Crystal Palace (From trainee on 2/12/1993)
FL 0+3*

*Bournemouth (Loaned on 14/10/1994) FL
6+4 Others 2*
Cardiff C (Loaned on 5/11/1996) FL 13+1
*Manchester C (£80,000 on 12/8/1997) FL
1+8*
Stoke C (Loaned on 27/1/1998) FL 7
*Queens Park R (£155,000 on 17/3/1998) FL
20+20/2 FLC 4+1 FAC 0+1*
*Cambridge U (Free on 9/7/2001) FL 20+11/2
FLC 0+1 FAC 2 Others 3*
*Southend U (Loaned on 1/11/2002) FL 8
FAC 4*
*Peterborough U (Loaned on 26/3/2003) FL
0+3*

SEAMAN David Andrew
Born: Rotherham, 19 September 1963
Height: 6'4" **Weight:** 14.10
Club Honours: Div 1 '91; PL '98, '02;
FAC '93, '98, '02, '03; FLC '93; ECWC
'94; CS '98, '02
International Honours: E: 75; B-6; U21-
10
In his 13th season at Arsenal, David was
appointed as vice-captain last term and
made his 700th league appearance at
home against Middlesborough in
December. However, his season was again
affected by irritating injuries. In November
he sustained a groin strain, and in
February a hip injury forced him to leave
the field in the Champions' League game
against Ajax. When fully fit, David
showed that he was still an excellent shot
stopper. His size and composure were
often crucial to the defence when under
pressure.
Leeds U (From apprentice on 22/9/1981)
*Peterborough U (£4,000 on 13/8/1982) FL
91 FLC 10 FAC 5*
*Birmingham C (£100,000 on 5/10/1984) FL
75 FLC 4 FAC 5*
*Queens Park R (£225,000 on 7/8/1986) FL
141 FLC 13 FAC 17 Others 4*
*Arsenal (£1,300,000 on 18/5/1990) F/PL 405
FLC 38 FAC 48 Others 73+1*

SEARLE Damon Peter
Born: Cardiff, 26 October 1971
Height: 5'11" **Weight:** 10.4
Club Honours: WC '92, '93; Div 3 '93
International Honours: W: B-1; U21-6;
Yth; Sch
Damon had a fine season at left back for
Southend last term, finishing as runner-up
in the club's 'Player of the Year' award. By
his own high standards the opening half
of his campaign was somewhat
inconsistent, although at the turn of the
year his familiar quality defending and
rampaging runs returned to the fore. This
was capped by a tremendous 35-yard
strike in the 2-1 home victory over

champions Rushden & Diamonds, which won the Supporter's Club 'Goal of the Season' trophy. Out of contract at the season's end, he was released as part of the club's cost-cutting measures.
Cardiff C (From trainee on 20/8/1990) FL 232+2/3 FLC 9/1 FAC 13 Others 29
Stockport Co (Free on 28/5/1996) FL 34+7 FLC 2+1 FAC 2 Others 1
Carlisle U (Free on 6/7/1998) FL 57+9/3 FLC 4 FAC 1 Others 4+1/1
Rochdale (Loaned on 17/9/1999) FL 13+1
Southend U (Free on 10/7/2000) FL 126+7/3 FLC 4 FAC 12 Others 9/1

SEDDON Gareth Jonathan
Born: Burnley, 23 May 1980
Height: 5'11" **Weight:** 11.2
Injury problems contributed to a virtually wasted season for this Bury striker, who missed pre- and early-season action due to a rare genetic blood disorder that affected his lower back and caused a spate of injuries throughout the campaign. Gareth attempted a comeback in October when he also started two league games, but was then sidelined until December. He was loaned out to Northwich Victoria in January, but lasted just 15 minutes of his debut before suffering further injury problems.
Bury (Free from RAF Codsall, via trial at Everton, ex Accrington Stanley, Atherstone U, on 9/8/2001) FL 25+14/6 FLC 1 FAC 1/1

SEDGEMORE Benjamin (Ben) Redwood
Born: Wolverhampton, 5 August 1975
Height: 5'11" **Weight:** 12.10
International Honours: E: Sch
This hard-working central midfield man was a regular in the Lincoln starting line-up last season before losing his place to Richard Butcher in March. He contributed three goals, two of which were from the penalty spot, and with better luck could have significantly increased his tally.
Birmingham C (From trainee on 17/5/1993)
Northampton T (Loaned on 22/12/1994) FL 1
Mansfield T (Loaned on 25/8/1995) FL 4+5 Others 1
Peterborough U (Free on 10/1/1996) FL 13+4 FAC 1
Mansfield T (Free on 6/9/1996) FL 58+9/6 FLC 1 FAC 2+1 Others 2
Macclesfield T (£25,000 on 19/3/1998) FL 84+18/6 FLC 8/2 FAC 7/1 Others 2
Lincoln C (Signed on 16/2/2001) FL 59+22/5 FLC 2 FAC 4 Others 2+1/1

SEDGWICK Christopher (Chris) Edward
Born: Sheffield, 28 April 1980
Height: 5'11" **Weight:** 10.10
A product of Rotherham's youth policy, this winger missed just a handful of games during a season in which he also learned that the defensive aspect of his game is just as important as attacking. A speedy player, he has the ability to turn past defenders and deliver good crosses but he will have been disappointed with his solitary goal especially in view of the fact that it came in the first game of the season.
Rotherham U (From trainee on 16/8/1997) FL 136+47/13 FLC 5+2 FAC 6+5 Others 2+2/1

SELLARS Scott
Born: Sheffield, 27 November 1965
Height: 5'8" **Weight:** 10.0
Club Honours: FMC '87; Div 1 '93, '97
International Honours: E: U21-3
This vastly experienced midfielder signed a five-month contract for Mansfield Town in the summer of 2002. He began the new season on the right-hand side of midfield, but was sent off at Wigan and was then suspended for a short period. Scott was then injured in the match against Colchester in November and did not return to fitness until the new year, by which time he was also helping out on the coaching side with the youth team.
Leeds U (From apprentice on 25/7/1983) FL 72+4/12 FLC 4/1 FAC 4 Others 2
Blackburn Rov (£20,000 on 28/7/1986) FL 194+8/35 FLC 12/3 FAC 11/1 Others 20/2
Leeds U (£800,000 on 1/7/1992) PL 6+1 FLC 1+1 Others 1
Newcastle U (£700,000 on 9/3/1993) F/PL 56+5/5 FLC 6+1/2 FAC 3 Others 4/1
Bolton W (£750,000 on 7/12/1995) P/FL 106+5/15 FLC 8+1 FAC 5/1 Others 0+1
Huddersfield T (Free on 30/7/1999) FL 29+19/1 FLC 1+2/1 FAC 1+1 (Free to Aarhus on 17/4/2001)
Port Vale (Free on 11/1/2002)
Mansfield T (Free on 22/3/2002) FL 17+3/3

SELLEY Ian
Born: Chertsey, 14 June 1974
Height: 5'10" **Weight:** 11.0
Club Honours: FLC '93; FAC '93; ECWC '94
International Honours: E: U21-3; Yth
Ian was a regular in the Wimbledon reserve team last term and once again enjoyed a loan spell at Southend United, staying three months on this occasion. A fine central midfielder he has excellent distribution and does not shy away from a tackle, however, the form of Kevin Maher and Jay Smith meant the offer of a permanent deal was not forthcoming and

he returned to the Dons. He was released in the summer.
Arsenal (From trainee on 6/5/1992) PL 35+6 FLC 5+1 FAC 3 Others 8+2/2
Southend U (Loaned on 3/12/1996) FL 3+1
Fulham (£500,000 on 17/10/1997) FL 3
Wimbledon (Free on 8/8/2000) FL 1+3
Southend U (Loaned on 13/2/2002) FL 14
Southend U (Loaned on 9/8/2002) FL 11

SEMPLE Ryan David
Born: Belfast, 4 July 1985
Height: 5'11" **Weight:** 10.11
A product of the Peterborough United youth set-up, Ryan came to prominence after netting four goals in an FA Youth Cup tie and went on to make his senior debut against Bristol City in November. He produced a promising display with some surging runs and nearly scored with a fierce shot that came back off the woodwork. The pacy wide man received two further outings before being sidelined by a broken leg.
Peterborough U (From trainee on 12/8/2002) FL 1+2

SENDA Daniel (Danny) Luke
Born: Harrow, 17 April 1981
Height: 5'10" **Weight:** 10.0
International Honours: E: Yth
Danny had another season as automatic-choice right back at Wycombe Wanderers in particular having a most impressive first half of the season. He was asked to play some of the time as right wing back and his crossing noticeably improved as the season wore on. This is one of the fastest players in the Second Division and his acceleration consistently catches out opponents who mistakenly believe they have more time on the ball.
Wycombe W (From Southampton juniors on 26/1/1999) FL 94+54/5 FLC 1+3 FAC 5+3 Others 4+4

SENIOR Philip (Phil) Anthony
Born: Huddersfield, 30 October 1982
Height: 5'11" **Weight:** 11.1
Phil made his Football League debut for Huddersfield Town as a substitute in the away defeat at Crewe, and was almost rewarded with a clean sheet for some breathtaking saves. He later had a regular stint between the sticks for the Terriers, proving to be an excellent shot stopper who handles the ball well. A promising young 'keeper, he produced a fine performance in the victory at Barnsley.
Huddersfield T (From trainee on 6/11/1999) FL 16+2

SETCHELL Gary John
Born: Kings Lynn, 8 May 1975
Height: 6'1" **Weight:** 14.0
Club Honours: NC '01
This left-sided player agreed a new one-year contract with Rushden & Diamonds in the summer of 2002, but he was released 12 months later after starting just seven league games, mostly as cover for skipper Paul Underwood. Gary is a hard-working utility man who figured mainly from late September until mid-November. He also suffered hamstring problems in the later stages of the campaign, which kept him out of action.
Rushden & Diamonds (Signed from Kettering T, ex Kings Lynn, Wisbech, Wakenham T, on 6/6/2000) FL 20+13/1 FLC 1 FAC 1+1 Others 1+1

SHAABAN Rami
Born: Stockholm, Sweden, 30 June 1975
Height: 6'4" **Weight:** 14.9
This agile goalkeeper joined Arsenal as cover for David Seaman and Stuart Taylor and made his first-team debut in the Champions' League match at home to PSV Eindhoven. His Premiership debut came in the very next game at home to Tottenham, and on both occasions his alert displays rewarded him with clean sheets. Unfortunately, his season was cut short when he sustained a fractured right leg in a freak training ground accident at the end of December. Rami is a popular player who settled into the squad quickly, and impressed with his bravery and handling of the ball.
Arsenal (Signed from Djurgaarden, Sweden, ex Saltsjobadens, Zamalek, Thadosman, Nacka FF, on 30/8/2002) PL 3 Others 2

SHACKELL Jason
Born: Stevenage, 27 August 1983
Height: 5'11" **Weight:** 11.9
This 19-year-old product of the Norwich City youth system signed his first professional contract last January and made his senior debut at Derby in April. He played at left back on that occasion and followed up with a composed display as one of three centre halves at Leicester in the penultimate game of the season. By preference Jason plays as a central defender where his height and ability in the air already make him a formidable opponent. However, he can also play at left back where his calm approach and sweet left foot allow him to combine his defensive skills with attacking forays into opposition territory.
Norwich C (From trainee on 28/1/2003) FL 2

SHANDRAN Anthony Mark
Born: Newcastle, 17 September 1981
Height: 5'11" **Weight:** 12.2
This promising youngster spent the final three months of the 2002-03 season on loan to Third Division York City. A bustling, hard-working striker he notched three goals for the Minstermen including an outstanding effort at Carlisle in a 1-1 draw when coming on as a substitute and the winner at Leyton Orient. After returning to Turf Moor Anthony was one of several players released by Burnley during the summer.
Burnley (From trainee on 13/11/2000) FL 0+1
York C (Loaned on 31/1/2003) FL 12+6/3

SHARP James
Born: Reading, 2 January 1976
Height: 6'1" **Weight:** 14.6
This powerfully built left-sided defender hardly got a look in at Hartlepool in the 2002-03 season due to the consistency of

Rami Shaaban

the regular first-team back line, with his only senior appearance being in the LDV Vans Trophy match at Tranmere. Although praised for maintaining a professional approach when playing in the reserves he was released shortly before the end of the season.
Hartlepool U *(Free from Andover on 10/8/2000) FL 44+5/2 FLC 2 Others 6+1*

SHARP Kevin Phillip
Born: Ontario, Canada, 19 September 1974
Height: 5'9" **Weight:** 11.11
Club Honours: FAYC '93; Div 3 '97; AMC '99
International Honours: E: Yth (UEFA-U18 '93); Sch
Signed initially by Huddersfield as cover for the defensive positions, Kevin was given a regular left-back position due to injuries. Both competent and confident on the ball he soon settled into the pace of the Second Division. He tackled well, was effective attacking down the flank and showed plenty of skill around the opposition penalty box.
Leeds U *(£60,000 from Auxerre, France on 20/10/1992) PL 11+6 Others 0+1*
Wigan Ath *(£100,000 on 30/11/1995) FL 156+22/10 FLC 7+2/1 FAC 7+3 Others 18+1/1*
Wrexham *(Free on 2/11/2001) FL 12+3*
Huddersfield T *(Free on 8/8/2002) FL 38+1 FLC 2 FAC 1 Others 1*

SHARP Neil Anthony
Born: Hemel Hempstead, 19 January 1978
Height: 6'1" **Weight:** 12.10
Neil missed the first couple of games of the season, but fought his way back into the Swansea line-up with some brave displays until he sprained his left ankle ligaments against Hartlepool in early September. He eventually underwent surgery, returning to fitness in February when he featured in a number of friendly games for the Swans.
Swansea C *(Free from Merthyr Tydfil, ex Kansas C, Hayes, Boreham Wood, Barry T, on 25/10/2001) FL 26+6/1*

SHARPE Lee Stuart
Born: Halesowen, 27 May 1971
Height: 6'0" **Weight:** 12.12
Club Honours: ECWC '91; FLC '92; PL '93, '94, '96; CS '94
International Honours: E: 8; B-1; U21-8
This experienced left-sided player joined Exeter City on a non-contract basis last August. The quality of his technique was very evident in his four appearances for

the club, but he quickly departed from St James' Park. Lee was reported to have signed for Icelandic club Grindavik in March.
Torquay U *(From trainee on 31/5/1988) FL 9+5/3 Others 2+3*
Manchester U *(£185,000 on 10/6/1988) F/PL 160+33/21 FLC 15+8/9 FAC 22+7/3 Others 18+2/3*
Leeds U *(£4,500,000 on 14/8/1996) PL 28+2/5 FLC 3/1 FAC 0+1 Others 1+2*
Bradford C *(£200,000 on 25/3/1999) P/FL 36+20/4 FLC 3+1 FAC 2+1 Others 3*
Portsmouth *(Loaned on 2/2/2001) FL 17*
Exeter C *(Free on 12/8/2002) FL 4/1*

SHARPS Ian William
Born: Warrington, 23 October 1980
Height: 6'4" **Weight:** 13.8
Ian is a central defender who uses his height to its best advantage, being both commanding in the air and tenacious on the ground. He possesses great vision and is an accurate distributor of the ball who really matured during last season, despite experiencing the set back of being dropped early on in the campaign. Restored to the Tranmere line-up in January, Ian was then an ever-present. He struck up a good understanding with Graham Allen and even helped himself to three goals.
Tranmere Rov *(From trainee on 5/7/1999) FL 55+5/3 FLC 2 FAC 2 Others 2*

SHAW Jonathan (Jon) Steven
Born: Sheffield, 10 November 1983
Height: 6'1" **Weight:** 12.9
A strong central striker who has come up through the ranks at Sheffield Wednesday, John was beginning to establish himself at reserve-team level last season. He was a surprise inclusion on the Owls' bench for the FA Cup tie at Gillingham, but came on and enjoyed himself even if he could not halt his side's exit from the competition. He added a further appearance as a substitute and will be looking to gain more senior experience in 2003-04.
Sheffield Wed *(Trainee) FL 0+1 FAC 0+1*

SHAW Paul
Born: Burnham, 4 September 1973
Height: 5'11" **Weight:** 12.4
International Honours: E: Yth
Paul produced his best form since joining Gillingham in the 2002-03 season. A skilful striker, he again performed most effectively when employed in a position just behind the front two, from where opponents had difficulty picking him up. He finished the campaign as the Gills'

leading scorer with 13 goals, and was named as the club's 'Players' Player of the Season'.
Arsenal *(From trainee on 18/9/1991) PL 1+11/2 FAC 0+1*
Burnley *(Loaned on 23/3/1995) FL 8+1/4*
Cardiff C *(Loaned on 11/8/1995) FL 6*
Peterborough U *(Loaned on 20/10/1995) FL 12/5 Others 2*
Millwall *(£250,000 on 15/9/1997) FL 88+21/26 FLC 6/2 FAC 2 Others 5+6*
Gillingham *(£450,000 on 11/7/2000) FL 98+16/21 FLC 3+3 FAC 7/3*

SHAW Richard Edward
Born: Brentford, 11 September 1968
Height: 5'9" **Weight:** 12.8
Club Honours: FMC '91; Div 1 '94
At the start of last season Richard looked set for a major challenge for his place in Coventry's back four. His early appearances were at right back, where although not ideally suited to the role he never let the side down. However, in December an injury to Calum Davenport meant a recall at centre back and his return coincided with City's best run of the campaign. He was a virtual ever-present after that, always putting in solid performances and was voted the 'Players' Player of the Year'. Richard never gives less than 100 per cent and remains the best man-to-man marker at the club.
Crystal Palace *(From apprentice on 4/9/1986) F/PL 193+14/3 FLC 28+2 FAC 18 Others 12+1*
Hull C *(Loaned on 14/12/1989) FL 4*
Coventry C *(£1,000,000 on 17/11/1995) P/FL 231+9 FLC 17+2 FAC 17+1*

SHEARER Alan
Born: Newcastle, 13 August 1970
Height: 6'0" **Weight:** 12.6
Club Honours: PL '95
International Honours: E: 63; B-1; U21 11; Yth
Newcastle United's skipper enjoyed another fine season in 2002-03, once again netting a respectable tally of goals, setting personal landmarks and collecting numerous awards. Age may be eroding his pace, but his enthusiasm and commitment remain undiminished. He is supreme leader of the attack and a master at holding up the ball and bringing colleagues into the game, whilst his shooting remains as ferocious and deadly as ever, as shown by his stunning volley against Everton in December which he rates as his best goal for the club. He became the first player to score 100 times for two Premiership clubs. Alan was voted by the PFA as the 'Player of the Decade'

the Premiership, while his colleagues
lso voted him into the PFA Premiership
eam of the season and he was selected
s 'Newcastle Sports Personality of the
ear' and Tyne Tees TV's 'North East Player
f the Year'.
outhampton *(From trainee on 14/4/1988)*
*. 105+13/23 FLC 16+2/11 FAC 11+3/4
thers 8/5*
lackburn Rov *(£3,600,000 on 24/7/1992)*
L 132+6/112 FLC 16/14 FAC 8/2 Others 9/2
ewcastle U *(£15,000,000 on 30/7/1996) PL
01+5/109 FLC 12/6 FAC 27/19 Others 25/11*

HEERAN Mark John
orn: Newcastle, 9 August 1982
eight: 6'0" **Weight:** 11.10
fter being something of a super-sub for
arlington during the previous season,
lark had a disappointing campaign in
002-03, only making five substitute
ppearances and failing to find the net at
l. A promising young striker, he is
apable of losing defenders with his
arting runs and has a good eye for goal.
arlington *(From trainee on 9/7/2002) FL
+25/6 Others 0+2*

HELDON Gareth Richard
orn: Birmingham, 31 January 1980
eight: 5'11" **Weight:** 12.0
his speedy direct winger joined Exeter
ity in the summer of 2002. However he
ceived few opportunities in the starting
ne-up and made most of his
ppearances from the bench. Gareth was
ne of several players at St James' Park
vhose fortunes were affected by the
arious changes in management that took
lace during the season.
cunthorpe U *(From trainee on 4/2/1999) FL
2+35/6 FLC 4 FAC 4+1/1 Others 3+4/4*
xeter C *(Free on 2/8/2002) FL 7+12/1 FAC
1 Others 1/1*

HELLEY Brian
orn: Dublin, 15 November 1981
eight: 6'0" **Weight:** 11.12
nternational Honours: RoI; U21-4
rian had a good first season at Carlisle in
002-03 when he featured regularly in
le line-up, usually at right back. His
ssets include speed and a committed
ttitude to his performances. Although
ot a renowned attacker, his only goal
as a long-range strike at Leyton Orient's
risbane Road.
arlisle U *(Free from Bohemians on
8/2002) FL 32+3/1 FAC 3 Others 5*

HERIDAN Darren Stephen
orn: Manchester, 8 December 1967
eight: 5'5" **Weight:** 11.5

Darren's tireless displays in central midfield
were key to Oldham Athletic's promotion
challenge last season. The veteran
playmaker produced a series of clinical
performances, showing he had lost none
of his passion for the game. Typically
sitting just in front of the back three,
Darren prodded and prompted a young
Latics side to the play-offs while also
managing to clean up his disciplinary
record. His contract contains an option for
one more year at Boundary Park and at
the time of writing he looked set to stay
on.
Barnsley *(£10,000 from Winsford U on
12/8/1993) F/PL 149+22/5 FLC 9+4/1 FAC
9+2/1 Others 1+1*
Wigan Ath *(Free on 2/7/1999) FL 50+8/3
FLC 5 FAC 1+2 Others 5/1*

Oldham Ath *(Free on 24/7/2001) FL 54+7/3
FLC 3+1 FAC 7 Others 6*

SHERIDAN John Joseph
Born: Stretford, 1 October 1964
Height: 5'10" **Weight:** 12.0
Club Honours: FLC '91; Div 1 '97
International Honours: RoI: 34; B-1;
U23-2; U21-2; Yth
John announced his decision to retire
from the game in April after a glittering
career spanning two World Cups and
some 700 senior outings. His appearances
for Oldham Athletic became increasingly
limited last season, mainly as a result of a
persistent knee injury that was the major
factor behind his decision to call it a day.
John will remains at Boundary Park in his
new role as reserve-team coach.

Brian Shelley

Teddy Sheringham

eds U (From Manchester C juniors on
3/1982) FL 225+5/47 FLC 14/3 FAC 11+1/1
hers 11/1
ottingham F (£650,000 on 3/8/1989)
C 1
effield Wed (£500,000 on 3/11/1989)
PL 187+10/25 FLC 24/3 FAC 17+1/3 Others
2
rmingham C (Loaned on 9/2/1996) FL 1+1
C 2
olton W (£180,000 on 13/11/1996) F/PL
*+8/2 FLC 2 FAC 2 (Free to Doncaster Rov in
98 close season)
dham Ath (Free on 20/10/1998) FL
3+10/9 FLC 2+1 FAC 12+1/2 Others 1

HERINGHAM Edward
Teddy) Paul
orn: Highams Park, 2 April 1966
eight: 5'11" **Weight:** 12.5
ub Honours: Div 2 '88; FMC '92; CS
7; PL '99, '00, '01; FAC '99; EC '99
ternational Honours: E: 51; U21-1;
h

ddy was in superb form at Tottenham
st season, looking as fit, intelligent and
nthusiastic on the field as he was ten
ars ago. He finished the campaign as
int-top scorer with young Robbie Keane,
etting 13 goals in all competitions and it
as therefore something of a surprise to
ours' fans when it was announced that
s contract was not to be renewed and
e was on his way from White Hart Lane.
illwall (From apprentice on 19/1/1984) FL
5+15/93 FLC 16+1/8 FAC 12/5 Others
+2/5
dershot (Loaned on 1/2/1985) FL 4+1
thers 1
ottingham F (£2,000,000 on 23/7/1991) FL
2/14 FLC 10/5 FAC 4/2 Others 6/2
ottenham H (£2,100,000 on 28/8/1992) PL
53+3/76 FLC 14/10 FAC 17/13
anchester U (£3,500,000 on 1/7/1997) PL
3+31/31 FLC 1/1 FAC 4+5/5 Others 23+16/9
ottenham H (Free on 16/7/2001) PL
7+3/22 FLC 6+1/3 FAC 3/1

HERON Michael (Mike)
igel
orn: St Helens, 11 January 1972
eight: 5'10" **Weight:** 11.13
ternational Honours: E: U21-16
like probably has the best footballing
rain at Barnsley and when he was on his
ame still looked a class above the
econd Division last term. He seemed to
ay his best football away from Oakwell
here he found a little more time and
ace. Although not a prolific scorer he
d manage some spectacular efforts, one
gainst Oldham being the most
emorable. Mike was out of contract at

the end of the season and his future was
uncertain at the time of writing.
Manchester C (From trainee on 5/7/1990)
F/PL 82+18/24 FLC 9+1/1 FAC 5+3/3 Others 1
Bury (Loaned on 28/3/1991) FL 1+4/1
Others 2
Norwich C (£1,000,000 on 26/8/1994) P/FL
19+9/2 FLC 6/3 FAC 4/2
Stoke C (£450,000 on 13/11/1995) FL
64+5/34 FLC 4/5 FAC 1 Others 2

Queens Park R (£2,750,000 on 2/7/1997) FL
57+6/19 FLC 2+2/1 FAC 2
Barnsley (£1,000,000 on 27/1/1999) FL
114+38/33 FLC 10+2/7 FAC 4+3 Others 1

SHERWOOD Timothy (Tim)
Alan
Born: St Albans, 6 February 1969
Height: 6'0" **Weight:** 12.9
Club Honours: PL '95; Div 1 '03

Mike Sheron

International Honours: E: 3; B-1; U21-4
This experienced midfielder was out of the first-team picture at Tottenham last season and he eventually moved on to join promotion candidates Portsmouth early in the new year. He added strength, guile and balance to the squad, and the club's fortunes took an immediate upturn, as the team won 23 points from the first ten games he played in. Tim contributed one goal for Pompey, netting in the 5-0 win at Millwall. He is a composed playmaker, able to calm the game down and deliver a devastating pass.

Watford *(From trainee on 7/2/1987) FL 23+9/2 FLC 4+1 FAC 9 Others 4+1*
Norwich C *(£175,000 on 18/7/1989) FL 66+5/10 FLC 7/1 FAC 4 Others 5+1/2*
Blackburn Rov *(£500,000 on 12/2/1992) F/PL 239+7/25 FLC 24+1/2 FAC 15+2/4 Others 12*
Tottenham H *(£3,800,000 on 5/2/1999) PL 81+12/12 FLC 6+3/2 FAC 13/1 Others 3/1*
Portsmouth *(Free on 29/1/2003) FL 17/1*

SHIELDS Anthony (Tony)
Gerald
Born: Londonderry, 4 June 1980
Height: 5'7" **Weight:** 10.10
This talented young midfielder secured a regular first-team place for Peterborough United in 2002-03 after spending the previous campaign on the fringes of the squad. A tough-tackling dynamo in the centre of the park, what he lacks in pace he makes up for in determination. Tony scored one goal during 2002-03, netting in the 1-1 draw with Swindon in April.
Peterborough U *(From trainee on 6/7/1998) FL 84+31/3 FLC 4+1/1 FAC 4+3/1 Others 1+2*

SHILTON Samuel (Sam) Roger
Born: Nottingham, 21 July 1978
Height: 5'10" **Weight:** 11.6
Given an opportunity by Kidderminster's new manager Ian Britton, Sam blossomed at left wing back last term and showed far greater ability than he had under the previous management. A crucial part of the side for much of the 2002-03 season he ended the campaign with ten assists – more than any other player in the squad. He was reported to have agreed a new 12 month contract in the summer.
Plymouth Arg *(Trainee) FL 1+2 FAC 0+1*
Coventry C *(£12,500 on 31/10/1995) PL 3+4 FLC 1+1 FAC 0+1*
Hartlepool U *(Free on 9/7/1999) FL 45+9/7 FLC 1+1 FAC 3 Others 3+1*
Kidderminster Hrs *(Free on 11/7/2001) FL 51+14/5 FLC 1+1 FAC 2+1 Others 4/1*

SHIPPERLEY Neil Jason
Born: Chatham, 30 October 1974
Height: 6'1" **Weight:** 13.12
International Honours: E: U21-7
Neil was given the captain's armband for Wimbledon at the start of last season, and clearly relished the responsibility. It took him four games to open his scoring account for the campaign, but from then on the goals flowed, particularly when strike partner David Connolly returned from injury. Both players were totally unselfish in their play and were leading contenders for the club's 'Player of the Year' award, Neil's ever-present season and leadership qualities deservedly swinging the decision his way. Despite his vast experience, Neil remains the low side of 30, plays to his strengths, never gives up and has become the focal point of the team's attacking play. In difficult times for the club he had an inspirational season, it was as simple as that.
Chelsea *(From trainee on 24/9/1992) PL 26+11/7 FLC 4+2/1 FAC 3/1 Others 2*
Watford *(Loaned on 7/12/1994) FL 5+1/1*
Southampton *(£1,250,000 on 6/1/1995) PL 65+1/12 FLC 5+1/2 FAC 10/5*
Crystal Palace *(£1,000,000 on 25/10/1996) F/PL 49+12/20 FLC 3 FAC 2 Others 5/1*
Nottingham F *(£1,500,000 on 22/9/1998) PL 12+8/1 FAC 1*
Barnsley *(£700,000 on 7/7/1999) FL 70+8/27 FLC 4+1/3 FAC 2 Others 3/1*
Wimbledon *(£750,000 on 25/7/2001) FL 82+5/32 FLC 4/3 FAC 4/1*

SHITTU Daniel (Danny)
Olusola
Born: Lagos, Nigeria, 2 September 1980
Height: 6'3" **Weight:** 16.0
International Honours: Nigeria: 1
This tall and solid central defender remained a favourite with the Queen's Park Rangers fans, and continued to produce some solid performances. He initially formed a useful partnership with Steve Palmer and then with the returning Clark Carlisle, both of which contributed to the club's fine defensive record. Danny contributed a total of seven goals, all from corners or set pieces, and was runner-up in the Supporters Club 'Player of the Year' vote.
Charlton Ath *(Free from Carshalton Ath on 15/9/1999)*
Blackpool *(Loaned on 16/2/2001) FL 15+2/2 Others 2*
Queens Park R *(£250,000 on 23/10/2002) FL 70/9 FLC 1 FAC 1 Others 3*

SHOREY Nicholas (Nicky)
Born: Romford, 19 February 1981
Height: 5'9" **Weight:** 10.10
Now recognised as one of the best your left-backs in the Nationwide League, Nicky missed only three first-team game for Reading last season, adding maturity and composure to his obvious skill. He scored his first-ever league goal in the 1 home win over Bradford City, and doubled his career tally in the 5-1 win against Preston North End. His goal in th game came from the 12-yard mark after he had taken over as the team's penalty-kick taker. Such was his improvement th he was tipped for an England U21 cap, and even though this has not yet happened, there is no doubt that he is s for a long and distinguished career in th game.
Leyton Orient *(From trainee on 5/7/1999) 12+3 FAC 1*
Reading *(£25,000 on 9/2/2001) FL 75/2 FL 3 FAC 4 Others 4*

SHORT Craig Jonathan
Born: Bridlington, 25 June 1968
Height: 6'1" **Weight:** 13.8
Club Honours: FLC '02
This brave and committed central defender featured regularly for Blackburr last term, looking most comfortable whe playing alongside Henning Berg. Players do not come more competitive or consistent than Craig Short, and despite concerns over his apparent lack of speed he again proved the doubters wrong, notably when outpacing Bolton's Bernar Mendy to earn a standing ovation from the Rovers' fans. His only goal of the season was a late header at the Reebok, which was important in keeping the momentum of the season going. Craig signed a further extension to his contrac that will keep him at Ewood Park for another 12 months.
Scarborough *(Free from Pickering T on 15/10/1987) FL 61+2/7 FLC 6 FAC 2 Others 7/1*
Notts Co *(£100,000 on 27/7/1989) FL 128 FLC 6/1 FAC 8/1 Others 16/2*
Derby Co *(£2,500,000 on 18/9/1992) FL 118/9 FLC 11 FAC 7/4 Others 7*
Everton *(£2,700,000 on 18/7/1995) PL 90+9/4 FLC 7 FAC 4 Others 3*
Blackburn Rov *(£1,700,000 + on 3/8/1999 PI/FL 99+2/2 FLC 4/1 FAC 5 Others 2*

SHTANIUK Sergei
Born: Minsk, Belarus, 13 August 1973
Height: 6'3" **Weight:** 12.11
International Honours: Belarus: 42
Sergei was undoubtedly Stoke City's 'Player of the Season' in 2002-03 when he produced a series of outstanding performances in the heart of the defence

was something of a mystery (albeit ~~pl~~easant) that come the transfer window was not snapped up by a club in a ~~hig~~her grade. Off the field his mid-season ~~fo~~rm was not helped when his family ~~re~~turned to Belarus after they failed to ~~se~~ttle in England, nevertheless he was ~~ab~~le to guide the Potters to First Division ~~sa~~fety.

~~St~~oke C *(£200,000 from Dinamo Moscow, ~~Ru~~ssia, ex Belarus Minsk, Dinamo Minsk, on ~~3/~~3/2001) FL 84/5 FLC 2 FAC 6 Others 3*

~~S~~HUKER Christopher (Chris)
~~I~~an

~~Bo~~rn: Liverpool, 9 May 1982
~~H~~eight: 5'5" **Weight:** 10.1

~~Th~~is diminutive striker started the 2002-~~0~~3 season brightly, finding himself on the ~~su~~bstitutes' bench for Manchester City ~~ea~~rly in the campaign and he made his ~~fir~~st Premiership start against Blackburn. ~~Th~~ereafter he continued his development ~~in~~ the club's reserve team before joining ~~Fir~~st Division Walsall on loan. Chris ~~cr~~eated a good impression with his pace ~~an~~d trickery during his spell at Bescot. ~~W~~hat he lacks in size he makes up in ~~he~~art.

~~M~~anchester C *(From trainee on 21/9/1999) ~~F~~L 1+4 FLC 0+1/1*
~~M~~acclesfield T *(Loaned on 27/3/2001) FL ~~1~~-3/1*
~~W~~alsall *(Loaned on 26/2/2003) FL 3+2*

~~SI~~BON Gerald
~~Bo~~rn: Dalen, Holland, 19 April 1974
~~H~~eight: 6'5" **Weight:** 13.5

~~Th~~e one player who could produce the ~~un~~expected in the Sheffield Wednesday ~~si~~de, Gerald had a steady if not ~~sp~~ectacular season, and was leading ~~sc~~orer in all competitions. He showed ~~su~~blime skills and demonstrated a ~~th~~underous, accurate shot as he found ~~th~~e net on nine occasions. He was ~~ev~~entually released and returned to the ~~N~~etherlands to sign for SC Heerenveen.

~~Sh~~effield Wed *(£2,000,000 from Ajax, ~~H~~olland, ex Twente, VVV Groningen, Roda ~~JC~~, on 16/7/1999) P/FL 98+31/36 FLC 11+2/4 ~~FA~~C 7+1/3*

~~SI~~DIBE Mamady
~~Bo~~rn: Mali, 18 December 1979
~~H~~eight: 6'4" **Weight:** 12.4
~~In~~ternational Honours: Mali

~~Af~~ter impressing in pre-season friendlies, ~~M~~amady signed terms for Gillingham in ~~th~~e summer of 2002. However, his season ~~w~~as interrupted by a series of injuries and ~~h~~e was never able to claim a regular first-

team place. His best spell came on his return from a knee ligament injury in mid-October when he scored after just two minutes against Watford and netted the winner the following week at Ipswich Town. He also notched the all-important equaliser in the televised FA Cup tie against Leeds United. Mamady made his debut in international football for Mali against Seychelles in an African Nations' Cup qualifier in October and featured in the national squad regularly thereafter.

Swansea C *(Free from CA Paris, France, ex Racing Club Paris, on 27/7/2001) FL 26+5/7 FLC 0+1 FAC 2/1 Others 1*
Gillingham *(Free on 9/8/2002) FL 24+6/3 FLC 1 FAC 2+1/1*

SIDWELL Steven (Steve)
James
Born: Wandsworth, 14 December 1982
Height: 5'10" **Weight:** 11.2

Club Honours: FAYC '00, '01
International Honours: E: U21-2; Yth
Unable to make any progress at Highbury, this promising teenaged midfielder joined Brighton on loan in November. Steve boosted his reputation sufficiently during his time on the South Coast for Reading to pay a hefty fee for his services in January. Once at the Madejski Stadium he renewed his midfield partnership with James Harper, the two having played together for the Gunners' junior sides, and made an immediate impact for the Royals. He scored twice in his second game, a 5-2 win at Burnley, but his main strength was as a fetcher and carrier. He covers every area of the pitch during games, and his high-level control and passing make him an excellent distributor of the ball. Aged just 20, his enthusiasm and potential earned him a deserved call-up for the England U21 squad.

Gerald Sibon

Mikael Silvestre

senal *(From trainee on 2/7/2001)*
entford *(Loaned on 23/10/2001) FL
+1/4 FAC 2 Others 3*
ighton & Hove A *(Loaned on 9/11/2002)
11+1/5*
ading *(£250,000 on 21/1/2003) FL 13/2
hers 2*

IGURDSSON Larus Orri
rn: Akureyri, Iceland, 4 June 1973
eight: 6'0" Weight: 13.11
ternational Honours: Iceland: 41;
21-16; Yth
rus started the season at the back
ngside Darren Moore and Phil Gilchrist
West Bromwich Albion fielded a 3-5-2
rmation. He lost his place briefly to
nnie Wallwork, but was soon recalled
ly to lose out again when Sean Gregan
as switched from midfield. He battled
despite an abdominal strain, and after
gaining full fitness he had a decent spell
ck in the line-up either side of
ristmas when he produced some fine
rformances. However, he then missed
ne out with an achilles problem before
turning for a third stint in the side.
rus continued to feature for Iceland at
ternational level during the season.
oke C *(£150,000 from Thor, Iceland on
/10/1994) FL 199+1/7 FLC 15 FAC 6+1
hers 6*
'est Bromwich A *(£325,000 on 17/9/1999)
FL 99+12/1 FLC 4 FAC 6+1 Others 0+1*

ILVESTRE Mikael Samy
rn: Tours, France, 9 August 1977
eight: 6'0" Weight: 13.1
ub Honours: PL '00, '01, '03
ternational Honours: France: 22; U21;
th (UEFA-U18 '96)
ikael is a stylish, pacy defender who
eeps a cool head under pressure, and
ombines as an attacking outlet down the
ank. Such were his performances in the
eart of the Manchester United defence
st term, the club must have been
elighted when the Frenchman signed a
xtension to his contract in early January.
ertainly his partnership with Wes Brown
as a huge bonus as United put an
different start behind them to mount
eir perennial quest for top honours.
ikael's great strength in defence will
ertainly pose Sir Alex Ferguson with a
eadache most other managers would
lish. In all honestly he's always coveted
centre-back slot, and last season he
roved he was most natural there.
erhaps in the coming season, it will be
nited's other star defenders who will
ave to follow his lead and become more
daptable themselves.

Manchester U *(£4,000,000 from Inter Milan,
Italy on 10/9/1999) PL 120+10/2 FLC 5 FAC 6
Others 43+6/1*

SIMMS Gordon Henry
Born: Larne, 23 March 1981
Height: 6'2" Weight: 12.6
International Honours: NI: U21-14; Yth;
Sch
This young Hartlepool central defender
made little impact in the 2002-03
campaign due to the consistency of the
regular first-team pairing. Gordon
continued to represent the Northern
Ireland U21 side, but at Hartlepool his
senior football was limited to just one
appearance in an LDV Vans Trophy tie,
plus one brief outing as a substitute in a
league game. Recognised as being surplus
to requirements, he was released shortly
before the end of the season.
Wolverhampton W *(From trainee on
9/4/1998)*
Hartlepool U *(Free on 10/3/2001) FL 6+5
FAC 1 Others 1*

SIMONSEN Steven (Steve)
Preben
Born: South Shields, 3 April 1979
Height: 6'3" Weight: 13.2
International Honours: E: U21-4; Yth
Steve had a testing 2002-03 season, a
combination of injury and the good form
of Richard Wright meaning that he failed
to regain the 'keeper's jersey for Everton.
He was given his chance following an
injury to Wright after just two games of
the season, but was then relegated back
to the substitutes' bench. A broken toe at
the turn of the year meant that he was
unable to take advantage of injuries to
Everton's other two goalkeepers and he
failed to make a further first-team
appearance. Steve is an excellent shot
stopper with good command of his area
and he can only improve.
Tranmere Rov *(From trainee on 9/10/1996)
FL 35 FLC 4 FAC 3*
Everton *(£3,300,000 on 23/9/1998) PL 27+2
FLC 2 FAC 5*

SIMPEMBA Ian Frederick
Born: Dublin, 28 March 1983
Height: 6'2" Weight: 12.8
International Honours: RoI: Yth
On the fringes of the first team at
Wycombe, this promising central defender
was loaned out to Conference side
Woking for three months in October.
There he was successfully converted to a
midfielder but he rejected a permanent
move, opting to return to Adams Park. He
finally made his first-team debut for the
Chairboys, coming on as a substitute in

the last home game against Colchester.
Ian was a member of the Republic of
Ireland U19 squad that finished fourth in
the UEFA championships in the summer
of 2002.
Wycombe W *(From trainee on 10/7/2001) FL
0+1*

SIMPKINS Michael (Mike)
James
Born: Sheffield, 28 November 1978
Height: 6'1" Weight: 12.0
This athletic central defender received few
chances at Cardiff last term, and his only
first-team appearances came in the LDV
Vans Trophy matches against Exeter and
Bournemouth. In September he joined
Exeter on loan as the management
sought to stem the flow of goals
conceded. Later in the year he linked up
with Cheltenham Town in a similar deal,
but soon after returning to Ninian Park he
was released from his contract.
Sheffield Wed *(From trainee on 4/7/1997)*
Chesterfield *(Free on 26/3/1998) FL 22+4
FLC 2+1 FAC 1 Others 2*
Cardiff C *(Free on 29/5/2001) FL 13+4 FLC 1
Others 2*
Exeter C *(Loaned on 20/9/2002) FL 4+1*
Cheltenham T *(Loaned on 23/12/2002) FL 2
FAC 0+1*

SIMPSON Fitzroy
Born: Trowbridge, 26 February 1970
Height: 5'8" Weight: 12.0
International Honours: Jamaica: 39
Fitzroy returned to the Walsall first team
initially as a non-contract player and was
not on the losing side in any of his first six
games. His thoughtful passes and
intelligent runs made him a most useful
asset in midfield. He netted in the penalty
shoot-out FA Cup win at Reading but
slipped out of the first-team scene after a
thigh injury at Stoke. Fitzroy also
continued to represent Jamaica, featuring
in the Gold Cup qualifying matches in
November and adding a further three
caps to his impressive tally.
Swindon T *(From trainee on 6/7/1988) FL
78+27/9 FLC 15+2/1 FAC 2+1 Others 3+2*
Manchester C *(£500,000 on 6/3/1992) P/FL
58+13/4 FLC 5+1 FAC 4+1*
Bristol C *(Loaned on 16/9/1994) FL 4*
Portsmouth *(£200,000 on 17/8/1995) FL
139+9/10 FLC 12+1 FAC 8*
Heart of Midlothian *(£100,000 on
8/12/1999) SL 7+4 SLC 0+1 SC 2*
Walsall *(Free on 2/3/2001) FL 45+18/4 FLC 4
FAC 3+1 Others 1*

SIMPSON Michael
Born: Nottingham, 28 February 1974
Height: 5'9" Weight: 10.8

Club Honours: AIC '95

Every season is an improvement on the last for Michael, and he was easily the most influential player at Wycombe Wanders in 2002-03. The supporters confirmed that view when he comfortably won all of the 'Player of the Year' awards going. With one of the highest work rates in the team, Michael is Wycombe's midfield general, setting up attacks with deft passes and relentlessly closing down opponents. Of his five goals, the most spectacular was at Northampton when a free kick wide on the left eluded everybody on the way to the net.

Notts Co (From trainee on 1/7/1992) FL 39+10/3 FLC 4+1 FAC 2+1 Others 7+3

Plymouth Arg (Loaned on 4/10/1996) FL 10+2

Wycombe W (£50,000 on 5/12/1996) FL 229+18/14 FLC 12+1 FAC 21+2/4 Others 1

SIMPSON Paul David

Born: Carlisle, 26 July 1966
Height: 5'6" **Weight:** 11.10
Club Honours: AMC '02
International Honours: E: U21-5; Yth

Paul was promoted to become Rochdale player-manager in the summer of 2002 and made a remarkable start to his new dual role as his side reached second place in the table, while he was finding the net regularly, his tally including a hat-trick in 5-2 win at Wrexham. When Dale hit a bad spell though, he eventually left himself out of the side in order to view things from the sidelines, only reappearing for cup-ties, before ending the campaign on the injured list. Still a class act, if not as mobile as in his prime, his long-range shooting gained him a double-figure goal tally. He resigned from his post at Spotland in May 2003.

Manchester C (From apprentice on 4/8/1983) FL 99+22/18 FLC 10+1/2 FAC 10+2/4 Others 8+3

Oxford U (£200,000 on 31/10/1988) FL 138+6/43 FLC 10/3 FAC 9/2 Others 5/2

Derby Co (£500,000 on 20/2/1992) P/FL 134+52/48 FLC 12+3/6 FAC 4+4/1 Others 14+2/2

Sheffield U (Loaned on 6/12/1996) FL 2+4

Wolverhampton W (£75,000 on 10/10/1997) FL 32+20/6 FLC 2+1 FAC 2+5

Walsall (Loaned on 17/9/1998) FL 4/1

Walsall (Loaned on 11/12/1998) FL 6

Blackpool (Free on 11/8/2000) FL 69+7/13 FLC 5+1 FAC 6/1 Others 4+2/1

Rochdale (Free on 25/3/2002) FL 37+5/15 FLC 1 FAC 3+1/1 Others 3/1

SINCLAIR Dean Michael

Born: Luton, 17 December 1984
Height: 5'9" **Weight:** 11.3

Dean received his Norwich City debut in tough away fixture at Gillingham in February, giving a terrific account of himself in a particularly combative encounter. He is a hard-working midfielder who combines a tenacious approach to winning the ball when not in possession with an eye for the telling pass when on the ball. His successful introduction into senior football was rewarded with his first professional contract, which he signed in May.

Michael Simpson

orwich C *(From trainee on 7/5/2003) FL*
-1

INCLAIR Frank Mohammed
orn: Lambeth, 3 December 1971
eight: 5'9" **Weight:** 12.9
ub Honours: FAC '97; FLC '98, '00
ternational Honours: Jamaica: 22
ank settled effectively into Micky
dams' back four at Leicester last season,
perating in both wide and central
ositions. He proved to be a crucial factor
the team's promotion challenge,
oring his first goal of the season at
iestfield. He suffered a calf injury late in
e campaign. Frank added a further cap
r Jamaica when he appeared in the
endly against Nigeria in May.
*helsea (From trainee on 17/5/1990) F/PL
3+6/7 FLC 17+1/2 FAC 18/1 Others 13/3*
*est Bromwich A (Loaned on 12/12/1991)
6/1*
*icester C (£2,000,000 on 14/8/1998) P/FL
2+8/2 FLC 18 FAC 9/1*

INCLAIR Trevor Lloyd
orn: Dulwich, 2 March 1973
eight: 5'10" **Weight:** 12.10
ternational Honours: E: 11; B-1; U21-
; Yth
eturning from the World Cup finals
evor suffered an early-season loss of
rm and was dropped by his country. The
cky West Ham midfielder found it
fficult to find his best form and was left
ut of the side for a couple of games in
e new year, but returned to the line-up
West Bromwich when he scored two
al goals to help restore his confidence.
ow playing with a belief and
etermination, further goals followed
cluding an unstoppable strike against
ston Villa and a low shot into the corner
gainst Middlesbrough. This impressive
rm saw him recalled into the England
uad for the friendly in South Africa over
e summer.
*ackpool (From trainee on 21/8/1990) FL
+28/15 FLC 8 FAC 6+1 Others 8+5/1*
*ueens Park R (£750,000 on 12/8/1993)
FL 162+5/16 FLC 13/3 FAC 10/2*
*est Ham U (£2,300,000 + on 30/1/1998)
175+2/37 FLC 10+1 FAC 8 Others 10/1*

INGH Harpal
orn: Bradford, 15 September 1981
eight: 5'7" **Weight:** 10.9
talented left-footed winger, who uses
s pace and skill to take on defenders,
arpal spent most of the 2002-03
eveloping in Leeds United's reserve team.
e had a month on loan with Bradford
ity but his spell at Valley Parade

coincided with a bad run of results for the
First Division side.
Leeds U (From trainee on 26/9/1998)
*Bury (Loaned on 11/9/2001) FL 11+1/2 FAC
2/1 Others 1*
Bristol C (Loaned on 8/3/2002) FL 3
Bradford C (Loaned on 8/11/2002) FL 3

SKELTON Aaron Matthew
Born: Welwyn Garden City, 22 November
1974
Height: 5'11" **Weight:** 12.6
Aaron had a rather frustrating time with
injuries at Luton last term and he was
restricted to just five starts in Second
Division matches. A versatile player who
can appear at centre back or in midfield,
he is very skilful on the ball and his
excellent positional sense helps him to
read the game.
*Luton T (From trainee on 16/12/1992) FL
5+3 FLC 0+1 FAC 2 Others 2*
*Colchester U (Free on 3/7/1997) FL
114+11/17 FLC 4 FAC 5+1 Others 5+1*
*Luton T (Free on 6/7/2001) FL 14+3/2 FAC 1
Others 1*

SKORA Eric
Born: France, 20 August 1981
Height: 6'1" **Weight:** 11.10
Eric produced some tremendous
performances on the right-hand side of
midfield for Preston in the early part of
the 2002-03 campaign, and scored his
only goal of the season at Macclesfield in
the Worthington Cup. However, he lost
his starting place in the new year only to
regain it towards the end of the
campaign. A tenacious tackler, Eric is
comfortable on the ball, passing well and
always looking to support the attack.
However, his powerful shooting has not
yet gained the rewards he deserves, as
shown by his status as the First Division
player with the highest number of shots
without scoring in the league!
*Preston NE (Free from Nancy, France on
22/10/2001) FL 32+8 FLC 2/1 FAC 3/1
Others 1*

SLABBER Jamie
Born: Enfield, 31 December 1984
Height: 6'2" **Weight:** 11.10
International Honours: E: Yth
This talented young striker enjoyed a
prolific season for Tottenham's reserve and
youth teams, and was rewarded with an
appearance from the first team from the
substitutes' bench. Jamie is a great
attacking prospect and has represented
England at U18 level.
*Tottenham H (From trainee on 3/1/2002) PL
0+1*

SLAVEN John
Born: Edinburgh, 8 October 1985
Height: 6'0" **Weight:** 10.11
This promising young striker continued his
development with the Carlisle United
reserve and youth teams last season. Still
only 17, he added another first-team
appearance from the substitutes' bench
during the campaign.
*Carlisle U (From juniors on 5/11/2002) FL
0+3*

SMICER Vladimir (Vlad)
Born: Czechoslovakia, 24 May 1973
Height: 5'11" **Weight:** 11.3
Club Honours: FLC '01, '03; FAC '01;
UEFAC '01
International Honours: Czech Republic:
64; U21-7. Czechoslovakia: 1
As in previous seasons the Czech
international winger or striker flattered to
deceive for Liverpool last season and
remained a peripheral rather than a key
player in the squad. Although confident
when running with the ball, he rarely
seemed to create goal-scoring
opportunities. He scored just one goal,
netting in the away match with Basle in
European Champions' League action.
*Liverpool (£3,750,000 from RC Lens, France,
ex SK Slavia Praha, on 14/7/1999) PL 52+39/7
FLC 12+2/4 FAC 8+1/1 Others 17+12/2*

SMITH Nathan **Adam**
Born: Huddersfield, 20 February 1985
Height: 6'0" **Weight:** 12.5
Adam will complete his Chesterfield
scholarship in 2003-04. His substitute
appearance at Port Vale in the LDV Vans
Trophy is as yet only his senior one to date, but
his time will come. He has both pace and
a striker's instinct, while his strength
improves all the time. A series of eye-
catching displays for the reserves kept him
on the fringe of first-team involvement
throughout the campaign.
Chesterfield (Trainee) Others 0+1

SMITH Adrian (Adie)
Jonathan
Born: Birmingham, 11 August 1973
Height: 5'10" **Weight:** 12.0
Club Honours: NC '00
International Honours: E: SP-3
Adie passed the 200-game milestone for
Kidderminster last season in his normal
reliable, consistent, fashion. As usual he
found himself playing in a number of
positions – at right back, in the centre of
the defence and at wing back on the
right-hand side. He managed to find the
net only once, in the draw with Swansea
at Aggborough in March.

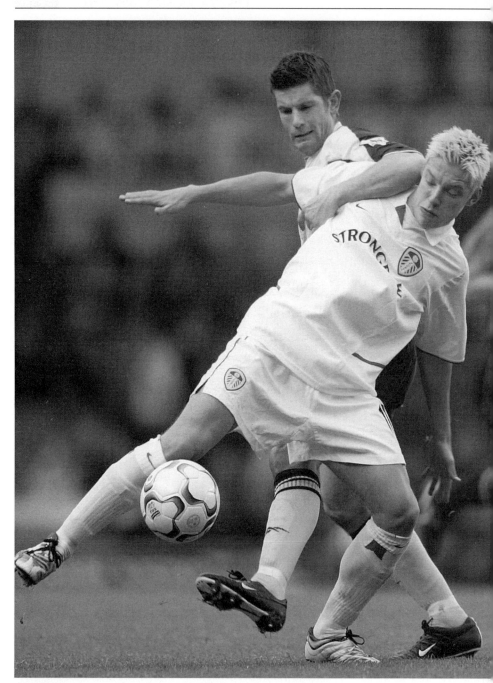

Alan Smith

dderminster Hrs *(£19,000 from romsgrove Rov on 17/6/1997) FL 93+7/8 C 1+1 FAC 4 Others 2/1*

MITH Alan

orn: Rothwell, 28 October 1980
eight: 5'9" **Weight:** 11.10
nternational Honours: E: 6; U21-10; th

his fiery striker appeared in a variety of les for Leeds United last term including the centre and on the right-hand side f midfield. The result was that he eveloped into a much more complete ayer as the season progressed. A ersonal highlight was netting all four of nited's goals in the UEFA Cup second leg ctory over Hapoel Tel Aviv. He only cored three times in the Premiership last erm, primarily as a result of playing in a nore withdrawn position, but is still reatly admired by the fans at Elland oad.

eeds U (From trainee on 26/3/1998) PL 13+24/29 FLC 2+2 FAC 10+4/4 Others 3+7/14

MITH Alexander (Alex)
hilip

orn: Liverpool, 15 February 1976
eight: 5'7" **Weight:** 11.10
lub Honours: AMC '01

. short nine-minute appearance as ubstitute in the 2-1 defeat at Leicester ity was Alex's only first-team outing for eading last term. He replaced Nicky horey, as manager Alan Pardew gambled n playing three at the back with the eam looking for a late equaliser. After nat it was a return to reserve-team ootball, although he later went out to hrewsbury where he featured at left ack during an extended loan period. lex certainly made a positive difference o the squad, especially with his forward uns, and played a part in the Shrews istoric FA Cup run.
verton (From trainee on 1/7/1994) windon T (Free on 12/1/1996) FL 17+14/1 luddersfield T (Free on 6/2/1998) FL 4+2 hester C (Free on 8/7/1998) FL 32/2 FLC 4/1 thers 1 ort Vale (£75,000 on 25/3/1999) FL 52+6/2 LC 2+1 FAC 2 Others 7/1 eading (Free on 19/7/2001) FL 12+2/2 FLC /1 FAC 1 Others 1 hrewsbury T (Loaned on 13/12/2002) FL 3 FAC 2 Others 3

MITH Christopher (Chris)
lan

orn: Derby, 30 June 1981
eight: 5'11" **Weight:** 11.6

This young central defender had a fine season with York City last term, featuring regularly in the line-up and showing consistent form. Powerful both on the ground and in the air his strengths are his composure, positional sense and a willingness to pass the ball out of defence.
Reading (From trainee on 22/6/1999) York C (Free on 2/7/2001) FL 45+6 FLC 1 FAC 4 Others 2

SMITH David

Born: Stonehouse, 29 March 1968
Height: 5'8" **Weight:** 10.7
Club Honours: AMC '98
International Honours: E: U21-10
David joined Swansea City during the 2002 close season and quickly slotted into the left-wing-back role, scoring in his first away appearance at Darlington. However, he injured his groin at Bury in the third game of season, and then a calf problem restricted him further. Prior to the Christmas period he had his contract paid up and he left the Vetch Field playing staff.
Coventry C (From apprentice on 7/7/1986) P/FL 144+10/19 FLC 17 FAC 6 Others 4+1 Bournemouth (Loaned on 8/1/1993) FL 1 Birmingham C (Signed on 12/3/1993) FL 35+3/3 FLC 4 FAC 0+1 Others 1 West Bromwich A (£90,000 on 31/1/1994) FL 82+20/2 FLC 4+2 FAC 1+3 Others 4+1 Grimsby T (£200,000 on 16/1/1998) FL 101+11/9 FLC 9+3/1 FAC 2+1 Others 7/1 Swansea C (Free on 8/7/2002) FL 3+1/1

SMITH David (Dave)
Christopher

Born: Liverpool, 26 December 1970
Height: 5'9" **Weight:** 12.9
After being released by Stockport County in the summer of 2002 Dave joined Eircom League outfit Drogheda United, before eventually linking up with Macclesfield Town early in the new year. The experienced midfielder only managed to make three first-team appearances for Macc before injuries sidelined him until the final two matches when he returned to the substitutes' bench.
Norwich C (From trainee on 4/7/1989) F/PL 13+5 FAC 2+1 Others 1+1 Oxford U (£100,000 on 5/7/1994) FL 193+5/2 FLC 23+1/1 FAC 9+1 Others 7 Stockport Co (Free on 4/2/1999) FL 64+7/3 FLC 3+1 FAC 2 (Freed during 2000 close season) Macclesfield T (Loaned on 1/2/2002) FL 8 Macclesfield T (Free from Drogheda U on 31/1/2003) FL 3

SMITH Dean

Born: West Bromwich, 19 March 1971
Height: 6'1" **Weight:** 12.10
Dean was again the Leyton Orient captain last season and played with a number of different central defensive partners, but always led by example. He was offered the chance to join Sheffield Wednesday's relegation fight and took the step up with ease. A good, robust old-fashioned centre half, dominant in the air and confident to battle his corner against all-comers, he was unable to prevent the Owls from dropping into the Second Division, but will be looking to contribute to their revival in 2003-04.
Walsall (From trainee on 1/7/1989) FL 137+5/2 FLC 10 FAC 4 Others 10 Hereford U (£75,000 on 17/6/1994) FL 116+1/19 FLC 10/3 FAC 7 Others 11+1/4 Leyton Orient (£42,500 on 16/6/1997) FL 239/32 FLC 18 FAC 19/4 Others 12/1 Sheffield Wed (Signed on 21/2/2003) FL 14

SMITH Grant Gordon

Born: Irvine, 5 May 1980
Height: 6'1" **Weight:** 12.7
Grant, although fully involved in Sheffield United's pre-season games, made just one start in the 2002-03 campaign, appearing as a striker against Wimbledon when things did not go his way. Occasionally on the bench, he was a regular in the Blades' successful reserve side and in March he joined Plymouth Argyle in a loan deal. He made his debut in midfield at Blackpool and went on to add a further four appearances, scoring at home to Brentford. Grant showed excellent pace and being good in the air, was a danger at set pieces.
Reading (Free from trainee at Wycombe W on 7/8/1998) Heart of Midlothian (Free on 19/3/1999) Livingston (Free on 4/7/2000) SL 0+2 SLC 1 Others 1 Clydebank (Free on 2/12/2000) SL 16+1/2 Sheffield U (Free on 13/7/2001) FL 2+8 FAC 0+1 Halifax T (Loaned on 7/9/2001) FL 11 Others 1 Plymouth Arg (Loaned on 10/3/2003) FL 4+1/1

SMITH Jack David

Born: Hemel Hempstead, 14 October 1983
Height: 5'11" **Weight:** 11.5
Jack is the younger brother of Watford striker Tommy Smith, but a central defender or midfield player rather than a striker. A product of the Hornets academy, he was a stalwart of the club's successful

reserve team and impressed with his mature attitude and application.   The Smiths became the third pair of brothers to play together for Watford since the war at Brighton towards the end of the season, when Jack made his first-team debut from the substitutes' bench.
Watford *(From trainee on 5/4/2002) FL 0+1*

SMITH James (Jamie) Jade Anthony
Born: Birmingham, 17 September 1974
Height: 5'7" **Weight:** 11.4

Dean Smith

Jamie eventually returned to action for Crystal Palace in March after almost a year out with injuries. However, he was stretchered off in only his second game back against Walsall, and spent the remainder of the campaign on the sidelines. When fully fit he is an exciting right back who is effective when pushing forward to deliver crosses into the opposition penalty area.
Wolverhampton W *(From trainee on 7/6/1993) FL 81+6 FLC 10+1 FAC 2 Others 4/1*
Crystal Palace *(Signed on 22/10/1997) P/FL 123+11/4 FLC 15/2 FAC 6+1 Others 1+1*
Fulham *(Loaned on 25/3/1999) FL 9/1*

SMITH Jason Leslie
Born: Bromsgrove, 6 September 1974
Height: 6'3" **Weight:** 13.7
Club Honours: Div 3 '00
International Honours: E: Sch
Jason started the season at the heart of the Swansea defence, but struggled to find his best form. He had a groin injury early on, and further problems with his ankle and hamstring saw him miss a number of matches throughout the campaign. A dominant player in the centre of defence on his day, Jason is particularly strong in aerial challenges.
Coventry C *(Signed from Tiverton T on 5/7/1993. Free to Tiverton T on 15/7/1995)*
Swansea C *(£10,000 on 1/7/1998) FL 141+1/8 FLC 7 FAC 9/1 Others 8/1*

SMITH Jay Alexander
Born: London, 24 September 1981
Height: 5'7" **Weight:** 10.6
Initially signed on loan from Aston Villa, Jay took Southend by storm with some excellent performances in the centre of midfield alongside captain Kevin Maher and it was a relief to secure his services on a permanent basis at the turn of the year. A gifted player with excellent distribution and great tactical awareness, he had a terrific campaign but unfortunately his season ended prematurely in March with a nasty groin injury.
Aston Villa *(From trainee on 7/7/2000)*
Southend U *(Free on 19/8/2002) FL 30+1/5 FLC 1 FAC 3+1 Others 1*

SMITH Jay Mark
Born: Hammersmith, 29 December 1981
Height: 5'11" **Weight:** 11.7
This stylish Brentford central midfielder showed what he could do with some good positional play and passing last season. He appeared in only around half of the games however, as he competed with Stephen Evans, Jamie Fullarton and Eddie Hutchinson for the two central midfield positions.
Brentford *(From trainee on 5/7/2000) FL 25+4 FAC 2 Others 2+2*

SMITH Jeffrey (Jeff)
Born: Middlesbrough, 28 June 1980
Height: 5'10" **Weight:** 11.8
A young and pacy winger, Jeff's only Bolton appearances last term came in the three domestic cup games. He impressed on each occasion and was particularly

utstanding in the FA Cup tie at home to
underland, when he gave a 'Man of the
Match' performance full of trickery and
nventiveness. That display certainly got
eff noticed after a period of some
nactivity since signing from Bishop
uckland, and he will be looking to build
pon that experience during the new
ampaign.
*artlepool U (From trainee on 3/7/1998) FL
+1 Others 1 (Free to Barrow in October
999)*
*olton W (Free from Bishop Auckland on
1/3/2001) P/FL 1+1 FLC 2 FAC 2*
*Macclesfield T (Loaned on 23/11/2001) FL
+1/2*

SMITH Martin Geoffrey
orn: Sunderland, 13 November 1974
Height: 5'11" **Weight:** 12.6
lub Honours: Div 1 '96
nternational Honours: E: U21-1; Yth;
ch
his skilful striker nearly single-handedly
ept Huddersfield Town in the Second
ivision last term. After a 17-month
bsence with injury Martin started the
rst game of the season on the wing,
efore suffering back and hamstring
roblems. He returned as a second-half
ubstitute in the 'derby' game with
arnsley and it was fitting that he netted
he winning goal. Once fully fit he
cored many a cracking goal as a result
f some great close control, tremendous
ace and a willingness to attack
pposing defences. A real threat at set
ieces, he adhered himself to the
upporters by turning down several
noves away from the club. Martin
inished the campaign as the Terriers'
eading scorer and also scooped the
Player of the Year' award.
*Sunderland (From trainee on 9/9/1992) P/FL
0+29/25 FLC 10+6/2 FAC 7+3/1
*heffield U (Free on 6/8/1999) FL 24+2/10
LC 3+1/4 FAC 3/1*
*Huddersfield T (£300,000 on 3/2/2000) FL
2+8/29 FLC 2+1 FAC 1 Others 1*

SMITH Ian Paul
orn: Easington, 22 January 1976
Height: 6'0" **Weight:** 13.3
aul is a strong left-sided player who is
nost effective running at the opposition
rom midfield. After playing so well for
lartlepool the previous season, he will be
lisappointed that his 2002-03 campaign
vas a constant personal struggle, while
he team did so well. Early in the season
e had to undergo a knee operation, and
ater he was out for a lengthy period with
nother leg injury.

*Burnley (From trainee on 10/7/1994) FL
79+33/5 FLC 3+1 FAC 6+1 Others 5*
*Oldham Ath (Loaned on 22/9/2000) FL 3+1
FLC 1*
*Hartlepool U (Free, via trial at Torquay U,
on 1/11/2001) FL 45+10/4 FAC 3 Others 2*

SMITH Paul Antony
Born: Hastings, 25 January 1976
Height: 5'11" **Weight:** 11.7
Paul started the 2002-03 season on the
right side of Lincoln's midfield but was
relegated to the substitutes' bench for
the middle part of the campaign. He
was brought back into the starting line-
up towards the end of the season when
he featured in a three-man strike force.
His ability to beat a defender set up
several chances and although he only
scored three goals these included a vital
strike in the home play-off win over
Scunthorpe.
*Nottingham F (£50,000 from Hastings T on
13/1/1995)*
*Lincoln C (£30,000 on 17/10/1997) FL
122+35/19 FLC 6+1/1 FAC 8+1/1 Others
11+1/1*

SMITH Paul Daniel
Born: Epsom, 17 December 1979
Height: 6'4" **Weight:** 14.0
Paul's first full season as Brentford's
number one goalkeeper concluded with
him winning the 'Player of the Year'
award, an honour he fully deserved
following some excellent performances.
He kept four clean sheets in the first four
games to set his standards for the
campaign. He also stopped a spot kick in
the Worthington Cup tie at
Bournemouth, adding two more saves in
the penalty shoot-out that decided the
match. Paul missed just three Second
Division games during the season.
*Charlton Ath (Free from Walton & Hersham
on 2/7/1998. Free to Walton & Hersham
during 1999 close season)*
*Brentford (Free from Carshalton Ath on
27/7/2000) FL 62+1 FLC 2 FAC 4 Others 6+1*

SMITH Paul William
Born: East Ham, 18 September 1971
Height: 5'11" **Weight:** 13.0
Once again Gillingham's captain was a
model of consistency in 2002-03, missing
just two games during the season. Paul
also made his 300th appearance for the
club in March, thus becoming only the
tenth Gills' player to achieve this feat. He
sustained a serious knee injury in the final
game of the season against Crystal
Palace, but is expected to be fit for the
start of the 2003-04 campaign.

*Southend U (From trainee on 16/3/1990) FL
18+2/1 Others 0+1*
*Brentford (Free on 6/8/1993) FL 159/11 FLC
12/1 FAC 12/3 Others 15/2*
*Gillingham (Signed on 25/7/1997) FL
267+1/18 FLC 15/1 FAC 17 Others 9+2/2*

SMITH Gareth Shaun
Born: Leeds, 9 April 1971
Height: 5'10" **Weight:** 11.0
This stalwart left-back became Third
Division Hull's seventh signing of the 2002
close season when he accepted a three-
year deal. His left-footed version of a
David Beckham style free-kick clinched
the Tigers first win of the season at
Cambridge but the arrival of Peter Taylor
as manager, plus the signing of Damien
Delaney, coincided with an untimely thigh
injury and subsequently struggled to
regain his place. Shaun made the 500th
appearance of his senior career when he
came off the substitutes' bench during
the Easter Monday visit to Darlington.
*Halifax T (From trainee on 1/7/1989) FL 6+1
Others 1 (Free to Emley in May 1991)*
*Crewe Alex (Free on 31/12/1991) FL
380+22/41 FLC 24+1/4 FAC 19+2/4 Others
19+2/3*
*Hull C (Free on 12/7/2002) FL 17+5/1 FLC 1
FAC 0+1*

SMITH Thomas (Tommy) William
Born: Hemel Hempstead, 22 May 1980
Height: 5'8" **Weight:** 11.4
International Honours: E: U21-1; Yth
Watford's senior striker had another hard
working and productive season in 2002-
03 except where it really matters: goal-
scoring. His return of nine goals was
disappointing for such a skilful player.
Tommy was outstanding in the club's FA
Cup run, scoring from a twice-taken
penalty at the Stadium of Light to beat
Sunderland. Soon afterwards, he suffered
whiplash injuries and cuts and bruises in a
car crash, and was touch and go to be fit
for the quarter-final against Burnley. In
the event, he played well and scored
again. He lost his place for the semi-final
to Michael Chopra, but came on as a
substitute. The season ended with Tommy
unable to agree a new contract at
Watford, leaving his future uncertain.
*Watford (From trainee on 21/10/1997) P/FL
114+35/33 FLC 7+3/1 FAC 5+3/2*

SOAMES David Michael
Born: Grimsby, 10 December 1984
Height: 5'5" **Weight:** 10.8
A product of the Grimsby Town youth
scheme, David emerged from a lengthy

struggle to recover from a cartilage problem and broke into the first team last season. He made several appearances from the substitutes' bench and showed his promise by scoring in only the third minute of his league career, when coming on in the closing stages at Pride Park. A young striker with speed and intelligence, he seems likely to get further opportunities as the Mariners adjust to life in the Second Division.
Grimsby T (Trainee) FL 0+10/1 FAC 2

SODJE Efetobore (Efe)
Born: Greenwich, 5 October 1972
Height: 6'1" **Weight:** 12.0
Club Honours: GMVC '96
International Honours: Nigeria: 10
After a successful campaign in the 2002 World Cup finals with Nigeria, Efe had another useful season with Crewe Alexandra last term. He featured in over half the club's games, playing in a variety of positions in the defence and contributing two goals. He made his 100th first team start for Alexandra in the final game of the season against Cardiff. Efe added a further cap for Nigeria when he played against Jamaica at the end of May.
Macclesfield T (£30,000 from Stevenage Borough on 11/7/1997) FL 83/6 FLC 6 FAC 6/1 Others 1
Luton T (Free on 12/8/1999) FL 5+4 FLC 1 FAC 2+1 Others 1
Colchester U (Free on 23/3/2000) FL 3
Crewe Alex (Free on 21/7/2000) FL 86+12/3 FLC 6+2 FAC 6+3/1 Others 2

SOLANO Nolberto (Nobby)
Albino
Born: Lima, Peru, 12 December 1974
Height: 5'8" **Weight:** 10.8
International Honours: Peru: 58; Yth
Nobby had another good season operating on the right side of Newcastle's midfield last term. Skilful on the ball he provides valuable width for the team and delivers telling crosses for his central strikers, but also recognises the importance of his defensive responsibilities and tracks back well when defending. He again collected his share of goals, some by exploiting his dead-ball expertise – notably a delightful free kick at home to Villa and his winning penalty in the 'derby' at Sunderland. Nobby passed 200 appearances for the club and continued to be selected for Peru.
Newcastle U (£2,763,958 from Boca Juniors, Argentina, ex Cristal Alianza Lima, Sporting, Deportivo Municipal, on 17/8/1998) PL 150+10/29 FLC 9+2 FAC 17/2 Others 23+3/6

SOLKHON Brett Michael
Born: Canvey Island, 12 September 1982
Height: 5'11" **Weight:** 12.6
This youngster's only appearance in the Football League last season came as a stand-in striker alongside Rushden & Diamonds skipper Paul Underwood for the first half at Hartlepool United in September. The former Nene Park youth-team captain was better known as a central defender and he joined Conference club Kettering Town later in the season.
Rushden & Diamonds (From Arsenal juniors on 7/7/2000) FL 1+1

SOLLITT Adam James
Born: Sheffield, 22 June 1977
Height: 6'0" **Weight:** 11.4
International Honours: E: SP-3
Adam completed a personal hat-trick of Northamptonshire clubs when he joined Rushden & Diamonds in the summer of 2002. However, the tall and agile goalkeeper had to wait until October for his first-team debut, replacing the injured Billy Turley. Adam then suffered a broken wrist towards the end of his home debut and this put him out of action for three months. He only returned to the substitutes' bench for the title decider against Hartlepool United on the last day of the season and was released shortly afterwards.
Barnsley (From trainee on 4/7/1995. Free to Gainsborough Trinity during 1997 close season)
Northampton T (£30,000 from Kettering T on 25/7/2000) FL 14+2 FLC 2 FAC 1 Others 1
Rushden & Diamonds (Free on 7/8/2002) FL 3 FAC 1 Others 1

SOLSKJAER Ole Gunnar
Born: Kristiansund, Norway, 26 February 1973
Height: 5'10" **Weight:** 11.10
Club Honours: PL '97, '99, '00, '01, '03; FAC '99; EC '99
International Honours: Norway: 58; U21-19
A supremely dedicated striker who is the most clinical of finishers, Ole Gunnar might well have bought a VIP Box at Old Trafford for his future entertainment, but he continued to thrill the Manchester United public with some wonderful goal poaching on the pitch. His 100th goal for the club was duly celebrated in United's opening Premiership fixture against West Bromwich Albion, whilst there were a further 13 contributions throughout an industrious campaign. For a player perennially noted as being United's 'Super

Sub', Ole Gunnar's superb strike rate and his ability to run at defences gave Sir Alex Ferguson more food for thought as the Reds fought Arsenal tooth and nail before clinching the the Premiership title at the close of the season.
Manchester U (£1,500,000 from Molde, Norway on 29/7/1996) PL 135+65/84 FLC 7+3/6 FAC 9+10/6 Others 38+43/18

SOLTVEDT Trond Egil
Born: Voss, Norway, 15 February 1967
Height: 6'1" **Weight:** 12.8
International Honours: Norway: 4
The 2002-03 season proved to be a frustrating time for this Sheffield Wednesday midfielder, lately turned central defender. Injury wrecked his campaign and he was ruled out of the side's relegation fight from mid-January onwards. His form before that had not been up to his past high standards, but he was sorely missed for his ability to drive on his fellow defenders in his role as club captain. He will be hoping to make a major contribution in 2003-04 as the Owls look to turn around their fortunes.
Coventry C (£500,000 from Rosenborg, Norway, ex Ny-Khronborg, Viking Stavanger, Brann, on 24/7/1997) PL 47+10/3 FLC 1+4/1 FAC 5+2
Southampton (£300,000 on 13/8/1999) PL 20+10/2 FLC 6/3 FAC 2+1
Sheffield Wed (Free on 13/2/2001) FL 74/2 FLC 6/2 FAC 1

SOMMEIL David
Born: Point-a-Pitre, Guadeloupe, 10 August 1974
Height: 5'11" **Weight:** 11.6
Signed during the January transfer window, this rugged, committed right-sided defender quickly blended in at Manchester City. He was an ever-present after making his debut against Fulham at the end of January and showed some fine defensive qualities. As he became more settled, so his form improved and towards the end of the season he switched to playing as a central defender. David also scored once for the Blues, netting in the away fixture at Tottenham.
Manchester C (£3,500,000 from Bordeaux, France, ex Caen, Rennes, on 27/1/2003) PL 14/1

SOMNER Matthew (Matt)
James
Born: Isleworth, 8 December 1982
Height: 6'0" **Weight:** 13.2
This solid Brentford defender established himself as a regular in the first team during the 2002-03 season. Although

ght footed he spent most of the ampaign at left back, however, he also nade some appearances at centre back nd, occasionally, at right back. Matt cored his first senior goal in the FA Cup e at Wycombe and followed up with rst league goal with a flick header gainst Northampton.

rentford (From trainee on 4/7/2001) FL 1+2/1 FLC 0+1 FAC 1+2/1 Others 1

5ONKO Ibrahima (Ibu)
orn: Bignona, Senegal, 22 January 1981
leight: 6'3" **Weight:** 13.7
nternational Honours: Senegal: U21
ɔu is a cool, composed Brentford centre
ack whose class impressed everyone last
eason. His reading of the game and
mely interceptions were the hallmarks of
is play and he eventually signed a

permanent contract for the Bees in December after being on non-contract terms from August. He scored twice against Blackpool in November. Ibu gained Senegal U21 caps against Guinea and Mali, and was also called up to the full international squad.

Brentford (Free from Grenoble, France, ex St Etienne, on 9/8/2002) FL 37/5 FLC 2/1 FAC 4 Others 2

SONNER Daniel (Danny) James
Born: Wigan, 9 January 1972
Height: 5'11" **Weight:** 12.8
International Honours: NI: 7; B-4
Signed by Walsall on a one-year contract in the summer of 2002, Danny battled to good effect in midfield in the first half of the season. He netted two penalties at Portsmouth in November and was 'Man

of the Match' in the game against Wolves in January. However, he slipped out of the first-team scene soon afterwards and was released in April after a final appearance against Pompey in which he gave his usual all-action display.

Burnley (From trainee at Wigan Ath on 6/8/1990) FL 1+5 FLC 0+1/1 Others 0+2 (Free to Preussen Koln, Germany during 1993 close season)

Bury (Loaned on 21/11/1992) FL 5/3 FAC 3 Others 1/1

Ipswich T (Free from FC Erzgebirge Aue, Germany on 12/6/1996) FL 28+28/3 FLC 6+4/1 FAC 1+1 Others 0+1

Sheffield Wed (£75,000 on 15/10/1998) PL 42+11/3 FLC 3+1/1 FAC 4+2

Birmingham C (Free on 4/8/2000) FL 32+9/2 FLC 12/1 FAC 1 Others 2

Walsall (Free on 5/8/2002) FL 20+4/4 FLC 2 FAC 2

SORENSEN Thomas
Born: Denmark, 12 June 1976
Height: 6'4" **Weight:** 13.10
Club Honours: Div 1 '99
International Honours: Denmark: 27; B-1; U21-6
Denmark's first choice goalkeeper is expected to leave Sunderland in the close season following the club's relegation to the Nationwide League, but he will depart the Stadium of Light as a player who will be fondly remembered by the Wearside faithful. An excellent shot stopper with fine positional sense, Thomas had a lot of competition for his position last season and missed three months of the campaign after dislocating an elbow at Arsenal in October. He returned to become the hero in the FA Cup fourth round replay win over Blackburn, saving two penalties in Sunderland's shoot-out triumph, and his performance against local rivals Newcastle, when he was only beaten by a penalty, was also outstanding.

Sunderland (£500,000 + from Odense BK, Denmark on 6/8/1998) P/FL 171 FLC 13 FAC 13

SORVEL Neil Simon
Born: Whiston, 2 March 1973
Height: 6'0" **Weight:** 12.9
Club Honours: GMVC '95, '97; FAT '96
Neil was once again a regular in midfield for Crewe Alexandra last term, proving to be a very capable and disciplined player. He scored the club's first goal of the season at Northampton and netted twice more, the best of which was at Barnsley – Alexandra's 100th of the campaign.

Crewe Alex (From trainee on 31/7/1991) FL 5+4 FAC 1+1 Others 4

Trond Egil Soltvedt

*Macclesfield T (Free on 21/8/1992) FL
79+7/7 FLC 4+1 FAC 5 Others 0+1*
*Crewe Alex (Free on 9/6/1999) FL
158+15/10 FLC 14 FAC 10+1 Others 4*

SOUTHALL Leslie **Nicholas (Nicky)**

Born: Stockton, 28 January 1972
Height: 5'10" **Weight:** 12.12
Nicky found himself out of the reckoning
at Bolton at the start of the 2002-03
campaign and in September he joined
Norwich City on loan. He was brought to
Carrow Road at a
time when City had suffered three
separate injuries to players who could
fulfil the wide-right-midfield role. Quietly
effective, his distribution was good and
he was unlucky not to get on the score
sheet on a couple of occasions. In
December Nicky rejoined Gillingham,
where he quickly slotted into the right-
wing-back position and it seemed he had
never been away. He showed he had lost
none of his appetite for the game and
was a major influence with his crossing
and powerful shooting.
*Hartlepool U (From Darlington juniors on
21/2/1991) FL118+20/24 FLC 6+1/3 FAC 4+4
Others 6+2*
*Grimsby T (£40,000 on 12/7/1995) FL
55+17/6 FLC 3+3/1 FAC 4+3/2*
*Gillingham (Free on 9/12/1997) FL
141+13/17 FLC 6+1/1 FAC 10/3 Others 12*
*Bolton W (Free on 2/7/2001) PL 10+8/1 FLC
4 FAC 2*
Norwich C (Loaned on 27/9/2002) FL 4+5
*Gillingham (Free on 6/12/2002) FL 22+2/1
FAC 3*

SOUTHERN Keith William

Born: Gateshead, 24 April 1981
Height: 5'10" **Weight:** 12.6
This young Everton midfielder initially
joined Blackpool on loan prior to the start
of the 2002-03 campaign. He settled in
well and was a regular in the line-up,
netting his first senior goal in the home
victory against Tranmere. Keith impressed
with his high work rate and
determination, but his campaign ended
due to an operation at the end of March.
Everton (From trainee on 21/5/1999)
*Blackpool (Free on 8/8/2002) FL 38/1 FLC 1
FAC 2 Others 1*

SOUTHGATE Gareth

Born: Watford, 3 September 1970
Height: 6'0" **Weight:** 12.8
Club Honours: Div 1 '94; FLC '96
International Honours: E: 55
Club captain Gareth was Middlesbrough's
'Mr Reliability' for yet another season. His

cool and composed displays at the heart
of the Boro' defence won the defender
many new admirers outside of Teesside
and his quick thinking can launch an
attack from defence in an instant. Gareth
and former Aston Villa defender Ugo
Ehiogu continued their almost telepathic
partnership at the Riverside and Gareth's
displays ensured his continued
appearance in the England team, winning
his 55th cap as recently as June against

Slovakia. He was, in his own words,
'chuffed to bits' to score only his second
goal for his country (in the first minute)
against South Africa at the King's Park
Stadium in Durban.
*Crystal Palace (From trainee on 17/1/1989)
F/PL 148+4/15 FLC 23+1/7 FAC 9 Others 6*
*Aston Villa (£2,500,000 on 1/7/1995) PL
191/7 FLC 17/1 FAC 20/1 Others 15*
*Middlesbrough (£6,500,000 on 14/7/2001)
PL 73/3 FLC 1 FAC 7*

Matt Sparrow

SPARROW Matthew (Matt)
Donald
Born: Wembley, 3 October 1981
Height: 5'11" Weight: 10.6
Matt made a clean sweep of Scunthorpe United's main 'Player of the Season' awards last term after having an excellent season on the right side of midfield. An attacking player, who loves to run at opposition defences, his performances were rewarded with nine goals – including several good strikes from outside the area. He scored twice in the 4-1 'derby' win over Hull in February and only missed four matches during the campaign. A competitive player, he is equally effective in the centre of the park.
*Scunthorpe U (From trainee on 30/7/2001)
L 73+15/14 FLC 1+3 FAC 4 Others 3+1*

SPEDDING Duncan
Born: Camberley, 7 September 1977
Height: 6'1" Weight: 11.1
Injury kept this left-sided defender out of the Northampton Town line-up for most of last season. At home either as a left back or in midfield he saw little first-team action after the first few weeks of the campaign and was released by the Cobblers in the summer.
*Southampton (From trainee on 24/5/1996)
L 4+3 FLC 0+1*
*Northampton T (£60,000 on 14/7/1998) FL
107+16/2 FLC 8+2 FAC 4+1 Others 5*

SPEED Gary Andrew
Born: Deeside, 8 September 1969
Height: 5'10" Weight: 12.10
Club Honours: Div 2 '90, Div 1 '92; CS 92
International Honours: W: 73; U21-3; Yth
After a delayed start due to a sprained ankle Gary had another fine season at the heart of Newcastle's midfield last term. His energy and reading of the game enabled him to protect his defence, whilst his vision and passing ability provided the springboard for prompting the attack. Hernia damage incurred against Tottenham in December required surgery and sidelined him for six weeks, and then in March he suffered a groin injury while playing for Wales against Azerbaijan which ended his season, his absence coinciding with a sharp decline in the Magpies' results. He continued to captain his country, sometimes from the unusual position of left back, and contributed vital goals in both the home and away Euro 2004 qualifying ties against Azerbaijan.

*Leeds U (From trainee on 13/6/1988) F/PL
231+17/39 FLC 25+1/11 FAC 21/5 Others
14+3/2*
*Everton (£3,500,000 on 1/7/1996) PL 58/16
FLC 5/1 FAC 2/1*
*Newcastle U (£5,500,000 on 6/2/1998) PL
169+6/26 FLC 9+1/1 FAC 20/5 Others 26/4*

SPENCER Damian Michael
Born: Ascot, 19 September 1981
Height: 6'1" Weight: 14.5
Damian joined Cheltenham Town in the summer of 2002 and went on to show a good deal of promise in his first-team appearances last season. A striker who possesses pace and awesome physical power, he has the ability to come alive in the penalty area, creating goal-scoring opportunities with his direct running and willingness to shoot from anywhere. His tally of six goals included excellent efforts in the 3-1 defeat at Blackpool and in the 3-0 win at Swindon Town. Damian showed enough potential during the season to be offered an extended two-year contract by manager Bobby Gould.
*Bristol C (From trainee on 14/6/2000) FL
8+5/1 FLC 0+1 Others 1+3/1*

Duncan Spedding

Exeter C (Loaned on 22/3/2001) FL 2+4
Cheltenham T (Free on 7/8/2002) FL 10+20/6 FAC 1+1 Others 1+1

SPENCER James Matthew
Born: Stockport, 11 April 1985
Height: 6'5" **Weight:** 15.2
Stockport County's youngest-ever goalkeeper made the most of his first opportunity last season when he kept a clean sheet in the LDV Vans Trophy victory against Darlington. He kept his place for the visit of Brentford but was then restricted to a place on the bench and did not add to his appearance total.
Stockport Co (From trainee on 19/4/2002) FL 2+1 Others 1

SPILLER Daniel (Danny)
Born: Maidstone, 10 October 1981
Height: 5'9" **Weight:** 12.3
Danny made a splendid full debut for Gillingham in the Worthington Cup game at Stockport last October. Selected just two hours before kick off, he was instrumental in creating both goals in a 2-1 victory. He was then given an extended run in the final five games of the season and created a favourable impression with his tireless running, tackling and shooting from distance. Danny signed an extension to his contract in March that will keep him at Priestfield until the summer of 2005.
Gillingham (From trainee on 10/7/2000) FL 5+6 FLC 1+1 FAC 0+1

SPRING Matthew John
Born: Harlow, 17 November 1979
Height: 5'11" **Weight:** 11.5
Matthew was once again a key figure in midfield for Luton Town last season, and forged an excellent partnership with Kevin Nicholls in the centre of the park. Despite his occasional loss of form he wrote his place in the Hatters' folklore by scoring a spectacular goal against local rivals Watford in the Worthington Cup. As well as netting vital goals, Matthew was also a key provider of chances for his colleagues.
Luton T (From trainee on 2/7/1997) FL 219+7/24 FLC 14/1 FAC 15+1/3 Others 3

STALLARD Mark
Born: Derby, 24 October 1974
Height: 6'0" **Weight:** 13.6
This talented striker had an excellent season with Notts County last term, finishing up as the club's leading scorer with 24 goals, a personal best tally. Despite this, he was completely unselfish around the penalty area, often forsaking the opportunity to score himself to pass

to a colleague in a more favourable position. A skilful striker who can turn defenders and shoot with either foot, Mark was deservedly selected as the Magpies' 'Player of the Year'.
Derby Co (From trainee on 6/11/1991) FL 19+8/2 FLC 2+1/2 FAC 2+2 Others 3/2
Fulham (Loaned on 23/9/1994) FL 4/3
Bradford C (£110,000 on 12/1/1996) FL 33+10/10 FLC 2/1 FAC 0+1 Others 3/2
Preston NE (Loaned on 14/2/1997) FL 4/1
Wycombe W (£100,000 on 7/3/1997) FL 67+3/23 FLC 5+1/1 Others 2/1

Mark Stallard

Notts Co (£10,000 on 3/3/1999) FL 150+13/63 FLC 11/6 FAC 8/3 Others 2

STAMP Darryn Michael
Born: Beverley, 21 September 1978
Height: 6'2" **Weight:** 12.0
The tall striker will always remember his Northampton debut for he was carried off after 21 minutes against Crewe. Darryn spent three months out of action, but when he returned he contributed a number of valuable goals. However, he then spent another lengthy period on the

idelines with an injury. Darryn is an ideal
arget man who is particularly effective in
he air.
*cunthorpe U (Signed from Hessle on
*/7/1997) FL 18+39/6 FLC 1+3 FAC 2+2
Others 3+1/1 (Free to Scarborough on
1/6/2001)
*Halifax T (Loaned on 18/2/2000) FL 5
*Northampton T (£30,000 + from
*carborough on 28/5/2002) FL 12+10/4 FAC
*+1/1

STAMPS Scott
Born: Birmingham, 20 March 1975
Height: 5'10" **Weight:** 11.10
Club Honours: NC '00
*cott's 2002-03 season at Kidderminster
*vas ruined by an ankle injury that forced
*him to miss over half of the campaign.
*After beginning in his usual reliable style
*he was injured in the LDV Vans Trophy
*ictory over Swindon in November and
*did not return until coming on as a
*ubstitute to a great ovation in the draw
*vith Swansea in March.
*Torquay U (From trainee on 6/7/1993) FL
*0+6/5 FLC 5 FAC 2 Others 2+1/1
*Colchester U (£10,000 on 26/3/1997) FL
*2+4/1 FLC 4 FAC 3+1 Others 1+1
*Kidderminster Hrs (Free on 17/9/1999) FL
*9+5 FLC 3 FAC 4 Others 3

STANDING Michael John
Born: Shoreham, 20 March 1981
Height: 5'10" **Weight:** 10.12
International Honours: E: Yth; Sch
Michael had a mixed season with
Bradford City last term. A talented
attacking midfield player, the highlight of
his season was a double strike in the 5-3
defeat by Wimbledon in November, but
these proved to be his only goals of the
campaign. He would have wanted to
make more outings in the first team as he
struggled to put a lengthy run of
appearances together.
*Aston Villa (From trainee on 26/3/1998)
*Bradford C (Free on 19/3/2002) FL 14+10/2
*FLC 1 FAC 1

STANFORD Edward (Eddie)
John
Born: Blackburn, 4 February 1985
Height: 5'7" **Weight:** 10.7
This young left-sided player was given a
surprise first-team chance for Coventry as
a substitute in the Worthington Cup
game with Rushden. The former
Manchester United academy player
performed well in defence with several
overlapping runs. He was also a regular in
the Sky Blues' reserve team for most of
the season.
*Coventry C (Trainee) FL 0+1 FLC 0+1

STANIC Mario
Born: Sarajevo, Yugoslavia, 10 April 1972
Height: 6'2" **Weight:** 12.12
Club Honours: CS '00
International Honours: Croatia: 49
The acquisition of another wide midfield
player in the shape of Quique De Lucas
seemed to limit the first-team chances of
Mario Stanic, but the doughty Croat
proved to be a versatile, and valuable,
member of the Chelsea squad. He
appeared in every position across the
Blues' four-man midfield, at right wing
back and for a spell in September as an
emergency left back. A useful
opportunistic goal-scorer, he netted twice
within four days in December, both
headers from corners and both against
Everton. Later, Premiership goals against
Arsenal, West Bromwich Albion and
Manchester City followed, plus the strike
that settled the FA Cup third round tie
against Middlesbrough. All in all, Mario
had a very satisfactory campaign in a
landmark season for the Blues.
*Chelsea (£5,600,000 from Parma, Italy, ex
*Zeljeznicar Sarajevo, Croatio Zagreb, Sporting
*Gijon, Benfica, Brugge, on 12/7/2000) PL
*39+18/7 FLC 3+1/1 FAC 7+2/2 Others 5

STANTON Nathan
Born: Nottingham, 6 May 1981
Height: 5'9" **Weight:** 11.3
International Honours: E: Yth
Nathan put his off-the-field problems to
one side to have another excellent
campaign in Scunthorpe's defence in
2002-03. A very quick, tigerish player, he
made the right-back spot his own but still
looked equally assured at centre back
when called upon. He only missed four
games all season as United finished fifth
and chose the first leg of the play-offs at
Lincoln to net his first goal in his 187th
appearance for the club.
*Scunthorpe U (From trainee on 19/3/1999)
*FL 145+16 FLC 5 FAC 12+1 Others 8+1/1

STAUNTON Stephen (Steve)
Born: Drogheda, Ireland, 19 January
1969
Height: 6'1" **Weight:** 12.12
Club Honours: FAC '89; Div 1 '90; FLC
'94, '96
International Honours: RoI: 102; U21-4;
Yth
Steve got off to a good start for Aston
Villa last term, scoring against FC Zurich
in the Intertoto Cup and featuring
regularly in the line-up in the first half of
the campaign. However, he underwent a
double hernia operation at the end of
December, and this was immediately

followed by ankle surgery to correct a
long-standing problem. Steve returned to
action in April, a little earlier than
expected. A vastly experienced and
versatile defender, he always gives 100
per cent for the team.
*Liverpool (£20,000 from Dundalk on
*2/9/1986) FL 55+10 FLC 6+2/4 FAC 14+2/1
*Others 1/1
*Bradford C (Loaned on 13/11/1987) FL 7+1
*FLC 2 Others 1
*Aston Villa (£1,100,000 on 7/8/1991) F/PL
*205+3/16 FLC 17+2/1 FAC 19+1/1 Others
*15+1
*Liverpool (Free on 3/7/1998) PL 38+6 FLC
*5/1 FAC 2 Others 5+2
*Crystal Palace (Loaned on 20/10/2000) FL 6/1
*Aston Villa (Free on 7/12/2000) PL 65+8 FLC
*5 FAC 4 Others 5/1

STEAD Jonathan (Jon)
Graeme
Born: Huddersfield, 7 April 1983
Height: 6'3" **Weight:** 11.7
Another youngster to progress through
the ranks at Huddersfield, Jon was
involved with the first-team squad
throughout the 2002-03 season. He
worked tirelessly as a striker, linking up
well with his fellow players and showing
good pace and an eye for goal. He scored
a total of six goals, including a fine
double in the home win against Notts
County.
*Huddersfield T (From trainee on
*30/11/2001) FL 28+14/6 FLC 2 FAC 1
*Others 1

STEELE Daniel (Danny)
Born: London, 11 October 1982
Height: 6'2" **Weight:** 13.6
This young centre half figured occasionally
for Colchester United during the first half
of the 2002-03 season, but he was sent
off in the 1-1 home draw against Barnsley
in late October and made just one more
appearance as a substitute. He left the
club in November. Danny is a fully
committed defender, who will no doubt
improve with age and experience.
*Millwall (From juniors on 1/2/2000)
*Colchester U (Free on 26/7/2002) FL 6+2
*Others 1

STEELE Lee Anthony James
Born: Liverpool, 7 December 1973
Height: 5'8" **Weight:** 12.7
Club Honours: Div 3 '01; Div 2 '02
Lee joined Oxford in the 2002 close
season, the intention being that he would
be the man to score the goals to get
promotion. However things did not start
well with an ankle injury keeping him out

for almost all the first half of the campaign. When he came in he scored from the bench against Exeter and hit two more at Torquay to show his goal-scoring ability. Unfortunately his season ended prematurely due to a cruciate knee ligament injury, which is likely to keep him out of action until the autumn.

Shrewsbury T (£30,000 + from Northwich Vic on 23/7/1997) FL 104+9/37 FLC 5/3 FAC 4+1 Others 3

Brighton & Hove A (Free on 19/7/2000) FL 24+36/11 FLC 1+1 FAC 1+4 Others 4/1

Oxford U (Free on 12/7/2002) FL 3+7/3 FAC 0+1

STEPANOVS Igors
Born: Ogre, Latvia, 21 January 1976
Height: 6'4" **Weight:** 13.7
International Honours: Latvia: 57
This big strong, imposing central defender, found it difficult to command a first-team place for Arsenal last term and his only appearances were due to injury to regular and established team members. He played regularly in the reserves with some success, and captained the team on occasions.

Arsenal (£1,000,000 from Skonto Riga, Latvia, ex FK Ventspils, on 5/9/2000) PL 17 FLC 4+1/1 FAC 4 Others 4+1

STEPHENS Kevin
Born: Enfield, 28 July 1984
Height: 5'10" **Weight:** 12.5
Kevin started last season as a regular at centre half in the Leyton Orient youth and reserve teams. A series of promising displays led to him being rewarded with his senior debut at York in November and he also added a couple more appearances in the new year. Kevin showed enough ability to be awarded a new contract and will be looking to challenge the more established players for a place in the side in 2003-04.

Leyton Orient (Trainee) FL 2+1

STEPHENS Ross
Born: Llandidloes, 28 May 1985
Height: 5'7" **Weight:** 8.6
This promising young striker took his first steps into senior football when he came on as substitute in Shrewsbury's last game of the season against Scunthorpe. Ross did well on that occasion and will be looking to receive more experience of first-team football in 2003-04.

Shrewsbury T (Trainee) FL 0+1

STEVENS Dean William
Born: Torbay, 7 February 1986
Height: 5'10" **Weight:** 12.0
A first-year scholarship boy at Torquay, Dean made his bow in senior football as a substitute against Cambridge in September and added two further appearances from the bench early in the new year. The promising young striker then returned to the Gulls' youth team to continue his development.

Torquay U (Trainee) FL 0+3

STEVENS Ian David
Born: Malta, 21 October 1966
Height: 5'10" **Weight:** 12.6
Club Honours: AMC '89
This experienced striker made a surprise return to Shrewsbury during the 2002 close season. Signed mainly as cover for Nigel Jemson, he was restricted to only four starts with the remainder of his appearances coming from the bench. Ian never really got a chance to put any consistency into his game and had a somewhat disappointing campaign. Nevertheless, his appetite for goals was still there as he got a late equaliser against Hull in October and another in a draw against Darlington in November. He was released in the summer.

Preston NE (From apprentice on 22/11/1984) FL 9+2/2 Others 1

Stockport Co (Free on 27/10/1986) FL 1+1 FAC 0+1 Others 0+1 (Free to Lancaster C on 27/11/1986)

Steve Staunton

olton W *(Free on 25/3/1987) FL 26+21/7*
LC 1+2 FAC 4/2 Others 3+1
ury (Free on 3/7/1991) FL 100+10/38 FLC
+1 FAC 2+2 Others 7+1/2
hrewsbury T (£20,000 on 11/8/1994) FL
4+17/37 FLC 2+1 FAC 4+2/2 Others
0+2/12
arlisle U (£100,000 on 13/5/1997) FL
4+14/26 FLC 2 FAC 2/1 Others 3/2
Vrexham (Free on 5/7/1999) FL 14+2/4 FLC
FAC 1+1
heltenham T (Loaned on 21/3/2000) FL 1
arlisle U (Free on 7/8/2000) FL 64+3/20 FLC
/1 FAC 5/4
hrewsbury T (Free on 3/7/2002) FL 4+14/2
LC 0+1 Others 0+4

STEVENSON Jonathan (Jon)
Ashlee
Born: Leicester, 13 October 1932
Height: 5'6" **Weight:** 11.11
This livewire young striking prospect was
involved regularly from the bench for
Leicester City during the 2002-03 season,
scoring in the drubbing at Portman Road.
Although he looked a fine prospect, Jon's
career will develop away from the Walkers
Stadium as he was released by the club in
preparation for the return to the
Premiership.
Leicester C (From trainee on 26/3/2001) P/FL
+12/2 FLC 0+2

STEWART Gareth John
Born: Preston, 3 February 1980
Height: 6'0" **Weight:** 12.8
International Honours: E: Yth; Sch
Gareth was expected to start the 2002-03
season as first choice 'keeper for
Bournemouth, but an injury two days
before the start of the campaign ruled
him out. He returned in December for
the FA Cup tie against Southend, but had
the misfortune to suffer a broken leg after
just 18 minutes play. Once fully fit he sat
on the substitutes' bench and it was not
until the final day of the season that he
featured in action for the Cherries.
Blackburn Rov (From trainee on 11/2/1997)
Bournemouth (Free on 2/7/1999) FL 83+1
LC 1 FAC 6+1

STEWART Jordan Barrington
Born: Birmingham, 3 March 1982
Height: 5'11" **Weight:** 11.12
International Honours: E: U21-1
This left-footed midfielder or full back is
very highly rated by everyone at Leicester
and captured the local headlines by
scoring the first goal for the Foxes at the
Walkers Stadium when he netted in a pre-
season friendly. His progress last term was
interrupted by the need for a hernia

operation but his first-team future still
looks promising. Jordan scored a couple
of quality strikes when cutting inside after
tricky runs, at Wimbledon and at home to
Rotherham, and had an excellent game in
the vital home win over Forest in April. He
was called up for the England U21 squad
in March, making his debut as a second
half substitute in Portugal.
Leicester C (From trainee on 22/3/2000) P/FL
37+13/4 FLC 2+1 FAC 3+2
Bristol Rov (Loaned on 23/3/2000) FL 1+3

STEWART William Paul **Marcus**
Born: Bristol, 7 November 1972
Height: 5'10" **Weight:** 11.0
International Honours: E: Sch
Marcus played in four of the first five
matches for Ipswich in 2002-03, scoring
a last-minute winner at Avenir Beggin,
before joining Sunderland just before the
August transfer window closed. A left-
sided striker, his appearances were
sporadic following two changes of
manager, but he still impressed
supporters and management alike. A
neat, clever player with excellent close
control who, although a clinical finisher,
can also create chances for team mates,
Marcus was the only Sunderland player
to score two goals in a game on more
than one occasion last term, bagging
braces at Cambridge and Arsenal, both
in the Worthington Cup.
Bristol Rov (From trainee on 18/7/1991) FL
137+34/57 FLC 11/5 FAC 7+1/4 Others
16+1/14
Huddersfield T (£1,200,000 + on 2/7/1996)
FL 129+4/58 FLC 18/7 FAC 9/3
Ipswich T (£2,500,000 on 1/2/2000) P/FL
65+10/27 FLC 4+2/1 FAC 4/2 Others 8/7
Sunderland (£3,250,000 on 30/8/2002) PL
9+10/1 FLC 3/4 FAC 2/1

STEWART Michael James
Born: Edinburgh, 26 February 1981
Height: 5'11" **Weight:** 11.11
International Honours: S: 3; U21-7; Sch
A Manchester United player who
combines midfield aggression and
technique in equal measure, young
Michael Stewart might be heralded as
one for the future, but he still has to play
the waiting game at Old Trafford. A
solitary Premiership appearance against
Liverpool in December was followed by a
Worthington Cup outing against Burnley,
otherwise he featured just twice more
from the bench. Sure to get his chance
again sooner rather than later, Michael
will hope that patience is a virtue.
Manchester U (From trainee on 19/3/1998)
PL 5+2 FLC 2+1 FAC 0+1 Others 0+2

STIENS Craig
Born: Swansea, 31 July 1984
Height: 5'8" **Weight:** 12.6
International Honours: W: Yth
This young striker or wide midfield player
joined Swansea City in a long-term loan
deal. Although he regularly appeared on
the bench early on, he made just three
first-team appearances, all as a substitute.
Craig also represented Wales at U19 level
during the season.
Leeds U (From trainee on 2/8/2001)
Swansea C (Loaned on 13/12/2002) FL 0+3

ST LEDGER-HALL Sean Patrick
Born: Birmingham, 28 December 1984
Height: 6'0" **Weight:** 12.0
A promising central defender who
developed through the ranks at
Peterborough, Sean made his bow in
senior football when he replace Simon
Rea in the first half of Posh's home game
with Wycombe Wanderers in April.
Effective in the air and a good reader of
the game, he will be hoping to gain more
first-team experience in 2003-04.
Peterborough U (Trainee) FL 0+1

STOCK Brian Benjamin
Born: Winchester, 24 December 1981
Height: 5'11" **Weight:** 11.2
International Honours: W: U21-2
This young midfielder showed glimpses of
why he is so highly rated by Bournemouth
last season, none more so than during the
live televised match against Hartlepool
when he ran the game with a
tremendous display. Brian won his first
international honours with Wales at U21
level and would have featured more if not
for an appendix operation and the form
of Marcus Browning.
Bournemouth (From trainee on 25/1/2000)
FL 37+22/4 FAC 4 Others 5+3

STOCKDALE David Adam
Born: Leeds, 20 September 1985
Height: 6'3" **Weight:** 13.4
A first-year trainee with York City this
young 'keeper made good progress last
term. He went on to make his senior
debut when replacing Michael Ingham at
half time in the final game of the season
at Oxford.
York C (Trainee) FL 0+1

STOCKDALE Robert
(Robbie) Keith
Born: Redcar, 30 November 1979
Height: 5'11" **Weight:** 11.3
International Honours: S: 4; E: U21-1
Robbie was given a new lease of life with
the arrival of new manager Steve
McClaren at the Middlesbrough in the

summer of 2001 but was forced to miss a lot of last season's games through injury. Despite playing initially for the England U21 side the cultured right back earned his full international spurs with Scotland because his grandparents were born there. However, last season Robbie, when he was fully fit, was competing with Stuart Parnaby for the right-back spot and it was England U21 player Stuart who just edged ahead.

Middlesbrough *(From trainee on 2/7/1998) P/FL 62+11/2 FLC 8+1 FAC 7*
Sheffield Wed *(Loaned on 13/9/2000) FL 6*

STOCKLEY Samuel (Sam) Joshua

Born: Tiverton, 5 September 1977
Height: 6'0" **Weight:** 12.0

Sam may have changed his hairstyle with great regularity last season, but he proved far more consistent as a trusty right back for Colchester United. He originally arrived at Layer Road on loan from Oxford United, and impressed to such an extent that the Essex club chose to sign him on a long-term deal, despite an initial hiccup (over a clause in his contract) that caused him to sit out the 4-2 defeat at Mansfield.

Sam weighed in with a goal in the 1-1 home draw against Barnsley.

Southampton *(From trainee on 1/7/1996)*
Barnet *(Free on 31/12/1996) FL 177+5/2 FLC 10 FAC 4 Others 11*
Oxford U *(£150,000 on 13/7/2001) FL 39+2 FLC 1 FAC 1 Others 1*
Colchester U *(Free on 30/8/2002) FL 31+2/1 FAC 1 Others 1*

STOCKWELL Michael (Mick) Thomas

Born: Chelmsford, 14 February 1965
Height: 5'9" **Weight:** 11.4
Club Honours: Div 2 '92

Mick announced his retirement as a professional footballer after more than 20 years in the game. He made his final first-team appearance as a substitute in Colchester United's 1-0 home defeat by Queen's Park Rangers on the final day of the 2002-03 season, when he was given the captain's armband by skipper Scott Fitzgerald. Mick celebrated his 38th birthday on Valentine's Day, and he can be proud of his last three years with the U's, after such a long career at Ipswich. He played as a right back, wing back, right-sided midfielder and front runner during the final season. He could also boast an incredible run of playing in 140 successive games for Colchester, before missing the 2-0 win over Northampton in March. Mick will now look to go into coaching.

Ipswich T *(From apprentice on 17/12/1982) F/PL 464+42/35 FLC 43+5/5 FAC 28+3/2 Others 22+4/2*
Colchester U *(Free on 27/7/2000) FL 121+10/22 FLC 7/1 FAC 4 Others 3+1/1*

STOLCERS Andrejs

Born: Latvia, 8 July 1974
Height: 5'10" **Weight:** 11.4
Club Honours: Div 1 '01
International Honours: Latvia: 67

Always a fringe player during his three seasons with Fulham, Andrejs again spent much of the 2002-03 season in the reserves where he tended to operate in a wide midfield role. A rare outing in the Worthington Cup tie against Bury saw him score two fine goals in the 3-1 victory. A tricky player with pace who can provide excellent crosses, one memorable effort led to Louis Saha's match winner against Sunderland. Despite his lack of first-team opportunities he continued to be selected for the Latvian national side.

Fulham *(£2,000,000 + from Shakhtjor Donetsk, Ukraine, ex Olympija Riga, Skonto Riga, on 7/12/2000) P/FL 8+17/2 FLC 2+1/2 FAC 0+2 Others 0+1*

Mick Stockwell

STONE Daniel (Danny) John Cooper

Born: Liverpool, 14 September 1982
Height: 5'11" **Weight:** 12.4

This young Notts County defender never really made a breakthrough to the first-team squad last term although he made the starting line-up on 11 occasions. When selected Danny was used either at right back or in the centre of defence and never let the team down when called upon. He was released by County in the summer.

Notts Co (Free from trainee at Blackburn Rov on 25/8/2001) FL 16+5 FAC 2+1 Others 2+1

STONE Steven (Steve) Brian

Born: Gateshead, 20 August 1971
Height: 5'8" **Weight:** 12.7
Club Honours: Div 1 '98, '03
International Honours: E: 9

Steve featured in the pre-season Intertoto Cup matches for Aston Villa last term, but was unable to win a place in the line-up when the Premiership started. He joined Portsmouth on loan in October as Harry Redknapp looked to strengthen his squad. His initial period at Fratton Park was cut short by a hamstring injury, but he later signed on a permanent basis in December. Steve proved a key figure for Pompey and his presence in the side helped the youngsters around him to clinch promotion. A combative attacking midfielder, he scored five goals from 19 appearances at Fratton Park.

Nottingham F (From trainee on 20/5/1989) PL 189+4/23 FLC 14+1/2 FAC 11 Others 12/2
Aston Villa (£5,500,000 on 12/3/1999) PL 46+24/4 FLC 5+3/1 FAC 5+5/2 Others 10+4
Portsmouth (Loaned on 24/10/2002) FL 5/1
Portsmouth (Free on 20/12/2002) FL 13/3 FAC 1/1

STONEBRIDGE Ian Robert

Born: Lewisham, 30 August 1981
Height: 6'0" **Weight:** 11.4
Club Honours: Div 3 '02
International Honours: E: Yth

This popular young striker, now in his fourth season with Plymouth Argyle, featured regularly in the starting line-up last season although he was disappointed with his tally of seven goals. Ian had to wait until October to notch his first goal against Wigan Athletic. His strengths include excellent link-up play with the midfield and some deft flicks and passes to his striking partners. He has signed a further two-year contract to keep him at Home Park until June 2005.

Plymouth Arg (From trainee at Tottenham H on 13/7/1999) FL 103+38/33 FLC 2+2/1 FAC 5+2/4 Others 3+2/1

STRACHAN Gavin David

Born: Aberdeen, 23 December 1978
Height: 5'11" **Weight:** 11.7
International Honours: S: U21-8; Yth

Gavin overcame a pre-season hernia injury to be in contention for a first-team place with Coventry City in the autumn, but although he appeared on the bench for several games he was called upon just once, in the 3-0 home win over Derby. He subsequently had trials with Blackpool and Sheffield Wednesday before having a brief spell at Peterborough where he made one start. Gavin then joined Southend United on non-contract terms on the transfer deadline where he slotted into a central midfield role alongside Kevin Maher. However, he seemed to find it difficult to adapt to the hurly-burly of Third Division football and was released by the Blues at the end of the season.

Coventry C (From trainee on 28/11/1996) P/FL 5+11 FLC 1+3/1 FAC 2+2
Dundee (Loaned on 27/1/1999) SL 4+2
Peterborough U (Free on 14/3/2003) FL 1+1
Southend U (Free on 27/3/2003) FL 6+1

STREET Kevin

Born: Crewe, 25 November 1977
Height: 5'10" **Weight:** 10.8

Kevin began the 2002-03 campaign with Conference outfit Northwich Victoria prior to joining Bristol Rovers last November. The hard-working midfielder was immediately drafted into action and his passing and ball-winning qualities were used to good effect as the club struggled to retain their Football League status. His

Steve Stone

only goal of the season was enough to earn Rovers a draw at Southend and in the closing stages of the campaign he had to be content with appearances from the substitutes' bench.

Crewe Alex *(From trainee on 4/7/1996) FL 57+58/9 FLC 4+3 FAC 1+1 (Free to Northwich Vic during 2002 close season)*
Luton T *(Loaned on 20/11/2001) FL 1+1*
Bristol Rov *(Free on 29/11/2002) FL 13+7/1*

STRINGER Christopher (Chris)
Born: Sheffield, 19 September 1983
Height: 6'6" **Weight:** 12.0
This young goalkeeper found himself third choice for Sheffield Wednesday last term following the arrival of Paul Evans at Hillsborough. Chris made just three first-team appearances, two of which were as a substitute. He looked to have plenty of promise, but really needs a lengthy run of senior football to enable his career to progress.
Sheffield Wed *(From trainee on 20/6/2000) FL 6+3 FLC 0+1 FAC 2*

STRONG Gregory (Greg)
Born: Bolton, 5 September 1975
Height: 6'2" **Weight:** 12.12
International Honours: E: Yth; Sch
Greg joined Third Division Hull in the summer of 2002 to partner former Livingston centre back John Anderson in the City defence. Named captain, things started to go wrong for the left-footed defender when he was sent off in his second game for the Tigers at Bristol Rovers. Greg then faced a two-month lay off after dislocating an elbow in training, during which time manager Jan Molby was replaced by Peter Taylor. He subsequently failed to regain his place in the side and had two spells out on loan, firstly at Cheltenham, in the opening weeks of Bobby Gould's reign as boss, and then at Scunthorpe, where he helped tighten the defence in the closing stages of the campaign.
Wigan Ath *(From trainee on 1/10/1992) FL 28+7/3 FLC 5 FAC 1 Others 3+1*
Bolton W *(Signed on 10/9/1995) P/FL 10+2/1 FLC 8+2*
Blackpool *(Loaned on 21/11/1997) FL 11/1 Others 1*
Stoke C *(Loaned on 24/3/1999) FL 5/1*
Motherwell *(Loaned on 17/3/2000) SL 11*
Motherwell *(£150,000 on 14/7/2000) SL 62+2/3 SLC 1/1 SC 2*
Hull C *(Free on 17/6/2002) FL 3*
Cheltenham T *(Loaned on 4/2/2003) FL 3+1*
Scunthorpe U *(Loaned on 25/3/2003) FL 7 Others 2*

STRUPAR Branko
Born: Croatia, 9 February 1970
Height: 6'3" **Weight:** 13.7
International Honours: Belgium: 17
After fulfilling an ambition by going to the World Cup finals with Belgium, Branko hoped for better fortune at club level with Derby County last term. There was no such luck and he was out of action from late September, requiring an operation on anterior cruciate knee ligaments. It was frustrating for player and club, as well as depriving supporters of one of their heroes, but injuries have dogged him since he joined Derby from KRC Genk. At his best, the striker has a sure touch in front of goal and can hit deadly free kicks but, taking his fitness record into account, it was no surprise when he was released at the end of his contract.
Derby Co *(£3,000,000 from KRC Genk, Belgium, ex Spansko, on 17/12/1999) P/FL 32+9/16 FLC 2*

STUART Graham Charles
Born: Tooting, 24 October 1970
Height: 5'9" **Weight:** 11.10
Club Honours: FAC '95; Div 1 '00
International Honours: E: U21-5; Yth
Graham started the 2002-03 campaign as club captain for Charlton, but suffered a cruciate ligament injury in only the second game when crossing the ball for Jason Euell to score the winning goal at Bolton. This virtually finished his season, although he made a brief comeback in the game at Middlesbrough and then had to wait until the final game of the season before he added another appearance, this time as a late substitute. Graham is a hard-working attacking midfielder who likes to play just behind the front two. He is a strong tackler and excellent distributor of the ball.
Chelsea *(From trainee on 15/6/1989) F/PL 70+17/14 FLC 11/2 FAC 5+2/1 Others 3+2/1*
Everton *(£850,000 on 19/8/1993) PL 116+20/22 FLC 9/3 FAC 10+3/5 Others 2+1/1*
Sheffield U *(£850,000 on 28/11/1997) FL 52+1/11 FLC 4 FAC 10+1/1 Others 0+1*
Charlton Ath *(£1,100,000 on 25/3/1999) P/FL 109+7/19 FLC 4 FAC 7/2*

STUART Jamie Christopher
Born: Southwark, 15 October 1976
Height: 5'10" **Weight:** 11.0
International Honours: E: U21-4; Yth
Jamie was generally regarded as the first choice left back at Bury throughout the 2002-03 campaign, but the tough-tackling defender never really found the

consistency that he had managed throughout the previous season. He headed the winner against Stoke City in the Worthington Cup for what was his only goal of the season, but he was also dismissed on two occasions.
Charlton Ath *(From trainee on 18/1/1995) F 49+1/3 FLC 8+1 FAC 3 Others 0+1*
Millwall *(Free on 25/9/1998) FL 42+3 FLC 2 FAC 1 Others 6*
Bury *(Free, via trial at Cambridge U, on 8/10/2001) FL 56+5/1 FLC 2+1/1 FAC 2+1 Others 4*

STUBBS Alan
Born: Liverpool, 6 October 1971
Height: 6'2" **Weight:** 13.10
Club Honours: SPD '98, '00; SLC '97, '9
International Honours: E: B-1
A rugged centre-half and lifelong Blue, Alan's consistent performances meant that he made more Premiership starts than any other Everton player last season and achieved a personal ambition when captaining the team for the first time at Tottenham. Having started the season well, Alan lost his place following a red card against Birmingham in August, only to force his way back into the side at West Ham in October, and from then on he was ever-present. A fine passer of the ball and dead-ball expert, Alan surprisingly failed to find the target last year, although his physical presence in the opposition penalty area was always a threat.
Bolton W *(From trainee on 24/7/1990) P/FL 181+21/9 FLC 23/4 FAC 16+2/2 Others 12+1*
Glasgow Celtic *(£3,500,000 on 10/7/1996) SL 101+5/3 SLC 8+1 SC 11 Others 16+1/2*
Everton *(Free on 13/7/2001) PL 63+3/2 FLC 2+1 FAC 6/1*

STURRIDGE Dean Constantine
Born: Birmingham, 27 July 1973
Height: 5'8" **Weight:** 12.1
Dean had been a prolific scorer in his first six months at Wolves, but was injured in a pre-season friendly with Newcastle. He soon eased his way into the team, yet the goals did not come quite so freely. An exception was the turn and shot against Preston which was a classic striker's goal. Dean reverted to the bench, before he capped a short run in the side with a dramatic headed winner against Nottingham Forest. Fitness problems hampered his progress early in 2003, and he rarely made the starting line-up thereafter.
Derby Co *(From trainee on 1/7/1991) P/FL 142+48/53 FLC 9+4/4 FAC 8/2 Others 2+1*
Torquay U *(Loaned on 16/12/1994) FL 10/5*

eicester C *(£350,000 on 19/1/2001) PL
0+2/6 FLC 1 FAC 2/1*
Wolverhampton W *(£375,000 on
3/11/2001) FL 44+22/30 FLC 1+1 FAC 1+1
Others 2+3/1*

STURROCK Blair David
Born: Dundee, 25 August 1981
Height: 6'0" **Weight:** 11.1
Club Honours: Div 3 '02
Blair once again struggled for regular
starting opportunities with Plymouth
Argyle last season and was used mainly
from the substitutes' bench. A pacy right-
sided midfielder who can also play up
front, he notched two goals during the
campaign. Blair will be aiming to feature
more regularly in the starting line-up in
2003-04. He is the son of Argyle manager
Paul Sturrock.
*Dundee U (From juniors on 5/9/1999)
Brechin C (Loaned on 8/8/2000) SL 20+7/6
FC 1+2 Others 3+1/3
Plymouth Arg (Free on 26/10/2001) FL
+30/2 FLC 1/1 FAC 0+5 Others 1*

SUKUR Hakan
Born: Sakarya, Turkey, 1 September 1971
Height: 6'3" **Weight:** 12.11
International Honours: Turkey: 84
This veteran Turkish international striker
joined Blackburn Rovers on a contract for
the remainder of the season last
December. He had the misfortune to
suffer a broken leg in training soon after
his arrival but worked his way back to
fitness and went on to make his bow in
the Premiership in the home game against
Manchester City in March. His mobility
and work rate were impressive while he
contributed two classic strikes in the 4-0
win at Fulham in April.
*Blackburn Rov (Free from Parma, Italy, ex
Sakaryaspor, Bursaspor, Galatasaray, Inter
Milan, on 6/12/2002) PL 7+2/2*

SUMMERBEE Nicholas
(Nicky) John
Born: Altrincham, 26 August 1971
Height: 5'11" **Weight:** 12.8
Club Honours: Div 1 '99
International Honours: E: B-1; U21-3
This elegant, skilful right winger initially
joined Leicester City in tandem with Billy
McKinlay in an agreement to play for free
to try to win a contract. Nicky's deal was
later extended to the end of the season
and he regularly contributed to the Foxes'
performances with a string of dangerous
crosses, creating several goals for Brian
Deane in particular. Mostly used from the
bench, he was particularly effective in the
way win at Turf Moor in March.
However, at the end of the season his
contract was not renewed.

Swindon T *(From trainee on 20/7/1989) F/PL
89+23/6 FLC 9+1/3 FAC 2+3 Others 7/1*
Manchester C *(£1,500,000 on 24/6/1994)
P/FL 119+12/6 FLC 11+2/2 FAC 12/2*
Sunderland *(£1,000,000 on 14/11/1997)
P/FL 87+6/7 FLC 6+1 FAC 4+1 Others 3/1*
Bolton W *(Free on 4/1/2001) FL 9+3/1 FAC 3*
Nottingham F *(Free on 9/11/2001) FL 17/2
FAC 1*
Leicester C *(Free on 9/8/2002) FL 7+22 FLC
1+1 FAC 2*

SUMMERBELL Mark
Born: Durham, 30 October 1976
Height: 5'9" **Weight:** 11.9
Signed by Carlisle United early on in the
2002-03 campaign, Mark is an 'engine
room' type of midfielder who works hard
as a ball winner and disrupter of opposing
attacks. A consistent performer who
always displayed total commitment in his
approach to his game, defensive duties
meant that he rarely featured in the
opposition's penalty area. However his
goal at Torquay at the end of April helped
secure a vital three points in United's
successful battle against the drop.
*Middlesbrough (From trainee on 1/7/1995)
F/PL 35+16/1 FLC 4+3/3
Bristol C (Loaned on 28/9/2001) FL 5
Portsmouth (Loaned on 28/3/2002) FL 5
Carlisle U (Free on 23/8/2002) FL 39/1 FLC 1
FAC 2 Others 5*

SUTCH Daryl
Born: Beccles, 11 September 1971
Height: 6'0" **Weight:** 12.0
International Honours: E: U21-4; Yth
This experienced campaigner failed to
make the Norwich City first team last
term and in February he joined Southend
United on a short-term contract, linking
up once more with former team mate
Rob Newman. Daryl performed well at full
back and his raiding runs down the flank
were a great benefit to the Blues,
although he sometimes struggled for pace
when occasionally asked to fill in at centre
back. Daryl was injured at York in March
and rarely figured as the season drew to a
close. He was not offered a new deal and
left Roots Hall at the season's end.
*Norwich C (From trainee on 6/7/1990) F/PL
255+50/9 FLC 24+3 FAC 10+3 Others 2+5
Southend U (Free on 3/1/2003) FL 16/1*

SUTTON John William Michael
Born: Norwich, 26 December 1983
Height: 6'0" **Weight:** 14.2
International Honours: E: Yth
This young striker managed to progress to
the Tottenham reserve team and in
October he spent time on loan at Carlisle

where he featured regularly in the line-up,
scoring once. However, soon after he
returned to White Hart Lane he was
released and he then had a short spell at
Swindon, where he made one appearance
as a substitute, coming on in the home
defeat by Crewe. However John was soon
on his way from the County Ground and
towards the end of the season he had a
trial at Southend. He is the younger
brother of Chris and the son of ex-
Carlisle, Norwich and Chester midfielder
Mike.
*Tottenham H (From trainee on 12/7/2001)
Carlisle U (Loaned on 4/10/2002) FL 7/1 FAC
1 Others 2
Swindon T (Free on 20/12/2002) FL 0+1*

SVARD Sebastian
Born: Hividovre, Denmark, 15 January
1983
Height: 6'1" **Weight:** 12.11
Club Honours: FAYC '01
International Honours: Denmark: "21-4;
Yth
Sebastian is an intelligent midfield player
who trained regularly with the Arsenal
first-team squad last term. His only senior
appearances came in the Worthington
Cup tie against Sunderland and in the FA
Cup against Oxford. Sebastian
represented Denmark at U21 level during
the season.
*Arsenal (Signed from FC Copenhagen,
Denmark on 1/11/2000) FLC 1+1 FAC 1*

SVENSSON Anders
Born: Sweden, 17 July 1976
Height: 5'10" **Weight:** 12.11
International Honours: Sweden: 38
Anders' performances for Sweden against
England and Argentina in the 2002 World
Cup finals fulfilled the promise that he
had shown throughout the preceding
season at Southampton. He continued to
show similar form in 2002-03, and from
time to time he showed flashes of genius.
He is capable of dextrous ball play in the
tightest situations from any position in the
Saints' midfield and possesses the ability
to thread the proverbial 'eye of the
needle' with his passes.
*Southampton (£750,000 from IF Elfsborg,
Sweden, ex Hestrafors, on 16/7/2001) PL
59+8/6 FLC 4/2 FAC 7+1/2*

SVENSSON Mathias (Matt)
Born: Boras, Sweden, 24 September
1974
Height: 6'0" **Weight:** 12.4
Club Honours: Div 1 '00
International Honours: Sweden: 3
Last term proved to be a rather frustrating
time for Matt, who started the season on

the bench for Charlton and then played a couple of games up front before being replaced by Shaun Bartlett. He rarely made the starting line-up after this and was mostly restricted to appearances as a substitute, many of which came too late in the game to make a difference. He was instrumental in creating Jonatan Johansson's late goal which went in off a defender against Aston Villa at the Valley in February, but that was as near as he got to a goal himself. Matt is a strong, aggressive striker who is excellent in the air, works very hard and is unselfish.
Portsmouth (£200,000 from Elfsborg, Sweden on 6/12/1996) FL 34+11/10 FLC 1/1 FAC 3+2/1 (£100,000 to Tirol Innsbruck, Austria on 15/7/1998)
Crystal Palace (£100,000 on 29/9/1998) FL 26+6/10 FLC 2 FAC 1
Charlton Ath (£600,000 on 28/1/2000) P/FL 41+26/7 FLC 0+1 FAC 2+4/1

SVENSSON Michael
Born: Sweden, 25 November 1975
Height: 6'2" **Weight:** 13.8
International Honours: Sweden: 20
Michael signed for Southampton on returning with the Sweden squad from the 2002 World Cup finals. Tall and willowy, he plays a lot harder than he looks from the sidelines and, being one of those central defenders who likes to get in his tackles and contest aerial balls early, he could be described as impetuous; a trait that has, occasionally, attracted the disapproval of match officials. He had many high points in his first Premiership season, but hitting the opening hit in the 4–0 defeat of Spurs in the third round of the FA Cup at St Mary's was certainly one, as was scoring the last-ever goal at Manchester City's Maine Road in Saints' 1–0 win there.
Southampton (£2,000,000 from Troyes, France, ex Halmstads BK, on 12/7/2002) PL 33+1/2 FLC 2/1 FAC 7/1

SWAILES Christopher (Chris)
William
Born: Gateshead, 19 October 1970
Height: 6'2" **Weight:** 12.11
This powerful central defender has a tremendous attitude to the game and never knows when he is beaten. Chris formed a formidable partnership at the back with Martin McIntosh for Rotherham as the pair more than held their own. His never-say-die approach epitomised the Millers' season and in addition to his defensive role, he also played a vital part in opposing penalty areas with his aerial strength proving to be useful in setting up chances.

Ipswich T (From trainee on 23/5/1989)
Peterborough U (£10,000 on 28/3/1991. Free to Boston U in August 1991)
Doncaster Rov (Free from Bridlington T on 27/10/1993) FL 49 FLC 2/1 FAC 1 Others 2
Ipswich T (£225,000 on 23/3/1995) P/FL 34+3/1 FLC 3 Others 2
Bury (£200,000 on 14/11/1997) FL 125+1/10 FLC 9 FAC 8 Others 3/1
Rotherham U (Free on 1/7/2001) FL 87/9 FLC 6/1 FAC 3

SWAILES Daniel (Danny)
Born: Bolton, 1 April 1979
Height: 6'3" **Weight:** 13.0
Danny enjoyed another solid season at the heart of the Bury defence in 2002-03. Dominant in the air, and also possessing the ability to move upfield and score important goals, only his distribution possibly prevents him from playing at a higher level. He broke his nose against Southend in October and also encountered mixed fortunes in the home game against Swansea City when he scored for both teams.
Bury (From trainee on 9/7/1997) FL 92+10/7 FLC 3+3 FAC 7+1 Others 8+2/1

SWEENEY Antony Thomas
Born: Stockton, 5 September 1983
Height: 6'0" **Weight:** 11.9
Antony is a young midfielder who looked to be on the verge of winning a first-team place at Hartlepool at the start of the 2002-03 season. He made the line-up for the opening league game at Carlisle, but was then rested as manager Chris Turner decided to go for experience. Unfortunately his big breakthrough at senior level did not materialise, but when he did make his rare appearances he did not let the side down.
Hartlepool U (From trainee on 10/1/2002) FL 2+4 Others 1

SWEENEY Peter Henry
Born: Glasgow, 25 September 1984
Height: 6'0" **Weight:** 12.0
International Honours: S: Yth
This promising young left-sided midfielder has great pace and can shoot with either foot. After developing through the Millwall academy sides he made his senior debut in the 2001-02 campaign, and last term he managed a handful more appearances for the senior team including his first start. He also scored a cracking goal in the 4-0 home win against Watford in January, cutting inside to find the net with a great right-foot shot. Peter represented Scotland at U19 level during the season, winning three caps.

Millwall (Free from juniors on 13/12/2000) FL 1+5/1 FAC 0+1

SWIERCZEWSKI Piotr
Born: Nowy Sacz, Poland, 8 April 1972
Height: 6'0" **Weight:** 12.1
International Honours: Poland: 69
Piotr joined Birmingham City on loan from Marseille during the transfer window but was unable to break up the Robbie Savage-Stephen Clemence central midfield partnership. His only Premiership appearance came as a second half substitute for Jeff Kenna against Chelsea in February, otherwise he proved to be a steady, reliable performer in the reserves. Lack of first-team action put his international place in jeopardy although he added a couple of caps to his impressive tally.
Birmingham C (£1,000,000 + from Marseilles, France, ex GKS Katowice, St Etienne, Bastia, on 23/1/2003) PL 0+1

SWONNELL Samuel (Sam)
Alfred
Born: Brentwood, 13 September 1982
Height: 5'10" **Weight:** 11.10
A central midfield player developed by the Watford academy, Sam faced strong competition for a first-team place but made his senior debut at Brighton. A busy and intelligent player, Sam's moment of glory came when he captained the club's reserves to a surprising success in the Barclaycard Premiership Reserve League South.
Watford (From trainee on 7/3/2001) FL 1+1

SYMONS Christopher (Kit)
Jeremiah
Born: Basingstoke, 8 March 1971
Height: 6'2" **Weight:** 13.7
Club Honours: Div 2 '99; Div 1 '01
International Honours: W: 36; B-1; U21-2; Yth
This experienced central defender missed the start of the 2002-03 campaign at Crystal Palace due to a recurrence of a knee injury. He returned to action in November and was a regular thereafter, quickly returning to his best form and even winning a recall to the Wales international squad, although he failed to add to his tally of caps.
Portsmouth (From trainee on 30/12/1988) FL 161/10 FLC 19 FAC 10 Others 13+1/1
Manchester C (£1,600,000 on 17/8/1995) P/FL 124/4 FLC 6 FAC 9
Fulham (Free on 30/7/1998) P/FL 96+6/13 FLC 15+1/1 FAC 12
Crystal Palace (£400,000 on 7/12/2001) FL 30+4 FLC 2 FAC 5

T

TABB Jay Anthony
Born: London, 21 February 1984
Height: 5'5" **Weight:** 9.7
This exciting left-footed attacking midfielder missed most of Brentford's season in 2002-03. Jay broke his foot during the pre-season, not returning until November, and then got injured in training in February before returning for the last few games of the campaign. He will be looking to make a breakthrough at first-team level in 2003-04.
Brentford (From trainee on 23/7/2001) FL 2+8 FAC 0+1 Others 1+1

TAGGART Gerald (Gerry) Paul
Born: Belfast, 18 October 1970
Height: 6'1" **Weight:** 13.12
Club Honours: Div 1 '97; FLC '00
International Honours: NI: 51; U23-2; Yth; Sch
This left-footed central defender quickly re-established his place at the heart of the Leicester City defence last season, and also earned an early recall to the Northern Ireland squad. Ever popular with the fans, Gerry was looking to renew his goal-scoring competition with fellow central defender Matt Elliott, having opened his account against Coventry. Like Elliott, his experience and reading of the game more than made up for any dwindling pace, particularly in the long unbeaten run late in the season that took the Foxes to promotion.
Manchester C (From trainee on 1/7/1989) FL 0+2/1 Others 1
Barnsley (£75,000 on 10/1/1990) FL 209+3/16 FLC 15/1 FAC 14/2 Others 6/1
Bolton W (£1,500,000 on 1/8/1995) F/PL 68+1/4 FLC 8/1 FAC 4
Leicester C (Free on 23/7/1998) P/FL 96+12/9 FLC 12+2/2 FAC 8+1 Others 2/1

TAIT Paul
Born: Newcastle, 24 October 1974
Height: 6'1" **Weight:** 11.10
This tall striker soon won over the supporters at Bristol Rovers last term after producing some hard-working performances. Displaying a good first touch and aerial ability Paul scored eight goals during the season including two fine match winners at Swansea City and Leyton Orient. He lost his place in the starting line-up for the last two months of the campaign but was recalled for the final match at Kidderminster when he scored an equaliser for Rovers.
Everton (From trainee on 8/7/1993)
Wigan Ath (Free on 22/7/1994) FL 1+4 (Free to Runcorn on 16/2/1996)
Crewe Alex (Signed from Northwich Vic on 9/6/1999) FL 31+32/6 FLC 0+1 FAC 1+1
Hull C (Loaned on 5/11/2001) FL 0+2
Bristol Rov (Free on 12/7/2002) FL 33+8/7 FLC 1 FAC 4/1

TALBOT Daniel Brian
Born: Enfield, 30 January 1984
Height: 5'9" **Weight:** 10.9
Club Honours: Div 3 '03
This young full back managed just seven starts for Rushden & Diamonds last term, but came off the bench to change the course of the game at Hartlepool and earn himself a contract extension. Daniel is the son of former England international Brian Talbot who is also the Diamonds' manager.
Rushden & Diamonds (From juniors on 10/2/2001) FL 7+9 FLC 1 Others 2

TALBOT Stewart Dean
Born: Birmingham, 14 June 1973
Height: 5'11" **Weight:** 13.7
This powerful Rotherham midfield player picked up an injury in the early part of the 2002-03 season and this kept him out of action for some time. On his return to fitness, Stewart had to be content with a place on the substitutes' bench, but he scored a vital goal in a great 2-1 win at Ipswich in a rare starting appearance. In order to get some first-team games under his belt, he went on loan to Shrewsbury Town, where he did well, contributing to a useful run of results in what was a poor season for the club. On his return to Millmoor Stewart appeared in a couple more games, adding much needed bite to the middle of the park.
Port Vale (Signed from Moor Green on 10/8/1994) FL 112+25/10 FLC 4+3 FAC 4+1 Others 2+3/1
Rotherham U (Free on 13/7/2000) FL 81+10/7 FLC 3 FAC 4+1
Shrewsbury T (Loaned on 11/2/2003) FL 5 Others 2

TALIA Francesco (Frank)
Born: Melbourne, Australia, 20 July 1972
Height: 6'1" **Weight:** 13.6
Club Honours: Div 2 '96
International Honours: Australia: Sch
This experienced goalkeeper left pre-season training at Bristol City to join Wycombe Wanderers on a short- term contract, as cover for the injured Martin Taylor. Although Taylor recovered in time for the season's start he only went two weeks before receiving another injury and Frank made his debut, ironically at Ashton Gate. In spite of the 3-0 defeat he impressed with his reflex saves and general all-round handling skills. The pair then alternated in short runs of games until manager Lawrie Sanchez made Frank first choice for the Boxing Day clash at Queen's Park Rangers and he was ever-present from then on.
Blackburn Rov (Free from Sunshine George Cross, Australia on 28/8/1992)
Hartlepool U (Loaned on 29/12/1992) FL 14 Others 1
Swindon T (£150,000 on 8/9/1995) FL 107 FLC 9 FAC 2
Sheffield U (Free, via trial at Wolverhampton W on 26/9/2000) FL 6 (Freed during 2001 close season)
Reading (Free from Royal Antwerp, Belgium on 15/3/2002)
Wycombe W (Free on 9/8/2002) FL 35 FLC 1 FAC 1 Others 1

TANN Adam John
Born: Kings Lynn, 12 May 1982
Height: 6'0" **Weight:** 11.5
International Honours: E: Yth
A pre-season injury kept this Cambridge United defender out of the line-up at the start of the campaign, but he soon forced his way back. He featured regularly from then on and scored his first goal for the club with an 18-yard header soon after returning to action.
Cambridge U (From trainee on 7/9/1999) FL 46+5/1 FAC 6/2 Others 12/1

TAPP Alexander (Alex) Nicholas
Born: Redhill, 7 June 1982
Height: 5'8" **Weight:** 11.10
Alex is a very competitive, tough-tackling left-sided midfielder who made his league debut for Wimbledon in the home match against Wolves last August. A run of ten consecutive games followed as he quickly settled in, and though he subsequently missed a few starts during the middle of the campaign, he had 11 more consecutive matches at the season's end. Not the tallest or indeed quickest of players, he compensates with good positional sense, and possesses a fearsome shot from the edge of the area. Alex was given an extended contract during the season and he has every chance of remaining a very useful member of the squad.
Wimbledon (From trainee on 10/1/2000) FL 23+1/2 FLC 2/1 FAC 1

Gerry Taggart

TARDIF Christopher (Chris) Luke

Born: Guernsey, 19 September 1979
Height: 5'11" **Weight:** 12.7
This young 'keeper joined Bournemouth on a 12-month loan deal from Portsmouth and started the 2002-03 season in the team after Gareth Stewart was sidelined by injury. A couple of hesitant performances saw Jamie Ashdown brought in, but Chris knuckled down and despite a couple of injuries he returned to play a hero's role in the FA Cup tie at Crewe. The arrival of Neil Moss meant that he made his last appearance in February and he returned to Fratton Park in the summer.
Portsmouth (From trainee on 3/7/1998) FL +2 FAC 1
Bournemouth (Loaned on 9/8/2002) FL 9 FLC 1 FAC 3+1 Others 1

TARICCO Mauricio Ricardo

Born: Buenos Aires, Argentine, 10 March 1973
Height: 5'9" **Weight:** 11.7
This tenacious defender put his disciplinary problems of 2001-02 behind him last season to become a regular for Tottenham, despite a recurring groin injury early in the campaign. Often used down the right, Mauricio is strong and confident on the ball and enjoys linking up with the midfield. He seemed happier on the left flank and was delighted to net his first Premiership goal last March.
Ipswich T (£175,000 from Argentinos Juniors, Argentina on 9/9/1994) FL 134+3/4 FLC 18/3 FAC 8 Others 7
Tottenham H (£1,800,000 on 4/12/1998) PL 84+4/1 FLC 9 FAC 7+2 Others 3

TATE Alan

Born: Easington, 2 September 1982
Height: 6'1" **Weight:** 13.9
This promising Manchester United central defender had spent the second half of the 2001-02 season on loan at Royal Antwerp, and last term he spent most of the campaign out on loan with Third Division strugglers Swansea City. Alan displayed good defensive awareness and accurate distribution skills at the Vetch Field. He took some time to adjust to the demands of the lower division football, but played a major role in the club's successful escape from relegation with his cool defensive play.
Manchester U (From trainee on 18/7/2000)
Swansea C (Loaned on 22/11/2002) FL 27

TATE Christopher (Chris) Douglas

Born: York, 27 December 1977
Height: 6'0" **Weight:** 11.10
Chris started the 2002-03 season in the Leyton Orient reserve team and in November he joined Chester City on loan. He was quickly recalled to Brisbane Road after scoring the winning goal in the FA Cup tie against Colchester and seemed to show a new lease of life. The experienced striker then remained a regular for the rest of the season, scoring his share of goals and showing his value at both ends of the pitch with his skills in the air.
Sunderland (From trainee at York C on 17/7/1996)
Scarborough (Free on 5/8/1997) FL 21+28/13 FLC 0+1 FAC 0+1 Others 2+1
Halifax T (£150,000 on 5/7/1999) FL 18/4 FLC 2 FAC 2/1 (£80,000 to Scarborough on 16/12/1999)
Leyton Orient (£25,000 on 3/11/2000) FL 29+23/9 FAC 1+2/1 Others 1+2/1

TAVLARIDIS Efstathios (Stathis)

Born: Greece, 25 January 1980
Height: 6'2" **Weight:** 12.11
International Honours: Greece: U21
This tall young central defender made only one first-team appearance for Arsenal last term, featuring in the Worthington Cup tie against Sunderland. He was a regular with the reserves and also had a spell on loan at Portsmouth. Although pitched straight into a difficult FA Cup tie at Old Trafford due to injury problems he performed competently and added a further four appearances for Pompey before returning to Highbury.
Arsenal (£600,000 from Iraklis, Greece on 21/9/2001) PL 0+1 FLC 4
Portsmouth (Loaned on 2/1/2003) FL 3+1 FAC 1

TAYLOR Christopher (Chris) James

Born: Swindon, 30 October 1985
Height: 5'8" **Weight:** 10.5
A regular member of the Swindon Town U19 side, this young midfielder made his league debut as a late substitute at Crewe last April. He was not overawed by the occasion, giving a mature display highlighted by his effective distribution of the ball. He repeated the performance when given a longer run during the next game and was also involved during the Robins' final two fixtures.
Swindon T (Trainee) FL 0+4

TAYLOR Cleveland Ken Wayne

Born: Leicester, 9 September 1983
Height: 5'8" **Weight:** 11.5
This attacking midfielder joined Exeter City in a long-term loan deal during the 2002 close season, but managed only three first-team appearances before returning to the Reebok. Later in the season he had another loan spell at Conference club Scarborough. Cleveland will be looking to gain further experience of senior football in 2003-04.
Bolton W (From trainee on 5/8/2002) FAC 0+1
Exeter C (Loaned on 9/8/2002) FL 1+2

TAYLOR Craig

Born: Plymouth, 24 January 1974
Height: 6'1" **Weight:** 13.2
Craig returned to full fitness after a long injury lay-off and enjoyed a spell on loan at Torquay early in the new year. Signed by the Gulls to shore up a jittery back four, his experience and organisational skills proved beneficial and the defence conceded just three goals in his five appearances. After returning to Plymouth he managed a single first-team appearance against Northampton Town in April. This tall, powerful centre half will be looking for more first-team opportunities in the 2003-04 campaign.
Exeter C (From trainee on 13/6/1992) FL 2+3 FLC 1 Others 2+2 (Free to Bath C on 18/3/1994)
Swindon T (£25,000 from Dorchester T on 15/4/1997) FL 47+8/2 FLC 0+1 FAC 3
Plymouth Arg (Loaned on 16/10/1998) FL 6/1
Plymouth Arg (£30,000 on 20/8/1999) FL 80+2/6 FLC 2 FAC 7 Others 1/1
Torquay U (Loaned on 24/2/2003) FL 5

TAYLOR Gareth Keith

Born: Weston super Mare, 25 February 1973
Height: 6'2" **Weight:** 13.8
International Honours: W: 12; U21-7
Burnley's supporters have been slow to take to Gareth, but 2002-03 saw the big striker finally gain full acceptance from the Turf Moor crowd as he was arguably the Clarets' most consistent performer of the season. A regular scorer, he showed much more of his all-round ability than before, often running himself into the ground in the team's cause, helping out in defence as well as being the main spearhead of the attack. Aerial ability remains his biggest asset, but his overall competitiveness was an example to those around him. Gareth's only hat-trick came in the home match against Watford, but was unfortunately overshadowed as Burnley were beaten 7-4!
Bristol Rov (From trainee at Southampton on 29/7/1991) FL 31+16/16 FLC 3+1 FAC 1+1 Others 5
Crystal Palace (£750,000 on 27/9/1995) FL 18+2/1 FAC 2/1

Sheffield U (Signed on 8/3/1996) FL 56+28/25 FLC 8+3/2 FAC 5+2 Others 1+2
Manchester C (£400,000 on 26/11/1998) FL 28+15/9 FLC 2+1/1 FAC 3 Others 1+3
Port Vale (Loaned on 21/11/2000) FL 4
Queens Park R (Loaned on 14/3/2000) FL 2+4/1
Burnley (Free on 20/2/2001) FL 88+7/36 FLC 4+1 FAC 6/1

TAYLOR Ian Kenneth
Born: Birmingham, 4 June 1968
Height: 6'1" **Weight:** 12.4
Club Honours: AMC '93; FLC '96
Ian had a disappointing season at Aston Villa last term when he struggled to combat a string of injuries. He scored in the first leg of the Intertoto Cup tie against Lille, but suffered a recurrence of his calf injury in the return match and this kept him out of action until the end of October. He then completed his longest spell in the side with a run of eight games (his return to the team just happened to coincide with Villa's best run of the season!) before limping off with a thigh strain in the Worthington Cup game against Preston. Finally a thigh muscle injury also kept him out for a while, restricting his appearances even further. A Villa man through and through, Ian's dedication, industry and work rate are second to none. He is one of that priceless breed of goal-scoring midfielders who can pop up from nowhere to stick the ball into the net.
Port Vale (£15,000 from Moor Green on 13/7/1992) FL 83/28 FLC 4/2 FAC 6/1 Others 13/4
Sheffield Wed (£1,000,000 on 12/7/1994) PL 9+5/1 FLC 2+2/1
Aston Villa (£1,000,000 on 21/12/1994) PL 202+31/28 FLC 20+2/8 FAC 14+3/2 Others 18+1/5

TAYLOR John Patrick
Born: Norwich, 24 October 1964
Height: 6'2" **Weight:** 13.12
Club Honours: Div 3 '91
Cambridge United's manager and all-time leading scorer made one more appearance during his testimonial season, coming off the bench for the final 20 minutes of the last match of the campaign against Boston United. In that time he came close to scoring on two occasions and showed that even with his advancing years he still had an eye for goal.
Colchester U (From juniors on 17/12/1982) FLC 0+1 (Freed during 1984 close season)
Cambridge U (Signed from Sudbury T on

24/8/1988) FL 139+21/46 FLC 9+2/2 FAC 21/10 Others 12+2/2
Bristol Rov (Signed on 28/3/1992) FL 91+4/44 FLC 4 FAC 3 Others 5
Bradford C (£300,000 on 5/7/1994) FL 35+1/11 FLC 4/2 FAC 2 Others 3
Luton T (£200,000 on 23/3/1995) FL 27+10/3 FLC 2 Others 1/1
Lincoln C (Loaned on 27/9/1996) FL 5/2
Colchester U (Loaned on 8/11/1996) FL 8/5 Others 1
Cambridge U (Free on 10/1/1997) FL 97+69/40 FLC 3+6/1 FAC 6+6/1 Others 1+2/1

TAYLOR Maik Stefan
Born: Hildeshein, Germany, 4 September 1971
Height: 6'4" **Weight:** 14.2
Club Honours: Div 2 '99; Div 1 '01
International Honours: NI: 29; B-1; U21-1
Although first choice for Northern Ireland throughout the 2002-03 season, Maik again started the domestic season as deputy to Edwin van der Sar at Fulham, making only rare appearances in the Intertoto and Worthington Cup matches. An injury to the Dutchman at Newcastle in December promoted Maik back to first choice and he grabbed the chance with both hands, giving a number of faultless performances. An excellent shot stopper and rarely second best in one-on-one situations, his finest display of the season came at Liverpool earning him the right to remain first choice when van der Sar was fit.
Barnet (Free from Farnborough on 7/6/1995) FL 70 FLC 6 FAC 6 Others 2
Southampton (£500,000 on 1/1/1997) PL 18
Fulham (£800,000 + on 17/11/1997) P/FL 183+1 FLC 22 FAC 20 Others 6

TAYLOR Martin
Born: Ashington, 9 November 1979
Height: 6'4" **Weight:** 15.0
Club Honours: FLC '02
International Honours: E: U21-1; Yth
Martin grew in maturity at Blackburn last season, beginning to realise some of his vast potential. Although still a little inconsistent, at times he looked the complete all-purpose centre back. He also showed his versatility when filling in adequately at full back when required. A regular at first-team level, he netted two goals, both coming in the 5-2 home victory over Newcastle in October.
Blackburn Rov (From trainee on 13/8/1997) P/FL 58+19/5 FLC 16 FAC 13+1/1 Others 3+1
Darlington (Loaned on 18/1/2000) FL 4
Stockport Co (Loaned on 23/3/2000) FL 7

TAYLOR Martin James
Born: Tamworth, 9 December 1966
Height: 6'0" **Weight:** 14.6
Martin only just made the opening game of the season for Wycombe last term after suffering a pre-season calf injury, but a back problem two weeks later saw him miss his first league games since January 2000. Short-term cover Frank Talia was more than an adequate replacement and although Martin eventually returned to the side, he lost his place again and made his final appearance for the Chairboys at Cheltenham in December. He joined Barnsley at the end of the season and played three matches but a recurrence of his back trouble forced an early return. Martin decided to retire from full-time professional football at the end of the season, and he later accepted a part-time contract with Conference side Telford.
Derby Co (Signed from Mile Oak Rov on 2/7/1986) F/PL 97 FLC 7 FAC 5 Others 11
Carlisle U (Loaned on 23/9/1987) FL 10 FLC 1 FAC 1 Others 2
Scunthorpe U (Loaned on 17/12/1987) FL 8
Crewe Alex (Loaned on 20/9/1996) FL 6
Wycombe W (Free on 27/3/1997) FL 238 FLC 14 FAC 23 Others 9
Barnsley (Loaned on 21/3/2003) FL 3

TAYLOR Matthew Simon
Born: Oxford, 27 November 1981
Height: 5'10" **Weight:** 11.10
Club Honours: Div 1 '03
International Honours: E: U21
This left wing back proved an excellent recruit for Portsmouth manager Harry Redknapp last season. He was a regular in the line-up until an ankle injury caused him to miss the closing stages and netted seven goals, including excellent long-range efforts against Nottingham Forest and Leicester City. Tenacious in the tackle, he also showed devastating turn of speed. Matthew was selected for the PFA Premiership team of the season.
Luton T (From trainee on 9/2/1999) FL 127+2/16 FLC 6 FAC 10/1 Others 1
Portsmouth (£400,000 + on 3/7/2002) FL 35/7 FLC 2 FAC 1

TAYLOR Michael John
Born: Liverpool, 21 November 1982
Height: 6'1" **Weight:** 12.13
Michael was one of several Premiership youngsters to enjoy a loan spell at Carlisle in the autumn. A commanding central defender, his best performance came in the goalless FA Cup tie at Scunthorpe in December. He returned to Ewood Park soon afterwards, later joining Rochdale,

lso on loan. Michael went straight into
the Dale line-up on the right-hand side of
the back three, but was more often used
s defensive cover on the bench.
Blackburn Rov (From trainee on
5/11/1999)
Carlisle U (Loaned on 27/9/2002) FL 10 FAC
Others 1
Rochdale (Loaned on 27/3/2003) FL 2

TAYLOR Robert (Bob)
Born: Horden, 3 February 1967
Height: 5'10" **Weight:** 12.12
This veteran striker played in just three
Premiership games for West Bromwich
Albion early on last season before being
sidelined with an achilles tendon injury.
Bob struggled to get fit, came back briefly
with the reserves, but then suffered a
relapse and was subsequently out of
action until January. He struggled
thereafter and failed to make the first-
team squad again until the final day of
the season when he made his farewell at
the Hawthorns against Newcastle.
Officially granted a testimonial by the club
in August 2002, he is now eighth in
Albion's all-time list of goal-scorers.
Leeds U (Free from Horden Colliery on
17/3/1986) FL 33+9/9 FLC 5+1/3 FAC 1
Others 4+1/1
Bristol C (£175,000 on 23/3/1989) FL
46+10/50 FLC 6+1/2 FAC 9+1/5 Others 3/1
West Bromwich A (£300,000 on 31/1/1992)
L 211+27/96 FLC 16/6 FAC 6+2/3 Others
6+3/8
Bolton W (Free on 8/1/1998) P/FL 57+20/21
FLC 6+5/2 FAC 4+1/2 Others 3/2
West Bromwich A (£90,000 on 23/3/2000)
P/FL 45+41/17 FLC 5+1 FAC 0+2/1 Others
+2

TAYLOR Robert Anthony
Born: Norwich, 30 April 1971
Height: 6'1" **Weight:** 13.8
This well travelled striker returned to
Grimsby on a non-contract basis for the
third time in only a few months last
season. Intended as cover for the injured
Steve Livingstone, he himself suffered a
damaged achilles tendon after just 20
minutes of his only game for the club. He
moved on to Scunthorpe in the new year
as he tried to rebuild his career and after
a brief run in the side looked to be
settling in. Unfortunately he was then
sidelined by a calf problem in early April.
When fully fit Robert is a useful striker
who is strong on the ball and has a good
touch.
Norwich C (From trainee on 26/3/1990)
Leyton Orient (Loaned on 28/3/1991) FL
4+3/1

Birmingham C (Signed on 31/8/1991)
Leyton Orient (Free on 21/10/1991) FL
54+19/20 FLC 1+1 FAC 2+1 Others 2+1
Brentford (£100,000 on 24/3/1994) FL
172+1/56 FLC 16/6 FAC 10/8 Others 14/4
Gillingham (£500,000 on 6/8/1998) FL
56+2/31 FLC 2+1/1 FAC 3/2 Others 7/5
Manchester C (£1,500,000 on 30/11/1999)
FL 14+2/5
Wolverhampton W (£1,550,000 on
15/8/2000) FL 5+4 FLC 3/3
Queens Park R (Loaned on 30/8/2001) FL
3+1
Gillingham (Loaned on 8/10/2001) FL 3+8
Grimsby T (Free on 18/1/2002) FL 5/1
Scunthorpe U (Free on 28/2/2003) FL 4+4

TAYLOR Ryan Anthony
Born: Liverpool, 19 August 1984
Height: 5'8" **Weight:** 10.4
International Honours: E: Yth
Ryan made his full first-team debut for
Tranmere last September and enjoyed a
dream start, scoring the winner in the
Worthington Cup tie against Hartlepool
with an excellent free kick. He played
most of his football at right back in the
reserves, but found himself pushed
forward into midfield following the arrival
of Sean Connelly. Ryan flourished in his
new position and featured regularly from
then on.
Tranmere Rov (From trainee on 3/4/2002) FL
18+7/1 FLC 2/1 FAC 2 Others 3/1

TAYLOR Scott James
Born: Chertsey, 5 May 1976
Height: 5'10" **Weight:** 11.4
Club Honours: AMC '02
Scott featured in almost every game for
Blackpool last term, although he was
often used from the substitutes' bench. A
striker who was also employed in a wide-
midfield role, he netted a respectable tally
of 16 goals in all competitions, scoring
regularly throughout the campaign.
Millwall (£15,000 from Staines on 8/2/1995)
FL 13+15 FLC 0+2/2 FAC 1+1
Bolton W (£150,000 on 29/3/1996) P/FL
2+10/1 FLC 0+4/1 FAC 1/1
Rotherham U (Loaned on 12/12/1997) FL
10/3 Others 1
Blackpool (Loaned on 26/3/1998) FL 3+2/1
Tranmere Rov (£50,000 on 9/10/1998) FL
78+30/17 FLC 16/5 FAC 2+5
Stockport Co (Free on 10/8/2001) FL 19+9/4
FLC 2/3 FAC 0+1
Blackpool (Free on 25/11/2002) FL 43+18/15
FLC 1 FAC 1+1/2 Others 3+2/3

TAYLOR Stuart James
Born: Romford, 28 November 1980
Height: 6'4" **Weight:** 13.4

Club Honours: PL '02; FAC '03
International Honours: E: U21-3; Yth
Stuart spent another frustrating season
living in David Seaman's shadows at
Arsenal. When called upon to deputise,
however, did so with great credit. A tall,
confident young goalkeeper, he has fine
reflexes, and he is an excellent shot
stopper. A broken finger sustained in
December put him out of action for some
weeks. Once given the chance of a
lengthy spell in the first team, Stuart
should develop into a top-class 'keeper.
Arsenal (From trainee on 8/7/1998) PL 16+2
FLC 4 FAC 3 Others 3+2
Bristol Rov (Loaned on 24/9/1999) FL 4
Crystal Palace (Loaned on 9/8/2000) FL 10
Peterborough U (Loaned on 15/2/2001) FL 6

TEALE Gary
Born: Glasgow, 21 July 1978
Height: 6'0" **Weight:** 11.6
Club Honours: Div 2 '03
After an uncertain start to the 2002-03
season Gary soon made the right-wing
position his own at Wigan Athletic. He
caused defenders all sorts of problems
with his blistering pace and mazy runs
and seemed to improve as the campaign
progressed, with his crosses providing a
vital supply line to the strikers. At his best
when running at defenders, he netted a
stunning strike in the home victory over
Chesterfield.
Clydebank (From juniors on 19/6/1996) SL
52+16/14 SLC 3+1 SC 1 Others 4
Ayr U (£70,000 on 2/10/1998) SL 94+7/13
SLC 5+1/1 SC 10/3 Others 4/1
Wigan Ath (£200,000 on 14/12/2001) FL
50+11/3 FLC 2+2 FAC 1+1 Others 2/2

TEBILY Olivier
Born: Ivory Coast, 19 December 1975
Height: 6'1" **Weight:** 13.4
Club Honours: SLC '99
International Honours: Ivory Coast: 4;
France: U21
A powerful defender whose robust play
made him difficult to get the better of,
Olivier was used at right back to provide
Birmingham City with strength and drive.
He featured regularly before suffering a
serious knee injury against Charlton at
Christmas, amazingly managing to
complete the game, before x-rays
revealed the damage. This effectively
ended his campaign and he made no
more senior appearances during the
season.
Sheffield U (£175,000 from Chateauroux on
24/3/1999) F+1
Glasgow Celtic (£1,250,000 on 8/7/1999) SL
29+9 SLC 4+1/1 SC 2+1 Others 5/1

Birmingham C (£700,000 on 22/3/2002) P/FL 19 FLC 1 Others 3

TELFER Paul Norman
Born: Edinburgh, 21 October 1971
Height: 5'9" **Weight:** 11.6
International Honours: S: 1; B-2; U21-3
A steady, industrious and intelligent player, Paul came to Southampton widely regarded as a right-sided midfielder. However, he replaced injured skipper Jason Dodd on the right side of the back four in the first week of the 2002-03 campaign, and was eventually to displace him on merit in December. He rarely got a chance to play in his customary midfield role, but formed a useful partnership down the flank with Fabrice Fernandes. One of the few exceptions was, notably, in the FA Cup final when he displaced Fernandes in the wide-right midfield position.
Luton T (From trainee on 7/11/1988) FL 136+8/19 FLC 5 FAC 14/2 Others 2/1
Coventry C (£1,500,000 on 11/7/1995) PL 178+13/6 FLC 15/2 FAC 15+4/4
Southampton (Free on 2/11/2001) PL 53+8/1 FLC 2 FAC 7

TEN HEUVEL Laurens
Born: Duivendrecht, Holland, 6 June 1976
Height: 6'0" **Weight:** 12.3
After joining Sheffield United in the 2002 close season, Laurens was injured as the new campaign began and failed to win a regular place in the Blades' line-up. A skilful striker with a hard shot he was successful in the reserves but was restricted to intermittent, usually brief, substitute appearances in the first team. In March he moved on loan to Bradford City and went straight into the side for the 3-2 defeat at Norwich, but generally failed to show his true ability in his appearances for the Bantams.
Barnsley (£75,000 from FC Den Bosch, Holland on 12/3/1996) FI/PL 1+7 FLC 0+1 (Freed to First Vienna, Austria during 1998 close season)
Sheffield U (Signed from Telstar U, Holland on 31/7/2002) FL 0+5 FLC 0+3 FAC 0+1
Bradford C (Loaned on 27/3/2003) FL 4+1

TERRY John George
Born: Barking, 7 December 1980
Height: 6'0" **Weight:** 12.4
Club Honours: FAC '00
International Honours: E: 1; U21-9
A bizarre pre-season injury that resulted in keyhole surgery to a knee cost fans' favourite John Terry his place in the Chelsea central defence. In his absence

the Gallic pairing of Marcel Desailly and William Gallas took over, establishing a superb partnership. Whenever John replaced Desailly during the season he was also awarded the captain's armband - a clear indication that he is being groomed as a future Chelsea skipper. After his setbacks of the previous 12 months, both off and on the field, he battled back magnificently, showing a maturity far beyond his years. Alongside his tigerish tackling, whole-hearted defending and raking long passes John showed the ability to link up with the Blues' extravagant attacking style and he notched six goals during the course of the season. The campaign certainly ended on a high for John as Champions' League qualification was bolstered by call-ups to the full England squad.
Chelsea (From trainee on 18/3/1998) PL 69+12/5 FLC 10+1 FAC 15+5/5 Others 6/2
Nottingham F (Loaned on 23/3/2000) FL 5+1

TESSEM Jo
Born: Orlandet, Norway, 28 February 1972
Height: 6'3" **Weight:** 12.10
International Honours: Norway: 8; B-1
Ostensibly a midfielder Jo more often than not found himself partnering James Beattie up front when called upon to start a game at Southampton in the 2002-03 season. His almost languid appearance disguises a hard-working, versatile approach to the game coupled with an ability to make life awkward for his direct opponent, whether he is marking or being marked. He is, however, not a natural goal-scorer, even though Saints' boss Gordon Strachan developed a taste for throwing him on late in games to liven things up a little. The ploy unfortunately did not pay off in the FA Cup final, although he did have a scoring opportunity with his first touch.
Southampton (£600,000 from Molde, Norway, ex Lyn, on 19/11/1999) PL 66+41/12 FLC 4+2/1 FAC 7+6/3

THATCHER Benjamin (Ben) David
Born: Swindon, 30 November 1975
Height: 5'10" **Weight:** 12.7
International Honours: E: U21-4; Yth
After a hip injury had ruled Ben out for a year, the left back found his form in the second half of 2002-03 campaign and eventually won a recall to the Tottenham side. Extremely strong and tenacious, his pace ensures that he can head off an attack from deep in the

middle of the field and still get back to form the last line of defence. Great at defending set pieces, Ben will be out to become a regular in the starting line-up in 2003-04.
Millwall (From trainee on 8/6/1992) FL 87+3/1 FLC 6 FAC 7 Others 4
Wimbledon (£1,840,00 on 5/7/1996) PL 82+4 FLC 12 FAC 5
Tottenham H (£5,000,000 on 12/7/2000) P 29+7 FLC 6+1 FAC 3

THEOBALD David John
Born: Cambridge, 15 December 1978
Height: 6'3" **Weight:** 12.0
This tall central defender missed the start of the season for Swansea, but made his debut shortly afterwards at Bury. David was never able to win a regular place in the Swans' line-up, however, and in January his contract was paid up. He subsequently joined Cambridge United on non-contract terms where he made a handful of appearances. He also featured for Dr Martens League club Cambridge City in the closing stages of the campaign.
Ipswich T (From trainee on 2/6/1997)
Brentford (Free on 8/7/1999) FL 26+5 Others 6
Swansea C (Free on 26/7/2002) FL 9+1 FAC 1 Others 1
Cambridge U (Free on 7/2/2003) FL 1+3

THEOKLITOS Michael
Born: Melbourne, Australia, 11 February 1981
Height: 6'0" **Weight:** 12.2
This promising young 'keeper joined Blackpool on a 12-month contract in the summer and spent the season as back up for Phil Barnes. He made his debut in the home match with Notts County and featured twice more during the campaign.
Blackpool (Free from Auckland Kingz, New Zealand, ex Bulleen Zebras, South Melbourne on 6/8/2002) FL 2 FAC 1

THIRLWELL Paul
Born: Washington, 13 February 1979
Height: 5'11" **Weight:** 11.4
International Honours: E: U21-1
Midfielder Paul enjoyed one of his longest runs in the Sunderland team last season, despite playing through the pain barrier caused by a persistent groin injury. Mainly operating in a central position, he is adept at playing the 'anchor man' role in midfield where he can win the ball with his strong tackling and distribute it sensibly and accurately. A prime example of this occurred at Charlton in November

hen a thunderous challenge set up Tore
ndre Flo for a goal. Paul underwent a
ernia operation in February and will be
oping to be fully fit for the start of the
ew season.
underland (From trainee on 14/4/1997)
FL 34+14 FLC 6+2/1 FAC 2+1
windon T (Loaned on 8/9/1999) FL 12

THOMAS Andrew Richard
orn: Stockport, 2 December 1982
eight: 5'8" **Weight:** 10.2
his young central defender had to wait
ntil January for his first opportunity of
e season for Stockport, coming on as a
ubstitute for the out-of-touch Carlton
almer in the 5-2 defeat against
windon. Andrew added another
ppearance, winning the 'Man of the
atch' award, the following month at
eterborough but was released at the
nd of the campaign.
ockport Co (From trainee on 11/7/2001) FL
+4

THOMAS Daniel (Danny)
ustin
orn: Leamington, 1 May 1981
eight: 5'7" **Weight:** 11.2
his lightning-quick left winger enjoyed a
ng run in the Bournemouth side last
ason, although he had to be content
ith a place on the bench in the latter
ages of the campaign. Danny was out
contract in the summer and at the time
writing his future was uncertain.
eicester C (From trainee at Nottingham F
13/5/1998) PL 0+3
ournemouth (Signed on 8/2/2002) FL
8+16/2 FLC 1/1 FAC 6/1 Others 4+2

THOMAS James Alan
orn: Swansea, 16 January 1979
eight: 6'0" **Weight:** 13.0
nternational Honours: W: U21-21
mes signed for his hometown club in
e summer of 2002 and began well,
oring two goals from his first three
ames. He showed pace and skill on the
ft-hand side of the attack and as the
ason progressed, he proved to have an
ve for half chances. Although troubled
an ankle ligament injury in the spring,
still finished the season as the Swans'
ading goal-scorer with 15 goals in all
ompetitions. James received a call up to
e full Welsh international squad for the
uro 2004 qualifying game in Azerbaijan,
hen he sat on the bench.
ackburn Rov (From trainee on 2/7/1996)
1+3/1 FLC 1/2
est Bromwich A (Loaned on 29/8/1997)
1+2

Blackpool (Loaned on 21/3/2000) FL 9/2
Sheffield U (Loaned on 24/11/2000) FL
3+7/1 FAC 0+1
Bristol Rov (Loaned on 22/3/2002) FL 7/1
Swansea C (Free on 9/7/2002) FL 34+5/13
FLC 1/1 FAC 1 Others 1/1

THOMAS Jerome William
Born: Wembley, 23 March 1983
Height: 5'10" **Weight:** 11.10
Club Honours: FAYC '00, '01
International Honours: E: Yth
This promising Arsenal youngster once
again linked up with Queen's Park
Rangers in a loan deal during the 2002-
03 season. He again produced some
reliable performances, but despite
manager Ian Holloway's attempts to
extend the loan period he returned to
Highbury to continue his development in
the club's reserve team. Jerome scored a
solitary goal for Rangers, netting in the
away game at Cheltenham.
Arsenal (From trainee on 3/7/2001)
Queens Park R (Loaned on 27/3/2002)
FL 4/1
Queens Park R (Loaned on 29/8/2002) FL
5+1/2

THOMAS Martin Russell
Born: Lymington, 12 September 1973
Height: 5'8" **Weight:** 12.6
Club Honours: Div 3 '00
Martin arrived at Exeter during the 2002
close season and made a central midfield
place his own before a change of
management in February limited his
chances. Experienced, competitive and
honest, he chipped in with three goals
during the campaign.
Southampton (From trainee on 19/6/1992)
Leyton Orient (Free on 24/3/1994) FL 5/2
Fulham (Free on 21/7/1994) FL 59+31/8 FLC
6+1 FAC 4/1 Others 7+1/2
Swansea C (Free on 30/7/1998) FL 70+21/8
FLC 8 FAC 5/2 Others 4/1
Brighton & Hove A (Free on 22/3/2001) FL
1+7
Oxford U (Free on 9/7/2001) FL 13+1/2
FLC 1
Exeter C (Free on 2/8/2002) FL 22+4/3 FLC 1
FAC 2 Others 0+1

THOMAS Stephen
Born: Hartlepool, 23 June 1979
Height: 5'10" **Weight:** 12.0
International Honours: W: U21-5; Yth
Stephen made the Wrexham starting line-
up for nearly half of their Football League
fixtures last term, including a run of 11
successive outings during January and
February, which ended when he picked
up a hamstring injury. Earlier in the season

he had been hampered by an ankle
problem, but got on the score sheet with
the winner against Southend in
November.
Wrexham (From trainee on 4/7/1997) FL
54+22/5 FLC 1+2 FAC 1 Others 4/2

THOMAS Wayne Junior Robert
Born: Gloucester, 17 May 1979
Height: 5'11" **Weight:** 11.12
In the opening stages of last term Wayne
failed to build on the progress he had
made at Stoke in the 2001-02 season and
the fans became restless at his
unexpected dip in form. However, he
responded positively to the faith put in
him by new manager Tony Pulis and by
the end of the campaign he had returned
to something like his best form. Wayne is
a promising young defender who can
appear at right back or in a more central
role.
Torquay U (From trainee on 4/7/1997) FL
89+34/5 FLC 2+1/1 FAC 7/1 Others 6+4
Stoke C (£200,000 + on 5/6/2000) FL
114+1/2 FLC 5+1 FAC 7 Others 10

THOME Emerson August
Born: Porto Alegre, Brazil, 30 March
1972
Height: 6'1" **Weight:** 13.4
A powerfully built centre back, Emerson's
constant battle against injury continued
last season and he made only five starts
during the campaign. Aerially dominant
and a natural leader, a persistent medial
ligament knee injury plagued him,
robbing the Black Cats of a pivotal figure,
even so it was somewhat surprising that
Sunderland decided to release Emerson in
the summer.
Sheffield Wed (Free from Benfica, Portugal
on 23/3/1998) PL 60+1/1 FLC 5+1 FAC 4/1
Chelsea (£2,700,000 on 23/12/1999) PL
19+2 Others 1
Sunderland (£4,500,000 on 1/9/2000) PL
43+1/2 FLC 4 FAC 5

THOMPSON Andrew (Andy)
Richard
Born: Cannock, 9 November 1967
Height: 5'5" **Weight:** 10.1
Club Honours: Div 4 '88, Div 3 '89; AMC
'88
This experienced right back was looking
to win a regular place in the
Shrewsbury line-up last term, but he
had the misfortune to miss most of the
season with an achilles problem. He
returned to action for the last few
matches, when he looked very effective
going forward, but was unable to
prevent the club from being relegated

to the Conference. Andy was released at the end of the season.

West Bromwich A *(From apprentice on 16/11/1985) FL 18+6/1 FLC 0+1 FAC 2 Others 1+1*
Wolverhampton W *(£35,000 on 21/11/1986) FL 356+20/43 FLC 22 FAC 20/1 Others 33/1*
Tranmere Rov *(Free on 21/7/1997) FL 91+5/4 FLC 13+1 FAC 5+1*
Cardiff C *(Free on 11/8/2000) FL 5+2 FAC 0+1 Others 2+1*
Shrewsbury T *(Loaned on 18/1/2002) FL 9+1*
Shrewsbury T *(Free on 28/3/2002) FL 20 FLC 1 FAC 1*

THOMPSON Christopher (Chris) Michael
Born: Warrington, 7 February 1982
Height: 5'11" **Weight:** 12.3
Out of favour at Blundell Park, this young Grimsby Town striker had few opportunities last term following the emergence of Darren Mansaram. Chris managed just a handful of first-team appearances, although he contributed a valuable goal during the 2-0 defeat of fellow strugglers Stoke. Chris was out of contract in the summer and his future was uncertain at the time of writing.

Grimsby T *(Free from trainee at Liverpool on 12/7/2001) FL 7+7/1 FAC 2+2*

THOMPSON David Anthony
Born: Birkenhead, 12 September 1977
Height: 5'7" **Weight:** 10.0
Club Honours: FAYC '96
International Honours: E: U21-7; Yth
David appeared in the first four games of the 2002-03 campaign for Coventry City before joining his old boss Graeme Souness at Blackburn. He proved a bargain signing for Rovers, full of fight and fire, capable of beating men and carrying play to the opposition, and possessor of a fine shot that brought crucial goals. More naturally at home in a central midfield position he played on either flank and he showed some excellent form. However, after forcing his way into the England squad he was sidelined for the last few months of the season following a knee operation to clear out some troublesome debris.

Liverpool *(From trainee on 8/11/1994) PL 24+24/5 FLC 5 FAC 0+1 Others 2*
Swindon T *(Loaned on 21/11/1997) FL 10*
Coventry C *(£3,000,000 on 8/8/2000) P/FL 61+5/15 FLC 3+1/1 FAC 2*
Blackburn Rov *(£1,500,000 on 28/8/2002) PL 23/4 FLC 4/1 FAC 2 Others 3/1*

THOMPSON Glyn William
Born: Telford, 24 February 1981
Height: 6'1" **Weight:** 12.4
This young Fulham goalkeeper arrived at Northampton last November and made his debut at home to Tranmere when he

Martin Thomas (centre)

avid Thompson

seemed to be all that stood between the opposition and a cricket score. Unfortunately his loan period coincided with the team's bad run of form and goals were being shipped in at an alarming rate. Nevertheless, he produced some creditable performances between the sticks and was signed permanently by the Cobblers on transfer deadline day.
Shrewsbury T (From trainee on 14/12/1998) FL 1 FLC 1
Fulham (£50,000 on 20/11/1999)
Mansfield T (Loaned on 21/11/2000) FL 16
Northampton T (Free on 29/11/2002) FL 11 FAC 1

THOMPSON John
Born: Dublin, 12 October 1981
Height: 6'1" **Weight:** 11.11
International Honours: RoI: U21-9; Yth
John was used in a variety of positions by Nottingham Forest throughout the 2002-03 season. He started out at right back, before being injured, and when he returned to the side on New Year's Day he featured in a central-midfield role from where he scored his first senior goal against Walsall. Then, when David Prutton moved on to Southampton, John took over his position on the right-hand side of midfield, eventually finishing up at centre half! John continued to add to his tally of caps for the Republic of Ireland U21s during the campaign.
Nottingham F (Signed from Home Farm, ex River Valley Rgrs, on 6/7/1999) FL 26+2/3 FLC 1+1 FAC 1 Others 1+1

THOMPSON Lee Jonathan
Born: Sheffield, 25 March 1983
Height: 5'7" **Weight:** 11.2
International Honours: E: Sch
This hard-working midfield player joined Boston United on loan from Sheffield United and proved an instant hit. He scored some spectacular long-range goals and netted the only hat-trick of the Pilgrims' season when he bagged all the goals in the 3-2 win at Darlington. Lee underwent a knee operation in February, which put him out of action for the remainder of the season.
Sheffield U (From juniors on 7/7/2000)
Boston U (Free on 4/10/2002) FL 12+3/4 FAC 1 Others 2/2

THOMPSON Neil
Born: Beverley, 2 October 1963
Height: 5'10" **Weight:** 13.8
Club Honours: GMVC '87; Div 2 '92
International Honours: E: SP-4
Boston United's manager was forced back into first-team action last term when an

early-season injury crisis left him with little option but to select himself. Neil performed solidly at left back but once players were fit again he was happy to resume his managerial role.
Hull C (From apprentice at Nottingham F on 28/11/1981) FL 29+2
Scarborough (Free on 1/8/1983) FL 87/15 FLC 8/1 FAC 3 Others 9/1
Ipswich T (£160,000 on 9/6/1989) F/PL 199+7/19 FLC 14+1/1 FAC 17/2 Others 8/2
Barnsley (Free on 14/6/1996) F/PL 27/5 FLC 4 FAC 1
Oldham Ath (Loaned on 24/12/1997) FL 8
York C (Free on 2/3/1998) FL 42/8 FLC 2/1 (Free to Scarborough on 17/2/2000)
Boston U (Free on 8/8/2002) FL 3 FLC 2

THOMPSON Tyrone
Born: Sheffield, 8 May 1982
Height: 5'9" **Weight:** 11.2
This midfield player joined Lincoln on loan last October, but found it difficult to break into the Imps' team. His only league experience came as a substitute for the final few minutes of the home clash with Bury, but he also started two LDV Vans Trophy matches before returning to Bramall Lane. Tyrone subsequently featured for Sheffield United in the FA Cup tie against Ipswich Town. He produced a hard-working performance in the centre of midfield, tackling and passing well, but the form of the senior players meant this was his only appearance. A regular in the successful reserve side, he moved on loan to Doncaster Rovers on transfer deadline day.
Sheffield U (From trainee on 10/7/2000) FLC 1+1 FAC 1
Lincoln C (Loaned on 18/10/2002) FL 0+1 Others 2

THOMSON Andrew (Andy)
Born: Motherwell, 1 April 1971
Height: 5'10" **Weight:** 10.13
This experienced striker was hampered by a string of injuries last term, which restricted him to just seven starts in Second Division matches. The main problem was a recurrence of an old back injury, but he also missed a period of six weeks with a hamstring problem. Andy spent the later stages of the campaign in the reserves, but returned to the starting line-up for the play-off semi-final against Oldham.
Queen of the South (Free from Jerviston BC on 28/7/1989) SL 163+12/93 SLC 8/3 SC 7+2/5 Others 9/8
Southend U (£250,000 on 4/7/1994) FL 87+35/28 FLC 4+1 FAC 3+2 Others 1+2

Oxford U (Free on 21/7/1998) FL 25+13/7 FLC 1 FAC 0+1
Gillingham (£25,000 on 5/8/1999) FL 32+20/14 FLC 5+1/3 FAC 5+1/4 Others 0+1
Queens Park R (Free on 22/3/2001) FL 43+24/28 FLC 1/1 FAC 2/1 Others 3+1

THOMSON Andrew (Andy) John
Born: Swindon, 28 March 1974
Height: 6'3" **Weight:** 14.12
Wycombe's big central defender was initially not a first choice when the 2002-03 season started, but a leaky defence saw him recalled five weeks into the campaign. From then on in Andy was a key member of the back line, dominant in the air and able to hustle opponents with his large frame. He goes about his business with a quiet authority and for such a big man is comfortable bringing the ball out of defence. His solitary goal was a far-post strike against Port Vale in December.
Swindon T (From trainee on 1/5/1993) P/FL 21+1 FLC 5/1 Others 3
Portsmouth (£75,000 on 29/12/1995) FL 85+8/3 FLC 4 FAC 6+1
Bristol Rov (£60,000 on 15/11/1999) FL 124+3/6 FLC 8 FAC 6 Others 5
Wycombe W (Free on 28/3/2002) FL 37+2/1 FLC 2 FAC 1 Others 3

THOMSON Steven (Steve)
Born: Glasgow, 23 January 1978
Height: 5'8" **Weight:** 10.4
International Honours: S: Yth
This busy, competitive midfielder again failed to win a regular place in the Crystal Palace line-up last season, although he proved to be a good squad player. He scored his only goal of the campaign with a great swerving shot in the 4-2 defeat of Wolves in September. Steve was released by the Eagles in the summer.
Crystal Palace (From trainee on 9/12/1995) FL 68+37/1 FLC 8+4/2 FAC 3+1/1 Others 1+1

THORNE Peter Lee
Born: Manchester, 21 June 1973
Height: 6'0" **Weight:** 13.6
Club Honours: Div 2 '96; AMC '00
Peter opened the door for Robert Earnshaw to score his record-breaking goals tally for Cardiff City last season. However, he didn't have his best season in front of goal, but still finished with a respectable total of 16 and the joint tally with Earnie was more than 50. The deft touches, supreme passes and fantastic flicks were again a joy to watch. Peter played a major role in promotion success and, along with Graham Kavanagh,

ismissed the possibility of four successive
lay-off failures. Both were in the Stoke
ity team to fall at the semi-final stage
or two years, and both were together in
he Cardiff team that lost to Stoke in
001-02.

lackburn Rov *(From trainee on 20/6/1991)*
thers 0+1
Wigan Ath *(Loaned on 11/3/1994) FL 10+1*
windon T *(£225,000 on 18/1/1995) FL*
5+11/27 FLC 5+1/4 FAC 4+2 Others 1+1/1
toke C *(£350,000 + on 25/7/1997) FL*
47+11/65 FLC 12+1/6 FAC 5+1 Others
+3/9
ardiff C *(£1,700,000 on 13/9/2001) FL*
9+3/21 FLC 1/1 FAC 4/1 Others 6/1

HORNLEY Benjamin (Ben)
indsay
orn: Bury, 21 April 1975
eight: 5'9" **Weight:** 11.12
lub Honours: FAYC '92
nternational Honours: E: U21-3; Sch
his skilful left winger featured in a
andful of games for Aberdeen at the
art of last season. He was subsequently
eleased and signed for Blackpool, making
s debut in the home game with
uddersfield on New Year's Day. Ben was
volved in the Seasiders' squad for the
est of the campaign, showing some neat
kills in the middle of the park or out
ide.
Manchester U *(From trainee on 29/1/1993)*
L 1+8 FLC 3 FAC 2
tockport Co *(Loaned on 6/11/1995) FL*
+2/1 Others 1
uddersfield T *(Loaned on 22/2/1996) FL*
2/2
uddersfield T *(£175,000 + on 3/7/1998) FL*
7+22/5 FLC 10 FAC 5/1
berdeen *(Signed on 1/8/2001) SL 17+13/3*
LC 2+1/1 SC 0+2/1
lackpool *(Free on 31/12/2002) FL 7+5*
AC 1

HORNTON Sean
orn: Drogheda, Ireland, 8 May 1983
eight: 5'10" **Weight:** 11.0
nternational Honours: RoI: U21-6; Yth
ean joined Sunderland as something of
n unknown quantity but ended the
ampaign as the Black Cats' 'Young Player
f the Year'. The central midfielder arrived
om Tranmere Rovers in the close season
nd, following a loan spell at Blackpool,
e made his debut in January in the FA
up third round replay victory over
olton, turning in an excellent and
onfident performance. A Republic of
eland U19 international, he also
raduated to U21 level last term. Sean's
rray of awards included the FAI U19

'Player of the Year' and the Sunderland
Echo 'Player of the Season', while his only
goal of the campaign was the Black Cats'
'Goal of the Season', a tremendous 20-
yard strike against Chelsea in April.
Tranmere Rov *(Trainee) FL 9+2/1 FAC 0+1*
Others 0+1
Sunderland *(Signed on 4/7/2002) PL 11/1*
FAC 3

Blackpool *(Loaned on 7/11/2002) FL 1+2*
Others 1

THORPE Anthony (Tony) Lee
Born: Leicester, 10 April 1974
Height: 5'9" **Weight:** 12.6
Tony returned to Luton Town once more
in the summer of 2002, this time on a
permanent basis. It didn't take him long

Peter Thorne

before he found his mark in the 5-2 defeat at Blackpool, but injuries and a loss of form restricted him in the first half of the season. However, he then established a fine partnership up front with Steve Howard and hit a rich scoring vein, netting nine goals in 11 games, until an injury put him out of the team until the very last match of the campaign when he scored against Swindon. Tony is a nippy striker with an excellent eye for goal.

Luton T *(From trainee at Leicester C juniors on 18/8/1992) FL 93+27/50 FLC 5+4/5 FAC 5+3/2 Others 4+3/3*
Fulham *(£800,000 on 26/2/1998) FL 5+8/3 Others 1+1*
Bristol C *(£1,000,000 on 23/6/1998) FL 102+26/50 FLC 5+2/4 FAC 6+1/3 Others 9/4*
Reading *(Loaned on 5/2/1999) FL 6/1*
Luton T *(Loaned on 25/3/1999) FL 7+1/4*
Luton T *(Loaned on 26/11/1999) FL 3+1/1*
Luton T *(Free on 1/7/2002) FL 28+2/13 FAC 1/1 Others 2/2*

THORPE Lee Anthony
Born: Wolverhampton, 14 December 1975
Height: 6'1" **Weight:** 12.4
This proven striker joined Leyton Orient during the 2002 close season but had a mixed campaign with the O's last term. He featured regularly in the squad, although often on the bench, but injuries and the absence of a regular striking partner seemed to hamper his progress. Nevertheless he finished as the club's leading scorer with a total of nine goals in all competitions.

Blackpool *(From trainee on 18/7/1994) FL 2+10 FLC 0+1 FAC 1 Others 1*
Lincoln C *(Free on 4/8/1997) FL 183+9/58 FLC 5+1/1 FAC 14/1 Others 9+1/7*
Leyton Orient *(Free on 3/5/2002) FL 27+11/8 FLC 2/1 Others 1*

THORRINGTON John
Born: Johannesburg, South Africa, 17 October 1979
Height: 5'8" **Weight:** 10.12
International Honours: USA: 1
This lively winger scored the first goal of the 2002-03 campaign for Huddersfield after coming on as a substitute at Plymouth. However, an ankle injury blighted part of his season, while a switch of formation meant that he was overlooked for a regular place in the line-up. Jon attacks with pace and purpose, and is a real threat with his close control and accurate crossing.

Manchester U *(Signed from Mission Viejos Pateadores, California, USA, on 7/10/1997)*

Free to Bayer Leverkusen, Germany during 1999 close season)
Huddersfield T *(Free on 16/3/2001) FL 45+17/7 FLC 0+2 FAC 0+1 Others 4*

THURGOOD Stuart Anthony
Born: Enfield, 4 November 1981
Height: 5'7" **Weight:** 11.8
After a super opening campaign at the

Lee Thorpe

John Thorrington

Li Tie

ub, Stuart had a somewhat
sappointing time at Southend last term.
e seemed consigned to the role of
ernal substitute following the arrival of
y Smith from Aston Villa, and when he
d come on he was often required to fill
at right back or wide right midfield
ther than in his usual central-midfield
le. He will be looking to regain his place
the starting line-up in 2003-04.
outhend U *(Free from Shimuzu-S-Pulse,
pan on 30/1/2001) FL 49+30/1 FLC 1 FAC
+1 Others 1+2*

IATTO Daniele (Danny)
madio
orn: Melbourne, Australia, 22 May 1973
eight: 5'7" **Weight:** 12.0
lub Honours: Div 1 '02
nternational Honours: Australia: 23;
23
his aggressive left-sided midfield player
ayed an effective role for Manchester
ity in the first half of last season and
as outstanding in the 'derby' match
gainst Manchester United, dominating
e midfield and running his socks off.
nfortunately he was sidelined by an
jury suffered on Boxing Day and failed
return to first-team action before the
ummer break.
toke C *(Loaned from FC Baden, Switzerland
n 25/11/1997) FL 11+4/1*
lanchester C *(£300,000 from FC Baden,
witzerland on 15/7/1998) P/FL 111+24/3 FLC
0/1 FAC 3+1 Others 1*

IDMAN Ola
orn: Sweden, 11 May 1979
eight: 6'2" **Weight:** 11.13
his Swedish goalkeeper arrived at
tockport in January from Belgian outfit
a Louviere and immediately won over the
ounty faithful. Ola made his debut in a
ough trip to high-flying Bristol City and
ade a series of fine saves to help his
ew side to a creditable 1-1 draw, a feat
ven more impressive considering the
atters played the majority of the game
vith ten men. After that he played in
very game showing some excellent form.
tockport Co *(Free from La Louviere,
elgium, ex BK Kick, Malmo FF, KAA Gent,
n 24/1/2003) FL 18*

IE Li
orn: Liaoning, China, 18 September
977
leight: 6'0" **Weight:** 11.10
nternational Honours: China: 79
egarded unfairly as being a makeweight
n the deal between Everton and their
hinese sponsors, this combative

midfielder surprised everybody by
appearing in 29 Premiership games until
tiredness resulting from 12 months of
consecutive football, including the 2002
World Cup finals, caught up with him.
Even so Li Tie can look back with pride on
his first season in English football, when
he quickly adapted to the pace and
physical demands placed upon any new
player. A feisty and industrious presence
in the Blues' midfield, he showed a keen
eye for a pass that led to several goals,
most notably for Tomasz Radzinski against
West Bromwich Albion and Leeds United.
Signed on a loan deal for one year, his
future was still uncertain at the time of
writing.
Everton *(Loaned from Liaoning Bodao, China
on 8/8/2002) PL 28+1 FLC 3 FAC 0+1*

TIERNEY Paul Thomas
Born: Salford, 15 September 1982
Height: 5'10" **Weight:** 12.10
International Honours: RoI: U21-7
This young Manchester United defender
joined Crewe Alexandra in the autumn
and made his senior debut at left back
against Brentford in November. Soon
afterwards he scored his first goal for the
club against Blackpool and he remained
at Gresty Road until the end of the
season. Paul also featured regularly for
the Republic of Ireland U21 side during
the campaign.
Manchester U *(From trainee on 18/7/2000)*
Crewe Alex *(Loaned on 8/11/2002) FL
14+3/1 FAC 2 Others 3*

TILER Carl
Born: Sheffield, 11 February 1970
Height: 6'3" **Weight:** 13.10
International Honours: E: U21-13
This experienced central defender was
mostly restricted to reserve-team football
for Portsmouth last term. His only first-
team outings came from the substitutes'
bench in the home games against Millwall
and Wimbledon and he finished the
campaign on the transfer list.
Barnsley *(From trainee on 2/8/1988) FL
67+4/3 FLC 4 FAC 4+1 Others 3+1*
Nottingham F *(£1,400,000 on 30/5/1991)
F/PL 67+2/1 FLC 10+1 FAC 6 Others 1*
Swindon T *(Loaned on 18/11/1994) FL 2*
Aston Villa *(£750,000 on 28/10/1995) PL
10+2/1 FLC 1 FAC 2*
Sheffield U *(£650,000 on 26/3/1997) FL
23/2 FLC 5 Others 3*
Everton *(£500,000 on 28/11/1997) PL 21/1
FLC 1 FAC 1*
Charlton Ath *(£700,000 on 30/9/1998) P/FL
38+7/2 FAC 1+1*
Birmingham C *(Loaned on 9/2/2001) FL 1*

Portsmouth *(£250,000 on 13/3/2001) FL
16+3/1 FAC 1*

TILLSON Andrew (Andy)
Born: Huntingdon, 30 June 1966
Height: 6'2" **Weight:** 12.10
This vastly experienced centre half had
impressed for Rushden & Diamonds in the
latter stages of the 2001-02 campaign,
but after featuring in a couple of early-
season games he lost his place in the line-
up. He returned for three games in
October, but shortly afterwards
announced his retirement from
professional football due to a back injury.
Andy was subsequently appointed as a
coach to FA Cup heroes Team Bath.
Grimsby T *(Free from Kettering T on
14/7/1988) FL 104+1/5 FLC 8 FAC 10 Others 5*
Queens Park R *(£400,000 on 21/12/1990)
FL 27+2/2 FLC 2 Others 1*
Grimsby T *(Loaned on 15/9/1992) FL 4
Others 1*
Bristol Rov *(£370,000 on 7/11/1992) FL
250+3/11 FLC 16/1 FAC 11 Others 19+1/2*
Walsall *(£10,000 on 9/8/2000) FL 50+1/2
FLC 4 FAC 4/2 Others 3*
Rushden & Diamonds *(Free on 8/2/2002) FL
19 Others 4*

TILSON Stephen (Steve)
Brian
Born: Wickford, 27 July 1966
Height: 5'11" **Weight:** 12.6
Club Honours: FAT '01
This veteran campaigner started the
2002-03 season as first-team coach at
Southend, with whom he also was
registered as a player. He made a handful
of first-team appearances to bring much
needed experience to a young side. His
consummate passing and exquisite left
foot were still a joy to watch and there
are few more deserving players of a
testimonial match. This long overdue
benefit took place against a former
England XI managed by Lawrie
McMenemy. Although Steve was replaced
as coach by Stewart Robson during the
season, he remained at Roots Hall in
charge of the club's academy.
Southend U *(Free from Witham T on
7/2/1989) FL 199+40/26 FLC 9+1 FAC 5
Others 12+2/4 (Free to Canvey Island on
18/7/1997)*
Brentford *(Loaned on 16/9/1993) FL 2*
Southend U *(Free on 7/10/2002) FL 2+1 FAC
0+2 Others 1*

TIMM Mads
Born: Odense, Denmark, 31 October
1984
Height: 5'9" **Weight:** 12.10

Club Honours: FAYC '03
International Honours: Denmark: Yth
An attacking young player who is also capable of playing in midfield or as an out-and-out striker a solitary run out in the 3-0 reverse to Maccabi Haifa was Mads' introduction to first-team life at Manchester United. Not that the youngster will let that worry him. Big things are expected of him, and he's sure to get more chances in the coming season.
Manchester U *(From juniors on 18/12/2001) Others 0+1*

TINDALL Jason

Born: Mile End, 15 November 1977
Height: 6'1" **Weight:** 11.10
Jason continued to play as a central defender for Bournemouth last season, bringing some style to the role. A regular in the line-up, he again showed improvement in his overall performances. Unfortunately he suffered a knee injury in the away game at Rushden & Diamonds in March and was forced to miss the remainder of the campaign.
Charlton Ath *(From trainee on 18/7/1996)*
Bournemouth *(Free on 3/7/1998) FL 122+19/6 FLC 4+2 FAC 8+1 Others 3+2*

TINKLER Mark Roland

Born: Bishop Auckland, 24 October 1974
Height: 5'11" **Weight:** 13.3
Club Honours: FAYC '93
International Honours: E: Yth (UEFA-U18 '93); Sch
Last term proved to be another excellent season for Hartlepool's hard-working midfielder who improved his game by becoming a much more regular goal-scorer. His most memorable appearance was against Wrexham in October when he netted his first ever hat-trick and also had another seemingly good goal disallowed. Mark was one of four Hartlepool players chosen in the PFA's Division Three team of the year.
Leeds U *(From trainee on 29/11/1991) PL 14+11 FLC 1 Others 0+1*
York C *(£85,000 on 25/3/1997) FL 88+2/8 FLC 6 FAC 5 Others 2*
Southend U *(£40,000 on 13/8/1999) FL 55+1/1 FLC 2+1 FAC 1 Others 1*
Hartlepool U *(Free on 2/11/2000) FL 112+1/25 FLC 2 FAC 3 Others 6/1*

TINNION Brian

Born: Stanley, 23 February 1968
Height: 6'0" **Weight:** 13.0
Club Honours: AMC '03

Brian improved on a disappointing 2001-02 season last term, but there were signs that Bristol City's great midfield servant is feeling the effect of ten years at Ashton Gate. The spark often wasn't there when required in the big games, although he was unfortunate with a great header in the second leg of the play-off semi-final against Cardiff City. With his contract up for renewal at the end of the campaign he intimated that he would be calling it a day if City didn't require his services. Fortunately he was offered a role as player-coach at Ashton Gate and hopefully his wonderful passing skills will be able to take the Robins to promotion in 2003-04.
Newcastle U *(From apprentice on 26/2/1986) FL 30+2/2 FLC 5 Others 1+1*
Bradford C *(£150,000 on 9/3/1989) FL 137+8/22 FLC 12/1 FAC 9/4 Others 7+1/2*
Bristol C *(£180,000 on 23/3/1993) FL 364+27/33 FLC 24 FAC 25+2/6 Others 18+6*

TINSON Darren Lee

Born: Birmingham, 15 November 1969
Height: 6'0" **Weight:** 13.7
Club Honours: GMVC '97
Once again captain of Macclesfield Town, this centre half was the linchpin in the defence last term when he missed just one first-team match. Physically strong and very effective in the air, Darren is the second longest-serving member of the squad. He played as one of the three central defenders and performed equally well as a centre back in the middle of the season when the manager adopted a 4-4-2 formation.
Macclesfield T *(£10,000 from Northwich Vic on 14/2/1996) FL 263/5 FLC 15 FAC 14 Others 5*

TIPTON Matthew John

Born: Bangor, Wales, 29 June 1980
Height: 5'10" **Weight:** 13.0
International Honours: W: U21-6; Yth
Matthew appeared regularly in the Macclesfield side last term until the end of March when on-loan strikers were often preferred. He partnered Kyle Lightbourne up front with some success and contributed a useful tally of 14 goals in all competitions, with his double strike in the home win against Leyton Orient probably being his best performance of the season.
Oldham Ath *(From trainee on 1/7/1997) FL 51+61/15 FLC 3+4 FAC 4+7/1 Others 3+3/1*
Macclesfield T *(Free on 13/2/2002) FL 40+9/12 FLC 2/1 FAC 3/2 Others 1/1*

TOD Andrew (Andy)

Born: Dunfermline, 4 November 1971
Height: 6'3" **Weight:** 12.0
Club Honours: S Div 1 '96
Andy played just five games for Bradford City last term before moving north of the border to join Dundee United on loan in January and he remained at Tannadice until the end of the season. A versatile player who initially joined the Bantams a a centre back, he featured as a striker an scored his only goal in the 1-1 draw at Crystal Palace.
Dunfermline Ath *(Signed from Kelty Heart on 4/11/1993) SL 211+15/35 FLC 14 SC 12+3/2 Others 8+1/2*
Stockport Co *(Loaned on 6/10/2000) FL 11*
Bradford C *(£100,000 on 21/8/2001) FL 29+6/5 FLC 2+1/2 FAC 1*
Heart of Midlothian *(Loaned on 28/3/200. SL 3/1*
Dundee U *(Loaned on 28/1/2003) SL 12+1/*

TODA Kazuyuki

Born: Tokyo, Japan, 30 December 1977
Height: 5'10" **Weight:** 10.11
International Honours: Japan: 15
Kazuyuki joined Spurs on a one-year loa deal from Shimizu S-Pulse in January, and impressed in the handful of appearances he made last season. A combative midfielder who is known almost as much for his ever-changing hairstyles as for his football, he will be looking to feature more regularly in the line-up in 2003-04.
Tottenham H *(Loaned from Shimizu S-Pulse Japan on 28/1/2003) PL 2+2*

TODD Andrew (Andy) John James

Born: Derby, 21 September 1974
Height: 5'10" **Weight:** 11.10
Club Honours: Div 1 '97, '00
This versatile defender was very much a fringe player at Blackburn last season. Although given the number 4 shirt he was injured early on and never found a regular starting place. When selected he showed a considerable ability to read the game, but needs to develop greater consistency. Andy opened his goal-scorin account for Rovers in the 3-2 win at Leeds in April.
Middlesbrough *(From trainee on 6/3/1992) FL 7+1 FLC 1+1 Others 5*
Swindon T *(Loaned on 27/2/1995) FL 13*
Bolton W *(£250,000 on 1/8/1995) P/FL 66+18/2 FLC 14+5/1 FAC 1 Others 3*
Charlton Ath *(£750,000 on 18/11/1999) P/FL 27+13/1 FLC 4 FAC 6+1*
Grimsby T *(Loaned on 21/2/2002) FL 12/3*

lackburn Rov (£750,000 on 31/5/2002) PL
+5/1 FLC 4 FAC 2 Others 1

ODD Christopher (Chris)
ichard
orn: Swansea, 22 August 1981
leight: 6'0" **Weight:** 11.4
his promising young central defender
howed maturity beyond his years when
alled up into the Exeter City first team by
ew manager Gary Peters last March. His
ace and awareness made him a popular
gure with the City faithful, and also
elped the team shore up the defence. It
vas no coincidence that the goals
topped leaking when Chris came into
he line-up.
wansea C (From trainee on 6/7/2000) FL
9+4/4 FLC 1 FAC 1 Others 1 (Freed during
*002 close season)
xeter C (Free from Drogheda U on
1/1/2003) FL 12

ODOROV Svetoslav
orn: Bulgaria, 30 August 1978
leight: 6'0" **Weight:** 11.11
:lub Honours: Div 1 '03
nternational Honours: Bulgaria: 29;
'th
his predatory striker had an excellent
ampaign at Portsmouth in 2002-03, finishing as the First Division's leading
oal-scorer and winning a recall to the
ulgarian international squad. Svetoslav's
ally of 26 goals included a hat-trick at
radford in the final game of the season.
.lthough not particularly tall, he has
ood technique on the ball and is able to
urn quickly. His ability to convert a half-
hance into a goal served him well and he
nade a major contribution to Pompey's
tle-winning side.
West Ham U (£500,000 + from Liteks
ovech, Bulgaria on 30/1/2001) PL 4+10/1
LC 1 FAC 0+2/1
ortsmouth (£750,000 on 20/3/2002) FL
6+2/27 FLC 2 FAC 1

ROFTING Stig
orn: Aarhus, Denmark, 14 August 1969
leight: 5'9" **Weight:** 12.0
nternational Honours: Denmark: 41
A massive cult hero among the Bolton
ans, Stig began the 2002-03 season
oming off the back of a successful World
:up with the Denmark national team.
lowever, off-the-field problems had a big
mpact on his campaign and he started
ust two Premiership games, although he
lso featured in three cup ties. A tough-
ackling battering ram of a midfielder, Stig
nade a handful of appearances from the
ench, although events away from the

football field ultimately resulted in his
leaving the club towards the end of the
season. He subsequently returned in a
commercial capacity and the response he
received when making a half-time
appearance proved that this passionate
and dedicated player will be afforded a
warm welcome should he ever return to
the Reebok Stadium.
Bolton W (£250,000 from Hamburger SV,
Germany, ex Aarhus GF, Hamburger SV,
Odense BK, Duisburg, on 8/2/2002) PL 8+6
FLC 1 FAC 2

TOGWELL Samuel (Sam)
Born: Beaconsfield, 14 October 1984
Height: 5'11" **Weight:** 12.4
This young Crystal Palace defender did
well in the club's reserves last term and
stepped up to make his senior debut in
the televised game at Rotherham shortly
before Christmas. He subsequently
returned to the second string, but had the
misfortune to suffer a broken leg playing
against Bristol Rovers in February and this
brought his campaign to a premature
end.
Crystal Palace (Trainee) FL 0+1

TOLLEY Glenn Anthony
Born: Knighton, 24 September 1984
Height: 5'8" **Weight:** 10.3
This promising Shrewsbury midfield player
did well in the reserve and youth teams
last term and made his bow in senior
football as a substitute in the home
match with Hartlepool last October. Glenn
is a cousin of his Shrewsbury colleague
Jamie Tolley.
Shrewsbury T (Trainee) FL 0+1

TOLLEY Jamie Christopher
Born: Ludlow, 12 May 1983
Height: 6'0" **Weight:** 11.3
International Honours: W: U21-6
Jamie enjoyed an excellent season for
Shrewsbury Town and his totally
committed style ensured he was the
backbone of the midfield. He has a
tremendous shot and scored four times,
adding another for Wales U21s against
Italy in Cardiff. It remains to be seen
whether the talented youngster will
remain at Gay Meadow following the
club's relegation to the Conference.
Shrewsbury T (From trainee on 9/1/2001) FL
79+9/6 FLC 1+1 FAC 3+3/1 Others 5+1

TOMLINSON Stuart
Born: Chester, 10 May 1985
Height: 6'0" **Weight:** 11.0
This promising young Crewe Alexandra
goalkeeper featured a number of times

on the substitutes' bench last term. He
stepped up to make his bow in senior
football when replacing the injured Danny
Milosevic early in the second half of the
game at Oldham in January and went on
to produce a more than competent
performance.
Crewe Alex (Trainee) FL 0+1

TONER Ciaran
Born: Craigavon, 30 June 1981
Height: 6'1" **Weight:** 12.4
International Honours: NI: 2; U21-17;
Yth; Sch
Ciaran joined Leyton Orient during the
2002 close season and featured regularly
for the first team during the 2002-03
campaign. An attacking midfielder who is
able to deliver telling passes, he captained
the Northern Ireland U21s and won his
first full caps in the end-of-season games
against Italy and Spain.
Tottenham H (From trainee on 14/7/1999)
Peterborough U (Loaned on 21/12/2001) FL
6 FAC 1
Bristol Rov (Free on 28/3/2002) FL 6
Leyton Orient (Free on 7/5/2002) FL 22+3/1
FLC 1 FAC 1 Others 2

TONGE Michael William
Born: Manchester, 7 April 1983
Height: 6'0" **Weight:** 11.10
International Honours: E: Yth
Following an impressive first season in
2001-02 for Sheffield United, Michael
continued to progress last term. Playing as
an attacking midfielder he had an
excellent campaign, showing great vision
with his passing and the ability to beat an
opponent down the flanks and produce
searching crosses. He showed a keen eye
for goal too, and his long-range brace
against Liverpool in the Worthington Cup
semi-final was particularly memorable.
Michael played for England U20 against
Italy and Switzerland during the season.
Sheffield U (From trainee on 16/3/2001) FL
68+8/9 FLC 7/2 FAC 6 Others 3

TONKIN Anthony
Born: Newlyn, 17 January 1980
Height: 5'11" **Weight:** 12.2
Club Honours: FAT '02
Following his arrival at Stockport from
eventual Conference champions Yeovil
Town for a bargain fee, Anthony was
thrown straight into a tough Cheshire
'derby' at Tranmere. He quickly adapted
to life in Division Two with some
confident performances and impressed
with his assured tackling and pacy runs
down the left flank.

Stockport Co (£50,000 from Yeovil T on 26/9/2002) FL 23+1 FLC 1 FAC 2

TORPEY Stephen (Steve)
David James
Born: Islington, 8 December 1970
Height: 6'3" **Weight:** 14.6
Club Honours: AMC '94
Scunthorpe United's target man had an excellent first half to the 2002-03 season netting 15 goals by New Year's Day including two hat-tricks in quick succession against Torquay and in the FA Cup tie at Northwich. Strong in the air, he held the ball up well and was a constant threat to opposition defences before a torn thigh muscle against Exeter in January ruled him out for three months. He returned for the last two games and the play-offs.
Millwall (From trainee on 14/2/1989) FL 3+4 FLC 0+1
Bradford C (£70,000 on 21/11/1990) FL 86+10/22 FLC 6 FAC 2+1 Others 8/6
Swansea C (£80,000 on 3/8/1993) FL 151+11/44 FLC 9+2/2 FAC 10/5 Others 18+3/6
Bristol C (£400,000 on 8/8/1997) FL 53+17/13 FLC 4+1/1 FAC 3 Others 3+1
Notts Co (Loaned on 7/8/1998) FL 4+2/1 FLC 1+1/1
Scunthorpe U (£175,000 on 3/2/2000) FL 118+4/34 FLC 3/2 FAC 11/4 Others 5+1/3

TOURE Kolo Abib
Born: Ivory Coast, 19 March 1981
Height: 5'10" **Weight:** 11.13
Club Honours: CS '02; FAC '03
International Honours: Ivory Coast
In his first season at Arsenal, the young Ivory Coast international showed great promise. A powerful runner with incredible upper body strength, he played in a variety of positions in the reserves. However, he prefers a midfield role, where his versatility, stamina and strength all come into play. Kolo featured at left back for the Gunners in Champions' League games against Valencia and PSV Eindhoven.
Arsenal (Signed from ASEC Mimosa, Ivory Coast on 18/2/2002) PL 9+17/2 FLC 1 FAC 3+2 Others 3+5

TOWN David Edward
Born: Bournemouth, 9 December 1976
Height: 5'8" **Weight:** 11.7
Club Honours: NC '02
This bustling striker was given few chances to shine in Boston United's first season of Third Division football. Early in the campaign he was loaned out to

Kettering Town for a month and on his return was mostly restricted to reserve football. David's only first-team appearances were from the substitutes' bench. He was released at the end of the season and was reported to have signed for Dr Martens League club Havant & Waterlooville.
Bournemouth (From trainee on 11/4/1995) FL 18+38/2 FLC 0+8 Others 0+2 (Free to Rushden & Diamonds on 5/6/1999)
Boston U (Free from Hayes on 28/3/2001) FL 0+8

TOWNSEND Benjamin (Ben)
Born: Reading, 8 October 1981
Height: 5'10" **Weight:** 11.3
This young Wycombe right back made just one solitary first-team appearance last season, coming on as a substitute in the LDV Vans Trophy tie at Torquay in October. A training injury put him out of contention for a month in November, but he then enjoyed a very successful spell on loan at Conference side Woking starting in January. He helped steer the club to safety and decided to accept their offer of a contract before the end of the season
Wycombe W (From trainee on 13/1/2001) FL 12+1 FAC 5+1 Others 2+1

TOWNSON Kevin
Born: Liverpool, 19 April 1983
Height: 5'8" **Weight:** 10.3
International Honours: E: Yth
After his sensational breakthrough in 2001-02, Kevin had a somewhat quieter time last term. He started the first two games but lost his place to the more physical Lee McEvilly and thereafter spent almost the whole of the season on the bench, managing just four more starts but being a substitute more than 40 times. His one goal came against Cambridge, when he came on to help Dale turn a 3-1 deficit into a 4-3 win.
Rochdale (Free from Everton juniors on 6/7/2000) FL 23+45/15 FLC 0+2/2 FAC 1+3 Others 4+1/1

TRAORE Djimi
Born: Paris, France, 1 March 1980
Height: 6'3" **Weight:** 13.10
Club Honours: FLC '03
International Honours: France: U21; Yth
After spending the previous season on loan to Lens, it seemed that the young French defender's days at Anfield were numbered but it now appears that Liverpool manager Gerald Houllier was grooming him for stardom. He started the season as first choice left back and held his place for much of the campaign,

standing in for the injured Stephane Henchoz in central defence for a while. Whilst not always convincing at the back his progress was clear to see.
Liverpool (£550,000 from Laval, France on 18/2/1999) PL 38+2 FLC 5+1 FAC 2 Others 14+2

TRAYNOR Robert (Rob)
Terence
Born: Burnham, 1 November 1983
Height: 5'9" **Weight:** 12.2
This exciting Brentford youngster established himself as a proven goal-scorer at U19 level. A talented outside right he made three substitute appearances for the first team in January. Rob will be looking to gain further senior experience for the Bees in 2003-04.
Brentford (From trainee on 9/7/2002) FL 0+ Others 0+1

TROLLOPE Paul Jonathan
Born: Swindon, 3 June 1972
Height: 6'0" **Weight:** 12.6
Club Honours: Div 2 '99
International Honours: W: 9; B-1
The defensive midfield player was appointed captain on his arrival at Northampton last season. Although the campaign started well, the team was disrupted by a run of injuries and Paul was called upon to adapt his game to suit the nature of the line-up. He looked useful going forward and netted a couple of much needed goals. Paul is the son of John Trollope the former Swindon Town defender.
Swindon T (From trainee on 23/12/1989)
Torquay U (Free on 26/3/1992) FL 103+3/16 FLC 9+1/1 FAC 7 Others 8+1
Derby Co (£100,000 on 16/12/1994) F/PL 47+18/5 FLC 3+2/1 FAC 3+1
Grimsby T (Loaned on 30/8/1996) FL 6+1/1
Crystal Palace (Loaned on 11/10/1996) FL 0+9
Fulham (£600,000 on 28/11/1997) FL 54+22/5 FLC 9+2 FAC 3+5 Others 4/1
Coventry C (Free on 22/3/2002) FL 5+1
Northampton T (Free on 31/7/2002) FL 41/2 FLC 1 FAC 3 Others 2

TRUNDLE Lee Christopher
Born: Liverpool, 10 October 1976
Height: 6'0" **Weight:** 13.3
With quick feet and no little skill Lee can be a real handful for any defence, and his trump card is his ability to turn his opponent in one movement and set off for goal. The predominantly left-footed player can also frustrate however, especially if he loses possession in promising situations. The talented striker

ored his quota of goals, a number of
em spectacular affairs, notably a 25-
rd strike at Kidderminster in April,
though he missed the Cambridge
ited match at the Racecourse when
omotion was clinched, the fans gave
m a hero's reception on his return for
e next match at Leyton Orient.
*rexham (£60,000 from Rhyl, ex
rscough, Chorley, Stalybridge Celtic,
uthport, on 16/2/2001) FL 73+21/27 FLC
-2 FAC 1 Others 4+1/3*

UDGAY Marcus
orn: Shoreham, 3 February 1983
eight: 6'3" **Weight:** 13.2
striker with good pace, Marcus made a
ries of substitute appearances for Derby
ounty before his first start in the FA Cup
it at Brentford. A severe ankle injury
ought a premature end to his season
d he was offered a monthly contract to
courage recovery. Even in the reserves,
arcus is not a prolific scorer, preferring
hold the ball and bring others into the
tion. He has to realise that strikers are
easured by their goals but showed
erby that there is something to work on
d develop.
*erby Co (From trainee on 16/7/2002) FL
-8 FAC 1*

UDOR Shane Anthony
orn: Wolverhampton, 10 February 1982
eight: 5'8" **Weight:** 11.2
ne of the stars of the season for
ambridge United, Shane featured
gularly in the line-up on the right wing,
eating chances for others and scoring
l goals himself. His strike against
ochdale in March was voted as 'Goal of
e Season', but it also proved his
ownfall, as he damaged his hamstring
d groin forcing him to miss the
mainder of the campaign. He was also
ted as the U's 'Young Player of the
ear'.
*/olverhampton W (From trainee on
8/1999) FL 0+1
ambridge U (Free on 22/11/2001) FL
7+2/12 FLC 2/1 FAC 7/1 Others 10/2*

TUGAY] KERIMOGLU Tugay
orn: Istanbul, Turkey, 24 August 1970
eight: 5'9" **Weight:** 11.6
lub Honours: SPD '00; SC '00; FLC '02
ternational Honours: Turkey: 86
ugay was very much the fulcrum of the
ackburn Rovers team last season, pulling
e strings in midfield, directing the
attern of play and ensuring the ball was
tained long enough to threaten
pposition defences. He was superb in

Shane Tudor

the UEFA cup tie against Celtic in Glasgow, the complete master of the game, and several other teams found him impossible to counter. His only goal proved to be the crucial strike that beat Arsenal and it was struck so well that one wonders why he scores so few.
Glasgow R *(Signed from Galatasaray, Turkey on 15/1/2000) SL 26+16/4 SLC 2+1 SC 3+4 Others 6*
Blackburn Rov *(£1,300,000 on 20/7/2001) PL 64+6/4 FLC 9+1 FAC 5+2 Others 4*

TURLEY William (Billy) Lee
Born: Wolverhampton, 15 July 1973
Height: 6'4" **Weight:** 15.0
Club Honours: NC '01; Div 3 '03
This highly rated goalkeeper enjoyed another excellent year with Rushden & Diamonds, helping the team win a second championship in three seasons. Once again Billy made a series of crucial saves at vital times throughout the campaign to play a key role in the title success. He missed only five games due to a groin injury just before Christmas and ensured that summer signing Adam Sollitt stayed as second choice.
Northampton T *(Free from Evesham on 10/7/1995) FL 28 FAC 2 Others 4*
Leyton Orient *(Loaned on 5/2/1998) FL 14*
Rushden & Diamonds *(£135,000 on 15/6/1999) FL 86+1 FLC 4 FAC 4 Others 4*

TURNER Andrew (Andy)
Peter
Born: Woolwich, 23 March 1975
Height: 5'10" **Weight:** 11.12
International Honours: RoI: U21-7. E: Yth; Sch
A winger turned midfielder, Andy was reunited with his former Portsmouth boss Terry Fenwick when he joined Northampton from Dr Martens League club Tamworth last season. However, he managed just three appearances from the substitutes' bench for the Cobblers. When Fenwick departed, Andy fell out of favour altogether and moved on to Conference club Northwich Victoria. No longer commanding the pace of his earlier days, he showed he still had the ability to hold the ball.
Tottenham H *(From trainee on 8/4/1992) PL 8+12/3 FLC 0+2/1 FAC 0+1 Others 1*
Wycombe W *(Loaned on 26/8/1994) FL 3+1*
Doncaster Rov *(Loaned on 10/10/1994) FL 4/1 Others 1/1*
Huddersfield T *(Loaned on 28/11/1995) FL 2+3/1*
Southend U *(Loaned on 28/3/1996) FL 4+2*
Portsmouth *(£250,000 on 4/9/1996) FL 34+6/3 FLC 2+2 FAC 1*

Crystal Palace *(Free on 27/10/1998) FL 0+2*
Wolverhampton W *(Free on 25/3/1999)*
Rotherham U *(Free on 1/7/1999) FL 29+7/1 FLC 2 Others 1*
Rochdale *(Loaned on 22/3/2001) FL 2+2*
Northampton T *(Free from Tamworth, ex Yeovil T, Nuneaton Borough, on 16/1/2003) FL 0+3*

TURNER John Andrew James
Born: Harrow, 12 February 1986
Height: 6'2" **Weight:** 11.0
This promising Cambridge striker made a dream of a debut after coming off the bench in the game at Exeter in April. Into stoppage time, he burst into the area to score the winning goal. Injury then cut his season short, but he will be hoping for more senior action in 2003-04.
Cambridge U *(Trainee) FL 0+1/1*

TURNER Michael Thomas
Born: Lewisham, 9 November 1983
Height: 6'4" **Weight:** 12.6
This tall and powerful central defender captained the Charlton Athletic reserve team for much of last season. In March he joined Third Division Leyton Orient on loan, soon settling into the team and scoring for the O's in the home win over Swansea City.
Charlton Ath *(From trainee on 6/3/2001)*
Leyton Orient *(Loaned on 26/3/2003) FL 7/1*

TUTTLE David Philip
Born: Reading, 6 February 1972
Height: 6'1" **Weight:** 12.10
Club Honours: FAYC '90
International Honours: E: Yth
David began the 2002-03 season as third-string central defender for Millwall, and his only first-team appearance came at Watford in August. A recurring back problem eventually forced him to give up first-team football and he has since been involved with the Lions' academy set-up. Very much 'Mr Dependable' David's experience at the back was always of great benefit to the team.
Tottenham H *(From trainee on 8/2/1990) F/PL 10+3 FLC 3+1 Others 1/1*
Peterborough U *(Loaned on 21/11/1993) FL 7*
Sheffield U *(£350,000 on 1/8/1993) P/FL 63/1 FLC 2 FAC 3*
Crystal Palace *(Signed on 8/3/1996) F/PL 73+8/5 FLC 7 FAC 2 Others 6*
Barnsley *(£150,000 on 18/8/1999) FL 11+1 FAC 1*
Millwall *(£200,000 on 2/3/2000) FL 19+4 FLC 2+1 Others 3*
Wycombe W *(Loaned on 22/2/2002) FL 4*

TWIGG Gary
Born: Glasgow, 19 March 1984
Height: 6'0" **Weight:** 11.12
Gary made a number of substitute appearances for Derby County early in the 2002-03 season and a first start in a heavy home defeat by Wolves, but was usually played in wide areas rather than his preferred position as a striker. His campaign was then disrupted by a hernia problem that required surgery, although he was able to return in the reserves. As one of Derby's brighter prospects, Gary hopes for greater progress in the season ahead.
Derby Co *(From trainee on 20/3/2001) P/FL 1+8*

TYLER Mark Richard
Born: Norwich, 2 April 1977
Height: 6'0" **Weight:** 12.9
International Honours: E: Yth
Rated by many as one of the finest goalkeepers in the lower divisions, Mark was first choice for Peterborough United until being sidelined by a broken arm in a friendly game with Arsenal in November. He returned to action in March and resumed his position as the club's number one 'keeper. Agile and a fine shot stopper, he is rumoured to have been tracked by a number of higher-level clubs.
Peterborough U *(From trainee on 7/12/1994) FL 225+1 FLC 11 FAC 18 Others 16*

TYSON Nathan
Born: Reading, 4 May 1982
Height: 5'10" **Weight:** 11.12
International Honours: E: Yth
The outstanding performance of the season from Nathan came not in a Reading shirt but in an England one, when he scored twice for the U20 team in a 2-1 victory against Germany in front of his home town crowd at the Madejski Stadium. His superlative display in that game, plus a series of exciting games in the outside-left position for his club, earned the academy graduate a two-year extension to his contract. Nathan scored his first league goal too, with a cross-shot in the 2-1 win against Derby County. He is by no means the finished article but his progress over the season was remarkable.
Reading *(From trainee on 18/3/2000) FL 9+16/1 FLC 0+1 FAC 2+1 Others 0+2*
Swansea C *(Loaned on 30/8/2001) FL 7+4/1*
Cheltenham T *(Loaned on 22/3/2002) FL 1+7/1*

UV

'DDIN Anwar

orn: Tower Hamlets, 1 November 1981
eight: 6'2" **Weight:** 13.0
is young central defender joined Bristol
overs during the summer of 2002 and
ter making his league debut on the
pening day of the season he quickly
pressed with his mature performances.
nwar was a regular in the line-up until
ovember when he picked up a groin
jury, which required an operation and
delined him for eight weeks. He
turned briefly but struggled to regain
ll match fitness and had to be content
ith a few reserve-team games.
'est Ham U (From trainee on 9/7/2001)
neffield Wed (Free on 28/2/2002)
ristol Rov (Free on 2/7/2002) FL 17+1/1
C 1 Others 1

DEZE Ifeanyi (Iffy)

orn: Nigeria, 21 July 1980
eight: 5'9" **Weight:** 11.8
ternational Honours: Nigeria:
well-proportioned attacking left-sided
ayer with a fair turn of speed, Iffy joined
Vest Bromwich Albion on loan in January
s back up for Neil Clement. He made his
emiership debut at left back in the 1-0
ome defeat by Charlton two weeks after
gning, but only made a handful of
opearances as an infuriating knee injury
terrupted his progress in April. Iffy
ontinued to represent Nigeria at
ternational level during the campaign.
'est Bromwich A (Loaned from PAOK
alonika, Greece, ex Benden Insurance,
avala, on 17/1/2003) PL 7+4

HLENBEEK Gustav (Gus)

einier
orn: Paramaribo, Surinam, 20 August
970
eight: 5'10" **Weight:** 12.6
lub Honours: Div 2 '99
powerful and pacy full back, Gus
nowed plenty of ability with Bradford last
eason. He was a virtual ever-present for
ne club and proved to be a shrewd buy
the transfer market. Although he posed
constant threat with his runs down the
ing, his only goal of the campaign was
the 4-2 home victory over Rotherham
t the end of August. Gus was out of
ontract in the summer and at the time of
riting his future was uncertain.
oswich T (£100,000 from Tops SV, Holland,
x Ajax, Cambuur, on 11/8/1995) FL 77+12/4
C 5+3 FAC 4+3 Others 7+1

Fulham (Free on 22/7/1998) FL 22+17/1 FLC
4+1 FAC 3+2 Others 1
Sheffield U (Free on 10/8/2000) FL 47+4 FLC
5 FAC 3
Walsall (Loaned on 28/3/2002) FL 5
Bradford C (Free on 9/8/2002) FL 42/1 FLC 1
FAC 1

ULLATHORNE Robert (Rob)

Born: Wakefield, 11 October 1971
Height: 5'8" **Weight:** 11.3
International Honours: E: Yth
Rob began the 2002-03 season as first
choice left wing back at Sheffield United,
using his pace and anticipation in defence
and linking up well when going forward
to produce some searching crosses. In
mid-October he had a double hernia
operation, which kept him out for much

longer than expected, but he returned to
reserve-team duty in April.
Norwich C (From trainee on 6/7/1990) F/PL
86+8/7 FLC 10+2/1 FAC 7+1 Others 1 (Free
to Osasuna, Spain during 1996 close season)
Leicester C (£600,000 on 18/2/1997) PL
28+3/1 FLC 8+1 FAC 2/1
Sheffield U (Free, following an injury and
trials at Huddersfield T, Real Zaragoza,
Tenerife, Newcastle, on 1/12/2000) FL 39+1
FLC 2 FAC 2

UNDERWOOD Paul Victor

Born: Wimbledon, 16 August 1973
Height: 5'11" **Weight:** 12.8
Club Honours: NC '01; Div 3 '03
International Honours: E: SP-4
The Rushden & Diamonds' 'Captain
Marvel' produced a series of consistent

Gus Uhlenbeek

performances at left back last season to guide the side to the Third Division title. He was a very influential figure on the pitch throughout the championship campaign and his form was recognised by his fellow professionals with fully deserved selection in the PFA's Division Three team of the season. Manager Brian Talbot's first signing at Nene Park, and arguably his best, Paul scored his first-ever Football League goal to snatch a last-gasp draw at Swansea City on the opening day of the season.

Rushden & Diamonds (£50,000 from Enfield, ex Kingstonian, Molesey, Sutton U, Carshalton Ath, on 6/6/1997) FL 80/1 FLC 3 FAC 5 Others 4

UNSWORTH David Gerald
Born: Chorley, 16 October 1973
Height: 6'1" **Weight:** 14.2
Club Honours: FAC '95; CS '95
International Honours: E: 1; U21-6; Yth
Another Everton player who looked fitter than for some time, David had a typically consistent and committed season in his testimonial year when he also reached 300 games for the club. Capable of playing in central defence as well as on the left-hand side, David was employed at left back for the majority of the campaign. He was as robust as ever and showed his usual adroitness from the penalty spot, equalling the club record of 23 successful spot-kicks in the game against Liverpool. There have been very few more honest performers in the game in the past few years and David was one of the deserved nominations for the Premiership's ten-year awards for his work with disabled players and the community.

Everton (From trainee on 25/6/1992) F/PL 108+8/11 FLC 5+2 FAC 7 Others 4/1
West Ham U (£1,000,000 + on 18/8/1997) PL 32/2 FLC 5 FAC 4
Aston Villa (£3,000,000 on 28/7/1998)
Everton (£3,000,000 on 22/8/1998) PL 142+20/20 FLC 9/1 FAC 13+1/4

UNSWORTH Lee Peter
Born: Eccles, 25 February 1973
Height: 5'11" **Weight:** 11.8
Lee found himself turning out at right wing back for Bury for much of last season, although he also occasionally filled in at his preferred role of centre half. He turned in consistent performances in both positions and managed to steer clear of injury throughout the campaign. He also popped up with important goals against Bournemouth and Carlisle. Lee was forced onto the substitutes' bench for the closing dozen or so games after

he lost his place to Lee Connell.
Crewe Alex (Signed from Ashton U on 20/2/1995) FL 93+33 FLC 10+1/1 FAC 5+1/1 Others 8+2
Bury (Free on 4/8/2000) FL 80+5/3 FLC 5 FAC 4 Others 7

UPSON Matthew James
Born: Stowmarket, 18 April 1979
Height: 6'1" **Weight:** 11.4
Club Honours: PL '02
International Honours: E: 3; U21-10; Yth
Despite his considerable talent and ability, Matthew was unable to break into the Arsenal first team. He enjoyed a very successful loan spell at Reading, where his arrival coincided with a run of six consecutive wins without conceding a goal. However, he was then sold to Birmingham City during the January transfer window for a bargain fee. Matthew quickly settled in and gave Kenny Cunningham in the Blues' defence and did so much to help them become a mean outfit during the battle against relegation. His decisive form earned the club's first England call-up in 25 years when he made his international debut against Australia in February.
Luton T (From trainee on 24/4/1996) FL 0+1 Others 1
Arsenal (£1,000,000 on 14/5/1997) PL 20+14 FLC 8 FAC 3+1 Others 8+2
Nottingham F (Loaned on 8/12/2000) FL 1
Crystal Palace (Loaned on 2/3/2001) FL 7
Reading (Loaned on 6/9/2002) FL 13+1 FLC 1/1
Birmingham C (£1,000,000 + on 23/1/2003) PL 14

VAESEN Nico Jos-Theodor
Born: Ghent, Belgium, 28 September 1969
Height: 6'3" **Weight:** 12.8
Nico was Birmingham City's regular goalkeeper until manager Steve Bruce rested him in January. He had done little wrong, however, and soon got his place back only to suffer a serious knee injury towards the end of the 2-0 'derby' win at Aston Villa in March. He showed excellent command of the air and made numerous key stops, especially in one-on-one situations in a number of games when the outcome was still in the balance.
Huddersfield T (£80,000 from SC Eendracht Aalst, Belgium on 10/7/1998) FL 134 FLC 12 FAC 7
Birmingham C (£800,000 on 19/6/2001) P/FL 49+1 FLC 2 FAC 1 Others 3

VALAKARI Simo
Born: Helsinki, Finland, 28 April 1973
Height: 5'10" **Weight:** 11.10

International Honours: Finland: 30; U21-1
Surgery on ruptured ankle ligaments caused Simo to miss the start of the 2002-03 season for Derby County but, although he returned to reserve football at the start of October, he never gained place in the squad while John Gregory was manager. At one stage, it looked likely that his contract would be paid up and, shortly before the League transfer deadline, he rejected a loan to Macclesfield Town. When George Burley was appointed as interim manager, Simo was straight into the side and responded with an exquisite lob to score at Wimbledon in an impressive victory. He is economically neat in midfield and should surely have played a part earlier. Once fit he regained his place in the Finland squad.
Motherwell (Signed from MyPa, Finland on 6/2/1997) SL 98+6 SLC 3+1 SC 7+2
Derby Co (Free on 6/7/2000) P/FL 20+6/3 FLC 4

VALENTINE Ryan David
Born: Wrexham, 19 August 1982
Height: 5'10" **Weight:** 11.11
International Honours: W: U21-8; Yth
This young Wales U21 international arrived at Darlington in the 2002 close season and made the left-back slot his own, missing just a handful of games. Ryan is quick into the tackle and loves to get forward, overlapping down the flank to link up with the midfield. These attacking forays, however, only produced one goal when he netted in the 2-2 draw at Bury in October.
Everton (From trainee on 1/9/1999)
Darlington (Free on 8/8/2002) FL 43/1 FLC FAC 3 Others 1

VAN BLERK Jason
Born: Sydney, Australia, 16 March 1968
Height: 6'1" **Weight:** 13.0
International Honours: Australia: 27; Yth
Jason signed for Shrewsbury Town during the 2002 close season and made his debut at full back in the opening fixture. He featured regularly early on, but as the campaign unfolded he became more of a squad player. Jason also featured in central defence and midfield and scored two goals, including one in the draw at Rochdale in September. He was released at the end of the season.
Millwall (£300,000 from Go Ahead Eagles, Holland on 8/9/1994) FL 68+5/2 FLC 5 FAC 6+1 Others 1+1
Manchester C (Free on 9/8/1997) FL 10+9 FLC 0+1 FAC 0+1

West Bromwich A (£250,000 on 13/3/1998)
FL 106+3/3 FLC 8+1 FAC 1 Others 2
Stockport Co (Free on 16/8/2001) FL 13
FLC 1
Hull C (Free on 3/1/2002) FL 10/1
Shrewsbury T (Free on 8/8/2002) FL 17+6/1
FLC 1 FAC 2/1 Others 4

VAN BRONCKHORST
Giovanni (Gio) Christiaan
Born: Rotterdam, Holland, 5 February
1975
Height: 5'10" **Weight:** 11.10
Club Honours: SPD '99, '00; SC '99, '00;
FLC '98; PL '02; FAC '03
International Honours: Holland: 29
This talented midfield player suffered a
cruciate ligament injury in February 2002,
which kept him out of action until last
December. Once fully fit he found it
difficult to command an automatic spot in
the Arsenal line-up and most of his
appearances were as cover for injured
players. Gio is a creative left-sided player
either at full back or in midfield, he gets
forward well and is a good crosser of the
ball.
Glasgow R (£5,000,000 from Feyenoord,
Holland on 15/7/1998) SL 72+1/13 SLC 6/1
SC 10+1/3 Others 28/5
Arsenal (£8,500,000 on 22/6/2001) PL
12+19/2 FLC 4 FAC 5+2 Others 8+3

VAN DER SAR Edwin
Born: Leiden, Holland, 29 October 1970
Height: 6'5" **Weight:** 13.6
International Honours: Holland: 72
Edwin is a goalkeeper whose vast
international and European experience
proved invaluable as Fulham made it
through to the third round of the UEFA
Cup. An excellent shot stopper who
dominates the penalty area with his size,
he started the 2002-03 season as first
choice and rarely missed out until
sustaining a foot injury at Newcastle in
December which kept him out of the
game for four months. Although he did
regain his place when fit he went straight
back into the Netherlands side for the
friendly against Portugal in late April.
Fulham (£7,000,000 from Juventus, Italy, ex
Noordwijk, Ajax, on 10/8/2001) PL 56 FAC 4
Others 11

VAN DEURZEN Jurgen
Born: Genk, Belgium, 26 January 1974
Height: 5'7" **Weight:** 11.0
This adaptable left-sided player re-
established his place in the Stoke City
line-up as a wide midfield player during
the first part of last season. However, the
poor general form of the side and a

change in managers did nothing for his
confidence and at the end of the year it
was decided to pay up his contract and
allow him to return to Belgium where he
signed for Second Division outfit KFC
Dessel Sport.
Stoke C (Signed from KFC Turnhout, Belgium
on 8/8/2001) FL 44+8/5 FLC 1 FAC 4 Others
0+3

VAN HEUSDEN Arjan
Born: Alphen, Holland, 11 December
1972
Height: 6'3" **Weight:** 14.7
This experienced goalkeeper signed a
short-term contract for Mansfield last
September when both the club's senior
'keepers were injured. Arjan's first job was
to pick the ball out of the net in the
second minute of his debut at
Northampton after he had given away a
penalty, but he recovered from this
mishap and performed well for the rest of
his short period at Field Mill. He
subsequently joined Torquay United,
where he got off to a good start, but
then succumbed to a thigh injury.
However, Arjan did well enough to earn
himself a contract for the Gulls and
eventually won his place back in the line-
up.
Port Vale (£4,500 from VV Noordwijk,
Holland on 15/8/1994) FL 27 FLC 4 Others 2
Oxford U (Loaned on 26/9/1997) FL 11 FLC
2
Cambridge U (Free on 4/8/1998) FL 41+1
FLC 6 FAC 1 Others 4
Exeter C (Free on 31/7/2000) FL 74 FLC 2
FAC 4 Others 1
Mansfield T (Free on 27/9/2002) FL 5
Torquay U (Free on 1/11/2002) FL 15 FAC 1

VAN NISTELROOY Rutgerus
(Ruud) Johannes Martinus
Born: Oss, Holland, 1 July 1976
Height: 6'2" **Weight:** 12.13
Club Honours: PL '03
International Honours: Holland: 25
An archetypal centre forward who is
blessed with all-round technique,
powerful in the air, and packing a
fearsome shot in either foot, Ruud's
influence on the goal-scoring front last
season was such he seemed determined
to smash every Manchester United record
going. In Europe alone, he notched a
remarkable 14 goals in 11 games, thus,
with the previous season's tally, eclipsing
the all-time club record previously held by
Andy Cole. He also notched 25 in
Premiership matches, including hat-tricks
against Newcastle, Fulham, and Charlton.
The sheer beauty of his goals had older

fans comparing him to Denis Law, but
even the 'King' would agree that Ruud
looks set to rewrite the Old Trafford
record books in double-quick time.
Manchester U (£19,000,000 from PSV
Eindhoven, Holland, ex Den Bosch,
Heerenveen, on 5/7/2001) PL 62+4/48 FLC
4/1 FAC 3+2/6 Others 25+1/25

VARGA Stanislav
Born: Czechoslovakia, 8 October 1972
Height: 6'2" **Weight:** 14.8
International Honours: Slovakia: 39
A giant Slovakian international centre
back, Stanislav made his only Sunderland
appearances last term in the Worthington
and FA Cups. Dangerous at set pieces,
where he is virtually unbeatable in the air,
he is also an excellent distributor of the
ball from defence. After beginning the
season as a player deemed surplus to
requirements, he was allowed to join
Celtic in January by mutual agreement.
However, Stanislav made his debut for the
Bhoys in the Scottish Cup debacle against
Inverness, and made only one more
appearance before the close of the
season.
Sunderland (£650,000 from SK Slovan
Bratislave, Slovakia, ex Tetran Presov, on
14/8/2000) PL 18+3/1 FLC 5+1 FAC 5+1
West Bromwich A (Loaned on 25/3/2002)
FL 3+1

VASSELL Darius
Born: Birmingham, 13 June 1980
Height: 5'7" **Weight:** 12.0
International Honours: E: 13; U21-10;
Yth
Darius struggled to find consistency in his
performances for Aston Villa last term,
despite the fact that he was a regular in
the line-up throughout the season. A
quick and skilful striker who loves to take
defences on, he has nifty footwork and is
lightning quick. His best goal-scoring form
came in November when he netted five
times in a run of six games. Darius
featured on a number of occasions for
the full England side, scoring a vital goal
in the Euro 2004 qualifier against Turkey.
He was voted as Villa's 'Young Player of
the Year'.
Aston Villa (From trainee on 14/4/1998) PL
64+45/24 FLC 4+7/3 FAC 3+4/1 Others
3+11/4

VAUGHAN Anthony (Tony)
John
Born: Manchester, 11 October 1975
Height: 6'1" **Weight:** 11.2
International Honours: E: Yth; Sch
Out of favour again with Nottingham

Edwin Van Der Sar

rest, this experienced central defender
ined neighbours Mansfield Town on
an to cover for injuries and suspension.
e produced some solid performances
n the left-hand side of the defence, but
turned to the City Ground with an
jury. In the new year he went out on
an again, this time to Motherwell
here he made 15 appearances, scoring
the 2-2 draw with Dundee United.
swich T (From trainee on 1/7/1994) P/FL
5+11/3 FLC 4+2 FAC 2 Others 4
anchester C (£1,350,000 on 9/7/1997) FL
4+4/2 FLC 6+1 FAC 3 Others 3+1
ardiff C (Loaned on 15/9/1999) FL 14
thers 1
ottingham F (£350,000 on 8/2/2000) FL
8+5/1 FLC 2 FAC 1
cunthorpe U (Loaned on 26/3/2002) FL 5
ansfield T (Loaned on 25/10/2002) FL 4
otherwell (Loaned on 31/1/2003) SL 12/1
C 3

VAUGHAN David Owen
orn: Rhuddlan, 18 February 1983
eight: 5'7" **Weight:** 10.10
ternational Honours: W: 1; U21-2; Yth
former member of the Crewe
lexandra youth team, David is a versatile
layer who can take any of the left-sided
ositions in the line-up. He had a good
eason at Gresty Road in 2002-03,
ecovering well from a minor operation
uring the campaign. David continued to
epresent Wales at U21 level and stepped
p to make his full international debut in
he friendly against the USA during the
ummer.
rewe Alex (From trainee on 6/2/2001) FL
0+6/3 FLC 1 FAC 7/1 Others 2/1

VENUS Mark
orn: Hartlepool, 6 April 1967
eight: 6'0" **Weight:** 13.11
lub Honours: Div 3 '89
knee injury that eventually required an
peration meant that Mark's appearances
or Ipswich Town were severely restricted
st season. He managed just a dozen
rst-team outings before being released in
he summer. Mark is confident that he
ill return to full fitness before the start
f the 2003-04 campaign and feels that
e has got at least another season in him
efore he has to hang up his boots.
artlepool U (From juniors on 22/3/1985) FL
Others 0+1
eicester C (Free on 6/9/1985) FL 58+3/1 FLC
FAC 2 Others 2+1
olverhampton W (£40,000 on 23/3/1988)
. 271+16/7 FLC 17+1/1 FAC 15+1 Others
7/2

Ipswich T (£150,000 on 29/7/1997) P/FL
144+4/16 FLC 18/3 FAC 4 Others 14

VERNAZZA Paolo Andrea Pietro
Born: Islington, 1 November 1979
Height: 6'0" **Weight:** 11.10
International Honours: E: U21-2; Yth
A skilful and creative midfield player,
Paolo adorns any team he plays for but
sometimes fails to impose himself as he
should. He made a slow start last season
after suffering cartilage trouble but
gained in strength and influence as he
developed match fitness. In the end he
made more than 20 appearances, but his
failure to score was a disappointment.
Arsenal (From trainee on 18/11/1997) PL
2+3/1 FLC 4 Others 1+2
Ipswich T (Loaned on 2/10/1998) FL 2
Portsmouth (Loaned on 14/1/2000) FL 7
Watford (£350,000 + on 15/12/2000) FL
54+13/2 FLC 3/1 FAC 7

VERNON Scott Malcolm
Born: Manchester, 13 December 1983
Height: 6'1" **Weight:** 11.6
A product of Oldham Athletic's youth
system, this young striker became an
instant hit on his first-team debut in
October, scoring twice as the Latics lost 3-
2 at home to Carlisle United in the LDV
Vans Trophy. He had further success the
following month, netting on his league
debut as a substitute against Stockport
County. The emergence of Wayne
Andrews and return to action of Clyde
Wijnhard restricted Scott's opportunities
thereafter and he spent most of his time
on the substitutes' bench.
Oldham Ath (From trainee on 3/7/2002) FL
2+6/1 FAC 0+1 Others 1/2

VERON Juan Sebastian
Born: Buenos Aires, Argentina, 9 March
1975
Height: 6'1" **Weight:** 12.7
Club Honours: PL '03
International Honours: Argentina: 52
A superbly balanced midfield playmaker,
with a range of sublime passing skills,
Juan Sebastian missed only four
Premiership games for Manchester United
from August to December, his goal
against Arsenal in December providing
one of the sweetest moments of the
campaign. There were several other
contributions worthy of note, particularly
in Europe with strikes against Maccabi
Haifa, Olympiakos and Bayer Leverkusen.
Sir Alex Ferguson, always vociferous in his
support, certainly gave him his head and
it was only in March when injury
prevented him from ending the campaign

as one of United's regular first-team stars.
Manchester U (£28,100,000 from Lazio,
Italy, ex Estudiantes, Boca Juniors, Sampdoria,
Parma, on 13/7/2001) PL 45+6/7 FLC 4+1
FAC 2 Others 24/4

VIANA Hugo Miguel Ferreira
Born: Barcelos, Portugal, 15 January 1983
Height: 5'9" **Weight:** 11.8
International Honours: Portugal: 7; B1;
U21-4; Yth
Hugo joined Newcastle after a superb
showing in the European U21 tournament
in the summer of 2002 following which he
joined the full Portugal squad at the World
Cup finals, although he did not play. Very
skilful on the ball with good vision and a
delightful left foot, he was used primarily
on the left flank of midfield, and once he
had adapted to the pace and physical
nature of the Premiership he became a
great favourite on Tyneside. After scoring a
couple of important goals in the
Champions' League his first Premiership
goal came in the penultimate match when
a free kick against Birmingham secured
third place for his club. Despite not starting
regularly for the Magpies he continued to
be capped by his country at both full and
U21 levels.
Newcastle U (£8,500,000 from Sporting
Lisbon, Portugal on 19/7/2002) PL 11+12/2
FLC 1 Others 5+5/2

VICKERS Stephen (Steve)
Born: Bishop Auckland, 13 October 1967
Height: 6'1" **Weight:** 12.12
Club Honours: AMC '90; Div 1 '95
This experienced defender had the
misfortune to suffer a rib injury on his first
Premiership start for Birmingham City at
West Bromwich Albion last October and
after recovering he damaged his ankle in
the Boxing Day game against Everton. He
managed just five first-team outings and
did not make the line-up at all after mid-
January. When selected, Steve organised
the Blues' defence soundly, but neverthe-
less he was released in the summer.
Tranmere Rov (Signed from Spennymoor U
on 11/9/1985) FL 310+1/11 FLC 20+1/5 FAC
19/3 Others 36/1
Middlesbrough (£700,000 on 3/12/1993)
P/FL 248+11/8 FLC 27+2/3 FAC 17+1
Others 2
Crystal Palace (Loaned on 21/9/2001) FL 6
FLC 1
Birmingham C (£400,000 on 16/11/2001)
P/FL 18+1/1 FLC 1 FAC 1 Others 2

VICTORY Jamie Charles
Born: Hackney, 14 November 1975
Height: 5'10" **Weight:** 12.0

433

Club Honours: FAT '98; NC '99
International Honours: E: SP-1
Jamie was once again virtually ever-present at left back for Cheltenham Town last season, missing just two first-team games. He put in a series of consistent performances from both a defensive and attacking standpoint, although he was occasionally exposed by some of the more highly rated right-sided players in Division Two. He ended the campaign on a high note and will be looking to regain his reputation as a goal-scoring defender next term.
West Ham U (From trainee on 1/7/1994)
Bournemouth (Free on 1/7/1995) FL 5+11/1 FLC 1+1 Others 1+1
Cheltenham T (Free on 1/7/1996) FL 139+1/14 FLC 6/1 FAC 10 Others 8/1

VIDMAR Anthony (Tony)
Born: Adelaide, Australia, 15 April 1969
Height: 6'1" **Weight:** 12.10

Club Honours: SPD '99, '00; SLC '99, '02; SC '99, '00, '02
International Honours: Australia: 69; Yth
This much-travelled and vastly experienced Australian international signed for Middlesbrough on a one-year contract from Glasgow Rangers last September, after spending the summer training at the Riverside. The transfer went ahead after the deadline had passed because the player was out of contract. Tony can play anywhere in defence, his preferred choice was at left back, and he made his debut in the 1-0 Premiership victory over Birmingham City later that month. He won his 68th Australian cap as a substitute at Upton Park in the Socceroos' surprise 3-1 win over England.
Glasgow R (Free from NAC Breda, Holland, ex Ekeren, Adelaide C, on 30/6/1997) SL 89+18/7 SLC 6+2 SC 15/2 Others 23+6/2
Middlesbrough (Free on 5/9/2002) PL 9+3 FLC 2 FAC 1

VIDUKA Mark Anthony
Born: Australia, 9 October 1975
Height: 6'2" **Weight:** 13.9
Club Honours: SLC '00
International Honours: Australia: 22; U23; Yth
This big, strong centre forward started with a bang for Leeds United last term, scoring in the first two games against Manchester City and West Bromwich Albion. After netting in the 2-0 win at Newcastle, Mark then went on something of a barren run and was dropped for a period in December, but came back and hit a rich scoring vein under new manager Peter Reid. He finished the season by netting 13 times in a run of nine games, including a hat-trick in the amazing 6-1 win at Charlton. Sublimely skilful for a big man, his ability to hold the ball up and link others into play is second to none. A highlight at international level was his appearance for Australia in their historic

Hugo Viana (right)

Mark Viduka (right)

win against England at Upton Park.
Glasgow Celtic (Signed from NK Croatia Zagreb, Croatia, ex Melbourne Knights, on 2/12/1998) SL 36+1/30 SLC 4/1 SC 3/3 Others 4/1
Leeds U (£6,000,000 on 25/7/2000) PL 96+4/48 FLC 3/1 FAC 7/4 Others 25/7

VIEIRA Patrick

Born: Dakar, Senegal, 23 June 1976
Height: 6'4" **Weight:** 12.5
Club Honours: PL '98, '02; FAC '98, 02; CS '98, '99, '02
International Honours: France: 62 (WC '98, UEFA '00)
The inspirational captain of Arsenal, Patrick took over the role from Tony Adams in commanding fashion. A world-class player in the centre of midfield, dominating most games from start to finish, he is a fantastic ball winner with the ability to take the game to the opposition with his strong driving runs through the centre of the field. Patrick combines skill and speed to use quick, short passes in one-two movements with support players in an attempt to create attacking situations. He was one of five Gunners selected for the PFA Premiership team of the season.
Arsenal (£3,500,000 from AC Milan, Italy, ex Cannes, on 14/8/1996) PL 211+7/19 FLC 5 FAC 35+2/2 Others 58/2

VIGNAL Gregory

Born: Montpellier, France, 19 July 1981
Height: 6'0" **Weight:** 12.4
Club Honours: FAC '01; UEFAC '01; ESC '01; FLC '03
International Honours: France: U21; Yth (UEFA-U18 '00)
The young Liverpool left back scarcely figured in the first team last season, starting only two games, both in the Worthington Cup, against Southampton and Ipswich. His only Premiership appearance was as a late substitute against Newcastle on New Year's Day whilst in the Champions' League he featured briefly as a substitute against Spartak Moscow.
Liverpool (£500,000 from Montpellier, France on 29/9/2000) PL 7+4 FLC 3 FAC 0+1 Others 4+1

VINE Rowan Lewis

Born: Basingstoke, 21 September 1982
Height: 6'1" **Weight:** 12.2
Portsmouth striker Rowan spent the whole of the 2002-03 season on loan at Brentford. He scored on his debut at Huddersfield and added two more against Swindon a couple of weeks later. He also

netted twice in the FA Cup tie at Wycombe, but the supply of goals dried up at the turn of the year and his form dipped. Rowan scored just twice in 2003, although the second was a wonderful left-footed 20-yarder at Luton in February.
Portsmouth (From trainee on 27/4/2001) FL 3+10
Brentford (Loaned on 7/8/2002) FL 37+5/10 FLC 1+1/1 FAC 3/2 Others 3

VINNICOMBE Christopher (Chris)

Born: Exeter, 20 October 1970
Height: 5'9" **Weight:** 10.12
Club Honours: SPD '91
International Honours: E: U21-12
Wycombe's left back started every game until suffering what was thought to be a groin strain in November. This turned into a tendon problem, which eventually kept him out for five months. Although a number of other players filled in capably, the team sorely missed his considerable presence. Chris is the most tidy of defenders, a dogged marker who uses his considerable stamina to push forward whenever possible to deliver, more often than not, an inswinging far-post cross.
Exeter C (From trainee on 1/7/1989) FL 35+4/1 FLC 5/1 Others 2
Glasgow R (£150,000 on 3/11/1989) SL 14+9/1 SLC 1+2 Others 1
Burnley (£200,000 on 30/6/1994) FL 90+5/3 FLC 9 FAC 2 Others 7+1/1
Wycombe W (Free on 6/8/1998) FL 181+4/2 FLC 12 FAC 17 Others 6

VIRGO Adam John

Born: Brighton, 25 January 1983
Height: 6'2" **Weight:** 13.7
A solid central defender, Adam turned out just four times for Brighton & Hove Albion in 2002-03. Although he played impressively during his short run in the side, he had to compete with Adam Hinshelwood and others for a back-up role and was allowed to join Exeter City in November for an extended loan spell. He was one of many players to occupy the troublesome centre half position for the Grecians and coped admirably before returning to the South Coast after nine appearances.
Brighton & Hove A (From juniors on 4/7/2000) FL 9+6 FLC 1 Others 1+2
Exeter C (Loaned on 29/11/2002) FL 8+1

VIVEASH Adrian Lee

Born: Swindon, 30 September 1969
Height: 6'2" **Weight:** 12.13
Adrian's first-team involvement for

Reading was restricted to a handful of games as a non-playing substitute until the final part of the campaign. He kept i shape with a two-month loan spell at Oxford United, helping the club to one c their best spells of the season. His know how at the back was very important and gave the U's the confidence to go forward. Adrian was recalled to the Royals' first team as a centre-back replacement for Steve Brown, then Adria Williams, when the first-choice defender were injured. He even captained the side in the last two league games against Watford and Stoke City. He played brave and well, and was rewarded at the end c the campaign with a one-year deal, whic will involve not just playing but also coaching the young defenders at the club.
Swindon T (From trainee on 14/7/1988) FL 51+3/2 FLC 6+1 FAC 0+1 Others 2
Reading (Loaned on 4/1/1993) FL 5 Others 1/1
Reading (Loaned on 20/1/1995) FL 6
Barnsley (Loaned on 10/8/1995) FL 2/1
Walsall (Free on 16/10/1995) FL 200+2/13 FLC 12 FAC 15/2 Others 13/1
Reading (Free on 6/7/2000) FL 62+1/3 FLC 3+1 FAC 5 Others 7
Oxford U (Loaned on 6/9/2002) FL 11 FLC . Others 1

VOLZ Moritz

Born: Siegen, Germany, 21 January 198?
Height: 5'11" **Weight:** 12.10
Club Honours: FAYC '00, '01
International Honours: Germany:
This pacy right back or midfield player made only one first-team appearance for Arsenal last season, coming on as a substitute in the Worthington Cup matcl against Sunderland. Moritz put in severa good performances with the reserves before joining Wimbledon on loan at the beginning of February. He went straight into the Dons' starting line-up at right back, scoring on his debut in the win at Brighton. Very composed and skilful on the ball, he quickly settled into the team though it became clear after a few game that he was far more comfortable going forward than putting in meaty defensive challenges. He ended his spell at Selhurs Park playing as a right-sided midfielder, but it is as a wing back that he will more than likely make his eventual mark in the game. Moritz captained the German U20 team during the season.
Arsenal (Free from Schalke 04, Germany on 25/1/2000) FLC 1+1
Wimbledon (Loaned on 3/2/2003) FL 10/1

WAINE Andrew Paul
Born: Manchester, 24 February 1983
Height: 5'9" **Weight:** 10.5
A competitive midfielder, Andrew made his Burnley debut from the bench in the home game against Gillingham near the end of the season. His short time on the pitch was enough to give evidence of his battling qualities, and he will be hoping to gain more senior experience in 2003-4
Burnley (From trainee on 17/7/2002) FL 0+2

WAINWRIGHT Neil
Born: Warrington, 4 November 1977
Height: 6'0" **Weight:** 11.5
Neil had a rather disappointing time at Darlington last term and only started about half the games, being used as a substitute in the majority of the rest. A talented right winger, he is at his best when running at defenders to cut in and head for goal. He scored just once during the campaign, heading home the final goal scored at Feethams in the Quakers' 3-2 with Leyton Orient on the emotional last day of the season.
Wrexham (From trainee on 3/7/1996) FL 4+3 FAC 1 Others 1
Sunderland (£100,000 + on 9/7/1998) FL 2 FLC 5+1
Darlington (Loaned on 4/2/2000) FL 16+1/4
Halifax T (Loaned on 13/10/2000) FL 13 FAC Others 2
Darlington (£50,000 on 17/8/2001) FL 3+15/5 FLC 0+1 FAC 6+1/2 Others 2

WAKE Brian
Born: Stockton, 13 August 1982
Height: 6'0" **Weight:** 11.2
A prolific striker with Northern League club Tow Law, Brian's Football League debut for Carlisle was marked with a timely taken goal. A month later, his hat-trick at home to Boston sparked one of United's best wins of the season. The majority of his appearances were off the bench, but after a lean spell in front of goal, he bagged five in three games in April including another hat-trick at Shrewsbury to secure Carlisle's league status. He thus became the first United player in over 30 years to score two hat-tricks in a season and the first since the 1963-64 season to achieve the feat both home and away.
Carlisle U (Signed from Tow Law T on 10/5/2002) FL 10+18/9 FLC 1 FAC 0+1 Others +3

WALKER Desmond (Des) Sinclair
Born: Hackney, 26 November 1965
Height: 5'11" **Weight:** 11.13
Club Honours: FLC '89, '90; FMC '89, '92
International Honours: E: 59; U21-7
A legendary figure in the modern history of Nottingham Forest, Des returned to the City Ground in the summer of 2002 after finishing the previous season training with the club. He was immediately appointed captain and his calming influence and experience helped many of his young team mates. Des's leadership qualities were missed when he was absent for a period of 17 games in mid-season through injury, but his eagerness to return to action cost him, as he twice came back from injury too early only to break down.
Nottingham F (From apprentice on 2/12/1983) FL 259+5/1 FLC 40 FAC 28 Others 14 (£1,500,000 to Sampodoria on 1/8/92)
Sheffield Wed (£2,700,000 on 22/7/1993) P/FL 307 FLC 28 FAC 24 Others 3 (Freed during 2001 close season)
Nottingham F (Free, via a spell at Burton A, on 9/7/2002) FL 29+2 Others 2

WALKER Ian Michael
Born: Watford, 31 October 1971
Height: 6'2" **Weight:** 13.1
Club Honours: FAYC '90; FLC '99
International Honours: E: 3; B-1; U21-9; Yth
This experienced goalkeeper often looked to be the classiest custodian in the First Division, although he just missed out to Shaka Hislop for PFA honours. Ian made a string of important saves in the early weeks to instil extra confidence into his back four, and also starred in the narrow home win over Palace in February when he made a couple of vital one-on-one saves. He finished the season with a healthy tally of clean sheets that was just short of the Leicester all-time record, and was the Foxes' only ever-present during the campaign.
Tottenham H (From trainee on 4/12/1989) F/PL 257+2 FLC 22+1 FAC 25 Others 6
Oxford U (Loaned on 31/8/1990) FL 2 FLC 1
Leicester C (£2,500,000 on 26/7/2001) P/FL 81 FLC 5 FAC 4

WALKER James Barry
Born: Sutton in Ashfield, 9 July 1973
Height: 5'11" **Weight:** 13.5
James enjoyed a highly successful tenth season with Walsall, taking his appearance tally well past the 400 mark and deservedly being awarded a testimonial. Although twice sent off by referees playing to the letter rather than the spirit of the law and suffering a cruel bounce on a divet that cost the game against Wolves, he made a vital penalty save to win the FA Cup shoot-out at Reading and his injury-time save from Gary McAllister against Coventry brought back memories of Gordon Banks, who incidentally was the guest speaker at Jimmy's testimonial dinner.
Notts Co (From trainee on 9/7/1991)
Walsall (Free on 4/8/1993) FL 358+2 FLC 22+1 FAC 29 Others 19

WALKER Justin Matthew
Born: Nottingham, 6 September 1975
Height: 5'11" **Weight:** 12.12
International Honours: E: Yth; Sch
Justin's tenacity and never-say-die attitude made him a favourite with all three of Exeter City's managers last season. This was borne out by the fact that he played in 39 League games. He played out of his skin in the tense end-of-season match at Swansea when he was rewarded with the Grecians' 1-0 victory. The skilful central midfield player was reported to have signed for Cambridge United during the summer
Nottingham F (From juniors on 10/9/1992)
Scunthorpe U (Signed on 26/3/1997) FL 126+6/2 FLC 8 FAC 6 Others 7/1
Lincoln C (Free on 12/7/2000) FL 68+8/4 FLC 1+2 FAC 3+1 Others 6/1
Exeter C (Free on 6/8/2002) FL 35+4/5 FLC FAC 3+1/1 Others 1

WALKER Richard Martin
Born: Birmingham, 8 November 1977
Height: 6'0" **Weight:** 12.0
Club Honours: AMC '02
A pacy striker who holds the ball up well, Richard featured regularly in the Blackpool squad last term although many of his appearances came from the bench. He scored four times in Second Division games, but also netted a hat-trick for the Seasiders' reserves in a 4-0 win at Wigan.
Aston Villa (From trainee on 13/12/1995) PL 2+4/2 FLC 1+1 FAC 0+1 Others 1
Cambridge U (Loaned on 31/12/1998) FL 7+14/3 Others 1+2/1
Blackpool (Loaned on 9/2/2001) FL 6+12/3 FAC 1/1
Wycombe W (Loaned on 13/9/2001) FL 10+2/3 FAC 1/1
Blackpool (£50,000 + on 21/12/2001) FL 35+18/12 FLC 0+1 FAC 1+2 Others 3+1/3

WALKER Richard Neil
Born: Derby, 9 November 1971
Height: 6'0" **Weight:** 12.0
Club Honours: NC '99
This left-footed defender was one of the

more consistent performers during a difficult start to the season for Cheltenham Town last term. He played alongside Michael Duff in a four-man defence and put in some stalwart performances as the Robins tried to adjust to life in Division Two against some tough opposition in the opening weeks. However, just as the team appeared to be turning the corner Richard suffered an injury to the base of the thigh-bone inside the knee joint during an LDV Vans Trophy match against Colchester United. This required corrective surgery and he spent the remainder of the campaign on the sidelines.
Notts Co (From trainee on 3/7/1990) FL 63+4/4 FLC 10 FAC 1+2 Others 8+1 (Free to Hereford U on 24/7/1997)
Mansfield T (Loaned on 23/3/1995) FL 4
Cheltenham T (Signed on 23/10/1998) FL 67+3/1 FLC 5 Others 4

WALKER Richard Stuart
Born: Stafford, 17 September 1980
Height: 6'2" **Weight:** 13.0
Last term proved to be the season when Richard broke into the Crewe Alexandra first team, and he went on to really make his mark in the defence. His confidence grew as the campaign progressed and he will be looking to consolidate his place in the line-up in 2003-04. Richard scored two goals during the season including one in the final home match against Cardiff City.
Crewe Alex (From trainee on 6/7/1999) FL 33+6/2 FLC 2 FAC 1+1 Others 4

WALLACE Rodney (Rod)
Seymour
Born: Greenwich, 2 October 1969
Height: 5'7" **Weight:** 11.6
Club Honours: Div 1 '92; CS '92; SPD '99, '00; SC '99, '00; SLC '98
International Honours: E: B-2; U21-11
Rod's campaign at Gillingham did not really get going until the end of September after he picked up a groin strain in pre-season training. However, once he got involved in first-team action he showed his ability both in front of goal and with his all-round play, and in the new year he netted seven goals in a run of eight games. He went on to finish up with a respectable total of 11 goals (from 19 first-team starts) to end the season as the Gills' second-top scorer.
Southampton (From trainee on 19/4/1988) FL 111+17/45 FLC 18+1/6 FAC 10/3 Others 3+1/2
Leeds U (£1,600,000 on 7/6/1991) F/PL 187+25/53 FLC 18+1/8 FAC 16+5/4 Others 1+4/1

Glasgow R (Free on 17/7/1998) SL 73+4/39 SLC 6/4 SC 10+1/4 Others 24+2/7
Bolton W (Free on 17/9/2001) PL 14+5/3 FLC 1+2/1 FAC 1
Gillingham (Free on 8/8/2002) FL 17+5/11 FLC 1 FAC 1+1

WALLWORK Ronald (Ronnie)
Born: Manchester, 10 September 1977
Height: 5'10" **Weight:** 12.9
Club Honours: FAYC '95; PL '01
International Honours: E: Yth
This versatile player joined West Bromwich Albion in the summer of 2002, becoming manager Gary Megson's first signing following promotion to the Premiership. Substitute for the opening three matches, he made his Baggies' debut in the 1-0 home win over Fulham, but failed to hold down a permanent place in the side during the campaign, although he did make the starting line-up in over half the club's Premiership matches. A hard-working midfielder, his best run in the line-up came late on in the season.
Manchester U (From trainee on 17/3/1995) PL 4+15 FLC 4+1 FAC 1+1 Others 1+1
Carlisle U (Loaned on 22/12/1997) FL 10/1 Others 2
Stockport Co (Loaned on 18/3/1998) FL 7
West Bromwich A (Free on 2/7/2002) PL 23+4 FLC 1 FAC 2

WALSH Gary
Born: Wigan, 21 March 1968
Height: 6'3" **Weight:** 15.10
Club Honours: ECWC '91; ESC '91; FAC '94
International Honours: E: U21-2
Gary had another unfortunate season with injuries in 2002-03, despite starting as Bradford City's number one 'keeper and playing in the first three games. He spent most of the campaign recovering from knee surgery and only returned to the squad at the end of February. By then Aidan Davison had secured a firm grip on the goalkeeper's jersey and Gary was forced to sit out the rest of the season from the bench. A tall and commanding goalkeeper who has been a good servant to the club, he was released at the end of the season.
Manchester U (From juniors on 25/4/1985) F/PL 49+1 FLC 7 Others 6
Airdrie (Loaned on 11/8/1988) SL 3 SLC 1
Oldham Ath (Loaned on 19/11/1993) PL 6
Middlesbrough (£500,000 on 11/8/1995) PL 44 FLC 9 FAC 4
Bradford C (£500,000 + on 26/9/1997) P/FL 131+1 FLC 7 FAC 4 Others 1
Middlesbrough (Loaned on 15/9/2000) PL 3

WALSH Michael Shane
Born: Rotherham, 5 August 1977
Height: 6'0" **Weight:** 13.2
Club Honours: AMC '01
This highly rated Port Vale defender once again had his season blighted by injury. After playing in the first eight games of the campaign he suffered a knee injury that kept him out until March when he returned at Notts County. Michael soon recovered the form that he is capable of and his partnership with Sam Collins and Peter Clarke went a long way to securing the club's escape from the relegation zone. He scored one goal, a header in the 3-2 victory over Northampton Town.
Scunthorpe U (From trainee on 3/7/1995) F 94+9/1 FLC 4 FAC 9 Others 5
Port Vale (£100,000 on 30/7/1998) FL 110+5/4 FLC 5+1 FAC 2 Others 7

WALSH Steven (Steve)
Born: Preston, 3 November 1964
Height: 6'3" **Weight:** 14.9
Club Honours: AMC '85; FLC '97, '00
The former Leicester central defender made two first-team appearances for Coventry City last term after impressing the management in a reserve game. However, he struggled against the speed Watford attack in his only start and returned to Tamworth as player-coach soon afterwards. He went on to assist th Lambs to the Dr Martens League title an also featured in their FA Trophy final defeat by Burscough.
Wigan Ath (From juniors on 11/9/1982) FL 123+3/4 FLC 7 FAC 6 Others 10+2
Leicester C (£100,000 on 24/6/1986) P/FL 352+17/53 FLC 39+1/4 FAC 16+1/1 Others 23/4
Norwich C (Free on 18/9/2000) FL 1+3 FLC
Coventry C (Free from Tamworth on 23/8/2002) FL 1+1

WALSHE Benjamin (Ben) Matthew
Born: Hammersmith, 24 May 1983
Height: 6'1" **Weight:** 12.12
A left-sided forward, Ben spent most of th 2002-03 campaign as a regular in the Queen's Park Rangers' reserve side. In February he joined Ryman League outfit Aldershot Town to gain some first-team action. On his return he made the starting line-up for the match at Chesterfield, but unfortunately suffered a leg injury before half time. Ben made it back into the reserv side but after three games he suffered a recurrence of the problem, which brought his season to a premature close.
Queens Park R (From trainee on 4/7/2000) FL 1+1

Ashley Ward

WALTERS Jonathan (Jon)
Ronald
Born: Birkenhead, 20 September 1983
Height: 6'1" **Weight:** 12.0
Jon made his Bolton debut as a substitute in the August home defeat against Charlton, featuring in a handful more games from the bench and receiving his first start in the Worthington Cup tie against Bury. A strong and powerful centre forward who was a prolific scorer in the Blackburn academy set-up, he joined Hull City on loan in February, a deal that was subsequently extended to the end of the season. Jon made an immediate impression on the Tigers as he scored twice on his debut in a 5-1 win at Carlisle – City's biggest away win since 1946! Praised by Hull boss Peter Taylor for his intelligent running off the ball, the marksman has undoubted potential and formed a useful partnership with his former Blackburn team mate Ben Burgess during his spell at the KC Stadium.
Blackburn Rov (From trainee on 3/8/2001)
Bolton W (Signed on 30/4/2002) PL 0+4 FLC 1 FAC 0+1
Hull C (Loaned on 24/2/2003) FL 11/5

WALTON David (Dave) Lee
Born: Bedlington, 10 April 1973
Height: 6'2" **Weight:** 14.8
Club Honours: Div 3 '94
After finally putting his injuries behind him, Dave proved to be a key member of the Crewe Alexandra team that gained promotion last term. A very capable central defender who is effective in the air, his experience proved invaluable to the side. Dave also contributed a rare goal against Mansfield Town on New Year's Day.
Sheffield U (Free from Ashington on 13/3/1992)
Shrewsbury T (Signed on 5/11/1993) FL 127+1/10 FLC 7 FAC 10/1 Others 11/1
Crewe Alex (£500,000 + on 20/10/1997) FL 146+9/3 FLC 8+1/1 FAC 7

WANLESS Paul Steven
Born: Banbury, 14 December 1973
Height: 6'1" **Weight:** 13.12
Cambridge United's hard-working and popular captain was again a force to be reckoned with in midfield. He suffered a nasty facial injury in an FA Cup tie which rendered him unconscious and in need of stitches, but still declared himself fit for action the following week. Paul featured regularly in the U's squad, although often from the bench, and scored seven valuable goals.

Oxford U (From trainee on 3/12/1991) FL 12+20 FLC 0+3/1 Others 2+2
Lincoln C (Free on 7/7/1995) FL 7+1 Others 2
Cambridge U (Free on 8/3/1996) FL 264+20/44 FLC 13 FAC 19+2/2 Others 16/3

WARBURTON Raymond (Ray)
Born: Rotherham, 7 October 1967
Height: 6'0" **Weight:** 13.6
Club Honours: NC '01
This experienced central defender gave some solid performances for Boston United in the opening months of the 2002-03 season before long-term injuries caught up with him. Ray chose to retire from the full-time game in January and subsequently signed for Aldershot Town, helping his new club to the Ryman League championship and promotion to the Conference.
Rotherham U (From apprentice on 5/10/1985) FL 3+1 FAC 2 Others 2
York C (Free on 8/8/1989) FL 86+4/9 FLC 8/1 FAC 6/1 Others 7
Northampton T (£35,000 on 4/2/1994) FL 186/12 FLC 10 FAC 7/1 Others 17/3
Rushden & Diamonds (£60,000 on 23/10/1998) FL 1
Boston U (Free on 22/3/2002) FL 16 FLC 2 FAC 1 Others 0+1

WARD Ashley Stuart
Born: Manchester, 24 November 1970
Height: 6'2" **Weight:** 13.10
A reliable target man, Ashley will be disappointed with his return of just three goals for Bradford City in the 2002-03 season. Despite the lack of strikes he was always a valuable member of the side, his experience and knowledge playing a key role in helping the youngsters to progress into the first team. However, Ashley missed the last two months of the campaign after failing to recover from a rib injury he picked-up in the Yorkshire 'derby' with Sheffield Wednesday.
Manchester C (From trainee on 5/8/1989) FL 0+1 FAC 0+2
Wrexham (Loaned on 10/1/1991) FL 4/2 Others 1
Leicester C (£80,000 on 30/7/1991) FL 2+8 FLC 2+1 FAC 0+1 Others 0+1
Blackpool (Loaned on 21/11/1992) FL 2/1
Crewe Alex (£80,000 on 1/12/1992) FL 58+3/25 FLC 4/2 FAC 2/4 Others 7/5
Norwich C (£500,000 on 8/12/1994) P/FL 53/18 FLC 6/3 FAC 1
Derby Co (£1,000,000 on 19/3/1996) F/PL 32+8/9 FLC 1+1 FAC 2/1
Barnsley (£1,300,000 + on 5/9/1997) P/FL 45+1/20 FLC 9/4 FAC 6/1

Blackburn Rov (£4,250,000 + on 31/12/1998) P/FL 52+2/13 FLC 2 FAC 4+1
Bradford C (£1,500,000 on 18/8/2000) P/FL 75+9/17 FLC 4+1/3 FAC 1

WARD Christopher (Chris)
Born: Preston, 28 April 1981
Height: 6'1" **Weight:** 11.3
Chris was given a chance to resurrect his full-time career when Lincoln signed him from Leigh RMI last October. He showed some neat ball skills up front and netted on his first league start at Carlisle, but only scored one further goal. An ankle injury kept him out of action in the closing weeks of the season and he was released in May.
Birmingham C (Signed from Lancaster C on 28/4/2001. Freed during 2002 close season)
Lincoln C (Free from Leigh RMI, ex Barrow, on 25/10/2002) FL 5+1/2 FAC 0+1 Others 1

WARD Darren
Born: Worksop, 11 May 1974
Height: 6'2" **Weight:** 14.2
Club Honours: Div 3 '98
International Honours: W: 4; B-1; U21-2
Darren continued to impress in goal for Nottingham Forest with his shot stopping ability last season. A near ever-present, h only absence was on the final day of the regular season when he was rested in preparation for the play-offs, thus bringing a run of 98 consecutive league and cup appearances to an end. Darren returned to the Wales international squad and added further caps against Bosnia and the USA during the campaign.
Mansfield T (From trainee on 27/7/1992) FL 81 FLC 5 FAC 5 Others 6
Notts Co (£160,000 on 11/7/1995) FL 251 FLC 18 FAC 23 Others 10
Nottingham F (Free on 21/5/2001) FL 91 FL 5 FAC 2 Others 2

WARD Darren Philip
Born: Harrow, 13 September 1978
Height: 6'0" **Weight:** 12.6
Darren consolidated his place in the Millwall line-up last term and apart from suspensions he was a near ever-present ir the team. He grew in confidence and began to produce some excellent footbal forging a great understanding with both Paul Robinson and Stuart Nethercott in the heart of the Lions' defence. Darren is a tall, strong central defender who is commanding in the air and reads the game well.
Watford (From trainee on 13/2/1997) P/FL 56+3/2 FLC 6/1 FAC 2 Others 0+1
Queens Park R (Loaned on 17/12/1999) FL 14 FAC 1

arren Ward (Nottingham Forest)

Millwall (£500,000 on 3/10/2001) FL 46+7/1 FLC 1 FAC 5 Others 2

WARD Gavin John
Born: Sutton Coldfield, 30 June 1970
Height: 6'3" **Weight:** 14.12
Club Honours: Div 3 '93; WC '93; AMC '00

Gavin had a thankless task as deputy to James Walker at Walsall, but he gave a sound display on his debut against his former club Stoke and was a key figure in the late-season win at Gillingham that took the Saddlers a huge stride towards First Division survival. Inevitably he was out of the team for the next game as Walker returned from suspension.
Shrewsbury T (From trainee at Aston Villa on 26/9/1988)
West Bromwich A (Free on 18/9/1989) FLC 1
Cardiff C (Free on 5/10/1989) FL 58+1 FAC 1 Others 7
Leicester C (£175,000 on 16/7/1993) F/PL 38 FLC 3 FAC 0+1 Others 4
Bradford C (£175,000 on 13/7/1995) FL 36 FLC 6 FAC 3 Others 2
Bolton W (£300,000 on 29/3/1996) F/PL 19+3 FLC 2 FAC 4
Burnley (Loaned on 14/8/1998) FL 17
Stoke C (Free on 25/2/1999) FL 79 FLC 7 FAC 2 Others 12
Walsall (Free on 9/8/2002) FL 5+2

WARD Iain Campbell
Born: Cleethorpes, 13 May 1983
Height: 6'0" **Weight:** 10.10
This young Grimsby defender once again found his chances restricted by the consistency of senior players in 2002-03. His total of nine league starts, however, certainly bettered his sole game of the previous season. He may well get more opportunities in 2003-04 as the Mariners regroup following relegation.
Grimsby T (From juniors on 22/11/2000) FL 10+2 FLC 0+1 FAC 0+1

WARD Mitchum (Mitch) David
Born: Sheffield, 19 June 1971
Height: 5'8" **Weight:** 11.7
Mitch was probably playing his best football for Barnsley when an ankle injury put him out of action until the start of February. He featured as anchor man in midfield where he used his experience to the full. A good tackler and distributor of the ball, the Reds were always a more efficient outfit with him in the team. He became captain when Chris Morgan was absent and was seen as such a good influence that he retained the post when

Morgan returned. Mitch was out of contract at the end of the season and his future was uncertain at the time of writing.
Sheffield U (From trainee on 1/7/1989) F/PL 135+19/11 FLC 8+3/2 FAC 7+2/2 Others 5+1/1
Crewe Alex (Loaned on 1/11/1990) FL 4/1 FAC 1/1 Others 2
Everton (£850,000 on 25/11/1997) PL 18+6 FLC 2+1 FAC 2
Barnsley (£20,000 on 14/7/2000) FL 68+9 FLC 5+1 FAC 2

WARDLEY Stuart James
Born: Cambridge, 10 September 1975
Height: 5'11" **Weight:** 12.7
Club Honours: Div 3 '03
This box-to-box midfielder's competitive style played a vital role in Rushden & Diamonds last term, breaking up opposition attacks, making tackles and covering the whole of the pitch. He also scored a few goals, including one at Carlisle United when Diamonds secured automatic promotion into Division Two. However, later in that game Stuart suffered a knee injury, which needed surgery bringing a premature end to his season and cruelly ruling him out of the championship finale plus, probably, the start of the new campaign.
Queens Park R (£15,000 from Saffron Walden T on 22/7/1999) FL 72+15/14 FLC 2 FAC 3+2/3 Others 1
Rushden & Diamonds (Loaned on 25/1/2002) FL 54+3/10 FLC 2 FAC 3/1 Others 3+1/1

WARHURST Paul
Born: Stockport,, 26 September 1969
Height: 6'1" **Weight:** 13.6
Club Honours: PL '95
International Honours: E: U21-8
Paul made a few early season appearances for Bolton last term, but he was disrupted by a series of hamstring and calf problems. Without a doubt one of the classiest and most versatile players in the Wanderers squad, the run of injuries took their toll on him and he eventually went out on loan to Stoke. Here he added a touch of class in the centre of the park and helped the Potteries club successfully retain their First Division status.
Manchester C (From trainee on 1/7/1988)
Oldham Ath (£10,000 on 27/10/1988) FL 60+7/2 FLC 8 FAC 5+4 Others 2
Sheffield Wed (£750,000 on 17/7/1991) F/PL 60+6/6 FLC 9/4 FAC 7+1/5 Others 5/3
Blackburn Rov (£2,700,000 on 17/8/1993) PL 30+27/4 FLC 6+2 FAC 2+1 Others 4+2

Crystal Palace (£1,250,000 on 31/7/1997) P/FL 27/4 FLC 2 FAC 1
Bolton W (£800,000 on 25/11/1998) P/FL 81+10 FLC 3+3 FAC 3+2 Others 2+2
Stoke C (Loaned on 27/3/2003) FL 4+1/1

WARNE Paul
Born: Norwich, 8 May 1973
Height: 5'9" **Weight:** 11.2
Paul started the 2002-03 campaign playing in a wide role on the left of midfield for Rotherham, and even though his true position is as a striker he tackled the job with great enthusiasm. He then had to settle for a spell on the bench before playing a handful of games up front during which time he netted his only league goal of the season in a draw at Gillingham. A good club man, Paul will always tackle any job asked of him with maximum effort.
Wigan Ath (£25,000 from Wroxham on 30/7/1997) FL 11+25/3 FLC 0+1 FAC 1 Others 1+2/1
Rotherham U (Free on 15/1/1999) FL 137+34/26 FLC 4+4/1 FAC 8/1 Others 5

WARNE Stephen (Steve) James
Born: Sutton in Ashfield, 27 February 1984
Height: 5'9" **Weight:** 10.12
Steve graduated from Chesterfield's youth ranks to earn a professional contract for 2003-04. A midfielder, he is equally adept at the defensive and attacking aspects of the game, and has the physical presence to make his mark on a match without ever losing the touch of a stylist. His early league appearances have promised much for the future.
Chesterfield (Trainee) FL 2+1 Others 0+1

WARNER Anthony (Tony) Randolph
Born: Liverpool, 11 May 1974
Height: 6'4" **Weight:** 13.9
Club Honours: Div 2 '01
Tony was an ever-present for Millwall for the second successive season and produced some excellent displays between the sticks for the Lions. Tall and commanding, he continued to grow in maturity and on many occasions kept his team in the game when they might otherwise have been dead and buried. Tony loves to thrill the crowd on occasion with his 'outstanding' footwork and is regularly called upon to remind the Millwall faithful what the score is. He was deservedly voted as the club's 'Player of the Year'.
Liverpool (From juniors on 1/1/1994)

windon T *(Loaned on 5/11/1997) FL 2*
lasgow Celtic *(Loaned on 13/11/1998) SL 3*
berdeen *(Loaned on 31/3/1999) SL 6*
lillwall *(Free on 16/7/1999) FL 172 FLC 9*
C 9 Others 5

WARNER Philip (Phil)
orn: Southampton, 2 February 1979
eight: 5'10" **Weight:** 11.10
his versatile defender played in every
osition across the back four for
ambridge United last term, but then lost
ut in the struggle for a first-team place
nd spent much of the remainder of the
ampaign on the bench. Phil made ten
ppearances for the U's, but has yet to
gister his first goal in senior football.
outhampton *(From trainee on 23/5/1997)*
. 5+1 FLC 1
rentford *(Loaned on 9/7/1999) FL 1+13 FLC*
+1 FAC 1
ambridge U *(Free on 4/6/2001) FL 18+2*
.C 2 FAC 1+1 Others 2

WARNER Scott
orn: Rochdale, 3 December 1983
eight: 5'11" **Weight:** 11.11
nother product of Rochdale's youth
stem, Scott figured in a 2002-03 pre-
eason game against the Isle of Man and
ent on to make his first senior
ppearance in midfield, when he came on
s substitute in Dale's 5-2 win at
Jrexham. His full debut came at
ournemouth after Christmas, when he
as handed the right-wing-back role as
ale experimented with a 3-5-2
ormation. His second full game was the
up win at Preston and he also figured in
he big televised game against Wolves.
ochdale *(Trainee) FL 6+1 FAC 2*

WARNOCK Stephen (Steve)
orn: Ormskirk, 12 December 1981
eight: 5'7" **Weight:** 12.1
nternational Honours: E: Yth; Sch
his highly rated Liverpool youngster
njoyed a successful loan spell with
radford City last term. Used mainly in a
vide-left midfield slot, he made his debut
n the 1-0 win at Walsall and scored his
nly goal in the Yorkshire 'derby' defeat
t Sheffield Wednesday in October. On
eturning to Anfield Steve continued his
evelopment in the club's reserves,
aptaining the side occasionally towards
he end of the season.
iverpool *(From trainee on 27/4/1999)*
radford C *(Loaned on 13/9/2002) FL 12/1*

WARREN Christer Simon
orn: Weymouth, 10 October 1974
eight: 5'10" **Weight:** 11.10

This left-sided midfield player joined
Bristol Rovers on a non-contract basis and
went on to make his debut as a substitute
against Macclesfield Town last October.
Christer made a further appearance from
the bench in the home game with Bury,
but failed to win a longer-term deal and
moved on to Wessex League outfit
Eastleigh
Southampton *(£40,000 from Cheltenham T
on 31/3/1995) PL 1+7 FLC 1*
Brighton & Hove A *(Loaned on 11/10/1996)
FL 3*
Fulham *(Loaned on 6/3/1997) FL 8+3/1*
Bournemouth *(£50,000 on 8/10/1997) FL
94+9/13 FLC 4+3 FAC 10/1 Others 7*

Queens Park R *(Free on 15/6/2000) FL
24+12 FLC 1 FAC 1*
Bristol Rov *(Free on 3/9/2002) FL 0+2*

WARREN Mark Wayne
Born: Clapton, 12 November 1974
Height: 6'0" **Weight:** 12.2
International Honours: E: Yth
This experienced defender deputised as
skipper for Colchester United during the
first half of the 2002-03 season due to
Scott Fitzgerald's absence through injury.
Mark's sound displays in a three-man
defence were unfortunately punctuated
by a couple of red cards, and then a long-
term groin problem sidelined him from

Mark Warren

the end of January. He was subsequently released at the end of the season.
Leyton Orient (From trainee on 6/7/1992) FL 134+18/5 FLC 8+1/2 FAC 5+1 Others 10+4/1
Oxford U (Loaned on 24/12/1998) FL 4
Notts Co (Signed on 28/11/1999) FL 76+8/1 FLC 9 FAC 1 Others 4
Colchester U (Free on 9/8/2002) FL 20 FAC 1

WATERMAN David (Dave) Graham
Born: Guernsey, 16 May 1977
Height: 5'10" **Weight:** 13.2
International Honours: NI: U21-14
Dave was a very reliable performer for Oxford United last term in whichever position he played. Most of his games were as the middle of three central defenders but he also featured as the 'holding' man in midfield. Dave contributed two goals during the campaign, including a close-range winner at Shrewsbury.
Portsmouth (From trainee on 4/7/1995) FL 60+20 FLC 4+1 FAC 3
Oxford U (Free on 28/3/2002) FL 31+3/1 FAC 3 Others 1/1

WATKIN Stephen (Steve)
Born: Wrexham, 16 June 1971
Height: 5'10" **Weight:** 11.10
Club Honours: WC '95; Div 3 '00
International Honours: W: B-2; Sch
Steve scored Swansea's equalising goal at Darlington early last season after coming on as substitute, but in the next game at Bury, which he started, he received a red card. He subsequently struggled to find consistency as the campaign progressed, although he was regularly used by Brian Flynn as a substitute. An influential striker on his day, Steve still possesses the ability to hold the ball up, and look for the half chances in the area.
Wrexham (From juniors on 24/7/1989) FL 167+33/55 FLC 11+3/3 FAC 16+6/12 Others 17+5/4
Swansea C (£108,000 on 26/9/1997) FL 167+39/44 FLC 8/1 FAC 6+4/2 Others 2+2/1

WATSON Alexander (Alex) Francis
Born: Liverpool, 5 April 1968
Height: 6'1" **Weight:** 13.0
Club Honours: CS '88
International Honours: E: Yth
This experienced central defender managed just three first-team appearances early on for Exeter before a change in management curtailed his opportunities. Alex is a powerful and commanding centre half who is particularly effective in the air.

Liverpool (From apprentice on 18/5/1985) FL 3+1 FLC 1+1 FAC 1+1 Others 1
Derby Co (Loaned on 30/8/1990) FL 5
Bournemouth (£150,000 on 18/1/1991) FL 145+6/5 FLC 14/1 FAC 12/1 Others 5
Gillingham (Loaned on 11/9/1995) FL 10/1
Torquay U (£50,000 on 23/11/1995) FL 201+1/8 FLC 11 FAC 10 Others 7/1
Exeter C (Free on 30/7/2001) FL 45+1/1 FLC 1 FAC 3 Others 1

WATSON Benjamin (Ben)
Born: London, 9 July 1985
Height: 5'10" **Weight:** 10.11
This promising midfielder did well in the Crystal Palace academy team last year and after progressing to the reserves he made his bow in senior football against Watford in April. He produced a fine performance, looking confident and passing the ball well, and he went on to add a handful more first-team appearances in the closing stages of the campaign.
Crystal Palace (Trainee) FL 3+2

WATSON Gordon William George
Born: Sidcup, 20 March 1971
Height: 5'11" **Weight:** 13.2
International Honours: E: U21-2
A fine opportunist goal-scorer, Gordon looked to have put his longstanding injury problems to rest in 2001-02 when he returned to league football with Hartlepool. He began 2002-03 where he had left off the previous season, and was soon among the leading scorers in Division Three. He was unlucky to suffer a broken leg in the home 'derby' match with Darlington. A speedy recovery was anticipated, but the injury turned out to be more troublesome than at first thought. He returned to make a number of first-team appearances in the later stages of the season, but he was unable to rediscover his scoring boots.
Charlton Ath (From trainee on 5/4/1989) FL 20+11/7 FLC 2/1 FAC 0+1 Others 1+1
Sheffield Wed (£250,000 on 20/2/1991) F/PL 29+37/15 FLC 6+5/5 FAC 5+2 Others 2+2/1
Southampton (£1,200,000 on 17/3/1995) PL 37+15/8 FLC 6+3/5 FAC 5+1/1
Bradford C (£550,000 on 17/11/1997) FL 8+13/5 FLC 1+3
Bournemouth (Free on 23/8/1999) FL 2+4 FLC 0+1 FAC 1+2 Others 0+1 (Free during 2000 close season)
Hartlepool U (Free after recovering from injury and trialling with Portsmouth, on 21/9/2001) FL 43+6/23 FAC 1 Others 3

WATSON Kevin Edward
Born: Hackney, 3 January 1974
Height: 6'0" **Weight:** 12.6
A permanent fixture in the Reading midfield for the first half of the campaign, Kevin's place became vulnerable after Steve Sidwell was signed from Arsenal, and he only made sporadic appearances, usually as substitute, thereafter. His main strength is in playing a neat, short-passing game, but Reading's 4-5-1 style dictates greater movement from the midfield players. His only goal of the season came with a 30-yard right-foot drive in the home game against Watford, and brought his team a 1-0 win.
Tottenham H (From trainee on 15/5/1992) PL 4+1 FLC 1+1/1 FAC 0+1 Others 4
Brentford (Loaned on 24/3/1994) FL 2+1
Bristol C (Loaned on 2/12/1994) FL 1+1
Barnet (Loaned on 16/2/1995) FL 13
Swindon T (Free on 15/7/1996) FL 39+24/1 FLC 2+2 FAC 1+2
Rotherham U (Free on 31/7/1999) FL 109/7 FLC 6/1 FAC 7 Others 3
Reading (Loaned on 2/11/2001) FL 6
Reading (£150,000 + on 14/3/2002) FL 30+8/2 Others 0+1

WATSON Paul Douglas
Born: Hastings, 4 January 1975
Height: 5'8" **Weight:** 10.10
Club Honours: Div 3 '99, '01; Div 2 '02
Although he missed just one senior game for Brighton last term, Paul will be the first to admit that he had a rather disappointing campaign. The left-footed right back, who had scored 18 goals in the previous three seasons, hardly came close to adding to that total as his dead-ball expertise inexplicably waned, and he struggled at times against the sharper attacks of the First Division. Although never giving less than total effort, he fared little better in a brief run at left back. In previous seasons Paul was often one of the Seagulls' most creative players and the Withdean fans will be hoping that he can rediscover his best form back in Division Two.
Gillingham (From trainee on 8/12/1992) FL 57+5/2 FLC 4 FAC 6 Others 5+3
Fulham (£13,000 on 30/7/1996) FL 48+2/4 FLC 3/1 FAC 2 Others 2
Brentford (£50,000 on 12/12/1997) FL 37 FLC 2 FAC 2 Others 0+1
Brighton & Hove A (£20,000 on 9/7/1999) FL 176+2/14 FLC 7/1 FAC 10/3 Others 5

WATSON Stephen (Steve) Craig
Born: North Shields, 1 April 1974
Height: 6'0" **Weight:** 12.7

International Honours: E: B-1; U21-12;
th

combination of injury and the good
rm of his team mates restricted Steve's
pportunities at Everton until January,
hen he emerged as a real goal threat
ter announcing his return to the team
ith four goals in four matches, including
brace at Bolton that incorporated an
xpertly executed right-footed overhead
ck. A consistent and versatile performer
every sense, comfortable with the ball
nd a good crosser, he made the right-
ded midfield spot his own during the
econd half of the season and now
egards this as his favourite position.
ewcastle U (From trainee on 6/4/1991) F/PL
79+29/12 FLC 10+6/1 FAC 13+4 Others
8+4/1
ston Villa (£4,000,000 on 15/10/1998) PL
9+2 FLC 8+1/1 FAC 4
verton (£2,500,000 on 12/7/2000) PL
2+5/9 FLC 3+1/1 FAC 2/1

WATTS Steven (Steve)
orn: Lambeth, 11 July 1976
leight: 6'1" **Weight:** 13.7
teve had a somewhat varied season last
erm when he played for five different
ootball League and Conference sides. He
nade a couple of early appearances for
eyton Orient, then joined Margate in
eptember, getting off to a good start
vith four goals in his first three games.
Jext stop was Lincoln, for whom he
roved an effective target man and
etted on his second appearance against
ork, A spell with Conference club
Jagenham & Redbridge followed, before
e finished by signing a long-term
ontract for Shrewsbury on transfer
leadline day. Steve competed with Nigel
emson for a place in the line-up but
ailed to get off the mark in his brief
eriod at Gay Meadow.
eyton Orient (Signed from Fisher on
4/10/1998) FL 69+63/29 FLC 5+2/2 FAC
8+3/4 Others 7+2/1
incoln C (Loaned on 12/12/2002) FL 5/1
Shrewsbury T (Free on 27/3/2003) FL 3+4

WEATHERSTONE Ross
Born: Reading, 16 May 1981
Height: 5'11" **Weight:** 12.0
Club Honours: NC '02
Ross only had a couple of first-team starts
for Boston United last term after finding it
difficult to break into the line-up.
However, when selected he was sharp in
the tackle with a thunderous shot. Ross,
brother of team mate Simon, moved on

before the transfer deadline joining
Conference club Nuneaton Borough.
Oxford U (From trainee on 29/10/1999) FL 4
FAC 1 Others 2
Boston U (Free on 16/2/2001) FL 2+6 FAC
0+1 Others 0+1

WEATHERSTONE Simon
Born: Reading, 26 January 1980
Height: 5'10" **Weight:** 12.0
Club Honours: NC '02
International Honours: E: SP-3
This skilful left-sided midfield man was
one of the successes of Boston United's
first season of Third Division football and
was always capable of unlocking
opposition defences with his precision
passing. Simon was also used as a striker
and netted eight league and cup goals
making him second-top scorer for the
Pilgrims. His brother Ross also played for
Boston.
Oxford U (From trainee on 27/3/1997) FL
25+27/3 FLC 1+3/1 Others 1
Boston U (Free on 16/2/2001) FL 43+2/6 FLC
2/1 Others 2/1

WEAVER Simon Daniel
Born: Doncaster, 20 December 1977
Height: 6'1" **Weight:** 10.7
Simon had the best possible start to his
career at Lincoln when he scored on his
debut at Kidderminster on the opening
day of the 2002-03 campaign. He
contributed a useful supply of goals but
his main role was in the middle of a five-
man defence that conceded the least
goals in Division Three. Simon showed a
tremendous attitude and produced some
excellent defensive performances.
Sheffield Wed (From trainee on 24/5/1996.
Freed during 1998 close season)
Doncaster Rov (Loaned on 14/2/1997) FL 2
Lincoln C (Free from Nuneaton Borough, ex
Ilkeston T, on 7/8/2002) FL 44/3 FAC 1
Others 5/1

WEBB Daniel (Danny) John
Born: Poole, 2 July 1983
Height: 6'1" **Weight:** 11.8
Club Honours: Div 2 '02
This hard-working striker joined Brighton
on loan in November, making three
appearances as a substitute. He
subsequently returned to Southend only
to rejoin his former manager Peter Taylor
at Hull City on a permanent basis shortly
afterwards. Two days after becoming a
Tiger, Danny earned a place in the club's
record books when he came on as a
substitute for John Anderson against
Darlington, thus becoming the last-ever
player to make his Hull debut at
Boothferry Park. Danny was allowed to go

out on loan to Lincoln later in the season,
where he scored one goal in four starts
before an ankle injury sidelined him.
Although he had the chance to spend a
second month with Lincoln, he chose to
return to Hull and fight to get back into
their first team. He is the son of former
Chelsea star Dave Webb.
Southend U (From trainee at Southampton
on 4/12/2000) FL 16+15/3 FLC 1 FAC 1+1
Others 3+2/1
Brighton & Hove A (Loaned on 12/12/2001)
FL 7+5/1 FAC 1
Brighton & Hove A (Loaned on 8/11/2002)
FL 0+3
Hull C (Free on 13/12/2002) FL 4+8
Lincoln C (Loaned on 14/3/2003) FL 4+1/1

WEBBER Daniel (Danny)
Vaughn
Born: Manchester, 28 December 1981
Height: 5'9" **Weight:** 10.8
International Honours: E: Yth
A quick-witted and highly mobile forward
who has the potential to become one of
the best young strikers in the Premiership,
Danny showed his goal-scoring potential
for Manchester United reserves for much
of last season. He was given only one run
out for the Reds in the Champions'
League game against Deportivo in March.
He began the season on loan at Watford
where he showed impressive form,
scoring an outstanding goal in the 5-2
win over Coventry City. Unfortunately, he
dislocated his shoulder against Sheffield
Wednesday in October and returned to
Old Trafford two weeks before schedule.
Manchester U (From trainee on 7/1/1999)
FLC 1+1 Others 0+1
Port Vale (Loaned on 23/11/2001) FL 2+2
Others 0+1
Watford (Loaned on 28/3/2002) FL 4+1/2
Watford (Loaned on 13/8/2002) FL 11+1/2

WEIR David (Davie) Gillespie
Born: Falkirk, 10 May 1970
Height: 6'2" **Weight:** 13.7
Club Honours: S Div 1 '94; B&Q '94; SC
'98
International Honours: S: 36
Davie had another solid and reliable
season at the heart of the Everton
defence, forming an effective central
defensive partnership with Alan Stubbs.
After starting the season well, Davie was
unlucky to receive a red card at Old
Trafford in October and lost his place in
the team following suspension. He was
recalled in December and remained there
until a further red card against Liverpool
ended his campaign. Davie continues to
be one of the most underrated defenders

in the Premiership and is an excellent reader of the game.

Falkirk *(From Celtic BC on 1/8/1992) SL 133/8 SLC 5 SC 6 Others 5*
Heart of Midlothian *(Signed on 29/7/1996) SL 92/8 SLC 10/2 SC 9/2 Others 6*
Everton *(£250,000 on 17/2/1999) PL 146+7/7 FLC 6 FAC 13*

Danny Webber

WELCH Keith James
Born: Bolton, 3 October 1968
Height: 6'2" **Weight:** 13.7
International Honours: S: Yth
Keith joined Tranmere on a short-term contract at the start of last season to cover for the suspended John Achterberg. However, his time at Prenton Park was dogged by ill luck. In the opening game he fell awkwardly and broke his collarbone, and then on his return at Crewe he dislocated his collarbone. Keith moved on to Torquay, again as cover, where he helped to calm a defence that had started to look somewhat panic-stricken. Finally he signed for Mansfield where he eventually won a contract to the end of the season. The experienced 'keeper celebrated with a penalty stop at Loftus Road, but once Kevin Pilkington regained full fitness Keith was relegated to the bench.

Rochdale *(From Bolton W juniors on 3/3/1987) FL 205 FLC 12 FAC 10 Others 12*
Bristol C *(£200,000 on 25/7/1991) FL 271 FLC 20 FAC 13 Others 14*
Northampton T *(Free on 7/7/1999) FL 117 FLC 3 FAC 4 Others 3*
Tranmere Rov *(Free on 8/8/2002) FL 2*
Torquay U *(Free on 21/11/2002) FL 3 FAC 1*
Mansfield T *(Free on 13/2/2003) FL 9*

WELCH Michael Francis
Born: Crewe, 11 January 1982
Height: 6'3" **Weight:** 11.12
International Honours: Rol: Yth
After breaking into the Macclesfield Town first team at the end of the 2001-02 season Michael missed few matches last term and scored his first senior goal with a spectacular 40-yard strike in the away win at Hull City in September. He made the majority of his appearances as a central defender in a back-five or back-four formation where his height and strength served him well, although he also played in midfield on several occasions where he performed adequately but did not look as comfortable as in his more accustomed defensive role.

Macclesfield T *(Free from trainee at Barnsley on 9/8/2001) FL 44+1/3 FLC 2 FAC 2 Others*

WELLENS Richard Paul
Born: Manchester, 26 March 1980
Height: 5'9" **Weight:** 11.6
Club Honours: AMC '02
International Honours: E: Yth
This promising midfielder was a regular for Blackpool last term. A player of immense skill and an expert at delivering set pieces, his only goal came in the 3-1 win over Cheltenham in October. Richard signed a new two-year deal for the Seasiders in the summer.

Manchester U *(From trainee on 19/5/1997) FLC 0+1*
Blackpool *(Signed on 23/3/2000) FL 106+13/10 FLC 5+1 FAC 6 Others 8+3/1*

WELLER Paul Anthony
Born: Brighton, 6 March 1975
Height: 5'8" **Weight:** 11.2

ow approaching ten years with Burnley, ul had a slightly less successful season ith the Clarets than in recent times, not ast because of several injuries which evented him really settling into the side. pre-season foot injury ruled him out of e preparations, and a recurring achilles oblem then disrupted his campaign. hen in the side, he remained a highly liable competitor, playing more often in ntral midfield than in his previously voured role on the right, and he was warded with the captaincy for a spell uring Steve Davis's absence. Paul is ldom spectacular, but his 'fetching and arrying' is essential and he remains a ear-automatic first choice when fit.

urnley (From trainee on 30/11/1993) FL 74+45/11 FLC 10+2 FAC 7+5/2 Others 7

WELSH Andrew (Andy)
orn: Manchester, 24 November 1983
eight: 5'8" **Weight:** 9.8
ndy made a huge impression during a x-week loan spell with Macclesfield last erm. Playing on the right wing his pace aused problems for opposition defences nd he scored his first senior goal at ochdale at the end of August. However, fter returning to Stockport he suffered a ernia strain that took much longer to eal than first anticipated. He eventually orced his way into the side and scored ith a fine header against champions-lect Wigan. The mercurial winger then rabbed another goal on the final day gainst Tranmere.

tockport Co (From trainee on 11/7/2001) FL 6+12/2 FAC 1 Others 0+1
Macclesfield T (Loaned on 30/8/2002) FL +2/2

WELSH John Joseph
orn: Liverpool, 10 January 1984
eight: 5'7" **Weight:** 11.6
nternational Honours: E: Yth
his young midfielder made his first-team ebut for Liverpool as a late substitute for ladimir Smicer in the Worthington Cup ourth round tie against Ipswich in ecember, a match won by the Reds in a enalty shoot-out after a 1-1 draw in xtra time. He will be looking to gain urther experience of senior football in *003-04.

iverpool (From trainee on 29/1/2001) FLC)+1

WEST Dean
Born: Morley, 5 December 1972
Height: 5'10" **Weight:** 12.2
Club Honours: Div 2 '97
urnley's 'Mr Consistency', Dean had

another fine campaign at right back for the Clarets. He remained solid at the back and more than useful going forward, particularly in support of Glen Little. His fourth season at Turf Moor also saw him finally find the net, which he did on five occasions, including a penalty against Millwall and an unstoppable effort from the edge of the box in a 5-2 home defeat by Reading. Although this was then upstaged by his stunning first-time shot from 25 yards out which proved to be the winner at Stoke. Dean started the season on a week-to-week contract with the club, and it was good news for all Burnley supporters when he stayed.

Lincoln C (From trainee on 17/8/1991) FL 93+26/20 FLC 11/1 FAC 6/1 Others 5+2/1
Bury (Signed on 29/9/1995) FL 100+10/8 FLC 6 FAC 3 Others 2+1
Burnley (Free on 26/7/1999) FL 120+6/4 FLC 4+1/1 FAC 11 Others 1

WESTCARR Craig Naptali
Born: Nottingham, 29 January 1985
Height: 5'11" **Weight:** 11.8
International Honours: E: Yth
This promising Nottingham Forest striker continued to learn his trade in the reserves for most of last season. He made a number of first-team appearances, mostly from the substitutes' bench, and scored his first senior goal for the club against Rotherham in the final match of the campaign. Craig will be aiming to win a regular place in the squad in 2003-04.

Nottingham F (From trainee on 31/1/2002) FL 2+17/1 FLC 1+1

WESTLAKE Ian John
Born: Clacton, 10 July 1983
Height: 5'10" **Weight:** 11.6
This promising left-sided midfield player was another of the young talents to be offered a first-team chance at Ipswich last term. He made his senior debut as a substitute in the home defeat by Gillingham in October when Tony Mowbray was looking after the team and made a handful more appearances from the bench later in the season.

Ipswich T (From trainee on 9/8/2002) FL 0+4 FLC 0+1

WESTON Rhys David
Born: Kingston, 27 October 1980
Height: 6'1" **Weight:** 12.3
International Honours: W: 4; U21-4; E: Yth; Sch
Rhys has shown great character since moving from Arsenal to Cardiff City although he initially struggled to adapt to the move from a Premiership club. He also

had to settle after being switched from his usual central position in defence to right back. Last term, however, he won over the Bluebirds' fans to establish himself in the team, and scored the first senior goals of his career, netting in successive home games against Tranmere Rovers and Peterborough. Rhys is a quick and agile full back who gets forward with increasing confidence. He also established himself in the full Wales squad during the campaign.

Arsenal (From trainee on 8/7/1999) PL 1 FLC 1+1
Cardiff C (£300,000 on 21/11/2000) FL 98+5/2 FLC 3 FAC 10+1 Others 7

WESTWOOD Ashley Michael
Born: Bridgnorth, 31 August 1976
Height: 6'0" **Weight:** 12.8
Club Honours: FAYC '95
International Honours: E: Yth
It was not until the middle of the 2002-03 season that Ashley won a regular place in the Sheffield Wednesday line-up, and then he found himself playing at right back rather than his favoured role in the centre of the defence. He produced a series of sound displays, showing himself to be calm and always giving 100 per cent effort for the cause.

Manchester U (From trainee on 1/7/1994)
Crewe Alex (£40,000 on 26/7/1995) FL 93+5/9 FLC 8 FAC 9/2 Others 10
Bradford C (£150,000 on 20/7/1998) P/FL 18+6/2 FLC 1 FAC 2 Others 10
Sheffield Wed (£150,000 + on 10/8/2000) FL 79+3/5 FLC 10+2/4 FAC 2

WESTWOOD Christopher (Chris) John
Born: Dudley, 13 February 1977
Height: 6'0" **Weight:** 12.2
Last term proved to be another good solid season for this Hartlepool central defender. He was ever-present in league games and formed a great partnership with Graeme Lee. A consistent player with a fine temperament, Chris can be considered a model professional. A rare goal-scorer, he scored just one goal, netting with a header in the last minute of the final league match of the season. It was an important strike for Hartlepool as it guaranteed them the runners-up position in Division Three after a disappointing spell looked to see them slipping behind Wrexham. Chris was chosen by his fellow professionals for the PFA Division Three team of the season, while he was also the recipient of a number of club awards.

Wolverhampton W (From trainee on

3/7/1995) FL 3+1/1 FLC 1+1 (Released during 1998 close season)
Hartlepool U *(Signed from Telford U on 24/3/1999) FL 163+5/3 FLC 4 FAC 6 Others 12*

WETHERALL David

Born: Sheffield, 14 March 1971
Height: 6'3" **Weight:** 13.12
International Honours: E: Sch
David again suffered a frustrating season with injuries in 2002-03. The veteran Bradford City defender struggled to shake off niggling hip and hamstring problems for most of the campaign. He eventually forced his way back into the side by the end of February and finished the season with a run of 17 consecutive appearances. His presence at the back, either on the right or in the centre, is always a major boost and David will be keeping his fingers crossed for an injury-free campaign for the 2003-04 season. His height and strength were again useful assets in the Bantams' attacking play.
Sheffield Wed *(From trainee on 1/7/1989)*
Leeds U *(£125,000 on 15/7/1991) F/PL 188+14/12 FLC 19+1/2 FAC 21+3/4 Others 4*
Bradford C *(£1,400,000 on 7/7/1999) P/FL 89+3/5 FLC 6/2 FAC 1 Others 3*

WHALEY Simon

Born: Bolton, 7 June 1985
Height: 5'11" **Weight:** 11.7
A product of Bury's youth policy, this young attacking midfield player made his first tentative steps into the first team last season, appearing in the final ten minutes of the LDV Vans Trophy game a Rochdale in October, and later making his Football League debut from the bench against Torquay in November. In January he was stretchered off in a reserve game with a knee injury that kept him sidelined for several weeks, but it did not stop the Shakers offering him an 18-month contract extension the following month. Simon is tricky on the ball and good at using his pace to take players on and deceive them.
Bury *(From trainee on 30/10/2002) FL 0+2 Others 0+3*

WHALLEY Gareth

Born: Manchester, 19 December 1973
Height: 5'10" **Weight:** 11.12
The loss of Gareth Whalley and Danny Gabbidon, both on the same day in November, was a major blow to Cardiff City's hopes of automatic promotion. Gareth was taken off on a stretcher after suffering a knee ligament injury. He was out for almost five months and City's

hopes of a top-two finish disappeared. He returned for the run-in and played a huge role in the Bluebirds earning promotion via the play-offs. Gareth's ability to unlock a defence proved crucial in the final against Queen's Park Rangers at the Millennium Stadium, when his lofted pass sent Andy Campbell free for the only goal of the game.
Crewe Alex *(From trainee on 29/7/1992) FL 174+6/9 FLC 11+1/1 FAC 15+1/3 Others 24/3*
Bradford C *(£600,000 on 24/7/1998) P/FL 99+4/3 FLC 10+2/2 FAC 2 Others 5+1*
Crewe Alex *(Loaned on 28/3/2002) FL 7*
Cardiff C *(Free on 9/7/2002) FL 17+2 FLC 1 Others 3*

WHEATCROFT Paul Michael

Born: Bolton, 22 November 1980
Height: 5'9" **Weight:** 9.11
International Honours: E: Yth; Sch
Paul became Scunthorpe United's only summer signing when joining from Bolton and was expected to be a key striker for the club last term. Good on the ball with fine finishing ability, he started the first two games of the season and came on twice as a substitute by the end of August. However, a groin injury sidelined him for two months and he was then released from his contract in January to join Conference outfit Southport.
Manchester U *(From trainee on 8/7/1998)*
Bolton W *(Free on 6/7/2000) FLC 0+1 FAC 0+2*
Rochdale *(Loaned on 27/9/2001) FL 6/3*
Mansfield T *(Loaned on 26/2/2002) FL 1+1*
Scunthorpe U *(Free on 9/8/2002) FL 2+2*

WHELAN Noel David

Born: Leeds, 30 December 1974
Height: 6'2" **Weight:** 12.3
Club Honours: FAYC '93
International Honours: E: U21-2; Yth (UEFA-U18 '93)
This experienced striker struggled to hold down a regular first-team place at Middlesbrough last term, only managing some 15 Premiership games (13 as substitute) all season. Realising that his career was stagnating at the Riverside, even more so with the arrival of Michael Ricketts and Malcolm Christie, Noel agreed to a loan deal with Crystal Palace in March. He scored on his debut for the Eagles at Bradford City and added two more goals before returning to Teesside with an injury.
Leeds U *(From trainee on 5/3/1993) PL 28+20/7 FLC 3+2/1 FAC 2 Others 3*
Coventry C *(£2,000,000 on 16/12/1995) PL 127+7/31 FLC 6/1 FAC 15+1/7*

Middlesbrough *(£2,200,000 on 4/8/2000) PL 33+28/6 FLC 4/2 FAC 5+3/3*
Crystal Palace *(Loaned on 7/3/2003) FL 7+1«*

WHELAN Philip (Phil) James

Born: Stockport, 7 March 1972
Height: 6'4" **Weight:** 14.7
International Honours: E: U21-3
This veteran centre half had a difficult time at Southend last term. After being dropped from the team following the 2-1 defeat at Leyton Orient he fought his wa« back in January only to suffer a severe knee ligament injury in the away game a« Carlisle and this kept him sidelined for th« remainder of the campaign. Phil was advised in March that his contract would not be renewed by the Blues.
Ipswich T *(From juniors on 2/7/1990) F/PL 76+6/2 FLC 6+1 FAC 3+1 Others 1*
Middlesbrough *(£300,000 on 3/4/1995) PL 18+4/1 FLC 5 FAC 3*
Oxford U *(£150,000 on 15/7/1997) FL 51+3/2 FLC 3/1 FAC 5 Others 3*
Rotherham U *(Loaned on 12/3/1999) FL 13/«*
Southend U *(Free on 4/7/2000) FL 96+4/6 FLC 2+2 FAC 7/1 Others 8/1*

WHING Andrew John

Born: Birmingham, 20 September 1984
Height: 6'0" **Weight:** 12.0
Andrew captained the Coventry City youth team last term and after only a handful of reserve-team games he was given a surprise senior debut in the home game with Burnley. He made an immediate impression at full back with hi« strong tackling and keenness to get forward and was a virtual ever-present fo« the rest of the season. He was rewarded with a two-year contract.
Coventry C *(From trainee on 7/4/2003) FL 13+1*

WHITAKER Daniel (Danny) Phillip

Born: Wilmslow, 14 November 1980
Height: 5'10" **Weight:** 11.2
Macclesfield's pacy midfielder finished the 2002-03 season as joint-top scorer with a« tally of 14 goals. A highlight of his campaign was scoring an extra-time hat-trick (the club's only triple strike of the campaign) in the Worthington Cup first round win over Barnsley and he went on to net with a spectacular 30-yard strike in« the FA Cup victory at Hull City. Danny works tirelessly and is capable of playing in any of the midfield positions. He was voted as Macclesfield's 'Players' Player of the Year'.
Macclesfield T *(Signed from Wilmslow Sports on 5/7/2000) FL 56+1/12 FLC 2/3 FAC 3/1 Others 1*

WHITBREAD Adrian Richard
Born: Epping, 22 October 1971
Height: 6'1" **Weight:** 12.12
Adrian was one of several defenders brought in on loan last season in a bid to plug the leaky Exeter defence. His experience and composure helped steady the ship before he headed back to Berkshire after seven games. However, he was out of favour at Reading, where he made no first-team appearances during the campaign.
Leyton Orient (From trainee on 13/11/1989) FL 125/2 FLC 10+1 FAC 11/1 Others 8
Swindon T (£500,000 on 29/7/1993) P/FL 35+1/1 FAC 2
West Ham U (£650,000 on 17/8/1994) PL 3+7 FLC 2+1 FAC 1
Portsmouth (Loaned on 9/11/1995) FL 13
Portsmouth (£250,000 on 24/10/1996) FL 133+1/2 FLC 8/1 FAC 3
Luton T (Loaned on 23/11/2000) FL 9 FAC 4
Reading (Free on 8/2/2001) FL 33 FLC 3 FAC 1
Exeter C (Loaned on 24/1/2003) FL 7

WHITE Alan
Born: Darlington, 22 March 1976
Height: 6'1" **Weight:** 13.2
Central defender Alan enjoyed his best-ever season with Colchester United last term. He only missed five games during the campaign, all due to suspension and was a tower of strength at the heart of the defence. He formed a superb partnership with skipper Scott Fitzgerald and won the supporters over with his no-nonsense displays.
Middlesbrough (From trainee on 8/7/1994) Others 1
Luton T (£40,000 on 22/9/1997) FL 60+20/3 FLC 3+3 FAC 2 Others 4
Colchester U (Loaned on 12/11/1999) FL 4 Others 1
Colchester U (Free on 19/7/2000) FL 98+8/3 FLC 5+1 FAC 1+1 Others 1

WHITE Andrew (Andy)
Born: Swanwick, 6 November 1981
Height: 6'4" **Weight:** 13.4
This talented youngster came on in leaps and bounds at Mansfield last term. Andy opened his season's account with a brace against Plymouth Argyle in the first match, then in October he was surprisingly sent out on loan to Crewe with Colin Little moving to Field Mill in a similar move. On his return to the club he partnered Iyseden Christie up front but found goals difficult to come by. Andy is a tall central striker, whose height and attitude make him an awkward opponent for most defenders.

Mansfield T (Signed from Hucknall T on 13/7/2000) FL 35+19/10 FLC 1+1/1 FAC 0+3 Others 0+1
Crewe Alex (Loaned on 24/10/2002) FL 0+2

WHITE Jason Lee
Born: Sutton in Ashfield, 28 January 1984
Height: 6'3" **Weight:** 12.7
Mansfield Town's youth-team goalkeeper was given his senior debut as substitute when Kevin Pilkington broke a bone in his wrist during the 2-0 home defeat by Cheltenham Town. After regular second-string 'keeper Mick Bingham was released as an economy measure Jason spent much of the remainder of the season on the substitutes' bench.
Mansfield T (From juniors on 9/8/2002) FL 0+1

WHITEHEAD Dean
Born: Oxford, 12 January 1982
Height: 5'11" **Weight:** 12.1
Dean struggled to establish himself in the Oxford United line-up last term, although

Dean Whitehead

he did win the title of 'Young Player of the Year'. A strong, energetic midfielder, he scored his only goal on Boxing Day in the win over Bournemouth. Dean has a very positive attitude and is excellent at delivering set pieces.

Oxford U (From trainee on 20/4/2000) FL 55+23/2 FLC 3+1 FAC 2+2 Others 1+2

WHITEHEAD Philip (Phil) Matthew
Born: Halifax, 17 December 1969
Height: 6'3" **Weight:** 15.10

Phil began the 2002-03 campaign as first choice 'keeper for Reading, but as soon as Marcus Hahnemann arrived from Fulham his place came under threat and after a short spell of games on the bench he dropped out of the first team reckoning altogether. He spent time on loan at Tranmere as cover for the injured John Achterberg and later at York, where he again covered for a crisis and performed well. Phil was made available on a free transfer by Reading in the summer.

Halifax T (From trainee on 1/7/1988) FL 42 FLC 2 FAC 4 Others 4
Barnsley (£60,000 on 9/3/1990) FL 16
Halifax T (Loaned on 7/3/1991) FL 9
Scunthorpe U (Loaned on 29/11/1991) FL 8 Others 2
Scunthorpe U (Loaned on 4/9/1992) FL 8 FLC 2
Bradford C (Loaned on 19/11/1992) FL 6 Others 4
Oxford U (£75,000 on 1/11/1993) FL 207 FLC 15 FAC 13 Others 3
West Bromwich A (£250,000 on 1/12/1998) FL 26 FLC 1 FAC 1
Reading (£250,000 on 7/10/1999) FL 94 FLC 5 FAC 6 Others 3
Tranmere Rov (Loaned on 27/9/2002) FL 2 FLC 1
York C (Loaned on 10/4/2003) FL 2

WHITEHEAD Stuart David
Born: Bromsgrove, 17 July 1976
Height: 5'11" **Weight:** 12.4

Stuart began the 2002-03 season in typical fashion at Carlisle, producing some authoritative defensive displays that earned him more than one 'Man of the Match' citation. However, Darlington had previously shown an interest in securing his services and he joined the Quakers in the autumn. He immediately slotted into the heart of the defence alongside Craig Liddle to form a very effective partnership, showing calm control and effective distribution. Unfortunately, a series of niggling injuries disrupted any lengthy run

in the team, while he is still searching for his first Darlington goal.

Bolton W (Signed from Bromsgrove Rov on 18/9/1995)
Carlisle U (Free on 31/7/1998) FL 148+4/2 FLC 7 FAC 4 Others 2
Darlington (Free on 3/10/2002) FL 23 FAC 1+1

WHITFIELD Paul Michael
Born: St Asaph, 6 May 1982
Height: 6'0" **Weight:** 12.8
International Honours: W: U21-1; Yth

Paul made his senior debut for Wrexham against Everton last October, the night new teenage sensation Wayne Rooney became the Toffees' youngest-ever goalscorer! Highly thought of at the Racecourse Paul made further progress, earning an extended run in the side from the end of October until mid-December, when a cartilage problem sidelined him. His display at Southend had no less a 'keeper than Nev Southall praising his display and helped ensured a much

Jim Whitley

heeded three points during a poor run. A steady custodian who radiates confidence to his defence he made his Wales U21 debut against Azerbaijan in March.
Wrexham (From trainee on 16/7/2001) FL 7+1 FLC 1 FAC 1 Others 2+1

WHITLEY James (Jim)
Born: Zambia, 14 April 1975
Height: 5'9" **Weight:** 11.0
International Honours: NI: 3; B-1
Jim's battling qualities in midfield were an essential feature of Wrexham's promotion campaign last term and on the rare occasions when he was out injured he was sorely missed. Always first on manager Denis Smith's team sheet, he did not get on the score sheet often, but netted an important goal in the 2-2 draw at Cambridge. Jim is the older brother of Jeff Whitley.
Manchester C (From juniors on 1/8/1994) FL 27+11 FLC 3+1/1 FAC 2+1 Others 0+1
Blackpool (Loaned on 20/8/1999) FL 7+1 FLC 1
Norwich C (Loaned on 24/8/2000) FL 7+1/1
Swindon T (Loaned on 15/12/2000) FL 2 FAC 1
Northampton T (Loaned on 27/2/2001) FL 13
Wrexham (Free on 11/10/2001) FL 78/1 FLC 2 FAC 2 Others 4

WHITLEY Jeffrey (Jeff)
Born: Zambia, 28 January 1979
Height: 5'8" **Weight:** 11.2
International Honours: NI: 6; B-2; U21-17
Jeff was out of the reckoning for a first-team place at Manchester City last term and in October he returned to Notts County on loan. He featured regularly in a three-month spell at Meadow Lane, before returning to City in January, and shortly afterwards he was released to allow him to find a new club. Jeff is a very dependable midfield anchor man who is capable in possession and rarely puts a foot wrong.
Manchester C (From trainee on 19/2/1996) P/FL 96+27/8 FLC 9+1 FAC 2+2 Others 4
Wrexham (Loaned on 14/11/1999) FL 9/2
Notts Co (Loaned on 21/3/2002) FL 6
Notts Co (Loaned on 18/10/2002) FL 12 FAC 1 Others 1

WHITLOW Michael (Mike)
William
Born: Northwich, 13 January 1968
Height: 6'0" **Weight:** 12.12
Club Honours: Div 2 '90, Div 1 '92; FLC '97
Bolton's 'Mr Reliable' and one of the club's longest-serving players, Mike began

the 2002-03 season in the first team as a centre back, but a series of injuries (notably a persistent groin problem) prevented him from becoming a regular in the line-up. Nevertheless, he still made 14 starts in the Premiership and eventually returned to first-team action after five months out for the crucial final-day victory over Middlesbrough. A tireless worker, Mike is also one of Bolton's most committed contributors to off-field activities and spends many hours supporting local charitable causes. One of the games genuine nice guys, he will be looking for a new contract with the club when his current deal expires in the summer.
Leeds U (£10,000 from Witton A on 11/11/1988) FL 62+15/4 FLC 4+1 FAC 1+4 Others 9
Leicester C (£250,000 on 27/3/1992) F/PL 141+6/8 FLC 12/1 FAC 6 Others 14
Bolton W (£500,000 + on 19/9/1997) P/FL 124+8/2 FLC 13+2 FAC 10+1 Others 2+3

WHITTINGHAM Peter
Born: Nuneaton, 8 September 1984
Height: 5'10" **Weight:** 10.5
Club Honours: FAYC '02
International Honours: E: Yth
This promising left back was a member of the Aston Villa team that defeated Everton to win the FA Youth Cup in 2001-02. He was handed a first-team squad number last term and after featuring on the bench, he received his first Premiership start in the final game of the season at Leeds. Peter also represented England at U19 level during the campaign.
Aston Villa (From trainee on 2/11/2002) PL 1+3

WHITTLE Justin Phillip
Born: Derby, 18 March 1971
Height: 6'1" **Weight:** 12.12
With the arrival of a new centre-back duo in the close season, Justin's future at Hull appeared bleak as the 2002-03 season commenced. However, despite further setbacks, subsequent events saw him restored to the club's captaincy in his familiar right-sided centre-back role and becoming the Tigers' current longest-serving player. Highly respected by staff, players and supporters alike, there was never any doubt about Justin's continuing commitment to the cause. As he approaches a career total of 300 appearances, a testing campaign merely proved that the no-nonsense defender remains a role model for his younger colleagues.

Glasgow Celtic (Free from Army during 1994 close season)
Stoke C (Free on 20/10/1994) FL 66+13/1 FLC 3+4 FAC 2 Others 2
Hull C (£65,000 on 27/11/1998) FL 169+6/2 FLC 8 FAC 7+2 Others 6/1

WHITWORTH Neil Anthony
Born: Wigan, 12 April 1972
Height: 6'2" **Weight:** 12.6
International Honours: E: Yth
This powerful central defender was unable to hold down a regular place in the Exeter City starting line-up last season and was mainly used as cover during suspensions and injuries. An experienced player who reads the game well, his cause was not helped by the various changes in management at St James' Park during the campaign.
Wigan Ath (Trainee) FL 1+1
Manchester U (£45,000 on 1/7/1990) FL 1
Preston NE (Loaned on 16/1/1992) FL 6
Barnsley (Loaned on 20/2/1992) FLC 1
Rotherham U (Loaned on 8/10/1993) FL 8/1 Others 2
Blackpool (Loaned on 10/12/1993) FL 3
Kilmarnock (£265,000 on 2/9/1994) SL /4+1/3 SLC 3 SC 4 Others 1
Wigan Ath (Loaned on 11/3/1998) FL 1+3
Hull C (Free on 16/7/1998) FL 18+1/2 FLC 4 FAC 1
Exeter C (Free on 4/8/2000) FL 53+4/1 FLC 3 FAC 1 Others 1

WIDDRINGTON Thomas (Tommy)
Born: Newcastle, 1 October 1971
Height: 5'9" **Weight:** 11.12
Club Honours: AMC '01
A hard-tackling defensive midfielder, Tommy returned to action in the 2002-03 pre-season build-up after having been sidelined through injury for over six months. A player who holds the ball well, he can be satisfied with his contribution to a Hartlepool team that gained promotion with several games to spare. He had a particularly good spell towards the end of the season, and had hoped to win a new contract, but was subsequently released by manager Mike Newell.
Southampton (From trainee on 10/5/1990) F/PL 67+8/3 FLC 3+1 FAC 11
Wigan Ath (Loaned on 12/9/1991) FL 5+1 FLC 2
Grimsby T (£300,000 on 11/7/1996) FL 72+17/8 FLC 10+3 FAC 3+1 Others 1
Port Vale (Free on 24/3/1999) FL 77+5/8 FLC 2 FAC 2 Others 3
Hartlepool U (Free on 30/7/2001) FL 50+6/5 FLC 1 FAC 1+1 Others 2

Clyde Wijnhard

WIEKENS Gerard
Born: Tolhuiswyk, Holland, 25 February 1973
Height: 6'0" **Weight:** 13.4
Club Honours: Div 1 '02
This defensive midfielder or centre back started the 2002-03 season out of favour at Manchester City, although he was used as a substitute in the Worthington Cup tie at Wigan. Four days later Gerard made his first start in the 'derby' match against Manchester United when he was outstanding, keeping Ruud Van Nistelrooy quiet, but a slight knock put him on the sidelines again. However after that he rarely featured in the line-up, often seeming to be overlooked even when things were going wrong at the back. He will be hoping for a better time in the 2003-04 campaign.
Manchester C (£500,000 from SC Veendam, Holland on 28/7/1997) P/FL 167+15/10 FLC 13+2 FAC 11+1 Others 3

WIJNHARD Clyde
Born: Surinam, 9 November 1973
Height: 5'11" **Weight:** 12.4
This experienced striker had a mixed season at Oldham Athletic last term. After surviving a near-fatal car crash, which sidelined him for 18 months, Clyde began in style for his new club, scoring 11 times in 16 games. However, the powerful hitman suffered cartilage problems in October and was later informed that he required surgery and another 18-month lay-off. A second opinion helped him return to action by March but the knee problem returned during the club's play-off campaign. Latics await the results of surgery before deciding whether to renew his contract in the summer.
Leeds U (£1,500,000 from Willem II, Holland, ex Ajax, Groningen, RKC Waelwijk, on 22/7/1998) PL 11+7/3 FLC 1 FAC 1+1/1 Others 1+3
Huddersfield T (£750,000 on 22/7/1999) FL 51+11/16 FLC 7/1 FAC 1 Others 1+1/1
Preston NE (Free on 22/3/2002) FL 6/3
Oldham Ath (Free on 30/8/2002) FL 24+1/1C FLC 3/2 FAC 2/1 Others 1

WILBRAHAM Aaron Thomas
Born: Knutsford, 21 October 1979
Height: 6'3" **Weight:** 12.4
A close-season operation to correct a back problem kept this Stockport County striker on the sidelines until late January. After several substitute appearances he hit top form during the run-in and his seven goals, from six games, went a long way to securing the

team's Second Division survival. Although he is only in his early 20s, Aaron is now the longest-serving player at Edgeley Park.

Stockport Co (From trainee on 29/8/1997) FL 36+45/27 FLC 4+2/1 FAC 3

WILCOX Jason Malcolm
Born: Farnworth, 15 July 1971
Height: 5'11" **Weight:** 11.10
Club Honours: PL '95
International Honours: E: 3; B-2
After limited appearances for Leeds United in the previous season, Jason did not enter the first-team picture last term until November, when he played in the Worthington Cup defeat at Sheffield United. He then maintained his place on the left-hand side of midfield, giving the team a better balance with Harry Kewell playing in a more direct striker's role. Jason scored a memorable goal in the 3-0 victory at Bolton in December, cutting in from the left flank before unleashing a powerful right-foot shot which flew in from outside the box.

Blackburn Rov (From trainee on 13/6/1989) F/PL 242+27/31 FLC 16+1/1 FAC 18+2/2 Others 7
Leeds U (£3,000,000 on 17/12/1999) PL 49+26/4 FLC 2 FAC 6+1 Others 9+6/2

WILD Peter
Born: Stockport, 12 October 1982
Height: 5'9" **Weight:** 11.12
This young midfielder struggled to break into the Stockport County first-team squad last season making just four substitute appearances. Although he was released at the end of the campaign Peter will be remembered for coming off the bench at Cheltenham and scoring a last-minute goal, his first for the club, to secure a memorable, and crucial, 2-0 victory.

Stockport Co (From trainee on 11/7/2001) FL 0+3/1 Others 0+1

WILDING Craig
Born: Birmingham, 30 October 1981
Height: 5'10" **Weight:** 11.13
This promising York City striker received two starts last term, featuring in the LDV Vans Trophy tie at Lincoln and in the home fixture with Wrexham soon afterwards, while he also added a handful of appearances from the substitutes' bench. He impressed with his pace and enthusiasm and will be aiming to feature more regularly in the 2003-04 campaign.

Chesterfield (From trainee on 28/7/2001)
York C (Free on 8/7/2002) FL 1+6 Others 1

WILDING Peter John
Born: Shrewsbury, 28 November 1968
Height: 6'1" **Weight:** 12.12
This hard-working player showed his versatility last season by playing in the centre of defence, midfield and at full back for Shrewsbury Town. Peter even managed a full appearance in goal for the reserves after Lee Kendall was injured in the warm-up against Chesterfield, and helped the Shrews to a 2-1 victory! A firm favourite with the club's supporters he always gave 100 per cent and his tally of five goals included a brace in the FA Cup tie against Stafford. Peter won the supporters' 'Player of the Year' award, and the accolade of keeping Wayne Rooney very quiet in the giant-killing victory over Everton.

Shrewsbury T (£10,000 from Telford on 10/6/1997) FL 170+23/7 FLC 8+1 FAC 9+1/3 Others 4+2/1

WILKINSON Shaun Frederick
Born: Portsmouth, 12 September 1981
Height: 5'8" **Weight:** 11.2
Having played as a full back, in midfield and up front for Brighton reserves, Shaun was given an early opportunity in the first team as a striker by manager Martin Hinshelwood last term and was rewarded with his first senior goal, a cracking effort against Exeter City. He performed gamely in the absence of more senior forwards, and chased many a lost cause on his own. A spell on loan with Chesterfield saw him add a further appearance from the subs' bench and he will be hoping to gain further senior experience with the Seagulls in 2003-04.

Brighton & Hove A (From trainee on 7/8/2001) FL 4+11 FLC 1/1
Chesterfield (Loaned on 27/11/2002) FL 0+1

WILKSHIRE Luke
Born: Wollongong, Australia, 2 October 1981
Height: 5'9" **Weight:** 11.5
International Honours: Australia: U23; Yth
Luke arrived at Middlesbrough back in 1998 after impressing the club's Australian scouts but failed to persuade manager Bryan Robson to give him a chance. The attacking midfielder's fortunes changed with the arrival of Steve McClaren and he featured regularly in the squad last term. A product of the New South Wales Institute of Sport development programme, Luke appeared for Australia U23s against Spain in April.

Middlesbrough (Signed from AIS, Australia on 12/5/1999) PL 13+8 FLC 2 FAC 1

WILLIAMS Adrian
Born: Reading, 16 August 1971
Height: 6'2" **Weight:** 13.2
Club Honours: Div 2 '94
International Honours: W: 13
This experienced centre back enjoyed one of the best seasons of his long and distinguished career, and despite passing the 30 mark, he still has all the ambition, fitness and enthusiasm of a youngster. He took over from Phil Parkinson as Reading's longest-serving player and club captain, and contributed a series of performances in which his level of play was never less than outstanding. Adrian only scored once, a clinical striker-type chip in the 3-1 victory at Sheffield United, but he reached two landmarks during the campaign. He made his 350th appearance for the Royals in the 5-2 win at Burnley in February, and was recalled to the Wales international team after an absence of three years, winning his 13th cap against the USA in May.

Reading (From trainee on 4/3/1989) FL 191+5/14 FLC 17/1 FAC 16/2 Others 14/2
Wolverhampton W (£750,000 on 3/7/1996) FL 26+1 FLC 3 FAC 2+2 Others 2/1
Reading (Loaned on 15/2/2000) FL 5/1 Others 1
Reading (Free on 26/3/2000) FL 86+2/2 FLC 3+1 FAC 1 Others 5

WILLIAMS Anthony Simon
Born: Bridgend, 20 September 1977
Height: 6'1" **Weight:** 13.5
International Honours: W: U21-16; Yth
Hartlepool's only experienced goalkeeper, Anthony was an ever-present in league games in 2002-03 as Pool gained automatic promotion from Division Three. He pulled off some great saves, and can look back proudly on a season when he was able to keep 16 clean sheets as part of an outstanding defence. A confident 'keeper, he has occasionally lacked consistency, but there is no doubting he has the ability to make his mark in the higher division.

Blackburn Rov (From trainee on 4/7/1996)
Macclesfield T (Loaned on 16/10/1998) FL 4
Bristol Rov (Loaned on 24/3/1999) FL 9
Gillingham (Loaned on 5/8/1999) FL 2 FLC 2
Macclesfield T (Loaned on 28/1/2000) FL 11
Hartlepool U (Free on 7/7/2000) FL 130 FLC 2 FAC 4 Others 8

WILLIAMS Benjamin (Ben) Philip
Born: Manchester, 27 August 1982
Height: 6'0" **Weight:** 13.4
International Honours: E: Sch
This young Manchester United goalkeeper

453

had a spell on loan at Coventry last autumn, featuring as an unused substitute, before joining Chesterfield in a similar capacity in the wake of 'keeper Carl Muggleton's injury. He showed well in his first month, being particularly brave, and a good shot-stopper. Two subsequent months saw him given rather too much practise at the latter, as the team declined towards the relegation zone! Muggleton's return came at the right time for the Spireites and Ben will have learned much from his experience.
Manchester U (From juniors on 3/7/2001)
Chesterfield (Loaned on 30/12/2002) FL 14

WILLIAMS Christopher (Chris) Jonathan
Born: Manchester, 2 February 1985
Height: 5'8" **Weight:** 9.6
Although scoring regularly for the reserves this young striker found first-team opportunities hard to come by at Stockport County last term. Chris's only taste of Second Division action came when he replaced Aaron Wilbraham late in the game at Crewe in March.
Stockport Co (From trainee on 5/3/2002) FL 1+5 FAC 0+1

WILLIAMS Daniel (Danny) Ivor Llewellyn
Born: Wrexham, 12 July 1979
Height: 6'1" **Weight:** 13.0
International Honours: W: U21-9
A firm favourite with the Kidderminster fans, Danny deservedly picked up the supporters' 'Player of the Year' award last term after a series of good displays in the heart of the midfield. Although not necessarily the most creative of players, he is strong in the tackle and an inspiration to those around him. His contract was up at the end of the season and at the time of writing it was unclear whether he would be offered a new one.
Liverpool (From trainee on 14/5/1997)
Wrexham (Free on 22/3/1999) FL 38+1/3 FLC 4 FAC 4/1 Others 1
Kidderminster Hrs (Free on 11/7/2001) FL 80+3/3 FLC 1 FAC 3 Others 4+1

WILLIAMS Darren
Born: Middlesbrough, 28 April 1977
Height: 5'10" **Weight:** 11.12
Club Honours: Div 1 '99
International Honours: E: B-1; U21-2
One of Sunderland's longest-serving players, Darren has seen many highs and lows during his time on Wearside, but can always be relied upon to give 100 per cent when called upon. He can operate at centre back, in midfield, or at full back,

and it was at right back that he enjoyed his most extended run in the side where his overlapping ability was apparent. A powerful tackler, Darren made his 200th appearance for the Black Cats against Newcastle in April.
York C (From trainee on 21/6/1995) FL 16+4 FLC 4+1 FAC 1 Others 3/1
Sunderland (£50,000 on 18/10/1996) F/PL 130+39/4 FLC 18+1/2 FAC 10+1 Others 3

WILLIAMS Eifion Wyn
Born: Anglesey, 15 November 1975
Height: 5'11" **Weight:** 11.12
International Honours: W: B-1
Hartlepool target man and front runner Eifion took over the main goal-scoring responsibilities following an early-season injury to Gordon Watson. A brave player, he fulfilled the confidence shown in him by manager Chris Turner, and displayed a great attitude throughout 2002-03. Late in the season he went 11 matches without scoring as Pool's fortunes declined, but he still finished as the club's top scorer with 16 league and cup goals.
Torquay U (£70,000 from Barry T on 25/3/1999) FL 84+27/24 FLC 4+1 FAC 3 Others 3
Hartlepool U (£30,000 on 6/3/2002) FL 49+4/19 FLC 1/1 FAC 2 Others 2/1

WILLIAMS Gareth Ashley
Born: Johannesburg, South Africa, 10 September 1982
Height: 5'10" **Weight:** 11.13
International Honours: W: U21-3; Yth
Gareth made his bow in senior football for Crystal Palace from the bench at Norwich last November, but mostly featured in the Eagles' reserve team, for whom he finished as leading scorer. In January the promising striker joined Colchester United on loan and proved to be a revelation. He netted six goals in his spell at Layer Road, including a hat-trick in the 4-1 defeat of Port Vale, the first treble-strike by a U's player in a league match since 1993. His form eventually earned him a recall to Selhurst Park and he added two appearances late on as a substitute. Gareth also featured for Wales at U21 level during the season.
Crystal Palace (From trainee on 9/7/2002) FL 0+5 FLC 1+1
Colchester U (Loaned on 24/1/2003) FL 6+2/6

WILLIAMS Gareth John
Born: Glasgow, 16 December 1981
Height: 5'11" **Weight:** 11.10
International Honours: S: 4; U21-4; Yth
This skilful midfield player added another

dimension to his play last season as his tackling improved immensely. Gareth captained the Nottingham Forest side on occasions and scored his first senior goal for the club against Coventry City. He also showed great courage by appearing in the play-offs against Sheffield United with a damaged shoulder which will require an operation in the summer. Gareth continued to represent Scotland at U21 level and added a further full cap when he appeared against Portugal.
Nottingham F (From trainee on 23/12/1998) FL 94+9/3 FLC 3 FAC 3 Others 2

WILLIAMS John Nelson
Born: Birmingham, 11 May 1968
Height: 6'1" **Weight:** 13.12
John went through a major fitness drive in the summer of 2002, losing over a stone in weight, and he showed his old sharpness in pre-season matches. He was mostly used from the substitutes' bench during the early part of the season where his pace was used to good effect. An experienced striker, he recovered from a groin strain in October to score only his second goal in two seasons at the Vetch Field in the 2-0 win over Lincoln City.
Swansea C (£5,000 from Cradley T on 19/8/1991) FL 36+3/11 FLC 2+1 FAC 3 Others 1
Coventry C (£250,000 on 1/7/1992) PL 66+14/11 FLC 4 FAC 2
Notts Co (Loaned on 7/10/1994) FL 3+2/2
Stoke C (Loaned on 23/12/1994) FL 1+3
Swansea C (Loaned on 3/2/1995) FL 6+1/2
Wycombe W (£150,000 on 15/9/1995) FL 34+14/9 FLC 4+1/2 FAC 5/4 Others 2
Hereford U (Free on 14/2/1997) FL 8+3/3
Walsall (Free on 21/7/1997) FL 0+1
Exeter C (Free on 29/8/1997) FL 16+20/4
Cardiff C (Free on 3/8/1998) FL 25+18/12 FLC 2 FAC 5/3 Others 1
York C (£20,000 on 12/8/1999) FL 29+13/3 FLC 2 FAC 0+1 Others 1
Darlington (Free on 21/12/2000) FL 23+1/3 Others 1
Swansea C (Free on 17/7/2001) FL 37+31/5 FLC 1+1 FAC 2+1/1 Others 1

WILLIAMS Lee
Born: Birmingham, 3 February 1973
Height: 5'7" **Weight:** 11.13
International Honours: E: Yth
One of the stars of Cheltenham Town's promotion campaign in 2001-02, last season was not a particularly successful one for this tricky wide-right player. He began the campaign in the line-up, and indeed hit the post in an early game against Tranmere, but he then lost out to Martin Devaney and found it difficult to

regain his place, although he did make one appearance as a right wing back in the 2-1 defeat at Cardiff. Following the arrival of new manager Bobby Gould Lee went out on loan to Dr Martens League outfit Halesowen Town, where he spent the final three months of the season before being given a free transfer.
Aston Villa (From trainee on 26/1/1991)
Shrewsbury T (Loaned on 8/11/1992) FL 2+1 FAC 1+1/1 Others 2
Peterborough U (Signed on 23/3/1994) FL 83+8/1 FLC 4+1 FAC 5+1/1 Others 7 (Free to Shamrock Rov during 1996 close season)
Mansfield T (Free on 27/3/1997) FL 149+28/9 FLC 8 FAC 4+2 Others 4+1
Cheltenham T (Free on 21/9/2001) FL 42+9/3 FLC 0+1 FAC 5+1 Others 4+1/1

WILLIAMS Mark Ross
Born: Chatham, 19 October 1981
Height: 5'9" **Weight:** 11.0
In his third season as a professional, Brentford's outside right was again a regular on the substitutes' bench last term. He is now the club record holder for league substitute appearances (62) beating Bees' legend Bob Booker. Mark provided his usual effort and supply of crosses, scoring his only goal of the campaign at Notts County. He was surprisingly released in the summer.
Brentford (From trainee on 2/11/2000) FL 10+62/4 FLC 0+3 FAC 0+3 Others 1+3

WILLIAMS Mark Stuart
Born: Stalybridge, 28 September 1970
Height: 6'0" **Weight:** 13.0
Club Honours: Div 3 '94
International Honours: NI: 19; B-1
After missing most of 2001-02 through injury, Mark began last season fully fit and in the Wimbledon first team. He quickly cemented his place, and displayed his usual rugged defensive qualities alongside a number of different central defensive partners. His experience was invaluable to his younger colleagues, but as the season progressed, so time marched on, and as his contract was coming to an end he was allowed an early release to join Stoke City's ultimately successful bid for Division One survival. He principally featured in away games as manager Tony Pulis resorted to three at the back, but Mark did not do enough to earn a longer contract at the end of the campaign and was released.
Shrewsbury T (Free from Newtown on 27/3/1992) FL 96+6/3 FLC 7+1 FAC 6 Others 6/1
Chesterfield (£50,000 on 7/8/1995) FL 168/12 FLC 10 FAC 13/1 Others 7/1

Watford (Free on 13/7/1999) P/FL 20+2/1 FLC 2
Wimbledon (Signed on 26/7/2000) FL 69+1/7 FLC 5/1 FAC 8/1
Stoke C (Free on 11/3/2003) FL 5+1

WILLIAMS Paul Darren
Born: Burton, 26 March 1971
Height: 6'0" **Weight:** 13.0
International Honours: E: U21-6
Paul began the 2002-03 season as the automatic choice to partner Claus Lundekvam in the centre of the Southampton back four, but after losing his place to Michael Svensson in September he took up near permanent residence on the substitutes' bench. He did, however, play four first-team matches in the new year and proved as solid and as quick as ever, showing a special talent for getting forward and winning 50:50 balls in midfield.
Derby Co (From trainee on 13/7/1989) FL 153+7/26 FLC 10+2/2 FAC 8/3 Others 14+1/2
Lincoln C (Loaned on 9/11/1989) FL 3 FAC 2 Others 1
Coventry C (£975,000 on 6/8/1995) P/FL 153+16/5 FLC 16+1/1 FAC 13
Southampton (Free on 26/10/2001) PL 37+2 FLC 1 FAC 2

WILLIAMS Robert (Robbie)
Born: Pontefract, 2 October 1984
Height: 5'10" **Weight:** 11.13
Another product of the Barnsley academy, Robbie is a left back of tremendous promise. He was given his chance in the Reds' first team last term after a number of impressive performances in the reserves and U19s. A strong player, he was seen at his best when going forward. Robbie possesses a fearsome shot and is a dead-ball specialist.
Barnsley (Trainee) FL 7+1 FAC 1 Others 0+1

WILLIAMS Ryan Neil
Born: Sutton in Ashfield, 31 August 1978
Height: 5'5" **Weight:** 11.4
International Honours: E: Yth
Although appearing to have dropped down the Hull pecking order when the 2002-03 campaign kicked off, Ryan was a regular feature in his familiar right-sided role in the early months of the season. The enthusiastic pint-sized midfielder suffered a setback in November though when he damaged knee ligaments in training and was sidelined for two months. Highly regarded by new Hull boss Peter Taylor, Ryan was used on the left of City's middle four before drifting out of the first-team scene as the season progressed.

Mansfield T (Trainee) FL 9+17/3 FLC 2 FAC 0+1
Tranmere Rov (£70,000 + on 8/8/1997) FL 2+3
Chesterfield (£80,000 on 10/11/1999) FL 69+6/13 FLC 3 FAC 1 Others 5+1/1
Hull C (£150,000 on 9/7/2001) FL 40+12/2 FLC 1 FAC 2+1 Others 3+1

WILLIAMS Thomas (Tommy) Andrew
Born: Carshalton, 8 July 1980
Height: 6'0" **Weight:** 11.8
This left-sided player who can play either in defence or midfield joined Queen's Park Rangers on a 12-month loan deal last season. He quickly made the left-back position his own, producing some strong performances, and was an ever-present until he suffered a serious leg injury in November. Although he regained fitness in March Tommy was then unable to dislodge Gino Padula from the starting line-up.
West Ham U (£60,000 from Walton & Hersham on 3/4/2000)
Peterborough U (Free on 22/3/2001) FL 32+4/2 FLC 1+1 FAC 4+1 Others 1
Birmingham C (£1,000,000 on 12/3/2002) FL 4
Queens Park R (Loaned on 8/8/2002) FL 22+4/1 FLC 1 FAC 2 Others 2+2

WILLIAMSON Lee Trevor
Born: Derby, 7 June 1982
Height: 5'10" **Weight:** 10.4
Lee was appointed team captain for Mansfield Town before the start of the 2002-03 campaign. However, this highly rated midfielder played his usual role for the Stags and his new responsibility did not stop him making a rash challenge in the Worthington Cup tie against Derby County, which resulted in a red card. He lost the captaincy after this, but continued to feature regularly for the Stags during the season.
Mansfield T (From trainee on 3/7/2000) FL 82+23/3 FLC 2+3 FAC 5+1 Others 3

WILLIS Adam Peter
Born: Nuneaton, 21 September 1976
Height: 6'1" **Weight:** 12.2
Adam began the 2002-03 season as first choice for one of the centre-back positions at Swindon and initially gave some solid performances. However, after a poor run of results he found himself out of the side and then found it difficult to win his place back. Apart from a few outings from the bench he was then limited to starts in the LDV Vans Trophy

games before eventually being recalled for his first league start at Barnsley at the beginning of February. Unfortunately he picked up an ankle injury early in the game and this sidelined him for the rest of the campaign. A steady, reliable central defender, he was released during the close season.

Coventry C *(From trainee on 1/7/1995)*
Swindon T *(Free on 21/4/1998) FL 76+16/1 FLC 2+1/1 FAC 3+1/1 Others 3*
Mansfield T *(Loaned on 25/3/1999) FL 10*

Tommy Williams

WILLIS Roger Christopher
Born: Sheffield, 17 June 1967
Height: 6'1" **Weight:** 12.0
Club Honours: GMVC '91
International Honours: E: SP-1
This veteran striker returned to Peterborough United early in the 2002-03 season, but failed to impress and only managed one start. He quickly moved on, firstly to Conference neighbours Kettering Town and shortly afterwards to Stevenage Borough.

Grimsby T *(Signed from Central Midland League side, Dunkirk, on 20/7/1989) FL 1+8 FLC 0+1*
Barnet *(£10,000 on 1/8/1990) FL 39+5/13 FLC 2 FAC 1+1 Others 1+4/1*
Watford *(£175,000 on 6/10/1992) FL 30+6/2 FAC 1*
Birmingham C *(£150,000 on 31/12/1993) FL 12+7/5 FAC 0+1*
Southend U *(Signed on 16/9/1994) FL 30+1/7 FAC 1 Others 1*
Peterborough U *(Free on 13/8/1996) FL 34+6/6 FLC 3 FAC 5+1 Others 5*
Chesterfield *(£100,000 on 11/7/1997) FL 68+67/21 FLC 12+4/2 FAC 4+3/1 Others 2+4*
Peterborough U *(Free on 16/8/2002) FL 1+3*

WILLIS Scott Leon
Born: Liverpool, 20 February 1982
Height: 5'10" **Weight:** 11.5
This hard-tackling midfield man quickly won over the Lincoln fans with his enthusiastic style after signing in the summer of 2002 from non-league Droylesden. Scott worked hard to overcome a reckless streak that led to early-season disciplinary problems. He scored a memorable winner against Exeter and after a spell on the sidelines was often used as a third striker in the second half of the season. He is the younger brother of Jimmy (ex-Leicester City) and Paul (formerly of Halifax and Darlington).

Mansfield T *(Free from trainee at Wigan Ath on 23/3/2000. Freed on 23/2/2001)*
Carlisle U *(Free from Doncaster Rov on 10/8/2001) FL 0+1 (Free to Bamber Bridge on 17/10/2001)*
Lincoln C *(Free from Droylesden on 7/8/2002) FL 23+7/3 FLC 1 FAC 1 Others 1+3*

WILLMOTT Christopher (Chris) Alan
Born: Bedford, 30 September 1977
Height: 6'2" **Weight:** 11.12
Chris started the first five games of the 2002-03 campaign alongside Mark Williams at the heart of the Wimbledon defence, but was benched after the 2-0 defeat at Nottingham Forest and from then on failed to start another game. His former club Luton Town took him on loan for the last three months of the season and he fitted in well at Kenilworth Road, featuring regularly in the line-up. An upright player, Chris always looks happiest starting as the right-central defender, but more often than not he has been asked to occupy the left-hand side for the Dons. He was released in the summer.

Luton T *(From trainee on 1/5/1996) FL 13+1*

*Wimbledon (£350,000 on 14/7/1999) P/FL
0+3/2 FLC 3+1 FAC 2
Luton T (Loaned on 1/2/2003) FL 7+1
Luton T (Loaned on 8/4/2003) FL 5*

WILLOCK Calum Daniel
Born: London, 29 October 1981
Height: 5'11" **Weight:** 12.7
International Honours: E: Sch
A promising young striker yet to fulfil his
full potential, Calum made only two
appearances in the Premiership last
season during an injury crisis which saw
him earn brief spells on the field in
consecutive games against Birmingham
and Newcastle. These rare first-team
opportunities came soon after a loan spell
at Queen's Park Rangers, where he made
three appearances. A regular member of
the successful Fulham reserve side, his
pace and direct approach to goal saw him
link well with Elvis Hammond and score
in eight occasions.
*Fulham (From ADT College, Putney on
8/7/2000) P/FL 0+5
Queens Park R (Loaned on 7/11/2002) FL 3*

WILLS Kevin Michael
Born: Torquay, 15 October 1980
Height: 5'8" **Weight:** 10.7
Club Honours: Div 3 '02
This attacking midfielder failed to win a
place in the Plymouth Argyle line-up last
term and initially joined Torquay United
on loan. He impressed during his spell at
Plainmoor and was subsequently offered
a longer deal. Although his best position
is in a free attacking role behind the main
strike force, he was often used as a
substitute, and scored within a minute of
coming on at home to Oxford.
*Plymouth Arg (From trainee on 16/7/1999)
FL 17+15/1 FLC 1 FAC 1+3 Others 2+1
Torquay U (Free on 29/11/2002) FL 5+15/1
FAC 0+1*

WILNIS Fabian
Born: Surinam, 23 August 1970
Height: 5'8" **Weight:** 12.6
After an indifferent start to the season
Fabian bounced back to become a vital
team player for Ipswich under Joe Royle's
leadership. Although sound defensively,
he is also a dangerous attacker, making
frequent sorties down the right flank and
scoring the odd goal too. He became a
hero of the fans when he netted the
opening goal of the Carrow Road 'derby',
firing home from around the penalty spot
after Dean Bowditch's cross was not
cleared properly to set Ipswich on the
road to victory.

*Ipswich T (£200,000 from De Graafschap,
Holland, ex NAC Breda, on 6/1/1999) P/FL
113+18/5 FLC 9+3 FAC 7 Others 9+1*

WILSON Brian Jason
Born: Manchester, 9 May 1983
Height: 5'10" **Weight:** 11.0
Brian started the 2002-03 campaign as a
regular member of Stoke City's first-team
squad understudying Wayne Thomas at
right back. However, as the season
progressed and results failed to improve,
management took him out of the side to
allow him to continue his development in
the reserves. Still a defender with a bright
future he was rewarded with the offer of
a new contract in the summer. He will be
looking to make further progress in
2003-04.
*Stoke C (From trainee on 5/7/2001) FL 1+3
Others 1*

WILSON Mark Antony
Born: Scunthorpe, 9 February 1979
Height: 5'11" **Weight:** 13.0
Club Honours: E: Yth; Sch
International Honours: E: U21-2; Yth;
Sch
Mark featured in six Premiership games
for Middlesbrough last season and also
played in the club's Worthington Cup
games, scoring in the 4-1 win against
Brentford. To gain further experience he
was allowed to join Stoke City on a
month's loan, linking up with Boro'
colleague Mark Crossley at the Britannia
Stadium. He made four appearances
during his time with the Potters but he
injured his shoulder in a 0-0 draw with
Gillingham and returned to Teesside when
the month was up.
*Manchester U (From trainee on 16/2/1996)
PL 1+2 FLC 2 Others 3+2
Wrexham (Loaned on 23/2/1998) FL 12+1/4
Middlesbrough (£1,500,000 on 9/8/2001)
PL 6+10 FLC 4/2 FAC 2+1
Stoke C (Loaned on 14/3/2003) FL 4*

WILSON Stephen (Steve) Lee
Born: Hull, 24 April 1974
Height: 5'10" **Weight:** 11.2
Macclesfield 'keeper Steve enjoyed a
good season despite the occasional slip-
up, again showing his ability as a shot
stopper by making some spectacular saves
which kept his side in the match on more
than one occasion. An excellent example
was his penalty stop at Torquay late in the
season. Without his overall contribution
there is no doubt that the number of
goals conceded by Macc would have
been much higher. Steve was the only

member of the squad to be ever-present
until injury sidelined him for two matches
towards the end of the campaign. He was
voted as the club's 'Player of the Year'.
*Hull C (From trainee on 13/7/1992) FL 180+1
FLC 13 FAC 13 Others 11+1
Macclesfield T (Free on 22/3/2001) FL 83
FLC 2 FAC 7 Others 2*

WILTORD Sylvain
Born: Paris, France, 10 May 1974
Height: 5'9" **Weight:** 12.2
Club Honours: FAC '02, '03; PL '02; CS
'02
International Honours: France: 55
(UEFA '00)
Sylvain started the 2002-03 season in
great style for Arsenal with six goals in
the opening six Premiership games. His
role in the side is very much as a right-
sided midfielder getting forward as an
additional striker to the front two. He is
very strong and lively with great ball
control and a willingness to work back
and help in defence when required.
Sylvain possesses an outstanding array of
skills, and can make goals as well as
being a consistent scorer. He became a
regular member of the French national
team and featured in the side that
defeated Cameroon to win the
Confederations Cup tournament over the
summer.
*Arsenal (£13,000,000 from Bordeaux,
France, ex Rennes, Girondins, on 31/8/2000)
PL 70+24/28 FLC 4/4 FAC 14+6/10 Others
22+15/3*

WINDASS Dean
Born: Hull, 1 April 1969
Height: 5'10" **Weight:** 12.6
This brave and forceful attacker featured
in only four games for Middlesbrough last
term (all away from the Riverside) and he
joined Sheffield United, initially on loan.
Dean was an instant hit, scoring on his
debut at Bradford and using his
experience and physical presence as a
striker to score and create opportunities
for others. His move to Bramall Lane
subsequently became permanent,
although he was in and out of the side
but his whole-hearted displays certainly
endeared him to the fans.
*Hull C (Free from North Ferriby on
24/10/1991) FL 173+3/57 FLC 11/4 FAC 6
Others 12/3
Aberdeen (£700,000 on 1/12/1995) SL
60+13/21 SLC 5+2/6 SC 7/3 Others 6/1
Oxford U (£475,000 on 6/8/1998) FL 33/15
FLC 2 FAC 3/3
Bradford C (£950,000 + on 5/3/1999) P/FL
64+10/16 FLC 6/2 FAC 2 Others 6/3*

Nigel Winterburn

Middlesbrough (£600,000 + on 15/3/2001)
L 16+21/3 FLC 2 FAC 4+3
heffield Wed (Loaned on 6/12/2001) FL 2
heffield U (Loaned on 11/11/2002) FL 4/3
heffield U (Signed on 16/1/2003) FL 16/3
Others 2

WINTERBURN Nigel

Born: Nuneaton, 11 December 1963
Height: 5'9" **Weight:** 11.4
Club Honours: Div 1 '89, '91; PL '98;
AC '93, '98; FLC '93; ECWC '94; CS '98
99
International Honours: E: 2; B-3; U21-1;
th

his veteran full back was once again a
model of consistency for West Ham
United last term. He rarely put a foot
wrong and was the top defender in
November with a gutsy display against
eeds. Unfortunately he sustained a
broken wrist in February, which required
n operation and meant he missed the
losing stages of the season. A great man
o have around the club especially for the
youngsters to learn from, he will be sorely
missed after being released by the
Hammers in the summer.
Birmingham C (From apprentice on
4/8/1981)
Wimbledon (Free on 22/9/1983) FL 164+1/8
LC 13 FAC 12 Others 2
Arsenal (£407,000 on 26/5/1987) F/PL
29+11/8 FLC 49/3 FAC 47 Others 50+1/1
West Ham U (£250,000 on 5/7/2000) PL
8+4/1 FLC 3+1 FAC 8

WINTERS Robert (Robbie)

Born: East Kilbride, 4 November 1974
Height: 5'10" **Weight:** 11.12
International Honours: S: 1
Robbie joined Luton Town on non-
contract forms in the summer of 2002
and was given his chance in the opening
game of the season, when he filled in on
he left wing, only to be substituted at
half time. He left Kenilworth Road soon
afterwards and subsequently signed a
long-term deal with Norwegian club
Brann Bergen.
Dundee U (Free from Muirhead Amateurs on
1/11/1992) SL 99+19/27 SLC 11+1/7 SC 11/5
Others 4+2/2
Aberdeen (£700,000 on 23/9/1998) SL
22+10/41 SLC 6+1/1 SC 9+2/2 Others 2/1
Luton T (Free on 9/8/2002) FL 1

WISE Dennis Frank

Born: Kensington, 15 December 1966
Height: 5'6" **Weight:** 10.10
Club Honours: FAC '88, '97, '00; FLC
98; ECWC '98; ESC '98; CS '00
International Honours: E: 21; B-3; U21-1

After leaving Leicester City under rather
controversial circumstances, Dennis
returned to London and signed for First
Division Millwall shortly after the start of
the 2002-03 campaign. He made an
instant impact on his debut against
Coventry, showing a great appetite for
the game, and went on to score his first
goal for the Lions against his former
club, Leicester. He eventually took on the
captain's armband and his experience
and skill helped no end in bringing on
the talented youngsters at the New Den.
Denis is a vastly experienced midfield
anchor man who has a whole-hearted
approach to every game.
Wimbledon (From trainee at Southampton
on 28/3/1985) FL 127+8/27 FLC 14 FAC 11/3
Others 5
Chelsea (£1,600,000 on 3/7/1990) F/PL
322+10/53 FLC 30/6 FAC 38/8 Others 44+1/8
Leicester C (£1,600,000 + on 23/6/2001) PL
15+2/1 FLC 1 FAC 1
Millwall (Free on 24/9/2002) FL 28+1/3
FAC 3

WISE Stuart

Born: Middlesbrough, 4 April 1984
Height: 6'1" **Weight:** 13.2
This powerful young defender added
three more starts for York City last term,
plus a handful of outings from the
substitutes' bench. However, he remains a
fine prospect and this was recognised
when he was offered a full professional
contract for the 2003-04 season.
York C (Trainee) FL 6+8

WOAN Ian Simon

Born: Heswall, 14 December 1967
Height: 5'10" **Weight:** 12.4
Club Honours: Div 1 '98
When Ian played well, Shrewsbury played
well last term. Perhaps his best
performance was in the FA Cup victory
over Everton when he delivered the free
kick that set Nigel Jemson up for the
winner. A talented midfield playmaker, his
passing and dead-ball kicks were of a
high quality and his tally of four goals
included one direct from a corner in the
3-3 draw at Wrexham. Ian was out of
contract in the summer and his future
was uncertain at the time of writing.
Nottingham F (£80,000 from Runcorn on
14/3/1990) F/PL 189+32/31 FLC 15+3/1 FAC
20/6 Others 13/2
Barnsley (Free on 25/8/2000) FL 2+1 FLC 3
Swindon T (Free on 27/10/2000) FL 21+1/3
FAC 3 (Free to Columbus Crew, USA during
2001 close season)
Shrewsbury T (Free on 31/1/2002) FL
47+3/7 FAC 2 Others 4

WOME Pierre Nlend

Born: Douala, Cameroon, 23 March 1979
Height: 5'11" **Weight:** 12.4
International Honours: Cameroon:
Pierre arrived at Fulham last August 2002
on a year's loan from Bologna, ironically
the Italian team that were Fulham's
Intertoto Cup final opponents, which
meant he did not play until the following
home game against Tottenham. His
tough-tackling style was immediately
evident in his appearances as an attacking
left back, and he also occasionally
featured in the centre of defence and on
the left-hand side of midfield. Overall,
though, he found his first-team
opportunities limited by the form of Rufus
Brevett and then Jon Harley. Pierre's only
goal of the campaign was a memorable
long-distance free kick in the 3-0 home
win over West Bromwich Albion.
Fulham (Loaned from Bologna, Italy, ex
Fogape, Canon Yaounde, Vicenza, Lucchese,
Roma, on 23/8/2002) PL 13+1/1 FLC 2 FAC
0+1 Others 1+1

WOOD Jamie

Born: Salford, 21 September 1978
Height: 5'10" **Weight:** 13.0
International Honours: Cayman
Islands: 2
Jamie showed up well for Swansea in the
early fixtures with his work rate and
speed off the mark. The hard-working
striker scored his first goal in the second
home game against Bournemouth, and
also netted against Hartlepool and
Wolves. He was then disrupted by
suspensions and soon afterwards he
limped off after coming on as a substitute
against Darlington, only to find out the
next day that he had broken a metatarsal
bone in his foot. In mid-April a training
ground injury saw him aggravate the
problem, leaving him sidelined for the
remainder of the season.
Manchester U (From trainee on 10/7/1997)
Hull C (Free on 21/7/1999) FL 15+32/6 FLC
2+3 FAC 3+2/1 Others 2+1
Halifax T (Free on 10/8/2001) FL 10+6 FLC 1
FAC 1/1 Others 0+1
Swansea C (Free on 26/7/2002) FL 13+4/2
FLC 1/1 FAC 1 Others 1

WOOD Leigh James

Born: York, 21 May 1983
Height: 6'1" **Weight:** 11.2
This highly rated young midfielder found
himself unable to win a regular place in
the York City line-up last season and was
mostly restricted to appearances from the
substitutes' bench. A mature player for his
age, he impressed with his passing skills
and all-round ability.

459

Dennis Wise (left)

ork C *(From trainee on 7/3/2002) FL 23+15
thers 1*

WOOD Richard Mark
orn: Wakefield, 5 July 1985
eight: 6'3" **Weight:** 11.11
his young central defender played well
or Sheffield Wednesday's reserve and
cademy teams last season. The result
vas that he received a call up to the first
eam in the closing stages of the
ampaign, making his debut as a
ubstitute in the last few minutes at
righton, before winning a place in the
tarting line-up for the trip to Burnley
vhen he scored in the Owls' remarkable
-2 victory. Richard will be looking to
uild on this promising start in 2003-04.
heffield Wed *(From trainee on 7/4/2003)
2+1/1*

WOODGATE Jonathan Simon
orn: Middlesbrough, 22 January 1980
Height: 6'2" **Weight:** 13.0
lub Honours: FAYC '97
nternational Honours: E: 4; U21-1; Yth
his talented central defender began the
002-03 campaign in excellent form for
eeds United and featured regularly in the
ne-up until financial considerations
orced a sale to Newcastle during the
anuary transfer window. After recovering
om the thigh strain he was carrying at
he time of his move, Jonathan made his
ebut in the victory at home to Chelsea
t the beginning of March and
nmediately looked at home, impressing
vith his calmness under pressure, his pace
nd his organising of the defence. Tall
nd effective in the air, he is just as
omfortable playing the ball on the
round, and has already become the
ornerstone of his team's defence.
onathan was called up by England for
ne Euro 2004 qualifiers against Slovakia
nd Macedonia.
eeds U *(From trainee on 13/5/1997) PL
00+4/4 FLC 7 FAC 11 Others 20*
Iewcastle U *(£9,000,000 on 31/1/2003)
'L 10*

WOODHOUSE Curtis
orn: Beverley, 17 April 1980
Height: 5'8" **Weight:** 11.0
nternational Honours: E: U21-4; Yth
urtis made one start for Birmingham
ity, in the Worthington Cup defeat of
eyton Orient in October, but could not
orce his way into the Premiership club's
ne-up. Nevertheless, he worked
xtremely hard in training and for the
eserves, getting into the best shape of

his career, before joining Rotherham on
loan. He brought experience and bite to
the Millers' midfield as he accepted the
chance to play some first-team football.
But his spell was brought to an early end
when he picked up an injury which kept
him out of action for the last few games
of the season.
Sheffield U *(From trainee on 31/12/1997) FL
92+12/6 FLC 5+3 FAC 10*
Birmingham C *(£1,000,000 on 2/2/2001)
P/FL 35+13/2 FLC 3+1 FAC 1 Others 2*
Rotherham U *(Loaned on 1/2/2003) FL 11*

WOODMAN Andrew (Andy) John
Born: Camberwell, 11 August 1971
Height: 6'3" **Weight:** 13.7
Club Honours: Div 3 '99
Andy was the regular Oxford goalkeeper
last term, missing just one game during
the season. He looked set to be an ever-
present but a nasty facial injury that led to
42 stitches being inserted, kept him out
for one game. He is a good shot stopper
and someone who always gees up his
team mates. His best game was possibly
the Worthington Cup tie at Charlton
when he kept out the Premiership
forwards and also saved several spot kicks
in the ensuing penalty shoot-out to lead
the U's to victory.
Crystal Palace *(From trainee on 1/7/1989)*
Exeter C *(Free on 4/7/1994) FL 6 FLC 1 FAC 1
Others 2*
Northampton T *(Free on 10/3/1995) FL 163
FLC 13 FAC 8 Others 13*
Brentford *(Signed on 22/1/1999) FL 61 FLC
1 FAC 2 Others 3*
Southend U *(Loaned on 8/8/2000) FL 17
FLC 2*
Colchester U *(Free on 10/11/2000) FL 54 FLC
2 FAC 2 Others 1*
Oxford U *(Free on 18/1/2002) FL 60 FLC 3
FAC 3 Others 1*

WOODMAN Craig Alan
Born: Tiverton, 22 December 1982
Height: 5'9" **Weight:** 9.11
Rather surprisingly this young left back
didn't feature regularly for Bristol City last
season. Nevertheless, Craig maintained
the promise shown the previous year by
creating a good impression in his limited
opportunities. He will be looking to gain a
regular place in the line-up in 2003-04.
Bristol C *(From trainee on 17/2/2000) FL
13+5 FLC 1 Others 6*

WOODS Stephen (Steve) John
Born: Northwich, 15 December 1976
Height: 5'11" **Weight:** 12.3
After being a near ever-present for

Torquay United during the previous
campaign, this reliable defensive organiser
suffered a frustrating time in the 2002-03
season. Ruled out by a knee injury until
December, he returned to take up his
favoured position as sweeper as the Gulls
temporarily reverted to a back five, only
for further knee problems to end his
season after ten appearances.
Stoke C *(From trainee on 3/8/1995) FL 33+1
FLC 2 FAC 2 Others 2*
Plymouth Arg *(Loaned on 26/3/1998) FL
4+1*
Chesterfield *(Free on 7/7/1999) FL 22+3 FLC
4 Others 0+1*
Torquay U *(Free on 17/8/2001) FL 43+4/2
FLC 1 FAC 2*

WOODTHORPE Colin John
Born: Ellesmere Port, 13 January 1969
Height: 5'11" **Weight:** 11.8
It was Colin's experience and ability to
play in numerous positions that made his
signature attractive to Bury manager Andy
Preece last August and he certainly did
not let his manager down during the
season. Whether he appeared in central
defence, at left back or in midfield he was
a reliable figure and proved to be an
excellent addition to the squad. Initially
signed on a three-month contract, this
was deservedly renewed several times
during the season.
Chester C *(From trainee on 23/8/1986) FL
154+1/6 FLC 10 FAC 8+1 Others 18/1*
Norwich C *(£175,000 on 17/7/1990) P/FL
36+7/1 FLC 0+2 FAC 6 Others 1+1*
Aberdeen *(£400,000 on 20/7/1994) SL
43+5/1 SLC 5+1/1 SC 4 Others 5+2*
Stockport Co *(£200,000 on 29/7/1997) FL
114+39/4 FLC 12+1/2 FAC 4+1/1*
Bury *(Free on 23/8/2002) FL 30+2 FLC 2+1
FAC 1 Others 6/1*

WOOZLEY David James
Born: Ascot, 6 December 1979
Height: 6'0" **Weight:** 12.10
Leadership qualities earned David the
Torquay United captaincy at the start of
the 2002-03 season, making it easy to
forget that he is still a relatively young
and inexperienced defender. In addition,
the Gulls reliance on an open passing
game meant that he led a back four
afforded less protection than most.
However, he stuck to the task and was an
ever-present throughout the campaign,
mostly featuring as a centre half although
he also had a spell as an orthodox left
back.
Crystal Palace *(From trainee on 17/11/1997)
FL 21+9 FLC 3+1 FAC 0+1*

Craig Woodman

Bournemouth *(Loaned on 15/9/2000) FL 6*
Torquay U *(Loaned on 28/8/2001) FL 12 FLC 1*
Torquay U *(Free on 27/3/2002) FL 48+2/3 FLC 1 FAC 2 Others 1*

WORRELL David
Born: Dublin, 12 January 1978
Height: 5'11" **Weight:** 12.4
Club Honours: Div 3 '02
International Honours: RoI: U21-17
David had another steady campaign at right back for Plymouth Argyle in 2002-03. He was rarely absent all season and put in some excellent defensive performances. His strengths lie in his positional play and good communication with his team mates. He also likes to support the midfield and often puts in dangerous crosses leading to goal-scoring opportunities for his colleagues. David is still looking for his first Argyle goal after over 100 appearances for the club.
Blackburn Rov *(Signed from Shelbourne on 12/1/1995)*
Dundee U *(Free on 30/3/1999) SL 13+4 SLC 2*
Plymouth Arg *(Signed on 23/11/2000) FL 9 FLC 1 FAC 8 Others 4*

WORTHINGTON Jonathan (Jon) Alan
Born: Dewsbury, 16 April 1983
Height: 5'9" **Weight:** 11.0
This young Huddersfield Town midfielder produced a 'Man of the Match' performance in his first home start against Wycombe Wanderers. Jon showed bags of enthusiasm and covered every blade of grass in a solid display of controlled passing and tackling. He continued to be on the fringe of first-team duties for the remainder of the season and held down a regular place in the last few games. Good in the air and with an added blend of pace and skill, Jon will be looking to gain further experience in 2003-04.
Huddersfield T *(From trainee on 10/9/2001) FL 10+12 FAC 1*

WOTTON Paul Anthony
Born: Plymouth, 17 August 1977
Height: 5'11" **Weight:** 12.0
Club Honours: Div 3 '02
Paul had another excellent season in the heart of Plymouth's defence in 2002-03. He has built up an excellent partnership with Graham Coughlan and as club captain leads by example. His ferocious free kicks once again proved effective, contributing to his total of 11 goals, a fine tally for a central defender. Paul was

warded for his efforts by being named the supporters' 'Player of the Year' for e season.

ymouth Arg (From trainee on 10/7/1995) FL 219+22/20 FLC 7 FAC 20/5 Others 7+1/2

RACK Darren

orn: Cleethorpes, 5 May 1976
eight: 5'9" **Weight:** 12.10

his fifth season with Walsall Darren ok his tally of league games beyond the)0 mark and showed splendid versatility. though playing soundly as a wing back e was never happier than when pushing rward from midfield and early in the ason got a last-minute winner at ottingham Forest. He also netted twice the brave 3-2 defeat at Ipswich in ecember and opened the scoring in the Cup replay at Reading.

erby Co (From trainee on 12/7/1994) FL -22/1 FLC 0+3 FAC 0+2
rimsby T (£100,000 + on 19/7/1996) FL -8/1 Others 0+1
rewsbury T (Loaned on 17/2/1997) FL -1 Others 1
alsall (Free on 6/8/1998) FL 174+30/31 FLC +1/1 FAC 12+1/2 Others 7+1/1

RIGHT Alan Geoffrey

orn: Ashton under Lyne, 28 September 971
eight: 5'4" **Weight:** 9.9
ub Honours: FLC '96
ternational Honours: E: U21-2; Yth; h

an had a somewhat disappointing ason for Aston Villa last term and only atured in a handful of first-team games. he emergence of JLloyd Samuel and the surgence of Gareth Barry meant a eatly reduced number of opportunities nd he lost his tag as first choice left ack. Nevertheless, Alan remained a ependable and consistent performer ho pushed up and down the touchline ith ease. He is small and pacy, but never acks out of a tackle.

ackpool (From trainee on 13/4/1989) FL +7 FLC 10+2 FAC 8 Others 11+2
ackburn Rov (£400,000 on 25/10/1991) PL 67+7/1 FLC 8 FAC 5+1 Others 3
ston Villa (£1,000,000 on 10/3/1995) PL 55+5/5 FLC 19 FAC 25 Others 26

RIGHT David

orn: Warrington, 1 May 1980
eight: 5'11" **Weight:** 10.8
ternational Honours: E: Yth

avid occupied the right-back slot for rewe Alexandra for most of the 2002-03 eason before suffering an injury against /ycombe Wanderers, which kept him on

the sidelines for the closing stages. He performed consistently well throughout the campaign and contributed a valuable goal in the away game at Chesterfield.
Crewe Alex (From trainee on 18/6/1997) FL 166+5/2 FLC 8+1 FAC 11 Others 3+1

WRIGHT Jermaine Malaki

Born: Greenwich, 21 October 1975
Height: 5'9" **Weight:** 11.9
International Honours: E: Yth

A versatile player who can appear at full back or in midfield, Jermaine always gave

Jermaine Wright

of his best for Ipswich Town last season He does not get on the score sheet very often but when he does the goals are usually memorable. His only goal last season was a case in point. Against one of his former clubs, Millwall, he picked up a loose ball in midfield, advanced a couple of strides and struck it into the net from outside the box.

Millwall (From trainee on 27/11/1992)
Wolverhampton W (£60,000 on 29/12/1994) FL 4+16 FLC 1+3/1 Others 0+1
Doncaster Rov (Loaned on 1/3/1996) FL 13
Crewe Alex (£25,000 on 19/2/1998) FL 47+2/5 FLC 5 FAC 1
Ipswich T (£500,000 on 23/7/1999) P/FL 105+34/5 FLC 13+2 FAC 6+1/1 Others 8+1

WRIGHT Mark Anthony
Born: Wolverhampton, 24 February 1982
Height: 5'11" **Weight:** 11.4
Mark's first-team chances were limited at Walsall last term, but he laid on an early-season goal for Moriera Herivelto against Wolves at Molineux and while always eager to go forward from a wide position was equally happy to help out in defence when required. The promising young midfielder also created a big impression at Filbert Street against promotion candidates Leicester in November.
Walsall (From trainee on 26/1/2001) FL 2+7 FLC 0+1 Others 2

WRIGHT Richard Ian
Born: Ipswich, 5 November 1977
Height: 6'2" **Weight:** 13.0
Club Honours: FAC '02; PL '02
International Honours: E: 2; U21-15; Yth; Sch
Following a nervous and uneasy start to his Everton career, the former Ipswich and Arsenal 'keeper found his feet and improved his performances to such an extent that he was recalled into the England squad for the friendly match against Australia. A shot stopper par excellence, Richard made late match-winning saves against Blackburn away (during a spell of over ten hours without conceding a Premiership goal) and in home games against Sunderland and Newcastle. He also made a crucial penalty stop in the victory at Sunderland and performed heroics in the penalty shoot-out win at Newcastle in the Worthington Cup. If Richard can reduce the lapses in concentration that sometimes affect his game, then he will be one of the leading candidates to replace David Seaman as his country's number one.
Ipswich T (From trainee on 2/1/1995) P/FL 240 FLC 27 FAC 13 Others 11

Arsenal (£6,000,000 on 13/7/2001) PL 12 FLC 1 FAC 5 Others 4
Everton (£3,500,000 + on 26/7/2002) PL 33 FLC 3 FAC 1

WRIGHT Stephen (Steve)
Born: Bellshill, 27 August 1971
Height: 5'10" **Weight:** 12.2
International Honours: S: 2; B-2; U21-14
This Scottish international right back answered emergency calls from Scunthorpe United on two occasions last term. He spent short spells with the club in September and November to cover for suspensions in defence with the club unable to offer him a longer deal. Excellent on the ball with good distribution and positional sense, he subsequently returned to a coaching post north of the Border.
Aberdeen (Free from Eastercraigs on 28/11/1987) SL 141+8/2 SLC 11+1 SC 13 Others 3
Glasgow R (Signed on 5/7/1995) SL 7 SLC 5 Others 6+1
Wolverhampton W (Loaned on 20/3/1998) FL 3
Bradford C (Free on 30/7/1998) FL 21+1 FLC 6 FAC 2
Dundee U (Signed on 21/8/2000) SL 13+2 SLC 2 SC 2
Scunthorpe U (Free on 6/9/2002) FL 2 FLC 1 FAC 1

WRIGHT Stephen John
Born: Liverpool, 8 February 1980
Height: 6'2" **Weight:** 12.0
Club Honours: UEFAC '01
International Honours: E: U21-6; Yth
A former England U21 international right back, Stephen joined Sunderland from Liverpool in the close season to fill what had become a problem position for the Black Cats. His combative style of play was immediately evident as he was booked in the first five minutes of his debut at Blackburn and he was to serve two suspensions during the season. However, he is also an intelligent passer of the ball and more than willing to cover vast acres of the pitch in support of his colleagues. A hamstring injury, sustained in March, brought a premature end to Stephen's campaign.
Liverpool (From trainee on 13/10/1997) PL 10+4 FLC 1+1 FAC 2 Others 2+1/1
Crewe Alex (Loaned on 6/8/1999) FL 17+6 FLC 1
Sunderland (£3,000,000 on 15/8/2002) PL 25+1 FAC 3

WRIGHT Thomas (Tommy)
Born: Kirby Muxloe, 28 September 198▨
Height: 6'0" **Weight:** 11.12
International Honours: E: Yth
A prolific striker with the Leicester Cit academy teams, Tommy was offered a professional contract in the summer o 2003. He appeared from the bench in the early-season home win over Reading, then later he netted his first senior goal for the Foxes as a substitute at Gillingham. He finally made his first senior start when injury and suspension ruled out both Brian Deane and Paul Dickov from the vital home clash with Nottingham Forest in April and duly celebrated with the on goal of the game. A typical piece of alertness, this strike effectively ensure promotion for the Foxes. Tommy also progressed further through the England junior ranks during the campaign, opening his scoring accoun at U19 level.
Leicester C (Trainee) P/FL 2+12/2 FAC 0+1

WRIGHT-PHILLIPS Shaun Cameron
Born: Greenwich, 25 October 1981
Height: 5'6" **Weight:** 10.1
Club Honours: Div 1 '02
International Honours: E: U21-4
Shaun coped well with the step up to top-flight football with Manchester City last term. He featured regularly in the starting line-up, mainly on the right-hand side as a wing back or midfielder, and netted his first Premiership goal with his first touch after coming off the bench against Fulham. An extremely tricky player with plenty of skill and the ability to take on players, he also appeared for England U21s during the campaign. Shaun is the son of the former Arsenal and England striker Ian Wright.
Manchester C (From trainee on 28/10/1998 P/FL 65+20/9 FLC 5+4 FAC 4

WROE Nicholas (Nicky)
Born: Sheffield, 28 September 1985
Height: 5'11" **Weight:** 10.7
Another product of the Barnsley academ Nicky is a midfield player of great promise. He was an used substitute in th Reds' first team on a couple of occasions last term before been given his debut in the final game of the season at champions Wigan, where he played the full 90 minutes. He will be looking to make even more progress in the 2003-04 season.
Barnsley (Trainee) FL 1

XYZ

XAVIER Abel
Born: Mozambique, 30 November 1972
Height: 6'2" **Weight:** 13.6
International Honours: Portugal: 20;
21; Yth (UEFA-U16 '89; U18 '90)
This Portuguese international seemed to
be an inspired signing by Liverpool
manager Gerald Houllier in the previous
season. However after starting last term
as first choice right back, some early
mistakes saw him dropped from the first
team. His only subsequent first-team
appearance came in December in the
Worthington Cup tie against Ipswich and
soon afterwards he was loaned out to
Galatasaray, for the remainder of the
season.
*Everton (£1,500,000 from PSV Eindhoven,
Holland on 8/9/1999) PL 39+4 FLC 2 FAC 4*
*Liverpool (£800,000 on 31/1/2002) PL
3+1/1 FLC 1 Others 6/1*

XALCIN Levent
Born: Middlesbrough, 25 March 1985
Height: 6'0" **Weight:** 12.2
Levent made his senior debut for York
City in the Worthington Cup tie at
Sheffield United last September when he
came on as a late substitute for Graham
Potter. A second-year scholarship boy, he
remained in the first-team squad adding
further appearances from the bench until
injury caused him to miss much of the
second half of the season. A promising
striker, he is a product of the
Minstermen's thriving youth system and
has been capped by Turkey at youth level.
York C (Trainee) FL 0+5 FLC 0+1

YATES Mark Jason
Born: Birmingham, 24 January 1970
Height: 5'11" **Weight:** 13.2
Club Honours: NC '99
International Honours: E: SP-2
Last term was an eventful time for
Cheltenham Town's long-serving central
midfielder. He began the season in the
line-up under the management of
Graham Allner but lost his place following
a run of poor results and the arrival of
Richard Forsyth from Peterborough
United. However, new manager Bobby
Gould was impressed with Mark's
attitude, work-rate and robust
performances, naming him captain and
selected him alongside John Finnigan for
the remainder of the campaign. The pair
complemented each other well and their
form in the closing weeks was a factor in

the Robins' brave but unsuccessful battle
to avoid the drop.
*Birmingham C (From trainee on 8/7/1988) FL
38+16/6 FLC 5/1 FAC 0+2 Others 5*
*Burnley (£40,000 on 30/8/1991) FL 9+9/1
FLC 1 FAC 0+2 Others 2+1*
Lincoln C (Loaned on 19/2/1993) FL 10+4
*Doncaster Rov (Signed on 30/7/1993) FL
33+1/4 FLC 2 FAC 1 Others 1 (Transferred to
Kidderminster Hrs on 13/8/1994)*
*Cheltenham T (Signed on 28/11/1999) FL
170+3/17 FLC 7 FAC 11+1/1 Others 7+2*

YATES Stephen (Steve)
Born: Bristol, 29 January 1970
Height: 5'11" **Weight:** 12.2
Club Honours: Div 3 '90
This versatile, reliable defender featured at
right wing back for Sheffield United in
pre-season matches. An injury to Robert
Page meant a move to central defence
and he produced a series of impressive,
unflappable performances, being
particularly good in the air. A groin injury
caused Steve to miss a few games and he
returned at left wing back. A training
injury then kept him out for three months
and on his first game back he pulled his
hamstring, which kept him out for the
rest of the season! Steve will be hoping
for better luck with injuries in 2003-04.
*Bristol Rov (From trainee on 1/7/1988) FL
196+1 FLC 9 FAC 11 Others 21*
*Queens Park R (£650,000 on 16/8/1993)
P/FL 122+12/2 FLC 8 FAC 7*
*Tranmere Rov (Free on 5/8/1999) FL
109+4/7 FLC 13+1/2 FAC 10/5*
*Sheffield U (Free on 4/7/2002) FL 11+1
FLC 1*

YEO Simon
Born: Stockport, 20 October 1973
Height: 5'10" **Weight:** 11.8
This striker was given the opportunity of
league football at a relatively late stage in
his career when Lincoln signed him from
Hyde United in the summer of 2002. He
made a promising start by scoring on his
home debut and his direct style and hard
work always caused danger for defences.
Simon's goals supply then seemed to dry
up, but he broke his drought in dramatic
style with a late equaliser in the final
game of the season to take the Imps into
the play-offs. His fairy-tale end to the
season continued when he netted twice
from the substitutes' bench in the home
play-off semi-final against Scunthorpe
followed by the winner in the second leg.
He came on at the Millennium Stadium
too, and was close to scoring again
before Lincoln finally went down to a 5-2
defeat.

*Lincoln C (Free from Hyde U on 7/8/2002) FL
22+15/5 FAC 1 Others 1+4/5*

YETTON Stewart David
Born: Plymouth, 27 July 1985
Height: 5'8" **Weight:** 10.3
A product of Plymouth Argyle's youth
academy, Stewart made his first-team
debut as a substitute for winger David
Beresford in the 2-0 defeat against
Swindon in April following an impressive
run of four goals in five reserve games.
The second year scholar was a regular
scorer in Plymouth's U19 side and will be
aiming to gain more senior experience in
2003-04.
Plymouth Arg (Trainee) FL 0+1

YOBO Joseph
Born: Kano, Nigeria, 6 September 1980
Height: 6'2" **Weight:** 11.6
International Honours: Nigeria:
Signed on an initial one-year contract, it
was clear from the first appearance that
Joseph was an international class player.
After a leg injury sustained in a pre-
season friendly and a freak training
ground incident had delayed his debut
until September, the Nigerian
international brought pace and a
muscular presence to the Everton
defence, with the added bonus of
composure on the ball and strong
heading ability. His consistently excellent
displays were rightfully rewarded with the
PFA Fans' Award for the November 'Player
of the Month'. Joseph was then deployed
at full back for several games where,
although effective, he failed to reach the
standards he had set earlier on. Restored
to the centre of defence for the final few
matches, he reminded everybody of the
class act he is and why Everton were keen
to tie up a permanent deal with him
during the summer.
*Everton (£4,500,000 from Marseilles, France,
ex Micheline, Standard Liege, on 6/8/2002) PL
22+2 FLC 2*

YORKE Dwight
Born: Canaan, Tobago, 3 November 1971
Height: 5'10" **Weight:** 12.4
Club Honours: FLC '96; FAC '99; PL '99,
'00, '01; EC '99
International Honours: Trinidad &
Tobago
Signed by Blackburn Rovers boss Graeme
Souness to renew his partnership with
Andy Cole, Dwight responded by finishing
the campaign as his club's joint-leading
scorer with 13 goals in all competitions.
Several of these were fine efforts, the best
being a thoughtful strike in the 2-1 win at

Highbury in October. An experienced striker, he showed a good understanding up front with Cole, particularly in the use of flicks and lay-offs inside the opposition penalty area.

Aston Villa (£120,000 from Signal Hill, Tobago on 19/12/1989) F/PL 195+36/73 FLC 20+2/8 FAC 22+2/14 Others 10/3
Manchester U (£12,600,000 on 22/8/1998) PL 80+16/48 FLC 3/2 FAC 6+5/3 Others 31+11/12
Blackburn Rov (£2,000,000 on 26/7/2002) PL 25+8/8 FLC 4/2 FAC 3/3 Others 3

Dwight Yorke

YOUDS Edward (Eddie) Paul
Born: Liverpool, 3 May 1970
Height: 6'2" **Weight:** 14.2
Club Honours: Div 1 '00
Eddie impressed in the heart of the Huddersfield Town defence last term, showing a no-nonsense attitude and some fine leadership skills. Effective in the air and with good distribution, his appearances were restricted by niggling hamstring problems, but when absent he was sorely missed. His importance to the Terriers was recognised when he was appointed club captain following the departure of Steve Jenkins.

Everton (From trainee on 10/6/1988) FL 5+ FLC 0+1 Others 1
Cardiff C (Loaned on 8/2/1990) FL 0+1 FAC 0+1
Wrexham (Loaned on 8/2/1990) FL 20/2
Ipswich T (£250,000 on 15/11/1991) F/PL 38+12/1 FLC 1+2 FAC 5+1
Bradford C (£175,000 on 2/1/1995) FL 85/8 FLC 7/2 FAC 3 Others 4
Charlton Ath (£550,000 on 26/3/1998) P/F 52+1/2 FLC 4/1 FAC 1+1 Others 3
Huddersfield T (Free on 25/7/2002) FL 25

YOUNG Alan James
Born: Swindon, 12 August 1983
Height: 5'6" **Weight:** 10.2
International Honours: E: Yth
Although well regarded by Swindon Town manager Andy King, Alan's only start last term was in the LDV Vans Trophy tie against Kidderminster when he netted in a 3-2 defeat. He was a regular on the substitutes' bench and again led the scoring for the club's reserve side. He is a slightly built, skilful forward who is happy to get involved in the action.
Swindon T (From trainee on 30/10/2000) FL 7+22/1 FAC 0+4/1 Others 2/1

YOUNG Gregory (Greg) James
Born: Doncaster, 25 April 1983
Height: 6'1" **Weight:** 12.3
This promising young Grimsby Town defender did enough to earn a call up to the first-team squad once the club's relegation to Division Two had been confirmed. Greg made his senior debut in the penultimate game of the season at Reading and will be aiming to gain more senior experience in 2003-04.
Grimsby T (Free from trainee at Sheffield Wed on 26/7/2002) FL 1

YOUNG Luke Paul
Born: Harlow, 19 July 1979
Height: 6'0" **Weight:** 12.4
Club Honours: FLC '99
International Honours: E: U21-16; Yth
Luke was a first choice for Charlton Athletic for most of last season and generally put in some steady performances. Comfortable either at right back or in the centre of defence, he was used mainly as an orthodox right back or right wing back depending on the formation employed. He is very confident on the ball, a good tackler and is able to put in an accurate cross from the by-line. He also possesses a very long throw. Luke played the last three games in the centre of defence and did extremely well in this

...sition, suggesting he could well be
...ed there again in the future.
...ttenham H *(From trainee on 3/7/1997) PL
+14 FLC 1+3 FAC 9+2 Others 2+1*
...arlton Ath *(£3,000,000 + on 27/7/2001)
63+3 FLC 3 FAC 3*

...OUNG Neil Anthony
...rn: Harlow, 31 August 1973
...ight: 5'9" **Weight:** 12.0
...il enjoyed a tremendous season at
...urnemouth last term when his fitness
...vels reached their highest for some time.
...loyal clubman, the experienced right

...ddie Youds

back was solid and dependable
throughout the campaign and excelled in
the play-off final against Lincoln at the
Millennium Stadium.
Tottenham H *(From trainee on 17/8/1991)*
Bournemouth *(Free on 11/10/1994) FL
286+6/4 FLC 19+1 FAC 20 Others 18*

YOUNG Scott
Born: Pontypridd, 14 January 1976
Height: 6'2" **Weight:** 12.6
International Honours: W: B-1; U21-5
Cardiff City's longest serving player, Scott
joined the Bluebirds as a schoolboy. He

has since made almost 350 first-team
appearances for the club. He suffered
with injuries in the 2002-03 season, but
showed his delight at promotion when he
raced onto the pitch to hug club-mates as
the final whistle blew. Scott had a similar
back problem to that suffered by Danny
Gabbidon and at one stage they were
seeing the same specialist in Luton. A
solid, efficient centre back, he is gearing
up for his testimonial season in 2003-04,
which kicks off with a match against
Charlton Athletic at Ninian Park.
Cardiff C *(From trainee on 4/7/1994) FL
257+20/22 FLC 13+1/1 FAC 21+1/2 Others
17+3/1*

YOUNGS Thomas (Tom)
Anthony John
Born: Bury St Edmunds, 31 August 1979
Height: 5'9" **Weight:** 10.4
Cambridge United's longest-serving
player worked tirelessly up front last
term, scoring regularly and creating
chances for his colleagues with his
unselfish play. He made a surprise move
to Northampton Town on transfer
deadline day where he featured on the
left-hand side as an attacking
midfielder, although he has yet to
register his first goal for the Cobblers.
Cambridge U *(From juniors on 3/7/1997) FL
118+32/43 FLC 3+3 FAC 10/3 Others 12+3/2*
Northampton T *(£50,000 on 27/3/2003)
FL 5*

YULU Christian
Born: Congo, 26 January 1978
Height: 5'10" **Weight:** 12.1
This young striker joined Coventry City on
loan last January and impressed when
scoring on his reserve-team debut. He
was subsequently offered a short-term
contract and made a handful of first-team
appearances but failed to create a big
impression at Highfield Road.
Coventry C *(Free from Rennes, France on
14/2/2003) FL 1+2*

ZAKUANI Gabriel
Born: Congo, 31 May 1986
Height: 6'0" **Weight:** 10.10
This highly rated right back was turning
out for the Leyton Orient U17s at the
start of last season, but made rapid
progress through the ranks and was
rewarded with his first-team debut when
he came on as a substitute at
Bournemouth in March. Gabriel showed
maturity beyond his years and will be
aiming to gain more senior experience in
2003-04.
Leyton Orient *(Trainee) FL 0+1*

ZAMORA Robert (Bobby)
Lester
Born: Barking, 16 January 1981
Height: 6'0" **Weight:** 11.0
Club Honours: Div 3 '01; Div 2 '02
International Honours: E: U21-6
Although by his own standards 2002-03 was a comparatively quiet season, this prolific striker still hit 14 First Division goals in a struggling side despite his campaign being disrupted by injury. His value to the Seagulls was demonstrated by the fact that just two points were gained in his absence, and while he perhaps needed to perform a touch more consistently the quality of his play was obvious. Blessed with pace, skill and all-round ability, Bobby also demonstrated a commitment to his colleagues with his enthusiasm for chasing alone up front and in tackling back. He scored tap-ins, headers, one-on-ones and pile-drivers, but still needs to have more confidence in his right foot. He also increased his tally of England U21 caps during the season.
Bristol Rov (From trainee on 1/7/1999) FL 0+4 FLC 0+1 FAC 0+1
Brighton & Hove A (Loaned on 11/2/2000) FL 6/6
Brighton & Hove A (£100,000 on 10/8/2000) FL 117+2/70 FLC 4/2 FAC 6/4 Others 1/1

ZAVAGNO Luciano
Born: Rosario, Argentina, 6 August 1977
Height: 6'0" **Weight:** 12.0
It is hard to find a Derby player not hampered by injuries last season and the Argentine left back was no exception. Knee ligament and thigh problems kept him out until the new year but he hit a good spell after returning as a substitute in the depressing FA Cup defeat at Brentford. Luciano scored his first goal in England with a point-saving penalty against Gillingham and, in the next game, headed the second in the important victory at Stoke. He is exciting and a force when he surges into attack but has to work on the defensive side of his game. He missed the last eight matches following a hernia operation.
Derby Co (Signed from ES Troyes, France, ex Santa Fe, Strasbourg, on 19/10/2001) P/FL 32+3/2 FAC 1+1

ZDRILIC David
Born: Sydney, Australia, 14 April 1974
Height: 6'0" **Weight:** 12.7
International Honours: Australia: 22
This Australian international made a great early-season impression with the Walsall fans after netting two powerfully struck

goals in his second full game against Rotherham. A few days later he headed a fine goal at Millwall and soon he was netting an injury-time effort in the Worthington Cup tie at Blackburn. David provided a quality finish to win the FA Cup tie against Wimbledon but faded from the first-team scene later in the season and was not retained.
Walsall (Free from Sp Vgg Unterhaching, Germany, ex Sydney U, Aarau, SSV Ulm, on 7/8/2002) FL 9+15/3 FLC 0+2/1 FAC 1+2/1

ZENDEN Boudewijn (Bolo)
Born: Maastricht, Holland, 15 August 1976
Height: 5'9" **Weight:** 11.5
International Honours: Holland: 45
Despite a bright start to the season Chelsea's flying left winger ultimately had a disappointing campaign, drifting intermittently in and out of the side. He bamboozled the Charlton defence to lay on the Blues' first goal of the season for Franco Zola and in the second match scored his only Premiership goal against Manchester United with a superb swerving left-footed drive. A succession of niggling injuries cost him his place, which was brilliantly filled by Graeme Le Saux. Bolo's second half of the season was restricted mainly to substitute appearances, but he still has a vital part to play as the Blues strive to make the most of their attacking options next term, particularly in the Champions' League where his considerable European experience could prove decisive.
Chelsea (£7,500,000 from Barcelona, Spain, ex PSV Eindhoven, on 10/8/2001) PL 24+19/4 FLC 2+3 FAC 1+6 Others 3+1

ZHIYI Fan
Born: Shanghai, China, 6 November 1969
Height: 6'2" **Weight:** 12.1
International Honours: China: 109
This experienced international spent the summer on loan in China with Shanghai Zhongyuan Huili and with the national team at the World Cup finals. He made a surprise move to Cardiff City at the end of the year and enjoyed a short run in the side, but never really established himself. He was hampered by a foot injury and after being switched from central defence to midfield he never managed to settle. A highlight was his goal with a cracking volley from 40 yards in a reserve match. He was released at the end of the season.
Crystal Palace (£500,000 from Shanghai Shenhua, China on 10/9/1998) FL 87+1/4 FLC 11/2 FAC 3

Dundee (£300,000 on 2/11/2001) SL 14/2 SC 4/1
Cardiff C (Free on 14/11/2002) FL 6 Others

ZIEGE Christian
Born: Germany, 1 February 1972
Height: 6'1" **Weight:** 12.12
Club Honours: FLC '01
International Honours: Germany: 71 (UEFA '96)
A left wing back of the highest quality, Christian has pace, accuracy and a fabulous eye for goal. After returning from a calf injury, he looked set to cement his reputation as one of the best defenders in the Premiership last season. However, an injury picked up at Charlton developed complications and restricted his appearances for Tottenham. Nevertheless, he produced some outstanding performances topped off when he scored with a 30-yard free kick against Arsenal at White Hart Lane.
Middlesbrough (£4,000,000 from AC Milan, Italy, ex Bayern Munich, on 6/8/1999) PL 29 FLC 3+1/1 FAC 1
Liverpool (£5,500,000 on 29/8/2000) PL 11+5/1 FLC 1+3/1 FAC 2+1 Others 6+3
Tottenham H (£4,000,000 on 1/8/2001) PL 37+2/7 FLC 4/1 FAC 2/1

ZOLA Gianfranco (Franco)
Born: Sardinia Italy, 5 July 1966
Height: 5'6" **Weight:** 10.10
Club Honours: FAC '97, '00; FLC '98; ECWC '98; ESC '98; CS '00
International Honours: Italy: 35
Chelsea's evergreen superstar trained harder than ever during the 2002 close season, and how his hard work paid off, as he featured in every Premiership match! Eight goals in the first ten matches took him to the top of the goal scoring charts and deservedly brought the Barclaycard Premiership 'Player of the Month' award for October. One sublime moment came against Birmingham when he played a wall pass against a defender's shin and slammed an unstoppable drive across the 'keeper. Franco had an unfortunate start to 2003, picking up a nasty calf injury, but he returned to give a veritable master class in the FA Cup at Gay Meadow to steer the Blues past Shrewsbury Town. Franco went on to top the Chelsea scoring charts with 16 goals but with his contract expiring at the end of the season his future was uncertain at the time of writing.
Chelsea (£4,500,000 from Parma, Italy, ex Napoli, Torres, Nuorese, on 15/11/1996) PL 185+44/59 FLC 10+3/1 FAC 28+3/11 Others 37+2/9

A Barclaycard Premiership and Nationwide League Clubs

ummary of Appearances and Goals for 2002-2003

EY TO TABLES: P/FL = Premier/Football League. FLC = Football League Cup. FAC = FA Cup. Others = Other first team appearances.
Left hand figures in each column list number of full appearances + appearances as substitute. Right hand figures list number of goals scored.

RSENAL (PREM: 2nd)

	P/FL App	Goals	FLC App	Goals	FAC App	Goals	Others App	Goals
JADIERE Jeremie	0 + 3				1			
ENTLEY David			0 + 1					
ERGKAMP Dennis	23 + 6	4			2 + 2	2	7 + 1	1
AMPBELL Sol	33	2			5	1	11	
OLE Ashley	30 + 1	1			3		10	
YGAN Pascal	16 + 2	1			2		9 + 2	
DU	12 + 6	2			5 + 1	1	2 + 3	
ARRY Ryan	1		0 + 1					
LBERTO SILVA	32 + 3				1 + 2		11 + 2	3
ENRY Thierry	37	24			2 + 3	1	13	7
OYTE Justin	0 + 1							
FFERS Francis	2 + 14	2	1	1	6	3	1 + 4	
ANU Nwankwo	9 + 7	5	1		1		2 + 6	1
EOWN Martin	22 + 2				5		5 + 1	
AUREN	26 + 1	1			6	2	10 + 1	
UNGBERG Freddie	19 + 1	6			3 + 1	1	7 + 1	2
UZHNY Oleg	11 + 6		1		2		3 + 1	
ARLOUR Ray	14 + 5				6		1 + 2	
ENNANT Jermaine	1 + 4	3	1				0 + 1	
RES Robert	21 + 5	14	1	1	5 + 1	1	8 + 1	
EAMAN David	28				5		10	
HAABAN Rami	3						2	
TEPANOVS Igors	2		1				1	
VARD Sebastian			1		1			
VLARIDIS Stathis	0 + 1		1					
AYLOR Stuart	7 + 1				2		1 + 1	
URE Kolo	9 + 17	2	1		3 + 2		3 + 5	
PSON Matthew					1			
AN BRONCKHORST Gio	9 + 11	1	1		3 + 2		2 + 2	
EIRA Patrick	24	3			5		13	1
OLZ Moritz			0 + 1					
ILTORD Sylvain	27 + 7	10			3 + 4	2	11 + 2	1

STON VILLA (PREM: 16th)

	P/FL App	Goals	FLC App	Goals	FAC App	Goals	Others App	Goals
LLBACK Marcus	9 + 11	5	0 + 2				3	1
LPAY	5							
NGEL Juan Pablo	8 + 7	1	0 + 3	1	1		1	
ARRY Gareth	35	3	4	1	1		4	
OATENG George							1	
OULDING Michael							2	1
OOKE Stephen	0 + 3							
ROUCH Peter	7 + 7						4	
E LA CRUZ Ulisses	12 + 8	1	2 + 1	1	1			
ELANEY Mark	12		1					
UBLIN Dion	23 + 5	10	4		4	1	2	
DWARDS Rob	7 + 1				1			
NCKELMAN Peter	33		3				3	
UDJONSSON Joey	9 + 2	2	1					
ADJI Moustapha	7 + 4		1				1 + 2	
ENDRIE Lee	22 + 5	4	3		1		1 + 2	
ITZLSPERGER Thomas	24 + 2	2	2 + 1	2			4	
OHNSEN Ronny	25 + 1		3					
ACHLOUL Hassan							0 + 1	
NSELLA Mark	15 + 4		2 + 2		1			
EONHARDSEN Oyvind	13 + 6	3	3 + 1		1			
ELLBERG Olof	38	1	2		1		3	
ERSON Paul							0 + 1	
OORE Stefan	7 + 6	1	1 + 1				0 + 2	
OSTMA Stefan	5 + 1		1		1		1	
IDGEWELL Liam					0 + 1			
AMUEL JLloyd	33 + 5		4				2	
TAUNTON Steve	22 + 4		3				3	1
TONE Steve							1 + 1	
AYLOR Ian	9 + 4		2	1	0 + 1		3	1
VASSELL Darius	28 + 5	8	3	3	0 + 1		1 + 1	
WHITTINGHAM Peter	1 + 3							
WRIGHT Alan	9 + 1				1		1	

BARNSLEY (DIV 2: 19th)

	P/FL App	Goals	FLC App	Goals	FAC App	Goals	Others App	Goals
AUSTIN Neil	32 + 2				1			
BARROWCLOUGH Carl	0 + 5							
BERTOS Leo	2 + 4	1						
BETSY Kevin	32 + 7	5	1		1		1	
CROOKS Lee	10 + 8							
CURLE Keith	11		1					
DONOVAN Kevin	20 + 2							
DYER Bruce	39 + 1	17			1	1	1	
FALLON Rory	18 + 8	7	0 + 1		1		1	
FLYNN Mike	13 + 1							
GHENT Matthew	7				0 + 1		1	
GIBBS Paul	23 + 3	1			1		1	
GORRE Dean	18 + 9						1	
HAYWARD Steve	6							
HOLT Andy	4 + 3		1					
JONES Gary	31		1				1	
JONES Griff	0 + 2						0 + 1	
KAY Antony	13 + 3						1	
LUMSDON Chris	21 + 4	3	1		1		1	
MARRIOTT Andy	36		1		1		1	
MORGAN Chris	36	2	1		1		1	
MULLIGAN David	30 + 3	1	1		1		1	
NEIL Alex	30 + 3		1		1		1	
O'CALLAGHAN Brian	12 + 2	1	1					
RANKIN Izzy	1 + 8	1	1	1				
SHERON Mike	28 + 6	9	0 + 1		0 + 1		1	
TAYLOR Martin	3							
WARD Mitch	22 + 4						1	
WILLIAMS Robbie	7 + 1				1		0 + 1	
WROE Nicky	1							

BIRMINGHAM CITY (PREM: 13th)

	P/FL App	Goals	FLC App	Goals	FAC App	Goals	Others App	Goals
BENNETT Ian	10		2					
CARTER Darren	3 + 9						1	
CISSE Aliou	21							
CLAPHAM Jamie	16							
CLEMENCE Stephen	15	2						
COLY Ferdinand	1				1			
CUNNINGHAM Kenny	31		1					
DEVLIN Paul	20 + 12	3			1			
DUGARRY Christophe	16	5						
FAGAN Craig	0 + 1		0 + 2		0 + 1			
GRAINGER Martin	8 + 1		1		1			
HORSFIELD Geoff	15 + 16	5	2		0 + 1			
HUGHES Bryan	10 + 12	2	1		0 + 1			
HUTCHINSON Joey	1		1					
JOHN Stern	20 + 10	5	1	3	0 + 1	1		
JOHNSON Damien	28 + 2	1	0 + 1		1			
JOHNSON Michael	5 + 1		1					
KENNA Jeff	36 + 1	1	1		1			
KIROVSKI Jovan	5 + 12	2	1 + 1		1			
LAZARIDIS Stan	17 + 13	2	2					
MARRIOTT Andy	1							
MOONEY Tommy	0 + 1							
MORRISON Clinton	24 + 4	6	1		1			
POWELL Darryl	3 + 8		2		1			
PURSE Darren	19 + 1	1	1					
SADLER Mat	2		2					
SAVAGE Robbie	33	4			1			
SWIERCZERSKI Piotr	0 + 1							
TEBILY Olivier	12							

	P/FL App	P/FL Goals	FLC App	FLC Goals	FAC App	FAC Goals	Others App	Others Goals
UPSON Matthew	14							
VAESEN Nico	27			1				
VICKERS Steve	5		1					
WOODHOUSE Curtis	0 + 3		1					
BLACKBURN ROVERS (PREM: 6th)								
BERG Henning	15 + 1	1			1		1 + 1	
BJORNEBYE Stig Inge		1						
COLE Andy	32 + 2	7	4	4	2	2	2 + 1	
CURTIS John	5				1			
DANNS Neil	1 + 1		2		1		1	
DOUGLAS Jonathan	0 + 1		0 + 1		1 + 2			
DUFF Damien	26	9	2	1			3	1
DUNN David	26 + 2	8	2		2		3 + 1	
FLITCROFT Garry	33	2	3 + 1		2	2	1	
FRIEDEL Brad	37		3		3		4	
GALLAGHER Paul	0 + 1							
GILLESPIE Keith	10 +15		2 + 2		0 + 2		0 + 3	
GRABBI Ciccio	1 +10	1	1 + 1	1	0 + 1		1	1
GRESKO Vratislav	10							
HIGNETT Craig	1 + 2	1						
JANSEN Matt	0 + 7		1 + 2		2	2	0 + 1	
JOHANSSON Nils-Eric	20 +10		2 + 1		1 + 1		4	
KELLY Alan	1		2					
McEVELEY Jay	9		3 + 1		2			
MAHON Alan	0 + 2		1					
NEILL Lucas	34		4		3		4	
OSTENSTAD Egil	8 + 9	1	0 + 2		1 + 2		2 + 1	1
PELZER Marc Sebastian			1					
RICHARDS Marc			0 + 1					
SHORT Craig	26 + 1	1	1				2	
SUKUR Hakan	7 + 2	2						
TAYLOR Martin	29 + 4	2	3		3		3	
THOMPSON David	23	4	4	1	2		3	1
TODD Andy	7 + 5	1	4		2		1	
TUGAY	32 + 5	1	4		2 + 1		4	
YORKE Dwight	25 + 8	8	4	2	3	3	3	
BLACKPOOL (DIV 2: 13th)								
BARNES Phil	44		1		2		2	
BLINKHORN Matthew	3 + 4	2					1	
BULLOCK Martin	34 + 4	1	0 + 1		2 + 1		1	
BURNS Jamie	4 + 3							
CLARKE Chris	12 + 5	1			3		1	
CLARKE Peter	16	3						
COID Danny	31 + 5	1	1		3		2	
COLLINS Lee	1 + 5		1		1 + 1		1	
DALGLISH Paul	20 + 7	1	1		2	1	0 + 1	
DOUGHTY Phil					0 + 1			
EVANS Paul	10	1						
FLYNN Mike	21							
GRAYSON Simon	44 + 1	3	1		3		1	
GULLIVER Phil	2 + 1				1			
HENDRY Colin	14							
HILLS John	20 + 7	5	1		2	1	1	
HUGHES Ian	13 + 5						1	
JASZCZUN Tommy	15 + 6	1	1		1		2	
McMAHON Stephen	3 + 3						1	
MILLIGAN Jamie	0 + 7	1					1	1
MURPHY John	33 + 2	16	0 + 1		3	2	1 + 1	1
O'KANE John	8 + 6		1		0 + 3		1	
REID Brian							1	
RICHARDSON Leam	20				1			
ROBINSON Paul	5 + 2	1						
SOUTHERN Keith	38		1		2		1	
TAYLOR Scott	30 +14	13	1		1 + 1	2	0 + 2	1
THEOKLITOS Michael	2				1			
THORNLEY Ben	7 + 5				1			
THORNTON Sean	1 + 2						1	
WALKER Richard	19 +13	4	0 + 1		1 + 2		2	
WELLENS Richard	36 + 3	1	1		3		0 + 2	

	P/FL App	P/FL Goals	FLC App	FLC Goals	FAC App	FAC Goals	Others App	Others Goals
BOLTON WANDERERS (PREM: 17th)								
AKIN Bulent	0 + 1		1		1			
ANDRE Pierre-Yves	0 + 9							
ARMSTRONG Chris			1					
BARNESS Anthony	21 + 4				1			
BERGSSON Gudni	31	1						
CAMPO Ivan	28 + 3	2	1		2			
CHARLTON Simon	27 + 4							
DJORKAEFF Youri	36	7			1			
FACEY Delroy	1 + 8	1			2			
FARRELLY Gareth	6 + 2	1			2			
FRANDSEN Per	34	2						
GARDNER Ricardo	31 + 1	2						
HOLDSWORTH David			1					
HOLDSWORTH Dean	5 + 4		0 + 1					
HUNT Nicky							1 + 1	
JAASKALAINEN Jussi	38							
JOHNSON Jermaine	0 + 2		1					
LAVILLE Florent	10							
LIVESEY Danny	0 + 2		1					
MENDY Bernard	20 + 1		1		1			
N'GOTTY Bruno	23				1			
NOLAN Kevin	15 +18	1	0 + 1		1 + 1			
OKOCHA Jay Jay	26 + 5	7			0 + 1			
PEDERSEN Henrik	31 + 2	7	0 + 1					
POOLE Kevin			1		2			
RICKETTS Michael	13 + 9	6			1		1	
SALVA	1 + 5							
SMITH Jeff			1		2			
TOFTING Stig	2 + 6		1		2			
WALTERS Jon	0 + 4		1		0 + 1			
WARHURST Paul	5 + 2				0 + 1			
WHITLOW Mike	14 + 3				1 + 1			
BOSTON UNITED (DIV 3: 15th)								
ANGEL Mark	24 + 7	5	2		1		2	
BALMER Stuart	21							
BASTOCK Paul	46		2		1		2	
BATTERSBY Tony	7 + 4	1			1	1	2	
BEEVERS Lee	0 + 1							
BENNETT Tom	29 + 4		2		1		2	
BURTON Steve	6 + 2		1 + 1	1				
CHAPMAN Ben	37				1		2	
CLARE Daryl	7		1	1				
CLIFFORD Mark	5 + 2		1				1	
COOK Jamie	6 +10	2	0 + 1		1			
COSTELLO Peter	13 + 5							
DOUGLAS Stuart	14 +15	7			0 + 1		0 + 1	
DUFFIELD Peter	12 + 4	4						
ELDING Anthony	3 + 5				0 + 1		0 + 1	
ELLENDER Paul	25 + 1		2	1				
GEORGE Liam	1 + 2							
GOULD James	10 +10	2						
GREAVES Mark	24 + 2	1					2	
HIGGINS Alex	13				1	1	2	
HOCKING Matt	44 + 1	1	1 + 1		1		2	
JONES Graeme	2 + 1	1						
LODGE Andy	1 + 1							
LOGAN Richard	26 + 1	10						
McCARTHY Paddy	11 + 1							
MONINGTON Mark	1							
MORLEY Ben	1 + 1							
REDFEARN Neil	27 + 4	6	1					
RODWELL Jim	2 + 1							
RUSK Simon	12 + 6	2	1		1		1	
THOMPSON Lee	12 + 3	4			1		2	
THOMPSON Neil	3		2					
TOWN David	0 + 8							
WARBURTON Ray	16		2		1		0 + 1	
WEATHERSTONE Ross	2 + 6				0 + 1		0 + 1	
WEATHERSTONE Simon	43 + 2	6	2	1			2	

OURNEMOUTH (DIV 3: 4th)

	P/FL App	P/FL Goals	FLC App	FLC Goals	FAC App	FAC Goals	Others App	Others Goals
SHDOWN Jamie	2							
LAYNEY Alan	2							
ROADHURST Karl	20 + 1	1	1		3	1	3	
ROWNING Marcus	40 + 3	1	1	1	3 + 1	1	5	
UXTON Lewis	15 + 2				1			
ONNELL Alan	10 + 3	6	1	1				
UMMINGS Warren	20							
LLIOTT Wade	39 + 5	4	1		6		6 + 1	1
RIBENNE Chukki	0 + 6							
EENEY Warren	11 +10	7			1 + 4		2 + 2	1
ETCHER Carl	42		1	1	6		7	3
ETCHER Steve	29 + 6	5			6	2	5 + 2	2
OYEWA Amos	0 + 1				0 + 2			
ULLIVER Phil	4 + 2				3			
AYTER James	35 +10	9	0 + 1		6	1	6 + 1	4
OLMES Derek	11 +18	3	1		0 + 4	1	2 + 2	
McDONALD Scott	3 + 4	1			0 + 1			
AHER Shaun	7 + 1	2	1					
OSS Neil	33				6			
ARADA	3 + 4				1 + 1		4	
'CONNOR Garreth	29 +12	8	0 + 1		6		6 + 1	2
URCHES Steve	43 + 1	3	1		6		7	2
IDGEWELL Liam	2 + 3							
TEWART Gareth	0 + 1				1 + 1			
TOCK Brian	14 +13	2			2		3 + 2	
ARDIF Chris	9				3 + 1	1		
HOMAS Danny	30 + 7	2	1	1	6	1	4 + 2	
NDALL Jason	24 + 3	1	1		3 + 1		1 + 1	
OUNG Neil	29 + 3	1	0 + 1		4		3	

RADFORD CITY (DIV 1: 19th)

	P/FL App	P/FL Goals	FLC App	FLC Goals	FAC App	FAC Goals	Others App	Others Goals
THERTON Peter	25	1						
ANKS Steve	8 + 1							
OWER Mark	36 + 1		1		1			
ADAMARTERI Danny	14 + 6		1	1				
ANKS Mark	0 + 3				0 + 1	1		
AVISON Aidan	33 + 1		1		1			
MANUEL Lewis	25 + 4				1			
VANS Paul	16 + 3	2	1					
ACEY Delroy	6	1						
ORREST Danny	10 + 7	3	1					
RANCIS Simon	24 + 1	1			1			
RAY Andy	44	15	1		1			
ACOBS Wayne	19 + 4							
ORGENSEN Claus	28 + 4	11	0 + 1		1			
UANJO	2 + 7		0 + 1		1			
EARNEY Tom	4							
AWRENCE Jamie	15 + 1	1						
EE Andy	0 + 1							
McHUGH Frazer	2							
OLENAAR Robert	28 + 1	1	1		1			
UIRHEAD Ben	5 + 3							
MYERS Andy	21 + 3		1					
MYHILL Boaz	2							
ENFORD Tom	0 + 3							
ROCTOR Michael	10 + 2	4						
EID Paul	7 + 1	2						
ANASY Kevin	0 + 1							
INGH Harpal	3							
TANDING Michael	14 +10	2	1		1			
EN HEUVEL Laurens	4 + 1							
OD Andy	4 + 1	1						
JHLENBEEK Gus	42	1	1		1			
WALSH Gary	3							
WARD Ashley	24	3	1					
WARNOCK Steve	12	1						
WETHERALL David	16 + 1							

RENTFORD (DIV 2: 16th)

	P/FL App	P/FL Goals	FLC App	FLC Goals	FAC App	FAC Goals	Others App	Others Goals
ANDERSON Ijah	9		2					
ANTOINE-CURIER Mickael	11	3						
BLACKMAN Lloyd	1							
CHORLEY Ben	2		1					
CONSTANTINE Leon	2 +15		1 + 1					
DOBSON Michael	45 + 1	1	2		4		2	
EVANS Steve	20 + 3	3	1 + 1		3		2	
FIELDWICK Lee	6 + 1							
FRAMPTON Andy	9 + 6				3		3	
FULLARTON Jamie	22 + 5	1	2		1		2	
HUGHES Steve	2 + 1				1 + 1		0 + 1	
HUNT Steve	41 + 1	7	1 + 1		4	2	2	1
HUTCHINSON Eddie	21 + 2		2				0 + 1	
JULIAN Alan	3						1	
LOVETT Jay	1							
McCAMMON Mark	31 + 6	7	1		3	1	1	1
MARSHALL Scott	22 + 2	1	1		4		3	1
O'CONNOR Kevin	44 + 1	5	2	2	4	1	2	1
PETERS Mark	3 + 8	1			0 + 1			
ROGET Leo	14		1		1		1	
ROWLANDS Martin	13 + 5	1			2		2	
SMITH Jay	23 + 3				2		2 + 1	
SMITH Paul	43		2		4		2	
SOMNER Matt	39 + 1	1	0 + 1		1 + 2	1	1	
SONKO Ibu	37	5	2	1	4		2	
TABB Jay	1 + 4				0 + 1		1 + 1	
TRAYNOR Rob	0 + 2						0 + 1	
VINE Rowan	37 + 5	10	1 + 1	1	3	2	3	
WILLIAMS Mark	4 +18	1	0 + 1		0 + 1			

BRIGHTON & HOVE ALBION (DIV 1: 23rd)

	P/FL App	P/FL Goals	FLC App	FLC Goals	FAC App	FAC Goals	Others App	Others Goals
BARRETT Graham	20 +10	1			1			
BEASANT Dave	16							
BLACKWELL Dean	18 + 3	2			0 + 1			
BROOKER Paul	32 + 5	6	2		1			
BUTTERS Guy	6		1					
CARPENTER Richard	42 + 2	2	2		1			
CULLIP Danny	44		2		2	1	1	
HAMMOND Dean	1 + 3		1	1				
HARDING Dan	0 + 1							
HART Gary	27 + 9	4	1					
HINSHELWOOD Adam	4 + 3							
INGIMARSSON Ivar	15							
JONES Nathan	16 +12	1	0 + 1		1			
KITSON Paul	7 + 3	2						
KUIPERS Michel	21				1			
McPHEE Chris	0 + 2		0 + 2					
MARNEY Danny	6 + 6		1					
MAYO Kerry	41		1		1			
MELTON Steve	6 + 2	1	1 + 1					
OATWAY Charlie	18 +11	1	2		1			
PACKHAM Will					0 + 1			
PETHICK Robbie	25 + 1		1		1	1		
PETTERSON Andy	6 + 1		2					
PIERCY John	1 + 3		1		0 + 1			
ROBERTS Ben	3							
RODGER Simon	27 + 2	2						
ROGERS Paul	1 + 3		0 + 1					
ROUGIER Tony	5 + 1	2						
SIDWELL Steve	11 + 1	5						
VIRGO Adam	3		1					
WATSON Paul	45				1			
WEBB Danny	0 + 3							
WILKINSON Shaun	4 + 8		1	1				
ZAMORA Bobby	35	14			1			

BRISTOL CITY (DIV 2: 3rd)

	P/FL App	P/FL Goals	FLC App	FLC Goals	FAC App	FAC Goals	Others App	Others Goals
AMANKWAAH Kevin	0 + 1						0 + 1	
BEADLE Peter	11 +13	4	0 + 1		0 + 2		1 + 4	
BELL Mickey	37 + 1	2			3		5	2
BROWN Aaron	21 +11	2			0 + 1		3 + 3	
BURNELL Joe	43 + 1		1		3		7	1
BUTLER Tony	38		1		3		9	

	P/FL App	Goals	FLC App	Goals	FAC App	Goals	Others App	Goals
CAREY Louis	21 + 3	1			0 + 1		7	1
CLIST Simon	0 + 3	1	0 + 1					
COLES Danny	38 + 1	2			3		6	1
CORREIA Albano							0 + 2	
DOHERTY Tommy	38		1		3		8 + 1	1
FAGAN Craig	5 + 1	1					1	
FORTUNE Clayton	7 + 3						2 + 1	
HILL Matt	39 + 3	3	1		3		7 + 1	
HULBERT Robin	2 + 5		1				2	
LITA Leroy	0 + 15	2			0 + 1	2	0 + 2	
MATTHEWS Lee	3 + 4	1	0 + 1					
MILLEN Keith	3							
MURRAY Scott	45	19	1		3	3	8	5
PEACOCK Lee	33 + 4	12	1		3		7	3
PHILLIPS Steve	46		1		3		9	
ROBERTS Christian	31 + 13	13	1		3	3	6 + 2	1
ROBINS Mark	6	4					1 + 1	1
ROSENIOR Liam	2 + 19	2			0 + 1		2 + 3	1
TINNION Brian	30 + 10	9	1		3		6 + 3	
WOODMAN Craig	7 + 3		1				2	

BRISTOL ROVERS (DIV 3: 20th)

	P/FL App	Goals	FLC App	Goals	FAC App	Goals	Others App	Goals
ALLEN Bradley	5 + 3	1			1 + 1	1		
ANDERSON Ijah	14							
ARNDALE Neil	1				1			
ASTAFJEVS Vitas	26 + 7	8			4			
AUSTIN Kevin	31 + 2				3 + 1			
BARRETT Adam	45	1	1		4	1	1	
BOXALL Danny	35 + 4		1		4		1	
BRYANT Simon	14 + 8	1			2 + 1		1	
CARLISLE Wayne	35 + 6	7	1		3 + 1	1		
CHALLIS Trevor	16		1		2			
CLARKE Ryan	2						1	
COOTE Adrian	4 + 1	1					1	
DI PIEDI Michele	3 + 2							
GALL Kevin	0 + 9				0 + 1		0 + 1	
GILROY David	3 + 8				0 + 1	1	0 + 1	
GRAZIOLI Giuliano	28 + 6	11	1		3	1		
HODGES Lee	7 + 1							
HOGG Lewis	8 + 9		1		0 + 2		1	
HOWIE Scott	44		1		4			
HYDE Graham	21	1			2			
LEE David	5						1	
LLEWELLYN Chris	14	3						
McKEEVER Mark	7 + 9		1		1		1	
PARKER Sonny	13 + 2				1			
PLUMMER Chris	2				2			
QUINN Rob	44	2	1		4		1	
RAMMELL Andy	7	4						
RICHARDS Justin	0 + 8							
ROSE Richard	9							
STREET Kevin	13 + 7	1						
TAIT Paul	33 + 8	7	1		4	1		
U'DDIN Anwar	17 + 1	1	1				1	
WARREN Christer	0 + 2							

BURNLEY (DIV 1: 16th)

	P/FL App	Goals	FLC App	Goals	FAC App	Goals	Others App	Goals
ARMSTRONG Gordon	1 + 5				0 + 1			
BERESFORD Marlon	33 + 1		4		5			
BLAKE Robbie	34 + 7	13	4	1	3 + 1	2		
BRANCH Graham	31 + 1		2 + 1		6			
BRISCOE Lee	32 + 1	2	4		4			
CHAPLOW Richard	2 + 3							
COOK Paul	21 + 2		1 + 2		5 + 1	1		
COX Ian	23 + 3	1	2		4 + 1			
DAVIS Steve	25 + 3	4	3		0 + 1	1		
DIALLO Drissa	14	1			4	1		
GNOHERE Arthur	31 + 2	2	4		3			
GRANT Tony	24 + 10	1	3 + 1		6			
JOHNROSE Lenny	5 + 1							
LITTLE Glen	28 + 5	5	2 + 1		1 + 3	2		
McGREGOR Mark	25 + 5	1	3		2 + 2			

	P/FL App	Goals	FLC App	Goals	FAC App	Goals	Others App	Goals
MAYLETT Brad	1 + 5							
MICHOPOULOS Nik	13				1			
MOORE Alan	14 + 13	1	1 + 2		5 + 1	2		
MOORE Ian	35 + 9	8	2		6	3		
O'NEILL Matt	2 + 5							
PAPADOPOULOS Demi	7 + 27	3	0 + 4	3	1 + 1			
PAYTON Andy	0 + 1				0 + 1			
RASMUSSEN Mark	0 + 2							
TAYLOR Gareth	38 + 2	16	3 + 1		4	1		
WAINE Andrew	0 + 2							
WELLER Paul	26 + 8		3		1 + 2	1		
WEST Dean	41	4	3	1	5			

BURY (DIV 3: 7th)

	P/FL App	Goals	FLC App	Goals	FAC App	Goals	Others App	Goals
ABBOTT Pawel	17	6	2				1	
BARRASS Matt	16		2		1		1	
BILLY Chris	33 + 5	4	2 + 1		1		4	
CLEGG George	28 + 3	5	2				3	
CONNELL Lee	13 + 1	2					2	
CRAMB Colin	17 + 1	3					2	
DUNFIELD Terry	28 + 1	2	3				1	
FORREST Martyn	22 + 7	1	2 + 1				2 + 1	
GARNER Glyn	46		3		1		6	
GEORGE Liam	3 + 5	1					2	
HILL Nicky	1 + 1						3	
JOHNROSE Lenny	5 + 1						2	
LAWSON Ian	3 + 4	3			1		3	
NELSON Michael	38 + 1	5	3		1		3	
NEWBY Jon	46	10	3	1	1		4	
NUGENT David	11 + 20	4	0 + 1		0 + 1		3 + 3	
O'SHAUGHNESSY Paul	6 + 10		0 + 1		1		3	
PORTER Chris	0 + 2							
PREECE Andy	11 + 18	4	1 + 2		0 + 1		0 + 3	
REDMOND Steve	26 + 1	2	0 + 1				5	
SEDDON Gareth	2 + 2							
STUART Jamie	32 + 5		2 + 1	1	1		2	
SWAILES Danny	38 + 1	3	3		1		4 + 2	
UNSWORTH Lee	34 + 1	2	3		1		4	
WHALEY Simon	0 + 2						0 + 3	
WOODTHORPE Colin	30 + 2		2 + 1		1		6	

CAMBRIDGE UNITED (DIV 3: 12th)

	P/FL App	Goals	FLC App	Goals	FAC App	Goals	Others App	Goals
ANGUS Stev	40		2		6		3	
BRENNAN Martin	1				0 + 1		0 + 1	
BRIDGES David	6 + 11	2	2		1 + 2		2 + 1	
CHILLINGWORTH Dan	11 + 19		0 + 1		1 + 4		2 + 3	
DUNCAN Andy	21 + 2		1	1	6		3	
FLEMING Terry	42 + 1	2	2		5		5 + 1	
GOODHIND Warren	34 + 3		1		5		4	
GUTTRIDGE Luke	39 + 4	3	0 + 1		2 + 1		4 + 1	
HEATHCOTE Jonathan	2							
IRIEKPEN Izzy	13	1						
JORDAN Steve	11						3	
KITSON Dave	44	20	2	1	6	1	3 + 1	
MARSHALL Shaun	45		2		6		6	
MURRAY Fred	25 + 4		1		1 + 1		3	
NACCA Franco	9 + 8		0 + 2		1 + 3		2 + 3	
NEWEY Tom	6						1	
OPARA Lloyd	0 + 2						0 + 1	
PAYNTER Owen							0 + 1	
REVELL Alex	0 + 9						0 + 2	
RIZA Omer	43 + 3	11	2		3 + 2	1	4 + 1	
SCULLY Tony	1 + 5		0 + 1				1	
TANN Adam	21 + 4	1			6	2	6	
TAYLOR John	0 + 1							
THEOBALD David	1 + 3							
TUDOR Shane	26 + 1	9	2		1	5	4	
TURNER John	0 + 1	1						
WANLESS Paul	27 + 12	5	1		6	1	5	
WARNER Phil	7 + 1		2					

	P/FL App	Goals	FLC App	Goals	FAC App	Goals	Others App	Goals
OUNGS Tom	31 + 4	10	2		6	2	5	1

ARDIFF CITY (DIV 2: 6th)

	P/FL App	Goals	FLC App	Goals	FAC App	Goals	Others App	Goals
INSWORTH Gareth	9							
LEXANDER Neil	40		1		4		3	
ARKER Chris	32 + 8		1		5		4	
OLAND Willie	40 + 1		2		4	1	3	
ONNER Mark	7 + 7						2 + 3	
OWEN Jason	7 + 4	3			5		1 + 1	1
AMPBELL Andy	10 +18	3	1 + 1		2 + 3	2	2 + 3	2
OLLINS James	0 + 2				2 + 1	2	2	
ROFT Gary	39 + 4	1	2		3 + 1		0 + 2	
ARNSHAW Robert	39 + 7	31	2	3	3 + 1	1	3	
ORTUNE-WEST Leo	7 +12	2	1 + 1		1 + 4	1	2	1
ABBIDON Danny	22 + 2		1				3	
ORDON Gavin	3 + 7	2					0 + 1	1
REEN Ryan							1	
AMILTON Des	2 + 4		0 + 1		2 + 1		2	
ENKINS Steve	4							
AVANAGH Graham	42 + 2	5	2		4	1	3	
EGG Andy	26 + 9	3	1 + 1		4 + 1		4	
AHON Alan	13 + 2	2						
ARGETSON Martyn	6		1		1		2	
AXWELL Layton	5 +11		1 + 1		1 + 2		1	
RIOR Spencer	35 + 2		2		4		3	
IMPKINS Mike							2	
HORNE Peter	46	13	1	1	4	1	4	1
ESTON Rhys	38		2		5		4	
HALLEY Gareth	17 + 2		1				3	
OUNG Scott	11 + 1	1			1 + 1			
HIYI Fan	6							

ARLISLE UNITED (DIV 3: 22nd)

	P/FL App	Goals	FLC App	Goals	FAC App	Goals	Others App	Goals
NDREWS Lee	11 + 4		0 + 1		0 + 1			
ALDACCHINO Ryan	11 +11				1 + 2		1 + 3	
IRCH Mark	21 + 3	1	1		2		2 + 1	
URNS John	4 + 1							
URT Jamie	4	1						
YRNE Des	9 + 1				0 + 1		1	
ILLON Dan	0 + 1							
ARRELL Craig	31 + 2	11			1	1	6 + 1	2
ORAN Richie	27 + 4	7			3	1	4 + 2	1
REEMAN David	3 + 1							
ALLOWAY Mick	4 + 5		1					
LENNON Matty	32				3		7	
REEN Stuart	9 + 1	2					3	
ULLIVER Phil	1							
EVICON Ryan	0 + 1							
UDSON Mark	14 + 1	1						
ACK Michael	3 + 4		0 + 1					
EEN Peter	13							
ELLY Darren	30 + 2	1	1		2		7	
McCARTHY Jon	19 + 2	1			2		4	1
McDONAGH Will	10 +14	2			2		4 + 2	3
McGILL Brendan	22 +12	3	1	1	2 + 1		3 + 2	
ADDISON Lee	18 + 3	1			3		2 + 2	
AGENNIS Mark	6						1	
OLLY Trevor	7	1	1					
URPHY Peter	38 + 2	2	1		3		7	
AISBITT Danny	1		1					
IXON Marc	3 + 4		1		0 + 1			
SMAN Leon	10 + 2	1					3	2
AVEN Paul	11						3	
ROBINSON Paul	1 + 4	1			2		0 + 1	1
RUNDLE Adam	19 + 2	1					3 + 1	1
RUSSELL Craig	7 + 6	1					3	
HELLEY Brian	32 + 3	1			3		5	
LAVEN John	0 + 1							
UMMERBELL Mark	39	1	1		2		5	
UTTON John	7	1					2	
AYLOR Michael	10				1		1	
WAKE Brian	10 +18	9	1		0 + 1		0 + 3	

	P/FL App	Goals	FLC App	Goals	FAC App	Goals	Others App	Goals
WHITEHEAD Stuart	9		1					

CHARLTON ATHLETIC (PREM: 12th)

	P/FL App	Goals	FLC App	Goals	FAC App	Goals	Others App	Goals
BARTLETT Shaun	25 + 6	4	1		2			
BART-WILLIAMS Chris	7 + 6	1					1 + 1	
BLOMQVIST Jesper	0 + 3				1			
BROWN Steve	0 + 3		0 + 1					
CAMPBELL-RYCE Jamal	0 + 1							
EL KHALEJ Tahar	2 + 1							
EUELL Jason	35 + 1	10	1		2	1		
FISH Mark	23		1		1			
FORTUNE Jon	22 + 4	1	1		1 + 1			
JENSEN Claus	32 + 3	6	1		1			
JOHANSSON JJ	10 +21	3	1		2	2		
KIELY Dean	38		1		2			
KISHISHEV Radostin	27 + 7	2	1		2			
KONCHESKY Paul	17 +13	3	1		2			
LISBIE Kevin	24 + 8	4			0 + 1			
MUSTOE Robbie	6		1					
PARKER Scott	28	4			1			
POWELL Chris	35 + 2							
ROBERTS Ben	0 + 1							
ROBINSON John	10 + 3		0 + 1					
ROWETT Gary	12	1						
RUFUS Richard	29 + 1	2	1		2			
SANKOFA Osei	0 + 1							
STUART Graham	3 + 1							
SVENSSON Matt	4 +11		0 + 1		0 + 2			
YOUNG Luke	29 + 3				2			

CHELSEA (PREM: 4th)

	P/FL App	Goals	FLC App	Goals	FAC App	Goals	Others App	Goals
BABAYARO Celestine	16 + 3	1	2		3			
BOGARDE Winston	0 + 1				0 + 1			
COLE Carlton	2 +11	3	1	2	0 + 2	1		
CUDICINI Carlo	36		3		5		2	
DE GOEY Ed	2				0 + 1			
DE LUCAS Quique	17 + 8		2 + 1		1 + 1		1	
DE OLIVEIRA Felipe	0 + 3		0 + 1				0 + 1	
DESAILLY Marcel	30 + 1	2			1		1	
FERRER Albert	3		1					
GALLAS William	36 + 2	4	3		5		2	
GRØNKJAER Jesper	20 +10	4	1 + 1		2 + 3	1	2	
GUDJOHNSEN Eidur	20 +15	10	0 + 2		3 + 2		1 + 1	
HASSELBAINK Jimmy Floyd	27 + 9	11	2	2	4	1	2	1
HUTH Robert	2				0 + 1		2	
KEENAN Joe	0 + 1							
LAMPARD Frank	37 + 1	6	3		5	1	1 + 1	1
LE SAUX Graeme	27 + 1	2	2		3		1	
MELCHIOT Mario	31 + 3		2		4 + 1		1	
MORRIS Jody	19 + 6		2 + 1		2 + 1	1	1 + 1	
PETIT Manu	23 + 1	1	1	1	5		1	
STANIC Mario	13 + 5	4	2	1	3	1	2	
TERRY John	16 + 4	3	3		5	2	1	
ZENDEN Bolo	11 +10	1	0 + 1		1 + 3		0 + 1	
ZOLA Franco	30 + 8	14	3		3		2	

CHELTENHAM TOWN (DIV 2: 21st)

	P/FL App	Goals	FLC App	Goals	FAC App	Goals	Others App	Goals
ALSOP Julian	32 + 5	10	2		2 + 1	1	1 + 1	1
BIRD David	12 + 2							
BOOK Steve	36		2		3		1	
BRAYSON Paul	14 + 6	1			2 + 1	1	2	2
BROUGH John	21 + 8	1			3		1	
BROWN Marvin	11 + 4	2					1	
COATES Jonathan							1	
DEVANEY Martin	35 + 5	6			2	1	2	
DUFF Michael	44	2	2		3		2	
DUFF Shane	15 + 3							
FINNIGAN John	34 + 3	1	2		3			
FORSYTH Richard	12	2			3		2	1
GRIFFIN Antony	8 + 3	1					0 + 1	
HIGGS Shane	10						1	
HOWARTH Neil	26 + 1	1	1		3		2	

	P/FL App	Goals	FLC App	Goals	FAC App	Goals	Others App	Goals
JONES Steve	5							
McAULEY Hugh	15 + 4	2	2	1	3		1	
McCANN Grant	27	6					2	1
MILTON Russell	15 + 6	2	2				0 + 1	
NAYLOR Tony	19 +11	6	2	2				
SIMPKINS Mike	2				0 + 1			
SPENCER Damian	10 +20	6			1 + 1		1 + 1	
STRONG Greg	3 + 1							
VICTORY Jamie	45	2	2		3		1	
WALKER Richard	15		2				1	
WILLIAMS Lee	6 + 7		0 + 1		0 + 1			
YATES Mark	34 + 3	2	2		2 + 1	1	1 + 1	

CHESTERFIELD (DIV 2: 20th)

	P/FL App	Goals	FLC App	Goals	FAC App	Goals	Others App	Goals
ALLOTT Mark	24 + 9		1 + 1	1	1		2	1
BLATHERWICK Steve	30 + 1				1			
BOOTY Martyn	35 + 3		2		1			
BRADLEY Shayne	1 + 8	2						
BRANDON Chris	35 + 1	7	1 + 1	1	1		2	2
BURT Jamie	11 + 5	1	1 + 1	1	1		2	
CLOSE Brian	8	1						
DAVIES Gareth	27 + 7	1	2		1	1	2	
DAWSON Kevin	26	1	2		1		2	
DOUGLAS Jonathan	7	1						
EBDON Marcus	21 + 3	4	2				0 + 1	
EDWARDS Robbie	25 + 4	2	0 + 1		1		1	
FOLAN Caleb	9 + 4	1						
HOWARD Jon	1 + 8				0 + 1		1 + 1	
HOWSON Stuart	32 + 1	2	2		1		2	
HUDSON Mark	23 + 1	3	1		0 + 1		0 + 1	
HURST Glynn	27 + 5	7			0 + 1			
INNES Mark	5 + 5							
MUGGLETON Carl	26		2		1		2	
O'HARE Alan	18 + 4						2	
PAYNE Steve	34	2	1		1		2	
REEVES David	36 + 4	8	2					
RICHARDSON Lee			0 + 1				1	
RICHMOND Andy	6 + 1							
ROWLAND Keith	0 + 3						1	
RUSHBURY Andy	23 + 7		2		1		0 + 1	
SMITH Adam							0 + 1	
WARNE Steve	2 + 1						0 + 1	
WILKINSON Shaun	0 + 1							
WILLIAMS Ben	14							

COLCHESTER UNITED (DIV 2: 12th)

	P/FL App	Goals	FLC App	Goals	FAC App	Goals	Others App	Goals
ATANGANA Simon	1 + 5				0 + 1			
BALDWIN Pat	13 + 7		1		1			
BOWRY Bobby	33 + 2	1	1		1		1	
BROWN Simon	26 + 1				1		0 + 1	
CANHAM Marc	2 + 1							
CHILVERS Liam	6							
COOTE Adrian	7 + 9							
DUGUID Karl	26 + 1	3	1		1		1	
EDWARDS Michael	3 + 2							
FITZGERALD Scott	26							
HALFORD Greg	1							
IZZET Kem	43 + 2	8	1		1		1	
JACKSON Johnnie	8							
JOHNSON Gavin	8		1					
KEEBLE Chris	0 + 3							
KEITH Joe	36	9	1		1		1	
McGLEISH Scott	38 + 5	8	1		1		1	1
McKINNEY Richard	20 + 1		1				1	
MAY Ben	4 + 2							
MORGAN Dean	22 +15	6	1		0 + 1			
ODUNSI Leke	3 + 3		0 + 1				0 + 1	
OPARA Lloyd	0 + 5		0 + 1					
PINAULT Thomas	32 +10	4	1		1		1	
RAPLEY Kevin	14 + 7	2	0 + 1		1		1	
RICHARDS Justin	0 + 2						0 + 1	
STEELE Danny	6 + 2				1			

	P/FL App	Goals	FLC App	Goals	FAC App	Goals	Others App	Goal
STOCKLEY Sam	31 + 2	1			1		1	
STOCKWELL Mick	30 + 9	2	1		1		1	
WARREN Mark	20				1			
WHITE Alan	41		1				1	
WILLIAMS Gareth	6 + 2	6						

COVENTRY CITY (DIV 1: 20th)

	P/FL App	Goals	FLC App	Goals	FAC App	Goals	Others App	Goal
BATES Tom	0 + 1							
BETTS Robert	1		1	1	1 + 1			
BOTHROYD Jay	24 + 9	8	0 + 3	2	3	1		
CALDWELL Gary	36		3		2			
CHIPPO Youssef	20 + 3		1 + 1					
COONEY Sean	0 + 1							
DAVENPORT Calum	26 + 6	3	2		2 + 1			
DEBEC Fabien	11		2					
DELORGE Laurent	2		1					
ENGONGA Vicente	5 + 3							
EUSTACE John	23 + 9	4	1 + 1		1			
FOWLER Lee	1				1 + 1	1		
GORDON Dean	30	1	2		3			
HIGNETT Craig	7 + 1	2	1					
HOLDSWORTH Dean	13 + 4				3			
HUGHES Lee	3 + 1	1						
HYLDGAARD Morten	27		1		3			
JANSEN Matt	8 + 1		2					
JEPHCOTT Avun	0 + 1							
JOACHIM Julian	10 + 1	2						
KERR Brian	2 + 1		1					
KONJIC Mo	42		3		3			
McALLISTER Gary	41	7	2	1	3			
MACKEY Ben	0 + 3							
McMASTER Jamie	2							
McSHEFFREY Gary	14 +15	4	2	4	1 + 1			
MILLS Lee	11 + 7	2	3	3	1	1		
MONTGOMERY Gary	8							
NOON Mark	0 + 2							
NORMANN Runar	2 + 1	1	0 + 1					
OSBOURNE Isaac	2							
PARTRIDGE Richie	23 + 4	4	2					
PEAD Craig	17 + 7	2			2			
PIPE David	11 +10	1	1 + 1		0 + 1			
QUINN Barry	13 + 5		1					
SAFRI Youssef	24 + 3		2					
SARA Juan	1 + 2	1			0 + 1			
SHAW Richard	27 + 2		1 + 1		2			
STANFORD Eddie	0 + 1		0 + 1					
STRACHAN Gavin	0 + 1							
THOMPSON David	4							
WALSH Steve	1 + 1							
WHING Andrew	13 + 1							
YULU Christian	1 + 2							

CREWE ALEXANDRA (DIV 2: 2nd)

	P/FL App	Goals	FLC App	Goals	FAC App	Goals	Others App	Goal
ASHTON Dean	24 +15	9	1		1 + 1	2	3	
BANKOLE Ade	2 + 1				0 + 1		4	
BELL Lee	3 +14	1			0 + 2		1 + 3	
BRAMMER Dave	41	1	2		4	1	2	
BURTON-GODWIN Sagi	1							
COLLINS Wayne							0 + 1	
EDWARDS Paul	0 + 2							
FOSTER Steve	35	4	1		3		4	
HULSE Rob	35 + 3	22	1	1	1		2	
INCE Clayton	43		2		2			
JACK Rodney	35 + 3	9	2	3	2		3	
JONES Steve	18 +13	9	0 + 1		2 + 1	1	2 + 2	
LITTLE Colin	3 + 3		1					
LUNT Kenny	46	7	2		4		4	
McCREADY Chris	6 + 2		1					
MILES John	0 + 5	1	1				0 + 2	
MILOSEVIC Danny	1							
OAKES Stef	3 + 4							
RIX Ben	17 + 6				2 + 1	1	1 + 1	

Player	P/FL App	Goals	FLC App	Goals	FAC App	Goals	Others App	Goals
ROBINSON James	0 + 1							
SODJE Efe	23 + 7	1	2		0 + 3	1	2	
SORVEL Neil	39 + 4	3	2		4		4	
TIERNEY Paul	14 + 3	1			2		3	
TOMLINSON Stuart	0 + 1							
VAUGHAN David	28 + 4	3	1		4		2	1
WALKER Richard	31 + 4	2	2		1 + 1		4	
WALTON Dave	27 + 1	1	0 + 1		4			
WHITE Andy	0 + 2							
WRIGHT David	31	1	1		4		3 + 1	

CRYSTAL PALACE (DIV 1: 14th)

Player	P/FL App	Goals	FLC App	Goals	FAC App	Goals	Others App	Goals
ADEBOLA Dele	32 + 7	5	5	2	4			
AKINBIYI Ade	2 + 8	1			0 + 4			
ANTWI Will	0 + 4		1 + 2					
AUSTIN Dean	0 + 3		1 + 1					
BERTHELIN Cedric	9				2 + 1			
BLACK Tommy	20 +16	6	3 + 1	2	3	2		
BORROWDALE Gary	8 + 5		0 + 2		0 + 1			
BUTTERFIELD Danny	46	1	4 + 1		4			
CLARKE Matt	6							
DERRY Shaun	36 + 3	1	2		4			
FLEMING Curtis	9 + 2		1		1			
FRAMPTON Andy	0 + 1		0 + 1					
FREEDMAN Dougie	22 + 7	9	3	2	0 + 2			
GRANVILLE Danny	30 + 5	3	4		2 + 2			
GRAY Julian	29 + 6	5	1 + 2	1	4	2		
HUNT David	2		0 + 1					
JOHNSON Andy	27 + 1	11	3	3	3			
KABBA Steve	0 + 4	1						
KOLINKO Alex	26 + 2		4		2			
MICHOPOULOS Nik	5		1 + 1					
MULLINS Hayden	43	2	5	1	4			
POPOVIC Tony	36	3	3	1	3			
POWELL Darren	39	1	5	1	2			
RIIHILAHTI Aki	15 +10	1	3		2			
ROUTLEDGE Wayne	13 +13	4	2		0 + 1			
RUBINS Andrejs	0 + 2							
SMITH Jamie	2							
SYMONS Kit	21 + 4		2		4			
THOMSON Steve	18 + 9	1	1 + 1		0 + 1			
TOGWELL Sam	0 + 1							
WATSON Ben	3 + 2							
WHELAN Noel	7 + 1	3						
WILLIAMS Gareth	0 + 5		1 + 1					

DARLINGTON (DIV 3: 14th)

Player	P/FL App	Goals	FLC App	Goals	FAC App	Goals	Others App	Goals
ALEXANDER John	0 + 1							
BETTS Simon	40	1			3		1	
CAMPBELL Paul	3 + 2						1	
CLARK Ian	23 +10	7	1		2 + 1	1	1	
CLARKE Matthew	35 + 3	3	1		2		1	
COLLETT Andy	38		1		1		1	
CONLON Barry	41	15	1		2	2	1	
CONVERY Mark							0 + 1	
CORBETT Jim	9 + 1	2						
CULLEN Jon	2 + 1		1					
FENTON Graham	4 + 2	1						
FORD Mark	10 + 1		1					
HADLAND Phil	4 + 2		1					
HODGSON Richard	22 + 5	2			3	1	1	
INGHAM Michael	3							
KELTIE Clark	27 + 3	3			3		1	
LIDDLE Craig	42	4	1		3		1	
LONERGAN Andy	2							
McGURK David	3 + 1		1				1	
MADDISON Neil	25 + 3	1	1					
MELLANBY Danny	6 + 7	4			0 + 1		1	
NAYLOR Glenn	1 +12	3	0 + 1				0 + 1	
NEWEY Tom	7		1					
NICHOLLS Ashley	40 + 1	6	0 + 1		3	1	1	
OFFIONG Richard	7	2			2	2		
PEARSON Gary	19 + 2	1			0 + 1			
PORTER Chris	2 + 1		2					
REED Adam	0 + 1							
RUNDLE Adam	3 + 2							
RUSSELL Sam	1							
SHEERAN Mark	0 + 4						0 + 1	
VALENTINE Ryan	43	1	1		3		1	
WAINWRIGHT Neil	21 +12	1	0 + 1		3			
WHITEHEAD Stuart	23				1 + 1			

DERBY COUNTY (DIV 1: 18th)

Player	P/FL App	Goals	FLC App	Goals	FAC App	Goals	Others App	Goals
BARTON Warren	39		2		1			
BOERTIEN Paul	42	1	2		1			
BOLDER Adam	38 + 7	6	2		1			
BURLEY Craig	20		3					
BURTON Deon	4 + 3	3						
CAMP Lee	0 + 1							
CARBONARI Horacio	2		1		1			
CHADWICK Nicky	4 + 2							
CHRISTIE Malcolm	24	8	2	1	1			
ELLIOTT Steve	21 + 2		1		1			
EVATT Ian	18 +12		0 + 2	1	1			
GRANT Lee	26 + 3				1			
GRENET Francois	2 + 1							
HIGGINBOTHAM Danny	22 + 1	2	2		1			
HOLMES Lee	0 + 2						0 + 1	
HUNT Lewis	7 + 3		0 + 2					
JACKSON Richard	16 + 5							
KINKLADZE Giorgi	22 + 6	4	0 + 1				0 + 1	
LEE Rob	34 + 1	2	2					
McLEOD Izzy	20 + 9	3	1					
MILLS Pablo	12 + 4							
MOONEY Tommy	7 + 1							
MORRIS Lee	26 + 4	8	1 + 1	1	1			
MURRAY Adam	17 + 7				1			
OAKES Andy	7							
O'NEIL Brian	3		1					
POOM Mart	13							
RAVANELLI Fabrizio	16 + 3	5						
RIGGOTT Chris	21 + 1	2	2					
RITCHIE Paul	7							
ROBINSON Marvin	0 + 1							
STRUPAR Branko	4 + 1	1	1					
TUDGAY Marcus	0 + 8				1			
TWIGG Gary	1 + 7							
VALAKARI Simo	5 + 1	2						
ZAVAGNO Luciano	6 + 3	2					0 + 1	

EVERTON (PREM: 7th)

Player	P/FL App	Goals	FLC App	Goals	FAC App	Goals	Others App	Goals
ALEXANDERSSON Niclas	4 + 3				0 + 1		1	
BAARDSEN Espen								
CAMPBELL Kevin	31 + 5	10	3		2			
CARSLEY Lee	21 + 3	3	2					
CHADWICK Nicky	0 + 1							
CLARKE Peter					1			
FENG Li Wei	1		1					
FERGUSON Duncan	0 + 7		0 + 1		1			
GEMMILL Scot	10 + 6		1 + 1		1			
GERRARD Paul	2							
GRAVESEN Thomas	30 + 3	1	1		1			
HIBBERT Tony	23 + 1		1		1			
LINDEROTH Tobias	2 + 3		1					
McBRIDE Brian	7 + 1	4						
McLEOD Kevin					0 + 1			
NAYSMITH Gary	24 + 4	1	2 + 1	1	1			
OSMAN Leon	0 + 2							
PEMBRIDGE Mark	19 + 2	1	1					
PISTONE Sandro	10 + 5		2					
RADZINSKI Tomasz	27 + 3	11	2 + 1		1			
RODRIGO	0 + 4							
ROONEY Wayne	14 +19	6	2 + 1	2	1			
TIE Li	28 + 1		3		0 + 1			

	P/FL App	Goals	FLC App	Goals	FAC App	Goals	Others App	Goals
SIMONSEN Steve	2							
STUBBS Alan	34 + 1		1 + 1		1			
UNSWORTH David	32 + 1	5	3	1	1			
WATSON Steve	14 + 4	5	0 + 1	1	1			
WEIR Davie	27 + 4		2		1			
WRIGHT Richard	33		3		1			
YOBO Joseph	22 + 2		2					

EXETER CITY (DIV 3: 23rd)

	P/FL App	Goals	FLC App	Goals	FAC App	Goals	Others App	Goals
ALCIDE Colin	1							
AMPADU Kwame	18 + 5		0 + 1		1		1	
BAKER Phil	5 + 1							
BARNARD Lee	3				1			
BRESLAN Geoff	0 +10		0 + 1					
BUXTON Lewis	4						2	
COPPINGER James	35 + 8	5	1		3		2	
CRONIN Glenn	28 +11		1		3		2	
CURRAN Chris	10 + 3		1				0 + 1	
DEVINE Sean	21 + 2	8						
FLACK Steve	39 + 1	13			4		2	
FRASER Stuart	0 + 1				1			
GAIA Santos	33	1	1		4	1	1	
GOODMAN Don	11 + 2	1	1					
HARRIES Paul	0 + 1		0 + 1					
HILEY Scott	37				4		2	
KILHEENEY Ciaran	0 + 4							
LOCK Matthew	1 + 2				0 + 2	1		
McCONNELL Barry	13 + 8		1	1	2 + 1	1	1 + 1	
MILLER Kevin	46		1		3		2	
MOOR Reinier	2 +15	3			1 + 3		0 + 1	
PARTRIDGE Scott	2 + 2	2			4		2	
PETTEFER Carl	30 + 1	1			4		2	
PILKINGTON George	7				4		1	
POWER Graeme	27 + 3		1				1	
ROSCOE Andy	23 +10	3	1		3			
SHARPE Lee	4	1						
SHELDON Gareth	7 +12	1			2	1	1	1
SIMPKINS Mike	4 + 1							
TAYLOR Cleveland	1 + 2							
THOMAS Martin	22 + 4	3	1		2		0 + 1	
TODD Chris	12							
VIRGO Adam	8 + 1							
WALKER Justin	35 + 4	5	1		3 + 1	1	1	
WATSON Alex	3							
WHITBREAD Adrian	7							
WHITWORTH Neil	7 + 1							

FULHAM (PREM: 14th)

	P/FL App	Goals	FLC App	Goals	FAC App	Goals	Others App	Goals
BOA MORTE Luis	25 + 4	2	0 + 1	1	2		10 + 2	2
BREVETT Rufus	20						10	
CLARK Lee	9 + 2	2	2	1			1 + 1	
COLLINS John	0 + 5		2		0 + 1		3 + 2	
DAVIS Sean	28	3	0 + 1		4		12	1
DJETOU Martin	22 + 3	1	1 + 1		4		3 + 1	
FINNAN Steve	32				3		5	
GOLDBAEK Bjarne	8 + 2		1		2 + 1	1	2 + 2	
GOMA Alain	29				3		13	
HAMMOND Elvis	3 + 7							
HARLEY Jon	11	1			4		4	
HAYLES Barry	4 +10	1	1				2 + 5	2
HERRERA Martin	1 + 1							
HUDSON Mark			0 + 1					
INAMOTO Junichi	9 +10	2	2		1 + 1		3 + 7	4
KNIGHT Zat	12 + 5				0 + 1		3 + 2	
LEACOCK Dean			1					
LEGWINSKI Sylvain	33 + 2	4			3		10 + 2	2
MALBRANQUE Steed	35 + 2	6			4	4	12 + 2	3
MARLET Steve	28	4			1 + 1		13 + 1	5
MELVILLE Andy	24 + 2		1		3		12	
OUADDOU Abdeslam	9 + 4		2		0 + 1		10	
SAHA Louis	13 + 4	5			3	1	5 + 4	1
SAVA Facundo	13 + 7	5	1 + 1		3 + 1	1	6	

	P/FL App	Goals	FLC App	Goals	FAC App	Goals	Others App	Goals
STOLCERS Andrejs	0 + 5		2	2			0 + 1	
TAYLOR Maik	18 + 1		2		4		3	
VAN DER SAR Edwin	19						11	
WILLOCK Calum	0 + 2							
WOME Pierre	13 + 1	1	2		0 + 1		1 + 1	

GILLINGHAM (DIV 1: 11th)

	P/FL App	Goals	FLC App	Goals	FAC App	Goals	Others App	Goals
ASHBY Barry	38		3		2			
AWUAH Jones	1 + 3							
BARTRAM Vince	7 + 1		1					
BROWN Jason	39		2		3			
CROFTS Andrew			0 + 1					
EDGE Roland	34		1		2			
EDUSEI Akwasi	0 + 2							
HESSENTHALER Andy	32 + 1	1	2	1	3			
HOPE Chris	46	1	3		3	1		
IPOUA Guy	22 +11	4	3	1	2 + 1	2		
JAMES Kevin	5 +10	3	1		1			
JOHNSON Leon	8 +10		1		1			
JOHNSON Tommy	12 +14	2	0 + 2	1	0 + 1			
KING Marlon	9 + 1	4	0 + 1	1	1	2		
NOSWORTHY Nyron	37 + 2	2	2		2			
OSBORN Simon	15 + 3	1						
PATTERSON Mark	1 + 1		1					
PENNOCK Adrian	2 + 1							
PERPETUINI David	13 +16	2	2 + 1		1			
ROSE Richard	0 + 2		0 + 1					
SAUNDERS Mark	28 + 6	3	2		2			
SHAW Paul	44	13	3		2			
SIDIBE Mamady	24 + 6	3	1		2 + 1	1		
SMITH Paul	45	3	3		2			
SOUTHALL Nicky	22 + 2	1			3			
SPILLER Danny	5 + 5		1 + 1		0 + 1			
WALLACE Rod	17 + 5	11			1 + 1			

GRIMSBY TOWN (DIV 1: 24th)

	P/FL App	Goals	FLC App	Goals	FAC App	Goals	Others App	Goals
BARNARD Darren	21 + 8	2			1			
BOLDER Chris	7 + 5				0 + 1			
BOULDING Michael	10 + 2	4						
CAMPBELL Stuart	45	6	1		2			
CHETTLE Steve	18 + 2	1	1		1 + 1			
COLDICOTT Stacy	26 + 5		1		1			
COOKE Terry	15 +10		1		2	1		
COYNE Danny	46		1		2			
FORD Simon	35 + 4	2			1			
GALLIMORE Tony	38		1		2			
GAVIN Jason	8 + 2							
GROVES Paul	32 + 4	3	1		1			
HOCKLESS Graham	1							
HUGHES Richard	12	1						
JEVONS Phil	0 + 3							
KABBA Steve	13	6	1					
KEANE Michael	7	2						
LIVINGSTONE Steve	21 + 9	3			1			
McDERMOTT John	35		1		1			
MANSARAM Darren	21 +13	2	0 + 1		2	1		
OSTER John	17	6			1			
PARKER Wes	1 + 4				1			
POUTON Alan	25	5	1					
RAVEN Paul	6 + 1							
ROBINSON Paul	5 + 7	1	1					
ROWAN Jonny	2 + 7		0 + 1		0 + 1			
SAGARE Jake	1							
SANTOS Georges	24 + 2	1			1			
SOAMES David	0 +10	1			2			
TAYLOR Robert	1							
THOMPSON Chris	3 + 3	1			0 + 2			
WARD Iain	9 + 2		0 + 1		0 + 1			
YOUNG Greg	1							

HARTLEPOOL UNITED (DIV 3: 2nd)

	P/FL App	Goals	FLC App	Goals	FAC App	Goals	Others App	Goals
ARNISON Paul	9 +10	1	1		1 + 1		1	

Player	P/FL App	P/FL Goals	FLC App	FLC Goals	FAC App	FAC Goals	Others App	Others Goals
BARRON Micky	42		1		2	1		
BARRY-MURPHY Brian	7				2			
BASS Jon	2 + 2						1	
BOYD Adam	11 +11	5	1		0 + 1	1		
CLARKE Darrell	45	7	1		1			
EASTER Jermaine	0 + 8						0 + 1	
HENDERSON Kevin	5 +25	2	0 + 1	1			1	
HUMPHREYS Richie	46	11	1		2			
ISTEAD Steven	0 + 6						0 + 1	
LEE Graeme	45	2	1		2			
McKENZIE Colin							1	
PROVETT Jim							1	
RICHARDSON Marcus	20 + 4	5			2	1		
ROBINSON Mark	38		1					
ROBSON Matty							1	
SHARP James							1	
SIMMS Gordon	0 + 1						1	
SMITH Paul	15 + 9				2			
SWEENEY Antony	2 + 2						1	
TINKLER Mark	45	13	1		2			
WATSON Gordon	12 + 5	5						
WESTWOOD Chris	46	1	1		2			
WIDDRINGTON Tommy	26 + 6	3			0 + 1	1	1	
WILLIAMS Eifion	44 + 1	15	1	1	2			
WILLIAMS Anthony	46		1		2			

HUDDERSFIELD TOWN (DIV 2: 22nd)

Player	P/FL App	P/FL Goals	FLC App	FLC Goals	FAC App	FAC Goals	Others App	Others Goals
ASHCROFT Lee	4							
BALDRY Simon	14 + 8	2	2	1			1	
BEVAN Scott	30		2		1		1	
BOOTH Andy	32 + 1	6						
BROWN Nat	36 + 2		1		1		1	
CLARKE Nathan	2 + 1							
DYSON Jon	2 + 1		2					
GALLACHER Kevin	5 + 2		1					
GAVIN Jason	10		1					
HEARY Thomas	14 + 6						1	
HOLLAND Chris	33 + 1		2		1		1	
IRONS Kenny	29 + 6	1	1				0 + 1	
JENKINS Steve	26		2		1			
LABARTHE Gianfranco	0 + 3							
MACARI Paul	0 + 5		0 + 1					
McCOMBE John	0 + 1							
McDONALD Scott	7 + 6	1	0 + 1					
MATTIS Dwayne	27 + 6	1	1 + 1		1		1	1
MIRFIN David	0 + 1							
MOSES Ade	40		1		1		1	
SCHOFIELD Danny	25 + 5	2	2		1		0 + 1	
SCOTT Paul	2 +11		0 + 1					
SENIOR Phil	16 + 2							
SHARP Kevin	38 + 1		2		1		1	
SMITH Martin	35 + 3	17	1 + 1		1		1	
STEAD Jon	28 +14	6	2		1		1	
THORRINGTON John	16 +15	1	0 + 1		0 + 1		1	
WORTHINGTON Jon	10 +12				1			
YOUDS Eddie	25							

HULL CITY (DIV 3: 13th)

Player	P/FL App	P/FL Goals	FLC App	FLC Goals	FAC App	FAC Goals	Others App	Others Goals
ALEXANDER Gary	21 + 4	6	1	1	1		1	
ANDERSON John	42 + 1	1	1		1			
APPLEBY Richie	6		1					
ASHBEE Ian	31	1	1	1	1			
BRADSHAW Gary	2 + 3				1			
BRANCH Michael	6 + 1	3						
BURGESS Ben	7	4						
BURTON Steve	2 + 9				1		1	
CHAPMAN Liam							1	
DELANEY Damien	30	1			1			
DONALDSON Clayton	0 + 2						0 + 1	1
DUDFIELD Lawrie	7 +14	1						
EDWARDS Michael	3 + 3							
ELLIOTT Stuart	30 + 6	12			0 + 1			
FETTIS Alan	17							
FORRESTER Jamie	11	3						
FRY Russell							0 + 1	
GLENNON Matty	9		1					
GREAVES Mark	3							
GREEN Stuart	27 + 1	6			1			
HEARD Jamie							1	
HOLT Andy	5 + 1							
JEVONS Phil	13 +11	3	1		1			
JOHNSON Simon	4 + 8	2	0 + 1					
JOSEPH Marc	22 + 1							
KEATES Dean	36	4	1					
KERR Scott							1	
MELTON Steve	19 + 6							
MORRISON Owen	1 + 1							
MUSSELWHITE Paul	20		1		1			
OTSEMOBOR John	8 + 1	3						
PEAT Nathan	0 + 1				0 + 1		1	
PETTY Ben	2							
PHILPOTT Lee	0 + 1						1	
PRICE Michael	1 + 2		0 + 1				1	
REEVES Martin	5 + 3	1						
REGAN Carl	33 + 5		1		1			
RUSSELL Simon	0 + 1						0 + 1	
SMITH Shaun	17 + 5	1	1		0 + 1		1	
STRONG Greg	3							
WALTERS Jon	11	5						
WEBB Danny	4 + 8							
WHITTLE Justin	34 + 5	1	1		1			
WILLIAMS Ryan	14 + 9		1		1		1	

IPSWICH TOWN (DIV 1: 7th)

Player	P/FL App	P/FL Goals	FLC App	FLC Goals	FAC App	FAC Goals	Others App	Others Goals
ABIDALLAH Nabil					0 + 1			
AMBROSE Darren	20 + 9	8	2	1	1 + 1	1	3 + 1	1
ARMSTRONG Alun	9 +10	1	0 + 1				4	1
BENT Darren	24 +11	12	3		0 + 2	3	1 + 3	1
BENT Marcus	25 + 7	11	0 + 1		2		2 + 1	1
BOWDITCH Dean	0 + 5						3	
BROWN Wayne	7 + 2		1				3	1
CLAPHAM Jamie	26		1		1	1	6	
COLLINS Aidan	0 + 1							
COUNAGO Pablo	28 +11	17	2	1	2		5	3
GAARDSOE Thomas	37	4	2		1	1	2 + 1	
GEORGE Finidi	3 + 7		1 + 1				1 + 4	
GERRARD Paul	5							
HOLLAND Matt	45	7	1		2		4 + 2	
HREIDARSSON Hermann	28		3		2		3	
LE PEN Ulrich	0 + 1						0 + 1	
LOGAN Richard	0 + 1							
McGREAL John	16	1	1				5	1
MAGILTON Jim	39 + 1	3	1 + 1		1		3 + 1	
MAKIN Chris	33		1		1		3	
MARSHALL Andy	40		2		2		6	
MILLER Tommy	24 + 6	6	2	1	1	1	3 + 1	2
MURRAY Antonio	0 + 1							
NAYLOR Richard	11 + 6	2	0 + 1		1			
PULLEN James	1		1					
REUSER Martijn	6 +10	2			0 + 1		1	
RICHARDS Matthew	10 + 3		0 + 1				1 + 1	
STEWART Marcus	3						1	1
VENUS Mark	8		2				2	
WESTLAKE Ian	0 + 4		0 + 1					
WILNIS Fabian	33 + 2	2	2		2		4	
WRIGHT Jermaine	25 +14	1	3		2		3	

KIDDERMINSTER HARRIERS (DIV 3: 11th)

Player	P/FL App	P/FL Goals	FLC App	FLC Goals	FAC App	FAC Goals	Others App	Others Goals
AYRES Lee	22 + 7	2	1		2		2 + 1	
BENNETT Dean	28 + 4	1			1 + 1		0 + 2	1
BISHOP Andy	22 + 7	5					0 + 1	
BROCK Stuart	35		1		2		3	
BROUGHTON Drewe	28 + 9	4	2		2	2	3	2
CLYDE Mark	4							

	P/FL App	Goals	FLC App	Goals	FAC App	Goals	Others App	Goals
COLEMAN Kenny	13 + 2				2		3	
DIGBY Fraser	11							
DOYLE Daire	1 + 4		0 + 1		0 + 1			
DUCROS Andy	2		1					
FLYNN Sean	45	2	1		1		3	
FOSTER Ian	7 +22	1	1		1 + 1		1 + 2	
HEATH Nick	0 + 1							
HENRIKSEN Bo	36 + 1	20	1		2		1 + 1	
HINTON Craig	44		1		2		3	
JOY Ian	2 + 4				0 + 1		1	
KHELA Inderpaul	0 + 1							
LEWIS Matt	0 + 2							
LOWER Scott			0 + 1					
McAULEY Hugh	0 + 4							
MELLIGAN JJ	28 + 1	10					3	2
MORGAN Wes	5		1					
PARRISH Sean	21 + 8	5	1		2		2 + 1	
SALL Abdou	4				1		1	1
SCOTT Dion	19	1						
SHILTON Sam	39 + 2	5	0 + 1		2		3	
SMITH Adie	28 + 2	1			1		1	
STAMPS Scott	19 + 4		1					
WILLIAMS Danny	43 + 2	2	1		2		2 + 1	

LEEDS UNITED (PREM: 15th)

	P/FL App	Goals	FLC App	Goals	FAC App	Goals	Others App	Goals
BAKKE Eirik	31 + 3	1	1		3 + 1	2	6	1
BARMBY Nicky	16 + 3	4	1		0 + 2		3	1
BOWYER Lee	15	3	1				5	
BRAVO Raul	5				1			
BRIDGES Michael	1 + 4		0 + 1				1 + 2	
BURNS Jacob	2							
DACOURT Olivier	4 + 3						2	
DUBERRY Michael	11 + 3		0 + 1		1 + 1		3 + 1	
FOWLER Robbie	2 + 6	2			0 + 1		0 + 1	
HARTE Ian	24 + 3	3	1		3		5	
JOHNSON Seth	3 + 6	1			3 + 1			
JOHNSON Simon	1 + 3							
KEANE Robbie	0 + 3	1						
KELLY Garry	24 + 1				4	1	6	
KEWELL Harry	31	14			4	1	5	1
KILGALLON Matthew	0 + 2						0 + 1	
LUCIC Teddy	16 + 1	1	1		2 + 1			
McMASTER Jamie	0 + 4							
McPHAIL Stephen	7 + 6		0 + 1				2 + 3	
MATTEO Dom	20				3		1	
MILLS Danny	32 + 1	1	1		4		2 + 1	
MILNER James	1 +17	2			0 + 4			
OKON Paul	15				5		1	
RADEBE Lucas	16 + 3				4		3	
RICHARDSON Frazer							0 + 1	
ROBINSON Paul	38		1		5		6	
SMITH Alan	33	3			4	1	6	5
VIDUKA Mark	29 + 4	20	1		4	2	2	
WILCOX Jason	23 + 2	1	1		4		3	
WOODGATE Jonathan	18		1		1		4	

LEICESTER CITY (DIV 1: 2nd)

	P/FL App	Goals	FLC App	Goals	FAC App	Goals	Others App	Goals
ASHTON Jon	0 + 2		0 + 1					
BENJAMIN Trevor	18 +17	8	2 + 1	1	0 + 1			
DAVIDSON Callum	28 + 2	1	3		1			
DEANE Brian	31 + 1	13			1			
DICKOV Paul	42	17	2		2	2		
ELLIOTT Matt	43 + 1	5	3		2	1		
FLOWERS Tim	0 + 1							
HEATH Matt	9 + 2	3	2		1 + 1			
IMPEY Andy	27 + 5		2		1			
IZZET Muzzy	38	4	3		1			
JONES Matt	3 + 3				0 + 2			
LEWIS Junior	5 + 4	1	2		1			
McKINLAY Billy	29 + 8	1	0 + 1		1			
MARSHALL Lee	1							
OAKES Stef	1 + 4		0 + 1					

	P/FL App	Goals	FLC App	Goals	FAC App	Goals	Others App	Goals
O'GRADY Chris	0 + 1							
PETRESCU Tomi	0 + 1							
REEVES Martin	0 + 3		1 + 1					
ROGERS Alan	41		3	2	2			
SCOWCROFT Jamie	43	10	3	1	1			
SINCLAIR Frank	31 + 2	1	2		2			
STEVENSON Jon	0 + 6	1	0 + 2					
STEWART Jordan	28 + 9	4	1 + 1		1 + 1			
SUMMERBEE Nicky	7 +22		1 + 1		2			
TAGGART Gerry	33 + 4	1						
WALKER Ian	46		3		2			
WRIGHT Tommy	2 +11	2			0 + 1			

LEYTON ORIENT (DIV 3: 18th)

	P/FL App	Goals	FLC App	Goals	FAC App	Goals	Others App	Goals
ALEXANDER Gary	12 + 5	2						
BARNARD Donny	22 + 7		0 + 2		1		2	1
BARRETT Scott	11				1 + 1			
BRAZIER Matthew	33	1	2		0 + 1		0 + 1	
CAMPBELL-RYCE Jamal	16 + 1	2	2	1				
CANHAM Scott	9 + 7	2			2		1	
DOWNER Simon	8							
EVANS Rhys	7							
FLETCHER Gary	7 + 5	1	1	1	2			
FORBES Boniek	0 + 3				0 + 1			
HARRIS Andy	43 + 2	1	2		1		1 + 1	
HARRISON Lee	6							
HATCHER Danny	1 + 5				1 + 1		1 + 1	
HEALD Greg	5		1					
HUTCHINGS Carl	21 + 7	1	2					
IBEHRE Jabo	11 +14	5	0 + 1	1	0 + 1		1	
IRIEKPEN Izzy	5		1		1		2	1
JONES Billy	22 + 2		1					
JOSEPH Matthew	37		1		1			
LOCKWOOD Matthew	42 + 1	5	1		2		2	1
McGHEE Dave	3		1					
McLEAN Aaron	0 + 8							
MARTIN John	21 +11	3	0 + 2		2	1	2	
MILLER Justin	19		1		2		2	
MORRIS Glenn	22 + 1		2		1		2	
NUGENT Kevin	10 + 9	3	1	1	2		1	
PURSER Wayne	7	3						
SMITH Dean	27	3	2		2		2	
STEPHENS Kevin	2 + 1							
TATE Chris	19 + 4	6						
THORPE Lee	27 +11	8	2	1			1	
TONER Ciaran	22 + 3	1	1		1		2	
TURNER Michael	7		1					
WATTS Steve	2 + 4				0 + 1		0 + 2	
ZAKUANI Gabriel	0 + 1							

LINCOLN CITY (DIV 3: 6th)

	P/FL App	Goals	FLC App	Goals	FAC App	Goals	Others App	Goals
BAILEY Mark	45		1		1		3	1
BATTERSBY Tony	1							
BIMSON Stuart	41 + 1	1	1		1		5	
BLACK Kingsley	0 + 1							
BLOOMER Matt	3 +10	1					0 + 1	
BRADLEY Shayne	3							
BUCKLEY Adam	0 + 3		0 + 1				1 + 1	1
BUTCHER Richard	23 + 3	3					3	
CAMM Mark	3 +10		0 + 1				2	
CORNELLY Chris	9 + 7						0 + 1	
CORNWALL Luke	1 + 2							
CROPPER Dene	24 + 5	3	1		1		3 + 1	
DYKES Daren	2 + 1							
FUTCHER Ben	41 + 2	8			1	1	5	2
GAIN Peter	43	5	1		1		3 + 1	
LOGAN Richard	10	1	1					
MARRIOTT Alan	46		1		1		3	
MAYO Paul	5 +10		1				3	1
MIKE Adie	5 +12	2	0 + 1	1	0 + 1		2	
MORGAN Paul	45		1		1		5	
PEARCE Allan	9 + 7	1						

	P/FL App	Goals	FLC App	Goals	FAC App	Goals	Others App	Goals
PETTINGER Paul							2	
SEDGEMORE Ben	23 + 5	2	1		1		1	1
SMITH Paul	21 +16	2	1		0 + 1		4 + 1	1
THOMPSON Tyrone	0 + 1						2	
WARD Chris	5 + 1	2			0 + 1		1	
WATTS Steve	5	1						
WEAVER Simon	44				1		5	1
WEBB Danny	4 + 1	1						
WILLIS Scott	23 + 7	3	1		1		1 + 3	
YEO Simon	22 +15	5			1		1 + 4	5

LIVERPOOL (PREM: 5th)

	P/FL App	Goals	FLC App	Goals	FAC App	Goals	Others App	Goals
BABBEL Markus	2		3				1 + 1	
BAROS Milan	17 +10	9	2 + 2	2	0 + 1		3 + 7	1
BERGER Patrik	0 + 2		1	1			0 + 1	
BISCAN Igor	3 + 3		2 + 1		0 + 1		0 + 3	
CARRAGHER Jamie	34 + 1		3 + 2		3		11	
CHEYROU Bruno	8 +11		1 + 1		2		3 + 3	1
DIAO Salif	13 +13	1	3 + 1		1 + 1		5 + 3	1
DIOUF El Hadji	21 + 8	3	5	3	3		6 + 4	
DUDEK Jerzy	30		2		1 + 1		12	
GERRARD Steven	32 + 2	5	6	2	2		13	
HAMANN Dietmar	29 + 1	2	1		1		8 + 2	
HENCHOZ Stephane	19		4		2		7	
HESKEY Emile	22 +10	6	2 + 3		2 + 1		11 + 1	3
HYYPIA Sami	36	3	4		3		13	2
KIRKLAND Chris	8		4		2		1	
MELLOR Neil	1 + 2		2	1	1			
MURPHY Danny	36	7	4	2	3	1	12 + 1	2
OTSEMOBOR John			1					
OWEN Michael	32 + 3	19	3 + 1	2	2		11 + 1	7
RIISE Jon Arne	31 + 6	6	4		2 + 1		11 + 1	
SMICER Vlad	10 +11		4 + 1		1		3 + 4	1
TRAORE Djimi	30 + 2		2 + 1		2		11 + 1	
VIGNAL Gregory	0 + 1		2				0 + 1	
WELSH John			0 + 1					
XAVIER Abel	4		1				1	

LUTON TOWN (DIV 2: 9th)

	P/FL App	Goals	FLC App	Goals	FAC App	Goals	Others App	Goals
BARNETT Leon							0 + 1	
BAYLISS David	7 + 6		1					
BECKWITH Robert	4							
BERTHELIN Cedric	9							
BOYCE Emmerson	33 + 1		2		2		1	
BRKOVIC Ahmet	29 + 7	3	1		2	2	3	3
COYNE Chris	38 + 2	1	1		2		1	
CROWE Dean	17 +10	2	1 + 1		1			
DAVIS Sol	34		2		1		1	
DEENEY Joe					2		1	
EMBERSON Carl	18 + 2		2		2		1	
FOLEY Kevin	0 + 2						1 + 1	
FORBES Adrian	3 + 2	1						
FOTIADIS Andy	8 + 9	6	1		1		0 + 1	
GRIFFITHS Carl	3	1						
HILLIER Ian	12 +10		0 + 1		0 + 1		2	
HIRSCHFELD Lars	5							
HOLMES Peter	8 + 9	1	1		1 + 1		2 + 1	1
HOWARD Steve	41	22	2		1	1		
HUGHES Paul	30 + 5	3	2		1		2	
IGOE Sammy	2							
JOHNSON Marvin							1 + 1	
JUDGE Matthew	0 + 1				0 + 1		1 + 1	
JUPP Duncan	2 + 3							
KIMBLE Alan	8 + 4		1				2 + 1	1
LEARY Michael							1 + 1	
MANSELL Lee	0 + 1						2	
NEILSON Alan	21 + 5		0 + 2		1 + 1			
NICHOLLS Kevin	35 + 1	5	1		1		1	
OKAI Parys							0 + 1	
OSBORN James							1	
OVENDALE Mark	5 + 1						2	
PERRETT Russ	19 + 1	2	2		1			

	P/FL App	Goals	FLC App	Goals	FAC App	Goals	Others App	Goals
ROBERTS Ben	5							
ROBINSON Steve	23 + 6	1	1 + 1		2		1	
SKELTON Aaron	5 + 3	1					1	
SPRING Matthew	41	5	2	1	2	1	1	
THORPE Tony	28 + 2	13			1	1	2	2
WILLMOTT Chris	12 + 1							
WINTERS Robbie	1							

MACCLESFIELD TOWN (DIV 3: 16th)

	P/FL App	Goals	FLC App	Goals	FAC App	Goals	Others App	Goals
ABBEY George	16 + 6	1			0 + 2			
ADAMS Danny	45	1	2		3		1	
ALDRIDGE Paul	0 + 1							
ASKEY John	1 + 8	2	0 + 1		0 + 1			
BRACKENRIDGE Steve	0 + 2							
BYRNE Chris	2 + 1	1	1		1			
CAME Shaun	1							
CARR Michael	4							
DUNNING Darren	17							
EATON David	8 +12	5			1 + 2		1	
GLOVER Lee	5	1						
HADDRELL Matt	2 + 2							
HARDY Lee	8 + 8		1		2		0 + 1	
HITCHEN Steve	32 + 1		2		3		1	
LIGHTBOURNE Kyle	39 + 5	11	2	1	3	2	1	
LITTLE Colin	4 + 2	1						
MACAULEY Steve	20		1		1			
MARTIN Lee	2							
MILES John	7 + 1	4						
MUNROE Karl	20 + 5		0 + 1		3		1	
NASH Martin	1 + 4							
O'NEILL Paul	11 + 1		1				0 + 1	
PRIEST Chris	34 + 3	2	2		7			
RIDLER Dave	16 + 1		1		1		1	
ROBINSON Neil	2 + 8		0 + 1					
ROSS Neil	6 + 2							
SMITH Dave	3							
TINSON Darren	45		2		3		1	
TIPTON Matthew	28 + 8	9	2	1	3	2	1	1
WELCH Michael	38 + 1	3	2		2		1	
WELSH Andy	4 + 2	2						
WHITAKER Danny	41	10	2	3	3	1	1	
WILSON Steve	44		2		3		1	

MANCHESTER CITY (PREM: 9th)

	P/FL App	Goals	FLC App	Goals	FAC App	Goals	Others App	Goals
ANELKA Nicolas	38	14	2		1			
BARTON Joey	7	1						
BELMADI Djemal	2 + 6							
BENARBIA Ali	21 +12	3	2		1			
BERKOVIC Eyal	27	1	1	1	0 + 1			
BISCHOFF Mikkel	1							
DISTIN Sylvain	34		1		1			
DUNNE Richard	24 + 1	1	1		1			
FOE Marc-Vivien	35	9	2		1			
FOWLER Robbie	12 + 1	2						
GOATER Shaun	14 +12	7	2		0 + 1			
HORLOCK Kevin	22 + 8		1 + 1		1			
HOWEY Steve	24	2	2					
HUCKERBY Darren	6 +10	1	0 + 2	1	0 + 1			
JENSEN Niclas	32 + 1	1	2		1			
JIHAI Sun	25 + 3	2	2		1			
JORDAN Steve	0 + 1							
MACKEN Jon	0 + 5							
METTOMO Lucien	3 + 1		1		1			
NASH Carlo	9		1					
SCHMEICHEL Peter	29		1					
SHUKER Chris	1 + 2							
SOMMEIL David	14	1						
TIATTO Danny	10 + 3							
WIEKENS Gerard	5 + 1		0 + 1		1			
WRIGHT-PHILLIPS Shaun	23 + 8	1	1 + 1		1			

Gregory Vignal (Liverpool)

MANCHESTER UNITED (PREM: 1st)

	P/FL		FLC		FAC		Others	
	App	Goals	App	Goals	App	Goals	App	Goals
ARTHEZ Fabien	30		4		2		10	
ECKHAM David	27 + 4	6	5	1	3	1	10 + 3	3
LANC Laurent	15 + 4				1		9	1
ROWN Wes	22		5		1 + 1		6	1
UTT Nicky	14 + 4		0 + 1		0 + 2		8	
ARROLL Roy	8 + 2		2		1		3	
HADWICK Luke	0 + 1		1				0 + 3	
ERDINAND Rio	27 + 1		4		3		11	
LETCHER Darren							2	
ORLAN Diego	7 +18	6	3 + 2	2	0 + 2		5 + 8	1
ORTUNE Quinton	5 + 4		1				3 + 3	
IGGS Ryan	32 + 4	8	4 + 1		3	2	13 + 2	4
EANE Roy	19 + 2		2		3		6	
YNCH Mark							1	
AY David	0 + 1		2				0 + 1	
ARDIELLO Danny			1				0 + 1	
EVILLE Gary	19 + 7		5		3		8 + 2	1
EVILLE Phil	19 + 6	1	4		2	1	10 + 2	
'SHEA John	26 + 6		3		1		12 + 4	
UGH Danny	0 + 1		1				1 + 2	
ICARDO	0 + 1						3 + 1	
ICHARDSON Kieran	0 + 2		0 + 1	1	1		2 + 3	
OCHE Lee	0 + 1						1	
CHOLES Paul	31 + 2	14	4 + 2	3	2 + 1	1	9 + 1	2
ILVESTRE Mikael	34		5		2		13	
OLSKJAER Ole Gunnar	29 + 8	9	1 + 3	1	1 + 1	1	9 + 5	4
TEWART Michael	0 + 1		1		0 + 1		0 + 1	
IMM Mads							0 + 1	
AN NISTELROOY Ruud	33 + 1	25	4	1	3	4	10 + 1	14
ERON Juan	21 + 4	2	4 + 1		1		11	4
WEBBER Danny							0 + 1	

MANSFIELD TOWN (DIV 2: 23rd)

	App	Goals	App	Goals	App	Goals	App	Goals
ACON Danny	0 + 6		0 + 1		1 + 1		0 + 1	
EARDSLEY Chris	1 + 4							
UXTON Jake	3						0 + 1	
HRISTIE Iyseden	29 + 8	18	1		2	1	1	
LARK Peter	2 + 1		1					
LARKE Jamie	17 + 4	1	1		2		1	
ORDEN Wayne	37 + 7	13	1		2		1	
URLE Keith	11 + 3							
URTIS Tom	23							
AY Rhys	23	1			1			
ELANEY Damien	7							
ISLEY Craig	39 + 3	4	1		2			
OANE Ben	11							
ATON Adam	20							
ADSBY Matthew	13 + 7				2			
LOVER Lee	0 + 2							
ANKEY Dean	0 + 1							
ASSELL Bobby	19 + 1							
OLYOAK Danny	0 + 2						1	
URST Mark	1		0 + 1				1	
ERVIS Dave	4 + 1				0 + 1			
OHN-BAPTISTE Alex	4							
ONES Andy	0 + 1							
ARKIN Colin	13 + 9	7			2		1	
AWRENCE Liam	40 + 3	10	1		1	2	1	
EVER Mark	15				1			
ITTLE Colin	5							
MacKENZIE Neil	16 + 8	1	1		2		1	
MENDES Junior	18	1						
MITCHELL Craig	3 +12	1						
MOORE Neil	18		1		1 + 1		1	
ILKINGTON Kevin	32		1		2		1	
EDDINGTON Stuart	5 + 2							
ELLARS Scott	12 + 2	2						
AN HEUSDEN Arjan	5							
AUGHAN Tony	4							
WELCH Keith	9							

	P/FL		FLC		FAC		Others	
	App	Goals	App	Goals	App	Goals	App	Goals
WHITE Andy	19 + 9	6	0 + 1				0 + 1	
WHITE Jason	0 + 1							
WILLIAMSON Lee	28 +12		1		1		1	

MIDDLESBROUGH (PREM: 11th)

	App	Goals	App	Goals	App	Goals	App	Goals
BOATENG George	28							
BOKSIC Alen	13 + 5	2			0 + 1			
CADE Jamie			0 + 1					
CHRISTIE Malcolm	11 + 1	4						
CLOSE Brian			0 + 1					
COOPER Colin	14 + 6		2		0 + 1			
CROSSLEY Mark			2					
DAVIES Andrew	1		1					
DORIVA	3 + 2							
DOVE Craig			0 + 2					
DOWNING Stewart	0 + 2		0 + 1	1				
EHIOGU Ugo	31 + 1	3						
EUSTACE John	0 + 1							
GAVIN Jason			1					
GEREMI	33	7			1			
GREENING Jonathan	38	2			1			
JOB Josephe-Desire	22 + 6	4			1			
JOHNSTON Allan			2					
JUNINHO	9 + 1	3						
MACCARONE Massimo	26 + 8	9						
MARINELLI Carlos	3 + 4		2	1				
MURPHY David	4 + 4							
NEMETH Szilard	15 +13	7	1		1			
PARNABY Stuart	21		1		1			
QUEUDRUE Franck	29 + 2	1	1		1	1		
RICKETTS Michael	5 + 4	1						
RIGGOTT Chris	4 + 1	2						
SCHWARZER Mark	38				1			
SOUTHGATE Gareth	36	2			1			
STOCKDALE Robbie	12 + 2		1					
VIDMAR Tony	9 + 3		2		1			
WHELAN Noel	2 +13	1	1	1	0 + 1			
WILKSHIRE Luke	7 + 7		2					
WILSON Mark	4 + 2		2	1	1			
WINDASS Dean	0 + 2		1		1			

MILLWALL (DIV 1: 9th)

	App	Goals	App	Goals	App	Goals	App	Goals
ASHIKODI Moses	0 + 5							
BALTACHA Sergei	1 + 1				0 + 1			
BRANIFF Kevin	5 + 5				1 + 1			
BULL Ronnie	9 + 3		0 + 1					
CAHILL Tim	9 + 2	3						
CLARIDGE Steve	31 +13	9	0 + 1		4	3		
CRAIG Tony	2		1					
DAVIES Kevin	6 + 3	3						
DOLAN Joe	2							
DUNNE Alan	3 + 1							
ELLIOTT Marvin	0 + 1							
HARRIS Neil	34 + 6	12			1			
HEARN Charley	6 + 3		0 + 1		2 + 2			
IFILL Paul	45	6	1		4	1		
JOHNSON Glen	7 + 1							
KINET Christophe	10 +10	2	1		1 + 1			
LAWRENCE Matt	31 + 2		1		4			
LIVERMORE David	41	2	1		4			
McCAMMON Mark	7	2						
MAY Ben	4 + 6	1	1		0 + 1			
NETHERCOTT Stuart	34 + 2	2	1		1			
PHILLIPS Mark	7							
REID Steven	19 + 1	6			4	1		
ROBERTS Andy	31 + 2	2	1					
ROBINSON Paul	12 + 2				3 + 1	1		
RYAN Robbie	36 + 5	2	1		4			
SADLIER Richard	2 + 3	1						
SWEENEY Peter	1 + 4	1			0 + 1			
TUTTLE David	1							

	P/FL App	P/FL Goals	FLC App	FLC Goals	FAC App	FAC Goals	Others App	Others Goals
WARD Darren	36 + 3	1	1		4			
WARNER Tony	46		1		4			
WISE Dennis	28 + 1	3			3			
NEWCASTLE UNITED (PREM: 3rd)								
ACUNA Clarence	2 + 2		1		1			
AMBROSE Darren	0 + 1							
AMEOBI Shola	8 +20	5			0 + 1		4 + 6	3
BELLAMY Craig	27 + 2	7			1		6	2
BERNARD Olivier	24 + 6	2	1		1		8 + 2	
BRAMBLE Titus	13 + 3						8	
CALDWELL Steve	12 + 2	1	1				1 + 1	
CHOPRA Michael	0 + 1		0 + 1				0 + 2	
CORT Carl	0 + 1		1				0 + 1	
DABIZAS Nikos	13 + 3		1		0 + 1		7 + 1	
DYER Kieron	33 + 2	2	1	2			11 + 1	2
ELLIOTT Robbie	0 + 2		1				0 + 1	
GIVEN Shay	38				1		13	
GRIFFIN Andy	22 + 5	1	1		1		11	1
HARPER Steve			1				1	
HUGHES Aaron	35	1			1		11 + 1	
JENAS Jermaine	23 + 9	6			1	1	8	
KERR Brian	4 + 4						1 + 1	
LUA LUA Lomano	5 + 6	2	1		0 + 1		5 + 4	2
McCLEN Jamie	0 + 1							
O'BRIEN Andy	26				1		11 + 1	
QUINN Wayne							0 + 1	
ROBERT Laurent	25 + 2	5	0 + 1		1		9 + 2	
SHEARER Alan	35	17			1	1	12	7
SOLANO Nobby	29 + 2	7	0 + 1		1		10 + 2	1
SPEED Gary	23 + 1	2					12	1
VIANA Hugo	11 +12	2	1				5 + 5	2
WOODGATE Jonathan	10							
NORTHAMPTON TOWN (DIV 2: 24th)								
ABBEY Nathan	4 + 1		1				2	
ASAMOAH Derek	20 +22	4	0 + 1		2 + 1	1	2	1
BURGESS Daryl	24 + 1	1	1		2		1	
CARRUTHERS Chris	26 + 7		1		3		0 + 1	
CHAMBERS Luke	0 + 1							
DUDFIELD Lawrie	8 + 2	1						
FORRESTER Jamie	18 + 7	5	1		3		2	2
FRAIN John	13 + 1						1	
GABBIADINI Marco	33 + 8	12	1		3	1	2	1
GILL Jerry	41		1		2		2	
HARGREAVES Chris	36 + 3		1		3	1	2	1
HARPER Lee	31				2		0 + 1	
HARSLEY Paul	41 + 4	2	1		3	1	1 + 1	
HOPE Richard	17 + 6	1			1 + 2		1 + 1	
JOHNSON Richard	5 + 1	1						
LINCOLN Greg	5 + 7							
McGREGOR Paul	17 + 6	2	1		0 + 2			
MARSH Chris	15							
MORISON Steve	4 + 9	1					0 + 2	
ONE Armand	6	1	0 + 1					
RAHIM Brent	6	1						
REID Paul	19							
RICKERS Paul	8 + 3		0 + 1		1		2	1
SAMPSON Ian	31 + 2	1			3		2	
SPEDDING Duncan	9 + 2		1		0 + 1			
STAMP Darryn	12 +10	4			1 + 1	1		
THOMPSON Glyn	11				1			
TROLLOPE Paul	41	2	1		3		2	
TURNER Andy	0 + 3							
YOUNGS Tom	5							
NORWICH CITY (DIV 1: 8th)								
ABBEY Zema	12 +18	5			1 + 2	1		
BRIGGS Keith	1 + 1							
BROMBY Leigh	5							
DRURY Adam	45	2	1		3			
EASTON Clint	23 + 3	2	1		0 + 1			

	P/FL App	P/FL Goals	FLC App	FLC Goals	FAC App	FAC Goals	Others App	Others Goal
EMBLEN Neil	5 + 7		0 + 1					
FLEMING Craig	28 + 2				3			
GREEN Robert	46		1		3			
HEALY David	10 + 3	2						
HECKINGBOTTOM Paul	7 + 8		0 + 1					
HENDERSON Ian	4 +16	1			0 + 2			
HOLT Gary	45		1		3			
JARVIS Ryan	2 + 1							
KENTON Darren	36 + 1	1	1					
LLEWELLYN Chris	2 + 3		0 + 1					
MACKAY Malky	35 + 2	6	1		3			
McVEIGH Paul	38 + 6	14			3	1		
MULRYNE Phil	31 + 2	6	1		3	2		
NEDERGAARD Steen	34 + 1	2	1		1			
NIELSEN David	11 +22	6	1		3			
NOTMAN Alex	2 + 6		1					
RIVERS Mark	28 + 2	4			2			
ROBERTS Iwan	33 +10	7	1		2 + 1			
RUSSELL Darel	16 + 5				3			
SHACKELL Jason	2							
SINCLAIR Dean	1 + 1							
SOUTHALL Nicky	4 + 5							
NOTTINGHAM FOREST (DIV 1: 6th)								
BOPP Eugene	10 + 3	2	2					
BRENNAN Jim	45	1	1		1		2	
CASH Brian	0 + 1		0 + 1					
DAWSON Michael	38	5	2		1		1	
DOIG Chris	4 + 6		2		1			
HALL Marcus	1							
HAREWOOD Marlon	42 + 2	20	1		1	1	2	
HJELDE Jon Olav	19 + 7		1				0 + 1	
HUCKERBY Darren	9	5					2	
JESS Eoin	17 +15	3	0 + 1					
JOHNSON David	40 + 2	25	2	2	1		2	
LESTER Jack	20 +13	7	1	2			0 + 1	
LOUIS-JEAN Matthieu	41	1	1		1		2	
OYEN Davy	0 + 4							
PRUTTON David	24	1	1		1			
REID Andy	22 + 8	1	1 + 1		1	1	2	
ROCHE Barry	1							
SCIMECA Ricardo	40	3	2	1	1		2	
THOMPSON John	18 + 2	3	1 + 1		1		1 + 1	
WALKER Des	29 + 2						2	
WARD Darren	45		2		1		2	
WESTCARR Craig	2 + 9	1	1 + 1					
WILLIAMS Gareth	39 + 1	3	1				2	
NOTTS COUNTY (DIV 2: 15th)								
ALLSOPP Danny	28 + 5	10	1		1	2	0 + 1	
ASHTON Jon	4							
BARACLOUGH Ian	33 + 1	2	1		0 + 1			
BOLLAND Paul	27 + 2	3					0 + 1	
BROUGH Michael	26 + 5	1			1		1	
CAS Marcel	10 + 8	2	1		1		1	
CASKEY Darren	33 + 6	3	1		1			
DEENEY Saul	7							
FENTON Nicky	40	3	1		1		1	
FRANCIS Willis	2 + 8							
GARDEN Stuart	18		1		1			
HACKWORTH Tony	4 + 5		0 + 1					
HARRAD Shaun	0 + 5							
HEFFERNAN Paul	25 +11	10	0 + 1	1	0 + 1		1	
HOLMES Richard	2 + 2						0 + 1	
IRELAND Craig	35 + 2	1	1		1			
JUPP Duncan	6 + 2				0 + 1			
LIBURD Richard	26 + 6	2	1				1	
McCARTHY Paddy	6							
MILDENHALL Steve	21						1	
NICHOLSON Kevin	34 + 3						1	
RAMSDEN Simon	21 +11		1		1			
RICHARDSON Ian	30 + 4	1	1				1	

	P/FL App	Goals	FLC App	Goals	FAC App	Goals	Others App	Goals
LEY Paul	2 + 1							
ALLARD Mark	43 + 2	24	1	1	1		1	
ONE Danny	11 + 4				1		1	
HITLEY Jeff	12				1		1	
LDHAM ATHLETIC (DIV 2: 5th)								
NDREWS Wayne	28 + 9	11	1 + 2		2 + 1		3	1
PPLEBY Matty	11 + 1							
RMSTRONG Chris	33	1	2		3		3	
AUDET Julien	21 + 3	2	2		1		1	
CHARALL Dave	30 + 2		4		3			
OSHELL Danny	2							
URGESS Ben	6 + 1							
ARSS Tony	16 +10	2	2	1			1 + 2	
EGG Michael	7 + 1		1				0 + 1	
RAZZIN Carlo	21 +18	4	2 + 2	1	1 + 2		0 + 2	
UXBURY Lee	16 +18	4	1		0 + 2		0 + 1	
YRE John	27 + 4	2	2		3		2 + 1	
RES David	40	13	4	1	3	1	2	1
INING Will	25 + 1	2	0 + 1		0 + 1	1	3	
LL Danny	0 + 2							
LL Fitz	40		4		3		2 + 1	
L Clint	17	1	4		2		2	
OLDEN Dean	2 + 4	2	0 + 1					
LEN Chris	11 +16	3	2 + 1	1	1 + 2		1	
URENCO	1 + 6	1	1 + 1				1	
W Josh	19 + 2	3	2		2	1	2	
SKELLY David	9 + 2		2				2	
JRRAY Paul	29 + 1	1	1		1		2	
GLIACOMI Les	37		2		3		1	
ERIDAN Darren	79 + 4	1	1 + 1		3		3	
ERIDAN John	3 + 2		1					
RNON Scott	2 + 6	1			0 + 1		1	2
JNHARD Clyde	24 + 1	10	3	2	2	1	1	
KFORD UNITED (DIV 3: 8th)								
ASHAM Steve	25 + 6	8	1		3		1	
OUND Matt	41		1		3		3	
ROSBY Andy	46	6	3		3		1	1
WARDS Christian	5 + 1							
LEY Dominic	4 + 2							
RD Bobby	31 + 6	1	2		2			
ORDON Gavin	3 + 3	1	0 + 1					
ACKETT Chris	1 +11		0 + 1				1	
NT James	39	1	3	1	2			
JNTER Roy	12 + 5	1			1		1	
DGE Alan	1							
UIS Jefferson	12 +22	6	1 + 1		1 + 2	1	1	
CARTHY Paul	6	1						
NIVEN Scott	44	1	3		3			
DFIELD David	19 + 9	2	2		2	1	0 + 1	
MOYIMNI Manny	4 +13	3	0 + 2		0 + 1			
WELL Paul	4 +10	4	0 + 2					
CKETTS Sam	0 + 2							
OBINSON Matt	42	1	3		3		0 + 1	
LL Abdou	0 + 1				0 + 1			
VAGE Dave	43		3		3		1	
OTT Andy	29 + 9	11	2		0 + 1			
EELE Lee	3 + 7	3			0 + 1			
VEASH Adrian	11		3				1	
ATERMAN Dave	27 + 2	1			3		1	1
HITEHEAD Dean	9 + 9	1	1		1 + 1		0 + 1	
OODMAN Andy	45		3		3		1	
TERBOROUGH UNITED (DIV 2: 11th)								
LEN Bradley	10 + 1	3					1	
RBER Mark	24 + 1	2						
UCAUD Andre	5 + 1							
LLARD Jimmy	26	3	1		1		1	
RTON-GODWIN Sagi	28 + 3		1		1			
ARKE Andy	41 + 4	16	0 + 1		1		1	1	1
ARKE Lee	0 + 1							

	P/FL App	Goals	FLC App	Goals	FAC App	Goals	Others App	Goals
CONNOR Dan	4							
DANIELSSON Helgi	15 + 3		1		1		0 + 1	
EDWARDS Andy	23	1			1		1	
FARRELL David	21 +16	3	1		0 + 1		1	
FENN Neale	8 + 6	1	1		0 + 1	1		
FORSYTH Richard	6 + 2							
FOTIADIS Andy	6 + 5	2						
GILL Matthew	41		0 + 1		1			
GREEN Francis	8 +11	2	1				0 + 1	
HARRISON Lee	12							
HENDON Ian	7	1						
HYDE Graham	8 + 1							
JELLEYMAN Gareth	30 + 2				1		1	
JOSEPH Marc	16 + 1		1		1		1	
LEE Jason	12 +13	3			1		0 + 1	
MacDONALD Gary	5 + 3		0 + 1					
McGOVERN Brian	1							
McKENZIE Leon	6 + 5	5						
MURPHY Brian	1							
NEWTON Adam	31 + 5	2	1		0 + 1		1	
PEARCE Dennis	2		1					
REA Simon	35 + 2	3	1				1	
SCOTT Richard	13 + 3	1						
SCULLY Tony	0 + 3							
SEMPLE Ryan	1 + 2							
SHIELDS Tony	29 + 4	1	1		1		1	
ST LEDGER-HALL Sean	0 + 1							
STRACHAN Gavin	1 + 1							
TYLER Mark	29		1		1		1	
WILLIS Roger	1 + 3							
PLYMOUTH ARGYLE (DIV 2: 8th)								
ADAMS Steve	36 + 1	2	1		4		1 + 1	
AIJOFREE Hasney	19		1		1		1	
BARRAS Tony	4							
BENT Jason	23 + 2	1			1 + 1			
BERESFORD David	6 +10						2	
BERNARD Paul	7 + 3							
BROAD Joe	1 + 1						2	
CAPALDI Tony	1							
CONNOLLY Paul	2						1	
COUGHLAN Graham	42	5	1		4			
EVANS Micky	35 + 7	4	0 + 1		4	1	0 + 1	1
FRIIO David	33 + 3	6	0 + 1		3 + 1	1		
HODGES Lee	38 + 1	2	1		3			
KEITH Marino	20 +17	11			3 + 1		1 + 1	1
LARRIEU Romain	43				4			
LOPES Osvaldo	4 + 5		1		1		2	
LOWNDES Nathan	6 +10	2	1				2	
McANESPIE Kieran	2 + 2							
McCORMICK Luke	2 + 1						2	
McGLINCHEY Brian	11 + 8	1			0 + 2		2	
MALCOLM Stuart	3						2	
MILOSEVIC Danny	1							
NORRIS David	29 + 4	6			3			
PHILLIPS Martin	14 +10	2	1		1 + 1		2	
SMITH Grant	4 + 1	1						
STONEBRIDGE Ian	30 + 7	5	0 + 1		4	2	0 + 1	
STURROCK Blair	5 +15	1	1	1	0 + 3		1	
TAYLOR Craig	1							
WORRELL David	43		1		4		1	
WOTTON Paul	41 + 2	8	1		4		3	
YETTON Stewart	0 + 1							
PORTSMOUTH (DIV 1: 1st)								
AYEGBINI Yakubu	12 + 2	7						
BRADBURY Lee	3		1					
BURCHILL Mark	4 +14	4	1 + 1					
BURTON Deon	11 + 4	4			0 + 1			
BUXTON Lewis	0 + 1							
CROWE Jason	7 + 9	4	1					
DE ZEEUW Arjan	35 + 3	1	1					

	P/FL		FLC		FAC		Others	
	App	Goals	App	Goals	App	Goals	App	Goals
DIABATE Lassina	16 + 9				1			
FESTA Gianluca	27	1	2					
FOXE Hayden	30 + 2	1			1			
HARPER Kevin	21 +16	4	1 + 1		1			
HEIKKINEN Markus	0 + 2							
HISLOP Shaka	46		2		1			
HOWE Eddie	1							
HUGHES Richard	4 + 2		1					
KAWAGUCHI Yoshi	0 + 1							
MERSON Paul	44 + 1	12	2		1			
O'NEIL Gary	11 +20	3	1		0 + 1			
PERICARD Vincent	18 +14	9	1 + 1	1	0 + 1			
PRIMUS Linvoy	39 + 1		2		1			
QUASHIE Nigel	42	5	1	1	1			
RITCHIE Paul	8 + 4		1					
ROBINSON Carl	11 + 4		1 + 1					
SHERWOOD Tim	17	1						
STONE Steve	18	4			1	1		
TAVLARIDIS Stathis	3 + 1				1			
TAYLOR Matthew	35	7	2		1			
TILER Carl	0 + 2							
TODOROV Svetoslav	43 + 2	26	2		1			

PORT VALE (DIV 2: 17th)

	P/FL		FLC		FAC		Others	
	App	Goals	App	Goals	App	Goals	App	Goals
ANGELL Brett	13 + 2	5	0 + 1				1	2
ARMSTRONG Ian	20 + 9	7	0 + 1		0 + 1		2 + 1	1
ASHCROFT Lee	3				1			
BIRCHALL Chris	0 + 2							
BOYD Marc	19 + 1	3	1		1		2	1
BRIDGE-WILKINSON Marc	29 + 2	9	1		1		1	
BRIGHTWELL Ian	34 + 1		1		1		1	
BRISCO Neil	23 + 1	1						
BROOKER Steve	21 + 5	5	1		1		0 + 2	
BROWN Ryan	0 + 1							
BURNS Liam	14 + 2				1		2	
BYRNE Paul	6 + 2						0 + 1	
CARRAGHER Matt	34 + 1		1		1		3	1
CHARNOCK Phil	14 + 4	1			1		3	
CLARKE Peter	13	1						
COLLINS Sam	44	5	1		1		3	
CUMMINS Micky	29 + 1	4	1		1		3	
DELANY Dean	10							
DURNIN John	25 + 3	1			1		1 + 1	
ELDERSHAW Simon	0 + 2							
GOODLAD Mark	36 + 1		1		1		3	
INGRAM Rae	3 + 1							
LITTLEJOHN Adrian	12 + 1	3						
McCARTHY Jon	5 + 3		1					
McCLARE Sean	9 + 8				0 + 1		0 + 3	
McPHEE Steve	35 + 5	3	1		1		3	
PAYNTER Billy	16 +15	5			0 + 1		2	
REID Levi	0 + 1							
ROWLAND Steve	22 + 3						2	
WALSH Michael	17	1	1					

PRESTON NORTH END (DIV 1: 12th)

	P/FL		FLC		FAC		Others	
	App	Goals	App	Goals	App	Goals	App	Goals
ABBOTT Pawel	6 +10	4			1			
ALEXANDER Graham	45	10	4	1	1			
ANDERSON Iain	0 + 8		1		0 + 1	1		
BAILEY John	0 + 1							
BARRY-MURPHY Brian	2							
BROOMES Marlon	21 + 7		3		1			
CARTWRIGHT Lee	13 + 9	1	0 + 2		0 + 1			
CRESSWELL Richard	42	16	3 + 1					
EATON Adam	0 + 1		1					
EDWARDS Rob	26		2					
ETUHU Dickson	33 + 6	6	4		1			
FULLER Ricardo	18	9	1 + 1	2				
GOULD Jonathan	13 + 1							
HEALY David	12 +12	5	4		1			
JACKSON Michael	21 + 1	1	1		1			
KEANE Michael	1 + 4		1					

	P/FL		FLC		FAC		Others	
	App	Goals	App	Goals	App	Goals	App	Goals
KOUMANTARAKIS George	10	3						
LEWIS Eddie	34 + 4	5	3 + 1	1	1			
LUCAS David	19 + 2		4					
LUCKETTI Chris	43	2	4		1			
LYNCH Simon	6 +11	1						
McKENNA Paul	39 + 2	3	3		1			
MEARS Tyrone	11 +11	1	1 + 1		0 + 1			
MOILAINEN Tepi	14 + 1		0 + 1		1			
MURDOCK Colin	24		1 + 1		1			
O'NEIL Brian	12 + 3							
RANKINE Mark	11 + 8		1 + 3					
SKORA Eric	30 + 6		2	1	1			

QUEENS PARK RANGERS (DIV 2: 4th)

	P/FL		FLC		FAC		Others	
	App	Goals	App	Goals	App	Goals	App	Goals
ANGELL Brett	8 + 5							
BEAN Marcus	4 + 3						0 + 1	
BIRCHAM Marc	34 + 2	2			2		3	
BURGESS Oliver	2 + 3				2		1	
CARLISLE Clarke	34 + 2	2	1		2		2	
CONNOLLY Karl	12 + 4	4	1		1 + 1		1	
COOK Lee	13	1						
CULKIN Nick	17							
DALY Wes	3 + 3						1	
DAY Chris	12						3	
DIGBY Fraser	1 + 2		1		2			
DOUDOU	3 + 7		0 + 1				0 + 1	
FORBES Terrell	38		1		1 + 1		2	
FURLONG Paul	27 + 6	13			1		3	
GALLEN Kevin	41 + 1	13	0 + 1	1	0 + 1		2	
GRIFFITHS Leroy	3 + 3							
KELLY Stephen	7						2	
LANGLEY Richard	38 + 1	9	1		1		2	
McLEOD Kevin	8	2					3	
MURPHY Danny	4 + 7				0 + 1			
OLI Dennis	8 +10		0 + 1		1 + 1		1	
PACQUETTE Richard	4 + 7	4	1				1 + 2	
PADULA Gino	17 + 4	1			1 + 1		2 + 1	
PALMER Steve	46	1	1		2		4	
PLUMMER Chris	0 + 2							
ROSE Matthew	25 + 3	2	1		1		2	
ROYCE Simon	16						1	
SHITTU Danny	43	7	1		1		3	
THOMAS Jerome	5 + 1	2						
THOMSON Andy	7 +14	3	1	1	2	1	2 + 1	
WALSHE Ben	1							
WILLIAMS Tommy	22 + 4	1	1		2		2 + 1	
WILLOCK Calum	3							

READING (DIV 1: 4th)

	P/FL		FLC		FAC		Others	
	App	Goals	App	Goals	App	Goals	App	Goals
ASHDOWN Jamie	1							
BROWN Steve	21	1			2		2	
BUTLER Martin	12 + 9	2	1		2			
CAMPBELL Darren	0 + 1							
CASTLE Peter	0 + 1							
CHADWICK Luke	15	1					1 + 1	
CURETON Jamie	13 +14	9	1		1 + 1		1 + 1	
FORSTER Nicky	35 + 5	16	1		1 + 1		1	
HAHNEMANN Marcus	41		1		2		2	
HARPER James	34 + 2	2			2		2	
HENDERSON Darius	1 +21	4			0 + 1		2	
HUGHES Andy	41 + 2	9	1		0 + 1		2	
IGOE Sammy	8 + 7		0 + 1		2			
LITTLE Glen	6	1					1	
MACKIE John	20 + 5		1		2			
MURTY Graeme	43 + 1				2		2	
NEWMAN Ricky	21 + 7		1		2		0 + 1	
PARKINSON Phil	0 + 6		1					
ROUGIER Tony	13 + 7	3	0 + 1		1		0 + 1	
SALAKO John	33 +10	4	1		0 + 2		1	
SHOREY Nicky	43	2	1		2		2	
SIDWELL Steve	13	2					2	
SMITH Alex	0 + 1							

	P/FL		FLC		FAC		Others	
	App	Goals	App	Goals	App	Goals	App	Goals
YSON Nathan	9 +14		1		2		0 + 1	
PSON Matthew	13 + 1		1	1				
VEASH Adrian	4 + 1							
ATSON Kevin	24 + 8	1					0 + 1	
HITEHEAD Phil	4							
ILLIAMS Adrian	38	1	0 + 1		2			

OCHDALE (DIV 3: 19th)

	App	Goals	App	Goals	App	Goals	App	Goals
NDREWS Lee	8							
EECH Chris	16 + 2	1			1	1		
ENNETT Neil	1							
SHOP Ian	5 + 3				1			
ANSDELL-SHERIFF Shane	3				1			
ONNOR Paul	30 + 9	12	1		5	3	0 + 1	
OUGHTY Matt	39 + 2		1		4		1	
UFFY Lee	19 + 3		1		3		1	
DWARDS Neil	26		1		5			
VANS Wayne	40		1		6			
ITCROFT Dave	40 + 1	2	1		5 + 1			
ILKS Matt	19 + 1				1		1	
RAND Simon	22 + 1	2			5			
RIFFITHS Gareth	41 + 1	6	1		3	1	1	
ILL Stephen	9 + 1				2			
OCKENHULL Darren	6 + 1	1						
ODGES Lee	3 + 4				1			
OBSON Richard	15 + 1		1		3			
ACAULEY Steve	6						1	
CCOURT Paddy	12 +14	2	0 + 1		0 + 2	1	0 + 1	
CEVILLY Lee	27 +10	15			4 + 1	1	1	
ELAUGH Gavin	17 + 2	1			5		1	
LIVER Michael	17 + 3	2	1		2		1	
TTERSON Rory	2 + 6						0 + 1	
LATT Clive	40 + 2	6	1		6	3		
MPSON Paul	30 + 5	10	1		3 + 1	1	1	
AYLOR Michael	2							
OWNSON Kevin	5 +19	1	0 + 1		0 + 2	1		
WARNER Scott	6 + 1				2			

OTHERHAM UNITED (DIV 1: 15th)

	App	Goals	App	Goals	App	Goals	App	Goals
ARKER Richie	23 +14	7	4	2	1			
ARKER Shaun	11							
EECH Chris	1 + 1		1					
RANSTON Guy	13 + 2	2	2					
RYAN Marvin	12 + 4		0 + 3		1			
YFIELD Darren	24 +13	13	0 + 1					
AWS Nick	30 + 3	1	3 + 1		1			
ARRELLY Gareth	6							
ARNER Darren	20 + 6	3	3		0 + 1			
RAY Ian	5 + 1							
URST Paul	44	1	3		1			
EE Alan	38 + 3	15	2	1	1			
cINTOSH Martin	42	5	2		1			
ONKHOUSE Andy	11 + 9		4	3				
ULLIN John	31 + 3	3	2		1			
OLLITT Mike	41		4		1			
OBINS Mark	6 +10	5	2 + 1	2	0 + 1			
COTT Rob	23		4					
EDGWICK Chris	42 + 1	1	3		1			
WAILES Chris	43	3	4	1	1			
ALBOT Stewart	8 + 7	1						
WARNE Paul	21 +19	1	1 + 3	1	1			
OODHOUSE Curtis	11							

USHDEN & DIAMONDS (DIV 3: 1st)

	App	Goals	App	Goals	App	Goals	App	Goals
ATTERSBY Tony	2 + 3							
ELL David	26 + 4	3	1		1 + 2		1	
GNOT Marcus	33		0 + 1		3		1	
URGESS Andy	19 + 8	1	0 + 1					
ARBY Duane	35 + 2	14	1		2 + 1		0 + 1	
EMPSTER John	11 + 5	1	1 + 1		1			
UFFY Robert	3 + 9				3	3	1	
DWARDS Andy	11 + 1	1						

	P/FL		FLC		FAC		Others	
	App	Goals	App	Goals	App	Goals	App	Goals
GRAY Stuart	34 + 4	7	2		3		1	
HALL Paul	44 + 1	16	2		2 + 1		0 + 1	
HOLDSWORTH Dean	4 + 3	2						
HUNTER Barry	40	1	1		2			
LOWE Onandi	38 + 1	15			1 + 1	1	1	
MILLS Danny	23 + 7		2		2		1	
MUSTAFA Tarkan	10 + 1		2					
PARTRIDGE Scott	2 + 5		1 + 1		0 + 1			
PETERS Mark	25 + 2	1	2		3		1	
SAMBROOK Andy	6 + 9							
SETCHELL Gary	7 + 4		1		1		1	
SOLKHON Brett	1							
SOLLITT Adam	3				1		1	
TALBOT Daniel	5 + 8		1				1	
TILLSON Andy	5						1	
TURLEY Billy	43 + 1		2		2			
UNDERWOOD Paul	40	1	1		3			
WARDLEY Stuart	36 + 3	6	2		3	1	0 + 1	

SCUNTHORPE UNITED (DIV 3: 5th)

	App	Goals	App	Goals	App	Goals	App	Goals
BALMER Stuart	6						1	
BARWICK Terry	1 + 4		0 + 1					
BEAGRIE Peter	29 + 5	5					2	
BROUGH Scott	10 +13	2	1		3 + 1		2	
BYRNE Cliff	13				3			
CALVO-GARCIA Alex	28 + 7	3	1		1 + 2		2	2
CARRUTHERS Martin	42 + 3	20	1		4	1	2 + 1	
COTTERILL James	7 + 2							
DALGLISH Paul	5 + 3	3					1 + 1	
DAWSON Andy	43		1		4		3	1
EVANS Tommy	46		1		4		3	
FEATHERSTONE Lee	10 +10				3		0 + 1	
GRAVES Wayne	35 + 6	1	1		3 + 1		1 + 1	
HAYES Paul	15 + 3	8					2	
JACKSON Mark	32 + 1		1		2		2	
KILFORD Ian	27 + 1	3			3 + 1		2	
McCOMBE Jamie	23 + 8	1			2		1 + 1	
O'CONNOR Aaron	0 + 3							
PARTON Andy	0 + 8		0 + 1		0 + 2		0 + 1	
RIDLEY Lee	9 + 2							
RYAN Leon	0 + 2							
SPARROW Matt	42	9	1		3		3	
STANTON Nathan	42		1		3		3	1
STRONG Greg	7						2	
TAYLOR Robert	4 + 4							
TORPEY Steve	26 + 2	10	1	1	4	3	2 + 1	
WHEATCROFT Paul	2 + 2							
WRIGHT Steve	2		1					

SHEFFIELD UNITED (DIV 1: 3rd)

	App	Goals	App	Goals	App	Goals	App	Goals
ALLISON Wayne	15 +19	6	6	1	2 + 2		0 + 2	
ASABA Carl	16 +12	11	4 + 1	1	0 + 1		3	
BOULDING Michael	3 + 3		1	1				
BROWN Michael	39 + 1	16	6 + 1	2	4	2	3	2
CAS Marcel	3 + 3							
CRYAN Colin	0 + 2							
CURTIS John	9 + 3				1		3	
DE VOGT Wilko					1			
DOANE Ben	2 + 3		1 + 1					
EDGHILL Richard	0 + 1							
HARLEY Jon	8 + 1	1	2					
JAGIELKA Phil	41 + 1		7	1	5	1	3	
JAVARY Jean-Phillipe	2 + 4				0 + 1			
KABBA Steve	19 + 6	7			5	3	1 + 2	1
KELLY Gary	1							
KENNY Paddy	45		7		4		3	
KOZLUK Rob	29 + 3	1	1 + 1		4		3	
McCALL Stuart	32 + 2		6		5		0 + 1	
McGOVERN Jon-Paul	11 + 4	1	2		1	1		
MONTGOMERY Nick	15 + 8		3 + 3	1	2 + 1		3	
MOONEY Tommy	2 + 1		0 + 1		2	1		
MORRISON Owen	3 + 5							

	P/FL App	P/FL Goals	FLC App	FLC Goals	FAC App	FAC Goals	Others App	Others Goals
MURPHY Shaun	42 + 1	2	7	1	3	1		
NDLOVU Peter	30 + 9	8	4 + 2	1	3	1	3	
ONUORA Iffy	7	1	1					
PAGE Robert	33 + 1		6		5		3	
PESCHISOLIDO Paul	4 +19	3	1 + 4	2	1 + 3	1	0 + 2	1
QUINN Wayne	6		2		2			
RANKINE Mark	5 + 1						3	
SMITH Grant	1 + 2				0 + 1			
TEN HEUVEL Laurens	0 + 5		0 + 3		0 + 1			
THOMPSON Tyrone					1			
TONGE Michael	40 + 4	6	7	2	4		3	
ULLATHORNE Rob	12		2					
WINDASS Dean	20	6					2	
YATES Steve	11 + 1		1					

SHEFFIELD WEDNESDAY (DIV 1: 22nd)

	P/FL App	P/FL Goals	FLC App	FLC Goals	FAC App	FAC Goals	Others App	Others Goals
ARMSTRONG Craig	17	1	2					
BARRY-MURPHY Brian	17							
BESWETHERICK Jon	5 + 1				1			
BRADBURY Lee	10 + 1	3						
BROMBY Leigh	26 + 1		2		1			
BURROWS David	13		2					
CRANE Tony	13 + 6	2			1			
DI PIEDI Michele	1 + 1							
DONNELLY Simon	10 + 5	2	0 + 1					
EVANS Paul	7							
EVANS Richard	3 + 1	1						
GEARY Derek	24 + 2		1 + 1					
GREEN Ryan	4							
HAMSHAW Matt	4 +11	1	0 + 2					
HASLAM Steven	18 + 8	1			1			
HENDON Ian	9		1					
HOLT Grant	3 + 4	1						
JOHNSTON Allan	12	2						
KNIGHT Leon	14 +10	3	2		0 + 1			
KUQI Shefki	34 + 6	8	2		1			
McLAREN Paul	31 + 5	4	1					
MADDIX Danny	22 + 1	1	2					
MONK Garry	15							
MORRISON Owen	0 + 1				1			
OWUSU Lloyd	12 +20	4	1 + 1					
POWELL Darryl	8							
PRESSMAN Kevin	38		2					
PROUDLOCK Adam	3 + 2	2						
QUINN Alan	33 + 4	5	2		1			
REDDY Michael	13 + 2	3						
ROBINSON Carl	4	1						
SHAW Jon	0 + 1				0 + 1			
SIBON Gerald	23 + 2	6	2	2	1	1		
SMITH Dean	14							
SOLTVEDT Trond Egil	21				1			
STRINGER Chris	1 + 2				1			
WESTWOOD Ashley	22 + 1	2	0 + 1		1			
WOOD Richard	2 + 1	1						

SHREWSBURY TOWN (DIV 3: 24th)

	P/FL App	P/FL Goals	FLC App	FLC Goals	FAC App	FAC Goals	Others App	Others Goals
AISTON Sam	11 +10	2			0 + 1		0 + 3	
ARTELL Dave	27 + 1	1			3		5	
ATKINS Mark	29 + 1	1	1		4		3	1
CARTWRIGHT Mark	13							
DRYSDALE Leon	11 + 8	1	1		2 + 2		2 + 1	
DUNBAVIN Ian	33		1		4		6	
EDWARDS David	0 + 1							
HEATHCOTE Mick	6							
HOLT Andy	9							
HULBERT Robin	4 + 3							
JAGIELKA Steve	12 +11	3			1 + 2		1 + 3	
JEMSON Nigel	38 + 2	11	1		4	5	6	1
LOWE Ryan	27 +12	9	1		3 + 1		5	4
MORTIMER Alex	0 + 1							
MOSS Darren	35 + 5	2	0 + 1		3		6	1
MURPHY Chris	0 + 3				0 + 1		0 + 1	

	P/FL App	P/FL Goals	FLC App	FLC Goals	FAC App	FAC Goals	Others App	Others Goal
MURRAY Karl	17 +11	2			1 + 1		2 + 2	
PARTRIDGE Scott	2 + 1							
REDMILE Matt	39	1	1		2		6	
RODGERS Luke	36	16	1		4		6	
SMITH Alex	13				2		3	
STEPHENS Ross	0 + 1							
STEVENS Ian	4 +14	2	0 + 1				0 + 4	
TALBOT Stewart	5						2	
THOMPSON Andy	16		1		1			
TOLLEY Glenn	0 + 1							
TOLLEY Jamie	38 + 1	3	1		3	1	4 + 1	
VAN BLERK Jason	17 + 6	1	1		2	1	4	
WATTS Steve	3 + 4							
WILDING Peter	28 + 5	3	0 + 1		3	2	1 + 2	
WOAN Ian	33 + 3	4			2		4	

SOUTHAMPTON (PREM: 8th)

	P/FL App	P/FL Goals	FLC App	FLC Goals	FAC App	FAC Goals	Others App	Others Goal
BAIRD Chris	1 + 2				1			
BEATTIE James	35 + 3	23	2		7	1		
BENALI Francis	2				2			
BRIDGE Wayne	34		1	2	4			
DAVIES Kevin	1 + 8	1			0 + 4	1		
DELAP Rory	22 + 2		1 + 1		3 + 1			
DELGADO Agustin	2 + 4		1	1				
DODD Jason	13 + 2		2		1 + 1			
EL KHALEJ Tahar	0 + 1							
FERNANDES Fabrice	35 + 2	3	1		5 + 2			
HIGGINBOTHAM Danny	3 + 6				1			
JONES Paul	13 + 1				1 + 1			
KANCHELSKIS Andrei	0 + 1		0 + 1					
LUNDEKVAM Claus	33		2		6			
MARSDEN Chris	30	1	2	1	6 + 1	1		
MONK Garry	1							
NIEMI Antti	25		2		6			
OAKLEY Matt	28 + 3		2		7	2		
ORMEROD Brett	22 + 9	5	1	3	5 + 2	1		
PAHARS Marian	5 + 4	1	0 + 1					
PRUTTON David	9 + 3							
SVENSSON Anders	26 + 7	2	1		6 + 1	2		
SVENSSON Michael	33 + 1	2	2		7	1		
TELFER Paul	26 + 7		1		6			
TESSEM Jo	9 +18	2	0 + 1		2 + 5	2		
WILLIAMS Paul	10 + 1				1			

SOUTHEND UNITED (DIV 3: 17th)

	P/FL App	P/FL Goals	FLC App	FLC Goals	FAC App	FAC Goals	Others App	Others Goal
BEARD Mark	29 + 7		1		4		0 + 1	
BELGRAVE Barrington	6 +15	3			1		1	
BRAMBLE Tes	31 + 3	9	1		4	2		
BROAD Steve	17		1		1			
CLARK Steve	20 +13		0 + 1		1 + 3		1	
CORT Leon	46	6	1		4	1	1	
DARBY Brett	6 + 4							
FLAHAVAN Darryl	41		1		4		1	
FOLEY Dominic	5							
GAY Danny	5							
HENRY Ronnie	3							
JENKINS Neil	29 + 5	7	1		1 + 1			
JONES Graeme	18 + 3	2	1		2 + 1		1	
JORDAN Tom	0 + 1						1	
KELLY Stephen	10							
KIGHTLY Michael	0 + 1							
McSWEENEY David	15 + 2				4		0 + 1	
MAHER Kevin	42	2	1		4			
MARNEY Danny	13 + 4							
MAYE Danny	0 + 2		0 + 1					
RAWLE Mark	33 + 1	9	1	1	3	2		
SALTER Mark	5 + 8	1					0 + 1	
SCULLY Tony	8				4			
SEARLE Damon	39 + 5	1	1		4		1	
SELLEY Ian	11							
SMITH Jay	30 + 1	5	1		3 + 1		1	
STRACHAN Gavin	6 + 1							

	P/FL App	Goals	FLC App	Goals	FAC App	Goals	Others App	Goals
UTCH Daryl	16	1						
HURGOOD Stuart	7 +20				1 + 1		1	
LSON Steve	2 + 1				0 + 2		1	
WHELAN Phil	13 + 1		0 + 1				1	

STOCKPORT COUNTY (DIV 2: 14th)

	P/FL App	Goals	FLC App	Goals	FAC App	Goals	Others App	Goals
ECKETT Luke	41 + 1	27	2	1	2	1	1	
LAYNEY Alan	2						1	
RIGGS Keith	13 + 6	1	2		2		2	1
URGESS Ben	17 + 2	4	0 + 1		1 + 1	2	2	
HALLINOR Dave	46	1	2		2		2	
LARE Rob	31 + 5		1	1			1	
LARK Peter	21	1						
ALY Jon	25 +10	7	1	1			0 + 1	
LLISON Kevin	17 + 6	1					1	
RADIN Karim	8 + 1				2		2	1
IBB Ally	43 + 2	1	2		2		1	
OODWIN Jim	22 +11	3	1		2		2	
REER Gordon	4 + 1	1						
ARDIKER John	19 + 4		2		1		2	
NGHAM Michael			1					
ONES Brad	1							
ONES Lee	24		1		2			
AMBERT Rickie	22 + 7	2	1					
ESCOTT Aaron	36 + 5	1	1 + 1		1 + 1		1	
McLACHLAN Fraser	18 + 4				2			
ALMER Carlton	22	1	2	1	1		0 + 1	
EMBERTON Martin	15 + 5		1 + 1					
OSS Neil	1 + 3	1	1 + 1		1		1 + 1	
PENCER James	1						1	
HOMAS Andrew	1 + 1							
IDMAN Ola	18							
ONKIN Anthony	23 + 1		1		2			
ELSH Andy	7 + 6	2					0 + 1	
ILBRAHAM Aaron	8 + 7	7						
ILD Peter	0 + 3	1					0 + 1	
ILLIAMS Chris	0 + 1							

STOKE CITY (DIV 1: 21st)

	P/FL App	Goals	FLC App	Goals	FAC App	Goals	Others App	Goals
KINBIYI Ade	4	2						
ANKS Steve	14				2			
LARKE Clive	27 + 4	3	1					
OMMONS Kris	6 + 2	1	1					
OOKE Andy	24 + 7	6	1					
ROSSLEY Mark	12							
UTLER Neil	20		1		1 + 1			
OODFELLOW Marc	6 +14	1	0 + 1		0 + 3			
REENACRE Chris	18 +12	4			3	2		
UDJONSSON Bjarni	25 +11	1	1		2 + 1			
UNNARSSON Brynjar	40	5	1		3			
ALL Marcus	23 + 1				3			
ANDYSIDE Peter	44		1		2			
ENRY Karl	15 + 3	1	0 + 1		2 + 1			
OEKSTRA Peter	26 + 4	4	0 + 1		2	1		
WELUMO Chris	15 +17	5	1		3	3		
ARTEINSSON Petur	7 + 5	2			1 + 1			
MILLS Lee	7 + 4	2						
OONEY Tommy	11 + 1	3						
EAL Lewis	7 + 9				1 + 2			
O'CONNOR James	43		1		3			
ICHARDSON Frazer	6 + 1							
HTANIUK Sergei	44	3	1		2			
HOMAS Wayne	41		1		3			
AN DEURZEN Jurgen	7 + 5	1						
ARHURST Paul	4 + 1	1						
ILLIAMS Mark	5 + 1							
ILSON Brian	1 + 2							
ILSON Mark	4							

SUNDERLAND (PREM: 20th)

	P/FL App	Goals	FLC App	Goals	FAC App	Goals	Others App	Goals
RCA Julio	7 + 6		1	1	4	1		
ABB Phil	26		1		3			

	P/FL App	Goals	FLC App	Goals	FAC App	Goals	Others App	Goals
BELLION David	5 + 6	1	2		0 + 1			
BJORKLUND Joachim	19 + 1				1 + 1			
BLACK Chris	2							
BUTLER Thomas	7		0 + 1					
CLARK Ben	0 + 1				1			
CRADDOCK Jody	25	1	1		4			
DICKMAN Jonjo	0 + 1							
EL KARKOURI Talal	8				0 + 1			
FLO Tore Andre	23 + 6	4	1	2	1 + 1			
GRAY Michael	32		1		4			
KILBANE Kevin	30	1	1		3			
KYLE Kevin	9 + 8		2	1	2 + 1			
McATEER Jason	9		1		1			
McCANN Gavin	29 + 1	1	2	1	3	1		
McCARTNEY George	16 + 8		2 + 1		1 + 2			
MACHO Jurgen	12 + 1		2		1			
MEDINA Nicolas					1			
MYHRE Thomas	1 + 1		1					
OSTER John	1 + 2				1 + 1			
PHILLIPS Kevin	32	6	0 + 1		4	3		
PIPER Matt	8 + 5		0 + 1					
POOM Mart	4							
PROCTOR Michael	11 +10	2	2		3 + 2	2		
QUINN Niall	0 + 8							
REYNA Claudio	11		1	1				
ROSSITER Mark			2		0 + 1			
RYAN Richie	0 + 2							
SCHWARZ Stefan			1 + 1					
SORENSEN Thomas	21				4			
STEWART Marcus	9 +10	1	3	4	2	1		
THIRLWELL Paul	12 ¦ 7		1 ¦ 1		1			
THOME Emerson	1		2		2			
THORNTON Sean	11	1			3			
VARGA Stanislav			2		0 + 1			
WILLIAMS Darren	12 + 4		3		2			
WRIGHT Stephen	25 + 1				3			

SWANSEA CITY (DIV 3: 21st)

	P/FL App	Goals	FLC App	Goals	FAC App	Goals	Others App	Goals
BRITTON Leon	25							
CASH Brian	5						1	
COATES Jonathan	2 + 1							
CUSACK Nick	4 + 1	1	1					
CUTLER Neil	13							
DE-VULGT Leigh	3 + 1							
DURKAN Kieron	4 + 2							
EVANS Terry	25 + 2		1		1			
FREESTONE Roger	33		1		1		1	
HOWARD Michael	36 + 2		1		1		1	
HYLTON Leon	7 + 1							
JACKSON Michael	0 + 1						0 + 1	
JENKINS Lee	26 + 6		1		1		1	
JOHNROSE Lenny	15	3						
JONES Stuart	5 + 1						1	
KEAVENY Jonathan	4 + 5							
LACEY Damian	7 + 3		0 + 1				1	
MARTINEZ Roberto	19	2						
MAYLETT Brad	6							
MOSS David	3 + 6	2	1					
MUMFORD Andrew	17 + 1	1			1			
MURPHY Matt	9 + 3	2			1	1	0 + 1	
NUGENT Kevin	15	5						
O'LEARY Kristian	29 + 4		1				1	
PHILLIPS Gareth	19 + 8		1		1			
REID Paul	18 + 2	1	1				1	
RICHARDS Marc	14 + 3	7						
SHARP Neil	4 + 3							
SMITH David	3 + 1	1						
SMITH Jason	27	3			1			
STIENS Craig	0 + 3							
TATE Alan	27							
THEOBALD David	9 + 1				1		1	

	P/FL App	P/FL Goals	FLC App	FLC Goals	FAC App	FAC Goals	Others App	Others Goals
THOMAS James	34 + 5	13	1	1	1		1	1
WATKIN Steve	15 +11	2			0 + 1			
WILLIAMS John	11 +16	1	0 + 1		0 + 1			
WOOD Jamie	13 + 4	2	1	1	1			

SWINDON TOWN (DIV 2: 10th)

	P/FL App	P/FL Goals	FLC App	FLC Goals	FAC App	FAC Goals	Others App	Others Goals
BAMPTON Dave	0 + 3				0 + 1			
BESWETHERICK Jon	3							
DAVIS Jimmy	10 + 3	2	1				1	1
DUKE David	44	2	1		2		1 + 1	
DYKES Daren	1 + 1		0 + 1				1 + 1	
EDDS Gareth	8 + 6		0 + 1		1		2	
EDWARDS Nathan	0 + 3							
FARR Craig	2						1 + 1	
GARRARD Luke	0 + 1							
GRIEMINK Bart	44		1		2		1	
GURNEY Andy	41	8	1		1	1	1 + 1	
HERRING Ian	2 + 2							
HEWLETT Matt	39 + 1	1	1		2			
HEYWOOD Matty	46	1	1		2		2	1
IFIL Jerel	5 + 4							
INVINCIBILE Danny	37 + 5	7			2		2	2
JACKSON Johnnie	12 + 1	1			2		2	1
LEWIS Junior	9							
MARNEY Dean	8 + 1							
MIGLIORANZI Stefani	39 + 2	3	1		1		2	1
NIGHTINGALE Luke	2 + 1							
PARKIN Sam	41 + 2	25	1		2		1 + 1	1
REEVES Alan	35 + 1	3	0 + 1		2		1	
ROBINSON Steve	42 + 2	2	1		1		1	
SABIN Eric	27 +12	4	1		2		0 + 1	
SUTTON John	0 + 1							
TAYLOR Chris	0 + 4							
WILLIS Adam	9 + 6		1	1	0 + 1		2	
YOUNG Alan	0 +11				0 + 1		1	1

TORQUAY UNITED (DIV 3: 9th)

	P/FL App	P/FL Goals	FLC App	FLC Goals	FAC App	FAC Goals	Others App	Others Goals
AMANKWAAH Kevin	6							
ASHINGTON Ryan	0 + 2				0 + 1		0 + 1	
ATTWELL Jamie	2 + 2				1			
BEDEAU Tony	38 + 2	6	1		2			
BENEFIELD Jimmy	0 + 8				0 + 1			
BOND Kain	0 + 1				0 + 1			
BROWN Marvin	2 + 2							
CAMARA Ben	0 + 2							
CANOVILLE Lee	36		1		1		1	
CLIST Simon	11	2						
DEARDEN Kevin	26 + 1		1					
DOUGLIN Troy	1 + 4						0 + 1	
DUNNING Darren	4 + 3	1			1			
FORRINTON Howard	1							
FOWLER Jason	40	4	1		2	1	0 + 1	
GRAHAM David	26 + 8	15	1		2		1	
GRITTON Martin	39 + 4	13	1		2	3	1	
HANKIN Sean	17 + 2	1	1		1			
HAZELL Reuben	46		1		1		1	
HILL Kevin	37 + 2	4	1		1		1	
HOCKLEY Matt	25 +15	2			1		1	
HOLMES Paul	7						1	
KILOUGHERY Graham	1 + 2							
OSEI-KUFFOUR Jo	18 +12	5			1 + 1	1	1	
PRINCE Neil	3 + 4		0 + 1					
RICHARDSON Marcus	3 + 6	2	0 + 1					
RUSSELL Alex	39	9	1		2	1	1	
STEVENS Dean	0 + 3							
TAYLOR Craig	5							
VAN HEUSDEN Arjan	15				1			
WELCH Keith	3				1			
WILLS Kevin	5 +15	1			0 + 1			
WOODS Steve	5 + 4				1			
WOOZLEY David	45 + 1	3	1		2		1	

	P/FL App	P/FL Goals	FLC App	FLC Goals	FAC App	FAC Goals	Others App	Others Goal
TOTTENHAM HOTSPUR (PREM: 10th)								
ACIMOVIC Milenko	4 +13		1					
ANDERTON Darren	18 + 2		0 + 1		0 + 1			
BLONDEL Jonathan	0 + 1							
BUNJEVCEVIC Goran	31 + 4		2					
CARR Stephen	30		1		1			
CLEMENCE Stephen			1					
DAVIES Simon	33 + 3	5	2		1			
DOHERTY Gary	7 + 8	1	0 + 2		0 + 1			
ETHERINGTON Matthew	15 + 8	1	2					
FERDINAND Les	4 + 7	2	1 + 1					
FREUND Steffen	13 + 4		1					
GARDNER Anthony	11 + 1	1	1					
IVERSEN Steffen	8 +11	1	1 + 1		0 + 1			
KEANE Robbie	29	13	1 + 1		1			
KELLER Kasey	38		2		1			
KING Ledley	25				1			
PERRY Chris	15 + 3	1	1		1			
POYET Gus	22 + 6	5	1	1	1			
REDKNAPP Jamie	14 + 3	3						
RICHARDS Dean	26		2		1			
SHERINGHAM Teddy	34 + 2	12	1	1	1			
SLABBER Jamie	0 + 1							
TARICCO Mauricio	21		1		1			
THATCHER Ben	8 + 4		1		1			
TODA Kazuyuki	2 + 2							
ZIEGE Christian	10 + 2	2						

TRANMERE ROVERS (DIV 2: 7th)

	P/FL App	P/FL Goals	FLC App	FLC Goals	FAC App	FAC Goals	Others App	Others Goal
ACHTERBERG John	38		1		2		3	
ALLEN Graham	40 + 1	3	2	1	2		2	
ANDERSON Iain	7	2						
BARLOW Stuart	19 +10	3	2		2	1	1 + 1	
CONNELLY Sean	33				1		3	
CURTIS Tom	8		2				1	
EDWARDS Christian	12		1		2		2	
FEUER Ian	2							
GRAY Kevin	9 + 1	1	1		1 + 1		1 + 1	
HARRISON Danny	7 + 5		1		0 + 1		1 + 1	
HAWORTH Simon	42	20	1		2	1	2	
HAY Alex	11 + 8	3	1		0 + 2			
HINDS Richard	6 + 2		0 + 1					
HOWARTH Russell	2 + 1				0 + 1			
HUME Iain	22 +13	6	0 + 1		0 + 1		0 + 2	
JACKSON Michael	6							
JONES Gary	40	6	2		2		3	
KOUMAS Jason	4	2						
LORAN Tyrone	16 + 1							
McGIBBON Pat	4							
MELLON Micky	29 + 5	1	2		2	1	3	
NAVARRO Alan	5							
NICHOLSON Shane	36 + 2	4			2		3	
NIXON Eric	0 + 2							
OLSEN James	1 + 2		0 + 1				0 + 1	
PARKINSON Andy	1 + 9		0 + 1					
PRICE Jason	14 +11	4						
PROUDLOCK Adam	5						1	
ROBERTS Gareth	34 + 3	4	2		2		3	
ROBINSON Andrew							0 + 1	
ROBINSON Marvin	1 + 5	1					0 + 1	
SHARPS Ian	30	3	1				1	
TAYLOR Ryan	18 + 7	1	2	1	2		3	
WELCH Keith	2							
WHITEHEAD Phil	2		1					

WALSALL (DIV 1: 17th)

	P/FL App	P/FL Goals	FLC App	FLC Goals	FAC App	FAC Goals	Others App	Others Goal
AINSWORTH Gareth	2 + 3	1						
ARANALDE Zigor	38 + 1	3	3	1	4			
BARRAS Tony	14 + 5		0 + 2		1			
BAZELEY Darren	41 + 2		3		4			
BIRCH Gary	6 +13	1	0 + 1					

	P/FL		FLC		FAC		Others	
	App	Goals	App	Goals	App	Goals	App	Goals
ARBON Matt	20 + 5	1	1		3			
ORICA Steve	33 + 8	4	3		2 + 1			
MBLEN Neil	3 + 2							
AY Danny	26 + 3		3		3			
ERIVELTO Moriera	0 + 4	1	0 + 1					
JNIOR	28 + 8	15	3	1	3			
AWRENCE Jamie	4 + 1							
EITAO Jorge	43 + 1	11	3	2	4			
ARTINEZ Roberto	1 + 5							
ATIAS Pedro	8 +15	3	0 + 2		0 + 3			
'CONNOR Martin	33 + 2	1	2		3			
OLLET Ludo	5							
OBINSON Carl	10 + 1	1						
ODRIGUES Dani	0 + 1							
OPER Ian	39 + 1		3		3 + 1			
AMWAYS Vinny	13							
HUKER Chris	3 + 2							
IMPSON Fitzroy	16 + 9	1	2		3 + 1			
ONNER Danny	20 + 4	4	2		2			
ALKER James	41		3		4			
ARD Gavin	5 + 2							
RACK Darren	43	6	2 + 1		4	1		
RIGHT Mark	2 + 3							
ORILIC David	9 +15	3	0 + 2	1	1 + 2	1		

ATFORD (DIV 1: 13th)

	P/FL		FLC		FAC		Others	
RDLEY Neal	42 + 1	2	1		5			
ROWN Wayne	12 + 1	1	1		1			
HAMBERLAIN Alec	42		1		5			
HOPRA Michael	4 + 1	5			1			
OOK Lee	3 + 1				0 + 1			
OX Neil	40	9	1		5			
OYLEY Lloyd	21 + 1		1		0 + 1			
YCHE Sean	23 + 1		1					
ISKEN Gary	3 + 1							
ITZGERALD Scott	1 + 3	1						
OLEY Dominic	6 + 9	3	1	1				
AYLE Marcus	30 + 1				5	1		
LASS Stephen	26 + 7	1	1		2	1		
ODFREY Elliott	0 + 1							
AND Jamie	20 + 3		1		0 + 1			
ELGUSON Heidar	28 + 2	11			5	2		
YDE Micah	37	4	1		1			
FIL Jerel	1							
OHNSON Richard	5 + 7							
EE Richard	4							
cNAMEE Anthony	1 +22		0 + 1					
AHON Gavin	13 + 4				4 + 1			
IELSEN Allan	31 + 3	3	1		3 + 1			
OEL-WILLIAMS Gifton	8 + 8				1 + 2			
ORVILLE Jason	6 + 6	1	0 + 1					
ENNANT Jermaine	12				2	1		
OBINSON Paul	37	3	1		4			
MITH Jack	0 + 1							
MITH Tommy	25 +10	7	1		3 + 2	2		
WONNELL Sam	1 + 1							
ERNAZZA Paolo	13 +10				5			
EBBER Danny	11 + 1	2						

EST BROMWICH ALBION (PREM: 19th)

	P/FL		FLC		FAC		Others	
ALIS Igor	27 + 1	2			0 + 1			
HAMBERS Adam	10 + 3				1 + 1			
HAMBERS James	2 + 6		1					
LEMENT Neil	34 + 2	3	0 + 1		2			
ICHIO Danny	19 + 9	5	1		2	3		
OBIE Scott	10 +21	5	0 + 1		0 + 2			
YER Lloyd			1					
ILCHRIST Phil	22				1 + 1			
REGAN Sean	36	1			2			
OULT Russell	37				2			
UGHES Lee	14 + 9		1	1				
OHNSON Andy	30 + 2	1			2			

	P/FL		FLC		FAC		Others	
	App	Goals	App	Goals	App	Goals	App	Goals
JORDAO	0 + 3		1					
KOUMAS Jason	27 + 5	4	1		2			
LYTTLE Des	2 + 2		1					
McINNES Derek	28 + 1	2			1			
MARSHALL Lee	4 + 5	1	1					
MOORE Darren	29	2			2			
MURPHY Joe	1 + 1		1					
ROBERTS Jason	31 + 1	3			2			
SIGURDSSON Larus	23 + 6		1		1 + 1			
TAYLOR Bob	2 + 2							
UDEZE Iffy	7 + 4							
WALLWORK Ronnie	23 + 4		1		2			

WEST HAM UNITED (PREM: 18th)

	P/FL		FLC		FAC		Others	
BOWYER Lee	10				1			
BREEN Gary	9 + 5		2		2			
BREVETT Rufus	12 + 1				1			
CAMARA Titi	0 + 4		1		0 + 1			
CARRICK Michael	28 + 2	1	2		2			
CISSE Edouard	18 + 7		1		2			
COLE Joe	36	4	2		2	1		
DAILLY Christian	23 + 3		1		1 + 1			
DEFOE Jermain	29 + 9	8	2	1	2	2		
DI CANIO Paolo	16 + 2	9	1					
FERDINAND Les	12 + 2	2						
GARCIA Richard			0 + 1		0 + 1			
HUTCHISON Don	0 +10							
JAMES David	38		2		2			
JOHNSON Glen	14 + 1				0 + 1			
KANOUTE Fredi	12 + 5	5						
LABANT Vladimir	0 + 1							
LOMAS Steve	27 + 2		2		1			
MINTO Scott	9 + 3		2		1			
MONCUR John	0 + 7							
PEARCE Ian	26 + 4	2	1		2			
REPKA Tomas	32		1		0 + 1			
SCHEMMEL Sebastien	15 + 1		1 + 1		1			
SINCLAIR Trevor	36 + 2	8	1		2			
WINTERBURN Nigel	16 + 2		0 + 1		1			

WIGAN ATHLETIC (DIV 2: 1st)

	P/FL		FLC		FAC		Others	
ASHCROFT Lee			0 + 1					
BAINES Leighton	6		1 + 1		2		1 + 1	
BEASANT Dave							1	
BRANNAN Ged	6						1	
BRECKIN Ian	7 + 2				2		1	
BULLARD Jimmy	17	1						
DE VOS Jason	43	8	5		1			
DINNING Tony	36 + 2	7	4		2			
EADEN Nicky	37		4		3		1	
EDGHILL Richard							1	
ELLINGTON Nathan	41 + 1	15	5	5	2 + 1	2	0 + 1	
FILAN John	46		5		3		1	
FLYNN Michael	3 +14	1	0 + 3		0 + 2	1	2	
GREEN Scott	14 + 3	2	3 + 1		3		2	
JACKSON Matt	45		5		3		2	
JARRETT Jason	25 +10		5	1	3		1 + 1	1
KENNEDY Peter	21 + 1	1	3		3		2	
LIDDELL Andy	32 + 5	16	2		1		1	
McCULLOCH Lee	33 + 5	6	2		0 + 1			
McMILLAN Steve	28 + 4		4					
MITCHELL Paul	13 +14		1 + 2		1 + 1		2	
ROBERTS Neil	25 +12	6	4 + 1	1	3		1	
TEALE Gary	28 +10	2	2 + 2		1 + 1		2	2

WIMBLEDON (DIV 1: 10th)

	P/FL		FLC		FAC		Others	
AGYEMANG Patrick	12 +21	5	1	1	1 + 1			
AINSWORTH Gareth	8 + 4	2	1 + 1		0 + 1			
ANDERSEN Trond	34 + 4	1	3	1	2			
CHORLEY Ben	8 + 2							
CONNOLLY David	28	24			2			
DARLINGTON Jermaine	32 + 3	2	1 + 1		1			

489

	P/FL App	Goals	FLC App	Goals	FAC App	Goals	Others App	Goals
DAVIS Kelvin	46		3		2			
FRANCIS Damien	29 + 5	6	2 + 1		2			
GIER Rob	27 + 2		3		1			
GORDON Michael	0 + 1							
GRAY Wayne	12 +18	2	1 + 1				0 + 1	
HAWKINS Peter	43		2		2			
HOLLOWAY Darren	14 + 2		3					
KAMARA Malvin	0 + 2							
KARLSSON Par	2 + 1							
LEIGERTWOOD Mikele	27 + 1		3	1	2			
LEWINGTON Dean	0 + 1							
McANUFF Jobi	29 + 2	4	2	1	1	1		
MORGAN Lionel	6 + 5	1	1		0 + 1	1		
NOWLAND Adam	10 +14	2	1 + 1					
REO-COKER Nigel	32	2	1 + 1		1 + 1			
SHIPPERLEY Neil	46	20	3	3	2	1		
TAPP Alex	23 + 1	2	2	1	1			
VOLZ Moritz	10	1						
WILLIAMS Mark	23	1			2			
WILLMOTT Chris	5							

WOLVERHAMPTON WANDERERS (DIV 1: 5th)

	P/FL App	Goals	FLC App	Goals	FAC App	Goals	Others App	Goals
ANDREWS Keith	2 + 7				1			
BLAKE Nathan	22 + 1	12	2	1			3	1
BUTLER Paul	31 + 1	1	2		4		3	
CAMERON Colin	29 + 4	7			4		3	
CLYDE Mark	15 + 2				0 + 1			
COLE Carlton	5 + 2	1						
COOPER Kevin	13 +13	3			0 + 1		0 + 1	
EDWORTHY Marc	18 + 4		1					
INCE Paul	35 + 2	2	1 + 1		3	1	3	
INGIMARSSON Ivar	10 + 3	2	2					
IRWIN Denis	43		2		1 + 1		3	
KENNEDY Mark	30 + 1	3			4	1	3	1
LESCOTT Joleon	44		1		4		3	
MELLIGAN JJ	0 + 2							
MILLER Kenny	35 + 8	19	1 + 1	1	4	3	3	1
MURRAY Matt	40		1		4		3	
NAYLOR Lee	31 + 1	1	2		4		3	1
NDAH George	17 + 8	7	1		3	4	3	
NEWTON Shaun	29 + 4	3	2	1	4		2 + 1	
OAKES Michael	6		1					
POLLET Ludo	2		1	1			0 + 1	
PROUDLOCK Adam	2 +15	2	0 + 1		0 + 3	1	0 + 1	
RAE Alex	30 + 8	3	2	2	0 + 2		0 + 1	1
STURRIDGE Dean	17 +22	10	1 + 1		0 + 1		0 + 3	

WREXHAM (DIV 3: 3rd)

	P/FL App	Goals	FLC App	Goals	FAC App	Goals	Others App	Goals
BARRETT Paul	22 + 4	1	2				3	
BENNETT Dan	14 + 4		1				2	
CAREY Brian	31 + 2	4	1		1		0 + 1	
DIBBLE Andy	33		1				1	
EDWARDS Carlos	43 + 1	8	2	1	1		2	1
EDWARDS Paul	33 + 5	4	2		0 + 1		2	
EVANS Mark	0 + 1							
FERGUSON Darren	41		2		1		3	
GREEN Scott	12 + 3	3						
HOLMES Shaun	13 +17		0 + 2		1		1 + 1	
JONES Lee	9 +14	4			0 + 1		2 + 1	2
JONES Mark	0 + 1							
LAWRENCE Denis	30 + 2	1	1				2	
MORGAN Craig	1 + 5	1					1	
MORRELL Andy	45	34	2	1	1		1	
PEJIC Shaun	23 + 4		2		1		2	
PHILLIPS Waynne	1							
ROBERTS Steve	39	2	1		1		2	1
ROGERS Kristian	6 + 1							
RUSSELL Kevin	1							
SAM Hector	8 +18	5	2		0 + 1		0 + 3	

	P/FL App	Goals	FLC App	Goals	FAC App	Goals	Others App	Goal
THOMAS Stephen	19 + 6	2	0 + 1		1		2	
TRUNDLE Lee	31 +13	11	0 + 2		1		3	
WHITFIELD Paul	7 + 1		1		1		2 + 1	
WHITLEY Jim	44	1	2		1		2	

WYCOMBE WANDERERS (DIV 2: 18th)

	P/FL App	Goals	FLC App	Goals	FAC App	Goals	Others App	Goal
ANDERSON Ijah	5							
BROWN Steve	33 + 4	5	0 + 2		1	1	1	
BULMAN Dannie	42	3	2		1		3	
COOK Lewis	4 +13				0 + 1		3	
CURRIE Darren	23 +15	4	2		0 + 1		2	
DEVINE Sean	13 + 5	5	1 + 1				1	
DIXON Jonny	14 + 8	5					0 + 2	
FAULCONBRIDGE Craig	29 + 5	6	2		1		3	
HARRIS Richard	5 +17	5	0 + 2	1	1		1	
HOLLIGAN Gavin	1 + 9	2						
JOHNSON Roger	26 + 7	3	1				0 + 1	
LEE Martyn	2 + 4							
McCARTHY Paul	22 + 2	1	2	2	1		2	
McSPORRAN Jermaine	6 + 3	1						
OLIVER Luke	0 + 2							
RAMMELL Andy	17 + 4	4			1	1		
ROBERTS Stuart	14 +14	4	2				0 + 1	
ROGERS Mark	31 + 5	1	1				2 + 1	
RYAN Keith	33 + 3	2	0 + 1		0 + 1		1	
SENDA Danny	39 + 2	2	1		1		2	
SIMPEMBA Ian	0 + 1							
SIMPSON Michael	42	5	2		1		3	
TALIA Frank	35		1		1		1	
TAYLOR Martin	11		1				2	
THOMSON Andy	34 + 2	1	1		1		3	
TOWNSEND Ben	0 + 1						0 + 1	
VINNICOMBE Chris	25		2		1		2	

YORK CITY (DIV 3: 10th)

	P/FL App	Goals	FLC App	Goals	FAC App	Goals	Others App	Goal
BERESFORD Marlon	6							
BRACKSTONE Steve	22 + 4	2	1		2			
BRASS Chris	40		1	1	2		0 + 1	
BULLOCK Lee	38 + 1	6	1		2	1		
CARVALHO Rogerio	0 + 4		0 + 1					
COOK Lee	7		1				1	
COOPER Richard	21 + 3	1	1					
COWAN Tom	31 + 2	1	1					
DUFFIELD Peter	28	13	1		2	2		
EDMONDSON Darren	37 + 1	5	1		2		1	
FETTIS Alan	21		1		2			
FOX Christian	6 + 5		1					
GRAYDON Keith	4 + 3	1						
HOBSON Gary	24 + 4		1		2		1	
HOWARTH Russell								
INGHAM Michael	17							
JONES Scott	19 + 1				1			
McCARTHY Jon	1							
MATHIE Alex	2 + 8							
MAZZINA Nicolas	0 + 3							
NOGAN Lee	39 + 7	5	1		2		1	
OKOLI James	1 + 2				1			
PARKIN Jon	37 + 4	10			2		1	
POTTER Graham	37 + 2	1	1		2		1	
REDDY Michael	10 + 1	2			1			
SHANDRAN Anthony	12 + 6	3						
SMITH Chris	33 + 3	3	1		1		1	
STOCKDALE David	0 + 1							
WHITEHEAD Phil	2							
WILDING Craig	1 + 6				1			
WISE Stuart	3 + 5							
WOOD Leigh	7 +12				1			
YALCIN Levent	0 + 5		0 + 1					

Where Did They Go?

Below is a list of all players who were recorded in the previous edition as making a first-team appearance in 2001-2002, but failed to make the current book. They are listed alphabetically and show their approximate leaving dates as well as their first port of call if known. Of course, they may well have moved on by now, but space does not allow further reference.

* Shows that the player in question is still with his named club but failed to make an appearance in 2002-2003, the most common reason being injury.

- Players retained by Halifax, who were relegated to the Conference.

Name	Club	Date	Destination
DAMCZUK Dariusz	Wigan Ath	11.01	Glasgow Rangers
DAMS Tony	Arsenal	06.02	Retired
DAMSON Chris	West Bromwich A	04.03	St Patricks Ath
FFUL Les	Exeter C	*	
GGREY Jimmy	Torquay U	12.01	Dover Ath
GOGO Junior	Queens Park R	07.02	Barnet
LDERTON Rio	Southend U	05.02	Gravesend & Northfleet
LLAN Jonny	Carlisle U	08.02	Northwich Victoria
NDERSON Mark	Scunthorpe U	07.02	Gainsborough Trinity
NDRE Carlos	Walsall	03.02	
NTONELIUS Tomas	Coventry C	02.02	FC Copenhagen (Denmark)
PPLETON Michael	West Bromwich A	*	
RPEXHAD Pegguy	Liverpool	06.03	
SHIER Alistair	Mansfield T	08.02	Halifax I
SHFORD Ryan	Torquay U	08.02	Weymouth
TKINSON Brian	Darlington	09.02	
TKINSON Graeme	Rochdale	07.02	Lancaster C
AIRD Andy	Wycombe W	08.02	Brackley T
AK Arek	Birmingham C	02.02	Polonia Warsaw
ALABAN Bosko	Aston Villa	08.02	Dinamo Zagreb (Croatia)
ALL Kevin	Burnley	06.02	Retired
ANGER Nicky	Torquay U	08.02	Woking
ANKS Chris	Cheltenham T	01.03	Retired
ARLOW Martin	Exeter C	09.02	Telford U
ARNETT Jason	Lincoln C	08.02	Lincoln U
ARR Hamid	Queens Park R	06.02	St Albans C
ARRETT Neil	Portsmouth	*	
ASHAM Mike	York C	02.03	Chelmsford C
ASSEDAS Christian	Newcastle U	03.03	Tenerife (Spain)
ATTY David	Leeds U	*	
AYES Ashley	Leyton Orient	08.02	Bohemians
EALL Billy	Leyton Orient	02.02	Cambridge C
EAUCHAMP Joey	Oxford U	08.02	Abingdon T
ELL Stuart	Carlisle U	08.02	Retired
EN ASKAR Aziz	Queens Park R	05.02	Stade Lavallois (France)
ERHALTER Gregg	Crystal Palace	08.02	Energie Cottbus (Germany)
ERKLEY Austin	Barnet	09.02	Chelmsford C
HUTIA Bhaichung	Bury	07.02	Mohun Bagen AC (India)
AGINI Leonardo	Portsmouth	03.02	Mallorca (Spain)
ANCALINI Frederic	Walsall	07.02	AS Nancy-Lorraine (France)
NGHAM Michael	Mansfield T	10.02	Hednesford T
RD Tony	Kidderminster Hrs	07.02	St Patricks Ath
ACKWOOD Michael	Wrexham	09.02	Stevenage Borough
AKE Mark	Kidderminster Hrs	12.02	Retired
ATSIS Con	Colchester U	07.02	Kacaclispor (Turkey)
EIDELIS Imants	Southampton	01.03	Viborg (Denmark)
ONDEAU Patrick	Watford	07.02	Creteil (France)
OBIC Fredi	Bolton W	07.02	Hannover 96 (Germany)
BOLLAND Phil	Oxford U	03.02	Chester C
BONNOT Alex	Queens Park R	02.02	France
BONVIN Pablo	Sheffield Wed	06.02	
BORLEY David	Bury	04.03	
BOSNICH Mark	Chelsea	01.03	
BRABIN Gary	Torquay U	11.01	Chester C
BRADSHAW Carl	Scunthorpe U	07.02	Alfreton T
BRADY Garry	Portsmouth	07.02	Dundee
BRADY Jon	Rushden & Diamonds	10.02	Chester C
BRAGSTAD Bjorn Otto	Derby Co	01.03	SW Bregenz (Austria)
BRANAGAN Keith	Ipswich T	11.02	Retired
BRAYLEY Bertie	Swindon T	08.02	Canvey Island
BRENNAN Dean	Luton T	03.02	Hitchin T
BRIGHTWELL David	Darlington	06.02	Retired
BRODIE Steve	Swansea C	06.02	Chester C
BROOKS Jamie	Oxford U	*	
BROWN David	Torquay U	12.01	Chester C
BROWN Grant	Lincoln C	07.02	Telford U
BRUCE Paul	Queens Park R	07.02	Dagenham & Redbridge
BRUMWELL Phil	Darlington	07.02	Blyth Spartans
BRYAN Del	Brentford	03.02	Welling U
BRYNGELSSON Fredrik	Stockport Co	01.02	Sweden
BUBB Alvin	Bristol Rov	09.02	Slough T
BUCHANAN Wayne	Bolton W	01.03	Lisburn Distillery
BUCKLE Paul	Exeter C	08.02	Aldershot T
BUKRAN Gabor	Wigan Ath	09.01	SV Solzburg (Austria)
BULLOCK Darren	Bury	10.01	Worcester C
BULLOCK Matthew	Stoke C	01.02	Leek T
BURGESS Richard	Port Vale	01.02	Nuneaton Borough
BURNETT Wayne	Grimsby T	09.02	Grays Ath
BURROWS Mark	Exeter C	09.02	Kings Lynn
BUSHELL Steve	Halifax T	+	
BUSSCHER Robby	Grimsby T	01.02	NAC Breda (Holland)
BUTLER Lee	Halifax T	01.02	Doncaster Rov
BUTTERWORTH Gary	Rushden & Diamonds	05.02	Farnborough T
BYRNE Mark	Stockport Co	01.03	Burscough
BYRNE Shaun	West Ham U	*	
CACERES Adrian	Hull C	05.02	Perth Glory (Australia)
CAMARA Mohamed	Wolverhampton W	06.03	
CAMERON Dave	Lincoln C	07.02	Chester C
CAMERON Martin	Bristol Rov	07.02	St Mirren
CAMPBELL Jamie	Exeter C	03.02	Stevenage Borough
CARASSO Cedric	Crystal Palace	06.02	Marseilles (France)
CARBONE Beni	Bradford C	06.02	Como (Italy)
CAREY Shaun	Rushden & Diamonds	02.02	Chester C
CARR Darren	Rushden & Diamonds	03.02	Retired
CARRATT Phil	Stockport Co	06.02	
CARROLL Dave	Wycombe W	03.02	Aldershot T
CASEY Ryan	Swansea C	10.02	St Patricks Ath
CASTLE Steve	Leyton Orient	06.02	St Albans C
CAVILL Aaron	Northampton T	*	

Name	Club	Date	Moved to
CENNAMO Luigi	Burnley	06.02	
CHALK Martyn	Wrexham	08.02	Rhyl
CHAMBERS Triston	Colchester U	02.03	Heybridge Swifts
CHARVET Laurent	Manchester C	10.02	Sochaux (France)
CHRISTIE Jeremy	Barnsley	12.02	Auckland Kingz (New Zealand)
CLARK Anthony	Southend U	*	
CLARK Simon	Colchester U	01.02	Woodlands (Singapore)
CLARKSON Ian	Kidderminster Hrs	06.02	Nuneaton Borough
CLARKSON Phil	Bury	08.02	Halifax T
CLELAND Alex	Everton	06.02	Retired
CLEMENTS Matt	Cambridge U	05.02	Cambridge C
COBIAN Juan	Swindon T	01.03	
COLEMAN Simon	Rochdale	08.02	Ilkeston T
COLOSIMO Simon	Manchester C	01.02	KRC Genk (Belgium)
COLUSSO Christian	Oldham Ath	05.02	Rosario (Argentina)
COMBE Alan	Bradford C	05.02	Dundee U
COOPER Shaun	Portsmouth	*	
CORBETT Andy	Kidderminster Hrs	11.02	Solihull Borough
CORBO Mateo	Barnsley	02.02	
COSTA Jorge	Charlton Ath	06.02	FC Porto (Portugal)
COURTOIS Laurent	West Ham U	01.03	Istres (France)
COUSINS Jason	Wycombe W	06.02	Aldershot T
CRICHTON Paul	Norwich C	*	
CROOKES Peter	Halifax T	07.02	Hyde U
CROUDSON Steve	Grimsby T	06.03	
D'AURIA David	Chesterfield	08.02	Newport Co
DADASON Rikki	Stoke C	07.02	Lillestrom (Norway)
DAINO Danny	Derby Co	11.02	AC Milan (Italy)
DALLA BONA Sam	Chelsea	07.02	AC Milan (Italy)
DANBY John	Kidderminster Hrs	*	
DARLOW Kieran	York C	07.02	Frickley Ath
DAVIES Ben	Kidderminster Hrs	06.02	Chester C
DAVIES Gareth	Swindon T	01.02	Chippenham T
DEBEVE Michael	Middlesbrough	07.02	Amiens (France)
DEMPSEY Paul	Northampton T	04.02	Auckland Kingz (New Zealand)
DE ORNELAS Fernando	Queens Park R	11.01	CS Maritimo (Portugal)
DIALLO Cherif	Exeter C	01.02	Hayes
DIAWARA Djibril	Bolton W	01.02	Torino (Italy)
DICKINSON Michael	Carlisle U	02.03	Gateshead
DIOMEDE Bernard	Liverpool	06.03	
DIXON Lee	Arsenal	06.02	Retired
D'JAFFO Laurent	Sheffield U	07.02	Aberdeen
DJORDJIC Bojan	Manchester U	08.02	AGF (Denmark)
DODD Ashley	Port Vale	06.02	Stafford R
DONNELLY Paul	Port Vale	06.02	
DORRIAN Chris	Leyton Orient	07.02	Harlow T
DRAPER Craig	Swansea C	06.02	
DRAPER Mark	Southampton	*	
DRYDEN Richard	Luton T	08.02	Scarborough
DSANE Roscoe	Southend U	12.01	Woking
DUCROCQ Pierre	Derby Co	05.02	Le Havre (France)
DUDLEY Craig	Oldham Ath	08.02	Burton A
DUFFY Richard	Swansea C	*	
DUNNE Joe	Colchester U	05.03	Retired
EDINBURGH Justin	Portsmouth	03.02	Retired
EKOKU Efan	Sheffield Wed	09.02	Retired
ELLIOTT Stuart	Exeter C	08.02	Halifax T
ELLIS Tony	Burnley	09.02	Mossley
EMBLEN Paul	Wycombe W	10.02	Tonbridge Angels
EMMERSON Scott	York C	07.02	Blyth Spartans
ESPARTERO Mario	Bolton W	04.02	Metz (France)
EVANS Gareth	Huddersfield T	06.03	
EVANS Gary	Bury	03.03	
EVANS Michael	York C	10.01	Holland

Name	Club	Date	Moved to
EVERS Sean	Plymouth Arg	08.02	Woking
EYRE Richard	Macclesfield T	03.02	Kidsgrove Ath
FALCONER Willie	Grimsby T	05.02	Retired
FARRELL Andy	Halifax T	+	
FERRARI Carlos	Birmingham C	03.02	Mirassol (Brazil)
FIELDING John	York C	07.02	Harrogate T
FINCH Keith	Darlington	03.02	Bishop Auckland
FITZPATRICK Ian	Halifax T	+	
FOLETTI Patrick	Derby Co	05.02	Luzern (Switzerland)
FOLLAND Rob	Oxford U	05.02	Port Talbot T
FORAN Mark	Bristol Rov	07.02	Telford U
FORBES Scott	Southend U	07.02	Canvey Island
FORD James	Bournemouth	07.02	Havant & Waterloovi
FORD Tony	Rochdale	11.01	Retired
FORSSELL Mikael	Chelsea	*	
FOSTER Steve	Bristol Rov	08.02	Doncaster Rov
FOX Ruel	West Bromwich A	06.02	Retired
FOY Keith	Nottingham F	11.02	Doncaster Rov
FRASER Stuart	Luton T	03.02	Stevenage Borough
FREESTONE Chris	Shrewsbury T	02.02	Rugby U
FRENCH Daniel	Peterborough U	02.03	Bedford T
FRIARS Sean	Carlisle U	12.01	Newry T
GALLI Filippo	Watford	06.02	Pro Sesta (Italy)
GAMBLE Joe	Reading	*	
GARNETT Shaun	Oldham Ath	10.02	Halifax T
GARROCHO Carlos	Walsall	06.02	Portugal
GASCOIGNE Paul	Burnley	06.02	Gansu Tianma (China
GIBBS Nigel	Watford	05.02	Retired
GIBSON Alex	Port Vale	07.02	Stafford R
GIBSON Robin	Wrexham	07.02	Stafford R
GILES Martyn	Cardiff C	06.03	
GILL Wayne	Oldham Ath	06.03	
GILLMAN Robert	Luton T	03.03	Enfield
GINOLA David	Everton	05.02	Retired
GOFF Shaun	Exeter C	06.03	
GOODEN Ty	Gillingham	06.03	
GOODING Scott	Crystal Palace	09.01	Hornchurch
GOODISON Ian	Hull C	04.02	Seba U (Jamaica)
GOODRIDGE Greg	Torquay U	06.02	
GORAM Andy	Oldham Ath	04.02	Queen of the South
GORE Shane	Wimbledon	*	
GOTTSKALKSSON Olafur	Brentford	11.02	Retired
GOUGH Neil	Leyton Orient	09.02	Heybridge Swifts
GRANT Gareth	Bradford C	05.02	Gainsborough Trinity
GRANT John	Crewe Alex	06.02	Hereford U
GRANT Kim	Scunthorpe U	10.01	Yeovil T
GRANT Lee	York C	07.02	Aston Villa (trainee)
GRAY Phil	Oxford U	07.02	Chelmsford C
GRAYSON Neil	Cheltenham T	06.02	Forest Green Rov
GREGG Matt	Crystal Palace	10.01	Bray W
GREGORY David	Colchester U	08.02	Canvey Island
GREYLING Anton	Torquay U	10.01	South Africa
GRIFFIN Adam	Oldham Ath	*	
GRIMANDI Gilles	Arsenal	06.02	Colorado Rapids (USA
GROSS Marcus	Exeter C	10.01	Tiverton T
GUDJONSSON Thordur	Preston NE	05.02	VFL Bochum (German
GUERET Willy	Millwall	*	
GUERRERO Ivan	Coventry C	10.02	CD Montagua (Honduras)
GUINAN Steve	Shrewsbury T	08.02	Hereford U
GUNBY Steve	Bury	*	
GUNNLAUGSSON Arnie	Stoke C	07.02	Dundee
GUYETT Scott	Oxford U	08.02	Chester C
HAALAND Alf-Inge	Manchester C	01.03	Retired
HAAS Bernt	Sunderland	08.02	FC Basel (Switzerland
HADDOW Alex	Carlisle U	06.02	

492

Name	Club	Date	Destination
ADLEY Stewart	Kidderminster Hrs	01.02	Worcester C
ADRAVA David	Colchester U	12.02	Heybridge Swifts
ALL Laurence	Stoke C	*	
ALLE Gunnar	Bradford C	06.02	Norway
ALLIDAY Kevin	Swindon T	06.03	
ALLIDAY Steve	Carlisle U	05.02	
ALLS John	Arsenal	08.02	Beveren (Belgium)
AMILTON Ian	Lincoln C	10.02	Woking
ANCOCK Glynn	Stockport Co	06.03	
ANLON Richie	Rushden & Diamonds	*	
ANSEN Bo	Bolton W	08.02	Midtjylland (Denmark)
ANSON Christian	Middlesbrough	10.02	Havant & Waterlooville
ARDY Niell	Stockport Co	05.02	Radcliffe Borough
ARDY Phil	Port Vale	06.02	
ARKIN Mo	Carlisle U	01.02	Nuneaton Borough
ARPER Steve	Darlington	09.02	Kidsgrove Ath
ARRIS Jason	Southend U	11.01	Nuneaton Borough
ARRISON Craig	Crystal Palace	06.03	
ATSWELL Wayne	Oxford U	06.02	Chester C
AWLEY Karl	Walsall	*	
AY Chris	Huddersfield T	08.02	St Johnstone
EALD Paul	Wimbledon	06.03	
EALY Brian	Darlington	02.02	Shildon
EALY Colin	Coventry C	05.02	Glasgow Celtic
EANEY Neil	Plymouth Arg	01.03	Retired
EDMAN Magnus	Coventry C	08.02	Glasgow Celtic
EINEMANN Nicky	Halifax T	+	
ELIN Petri	Stockport Co	05.02	Denizlispor (Turkey)
ENRY Nick	Tranmere Rov	06.02	Scarborough
ERBERT Robert	Halifax T	+	
ERRERA Robbie	Leyton Orient	11.01	Taunton T
EWILL Jamie	Chesterfield	06.02	Retired
EWS Chay	Carlisle U	10.01	IF Sylvia (Sweden)
ILL Keith	Cheltenham T	07.02	Morecambe
ILLIER David	Bristol Rov	08.02	Barnet
INCHCLIFFE Andy	Sheffield Wed	03.02	Retired
ODGE John	Northampton T	06.02	Retired
OLLUND Martin	Hartlepool U	06.02	Lov Hom (Norway)
OLMES Steve	Lincoln C	08.02	Dunston FB
OLNESS Dean	Southend U	09.01	
OLT David	Stockport Co	*	
OOPER Dean	Peterborough U	05.02	Aldershot T
OPKIN David	Crystal Palace	08.02	Morton
OPKINS Gareth	Cheltenham T	06.02	Cirencester T
OPPER Tony	Carlisle U	06.02	Workington
ORE John	Carlisle U	06.02	Gretna
ORRIGAN Darren	Lincoln C	*	
OTTE Mark	Oldham Ath	01.02	Scarborough
OUGHTON Scott	Halifax T	03.02	Stevenage Borough
OWE Bobby	Swindon T	08.02	Havant & Waterlooville
OWELLS Lee	Cheltenham T	*	
UCK William	Bournemouth	06.02	Angers (France)
UDSON Danny	Rotherham U	06.03	
UGHES David	Cardiff C	04.03	
UGHES Michael	Wimbledon	06.03	
UGHES Mark	Blackburn Rov	06.02	Retired
UGHES Stephen	Watford	12.02	Retired
LIC Sasa	Charlton Ath	06.02	Zalacgerszog (Hungary)
NGLEDOW Jamie	Chesterfield	09.02	Stocksbridge PS
SSA Pierre	Watford	08.02	Beirut (Lebanon)
ONGA Carlin	Arsenal	06.02	Oxford U (N/C)
ACKMAN Daniel	Aston Villa	*	
ACKSON Justin	Rushden & Diamonds	09.01	Doncaster Rov
ACKSON Kirk	Darlington	01.02	Stevenage Borough
EANNE Leon	Cardiff C	07.02	Newport Co
EANNIN Alex	Darlington	01.02	France
JEFFREY Mike	Grimsby T	06.02	
JENKINS Iain	Shrewsbury T	12.01	Chester C
JENSEN Brian	West Bromwich A	06.03	
JOHNSON Ross	Colchester U	09.02	Canvey Island
JOHNSSON JJ	Hull C	07.02	B36 (Faeroes)
JOKANOVIC Slavisa	Chelsea	06.02	Retired
JONES Darren	Bristol C	*	
JONES Gary	Halifax T	06.02	Nuneaton Borough
JONES Jason	Swansea C	06.02	Llanelli
JONES Keith	Reading	06.02	Retired
JONES Mark	Chesterfield	11.01	Raith Rov
JONES Gethin	Cardiff C	06.03	
JONES Steve	Bristol C	07.02	Hornchurch
JORGENSEN Henrik	Notts Co	04.02	B1909 (Denmark)
JUAN	Arsenal	*	
JULES Mark	Halifax T	07.02	Alfreton T
KANDOL Tresor	Bournemouth	07.02	Chesham U
KEEGAN Michael	Swansea C	02.02	Marine
KEEN Kevin	Macclesfield T	06.02	Retired
KELL Richard	Scunthorpe U	06.03	
KELLY David	Mansfield T	07.02	Derry C
KELLY Leon	Cambridge U	06.02	Ilkeston T
KENDALL Lee	Cardiff C	08.02	Shrewsbury T
KERR Dylan	Exeter C	08.02	Gateshead
KERR Stewart	Wigan Ath	09.02	
KERRIGAN Danny	Southend U	07.02	Billericay T
KERRIGAN Steve	Halifax T	01.03	Stirling A
KETSBAIA Temuri	Wolverhampton W	10.01	Dundee
KIDD Ryan	Preston NE	11.01	Retired
KILLEEN Lewis	Sheffield U	06.03	
KILTY Mark	Darlington	*	
KING Simon	Oxford U	*	
KIPPE Frode	Liverpool	03.02	Lillestrom (Norway)
KITAMIRIKE Joel	Chelsea	*	
KNIGHT Richard	Oxford U	05.02	
KOEJOE Sammy	Queens Park R	08.02	SC Lustenau (Austria)
KONSTANTINIDIS Kostas	Bolton W	07.02	Hannover 96 (Germany)
LASLANDES Lilian	Sunderland	07.02	Bastia (France)
LAURSEN Jacob	Leicester C	01.03	Denmark
LAVIN Gerard	Northampton T	04.03	
LAW Gareth	Torquay U	12.01	Barnstaple T
LEABURN Carl	Queens Park R	06.02	Grays Ath
LEACH Marc	Wycombe W	07.02	Chesham U
LEE Christian	Rushden & Diamonds	10.01	Farnborough T
LEHMANN Dirk	Brighton & Hove A	01.02	Motherwell
LE TISSIER Matt	Southampton	06.02	Retired
LIBBRA Marc	Norwich C	08.02	Creteil (France)
LITMANEN Jari	Liverpool	08.02	Ajax (Holland)
LOCKE Adam	Luton T	09.02	Hornchurch
LOCKE Gary	Bradford C	08.02	Kilmarnock
LOPEZ Carlos	Wycombe W	01.02	
LOPEZ Rik	Bristol Rov	05.02	
LORMOR Anth	Hartlepool U	06.02	Telford U
LOVELL Steve	Portsmouth	08.02	Dundee
LUDDEN Dominic	Halifax T	08.02	Leigh RMI
LUNAN Daniel	Southend U	*	
LUNTALA Tresor	Birmingham C	04.03	
McANESPIE Steve	Cambridge U	03.02	Partick Thistle
McAREAVEY Paul	Swindon T	06.02	Portadown
McAUGHTRIE Craig	Carlisle U	07.02	Stafford R
McAULEY Sean	Rochdale	08.02	Halifax T
McAVOY Andy	Macclesfield T	08.02	Spennymoor U
McCALDON Ian	Oxford U	06.03	
McCARTHY Sean	Exeter C	06.03	Retired
McCULLOCH Scott	Cardiff C	03.02	Forfar Ath

Name	Club	Date	Destination
MacDONALD Charlie	Charlton Ath	09.02	Stevenage Borough
McELHATTON Mike	Rushden & Diamonds	08.02	Retired
McELHOLM Brendan	Leyton Orient	01.02	Omagh T
McEWEN Dave	Queens Park R	01.02	
McLOUGHLIN Alan	Rochdale	07.02	Forest Green Rov
McNAMARA Niall	Notts Co	08.02	Belper T
McNEIL Martin	Torquay U	01.02	Kings Lynn
McSWEGAN Gary	Luton T	03.02	Kilmarnock
MAKEL Lee	Bradford C	12.01	Livingston
MALEY Mark	Sunderland	03.03	Retired
MALLON Ryan	Sheffield U	06.03	
MARCELLE Clint	Darlington	07.02	Harrogate T
MARCELO	Walsall	07.02	Academica Coimbra (Portugal)
MARSH Adam	Darlington	08.02	Buxton
MARSHALL Ian	Blackpool	06.02	Retired
MARTIN Andy	Torquay U	10.02	Hornchurch
MARTINEZ Jairo	Coventry C	10.02	CD Montagua (Honduras)
MARTYN Nigel	Leeds U	*	
MATTHEWS Rob	Hull C	10.02	Northwich Victoria
MAUGE Ronnie	Bristol Rov	09.02	Aldershot T
MAYBURY Alan	Leeds U	10.01	Heart of Midlothian
MBOMA Patrick	Sunderland	04.02	Al Ittihad (Saudi Arabia)
MEDOU-OTYE Parfait	Kidderminster Hrs	09.02	Stourport Swifts
MENETRIER Mickael	Bournemouth	07.02	France
MIDDLETON Craig	Halifax T	07.02	Bedworth U
MIDGLEY Craig	Halifax T	+	
MIKE Leon	Manchester C	02.02	Aberdeen
MILD Hakan	Wimbledon	09.02	Göteborg (Sweden)
MILLER Willie	Wrexham	10.02	Dundee
MILLIGAN Mike	Blackpool	03.02	Retired
MINTON Jeff	Leyton Orient	08.02	Canvey Island
MIRANDA Jose	Rotherham U	12.02	Portugal
MITCHELL Graham	Halifax T	06.02	Bradford Park Ave
MOHAN Nicky	Hull C	10.02	Gateshead
MOODY Adrian	Wrexham	08.02	Colwyn Bay
MOODY Paul	Oxford U	08.02	Aldershot T
MOORE David	Wigan Ath	*	
MOORE Joe-Max	Everton	01.03	New England (USA)
MORGAN Alan	Tranmere Rov	05.02	Doncaster Rov
MORGAN Simon	Brighton & Hove A	06.02	Retired
MORLEY David	Oxford U	06.02	Doncaster Rov
MURPHY Neil	Blackpool	07.02	Altrincham
MUSCAT Kevin	Wolverhampton W	07.02	Glasgow Rangers
MUSTOE Neil	Cambridge U	08.02	Gloucester C
N'DIAYE Seyni	Tranmere Rov	02.02	Dunfermline Ath
NEGOUAI Christian	Manchester C	*	
NEWMAN Rob	Southend U	03.03	Retired
NICHOLLS Mark	Torquay U	11.01	Clydebank
NILSSON Roland	Coventry C	06.02	Retired
NISHIZAWA Akinori	Bolton W	01.02	Cerezo Osaka (Japan)
NOBLE David	Arsenal	01.03	West Ham U
NOLAN Ian	Wigan Ath	10.02	Southport
OAKES Scott	Leyton Orient	07.02	St Albans
O'BRIEN Mick	Torquay U	09.01	Chester C
O'CALLAGHAN George	Port Vale	03.02	Cork C
O'DONNELL Phil	Sheffield Wed	06.03	
OFORDILE Adolfus	Walsall	04.02	St Pauli (Germany)
O'HALLORAN Keith	Swindon T	*	
O'KANE Aidan	York C	03.03	
OLEKSEWYCZ Steve	Halifax T	07.02	Ossett T
OMMEL Sergio	Bristol Rov	07.02	Telstar (Holland)
O'NEILL Keith	Coventry C	06.03	
ORMEROD Anthony	Middlesbrough	07.02	Scarborough
OSBORN Mark	Wycombe W	05.03	Farnborough T
OULARE Souleymane	Stoke C	09.02	
OWERS Gary	Notts Co	07.02	Forest Green Rov
PANAYI Jimmy	Watford	07.02	Apollon Limassol (Cyprus)
PANOPOULOS Mike	Portsmouth	04.02	Greece
PARKER Kevin	Torquay U	09.01	Weymouth
PARKINSON Gary	Blackpool	06.02	Retired
PARTRIDGE David	Leyton Orient	07.02	Motherwell
PATMORE Warren	Rushden & Diamonds	09.01	Woking
PATTERSON Darren	Oxford U	04.02	Retired
PEACOCK Gavin	Queens Park R	07.02	Retired
PEARCE Greg	Chesterfield	06.02	Stalybridge Celtic
PEARCE Stuart	Manchester C	06.02	Retired
PENDLEBURY Ian	Wigan Ath	03.03	Leigh RMI
PENNOCK Tony	Rushden & Diamonds	07.02	Farnborough T
PEPPER Nigel	Scunthorpe U	06.02	Retired
PERALTO Sixto	Ipswich T	05.02	Racing Club (Argentina)
PEREZ Lionel	Cambridge U	09.02	Enfield
PERRY Mark	Queens Park R	06.02	
PETRESCU Dan	Southampton	07.02	National Bucharest (Romania)
PHELAN Leeyon	Wycombe W	06.02	Hayes
PHELAN Terry	Sheffield U	11.01	Charleston (USA)
PITCHER Geoff	Brighton & Hove A	02.03	Farnborough T
PITT Courtney	Portsmouth	*	
PLUMMER Dwayne	Bristol Rov	01.03	Aylesbury U
PREECE David	Torquay U	07.02	Enfield
PRENDERVILLE Barry	Oldham Ath	01.02	Shelbourne
PRINGLE Martin	Grimsby T	11.02	Retired
PRITCHARD Dave	Bristol Rov	10.01	Retired
PROKAS Richard	Cambridge U	07.02	Workington
PROSINECKI Robert	Portsmouth	04.02	Olimpic Ljubljana (Slovenia)
QUAILEY Brian	Scunthorpe U	09.02	Halifax T
QUINN James	West Bromwich A	06.02	Willem II (Holland)
RACHUBKA Paul	Manchester U	05.02	Charlton Ath
RAMSAY Scott	Brighton & Hove A	06.02	Eastbourne Borough
READ Paul	Exeter C	06.02	
REBROV Sergei	Tottenham H	01.03	Fenerbahce (Turkey)
REES Jason	Torquay U	07.02	Tiverton T
REILLY Alan	Halifax T	06.02	Bohemians
RHODES Ben	York C	08.02	Pickering T
RICARD Hamilton	Middlesbrough	03.02	CSKA Sofia (Bulgaria)
RICHARDS Tony	Southend U	09.02	
RICHARDSON Barry	Halifax T	07.02	Gainsborough Trinity
RICHARDSON Jay	Exeter C	09.02	Enfield
RICHARDSON Jon	Oxford U	05.02	Forest Green Rov
RICHARDSON Nick	York C	06.02	Harrogate T
RICKETTS Rohan	Arsenal	07.02	Tottenham H
RIDEOUT Paul	Tranmere Rov	06.02	Retired
RIOCH Greg	Shrewsbury T	06.02	Northwich Vic
RIPLEY Stuart	Southampton	06.02	Retired
RISBRIDGER Gareth	Southend U	02.02	Aylesbury U
ROACH Neville	Torquay U	12.01	Slough T
ROBERTS Sean	Sheffield Wed	09.02	Harrow Borough
ROBINSON Les	Mansfield T	07.02	Hednesford T
ROBINSON Mark	Swindon T	07.02	Chippenham T
ROGERS Dave	Carlisle U	06.02	Cambuur (Holland)
ROMO David	Swansea C	05.02	France
ROOKE Steve	Carlisle U	06.02	Gretna
ROSE Karl	Rochdale	12.01	Scarborough
ROSLER Uwe	Southampton	01.02	Unterhaching (Germany)

Name	Club	Date	Destination
USSEL Cedric	Wolverhampton W	07.02	RAEC Mons (Belgium)
VDE Marius	Wrexham	04.02	Lillestrom (Norway)
WE Rodney	Hull C	07.02	Wakefield & Emley
WSON David	Stoke C	01.03	Partick Thistle
DDOCK Neil	Swindon T	01.03	Retired
DONJA Mladen	Portsmouth	04.02	Olimpic Ljubljana (Slovenia)
SSELL Lee	Torquay U	03.02	Forest Green Rov
LVATI Marc	York C	06.02	Whitby T
NCHEZ-LOPEZ Carlos	Bristol Rov	01.02	
ND Peter	Barnsley	02.02	Stabaek (Norway)
NDFORD Lee	Sheffield U	08.02	Woking
NTUS Paul	Wigan Ath	06.03	
VAGE Bas	Reading	*	
VARESE Giovanni	Millwall	11.01	Venezuela
OTHERN Ashley	Barnsley	*	
NIOR Michael	Huddersfield T	08.02	Halifax T
RENI Matteo	Ipswich T	07.02	Brescia (Italy)
AIL Mark	Kidderminster Hrs	01.02	Worcester C
IELDS Greg	Charlton Ath	03.02	Kilmarnock
ORE Drew	Bristol Rov	12.02	Bath C
UTTLEWORTH Barry	Macclesfield T	02.02	Altrincham
GERE Jean-Michel	Rushden & Diamonds	10.01	Stevenage Borough
NTON Andy	Wolverhampton W	08.02	Burton A
NNER Steve	Carlisle U	11.01	Gretna
ART Allan	Oldham Ath	07.02	Dundee
ITH Ben	Southend U	07.02	Hereford U
ITH Craig	Halifax T	+	
ITH Danny	Bournemouth	07.02	Winchester C
ITH Mark	Bristol Rov	06.02	
ITH Neil	Reading	10.02	Woking
EEKES Richard	Hull C	05.02	Herfolge (Denmark)
LEY Steve	Carlisle U	06.02	Southport
MA Ragnvald	West Ham U	08.02	Bryne (Norway)
NG Rigobert	West Ham U	07.02	RC Lens (France)
AM Jaap	Manchester U	08.01	Lazio (Italy)
AMP Neville	York C	08.02	Basingstoke T
AMP Phil	Middlesbrough	08.02	Heart of Midlothian
EELE Luke	Peterborough U	05.02	Manchester U
EPHENSON Paul	Hartlepool U	06.02	Retired
LLIE Derek	Wigan Ath	07.02	Dunfermline Ath
RLING Jude	Luton T	02.02	Stevenage Borough
ONEMAN Paul	Halifax T	+	
OWELL Mike	Bristol C	06.03	Retired
FFO Patrick	Sheffield U	04.02	Numancia (Spain)
LLIVAN Neil	Tottenham H	*	
VALES Steve	Halifax T	07.02	Whitby T
ROS George	Bury	12.01	Akratitos (Greece)
MID Marek	Southend U	06.02	Sutton Coldfield T
T Paul	Oxford U	07.02	Salamina (Cyprus)
L Idan	Everton	09.02	Rayo Vallecano (Spain)
NKARD Allen	Mansfield T	02.03	Retired
YLOR Scott	Cambridge U	02.02	Hayes
ELWELL Alton	Tottenham H	06.03	
OGERSEN Thomas	Portsmouth	05.02	Denmark
OM Stuart	Scunthorpe U	12.02	Barrow
OMAS Geoff	Crewe Alex	06.02	Retired
OMAS Mitchell	Burnley	06.02	Retired
OMPSON Chris	Northampton T	06.02	Gloucester C
OMPSON Phil	Blackpool	08.02	Squires Gate
OMSON Peter	Luton T	01.02	Chester C
ORDARSON Stefan	Stoke C	08.02	IA Akranes (Iceland)
URSTAN Mark	Carlisle U	08.02	
WAITES Adam	Carlisle U	08.02	Gretna
NKLER Eric	Barnsley	03.02	South Africa
DD Lee	Rochdale	06.02	

Name	Club	Date	Destination
TOMLINSON Graeme	Exeter C	06.02	Stevenage Borough
TORPEY Steve	Port Vale	08.02	Prescot Cables
TOURE Alioune	Manchester C	06.02	Paris Saint Germain (France)
TRACEY Richard	Macclesfield T	03.02	Scarborough
TRACEY Simon	Sheffield U	06.03	
TRAORE Demba	Cambridge U	09.02	Enfield
TRAYNOR Greg	Wigan Ath	*	
TRETTON Andy	Shrewsbury T	06.02	Hereford U
TROUGHT Mike	Bristol Rov	07.02	Bath C
TULLY Steve	Torquay U	07.02	Weymouth
TURNER Sam	Stockport Co	06.02	Southall
UNSAL Hakan	Blackburn Rov	06.02	Galatasaray (Turkey)
VALOIS Jean-Louis	Luton T	08.02	Heart of Midlothian
VAN DER GEEST Frank	Darlington	01.02	ADO '20 (Holland)
VAN DER GOUW Rai	Manchester U	07.02	West Ham U
VEGA Ramon	Watford	08.02	Creteil (France)
VIANDER Jani	Stoke C	03.03	Midtjylland (Denmark)
VINCENT Jamie	Portsmouth	*	
WALKER Andy	Exeter C	10.01	Tonbridge Angels
WALKER Joshua	Shrewsbury T	06.02	Moor Green
WALLACE Adam	Southend U	06.02	Salisbury C
WALLING Dean	Cambridge U	07.02	Gainsborough Trinity
WALSH Danny	Chesterfield	06.02	Kettering T
WALSH Dave	Wrexham	07.02	Connahs Quay Nomads
WALTERS Mark	Bristol Rov	08.02	Ilkeston T
WALTON Mark	Cardiff C	06.03	
WANCHOPE Paulo	Manchester C	*	
WARD Mark	Sheffield U	09.02	Belper T
WARE Paul	Rochdale	07.02	Hednesford T
WARREN David	Wrexham	06.02	
WEARE Ross	Bristol Rov	06.02	Retired
WEAVER Luke	Carlisle U	06.03	
WEAVER Nicky	Manchester C	*	
WESTERVELD Sander	Liverpool	12.01	Real Sociedad (Spain)
WHITE Jason	Cheltenham T	08.02	Mansfield T
WHITEHEAD Damien	Macclesfield T	07.02	Leigh RMI
WHITMORE Theo	Hull C	04.02	Seba U (Jamaica)
WICKS Matthew	Hull C	02.03	
WILCOX Russ	Scunthorpe U	05.02	Retired
WILKIE Lee	Notts Co	09.01	Dundee
WILKINSON Andy	Stoke C	*	
WILLEMS Menno	Grimsby T	05.02	Haarlem (Holland)
WILLIAMS Danny	Chesterfield	07.02	Hereford U
WILLIAMS James	Swindon T	06.02	
WILLIAMSON Mike	Southampton	*	
WILLIAMSON Tom	Leicester C	*	
WILSON Che	Bristol Rov	08.02	Cambridge C
WILSON Scott	Portsmouth	07.02	Dunfermline Ath
WINDER Nathan	Halifax T	10.02	Chesterfield
WINSTANLEY Mark	Carlisle U	07.02	Southport
WISS Jarkko	Stockport Co	01.02	Hibernian
WOLLEASTON Robert	Chelsea	06.03	Bradford C
WOODWARD Andy	Halifax T	08.02	Northwich Victoria
WOOLLEY Matt	Macclesfield T	03.03	
WOOTER Nordin	Watford	06.02	Roosendal BC (Holland)
WORMULL Simon	Rushden & Diamonds	10.01	Stevenage Borough
WRIGHT Peter	Halifax T	07.02	Burscough
YORDI	Blackburn Rov	05.02	Real Zaragoza (Spain)
ZABEK Lee	Exeter C	06.02	
ZAMPERINI Alessandro	Portsmouth	07.02	Modena (Italy)
ZUNIGA Ysrael	Coventry C	07.02	Estudiantes (Argentina)

PFA AWARDS 2003

Player of the Year
THIERRY HENRY
(ARSENAL)

Young Player of the Year
JERMAINE JENAS
(NEWCASTLE UNITED)

Special Merit Award
SIR BOBBY ROBSON

Player of the Decade
ALAN SHEARER
(NEWCASTLE UNITED)

DIVISIONAL AWARDS

FA Barclaycard Premiership

Brad Friedel	Blackburn Rovers
Stephen Carr	Tottenham Hotspur
Ashley Cole	Arsenal
Sol Campbell	Arsenal
William Gallas	Chelsea
Patrick Vieira	Arsenal
Paul Scholes	Manchester United
Robert Pires	Arsenal
Kieron Dyer	Newcastle United
Alan Shearer	Newcastle United
Thierry Henry	Arsenal

Nationwide League Division One

Shaka Hislop	Portsmouth
Denis Irwin	Wolverhampton Wanderers
Michael Dawson	Nottingham Forest
Joleon Lescott	Wolverhampton Wanderers
Matthew Taylor	Portsmouth
Michael Brown	Sheffield United
Muzzy Izzet	Leicester City
Paul Merson	Portsmouth
Michael Tonge	Sheffield United
David Johnson	Nottingham Forest
Paul Dickov	Leicester City

Nationwide League Division Two

John Filan	Wigan Athletic
Nicky Eaden	Wigan Athletic
Jason De Vos	Wigan Athletic
Fitz Hall	Oldham Athletic
Micky Bell	Bristol City
Scott Murray	Bristol City
Jimmy Bullard	Wigan Athletic
Graham Kavanagh	Cardiff City
Martin Bullock	Blackpool
Robert Earnshaw	Cardiff City
Rob Hulse	Crewe Alexandra

Nationwide League Division Three

Alan Fettis	Hull City
Carlos Edwards	Wrexham
Graeme Lee	Hartlepool United
Chris Westwood	Hartlepool United
Paul Underwood	Rushden & Diamonds
Richie Humphreys	Hartlepool United
Mark Tinkler	Hartlepool United
Paul Hall	Rushden & Diamonds
Alex Russell	Torquay United
Andy Morrell	Wrexham
Dave Kitson	Cambridge United